SCANDINAVIA

10TH EDITION

Where to Stay and Eat
for All Budgets

Must-See Sights
and Local Secrets

Ratings You Can Trust

Portions of this book appear in *Fodor's Denmark, Norway,* and *Sweden*

Fodor's Travel Publications   New York, Toronto, London, Sydney, Auckland
www.fodors.com

FODOR'S SCANDINAVIA

Editor: Nuha E. Ansari

Editorial Production: David Downing
Editorial Contributors: Charles Ferro, Rob Hincks, Satu Hummasti, Michael Kissane, Christina Knight, Joan Lofgren, Eduardo López de Luzuriaga, Tom Mercer, Karin Palmquist, Sonya Procenko, Lars Ursin
Maps: David Lindroth *cartographer;* Bob Blake and Rebecca Baer, *map editors*
Design: Fabrizio La Rocca, *creative director;* Guido Caroti, *art director;* Melanie Marin, *senior photo editor*
Production/Manufacturing: Angela L. McLean
Cover Photo (Dettifoss Waterfall, North Iceland): Harald Sund/The Image Bank

Tenth Edition

ISBN 1–4000–1340–2

ISSN 0071–6529

SPECIAL SALES

This book is available for special discounts for bulk purchases for sales promotions or premiums. Special editions, including personalized covers, excerpts of existing books, and corporate imprints, can be created in large quantities for special needs. For more information, write to Special Markets/Premium Sales, 1745 Broadway, MD 6-2, New York, New York 10019 or e-mail specialmarkets@randomhouse.com. Inquiries from Canada should be directed to your local Canadian bookseller or sent to Random House of Canada, Ltd., Marketing Department, 2775 Matheson Boulevard East, Mississauga, Ontario L4W 4P7. Inquiries from the United Kingdom should be sent to Fodor's Travel Publications, 20 Vauxhall Bridge Road, London SW1V 2SA, England.

AN IMPORTANT TIP & AN INVITATION

Although all prices, opening times, and other details in this book are based on information supplied to us at press time, changes occur all the time in the travel world, and Fodor's cannot accept responsibility for facts that become outdated or for inadvertent errors or omissions. So **always confirm information when it matters,** especially if you're making a detour to visit a specific place. Your experiences—positive and negative—matter to us. If we have missed or misstated something, **please write to us.** We follow up on all suggestions. Contact the Scandinavia editor at editors@fodors.com or c/o Fodor's at 1745 Broadway, New York, New York 10019.

PRINTED IN THE UNITED STATES OF AMERICA

10 9 8 7 6 5 4 3 2 1

DESTINATION SCANDINAVIA

The islands of Stockholm mirrored in the water, the ships and Little Mermaid of Copenhagen, Oslo and its majestic fjord, the bay and peninsulas of Helsinki, Reykjavík with its busy, deep-blue harbor: the capitals of Scandinavia are unthinkable without the water that surrounds and sustains them. What is true of the capitals is equally true of the countries. Denmark consists of one peninsula and more than 400 islands, half of them inhabited. Finland and Sweden used to dispute which country was really "the land of a thousand lakes." Finland settled it, after counting almost 190,000. An island summer in the archipelago is part of every Stockholmer's childhood memory. The mail packets of Norway's *Hurtigruten* sail north from Bergen along the fjord-indented coast and turn around at Kirkenes on the Russian border, 2,000 km (1,242 mi) later. Iceland is so dependent on the surrounding sea that it has been known to take on the British navy to protect its fishing limits. Every corner of Scandinavia richly rewards those who take the time to get to know it better. Have a fabulous trip!

Karen Cure, Editorial Director

CONTENTS

Understanding Scandinavia 708

Vocabulary 727

Index 737

Maps

CloseUps

ABOUT THIS BOOK

There's no doubt that the best source for travel advice is a like-minded friend who's just been where you're headed. But with or without that friend, you'll have a better trip with a Fodor's guide in hand. Once you've learned to find your way around its pages, you'll be in great shape to find your way around your destination.

SELECTION

Our goal is to cover the best properties, sights, and activities in their category, as well as the most interesting communities to visit. We make a point of including local food-lovers' hot spots as well as neighborhood options, and we avoid all that's touristy unless it's really worth your time. You can go on the assumption that everything you read about in this book is recommended wholeheartedly by our writers and editors. Flip to **On the Road with Fodor's** to learn more about who they are. It goes without saying that no property mentioned in the book has paid to be included.

RATINGS

Orange stars ★ denote sights and properties that our editors and writers consider the very best in the area covered by the entire book. These, the best of the best, are listed in the **Fodor's Choice** section in the front of the book. Black stars ★ highlight the sights and properties we deem **Highly Recommended**, the don't-miss sights within any region. Fodor's Choice and Highly Recommended options in each region are usually listed on the title page of the chapter covering that region. Use the index to find complete descriptions. In cities, sights pinpointed with numbered map bullets ❶ in the margins tend to be more important than those without bullets.

SPECIAL SPOTS

Pleasures & Pastimes focuses on types of experiences that reveal the spirit of the destination. Watch for **Off the Beaten Path** sights. Some are out of the way, some are quirky, and all are worth your while. If the munchies hit while you're exploring, look for **Need a Break?** suggestions.

TIME IT RIGHT

Wondering when to go? Check **On the Calendar** up front and chapters' **Timing** sections for weather and crowd overviews and best days and times to visit.

SEE IT ALL

Use Fodor's exclusive **Great Itineraries** as a model for your trip. (For a good overview of the entire destination, follow those that begin the book, or mix regional itineraries from several chapters.) In cities, **Good Walks** guide you to important sights in each neighborhood; ☞ indicates the starting points of walks and itineraries in the text and on the map.

BUDGET WELL

Hotel and restaurant price categories from ¢ to $$$$ are defined in the opening pages of each chapter—expect to find a balanced selection for every budget. For attractions, we always give standard adult admission fees; reductions are usually available for children, students, and senior citizens. Look in **Discounts & Deals** in Smart Travel Tips for information on destination-wide ticket schemes. Want to pay with plastic? **AE, DC, MC, V** following restaurant and hotel listings indicate whether American Express, Diner's Club, MasterCard, or Visa are accepted.

BASIC INFO

Smart Travel Tips lists travel essentials for the entire area covered by the book; city- and region-specific basics end each chapter. To find the best way to get around, see the transportation section; see individual modes of travel ("By Car," "By Train") for details. We assume you'll check Web sites or call for particulars.

ON THE MAPS   Maps throughout the book show you what's where and help you find your way around. Black and orange numbered bullets ❶ ❶ in the text correlate to bullets on maps.

BACKGROUND   In general, we give background information within the chapters in the course of explaining sights as well as in CloseUp boxes and in Understanding Scandinavia at the end of the book. To get in the mood, review the suggestions in Books & Movies. The glossary can be invaluable.

FIND IT FAST   Within the book, chapters are arranged in alphabetical order by country. Individual country chapters are divided into small regions, within which towns are covered in logical geographical order; attractive routes and interesting places between towns are flagged as En Route. Heads at the top of each page help you find what you need within a chapter.

DON'T FORGET   Restaurants are open for lunch and dinner daily unless we state otherwise; we mention dress only when there's a specific requirement and reservations only when they're essential or not accepted—it's always best to book ahead. Hotels have private baths, phone, TVs, and air-conditioning and operate on the European Plan (a.k.a. EP, meaning without meals). We always list facilities but not whether you'll be charged extra to use them, so when pricing accommodations, find out what's included.

SYMBOLS

Many Listings

★ Fodor's Choice
★ Highly recommended
⊠ Physical address
✦ Directions
🗇 Mailing address
☎ Telephone
🖷 Fax
⊕ On the Web
✉ E-mail
🎫 Admission fee
⊙ Open/closed times
► Start of walk/itinerary
Ⓜ Metro stations
⊟ Credit cards

Outdoors

🏌 Golf
⛺ Camping

Hotels & Restaurants

🏨 Hotel
🛏 Number of rooms
♨ Facilities
🍽 Meal plans
✕ Restaurant
⚓ Reservations
🏛 Dress code
🚬 Smoking
🍷 BYOB
✕🏨 Hotel with restaurant that warrants a visit

Other

🐾 Family-friendly
🛈 Contact information
⇨ See also
⊠ Branch address
☞ Take note

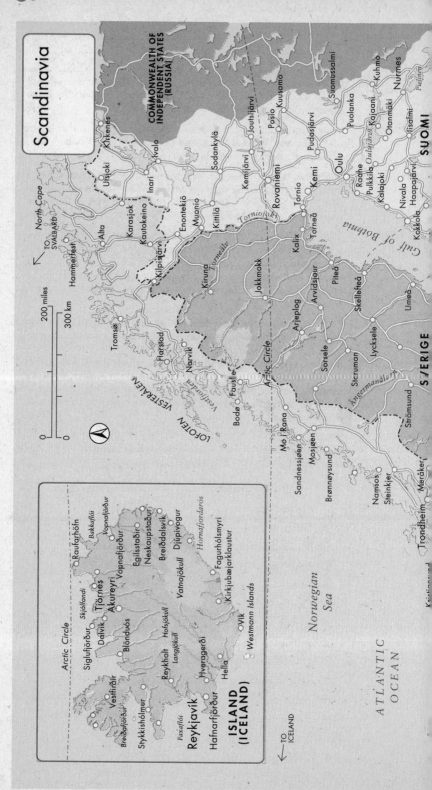

Scandinavia

KEY

- - - Ferry lines

Faroe
Islands
(Denmark)

ON THE ROAD WITH FODOR'S

A trip takes you out of yourself. Concerns of life at home completely disappear, driven away by more immediate thoughts—about, say, what marvels will beguile the next day, or where you'll have dinner. That's where Fodor's comes in. We make sure that you know all your options, so that you don't miss something that's around the next bend just because you didn't know it was there. Because the best memories of your trip might well have nothing to do with what you came to Scandinavia to see, we guide you to sights large and small all over the region. You might set out to laze on the beach, but back at home you find yourself unable to forget exploring the fjords on Norway's west coast, or dogsledding in Samíland. With Fodor's at your side, serendipitous discoveries are never far away.

Our success in showing you every corner of Scandinavia is a credit to our extraordinary writers. Although there's no substitute for travel advice from a good friend who knows your style, our contributors are the next best thing—the kind of people you would poll for travel advice if you knew them.

Greenland updater **Charles Ferro**, a freelance journalist, has lived in Copenhagen since 1977. A highlight of his journalism career was an interview with the late Danish comedian and pianist Victor Borge. He writes for travel and entertainment publications, as well as a number of consumer magazines. Charles is also the author of 14 books for teens.

British journalist **Rob Hincks** wrote about Sweden for this edition. He primarily writes and edits for food and travel magazines in Sweden and England. Rob has lived in Stockholm since 2000, but through his Swedish wife, Mikaela, his associations with the country go back much further.

Michael J. Kissane has lived nearly 20 years in Iceland, where he travels widely. He has contributed to *Barron's–Wall Street Journal* and other publications.

Finland updater **Joan Lofgren** has a social science doctorate from Columbia University in New York, specializing in the Baltic region. Currently based in Tampere, Finland, she has also worked as a freelance writer and teacher, drawing on her experiences living and working in Sweden, Estonia, and Russia.

After freelancing for several years in both Cologne, Germany, and London, our Sjaelland and Faroe Islands updater **Eduardo López de Luzuriaga** moved to Copenhagen in 1997. He has worked regularly for the Spanish news agency EFE and is a correspondent for the European Press Network, an international news agency.

Norwegian-Canadian journalist **Sonya Procenko** covers Norway and the Nordic countries for European and North American publications. In 1998, Sonya returned to her roots by moving back to Norway, where she hikes, climbs, skis, and writes.

Our Sweden updater, **Karin Palmquist** is a journalist who has written for the *Washington Post* and the *Washington Times* among other publications. She grew up in Sweden, and has traveled extensively throughout Scandinavia.

Norway updater **Lars Ursin** has worked as a freelance journalist and translator. He has traveled extensively in Norway, partly for his journalistic assignments, but mainly to satisfy his addiction to everything mountain-related, especially hiking, skiing, and snowboarding.

1 Denmark

The Kingdom of Denmark dapples the Baltic Sea in an archipelago of some 450 islands and the arc of one peninsula. Measuring 43,069 square km (16,628 square mi), with a population of 5.3 million, it is the geographical link between Scandinavia and Europe.

The island of Sjælland, the largest of the Danish isles, is the most popular tourist destination. Here you'll find Copenhagen, Scandinavia's most populous city (population 1.7 million), Denmark's capital, and the seat of the oldest kingdom in the world. The city's, if not Denmark's, best-known attraction is Tivoli Gardens, a bewitching blend of blooming gardens, fun fair rides, pantomime theater, stylish restaurants, and concerts. To the north of Copehnagen are royal castles (including Helsingør's Kronborg of Hamlet fame), ritzy beach towns, and top-notch museums. The modern-art museum Louisiana, set in a spectacular seaside location on Sjaelland's northeastern coast, has a superb collection of modern European and American art, from Warhol to Giacometti. To the west, Roskilde holds relics of medieval Denmark; it also hosts Northern Europe's largest music festival, usually at the end of June, which draws more than 70,000 revelers who come to groove to rock, pop, jazz, and folk music. And to the west and south, rural towns and farms edge up to beach communities and fine white beaches, often surrounded by forests. On the southeast island of Møn, 75-million-year-old chalk cliffs plunge dramatically to the sea.

Fyn (Funen), the smaller of the country's two main islands, is the site of Denmark's third-largest city, Odense, the birthplace of Hans Christian Andersen. It's no wonder this area inspired many fairy tales: 1,120 km (700 mi) of coastline and lush stretches of vegetable and flower gardens are punctuated by manor houses, beech glades, castles, swan ponds, and thatch-roof homes. In the south is the Egeskov Slot, a well-preserved Renaissance castle that even has a moat. Myriad islands speckle the sea south of Fyn, including verdant Ærø, called the Jewel of the Archipelago. In the island's port town, narrow cobbled streets wind among beautifully preserved half-timber houses.

Jylland, Denmark's western peninsula, shares its southern border with Germany. At the northern tip lies Skagen, a luminous, dune-covered point, and just below it are Århus and Aalborg, two of Denmark's largest cities. Home to a major university, Århus pulsates with a lively nightlife and café scene that rivals Copenhagen's. The heart of the peninsula, mostly lakeland and beech forests, is dotted with castles and parklands and is home to the famed Legoland. Along the east coast, deep fjords are rimmed by forests. The south holds marshlands; gabled houses; and Ribe, Denmark's oldest town. The islands of Fanø and Rømø, with silky sand beaches and windswept dunes, draw scores of vacationing Northern Europeans.

The island of Bornholm, 177 km (110 mi) southeast of Sjælland, has a temperate climate that distinguishes it from the rest of Denmark. Its old-fashioned towns and exuberant natural beauty have earned it the title of Pearl of the Baltic.

The 18 Faroe Islands dot the North Atlantic 1,300 km (812 mi) northwest of Denmark. Granted home rule in 1948, the native Faroese live by fishing and shepherding amid rugged pastureland that is home to more than 120 migratory species of birds. Villages of thatch-roof houses nestle up to mossy hillsides, and harbors bustle with the comings and goings of fishing boats.

Last but not least, there's Greenland, the second-largest island in the world (after the continent of Australia). Greenland's allure is its savage landscape of jagged fjords and gargantuan icebergs. Its wild and raw nature is the biggest and best sight of all. It's a land where tourism is still new and travel is limited to helicopters, coastal boats, or dogsleds that traverse the bright-white frozen plains. Greenland's second largest town, Sisimiut, is the center for winter tourism.

(2) Finland

Finland is one of the world's northernmost countries, with its entire Lapland region above the Arctic Circle. It's a country of beautiful scenery and strong, spirited citizens. Sweden and Russia fought over the land for centuries, but the Finns themselves are neither Scandinavian nor Slavic. Finnish, a non–Indo-European language, is closely linked to Estonian and more distantly to Hungarian. It has no relation to Swedish, the second national language. Helsinki, the capital since 1812, is a meeting ground for eastern and western Europe. Built on peninsulas and islands along the Baltic coast, the city's streets curve around bays, and bridges arch across to nearby islands. Stunning architecture abounds, from 19th-century neoclassical buildings to sleek, modern high-rises. Helsinki is the country's cultural hub and home to one-sixth of the nation's population.

In the southwest lies Turku, the former capital. Founded more than 750 years ago, the city was the main gateway through which cultural influences reached Finland over the centuries. It remains a busy harbor, from which you can sail for the rugged and fascinating Åland Islands. Encompassing some 6,500 of the more than 30,000 islands that form the magnificent archipelago along Finland's coastline, the Ålands were long the subject of a territorial dispute between Finland and Sweden. The islands are home to many families that fish or run small farms.

Eastern and central Finland are dimpled with nearly 200,000 lakes, most fringed with tiny cabins—Finnish vacation institutions. Amid the many delightful small towns of the Lakelands, the larger Savonlinna is hugged by gigantic Lake Saimaa and is worth a visit for its waterbound scenery and cultural life. Opera, drama, ballet, and instrumental performances fill the month of July at the Savonlinna Opera festival.

Tampere, the largest city in the region, is famous for its history as a textile factory town nestled between two large lakes. Now it is a busy university city, with a variety of festivals throughout the year, including an international short film festival in March. Lapland, north of the Arctic Circle, remains unspoiled wilderness. Summer is a time of round-the-clock daylight, whereas the winter landscape is lit only by reflections on the snow. As the area has become more accessible, comfortable hotels and modern amenities have popped up, but nature is the star attraction: reindeer, great forests, crystal-clear streams, and the midnight sun's reflection on a lake's dark water.

③ Iceland

Iceland is the westernmost outpost of Europe, 800 km (500 mi) from the nearest European landfall in Scotland, and more than 80% of its 103,000 square km (40,000 square mi) remains uninhabited. It has the world's oldest functioning parliament—the Alþingi (founded in AD 930); Europe's largest glacier, Vatnajökull; and the namesake of all spouting hot springs, Geysir. The thundering Dettifoss is also Europe's most powerful waterfall and the magnificent Gullfoss Europe's tallest.

Icelanders gained a sort of notoriety when a European survey showed them to be Europe's champion optimists. What else would you call a country perched on the Arctic Circle that sets its First Day of Summer in April, or folks who occupy the same island for more than 1,100 years, despite the intrusion of volcanic eruptions almost as frequent as other nations hold political elections?

Reykjavík, the capital, is home to half the island's 275,000 citizens. Along with most of the island, it enjoys pollution-free warmth from geothermal hot springs, which also heat many popular swimming pools. The thriving arts scene here includes the Reykjavík Arts Festival, theater, ballet, symphonies, museums, and private galleries. An hour's drive from Reykjavík is Þingvellir, a national park and, as site of the original Alþingi (parliament), a symbol of the nation's heritage. In the north, Akureyri, Iceland's second-largest city, offers several museums and the Lystigarðurinn, a botanical garden. The inland east's Hallormsstaður Forestry Reserve has camping spots in the country's largest forest, on the shore of Lake Lögurinn, which some claim is home to a large serpent. Oh yes, Icelanders, who really do divert highways for the *Huldufólk* (Hidden People), tend to believe in the supernatural rather more than most people.

④ Norway

Norway, roughly 400,000 square km (155,000 square mi), is about the same size as California. Approximately 30% of this long, narrow country is covered with clear lakes, lush forests, and rugged mountains. Western Norway, bordered by the Norwegian Sea and the Atlantic Ocean, is the fabled land of the fjords—few places on earth can match its power and splendor. The magnificent Sognefjord, the longest inlet in western Norway, is only one of many fjords found here, including the Hardangerfjord, Geirangerfjord, Lysefjord, and Nordfjord.

Bergen, often hailed as the "Fjord Capital of Norway," is the second-largest city in the country. The cobblestone streets, well-preserved buildings at the Bryggen, and seven mountains that surround the city all add to its storybook charm.

Eastern Norway, bordered by Sweden, and by Finland and Russia to the north, is punctuated by rolling hills, abundant valleys, and fresh lakes—much more subdued than the landscape of the west. Near Gudbrandsdalen (Gudbrands Valley) you'll find Lillehammer. Almost directly south, rising from the shores of the Oslofjord, is the capital of Norway—Oslo. With a population of about a half million, Oslo is a friendly, manageable city.

If you follow the coast south, you'll come to Kristiansand, one of Sør-landet's (the Southland's) leading cities. Sørlandet is known for its long stretches of unspoiled, uncrowded beach. Stavanger, farther west, is one of the most cosmopolitan cities in Scandinavia—its oil and gas industry draws people from around the globe.

Halfway between Oslo and Bergen lies Hardangervidda (Hardanger Plateau), Norway's largest national park. At the foot of the plateau is Geilo, one of the country's most popular ski resorts. Almost directly north is the bustling city of Trondheim.

From here, a thin expanse of land stretches up to the Nordkapp (North Cape). Known as the Land of the Midnight Sun (the display of the northern lights in the winter is pretty amazing, too), this region is marked with exquisite landscapes: glaciers, fjords, and rocky coasts. Narvik, a major Arctic port, is the gateway to the Lofoten Islands, where puffins march about. Even farther north is one of Norway's major universities, Tromsø, the lifeline to settlements and research centers at the North Pole. At the very top of Norway is the county of Finnmark, where many Sámi (native Laplanders) live. Access to the area is primarily through Hammerfest, Europe's northernmost city, where the sun is not visible from November 21 to January 21, but is uninterrupted May 17 through July 29.

5 Sweden

In Sweden, streamlined, ultramodern cities give way to lush forests and timbered farmhouses, and modern western European democracy coexists with strong affection for a monarchy. With 449,963 square km (173,731 square mi) for only 8.9 million residents, almost all have room to live as they choose.

Stockholm, one of Europe's most beautiful capitals, is built on 14 small islands. Bustling, skyscraper-lined boulevards are a short walk from twisting medieval streets in this modern yet pastoral city. South of the city, in the densely forested Småland province, are isolated villages whose names are bywords when it comes to fine crystal glassware: Kosta, Boda and Orrefors.

Skåne, the country's southernmost province, and the other southern provinces have a significantly different heritage than the rest of the country. Part of Denmark until 1658, the area still has its own distinct dialect. Known as Sweden's best area for crops, this is a lush, expansive countryside with many farms. It is a place of exceptional beauty, ranging from the coastal headlands of Mölle and the Kullaberg national park, to lovely nature reserves and the urban capital, Malmö. Historic castles abound, reminding you that there has always been an aristocracy in Sweden.

Sweden's second-largest city, Göteborg, is on the west coast. A Viking port in the 11th century, today the city is home to the Scandinavium indoor arena; Nordstan, one of Europe's largest indoor shopping malls; and Liseberg, Scandinavia's largest amusement park. A cruise on the Göta Canal provides a notable coast-to-coast journey through the Swedish countryside.

Dalarna, the central region of Sweden, is considered the most typically Swedish of all the country's 24 provinces, a place of forests, mountains, and red-painted wooden farmhouses and cottages by the shores of pristine, sun-dappled lakes. The north of Sweden, Norrland, is a place of wide-open spaces. Eagles soar above snowcapped crags; huge salmon fight their way up wild, tumbling rivers; rare orchids bloom in Arctic heathland; wild rhododendrons splash the land with color. The Bothnian Coast is a rugged, windswept finger of land that runs up the eastern side of Sweden between Stockholm and Norrland. Its grand 19th-century towns and cities testify to the wealth that industry brought in the recent past, while its tiny fishing villages and ancient communities point to the more isolated times that preceded it.

Our itineraries suggest ways in which Scandinavian destinations can be combined; note they tend to allow the minimum amount of time needed in various destinations. Elements from different itineraries can be combined to create an itinerary that suits your interests.

Sand, Surf & Ships, Scandinavia-Style
2 weeks

Scandinavia is defined by water. Glaciers, rivers, and sea tides determine the geography; oceans shape the history and culture. Tiny Denmark, for example, would probably not exist as a country today, except for the way it sticks up like a cork in the bottleneck entrance to the Baltic Sea. Its shape makes it strategically important for such major shipping and trading countries as England, which has both attacked and defended the country over trading issues during the past 400 years. What better way, then, to see the land of the Vikings than by water?

DENMARK 3 days. Fly to Copenhagen. Explore the city and its waterways: Nyhavn's tall ships and myriad restaurants; Christianshavn, with its encircling moat and canals reflecting colorful old buildings; and the canal-ringed palace of Christiansborg, where you can visit the Danish Parliament and the royal reception rooms. Enjoy the twinkling lights and happy atmosphere of Tivoli from mid-April through mid-September and its frostier but less crowded attributes several weeks before Christmas. Take a harbor cruise, passing *Den Lille Havfrue (The Little Mermaid)*, perched on her rock. Sun on the beaches north of town or sail the Øresund—maybe even all the way around Sjælland. You'll love the castle of Frederiksborg, set in its lake a little less than an hour north of Copenhagen, and the Karen Blixen Museum at Rungstedlund. Continue by air to Stockholm.

SWEDEN 6 days. Beautiful Stockholm is made up of 14 islands surrounded by sparkling water, clean enough for fishing and swimming even in the city center. You can take ferries all around town and out into the enchanting archipelago, with its 24,000 islands. Don't miss the picturesque Old Town; the museum for the salvaged 17th-century warship *Vasa*; or Skansen, the world's oldest open-air museum.

From Stockholm, take the train across Sweden to Göteborg, where you can explore the west-coast beaches warmed by the Gulf Stream. Try sea fishing or windsurfing, and visit the 17th-century fortress of Elfsborg, which guards the harbor entrance. Take a ferry to Oslo.

NORWAY 5 days. In Oslo, visit the Viking Ship and Kon-Tiki museums and the fabulous Vigeland sculpture park. The Bergen Railway will carry you across the roof of Norway in 6½ dramatic hours. If you can spare an extra day, stop in Myrdal for a side trip on the Flåm Railway and a short cruise on the beautiful Aurland Fjord before continuing to Bergen. Here you can explore Bryggen, a collection of reconstructed houses dating from the Hansa period in the 14th century, the famous fish market, and funicular. View the magnificent, ever-changing Norwegian coastline aboard a Coastal Express ship to Trondheim, where you can fly to Oslo or Copenhagen, then home.

BORNHOLM & GOTLAND Alternate days. If you already know Copenhagen and Stockholm, consider visiting the beautiful islands of Bornholm in Denmark or Sweden's Gotland. Bornholm is graced by beaches perfect for surfing and sailing; excellent golf courses; one of the largest castle ruins in Scandinavia; and some memorable architecture, including the famous round churches from the 12th and 13th centuries. You can reach it by ferry from Copenhagen or from Ystad, in southern Sweden, bringing your car if you like. Alternatively, you can fly to Rønne, the capital of Bornholm, directly from Copenhagen in about 30 minutes.

Gotland is the largest island in the Baltic, with peaceful little towns and fishing villages, and a striking capital, Visby, with a medieval flavor and a well-preserved city wall dating from the 14th and 15th centuries. "Medieval Week" in early August is celebrated with mummers, knights, tournaments, and lots of other special attractions. Ferries sail from Stockholm and several other Swedish ports.

Scandinavian Mountains
2 weeks

If you like snow-clad mountains, Scandinavia has plenty of terrain for you: glacier climbing, reindeer- and dogsledding, cross-country skiing, and even just hiking amid gorgeous surroundings.

NORWAY **5 days.** Fly to Oslo and then on to Bodø or another destination in northern Norway. Some of the country's most striking ranges are the Lofoten and Vesterålen islands, near Bodø, along with the Lyngen Peninsula in Tromsø. Begin with a four-day hiking tour or a glacier walk. From Bodø, fly to Narvik; then take the train to Kiruna, Sweden, the largest town in Swedish Lapland.

SWEDEN **5 days.** Welcome to the Arctic Circle, the land of the midnight sun, where the sun stays above the horizon 24 hours during the summer solstice. In Kiruna, join a three-day whitewater canoeing trip. Take a rest, rent a car, and go see the waterfall and trails at Muddus National Park and the fine collection of Sámi (Lapp) art in Jokkmokk. Drive or take the train to Rovaniemi, Finland, about 323 km (200 mi) from Kiruna, a five- or six-hour drive. Watch out for deer and other animals on the road.

FINLAND **4 days.** Rovaniemi is an end point for the Road of the Four Winds, or, simply, the Arctic Road, which runs 1,000 km (625 mi) north from Helsinki. In summer, look for the salmon-fishing competition, reindeer herding, gold panning, logging, and the Russian Orthodox Skolt Sámi festivals that are held throughout the region. Fly from Rovaniemi to Helsinki and then home.

Tracing the Vikings
10 days

Traces can still be found of the seafaring warriors who, from the 8th through the 11th century, traded with, settled in, or raided the parts of the world that became known as Western Europe, Iceland, Greenland, Labrador, Newfoundland, and Russia. The Vikings' 1,000-year-old remains are scattered throughout Scandinavia and provide a fascinating record of their culture.

DENMARK **3 days.** Begin in Copenhagen with a visit to the Nationalmuseet, which has many Viking exhibits labeled in English; one exhibit shows how the Vikings could navigate their ships across vast oceans at a time when most people believed the world was flat. Take the hour-long train ride to the Vikingeskibshallen (Viking Ship Museum) in Roskilde, where five ships found in the Roskilde Fjord and dating from around AD 1000 have been restored. At the nearby Lejre Forsøgscenter (Lejre Archaeological Research Center), you can see how the Vikings lived. On the way back, if you are a true Viking buff, visit Trælleborg, in western Sjælland, where you'll find the remains of a staging area for troops led by Knud (Canute), the 11th-century king who ruled England, Denmark, Norway, and part of Sweden. In June you can enjoy the colorful Viking Games in the lovely park at Frederikssund, northwest of Copenhagen.

Rent a car or take a train and stay overnight in Vejle, on the large peninsula of Jylland; then head for Jelling, where two Viking kings—Gorm the Old and his son, Harald Bluetooth, Knud's great-grandfather—reigned. They left two large burial mounds and two runic stones, dating from around AD 950.

If you have more time, you can visit many other Viking sites in Denmark: Ribe, Denmark's oldest town and site of a Viking village open-air museum; Lindholm Høje, where graves are marked by 4-foot-tall stones placed in the pattern of a ship; Moesgård museum near Århus; and Viborg. Return to Copenhagen and fly to Oslo.

NORWAY **3 days.** Go straight to Oslo's Vikingskiphuset (Viking Ship Museum), which has the finest single collection of excavated and preserved Viking ships, once used as tombs for nobles. The next day, in Oslo's Historisk Museum, you'll find beautiful jewelry from the 9th century: gold necklaces, silver ornaments, and "gripping beasts"—whimsical monsters fashioned from amber and other materials. Fly to Stockholm.

SWEDEN **4 days.** In the Historiska Museet you'll find swords, saddlery, and wonderful Viking gold jewelry, including amulets shaped as hammers, the symbol of Thor, the thunder god. At Gamla Uppsala (Old Uppsala), an easy drive north of Stockholm, burial grounds for three 6th-century Viking monarchs remain. Take the ferry to the island of Gotland. In the Fornsal Museum, you'll find silver hoards and other Viking valuables. Scattered around the island of Gotland are Viking burial sites, picture stones and deserted Iron Age homesteads and trading places. If time permits, visit some of these burial sites, and then stop in Tofta, 17 km (11 mi) south of Visby. In Vikingabyn i Tofta, a Viking village reconstruction, visitors can participate in such everyday Viking activities as grinding flour on a millstone, baking bread over an open fire, and making hooks and simple tools with a Viking blacksmith. Return to Stockholm and then home.

Architecture & Crafts
10 days

Scandinavian design—furniture, architecture, and crafts—is world renowned.

DENMARK **3 days.** Strolling through Copenhagen you'll be amazed by the number of beautiful buildings, punctuated by green copper spires and gentle fountains. Don't miss the 15th-century Helligånds Kirken (Church of the Holy Ghost) and the Gothic Vor Frelsers Kirken (Church of Our Saviour). Brick Renaissance buildings date from the reign of King Christian IV. The Børsen (Stock Exchange) is topped by a spire of twisting dragon tails. The exquisite Rosenborg Slot (Rosenborg Castle) houses the crown jewels, royal art, and furniture, including the famous life-size silver lions. From the Rundetårn (Round Tower), Copenhagen's first observatory, you'll see the old town spread out like a map. Enjoy charming Gråbrødretorv (Grey Friars' Square) and the colorful old buildings reflected in the canals that front Nyhavn and Christianshavn. Amalienborg, home of the royal family, and Christiansborg Slot, which houses the Parliament and royal reception rooms, are both monumental. Examples of *modern* monumentality are the exciting Black Diamond, an annex to the Kongelige Bibliotek (Royal Library) made of polished black Zimbabwean granite reflecting the sea and the sky, and the expansion of the Statens Museum for Kunst (the National Art Gallery). An hour north of Copenhagen, visit two castles: Frederiksborg in Hillerød and Kronborg (Hamlet's castle) in Helsingør.

In Copenhagen, visit Illums Bolighus, packed with all kinds of home furnishings, and have a gourmet lunch at Paustian, where refined contemporary furniture and accessories are installed in a building by the Danish architect Jørn Utzon (of Sydney Opera House fame). Enjoy the porcelain on display at Royal Copenhagen and Bodum Hus. Watch exquisite glass being blown at the Holmegaard Glass factory, about an hour south of town, or porcelain being hand-painted at the Smallegade factory of Royal Copenhagen in Frederiksberg, just north of central Copenhagen. Visit the Georg Jensen Museum, next door to the shop at Amagertorv 4, and the Kunstindustrimuseet (Museum of Decorative Art), with its rococo buildings, fine exhibits of European and Asian crafts, and excellent library.

Make a point of asking at the tourist board about any special exhibitions that might highlight the streamlined furniture-making traditions of Denmark in the '30s and '40s; true aficionados will want to overnight at the Radisson SAS Royal Hotel, which master architect Arne Jacobsen designed in 1960. Although it's filled with his trademark "egg" chairs, the feeling is even more intense in Suite 606, which is totally furnished in cool green Jacobsen furniture, including original swan and egg chairs. Make a point of stopping by the Dansk Design Center, close to the Townhall Square, which is a showcase for industrial design. Take the overnight train or fly to Stockholm.

SWEDEN **2 days.** Stroll around Stockholm's Gamla Stan (Old Town) and visit the 608-room Kungliga Slottet (Royal Palace). Be sure to walk over to Riddarholmen for a view of the 700-year-old Riddarholmskyrkan (Riddarholm Church). From the tower of the beautiful early 20th-century Stadshuset (City Hall)—with its handmade brickwork and golden mosaics—gaze over Stockholm's 14 islands and glittering, clean waters. Visit Skansen's open-air museum with 150 regional buildings and handicraft shops, ending with dinner, a concert, or outdoor entertainment. The Nationalmuseum has a fine collection of Scandinavian applied arts, while the Nordiska Museet documents daily life from the past 500 years. Noteworthy is the Vasamuseet's fabulous warship, raised from where it sank on its maiden voyage in 1628. Slightly outside the city, visit Ulriksdals Slott and park, or Millesgården, the Carl Milles Sculpture Garden, in Lidingö. If you can spend an extra day, take a ferry or drive to Gripsholms Slott or Drottningholms Slott, the royal residence. Alternatively, take a train to Växjö and see the Småland Museum's glass collection, which includes some amazing Swedish designs done in crystal. From Stockholm, take the overnight ferry to Helsinki.

FINLAND **5 days.** The Taideteollisuusmuseo (Museum of Art and Design) will give you an overview of the development of Finnish architecture and design. See the fine neoclassical Senaatintori (Senate Square) and the art nouveau buildings at Eira and Katajanokka, as well as Eliel Saarinen's Helsinki railway station from 1914. Don't miss Finlandiatalo, the concert hall designed by Finland's greatest architect, Alvar Aalto; the

Temppeliaukio Kirkko, hollowed out from rock with only its dome show-ing; or the magnificent sculpture commemorating the composer Jean Sibelius. The Gallen-Kallela Estate is a studio-castle in the National Ro-mantic style built on a rocky peninsula. It was designed by the artist Ak-seli Gallen-Kallela for his paintings, drawings, sculpture, textiles, and furniture. Fine china and pottery are displayed at the Hackman Factory Shop Arabia, and you can see fine textiles being made at the Marimekko factory. Rent a car to visit the Suomen Lasimuseo (Finnish Glass Mu-seum), 50 km (31 mi) north of Helsinki in Riihimäki, with permanent exhibits on glass-making and exhibitions of old Finnish glassware and crystal as well as works by contemporary designers. Stop by Hvitträsk, a turn-of-the-20th-century studio designed by and for three Finnish ar-chitects as a laboratory for their aesthetic principles.

From Helsinki take a ferry to Suomenlinna, a former island fortress from 1748, from which Taidekeskus Retretti (Retretti Art Center) is accessi-ble by boat. Also stop in at Tapiola, a Helsinki suburb designed by the top Finnish architects of the 1950s, whose planners sought to meld its architecture with its surroundings.

The Scandinavian tourist season peaks in June, July, and August, when daytime temperatures are often in the 70s (21°C to 26°C) and sometimes rise into the 80s (27°C to 32°C). Detailed temperature charts are below. In general, the weather is not overly warm, and a brisk breeze and brief rainstorms are possible anytime. Nights can be chilly, even in summer.

Visit in summer if you want to experience the delightfully long summer days. In June, the sun rises in Copenhagen at 4 AM and sets at 11 PM. Daylight lasts even longer farther north, making it possible to continue your sightseeing into the balmy evening. Many attractions extend their hours in summer, and many shut down altogether when summer ends. Fall, spring, and even winter are pleasant, despite the area's reputation for gloom. The days become shorter quickly, but the sun casts a golden light not seen farther south. On dark days, fires and candlelight will warm you indoors.

The Gulf Stream warms Denmark, the western coast of Norway, and Iceland, making winters in these areas similar to those in London. Even the harbor of Narvik, far to the north in Norway, remains ice-free year-round. Away from the protection of the Gulf Stream, however, northern Norway, Sweden, and Finland experience very cold, clear weather that attracts skiers; even Stockholm's harbor, well south in Sweden but facing the Baltic Sea, freezes over completely.

Climate

Below are average daily maximum and minimum temperatures for major Scandinavian cities.

🔁 Forecasts **Weather Channel Connection** ⊕ www.weather.com.

COPENHAGEN

Month	°F	°C	Month	°F	°C	Month	°F	°C
Jan.	36F	2C	May	61F	16C	Sept.	64F	18C
	28	– 2		46	8		52	11
Feb.	36F	2C	June	66F	19C	Oct.	54F	12C
	27	– 3		52	11		45	7
Mar.	41F	5C	July	72F	22C	Nov.	45F	7C
	30	– 1		57	14		37	3
Apr.	52F	11C	Aug.	70F	21C	Dec.	39F	4C
	37	3		57	14		34	1

HELSINKI

Month	°F	°C	Month	°F	°C	Month	°F	°C
Jan.	30F	– 1C	May	64F	18C	Sept.	53F	11C
	26	– 3		49	9		39	4
Feb.	34F	1C	June	60F	16C	Oct.	46F	8C
	24	– 4		48	9		36	2
Mar.	36F	2C	July	68F	20C	Nov.	32F	0C
	26	– 3		55	13		26	– 3
Apr.	46F	8C	Aug.	64F	18C	Dec.	32F	0C
	32	0		53	12		24	– 4

REYKJAVÍK

Month	°F	°C	Month	°F	°C	Month	°F	°C
Jan.	36F	2C	May	50F	10C	Sept.	52F	11C
	28	– 2		39			43	6
Feb.	37F	3C	June	54F	12C	Oct.	45F	7C
	28	– 2		45	7		37	3
Mar.	39F	4C	July	57F	14C	Nov.	39F	4C
	30	– 1		48	9		32	0
Apr.	43F	6C	Aug.	57F	14C	Dec.	36F	2C
	34	1		46	8		28	– 2

OSLO

Jan.	28F	– 2C	May	61F	16C	Sept.	60F	16C
	19	– 7		43	6		46	8
Feb.	30F	– 1C	June	68F	20C	Oct.	48F	9C
	19	– 7		50	10		38	3
Mar.	39F	4C	July	72F	22C	Nov.	38F	3C
	25	– 4		55	13		31	– 1
Apr.	50F	10C	Aug.	70F	21C	Dec.	32F	0C
	34	1		54	12		25	– 4

STOCKHOLM

Jan.	30F	– 1C	May	57F	14C	Sept.	59F	15C
	23	– 5		43	6		48	9
Feb.	30F	– 1C	June	66F	19C	Oct.	48F	9C
	23	– 5		52	11		41	5
Mar.	37F	3C	July	72F	22C	Nov.	41F	5C
	25	– 4		57	14		34	1
Apr.	46F	8C	Aug.	68F	20C	Dec.	36F	2C
	34	1		55	13		28	– 2

ON THE CALENDAR

DENMARK	
Mar.	The Snow Festival that takes place in Nuuk, Greenland, is best known for its snow-sculpture contest.
	The Nuuk Marathon draws a hardy crowd of runners.
	In Copenhagen, Denmark's—and the world's—oldest amusement park, Bakken, opens with much fanfare and a motorcycle parade through the city.
Apr.	Near the start of the month, the Drambuie World Ice Golf Championship takes place in Uummannaq, Greenland. Its 35 or so participants include some of the world's best.
	The Arctic Circle Race takes place for three days just outside Sisimiut.
Apr. 16	The Queen's Birthday is celebrated with the royal guard in full ceremonial dress as the royal family appears before the public on the balcony of Amalienborg.
Mid-Apr.–Sept.	Tivoli in Copenhagen twinkles with rides, concerts, and entertainment.
May	The Copenhagen Carnival includes boat parades in Nyhavn and costumed revelers in the streets.
June	The Around Fyn Regatta starts in Kerteminde.
	The Round Zealand Regatta, one of the largest yachting events in the world, starts and ends in Helsingør.
	The Aalborg Jazz Festival fills the city with four days of indoor and outdoor concerts, many of them free.
	The Viking Festival in Frederikssund, northwest of Copenhagen, includes open-air performances of a Viking play.
	On Midsummer's Night, Danes celebrate the longest day of the year with bonfires and picnics.
	Jazz fans descend on Silkeborg for the four-day Riverboat Jazz Festival, featuring international and local jazz bands.
June & July	The Roskilde Festival, the largest rock concert in northern Europe, attracts dozens of bands and more than 75,000 fans.
June 21	Greenland National Day celebrates the anniversary of Home Rule.
Late June	The luminous, northern tip of Denmark is at its liveliest during the annual Skagen Festival, showcasing international and local folk music.
July	The Copenhagen Jazz Festival gathers international and Scandinavian jazz greats for a week of concerts, many of them free.
July 4	The Fourth of July celebration in Rebild Park, near Aalborg, sets off the only foreign-sponsored American Independence Day festivities.
Mid-July	The Århus International Jazz Festival gathers world-renowned names for indoor and outdoor concerts.
	On the island of Fanø, off the coast of Jylland, the Sønderhodag Festival gets underway with dancing and music performed by locals in traditional garb.

Late Aug.	Folk music lovers from around the world head to the south of Jylland for the Tønder Folk Music Festival, which has been going strong since 1974. It features everything from blues, zydeco, and gospel to traditional Irish, Scottish, and American folk tunes.
Sept.	The 10-day Århus Festival, Denmark's most comprehensive fête, fills the city with concerts, sports, and theater.
	The Golden Days Festival celebrates the 19th-century cultural blossoming of Denmark through exhibits, readings, and performances.
Nov.	Fans of new and avant-garde concert music swarm to Odense for the annual Musikhøst (Music Harvest) festival, when concerts are held throughout the city.
Nov. & Dec.	Tivoli Gardens features its annual Christmas Market, with lots of decorations, gift ideas, and seasonal treats.
Dec. 24	If there's a time when Denmark is at its most *hygellig* (roughly translated, warm and cozy), it's during Christmas, a holiday that the Danes celebrate in great style. For Danes, it's Christmas Eve that's the main day. They dance around the tree while singing carols, and then feast on roast duck or goose with *ris à l'amande* (almond rice pudding) for dessert; an almond is hidden inside the pudding and whoever finds it receives a gift.
Dec. 31	Fireworks at the Town Hall Square are set off by local revelers.

FINLAND

Jan.	The Arctic Lapland Rally gets into gear in Rovaniemi.
Feb.	Shrove Tuesday celebrations throughout Finland include skiing, skating, and tobogganing events.
	Finlandia-hiihto is a 60-km (37-mi) ski event that begins and ends in Lahti.
	Weather permitting, the LumiLinna, the "world's biggest snow castle," is erected in the small town of Kemi, with concerts and church services held inside the structure.
Mar.	The Tar Ski Race in Oulu is the oldest cross-country ski trek (75 km[47 mi]) in the country.
	At the Oulu Music Festival for classical music, soloists and orchestras perform.
	The Porokuninkuusajot Reindeer Races are run in Inari at the end of the month.
	The Maria's Day church festival in Enontekiö includes reindeer racing and lassoing competitions.
	The Tampere International Short Film Festival features some of the best film in its category.
Apr.	April Jazz Espoo features foreign and Finnish performers in this Helsinki suburb.
	Rovaniemi hosts the World Cup in Ski Orienteering.

	The Tampere Biennale, held in even-number years, is a festival of contemporary music.
May	Vapunaatto and Vappu (May Day Eve and May Day) celebrations occur nationwide and include picnicking—and much drinking. There are joint student and worker celebrations.
	Native and foreign musicians come to jam at Kainuu Jazz Spring, which lasts for four days in Kajaani.
June	The Kuopio Dance Festival is the largest annual festival of dance art in the Nordic countries.
	The Naantali Music Festival soothes the ears of chamber music lovers in concerts at the medieval Abbey and other churches.
	Juhannus (Midsummer) is celebrated nationwide with bonfires and all-night boat cruises, starting on Midsummer Eve.
	Jutajaiset: The International Folklore Festival of Nightless Nights, in Rovaniemi, has traditional dance, music, and song during the season of the midnight sun.
	Avanti! Summer Sounds fest in Porvoo focuses on baroque and contemporary music.
	The Midnight Sun Film Festival unites established moviemakers and young celluloid hopefuls in Sodankylä, north of the Arctic Circle.
	The Big Band Festival, in Imatra near the Russian border, is a cheerful lakeside meeting of bands from all over the world, with plenty of free outdoor concerts.
	St. Petersburg's famed Mariinsky Theater regularly sends its performers to the Mikkeli Music Festival.
	At the end of the month, the Lakeside Blues Festival in Järvenpää enjoys the lively presence of many international stars, plus family events centered around Blues Street, downtown.
July	The Savonlinna Opera Festival, on a grand scale and a month long, is a festival of international opera staged at Olavinlinna Castle, Savonlinna.
	Around the first week of July, the Sata-Häme Accordion Festival in Ikaalinen (near Tampere), brings in 800 Finnish and foreign performers, with styles ranging from French musette to zydeco and Latin American.
	The Hanko Regatta is a popular open-sea sailing competition.
	Pori Jazz, Finland's premier international jazz festival offers a wide range of styles, including blues, in 100 concerts.
	The Kuhmo Chamber Music Festival brings international artists to eastern Finland for a week of music that's often thematically organized.
	The Kaustinen Folk Music Festival, in western Finland, also often includes dance events.
	The Ruisrock Festival, held in Turku's Kansanpuisto (People's Park), is Finland's oldest and largest rock festival.

	Finland's tango capital, Seinäjoki in Ostrobothnia, is the venue for the annual Tango Festival, where tango kings and queens are selected.
	The Lahti Organ Festival examines every aspect—not just ecclesiastical—of this versatile instrument.
	The Jyväskylä Arts Festival is one of the Finland's longest-established cultural events, with the country's oldest multi-art discussion forum.
Aug.	The Häme Castle Children's Festival in Hämeenlinna, focuses on a broad spectrum of arts events—drama, puppet theater, dance, concerts, and films—in the medieval castle and its grounds.
	Baroque through contemporary performances are put on during the Turku Music Festival.
	The Helsinki Festival means two weeks of dance, music, drama, and children's shows in the capital and its environs.
Oct.	The Baltic Herring Festival is the biggest market for fishermen's catches, held for one weekend on the quayside in Helsinki.
Nov.	Kaamos Jazz, a jazz fest, is held in Lapland's winter twilight, at Saariselkä/Tankavaara, near Ivalo.
Dec.	Independence Day (December 6) brings a parade to the candlelit Senate Square in Helsinki.
	Lucia Day is celebrated in Helsinki on December 13 with a concert at Finlandiatalo.
	New Year's celebrations vary, but the fireworks can be seen every year from Senate Square in Helsinki.
ICELAND	
Jan. 19–mid-Feb.	Traditional Icelandic foods and drinks are served at Þorri Banquets around the country.
Mar.–Apr.	From Palm Sunday to Easter Monday, fjord cruises, jazz concerts, and dances accompany a week of skiing at the Ski Festival in Ísafjörður.
Mid-May–mid-June	The biennial Reykjavík Arts Festival, held in even-number years, has hosted many renowned artists over its 30-year history.
First Sun. in June	Many coastal towns celebrate Sjómannadagur (Seamen's Day); in Reykjavík there are harborfront markets, rescue demonstrations, and rowing and swimming competitions.
June 17	Iceland National Day is cause for a nationwide party, with parades and outdoor dancing downtown in Reykjavík, Akureyri, and other towns.
Late June	The Arctic Open Golf Tournament is held, in the midnight sun, on the 18-hole golf course at Akureyri.
June & July	Just south of Reykjavík in Hafnarfjörður, the International Viking Festival celebrates the country's Viking heritage with a Viking village, living-history demonstrations, battle enactments, and cruises aboard a full-size Viking ship.

July & Aug.	The Skálholt Music Festival, at the south's Skálholt Cathedral, includes concerts of baroque and contemporary music every weekend.
First Mon. in Aug.	Bank Holiday Weekend draws large crowds for outdoor celebrations throughout the country. In Vestmannaeyjar (the Westman Islands) it's called *Þjóðhátíð* with an atmosphere akin to that of Rio's Carnival.
Mid-Aug.	Icelandic and European musicians give performances during the Kirkjubæjarklaustur Chamber Music Festival.
	The Reykjavík Marathon sends world-class distance runners on their annual race around the city.

NORWAY

Jan.	The Tromsø International Film Festival, Norway's largest and the world's most northerly such festival presents a cutting-edge program of feature movies and short films from around the world.
Feb.	Lillehammer's Winter Arts Festival has music, theater, and art exhibitions.
	The Røros Fair has been an annual tradition since 1854.
Mar.	Europe's largest dogsledding competition, the Finnmarksløpet (Finnmark Race) follows old mail routes across Finnmarksvidda.
	The Birkebeiner Race commemorates a centuries-old cross-country ski race from Lillehammer to Rena.
	In Oslo, the Holmenkollen Ski Festival features Nordic skiing events as well as breathtaking ski-jumping feats.
Mar. & Apr.	The Karasjok Easter Festival features a variety of concerts, theater performances, art exhibits, snowmobile rallies, and husky dog and reindeer races.
May	The Grete Waitz Race is a 5-km (3-mi), women-only race in Oslo.
	The festivities of the annual Bergen International Festival, customarily opened by the king, include dance, music, and theater performances.
May 17	Constitution Day brings out every Norwegian flag and crowds of marchers for parades and celebrations throughout the country.
June 23	Midsummer Night, called *Sankt Hans Afton*, is celebrated nationwide with bonfires, fireworks, and outdoor dancing.
	Meet fellow Norwegian Americans and Norwegians at the annual Emigration Festival in Stavanger.
	The Festspillene i Nord-Norge (North Norway Cultural Festival) in Harstad features a feast of cultural activities, including performance art, exhibitions, music, theater, and youth events.
July	The plays, exhibitions, concerts, and historic walking tours of the Kristindagene (Kristin Festival) pay tribute to the subject of *Kristin Lavransdatter*, the novel by Nobel prize–winning Sigrid Undset.

	Jazzaholics and international stars descend on Norway's west coast for the Molde International Jazz Festival, one of the longest-established in Europe. As well as theater performances and art exhibitions, there are over 50 free-of-charge concerts.
	The ExxonMobil Bislett Games attract leading international track and field athletes to the Bislett Stadium in Oslo.
Aug.	You'll find Scandinavian and international folk music, folk dancing, and folk songs at the Telemark International Folk Festival in the town of Bø, as well as jazz and blues concerts.
	The Peer Gynt Festival in Gudbrandsdalen brings art exhibits, children's activities, and open-air theater performances of Henrik Ibsen's *Peer Gynt*—as well as Edvard Grieg's music.
	The International Chamber Music Festival stages classical concerts at different venues in and around Stavanger.
	Near the end of the month, the Ibsen Stage Festival gets underway in Oslo, with stars from overseas participating. The festival is held in even-number years.
Sept.	The Oslo Marathon stretches 42 km (26 mi) through the streets of Oslo.
	For art lovers, the annual Høstutstillingen (Fall Exhibition) at Kunstnernes Hus (the Artists' House) is worth a visit.
Dec. 10	The Nobel Peace Prize is awarded—by invitation only—in Oslo.
SWEDEN	
Jan. 13	Knut signals the end of Christmas festivities and the "plundering" of the Christmas tree: Trinkets are removed from the tree, edible ornaments gobbled up, and the tree itself thrown out.
Feb.	A market held in Jokkmokk features both traditional Sámi (Lapp) artifacts and plenty of reindeer. It begins on the first Thursday and runs through Saturday.
	On Shrove Tuesday special buns called *semlor*—lightly flavored with cardamom, filled with almond paste and whipped cream—are traditionally placed in a dish of warm milk, topped with cinnamon, and eaten.
First Sun. in Mar.	The Vasalopp Ski Race goes 90 km (56 mi) from Sälen to Mora in Dalarna, and attracts entrants from all over the world.
Apr.	On Maundy Thursday, which marks the beginning of Easter celebrations, small girls dress up as witches and hand out "Easter letters" for small change or candy.
	On April 30, for the Feast of Valborg, bonfires are lit to celebrate the end of winter. The liveliest celebrations involve the students of the university cities of Uppsala and Lund.
May 1	Labor Day marches and rallies are held nationwide, and politicians give speeches at the town square.
	Tjejtrampet, one of the world's largest bicycle races for women, takes place in May as well.

June	In early June, the Restaurant Festival fills Stockholm's Kungsträdgården with booths offering inexpensive international and Swedish cuisine.
	Also in June is the Stockholm Marathon.
June 6	National Day is celebrated, with parades, speeches, and band concerts nationwide.
Mid–Late June	In mid-June comes the Hultsfred Festival, in southern Sweden. It's the country's largest, and wildest, rock festival, with major acts from all over the world.
	Midsummer Eve and Day celebrations are held on the Friday evening and Saturday that fall between June 20 and 26.
July	Since 1983 the Stockholm Jazz Festival has brought in the world's best jazz and blues musicians for a five-day festival of music and good cheer. It's held on Skeppsholmen, on a stage behind the Moderna Museet.
Aug.	Crayfish are a delicacy in Sweden, and the second Wednesday of August marks the Crayfish Premiere, when friends gather to eat them at outdoor parties.
Nov.	The Stockholm Film Festival brings world-class films, directors, and actors to the city.
	The Stockholm Open tennis tournament attracts top players for an indoor tournament at the Kungliga Tennishallen.
	The Stockholm International Horse Show, held at the Globen sports center, is a big draw.
Nov. 11	St. Martin's Day is celebrated primarily in the southern province of Skåne. Roast goose is served, accompanied by *svartsoppa*, a bisque made of goose blood and spices.
Dec.	For each of the four weeks of Advent, which leads up to Christmas, a candle is lit in a four-prong candelabra.
Dec. 10	Nobel Day sees the presentation of the Nobel prizes by the King of Sweden at a glittering banquet held in Stadshuset, Stockholm's City Hall.
Dec. 13	On Santa Lucia Day young girls are selected to be "Lucias"; they wear candles in their hair and sing hymns at ceremonies around the country.
Dec. 24	Christmas Eve is the principal day of Christmas celebration. Traditional Christmas dishes include ham, rice porridge, and *lutefisk* (dried cod soaked in lye and then boiled).
Dec. 31	New Year's Eve is the Swedes' occasion to set off an astounding array of fireworks. Every household has its own supply, and otherwise quiet neighborhood streets are full of midnight merrymakers.

FODOR'S CHOICE

The sights, restaurants, hotels, and other travel experiences on these pages are our editors' top picks—our Fodor's Choices. They're the best of their type in the area covered by the book—not to be missed and always worth your time. In the destination chapters that follow, you will find all the details.

LODGING

DENMARK

D'Angleterre, Copenhagen. This grande dame has hosted everyone from royalty to rock stars. Victor Borge was a regular and stayed in a suite bearing his name. The prim and proper staff is renowned for its attentiveness. $$$$

Hesselet, Nyborg, Fyn. Within the brick walls of this refined Anglo-Asian sanctuary, many rooms have a splendid view onto the nearby Storebæltsbro. $$$$

Radisson SAS Royal, Copenhagen. Towering over the heart of Copenhagen, this luxury hotel was designed "right down to the door handles" by the legendary Arne Jacobsen in 1960; the light-filled rooms and high-ceiling lobby are living museums to Jacobsen's chairs, lamps, and other furnishings. $$$$

Schackenborg Slotskro, Møgeltønder, Jylland. An intimate hotel with richly colored rooms, this is the official royal inn of nearby Schackenborg Castle, home to Prince Joachim and Princess Alexandra. $$$–$$$$

Hotel Dagmar, Ribe, Jylland. Denmark's oldest hotel has 16th-century charm to spare; half-timber walls, sloping wooden floors, and stained-glass windows in the lobby lead to the antique canopy beds and chaise longues in the bedrooms. $$–$$$

FINLAND

Hilton Helsinki Strand. The contemporary design of this Hilton, with its granite and marble atrium, and the beautiful waterfront vistas outside make this a grand place to spend your visit. $$$$

Radisson SAS Plaza Hotel, Helsinki. This Renaissance-style former office building is now a beautifully designed, contemporary hotel with a sophisticated restaurant and bar. $$$$

Scandic Hotel Continental, Helsinki. Popular with business travelers, this Helsinki institution is an efficient, modern hotel close to Finlandia Hall and the Finnish National Opera. $$$–$$$$

Kalastajatorppa, Helsinki. In the western Munkkiniemi neighborhood, just outside Helsinki, this hotel makes a wonderful Nordic seaside retreat. $$$

Lord Hotel, Helsinki. Fit for a king, this hotel is central and cozy, with a remarkable romantic art nouveau exterior and interior. $$$

Rantasipi Aulanko, Hämeenlinna. This hotel is the lap of luxury beside a lake in a beautifully landscaped park just outside town. $$$

Rivoli Jardin, Helsinki. A classy hotel in a town house, the Rivoli Jardin is in the heart of Helsinki's shopping and business center, but tranquil and free from traffic noise. $$$

ICELAND	**Hótel Borg,** Reykjavík. This art deco gem has tastefully decorated rooms and many quality amenities, from a generous breakfast to down comforters in all the guest rooms. $$$$
	Hótel Holt, Reykjavík. The luxuriously appointed rooms are a bit small, but the excellent service, fine restaurant, and central location more than compensate. $$$$
NORWAY	**Hotel Continental,** Oslo. With its elegant early-20th-century facade, the Continental is an Oslo landmark that continues to attract with gracious service and wonderful restaurants. $$$–$$$$
	Skarsnuten Hotell, Hemsedal. Perched like an eagle's nest, this mountainside hotel has spectacular views and many activities for kids and their parents. $$$–$$$$
	Dagali Hotell, Dagali. This charming chalet-style hotel, 2,870 feet above sea level is peaceful and secluded, with a wonderful, traditional kitchen and skiing facilities nearby. $$–$$$
	Landego Fyr, Bodø. Braving Vestfjord's pounding waves on Fyrholmen lighthouse rock is this red-and-white cast-iron lighthouse that dates from 1902. $–$$$
	Venabu Fjellhotell, Ringebu. There are no room televisions at this typically Norwegian, country hotel. Guests spend their time outdoors or socializing in the lounges. $$
SWEDEN	**Grand Hotel,** Stockholm. The city's showpiece, an 1874 landmark, is luxurious and has a glassed-in veranda overlooking the harbor. $$$$
	Berns, Stockholm. Discreet lighting; modern Italian furniture; and swank marble, granite, and wood inlays all work together to bring art-deco style to Berns, which has been open for business since the days of Strindberg. $$$–$$$$
	Diplomat, Stockholm. You never feel the Diplomat has to try too hard; Euro-chic meets quiet efficiency in an effortlessly stylish art-nouveau showpiece. $$$–$$$$
	Radisson SAS Grand Hotel, Saltsjöbaden. A white-stone confection in the fashionable Victorian resort outside Stockholm. The grandeur is pleasantly faded, the service perfectly deft. $$$
	Villa Källhagen, Stockholm. Peaceful grace, natural light, an affinity with the changing seasons and one of Sweden's best restaurants—all this is just minutes from bustling downtown Stockholm. $–$$$
	Elite Plaza, Göteborg. The palatial 1889 exterior encloses a stylish modern hotel with luxury and quiet elegance. All the original details remain, from stucco ceilings to the English mosaic floor. $$
	Hotel Continental, Malmö. The Continental is grand inside and out. The remarkable foyer has marble chandeliers and marble pillars and stairs. Every room is bright, modern, and unique. $$
	Grand Hotel, Mölle. It's not the plushest hotel in the world, but the turreted Grand has a cordial staff and an unrivaled view of the town below. The hotel's restaurant is also excellent. $–$$

BUDGET LODGING

DENMARK

Skovshoved, Copenhagen. Some of the larger rooms overlook the sea at this art-filled inn in Charlottenlund, only a short drive north of the Danish capital. $$

Den Gamle Arrest, Ribe, Jylland. This "Old Jail" served as Ribe's main prison from 1893 to 1989. The tiny cell windows and wrought iron gates have been preserved, but the rooms themselves have been creatively and comfortably refashioned. $–$$

Hotel Vallø Slotskro, Vallø, Sjælland. South of Køge, this rural inn has charming rooms and personable service only a short walk over a moat and through a manicured park from fairytale Vallø Slot. $

Hotel Ydes, Odense, Fyn. This hotel maintains comfortable rooms for travelers in town to see the Hans Christian Andersen sights. ¢

Skansin Guesthouse, Tórshavn, Faroe Islands. Faorese hospitality reigns at this private home, which occupies a central location on the archipelago. ¢

NORWAY

Rainbow Hotel Bristol, Bergen. The Bristol is minutes away from many popular attractions, with rooms that are small but comfortable. ¢–$$

Rainbow Cecil, Oslo. An inexpensive hotel right in the center of town, with basic rooms for the on-the-go traveler. $

SWEDEN

Columbus Hotel, Stockholm. Ideal for a quiet vacation, the Columbus is an oasis of calm in the busy urban streets of Södermalm. ¢–$$

Hotel Gustav Wasa, Stockholm. Right next to Odenplan Square, the Gustav Wasa is a great budget option, a friendly hotel in the heart of downtown. $

Hotel Winn, Falun. Built in rustic Dalarna style, this small, cozy hotel in the town center is the place to unwind after a long day's sightseeing. $

Marina Plaza, Helsingborg. The use of space, style, and elegance—especially in the loftlike atrium—lends a decidedly modern appeal to this lodging. $

Pärlan, Stockholm. Entering the Pearl, a bed-and-breakfast on a quiet street in Östermalm, is like walking into a home from the 19th century. $

Royal, Göteborg. Small, family owned, and traditional, the Royal is a taste of old-fashioned Swedish elegance in the center of bustling Göteborg. $

Hotel Dalecarlia, Tällberg. There's a homey feel to this first-class hotel, which has good lake views, a spa and fitness center, and wonderful food. ¢

Rum i Backen, Vaxholm. This pretty, early-20th-century wooden house on Vaxholm's main street is a charming, family-run B&B with just one guest room. ¢

RESTAURANTS	
DENMARK	**Falsled Kro,** Millinge, Fyn. This former smuggler's hideaway is now an utterly romantic and elegant inn with a fabulous French-Danish restaurant. This is one of the most sought-after spots in the country and reservations are imperative. *$$$$*
	Kommandanten, Copenhagen. The ever-changing menu here is inventive and fresh with unusual combinations such as oxtail and lobster stew as well as pigeon on a bed of vegetables and fava beans. *$$$$*
	Marie Louise, Odense, Fyn. Renowned for its French cuisine, Marie Louise serves superb concoctions that include salmon scallop with bordelaise sauce and grilled veal with lobster-cream sauce. *$$$–$$$$*
	Seafood, Århus, Jylland. This harborside seafood restaurant is famous for its bouillabaisse heaped with tiger prawns, squid, Norwegian lobster, and mussels. Aioli comes on the side. *$$–$$$$*
	Reinwalds, Copenhagen. Open, airy, and cozy, this spot serves fine neo-European food to equal some of the best spots in town, but at lower prices. Wines are superb, yet reasonable, and the service is envied by other eateries. *$$$*
	Skipperhuset, Fredensborg, Sjælland. At this 18th-century former boathouse on the grounds of the queen's summer residence, meals eaten alfresco on the shore of Lake Esrum at sunset are a special delight. The wild Baltic salmon is a favorite for lunch and dinner. *$$–$$$*
	Ida Davidsen, Copenhagen. More than 100 years old, this Copenhagen institution serves an elaborate menu of smørrebrød that knows no rival. *$$*
FINLAND	**Alexander Nevski,** Helsinki. Czarist-era dishes are the specialty at this Russian restaurant. Try the roast bear in a pot. *$$$$*
	Havis Amanda, Helsinki. Across the street from the Havis Amanda statue, its namesake restaurant specializes in fish dishes with central European accents. *$$$–$$$$*
	Bridges, Helsinki. This atrium restaurant in the Hilton Helsinki Strand serves steaks and burgers alongside Finnish classics like smoked Arctic char. *$–$$*
	Kosmos, Helsinki. This cozy restaurant is a lunchtime favorite for its hearty Finnish meat-and-potatoes dishes. *$–$$*
	Töölönranta, Helsinki. You can watch the water-cooled wok in the open kitchen turn out stir-fried specials, or opt for more traditional arctic char, wild duck, and lamb dishes at Töölönranta. *$–$$*
	Kynsilaukka, Helsinki. Beautifully prepared dishes highlight garlic at this cozy restaurant. The garlic cream soup is a winner. *¢–$$*
ICELAND	**Gallery Restaurant,** Reykjavík. The wild game and seafood here is expertly prepared. Try the gravlax, the reindeer carpaccio, and the rack of lamb. *$$$–$$$$*

Hjá Sigga Hall á Oðinsvé, Reykjavík. Iceland's celebrity chef Siggi Hall is adventurous with his fish, lamb, and game dishes, meticulously prepared and beautifully presented to his hungry patrons. $$$–$$$$

Við Tjörnina, Reykjavík. Innovative dishes and good lunchtime prices make this restaurant one of the best in town for seafood. $$$

NORWAY

Bagatelle, Frogner. Widely recognized as one of the city's best restaurants Chef Eyvind Hellstrøm's modern Norwegian cuisine and superb service attracts the who's who of Oslo society. $$$$

De Fem Stuer, Holmenkollen. Near the famous Holmenkollen ski jump, this restaurant has first-rate views and food with strong classic roots by Chef Jorn Dahl. $$$$

Bølgen & Moi Briskeby, Oslo. Modern and innovative, restaurant duo Toralf Bølgen and Trond Moi keep harvesting culinary successes, from Oslo to Stavanger. $$$–$$$$

Kafé Kristall, Bergen. This small, intimate restaurant is one of the most fashionable in town, serving modern interpretations of traditional Norwegian dishes. $$$–$$$$

Magma, Oslo. Sonja Lee and partner Laurent Surville bring their Provence and London experience to their sun-kissed Mediterranean restaurant and its sumptuous seasonal dishes. $$$–$$$$

Oro, Oslo. Terje Ness's Mediterranean-style restaurant is one of Norway's most celebrated restaurants. The next-door tapas bar, Plata, is great for a lighter meal. $$$–$$$$

Lubbenes, Molde. In a Swiss-style chalet, this is one of the best restaurants in the region, with a special emphasis on seafood. $$$

N. B. Sørensen's Dampskibsexpedition, Stavanger. Norwegian emigrants waited here before boarding steamships crossing the Atlantic to North America 150 years ago. The historic wharfhouse is now a restaurant and bar with an exciting Norwegian and international menu. $–$$$

Værtshuset Bærums Verk, Bærum. Norway's oldest restaurant, specializing in traditional Norwegian cuisine is a must on any itinerary that includes the neighboring iron works in this suburb of Oslo. $$

SWEDEN

Edsbacka Krog, Stockholm. Traditional Swedish cuisine is taken to new heights at this phenomenal restaurant in an old inn just outside town. $$$–$$$$

Wedholms Fisk, Stockholm. The traditional Swedish fare here, especially the fresh fish, is simple but outstanding. $$$–$$$$

Bon Lloc, Stockholm. Enjoy Mediterranean-influenced Swedish cuisine at this elegant restaurant. $$$

Fredsgatan 12, Stockholm. The city's politicians and style mavens gather here for the Swedish-Asian fare, which is some of the best grub in town. $$$

Le Village, Göteborg. The food here is exceptional, especially the seasonal meat dishes. If you like any of the furnishings, you can buy them from the store next door. *$$$*

Tranan, Stockholm. The food here is Swedish with a touch of French, and is so good it'll make you want to keep coming back. *¢–$$$*

Cyrano, Göteborg. A little piece of southern France in Sweden, this superb, authentically Provençal bistro is an absolute must. *$–$$*

Salt & Brygga, Malmö. Not only is the Mediterranean cooking here done with organic produce, but ecologically friendly materials have been used for everything from the wall paint to the table linens and the staff's uniforms. *$–$$*

BUDGET RESTAURANTS

DENMARK

Told & Snaps, Copenhagen. The long menu of Danish smørrebrød delights prices out more reasonably than at the iconic Ida Davidsen. *$$*

Riz Raz, Copenhagen. This crowded Middle Eastern joint near Strøget maintains an inexpensive all-you-can-eat buffet full of spicy fare. *$–$$*

Bregninge Mølle, Tåsinge, Fyn. Although the traditional Danish dishes here are enjoyable, the real attraction is the 360-degree view of the surrounding sea, islands, and countryside from this converted windmill. *¢–$$*

Bryggeriet Sct. Clemens, Århus, Jylland. This local haunt is primarily a watering hole, but food is served and this is a great place to meet some Århus residents and students. *¢–$$*

NORWAY

Fjellstua, Ålesund. This traditional, mountaintop restaurant has tremendous views over the surrounding peaks, islands, and fjords. Try the Norwegian salmon, and lamb. *$*

Brasserie 45, Oslo. This romantic, candlelit brasserie on the second floor overlooks the fountain on Karl Johans Gate. *¢–$*

Pizza da Mimmo, Oslo. Named for owner Domenico Giardina, a.k.a. Mimmo, this is Oslo's best pizzeria. *¢–$*

SWEDEN

Pelican, Stockholm. This traditional, working-class drinking hall serves hearty Swedish fare and lots of beer. *¢–$$*

Lottas, Ystad. The steak is beautifully cooked and presented at this typical southern Swedish restaurant. *$*

Herman's, Stockholm. Try the buffet-style vegetarian meals at this Södermalm institution. *¢–$*

Il Forno, Stockholm. Go to Il Forno for some of the best brick-oven pizza north of the Mediterranean—be sure to sit outside in summer. *¢–$*

Jukkasjärvi Wärdshus, Jukkasjärvi. The Norrland cuisine—characterized by reindeer, wild berries, mushrooms, dried and smoked meats, salted fish, fermented herring, and rich sauces using thick creams—is superb at this hotel restaurant. ¢

Köpmangården, Sunne. If you blink, you may miss this tiny bar and restaurant on a residential street, serving delicious, hearty meals. ¢

CASTLES & CHURCHES

DENMARK

Christiansborg Slot, Copenhagen. The seat of Parliament, and once a year the queen of Denmark still receives guests in this 12th-century castle. Parts of the building are open to the public.

Domkirke, Roskilde, Sjælland. Once the capital of Denmark, Roskilde still has its magnificent 15th-century cathedral, where Danish royalty has been buried for the past half millennium.

Egeskov Slot, Kværndrup, Fyn. One of the best preserved island-castles in Europe, Egeskov Slot is topped with copper spires and ringed by lush Renaissance and baroque gardens. One of the world's largest mazes is also here.

Kronborg Slot, Helsingør, Sjælland. William Shakespeare never saw this castle, but that didn't stop him from using it as the setting for Hamlet. Don't miss the Flemish tapestries displayed in the "small room."

Østerlars Kirke, Bornholm. The largest of Bornholm's unique round churches—considered some of the finest specimens of Scandinavian medieval architecture—this whitewashed marvel was built of boulders and slabs of limestone.

Rosenborg Slot, Copenhagen. The only castle still owned by Denmark's royal family, Rosenborg Slot is home to the crown jewels and many other treasures. The castle is surrounded by the royal gardens, and delightful walks are offered in summer.

Tilsandede Kirke, Skagen, Jylland. Perched at Denmark's northernmost, wave-thrashed tip, the 18th-century Sand-Buried Church is covered by dunes.

Valdemars Slot, Troense, Fyn. One of Denmark's largest castles not owned by the state, the regal Valdemars Slot has sumptuous, richly decorated rooms and libraries as well as a yachting museum.

FINLAND

Temppeliaukio Kirkko, Helsinki. A copper dome is the only part of this modern church visible from aboveground, since the church itself is carved into the rock outcropping.

Tuomiokirkko, Tampere. The cathedral houses some of the best-known masterpieces of Finnish art.

Uspenskin Katedraali, Helsinki. Glistening onion domes top this Russian Orthodox cathedral, built in 1868 in the Byzantine-Slavonic style.

ICELAND

Dómkirkjan, Reykjavík. A place of worship has existed on this site of this Lutheran cathedral since AD 1200. Among the treasured items inside is a baptismal font carved and donated by the famous 19th-century master sculptor Bertel Thorvaldsen.

Hallgrímskirkja, Reykjavík. Named for 17th-century hymnist Rev. Hallgrímur Pétursson, Hallgrím's Church has a high tower that's a city landmark.

NORWAY

Akershus Slott og Festning, Oslo. On the brow of the Oslo fjord, this stone fortress, castle, and royal residence dates to the 1300s.

Det Kongelige Slottet, Oslo. A neoclassical beauty in vanilla and cream, the Royal Palace can only be visited on summer tours. Come here early on May 17th and watch the royal family wave to a sea of its subjects.

Ishavskatedralen, Tromsø. A symbol of Tromsø, the cathedral is meant to represent North Norwegian nature, culture, and faith. The cathedral's shape evokes a Sámi tent and the iciness of a glacier.

Nidaros Cathedral, Trondheim. Since the Middle Ages, Norway's kings have been crowned and blessed here. Princess Martha Louise married Ari Behn here in spring 2002.

Stave churches, around Norway. A distinctive symbol of Norway's culture, these medieval churches are always worth a visit. Those in Bergen and Ål and at the Norsk Folkemuseum in Oslo are standouts.

SWEDEN

Drottningholms Slott, Stockholm. One of the most delightful European palaces, this is a kind of miniature Versailles, full of insights into how mid-18th-century royalty lived.

Kalmar Slott, Småland. Sweden's best-preserved Renaissance castle is set on a commanding site on the Baltic shore. Sections of it date back 800 years.

Kungliga Slottet, Stockholm. In this magnificent granite edifice you can tour the State Apartments; the Royal Armory; and the Treasury, where the crown jewels are kept.

Tjolöholms Slott, Tjolöholm, Swedish Riviera. This eccentric castle, built at the turn of the 20th century by a Scottish manufacturer, has amazing interiors full of what were then state-of-the-art touches.

MUSEUMS & MONUMENTS

DENMARK

Brandts Klædefabrik, Odense, Fyn. Inside an impressively refurbished textile factory is a complex of museums covering three main areas: photography, graphic art, and fine art.

Lejre Forsøgscenter, near Roskilde, Sjælland. This living open-air museum has many hands-on activities that convey the character of daily life for the Vikings.

Louisiana, Humlebæk, Sjælland. A half-hour drive north of Copenhagen, this world-class modern-art collection displays the likes of Warhol and Picasso and even has a thoughtfully laid out children's wing.

Ny Carlsberg Glyptotek, Copenhagen. The best collection of Etruscan art outside Italy and Europe's finest gathering of Roman portraits are both here. There's also an impressive collection of rare pre-impressionist works by such masters as Gauguin and Rodin.

Ordrupgaard, Charlottenlund, Sjælland. Housed in a 1918 manor house just north of Copenhagen, this antiques-filled museum showcases one of the largest collections of French impressionism in Europe outside of France; also impressive is their extensive collection of Danish Golden Age painters.

Trapholt Museum for Moderne Kunst, Kolding, Jylland. Sprawling along the banks of the Kolding Fjord, the light-filled Trapholt is one of the largest modern-art museums outside Copenhagen.

FINLAND

Lusto Finnish Forest Museum, Punkaharju. Every aspect of Finland's close relationship with its most abundant natural resource is examined here.

Nykytaiteenmuseo (Kiasma), Helsinki. American architect Steven Holl's controversial arc design for the Museum of Contemporary Art provides a striking background to the statue of General Mannerheim in the heart of the city.

Ortodoksinen Kirkkomuseo, Kuopio. Religious art from monasteries was brought to Kuopio after World War II, creating a rare collection of Orthodox art in this small town in the Lakelands.

Seurasaaren Ulkomuseo, Helsinki. Old farmhouses and barns were brought from all over Finland to create this outdoor museum of Finnish rural architecture.

Taidekeskus Retretti, Punkaharju. This uniquely designed modern art complex, with a cavern section built into the Punkaharju ridge, is the setting for outdoor summer concerts.

ICELAND

Árbæjarsafn, Reykjavík. Tour this outdoor village of 18th- and 19th-century houses that are furnished with period antiques and display household utensils and tools.

Þjóðleikhús, Reykjavík. Construction on the basalt-black edifice of the National Theater began in 1928. The concrete interior ceiling—an amazing architectural accomplishment in its day—mimics polygonal basalt columns occurring in Icelandic nature.

NORWAY

Munchmuseet, Oslo. Pay homage here to Norway's most famous artist, Edvard Munch, who painted that 20th-century icon, *The Scream.* He bequeathed thousands of his works to Oslo upon his death in 1944.

Norsk Fjellmuseum, Lom. In the picturesque mountain town of Lom, the Norwegian Mountain Museum pays tribute to the Norway's mountainous landscape and history. It covers topics such as early mountaineering, hunting, and mountain railway- and road-building.

Norsk Folkemuseum, Bygdøy, Oslo. See Norway in a day at one of Europe's largest open-air museums. An original stave church, sod houses, and other buildings span the country's past.

Norsk Oljemuseum, Stavanger. The Petroleum Museum lays out the story of Norway's oil industry, showing the impact the commodity has had on the country's recent history.

Troldhaugen, outside Bergen. Composer Edvard Grieg played host to European luminaries here in his home, whose name means Hill of the Trolls. The salon seems frozen in time; you may think for a moment that the maestro might walk through the door.

Vikingskiphuset, Oslo. In a white-stone building resembling a Viking burial mound, the Vikings Ship Museum has three well-preserved ships and other relics that tell the story of these seafaring peoples.

SWEDEN

Carl Larsson Gården, Sundborn. The cottage here contains an exceptional assortment of beautiful rooms and works of art.

Marinmuseum, Karlskrona. One of the oldest museums in Sweden, opened in 1752, the Naval Museum is a UNESCO Heritage Site.

Motala Motormuseum. Packed with pristine cars and the paraphernalia of bygone days, the Motor Museum brings the past to life with music and a sense of fun.

Nationalmuseum, Stockholm. The museum's collection of paintings and sculptures is made up of about 12,500 works, with an emphasis on Swedish and Nordic art.

Skansen, Stockholm. Farmhouses, windmills, barns, and churches are just some of the buildings brought from around the country and preserved in this museum.

Stadshuset, Stockholm. A trip to the top of the tower of this ornate building, is rewarded by a breathtaking panorama of the city and Riddarfjärden.

Vasamuseet, Stockholm. The *Vasa,* a warship that sank on its maiden voyage in 1628, was raised nearly intact in 1961 and now has its own museum.

Zorn Museet, Mora. Many fine paintings by Anders Zorn (1860–1920), Sweden's leading impressionist painter, are displayed in this museum next to the beautiful house he built in his hometown.

QUINTESSENTIAL SCANDINAVIA

DENMARK

Legoland, Billund, Jylland. This paean to the modular Danish building blocks offers lots of fun for the kids, but the exhibits and general construction of the park provides plenty of interesting aspects for people of all ages.

Setting Foot on Greenland's Ice Cap, Greenland. Whether you get there by foot or skis, dogsled or helicopter, you must stand for a few moments on the massive ice sheet that covers all but the thin rocky crescents of the subcontinent's coast. The scale and grandeur of the frozen landscape is this remote destination's biggest attraction.

Tivoli Gardens, Copenhagen. The magnificent flower beds and wonderful fairy-tale architecture make this park the international icon and tourist attraction it is. There's no need to try the roller coaster; just walking around the meticulously kept grounds is a treat.

FINLAND

Cloudberry-picking, Lapland. A traditional activity in August, it's a good way to get outside and experience the vast wilderness that is Lapland.

The fall colors in Lapland are known as *ruska*. The colors are at their most warm and vibrant in early September, if you're fortunate enough to be in the region at this time.

ICELAND

Basking in the warmth of a huge New Year's Eve bonfire and wondering which is more spectacular—the man-made nationwide, fireworks celebration, or the serene, supernatural beauty of the iridescent northern lights

NORWAY

Bergen's seven mountains are a magical escape from the bustle of the city—you can hike up to the top of Ulriken, the tallest mountain, for some gorgeous views of the city.

The midnight sun at the Nordkapp (North Cape) attracts thousands of visitors a year, who come to bask in its glow.

Riding horseback across Hardangervidda, Europe's largest mountain plateau, you will see lakes, hills, and arctic plants and wildlife.

Walking on Jostedalsbreen, Europe's largest glacier, should only be attempted in summer, with a qualified guide, but is a fantastic way to experience the unique geography of this region.

SWEDEN

Cruising on a steamship around the Stockholm archipelago, which has more than 25,000 islands and skerries, is a timeless delight in the summer months.

Dogsledding, Norrland. You can take a combined dogsledding and skiing trip in Norrland—a popular destination is the Kebnekaise mountains, but it's only suitable for the really hardy and adventuresome.

Hiking, Ørland. The island of Ørland is an excellent place for a wander, with its ancient runic stones, nature reserve, and extraordinary birdlife.

Midsummer celebrations around Lake Siljan attract thousands of people every year. A good place to be based during the festivities is Leksand.

SMART TRAVEL TIPS

Finding out about your destination before you leave home means you won't squander time organizing everyday minutiae once you've arrived. You'll be more streetwise when you hit the ground as well, better prepared to explore the aspects of Scandinavia that drew you here in the first place. The organizations in this section can provide information to supplement this guide; contact them for up-to-the-minute details, and consult the A to Z sections that end each chapter for facts on the various topics as they relate to the countries of Scandinavia. Happy landings!

AIR TRAVEL

BOOKING

When you book **look for nonstop flights** and **remember that "direct" flights stop at least once.** Try to avoid connecting flights, which require a change of plane. For more booking tips and to check prices and make on-line flight reservations, log on to www. fodors.com.

CARRIERS

▶ Major Airlines **American** ☎ 800/433-7300 ⊕ www.aa.com to Stockholm. **Delta** ☎ 800/221-1212 ⊕ www.delta.com to Copenhagen. **Finnair** ☎ 800/950-5000 ⊕ www.finnair.com to Helsinki, Stockholm, Copenhagen, Reykjavík, Oslo. **Icelandair** ☎ 800/223-5500 ⊕ www.icelandair.com to Reykjavík. **SAS** ☎ 800/221-2350 ⊕ www.scandinavian.net.

CHECK-IN & BOARDING

Assuming that not everyone with a ticket will show up, airlines routinely overbook planes. When everyone does, airlines ask for volunteers to give up their seats. In return, these volunteers usually get a certificate for a free flight and are rebooked on the next flight out. If there are not enough volunteers, the airline must choose who will be denied boarding. The first to get bumped are passengers who checked in late and those flying on discounted tickets, so **get to the gate and check in as early as possible,** especially during peak periods.

Always **bring a government-issued photo I.D. to the airport;** even when it's not required, a passport is best.

CUTTING COSTS

The **SAS Visit Scandinavia/Europe Air Pass** offers up to eight flight coupons for one-way travel within and between Scandinavian cities (and participating European cities such as Frankfurt, Paris, and London). Most one-way tickets for domestic travel within each Scandinavian country cost $65; one-way fares between Scandinavian countries are usually $75, unless you are venturing into the far north, Lapland, Iceland, or Greenland (these flights range from $115 to $225). These passes can only be bought in conjunction with a round-trip ticket between North America and Europe on SAS and must be used within three months of arrival. SAS also provides family fares—children between 2 and 17 and a spouse can receive 50% off the full fare of business class tickets with the purchase of one full-fare business class ticket. Contact SAS for information.

The least expensive airfares to Scandinavia must usually be purchased in advance and are nonrefundable. It's smart to **call a number of airlines,** and when you are quoted a good price, **book it on the spot—** the same fare may not be available the next day. Always **check different routings** and look into using different airports. Travel agents, especially low-fare specialists (⇨ Discounts), are helpful.

Consolidators are another good source. They buy tickets for scheduled international flights at reduced rates from the airlines, then sell them at prices that beat the best fare available directly from the airlines, usually without restrictions. Sometimes you can even get your money back if you need to return the ticket. Carefully read the fine print detailing penalties for changes and cancellations, and **confirm your consolidator reservation with the airline.**
🛃 Consolidators **Cheap Tickets** ☎ 800/377-1000. **Discount Airline Ticket Service** ☎ 800/576-1600. **Unitravel** ☎ 800/325-2222. **Up & Away Travel** ☎ 212/889-2345. **World Travel Network** ☎ 800/409-6753.

ENJOYING THE FLIGHT

For more legroom, **request an emergency-aisle seat.** Don't sit in the row in front of the emergency aisle or in front of a bulkhead, where seats may not recline. If you have dietary concerns, **ask for special meals when booking.** These can be vegetarian, low-cholesterol, or kosher, for example. On long flights, try to maintain a normal routine, to help fight jet lag. At night, **get some sleep.** By day, **eat light**

meals, **drink water** (not alcohol), and **move around the cabin** to stretch your legs. For additional jet-lag tips consult *Fodor's FYI: Travel Fit & Healthy* (available at bookstores everywhere).

FLYING TIMES

Flying time from New York to Reykjavík is 5½ hours; to Copenhagen, 7¾ hours; to Stockholm, 8 hours; to Oslo, 7½ hours; to Helsinki, 8 hours. From Los Angeles to Copenhagen, flying time is 9¾ hours; to Helsinki, 11¼ hours. From London's Heathrow Airport, flying time to Helsinki is 3 hours; to Stockholm, 2¼ hours; to Reykjavík, 3 hours. From Sydney and major cities in New Zealand, the flight to any Scandinavian country will be more than 20 hours, and will require at least one transfer.

HOW TO COMPLAIN

If your baggage goes astray or your flight goes awry, complain right away. Most carriers have representatives in departure terminals and baggage collection halls and require that you **file a claim immediately.**
🛃 Airline Complaints **U.S. Department of Transportation Aviation Consumer Protection Division** ✒ C-75, Room 4107, Washington, DC 20590 ☎ 202/366-2220 ⊕ www.dot.gov/airconsumer. **Federal Aviation Administration Consumer Hotline** ☎ 800/322-7873.

WITHIN SCANDINAVIA

Scandinavia is larger than it looks on a map, and many native travelers choose to fly between the capital cities, using trains and buses for domestic travel. Flying times between Copenhagen, Helsinki, Oslo, and Stockholm range between one and two hours; a direct flight from Copenhagen or Stockholm to Reykjavík is approximately three hours.

If you are traveling from south to north in Norway, Sweden, or Finland, flying is often a necessity: Stavanger in southern Norway is as close to Rome, Italy, as it is to the northern tip of Norway.

For international travelers, one or two stopovers can often be purchased more cheaply along with an international ticket. Icelandair, which connects all of the Scandinavian capitals with North America, gives the option to extend a layover in Reykjavík for up to three days at no extra charge; Icelandair also arranges Fly and

Drive specials, which offer discounts on car rental and hotel fees if booking a flight to one of the Scandinavian capitals.

The cheapest tickets that SAS sells are round-trip, include a Saturday night lay-over, and must be bought within Scandi-navia three weeks ahead of time. Ask about low rates and discounts for hotels and car rental in connection with SAS tick-ets. Low-price round-trip weekend excur-sions from one Scandinavian capital to another (minimum three-day stay) can be bought one day in advance from SAS.

AIRPORTS

Major gateways to Scandinavia include Denmark's **Kastrup International Airport** 10 km (6 mi) southeast of Copenhagen; Finland's **Helsinki-Vantaa International Airport,** 20 km (14 mi) north of Helsinki; Iceland's **Keflavík International Airport,** 50 km (31 mi) southwest of Reykjavík; Norway's **Gardermoen Airport,** about 53 km (33 mi) northeast of Oslo; and Swe-den's **Arlanda International Airport** 41 km (26 mi) north of Stockholm.

F Arlanda International Airport ☎ 46/87976100 ⊕ www.lfv.se/eng/index.asp. Helsinki-Vantaa In-ternational Airport ☎ 358/200-4636, €0.60 per minute ⊕ www.ilmailulaitos.com. Kastrup Interna-tional Airport ☎ 45/32-31-32-31 ⊕ www.cph.dk. Keflavík International Airport ☎ 354/425-0600 for airport information, 011-354-425-0200 for flight information [Icelandair] ⊕ www.randburg.com/airport. Gardermoen Airport ☎ 47/815-50-250 ⊕ www.osl.no/english.

BIKE TRAVEL

BIKES IN FLIGHT

Most airlines accommodate bikes as lug-gage, provided they are dismantled and boxed. Airlines sell bike boxes, which are often free at bike shops, for about $5 (it's at least $100 for bike bags). Interna-tional travelers can sometimes substitute a bike for a piece of checked luggage at no charge; otherwise, the cost is about $100. Domestic and Canadian airlines charge $25–$50.

BOAT & FERRY TRAVEL

Taking a ferry isn't only fun, it's often nec-essary in Scandinavia. Many companies arrange package trips, some offering a rental car and hotel accommodations as part of the deal. The word "ferry" can be

deceptive; generally, the ferries are more like small-scale cruise ships, with several dining rooms, sleeping quarters, shopping, pool and sauna, and entertainment.

Ferry crossings often last overnight. The trip between Copenhagen and Oslo, for example, takes approximately 16 hours; most lines leave at about 5 PM and arrive about 9 the next morning. The direct cruise between Stockholm and Helsinki takes 12 hours, usually leaving at about 6 PM and arriving the next morning at 9. Trips from Germany to Oslo and Helsinki generally take about 20 hours; crossings to Reykjavík from Bergen tend to last about two days (25 hours to the Faroe Islands, and another 24 hours to Iceland). The shortest ferry route runs between Hels-ingør, Denmark, and Helsingborg, Swe-den; it takes only 20 minutes.

CAR FERRIES

Travel by car in Scandinavia often necessi-tates travel by ferry. Some well-known ve-hicle and passenger ferries run between Copenhagen, Denmark, and Malmö, Sweden; between Helsingør, Denmark, and Helsingborg, Sweden; between Copenhagen and Göteborg, Sweden; and between Stockholm, Sweden, and Helsinki, Finland. Taking a car on the Helsingør/Helsingborg ferry costs between SKr 255 and SKr 275 (about $24–$26 or £16–£18.50) one-way.

Transporting a car between Stockholm and Helsinki costs about € 52 during high season and € 29 during low season (about $47 and $26 or £32 and £18). Round-trip fares are cheaper, and on weekends the Øresund Runt pass (for crossing between Copenhagen and Malmö one way and Helsingborg and Helsingør the other way) costs only SKr 475 (about $45 or £31).

FARES & SCHEDULES

F Color Line ⊘ Box 30, DK-9850 Hirsthals, Denmark ☎ 45/99-56-20-00 ☐ 45/99-56-20-20 ✉ Hjortneskaia, Box 1422 Vika, N-0115 Oslo, Norway ☎ 47/22-94-44-00 ☐ 47/22-83-04-30 ✉ Color Scandi Line, Torksholmen, S-45 200 Strømstad, Sweden ☎ 46/52662000 ☐ 46/52614669 ✉ Color Line GmbH, Postfach 6080, 24121 Kiel, Germany ☎ 49/431-7300-300 ☐ 49/431-7300-400 ⊕ www.colorline.no. ScandLines ⊘ Box 1, DK-3000 Helsingør, Denmark ☎ 45/33-15-15-15 ☐ 45/33-15-10-20 ✉ Knutpunkten 43, S-252 78 Helsingborg, Sweden ☎ 46/42186100 ☐ 46/42186049 ⊕ www.scandlines.com.

FERRIES FROM ENGLAND

The chief operator between England and many points within Scandinavia, Holland, and Germany is DFDS Seaways, with ships connecting Harwich and Newcastle to Esbjerg, Denmark; Kristiansand, Norway; and Amsterdam. Fjord LineFjordline offers the only direct service from England to Bergen and northern Norway.

🚢 Major Operators **DFDS Seaways** ✉ Sankt Annae Plads 30, DK-1295 Copenhagen, Denmark ☎ 45/33-42-33-42 📠 45/33-42-33-41 ✉ DFDS Seaways Travel Centre, Scandinavia House, Parkeston Quay, Harwich, Essex, U.K. CO12 4QG ☎ 44/8705-333-000 📠 44/1255-244-382 ✉ DFDS Seaways USA Inc., 6555 NW 9th Ave., Suite 207, Fort Lauderdale, FL 33309 ☎ 800/533-3755 📠 954/491-7958 ✉ Box 8895, Scandiahamnen, S-402 72 Göteborg, Sweden ☎ 46/31650610 ⊕ www.seaeurope.com. **Fjord Line** ⚓ Skoltegrunnskaien, Box 7250, N-5020 Bergen, Norway ☎ 47/55-54-88-00 📠 47/55-54-86-01 ✉ Tyne Commission Quay, North Shields NE29 6EA, Newcastle, U.K. ☎ 44/191-296-1313 📠 44/191-296-1540 ⊕ www.fjordline.co.ukwww.fjordline.com.

PLYING SCANDINAVIAN WATERS

Connections from Denmark to Norway and Sweden are available through DFDS and the Stena Line. Fjord Line sails along the magnificent west coast of Norway. Connections to the Faroe Islands and Iceland from Norway and Denmark are available through the Smyril Line. Silja Line and Viking Line offer a variety of cruises to Finland, with departures from Stockholm to Mariehamn in the Åland archipelago, Turku (Åbo) and Helsinki (Helsingfors), and a crossing from Umeå to Vaasa.

🚢 Major Operators **DFDS Seaways** (⇨ Ferries from England). **Fjord Line** (⇨ Ferries from England). **Silja Line** ✉ Mannerheimintie 2, 00100 Helsinki, Finland ☎ 358/9-18041 📠 358/9-1804279 ✉ Kungsgatan 2, S-111 43 Stockholm, Sweden ☎ 46/86663512 or 46/8222140 📠 46/86119162 or 46/92316066 ✉ C/o DFDS Seaways, Scandinavia House, Parkeston Quay, Harwich, Essex, U.K. England CO12 4QG ☎ 44/1255-240-240 📠 44/255-244-382 ✉ c/o Norwegian Coastal Voyage, Inc./Bergen Line Service, 405 Park Ave., New York, NY 10022 ☎ 212/319-1300 or 800/323-7436 📠 212/319-1390 ⊕ www.silja.com/english. **Smyril Line** ✉ J. Brocksgøta 37, Box 370, FO-110 Tórshavn, Faroe Islands ☎ 298/34-59-00 📠 298/34-59-50 ✉ Slottsgate 1, Box 4135 Dreggen, N-5835 Bergen, Norway ☎ 47/55-32-09-70 📠 47/55-96-02-72

⊕ www.smyril-line.com. **Stena Line** ✉ Trafikhamnen, DK-9900 Frederikshavn, Denmark ☎ 45/96-20-02-00 📠 45/96-20-02-80 ✉ PB 764, Sentrum, N-0106 Oslo, Norway ☎ 47/23-17-91-00 📠 47/23-17-90-60 ✉ Stena Line AB, S-405 19 Göteborg, Sweden ☎ 46/317040000 📠 46/31858595 ⊕ www.stenaline.com. **Viking Line** ✉ Mannerheimintie 14, 00100 Helsinki, Finland ☎ 358/9-12351 📠 358/9-647075 ⊕ www.vikingline.fi.

BUS TRAVEL

Bus tours can be effective for smaller regions within Norway, Sweden, Finland, and Denmark, but all have excellent train systems, which offer much greater coverage in less time than buses. Buses do, however, tend to be a less expensive mode of transport in Scandinavia, and are necessary if you're traveling without a car between smaller towns in Lapland, the Danish islands, and Iceland. Detailed information on bus routes is available through local tourist offices.

CUTTING COSTS

Eurolines offers 15-, 30-, and 60-day passes for unlimited travel between Stockholm, Copenhagen, and Oslo, and more than 20 destinations throughout Europe.

CAMERAS & PHOTOGRAPHY

The *Kodak Guide to Shooting Great Travel Pictures* (available at bookstores everywhere) is loaded with tips.

🚢 Photo Help **Kodak Information Center** ☎ 800/242-2424.

EQUIPMENT PRECAUTIONS

Don't pack film and equipment in checked luggage, where it is much more susceptible to damage. X-ray machines used to view checked luggage are becoming much more powerful and therefore are much more likely to ruin your film. Always **keep film and tape out of the sun.** Carry an extra supply of batteries, and **be prepared to turn on your camera or camcorder** to prove to security personnel that the device is real. Always **ask for hand inspection of film,** which becomes clouded after repeated exposure to airport X-ray machines, and **keep videotapes away from metal detectors.**

CAR RENTAL

Rates in Stockholm begin at $60 a day and $175 a week for a manual economy car without air-conditioning and with unlimited mileage. Rates in Oslo begin at $70 a day and $284 a week. Rates in Helsinki begin at $70 a day and $287 a week, and in Copenhagen, car rentals can begin at $60 a day and $190 a week. This does not include tax on car rentals, which is 25% in Sweden and Denmark, 24% in Norway and Iceland, and 22% in Finland. A service charge is usually added, which ranges from $15–$25.

Major Agencies Alamo ☎ 800/522-9696, 020/8759-6200 in the U.K. ⊕ www.alamo.com. **Avis** ☎ 800/331-1084, 800/879-2847 in Canada, 02/9353-9000 in Australia, 09/525-1982 in New Zealand, 0870/606-0100 in U.K. ⊕ www.avis.com. **Budget** ☎ 800/527-0700, 0870/156-5656 in U.K. ⊕ www.budget.com. **Dollar** ☎ 800/800-6000, 0124/622-0111 in U.K. where it's affiliated with Sixt, 02/9223-1444 in Australia ⊕ www.dollar.com. **Hertz** ☎ 800/654-3001, 800/263-0600 in Canada, 020/8897-2072 in U.K., 02/9669-2444 in Australia, 09/256-8690 in New Zealand ⊕ www.hertz.com **National Car Rental** ☎ 800/227-7368, 020/8680-4800 in U.K. ⊕ www.nationalcar.com.

CUTTING COSTS

To get the best deal, **book through a travel agent who will shop around.** Do **look into wholesalers,** companies that do not own fleets but rent in bulk from those that do and often offer better rates than traditional car-rental operations. Payment must be made before you leave home.

Wholesalers Auto Europe ☎ 207/842-2000 or 800/223-5555 ⎙ 207/842-2222 ⊕ www.autoeurope.com. **Europe by Car** ☎ 212/581-3040 or 800/223-1516 ⎙ 212/246-1458 ⊕ www.europebycar.com. **DER Travel Services** ✉ 9501 W. Devon Ave., Rosemont, IL 60018 ☎ 800/782-2424 ⎙ 800/282-7474 information, 800/860-9944 brochures ⊕ www.dertravel.com. **Kemwel Holiday Autos** ☎ 800/678-0678 ⎙ 914/825-3160 ⊕ www.kemwel.com.

INSURANCE

When driving a rented car you are generally responsible for any damage to or loss of the vehicle. Before you rent, see what coverage your personal auto-insurance policy and credit cards provide.

Before you buy collision coverage, check your existing policies—you may already be covered. However, collision policies that car-rental companies sell for European rentals usually do not include stolen-vehicle coverage.

REQUIREMENTS & RESTRICTIONS

Ask about age requirements: Several countries require drivers to be over 20 years old, but some car-rental companies require that drivers be at least 25. In Scandinavia your own driver's license is acceptable for a limited time; check with the country's tourist board before you go. An International Driver's Permit is a good idea; it's available from the American or Canadian Automobile Association, or, in the United Kingdom, from the Automobile Association or Royal Automobile Club.

SURCHARGES

Before you pick up a car in one city and leave it in another, **ask about drop-off charges or one-way service fees,** which can be substantial. Note, too, that some rental agencies charge extra if you return the car before the time specified in your contract. To avoid a hefty refueling fee, **fill the tank just before you turn in the car,** but be aware that gas stations near the rental outlet may overcharge.

CAR TRAVEL

Excellent, well-marked roads make driving a great way to explore Scandinavia, but it can be an expensive choice. Ferry costs can be steep, and reservations are vital. Tolls on some major roads add to the expense, as do the high fees for city parking; tickets for illegal parking are painfully costly.

Also be aware that there are relatively low legal blood-alcohol limits and tough penalties for driving while intoxicated in Scandinavia; Iceland, Finland and Sweden have zero-tolerance laws. Penalties include suspension of the driver's license and fines or imprisonment and are enforced by random police roadblocks in urban areas. In addition, an accident involving a driver with an illegal blood-alcohol level usually voids all insurance agreements, so the driver becomes responsible for his own medical bills and damage to the cars.

In a few remote areas, especially in Iceland and northern Norway, Sweden, and Finland, road conditions can be unpredictable, and careful planning is required for safety's sake. Several mountain and highland roads in these areas close during winter—when driving in remote areas like these, especially in winter, it is best to let someone know your travel plans. It is also wise to **use a four-wheel-drive vehicle** and to **travel with at least one other car** in these areas.

Keep your headlights on at all times; this is required by law in most of Scandinavia. Also by Scandinavian law, everyone, including infants, must **wear seat belts.**

AUTO CLUBS

▶ In Australia **Australian Automobile Association** ☎ 02/6247–7311.
▶ In Canada **Canadian Automobile Association CAA** ☎ 613/247–0117.
▶ In New Zealand **New Zealand Automobile Association** ☎ 09/377–4660.
▶ In the U.K. **Automobile Association AA** ☎ 0990/500–600. **Royal Automobile Club RAC** ☎ 0990/722–722 membership, 0345/121–345 insurance.
▶ In the U.S. **American Automobile Association** ☎ 800/564–6222.

GASOLINE

Gasoline in Scandinavia costs roughly four times the typical U.S. price.

CHILDREN IN SCANDINAVIA

In Scandinavia children are to be seen *and* heard and are genuinely welcome in most public places.

If you are renting a car, don't forget to **arrange for a car seat** when you reserve. For general advice about traveling with children, consult *Fodor's FYI: Travel with Your Baby* (available in bookstores everywhere).

DISCOUNTS

Children are entitled to discount tickets (often as much as 50% off) on buses, trains, and ferries throughout Scandinavia, as well as reductions on special City Cards. Children under age 12 pay 75% of the adult fare and children under age 2 pay 10% on SAS round-trips. There are no restrictions on the children's fares when booked in economy class. "Family fares," only available in business class, are also worth looking into (⇨ Cutting Costs *in* Air Travel).

With the Scanrail Pass (⇨ Train Travel)— good for rail journeys throughout Scandinavia—children under age 4 (on lap) travel free; those ages 4–11 pay half-fare and those ages 12–25 can get a Scanrail Youth Pass, providing a 25% discount off the adult fare.

FLYING

If your children are age 2 or older, **ask about children's airfares.** As a general rule, infants under 2 not occupying a seat fly at greatly reduced fares or even for free. When booking, **confirm carry-on allowances** if you're traveling with infants. In general, for babies charged 10% of the adult fare you are allowed one carry-on bag and a collapsible stroller; if the flight is full, the stroller may have to be checked or you may be limited to less.

Experts agree that it's a good idea to use safety seats aloft for children weighing less than 40 pounds. Airlines set their own policies: U.S. carriers usually require that the child be ticketed, even if he or she is young enough to ride free, since the seats must be strapped into regular seats. Do **check your airline's policy about using safety seats during takeoff and landing.** And since safety seats are not allowed everywhere in the plane, get your seat assignments early.

When reserving, **request children's meals or a freestanding bassinet** if you need them. But note that bulkhead seats, where you must sit to use the bassinet, may lack an overhead bin or storage space on the floor. For all airlines servicing Scandinavia, it is necessary to reserve children's and baby meals at least 24 hours in advance; travel of an unaccompanied minor should be confirmed at least three days prior to the flight.

LODGING

Most hotels in Scandinavia allow children under a certain age to stay in their parents' room at no extra charge, but others charge for them as extra adults; be sure to **find out the cutoff age for children's discounts.**

SIGHTS & ATTRACTIONS

Places that are especially appealing to children are indicated by a rubber-duckie icon (☺) in the margin.

CONSUMER PROTECTION

Whenever shopping or buying travel services in Scandinavia, **pay with a major credit card,** if possible, so you can cancel payment or get reimbursed if there's a problem. If you're doing business with a particular company for the first time, **contact your local Better Business Bureau and the attorney general's offices** in your state and (for U.S. businesses) the company's home state as well. Have any complaints been filed? Finally, if you're buying a package or tour, always **consider travel insurance** that includes default coverage (⇨ Insurance).

⏹ BBBs Council of Better Business Bureaus ✉ 4200 Wilson Blvd., Suite 800, Arlington, VA 22203 ☎ 703/276-0100 🖷 703/525-8277 ⊕ www.bbb.org.

CRUISE TRAVEL

To learn how to plan, choose, and book a cruise-ship voyage, consult *Fodor's FYI: Plan & Enjoy Your Cruise* (available in bookstores everywhere).

⏹ Cruise Lines DFDS Seaways ✉ Sankt Annae Plads 30, DK-1295 Copenhagen, Denmark ☎ 45/33-42-33-42 🖷 45/33-42-33-41 ✉ DFDS Seaways Travel Centre, Scandinavia House, Parkeston, Harwich, Essex, U.K. CO12 4QG ☎ 44/8705-333-000 🖷 44/1255-244-382 ✉ DFDS Seaways USA Inc., 6555 NW 9th Ave., Suite 207, Fort Lauderdale, FL 33309 ☎ 800/533-3755 🖷 954/491-7958 ✉ Box 8895, Scandiahamnen, S-402 72 Göteborg, Sweden ☎ 46/3165060 ⊕ www.seaeurope.com. **Fjord Line** ⏏ Skoltegrunnskaien, Box 7250, N-5020 Bergen, Norway ☎ 47/55-54-88-00 🖷 47/55-54-86-01 ✉ Tyne Commission Quay, North Shields NE29 6EA, Newcastle, U.K. ☎ 44/191-296-1313 🖷 44/191-296-1540 ⊕ www.fjordline.co.uk

CUSTOMS & DUTIES

When shopping, **keep receipts** for all purchases. Upon reentering the country, **be ready to show customs officials what you've bought.** If you feel a duty is incorrect or object to the way your clearance was handled, note the inspector's badge number and ask to see a supervisor. If the problem isn't resolved, write to the appropriate authorities, beginning with the port director at your point of entry.

IN AUSTRALIA

Australian residents who are 18 or older may bring home $A400 worth of souvenirs and gifts (including jewelry), 250 cigarettes or 250 grams of tobacco, and 1,125 ml of alcohol (including wine, beer, and spirits). Residents under 18 may bring back $A200 worth of goods. Prohibited items include meat products. Seeds, plants, and fruits need to be declared upon arrival.

⏹ Australian Customs Service Regional Director ⏏ Box 8, Sydney, NSW 2001, Australia ☎ 02/9213-2000 🖷 02/9213-4000 ⊕ www.customs.gov.au.

IN CANADA

Canadian residents who have been out of Canada for at least seven days may bring home C$750 worth of goods duty-free. If you've been away fewer than seven days but more than 48 hours, the duty-free allowance drops to C$200; if your trip lasts 24–48 hours, the allowance is C$50. You may not pool allowances with family members. Goods claimed under the C$750 exemption may follow you by mail; those claimed under the lesser exemptions must accompany you. Alcohol and tobacco products may be included in the seven-day and 48-hour exemptions but not in the 24-hour exemption. If you meet the age requirements of the province or territory through which you reenter Canada, you may bring in, duty-free, 1.14 liters (40 imperial ounces) of wine or liquor *or* 24 12-ounce cans or bottles of beer or ale. If you are 19 or older you may bring in, duty-free, 200 cigarettes and 50 cigars. Check ahead of time with the Canada Customs Revenue Agency or the Department of Agriculture for policies regarding meat products, seeds, plants, and fruits.

You may send an unlimited number of gifts worth up to C$60 each duty-free to Canada. Label the package UNSOLICITED GIFT—VALUE UNDER $60. Alcohol and tobacco are excluded.

⏹ Canada Customs and Revenue Agency ✉ 2265 St. Laurent Blvd. S, Ottawa, Ontario K1G 4K3, Canada ☎ 204/983-3500 or 506/636-5064, 800/461-9999 in Canada ⊕ www.ccra-adrc.gc.ca.

IN NEW ZEALAND

Homeward-bound residents 17 or older may bring back $700 worth of souvenirs and gifts. Your duty-free allowance also includes 4.5 liters of wine or beer; one 1,125-ml bottle of spirits; and either 200 cigarettes, 250 grams of tobacco, 50 cigars, or a combination of the three up to 250 grams. Prohibited items include meat products, seeds, plants, and fruits.

⏹ New Zealand Customs Custom House ✉ 50 Anzac Ave., Box 29, Auckland, New Zealand ☎ 09/300-5399 🖷 09/359-6730 ⊕ www.customs.govt.nz.

IN SCANDINAVIA

Limits on what you can bring in duty-free vary from country to country. **Check with individual country tourist boards for limits on alcohol, cigarettes, and other items.** Also be careful to check before bringing food of any kind into Iceland: uncooked meat and uncooked milk and egg products are all prohibited.

IN THE U.K.

If you are a U.K. resident and your journey was wholly within the European Union (EU), you won't have to pass through customs when you return to the United Kingdom. If you plan to bring back large quantities of alcohol or tobacco, check EU limits beforehand. From countries outside the European Union, including Iceland and Norway, you may bring home, duty-free, 200 cigarettes or 50 cigars; 1 liter of spirits or 2 liters of fortified or sparkling wine or liqueurs; 2 liters of still table wine; 60 ml of perfume; 250 ml of toilet water; plus £145 worth of other goods, including gifts and souvenirs. If returning from outside the EU, prohibited items include meat products, seeds, plants, and fruits.

🗂 **HM Customs and Excise** ✉ St. Christopher House, Southwark, London, SE1 OTE, U.K. ☎ 020/ 7928-3344 🌐 www.hmce.gov.uk.

IN THE U.S.

U.S. residents who have been out of the country for at least 48 hours (and who have not used the $400 allowance or any part of it in the past 30 days) may bring home $400 worth of foreign goods duty-free.

U.S. residents age 21 and older may bring back 1 liter of alcohol duty-free. In addition, regardless of your age, you are allowed 200 cigarettes and 100 non-Cuban cigars. Antiques, which the U.S. Customs Service defines as objects more than 100 years old, enter duty-free, as do original works of art done entirely by hand, including paintings, drawings, and sculptures.

You may also mail or ship packages home duty-free: up to $200 worth of goods for personal use, with a limit of one parcel per addressee per day (except alcohol or tobacco products or perfume worth more than $5); label the package PERSONAL USE and attach a list of its contents and their retail value. Do not label the package UNSOLICITED GIFT or your

duty-free exemption will drop to $100. Mailed items do not affect your duty-free allowance on your return.

🗂 **U.S. Customs Service** ✉ 1300 Pennsylvania Ave. NW, Room 6.3D, Washington, DC 20229 🌐 www.customs.gov ☎ 202/354-1000 inquiries ✉ Complaints c/o 1300 Pennsylvania Ave. NW, Room 5.4D, Washington, DC 20229 ✉ Registration of equipment c/o, Office of Passenger Programs ☎ 202/927-0530.

EATING & DRINKING

Scandinavia's major cities offer a full range of dining choices, from traditional to international restaurants. The restaurants we list are the cream of the crop in each price category. Properties indicated by an ✕▢ are lodging establishments whose restaurant warrants a special trip.

Restaurant meals are a big-ticket item throughout Scandinavia, but there are ways to keep the cost of eating down. Take full advantage of the large buffet breakfast often included in the cost of a hotel room. At lunch, look for the "menu" that offers a set two- or three-course meal for a set price, or limit yourself to a hearty appetizer. Some restaurants now include a trip to the salad bar in the dinner price. At dinner, pay careful attention to the price of wine and drinks, since the high tax on alcohol raises these costs considerably. For more information on affordable eating, *see* Money Matters.

MEALS & SPECIALTIES

The surrounding oceans and plentiful inland lakes and streams provide Scandinavian countries with an abundance of fresh fish and seafood: salmon, herring, trout, and seafood delicacies are mainstays, and are prepared in countless ways. Elk, deer, reindeer, and lamb feed in relatively unspoiled areas in Iceland and northern Norway, Sweden, and Finland, and have the succulent taste of wild game. Berries and mushrooms are still harvested from the forests; sausage appears in a thousand forms, as do potatoes and other root vegetables such as turnips, radishes, rutabaga, and carrots. Some particular northern tastes can seem unusual, such as the fondness for pickled and fermented fish—to be sampled carefully at first—and a universal obsession with sweet pastries, ice cream, and chocolate.

Other novelties for the visitor might be the use of fruit in main dishes and soups, or sour milk on breakfast cereal, or preserved fish paste as a spread for crackers, or the prevalence of tasty, whole-grain crisp breads and hearty rye breads. The Swedish *smörgåsbord* (a kind of buffet meal) and its Scandinavian cousins are less common these days, but are still the traveling diner's best bet for breakfast. A smörgåsbord usually comes with a wide range of cheeses, fresh fish, and vegetables alongside meat and breads and other starches.

MEALTIMES

Unless otherwise noted, the restaurants listed in this guide are open daily for lunch and dinner. Meals in Scandinavia are taken early and many restaurants, particularly in rural areas, will close mid-evening.

RESERVATIONS & DRESS

Reservations are always a good idea: we mention them only when they're essential or not accepted. Book as far ahead as you can, and reconfirm as soon as you arrive. We mention dress only when men are required to wear a jacket or a jacket and tie.

WINE, BEER & SPIRITS

Restaurants' markups on alcoholic beverages are often very high in Scandinavia: as much as four times that of a standard retail price.

DISABILITIES & ACCESSIBILITY

Facilities for travelers with disabilities in Scandinavia are generally good, and most of the major tourist offices offer special booklets and brochures on travel and accommodations. Most Scandinavian countries have organizations that offer advice to travelers with disabilities, and can give information on public and local transportation, sights and museums, hotels, and special interest tours. Notify and make all local and public transportation and hotel reservations in advance to ensure a smooth trip. ⚑ Local Resources **Rullaten ry** ✉ Pajutie 7, FIN-02770 Espoo, Finland ☎ 358/9-805-7393 ⊕ www.rullaten.fi. **DHR De Handikappades Riksförbund** ✆ Box 47305, Katrinebergsvägen 6, 100 74 Stockholm, Sweden ☎ 46/86858000 ⊕ www.dhr.se/english.htm. **The Norwegian Association of the Disabled** ✆ Box 9217 Gronland, N-0134 Oslo,

Norway ☎ 47/22-17-02-55 ✆ 47/22-17-61-77 ⊕ www.nhf.no.

LODGING

Best Western offers properties with wheelchair-accessible rooms in Helsinki, Oslo, Stockholm, and just outside Copenhagen. If wheelchair-accessible rooms on other floors are not available, ground-floor rooms are provided. ⚑ Wheelchair-Friendly Chain **Best Western** ☎ 800/528-1234.

RESERVATIONS

When discussing accessibility with an operator or reservations agent, **ask hard questions.** Are there any stairs, inside *or* out? Are there grab bars next to the toilet *and* in the shower/tub? How wide is the doorway to the room? To the bathroom? For the most extensive facilities, **opt for newer accommodations.**

SIGHTS & ATTRACTIONS

Although most major attractions in the Scandinavian capitals present no problems, winding cobblestone streets in the older sections of cities may be challenging for travelers with disabilities, especially in Stockholm's Gamla Stan (Old Town).

TRANSPORTATION

With advance notice, most airlines, buses, and trains can arrange assistance for those requiring extra help with boarding. Contact each individual company at least one week in advance, or ideally at the time of booking.

Confirming ahead is especially important when planning travel to less populated regions. The smaller planes and ferries often used in such areas are not all accessible. ⚑ Complaints **Aviation Consumer Protection Division** (⇨ Air Travel) for airline-related problems. **Civil Rights Office** ✉ U.S. Department of Transportation, Departmental Office of Civil Rights, S-30, 400 7th St. SW, Room 10215, Washington, DC 20590 ☎ 202/366-4648 ✆ 202/366-9371 ⊕ www.dot.gov/ost/docr/index.htm for problems with surface transportation. **Disability Rights Section** ✆ U.S. Department of Justice, Civil Rights Division, Box 66738, Washington, DC 20035-6738 ☎ 202/514-0301 or 800/514-0301, 202/514-0383 TTY, 800/514-0383 TTY ✆ 202/307-1198 ⊕ www.usdoj.gov/crt/ada/adahom1.htm for general complaints.

TRAVEL AGENCIES

In the United States, the Americans with Disabilities Act requires that travel firms serve the needs of all travelers. Some agencies specialize in working with people with disabilities.

⚑ Travelers with Mobility Problems **Access Adventures** ✉ 206 Chestnut Ridge Rd., Scottsville, NY 14624 ☎ 716/889-9096 ✎ dltravel@prodigy.net, run by a former physical-rehabilitation counselor. **CareVacations** ✉ No. 5, 5110-50 Ave., Leduc, Alberta T9E 6V4, Canada ☎ 780/986-6404 or 877/478-7827 🖷 780/986-8332 ⊕ www.carevacations.com, for group tours and cruise vacations. **Flying Wheels Travel** ✉ 143 W. Bridge St., Box 382, Owatonna, MN 55060 ☎ 507/451-5005 or 800/535-6790 🖷 507/451-1685 ⊕ www.flyingwheelstravel.com.

DISCOUNTS & DEALS

Be a smart shopper and **compare all your options** before making decisions. A plane ticket bought with a promotional coupon from travel clubs, coupon books, and direct-mail offers or on the Internet may not be cheaper than the least expensive fare from a discount ticket agency. And always keep in mind that what you get is just as important as what you save.

DISCOUNT RESERVATIONS

To save money, **look into discount reservations services** with toll-free numbers, which use their buying power to get a better price on hotels, airline tickets, even car rentals. When booking a room, always **call the hotel's local toll-free number** (if one is available) rather than the central reservations number—you'll often get a better price. Always ask about special packages or corporate rates.

When shopping for the best deal on hotels and car rentals, **look for guaranteed exchange rates,** which protect you against a falling dollar. With your rate locked in, you won't pay more, even if the price goes up in the local currency.

⚑ Airline Tickets ☎ 800/247-4537.
⚑ Hotel Rooms **International Marketing & Travel Concepts** ☎ 800/790-4682 ⊕ www.imtc-travel.com. **Players Express Vacations** ☎ 800/458-6161 ⊕ www.playersexpress.com. **Steigenberger Reservation Service** ☎ 800/223-5652 ⊕ www.srs-worldhotels.com. **Travel Interlink** ☎ 800/888-5898 ⊕ www.travelinterlink.com. **Turbotrip.com** ☎ 800/473-7829 ⊕ www.turbotrip.com.

PACKAGE DEALS

Don't confuse packages and guided tours. When you buy a package, you travel on your own, just as though you had planned the trip yourself. Fly–drive packages, which combine airfare and car rental, are often a good deal. If you **buy a rail–drive pass,** you may save on train tickets and car rentals. All Eurail- and Europass holders get a discount on Eurostar fares through the Channel Tunnel. Also check rates for Scanrail Passes (⇨ Train Travel).

ELECTRICITY

To use electric-powered equipment purchased in the United States or Canada, **bring a converter and adapter.** The electrical current in Scandinavia is 220 volts, 50 cycles alternating current (AC); wall outlets take Continental-type plugs, with two round prongs.

If your appliances are dual-voltage, you'll need only an adapter. Don't use 110-volt outlets marked FOR SHAVERS ONLY for high-wattage appliances such as blow-dryers. Most laptops operate equally well on 110 and 220 volts and so require only an adapter.

EMERGENCIES

Ambulance, fire, and police assistance is available 24 hours in Scandinavia.
⚑ Denmark, Finland, Iceland, Norway, Sweden ☎ 112.

GAY & LESBIAN TRAVEL

Just as many Scandinavian countries were at the forefront of women's rights at the turn of the 20th century (Finland, for instance, was the first European country to grant women the right to vote, in 1906), Scandinavia has also had a liberal attitude toward gays and lesbians. The governments of Denmark, Sweden, Finland, and Norway grant to same-sex couples the same, or nearly the same, rights as their heterosexual counterparts, and Iceland allows gay couples joint custody of a child.

Reykjavík, Copenhagen, and Stockholm in particular have active, although not large, gay communities and nightlife.
⚑ Gay- & Lesbian-Friendly Travel Agencies **Different Roads Travel** ✉ 8383 Wilshire Blvd., Suite 902, Beverly Hills, CA 90211 ☎ 323/651-5557 or 800/429-8747 🖷 323/651-3678 ✎ lgernert@tzell.

com. **Kennedy Travel** ⊠ 314 Jericho Turnpike, Floral Park, NY 11001 ☎ 516/352-4888 or 800/237-7433 🖷 516/354-8849 ⊕ www.kennedytravel.com. **Now Voyager** ⊠ 4406 18th St., San Francisco, CA 94114 ☎ 415/626-1169 or 800/255-6951 🖷 415/626-8626 ⊕ www.nowvoyager.com. **Skylink Travel and Tour** ⊠ 1006 Mendocino Ave., Santa Rosa, CA 95401 ☎ 707/546-9888 or 800/225-5759 🖷 707/546-9891 ⊕ www.skylinktravel.com, serving lesbian travelers.

HOLIDAYS

In general, all Scandinavian countries celebrate New Year's Eve and Day, Good Friday, Easter and Easter Monday, May Day (May 1; celebrated as Labor Day for many of the countries), Midsummer Eve and Day (although its date varies by country), Christmas (as well as Christmas Eve and Boxing Day, the day after Christmas).

On major holidays such as Christmas, most shops close or operate on a Sunday schedule. On the eves of such holidays, many shops are also closed all day or are open with reduced hours.

On May Day, the city centers are usually full of people, celebrations and parades. During Midsummer, at the end of June, locals flock to the lakes and countryside to celebrate the beginning of long summer days with bonfires and other festivities.

The following holidays are not celebrated throughout Scandinavia entirely, only in particular countries.

Denmark: Maundy Thursday; First Day of Summer, Apr. 25; National Day, June 17; Bank Holiday Monday, Aug. 5.

Finland: Epiphany, Jan. 6; May Day Eve, Apr. 30; All Saint's Day, Nov. 1; Independence Day, Dec. 6.

Iceland: Maundy Thursday; First Day of Summer, Apr. 25; Pentecost, May 19; Independence Day, June 17; Worker's Day, Aug. 5.

Norway: Maundy Thursday; Constitution Day, May 17; Pentecost; St. Olav's Day, July 29.

Sweden: Epiphany, Jan. 6; Ascension; Pentecost Monday, All Saint's Day (observed the first Sat. after Oct. 30).

INSURANCE

The most useful travel-insurance plan is a comprehensive policy that includes coverage for trip cancellation and interruption, default, trip delay, and medical expenses (with a waiver for pre-existing conditions).

Without insurance you will lose all or most of your money if you cancel your trip, regardless of the reason. Default insurance covers you if your tour operator, airline, or cruise line goes out of business. Trip-delay covers expenses that arise because of bad weather or mechanical delays. Study the fine print when comparing policies.

If you're traveling internationally, a key component of travel insurance is coverage for medical bills incurred if you get sick on the road. Such expenses are not generally covered by Medicare or private policies. U.K. residents can buy a travel-insurance policy valid for most vacations taken during the year in which it's purchased (but check pre-existing-condition coverage). British and Australian citizens need extra medical coverage when traveling overseas.

Always **buy travel policies directly from the insurance company**; if you buy them from a cruise line, airline, or tour operator that goes out of business you probably will not be covered for the agency or operator's default, a major risk. Before making any purchase, **review your existing health and homeowner's policies** to find what they cover away from home.

🚩 Travel Insurers In the U.S.: **Access America** ⊠ 6600 W. Broad St., Richmond, VA 23230 ☎ 800/284-8300 🖷 804/673-1491 ⊕ www.etravelprotection.com. **Travel Guard International** ⊠ 1145 Clark St., Stevens Point, WI 54481 ☎ 715/345-0505 or 800/826-1300 🖷 800/955-8785 ⊕ www.travelguard.com.

🚩 Insurance Information In the U.K.: **Association of British Insurers** ⊠ 51-55 Gresham St., London EC2V 7HQ, U.K. ☎ 020/7600-3333 🖷 020/7696-8999 ⊕ www.abi.org.uk. In Canada: **RBC Travel Insurance** ⊠ 6880 Financial Dr., Mississauga, Ontario L5N 7Y5, Canada ☎ 905/791-8700, 800/668-4342 in Canada 🖷 905/816-2498 ⊕ www.royalbank.com. In Australia: **Insurance Council of Australia** ⊠ Level 3, 56 Pitt St., Sydney NSW 2000 Australia ☎ 02/9253-5100 🖷 02/9253-5111 ⊕ www.ica.com.au. In New Zealand: **Insurance Council of New Zealand** ⊠ Level 7, 111-115 Customhouse Quay, Box 474, Wellington, New Zealand ☎ 04/472-5230 🖷 04/473-3011 ⊕ www.icnz.org.nz.

LANGUAGE

Despite the fact that four of the five Scandinavian tongues are in the Germanic family of languages, it is a myth that someone who speaks German can understand Danish, Icelandic, Swedish, and Norwegian. Fortunately, English is widely spoken in Scandinavia. German is the most common third language. English becomes rarer outside major cities, and it's a good idea to **take along a dictionary or phrase book.** Even here, however, anyone under the age of 50 is likely to have studied English in school.

Danish, Norwegian, and Swedish are similar, and fluent Norwegian and Swedish speakers can generally understand each other. While Finns must study Swedish (the second national language) in school, they much prefer to speak English with their Scandinavian counterparts.

Characters special to these three languages are the Danish "ø" and the Swedish "ö," pronounced a bit like a very short "er," similar to the French "eu"; "æ" or "ä," which sounds like the "a" in "ape" but with a glottal stop, or the "a" in "cat," depending on the region, and the "å" (also written "aa"), which sounds like "or". The important thing about these characters isn't that you pronounce them correctly—foreigners usually can't—but that you know to look for them in the phone book at the very end. Mr. Søren Åstrup, for example, will be found after "Z." Æ or Ä and Ø or Ö follow. The Swedish letter "K" softens to a "sh" sound next to certain vowels such as the Ö—beware when pronouncing place names such as Enköping (sounds like "Enshöping").

Icelandic, because of its island isolation, is the language closest to what the Vikings spoke 1,000 years ago. Although Norwegian, Danish, and Swedish have clearly evolved away from the roots common to all four languages, Icelandic retains a surprising amount of its ancient heritage, and Icelanders want to keep it that way: a governmental committee in Iceland has the express task of coming up with Icelandic versions of more modern words such as *computer.* Two characters are unique to Icelandic and Faroese: the "Þ," which is pronounced like the "th" in "thing"; and the "ð," which is pronounced like the "th" in "the."

Finnish is a non-Germanic language more closely related to Estonian and Hungarian than to the other Scandinavian languages. A visitor isn't likely to recognize anything on the average newspaper's front page. A linguistic cousin to Finnish is still spoken by the Sámi (Lapps), who inhabit the northernmost parts of Norway, Sweden, Finland, and Russia.

LODGING

The lodgings we list are the cream of the crop in each price category. We always list the facilities that are available—but we don't specify whether they cost extra: When pricing accommodations, always ask what's included and what costs extra.

In the larger cities, lodging ranges from first-class business hotels run by SAS, Sheraton, and Scandic; to good-quality tourist-class hotels, such as RESO, Best Western, Scandic Budget, and Sweden Hotels; to a wide variety of single-entrepreneur hotels. In the countryside, look for independently run inns and motels. In Denmark they're called *kroer;* in Norway, *fjellstuer* or *pensjonat;* in Finland, *kienvari;* and elsewhere, guest houses. "Mökki" holidays, in summer cottages or farmhouses, have become popular with foreign visitors to Finland; farm holidays have also become increasingly available to tourists in the other Scandinavian countries, all of which have organizations that can help organize stays in the countryside.

Before you leave home, **ask your travel agent about discounts,** including summer hotel checks for Best Western, Scandic, and Inter Nor hotels, a summer Fjord pass in Norway, and enormous year-round rebates at SAS hotels for travelers over 65. All EuroClass (business class) passengers can get discounts of at least 10% at SAS hotels when they book through SAS.

Two things about hotels usually surprise North Americans: the relatively limited dimensions of Scandinavian beds and the generous size of Scandinavian breakfasts. Scandinavian double beds are often about 60 inches wide or slightly less, close in size to the U.S. queen size. King-size beds (72 inches wide) are difficult to find and, if available, require special reservations.

Older hotels may have some rooms described as "double," which in fact have one double bed plus one foldout sofa big enough for two people. This arrangement is occasionally called a combi-room but is being phased out.

Many older hotels, particularly the country inns and independently run smaller hotels in the cities, do not have private bathrooms. Ask ahead if this is important to you.

Scandinavian breakfasts resemble what many people would call lunch, usually including breads, cheeses, marmalade, hams, lunch meats, eggs, juice, cereal, milk, and coffee. Generally, the farther north you go, the larger the breakfasts become. Breakfast is usually included in hotel rates.

Make reservations whenever possible. Even countryside inns, which usually have space, are sometimes packed with vacationing Europeans.

Ask about high and low seasons when making reservations, since different countries define their tourist seasons differently. Some hotels lower prices during tourist season, whereas others raise them during the same period.

Assume that hotels operate on the **European Plan** (EP, with no meals) unless we specify that they use the **Continental Plan** (CP, with a Continental breakfast), **Modified American Plan** (MAP, with breakfast and dinner), or the **Full American Plan** (FAP, with all meals).

APARTMENT & VILLA RENTALS

If you want a home base that's roomy enough for a family and comes with cooking facilities, **consider a furnished rental.** These can save you money, especially if you're traveling with a group. Home-exchange directories sometimes list rentals as well as exchanges.

🚩 International Agents **Drawbridge to Europe** ✉ 98 Granite St., Ashland, OR 97520 ☎ 541/482-7778 or 888/268-1148 🖶 541/482-7779 ⊕ www.drawbridgetoeurope.com.

CAMPING

Campsites are plentiful in the Scandinavian countries, and are often near a lake or by the sea. Central Iceland and Lapland hold some of the most pristine forests and highland areas in Europe, with exceptional camping for those wanting to make the extra effort to find less inhabited, back-country areas. Contact the local tourist boards for details.

FARM & COTTAGE HOLIDAYS

The old-fashioned farm or countryside holiday, long a staple for Scandinavian city dwellers, is becoming increasingly available to tourists. In general, you can choose to stay on the farm itself, and even participate in daily activities, or you can opt to rent a private, housekeeping cottage. In Finland, lakeside cottages, where many Finns spend their summers, are as common as the sauna; in Norway, seaside fisherman's cabins or *rorbuer* are available, particularly in the Lofoten Islands (most Scandinavian cottages will be near a lake or by the sea). Contact the local tourist board, or one of the organizations specializing in farm and cottage holidays, for details.

🚩 **Icelandic Farm Holidays** ✉ Síðumúli 13, IS-108 Reykjavík, Iceland ☎ 354/570-2700 🖶 354/570-2799 ⊕ www.farmholidays.is. **Landsforeningen for Landboturisme** ✉ Lerbakken 7, Foelle, DK-8410 Rønde, Denmark ☎ 45/87-91-20-00 ⊕ www.bondegaardsferie.dk. **Swedish Farm Holidays** ⌂ Box 8, S-668 21 Ed, Sweden ☎ 46/53412075 🖶 46/53461011 ⊕ www.bopalantgard.org.

HOME EXCHANGES

If you would like to exchange your home for someone else's, **join a home-exchange organization,** which will send you its updated listings of available exchanges for a year and will include your own listing in at least one of them. It's up to you to make specific arrangements.

🚩 Exchange Clubs **HomeLink International** ⌂ Box 47747, Tampa, FL 33647 ☎ 813/975-9825 or 800/638-3841 🖶 813/910-8144 ⊕ www.homelink.org ✉ $106 per year. **Intervac U.S.** ⌂ Box 590504, San Francisco, CA 94159 ☎ 800/756-4663 🖶 415/435-7440 ⊕ www.intervacus.com ✉ $93 yearly fee includes one catalog and online access.

HOSTELS

No matter what your age, you can **save on lodging costs by staying at hostels.** In some 4,500 locations in more than 70 countries around the world, Hostelling International (HI), the umbrella group for a number of national youth-hostel associations, offers single-sex, dorm-style beds and, at many hostels, rooms for couples and family accommodations. Membership in any HI national hostel association, open to travelers of all ages, allows you to stay in HI-affiliated hostels at member rates; one-year membership is about $25 for adults (C$35 in Canada, £12.50 in the U.K., $52 in Australia, and $40 in New Zealand); hostels run about $10–$25 per night. If a hostel has nearly filled up, members have priority over others; members are also eligible for discounts around the world, even on rail and bus travel in some countries.

⁊ Organizations Hostelling International– American Youth Hostels ⊠ 733 15th St. NW, Suite 840, Washington, DC 20005 ☎ 202/783-6161 🖷 202/783-6171 ⊕ www.hiayh.org. **Hostelling International–Canada** ⊠ 400-205 Catherine St., Ottawa, Ontario K2P 1C3, Canada ☎ 613/237-7884, 800/663-5777 in Canada 🖷 613/237-7868 ⊕ www. hostellingintl.ca. **Youth Hostel Association of England and Wales** ⊠ Trevelyan House, 8 St. Stephen's Hill, St. Albans, Hertfordshire AL1 2DY, U.K. ☎ 0870/8708808 🖷 01727/844126 ⊕ www. yha.org.uk. **Youth Hostel Association Australia** ⊠ 10 Mallett St., Camperdown, NSW 2050, Australia ☎ 02/9565-1699 🖷 02/9565-1325 ⊕ www.yha. com.au. **Youth Hostels Association of New Zealand** ⊠ Level 3, 193 Cashel St., Box 436, Christchurch, New Zealand ☎ 03/379-9970 🖷 03/365-4476 ⊕ www.yha.org.nz.

HOTELS

All hotels listed have private baths unless otherwise noted.

All five Scandinavian countries offer Inn Checks, or prepaid hotel vouchers, for accommodations ranging from first-class hotels to country cottages. These vouchers, which must be purchased from travel agents or from the Scandinavian Tourist Board (⇨ Visitor Information) before departure, are sold individually and in packets for as many nights as needed and offer savings of up to 50%. Most countries also offer summer bargains for foreign tourists; winter bargains can be even greater. For further information about Scandinavian hotel vouchers, contact the Scandinavian Tourist Board.

ProSkandinavia checks can be used in 400 hotels across Scandinavia (excluding Iceland) for savings up to 50%, for reservations made usually no earlier than 24 hours before arrival, although some hotels allow earlier bookings. One check costs about $40. Two checks will pay for a double room at a hotel, one check for a room in a cottage. The checks can be bought at many travel agencies in Scandinavia or ordered from **ProSkandinavia** (⊠ Akersgt. 11, N-0158 Oslo, Norway ☎ 47/22–41–13–13 🖷 47/22–42–06–57 ⊕ www.proskandinavia.com).

⁊ Toll-Free Numbers Best Western ☎ 800/528-1234 ⊕ www.bestwestern.com. **Choice** ☎ 800/221-2222 ⊕ www.choicehotels.com. **Comfort** ☎ 800/228-5150 ⊕ www.comfortinn.com. **Hilton** ☎ 800/445-8667 ⊕ www.hilton.com. **Holiday Inn** ☎ 800/465-4329 ⊕ www.basshotels.com. **Inter-Continental** ☎ 800/327-0200 ⊕ www. intercontinental.com. **Le Meridien** ☎ 800/543-4300 ⊕ www.lemeridien.com. **Ramada** ☎ 800/228-2828, 800/854-7854 international reservations ⊕ www.ramada.com or www.ramadahotels. com. **Quality Inn** ☎ 800/228-5151 ⊕ www. qualityinn.com. **Radisson** ☎ 800/333-3333 ⊕ www.radisson.com. **Sheraton** ☎ 800/325-3535 ⊕ www.starwoodhotels.com.

MONEY MATTERS

Prices throughout this guide are given for adults. Substantially reduced fees are almost always available for children, students, and senior citizens. For information on taxes, *see* Taxes.

Costs are high in Denmark, Norway, and Sweden, higher still in Finland, and highest in Iceland, where so many things must be imported. Basic sample prices are listed in the Country A to Z section at the end of each chapter. Throughout the region, be aware that sales taxes can be very high, but foreigners can get some refunds by shopping at tax-free stores (⇨ Taxes). City cards can save you transportation and entrance fees in many of the larger cities.

You can **reduce the cost of food by planning.** Breakfast is often included in your hotel bill; if not, you may wish to buy fruit, sweet rolls, and a beverage for a picnic breakfast. Electrical devices for hot coffee or tea should be bought abroad, though, to conform to the local current.

Opt for a restaurant lunch instead of dinner, since the latter tends to be significantly more expensive. Instead of beer or wine, **drink tap water**—liquor can cost four times the price of the same brand in a store—but do specify tap water, as the term "water" can refer to soft drinks and bottled water, which are also expensive.

Throughout Scandinavia, the tip is included in the cost of your meal.

In most of Scandinavia, liquor and strong beer (over 3% alcohol) can be purchased only in state-owned shops, at very high prices, during weekday business hours, usually 9:30 to 6 and in some areas on Saturday until mid-afternoon. A midsize bottle of whiskey in Sweden, for example, can easily cost SKr 250 (about $35). Denmark takes a less restrictive approach, with liquor and beer available in the smallest of grocery stores, open weekdays and Saturday morning—but Danish prices, too, are high. (When you visit friends or relatives in Scandinavia, a bottle of liquor or fine wine bought duty-free on the trip over is often much appreciated.) Weaker beers and ciders are usually available in grocery stores in Scandinavia.

ATMS

🄵 **ATM Locations** Cirrus ☎ 800/424-7787.

CREDIT CARDS

Throughout this guide, the following abbreviations are used: **AE,** American Express; **DC,** Diners Club; **MC,** MasterCard; and **V,** Visa.

CURRENCY

Finland is the only Scandinavian country that has switched to the Euro. The FM (Finnish mark) is no longer accepted as currency. Denmark and Sweden, both EU countries like Finland, are still using their currencies, the DKr (Danish kroner) and SKr (Swedish kronor). Norway and Iceland, non-EU countries, are keeping their currencies, the NKr (Norwegian kroner) and the IKr (Icelandic kroner). In individual countries you may see prices indicated with Kr only, and you may see exchange rates in banks quoted for DKK, EUR, ISK, NOK, and SEK. Currency-exchange rates at press time are listed in the Country A to Z sections at the end of each chapter, but **since rates fluctuate daily, you should check them at the time of your departure.**

CURRENCY EXCHANGE

For the most favorable rates, **change money through banks.** Although ATM transaction fees may be higher abroad than at home, ATM rates are excellent because they are based on wholesale rates offered only by major banks. You won't do as well at exchange booths in airports or rail and bus stations, in hotels, in restaurants, or in stores. To avoid lines at airport exchange booths, **get a bit of local currency before you leave home.**

🄵 **Exchange Services** International Currency Express ☎ 888/278-6628 for orders ⊕ www.foreignmoney.com. Thomas Cook Currency Services ☎ 800/287-7362 for telephone orders and retail locations ⊕ www.us.thomascook.com.

TRAVELER'S CHECKS

Do you need traveler's checks? It depends on where you're headed. If you're going to rural areas and small towns, go with cash; traveler's checks are best used in cities. Lost or stolen checks can usually be replaced within 24 hours. To ensure a speedy refund, buy your own traveler's checks—don't let someone else pay for them: irregularities such as this can cause delays. The person who bought the checks should make the call to request a refund.

PACKING

Bring a folding umbrella and a lightweight raincoat, as it is common for the sky to be clear at 9 AM, rainy at 11 AM, and clear again in time for lunch. **Pack casual clothes,** as Scandinavians tend to dress more casually than their Continental brethren. If you have trouble sleeping when it is light or are sensitive to strong sun, **bring an eye mask and dark sunglasses;** the sun rises as early as 4 AM in some areas, and the far-northern latitude causes it to slant at angles unseen elsewhere on the globe. **Bring bug repellent** if you plan to venture away from the capital cities; large mosquitoes can be a real nuisance on summer evenings throughout Scandinavia.

In your carry-on luggage, **pack an extra pair of eyeglasses or contact lenses and enough of any medication** you take to last the entire trip. You may also ask your doctor to write a spare prescription using the drug's generic name, since brand names may vary from country to country. In luggage to be checked, **never pack prescription drugs or valuables.** To avoid customs delays, carry medications in their original packaging. And don't forget to carry with you the addresses of offices that handle refunds of lost traveler's checks. Check

Fodor's How to Pack (available in bookstores everywhere) for more tips.

CHECKING LUGGAGE

You are allowed one carry-on bag and one personal article, such as a purse or a laptop computer. Make sure that everything you carry aboard will fit under your seat or in the overhead bin. Get to the gate early, so you can board as soon as possible.

If you are flying internationally, note that baggage allowances may be determined not by piece but by weight—generally 88 pounds (40 kilograms) in first class, 66 pounds (30 kilograms) in business class, and 44 pounds (20 kilograms) in economy.

Airline liability for baggage is limited to $1,250 per person on flights within the United States. On international flights it amounts to $9.07 per pound or $20 per kilogram for checked baggage (roughly $640 per 70-pound bag) and $400 per passenger for unchecked baggage. You can buy additional coverage at check-in for about $10 per $1,000 of coverage, but it excludes a rather extensive list of items, shown on your airline ticket.

Before departure, **itemize your bags' contents** and their worth, and label the bags with your name, address, and phone number. (If you use your home address, cover it so potential thieves can't see it readily.) Inside each bag, **pack a copy of your itinerary.** At check-in, **make sure that each bag is correctly tagged** with the destination airport's three-letter code. If your bags arrive damaged or fail to arrive at all, file a written report with the airline before leaving the airport.

PASSPORTS & VISAS

When traveling internationally, **carry your passport** even if you don't need one (it's always the best form of I.D.) and **make two photocopies of the data page** (one for someone at home and another for you, carried separately from your passport). If you lose your passport, promptly call the nearest embassy or consulate and the local police.

ENTERING SCANDINAVIA

All U.S. citizens, even infants, need only a valid passport to enter any Scandinavian country for stays of up to three months.

PASSPORT OFFICES

The best time to apply for a passport or to renew is in fall and winter. Before any trip, check your passport's expiration date, and, if necessary, renew it as soon as possible.

🇦🇺 Australian Citizens **Australian Passport Office** ☎ 131-232 🌐 www.dfat.gov.au/passports.

🇨🇦 Canadian Citizens **Passport Office** ☎ 819/994-3500, 800/567-6868 in Canada 🌐 www.dfait-maeci.gc.ca/passport.

🇳🇿 New Zealand Citizens **New Zealand Passport Office** ☎ 04/494-0700 🌐 www.passports.govt.nz.

🇬🇧 U.K. Citizens **London Passport Office** ☎ 0870/521-0410 🌐 www.ukpa.gov.uk for fees and documentation requirements and to request an emergency passport.

🇺🇸 U.S. Citizens **National Passport Information Center** ☎ 877/487-2778 or 900/225-5674 🌐 www.travel.state.gov/npicinfo.html.

SENIOR-CITIZEN TRAVEL

To qualify for age-related discounts, **mention your senior-citizen status up front** when booking hotel reservations (not when checking out) and before you're seated in restaurants (not when paying the bill). When renting a car, ask about promotional car-rental discounts, which can be cheaper than senior-citizen rates.

TRAIN TRAVEL

Seniors over 60 are entitled to discount tickets (often as much as 50% off) on buses, trains, and ferries throughout Scandinavia, as well as reductions on special City Cards. Eurail offers discounts on Scanrail and Eurail train passes (⇨ Train Travel).

🇪🇺 Educational Programs **Elderhostel** ⊠ 11 Ave. de Lafayette, Boston, MA 02111-1746 ☎ 877/426-8056 🖷 877/426-2166 🌐 www.elderhostel.org.

SHOPPING

Prices in Scandinavia are never low, but quality is high, and specialties are sometimes less expensive here than elsewhere. Scandinavian design in both furniture and glassware is world-renowned. Swedish crystal, Icelandic sweaters, Danish Lego blocks and furniture, Norwegian furs, and Finnish fabrics—these are just a few of the items to look for. Keep an eye out for sales, called *udsalg* in Danish, *rea* in Swedish, and *ale* in Finnish.

STUDENTS IN SCANDINAVIA

F **I.D.s & Services Council Travel (CIEE)** ✉ 205 E. 42nd St., 15th fl., New York, NY 10017 ☎ 212/822–2700 or 888/268–6245 🖷 212/822–2699 ⊕ www. councilexchanges.org for mail orders only, in the United States. **Travel Cuts** ✉ 187 College St., Toronto, Ontario M5T 1P7, Canada ☎ 416/979–2406, 800/667–2887 in Canada 🖷 416/979–8167 ⊕ www. travelcuts.com.

TAXES

VALUE-ADDED TAX

Specific information on V.A.T. (value-added taxes) can be found in the Country A to Z section at the end of each chapter.

One way to beat high prices is to **take advantage of tax-free shopping.** Throughout Scandinavia, you can make major purchases free of tax if you have a foreign passport. Ask about tax-free shopping when you make a purchase for $50 (about £32) or more. When your purchases exceed a specified limit (which varies from country to country), you receive a special export receipt. Keep the parcels intact and take them out of the country within 30 days of purchase.

You can claim a V.A.T. refund from Finland, Sweden, and Denmark when you leave the last EU country visited; the V.A.T. refund (called *moms* all over Scandinavia) can be obtained in cash from a special office at the airport, or, upon arriving home, you can send your receipts to an office in the country of purchase to receive your refund by mail. Citizens of EU countries are not eligible for the refund.

In Sweden, for non-EU citizens, the refund is about 18%; in Finland, 10% to 16%; in Norway, 11% to 18%; in Denmark, 13% to 19%; in Iceland, up to 15% for purchases over IKr 4,000.

Note: Tax-free sales of alcohol, cigarettes, and other luxury goods have been abolished among EU countries, with Sweden, Finland, and Denmark among the last to adopt these regulations. Finland's Åland Islands have some special rights under the EU and therefore allow tax-free sales for ferries in transit through its ports. All Sweden–Finland ferry routes now pass through the islands, de facto continuing the extremely popular tax-free sales for tourists. Air travel to the Scandinavia EU member states (Sweden, Finland, Denmark), as well as Norway, no longer allows tax-free sales.

Global Refund is a V.A.T. refund service that makes getting your money back hassle-free. The service is available Europe-wide at 130,000 affiliated stores. In participating stores, **ask for the Global Refund form** (called a Shopping Cheque). Have it stamped like any customs form by customs officials when you leave the European Union (be ready to show customs officials what you've bought). Then take the form to one of the more than 700 Global Refund counters—conveniently located at every major airport and border crossing—and your money will be refunded on the spot in the form of cash, check, or a refund to your credit-card account (minus a small percentage for processing).

F **Global Refund** ✉ 99 Main St., Suite 307, Nyack, NY 10960 ☎ 800/566–9828 🖷 845/348–1549 ⊕ www.globalrefund.com.

TELEPHONES

AREA & COUNTRY CODES

The country code for Denmark is 45; for Finland, 358; for Iceland, 354; for Norway, 47; and for Sweden, 46. In this chapter, phone numbers outside the United States and Canada include country codes; in all other chapters only the area codes are listed.

The country code is 1 for the United States and Canada, 61 for Australia, 64 for New Zealand, and 44 for the United Kingdom.

INTERNATIONAL CALLS

When dialing from outside the country you're trying to reach, drop the initial 0 from the local area code.

LONG-DISTANCE SERVICES

AT&T, MCI, and Sprint access codes make calling long distance relatively convenient, but you may find the local access number blocked in many hotel rooms. First ask the hotel operator to connect you. If the hotel operator balks, ask for an international operator, or dial the international operator yourself. One way to improve your odds of getting connected to your long-distance carrier is to travel with more than one company's calling card (a hotel may block

Sprint, for example, but not MCI). If all else fails, call from a pay phone.

Access Codes AT&T Direct ☎ 8001/0010 Denmark, 9800/10010 Finland, 800/9001 Iceland, 800/19011 Norway, 020/795611 Sweden. **MCI WorldPhone** ☎ 8001/0022 Denmark, 9800/10280 Finland, 800/9002 Iceland, 800/10912 Norway, 020/795922 Sweden. **Sprint International Access** ☎ 800/10877 Denmark, 9800/10284 Finland, 800/9003 Iceland, 800/19877 Norway, 020/799011 Sweden.

MOBILE PHONES

Scandinavia has been one of the world leaders in mobile phone development; almost 90% of the population in Scandinavia owns a mobile phone. Although standard North American cellular phones will not work in Scandinavia, most Scandinavian capitals have several companies that rent cellular phones to tourists. Contact the local tourist offices for details.

TIME

Scandinavia falls into two time zones. Denmark, Norway, and Sweden are one hour ahead of Greenwich Mean Time (GMT) and six hours ahead of Eastern Standard Time (EST). Since Iceland does not observe Daylight Savings Times, the country is one hour ahead of GMT and five hours ahead of EST in the summer but in the same time zone as Denmark, Norway, and Sweden the rest of the year.

Finland is two hours ahead of GMT and seven hours ahead of EST.

TIPPING

When taking a taxi, a 10% tip is appreciated but not essential.

TOURS & PACKAGES

Because everything is prearranged on a prepackaged tour or independent vacation, you spend less time planning—and often get it all at a good price.

BOOKING WITH AN AGENT

Travel agents are excellent resources. But it's a good idea to collect brochures from several agencies as some agents' suggestions may be influenced by relationships with tour and package firms that reward them for volume sales. If you have a special interest, **find an agent with expertise in that area**; the American Society of

Travel Agents (ASTA; ⇨ Travel Agencies) has a database of specialists worldwide.

Make sure your travel agent knows the accommodations and other services of the place being recommended. Ask about the hotel's location, room size, beds, and whether it has a pool, room service, or programs for children, if you care about these. Has your agent been there in person or sent others whom you can contact?

Do some homework on your own, too: local tourism boards can provide information about lesser-known and small-niche operators, some of which may sell only direct.

Tour-Operator Recommendations American Society of Travel Agents (⇨ Travel Agencies). **National Tour Association** (NTA) ✉ 546 E. Main St., Lexington, KY 40508 ☎ 859/226–4444 or 800/682–8886 ⊕ www.ntaonline.com. **United States Tour Operators Association** (USTOA) ✉ 342 Madison Ave., Suite 1522, New York, NY 10173 ☎ 212/599–6599 or 800/468–7862 🖷 212/599–6744 ⊕ www.ustoa.com.

BUYER BEWARE

Each year consumers are stranded or lose their money when tour operators—even large ones with excellent reputations—go out of business. So **check out the operator.** Ask several travel agents about its reputation, and try to **book with a company that has a consumer-protection program.** (Look for information in the company's brochure.) In the United States, members of the National Tour Association and the United States Tour Operators Association are required to set aside funds to cover your payments and travel arrangements in the event that the company defaults. It's also a good idea to choose a company that participates in the American Society of Travel Agents' Tour Operator Program (TOP); ASTA will act as mediator in any disputes between you and your tour operator.

Remember that the more your package or tour includes the better you can predict the ultimate cost of your vacation. Make sure you know exactly what is covered, and **beware of hidden costs.** Are taxes, tips, and transfers included? Entertainment and excursions? These can add up.

TRAIN TRAVEL

Consider a Scanrail Pass, available for travel in Denmark, Sweden, Norway, and

Finland for both first- and second-class train travel: you may have five days of unlimited travel in any two-month period ($366 first-class, $271 second-class); 10 days of unlimited travel in two months ($488, $362) or 21 days of consecutive day unlimited train travel ($567, $420). With the Scanrail Pass, you also enjoy travel bonuses, including free or discounted ferry, boat, and bus travel and a Hotel Discount Card that allows 10%–30% off rates for select hotels June–August.

Passengers ages 12–25 can **buy Scanrail Youth Passes** ($254 first-class, $188 second-class, five travel days in two months; $341or $253 for 10 travel days in two months; $394or $292 for 21 days of unlimited travel).

Those over age 60 can **take advantage of the Scanrail Senior Pass**, which offers the travel bonuses of the Scanrail Pass and discounted travel ($324 first-class, $240 second-class, five days; $434or $322 10 days; $502or $372 for 21 consecutive days). Buy Scanrail passes through Rail Europe and travel agents.

For car and train travel, price the Scanrail'n Drive Pass: in 15 days you can get five days of unlimited train travel and two days of car rental (choice of three car categories) with unlimited mileage in Denmark, Norway, and Sweden. You can purchase extra car rental days and choose from first- or second-class train travel. Individual rates for two adults traveling together (compact car $385 first-class, $308 second-class) are considerably lower (about 25%) than for single adults; the third or fourth person sharing the car only needs to purchase a Scanrail pass.

In Scandinavia, you can **use EurailPasses,** which provide unlimited first-class rail travel, in all of the participating countries, for the duration of the pass. If you plan to rack up the miles, get a standard pass. These are available for 15 days ($580), 21 days ($762), one month ($946), two months ($1,338), and three months ($1,654). Eurail- and EuroPasses are available through travel agents and Rail Europe.

If you are an adult traveling with a youth under age 26 and/or a senior, consider buying a **EurailSaver Pass**; this entitles you to second-class train travel at the discount

youth or senior fare, provided that you are traveling with the youth or senior at all times. A Saver pass is available for $498 (15 days), $648 (21 days), and $804 (one month); two- and three-month fares are also available.

In addition to standard EurailPasses, **ask about special rail-pass plans.** Among these are the Eurail YouthPass (for those under age 26), a Eurail FlexiPass (which allows a certain number of travel days within a set period), the Euraildrive Pass, and the EuroPass Drive (which combines travel by train and rental car).

Whichever pass you choose, remember that you must **purchase your pass before you leave** for Europe.

Many travelers assume that rail passes guarantee them seats on the trains they wish to ride. Not so. You need to **book seats ahead even if you are using a rail pass;** seat reservations are required on some European trains, particularly high-speed trains, and are a good idea on trains that may be crowded—particularly in summer on popular routes. You will also need a reservation if you purchase sleeping accommodations.

🚆 Where to Buy Rail Passes **CIT Tours Corp.** ✉ 342 Madison Ave., Suite 207, New York, NY 10173 ☏ 212/697-2100 or 800/248-8687, 800/248-7245 in western U.S. ⊕ www.cit-tours.com. **DER Travel Services** 🖉 Box 1606, Des Plaines, IL 60017 ☏ 800/782-2424 🖶 800/282-7474 ⊕ www. dertravel.com. **Rail Europe** ✉ 226-230 Westchester Ave., White Plains, NY 10604 ☏ 800/438-7245, 914/682-5172, or 416/602-4195 ✉ 2087 Dundas E, Suite 105, Mississauga, Ontario L4X 1M2, Canada ☏ 800/438-7245, 914/682-5172, or 416/602-4195 ⊕ www.raileurope.com.

CUTTING COSTS

Rail passes may help you save money, but be aware that if you don't plan to cover many miles you may come out ahead by buying individual tickets.

TRANSPORTATION AROUND SCANDINAVIA

Vast distances between cities and towns make air transportation a cost-efficient mode of travel in Scandinavia. SAS is Scandinavia's major air carrier; it also operates domestic lines in Norway, Sweden, and Denmark. SAS offers discount packages for travel among the Scandinavian capitals, as well as reduced domestic fares in the summer. Finnair is also expanding its routes in Scandinavia.

Trains—comfortable, clean, and fast—are also good for covering the large distances here. Remember to specify a smoking or no-smoking seat or compartment. You should inquire with your travel agent about Scanrail Passes, or individual country passes, for travel within the region.

Another means of getting around Scandinavia's countries is to go by ferry. These huge vessels offer a combination of efficient travel (you sleep aboard and wake up in your destination the next morning) and amenities approaching what you might expect on a cruise ship: luxury dining, gambling, a sauna and pool, and entertainment. Travelers should beware, however, that the noise level may be high and the crowd is usually very lively.

If you prefer the freedom of planning an itinerary and traveling at your own pace, a rental car is a good, albeit expensive, alternative. Most major car rental companies operate in Scandinavia. Roads are generally good, but allow plenty of time for navigating the region's winding highway network. Scandinavia enforces some of the most strict drinking-and-driving laws in the world—a drunk driver could end up in jail after one offense.

Public transportation in Scandinavia's cities is safe, fast, and inexpensive. Some cities, including the capitals, offer day passes reducing the cost of buses and train travel.

Taxis in Scandinavia are safe, clean, *and* expensive. All taxis should be clearly marked and have a meter inside; unmarked taxis—usually operated illegally by unlicensed drivers—are not recommended. A 10% tip is a friendly gesture, but by no means necessary. Most taxis accept major credit cards and cash.

TRAVEL AGENCIES

A good travel agent puts your needs first. Look for an agency that has been in business at least five years, emphasizes customer service, and has someone on staff who specializes in your destination. In addition, **make sure the agency belongs to a professional trade organization.** The American Society of Travel Agents

(ASTA)—the largest and most influential in the field with more than 26,000 members in some 170 countries—maintains and enforces a strict code of ethics and will step in to help mediate any agent-client dispute if necessary. ASTA (whose motto is "Without a travel agent, you're on your own") also maintains a Web site that includes a directory of agents. (If a travel agency is also acting as your tour operator, *see* Buyer Beware *in* Tours & Packages).

Local Agent Referrals American Society of Travel Agents (ASTA) ⊠ 1101 King St., Suite 200, Alexandria, VA 22314 ☎ 800/965-2782 24-hr hotline 🖷 703/739-7642 ⊕ www.astanet.com. **Association of British Travel Agents** ⊠ 68-71 Newman St., London W1T 3AH, U.K. ☎ 020/7637-2444 🖷 020/7637-0713 ⊕ www.abtanet.com. **Association of Canadian Travel Agents** ⊠ 130 Albert St., Suite 1705, Ottawa, Ontario K1P 5G4, Canada ☎ 613/237-3657 🖷 613/237-7052 ⊕ www.acta.net. **Australian Federation of Travel Agents** ⊠ Level 3, 309 Pitt St., Sydney NSW 2000, Australia ☎ 02/9264-3299 🖷 02/9264-1085 ⊕ www.afta.com.au. **Travel Agents' Association of New Zealand** ⊠ Level 5, Paxus House, 79 Boulcott St., Box 1888, Wellington 10033, New Zealand ☎ 04/499-0104 🖷 04/499-0827 ⊕ www.taanz.org.nz.

VISITOR INFORMATION

Scandinavian Tourist Board In the U.S.: **Scandinavian Tourist Board** ⊠ 655 3rd Ave., New York, NY 10017 ☎ 212/885-9700 🖷 212/855-9710.

In the U.K.: **Danish Tourist Board** ⊠ 55 Sloan St., London SW1X 9SY ☎ 44/20-7259-5959 🖷 44/20-7259-5955. **Finnish Tourist Board** ⊡ Box 33213, London W6 8JX ☎ 44/20-7365-2512. **Iceland Tourist Board/Icelandair** ⊠ 172 Tottenham Court Rd., London W1P 7LY ☎ 44/207-874-1000 🖷 44/207-874-1001. **Norwegian Tourist Board** ⊠ Charles House, 5 [Lower] Regent St., London SW1Y 4LR ☎ 44/207-839-6255 🖷 44/207-839-6014. **Swedish Travel and Tourism Council** ⊠ 11 Montagu Pl., London W1H 2AL ☎ 0207/870-5600 🖷 0207/724-5872.

U.S. Government Advisories U.S. Department of State ⊠ Overseas Citizens Services Office, Room 4811 N.S., 2201 C St. NW, Washington, DC 20520 ☎ 202/647-5225 for interactive hot line. ⊕ travel.state.gov/travel.html; enclose a business-size SASE.

WEB SITES

Do check out the World Wide Web when planning your trip. You'll find everything from weather forecasts to virtual tours of famous cities. Be sure to **visit Fodors.com**

(⊕ www.fodors.com), a complete travel-planning site. You can research prices and book plane tickets, hotel rooms, rental cars, vacation packages, and more. In addition, you can post your pressing questions in the Travel Talk section. Other planning tools include a currency converter and weather reports, and there are loads of links to travel resources.

DANISH RESOURCES

Danish Tourist Board (general ⊕ www.dt.dk ✉ For North Americans ⊕ www.visitdenmark.dt.dk ✉ For those in Ireland and the U.K. ⊕ www.dtb.dt.dk). **Wonderful CopenhagenCopenhangen** (Copenhagen Tourist Board; ⊕ www.woco.dk). **Danish Meteorological Institute** (includes weather forecasts; ⊕ www.dmi.dk).

FINNISH RESOURCES

Finland Tourist Board (⊕ www.mek.fi); **Virtual Finland** (Ministry for Foreign Affairs of Finland; ⊕ virtual.finland.fi). **City of Helsinki** (⊕ www.hel.fi/english).

ICELANDIC RESOURCES

Tourist Boards (North Atlantic ⊕ www.goiceland.org ✉ Iceland ⊕ www.icetourist.is). **What's on in Iceland** (entertainment and cultural events ⊕ www.whatson.is). **Reykjavík Events** (⊕ www.reykjavik.com).

NORWEGIAN RESOURCES

Norwegian Tourist Board (⊕ www.visitnorway.com). **Oslo Visitors and Convention Bureau** (⊕ www.oslopro.no). **Royal Norwegian Embassy in the United States** (⊕ www.norway.org).

SWEDISH RESOURCES

Swedish Travel & Tourism Council (⊕ www.visitsweden.org). **City of Stockholm** (⊕ www.stockholm.se/english).

DENMARK

FODOR'S CHOICE

Brandts Klædefabrik, *museum in Odense, Fyn*

Christiansborg Slot, *seat of Parliament in Copenhagen*

Domkirke, *former capital in Roskilde, Sjælland*

Egeskov Slot, *island-castle in Kværndrup, Fyn*

Greenland's Ice Cap

Kronborg Slot, *castle in Helsingør, Sjælland*

Legoland, *Billund, Jylland*

Lejre Forsøgscenter, *open-air museum near Roskilde, Sjælland*

Louisiana, *museum in Humlebæk, Sjælland*

Ny Carlsberg Glyptotek, *museum in Copenhagen*

Ordrupgaard, *museum in Charlottenlund, Sjælland*

Østerlars Kirke, *church in Bornholm*

Rosenborg Slot, *castle in Copenhagen*

Tilsandede Kirke, *sand-buried church in Skagen, Jylland*

Tivoli Gardens, *Copenhagen*

Trapholt Museum for Moderne Kunst, *Kolding, Jylland*

Valdemars Slot, *castle in Troense, Fyn*

Many other great sights, restaurants, and hotels enliven this area.
For other favorites, look for the stars as you read this chapter.

Updated by
Charles Ferro
and Eduardo
López de
Luzuriaga

THE KINGDOM OF DENMARK dapples the Baltic Sea in an archipelago of some 450 islands and the crescent of one peninsula. Measuring 43,069 square km (17,028 square mi) and with a population of 5 million, it is the geographical link between Scandinavia and Europe. Half-timber villages and tidy agriculture hamlets rub shoulders with provincial towns and a handful of cities, where pedestrians set the pace, not traffic. Mothers safely park baby carriages outside bakeries while outdoor cafés fill with cappuccino-sippers, and lanky Danes pedal to work in lanes thick with bicycle traffic. Clearly this is a land where the process of life is the greatest reward.

While in Denmark, visitors pinch themselves in disbelief and make long lists of resolutions to emulate the natives. The Danes' lifestyle is certainly enviable, not yet the pressure-cooked life of some other Western countries. Long one of the world's most liberal nations, Denmark has a highly developed social-welfare system. Hefty taxes are the subject of grumbles and jokes, but Danes are proud of their state-funded medical and educational systems and high standard of living. They enjoy more than five weeks of annual vacation, 7½-hour workdays, and overall security. In 1989 Denmark made headlines worldwide when it became the first country to legally recognize gay partnerships. For the open-minded Danes, it was just a matter of course, while to the rest of the world it was a strong reminder of Denmark's progressive stance toward personal rights.

Educated, patriotic, and keenly aware of their tiny international position, most Danes travel extensively and have a balanced perspective of their nation's benefits and shortfalls. As in many other provincial states, egalitarianism is often a constraint for the ambitious. In Denmark, the Jante law, which refers to a literary principle penned in the early 20th century by Axel Sandemose, essentially means "Don't think you're anything special"—and works as an insidious cultural barrier to talent and aspiration. On the other hand, free education and state support give refugees, immigrants, and the underprivileged an opportunity to begin new, often prosperous lives.

Despite its relatively small population, Denmark has long played a feature role in the world stage of arts and letters—and it continues to do so. Writers Hans Christian Andersen and Karen Blixen (whose pen name was Isak Dinesen, and whose life story was made into the film *Out of Africa*) and existential philosopher Søren Kierkegaard may be the cornerstone contributors, but there's a new crop of artists leading the way, including writer Peter Høeg, and filmmaker Lars Von Trier, whose disturbing and unforgettable films have garnered vociferous praise and criticism in almost equal measure.

The Øresund Bridge, consisting of a 4-km (2½-mi) underground tunnel (one of the longest in Europe) that connects to an 8-km (5-mi) bridge via a man-made island, is an engineering masterpiece. Nine years in the making—at the staggering cost of Dkr 24 billion ($3 billion)—the Øresund Fixed Link made its splashy debut in July 2000, linking Denmark and Sweden across the 20-km (12-mi) Øresund Strait for the first time in more than 7,000 years. To many Scandinavians, however, the bridge was not so much an engineering feat as a cultural one. Malmö, Sweden's third-largest city, is now a 35-minute train- or car-ride from Copenhagen, just a little farther than some of Copenhagen's outlying suburbs. Indeed, many of Copenhagen's magazines and tourist literature feature Malmö's shops and sights as part of the Copenhagen itinerary. The bridge is an uncontested success; more than double the amount of people cross the bridge daily than previously took the ferry.

Denmark is divided into three regions: the two major islands of Sjælland and Fyn, and the peninsula of Jylland. To the east, Sjælland is Denmark's largest and most populated island, with Copenhagen its focal point. Denmark's second largest island, Fyn, is a pastoral, undulating land dotted with farms and summer-house beach villages, with Odense as its one major town. To the west, the relatively vast Jylland connects Denmark to the European continent; here you find the towns of Århus and Aalborg.

1

If you have
3 days

Take at least two days to explore and enjoy **Copenhagen.** The third day, head north of the city, first to **Rungsted** to see Karen Blixen's manor house and the lush garden surrounding it, then to the Louisiana modern-art museum in **Humlebæk.**

If you have
5 days

After two days and nights in **Copenhagen,** head north to **Rungsted** and **Humlebæk;** then spend the third night in **Helsingør.** The next day, visit the castles of Helsingør and **Hillerød,** and spend the night in medieval **Roskilde.** Day 5, venture southeast to enjoy the dramatic nature and history of **Møn** and the villages and beaches of Lolland and Falster. An alternative last-day tour is to head west to Hans Christian Andersen's birthplace of **Odense,** on Fyn.

If you have
7 days

In a week you can see Copenhagen and environs and explore Fyn and Jylland. Rent a car for the latter—it's the quickest way to make it from the historic cities of **Århus** and **Aalborg** to the blond beaches of **Skagen,** with time left over to meander through a couple of smaller villages. Keep in mind that to take in Greenland or the Faroe Islands in addition to seeing mainland Denmark, you'll need more than a week—ideally two.

As for its cultural ramifications, only time will tell whether the newly named Øresund region, anchored by Copenhagen and Malmö, with a joint population of 3 million, will continue to merge together or remain nothing more than two cities connected by a bridge.

The history of this little country stretches back 250,000 years, when Jylland was inhabited by nomadic hunters, but it wasn't until AD 500 that a tribe from Sweden, called the Danes, migrated south and christened the land Denmark. The Viking expansion that followed was based on the country's strategic position in the north. Struggles for control of the North Sea with England and western Europe; of the Skagerrak (the strait between Denmark and Norway) with Norway and Sweden; and of the Baltic Sea with Germany, Poland, and Russia ensued. With high-speed ships and fine-tuned warriors, intrepid navies navigated to Europe and Canada, invading and often pillaging, until, under King Knud (Canute) the Great (995–1035), they captured England by 1018.

After the British conquest, Viking supremacy declined as feudal Europe learned to defend itself. Internally, the pagan way of life was threatened by the expansion of Christianity, introduced under Harald Bluetooth, who in AD 980 "baptized" the country, essentially to avoid war with Germany. For the next several hundred years, the country tried to maintain its Baltic power with the influence of the German Hanseatic League. Under the leadership of Valdemar IV (1340–75), Sweden, Norway, Iceland, Greenland, and the Faroe Islands became a part of Denmark. Sweden broke away by the mid-15th century and battled Denmark for much of the next several hundred years, whereas Norway remained under Danish rule until 1814, Iceland until 1943. Greenland and the Faroe Islands are still self-governing Danish provinces.

Denmark prospered again in the 16th century, thanks to the Sound Dues, a levy charged to ships crossing the Øresund. Under King Christian IV, a construction boom crowned the land with what remain architectural gems today, but his fantasy spires and castles, compounded with the Thirty Years' War in the 17th century, led to state bankruptcy.

By the 18th century, absolute monarchy had given way to representative democracy, and culture flourished. Then—in a fatal mistake—Denmark sided with France and refused to surrender its navy to the English during the Napoleonic Wars. In a less than valiant episode of British history, Lord Nelson turned his famous blind eye to the destruction and bombed Copenhagen to bits. The defeated King Frederik VI handed Norway to Sweden. Denmark's days of glory were over.

Though Denmark was unaligned during World War II, the Nazis invaded in 1940. Against them, the Danes used the only weapons they had: a cold shoulder and massive underground resistance. After the war, Denmark focused inward, refining its welfare system and concentrating on its main industries of agriculture, shipping, and financial and technical services. It is an outspoken member of the European Union (EU), championing environmental responsibility and supporting development in emerging economies. And, expensive as it is, Denmark is in many ways less pricey than the rest of Scandinavia.

Copenhagen fidgets with its modern identity as both a Scandinavian–European link and cozy capital. The center of Danish politics, culture, and finance, it copes through balance and a sense of humor with a taste for the absurd. Stroll the streets and you'll pass classic architecture painted in candy colors, and businessmen clad in jeans and T-shirts.

The surrounding countryside in the rest of Sjælland is not to be missed. Less than an hour from Copenhagen, fields and half-timber cottages checker the land. Roskilde, to the east, has a 12th-century cathedral, and in the north, the Kronborg Castle of *Hamlet* fame crowns Helsingør. Beaches, some chic, some deserted, are powdered with fine white sand.

Fyn rightly earned its storybook reputation by making cuteness a local passion. The city of Odense, Hans Christian Andersen's birthplace, is cobbled with crooked old streets and Lilliputian cottages. Jylland's landscape is the most severe, with Ice Age–chiseled fjords and hills, sheepishly called mountains by the Danes. In the cities of Århus and Aalborg, you can find museums and nightlife rivaling Copenhagen's.

The best way to discover more of Denmark is to strike up a conversation with an affable and hospitable Dane. *Hyggelig* defies definition but comes close to meaning a cozy and charming hospitality. A summertime beach picnic can be as hyggelig as tea on a cold winter's night. The only requirement is the company of a Dane.

Exploring Denmark

Denmark is divided into three regions: the two major islands of Sjælland and Fyn, and the peninsula of Jylland. To the east, Sjælland is Denmark's largest and most populated island, with Copenhagen its focal point. Denmark's second largest island, Fyn, is a pastoral, undulating land dotted with farms and summer-house beach villages, with Odense

1

Beaches

In this country of islands, coastline, and water, beaches come in many breeds. In Sjælland, a series of chic strands stretches north and south of Copenhagen along Strandvejen—the old beach road—pinned down by a string of lovely old seaside towns; this is where the city's youth goes to strut and preen. Fyn's gentle, golden beaches are less a showplace than a quiet getaway for a largely northern European crowd. Windswept Jylland has the country's most expansive and dramatic shorelines—at its northern tip you can even see the line in the waves where the Kattegat meets the Skagerrak Sea. Even more remote, Bornholm's silky, white-sand beaches unfold against a backdrop of wild dunes along the southern edge of the island, while the rocky margins of the Faroe Archipelago are more suitable to distant admiration than leisurely recreation.

Biking

Without a doubt, Denmark is one of the best destinations in the world for biking. More than half the population pedals along city streets that effectively coordinate public transportation and cycle traffic, and along the country paths laced through Jylland and the island of Bornholm. Be sure to contact local or central tourist offices to inquire about biking opportunities. Roughly half of all city streets have been adjusted to accommodate bike traffic and many country routes have bicycle paths running parallel to them. Visitors can plan shorter day trips, or longer itineraries with lodging along the way. Bicyclists must observe all traffic laws, meaning they must signal, stop at stop lights and signs, and use proper lighting from 20 minutes after sunset until 20 minutes before sunrise. The police fine bicyclists Dkr 500 for each traffic infraction.

Boating & Sailing

Well-marked channels and nearby anchorages make sailing and boating easy and popular along the 7,300-km (4,500-mi) coastline. Waters range from the open seas of the Kattegat and the Baltic to Smålandshavet (between Sjælland, Lolland, and Falster) and the calm Limsfjord in Jylland. The country's calm streams are navigable for canoes and kayaks. In Copenhagen, the historic harbors of Christianshavn and Nyhavn and scores of marinas bristling with crisp, white sails are lined with old wooden houseboats, motorboats, yachts, and their colorful crews. And it's not only the well-heeled taking up this pastime: tousle-haired parents and babes, partying youths, and leathery pensioners tend to their boats and picnics, lending a festive, community spirit to the marinas.

Danish Design

Danish design has earned an international reputation for form and function; you will probably recognize the Arne Jacobsen furniture and Bang & Olufsen audio equipment you encounter in Copenhagen's shop windows and designer hotels. The best sales take place after Christmas and last until February, and there you can snatch up glassware, stainless steel, pottery, ceramics, and fur at reasonable prices. Summer clearance sales usually begin at the end of July, but the best bargains pop up in mid-August. Danish antiques and silver are also much cheaper here than in the United States. For major purchases—Bang & Olufsen products, for example—check prices stateside first so you can spot a good buy.

as its one major town. To the west, the relatively vast Jylland connects Denmark to the European continent; here you find the towns of Århus and Aalborg.

Numbers in the text correspond to numbers in the margin and on the maps.

About the Restaurants

Denmark's major cities have a good selection of restaurants serving both traditional Danish and international cuisines. The restaurants we list are the cream of the crop in each price category. Properties indicated by an ✕⊡ are lodging establishments whose restaurant warrants a special trip.

You can reduce the cost of food by planning. Breakfast is often included in your hotel bill; if not, you may wish to buy fruit, sweet rolls, and a beverage for a picnic breakfast. Bakeries abound and offer all the fixings for breakfast, except coffee or tea. In recent years many corner convenience stores have begun to sell hot drinks. Opt for a restaurant lunch instead of dinner, since the latter tends to be significantly more expensive. Instead of beer or wine, drink tap water—liquor can cost four times the price of the same brand in a store—but do specify tap water, as the term "water" can refer to soft drinks and bottled water, which are also expensive.

Danes start the workday early, which means they generally eat lunch at noon and consume their evening meal on the early side. Make sure you make your dinner reservations for no later than 9 PM. Bars and cafés stay open later, and most offer at least light fare. Unless otherwise noted, the restaurants listed in this guide are open daily for lunch and dinner.

Restaurants' markups on alcoholic beverages are often very high in Denmark: as much as four times that of a standard retail price.

About the Hotels

In the larger cities, lodging ranges from first-class business hotels run by SAS, Sheraton, and Scandic; to good-quality tourist-class hotels, such as RESO, Best Western, and Scandic Budget; to a wide variety of single-entrepreneur hotels. In the countryside, look for independently run inns and motels called *kroer*.

Before you leave home, **ask your travel agent about discounts,** including summer hotel checks for Best Western and Scandic, and enormous year-round rebates at SAS hotels for travelers over 65. All EuroClass (business class) passengers can get discounts of at least 10% at SAS hotels when they book through SAS.

Two things about hotels usually surprise North Americans: the relatively limited dimensions of Scandinavian beds and the generous size of Scandinavian breakfasts. Scandinavian double beds are often about 60 inches wide or slightly less, close in size to the U.S. queen size. King-size beds (72 inches wide) are difficult to find and, if available, require special reservations.

Older hotels may have some rooms described as "double," which in fact have one double bed plus one foldout sofa big enough for two people. This arrangement is occasionally called a combi-room but is being phased out.

Make reservations whenever possible. Even countryside inns, which usually have space, are sometimes packed with vacationing Europeans.

Denmark

Skagerrak

North Sea

SWEDEN

Skagen
Hirtshals
Hjørring
Frederikshavn
Sæby

TO GREENLAND
TO FAROE ISLANDS

Brønderslev
Hanstholm
Limfjord
Aalborg
Læsø
Thisted
Limfjord
Aalborg Bugt
Kattegat
Nykøbing
Hadsund
Lemvig
Skive
Anholt
Struer
Viborg
Holstebro
Randers
16
Grenå
Jylland
Silkeborg
Ringkøbing
Herning
Århus
Ebeltoft
Skanderborg
Tisvildeleje
Hornbæk
Grindsted
Horsens
Samsø
Nykøbing
Helsingør
Hillerød
Skjern
Billund
Vejle
Frederikssund
Humlebæk
Esbjerg
Holsted
Fredericia
Kalundborg
Holbæk
Copenhagen
Fanø
Kolding
Middelfart
Jyderup
Roskilde
Amager
Store bælt
Slagelse
Sjælland
Køge Bugt
Ribe
Vojens
Odense
Kerteminde
Rømø
Assens
Fyn
Nyborg
Ringsted
Køge
Skærbæk
Haderslev
Fåborg
Næstved
St. Heddinge
Tønder
Åbenrå
Lillebælt
Svendborg
Karrebæksminde
Sønderborg
Als
Langeland
Tranekær
Vordingborg
Stege
Ærøskøbing
Troense
Rudkøbing
Møn
Ærø
Marstal
Nakskov
Nykøbing
Rødby
Maribo
Falster
Nysted
Lolland
TO BORNHOLM
Ostsee

GERMANY

SWEDEN
Baltic Sea

Bornholm
Rønne

0 ————— 50 miles
0 ————— 75 km

WHAT IT COSTS In Danish Kroner				
$$$$	**$$$**	**$$**	**$**	**¢**
MAIN CITIES				

	$$$$	**$$$**	**$$**	**$**	**¢**
RESTAURANTS	over 200	151–200	121–150	90–120	under 90
HOTELS	over 1,700	1,400–1,700	1,000–1,400	700–1,000	under 700
	ELSEWHERE				
RESTAURANTS	over 180	141–180	121–140	90–120	under 90
HOTELS	over 1,500	1,200–1,500	1,000–1,200	700–1,000	under 700

Restaurant prices are for a main course at dinner, excluding tip. Hotel prices are for two people in a standard double room in high season.

Timing

Summertime—when the lingering sun of June, July, and August brings out the best in the climate and the Danes—is the best time to visit. In July most Danes flee to their summer homes or go abroad. If you do go in winter, the weeks preceding Christmas are a prime time to explore Tivoli. Although the experience is radically different from the flower-filled summertime park, the winter park has a charm all its own. Much of Tivoli is closed during these weeks, but you can still experience some of the shops, restaurants, a handful of rides, an "elf house," and some Danish theater.

Mainland Denmark and its surrounding islands have a cool maritime climate with mild to warm summers and cold (but not frigid) winters. Late summer and early fall is the rainiest season, but even then, precipitation is rarely heavy. In summer, Bornholm tends to stay warmer and sunnier longer than elsewhere; this is also the best time to visit Greenland and the Faroe Islands. Winter is dark and misty, but it's a great time to visit museums, libraries, and the countless atmospheric meeting places in which the Danes take refuge.

COPENHAGEN

Copenhagen—København in Danish—has no glittering skylines, few killer views, and only a handful of meager skyscrapers. Bicycles glide alongside manageable traffic at a pace that's utterly human. The early-morning air in the pedestrian streets of the city's core, Strøget, is redolent of freshly baked bread and soap-scrubbed storefronts. If there's such a thing as a cozy city, this is it.

Extremely livable and relatively calm, Copenhagen is not a microcosm of Denmark, but rather a cosmopolitan city with an identity of its own. Denmark's political, cultural, and financial capital is inhabited by 1.5 million Danes, a fifth of the national population, as well as a growing immigrant community. Filled with museums, restaurants, cafés, and lively nightlife, the city has its greatest resource in its spirited inhabitants. The imaginative, unconventional, and affable Copenhageners exude an egalitarian philosophy that embraces nearly all lifestyles and leanings.

The town was a fishing colony until 1157, when Valdemar the Great gave it to Bishop Absalon, who built a castle on what is now Christiansborg. It grew as a center on the Baltic trade route and became known as *købmændenes havn* (merchants' harbor) and eventually København. In the 15th century it became the royal residence and the capital of Norway and Sweden. A hundred years later, Christian IV, a Renaissance king obsessed with fine architecture, began a building boom that crowned the city with towers and castles, many of which still stand. They are almost all that remain of the city's 800-year history; much of Copenhagen was destroyed by two major fires in the 18th century and by British bombing during the Napoleonic Wars.

Despite a tumultuous history, Copenhagen survives as the liveliest Scandinavian capital. With its backdrop of copper towers and crooked rooftops, the venerable city is amused by playful street musicians and performers, soothed by one of the highest standards of living in the world, and spangled by the thousand lights and gardens of Tivoli.

Exploring Copenhagen

The sites in Copenhagen rarely jump out at you; the city's elegant spires and tangle of cobbled one-way streets are best sought out on foot at an unhurried pace. Excellent bus and train systems can come to the rescue of weary legs. The city is not divided into single-purpose districts; people work, play, shop, and live throughout the central core of this multilayered, densely populated capital.

Be it sea or canal, water surrounds Copenhagen. A network of bridges and drawbridges connects the two main islands—Sjælland and Amager—on which Copenhagen is built. The seafaring atmosphere is indelible, especially around Nyhavn and Christianshavn.

Some Copenhagen sights, especially churches, keep short hours, particularly in fall and winter. It's a good idea to call directly or check with the tourist offices to confirm opening times.

Rådhus Pladsen, Christiansborg Slot & Strøget

In 1728 and again in 1795, fires broke out in central Copenhagen with devastating effect. Disaster struck again in 1807, when the British fleet, under the command of Admiral Gambier, unleashed a heavy bombardment on the city and destroyed many of its oldest and most beautiful buildings. The attack also inflicted hundreds of civilian casualties. These events still shape modern Copenhagen, which was rebuilt with wide, curved-corner streets—making it easier for fire trucks to turn—and large, rectangular apartment buildings centered on courtyards. Arguably the liveliest area of the city, central Copenhagen is packed with shops, restaurants, businesses, and apartment buildings, as well as the crowning architectural achievements of Christian IV—all of it overflowing with Danes and visitors. Copenhagen's central spine consists of the five consecutive pedestrian strands known as Strøget and the surrounding tangle of roads and courtyards—less than a mile square in total. Across the capital's main harbor is the smaller, 17th-century Christianshavn. In the early 1600s, this area was mostly a series of shallows between land, which were eventually dammed. Today Christianshavn's colorful boats and postcard maritime character make it one of the toniest parts of town.

a good walk

The city's heart is the Rådhus Pladsen, home to the baroque-style **Rådhus** ❶ ▶ and its clock tower. On the east side of the square is the landmark **Lurblæserne** ❷. Off the square's northeastern corner is Frederiksberggade, the first of the five pedestrian streets making up **Strøget** ❸, Copenhagen's shopping district. Walk northeast past the cafés and trendy boutiques to the double square of Gammeltorv and Nytorv.

Down Rådhusstræde toward Frederiksholms Kanal, the **Nationalmuseet** ❹ contains an amazing collection of Viking artifacts. Cross Frederiksholms Kanal to Christiansborg Slotsplads, a small atoll divided by the canal and dominated by the burly **Christiansborg Slot** ❺. North of the castle is **Thorvaldsens Museum** ⑥, devoted to the works of one of Denmark's most important sculptors, Bertel Thorvaldsen. On the south end of Downtown is the three-story Romanesque **Kongelige Bibliotek** ⑦, edged by carefully tended gardens and tree-lined avenues. To the south, on the harbor side of the royal library, is its glass and granite annex, nicknamed the "Black Diamond." The newest addition to the library complex is the **Dansk Jødisk Museum** ⑧. Back on the south face of Christiansborg are the **Teatermuseet** ⑨ and the **Kongelige Stald** ⑩.

On the street that bears its name is the **Tøjhusmuseet** ⑪, and a few steps away is the architecturally marvelous **Børsen** ⑫ and the **Holmens Kirke** ⑬. To the southeast is **Christianshavn,** connected to downtown by the drawbridge Knippelsbro. Farther north, the former shipyard of Holmen is marked by expansive venues and several departments of the Københavns Universitet.

From nearly anywhere in the area, you can see the green-and-gold spire of **Vor Frelsers Kirken** ⑭. Northwest of the church, the **Dansk Arkitektur Center** ⑮ occupies a hulking old warehouse on Strandgade. Back across the Knippels Torvegade Bridge, about 1½ km (less than a mile) down Børgsgade through Højbroplads, is Amagertorv, one of Strøget's five streets. Here stands **W. Ø. Larsens Tobakmuseet** ⑯, and farther west down the street is the 18th-century **Helligaandskirken** ⑰. On Strøget's Østergade, the massive spire of **Nikolaj Kirken** ⑱ looks many sizes too large for the tiny cobble streets below.

TIMING The walk itself takes about two hours. Typically, Christiansborg Slot and its ruins and the Nationalmuseet both take at least 1½ hours to see—even more for Viking fans. The hundreds of shops along Strøget are enticing, so plan extra shopping and café time—at least as much as your wallet can spare. Note that many attractions on this walk are closed Sunday or Monday, and some have odd hours; always call ahead or check with the tourist information office.

WHAT TO SEE **Børsen** (Stock Exchange). This masterpiece of fantasy and architecture
⑫ is the oldest stock exchange in Europe. The Børsen was built between 1619 and 1640, with the majority of construction in the 1620s. Christian IV commissioned the building in large part because he wanted to make Denmark the economic superpower and crossroads of Europe. Rumor has it that when it was being built, he was the one who twisted the dragons' tails on the spire that tops the building. When it was first opened, it was used as a sort of medieval mall, filled with shopping stalls. Though parts of the Børsen still operate as a stock exchange, the bulk of the building houses the Chamber of Commerce, and therefore it's open only to accredited members and brokers. ⊠ *Christiansborg Slotspl., Downtown.*

off the beaten path **CHRISTIANIA** – If you are nostalgic for 1960s counterculture, head to this anarchists' commune on Christianshavn. Founded in 1971, when students occupied army barracks, it is now a peaceful community of nonconformists who run a number of businesses, including a bike shop, bakery, rock-music club, and communal bathhouse. Wall cartoons preach drugs and peace, but the inhabitants are less fond of cameras—picture-taking is forbidden. ⊠ *Prinsesseg. and Bådsmandsstr., Christianshavn* ☎ *32/57–96–70 guided tours* ⊕ *www.christiania.org.*

⑤ **Christiansborg Slot** (Christiansborg Castle). Surrounded by canals on
Fodor'sChoice three sides, the massive granite castle is where the queen officially receives guests. From 1441 until the fire of 1795, it was used as the royal

residence. Even though the first two castles on the site were burned, Christiansborg remains an impressive baroque compound, even by European standards. Free tours of the **Folketinget** (Parliament House; ☎ 33/37–55–00) are given Monday through Saturday from June to mid-August, as well as Sunday from July to mid-August; tours run Sunday to Friday from mid-August through September, and on weekdays from October through April. English-language groups embark at 2. At the **Kongelige Repræsantationlokaler** (Royal Reception Chambers; ☎ 33/92–64–92), you're asked to don slippers to protect the floors. Admission is Dkr 40; entry is via guided tour only. Tours are given daily May through September, and Tuesday, Thursday, and weekends from October through April; English tours are at 11 and 3. The **Højesteret** (Supreme Court), on the site of the city's first fortress, was built by Bishop Absalon in 1167. The guards at the entrance are knowledgeable and friendly; call them first to double-check the court's complicated opening hours.

While the castle was being rebuilt around 1900, the Nationalmuseet excavated the **ruins** (☎ 33/92–64–92) beneath it. The resulting dark, subterranean maze contains fascinating models and architectural relics. The ruins are open daily 9:30–3:30, May through September; and Tuesday, Thursday, and weekends the rest of the year. Admission is Dkr 20.

Wander around **Højbro Plads** and the delightful row of houses that borders the northern edge of Slotsholmen. The quays here were long ago Copenhagen's fish market, but today most fresh fish is transported directly from boats to the city's fish shops and supermarkets. However, one lone fisherwoman still hawks fresh fish, marinated herring, and eel in the early morning. She is the last fishmonger you'll see carrying on the tradition. ✉ *Prins Jørgens Gård 1, Downtown* ☎ *33/63–27–50.*

Christianshavn. Cobbled avenues, antique street lamps, and Left Bank charm make up one of the oldest neighborhoods in the city. Even the old system of earthworks—the best preserved of Copenhagen's original fortification walls—still exists. In the 17th century, Christian IV offered what were patches of partially flooded land for free, and with additional tax benefits; in return, takers would have to fill them in and construct sturdy buildings for trade, commerce, housing for the shipbuilding workers, and defense against sea attacks. Gentrified today, the area harbors restaurants, cafés, and shops, and its ramparts are edged with green areas and walking paths, making it the perfect neighborhood for an afternoon or evening amble. The central square, Christianshavn Torv, is where all activity emanates from, and Torvegade, a bustling shopping street, is the main thoroughfare. For a pleasant break, relax at one of the cafés along Wilders Canal, which streams through the heart of town.

⓯ Dansk Arkitektur Center. The Danish Architecture Center occupies an old wharfside warehouse built in 1880. The hulking structure fell into a state of disrepair after lying fallow for many years, but was rescued, renovated, and reopened in 1986. The center hosts rotating exhibitions that cover trends and trendsetters in Danish architecture and architectural design. ✉ *Strandg. 27B, Christianshavn* ☎ *32/57–19–30* ⊕ *www.dac. dk* ✇ *Dkr 30, exhibitions vary* ☉ *Weekdays 10–5.*

❽ Dansk Jødisk Museum (Danish Jewish Museum). At this writing, the museum, in a wing of the Royal Library is nearing completion of the first stage of construction. A date has not been set for the museum's opening. The site was designed by Daniel Libeskind, the architect behind the winning design proposal for the World Trade Center site in New York City. Along with a general overview of Jewish history in Denmark, the museum will give extensive coverage to the Danish resistance movement,

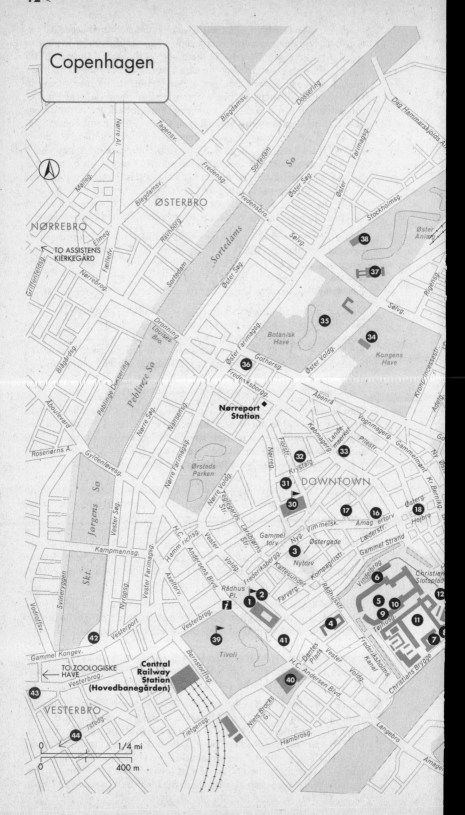

Copenhagen

ØSTERBRO

NØRREBRO

TO ASSISTENS
KIERKEGÅRD

Botanisk
Have

Øster
Anlæg

Kongens
Have

38

37

35

34

36

Nørreport
Station

DOWNTOWN

Ørsteds
Parken

32

33

31

30

17   16

18

3

Gammel
torv   Nyg.   Østergade

Nytorv

Christian
Slotsplad

6

5   10

9

11

7

12

Rådhus
Pl.

1   2

4

Tivoli

39

41

40

TO ZOOLOGISKE
HAVE

Central
Railway
Station
(Hovedbanegården)

42

43

VESTERBRO

44

0   1/4 mi

0   400 m

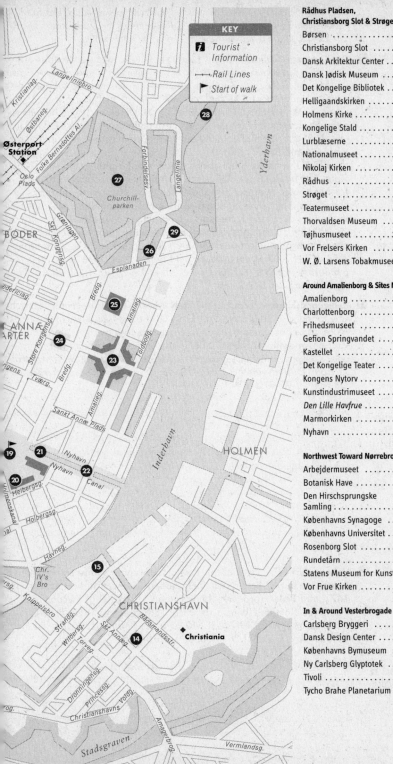

13

KEY

i *Tourist Information*

⊢—+ *Rail Lines*

▶ *Start of walk*

whose work during World War II helped bring nearly all of Denmark's 7,000 Jews to safety in Sweden. ⊠ *Købmagerg. 5, Downtown* ☎ *33/11–22–18* ⊕ *www.jewmus.dk* ⊙ *Hrs to be determined.*

❼ Det Kongelige Bibliotek (Royal Library). The Royal Library houses the country's largest collection of books, newspapers, and manuscripts. Among the more than 2 million volumes are accounts of Viking journeys to America and Greenland and original manuscripts by Hans Christian Andersen and Karen Blixen (Isak Dinesen). If you happen to be in the area, ramble around the statue of philosopher Søren Kierkegaard (1813–55), the formal gardens, and tree-lined avenues surrounding the scholarly building. The library's massive glass-and-granite annex, called the Black Diamond, looms between the main building and the waterfront. The Black Diamond hosts temporary historical exhibits that often feature books, manuscripts, and artifacts culled from the library's extensive holdings. The **National Museum of Photography,** also housed in the Black Diamond, contains a far-reaching collection of more than 25,000 Danish and international photographs, from which temporary exhibits display selections. ⊠ *Søren Kierkegaards Pl. 1, Downtown* ☎ *33/47–47–47* ⊕ *www.kb.dk* ⊠ *Library free, admission varies for temporary exhibits* ⊙ *Library weekdays 10–7, Sat. 10–2; Black Diamond Mon.–Sat. 10–5.*

⑰ Helligaandskirken (Church of the Holy Ghost). This 18th-century church was founded as an abbey of the Holy Ghost and is still one of the city's oldest places of worship. Its choir contains a font by the sculptor Thorvaldsen, and more-modern art is found in the large exhibition room—once a hospital—that faces Strøget. ⊠ *Niels Hemmingseng. 5, Amagertorv section, Downtown* ☎ *33/18–16–45* ⊕ *www.helligaandskirken.dk* ⊠ *Free* ⊙ *Weekdays 9–1, Sat. 10–noon.*

off the beaten path

HOLMAN – Previously isolated from central Copenhagen, this former navy base north of Christianshavn produced ships and ammunition until the 1980s. It was formally opened as the site of the 1995 United Nations Summit on Human Development and played an important role as a cultural area during Copenhagen's 1996 reign as the Cultural Capital of Europe. Today, among its several cultural venues is the city's biggest performance space, the Torpedo Hall, where torpedoes were actually assembled. You'll also find the Danish Art Academy's Architecture School, the National Theater School, the Rhythmic Music Conservatory, and the Danish Film School, which all host special activities.

⑬ Holmens Kirke (Islet's Church). Two of the country's most revered naval heroes are buried here: Niels Juel crushed the Swedish fleet at Køge in 1677, and Peder Tordenskjold defeated Charles XII of Sweden during the Great Northern War in the early 18th century. ⊠ *Holmenskanal, Christianshavn* ☎ *33/11–37–40* ⊕ *www.holmenskirke.dk* ⊠ *Free* ⊙ *Weekdays 9–2, Sat. 9–noon, Sun. during services.*

need a break?

Øieblikket Espresso Bar m.m. (⊠ Søren Kierkegaards Pl. 1, Downtown ☎ 33/47–49–50) operates out of a prime corner on the ground floor of the Royal Library's Black Diamond. The "m.m." in the name means "and more." It's named after a literary journal to which philosopher Søren Kierkegaard once contributed—and you too may be inspired to wax poetic as you gaze out over the harbor and bask in the sunlight streaming through the soaring glass walls. In summer, the café sets up outdoor tables. When the summer days turn nippy, you can stay snug indoors, while enjoying the illusion of being outside, thanks to the natural light that floods in at all angles. The simple fare includes croissants, brownies, and sandwiches made on fluffy round buns.

⑩ Kongelige Stald (Royal Stables). Between 9 and noon, time seems to stand still while riders, elegantly clad in breeches and jackets, exercise the horses. The vehicles, including coaches and carriages, and harnesses on display have been used by the Danish monarchy from 1778 to the present. ✉ *Christiansborg Ridebane 12, Downtown* ☎ *33/40–26–77* ☞ *Dkr 10* ⏲ *May–Sept., Fri.–Sun. 2–4; Oct.–Apr., weekends 2–4.*

❷ Lurblæserne (Lur Blower Column). Topped by two Vikings blowing an ancient trumpet called a *lur*, this column displays a good deal of artistic license—the lur dates from the Bronze Age, 1500 BC, whereas the Vikings lived a mere 1,000 years ago. City tours often start at this important landmark, which was erected in 1914. ✉ *East side of Rådhus Pl., Downtown.*

★ ☺ ❹ Nationalmuseet (National Museum). An 18th-century royal residence, peaked by massive overhead windows, has contained—since the 1930s—what is regarded as one of the best national museums in Europe. Extensive permanent exhibits chronicle Danish cultural history from prehistoric to modern times—included is one of the largest collections of Stone Age tools in the world—and Egyptian, Greek, and Roman antiquities are on display. The children's museum, with replicas of period clothing and all sorts of touchable items, transforms history into something to which children under age 12 can relate. ✉ *Ny Vesterg. 10, Downtown* ☎ *33/13–44–11* ⊕ *www.natmus.dk* ☞ *Dkr 50, free Wed.* ⏲ *Tues.–Sun. 10–5.*

⑱ Nikolaj Kirken (Nicholas Church). Though the green spire of the imposing church—named for the patron saint of seafarers—appears as old as the surrounding medieval streets, it is actually relatively young. The current building was finished in 1914; the previous structure, which dated from the 13th century, was destroyed by the 1795 fire. Today the church is a contemporary art gallery and exhibition center that often shows experimental work. ✉ *Nikolaj Pl. 10, Downtown* ☎ *33/93–16–26* ⊕ *www.nikolaj-ccac.dk* ☞ *Dkr 20, free Wed.* ⏲ *Daily noon–5.*

need a break? **Café Nikolaj** (✉ Nikolajpl., Downtown ☎ 33/93–16–26), inside Nikolaj Kirken, is a reliable, inexpensive café with good pastries and light meals. It's open noon to 3 for lunch and until 5 for cakes and drinks. From June through August, you can eat on the open terrace.

▶ ❶ Rådhus (City Hall). Completed in 1905, the mock-Renaissance building dominates **Rådhus Pladsen** (City Hall Square), the hub of Copenhagen's commercial district. Architect Martin Nyrop's creation was popular from the start, perhaps because he envisioned that it should give "gaiety to everyday life and spontaneous pleasure to all . . ." A statue of Copenhagen's 12th-century founder, Bishop Absalon, sits atop the main entrance.

Besides being an important ceremonial meeting place for Danish VIPs, the intricately decorated Rådhus contains the first **World Clock.** The multidial, superaccurate astronomical timepiece has a 570,000-year calendar and took inventor Jens Olsen 27 years to complete before it was put into action in 1955. If you're feeling energetic, take a guided tour up the 350-foot bell tower for the panoramic, but not particularly inspiring, view.

The modern glass and gray-steel **bus terminal** flanking the square's northwest side has French granite floors, pear-tree-wood shelving, and underground marble bathrooms. The $2.8 million creation proved so architecturally contentious—more for its placement than for its design—that there was serious discussion of moving it.

Look up to see one of the city's most charming bronze sculptures, created by the Danish artist E. Utzon Frank in 1936. Diagonally across Rådhus Pladsen, atop a corner office building, are a **neon thermometer** and a **gilded barometer.** On sunny days there's a golden sculpture of a girl on a bicycle; come rain, a girl with an umbrella appears. ⊠ *Rådhus Pl., Downtown* ☎ *33/66–33–66* ☒ *Tower tours Dkr 20* ☉ *Rådhus weekdays 8–5. Tours Oct.–May, Mon.–Sat. at noon; June–Sept., weekdays 10, noon, and 2. Sat. at noon.*

need a break?

Vandkunsten (⊠ Rådhusstr. 17, Downtown ☎ 33/13–90–40) is a mom-and-pop joint that makes great Italian-inspired sandwiches and salads, and they offer free coffee while you wait. The shop is tiny, but the efficient service keeps customers moving. There is only one table inside and it's usually surrounded by customers; so long as the weather is nice, get something to go and seek out a sunny spot for munching.

★ ❸ **Strøget.** Though it is referred to by one name, the city's pedestrian spine, pronounced *Stroy*-et, is actually a series of five streets: Frederiksberggade, Nygade, Vimmelskaftet, Amagertorv, and Østergade. By mid-morning, particularly on Saturday, it is congested with people, baby strollers, and street performers. Past the swank and trendy, and sometimes flashy and trashy, boutiques of **Frederiksberggade** is the double square of **Gammeltorv** (Old Square) and **Nytorv** (New Square), in summer often crowded with street vendors selling cheap jewelry.

In 1728 and again in 1795, much of Strøget was heavily damaged by fire. When rebuilding, the city fathers straightened and widened the streets. You can still see buildings from this reconstruction period, as well as a few that survived the fires.

In addition to shopping, you can enjoy Strøget for strolling, as hundreds do. Outside the posh fur and porcelain shops and bustling cafés and restaurants, the sidewalks have a festive street-fair atmosphere.

❾ **Teatermuseet** (Theater Museum). After you brush up on theater and ballet history, wander around the boxes, stage, and dressing rooms of the **Royal Court Theater** of 1767, which King Christian VII had built as the first court theater in Scandinavia. Tours can be arranged. ⊠ *Christiansborg Ridebane 10/18, Downtown* ☎ *33/11–51–76* ⊕ *www. teatermuseet.dk* ☒ *Dkr 30* ☉ *Wed. 2–4, weekends noon–4.*

❻ **Thorvaldsens Museum.** The 19th-century artist Bertel Thorvaldsen (1770–1844) is buried at the center of this museum in a simple, ivy-covered tomb. Strongly influenced by the statues and reliefs of classical antiquity, he is recognized as one of the world's greatest neoclassical artists, having completed commissions all over Europe. The museum, once a coach house to Christiansborg, now houses Thorvaldsen's interpretations of classical and mythological figures, and an extensive collection of paintings and drawings by other artists that Thorvaldsen assembled while living— for most of his life—in Rome. The outside frieze by Jørgen Sonne depicts the sculptor's triumphant return to Copenhagen after years abroad. ⊠ *Bertel Thorvaldsen Pl. 2, Downtown* ☎ *33/32–15–32* ⊕ *www. thorvaldsensmuseum.dk* ☒ *Dkr 20* ☉ *Tues.–Sun. 10–5.*

⑪ Tøjhusmuseet (Royal Danish Arsenal Museum). This Renaissance structure—built by King Christian IV and one of central Copenhagen's oldest—contains impressive displays of uniforms, weapons, and armor in a 600-foot-long arched hall. ✉ *Tøjhusg. 3, Downtown* ☎ *33/11–60–37* ⊕ *www.thm.dk* 🎫 *Dkr 40* ⊙ *Tues.–Sun. noon–4.*

⑭ Vor Frelsers Kirken (Church of Our Savior). The green-and-gold spire of this baroque church has dominated the Christianshavn area since it was completed in 1752. Local legend has it that the staircase encircling it was built curling the wrong way around, and that when its architect, Laurids de Thurah, reached the top and realized what he'd done, he jumped. In this case, however, legend is erroneous: de Thurah died in his own bed in 1759. ✉ *Skt. Annæg. 29, Christianshavn* ☎ *32/57–27–98* ⊕*www.vorfrelserskirke.dk* ⊙ *Apr.–Aug., daily 11–4:30; Sept.–Mar., daily 11–3:30* ⊙ *Tower closed Nov.–Mar. and in inclement weather.*

⑯ W. Ø. Larsens Tobakmuseet (W. Ø. Larsens Tobacco Museum). The Tobacco Museum has a full-fledged collection of pipes made in every conceivable shape from every possible material. Look for the tiny pipe that's no bigger than an embroidery needle. There are also paintings, drawings, and an amazing array of smoking implements. ✉ *Amagertorv 9, Downtown* ☎ *33/12–20–50* 🎫 *Free* ⊙ *Mon.–Thurs. 10–6, Fri. 10–7, Sat. 10–5.*

Around Amalienborg & Sites North

The Sankt Annæ district of the city was dubbed New Copenhagen when King Christian IV began to expand the city northeastward in the 17th century, building Sankt Annæ Fort (now the Churchillsparken and Kastellet) in the process. The district takes its name from the Sankt Annæ religious order, which valiantly staffed a 16th-century syphilis ward in the area.

North of Kongens Nytorv, the city becomes a fidgety grid of parks and wider boulevards pointing northwest across the canal toward upscale Østerbro—wreathed by manors commissioned by wealthy merchants and blue bloods. In the mid-1700s, King Frederik V donated parcels of this land to anyone who agreed to build from the work of architect Niels Eigtved, who also designed the Kongelige Theater. The jewel of this crown remains Amalienborg and its rococo mansions.

a good walk

At the end of Strøget, **Kongens Nytorv** ⑲ ⌐ is flanked on its south side by the **Kongelige Teater** ⑳, and backed by **Charlottenborg** ㉑, which contains the Danish Academy of Fine Art (call to see if an exhibition has opened the castle to the public). The street leading southeast from Kongens Nytorv is **Nyhavn** ㉒, a onetime sailors' haunt and now a popular waterfront hub. From the south end of the harbor (and the north end of Havnegade) high-speed craft leave for Malmö, Sweden; farther north, Kvæsthusbroen—at the end of Skt. Annæ Plads—is the quay for boats to Oslo, Norway, and Bornholm, Denmark; farther north still, just before the perch of *The Little Mermaid*, ships depart for Swinoujscie, Poland.

West of the harbor front is the grand square called Skt. Annæ Plads. Perpendicular to the oblong square is Amaliegade, its wooden colonnade bordering the cobbled square of **Amalienborg** ㉓, the royal residence with a pleasant garden on its harbor side. Steps west from the square is Bredgade, where the baroque **Marmorkirken** ㉔ flaunts its Norwegian marble structure. Farther north off Bredgade is the rococo **Kunstindustrimuseet** ㉕. Continuing north on Bredgade (you can also take the more colorful, café-lined Store Kongensgade, just west), turn right onto Esplanaden and you'll see the enormously informative **Frihedsmuseet** ㉖. At the Churchillparken's entrance stands the English church, St. Albans.

In the park's center, the **Kastellet** ㉗ serves as a reminder of the city's grim military history. At its eastern perimeter is Langelinie, a waterfront promenade with a view of Denmark's best-known pinup, **Den Lille Havfrue** ㉘. Wending your way back toward Esplanaden and the town center, you'll pass the **Gefion Springvandet** ㉙.

TIMING This walk amid parks, gardens, canals, and building exteriors should take a full day. If the weather is nice, linger in the parks, especially the Kastellet and Amalienhaven, and plan on a long lunch at Nyhavn. The Kunstindustrimuseet merits about an hour, more if you plan on perusing the design books in the museum's well-stocked library. The Frihedsmuseet may require more time: its evocative portrait of Danish life during World War II intrigues even the most history-weary teens. Avoid taking this tour Monday, when some sites are closed.

WHAT TO SEE **Amalienborg** (Amalia's Castle). The four identical rococo buildings oc-
㉓ cupying this square have housed the royals since 1784. The Christian VIII palace across from the Queen's residence houses the **Amalienborg Museum,** which displays the second part of the Royal Collection (the first is at Rosenborg Slot) and chronicles royal lifestyles between 1863 and 1947. Here you can view the study of King Christian IX (1818–1906) and the drawing room of his wife, Queen Louise. Rooms are packed with family gifts and regal baubles ranging from tacky knickknacks to Fabergé treasures, including a nephrite-and-ruby table clock, and a small costume collection.

In the square's center is a magnificent equestrian statue of King Frederik V by the French sculptor Jacques François Joseph Saly. It reputedly cost as much as all the buildings combined. Every day at noon, the Royal Guard and band march from Rosenborg Slot through the city for the changing of the guard. At noon on Queen Margrethe's birthday, April 16, crowds of Danes gather to cheer their monarch, who stands and waves from her balcony. On Amalienborg's harbor side are the trees, gardens, and fountains of **Amalienhaven.** ✉ *Christian VIII's Palace–Amalienborg Pl., Sankt Annæ Kvarter* ☎ *33/12–08–08* ✉ *Dkr 40* ☉ *May–Oct., daily 11–4; Nov.–Apr., Tues.–Sun. 11–4.*

㉑ **Charlottenborg** (Charlotte's Castle). This Dutch baroque–style castle was built by Frederik III's half brother in 1670. Since 1754 the garden-flanked property has housed the faculty and students of the Danish Academy of Fine Art. It is open only during exhibits, which occur year-round. ✉ *Nyhavn 2, Downtown* ☎ *33/13–40–22* ⊕ *www. charlottenborg-art.dk* ✉ *Dkr 40* ☉ *During exhibitions, daily 10–5 (Wed. until 7).*

㉖ **Frihedsmuseet** (Resistance Museum). Evocative, sometimes moving displays commemorate the heroic Danish resistance movement, which saved 7,000 Jews from the Nazis by hiding and then smuggling them to Sweden. The homemade tank outside was used to spread the news of the Nazi surrender after World War II. ✉ *Churchillparken, Sankt Annæ Kvarter* ☎ *33/13–77–14* ⊕ *www.natmus.dk* ✉ *Dkr 40, free Wed.* ☉ *May–mid-Sept., Tues.–Sat. 10–4, Sun. and holidays 10–5; mid-Sept.–Apr., Tues.–Sat. 11–3, Sun. and holidays 11–4.*

㉙ **Gefion Springvandet** (Gefion Fountain). Not far from *The Little Mermaid* yet another dramatic myth is illustrated. The goddess Gefion was promised as much of Sweden as she could plough in a night. The story goes that she changed her sons to oxen and used them to portion off what is now the island of Sjælland. ✉ *East of Frihedsmuseet, Sankt Annæ Kvarter.*

㉗ Kastellet (Citadel). At Churchill Park's entrance stands the spired English church **St. Albans.** From there, walk north on the main path to reach the Citadel. The structure's smooth, peaceful walking paths, marina, and greenery belie its fierce past as a city fortification. Built in the aftermath of the Swedish siege of the city on February 10, 1659, the double moats were among the improvements made to the city's defense. The Citadel served as the city's main fortress into the 18th century; in a grim reversal during World War II, the Germans used it as headquarters during their occupation. ⊠ *Center of Churchill Park, Sankt Annæ Kvarter* ⊠ *Free* ⊙ *Daily 6* AM–*sunset.*

⑳ Det Kongelige Teater (The Royal Danish Theater). The stoic, pillared, and gallery-front theater is the country's preeminent venue for music, opera, ballet, and theater. Nearly all theater works performed are in the Danish language, while operas are in their original language with Danish over-titles on a screen above the stage. The Royal Danish Ballet performs on the older stage in the main building; its repertoire ranges from classical to modern works. At this writing, a new opera house was under construction at the harborfront in the former naval base Holmen located in the Christianshavn district. The new facility is scheduled to open in 2005.

The current building was opened in 1874, though the annex, known as **Stærekassen** (Nesting Box) was not inaugurated until 1931. The Nesting Box got its name due to an obscure likeness to a birdhouse. Statues of Danish poet Adam Oehlenschläger and author Ludvig Holberg—whose works remain the core of Danish theater—flank the facade. Born in Bergen, Norway, in 1684, Holberg came to Denmark as a student and stayed. Often compared to Molière, he wrote 32 of his comedies in a "poetic frenzy" between 1722 and 1728, and, legend has it, he complained of interminable headaches the entire time. He published the works himself, made an enormous fortune, and invested in real estate. In the mid-'90s, an annex designed by Norwegian architect Sverre Fehn was planned for construction on the eastern side of the theater. The renovations have been half-finished and half-abandoned in light of the new opera house project. The theater closes for the summer months. ⊠ *Tordenskjoldsg. 3, Downtown* ☎ *33/69–69–33, 33/69–69–69 tickets* ⊕ *www.kgl-teater. dk* ⊠ *Guided tours 75 Dkr* ⊙ *Guided tours Sun. 11; no tours May 27–Aug. 5.*

▶ **⑲ Kongens Nytorv** (King's New Square). A mounted statue of Christian V dominates the square. Crafted in 1688 by the French sculptor Lamoureux, the subject is conspicuously depicted as a Roman emperor. Every year, at the end of June, graduating high school students arrive in horse-drawn carriages and dance beneath the furrowed brow of the sober statue. ⊠ *Between Gothersg., Holmenskanal, and Tordenskjoldsg., Downtown.*

> **need a break?** Dozens of restaurants and cafés line Nyhavn. **Cap Horn** (⊠ Nyhavn 21, Downtown ☎ 33/12–85–04) is among the best, with moderately priced and completely organic Danish treats served in a cozy, art-filled dining room that resembles a ship's galley. Try the fried plaice, swimming in a sea of parsley butter with boiled potatoes. In the summertime, try to grab a sidewalk table, the perfect place to enjoy an overstuffed focaccia sandwich and a Carlsberg.

㉕ Kunstindustrimuseet (Museum of Decorative Art). Originally built in the 18th century as a royal hospital, the fine rococo museum houses a large selection of European and Asian crafts. Also on display are ceramics, silverware, tapestries, and special exhibitions that often focus on contemporary design. The museum's excellent library is stocked with design books and magazines. A small café also operates here. ⊠ *Bredg. 68, Sankt Annæ Kvarter* ☎ *33/18–56–56* ⊕ *www.kunstindustrimuseet. dk* ⊠ *Dkr 40, additional fee for some special exhibits* ☉ *Permanent collection Tues.–Fri. 1–4, weekends noon–4; special exhibits Tues.–Fri. 10–4, weekends noon–4.*

❷❽ **Den Lille Havfrue** (*The Little Mermaid*). On the Langelinie promenade, this somewhat overhyped 1913 statue commemorates Hans Christian Andersen's lovelorn creation, and is the subject of hundreds of travel posters. Donated to the city by Carl Jacobsen, the son of the founder of Carlsberg Breweries, the innocent waif has also been the subject of some cruel practical jokes, including decapitation and the loss of an arm, but she is currently in one piece. Especially on a sunny Sunday, the Langelinie promenade is thronged with Danes and visitors making their pilgrimage to see the statue. On this occasion, you may want to read the original Hans Christian Andersen tale; it's a heart-wrenching story that's a far cry from the Disney animated movie. ⊠ *Langelinie promenade, Østerbro.*

❷❹ **Marmorkirken** (Marble Church). Officially the Frederikskirke, this ponderous baroque sanctuary of precious Norwegian marble was begun in 1749 and remained unfinished from 1770 to 1874 due to budget constraints. It was finally completed and consecrated in 1894. Around the exterior are 16 statues of various religious leaders from Moses to Luther, and below them stand sculptures of outstanding Danish ministers and bishops. The hardy can scale 273 steps to the outdoor balcony. From here you can walk past the exotic gilded onion domes of the **Russiske Ortodoks Kirke** (Russian Orthodox Church), just to the north of the Marmorkirken. ⊠ *Frederiksg. 4, off Bredg., Sankt Annæ Kvarter* ☎ *33/ 15–01–44* ⊕ *www.marmorkirken.dk* ⊠ *Free; balcony Dkr 20* ☉ *Mon., Tues., and Thurs. 10–5; Wed. 10–6; weekends noon–5. Guided tours mid-June–Aug., daily 1–3; Sept.–mid-June, weekends 1–3.*

★ ❷❷ **Nyhavn** (New Harbor). This harbor-front neighborhood was built 300 years ago to attract traffic and commerce to the city center. Until 1970, the area was a favorite haunt of sailors. Though restaurants, boutiques, and antiques stores now outnumber tattoo parlors, many old buildings have been well preserved and have retained the harbor's authentic 18th-century maritime character; you can even see a fleet of old-time sailing ships from the quay. Hans Christian Andersen lived at various times in the Nyhavn houses at numbers 18, 20, and 67.

Northwest Toward Nørrebro

By the 1880s many of the buildings that now line Nørrebro were being hastily thrown up as housing for area laborers. Many of these flats—typically decorated with a row of pedimented windows and a portal entrance—have been renovated through a massive urban-renewal program. But to this day, many share hall toilets, have no showers, and are heated only by kerosene heaters. On the Nørrebrogade and Skt. Hans Torv of today, you'll discover a fair number of cafés, restaurants, clubs, and shops.

a good walk

Take the train from Østerport Station, off Oslo Plads, to Nørreport Station on Nørre Voldg. and walk down Fiolstræde to **Vor Frue Kirken** ❸⓪ ⌐. The church's tall copper spire and four shorter ones crown the area. Backtrack north on Fiolstræde, to the main building of **Københavns Universitet** ❸❶; on the corner of Krystalgade is the **Københavns Synagoge** ❸❷.

Fiolstræde ends at the Nørreport train station. Perpendicular to Nørre Voldgade is Frederiksborggade, which leads northwest to the neighborhood of Nørrebro; to the southeast after the Kultorvet, or Coal

Square, Frederiksborggade turns into the pedestrian street Købmagergade. From anywhere in the area, you can see the stout **Rundetårn** ㉝:
the round tower stands as one of Copenhagen's most beloved landmarks,
with an observatory open on autumn and winter evenings. North from
the Rundetårn on Landemærket, Gothersgade gives way to **Rosenborg
Slot** ㉞, its Dutch Renaissance design standing out against the vivid
green of the well-tended Kongens Have. For a heavier dose of plants
and living things, head across Øster Voldgade to the 25-acre **Botanisk
Have** ㉟. South of the garden is the **Arbejdermuseet** ㊱, which profiles the
lives of workers from the late 1800s to the present.

Leave the garden's north exit to reach the **Statens Museum for Kunst** ㊲,
notable for exceptional Matisse works. An adjacent building houses **Den
Hirschsprungske Samling** ㊳, with 19th-century Danish art on display.
Nearby, on the east side of Øster Voldgade, is **Nyboder,** a neighborhood
full of tidy homes built by Christian IV for the city's sailors.

TIMING All of the sites on this tour are relatively close together and can be seen
in roughly half a day. Note that some sites close Monday or Tuesday;
call ahead. The tour can be easily combined with the one that follows—
just head back to Nørreport station and catch a train to Hovedbanegården.

WHAT TO SEE **Arbejdermuseet** (Workers' Museum). The vastly underrated museum
㊱ chronicles the working class from 1870 to the present, with evocative
life-size "day-in-the-life-of" exhibits, including reconstructions of a city
street and tram and an original apartment once belonging to a brewery
worker, his wife, and eight children. Changing exhibits focusing on
Danish and international social issues are often excellent. The museum
also has a 19th-century–style restaurant serving old-fashioned Danish
specialties and a '50s-style coffee shop. ✉ *Rømersg. 22, Downtown* ☎ *33/
93–25–75* ⊕ *www.arbejdermuseet.dk* ✉ *Dkr 50* ☉ *July–Oct., daily 10–4;
Nov.–June, Tues.–Sun. 10–4.*

off the
beaten
path

★

ASSISTENS KIRKEGÅRD (Assistens Cemetery) – This peaceful, leafy
cemetery in the heart of Nørrebro is the final resting place of
numerous great Danes, including Søren Kierkegaard (whose last
name means "church garden," or "cemetery"), Hans Christian
Andersen, and physicist Niels Bohr. In summer, the cemetery takes on
a cheerful, city-park air as picnicking families, young couples, and
sunbathers relax on the sloping lawns amid the dearly departed.
✉ *Kapelvej 2, Nørrebro* ☎ *35/37–19–17* ⊕ *www.assistens.dk*
✉ *Free* ☉ *May–Aug., daily 8–8; Sept.–Oct. and Mar.–Apr., daily
8–6; Nov.–Feb., daily 8–4.*

need a
break?

At the bar–café–restaurant combo **Barstarten** (✉ Kapelvej 1,
Nørrebro ☎ 35/24–11–00) you can get three squares, snacks, and a
dizzying array of beverages. The kitchen whips up simple French-
Italian country cooking and a new menu appears every two weeks. A
favorite is *Barstarten's Menu,* a three-course affair with a wine list to
accompany the food. DJs liven up the scene late on weekend nights
with a soul-and-funk repertoire.

㉟ **Botanisk Have** (Botanical Garden). Trees, flowers, ponds, sculptures,
and a spectacular 19th-century Palmehuset (Palm House) of tropical and
subtropical plants blanket the garden's 25-plus acres. There's also an
observatory and a geological museum. Take time to explore the gardens
and watch the pensioners feed the birds. Some have been coming here
so long that the birds actually alight on their fingers. ✉ *Gothersg. 128,*

Sankt Annæ Kvarter ☎ 35/32–22–40 ⊕ *www.botanic-garden.ku.dk* ✉ *Free* ☉ *Grounds May–Sept., daily 8:30–6; Oct.–Apr., Tues.–Sun. 8:30–4. Palm House daily 10–3.*

㊳ Den Hirschsprungske Samling (The Hirschsprung Collection). This museum showcases paintings from the country's Golden Age—Denmark's mid-19th-century school of naturalism—as well as a collection of paintings by the late-19th-century artists of the Skagen School. Their luminous works capture the play of light and water so characteristic of the Danish countryside. ✉ *Stockholmsg. 20, Østerbro* ☎ 35/42–03–36 ⊕ *www.hirschsprung.dk* ✉ *Dkr 35, free Wed.* ☉ *Thurs.–Mon. 11–4, Wed. 11–9.*

㉜ Københavns Synagoge (Copenhagen Synagogue). The contemporary architect Gustav Friedrich Hetsch borrowed from the Doric and Egyptian styles in creating this arklike synagogue. ✉ *Krystalg. 12, Downtown* ☎ 33/12–88–88 ☉ *Daily services 4:15.*

㉛ Københavns Universitet (Copenhagen University). The main building of Denmark's leading institution for higher learning was constructed in the 19th century on the site of a medieval bishop's palace. The university was founded nearby in 1479. ✉ *Nørreg. 10, Downtown* ☎ 35/32–26–26 ⊕ *www.ku.dk.*

need a break?
Near Copenhagen University is **Sømods Bolcher** (✉ Nørreg. 24 or 36, Downtown ☎ 33/12–60–46), a Danish confectioner that has been on the scene since the late 19th century. Children and candy-lovers relish seeing the hard candy pulled and cut by hand.

Nyboder. Tour the neat, mustard-color enclave of Nyboder, a perfectly laid-out compound of flat, long, former sailors' homes built by Christian IV. Like Nyhavn, the area was seedy and boisterous at the beginning of the 1970s, but today has become one of Copenhagen's more fashionable neighborhoods. At **Nyboder Mindestuer** (✉ Skt Paulsg. 24 ☎ 33/32–10–05 ✉ Dkr 10) you can view an exhibition of everyday life in Nyboder from its inception in 1631 to the present day. The people at the exhibition center also arrange guided tours of the neighborhood. ✉ *West of Store Kongensg. and east of Rigensg., Sankt Annæ Kvarter.*

㉞ Rosenborg Slot (Rosenborg Castle). This Dutch Renaissance castle contains ballrooms, halls, and reception chambers, but for all of its grandeur, there's an intimacy that makes you think the king might return any minute. Thousands of objects are displayed, including beer glasses, gilded clocks, golden swords, family portraits, a pearl-studded saddle, and gem-encrusted tables; an adjacent treasury contains the royal jewels. The castle's setting is equally welcoming: it's in the middle of the **Kongens Have** (King's Garden), amid lawns, park benches, and shady walking paths.

FodorsChoice ★

King Christian IV built the Rosenborg Castle as a summer residence but loved it so much that he ended up living and dying here. In 1849 when the absolute monarchy was abolished, all the royal castles became state property, except for Rosenborg, which is still passed down from monarch to monarch. Once a year, during the fall holiday, the castle stays open until midnight, and visitors are invited to explore its darkened interior with bicycle lights. ✉ *Øster Voldg. 4A, Sankt Annæ Kvarter* ☎ 33/15–32–86 ✉ *Dkr 50* ☉ *Nov.–Apr., Tues.–Sun. 11–2; May and Sept., daily 10–4; June–Aug., daily 10–5; Oct., daily 11–3.*

★ **㉝ Rundetårn** (Round Tower). Instead of climbing the stout Round Tower's stairs, visitors scale a smooth, 600-foot spiral ramp on which—legend has it—Peter the Great of Russia rode a horse alongside his wife, Catherine, who took a carriage. From its top, you enjoy a panoramic view of the twisted streets and crooked roofs of Copenhagen. The unusual building was constructed as an observatory in 1642 by Christian IV and is still maintained as the oldest such structure in Europe.

The art gallery has changing exhibits, and occasional concerts are held within its massive stone walls. An observatory and telescope are open to the public evenings mid-October through March, and an astronomer is on hand to answer questions. ⊠ *Købmagerg. 52A, Downtown* ☎ *33/73–03–73* ⊕ *www.rundetaarn.dk* ⊡ *Dkr 20* ☉ *Sept.–May, Mon.–Sat. 10–5, Sun. noon–5; June–Aug., Mon.–Sat. 10–8, Sun. noon–8. Observatory mid-Oct.–Mar., Tues. and Wed. 7 PM–10 PM.*

㉗ Statens Museum for Kunst (National Art Gallery). Old Master paintings—including works by Rubens, Rembrandt, Titian, El Greco, and Fragonard—as well as a comprehensive array of antique and 20th-century Danish art make up the gallery collection. Also notable is the modern art, which includes pieces by a very small but select group of artists, including Henri Matisse, Edvard Munch, Henri Laurens, Emil Nolde, and Georges Braque. The space also contains a children's museum, an amphitheater, a documentation center and study room, a bookstore, and a restaurant. A sculpture garden filled with classical, modern, and whimsical pieces flanks the building. ⊠ *Sølvg. 48–50, Sankt Annæ Kvarter* ☎ *33/74–84–94* ⊕ *www.smk.dk* ⊡ *Dkr 50, free Wed.* ☉ *Tues. and Thurs.–Sun. 10–5, Wed. 10–8.*

㉚ Vor Frue Kirken (Church of Our Lady). The site of this cathedral has drawn worshipers since the 13th century, when Bishop Absalon built a chapel here. Today's church is actually a reconstruction: the original church was destroyed during the Napoleonic Wars. Five towers top the neoclassical structure. Inside you can see Thorvaldsen's marble sculptures depicting Christ and the 12 Apostles, and Moses and David cast in bronze. ⊠ *Nørreg., Frue Pl., Downtown* ☎ *33/37–65–40* ⊕ *www.koebenhavnsdomkirke.dk* ⊡ *Free* ☉ *Daily 8–5.*

In & Around Vesterbrogade

To the southwest of the city are the vibrant working-class and immigrant neighborhoods of Vesterbro, where you'll find a good selection of inexpensive ethnic restaurants and shops. Like the area around Nørrebro, the buildings date from the late 1800s and were constructed for workers. From Vesterbro, Vesterbrogade leads further west to the neighborhood of Frederiksberg. Originally a farming area that supplied the royal households with fresh produce, Frederiksberg is now lined with residences of the well-heeled and home to the zoo and a vibrant theater district.

a good walk

Begin your tour from Copenhagen's main station, Hovedbanegården. When you exit on Vesterbrogade, take a right and you can see the city's best-known attraction, **Tivoli** ㊴ ▶. Southeast of the gardens, on Hans Christian Andersens Boulevard, the neoclassical **Ny Carlsberg Glyptotek** ㊵ contains one of the most impressive collections of antiquities and sculpture in northern Europe. North on Hans Christian Andersens Boulevard, across the street from Tivoli's eastern side, is the sleek **Dansk Design Center** ㊶, with innovative temporary exhibits that showcase Danish and international design. To the west of the main station and tucked between Skt. Jørgens Sø (St. Jørgens Lake) and the main arteries of Vestersøgade and Gammel Kongevej is the **Tycho Brahe Planetarium** ㊷, with an Omnimax Theater.

Vesterbro, which resembles New York's Lower East Side for its bohemian vibe and ethnically diverse population, is along Vesterbrogade near Tivoli. Running parallel to the south is **Istedgade,** Copenhagen's half-hearted red-light district.

Farther west on Vesterbrogade is **Københavns Bymuseum** ④, its entrance flanked by a miniature model of medieval Copenhagen. Beer enthusiasts can head south on Enghavevej and take a right on Ny Carlsbergvej to see the **Carlsberg Bryggeri** ④. The visitor center, nearby on Gamle Carslbergvej, has exhibits on the brewing process and Carlsberg's rise to fame.

TIMING These sights can be seen in half a day, and could be combined easily with a walk around Nørrebo. Tivoli offers charms throughout the day; visit in the late afternoon, and stay until midnight, when colored electrical bulbs and fireworks (on Wednesday and weekend nights) illuminate the park. Be sure to call ahead, since some places may be closed on Monday or Tuesday.

WHAT TO SEE **Carlsberg Bryggeri** (Carlsberg Brewery). As you approach the world-famous Carlsberg Brewery, the unmistakable smell of fermenting hops greets
④ you, a pungent reminder that this is beer territory. (Indeed, near the Brewery is the appealing little neighborhood of Humleby; "humle" means "hops.") Four giant Bornholm-granite elephants guard the brewery's main entrance on Ny Carlsbergvej. Nearby, on Gamle Carslbergvej, is the visitor center, in an old Carlsberg brewery. Colorful displays take you step by step through the brewing process. You can also walk through the draft horse stalls; at the end of your visit, you're rewarded with a few minutes to quaff a complimentary beer. The free **Carlsberg Museum** (✉ Valby Langgade 1, Vesterbro ☎ 33/27–12–74), open weekdays 10 to 3, offers a further look into the saga of the Carlsberg family, and how it managed to catapult Carlsberg from a local name into one of the most famous beers in the world. ✉ *Gamle Carlsbergvej 11, Vesterbro* ☎ *33/27–12–82* ⊕ *www.carlsberg.dk* ✉ *Free* ☉ *Tues.–Sun. 10–4.*

④ **Dansk Design Center** (Danish Design Center). This sleek, glass-panel structure looms in sharp contrast to the old-world ambience of Tivoli just across the street. More of a design showroom than a museum, the center's highlights are the innovative temporary exhibits on the main floor. Past exhibits have included "75 years of Bang & Olufsen," which covered the famed Danish audio-system company, and "Tooltoy," a playful, interactive exhibit of toys over the last century. One-third of the temporary exhibits showcase Danish design; the rest focus on international design. The semi-permanent collection on the ground floor (renewed every other year) often includes samples from the greats, including chairs by Arne Jacobsen, several artichoke PH lamps (designed by Poul Henningsen), and Bang & Olufsen radios and stereos. Note how the radios they made in the '50s look more modern than many of the radios today. The center's shop carries a wide range of Danish design items and selected pieces from the temporary exhibits. You can enjoy light meals in the atrium café, sitting amid the current exhibits. ✉ *H. C. Andersens Blvd. 27, Downtown* ☎ *33/69–33–69* ⊕ *www.ddc.dk* ✉ *Dkr 40* ☉ *Mon., Tues., Thurs., and Fri. 10–5, Wed. 10–9, weekends 11–4.*

Istedgade. In what passes for a red-light district in Copenhagen, mom-and-pop kiosks and ethnic restaurants stand side by side with porn shops and shady outfits aiming to satisfy all proclivities. Istedgade, like neighboring Vesterbrogade, has diversified over the past several years, drawing artists and students. Thanks to the city's urban-renewal projects, cafés and businesses are also moving in, mostly on the southwest end of Istedgade, around Enghave Plads (Enghave Square). Mama Lustra, at No. 96–98, is a laid-back café with comfy armchairs and a mixed crowd of students and older artsy types. Though Istedgade is relatively safe, you may want to avoid the area near the Central Station late at night. ⊠ *South of and parallel to Vesterbrogade, running southwest from the Central Station, Vesterbro.*

⑬ Københavns Bymuseum (Copenhagen City Museum). For a surprisingly evocative collection detailing Copenhagen's history, head to this 17th-century building in the heart of Vesterbro. A meticulously maintained model of 16th-century Copenhagen is kept outdoors from May through September; inside there is also a memorial room for philosopher Søren Kierkegaard, the father of existentialism. ⊠ *Vesterbrog. 59, Vesterbro* ☎ *33/21–07–72* ⊕ *www.kbhbymuseum.dk* ⊠ *Dkr 20, free Fri.* ☉ *May–Sept., Wed.–Mon. 10–4; Oct.–Apr., Wed.–Mon. 1–4.*

⑳ Ny Carlsberg Glyptotek (New Carlsberg Museum). Among Copenhagen's most important museums—thanks to its exquisite antiquities and Gauguins and Rodins—the neoclassical New Carlsberg Museum was donated in 1888 by Carl Jacobsen, son of the founder of the Carlsberg Brewery. Surrounding its lush indoor garden, a series of nooks and chambers houses works by Degas and other impressionists, plus an extensive assemblage of Egyptian, Greek, Roman, and French sculpture, not to mention Europe's finest collection of Roman portraits and the best collection of Etruscan art outside Italy. A modern wing, designed as a three-story treasure chest by the acclaimed Danish architect Henning Larsen, houses an impressive pre-impressionist collection that includes works from the Barbizon school; impressionist paintings, including works by Monet, Alfred Sisley, and Pissarro; and a postimpressionist section, with 50 Gauguin paintings plus 12 of his very rare sculptures. ⊠ *Dantes Pl. 7, Vesterbro* ☎ *33/41–81–41* ⊕ *www.glyptoteket.dk* ⊠ *Dkr 40, free Wed. and Sun.* ☉ *Tues.–Sun. 10–4.*

⑲ Tivoli. Copenhagen's best-known attraction, conveniently next to its main train station, attracts an astounding number of visitors: 4 million people from mid-April to mid-September. Tivoli is more sophisticated than a mere funfair: among its attractions are a pantomime theater, an open-air stage, 24 restaurants (some of them quite elegant), and frequent concerts, which cover the spectrum from classical to rock to jazz. Fantastic flower exhibits color the lush gardens and float on the swan-filled ponds.

The park was established in the 1840s, when Danish architect George Carstensen persuaded a worried King Christian VIII to let him build an amusement park on the edge of the city's fortifications, rationalizing that "when people amuse themselves, they forget politics." On Wednesday and weekend nights, elaborate fireworks are set off, and every day the Tivoli Guard, a youth version of the Queen's Royal Guard, performs. Try to see Tivoli at least once by night, when 100,000 colored lanterns illuminate the Chinese pagoda and the main fountain. Call to double-check prices, which vary throughout the year and often include family discounts at various times during the day. Tivoli is also open from late November to Christmas. ⊠ *Vesterbrog. 3, Vesterbro* ☎ *33/15–10–01* ⊕ *www.tivoli.dk* ⊠ *Dkr 45, plus Dkr 10 per attraction-ticket (each attraction requires 1–5 tickets)* ☉ *Mid-Apr.–mid-Sept., Sun.–Tues. 11–11, Wed. and Thurs. 11 AM–midnight, Fri. and Sat. 11 AM–1 AM; late Nov.–Dec. 23, Sun.–Wed. 11–9, Fri. and Sat. 11–10.*

⑫ Tycho Brahe Planetarium. This modern, cylindrical planetarium, which appears to be sliced at an angle, features astronomy exhibits. The **Omnimax Theater** takes you on visual odysseys as varied as journeys through space and sea, the stages of the Rolling Stones, or Kuwaiti fires from the first Persian Gulf War. These films are not recommended for

children under age 7. ⊠ *Gammel Kongevej 10, Vesterbro* ☏ *33/
12–12–24* ⊕ *www.planetarium.dk* ✉ *Dkr 85* ⊙ *Mon., Tues., Fri., and
Sat. 10:30–9; Wed. 9:45–9; Thurs. 9:30–9; Sun. 10:45–9.*

Vesterbro. Students, union workers, and immigrants (who account for
15% of Vesterbro's population) populate this area. It's a great place to
find ethnic groceries, discount shops, and cheap international restaurants. The face of Vesterbro, however, slowly has been gentrifying. Due
to the city's ongoing urban-renewal and clean-up efforts, the spruced-
up Vesterbro is starting to attract chic cafés and eateries, along with their
arty customers. The minimalist fusion restaurant-bar Delicatessen, on
Vesterbrogade, has drawn a steady stream of Copenhageners since it joined
the neighborhood. The shiny First Hotel Vesterbro is only a five-minute
walk from Tivoli on Vesterbrogade. ⊠ *At the southwestern end of
Vesterbrogade.*

off the beaten path

ZOOLOGISK HAVE – Children love the Zoological Gardens, which
are home to more than 2,000 animals. The small petting zoo and
playground includes cows, horses, rabbits, goats, and hens. The
indoor rain forest has butterflies, sloths, alligators, and other tropical
creatures. Sea lions, lions, and elephants are fed in the early
afternoon. Be warned: on sunny weekends, the line to enter runs far
down Roskildevej; get here early. ⊠ *Roskildevej 32, Frederiksberg*
☏ *70/20–02–00* ⊕ *www.zoo.dk* ✉ *Dkr 90* ⊙ *June–Aug., daily 9–6;
Sept. and Oct., daily 9–5; Apr. and May, weekdays 9–5, weekends
9–6; Nov.–Feb., daily 9–4; Mar. weekdays 9–4, weekends 9–5.*

Where to Eat

In Copenhagen, with its more than 2,000 restaurants, traditional Danish fare spans all price categories: you can order a light lunch of traditional smørrebrød, munch alfresco from a street-side *pølser* (sausage)
cart, or dine out on Limfjord oysters and local plaice. Even the most
upscale restaurants have moderate-price fixed menus. Though few Danish restaurants require reservations, it's best to call ahead to avoid a wait.
The city's more affordable ethnic restaurants are concentrated in Vesterbro, Nørrebro, and the side streets off Strøget. And for less-expensive,
savory noshes in stylish surroundings, consider lingering at a café.

WHAT IT COSTS In kroner				
	$$$$	$$$	$$	$	¢
AT DINNER	over 200	151–200	121–150	90–120	under 90

Prices are for a main course at dinner.

Christianhavn, Holmen & Amager

★ $$$$ ✕ **Era Ora.** This has long been the premier Italian restaurant in the city,
if not the country. Era Ora is outfitted perfectly—cozy and warm—for
a slow, Italian-style feast of many courses from the dazzling menu. The
wine list is quite long and distinguished and the menu is composed of
the best of fresh ingredients available in every season. ⊠ *Overgaden neden
Vandet 33-B, Christianshavn* ☏ *32/54–06–93* ♣ *Reservations essential* ⊟ *AE, DC, MC, V* ⊙ *Closed Sun.*

$$–$$$ ✕ **Spiseloppen.** Round out your visit to the Free State of Christiania with
a meal at Spiseloppen, a 160-seat warehouse restaurant that was a military storage facility and an army canteen in its former life. Upon entering Christiania, wind your way past shaggy dogs, their shaggy owners,
graffiti murals, and wafts of patchouli. (There are few street signs, so

DENMARK: ON THE MENU

FROM THE HEARTY MEALS of Denmark's fishing heritage to the inspired creations of a new generation of chefs, Danish cuisine combines the best of tradition and novelty. Though the country has long looked to the French as a beacon of gastronomy, chefs have proudly returned to the Danish table, emphasizing fresh, local ingredients and combining them with fusion trends. Many of Denmark's young, up-and-coming chefs are fully homegrown, completing all their training locally at the country's expanding list of superb, internationally recognized restaurants. Sample fresh fish and seafood from the Baltic; beef and pork from Jylland; and more-exotic delicacies, such as reindeer, caribou, seal meat, and whale from Greenland. Denmark's famed dairy products—sweet butter and milk among them—as well as a burgeoning organic foods industry, contribute to the freshness of the modern Danish kitchen.

Lunchtime is reserved for smørrebrød. You'll find the best, most traditional sampling of these open-face sandwiches in modest family-run restaurants that focus on generous—though never excessive—portions and artful presentation. If you find yourself fixing your gaze on tender mounds of roast beef topped with pickles or baby shrimp piled high on a slice of French bread, you are experiencing a slice of authentic Danish culture. Another specialty is wienerbrød, a confection far superior to anything billed as "Danish pastry" elsewhere. The European flatfish plaice, which appears on many restaurant menus, is caught off the Scandinavian coast, and its mild meat goes well with many types of sauces (hence its popularity). All Scandinavian countries have versions of the cold table, but Danes claim that theirs, det store kolde bord, is the original and the best.

As for beer, the ubiquitous Carlsberg and Tuborg are facing international competition. But you can't do better than to stick with the Danish brands, which happily complement the traditional fare better than high-priced wine. For Christmas and Easter, Carlsberg and Tuborg release their perennially popular—and potent—Jul (Christmas) and Påske (Easter) brews. If you go for the harder stuff, try the famous snaps, the aquavit traditionally savored with cold food. For an evening tipple, have a taste of the uniquely Danish Gammel Dansk, a bitter that is consumed in small quantities.

just ask; Spiseloppen is the neighborhood's best-known restaurant.) From the outside, this run-down warehouse with splintered windows may seem a bit foreboding, but inside it's a different story. Climb up rickety stairs to the second floor and you're rewarded with a loft-size dining room with low, wood-beam ceilings and candles flickering on the tables. The menu highlights are fresh and inventive vegetarian and fish dishes, which might include artichokes stuffed with eggplant or Portobello mushrooms served with squash, mango, and papaya. One floor down is Loppen, a club that hosts midweek jazz sessions and DJ dance nights on the weekends. ⊠ *Bådmandsstr. 43, Christianshavn* ☎ *32/57–95–58* ⊟ *MC, V* ☯ *Closed Mon. No lunch.*

$–$$$ ╳ **Krunch.** The motto here is "gastronomy within ecology." Krunch serves natural, organic foods from reliable sources and attempts to integrate an environmentally friendly spirit into every facet of the experience. Within these guiding principles, the objective of the owners is to create authentic French-bistro atmosphere and cuisine. The four-course menu changes seasonally; it typically consists of a choice of a fish, meat, or vegetarian main course and an assortment of side dishes. Krunch is also a fine spot for kids. ⊠ *Øresundsvej 14, Amager* ☎ *32/84–50–50* ⊟ *MC, V* ☯ *Closed Mon. No lunch.*

Downtown

$$$$ ╳ **Kommandanten.** Fancifully decorated by master florist Tage Andersen with brushed iron-and-copper furniture, down pillows, and foliage-flanked lights, this is among the city's most exclusive dinner spots, attracting well-heeled businesspeople and local celebrities. The adventuresome international fare might include dishes such as rabbit with bouillon-cooked lentils, herbs, and bacon, and marinated salmon with oysters and parsley. Jackets are recommended. ⊠ *Ny Adelg. 7, Downtown* ☎ *33/12–09–90* ⊟ *AE, DC, MC, V* ☯ *Closed Sun.*

FodorsChoice ★

★ **$$$$** ╳ **Kong Hans Kælder.** Five centuries ago this was a Nordic vineyard—now it's one of Scandinavia's finest restaurants. Chef Thomas Rode Andersen's French-Danish-Asian–inspired dishes employ the freshest local ingredients and are served in a mysterious subterranean space with whitewashed walls and vaulted ceilings. Try the foie gras with raspberry-vinegar sauce or the warm oysters in vichyssoise with smoked cheese and lemon. ⊠ *Vingårdstr. 6, Downtown* ☎ *33/11–68–68* ⊟ *AE, DC, MC, V* ☯ *Closed Sun. No lunch.*

$$$$ ╳ **Krogs.** This elegant canal-front restaurant has developed a loyal clientele—both foreign and local—for its old-fashioned atmosphere and its innovative fish dishes. Pale-green walls are simply adorned with paintings of old Copenhagen. The menu includes such specialties as pan-grilled lobster flavored with vanilla oil and monkfish fillets in a beurre-blanc sauce flavored with arugula and tomato. Jackets are recommended. ⊠ *Gammel Strand 38, Downtown* ☎ *33/15–89–15* ⌖ *Reservations essential* ⊟ *AE, DC, MC, V* ☯ *Closed Sun.*

★ **$$$$** ╳ **Tyvenkokkenhanskoneoghendeselsker.** If you've seen Peter Greenaway's dark and brilliant film *The Cook, the Thief, His Wife, and Her Lover* (with its macabre feast scenes), you may wonder what lies in store at this half-timber town-house restaurant with the same name. It's worth finding out. The same daring humor that inspired the unusual name is exhibited in the innovative seven-course menu, which changes every few weeks. You might be served baked cod in an aromatic coffee sauce or warm rooster simmered in spices and served with horseradish sauce. Desserts include pineapple with mint tortellini. Sit upstairs for a view of the cheery, orange-and yellow-walled old houses that lean against each other just across the narrow street. ⊠ *Magstr. 16, Downtown* ☎ *33/16–12–92* ⌖ *Reservations essential* ⊟ *DC, MC, V* ☯ *Closed Sun. No lunch.*

★ **$$$–$$$$** ✕ **Konrad.** Elegant and minimalist, this restaurant attracts young people and stars, many of whom look like they just walked off a fashion runway. Considering its linear, beige decor, the restaurant seems as geared for people-watching as dining. The French-international menu is inventive without being off-the-wall, with offerings such as potato tortellini filled with oysters and white cream sauce. ⊠ *Pilestr. 12–14, Downtown* ☎ *33/93–29–29* ⚱ *Reservations essential* ⊟ *AE, DC, MC, V* ⊗ *Closed Sun.*

$$$–$$$$ ✕ **L'Alsace.** Set in the cobbled courtyard of Pistolstræde and hung with paintings by Danish surrealist Wilhelm Freddie, this restaurant is peaceful and quiet, and has attracted such diverse diners as Queen Margrethe, Elton John, and Pope John Paul II. The hand-drawn menu lists oysters from Brittany, terrine de foie gras, and *choucroûte à la Strasbourgeoise* (a hearty mélange of cold cabbage, homemade sausage, and pork). Try the superb fresh-fruit tarts and cakes for dessert, and ask to sit in the patio overlooking the courtyard. ⊠ *Ny Østerg. 9, Downtown* ☎ *33/14–57–43* ⊟ *AE, DC, MC, V* ⊗ *Closed Sun.*

$–$$$$ ✕ **Café Ketchup.** You have a choice at this informal, upbeat eatery: for light meals (at light prices), try the lively front café, where you can settle into a red-and-white wicker chair next to the large picture windows and watch the world go by on chic Pilestræde. Try the spring rolls with smoked salmon and cod, flavored with ginger and coriander. The café also serves a tasty brunch (yogurt with muesli, toast with turkey, mozzarella, and bacon, and black currant–fig marmalade) from 10 to 1. For more-substantial fare, venture into the restaurant decorated with old French Perrier ads and lit with white candles. Starters include a potato-and-wasabi soup served with a spicy crab cake, and bruschetta topped with a mango salsa. Main dishes range from halibut stuffed with crabmeat and herbs to marinated duck breast served with sun-dried tomatoes and fennel salad sprinkled with pine nuts. By night, the place turns into a lively bar and club. There is also a Café Ketchup in Tivoli, with a large terrace and a similar menu. ⊠ *Pilestr. 19, Downtown* ☎ *33/32–30–30* ⊟ *DC, MC, V* ⊗ *Closed Sun.*

$$$ ✕ **El Mesón.** Smoothly worn wooden tables, earthen crockery, and dim lighting characterize the dining room of this Spanish restaurant. The knowledgeable waitstaff serves generous portions of beef spiced with spearmint, lamb with honey sauce, and paella Valenciano—a mixture of rice, chicken, ham, shrimp, lobster, squid, green beans, and peas—for two. ⊠ *Hauser Pl. 12, behind Kultorvet, Downtown* ☎ *33/11–91–31* ⊟ *AE, DC, MC, V* ⊗ *Closed Sun. No lunch.*

$$$ ✕ **Reinwalds.** The comfortable black teak chairs with blue upholstery
Fodor'sChoice signal the beginning of a series of delightful encounters with comfort
★ and fine food in a pleasant, modern setting. The tables spread out at sufficient intervals to prevent intrusions of privacy or overlap of conversations with neighboring diners. The informative waitstaff ensure that service is far above the norm and is adept at complementing selected dishes with a fine wine. The three- to five-course menus change monthly, according to the season's harvest. You might find offerings like creamy curry soup with rooster and quail eggs or baked sea bream with almond pesto. ⊠ *Farveg. 15, Downtown* ☎ *33/91–82–80* ⊟ *AE, DC, MC, V* ⊗ *Closed Sun.*

$$$ ✕ **Søren K.** Occupying a bright corner of the Royal Library's modern Black Diamond extension, this cool-tone restaurant, with clean lines, blond-wood furnishings, and recessed ceiling lights, serves bold French-Scandinavian concoctions using no cream, butter, or stock. The result is a menu of flavorful dishes that please the palate without weighing you down. A popular selection is the five-course menu entitled "a couple of hours in the company of fish," which has featured items such as tuna

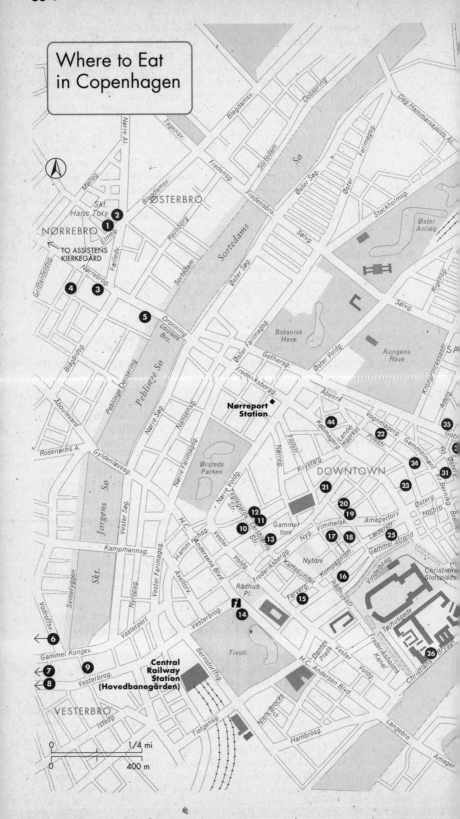

Where to Eat in Copenhagen

ØSTERBRO

NØRREBRO

Skt. Hans Torv

TO ASSISTENS KIERKEGÅRD

Dronning Louises Bro.

Botanisk Have

Kongens Have

Øster Anlæg

Peblinge Sø

Sortedams Sø

Nørreport Station

Ørsteds Parken

DOWNTOWN

Sct. Jørgens Sø

Rådhus Pl.

Tivoli

Central Railway Station (Hovedbanegården)

VESTERBRO

Christians Slotsplads

0   1/4 mi
0   400 m

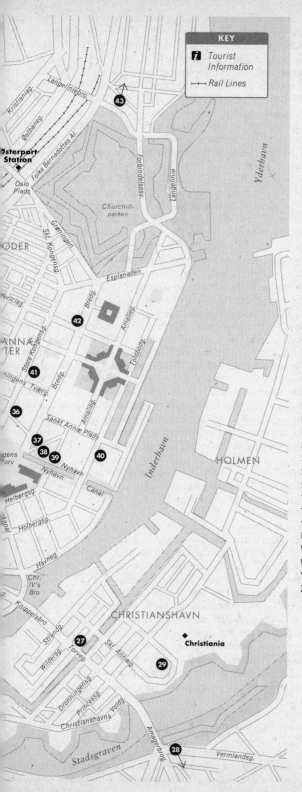

in soy and sesame sauce or mussels drizzled with lemon and thyme. Vegetarian dishes include tofu marinated with red wine and topped with roasted sesame seeds, radishes, and passion fruit. For waterfront views, choose one of the many tables that sit flush up against the Black Diamond's looming glass walls. In summer, you can enjoy your meal on the outside terrace. ⊠ *Søren Kierkegaards Pl. 1, inside the Black Diamond, Downtown* ☎ *33/47–49–50* 🖃 *DC, MC, V* ☉ *Closed Sun.*

$$$ ✕ **Sult.** Norwegian author Knut Hamsun's novel *Sult* now shares its moniker with this restaurant on the premises of the Danish Film Institute. The cuisine is Mediterranean, with strong North African and Asian influences. Try the mussels with carrots in a cream sauce or roast Guinea fowl with sweet potatoes. The wine list is impressive. ⊠ *Vognmagerg. 8B, Downtown* ☎ *33/74–34–17* 🖃 *MC, V* ☉ *Closed Mon.*

$$$ ✕ **Wiinblad.** This restaurant in the D'Angleterre hotel doubles as a gallery for the work of contemporary Danish artist Bjørn Wiinblad. Almost everything—tiles, wall partitions, plaques, candlesticks, vases, and even some tables—has been made by the great Dane, and the effect is bright, cheerful, and very elegant. The eatery offers an ample breakfast buffet, lunch, a fabulous and surprisingly affordable tea, and grilled specialties for dinner. Try the pickled herring with new potatoes topped with sour cream, or the breast of duck in cranberry cream sauce. ⊠ *D'Angleterre, Kongens Nytorv 34, Downtown* ☎ *33/37–06–19* 🖃 *AE, DC, MC, V.*

$–$$$ ✕ **Peder Oxe.** On a 17th-century square, this lively, countrified bistro has rustic tables and 15th-century Portuguese tiles. All entrées—among them grilled steaks, fish, and the best fancy burgers in town—come with an excellent self-service salad bar. Damask-covered tables are set with heavy cutlery and opened bottles of hearty Pyrénées wine. A clever call-light for the waitress is above each table. In spring, when the high northern sun is shining but the warmth still has not kicked in, you won't do badly sitting outside in the Gråbrødretorv (Gray Friars' Square) sipping drinks while wrapped in blankets left thoughtfully for patrons in wicker chairs. ⊠ *Gråbrødretorv 11, Downtown* ☎ *33/11–00–77* 🖃 *DC, MC, V.*

$–$$ ✕ **Flyvefisken.** Silvery stenciled fish swim along blue-and-yellow walls in this Thai eatery. Spicy dishes include chicken with cashew nuts and herring shark in basil sauce. ⊠ *Larsbjørnsstr. 18, Downtown* ☎ *33/14–95–15* 🖃 *DC, MC, V* ☉ *Closed Sun. No lunch.*

$–$$ ✕ **Københavner Caféen.** You know you're in for a real Danish meal when you can smell the vinegary *rød kål* (red cabbage, a Danish staple) upon entering. Dimly lit and warm, with a dark wood and burgundy color scheme, this local favorite just oozes with *hygge* (coziness). Old photographs of Danish royalty line the walls, and a 1798 street lamp stands alongside the inviting bar. Choose from a wide range of smørrebrød selections and also a formidable lineup of down-home Danish dishes such as *frikkedeller* (pork meatballs) and butter-fried salmon with boiled potatoes. In the summer the kitchen offers a traditional Danish Christmas meal "so that everyone can experience Denmark's Christmas traditions." The meal includes roast pork with red cabbage and the much-loved *ris à l'amande* (rice pudding) for dessert. Hidden inside is an almond, and whoever finds it receives a small present. These summer Christmas meals have become so popular that they are generally offered only to tour groups, but it's worth asking when you reserve. ⊠ *Badstuestr. 10, Downtown* ☎ *33/32–80–81* ⌖ *Reservations essential* 🖃 *MC, V.*

$–$$ ✕ **Riz Raz.** This Middle Eastern restaurant hops with young locals, families, couples, and anyone who appreciates good value and spicy fare. The inexpensive all-you-can-eat buffet is heaped with lentils, tomatoes, potatoes, olives, hummus, warm pita bread, yogurt and cucumbers, pickled vegetables, and bean salads. Don't be put off by the hordes—just join them, either in the restaurant's endless labyrinth of dining rooms or in the jam-packed summertime patio. The main location is on Kompagnistræde, between Christiansborg Slot and Strøget; there's a second branch behind Vor Frue Kirken. ⊠ *Kompagnistr. 20, Downtown* ☎ *33/15–05–75* ⊠ *Store Kannikestr. 19* ☎ *33/32–33–45* ⚫ *Reservations essential* ▤ *DC, MC, V.*

$–$$ ✕ **Victor.** Excellent people-watching and good bistro fare are the calling cards at this French-style corner café. It's best during weekend lunches, when young and old gather for such specialties as rib roast, homemade pâté, and smoked salmon and cheese platters. Come here for one of the best brunches in town. Be warned however that the formal restaurant in the back of the space is quite expensive—order from the front café side for a less expensive meal. ⊠ *Ny Østerg. 8, Downtown* ☎ *33/13–36–13* ▤ *AE, DC, MC, V.*

¢–$$ ✕ **Husmanns Vinstue.** Founded in 1888, this warmly lit basement restaurant is housed in a former stable dating from 1727, which accounts for the low ceilings. If you're looking for old-world Denmark, this is it. Beer mugs dangle above the bar, dark-green lamps shed light onto the heavy wooden tables, and black-and-white photographs of Copenhagen hang on the walls. Until 1981, women were allowed to enter only if accompanied by a male, a rule established by one of the restaurant's female owners. For more than 100 years, Husmanns has proudly served hearty Danish smørrebrød to everyone from Walt Disney to the Danish royal family. While other Danish lunch spots may serve salads and lighter cuisine, at Husmanns Vinstue you can feast on all types of herring (fried, curried, marinated, and spiced), smoked eel with scrambled eggs, beef tartare with egg yolk, homemade sausage, and roast beef with potato salad, all served on your choice of rye or white bread. ⊠ *Larsbjørnsstr. 2, Downtown* ☎ *33/11–58–86* ⚫ *Reservations essential* ▤ *AE, DC, MC, V* ☺ *No dinner.*

¢–$$ ✕ **Pasta Basta.** This bright, casual eatery just off the Strøget is always crammed with happy diners. Pasta Basta has all the ingredients for its well-deserved success: an all-you-can-eat fresh pasta and salad bar for a refreshingly low price (Dkr 79). The cheerful staff navigates a dining area marked by orange walls, an innovative mural, and glass-top tables painted in green and blue swirls. Main courses on the changing menu may include pasta with prawns, spinach, and chili peppers, or smoked salmon served with pasta in a creamy sauce of scallops, spinach, and herbs. Pasta Basta is one of the city's only restaurants (barring fast-food and shawarma joints) that serves food until 3 AM (and until 5 AM on Friday and Saturday). During these early morning hours, the restaurant is popular with dancers and musicians from the Royal Theater and other venues, who come in to relax and dine after their evening performances. ⊠ *Valkendorfsg. 22, Downtown* ☎ *33/11–21–31* ▤ *DC, MC, V.*

$ ✕ **Atlas Bar.** The health-food café Atlas Bar in the basement of restaurant Flyvefisken serves excellent food to a steady stream of students and hipsters. The snug eatery serves Oriental-inspired and fusion dishes, such as Manila chicken (chicken breasts in a tomato sauce with garlic, ginger, and chili) and medallions of venison. Atlas is also a favorite of vegetarians for its tempting menu of healthful, tasty dishes. ⊠ *Larsbjørnsstr. 18, Downtown* ☎ *33/15–03–52* ▤ *DC, MC, V* ☺ *Closed Sun.*

¢ ✕ **La Galette.** Tucked into a bright little courtyard, this cheery creperie serves an array of savory crepes, including the Asterix, stuffed with ratatouille, egg, and chives, and the Quimper, with spinach, egg, bacon, and cheese. The luscious lineup of sweet crepes includes everything from banana and chocolate to flambéed caramel apples. ⊠ *Larbjørnsstr. 9, Downtown* ☎ *33/32–37–90* ▭ *MC, V* ☺ *No lunch Sun.*

Nørrebro

$-$$ ✕ **Molevitten.** This spacious café–restaurant–club combination serves Asian-inspired dishes. A house favorite is *laksasuppe,* a Malaysian-style salmon soup. Brunch, lunch, and dinner crowds pack the three-level restaurant, and on weekend evenings the music cranks up and the dance-club revelers arrive. ⊠ *Nørrebrog. 13, Nørrebro* ☎ *35/39–49–00* ▭ *MC, V.*

$ ✕ **Pussy Galore's Flying Circus.** Done up with a few Arne Jacobsen swan chairs, naive wall paintings, and tables smashed up against each other, this trendy gathering place is supposed to be as kitsch as its name. While the mix of decor is retro and does a good job of setting a '60s stage, the regulars who come here make it feel more like a low-key neighborhood bar. Frequented by both young families and black-clad poseurs, this place serves surprisingly down-to-earth and affordable fare, with eggs and bacon and other brunch items along with hefty burgers and wok-fried delectables. ⊠ *Skt. Hans Torv 30, Nørrebro* ☎ *35/24–53–00* ▭ *DC, MC, V.*

$ ✕ **Sebastopol.** Students and locals crowd this laid-back eatery for brunch and on weekend evenings, but it's a good choice if you want to get off the beaten tourist path. The menu is varied with lots of salads, warm sandwiches, and burgers—and just about the most American-style brunch in the city. When it's warm, tables are set outside on the square, where there's great people-watching. ⊠ *Skt. Hans Torv 32, Nørrebro* ☎ *35/36–30–02* ⌘ *Reservations not accepted* ▭ *AE, DC, MC, V.*

¢–$ ✕ **Kashmir.** The quiet, carpet-shrouded Indian restaurant is a favorite with locals, who come for the unusual vegetarian and fish menu. Specialties include tandoori-fried salmon, a hearty lentil soup, and the basic side dishes—such as *bhajis* (fried vegetables patties); *raita* (yogurt and cucumbers); and naan, Indian flat bread cooked in the tandoori oven. ⊠ *Nørrebrog. 35, Nørrebro* ☎ *35/37–54–71* ▭ *DC, MC, V.*

¢ ✕ **Tibet.** Here is a place that comes close to making authentic Tibetan fare, although they have replaced traditional yak meat and milk dishes with beef and organic cows' milk. National favorites *momo* (steamed dumplings with vegetable or meat filling) and *thentuk* (rice noodles with lamb or beef) share the menu with a selection of dishes from the Szechuan province of China. ⊠ *Blågårds Plads 10, Nørrebro* ☎ *35/36–85–05* ▭ *No credit cards* ☺ *Closed Mon.*

Sankt Annæ Kvarter & Østerbro

★ $$$$ ✕ **Godt.** The name says it all: this elegant little two-story restaurant with cool gray walls, silvery curtain partitions, and tulips in clear-glass bottles is *godt* (good). Actually, it's very, very good—so good that Godt has become the buzz of the town. The superb French-Danish menu showcases Chef Colin Rice's commitment to fresh ingredients and seasonal produce, which he buys every morning. Rice prepares a set daily menu, and you can choose to have three, four, or five courses. Dishes may include a black-bean and crab soup or a fillet of venison drizzled with truffle sauce. ⊠ *Gothersg. 38, Sankt Annæ Kvarter* ☎ *33/15–21–22* ⌘ *Reservations essential* ▭ *DC, MC, V* ☺ *Closed Sun. and Mon. No lunch.*

$$$ ✕ **Els.** When it opened in 1853, the intimate Els was the place to be seen before the theater, and the painted Muses on the walls still watch diners rush to make an eight o'clock curtain. Antique wooden columns complement the period furniture, including tables inlaid with Royal Copenhagen tile work. The nouvelle French four-course menu changes every two weeks, always incorporating game, fish, and market produce. Jackets are recommended. ⊠ *Store Strandstr. 3, Sankt Annæ Kvarter*

☎ *33/14–13–41* ♨ *Reservations essential* ▭ *AE, DC, MC, V* ☉ *No lunch Sun.*

★ **$$$** ✕ **Le Sommelier.** The grande dame of Copenhagen's French restaurants is appropriately named. The cellar boasts more than 800 varieties of wine, and you can order many of them by the glass. Exquisite French dishes are complemented by an elegant interior of pale yellow walls, rough-hewn wooden floors, brass chandeliers, and hanging copper pots. Dishes include guinea fowl in a foie gras sauce or lamb shank and crispy sweetbreads with parsley and garlic. While waiting for your table, you can sidle up to the burnished dark-wood and brass bar and begin sampling the wine. ⊠ *Bredg. 63–65, Sankt Annæ Kvarter* ☎ *33/11–45–15* ▭ *AE, DC, MC, V.*

$$$ ✕ **Zeleste.** This restaurant specializes in an inventive and refreshing strain of fusion cuisine. Outfitted with a short but well-worn bar, a covered and heated atrium, and—upstairs—a U-shape dining room, it serves as a soothing respite to Nyhavn's canal-front party. Although the food is usually excellent, if you're ravenous, ask specifically about portions—otherwise, you could end up with some tiny slivers of fried foie gras or a few tortellini. For lunch, the famished will do well with either the focaccia sandwich or the lobster salad served with toast and an excellent roux dressing; if the latter is not at your table within five minutes, you get a free glass of champagne. ⊠ *Store Strandstr. 6, Sankt Annæ Kvarter* ☎ *33/16–06–06* ♨ *Reservations essential* ▭ *DC, MC, V.*

$$–$$$ ✕ **Le Saint Jacques.** The tiny dining room here barely accommodates a dozen tables, but whenever the sun shines, diners spill out from its icon-filled spaces to occupy tables facing busy Østerbrogade. The chef and owners come from some of the finest restaurants in town, but claim they started this place to slow down the pace and enjoy the company of their customers. The fare changes according to what is available at the market, but expect fabulous culinary combinations—smoked salmon with crushed eggplant, Canadian scallops with leeks and salmon roe in a beurre blanc sauce, sole with basil sauce and reduced balsamic glaze, and a savory *poussin* (young, small chicken) with sweetbreads scooped into phyllo pastry atop a bed of polenta and lentils. ⊠ *Skt. Jakobs Pl. 1, Østerbro* ☎ *35/42–77–07* ♨ *Reservations essential* ▭ *DC, MC, V.*

$$–$$$ ✕ **Nyhavns Færgekro.** Locals pack into this waterfront café every day at lunchtime, when the staff unveils a buffet with 10 kinds of herring. An unsavory sailors' bar when Nyhavn was the city's port, the butter-yellow building retains a rustic charm. Waiters duck under rough wood beams when they deliver your choice of the delicious dinner specials, which might be salmon with dill sauce or steak with shaved truffles. In summer, sit outside and order an aquavit, the local spirit that tastes like caraway seeds. ⊠ *Nyhavn 5, Sankt Annæ Kvarter* ☎ *33/15–15–88* ▭ *DC, MC, V.*

$$ ✕ **Ida Davidsen.** Five generations old, this world-renowned lunch spot
FodorśChoice is synonymous with smørrebrød, and the reputation has brought crowds.
★ The often-packed dining area is dimly lit, with worn wooden tables and news clippings of famous visitors on the walls. Creative sandwiches include the H. C. Andersen, with liver pâté, bacon, and tomatoes. The terrific smoked duck is smoked by Ida's husband, Adam, and served alongside a horseradish-spiked cabbage salad. ⊠ *Store Kongensg. 70, Sankt Annæ Kvarter* ☎ *33/91–36–55* ♨ *Reservations essential* ▭ *AE, DC, MC, V* ☉ *Closed weekends and July. No dinner.*

$$ ✕ **Told & Snaps.** This authentic Danish smørrebrød restaurant adheres to
FodorśChoice tradition by offering a long list of Danish delights, and the fare is some-
★ what cheaper than the city's benchmark smørrebrød restaurant Ida Davidsen. The butter-fried sole with remoulade is a treat, as is the steak tartare.

Wine is of course an option, but as this is true Danish cuisine, why not beer and *snaps* (Danish grain alcohol)? ⊠ *Toldbodg. 2, Sankt Annæ Kvarter* ☎ *33/93–83–85* ▤ *No credit cards* ⊘ *Closed Sun. No dinner.*

$ ✕ **Lai Hoo.** Denmark's Princess Alexandra, a native of Hong Kong, was a fan of this Chinese restaurant near the city's main square when she lived in Copenhagen. The lunch specialty is an inspired variety of steamed dumplings (dim sum), and the best bet at dinner is the fixed menu—try the salt-baked prawns in pepper or the luscious lemon duck. ⊠ *Store Kongensg. 18, Sankt Annæ Kvarter* ☎ *33/93–93–19* ▤ *MC, V* ⊘ *No lunch Mon.–Wed.*

Vesterbro & Frederiksberg

$$$$ ✕ **Formel B.** The name stands for "basic formula," but this French-Danish fusion restaurant is anything but basic. Kirk, a third-generation chef, is fanatical about freshness, and this comes through in every dish. Dishes might include mussel soup flavored with wood sorrel; smoked salmon with dill seeds, spinach, and bacon; or panfried chicken with parsley root and horseradish, accompanied by all its parts—the liver, the heart, the craw, and the red comb—served on an array of small plates. Dessert is a work of art: a collection of individual delicacies are arranged on a large white eye-shape platter, and drizzled with a passion-fruit glaze and pine nuts. Kirk prepares a six-course menu (Dkr 550) daily, depending on what seasonal ingredients are available. There is no à la carte menu. ⊠ *Vesterbrog. 182, Frederiksberg* ☎ *33/25–10–66* ▤ *AE, DC, MC, V* ♨ *Reservations essential* ⊘ *Closed Sun. No lunch.*

$$$–$$$$ ✕ **Passagens Spisehus.** Tucked into a *passagens* (passageway) just steps from the Det Ny Teater (New Theater), this restaurant is leading the rediscovery of Scandinavia's culinary roots. Starters include smoked heart of reindeer, thinly sliced, served on a bed of marinated onions and beans, and a cream soup with potatoes, carrots, dill, and Baltic salmon. For your main dish, you can carve into bear from the Swedish woods with stuffed cabbage, potatoes, and sweetened beets or fillet of Lapland reindeer with seasonal vegetables. The elegant interior has dark-wood walls, black leather chairs, and soft white globes of light hanging over every table. It's popular with theatergoers who come for the fixed-price theater menu, which includes two or three courses and changes daily. ⊠ *Vesterbrog. 42, Vesterbro* ☎ *33/22–47–57* ▤ *MC, V* ⊘ *Closed Sun. No lunch.*

$–$$$ ✕ **Copenhagen Corner.** Diners here feast on superb views of the Rådhus Pladsen and terrific smørrebrød, which compensate for the uneven pace of the harried but hard-working staff and some of the less appealing dishes on the menu. Specialties include fried veal with bouillon gravy and fried potatoes; entrecôte in garlic and bordelaise sauce with creamed potatoes; and a herring plate with three types of spiced, marinated herring and boiled potatoes. ⊠ *Vesterbrog. 1, Vesterbro* ☎ *33/91–45–45* ▤ *AE, DC, MC, V.*

$–$$ ✕ **Delicatessen.** Happily defying labels, this casual diner–café–bar is done up in Dansk design—silver-gray bucket seats and a stainless steel-top bar—and serves hearty brunches and global cuisine by day, and cocktails and DJ-spun dance tunes by night. Linger over scrambled eggs with bacon and a steaming cup of coffee (served from 11 AM), or tuck into the international cuisine of the month, which runs from North African to Thai to Italian. The menu might include pad thai; lamb curry with basmati rice, mint, and yogurt; or roast pork with thyme and zucchini. A trip to the bathroom is good for grins: On your way you pass by two fun-house mirrors; look to one side, and you're squat and fat. Look to the other, and you're slender and tall. ⊠ *Vesterbrog. 120, Vesterbro* ☎ *33/22–16–33* ▤ *V.*

¢–$$ ✕ **Yan's Wok.** The former chef of Lai Hoo mans the wok here, serving Hong Kong–style cuisine, as well as peppery dishes from the Szechuan province. The theater menu is a great deal and runs from 4 to 6, while a slightly higher-price card is offered during dinner hours. Regardless of the hour, you can be sure of getting tasty meals at bargain prices. ⊠ *Bagerstr. 9, Vesterbro* ☎ *33/23–73–33* ▤ *DC, MC, V* ⊘ *Closed Mon. No lunch.*

Where to Stay

Copenhagen is well served by a wide range of hotels, overall among Europe's most expensive. The hotels around the somewhat run-down red-light district of Istedgade—which looks more dangerous than it is—are the least expensive. Copenhagen is a compact, eminently walkable city, and most of the hotels are in or near the city center, usually within walking distance of most of the major sights and thoroughfares.

Breakfast is almost always included in the room rate. Rooms have bath or shower at the following hotels unless otherwise noted. Note that in Copenhagen, as in the rest of Denmark, half (to three-fourths) of the rooms usually have showers only (while the rest have showers and bathtubs) so make sure to state your preference when booking.

WHAT IT COSTS In kroner				
	$$$$	$$$	$$	$	¢
FOR 2 PEOPLE	over 1,700	1,400–1,700	1,000–1,400	700–1,000	under 700

Prices are for two people in a standard double room, including service charge and tax.

Amager & Kastrup

$$$$ ▦ **Hilton Copenhagen Airport.** Half the rooms at this modern business hotel have views of the city's skyline; the other half look out onto the airport. Rooms are done in a modern Scandinavian style with wooden furniture, light colors, and broad windows. The Copenhagen airport's main terminal is across the street. ⊠ *Ellehammersvej 20, Copenhagen Airport, DK–2770 Kastrup* ☎ *32/50–15–01* 🖶 *32/52–85–28* ⊕ *www.hilton.dk* ⇆ *382 rooms, 8 suites* ⚘ *3 restaurants, indoor pool, gym, sauna, bar, meeting rooms, some pets allowed, no-smoking rooms* ▤ *AE, DC, MC, V.*

$$$$ ▦ **Radisson SAS Scandinavia.** South across the Stadsgraven from Christianshavn, this is one of northern Europe's largest hotels, and Copenhagen's token skyscraper. An immense lobby, with cool, recessed lighting and streamlined furniture, gives access to the city's first (and only) casino. Guest rooms are large and somewhat institutional but offer every modern convenience, making this a good choice if you prefer familiar comforts over character. The hotel's Dining Room restaurant, overlooking Copenhagen's copper towers and skyline, is a fine site for a leisurely lunch, while the dinner menu tempts guests with a changing list of six main courses concocted from fresh seasonal ingredients. The restaurant is closed on Sunday. ⊠ *Amager Blvd. 70, Amager DK–2300* ☎ *33/96–50–00* 🖶 *33/96–55–00* ⊕ *www.radissonsas.com* ⇆ *542 rooms, 43 suites* ⚘ *4 restaurants, cable TV, indoor pool, Internet, meeting rooms* ▤ *AE, DC, MC, V.*

¢ ▦ **Amager Danhostel.** This simple lodging is 4½ km (3 mi) outside town, close to the airport. The hostel is spread over nine interconnecting buildings, all laid out on one story. The student backpackers and families who stay here have access to the communal kitchen or can buy breakfast and dinner from the restaurant. The hostel is also wheelchair-accessible. Before 5 PM on weekdays, take Bus 46 from the main station directly to the hostel. After 5, from Rådhus Pladsen or the main station, take Bus 250 to Sundbyvesterplads, and change to Bus 100. Ask the driver to signal your stop. ⊠ *Vejlands Allé 200, Amager DK–2300* ☎ *32/52–29–08* 🖷 *32/52–27–08* ⊕ *www.copenhagenyouthhostel.dk* ⤴ *64 rooms with 2 beds, 80 family rooms with 5 beds, 4 large communal bathrooms* ⚫ *Restaurant, laundry facilities, Internet* ☰ *MC, V.*

Downtown

$$$$
Fodor'sChoice
★

D'Angleterre. The grande dame of Copenhagen welcomes royalty, politicians, and rock stars—from Margaret Thatcher to Madonna—in palatial surroundings: an imposing New Georgian facade leads into an English-style sitting room. Standard guest rooms are furnished in pastels, with overstuffed chairs and a mix of modern and antique furniture. The spit-and-polish staff accommodates every wish. The elegant Wiinblad restaurant serves excellent French-Danish dishes. In winter the square in front of the hotel is converted into a skating rink. ⊠ *Kongens Nytorv 34, Downtown DK–1021* ☎ *33/12–00–95* 🖷 *33/12–11–18* ⊕ *www.remmen.dk* ⤴ *118 rooms, 19 suites* ⚫ *Restaurant, indoor pool, bar, Internet, meeting rooms* ☰ *AE, DC, MC, V.*

$$$$
Skt. Petri. For the better part of a century, a beloved department store nicknamed Dalle Valle occupied this site. It has been supplanted by this luxury hotel cast in a modern style. The individual rooms, designed and decorated by Per Arnoldi, are functional, decorated in a spare, modern aesthetic with bright and cheery colors. Most units have a terrace or balcony. The hotel envelops an atrium garden and terrace. ⊠ *Krystalg. 22, Downtown DK–1172* ☎ *33/45–91–00* 🖷 *33/45–91–10* ⊕ *www. hotelsktpetri.com* ⤴ *270 rooms, 27 suites* ⚫ *Restaurant, café, free parking* ☰ *AE, DC, MC, V.*

$$$–$$$$
Strand. You can't stay closer to the harbor than here: just a five-minute walk from Nyhavn, this pleasant hotel is housed in a waterfront warehouse dating from 1869. The cozy lobby has brown leather couches and old maritime pictures on the walls. The rooms are small but comfortable, with blue-and-yellow bedspreads and sparkling bathrooms. ⊠ *Havneg. 37, Downtown DK–1058* ☎ *33/48–99–00* 🖷 *33/48–99–01* ⊕ *www.copenhagenstrand.dk* ⤴ *174 rooms, 2 suites* ⚫ *Restaurant, bar, meeting rooms, some pets allowed, no-smoking rooms* ☰ *AE, DC, MC, V.*

$$$
Ascot. This charming downtown hotel's two outstanding features are a wrought-iron staircase and an excellent breakfast buffet. The lobby is classic, with marble and columns, and the guest rooms and apartments are comfy, with modern furniture and bright colors; some have kitchenettes. ⊠ *Studiestr. 61, Downtown DK–1554* ☎ *33/12–60–00* 🖷 *33/14–60–40* ⊕ *www.ascothotel.dk* ⤴ *161 rooms, 4 suites* ⚫ *Cable TV, bar, meeting room, free parking, some pets allowed* ☰ *AE, DC, V.*

$$
Ibsens Hotel. This winsome, family-owned hotel near the Nørreport station has cozy, immaculate rooms and a lovely courtyard. The friendly staff is particularly attentive and goes out of its way to help. The attention to detail is evident in the hotel's decor, as well. Each floor has its own theme. The Scandinavian floor showcases cool and modern local designs while the Bohemian floor is filled with antique furnishings. The breakfast room is a lovely place to start your morning. ⊠ *Vendersg. 23, Downtown DK–1363* ☎ *33/13–19–13* 🖷 *33/13–19–16* ⊕ *www. ibsenshotel.dk* ⤴ *118 rooms, 3 suites* ⚫ *Restaurant, bar, some pets allowed, no-smoking rooms* ☰ *AE, DC, MC, V.*

Sankt Annæ & North

$$$$
Clarion Neptun. This elegant, central hotel was bought years ago with the intention of making it the bohemian gathering place of Copen-

hagen, but these days it is more practical than artsy and welcomes business guests, tourists, and even large tour groups. The lobby and lounge are light, with classical furnishings and pale tones, and guest rooms have a tasteful modern decor. Many rooms face an interior covered courtyard. Next door is the Restaurant Gendarmen, run by a group of young restaurateurs who have created a dinner menu on the concept of old-meets-new, marrying traditional Danish dishes (roast pork or cod) with nouveau touches, such as a light truffle or blueberry sauce. The traditional lunch menu consists of good old Danish fare, smørrebrød and the like. ⊠ *Skt. Annæ Pl. 18–20, Sankt Annæ Kvarter DK–1250* ☎ *33/96–20–00* 🖷 *33/96–20–66* ⊕ *www.clarionhotel.com* 🖘 *133 rooms* ⚫ *Restaurant, bar, baby-sitting, meeting rooms, free parking* ▭ *AE, DC, MC, V.*

★ **$$$$** 🏨 **Nyhavn 71.** In a 200-year-old warehouse, this quiet, soothing hotel is a good choice for privacy-seekers. It overlooks the old ships of Nyhavn, and its nautical interiors have been preserved with their original thick plaster walls and exposed brick. The rooms are tiny but cozy, with warm woolen spreads, dark woods, soft leather furniture, and crisscrossing timbers. ⊠ *Nyhavn 71, Sankt Annæ Kvarter DK–1051* ☎ *33/43–62–00* 🖷 *33/43–62–01* ⊕ *www.71nyhavnhotelcopenhagen.dk* 🖘 *150 rooms, 3 suites* ⚫ *Restaurant, bar, meeting rooms, free parking, some pets allowed, no-smoking rooms* ▭ *AE, DC, MC, V.*

$$$$ 🏨 **Phoenix.** This luxury hotel has automatic glass doors, crystal chandeliers, and gilt touches everywhere. Originally built in the 1680s, the hotel was then torn down and rebuilt into a plush, Victorian-style hotel in 1847, rising from its rubble just like the mythical Phoenix rose from its ashes, and thus its name. The suites and business-class rooms are adorned with faux antiques and 18-carat gold–plated bathroom fixtures; the standard rooms are very small, measuring barely 9 feet by 15 feet. It's so convenient to city-center attractions that the hotel gets a fair amount of street noise; light sleepers should ask for rooms above the second floor. Downstairs is Murdoch's Books & Ale, a snug pub done up in mahogany and brass, with antique Danish tomes lining its bookshelves. The pub serves smørrebrød and light meals, including a green salad topped with chicken marinated in balsamic vinegar and a ham-and-onion quiche. It's closed on Sunday. ⊠ *Bredg. 37, Sankt Annæ Kvarter DK–1260* ☎ *33/95–95–00* 🖷 *33/33–98–33* ⊕ *www.phoenixcopenhagen.dk* 🖘 *206 rooms, 7 suites* ⚫ *Restaurant, bar, parking (fee), some pets allowed, no-smoking rooms* ▭ *AE, DC, MC, V.*

★ **$$$** 🏨 **Admiral.** A five-minute stroll from Nyhavn, overlooking old Copenhagen and Amalienborg, the monolithic Admiral was once a grain warehouse but now affords travelers no-nonsense accommodations. With massive stone walls—broken by rows of tiny windows—it's one of the less-expensive top hotels, cutting frills and prices. Its guest rooms are spare, with jutting beams and modern prints. ⊠ *Toldbodg. 24–28, Sankt Annæ Kvarter DK–1253* ☎ *33/74–14–14* 🖷 *33/74–14–16* ⊕ *www.admiralhotel.dk* 🖘 *314 rooms, 52 suites* ⚫ *Restaurant, bar, nightclub, meeting room, free parking, some pets allowed, no-smoking rooms* ▭ *AE, DC, V.*

$$ 🏨 **Skovshoved.** This delightful, art-filled inn is 8 km (5 mi) north of town, near a few old fishing cottages beside the yacht harbor. Licensed since 1660, it has retained its provincial charm. Larger rooms overlook the sea, smaller ones rim the courtyard; all have both modern and antique furnishings. The best way to get here is to take Bus 6 from Rådhus Pladsen or the S-train to Charlottenlund and walk 10 minutes from the station. ⊠ *Strandvejen 267, DK–2920 Charlottenlund* ☎ *39/64–00–28* 🖷 *39/64–06–72* 🖘 *23 rooms, 3 suites* ⚫ *Restaurant, billiards, bar, meeting rooms* ▭ *AE, DC, MC, V.*

Fodor's Choice ★

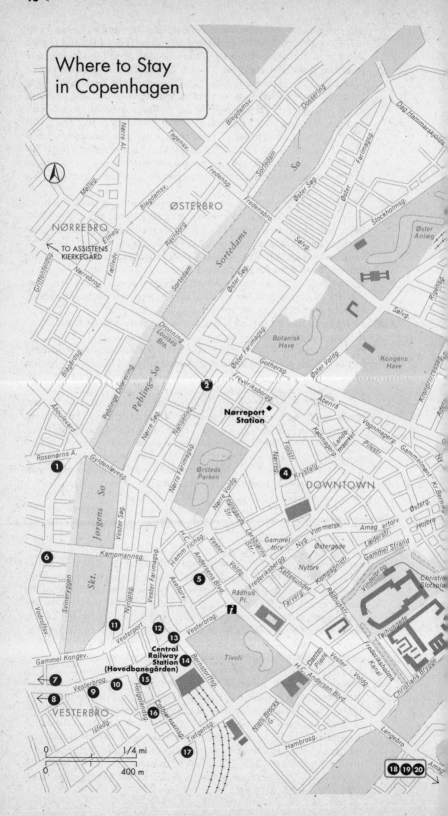

Where to Stay
in Copenhagen

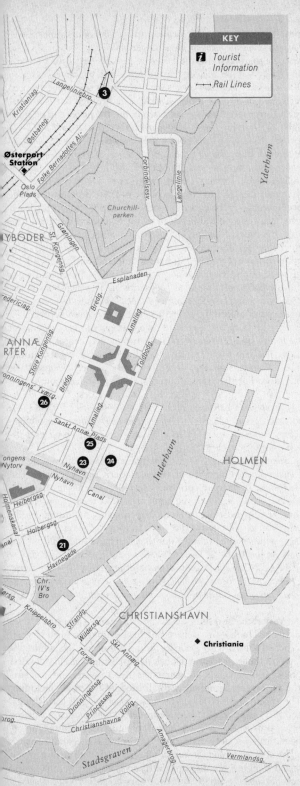

Vesterbro & Frederiksberg

$$$$ ⌹ **Plaza Sofitel.** With its convenient location and plush homey atmosphere, this hotel has attracted the likes of Tina Turner and Keith Richards. Close to Tivoli and the main station, the building puts its best foot forward with a stately lobby and the adjacent Plaza Restaurant, which serves haute French-Italian cuisine. The older rooms are scattered with antiques; newer ones are furnished in a more modern style. The Library Bar is an elegantly cozy and atmospheric place for a drink, but the prices can be staggeringly high. ⊠ *Bernstorffsg. 4, Vesterbro DK–1577* ☎ *33/14–92–62* 🖷 *33/93–93–62* ⊕ *www.sofitel.com* 🖙 *93 rooms, 6 suites* ⟁ *Restaurant, room service, bar, concierge, meeting rooms, parking (fee), some pets allowed, no-smoking rooms* ▤ *AE, DC, MC, V.*

$$$$ ⌹ **Radisson SAS Royal.** Towering over the heart of town, this high-rise
Fodor'sChoice   hotel was originally designed by Arne Jacobsen in 1960. Recently the own-
★   ers spent several years—and plenty of kroner—in reembracing its Jacobsen look, and the result is a veritable paean to the legendary designer. The graceful lobby has blue and white Jacobsen swan and egg chairs that are arranged in circles and illuminated by the ceiling's recessed lights. The soothing hotel rooms are paneled in light maple and outfitted with Jacobsen chairs and lamps. Even the heavy door handles, functionally designed to fill the palm, were created by Jacobsen. The headboards are inlaid with pale green and lavender kidney shapes. The most famous room is 606, which looks just like it did in 1960, with all the original furnishings, including a nifty desktop that opens to reveal a lighted makeup mirror. Many of the rooms boast views over Tivoli and the city center's coppertop buildings. The top-floor restaurant, Alberto K, serves top-notch Scandinavian-Italian cuisine. You don't have to be a hotel guest to bask in Jacobsen's aura. For the price of a cocktail, you can hang out in the elegant hotel bar, sitting on—and amid—Jacobsen designs. ⊠ *Hammerichsg. 1, Vesterbro DK–1611* ☎ *33/42–60–00* 🖷 *33/42–61–00* ⊕ *www.radissonsas.com* 🖙 *260 rooms, 6 suites* ⟁ *Restaurant, room service, gym, bar, Internet, meeting rooms, parking (fee), some pets allowed, no-smoking rooms* ▤ *AE, DC, MC, V.*

$$$$ ⌹ **Scandic Copenhagen.** Rising over Copenhagen's lakes, alongside the cylindrical Tycho Brahe Planetarium, is this modern high-rise hotel. The comfortable rooms, done up in cool tones and blond-wood furnishings, have splendid views. One side of the hotel overlooks the peaceful lakes, and the other side the bustling heart of Copenhagen, including Tivoli. The higher up you go, the better the view, so inquire about a room on the 17th floor, which is the highest floor that still has standard doubles; it's suites-only on the 18th. ⊠ *Vester Søg. 6, Vesterbro DK–1601* ☎ *33/14–35–35* 🖷 *33/32–12–23* ⊕ *www.scandic-hotels.com* 🖙 *472 rooms, 6 suites* ⟁ *Restaurant, room service, gym, sauna, bar, concierge, meeting rooms, parking (fee), some pets allowed, no-smoking rooms* ▤ *AE, DC, MC, V.*

$$$–$$$$ ⌹ **First Hotel Vesterbro.** Looming over Vesterbrogade—and just a five-minute walk from Tivoli—this deluxe hotel is Denmark's third largest. The sun-drenched lobby, with floor-to-ceiling windows, has white pillars, blond-wood tables, and gray Dansk design armchairs. It's the first hotel to be newly built in Copenhagen in the past 15 years and, not surprisingly, the rooms are equipped with all the latest gizmos, including Web TV. The rooms have pale yellow walls, cherrywood furnishings, and contemporary lithographs. Female travelers may want try out the "First Lady" rooms, which include adjustable mirrors and makeup remover in the bathrooms, fluffy bathrobes, an electric kettle, and women's magazines. The hotel's highlight is its magnificent brick-wall atrium awash in sunlight and hanging plants, and outfitted with marble tables and rounded wicker chairs; the ample complimentary breakfast buffet is served here. Later in the day the handsome Alex Vinbar & Kokken restaurant, presided over by an up-and-coming Swedish chef, serves contemporary Scandinavian cuisine and offers more than 250 wines, any of which can be ordered by the glass. ⊠ *Vesterbrog. 23–29, Vesterbro DK–1620* ☎ *33/78–80–00* 🖷 *33/78–80–80* ⊕ *www.firsthotels.com* 🛏 *403 rooms, 1 suite* ⚒ *Restaurant, gym, bar, meeting rooms, parking (fee), some pets allowed, no-smoking rooms* ☰ *AE, DC, MC, V.*

$$$–$$$$ 🏨 **Grand Hotel.** In operation since the turn of the 20th century, the Grand Hotel has a faded elegance that can be comforting. From its old-style lobby, presided over by a crystal chandelier, to its narrow stairs and uneven hallways, this hotel stands as the proud antithesis to all that's sleek and shiny. The rooms are a blend of old and new, with blue-and-gold curtains, traditional cherrywood furnishings, and all the modern conveniences, such as satellite TV and minibars. The drawback is that some of the rooms have tiny bathrooms, so inquire about this when booking. ⊠ *Vesterbrog. 9, Vesterbro DK–1620* ☎ *33/27–69–00* 🖷 *33/27–69–01* ⊕ *www.grandhotelcopenhagen.dk* 🛏 *161 rooms, 2 suites* ⚒ *Restaurant, room service, bar, concierge, meeting rooms, parking (fee), no-smoking rooms* ☰ *AE, DC, MC, V.*

$$$ 🏨 **DGI Byen.** "An unusual meeting place" is how the DGI Byen presents itself, and it's a thoroughly apt description. This state-of-the-art recreation and sports center, behind the Central train station, boasts a bowling alley, climbing wall, shooting range, swimming pool, spa, and 104-room hotel. The hotel rooms are an exquisite blend of Danish design. Dark blue furnishings and blond-wood floors are softly illuminated by cylindrical lamps. Short poems by the much-loved Danish philosopher Piet Hein grace the cool gray walls. Though most rooms have doubly insulated windows, you can sometimes hear the distant rumble of trains entering the station. The last train passes by at around 12:30 AM, so ask for a quiet room if you're a light sleeper. The pool is free to hotel guests; nonguests pay Dkr 46. You can pamper yourself with a range of soothing treatments at the full-service spa, but it costs extra. Ask about the substantially lower weekend rates. ⊠ *Tietgensg. 65, Vesterbro DK–1704* ☎ *33/29–80–00* 🖷 *33/29–80–80* ⊕ *www.dgi-byen.dk* 🛏 *104 rooms* ⚒ *Restaurant, café, pool, sauna, spa, bowling, meeting rooms, parking (fee), no-smoking rooms* ☰ *AE, DC, MC, V.*

$$ 🏨 **Guldsmeden.** This family hotel, in a 19th-century Vesterbro building, has rooms decorated and restored in French-colonial style with wood paneling, stucco, and high ceilings. The amenities of the rooms differ; some have four-poster beds, bathtubs, fireplaces, or furnished balconies. Every room has original art on the walls and hand-picked teak furniture. ⊠ *Vesterbrog. 66, Vesterbro DK–1620* ☎ *33/22–15–00* 🖷 *33/22–15–55* ⊕ *www.hotelguldsmeden.dk* 🛏 *64 rooms, some with bath, 4 suites* ⚒ *Café, some pets allowed* ☰ *AE, D, MC, V.*

$ 🏨 **Crown.** Tucked into a small brick courtyard off busy Vesterbrogade, this simple hotel has small but comfortable rooms with pale-yellow walls and light-green curtains. Some rooms overlook Vesterbrogade and the rest face the interior courtyard. The rooftop breakfast room floods with sunlight in summer and offers pleasant bird's-eye views of the Vesterbro neighborhood. ⊠ *Vesterbrog. 41, Vesterbro DK–1620* ☎ *33/21–21–66* 🖷 *33/21–00–66* ⊕ *www.ibishotel.dk* 🛏 *80 rooms* ⚒ *Meeting rooms, some pets allowed, no-smoking rooms* ☰ *AE, DC, MC, V.*

$ 🏨 **Saga.** This is one of the newer, refurbished hotels in the vicinity of the central train station. Some rooms have just a sink, while others have full bathrooms. Breakfast is included in the price, and the hotel is good for families. ⊠ *Colbjørnsensg. 18–20, Vesterbro DK–1652* ☎ *33/24–49–44* 🖷 *33/24–60–33* ⊕ *www.sagahotel.dk* 🛏 *79 rooms, 31 with bath* ⚒ *Some pets allowed* ☰ *AE, DC, MC, V.*

$ ▦ **Triton.** Despite seedy surroundings, this streamlined hotel attracts a cosmopolitan clientele thanks to a central location in Vesterbro. The large rooms, in blond-wood and warm tones, all include modern bathroom fixtures. The buffet breakfast is exceptionally generous and the staff friendly. There are also family suites with a bedroom and a sitting area with a sofabed. ✉ *Helgolandsg. 7–11, Vesterbro DK–1653* ☎ *33/ 31–32–66* 🖷 *33/31–69–70* ⊕ *www.ibishotel.dk* ↩ *123 rooms* ⚭ *Bar, some pets allowed* ▭ *AE, DC, MC, V.*

¢ ▦ **Cab–Inn Scandinavia.** This bright hotel is west of the lakes and Vester-port Station. Its impeccably maintained rooms are distinctly small, but designed with super efficiency to include ample showers; fold-away and bunk beds; and even electric water kettles. The hotel is popular with business travelers in winter and kroner-pinching backpackers and families in summer. Its sister hotel, the **Cab–Inn Copenhagen,** is around the corner, at Danasvej 32–34, but it's open only from April through September. ✉ *Vodroffsvej 55, Frederiksberg DK–1900* ☎ *35/36–11–11, 33/ 21–04–00 Cab–Inn Copenhagen* 🖷 *35/36–11–14, 33/21–74–09 Cab–Inn Copenhagen* ⊕ *www.cabinn.dk* ↩ *201 rooms with shower* ⚭ *Bar, meeting rooms, parking (fee)* ▭ *AE, DC, MC, V.*

¢ ▦ **Euroglobe.** A no-frills spot for the traveler who's looking for a comfortable bed with a roof overhead. Rooms are minimal, and guests share two common bathrooms on each floor. There's a little kitchen area on each floor where coffee, tea, or soups can be prepared. With breakfast included, this spot is a fine choice for the frugal. ✉ *Niels Ebbesensvej 20, Frederiksberg DK–1911* ☎ *33/79–79–54* ⊕ *www.euroglobe.dk* ↩ *47 rooms without bath* ⚭ *Some pets allowed* ▭ *No credit cards.*

¢ ▦ **Sct. Thomas.** A short walk from the center of town in Fredericksberg's theater district, this hotel is a true bargain and just off the beaten path. In a sitting room area for guests, the hotel provides free Internet access. There is free parking in an adjacent garage. ✉ *Frederiksberg Allé, Vesterbro DK–1621* ☎ *33/21–64–64* 🖷 *33/25–64–60* ⊕ *www. hotelsctthomas.dk* ↩ *34 rooms, 26 with bath* ⚭ *Internet, free parking, no-smoking rooms* ▭ *V.*

Nightlife & the Arts

Nightlife

Most nightlife is concentrated in the area in and around Strøget, though there are student and "leftist" cafés and bars in Nørrebro and more up-scale spots in Østerbro. Vesterbro, whose main drags are Vesterbrogade and Istedgade, is a budding nighttime neighborhood, with a clutch of hip bars and cafés. Many restaurants, cafés, bars, and clubs stay open after midnight, a few until 5 AM. Copenhagen used to be famous for jazz, but unfortunately that has changed, with many of the best clubs closing down. However, you can find nightspots catering to almost all musical tastes, from bop to ballroom music to house, rap, and techno, in trendy clubs soundtracked by local DJs. The area around Nikolaj Kirken has the highest concentration of trendy discos and dance spots. Copenhagen's clubs can be a fickle bunch; new nighttime venues crop up regularly, often replacing last year's red-hot favorites. Call ahead or check out *Copenhagen This Week* (⊕ www.ctw.dk) for current listings. The stylish, biannual magazine *Scandinavian Living* (⊕ www.cphliving.dk) includes informative listings on the latest bars, restaurants, and shops. It also features articles on Danish culture, food, and architecture and is available at stores, hotels, and the tourist office.

BARS & LOUNGES　Copenhagen is peppered with hip restaurants that get even hipper in the evening, when they morph into lively nightspots. **Bang & Jensen** (✉ Ist-edg. 130, Vesterbro ☎ 33/25–53–18), in the spotty-but-becoming-gentrified Vesterbro neighborhood, is a regular café during the day. From 9 PM until 2 AM, however, it turns into a cocktail bar jamming with loud music and a disco ambience. The **D'Angleterre Hotel** (⊠ Kongens Nytorv 34, Downtown ☎ 33/37–06–64) is home to a tiny English-style bar that's just the place to soak up the posh hotel's ambience without forking over the kroner to stay here. When the hotel restaurant closes at 10 PM, bar guests can sit at tables by windows looking out on Copenhagen's most beautiful square, Kongens Nytorv. Moreover, after a peaceful drink or two, you will be within walking distance of a slew of other, more raucous nighttime spots. **Delicatessen** (⊠ Vesterbrog. 120, Vesterbro ☎ 33/22–16–33) serves international cuisine by day, but after 11 PM Thursday through Saturday, it's time for cocktails and dancing to DJ-spun house, hip-hop, and rock. **Café Ketchup** (⊠ Pilestr. 19, Downtown ☎ 33/32–30–30), just off the Strøget, draws an informal—though not unsavvy—crowd that gabs and grooves to the sounds of funk, house, hip-hop, and African music. It gets cooking after 11 PM on the weekends, once cocktails start replacing coffee. **Charlie's Bar** (⊠ Pilestr. 33, Downtown ☎ 33/32–22–89) insists that there are other beers in Copenhagen besides the omnipresent Carlsberg and Tuborg, and serves more than 46 draft and bottled beers to prove it. You can sample a handful of Danish microbreweries or Hoegaarden beer from Belgium. Indeed, there's no better place to enjoy such diversity than at this bar, which calls itself "proudly independent, independently proud" because it doesn't kowtow to the two big Danish brands. The dark room with low ceilings, owned by a transplanted Scotsman, is refreshingly unpretentious, with a laid-back crowd of regulars, both locals and expats.

Hviids Vinstue (⊠ Kongens Nytorv 19, Downtown ☎ 33/15–10–64) dates from the 1730s and attracts all kinds, young and old, singles and couples, for a glass of wine or cognac. **Konrad** (⊠ Pilestr. 12–14, Downtown ☎ 33/93–29–29) attracts a chic crowd that gathers around the classy see-and-be-seen bar. The **Library** (⊠ Bernstorffsg. 4, Vesterbro ☎ 33/14–92–62), in the Plaza, is an elegant spot for a quiet but pricey drink. **"90"** ("halvfems" in Danish; ⊠ Gammel Kongevej 90, Frederiksberg ☎ 33/31–84–90), which goes only by its street number, is the only watering hole that many Copenhagen old-timers trust for a "real beer." Unfortunately, it can take up to 15 minutes for the harried bartender to pull your draft pint. The small, atmospheric bar with dark orange walls and heavy wooden tables is the second home to a cast of crusty Copenhagen characters and outspoken barflies. At lunch, do as the locals do and buy smørrebrød from around the corner, and then bring it into the bar where you can settle in at one of the tables and enjoy your meal with one of the famous drafts. (There's a Dkr 5 charge just to sit at the table.) **Peder Oxe's basement** (⊠ Gråbrødretorv 11, Downtown ☎ 33/11–11–93) is casual and young, though nearly impossible to squeeze into on weekends.

CAFÉS   Café life appeared in Copenhagen in the '70s and quickly became a compulsory part of its urban existence. The cheapest sit-down eateries in town, where a cappuccino and sandwich often cost less than Dkr 60, cafés are lively and relaxed at night, the crowd usually an interesting mix. Once run-down and neglected, the up-and-coming Istedgade strip is beginning to sprout cheery cafés and restaurants.

Amokka Kaffehus (⊠ Dag Hammarskjölds Allé 36–40, Østerbro ☎ 35/25–35–35), a 10-minute walk from the Østerport train station, is a coffee-lover's dream. Specialty java is served alongside inventive sandwiches and salads. **Bjørg's** (⊠ Vester Voldg. 19, Downtown ☎ 33/14–53–20) has a zinc bar, red seating, and lots of large windows. Guests slouch over huge burgers, club sandwiches, and excellent coffees. **Dan Turrell** (✉ Store Regneg. 3–5, Downtown ☎ 33/14–10–47), an old café, has become terribly chic of late, partly due to its good food and candlelight. At the fashionable **Europa** (✉ Amagertorv 1, Downtown ☎ 33/14–28–89), people-watching and coffee naturally go together. **Krasnapolsky** (✉ Vesterg. 10, Downtown ☎ 33/32–88–00) packs a young, hip, and painfully well-dressed audience at night, while a more mixed group populates its confines on placid afternoons.

Mama Lustra (✉ Istedg. 96, Vesterbro ☎ 33/25–26–11) looks like it could be a corner of your grandma's attic, with mismatched chairs, old wooden tables, and brass candle holders. Sink into a stuffed chair and sip a coffee or glass of Spanish wine while gazing out over busy Istedgade. The place also serves a simple but tasty brunch with cured ham, Italian sausages, and scrambled eggs, and an assortment of sandwiches including a vegetarian favorite—sun-dried tomatoes, pesto, and arugula. On Sunday, it hosts storytelling and spoken-word sessions. **Norden** (✉ Østerg. 61, Downtown ☎ 33/11–77–91) resides at the intersection of Købmagergade and Strøget. Substantial portions make up for minimal table space at this art nouveau–style café. **Rust** (✉ Guldbergsg. 8, Nørrebro ☎ 35/24–52–00) is a constantly crowded all-in-one rock club–restaurant–café on Nørrebro's main square, Skt. Hans Torv. Hearty, fresh dishes are served inside, while grill food is served on the terrace. **Sebastopol** (✉ Skt. Hans Torv 32, Nørrebro ☎ 35/36–30–02) teems with gussied-up locals in the evening and serves an ample weekend brunch. **Sommersko** (✉ Kronprinsensg. 6, Downtown ☎ 33/14–81–89) is the granddaddy of Copenhagen cafés, with a surprisingly varied menu (try the delicious french fries with pesto or the wok specialties) and an eclectic crowd. **Victor** (✉ Ny Østerg. 8, Downtown ☎ 33/13–36–13) is all brass and dark wood, lovely for a light lunch.

CASINO   The **Casino Copenhagen** (✉ Amager Blvd. 70, Amager ☎ 33/96–59–65), at the SAS Scandinavia Hotel, has American and French roulette, blackjack, baccarat, and slot machines. Admission is Dkr 80 (you must be 18 years old and show a photo I.D.), and a dress code (jackets required; no athletic clothing or jeans) is enforced. Outerwear must be left at the wardrobe, for a fee. The dealers and croupiers are not shy about reminding winners that a tip of a certain percentage is customary, even after hitting just one number on the roulette wheel. The casino is open 2 PM to 4 AM.

DISCOS, DANCING   Most discos open at 11 PM, charging covers of about Dkr 50–Dkr 100
& LIVE MUSIC   and selling drinks at steep prices. **Absalon** (✉ Frederiksbergg. 38, Downtown ☎ 33/16–16–98), popular with nearly everyone, has lively live music on the ground floor and a disco above. **Baron & Baroness** (✉ Vesterbrog. 2E, Vesterbro ☎ 33/16–01–01) has medieval interiors and draws loads of young people almost every night with retro '80s music. The dance floor is one flight up from ground level. **Columbus** (✉ Nørrebrog. 22, Nørrebro ☎ 35/37–00–51) is a lively salsa club where the activity gets hot as a chili pepper on a good night. Excellent salsa lessons are available to the uninitiated and out-of-practice. **Level CPH** (✉ Skinderg. 45, Downtown ☎ 33/13–26–25) pulsates to '80s dance tunes and features a roomy dance floor and a reconstructed airport–loungelike area, outfitted with real airplane seats. **Luft Kastellet** (✉ Strandg. 100–B, Christianshavn ☎ 70/26–26–24) fosters a beachlike atmosphere with its indoor-outdoor layout and harborside location. Guests often dance barefoot on the sand-covered floors to modern jazz, funk or lounge-inspired chill-out tunes. **Nasa** (✉ Gothersg. 8F, Boltens Gård, Sankt Annæ Kvarter ☎ 33/93–74–15) has an exclusive "members only" policy,

which has earned it legendary status among Copenhagen's nightclubs. The choosy doorman screens the throngs outside based on his impression of their looks, clothes, and attitude. Luckily, rumor has it that Nasa is relaxing its door policy. Once inside, you get to hobnob in cool, white interiors with the city's chic and moneyed set and local celebrities (Prince Frederik occasionally drops by). Underneath Nasa are two other clubs, Club Bahia and Blue Buddha, with a more casual vibe and much more lax door policies.

Park Café (⊠ Østerbrog. 79, Østerbro ☎ 35/42–62–48) offers an old-world café with live music downstairs, a disco upstairs, and a movie theater just next door. **Den Røde Pimpernel** (⊠ Bernstorffsg. 3, Vesterbro ☎ 33/75–07–60) draws an adult audience for dancing to live orchestras, trios, and old-time music. The very popular English-style **Rosie McGees** (⊠ Vesterbrog. 2A, Vesterbro ☎ 33/32–19–23) pub serves American and Mexican eats and encourages dancing. **Sabor Latino** (⊠ Vester Voldg. 85, Downtown ☎ 33/11–97–66) is the United Nations of discos, with an international crowd dancing to salsa and other Latin rhythms. **Sofie Kælder** (⊠ Overgaden oven Vandet 32, Christianshavn ☎ 32/57–27–87) is a veteran of the Copenhagen night scene and serves as a frequent hang-out for local musicians. Live music plays on Thursday, a DJ spins on Friday, and live jazz on Saturday afternoons gives way to piano-bar tunes in the evening. The kitchen serves simple fare to accompany cocktails. **Stereo Bar** (⊠ Linnésg. 16A, Downtown ☎ 33/13–61–13) has lava lamps and '70s furnishings; plays house, soul, and funk music; and draws an eclectic crowd, from design students to writers, providing your best chance for an interesting conversation in Copenhagen's club scene. The **Søpavillionen** (⊠ Gyldenløvsg. 24, Vesterbro ☎ 33/15–12–24) invariably inspires first-time visitors to ask, "what *is* that building?" The ornate white wooden structure next to Copenhagen's lakes was built in 1894. The pavilion hosts seminars and private events on weekdays and functions as a dance club until 5 AM on weekends, featuring live music and DJs. **Woodstock** (⊠ Vesterg. 12, Downtown ☎ 33/11–20–71) is among the city's most enduring clubs. A mixed audience grooves to music from the '50s to the '80s.

GAY BARS & ESTABLISHMENTS Given Denmark's long-time liberal attitudes toward homosexuality, it's not surprising that Copenhagen has a thriving and varied gay nightlife scene. In August, Copenhagen celebrates "Mermaid Pride," its boisterous annual gay-pride parade.

Amigo Bar (⊠ Schønbergsg. 4, Downtown ☎ 33/21–49–15) is popular with men of all ages. For a show-tune showdown, head for the piano bar at **Café Intime** (⊠ Allég. 25, Frederiksberg ☎ 38/34–19–58), where you can sip cocktails to Miss Monica's spirited renditions of standards. It's easy to meet mostly men at **Can Can** (⊠ Mikkel Bryggesg. 11, Downtown ☎ 33/11–50–10), a small place with a friendly bartender.

The small **Central Hjørnet** (⊠ Kattesundet 18, Downtown ☎ 33/11–85–49) has been around for about 60 years. The dark, casual **Cosy Bar** (⊠ Studiestr. 24, Downtown ☎ 33/12–74–27) is the place to go in the wee hours (it usually stays open until 8 AM). **Heaven Café** (⊠ Kompagnistr. 18, Downtown ☎ 33/15–19–00) is the latest addition to the gay café scene, serving light meals to a casual crowd of locals and foreigners. **Jeppes Club** (⊠ Allég. 25, Frederiksberg ☎ 38/87–32–48) is patronized mainly by gay women and opens on the first and last Friday of every month. **Masken Bar & Café** (⊠ Studiestr. 33, Downtown ☎ 33/91–09–37) is a relaxed bar welcoming both men and women. **Men's Bar** (⊠ Teglgård-str. 3, Downtown ☎ 33/12–73–03) is men-only with a leather-and-rubber dress code; the decor is dark and casual. **Never Mind** (⊠ Nørre

Voldg. 2, Downtown ☎ 33/11–88–86), across the street from a park where gay men cruise, is popular among gay persons of all ages and both genders. **Oscar Café & Bar** (✉ Rådhus Pl. 77, Downtown ☎ 33/12–09–99) is a relaxed spot for a drink or a cup of coffee. **Pan Caféen** (✉ Knabrostr. 3, off Strøget, Downtown ☎ 33/11–37–84) packs men and women into its three floors of coffee and cocktail bars; the disco is open Wednesday through Saturday.

For more information, call or visit the **Landsforeningen for Bøsser og Lesbiske** (Gay and Lesbian Association; ✉ Teglgårdstr. 13, Boks 1023, Downtown DK–1007 ☎ 33/13–19–48 ⊕ www.lbl.dk), which has a library and more than 45 years of experience. Check out the free paper *Panbladet* (⊕ www.panbladet.dk), or the gay guides *Gayguide* (⊕ www.gayguide.dk) and *Copenhagen Gay Life* (⊕ www.copenhagen-gay-life.dk) for listings of nightlife events and clubs, and other topical information of special interest to the gay individual.

JAZZ CLUBS Hard times have thinned Copenhagen's once-thriving jazz scene. Most of the clubs still open headline local talents, but European and international artists also perform, especially in July, when the Copenhagen Jazz Festival spills over into the clubs. Many jazz clubs host Sunday afternoon sessions that draw spirited crowds of Danes. **Copenhagen Jazzhouse** (✉ Niels Hemmingsensg. 10, Downtown ☎ 33/15–26–00) attracts European and some international names to its chic, modern, barlike interior. **Drop Inn** (✉ Kompagnistr. 34, Downtown ☎ 33/11–24–04) draws a capacity crowd for its popular Sunday afternoon jazz sessions. The bar was designed with the audience in mind. The stage faces an informal semicircle of chairs and booths so there isn't a bad seat in the house. The eclectic decor includes wrought-iron, wreath-shape candelabras, iron statues of winged bacchanalian figures, and an M. C. Escher–style ceiling fresco. **Jazzhuset** (✉ Rådhusstr. 13, Downtown ☎ 33/15–63–53), with exposed concrete walls decorated with local art, showcases traditional New Orleans–style jazz acts on Friday and Saturday. (It's closed on Sunday.) During the day, it functions as a café, in whose sunlit back room you can enjoy coffee, beer, and light sandwiches. An adjoining theater features everything from Shakespeare to experimental plays. **La Fontaine** (✉ Kompagnistr. 11, Downtown ☎ 33/11–60–98) is Copenhagen's quintessential jazz dive, with sagging curtains, impenetrable smoke, and hep cats. This is a must for jazz lovers.

ROCK CLUBS Copenhagen has a good selection of rock clubs, most of which cost less than Dkr 50. Almost all are filled with young, fashionable crowds. Clubs tend to open and go out of business with some frequency, but you can get free entertainment newspapers and flyers advertising gigs at almost any café.

Lades Kælder (✉ Kattesundet 6, Downtown ☎ 33/14–00–67), a local hangout just off Strøget, hosts bands that play good old-fashioned rock and roll. **Loppen** (✉ Bådsmandsstr. 43, Christianshavn ☎ 32/57–84–22), in Christiania, is a medium-size concert venue featuring some of the bigger names in Danish music (pop, rock, urban, and jazz) and budding artists from abroad. The **Pumpehuset** (✉ Studiestr. 52, Downtown ☎ 33/93–19–60) is the place for soul and rock. **Rust** (✉ Guldbergsg. 8, Nørrebro ☎ 35/24–52–00) is a smaller club, mainly featuring rock, pop, and urban acts. **Stengade 30** (✉ Steng. 18, Nørrebro ☎ 35/36–09–38), named for an address right down the street from the actual club, is a smallish rock venue doubling as a bar that remains open through the night. **Vega** (✉ Enghavevej 40, Vesterbro ☎ 32/25–70–11) has evening rock bands, after which the dance club plays house and techno, dragging action into the wee hours.

The Arts

The most complete English calendar of events is listed in the tourist magazine *Copenhagen This Week* (www.ctw.dk), and includes musical and theatrical events as well as films and exhibitions. Copenhagen's main theater and concert season runs from September through May, and tickets can be obtained either directly from theaters and concert halls, or from ticket agencies. **Billetnet** (☎ 70/15–65–65 ⊕ www.billetnet.dk), a box-office service available at all post offices, has tickets for most major events. The main phone line is often busy; for information go in person to any post office. There's one on Købmagergade, just off Strøget. Same-day purchases at the box office at **Tivoli** (✉ Vesterbrog. 3, Downtown ☎ 33/15–10–12) are half price if you pick them up after noon; the half-price tickets are for shows all over town, but the ticket center also has full-price tickets for the park's own performances. The box office is open Monday through Friday, 11 to 5.

FILM   Films open in Copenhagen a few months to a year after their U.S. premieres. The Danes are avid viewers, willing to pay Dkr 70 per ticket, wait in lines for premieres, and read subtitles. Call the theater for reservations, and pick up tickets (with assigned seat numbers) an hour before the movie. Most theaters have a café. **Cinemateket** (✉ Gothersg. 55, Downtown ☎ 33/74–34–00), in the Danish Film Institute building, runs art films—often a series with a theme—and houses an excellent gift shop and café. **Gloria** (✉ Rådhus Pl. 59, Downtown ☎ 33/12–42–92) plays recent independent releases and art-house favorites. **Grand Teatret** (✉ Mikkel Bryggersg. 8, Downtown ☎ 33/15–16–11) shows new foreign and art films, and is next door to its sister café. **Vester Vov Vov** (✉ Absalonsg. 5, Vesterbro ☎ 33/24–42–00) is an alternative venue for art-house and second-run films.

OPERA, BALLET, THEATER & MUSIC   Concert and festival information is available from the **Dansk Musik Information Center** (DMIC; ✉ Gråbrødre Torv 16, Downtown ☎ 33/11–20–66 ⊕ www.mic.dk).

Det Kongelige Teater (The Royal Theater) (✉ Kongens Nytorv, Downtown ✆ Box 2185, 1017 Kobenhavn K ☎ 33/69–69–33 ⊕ www.kgl-teater.dk), where the season runs October to May, is home to the Royal Danish Ballet, one of the premier companies in the world. Not as famous, but also accomplished, are the Royal Danish Opera and the Royal Danish Orchestra, the latter of which performs in all productions. Plays are exclusively in Danish. For information and reservations, call the theater. Beginning at the end of July, you can order tickets for the next season by writing to the theater.

If you are in search of experimental opera then **Den Anden Opera** (✉ Kronprinsensg. 7, Downtown ☎ 33/32–38–30 ⊕ www.denandenopera.dk) is worth a visit. **Dansescenen** (✉ Øster Fælled Torv 34, Østerbro ☎ 34/35–83–00 ⊕ www.dansescenen.dk) hosts various modern and experimental dance performances, some of which are put together by their choreographer-in-residence. **Kanonhallen** (✉ Øster Fælled Torv 37 Østerbro ☎ 70/15–65–65 ⊕ www.kanonhallen.net) runs a modern dance troupe in the city. **Nyt Dansk Danseteater** (✉ Guldbergsg. 29A, Nørrebro ☎ 35/39–87–87 ⊕ www.nddt.dk) has a modern dance company but not a performance space; Copenhagen performances are held at other venues.

Tivoli Concert Hall (✉ Tietensg. 20, Downtown ☎ 33/15–10–12) offers more than 150 concerts each summer, presenting a host of Danish and foreign soloists, conductors, and orchestras.

London Toast Theatre (✉ Kochsvej 18, Frederiksberg ☎ 33/22–86–86 ⊕ www.londontoast.dk) hosts English-language theater productions.

Københavns Internationale Teater (KIT) (Copenhagen International Theatre) (✉ Vesterg. 5, 3rd fl., Downtown ☎ 33/15–15–64 ⊕ www.kit.dk) offers an interesting lineup of entertainment for all ages between June and August. Under the title "Summerscene," KIT presents international contemporary theater, dance, inventive circus-style shows, and myriad other performances.

Sports & the Outdoors

Beaches

North of Copenhagen along the old beach road, **Strandvejen** is a string of lovely old seaside towns and beaches. **Bellevue Beach** (✉ Across the street from Klampenborg Station, Klampenborg) is packed with locals and has cafés, kiosks, and surfboard rentals. **Charlottenlund Fort** (Bus 6 from Rådhus Pl.) is a bit more private, but you have to pay (about Dkr 20) to swim off the pier. The beaches along the tony town of **Vedbæk**, 18 km (11 mi) north of Copenhagen, are not very crowded as they are not as close to Copenhagen nor as easily accessible by public transportation.

Closest to the city, the route along **Amager Strandvej** to and from the airport is a 12-km (7½-mi) stretch of beaches and wooded areas. Helgoland beach, on the north end of this strand, has bathhouses and a long dock and requires a token entrance fee.

Biking

Bike rentals are available throughout the city, and most roads have bike lanes. You might also be lucky and find an advertisement-flanked "city bike," parked at busy points around the city including Kongens Nytorv and the Nørreport train station. Deposit Dkr 20 and pedal away; your money is returned when you return the bike. The city bikes are out and about from May to September. The Wonderful Copenhagen tourist information office has city bike maps with suggested bike routes including a route of the city's ramparts or of the Copenhagen harbor. Follow all traffic signs and signals; bicycle lights and reflectors must be used at night. The **Danish Cyclist Federation** (✉ Rømersg. 7, Downtown ☎ 33/32–31–21 ⊕ www.dcf.dk) has information about biking in the city. **Wonderful Copenhagen** (✉ Gammel Kongevej 1, Downtown ☎ 33/25–74–00 ⊕ www.woco.dk) can provide information about bike rental companies and routes throughout the city.

Canoeing

About 15 km (10 mi) north of Copenhagen, especially in the Lyngby area, several calm lakes and rivers are perfect for canoeing: the Mølleå (Mølle River) and the Bagsværd, Lyngby, and Furesø (Bagsværd, Lyngby, and Fur lakes). Hourly and daily rentals and package canoe tours are available throughout the region.

Golf

Although almost all courses in Denmark are run by private clubs, anybody who is a member of a club approved by a recognized authority—such as USPGA or R & A—can play. You will generally be asked to present a handicap card, something many American golfers do not carry around with them. It might be a good idea to have some proof of membership with you when you go to sign in. Otherwise, you will need to convince the staff you are indeed a golfer. It would be wise to call beforehand to find out if and when it is possible to play. Most golf course staffs are accommodating, especially for visitors. At this writing, there were only three pay-and-play courses within a 20-mi (30 km) radius of Copenhagen, and they tend to be crowded. They also follow varying restrictions that tend to be as strict as those of private clubs. Most courses have handicap limits, normally around 28, for prospective players. Clubs, bags, and handcarts can be rented at virtually all courses, but carts are a rarity. With few exceptions, carts may not be used without a letter from a doctor stating it is necessary. Some clubs do not accept reservations; call for details. **Copenhagen Golf Center** (⊠ Golfsvinget 16–20, Vallenbæk ☎ 43/64–92–93) is one of the publicly accessible courses close to the city center. The 18-hole course is rather flat but challenging; there is a variety of practice facilities, including a driving range. **Copenhagen Indoor Golf Center** (⊠ Refshalevej 177–B, Holmen ☎ 32/66–11–00) is a newly expanded indoor practice center in what was once the huge B & W shipbuilding plant. Pros are on hand to give lessons at the driving and chipping ranges, or the practice green. The 18-hole course at **Københavns Golf Klub** (⊠ Dyrehaven 2, Lyngby ☎ 39/63–04–83) is said to be Scandinavia's oldest. It is located on the former royal hunting grounds, which is now a public park, so golfers must yield to people out strolling and to the herds of wild deer who live in the park. Greens fees cost about Dkr 280; check local rules about obstructions. One of Denmark's best courses, a frequent host of international tournaments, is the 18-hole **Rungsted Golf Klub** (⊠ Vestre Stationsvej 16, Rungsted Kyst ☎ 45/86–34–44). A 30 handicap for all players is required on weekdays; on weekends and holidays the required handicap is 24 for men and a 29 for women. In 2003 **Simons Golf Club** (⊠ Nybovej 5, Kvistgård ☎ 49/19–14–78) became the first course in Denmark to host European Tour competition. One of the finest in the country, the course was made even more challenging for the professionals who played there. There are fine practice facilities; call to check about the handicap requirement.

Horseback Riding
You can ride at the Dyrehavebakken (Deer Forest Hills) at **Fortunens Ponyudlejning** (⊠ Ved Fortunen 33, Lyngby ☎ 45/87–60–58). A one-hour session (English saddle), in which both experienced and inexperienced riders go out with a guide, costs about Dkr 100.

Running
The 6-km (4-mi) loop around the three lakes just west of city center—Skt. Jørgens, Peblinge, and Sortedams—is a runner's nirvana. There are also paths at the Rosenborg Have; the Frederiksberg Garden (near Frederiksberg Station, corner of Frederiksberg Allé and Pile Allé); and the Dyrehaven, north of the city near Klampenborg.

Soccer
Danish soccer fans call themselves Rooligans, which loosely translates as well-behaved fans, as opposed to hooligans. These Rooligans idolize the national team's soccer players as superstars. When the rivalry is most intense (especially against Sweden and Norway), fans don face paint, wear head-to-toe red and white, incessantly wave the Dannebrog (Danish flag), and have a good time whether or not they win. The biggest stadium in town for national and international games is **Parken** (⊠ Øster Allé 50, Østerbro ☎ 35/43–31–31). **Billetnet** (☎ 70/15–65–65) sells tickets for all matches. Prices are about Dkr 140 for slightly obstructed views at local matches, Dkr 220–Dkr 320 for unobstructed; international matches are more expensive.

Swimming
Swimming is very popular here, and the pools (all of which are indoor) are crowded but well maintained. Separate bath tickets can also be purchased. Admission to local pools (Dkr 20–Dkr 50) includes a locker key, but you have to bring your own towel. Most pools are 25 meters long.

The **DGI Byen Swim Center** (⊠ Tietgensg. 65, Vesterbro ☎ 33/29–80–00) contains a massive oval pool with 100-meter lanes and a nifty platform in the middle that can be raised for parties and conferences. The swim center also has a children's pool and a "mountain pool," with a climbing wall, wet trampoline, and several diving boards. Admission to the swim center is Dkr 50. During the popular monthly "spa night," candles are placed around the pool; dinner and wine are served on the raised pool platform; and massages and other spa services are offered. The beautiful **Frederiksberg Svømmehal** (⊠ Helgesvej 29, Frederiksberg ☎ 38/14–04–00) maintains its old art-deco decor of sculptures and decorative tiles. The 50-meter **Lyngby Svømmehal** (⊠ Lundtoftevej 53, Lyngby ☎ 45/97–39–60) has a separate diving pool. In the modern concrete **Vesterbro Svømmehal** (⊠ Angelg. 4, Vesterbro ☎ 33/22–05–00), many enjoy swimming next to the large glass windows.

Shopping

A showcase for world-famous Danish design and craftsmanship, Copenhagen seems to have been designed with shoppers in mind. The best buys are such luxury items as crystal, porcelain, silver, and furs. Look for offers and sales (*tilbud* or *udsalg* in Danish) and check antiques and secondhand shops for classics at cut-rate prices. Although prices are inflated by a hefty 25% value-added tax (Danes call it *moms*), non–European Union citizens can receive about an 18% refund. For more details and a list of all tax-free shops, ask at the tourist office for a copy of the *Tax-Free Shopping Guide*.

The **Information Center for Danish Crafts and Design** (⊠ Amagertorv 1, Downtown ☎ 33/12–61–62 ⊕ www.danishcrafts.dk) provides helpful information on the city's galleries, shops, and workshops specializing in Danish crafts and design, from jewelry to ceramics to wooden toys to furniture. Its Web site has listings and reviews of the city's best crafts shops.

Shopping Districts & Malls

The pedestrian-only **Strøget** and adjacent Købmagergade are *the* shopping streets, but wander down the smaller streets for lower-price, offbeat stores. The most exclusive shops are at the end of Strøget, around Kongens Nytorv, and on Ny Adelgade, Grønnegade, and Pistolstræde. **Kronprinsensgade** has become the in-vogue fashion strip, where a number of young Danish clothing designers have opened boutiques. **Bredgade,** just off Kongens Nytorv, is lined with elegant antiques and silver shops, furniture stores, and auction houses. **Scala,** a city-center mall across the street from Tivoli, has several clothing stores, a couple of boisterous pubs, and a main-floor food court for the famished. Copenhagen's latest mall is the gleaming **Fisketorvet Shopping Center,** built in what was Copenhagen's old fish market. It's near the canal, south of the city center, within walking distance to the Dybbølsbro station. It includes all the usual mall shops, from chain clothing stores (Mango, Hennes & Mauritz) and shoe shops (including the ubiquitous Ecco) to a smattering of jewelry, watch, and stereo retailers, such as Swatch and Bang & Olufsen. Fast-food outlets abound. In the south part of the city, on **Vesterbrogade,** you can find discount stores—especially leather and clothing shops.

Department Stores

Hennes & Mauritz (⊠ Amagertorv 21–24, Downtown ☎ 33/73–70–90), H & M for short, has stores all over town. They offer reasonably priced clothing and accessories for men, women, and children; best of all are the to-die-for baby clothes. **Illum** (⊠ Østerg. 52, Downtown ☎ 33/14–40–02), not to be confused with Illums Bolighus, is well stocked, with a lovely rooftop café and excellent basement grocery. **Magasin** (⌧ Kongens Nytorv 13, Downtown ☎ 33/11–44–33), Scandinavia's largest department store, also has a top-quality basement marketplace.

Specialty Stores

ANTIQUES For silver, porcelain, and crystal, the well-stocked shops on **Bredgade** are upscale and expensive. **Danborg Gold and Silver** (⌧ Holbergsg. 17, Downtown ☎ 33/32–93–94) is one of the best places for estate jewelry and silver flatware. **Dansk Møbelkunst** (⌧ Bredg. 32, Sankt Annæ Kvarter ☎ 33/32–38–37) is spacious and elegant, and home to one of the city's largest collections of vintage Danish furniture. Some of the pieces are by Arne Jacobsen, Kaare Klimt, and Finn Juhl, whose lustrous, rosewood furnishings are some of the finest examples of Danish design. **H. Danielsens** (⌧ Læderstr. 11, Downtown ☎ 33/13–02–74) is a good bet for silver, Christmas plates, and porcelain. **Kaabers Antikvariat** (⌧ Skinderg. 34, Downtown ☎ 33/15–41–77) is an emporium for old and rare books, prints, and maps. The dozens of **Ravnsborggade** (⌧ Nørrebro) stores carry traditional pine, oak, and mahogany furniture, and smaller items such as lamps and tableware. Some of them sell tax-free items and can arrange shipping. **Royal Copenhagen** (⌧ Amagertorv 6, Downtown ☎ 33/13–71–81), along Strøget, carries old and new china, porcelain patterns, and figurines, as well as seconds.

AUDIO EQUIPMENT For high-tech design and acoustics, **Bang & Olufsen** (⌧ Østerg. 3, Downtown ☎ 33/15–04–22) is so renowned that its products are in the permanent design collection of New York's Museum of Modern Art. (Check prices at home first to make sure you are getting a deal.)

CLOTHING It used to be that Danish clothing design took a back seat to the famous Dansk-designed furniture and silver, but increasingly that's no longer the case. If you're on the prowl for the newest Danish threads, you'll find a burgeoning number of cooperatives and designer-owned stores around town, particularly along Kronprinsensgade, near the Strøget.

Artium (⌧ Vesterbrog. 1, Vesterbro ☎ 33/12–34–88) offers an array of colorful, Scandinavian-designed sweaters and clothes alongside useful and artful household gifts. **Bruuns Bazaar** (⌧ Kronprinsensg. 8, Downtown ☎ 33/32–19–99) has its items hanging in the closet of almost every stylish Dane. Here you can buy the Bruuns label—inspired designs with a classic, clean-cut Danish look—and other high-end names, including Gucci. **Companys** (⌧ Frederiksbergg. 24, Downtown ☎ 33/11–35–55) carries a trendy, youthful style, typified by the Danish Matinique label. **Mett-Mari** (⌧ Vesterg. 11, Downtown ☎ 33/15–87–25) is among the most inventive handmade women's clothing shops. **Munthe plus Simonsen** (⌧ Kronprinsensg. 11, Downtown ☎ 33/32–03–12) sells innovative and playful—and pricey—Danish designs. **Petitgas Herrehatte** (⌧ Købmagerg. 5, Downtown ☎ 33/13–62–70) is a venerable shop for old-fashioned men's hats. The **Sweater Market** (⌧ Frederiksbergg. 15, Downtown ☎ 33/15–27–73) specializes in thick, traditional, patterned, and solid Scandinavian sweaters.

CRYSTAL & PORCELAIN Minus the V.A.T., such Danish classics as Holmegaards crystal and Royal Copenhagen porcelain usually are less expensive than they are back home. Signed art glass is always more expensive, but be on the lookout for seconds as well as secondhand and unsigned pieces. **Bodum Hus** (⌧ Østerg. 10, on Strøget, Downtown ☎ 33/36–40–80) shows off a wide variety of reasonably priced Danish-designed functional, and especially kitchen-oriented, accoutrements; the milk foamers are indispensable for cappuccino lovers. **Royal Copenhagen** (⌧ Amagertorv 6, Downtown ☎ 33/13–71–81) has firsts and seconds of its famous porcelain ware.

The **Royal Copenhagen Factory** (✉ Smalleg. 47, Frederiksberg ☎ 38/14–92–97) offers a look at the goods at their source. The factory runs tours through its facilities on weekdays 9, 10, and 11 from mid-September through April, and weekdays at 9, 10, 11, 1, and 2 from May to mid-September. Holmegaards Glass can be purchased at either the Royal Copenhagen store on Amagertorv or at the factory on Smallegade (for seconds). Alternatively, you can travel to their dedicated factory **Holmegaards Glasværker** (✉ Glasværkvej 45, Holme-Olstrup ☎ 55/54–50–00), 97 km (60 mi) south of Copenhagen near the town of Næstved. **Rosenthal Studio-Haus** (✉ Frederiksberg. 21, on Strøget, Downtown ☎ 33/14–21–01) offers the lead-crystal wildlife reliefs of Mats Johansson as well as the very modern functional and decorative works of many other Italian and Scandinavian artisans. **Skandinavisk Glas** (✉ Ny Østerg. 4, Downtown ☎ 33/13–80–95) has a large selection of Danish and international glass and a helpful, informative staff.

FUR   Denmark, the world's biggest producer of ranched minks, is the place to go for quality furs. Furs are ranked into four grades: Saga Royal (the best), Saga, Quality 1, and Quality 2. **Birger Christensen** (✉ Østerg. 38, Downtown ☎ 33/11–55–55), purveyor to the royal family and Copenhagen's finest furrier, deals only in Saga Royal quality. The store presents a new collection yearly from its in-house design team. Expect to spend about 20% less than in the United States for same-quality furs ($5,000–$10,000 for mink, $3,000 for a fur-lined coat) but as always, it pays to do your homework before you leave home. Birger Christensen is also among the preeminent fashion houses in town, carrying labels like Donna Karan, Chanel, Prada, Kenzo, Jil Sander, and Yves Saint Laurent. **A. C. Bang** (✉ Lyngby Hovedg. 55, Lyngby ☎ 45/88–00–54) carries less expensive furs than Birger Christensen, but has an old-world, old-money aura and very high quality.

FURNITURE &   **Gubi Design** (✉ Grønnegade 10, Downtown ☎ 33/32–63–68) is where
DESIGN   to go for the super-clean *Wallpaper* look. The chic kitchens are amazing and amazingly priced, but if you can't afford to move one back home, you can at least gain inspiration before you remodel your own kitchen. **Illums Bolighus** (✉ Amagertorv 10, Downtown ☎ 33/14–19–41) is part gallery, part department store, showing off cutting-edge Danish and international design—art glass, porcelain, silverware, carpets, and loads of grown-up toys. **Lysberg, Hansen & Therp** (✉ Bredg. 75, Sankt Annæ Kvarter ☎ 33/14–47–87), one of the most prestigious interior-design firms in Denmark, has sumptuous showrooms done up in traditional and modern styles. **Paustian** (✉ Kalkbrænderiløbskaj 2, Østerbro ☎ 39/16–65–65) offers you the chance to peruse elegant contemporary furniture and accessories in a building designed by Dane Jørn Utzon, the architect of the Sydney Opera House. You can also have a gourmet lunch at the Restaurant Paustian (it's open only for lunch). **Tage Andersen** (✉ Ny Adelg. 12, Downtown ☎ 33/93–09–13) has a fantasy-infused floral gallerylike shop filled with one-of-a-kind gifts and arrangements; browsers (who generally don't purchase the expensive items) are charged a Dkr 45 admission.

SILVER   Check the silver standard of a piece by its stamp. Three towers and "925S" (which means 925 parts out of 1,000) mark sterling. Two towers are used for silver plate. The "826S" stamp (also denoting sterling, but less pure) was used until the 1920s. Even with shipping charges, you can expect to save 50% versus American prices when buying Danish silver (especially used) at the source. **Georg Jensen** (✉ Amagertorv 4, Downtown ☎ 33/11–40–80) is one of the most recognized names in international silver and his elegant, austere shop is aglitter with sterling. Jensen has its own museum next door. **Danish Silver** (✉ Bredg. 22, Sankt Annæ Kvarter ☎ 33/11–52–52), owned by long-time Jensen collector Gregory Pepin, houses a remarkable collection of classic Jensen designs from holloware and place settings to art deco jewelry. Pepin, an American who has lived in Denmark for more than a decade, is a font of information on Danish silver design, so if you're in the market, it's well worth a visit. The **English Silver House** (✉ Pilestr. 4, Downtown ☎ 33/14–83–81) is an emporium of used estate silver. **Ira Hartogsohn** (✉ Palæg. 8, Sankt Annæ Kvarter ☎ 33/15–53–98) carries all sorts of silver knickknacks and settings. **Sølvkælderen** (✉ Kompagnistr. 1, Downtown ☎ 33/13–36–34) is the city's largest (and brightest) silver store, carrying an endless selection of tea services, place settings, and jewelry.

Street Markets

Check with the tourist office or the tourist magazine *Copenhagen This Week* (www.ctw.dk) for flea markets. Bargaining is expected. When the weather gets warm it's time for outdoor flea markets in Denmark and the adventure of finding treasure among a vast amount of goods. Throughout the summer and into the autumn, there are six major flea markets every weekend. Two of the sites are right downtown. Along the walls of the cemetery **Assistens Kirkegård** (✉ Nørrebro), where Hans Christian Andersen and Søren Kierkegaard are buried, there is a flea market on Saturdays with vendors who carry cutlery, dishes, clothes, books, and various other wares. At **Gammel Strand** on Friday and Saturday, the "market" is more of an outdoor antique shop; you might find porcelain and crystal figurines, silver, or even, on occasion, furniture. **Kongens Nytorv** hosts a Saturday flea market in the shadow of the Royal Theater; the pickings are not so regal, but if you arrive early enough, you might nab a piece of jewelry or some Danish porcelain. **Israel Plads** (✉ Near Nørreport Station) has a Saturday flea market from May through October, open 8–2. More than 100 professional dealers vend classic Danish porcelain, silver, jewelry, and crystal, plus books, prints, postcards, and more. The side street **Ravnsborggade** (✉ Nørrebro) is dotted with antiques shops that move their wares outdoors on Sunday.

Copenhagen A to Z

ADDRESSES

Copenhagen began as Havnen (the harbor) with the seat of local government being near what is now Gammel Torv, off the main pedestrian thoroughfare Strøget. Much of what is now the northeastern section of the downtown area was once under water. The harbor was dotted with islands. Through the centuries, various kings filled in the shallow waters and joined the islands to the mainland of Sjælland. During those years, the ramparts of the city were constructed and a system of moats and other water defenses were created. Most maps of the city still reveal the general plan of older defense measures.

Copenhagen grew up within and, eventually, beyond these fortified ramparts. Many of the main neighborhood districts are named after what were once the few points of entry to the city. What can confuse some visitors is the districts are named after points on the compass, but do not lie in that direction in relation to the city center. For instance, Vesterport means "western bridge" (the bridge was the western entry to Copenhagen), while the district lies southwest of downtown.

Nowadays downtown Copenhagen (indicated by a KBH K in mailing addresses) is concentrated around Strøget, in a one-square-km area containing lots of stores, cafés, restaurants, office buildings and galleries, with residential properties on the upper floors. Ten years ago, the center of town (including its northeastern subdistrict Sankt Annæ Kvarter) was the absolute center of all shopping, dining and nightlife activity. It's still thriving, but some of the action has moved to neighboring districts.

A couple of centuries ago the districts of Vesterbro (KBH V), Nørrebro (KBH N) and Østerbro (KBH Ø) were once the outskirts of Copenhagen, named after the ports for entering the city. In the past decade, nightlife and shops have moved into these districts to make them much sought-after spots to live and play. Halmtorv in Vesterbro was once a haunt for street walkers and other urchins, but has become an "in" and increasingly gentrified neighborhood in recent years. The area of Nørrebro closest to downtown was once the working-class area of the city, but now contains some of the hottest property in town after cafés and shops sprouted in the area. Østerbro was mostly a bourgeois bastion, but has turned into a center for young families with lots of opportunity for shopping and recreation.

The man-made island of Christianshavn (KBH K) was filled and raised between Copenhagen and Amager island by King Christian IV to bolster the city's defense installations. Many of the military fortifications can still be seen, such as the Holmen naval base, which has become a thriving spot for creative offices, nightlife, and new residential growth. To the south Amager Island (KBH S) is a main focus of development and expansion plans for the Copenhagen metropolitan region.

AIRPORTS & TRANSFERS
Copenhagen Airport, 10 km (6 mi) southeast of downtown in Kastrup, is the gateway to Scandinavia and the rest of Europe.
🚩 **Kastrup International Airport** ☎ 32/31-32-31 ⊕ www.cph.dk.

TRANSFERS Although the 10-km (6-mi) drive from the airport to downtown is quick and easy, public transportation is excellent and much cheaper. The airport's sleek subterra nean train system takes less than 12 minutes to zip passengers into Copenhagen's main train station. Buy a ticket (Dkr 22.50) upstairs in the airport train station at terminal three; a free airport bus connects the international terminal with the domestic terminal. Three trains an hour leave for Copenhagen, while a fourth travels to Roskilde. Trains also travel from the airport directly to Malmö, Sweden (Dkr 60), via the Øresund Bridge, leaving every 20 minutes and taking 35 minutes in transit. Trains run on weekdays from 5 AM to midnight, on Saturday from 6 AM to midnight, and on Sunday from 6 AM to 11 PM.

SAS coach buses leave the international arrivals terminal every 15 minutes from 5:45 AM to 9:45 PM, cost Dkr 50, and take 25 minutes to reach Copenhagen's main train station on Vesterbrogade. Another SAS coach from Christiansborg, on Slotsholmsgade, to the airport runs every 15 minutes between 8:30 AM and noon, and every half-hour from noon to 6 PM. HT city buses depart from the international arrivals terminal every 15 minutes from 4:30 AM (Sunday 5:30 AM) to 11:45 PM, but take a long, circuitous route. Take Bus 250S for the Rådhus Pladsen and transfer. One-way tickets cost about Dkr 22.50.

The 20-minute taxi ride downtown costs around Dkr 170, though slightly more after 4 PM and weekends. Lines form at the international arrivals terminal. In the unlikely event there is no taxi available, there are several taxi companies you can call including Københavns Taxa.
🚩 **Københavns Taxa** ☎ 35/35-35-35.

BIKE TRAVEL
Bikes are delightfully well suited to Copenhagen's flat terrain and are popular among Danes as well as visitors. Bike rental costs Dkr 35–Dkr

70 a day, with a deposit of Dkr 100–Dkr 300. You may also be lucky enough to find a free city bike chained up at bike racks in various spots throughout the city, including Nørreport and Nyhavn. Insert a Dkr 20 coin, which will be returned to you when you return the bike.

Københavns Cykler ⊠Central Station, Reventlowsg. 11, Vesterbro ☎33/33-86-13 ⊕www. rentabike.dk. **Østerport Cykler** ⊠ Oslo Pl. 9, Østerbro ☎ 33/33-85-13 ⊕ www.rentabike. dk. **Urania Cykler** ⊠ Gammel Kongevej 1, Vesterbro ☎ 33/21-80-88 ⊕ www.urania.dk.

CAR RENTAL

All major international car-rental agencies are represented in Copenhagen; most are at Copenhagen Airport or near the Vesterport Station.

Avis ⊠ Copenhagen Airport, Kastrup ☎ 32/51-22-99 or 32/51-20-99 ⊠ Kampmannsg. 1, Vesterbro ☎ 33/73-40-99 ⊕ www.avis.dk. **Budget** ⊠ Copenhagen Airport, Kastrup ☎ 32/52-39-00 ⊕ www.budget.com. **Europcar-Pitzner Auto** ⊠ Copenhagen Airport, Kastrup ☎ 32/50-30-90 or 32/50-66-60 ⊠ Gammel Kongevej 13A, Vesterbro ☎ 33/55-99-00 ⊕ www.europcar.com. **Hertz** ⊠ Copenhagen Airport, Kastrup ☎ 32/50-93-00 or 32/50-30-40 ⊠ Vester Farimagsg. 1, Vesterbro ☎ 33/17-90-00 ⊕ www.hertzdk.dk.

CAR TRAVEL

The E20 highway, via bridges, connects Fredericia (on Jylland) with Middelfart (on Fyn), a distance of 16 km (10 mi), and goes on to Copenhagen, another 180 km (120 mi) east. Farther north, from Århus (in Jylland), you can get direct auto-catamaran service to Kalundborg (on Sjælland). From there, Route 23 leads to Roskilde, about 72 km (45 mi) east. Take Route 21 east and follow the signs to Copenhagen, another 40 km (25 mi). Make reservations for the ferry in advance through the Danish State Railways. Since the inauguration of the Øresund Bridge in 2000, Copenhagen is now linked to Malmö, Sweden. The trip takes about 30 minutes, and the steep bridge toll stands at Dkr 225 per car at this writing, though prices are likely to decrease to encourage more use.

If you are planning on seeing the sites of central Copenhagen, a car is not convenient. Parking spaces are at a premium and, when available, are expensive. A maze of one-way streets, relatively aggressive drivers, and bicycle lanes make it even more complicated. If you are going to drive, choose a small car that's easy to parallel park, bring a lot of small change to feed the meters, and be very aware of the cyclists on your right-hand side: they always have the right-of-way. For emergencies, contact Falck.

Auto Rescue/Falck ☎ 70/10-20-30 ⊕ www.falck.dk. **Danish State Railways** (DSB) ⊠ Hovedbanegården (main train station), Vesterbro ☎ 70/13-14-15.

EMERGENCIES

Denmark's general emergency number is ☎ 112. Emergency dentists, near Østerport Station, are available weekdays 8 PM–9:30 PM and weekends and holidays 10–noon. The only acceptable payment method is cash. For emergency doctors, look in the phone book under *læge*. After normal business hours, emergency doctors make house calls in the central city and accept cash only; night fees are approximately Dkr 300–Dkr 400. You can also contact the U.S., Canadian, or British embassies for information on English-speaking doctors.

Doctors & Dentists Casualty Wards-Skadestuen ⊠ Italiensvej 1, Amager ☎ 32/34-35-00 ⊠ Niels Andersens Vej 65, Hellerup ☎ 39/77-37-64 or 39/77-39-77. **Doctor Emergency Service** ☎ 70/13-00-41 or 44/53-44-00, daily 4 PM–8 AM. **Tandlægevagt** (Dental Emergency Service) ⊠ 14 Oslo Pl., Østerbro ☎ No phone.

Emergency Services Police, fire, and ambulance ☎ 112.

Hospitals Frederiksberg Hospital ⊠ Nordre Fasanvej 57, Frederiksberg ☎ 38/16-38-16. **Rigshospitalet** ⊠ Blegdamsvej 9, Østerbro ☎ 35/45-35-45.

24-Hour Pharmacies Steno Apotek ⊠ Vesterbrog. 6C, Vesterbro ☎ 33/14-82-66. **Sønderbro Apotek** ⊠ Amangerbrog. 158, Amager ☎ 32/58-01-40.

ENGLISH-LANGUAGE MEDIA

BOOKS Boghallen, the bookstore of the Politiken publishing house, offers a good selection of English-language books. Arnold Busck has an excellent selection, and also textbooks, CDs, and comic books. Gad Boglader runs shops in various parts of the city, including one on Strøget and another in the new Royal Library, and offers a broad assortment of English-language volumes, fiction and non-fiction, along with other items of interest. Most of these stores have a large section devoted to Denmark and Danish literature. Another option for the bookworm would be to browse the many used-book shops that dot many areas of the city. **Arnold Busck** ⊠ Kobmagerg. 49, Downtown ☎ 33/73-35-00. **Boghallen** ⊠ Rådhus Pl. 37, Downtown ☎ 33/47-25-60. **Gad Boglader** ⊠ Vimmelskaftet 32, Downtown ☎ 33/15-05-58.

NEWSPAPERS & MAGAZINES *The Copenhagen Post* (www.cphpost.dk) is a weekly newspaper that covers Danish news events in English. Particularly helpful is its insert, *In & Out,* with reviews and listings of restaurants, bars, nightclubs, concerts, theater, temporary exhibits, flea markets, and festivals in Copenhagen. Anyone planning on staying in Copenhagen for a long period should peruse the classified ads listing apartment-rental agencies and jobs for English-speakers. It's available at select bookstores, some hotels, and tourist offices. The biannual magazine *Scandinavian Living* (www.scandinavianliving.com) includes articles on Scandinavian culture, food, and architecture and also lists the latest bars, restaurants, and shops. It's sold at the tourist office, as well as some stores and hotels.

LODGING

LOCAL AGENTS In summer, reservations are recommended, but should you arrive without one, try the hotel booking desk at the Wonderful Copenhagen tourist information office. The desk offers same-day, last-minute prices (if available) for remaining rooms in hotels and private homes. A fee of Dkr 50 is applied to each booking. You can also reserve private-home accommodations at Meet the Danes. The agency Hay4You has a selection of fully furnished apartments for rent to visitors staying in the city for a week or more. Young travelers looking for a room should head for Use It, the student and youth budget travel agency. **Hay4You** ⊠ Vimmelskaftet 49, Downtown ☎ 33/33-08-05 ⊟ 33/32-08-04 ⊕ www.hay4you.dk. **Hotel booking desk** ⊠ Bernstorffsg. 1, Downtown ☎ 70/22-24-42 ⊕ www.woco.dk. **Meet the Danes** ⊠ Ravnsborgg. 2, 2nd fl., Nørrebro ☎ 33/46-46-46 ⊟ 33/46-46-47 ⊕ www.meetthedanes.dk. **Use It** ⊠ Rådhusstr. 13, Downtown ☎ 33/73-06-20 ⊕ www.useit.dk.

MONEY MATTERS

ATMS ATMs are located around town. Look for the red logos "Kontanten/Dankort Automat." Here you can use Visa, Plus, Mastercard/Eurocard, Eurochequecard and sometimes JCB cards to withdraw money. Machines are usually open 24 hours but some are closed at night.

CURRENCY EXCHANGE Almost all banks (including the Danske Bank at the airport) exchange money. Most hotels cash traveler's checks and exchange major foreign currencies, but they charge a substantial fee and give a lower rate. The exception to the rule—if you travel with cash—are the several locations of Forex (including the main train station and close to the Nørreport station). For up to $500, Forex charges only Dkr 20 for the entire transaction. Keep your receipt and it will even change any remaining kroner you may still have back to dollars or another currency for free. For traveler's checks, it charges Dkr 10 per check. Den Danske Bank exchange is open during and after normal banking hours at the main railway station, daily June through August 7 AM–10 PM, and daily September through May, 7 AM–9 PM. American Express is open weekdays 9–5 and

Saturday 9–noon. The Change Group—open April through October daily 10–8, November through March daily 10–6—has several locations in the city center. Tivoli also exchanges money; it is open May through September, daily noon–11 PM.

📕 **American Express Corporate Travel** ✉ Nansensg. 19, Downtown ☎ 70/23-04-60. **The Change Group** ✉ Vimmelskaftet 47, Downtown ☎ 33/93-04-18, ✉ Frederiksbergg. 5, Downtown ☎ 33/93-04-15 ✉ Østerg. 61, Østerbro ☎ 33/93-04-55 ✉ Vesterbrog. 9A, Vesterbro ☎ 33/24-04-47. **Den Danske Bank** ✉ Banegårdspl. (main train station), Vesterbro ☎ 33/12-04-11 ✉ Copenhagen Airport, Kastrup ☎ 32/46-02-80. **Forex** ✉ Hovedbanegården 22 (main train station), Vesterbro ☎ 33/11-22-20 ✉ Nørre Voldg. 90, Downtown ☎ 33/32-81-00. **Tivoli** ✉ Vesterbrog. 3, Vesterbro ☎ 33/15-10-01.

TAXIS

The shiny computer-metered Mercedes and Volvo cabs are not cheap. The base charge is Dkr 15, plus Dkr 8–Dkr 10 per km. A cab is available when it displays the sign FRI (free); one can be hailed or picked up in front of the main train station or at taxi stands, or by calling the numbers below. Outside the city center, always call for a cab, as your attempts to hail one will be in vain. Try Kobenhavns Taxaor Amager Øbro Taxi. A 40% surcharge applies if you order a cab at night or on the weekend.

📕 **AmagerØbro Taxi** ☎ 32/52-31-11. **Kobenhavns Taxa** ☎ 35/35-35-35.

TOURS

The tourist office monitors all tours and has brochures and information. Most tours run through the summer until September.

BIKE TOURS Basic bicycle tours of Copenhagen with City Safari run around 2½ hours and cover the main sights of the city, while there is a more comprehensive trip (4½ hours) with lunch included. The guides not only point out the main attractions of Copenhagen and provide helpful information for travelers, but also give some insight into the daily routines of the Danes. Special theme tours are also available, such as a trip through historical Copenhagen, a tour to and around the Carlsberg brewery, a junket showing modern architecture, a route following the footsteps of Hans Christian Andersen, and an exciting Copenhagen-by-night trip. Prices range from Dkr 150 to Dkr 350 (lunch included).

If you would prefer that someone else do the peddling, an increasingly popular sightseeing method is provided by Quickshaw, one of the city's many cycle-taxi and -tour companies. Quickshaw bicycle chauffeurs can accommodate two passengers and offer two best-of-Copenhagen sightseeing routes or allow you to dictate your own trip; they will even wait out front while you visit museums or other points of interest. The cyclist-drivers are comfortable and adept as tour guides, narrating as they pedal. The cycle-taxis in service are parked at 18 strategic sites in the inner city.

📕 **City Safari** ✉ Dansk Arkitektur Center (Gammel Dok) Strandg. 27B, Christianshavn ☎ 33/23-94-90 ⊕ www.citysafari.dk. **Quickshaw** ✉ Esplanaden 8D, Downtown ☎ 70/20-13-75 ⊕ www.quickshaw.dk.

BOAT TOURS The Harbor and Canal Tour (one hour) leaves from Gammel Strand and the east side of Kongens Nytorv from May to mid-September. Contact Canal Tours or the tourist office for times and rates. The City and Harbor Tour (2½ hours) includes a short bus trip through town and sails from the Fish Market on Holmens Canal through several more waterways, ending near Strøget. Just south of the embarkation point for the City and Harbor Tour is the equally charming Netto Boats, which also offers hour-long tours for about half the price of its competitors.

📕 **Canal Tours** ☎ 33/42-33-20 ⊕ www.canal-tours.dk. **Netto Boats** ☎ 32/54-41-02 ⊕ www.havnerundfart.dk.

BUS TOURS The Grand Tour of Copenhagen (2½ hours) includes Tivoli, the New Carlsberg Museum, Christiansborg Castle, the Stock Exchange, the Danish Royal Theater, Nyhavn, Amalienborg Castle, Gefion Fountain, Grundtvig Church, and Rosenborg Castle. The City Tour (1½ hours) is more general, passing the New Carlsberg Museum, Christiansborg Castle, the Thorvaldsen Museum, the National Museum, the Stock Exchange, the Danish Royal Theater, Rosenborg Castle, the National Art Gallery, the Botanical Gardens, Amalienborg Castle, Gefion Fountain, and The Little Mermaid. The Open Top Tours (about 1 hour), which are given on London-style double-decker buses, include stops at Amalienborg, the Stock Exchange, Christiansborg, The Little Mermaid, Louis Tussaud's Wax Museum, the National Museum, the New Carlsberg Museum, Nyhavn, the Thorvaldsen Museum, and Tivoli. This tour gives attendees the option to disembark and embark on a later bus. Only the Grand Tour of Copenhagen, which covers the exteriors of the major sites, and the Open Top Tour, which covers less ground but more quickly, operate year-round. It's always a good idea to call first to confirm availability. Several other sightseeing tours leave from the Lur Blowers Column in Rådhus Pladsen 57, late March through September. For tour information call Copenhagen Excursions or Open Top Tours.

Copenhagen Excursions ☎ 32/54-06-06 ⊕ www.cex.dk. **Open Top Tours** ☎ 32/66-00-00 ⊕ www.sightseeing.dk.

WALKING TOURS Due to its manageable size and meandering avenues, Copenhagen is a great city for pedestrians. A number of companies offer walking tours of parts of the city, some catering to Danes and others offering outings in various languages. One of the best companies is Copenhagen Walking Tours, which schedules 10 different English-language guided tours. In addition to tours related to culture and city history, the service offers a Copenhagen shopping primer and a tour of Jewish Copenhagen. The outings begin at the Wonderful Copenhagen tourist information office on weekends—from June through August there are tours from Thursday through Sunday. In addition, there is also a special tour of Rosenborg Castle beginning in front of the palace at 11:30 on Tuesday.

Two-hour walking tours organized by Copenhagen Walks begin in front of the Wonderful Copenhagen office at 10:30 Monday through Saturday from May to September (call to confirm). There are three different routes: uptown on Monday and Thursday, crosstown on Tuesday and Friday, and downtown on Saturday. Richard Karpen, an American who has been living in Denmark for 14 years, leads the tours, offering information on both the interiors and exteriors of buildings and giving insight into the lifestyles, society, and politics of the Danes. His tour of Rosenborg Castle, including the treasury, meets at the castle at 1:30 Monday through Thursday from May to September.

Copenhagen Walking Tours ☎ 40/81-12-17 ⊕ www.copenhagen-walkingtours.dk. **Copenhagen Walks** ☎ 32/84-74-35 ⊕ www.copenhagenwalks.com. **Wonderful Copenhagen** ✉ Bernstorffsg. 1, Vesterbro ☎ 70/22-24-42 ⊕ www.woco.dk.

TRAIN TRAVEL
Copenhagen's Hovedbanegården (Central Station) is the hub of the DSB network and is connected to most major cities in Europe. Intercity trains leave every hour, usually on the hour, from 6 AM to 10 PM for principal towns in Fyn and Jylland. To find out more, contact the DSB. You can make reservations at the central station, at most other stations, and through travel agents.

DSB Information ☎ 70/13-14-15 ⊕ www.dsb.dk. **Hovedbanegården** ✉ Banegård-spl. 1 ☎ 33/14-17-01 ⊕ www.hovedbanen.dk.

TRANSPORTATION AROUND COPENHAGEN

Copenhagen is small, with most sights within one square mi at its center. Wear comfortable shoes and explore downtown on foot. Or follow the example of the Danes and rent a bike. For those with aching feet, an efficient transit system is available.

The Copenhagen Card offers unlimited travel on buses, metro and suburban trains (S-trains) as well as admission to some 60 museums and sights throughout both metropolitan Copenhagen and Malmö, Sweden. They're valid for a limited time, though, and therefore only worthwhile if you're planning a nonstop, intense sightseeing tour. The card costs Dkr 225 (24 hours), Dkr 375 (48 hours), or Dkr 500 (72 hours) and is half-price for children ages 5 to 11. It can be purchased at bus and train stations, tourist offices, and hotels, or from travel agents.

Trains and buses operate from 5 AM (Sunday 6 AM) to midnight. After that, night buses run every half hour from 1 AM to 4:30 AM from the main bus station at Rådhus Pladsen to most areas of the city and surroundings. Trains and buses operate on the same ticket system and divide Copenhagen and surrounding areas into three zones. Tickets are validated on a time basis: on the basic ticket, which costs about Dkr 11 per hour, you can travel anywhere in the zone in which you started. A discount *klip kort* (clip card), good for 10 rides, costs Dkr 85 and must be stamped in the automatic ticket machines on buses or at stations. (If you don't stamp your clip card, you can be fined up to Dkr 500.) Get zone details for S-trains on the information line. The buses have a Danish information line with an automatic answering menu that is not very helpful, but try pressing the number 1 on your phone and wait for a human to pick up. The phone information line operates daily 7 AM–9:30 PM. You might do better by asking a bus driver or stopping by the HT Buses main office (open weekdays 9–7, Saturday 9–3) on the Rådhus Pladsen, where the helpful staff is organized and speaks enough English to adequately explain bus routes and schedules to tourists.

The HT harbor buses are ferries that travel up and down the canal, embarking from outside the Royal Library's Black Diamond, with stops at Knippelsbro, Nyhavn, and Holmen, and then back again, with lovely vistas along the way. The harbor buses run 6 times an hour, daily from 6 AM to 6:25 PM, and tickets cost around Dkr 25. If you have a klip kort, you can use it for a trip on the harbor bus.

The metro system runs regularly from 5 AM to 1 AM, and all night on weekends. Until the end of 2007 only two metro lines are in operation linking the northern neighborhood of Vanløse to the beginning of southern Amager through the downtown area.

Bus information ☎ 36/13-14-15 ⊕ www.ht.dk. **Metro information** ☎ 70/15-16-15 ⊕ www.m.dk. **S-train information** ☎ 70/13-14-15 ⊕ www.rejseplan.dk.

TRAVEL AGENCIES

For student and budget travel, try Kilroy Travels Denmark. For charter packages, stick with Spies. Star Tours also handles packages.

American Express Corporate Travel ✉ Nansensg. 19, Downtown ☎ 70/23-04-60 ⊕ www.nymans.dk. **Carlson Wagonlit** ✉ Vester Farimagsg. 7, 2nd fl., Vesterbro ☎ 33/63-78-78 ⊕ www.cwt.dk. **DSB Travel Bureau** ✉ Hovedbanegården (main train station), Vesterbro ☎ 33/13-14-18 ⊕ www.dsb.dk/rejsebureau. **Kilroy Travels Denmark** ✉ Skinderg. 28, Downtown ☎ 70/80-80-15 ⊕ www.kilroytravels.dk. **Spies** ✉ Nyropsg. 41, Vesterbro ☎ 70/10-42-00 ⊕ www.spies.dk. **Star Tour** ✉ H. C. Andersens Blvd. 12, Vesterbro ☎ 70/11-10-50 ⊕ www.startour.dk.

VISITOR INFORMATION

The Wonderful Copenhagen tourist information office is open May through the first two weeks of September, daily 9–8; the rest of September through April, weekdays 9–4:30 and Saturday 9–1:30. Note that the tourist office hours vary slightly from year to year, so you may want to call ahead. Its well-maintained Web site includes extensive listings of sights and events. Youth information in Copenhagen is available from Use It. Listings and reviews of Copenhagen's museums (including temporary exhibits), sights, and shops are included on www.aok.dk. The Danish Tourist Board's Web site has listings on hotels, restaurants, and sights in Copenhagen and around Denmark; AOK also has an excellent Web site on Copenhagen. For more information on the outlying fishing village of Dragør, visit the office or Web site of Dragør Tourist Information.

AOK ⊕ www.aok.dk. **Danish Tourist Board** ⊕ www.visitdenmark.com. **Dragør Tourist Information** ⊠ Havnepladsen 2, Dragør ☎ 32/53–41–06 ⊕ www.dragoer-information.dk. **Use It** ⊠ Rådhusstr. 13, Downtown ☎ 33/73–06–20 ⊕ www.useit.dk. **Wonderful Copenhagen** ⊠ Bernstorffsg. 1, Vesterbro ☎ 70/22–24–42 ⊕ www.woco.dk.

SIDE TRIPS FROM COPENHAGEN

Experimentarium

8 km (5 mi) north of Copenhagen.

In the beachside town of Hellerup is the user-friendly **Experimentarium,** where more than 300 exhibitions are clustered in various "Discovery Islands," each exploring a different facet of science, technology, and natural phenomena. A dozen body- and hands-on exhibits allow you to take skeleton-revealing bike rides, measure your lung capacity, stir up magnetic goop, play ball on a jet stream, and gyrate to gyroscopes. Once a bottling plant for the Tuborg Brewery, this center organizes one or two special exhibits a year; past installations have included interactive exhibits of the brain and tongue-wagging, life-size dinosaurs. Take Bus 6 or 650S from Rådhus Pladsen or the S-train to Hellerup; transfer to Bus 21 or 650S. Alternatively, take the S-train to Svanemøllen station, then walk north for 10 minutes. ⊠ *Tuborg Havnevej 7, Hellerup* ☎ *39/27–33–33* ⊕ *www.experimentarium.dk* ⊠ *Dkr 95* ⊙ *Mon. and Wed.–Fri. 9–5, Tues. 9–9, weekends and holidays 11–5.*

Charlottenlund

10 km (6 mi) north of Copenhagen (take Bus 6 from Rådhus Pladsen or S-train to Charlottenlund station).

North of Copenhagen is the leafy, affluent coastal suburb of Charlottenlund, with a small, appealing beach that gets predictably crowded on sunny weekends. A little farther north is Charlottenlund Slot (Charlottenlund Palace), a graceful mansion that has housed various Danish royals since the 17th century. Today, it houses only offices and is not open to the public. The surrounding peaceful palace gardens, however, are open to all, and Copenhageners enjoy coming up here for weekend ambles and picnics.

A favorite with families is the nearby **Danmarks Akvarium** (Danmarks Aquarium), a sizeable, well-designed aquarium near the palace with all the usual aquatic suspects, from gliding sharks to brightly colored tropical fish to snapping crocodiles. ⊠ *Kavalergården 1, Charlottenlund* ☎ *39/62–32–83* ⊕ *www.akvarium.dk* ⊠ *Dkr 70* ⊙ *Nov.–Jan., daily 10–4; Feb.–Apr., daily 10–5; May–Aug., daily 10–6; Sept. and Oct., daily 10–5.*

Fodor's Choice ★ While in Charlottenlund, don't miss the remarkable **Ordrupgaard,** one of the largest museum collections of French impressionism in Europe outside of France. Most of the great 19th-century French artists are represented, including Manet, Monet, Matisse, Cezanne, Renoir, Degas, Gauguin, Alfred Sisley, Delacroix, and Pissarro. Particularly noteworthy is Delacroix's 1838 painting of George Sand. The original painting depicted Sand listening to her lover Chopin play the piano. For unknown reasons, the painting was divided, and the half portraying Chopin now hangs in the Louvre. The Ordrupgaard also has a superb collection of Danish Golden Age painters, from Christen Købke to Vilhelm Hammershøj, who has been called "the Danish Edward Hopper" because of the deft use of light and space in his haunting, solitary paintings. Perhaps best of all is that much of the magnificent collection is displayed, refreshingly, in a non-museumlike setting. The paintings hang on the walls of what was once the home of museum founder and art collector Wilhelm Hansen. The lovely interior of this graceful manor house dating from 1918 has been left just as it was when Hansen and his wife Henny lived here. The white-and-gold ceiling has intricate flower moldings, and the gleaming dark-wood tables are set with Royal Copenhagen Flora Danica porcelain. Interspersed among the paintings are windows that provide glimpses of the surrounding lush, park-size grounds of beech trees, sloping lawns, a rose garden, and an orchard. Note that the museum may be closed for renovations, so call ahead. ⊠ *Vilvordevej 110, Charlottenlund* ☎ *39/64–11–83* ⊕ *www.ordrupgaard.dk* ✎ *Dkr 35, Dkr 55 for special exhibits* ☉ *Tues.–Sun. 1–4.*

need a break? Before or after your visit to the Ordrupgaard museum, wind down next door at the soothing **Ordrupgaard Café** (⊠ Vilvordevej 110, Charlottenlund ☎ 39/63–00–33), housed in the former stable of the manor house–turned–museum. Large picture windows overlook the wooded grounds, and museum posters of French and Danish artists line the café's whitewashed walls. Sink into one of the rustic cane chairs and enjoy the daily changing menu of light Danish-French dishes, such as the smoked salmon drizzled with lime sauce or a fluffy ham quiche served with fresh greens. For an afternoon snack, try a pastry along with a pot of coffee that you can refill as often as you wish. On Sunday from noon to 2, it serves a hearty brunch of eggs, bacon, smoked ham, and rye bread. The café is open Tuesday through Sunday, noon–5. Credit cards are not accepted.

Dragør

★ 22 km (14 mi) southeast of Copenhagen (take Bus 30 or 33 from Rådhus Pladsen).

On the island of Amager, less than a half hour from Copenhagen, the quaint fishing town of Dragør (pronounced *drah*-wer) feels far away in distance and time. The town is set apart from the rest of the area around Copenhagen because it was settled by Dutch farmers in the 16th century. King Christian II ordered the community to provide fresh produce and flowers for the royal court. Today, neat rows of terra-cotta–roof houses trimmed with wandering ivy, roses, and the occasional waddling goose characterize the still meticulously maintained community. If there's one color that characterizes Dragør, it's the lovely pale yellow (called Dragør gul, or Dragør yellow) of its houses. According to local legend, the former town hall's chimney was built with a twist so that meetings couldn't be overheard.

As you're wandering around Dragør, notice that many of the older houses have an angled mirror contraption attached to their street-level windows. This *gade spejl* (street mirror), unique to Scandinavia, was— and perhaps still is—used by the occupants of the house to "spy" on the street activity. Usually positioned at seat-level, this is where the curious (often the older ladies of town) could pull up a chair and observe all the comings and goings of the neighborhood from the warmth and privacy of their own homes. You can see these street mirrors all across Denmark's small towns and sometimes in the older neighborhoods of the bigger cities.

The **Dragør Museum,** in one of the oldest houses in town, sits near the water on Dragør's colorful little harbor. The collection includes furniture from old skipper houses, costumes, drawings, and model ships. The museum shop has a good range of books on Dragør's history. ⊠ *Havnepl., Dragør* ☎ *32/53–41–06* ⊕ *www.dragoermuseum.dk* ⊠ *Dkr 30* ☉ *May–Sept., Tues.–Sun. 2–5, noon–4.*

A ticket to the Dragør Museum also affords entrance to the **Mølsted Museum,** which displays paintings by the famous local artist Christian Mølsted, whose colorful canvases capture the maritime ambience of Dragør and its rich natural surroundings. ⊠ *Dr. Dichs Pl. 1, Dragør* ☎ *32/53–41–06* ⊕ *www.dragoermuseum.dk* ⊠ *Dkr 30* ☉ *May–Aug., weekends noon–4.*

You can swing by the **Amagermuseet** in the nearby village of Store Magleby, 2 km (1 mi) west of Dragør. The museum is housed in two thatch-roof, whitewashed vintage farmhouses, which were once the home of the Dutch farmers and their families who settled here in the 16th century. The farmhouses are done up in period interiors, with original furnishings and displays of traditional Dutch costumes. Round out your visit with an outdoor stroll past grazing dairy cows and through well-tended vegetable gardens flourishing with the same vegetables that the settlers grew. ⊠ *Hovedg. 4 and 12, Dragør* ☎ *32/53–93–07* ⊕ *www. amagermuseet.dk* ⊠ *Dkr 30* ☉ *May–Sept., Tues.–Sun. noon–4; Oct.–Apr., Wed. and Sun. noon–4.*

Where to Stay & Eat

$$$ ✕ **Restaurant Beghuset.** This handsome restaurant with rustic stone floors and green-and-gold painted doors is named Beghuset (Pitch House), because this is where Dragør's fishermen used to boil the pitch that waterproofed their wooden ships. The creative Danish cuisine includes fried pigeon with mushrooms, grapes, and potatoes drizzled with a thyme-and-balsamic-vinegar dressing. The front-room café was once an old dry-foods store, hence all the old wooden shelves and drawers behind the bar. Here you can order simple (and inexpensive) dishes such as a beef patty with onions and baked potatoes, and wash them down with a cold beer. ⊠ *Strandg. 14, Dragør* ☎ *32/53–01–36* ⊟ *AE, DC, MC, V* ☉ *Closed Mon.*

$$–$$$ ✕ **Dragør Strandhotel.** Dragør's harborside centerpiece is this spacious, sunny restaurant and café, its exterior awash in a cool yellow like so many of the buildings in town. The Strandhotel started life as an inn, nearly 700 years ago, making it one of Denmark's oldest inns. Danish royalty used to stay here in the 1500s, after going swan hunting nearby, and in the 1800s, Søren Kierkegaard was a regular guest. Though it has kept the "hotel" in its name, today it is only a restaurant. Owned and run by the Helgstrand family for the past 25 years, the Strandhotel has retained its former charms—vintage wooden cupboards and colored ceramics—with views of Dragør's small, bustling harbor. The menu is, disappointingly, tourist-driven (with items such as Mexi-burgers and Caesar salads), but the restaurant also serves Danish fare, including *frikadeller* (pork meatballs) with potato salad; fillet of sole with *remoulade* (a creamy sauce); and cod with red beets, mustard sauce, and chopped boiled egg. ⊠ *Strandlinien 9, Dragør* ☎ *32/52–00–75* ▤ *DC, MC, V* ⊘ *Closed mid-Oct.–mid-Mar.*

$ 🏨 **Dragør Badehotel.** Built in 1907 as a seaside hotel for vacationing Copenhageners, this plain, comfortable hotel is still geared to the summer crowds, yet manages to maintain its wonderfully low prices (you'd easily pay twice the price in Copenhagen). The basic rooms have dark-green carpets and simple furniture; half the rooms include little terraces that face toward the water, so make sure to ask for one when booking. The bathrooms are small and basic, with a shower only (no bathtubs). Breakfast, which is included in the price, is served on the outside terrace during the summer. ⊠ *Drogdensvej 43, DK–2791 Dragør* ☎ *32/53–05–00* 🖷 *32/53–04–99* ⊕ *www.badehotellet.dk* ➱ *34 rooms* ⚫ *Restaurant, bar, meeting room, some pets allowed* ▤ *AE, DC, MC, V.*

Klampenborg, Bakken & Dyrehaven

15 km (9 mi) north of Copenhagen (take Bus 6 from Rådhus Pladsen or S-train to Klampenborg station).

As you follow the coast north of Copenhagen, you'll come upon the wealthy enclave of Klampenborg, whose residents are lucky enough to have the pleasant **Bellevue Beach** nearby. In summer, this luck may seem double-edged, when scores of city-weary sun-seekers pile out at the Klampenborg S-train station and head for the sand. The Danes have a perfect word for this: they call Bellevue a *fluepapir* (flypaper) beach. Still and all, Bellevue is an appealing seaside spot to soak up some rays, especially considering that it's just a 20-minute train ride from Copenhagen.

Klampenborg is no stranger to crowds. Just a few kilometers inland, within the peaceful Dyrehaven, is **Bakken,** the world's oldest amusement park—and one of Denmark's most popular attractions. If Tivoli is champagne in a fluted glass, then Bakken is a pint of beer. Bakken's crowd is working-class Danes, and lunch is hot dogs and cotton candy. Of course, Tivoli, with its trimmed hedges, dazzling firework displays, and evening concerts is still Copenhagen's reigning queen, but unpretentious Bakken makes no claims to the throne; instead, it is unabashedly about having a good time—being silly in the bumper cars, screaming at the top of your lungs on the rides, and eating food that's bad for you. There's something comfortable and nostalgic about Bakken's vaguely dilapidated state. Bakken has more than 100 rides, from quaint, rickety roller coasters (refreshingly free of that Disney gloss) to newer, faster rides to little-kid favorites such as Kaffekoppen, the Danish version of twirling teacups, where you sit in traditional Royal Copenhagen–style blue-and-white coffee cups. Bakken opens in the last weekend in March, with a festive ride by motorcyclists across Copenhagen to Bakken. It closes in late August, because this is when the Dyrehaven park animals begin to mate, and during their raging hormonal stage, the animals can be dangerous around children. To get there, take the S-train to Klampenborg Station. ⊠ *Dyrehavevej 62, inside Dyrhaven, Klampenborg* ☎ *39/63–73–00* ⊕ *www.bakken.dk* 🎫 *Free, rides cost Dkr 10–Dkr 25; Dkr 200 for a day pass to all rides* ⊘ *Late Mar.–late Aug., 2 PM–midnight.*

★   Bakken sits within the verdant, 2,500-acre **Dyrehaven** (Deer Park), where herds of wild deer roam freely. Once the favored hunting grounds of Danish royals, today Dyrehaven has become a cherished weekend oasis for Copenhageners. Hiking and biking trails traverse the park, and lush fields beckon to nature-seekers and families with picnic hampers. The deer are everywhere; in the less-trafficked regions of the park, you may find yourself surrounded by an entire herd of deer delicately stepping through the fields. The park's centerpiece is the copper-top, 17th-century **Eremitagen,** formerly a royal hunting lodge. It is closed to the public. Today, the Royal Hunting Society gathers here for annual lunches and celebrations, most famously on the first Sunday in November, when the society hosts a popular (and televised) steeplechase event in the park. The wet and muddy finale takes place near the Eremitagen when the riders attempt to make it across a small lake. Dyrehaven is a haven for hikers and bikers, but you can also go in for the royal treatment and enjoy it from the high seat of a horse-drawn carriage. The carriages gather at the park entrance near the Klampenborg S-train station. The cost is around Dkr 40 for 15 minutes, Dkr 60 to Bakken, Dkr 250 to the Eremitagen, and Dkr 400 for an hour. ⊠ *Park entrance is near Klampenborg S-train station, Klampenborg* ☎ *39/63–39-00.*

Where to Eat

★ **$$$$** ✕ **Strandmøllekroen.** The 200-year-old beachfront inn is filled with antiques and hunting trophies. The best views are of the Øresund from the back dining room. Elegantly served seafood and steaks are the mainstays, and for a bit of everything, try the seafood platter, with lobster, crab claws, and Greenland shrimp. ⊠ *Strandvejen 808, Klampenborg* ☎ *39/63–01–04* ▭ *AE, DC, MC, V.*

Frilandsmuseet

16 km (10 mi) northwest of Copenhagen.

North of Copenhagen is Lyngby, its main draw the Frilandsmuseet, an open air museum. About 50 farmhouses and cottages representing various periods of Danish history have been painstakingly dismantled, moved here, reconstructed, and filled with period furniture and tools. Trees and gardens surround the museum; bring lunch and plan to spend the day. To get here, take the S-train to the Sorgenfri Station, then walk right and follow the signs. ⊠ *Kongevejen, Lyngby* ☎ *33/13–44–41* ⊕ *www.frilandsmuseet.dk* ⊠ *Dkr 50, free Wed.* ☉ *Easter–Sept., Tues.–Sun. 10–5.*

Museet for Moderne Kunst (Arken)

20 km (12 mi) southwest of Copenhagen (take the S-train in the direction of either Hundige, Solrød Strand, or Køge to Ishøj Station, then pick up Bus 128 to the museum).

Architect Søren Robert Lund was 25 when awarded the commission for this forward-looking museum, which he designed in metal and white concrete set against the flat coast southwest of Copenhagen. The museum, also known as the *Arken,* opened in March 1996 to great acclaim, both for its architecture and its collection. Unfortunately, for a couple of years following its opening, it was plagued with a string of stranger-than-fiction occurrences, including a director with an allegedly bogus resume. The situation has greatly improved and today the museum's massive sculpture room exhibits both modern Danish and international art, as well as experimental works. Dance, theater, film, and multimedia exhibits are additional attractions. ⊠ *Skovvej 100, Ishøj* ☎ *43/54–02–22* ⊕ *www.arken.dk* ⊠ *Dkr 55* ☉ *Tues.–Sun. 10–5, Wed. 10–9.*

SJÆLLAND & ITS ISLANDS

The goddess Gefion is said to have carved Sjælland (Zealand) from Sweden. If she did, she must have sliced the north deep with a fjord, while she chopped the south to pieces and left the sides bowing west. Though the coasts are deeply serrated, Gefion's myth is more dramatic than the flat, fertile land of rich meadows and beech stands.

Slightly larger than the state of Delaware, Sjælland is the largest of the Danish islands. From Copenhagen, almost any point on it can be reached in an hour and a half, making it the most traveled portion of the country—and it is especially easy to explore thanks to the extensive road network. North of the capital, ritzy beach towns line up between Hellerup and Humlebæk. Helsingør's Kronborg, which Shakespeare immortalized in *Hamlet,* and Hillerød's stronghold of Frederiksborg, considered one of the most magnificent Renaissance castles in Europe, also lie to the north. To the west of Copenhagen is Roskilde, medieval Denmark's most important town, with an eclectic cathedral that served as northern Europe's spiritual center 1,000 years ago.

West and south, rural towns and farms edge up to seaside communities and fine white beaches, often encompassed by forests. Beaches with summer cottages, white dunes, and calm waters surround Gilleleje and the neighboring town of Hornbæk. The beach in Tisvildeleje is quieter and close to woods. Even more unspoiled are the lilliputian islands around southern Sjælland, virtually unchanged over the past century.

Biking
Sjælland's flat landscape allows easy biking. Most roads have cycle lanes, and tourist boards stock maps detailing local routes.

Canoeing
About 15 km (10 mi) north of Copenhagen, especially in the Lyngby area, several calm lakes and rivers are perfect for canoeing: the Mølleå (Mølle River) and the Bagsværd, Lyngby, and Furesø (Bagsværd, Lyngby, and Fur lakes). Hourly and daily rentals and package canoe tours are available throughout the region.

Fishing
Sjælland's lakes, rivers, and coastline teem with plaice, flounder, cod, and catfish. You can buy a fishing license for one day for Dkr 25; for one week, Dkr 75; or a one-year license for Dkr 100. Along Sjælland's coast it can be bought at any post office. Elsewhere, check with the local tourist office for license requirements. It is illegal to fish within 1,650 ft of the mouth of a stream.

Shopping
Shopping on Sjælland can be considerably cheaper outside Copenhagen. Pedestrian streets run through the center of most towns, and flea markets are usually held Saturday morning.

Rungsted

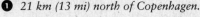 *21 km (13 mi) north of Copenhagen.*

Between Copenhagen and Helsingør is **Rungstedlund,** the elegant, airy former manor of Baroness Karen Blixen, who wrote *Out of Africa* and several accounts of aristocratic Danish life under the pen name Isak Dinesen. The manor house, where she lived as a child and to which she returned in 1931, is open as a museum and displays manuscripts, photographs, paintings, and memorabilia documenting her years in Africa and Denmark. Leave time to wander around the gardens. ⊠ *Rungsted Strandvej 111, Rungsted Kyst* ☎ *45/57–10–57combined train and admission tickets, 70/13–14–16 international, 70/13–14–15 domestic* 🖶 *45/57–10–58* ⊕ *www.karen-blixen.dk* ✆ *Dkr 35* ☉ *May–Sept., Tues.–Sun. 10–5; Oct.–Apr., Wed.–Fri. 1–4, weekends 11–4.*

★ **$$$** ✕ **Nokken.** The terrace, stretching from the base of the harbor to the waters of Øresund, provides a view of the sailboats returning to port as well as a tranquil skyline in the evening. The elegant Italian-style interior pleasantly contradicts the classic French cuisine served. Seafood fresh from the sound is the main attraction but tournedos and other succulent meat dishes are also available. French reserves dominate the wine menu. ⊠ *Rungsted Havn 44, Rungsted Kyst* ☎ *45/57–13–14* ▭ *AE, DC, MC, V.*

Humlebæk

❷ *10 km (6 mi) north of Rungsted, 31 km (19 mi) north of Copenhagen.*

Historically a fishing village, this elegant seaside town, with a population of about 6,000, has of late become a suburb of both Copenhagen and Helsingør. In summer the town's many cottages fill with vacationers and the gardens come alive with vibrant colors. The town takes its name from the plant *humle* (hops), which is abundant in the area.

☞ Humlebæk is home of the must-see **Louisiana,** a modern-art museum as
FodorśChoice famed for its stunning location and architecture as for its collection. Even
★ if you can't tell a Monet from a Duchamp, you should make the 30-minute trip from Copenhagen to see its elegant rambling structure, surrounded by a large park. Housed in a pearly 19th-century villa surrounded by dramatic views of the Øresund waters, the permanent collection includes modern American paintings and Danish paintings from the COBRA (a trend in northern European painting that took its name from its active locations, Copenhagen, Brussels, and Amsterdam) and deconstructionism movements. Be sure to see the haunting collection of Giacomettis backdropped by picture windows overlooking the sound. The children's wing has pyramid-shape chalkboards, child-proof computers, and weekend activities under the guidance of an artist or museum coordinator. To get here from the station, walk north about 10 minutes. ⊠ *Gammel Strandvej 13, Humlebæk* ☎ *49/19–07–19* ⓕ *49/19–35–05* ⊕ *www.louisiana. dk* ⊡ *Dkr 75* ⊙ *Thurs.–Tues. 10–5, Wed. 10–10.*

Helsingør

☞ **❸** *14 km (8½ mi) north of Humlebæk, 45 km (28 mi) north of Copenhagen.*

Helsingør dates back to the early 13th century. It wasn't until the 1400s when Erik of Pomerania established a tariff for all ships passing through the sound that the town began to prosper. Perhaps Helsingør is best known as the home of Shakespeare's fictional Hamlet. Today more than 55,000 people populate the city.

At the northeastern tip of the island, Helsingør is the departure point
for ferries to the Swedish town of Helsingborg, and it's the site of
FodorśChoice **Kronborg Slot** (Kronborg Castle), which was added to UNESCO's World
★ Heritage List in 2000. William Shakespeare based *Hamlet* on Danish mythology's Amleth, and used this castle as the setting even though he had probably never seen it. Built in the late 16th century, it is 600 years younger than the Elsinore we imagine from the tragedy. It was built as a Renaissance tollbooth: from its cannon-studded bastions, forces collected Erik of Pomerania's much-hated Sound Dues, a tariff charged to all ships crossing the sliver of water between Denmark and Sweden. Coming through the entrance arch decorated in Flemish style, you see the castle lawn in front of an octagonal tower, the Trumpeters Tower, whose decoration stands out from the whole.

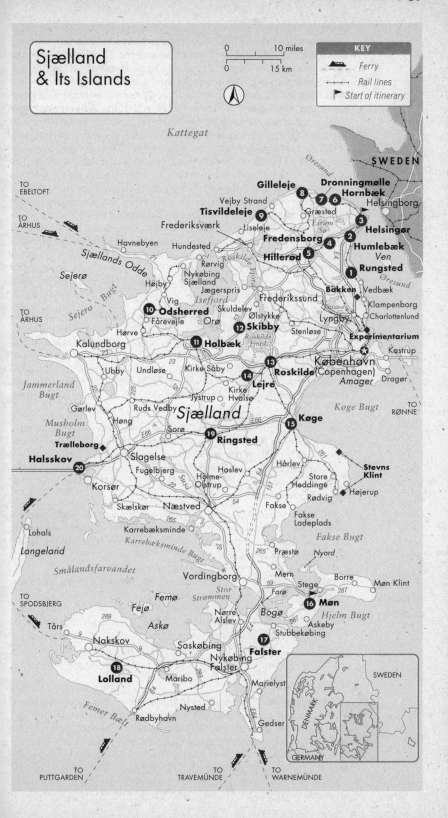

Sjælland & Its Islands

KEY

Ferry

Rail lines

Start of itinerary

0 — 10 miles
0 — 15 km

Kattegat

SWEDEN

Øresund

TO EBELTOFT

TO ÅRHUS

Gilleleje 8

Dronningmølle
Hornbæk 7 6

Helsingborg

Vejby Strand

Græsted

Esrum Sø

Tisvildeleje 9

Frederiksværk

Tiseleje

3 **Helsingør**

Havneby

Hundested

Fredensborg

4 2

Humlebæk

Ven

Sjællands Odde

Rørvig

Hillerød 5

1 **Rungsted**

Øresund

Sejerø

Nykøbing Sjælland

Højby

Jægerspris

Bakken

Vedbæk

Sejerø Bugt

Vig

Isefjord

Frederikssund

Klampenborg

TO ÅRHUS

10 **Odsherred**

Fåreveile

Skuldelev

Ølstykke

Furesø

Charlottenlund

Orø

Lyngby

Hørve

12 **Skibby**

Stenløse

Experimentarium

Kalundborg

11 **Holbæk**

Roskilde Fjord

Kastrup

23

Jammerland Bugt

Ubby

Undløse

Kirke Såby

13 **Roskilde** (Copenhagen)

København

Amager

Dragør

Gørlev

Ruds Vedby

14 **Lejre**

Kirke Hyalsø

Jystrup

Sjælland

Køge Bugt

TO RØNNE

Musholm Bugt

Høng

Sorø

E66

15 **Køge**

S346

Trælleborg

19 **Ringsted**

Halsskov

20

Slagelse

Fugelbjerg

Haslev

Hårlev

Stevns Klint

Korsør

Holme-Olstrup

Store Heddinge

Højerup

Skælskør

Næstved

Fakse

Rødvig

Lohals

Karrebæksminde

Fakse Ladeplads

Fakse Bugt

Langeland

Karrebæksminde Bugt

Præstø

Nyord

Smålandsfarvandet

Vordingborg

Mern

Stege

Borre

Møn Klint

TO SPODSBJERG

Femø

Stor Strømmen

Farø

16 **Møn**

Hjelm Bugt

Fejø

Nørre Alslev

Bogø

Askeby

Tårs

Askø

Stubbekøbing

Nakskov

Saskøbing

17 **Falster**

Nykøbing Falster

18 **Lolland**

Maribo

Marielyst

SWEDEN

DENMARK

Nysted

Rødbyhavn

Gedser

GERMANY

From the yard there is access to the royal chapel. Still true to its original Renaissance style from 1582, the chapel accommodates the royal throne, which has multicolor carved wood. Among the 27 rooms open to the public are two deserving of more attention: the so-called "lille sal" (small room) and the king's bedroom. In the "small room," on the second floor, hang seven tapestries made of silk and wool and created by the Flemish painter Hans Knieper between 1581 and 1586. What makes these tapestries exceptional is not merely their artistic quality but also their subject matter. The tapestries portray several Danish kings against backgrounds of stately buildings and luxuriant scenery with German translations accompanying Danish verses describing their respective achievements. The ceiling of the king's bedroom is worth a couple of extra minutes. If you crane your neck, you can see four scenes of royal life painted by the Dutch artist Gerrit van Honthorst in 1630. Also well worth seeing are the 200-foot-long dining hall and the dungeons, where there is a brooding statue of Holger Danske (Ogier the Dane). According to legend, the Viking chief sleeps, but will awaken to defend Denmark when it is in danger. (The largest Danish resistance group during World War II called itself Holger Danske after its fearless forefather.) ⊠ *At the point on the harborfront* ☎ *49/21–30–78* ⊕ *www.kronborg.dk* ⊠ *Dkr 60* ☉ *May–Sept., daily 10:30–5; Oct. and Apr., Tues.–Sun. 11–4; Nov.–Mar., Tues.–Sun. 11–3.*

Thanks to the hefty tolls collected by Erik of Pomerania, Helsingør prospered. Stroll past the carefully restored medieval merchants' and ferrymen's houses in the middle of town. On the corner of Stengade and Skt. Annæ gade near the harbor is **Skt. Olai Kirke** (St. Olaf's Church), the country's largest parish church and worth a peek for its elaborately carved wooden altar. ⊠ *Skt. Olai G. 51* ☎ *49/21–04–43, 9–noon* ⊕ *www. helsingordomkirke.dk* ⊠ *Free* ☉ *May–Sept., daily noon–3; Oct.–Apr., daily noon–2.*

Close to Skt. Olai Kirke is Skt. Marie Kirke with the 15th-century **Carmelite Kloster** (Carmelite Convent), one of the best-preserved examples of medieval architecture in Scandinavia. After the Reformation it was used as a hospital, and by 1630 it had become a poorhouse. ⊠ *Skt. Annæ G. 38* ☎ *49/21–17–74* ⊠ *Dkr 15* ☉ *Mid-May–mid-Sept., tour daily at 2, call ahead.*

If you want to know more about Helsingør, head to the modest **By Museum** (Town Museum), which has exhibits of 19th-century handicrafts, dolls, and a model of the town. ⊠ *Skt. Annæ G. 36* ☎ *49/28–18–00* ⊠ *Dkr 15* ☉ *Weekdays noon–4.*

off the beaten path

MARIENLYST SLOT – One kilometer (½ mi) north of Helsingør is the Louis XVI–style Marienlyst Castle. Built in 1587, it provided King Frederik II with a garden, as well as a delicate change of scenery from the militant Kronborg. Today the castle has been renovated and the gardens replanted. Inside are paintings by north Sjælland artists and a gallery with changing arts and crafts exhibitions. ⊠ *Marienlyst Allé* ☎ *49/28–37–91* ☎ *49/21–20–06* ⊠ *Dkr 25* ☉ *Daily noon–4.*

Where to Stay & Eat

$$ ✕⊡ **Hotel Hamlet.** A few minutes from the harbor, this overly renovated hotel has lost some of its charm but makes an attempt at character with raw timbers and deep-green walls. The rooms are furnished in rose schemes and dark wood, and all are comfortable, if nondescript. Downstairs, the Ophelia Restaurant serves traditional Danish seafood, steaks, and open-face sandwiches. ⊠ *Bramstr. 5, DK–3000* ☎ *49/21–05–91* ☎ *49/ 26–01–30* ⌐ *36 rooms with bath* ☆ *Restaurant, bar, some pets allowed, no-smoking rooms* ⊟ AE, DC, MC, V.

★ **$$$$** 🏨 **Hotel Marienlyst.** The rooms in this hotel full of flashy neon lights, bolts of drapery, and glass are all plush and pastel and include plenty of conveniences. Those situated on the sound side present a magnificent view of Kronborg Castle and the Swedish coastline, weather permitting. Of course these rooms with scenic views are more expensive. The hotel offers live music on Friday and Saturday. ⊠ *Nordre Strandvej 2, DK–3000* ☎ *49/21–40–00* 🖷 *49/21–49–00* ⊕ *www.marienlyst.dk* ➿ *224 rooms, 17 suites* ⚘ *Restaurant, cafeteria, indoor pool, gym, bar, casino, nightclub, meeting rooms, some pets allowed, no-smoking rooms* ⊟ *AE, DC, MC, V.*

¢ 🏨 **Villa Moltke Vandrerhjem.** This youth hostel faces the sound and has a private beach. It is located 2 km (1 mi) from the city center, but is well served by both bus and train. ⊠ *Nordre Strandvej 24, DK–3000* ☎ *49/21–16–40* 🖷 *49/21–13–99* ⊕ *www.helsingorhostel.dk* ➿ *180 beds* ⚘ *Cafeteria, fishing, badminton, Ping-Pong, soccer, library, laundry facilities* ⊟ *MC, V.*

Nightlife & the Arts

In summer, Kronborg Castle is the site of the **Hamlet Festival** (⊠ Havnepl. 1 ☎ 49/28–20–45 ⊕ www.hamletsommer.dk), during which internationally renowned theater companies offer outdoor performances of *Hamlet.* The schedule varies from year to year.

Sports & the Outdoors

GOLF The **Helsingør Golf Klub** (⊠ Gamle Hellebækvej 73 ☎ 49/21–29–70) has 18 holes on a lush green course flanked by trees and, on clear days, views across the sound to Sweden. A weekday handicap of 36 for men and women, and a weekend handicap of 24 for men and 36 for women, is expected.

Fredensborg

❹ *15 km (9 mi) southwest of Helsingør, 33 km (20 mi) northwest of Copenhagen.*

Fredensborg means "town of peace," and it was here that the Great Nordic War peace treaty was commemorated in 1722. The excellent Fredensborg Castle is a major draw, but the town also accommodates those who come to enjoy the great outdoors.

Commanding the town is the **Fredensborg Slot** (Castle of Peace), built by Frederik IV to commemorate the 1720 peace treaty with Sweden. The castle, with a towering domed hall in the center, was originally inspired by French and Italian castles, but 18th-century reconstructions, concealing the original design, instead serve as a review of domestic architecture. The castle became a favorite of Frederik V, who lined the gardens with marble sculptures of ordinary people. It is now the summer residence of the royal family, and interiors are closed except in July. Queen Margrethe II resides in the castle some months every year, usually in the spring and autumn. When the Queen is present, the Royal Life Guards perform reveille at 8 AM and sound the tattoo (taps) at 10 PM. At noon there is the changing of the guard.

The stately **Slotshave** (castle garden), inspired by the French gardens of Versailles, is Denmark's largest historical garden and well worth a stroll. The garden is open to the public all year with the exception of *den reserverede have* (the reserved garden), which is used privately by the Danish Royal Family but open to the public in July. The reserved garden includes a flower garden, an herb garden, and the orangerie where Denmark's oldest myrtles, which date back to the 1750s, are preserved. ⊠ *Fredensborg* ☎ *33/40–31–87* ⊕ *www.ses.dk* 🎫 *Castle Dkr 35, reserved gardens Dkr 35, common ticket Dkr 55* ☉ *Castle July, daily 1–5; reserved gardens July, daily 9–5.*

> **off the beaten path**

GRIBSKOV – On the opposite side of Lake Esrum from Fredensborg is Gribskov, the largest forest in Sjælland (14,079 acres). This former royal hunting ground has kept its natural shape since the times of Valdemar II in the 13th century, except for the clearing works done after the hurricane of 1981. Gribskov is one of the few places in Denmark where visitors can have a sense of natural solitude while being immersed in a wooded cloak of mystery. Black woodpeckers, woodcocks, sandpipers, buzzards, goshawks, and deer can be seen among the oaks and flowering trees.

Where to Stay & Eat

$$–$$$
Fodor'sChoice
★

✕ **Skipperhuset.** On the grounds of the royal summer residence of Fredensborg Slot, this 18th-century former royal boathouse is on the shore of Lake Esrum. When weather permits, an alfresco meal as the sun sets across the lake is pure enchantment. The three-course menu changes every two weeks. Warm-smoked wild Baltic salmon served with spinach flash-fried in soy sauce and balsamic vinegar is a delightful favorite and a fabulous buy for the money. ✉ *Skipperallé 6* ☎ *48/48–17–17* ▭ *MC, V* ✆ *Closed mid-Oct.–Easter.*

★ $$$$
✕▣ **Hotel Store Kro.** Built by King Frederik IV, this magnificent Renaissance annex to Fredensborg Castle is the archetypal stately inn. Inside are European antiques and paintings; outside, glass gazebos and classical statues overlook a lovely garden. The rooms are equally sumptuous, with delicately patterned wallpapers and antiques. The romantic restaurant, specializing in French fare, has a fireplace and grand piano. ✉ *Slotsg. 6, DK–3480* ☎ *48/40–01–11* ▤ *48/48–45–61* ⊕ *www.storekro.dk* ⤳ *49 rooms, 6 suites* ↻ *Restaurant, minibars, sauna, bar, meeting room* ▭ *AE, DC, MC, V.*

¢
▣ **Fredensborg Vandrerhjem.** This youth and family hostel offers a wide selection of sleeping arrangements. Both shared and private rooms (accommodating up to six people) are available. Breakfast can be ordered for Dkr 45. The restaurant serves lunch and dinner for groups only; however, the kitchen is available to all guests. ✉ *Østrupvej 3, DK–3480* ☎ *48/48–03–15* ▤ *48/48–16–56* ⊕ *www.fredensborghostel.dk* ⤳ *42 rooms without bath* ↻ *Ping-Pong, playground* ▭ *No credit cards.*

Sports & the Outdoors

Magnificent displays of hawks and eagles in flight can be seen at **Falkonergården.** Located 1 km (½ mi) northeast of Fredensborg, this former farm keeps alive the Danish tradition of hunting with hawks, a method used from the time of the Vikings until early in the 19th century. Falcons swooping at speeds approaching 300 kph (186 mph) can be witnessed in the hour-long shows. ✉ *Davidsvænge 11* ☎ *48/48–25–83* ⊕ *www.falkonergaarden.dk* ✉ *Dkr 65* ✆ *Showtimes: Apr. and May, Sun. at 2; June, Sept., and Oct., weekends at 2; July, Wed. at 10 and 5, Thurs. at 10, weekends at 5; Aug., Wed. and weekends at 5.*

The **Fredensborg Golf Club** (✉ Skovsvinget 25 ☎ 48/47–56–59) has 18 holes surrounded by woodlands. Men are required to have a handicap of 38 on weekdays and 24 on weekends whereas women need a handicap of 43 and 30, respectively.

Hillerød

❺ *10 km (6 mi) southwest of Fredensborg, 40 km (25 mi) northwest of Copenhagen.*

Hillerød is the main town of Frederiksborg County and appropriately enough is at its center. The town, founded in the 15th century, has developed itself around the Frederiksborg Castle and nowadays is an important industrial area.

★ Hillerød's **Frederiksborg Slot** (Frederiksborg Castle) is probably Denmark's most beautiful royal residence. Acquired in 1560, the castle was rebuilt by King Frederik II, who gave his name to the building. That structure was eventually demolished by his son, king-cum-architect Christian IV, who rebuilt it as one of Scandinavia's most magnificent castles. With three wings and a lower portal entrance, the Dutch Renaissance building is enclosed by a moat, covers three islets, and is peaked with dozens of gables, spires, and turrets. The two-story marble gallery known as the **Great Hall,** with its audacious festooning of drapery, paintings, and reliefs, sits on top of the vaulted chapel where monarchs were crowned for more than 200 years. Devastated by a fire in 1859, the castle was reconstructed with the support of the Carlsberg Foundation and now includes the **Nationalhistoriske Museum** (National History Museum). Frederiksberg Slot has 69 rooms, all of them decorated as they were before the fire. Those works of art that had been destroyed were substituted by other private pieces from the Danish aristocracy. The castle has an admirable Renaissance chapel, **Slotskirke,** with abundant ornamentation. The three-aisle chapel has a wide gallery with large windows. Between them hang Denmark's most important coat of arms, the knights of the Elephant Order, and the Great Cross of Dannebrog. Look for the 17th-century aisle seats as well as the altarpiece and the pulpit made of mahogany with gold and silver panels. The carved organ, made in 1610 and restored in 1988, still proudly carries its original tubes and manual bellows. The lovely **Baroque Gardens,** rebuilt according to J. C. Krieger's layout from 1725, include a series of wide, horizontal waterfalls that make the neatly trimmed park a lovely place for a stroll. ⊠ *Hillerød* ☏ *48/26–04–39* ⊕ *www.frederiksborgmuseet.dk* ✍ *Dkr 60; Baroque Gardens free* ☾ *Castle Apr.–Oct., daily 10–5; Nov.–Mar., daily 11–3. Baroque Gardens May–Aug., daily 10–9; Sept., Oct., Mar., and Apr., daily 10–7; Nov.–Feb., daily 10–4.*

> off the
> beaten
> path

ESRUM KLOSTER – Fifteen km (10 mi) north of Hillerød is the Cistercian monastery of Esrum. Originally built in the 1140s by the Benedictine monks, the monastery was abandoned by this order and occupied by Cistercian monks in 1151. After the Lutheran reformation, the church was demolished and the building materials were used to erect the Castle of Kronborg in Helsingør. The oldest remains are from the late Middle Ages. ⊠ *Klosterg. 11, Esrum, DK-3230 Græsted* ☏ *48/36–04–00* 🖷 *48/39–80–16* ⊕ *www.esrum. dk/kloster* ✍ *Dkr 40* ☾ *May–mid-June and mid-Aug.–mid-Oct., Tues.–Sun. 10–4; mid-June–mid-Aug., Tues.–Sun. 10–5; mid-Oct.–Apr., Thurs.–Sun. 10–4.*

Where to Stay & Eat

$$$ ✕ **La Perla.** Simple but good Italian food is served in this beautiful old house in the very center of town. The decor is an interesting mix of Italian and Danish styles, a thoroughly modern twist on the Mediterranean. ⊠ *Torvet 1* ☏ *48/24–35–33* 🖒 *Reservations essential* ⊟ *AE, DC, MC, V.*

$$$ ✕ **Slotskroen.** Functioning as an inn since 1795, Slotskroen is one of the oldest buildings of this royal town. The restaurant has been completely renovated, but it maintains its antique flavor and stands out for its veal and ox dishes. ⊠ *Slotsg. 67* ☏ *48/26–01–82* ⊟ *AE, DC, MC, V.*

$–$$ ✕ **Spisestedet Leonora.** In the shadow of Frederiksborg Castle, this family restaurant bustles in what used to be the castle stables. Antique on the outside and bright orange on the inside with hanging prints and paintings of royalty and the castle, it is a popular stopover for castle visitors. The Danish menu ranges from quick open-face sandwiches to savory stews, soups, and steaks. ⊠ *Frederiksborgslot 5* ☎ *48/26–75–16* ⊟ *DC, MC, V.*

$$ 🏨 **Hotel Hillerød.** In a typically Scandinavian fashion, this hotel's decor is furnished with sensible Danish designs and luxurious lighting accessories. The hotel's attentiveness extends to providing some rooms specifically for nonsmokers. The hotel is wheelchair accessible. Packages that include greens fees at a local golf course can be arranged. ⊠ *Milnersvej 41, DK–3400* ☎ *48/24–08–00* 🖷 *48/24–08–74* ⊕ *www.hotelhillerod. dk* 🛏 *74 rooms* ♿ *Restaurant, meeting room, some pets allowed, no-smoking rooms* ⊟ *AE, DC, MC, V.*

Hornbæk

❻ *27 km (17 mi) northeast of Hillerød, 47 km (29 mi) north of Copenhagen.*

Hornbæk is Denmark's answer to France's Riviera. Danish society's upper echelon maintains palatial summer homes here that line the streets closest to the water and are discreetly tucked away behind protective sand dunes. Regardless of your social standing, the bustling town offers lovely shopping opportunities and exciting nightlife year round. Summer brings the expansive beach alive with parties, volleyball tournaments, and more.

Where to Stay & Eat

$$$$ ✕ **Le Provençal.** On the "Danish Riviera," Le Provençal lives up to its name. The restaurant's south-of-France atmosphere is created with Limoges and Valdrôme porcelain along with gorgeous glass, expensive cutlery, and handmade chairs. The best seating on a warm afternoon is outside on the rustic terrace, where you can sip a glass of Corsican or Rhône wine. Main dishes include *filet de sandre* (a fillet of pike perch with aïoli and tomato confit), and *cailles aux raisins* (oven-roasted quails in grape sauce with roasted potatoes and chanterelles). ⊠ *Havnevej 1* ☎ *49/76–11–77* ⊟ *AE, DC, MC, V.*

★ $$$$ ✕ **Novo Latino.** The elegant restaurant is decorated in light, soft tones, but the terrace takes the cake with its outdoor fireplace. Inspired by classic Latin American cooking, Novo Latino modernizes the cuisine by adding its own touches. The chef here travels every autumn to the tropics to collect recipes and inspiration, which determine the menu for each coming year. For about Dkr 500 the restaurant offers a six-course menu that keeps pace with seasonal products. This is the ideal place to try innovative dishes such as fish with chocolate sauce. A wide range of excellent wines from the New and Old Worlds is on hand at prices starting from Dkr 300. ⊠ *Nordre Strandvej 154, 5 km (3 mi) east of Hornbæk, Ålsgårde* ☎ *49/ 70–90–03* ⊟ *AE, DC, MC, V* ☉ *Closed Mon. and Oct.–Mar.*

★ $$ ✕ **Hansen's Café.** This intimate restaurant, in a national trust building constructed in 1783, is a few steps from the harbor. The Danish art hanging from the timber walls provides a cozy ambience for a casual crowd that often lingers for drinks well after dinner. The daily menu is short but provides a taste of what's fresh—especially seafood. Try the lumpfish roe for a tasty local treat. Business hours vary so it's wise to call in advance. ⊠ *Havnevej 19* ☎ *49/70–04–79* ⊟ *DC, MC, V.*

$$$$ 🏨 **Havreholm Slot.** A few miles southwest of Hornbæk beach, this small former castle is surrounded by wooded grounds, which hide a couple of fair-size ponds in their midst. The guest houses' rooms and suites are decorated with Bang & Olufsen televisions and design furniture; most open onto balconies or terraces. Rowboats are available for use on the ponds, as is fishing gear—just remember to get your fishing permit first. There

are also tennis courts and a 9-hole par-3 golf course. The restaurant produces elaborate French cuisine at dinner and serves smørrebrød and Danish comfort food at lunch. ⊠ *Klosterrisvej 4, Havreholm, DK–3100* ☎ *49/75–86–00* 🖷 *49/75–80–23* ⊕ *www.havreholm.dk* ⇝ *32 rooms, 3 suites* ⚐ *Restaurant, 9-hole golf course, indoor-outdoor pool, sauna, fishing, billiards, Ping-Pong, squash, meeting rooms* ☰ *AE, DC, MC, V.*

$$$ 🏨 **Hotelpension Ewaldsgaarden.** This seaside pension is a few blocks from the marina and the beach in a residential neighborhood off one of the town's main (though quiet) streets. An informal family hotel, it is very casual, extremely well kept and service is provided with commendable pride. Inside the restaurant the Danish food is not fancy, but it's authentic and exceptionally good. Breakfast is included. ⊠ *Johannes Ewaldsvej 5, DK–3100* ☎ *49/70–00–82* 🖷 *49/70–00–82* ⊕ *www. ewaldsgaarden.dk* ⇝ *12 rooms* ⚐ *Restaurant* ☰ *No credit cards.*

¢ 🏨 **Hornbæk Bed & Breakfast.** Owned by an American-Danish couple, this country villa sits at the edge of the woods 100 meters from the Danish Riviera. On fair days you can see the Swedish coastline out the window. The rooms are a decent size for the reasonable price, and guests are allowed use of the kitchen. ⊠ *Skovvej 15C, DK–3100* ☎ *49/76–19–10* 🖷 *49/76–19–11* ⊕ *www.hornbaekbandb.dk* ⇝ *7 rooms without bath* ⚐ *Kitchen, no-smoking rooms* ☰ *No credit cards.*

Dronningmølle

❼ *10 km (6 mi) west of Hornbæk, 57 km (35 mi) north of Copenhagen.*

There's little more than a camping ground flanked by a very clean beach and a sculpture museum in Dronningmølle. The beauty of the area lies in the fact that it is largely undiscovered so it's quite easy to find a spot on the sand away from the crowds.

In 1916 Rudolph Tegner began to buy adjacent parcels of land to realize his dream of a museum and sculpture park dedicated to his own work.
★ The centerpiece of the resultant **Rudolph Tegners Museum** is the 36-foot-high octagonal building in the center of which Rudolph Tegner is buried. On display here are 191 of his sculptures in plaster, marble, and bronze; works in other media are represented including 12 paintings, many drafts, and several pieces of furniture he constructed. Tegner withstood the pressure towards normality in Danish society during his era and his best works are both provocative and disquieting. ⊠ *Museumsvej 19* ☎ *49/71–91–77* ⊕ *www.rudolphtegner.dk* 🎟 *Dkr 25* ⊙ *Mid-Apr.–May and Sept.–mid-Oct., noon–5; June–Aug., 9:30–5* ⊙ *Closed Mon.*

Where to Stay

¢ ⛺ **Dronningmølle Strandcamping.** Camp right on the sand and enjoy the best of the Danish Riviera without the crowds and high prices of other, better known coastal towns in north Sjælland. The surrounding countryside is a nature conservation area and has trails and bicycle paths. Kitchen facilities are available. ⊠ *Strandkrogen 2B, DK–3120* ☎ *49/ 71–92–90* 🖷 *49/71–98–93* ⊕ *www.dronningmolle.dk* ⚐ *Restaurant, cafeteria, sauna, miniature golf, shop, laundry* ☰ *No credit cards* ⊙ *Closed mid-Sept.–mid-Apr.*

Gilleleje

❽ *3 km (2 mi) north of Dronningmølle, 58 km (36 mi) northwest of Copenhagen.*

At the northern tip of Sjælland, Gilleleje was once a small fishing community. These days the population explodes every summer when northern Europeans take to its woods and fine, sandy beaches. It was a favorite getaway of philosopher Søren Kierkegaard, who wrote: "I often stood there and reflected over my past life. The force of the sea and the struggle of the elements made me realize how unimportant I was." The less existential can go for a swim and visit the philosopher's monument on a nearby hill. The old part of town, with its thatch-roof, colorfully painted houses, is good for a walk.

> **off the beaten path**
>
> **NORDSJÆLLANDS SOMMERPARK** – Situated 30 km (18 mi) west of Helsingør, this amusement park mixes water recreation with other attractions such as theater, concerts, and a mini zoo. The Sommerpark bus departs from the Gilleleje or Helsingør train station at 9:30 AM. ⊠ *Kirkevej 33, Græsted* ☎ *48/71–41–41* 🖷 *48/ 71–66–05* ⊕ *www.forlystelsespark.dk* 🎟 *Dkr 50* ☉ *Mid-June–July, daily 10–9; mid-May–mid-June and Aug., daily noon–8.*

Tisvildeleje

❾ *28 km (17 mi) west of Gilleleje, 65 km (40 mi) northwest of Copenhagen.*

Tisvildeleje is one of the most popular beaches in north Sjælland. There is more than 1 km (½ mi) of sandy beach backed by woods.

Where to Stay & Eat

$ ✕🏠 **Havgården.** The refurbished old manor house offers comfortable lodging within a typical Danish building. Dinner, served from 6 PM, is primarily Danish—John Dory is the house specialty. The site also rents out vacation cottages, fully furnished with all the comforts of home. Payment with credit card is subject to a 6% surcharge. ⊠ *Strandlyvej 1, Vejby Strand, DK–3210* ☎ *48/70–57–30* 🖷 *48/70–57–72* ⊕ *www. havgaarden.dk* 🛏 *13 rooms* ⅋ *Restaurant* ▤*MC, V* ☉ *Restaurant closed Sept.–May.*

¢ 🏠 **Skt. Helene Vandrerhjem.** This youth hostel is a 10-minute walk from the beach. The property also houses 28 chalets accommodating four to five people each. The whole complex is ecofriendly, with a farm, and organic food on offer. Guests are welcome to pitch in. There are also 15 apartments with kitchen and bath for rent. ⊠ *Bygmarken 30, DK–3220* ☎ *48/70–98–50* 🖷 *48/70–98–97* ⊕ *www.helene.dk* 🛏 *40 rooms* ⅋ *Restaurant, cafeteria, miniature golf, tennis court, basketball, soccer, volleyball, laundry facilities.*

Odsherred

❿ *45 km (28 mi) southwest of Gilleleje, 80 km (50 mi) northwest of Copenhagen (via Roskilde).*

With steep cliffs, white-sand dunes, and acres of forests to admire, the Odsherred peninsula is a big draw to people who want to relax in beautiful surroundings. The long beaches have silky sand and offer plenty of opportunities to take a refreshing swim in Sejerø Bugt (Sejerø Bay). This hammer-shape peninsula, which curves around Sejerø Bugt, is dotted with hundreds of burial mounds. You can get here either by driving around the fjords to the south and through the town of Holbæk, or by driving to Hundested and catching the 25-minute ferry ride to Rørvig.

If you are a devotee of ecclesiastical art, make a pilgrimage to explore the frescoes of the Romanesque-Gothic-Renaissance **Højby Kirke** (Højby Church) in the town of Højby, near Nykøbing Sjælland. In the town of Fårevejle is the Gothic **Fårevejle Kirke**, with the Earl of Bothwell's chapel.

Fewer than 5 km (3 mi) south of Nykøbing Sjælland, more than 500 animals of 85 different species can be seen at **Odsherreds Zoo Dyrepark.**

Children love the monkey house. Other attractive inhabitants include raccoons, llamas, reptiles, exotic birds, and the unique black swan. On weekends children can ride ponies. ⊠ *Esterhøjvej 94–96, Asnæs* ☎ *59/ 65–12–31* 🖷 *59/65–12–28* ⊕ *www.odsherreds-zoo.dk* 🖃 *Dkr 50* ◷ *Apr., Sept.–mid-Oct., daily 10–3:30; May, June, and Aug., daily 10–5; July, daily 10–6.*

Sjællands Odde (Zealand's Tongue), the tiny strip of land north of the Sejerø Bay, offers slightly marshy but secluded beach strands. Inside the bay, the beaches are once again smooth and blond. From here there is access to Århus and Ebeltoft in Jylland by ferry.

☾ **Sommerland Sjælland,** Zealand's amusement park, caters to visitors of all ages. The dozens of activities include a roller coaster, an aquapark, and a small zoo with pony rides. Children under 10 especially enjoy *Mini-land.* ⊠ *Gammel Nykøbingvej 169, Nykøbing Sjælland* ☎ *59/31–21–00* ⊕ *www.sommerlandsj.dk* 🖃 *Dkr 130* ◷ *Mid-May–mid-June and mid-Aug.–Sept., weekends 10–6; mid-June–mid-Aug., daily 10–7.*

Where to Stay & Eat

¢ ✕ **Den Gyldne Hane.** Built at the beginning of the 19th century by a community of fishermen, Den Gyldne Hane is a family hotel best known for the fish dishes served in its restaurant. The view of the harbor overlooking the fishing boats makes for an enjoyable meal. ⊠ *Vestre Havnevej 34, DK–4583 Sjællands Odde* ☎ *59/32–63–86* 🖷 *59/32–65–52* ⊕ *www.dengyldnehane.dk* ▭ *DC, MC, V* ◷ *Closed Dec.–Mar. No lunch.*

$$$ 🖽 **Dragsholm Slot.** Ideally located at Nekselø Bay, close to the forest and the beach, Dragsholm Castle, originally built in the 12th century, has been a home since the 18th century. Today the owners cultivate the land and raise their own livestock to provide wholesome ingredients for the restaurant on the premises. ⊠ *Dragsholm Allé 1, DK–4534 Hørve* ☎ *59/65–33–00* 🖷 *59/65–30–33* ⊕ *www.dragsholm-slot.dk* 🖙 *30 rooms with bath, 2 suites* ♨ *Restaurant* ▭ *AE, DC, MC, V.*

Holbæk

⑪ *83 km (51½ mi) southwest of Tisvildeleje (via Odsherred), 67 km (41½ mi) west of Copenhagen.*

Expanding out from the old fortress built in the 13th century by Valdemar II to defend Denmark against its attacking enemies, Holbæk is today an industrial and commercial town.

Situated close to the neo-Gothic Skt. Nicolaj Kirke, the **Holbæk Museum** consists of three wooden buildings from the 17th century and another two from the 19th century. The museum collection showcases handicrafts, archaeological artifacts, and objects from the town's contemporary history, such as household equipment from typical urban and rural houses of the 17th and 18th centuries. ⊠ *Klosterstr. 18* ☎ *59/43–23–53* 🖷 *59/43–24–52* ⊕ *www.holbmus.dk* 🖃 *Dkr 30* ◷ *Tues.–Fri. 10–4, weekends noon–4.*

off the beaten path

CHURCHES OF HOLBÆK FJORD – A 2 km (1 mi) drive south of Holbæk down the A57 delivers you to **Tveje Merløse,** built in the 13th century and restored at the end of the 19th century. Luckily, you can still see the 13th-century frescoes here. Just 4 km (2½ mi) to the southwest stands the 12th-century **Søstrup Kirke,** with Byzantine-style frescoes. West along road 155 another 4 km (2½ mi) stands **Tuse Kirke,** a typical example of a rural church from the 13th century. Inside the church are Gothic frescoes from the 15th century. North on road A21 is the 12th-century **Hagested Kirke,** which has 13th-century frescoes.

Where to Stay & Eat

¢ ✕🍽 **Hotel Orø Kro.** On the tiny island of Orø, this hotel radiates tranquility with the blue of Isefjord on one side and green fields on the other. The restaurant stands out for its simple and tasty fish specialties. On a warm summer evening, the inn's terrace is a delightful place to sit. The restaurant is closed on Monday. ⊠ *Byg. 57, Orø, DK–4300* ☎ *59/47–00–06* 🖷 *59/47–01–99* ⊕ *www.oroe.dk/kro* 🛏 *21 rooms* ♿ *Restaurant, some pets allowed* 🖃 *AE, MC, V.*

$$ 🍽 **Hotel Strandparken.** Beach and forest are the two views offered from the rooms of this hotel from its scenic location in the middle of a park just south of Holbæk Fjord. The pastel rooms are filled with flower prints and landscape paintings. Service is warm and attentive. ⊠ *Kalundborgvej 58, DK–4300* ☎ *59/43–06–16* 🖷 *59/43–32–76* ⊕ *www.hotelstrandparken.dk* 🛏 *31 rooms* ♿ *Restaurant, billiards, meeting room* 🖃 *AE, MC, V.*

Skibby

⓬ *26 km (16 mi) northeast of Holbæk, 65 km (40 mi) northwest of Copenhagen.*

Skibby is the main town of the little peninsula situated between Roskilde Fjord and Isefjord.

Four kilometers (2½ mi) east of Skibby is **Selsø Slot** (Selsø Castle), constructed in 1576 and reworked in 1734. The castle portrays life as it was for the aristocrats and their servants in the 1800s. The museum here displays original 17th-century interiors, as well as Renaissance furniture, weapons, clothes, domestic items, toys, and a collection of drawings. The altarpiece from 1605 and the pulpit from 1637 in the castle church exhibit Renaissance elements. ⊠ *Selsøvej 30A* ☎ *47/52–01–71* ⊕ *www.selsoe.dk* 🎟 *Dkr 40* ⊙ *May–mid-June and mid-Aug.–Oct., weekends 1–4; mid-June–mid-Aug., daily 11–4.*

> off the beaten path

JÆGERSPRIS SLOT – At the north end of the peninsula stands this medieval castle. The baroque southern wing is from the 17th century and the rest of the castle, save for the 15th-century northern wing, is from 1722 to 1746. King Frederik VII maintained his residence here in the 19th century and the decor in the southern wing reflects this. The tomb of his wife, the Countess Danner, is in the castle's park. To the north extends Nordskoven, a forest of 100-year-old oaks. To see the castle, you must join a guided tour and may not simply walk around on your own. Tours begin at the top of the hour and last for 50 minutes. ⊠ *Slotsgården 15, Jægerspris* ☎ *47/53–10–04* ⊕ *www.museer.fa.dk* 🎟 *Dkr 35* ⊙ *Apr.–Oct., Tues.–Sun. 11–4.*

Where to Stay & Eat

$$–$$$ ✕ **Sønderby Kro.** This typical countryside inn sits next to the village's duck pond and serves remarkably tasty veal dishes, curried herring, shrimp. The restaurant is perhaps best known for its smørrebrød. ⊠ *Sønderby Bro 2* ☎ *47/52–01–33* 🖃 *No credit cards* ⊙ *Closed Mon.*

$ 🍽 **Hotel Skuldelev Kro.** In the middle of the countryside, this inn has a peaceful environment in a beautiful location. Rooms are adequate even for families. Some rooms are available for nonsmokers. ⊠ *Østerg. 2B, DK–4050 Skuldelev* ☎ *47/52–03–08* 🖷 *47/52–08–93* ⊕ *www.hotelskuldelevkro.dk* 🛏 *32 rooms with bath* ♿ *Restaurant, outdoor pool, some pets allowed, no-smoking rooms* 🖃 *AE, DC, MC, V.*

Roskilde

⑬ *31 km (19 mi) southeast of Skibby, 36 km (22 mi) west of Copenhagen (on Rte. 156).*

Roskilde is Sjælland's second-largest town and one of its oldest, having been founded in 998. The town is named for Roars Kilde, a Viking king. Today Roskilde has a bustling smelting and machinery industry and two prominent academic institutions, Roskilde University and the Danish Center for Energetic Research of Risø.

Fodor'sChoice
★

Roskilde was the royal residence in the 10th century and became the spiritual capital of Denmark and northern Europe in 1170, when Bishop Absalon built the **Domkirke** (cathedral) on the site of a church erected 200 years earlier by Harald Bluetooth, the Viking founder of the town. Overwhelming the center of town, the current structure took more than 300 years to complete and thus provides a one-stop crash course in Danish architecture. Inside are an ornate Dutch altarpiece and the tombs—ranging from opulent to modest—of 38 Danish monarchs. Predictably, Christian IV is interred in a magnificent chapel with a massive painting of himself in combat and a bronze sculpture by Thorvaldsen. In modest contrast is the newest addition, the simple brick chapel of King Frederik IX, who died in 1972, outside the church. In November 2000, his wife Queen Ingrid joined him in his tomb at the foot of the cathedral. On the interior south wall above the entrance is a 16th-century clock depicting St. George charging a dragon, which hisses and howls, echoing throughout the church and causing Peter Døver, "the Deafener," to sound the hour. A squeamish Kirsten Kiemer, "the Chimer," shakes her head in fright but manages to strike the quarter-hours. Around the altar are the Kannikekoret, the wooden choir stalls carved in 1420. Each seat is topped with a panel depicting a Biblical scene. Behind the altarpiece is the alabaster and marble sarcophagus of Queen Margrethe I, who died in 1412. ⊠ *Domkirkestr. 10* ☎ *46/35–16–24* ⊕ *www. roskildedomkirke.dk* ⊡ *Dkr 15* ☉ *Apr.–Sept., weekdays 9–4:45, Sat. 9–noon, Sun. 12:30–4:45; Oct.–Mar., Tues.–Sat. 10–3:45, Sun. 12:30–3:45.*

Less than 1 km (½ mi) north of the cathedral, on the fjord, is the modern **Vikingeskibshallen** (Viking Ship Museum), containing five Viking ships sunk in the fjord 1,000 years ago. Submerged to block the passage of enemy ships, they were discovered in 1957. The painstaking recovery involved building a watertight dam and then draining the water from that section of the fjord. The splinters of wreckage were then preserved and reassembled. A deep-sea trader, warship, ferry, merchant ship, and fierce 92½-foot man-of-war attest to the Vikings' sophisticated and aesthetic boat-making skills. ⊠ *Vindeboder 12* ☎ *46/30–02–00* ⊕ *www. vikingeskibsmuseet.dk* ⊡ *Dkr 60* ☉ *Daily 10–5.*

Where to Stay & Eat

$$$ ✕ **Svogerslev Kro.** Three kilometers (2 mi) west of Roskilde is the village of Svogerslev, a peaceful location for this traditional thatch-roof Danish inn. Exposed wooden beams make the interior a cozy place to tuck into the hearty Danish fare. The menu includes a vegetarian option as well as some international dishes such as Wiener schnitzel and steak. ⊠ *Hovedg. 45, Svogerslev* ☎ *46/38–30–05* ▭ *AE, DC, MC, V.*

★ $ ✕ **Club 42.** This popular Danish restaurant spills out onto the sidewalk in summer while inside the roof opens over the dining room. The fare is typically Danish, including smørrebrød and spare ribs, which are simply prepared and served with potato salad. ⊠ *Skomagerg. 42* ☎ *46/ 35–17–64* ▭ *MC, V.*

$$$$ 🖼 **Hotel Prindsen.** In downtown Roskilde, this 100-year-old hotel is popular with business guests for its convenient location. The elegant dark-wood lobby leads to the plain but homey and comfortable rooms. Downstairs, the restaurant and grill La Bøf serves up fish, and next door there is a cushy bar. ✉ *Alg. 13, DK–4000* 📠 *46/30–91–00* 📠 *46/30–91–50* ⊕ *www.prindsen.dk* ⇆ *76 rooms, 3 suites* ⚒ *Restaurant, cafeteria, minibars, bar, meeting rooms, some pets allowed, no-smoking rooms* 🚪 *AE, DC, MC, V.*

¢ 🖼 **Roskilde Vandrerhjem.** This youth hostel, perfect for budget travelers, is on Roskilde Fjord, which is close to the town's green areas. Guests have use of the kitchen. ✉ *Vinderboder 7, DK–4000* 📠 *46/35–21–84* 📠 *46/32–66–90* ⊕ *www.rova.dk* ⇆ *152 beds, 40 showers* ⚒ *Restaurant, laundry facilities* 🚪 *No credit cards.*

Nightlife & the Arts

For one weekend at the end of June, Roskilde holds one of Europe's biggest rock-music gatherings, the **Roskilde Festival** (⊕ www.roskilde-festival.dk). Some 75,000 people show up every year to enjoy the outdoor concerts.

When town's youth are in the mood for live rock, they head to **Gimle** (✉ Ringstedg. 30 📠 46/35–12–13) on the weekends. At **Bryggergården** (✉ Alg. 15 📠 46/35–01–03), or the Draft Horse, adults have a late supper and beer in cozy surroundings. In summer, **Café Mulle Rudi** (✉ Djalma Lunds Gård 7 📠 46/37–03–25) is an arty spot with indoor and outdoor seating and live jazz.

Sports & the Outdoors

GOLF **Roskilde Golf Klub** (✉ Margrethehåbvej 116 📠 46/37–01–81) has an 18-hole golf course with views of the twin peak Roskilde Cathedral and the surrounding forest.

TOURS Boat excursions depart from the town's docks for dual-purpose (sightseeing and transportation) routes on Roskilde Fjord. The boats occasionally make stops at Frederikssund and Frederiksværk, but most passengers are there for a fun and scenic boat ride. Some refreshments can be purchased onboard. **Saga Fjord** (📠 46/75–64–60 ⊕ www.sagafjord.dk) operates more-sightseeing-oriented trips. **Viking Ruten** (📠 47/38–87–50 ⊕ www.vikingruten.dk) operates a regular run up to Frederikssund with stops along the way.

Shopping

CRAFTS Between Roskilde and Holbæk is **Galleri Kirke Sonnerup** (✉ Englerupvej 62, Såby 📠 46/49–25–77), with a good selection of pottery, glass, clothing, and woodwork produced by more than 50 Danish artists.

Lejre

14 *10 km (6 mi) west of Roskilde, 40 km (25 mi) west of Copenhagen.*

Archaeological digs unearthing the times of the Vikings show that Lejre has had a glorious past. During the 10th century the town reigned as the kingdom's most sacred place.

☾ The 50-acre **Lejre Forsøgscenter** (Lejre Archaeological Research Center)
Fodor'sChoice compound contains a reconstructed village dating from the Iron Age and
★ two 19th-century farmhouses. In summer a handful of hardy Danish families live here under the observation of researchers; they go about their daily routine—grinding grain, herding goats, eating with their hands, and wearing furs and skins—providing a clearer picture of ancient ways of life. In Bodalen (Fire Valley), children can try their own hand at such tasks as grinding corn, filing an ax, and sailing in a dugout canoe.

✉ *Slangealleen 2* ☎ *46/48–08–78* ⊕ *www.lejre-center.dk* ✆ *Dkr 75* ☉ *May–mid-June and mid-Aug.–mid-Sept., Tues.–Fri. 10–4, weekends 10–5; mid-June–mid-Aug., daily 10–5.*

Ledreborg Slot is one of Denmark's finest examples of 18th-century building and landscape architecture. Built in 1742, Ledreborg Castle is now owned by the eighth generation of the Holstein-Ledreborg family. The main building contains a remarkable collection of paintings and furniture from when it was first built. At the southern part there is an elaborate terraced garden in the 18th-century French style. ✉ *Ledreborg Allé 2* ☎ *46/48–00–38* ⊕ *www.ledreborgslot.dk* ✆ *Dkr 60* ☉ *May–mid-June and Sept., Sun. 11–5; mid-June–Aug., daily 11–5.*

Køge

🕕 *20 km (13 mi) southeast of Lejre, 47 km (29 mi) southwest of Copenhagen.*

The well-preserved medieval town of Køge began its existence as a fishing village dependent on the herring trade. Køge is also known for the witch hunts that took place in the early 17th century. Today, with about 40,000 inhabitants, this satellite town of Copenhagen exists as a center of trade. It links to the big city by suburban train.

In the 17th century and later during the Napoleonic wars, Køge was witness to many naval battles. The Danish and Swedish fleets clashed repeatedly in order to gain control over the sound, which was the gateway to trade with the Baltic Sea.

Køge Museum is in a centrally located 17th-century merchant's house. On display are mementos and items belonging to Hans Christian Andersen, local costumes, and artifacts including an executioner's sword and a 13th-century stone font. The legend of the font is that it had to be removed from the town church after a crippled woman committed an unsavory act into it, hoping her bizarre behavior would cure her. Also on exhibit are 16th-century silver coins from a buried treasure containing more than 2,000 coins. The stash was found in the courtyard of Langkildes Gård. ✉ *Nørreg. 4* ☎ *56/63–42–42* ✆ *Dkr 25* ☉ *June–Aug., daily 11–5; Sept.–May, Tues.–Fri. 1–5, Sat. 11–3, and Sun. 1–5.*

Kunstmuseet Køge Skitsesamling (Art Museum Køge Sketches Collection) has changing exhibitions and an extensive permanent collection of sketches, sculpture, and other modern Danish art. ✉ *Nørreg. 29* ☎ *56/67–60–20* ✆ *Dkr 30* ☉ *Tues.–Sun. 10–5;, Wed. 10–8.*

The old part of Køge is filled with 300 half-timber houses, all protected by the National Trust; it is a lovely area for a stroll. At the end of Kirkestræde is the 15th-century **Skt. Nicolai Kirke** (St. Nicholas Church). Once a lighthouse, its floor is now covered with more than 100 tombs of Køge VIPs. Carved angels line the church's walls, but most have had their noses struck off—a favorite pastime of drunken Swedish soldiers in the 1700s. ✉ *Kirkestr. 26* ☎ *56/65–13–59* ✆ *Free* ☉ *Mid-June–Aug., weekdays 10–4, Sat. 10–noon; Sept.–mid-June, weekdays 10–noon. Tower tours mid-June–mid-Aug., weekdays every 30 min. 10–1:30.*

off the beaten path

VALLØ SLOT – About 8 km (5 mi) south of Køge stands Vallø Slot, a large castle in Renaissance style from 1586. It was burnt down by a fire in 1893 and promptly rebuilt. The castle is surrounded by moats and reinforced with towers. Since 1737 noble families have used Vallø Slot for rest and relaxation. The gardens, the only part open to the public, are known for their roses and exotic plants. ✉ *Slotsg. 3, Vallø* ☎ *56/26–74–13* ✆ *Free* ☉ *Daily 8–sunset.*

Where to Stay & Eat

$$$$ ✕ **Horizonten Restaurant.** For a great view, sit at the terrace overlooking the harbor. Horizonten's interior is modern and often decorated with exhibitions of local artists. The food here includes a mixture of Italian, French, Spanish, and Danish cuisine. Any of the grilled-fish dishes on the menu are a good option, but the seafood-and-fish platter is the highlight. Lunch is served only by prior reservation. ⊠ *Havnen 29A* ☎ *56/ 63–86–28* ▤ *MC, V* ⊘ *Closed Mon.; Jan. and Feb., closed Sun.*

$$$ ▥ **Hotel Hvide Hus.** Built in 1966 and overlooking the Bay of Køge, the White House Hotel has fantastic views. The hotel is brightly decorated in a contemporary Danish style. ⊠ *Strandvejen 111, DK–4600* ☎ *56/ 65–36–90* ▤ *56/66–33–14* ⊕ *www.hotelhvidehus.dk* ⊸ *127 rooms, 1 suite* ⚉ *Restaurant, cafeteria, sauna, bar, meeting room, some pets allowed, no-smoking rooms* ▤ *AE, DC, MC, V.*

$ ▥ **Hotel Vallø Slotskro.** Near Vallø Slot and surrounded by the castle's beautifully landscaped grounds, this rural inn is a pleasant place to spend a couple of days. The rooms are charming, some of them have beds with canopies, and the service is personable. ⊠ *Slotsg. 1, DK–4600* ☎ *56/ 26–70–20* ▤ *56/26–70–71* ⊕ *www.valloeslotskro.dk* ⊸ *11 rooms, 7 with bath* ⚉ *Restaurant, bar, some pets allowed, no-smoking rooms* ▤ *AE, DC, MC, V.*

Fodor'sChoice ★

Nightlife & the Arts

Even if the name suggests another thing, **Hugo's Vinkælder** (Hugo's Winecellar; ⊠ Brog. 19, courtyard ☎ 56/65–58–50) is an old beer pub, which was opened in 1968 on the ruins of a medieval monastery cellar. It is a favorite gathering spot for locals. There are beers from all over the world and sandwiches to go with them. On Saturday there is live jazz until midnight. It's closed Sunday.

en route | Twenty-four kilometers (15 mi) south of Køge near Rødvig, the Stevns Klint chalk cliffs make a good stop. The 13th-century **Højerup Kirke** sits on the cliffs. Over time as the cliffs eroded, first the cemetery and then part of the church toppled into the sea. The church has now been restored and the cliffs below have been bolstered by masonry to prevent further damage. ⊠ *Højerup Byg., Stevns Klint, Store Heddinge* ☎ *56/50–36–88* ▱ *Dkr 15* ⊘ *Daily 11–5.*

Møn

⚑ **16** *77 km (47 mi) south of Køge, 122 km (75 mi) south of Copenhagen.*

The whole island of Møn is pocked with nearly 100 Neolithic burial mounds, but it is most famous for its dramatic chalk cliffs, the northern **Møns Klint**, which is three times as large as Stevns Klint. Circled by a beech forest, the milky-white 75-million-year-old bluffs plunge 400 feet to a small, craggy beach—accessible by a path and more than 500 steps. Wear good walking shoes and take care; though a park ranger checks the area for loose rocks, the cliffs can crumble suddenly. Once there, Danish families usually hunt for fossils of cuttlefish, sea urchins, and other sea life. The cliffs are an important navigational marker for ships as an unusual landmark on south Sjælland's otherwise flat topography.

Inland from the northern section of the Møns Klint is **Liselund Slot**, a delightful 18th-century folly. Antoine de la Calmette, the island's sheriff and a royal chamberlain, took his inspiration from Marie-Antoinette's *Hameau* (Hamlet) at Versailles and built the Liselund Castle in 1792 for his beloved wife. The thatch-roof palace, complete with English gardens, combines a Norwegian country facade with elegant Pompeiian interiors. In this lovely setting, Hans Christian Andersen wrote his fairy tale *The Tinder Box*. The palace has been open to the public since 1938. This castle is not to be confused with a hotel of the same name. ⊠ *Langebjergvej 4, Borre* ☎ *55/81–21–78* ☎ *Dkr 30* ⊙ *Tours, Danish and German only, May–Oct., Tues.–Fri. 10:30, 11, 1:30, and 2; weekends also 3 and 3:30.*

Møn's capital, **Stege**, received its town charter in 1268. A third of the island's 11,500 inhabitants live here. Stege began as a small fishing village and it expanded slowly around a castle erected in the 12th century. By the 15th century, Stege was a commercial center for fishermen, peasants, and merchants. It was in this wealthy period that the town was encircled with moats and ramparts. The fortified town had three entranceways, each of them controlled with the help of a gate tower. One of these gates, **Mølleporten**, raised around 1430, is still standing.

The **Møns Museum** in Stege showcases antiques and local-history exhibitions and is well worth a stop. ⊠ *Storeg. 75, Stege* ☎ *55/81–40–67* ⊕ *www.aabne-samlinger.dk/moens* ☎ *Dkr 30* ⊙ *May–Oct., daily 10–4.*

One of the island's medieval churches noted for its naive frescoes, **Fanefjord Kirke** may have been completed by a collaborative group of artisans. The whimsical paintings include scholastic and biblical doodlings. The church also maintains an original 13th-century aisle. The Fanefjord church is 12½ km (8 mi) southwest of Stege. Other churches in the area famed for their frescoes include the ones in Elmelunde and Keldby. ⊠ *Fanefjord Kirkevej 51, Askeby* ☎ *55/81–70–05* ⊙ *Apr.–Sept., daily 7–4; Oct.–Mar., daily 8–4.*

Ten kilometers (6 mi) west of Stege is **Kong Asgers Høj** (King Asger's Hill), Denmark's biggest passage grave (a collection of upright stones supporting a horizontal stone slab to make a tomb) that dates from the early Stone Age. A 26-foot-long hall precedes the 32-foot grave chamber. During its history, the passage grave has periodically been used as a common grave for locals.

Where to Stay & Eat

$–$$ ✕⊡ **Præstekilde Hotel.** On a small island close to the capital, this hotel has a splendid view of Stege Bay from the middle of the golf course. The service is efficient while maintaining the warmth of rural areas. The restaurant serves good French-inspired Danish food. The small, simply equipped rooms are decorated in light colors, giving a bright impression on sunny days. ⊠ *Klintevej 116, DK–4780 Keldby* ☎ *55/86–87–88* ☎ *55/81–36–34* ⊕ *www.praestekilde.dk* ⇗ *46 rooms with bath, 4 suites* ⚅ *Restaurant, minibars, 18-hole golf course, indoor pool, sauna, billiards, meeting rooms, some pets allowed, no-smoking rooms* ⊟ *AE, DC, MC, V.*

★ **$$** ⊡ **Liselund Ny Slot.** In a grand old manor on an isolated estate, this modern hotel offers refined accommodations without being stodgy. The staircase and frescoed ceilings have been preserved and the rooms are fresh and simple, with wicker furnishings and pastel color schemes. Half the rooms overlook the forest and a pond filled with swans. The downstairs restaurant serves Danish cuisine. ⊠ *Langebjergvej 6, DK–4791 Borre* ☎ *55/81–20–81* ☎ *55/81–21–91* ⇗ *15 rooms* ⚅ *Restaurant, meeting room* ⊟ *AE, DC, MC, V.*

¢ ⊡ **Pension Bakkegården.** Between the view of the Baltic Sea and the Klinteskov forest, this small hotel possesses the best qualities of the island. From here it is a simple and relaxing 20-minute stroll through the beech forest to see the cliffs of Møn. Partial board is available upon request. ⊠ *Busenevej 64, Busene, DK–4791 Borre* ☎ *55/81–93–01* 🖷 *55/ 81–94–01* ⊕ *www.bakkegaarden64.dk* ⇨ *12 rooms without bath* ♨ *Billiards* ▭ *No credit cards.*

Falster

⑰ *3 km (2 mi) south of Bogø; Nykøbing Falster is 49 km (30 mi) southeast of Stege, 134 km (83 mi) south of Copenhagen.*

Accessible by way of the striking Farø Bridge or the parallel Storstrømsbroen (Big Current Bridge) from Fredensborg, Falster is shaped like a tiny South America and has excellent blond beaches to rival those of its continental twin. Among the best are the southeastern Marielyst and southernmost Gedser. Almost everywhere on the island are cafés, facilities, and water-sports rentals. Falster is also one of the country's major producers of sugar beets.

☙ The **Middelaldercentret** (Center for the Middle Ages), a reconstructed medieval village, invites school classes to dress up in period costumes and experience life a millennium ago. Daytime visitors can participate in activities that change weekly—from cooking to medieval knife-making to animal herding and, on weekends, folk dances and other cultural happenings. ⊠ *Ved Hamborgskoven 2, Nykøbing Falster* ☎ *54/86–19–34* ⊕ *www.middelaldercentret.dk* 🖭 *Dkr 80* ☉ *May–Sept., daily 10–4.*

Where to Stay & Eat

$$$–$$$$ ✕ **Czarens Hus.** This stylish old inn dates back more than 200 years, when it was a guest house and supply store for area farmers and merchants. Deep-green walls, gold trim, and chandeliers set the backdrop for antique furnishings. The specialty of the house is Continental European–Danish cuisine, which translates as creative beef and fish dishes, often served with cream sauces. Try the Zar Beuf (calf tenderloin in a mushroom-and-onion cream sauce). ⊠ *Langg. 2, Nykøbing Falster* ☎ *54/85–28–29* ▭ *AE, DC, MC, V* ☉ *Closed Sun.*

$$–$$$ 🏨 **Hotel Falster.** This sleek and efficient hotel accommodates conference guests as well as vacationers with its comfortable yet businesslike demeanor. Rustic brick walls and Danish antiques mix with sleek Danish-design lamps and sculpture. Rooms are done in dark wood and modular furniture. ⊠ *Stubbekøbingvej 150, DK–4800 Nykøbing Falster* ☎ *54/ 85–93–93* 🖷 *54/82–21–99* ⊕ *www.hotel-falster.dk* ⇨ *68 rooms, 1 suite* ♨ *Restaurant, gym, bar, meeting room, some pets allowed, no-smoking rooms* ▭ *AE, DC, MC, V.*

Sports & the Outdoors

GOLF The 18-hole **Sydsjælland Golf Klub** (⊠ Præstø Landevej 39–Mogenstrup, DK–4700 Næstved ☎ 55/76–15–55) is more than 25 years old, and the park course is lined with a number of small lakes and streams. The highest accepted handicap is 36.

Lolland

⑱ *Sakskøbing is 19 km (12 mi) west of Nykøbing Falster and 138 km (85 mi) southwest of Copenhagen.*

The history of Lolland dates back more than 1,000 years, to a man named Saxe, who sat at the mouth of the fjord and collected a toll. He later cleared the surrounding land and leased it. It became known as Saxtorp and eventually Sakskøbing, the island's capital. Though most people head straight for the beaches, the area (accessible by bridge from Nykøbing

Falster) has a few sights, including a water tower with a smiling face and an excellent car museum near the central 13th-century Ålholm Slot (closed to the public). The **Ålholm Automobile Museum** is northern Europe's largest, with more than 200 vehicles. ⊠ *Ålholm Parkvej 17, Nysted* ☎ *54/87–19–11* ⊕ *www.aalholm.dk* ⊠ *Dkr 75* ☉ *Mid-May–Aug., daily 10–5; Sept.–mid-Oct., weekends 10–4.*

The **Knuthenborg Safari Park,** 8 km (5 mi) west of Sakskøbing and also on Lolland, has a drive-through range where you can rubberneck at tigers, zebras, rhinoceroses, giraffes, and areas where you can mingle with and pet camels, goats, and ponies. Besides seeing 20 species of animals, children can marvel at Småland's to-scale relief map of southern Sjælland or play on the jungle gym, minitrain, and other rides. ⊠ *Birketvej 1, Maribo, Bandholm* ☎ *54/78–80–88* ⊕ *www.knuthenborg.dk* ⊠ *Dkr 95* ☉ *Late Apr.–late Sept., daily 9–5; late Sept.–late Oct., weekends 9–5.*

Where to Stay

$$ 🏨 **Lalandia.** This massive water-park hotel has an indoor pool, beach-side view, and lots of happy families. On the southern coast of Lolland, about 27 km (16 mi) southwest of Sakskøbing, the modern white apartments, with full kitchen and bath, accommodate up to eight people. There are three family-style restaurants—a steak house, Italian buffet, and pizzeria. ⊠ *Rødbyhavn, DK–4970 Rødby* ☎ *54/61–05–00* 🖷 *54/61–05–01* ⊕ *www.lalandia.dk* ⟿ *636 apartments* ♨ *3 restaurants, 9-hole golf course, 5 tennis courts, indoor pool, health club, sauna, bar, playground, meeting room* ▤ *AE, DC, MC, V.*

¢ 🏨 **Hotel Saxkjøbing.** Behind its yellow half-timber facade, this comfortable hotel is short on character and frills, but the rooms are bright, sunny, and modern, if very simply furnished. In the town center, the hotel is convenient to everything. Its family-style restaurant serves pizzas, steaks, and salads. ⊠ *Torvet 9, DK–4990 Sakskøbing* ☎ *54/70–40–39* 🖷 *54/ 70–53–50* ⟿ *24 rooms with bath* ♨ *Restaurant, billiards, bar, meeting room* ▤ *AE, DC, MC.*

Ringsted

⑲ *95 km (59 mi) north of Sakskøbing (Lolland), 68 km (42 mi) south-west of Copenhagen (via Køge).*

During the Middle Ages Ringsted became one of the most important Danish towns by growing around a church and a nearby 12th-century Benedictine abbey. The abbey was partially destroyed by a fire in the beginning of the 1900s. Nowadays Ringsted is known for being "the town in the middle," the traffic junction of Sjælland.

The spirit of fairy tales is tangible at **Eventyrlandet** (Fantasy World), where a life-size, animated model of Hans Christian Andersen tells his stories via a recorded tape playing in Danish, English, and German. Children enjoy Santa World and Cowboy Land while adults can discover the Adventure Gardens, where Moorish, Japanese, and Roman ornaments dot the well-preserved gardens. ⊠ *Eventyrvej 13, DK–4100 Ringsted* ☎ *57/ 61–19–30* ⊕ *www.fantasy-world.dk* ⊠ *Dkr 70* ☉ *June–Aug., Oct.–Dec., 2nd wk of Feb., and Easter, daily 10–5.*

Sct. Bendts Kirke (St. Benedict's Church) is the only evidence left of the existence of the Benedictine monastery that thrived here in the 12th century. Inside, four Danish kings are buried, including Valdemar I who died in 1182. ⊠ *Sct. Bendtsg. 3* ☎ *57/61–40–19* ☉ *May–mid-Sept., daily 10–noon and 1–5; mid-Sept.–Apr., daily 1–3.*

> **off the beaten path**
> ★

SORØ – Eighteen kilometers (11 mi) west of Ringsted is the town of Sorø, known for **Akademiet,** founded in 1623 by King Christian IV. The Academy was established in the abbey, which had been built by Bishop Absalon in 1142 and abandoned after the Lutheran reformation. The educational importance of the town increased thanks to the Danish writer Ludvig Holberg, who donated his whole inheritance to the academy after his death in 1754. The academy is on the banks of Sorø Sø (Lake Sorø) inside an extensive park. Not far from here is **Klosterkirke,** a Roman church built in the 12th century as a part of a Cistercian abbey. In this church are the remains of Bishop Absalon.

BONBON-LAND – Children adore this park in the tiny southern Sjælland town of Holme-Olstrup between Rønnede and Næstved, 30 km (19 mi) south of Ringsted. Filled with rides and friendly costumed grown-ups, BonBon-Land is an old-fashioned playland, with a few eating and drinking establishments thrown in for adults. ⊠ *Gartnervej 2, DK–4684 Holme-Olstrup* ☎ *55/53–07–00* ⊕ *www. bonbonland.dk* ⊠ *Dkr 150* ⊙ *Mid-May–mid-June and Aug., daily 9:30–5; mid-June–July, daily 9:30–8.*

Where to Stay

$$ ⊞ **Skjoldenæseholm.** Any point of the island can be reached by car within an hour from this luxurious hotel in the very center of Sjælland. Luxury prevails, from the Jacuzzi in the suites to the surrounding lush park and forest. Cottages for groups and families, one of them placed by the 15th hole in the nearby golf course, are available to rent. ⊠ *Skjold-enæsvej 106, DK–4174 Jystrup Midsjælland* ☎ *57/52–81–04* 🖷 *57/ 52–88–55* ⊕ *www.skj.dk* ⇆ *38 rooms, 5 suites* 🍴 *Restaurant, billiards, bar, meeting room* ▭ *AE, DC, MC, V.*

Sports & the Outdoors

CANOEING Just 8 km (5 mi) south of Sorø is the Suså (Sus River) where you can arrange canoe trips that last an hour, a day, or as long as a week. Call **Suså Kanoudlejning** (☎ 57/64–61–44) for more information on canoe rentals.

Shopping

In Næstved, 25 km (16 mi) south of Ringsted, the **Holmegaards Glassværker** (Glass Workshop; ⊠ Glassværksvej 52–Fensmark, Næstved ☎ 55/ 54–62–00) sells seconds of glasses, lamps, and occasionally glass art, with reductions of up to 50%.

Halsskov

➁ *48 km (30 mi) west of Ringsted, 110 km (69 mi) southwest of Copenhagen.*

Europe's third-longest tunnel-bridge, Storebæltsbro—the entire fixed-link length of which is 18 km (11 mi)—links Halsskov, on west Sjælland, to Nyborg, on east Fyn. Rail traffic traverses the west bridge and tunnel while auto traffic passes on the east-and-west bridge.

The **Storebæltsbro og Naturcenter** (Great Belt Bridge and Nature Center), which details the tunnel-bridge construction process, includes videos and models and makes for an informative stop. ⊠ *Storebæltsvej 88, Halsskov Odde, Korsør* ☎ *58/35–01–00* ⊠ *Dkr 25* ⊙ *Mid-Apr.–mid-Oct., daily 10–5.*

> **off the beaten path**
>
> **TRÆLLEBORG** – Viking enthusiasts will want to head 18 km (11 mi) northeast from Halsskov to Slagelse to see its excavated Viking encampment with a reconstructed army shelter. No longer content to rely on farmer-warriors, the Viking hierarchy designed the geometrically exact camp within a circular, moated rampart, thought to be of Asian inspiration. The 16 barracks, of which there is one model, could accommodate 1,300 men. ⊠ *Trælleborg Allé 4, Hejninge, Slagelse* ☎ *58/54–95–16* ⌨ *Dkr 35* ⊙ *Apr.–mid-Oct., Sat.–Thurs. 10–5.*

Sjælland & Its Islands A to Z

AIRPORTS

🛈 **Kastrup International Airport** ☎ 32/31-32-31 ⊕ www.cph.dk is Sjælland's only airport.

BIKE TRAVEL

Sjælland's flat landscape allows easy biking, and in summer, touring this way can be a delightful experience. Most roads have cycle lanes, and tourist boards stock maps detailing local routes. For more biking information, call the Danish Cycling Association, the Danish Tourist Board, or the bicycle tour operator Bike Denmark.

🛈 **Bike Denmark** ⊠ Olaf Poulsens Allé 1A, DK-3480 Fredensborg ☎ 48/48-58-00 🖷 48/48-59-00 ⊕ www.bikedenmark.com. **Danmarks Turistråd** (Danish Tourist Board) ⊠ Vesterbrog. 6D, Vesterbro, DK-1620 Copenhagen ☎ 33/11-14-15 🖷 33/93-14-16 ⊕ www.visitdenmark.com. **Dansk Cyklist Forbund** (Danish Cyclist Federation) ⊠ Rømersg. 7, Downtown DK-1362 Copenhagen ☎ 33/32-31-21 🖷 33/32-76-83 ⊕ www.dcf.dk.

BOAT & FERRY TRAVEL

There are several DSB and Scandlines car ferries from Germany. They connect Kiel to Bagenkop, on the island of Langeland (from there, drive north to Spodsbjerg and take another ferry to Lolland, which is connected to Falster and Sjælland by bridges); Puttgarden to Rødbyhavn on Lolland; and Travemünde and Warnemünde to Gedser on Falster. If you are driving from Sweden, take a car ferry from Hälsingborg to Helsingør. Molslinien runs routes between Jylland and Sjælland, linking Kalundborg and Havnebyen to Århus, and Havnebyen to Ebeltoft.

The ScanRail Pass, for travel anywhere within Scandinavia (Denmark, Sweden, Norway, and Finland), and the Interail and EurailPasses are valid on some ferry crossings. Call the DSB Travel Office for information.

🛈 **DSB** ☎ 70/13-14-16 international, 70/13-14-15 domestic ⊕ www.dsb.dk. **Mols-Linien** ☎ 70/10-14-18 🖷 89/52-52-90 ⊕ www.molslinien.dk. **Scandinavian Seaways Ferries** (DFDS) ⊠ Skt. Annæ Pl. 30, Sankt Annæ DK-1295 Copenhagen ☎ 33/42-33-42 🖷 33/42-33-41 ⊕ www.dfds.com. **Scandlines** ☎ 33/15-15-15 🖷 35/29-02-01 ⊕ www.scandlines.dk.

CAR TRAVEL

Highways and country roads throughout Sjælland are excellent, and traffic—even around Copenhagen—is manageable most of the time. As elsewhere in Denmark, take care to give right-of-way to the bikes driving to the right of the traffic. Sjælland is connected to Fyn, which is connected to Jylland, by the Storebæltsbroen, and it is connected to Malmö in Sweden by Øresund Bridge, which ends in Copenhagen.

BRIDGES 🛈 **Storebæltsbroen** ⊠ Storebæltsvej 70, DK-4220 Korsør ☎ 70/15-10-15 🖷 58/30-30-80. **Øresundsbroen** ⊠ Vester Søg. 10, Downtown DK-1601 Copenhagen ☎ 33/41-60-00 🖷 33/93-52-04.

EMERGENCIES

For police, fire, or ambulance assistance anywhere in Denmark, dial 112.

🏥 Major Hospitals **Helsingør Sygehus** ✉ Esrumvej 145, Helsingør ☎ 48/29-29-29. **Køge Amts Sygehus** ✉ Lykkebækvej 1, Køge ☎ 56/63-15-00. **Roskilde Amts Sygehus** ✉ Køgevej 7-13, Roskilde ☎ 46/32-32-00.

🏥 24-Hour Pharmacies **Hillerød** ✉ Slotsg. 26 ☎ 48/26-56-00 🖶 48/24-23-85. **Roskilde** ✉ Dom Apotek, Alg. 52 ☎ 46/32-32-77 🖶 46/32-88-22.

SPORTS & THE OUTDOORS

FISHING Sjælland's lakes, rivers, and coastline teem with plaice, flounder, cod, and catfish. You can buy a fishing license for one day for Dkr 25; for one week for Dkr 75; or for one year for Dkr 100. Along Sjælland's coast it can be bought at any post office. Elsewhere, check with the local tourist office for license requirements. It is illegal to fish within 1,650 feet of the mouth of a stream.

TOURS

The turn-of-the-20th-century *Saga Fjord* gives tours of the waters of the Roskildefjord from April through September; meals are served on board. Schedules vary; call ahead for schedules and information. Another option is *Viking Ruten*.

Check with the local tourism boards for general sightseeing tours in the larger towns or for self-guided walking tours. Most tours of Sjælland begin in Copenhagen. For information, call Copenhagen Excursions. The Afternoon Hamlet Tour (5 hours) includes Frederiksborg Castle and the exterior of Fredensborg Palace and Kronborg Castle. The seven-hour Castle Tour of North Sjælland visits Frederiksborg Castle and the outside of Fredensborg Palace, and stops at Kronborg Castle. The six-hour Roskilde Vikingland Tour includes the market and cathedral, Christian IV's Chapel, and the Viking Ship Museum.

🏛 **Copenhagen Excursions** ✉ Artillerivej 147, DK-2300 Copenhagen ☎ 32/54-06-06 🖶 32/57-49-05 ⊕ www.cex.dk. **Saga Fjord** ✉ Store Valbyvej 154, DK-4000 Roskilde ☎ 46/75-64-60 🖶 46/75-63-60 ⊕ www.sagafjord.dk. **Viking Ruten** ✉ Sydkajen, DK-3600 Frederikssund ☎ 47/38-87-50 🖶 47/38-87-51 ⊕ www.vikingruten.dk.

TRAIN TRAVEL

Sjælland's extensive rail network will get you where you need to go in much less time than the cumbersome bus system. Most train routes, whether international or domestic, are directed to and through Copenhagen. Routes to north and south Sjælland almost always require a transfer at Copenhagen's main station. Every town in Sjælland has a central train station, usually within walking distance of hotels and sights. The only part of the island not connected to the DSB network is the sliver of northwestern peninsula known as Sjællands Odde. Trains leave from Holbæk to Højby, where you can bus to the tip of the point. For information, call the private railway company Arriva. Two vintage trains dating from the 1880s run from Helsingør and Hillerød to Gilleleje.

The Copenhagen Card, which includes train and bus transport as well as admission to some museums and sites, is valid within the HT bus and rail system, which extends north to Helsingør, west to Roskilde, and south to Køge. However, the Copenhagen Card is valid for a limited time, so it's only worthwhile if you're planning a nonstop, intense sightseeing tour.

🚆 **Arriva** ☎ 70/27-74-82 ⊕ www.arrivatog.dk. **DSB** ☎ 70/13-14-16 international, 70/13-14-15 domestic ⊕ www.dsb.dk. **HT Bus** ✉ Gammel Køge Landevej 3, DK-2500 Valby ☎ 36/13-14-15 🖶 36/13-18-97 ⊕ www.ht.dk. **Vintage trains** ☎ 48/30-00-30.

VISITOR INFORMATION

The Fiskeridirektoratet has information about fishing licenses and where to buy them.

Danmarks Turistråd (Danish Tourist Board) ⊠ Vesterbrog. 6D, Vesterbro, DK-1620 Copenhagen ☎ 33/11-14-15. **Det grønne Sjælland** (Zealand Naturally) ⊕ www.sjaelland.com. **Fiskeridirektoratet** ⊠ Stormg. 2, Downtown, DK-1470 Copenhagen ☎ 33/96-30-00 🖨 33/96-39-03 ⊕ www.fd.dk. **Fredensborg Turistinformation** ⊠ Slotsg. 2, DK-3480 ☎ 48/48-21-00 🖨 48/48-04-65 ⊕ www.visitfredensborg.dk. **Frederiksdal Kanoudlejning** ⊠ Nybrovej 520, DK-2800 Lyngby ☎ 45/85-67-70 🖨 45/83-02-91. **Helsingør Turistbureau** ⊠ Havnepl. 3, DK-3000 ☎ 49/21-13-33 🖨 49/21-15-77 ⊕ www.visithelsingor.dk. **Hillerød Turistbureau** ⊠ Slangerupg. 2, DK-3400 ☎ 48/24-26-26 🖨 48/24-26-65 ⊕ www.hillerodturist.dk. **Holbæk Turistbureau** ⊠ Jernbanepl. 3, DK-4300 ☎ 59/43-11-31 🖨 59/44-27-44 ⊕ www.holbaek-info.dk. **Hornbæk Turistinformation** ⊠ Vestre Stejlebakke 2A, DK-3100 ☎ 49/70-47-47 🖨 49/70-41-42 ⊕ www.hornbaek.dk. **Køge Turistbureau** ⊠ Vesterg. 1, DK-4600 ☎ 56/67-60-01 🖨 56/65-59-84 ⊕ www.koegeturist.dk. **Nykøbing Falster Turistinformation** ⊠ Østergåg. 7, DK-4800 ☎ 54/85-13-03 🖨 54/85-10-05 ⊕ www.tinf.dk. **Møn Turistbureau** ⊠ Storeg. 2, DK-4780 Stege ☎ 55/86-04-00 🖨 55/81-48-46 ⊕ www.moen-touristbureau.dk. **Næstved Turistbureau** ⊠ Det Gule Pakhus, Havnen 1, DK-4700 ☎ 55/72-11-22 🖨 55/72-16-67 ⊕ www.visitnaestved.com. **Odsherreds Turistbureau** ⊠ Svanestr. 9, DK-4500 Nykøbing Sjælland ☎ 59/91-08-88 🖨 59/93-00-24 ⊕ www.odsherred.com. **Midtsjællands Turistcenter** ⊠ Sct. Bendtsg. 6, DK-4100 Ringsted ☎ 57/62-66-00 🖨 57/62-66-10 ⊕ www.met-2000.dk. **Roskilde Festival** ⊠ Havsteensvej 11, DK-4000 Roskilde ☎ 46/36-66-13 🖨 46/32-14-99 ⊕ www.roskilde-festival.dk. **Roskilde Turistbureau** ⊠ Gullandsstr. 15, DK-4000 ☎ 46/31-65-65 🖨 46/31-65-60 ⊕ www.destination-roskilde.dk. **Sakskøbing Turistbureau** ⊠ Torveg. 4, DK-4990 ☎ 54/70-56-30 🖨 54/70-53-90 ⊕ www.lolland-falster.dk. **Slagelse Turistbureau** ⊠ Løveg. 7, DK-4200 ☎ 58/52-22-06 🖨 58/52-86-87 ⊕ www.vikingelandet.dk.

FYN & THE CENTRAL ISLANDS

Christened the Garden of Denmark by its most famous son, Hans Christian Andersen, Fyn (Funen) is the smaller of the country's two major islands. A patchwork of vegetable fields and flower gardens, the flat-as-a-board countryside is relieved by beech glades and swan ponds. Manor houses and castles pop up from the countryside like magnificent mirages. Some of northern Europe's best-preserved castles are here: the 12th-century Nyborg Slot, travel pinup Egeskov Slot, and the lavish Valdemars Slot. The fairy-tale cliché often attributed to Denmark springs from this provincial isle, where the only place with modern vigor or stress seems to be Odense, its capital. Trimmed with thatch-roof houses and green parks, the city makes the most of the Andersen legacy but surprises with a rich arts community at the Brandts Klædefabrik, a former textile factory turned museum compound.

Towns in Fyn are best explored by car. It's even quick and easy to reach the smaller islands of Langeland and Tåsinge—both are connected to Fyn by bridges. Slightly more isolated is Ærø, where the town of Ærøskøbing, with its colorfully painted half-timber houses and winding streets, seems caught in a delightful time warp.

Nyborg

▶ ❶ *136 km (85 mi) southwest of Copenhagen (including the bridge across the Great Belt), 30 km (19 mi) southeast of Odense.*

Like most visitors, you should begin your tour of Fyn in Nyborg, a 13th-century town that was Denmark's capital during the Middle Ages. The city's major landmark, the moated 12th-century **Nyborg Slot** (Nyborg Castle), was the seat of the Danehof, the Danish parliament from 1200 to 1413. It was here that King Erik Klipping signed the country's first constitution, the Great Charter, in 1282. In addition to geometric wall murals and an armory collection, the castle houses changing art exhibits. ⊠ *Slotsg. 34* ☎ *65/31–02–07* ⊕ *www.museer-nyborg.dk* ⊠ *Dkr 30, Dkr 45 combined ticket with Nyborg Museum* ☉ *Mar.–May and Sept.–mid-Oct., Tues.–Sun. 10–3; June and Aug., Tues.–Sun. 10–4; July, Tues.–Sun. 10–5.*

The **Nyborg Museum** occupies Mads Lerches Gård, a half-timber merchant's house from 1601, and provides an insight into 17th-century life. In addition to furnished period rooms, there's a small brewery. ⊠ *Slotspl. 11* ☎ *65/31–02–07* ⊕ *www.museer-nyborg.dk* ⊠ *Dkr 30, Dkr 45 combined ticket with Nyborg Slot* ☉ *Mar.–May and Sept. and Oct., Tues.–Sun. 10–3; June and Aug., Tues.–Sun. 10–4; July, Tues.–Sun. 10–5.*

Every Tuesday at 7 PM in July and August, look and listen for the **Nyborg Tappenstreg** (Nyborg Tattoo), a military march accompanied by music that winds through the streets in the center of town. This ceremony dates from the mid-17th century, when officers would march through the streets, rounding up all the soldiers from the bars and beer halls to return them to the barracks. The word "tattoo" has its roots in the old Dutch word "taptoo" (or "taptoe"), which means to close the tap of a barrel; the variant "taps" obviously claims the same etymology.

Where to Stay & Eat

$–$$$ ✕ **Central Cafeen.** In a 200-year-old town house in the center of town, this warm-tone restaurant with velvet seats has been open since 1854. To many a Nyborg native, there's nowhere better in town for a Danish smørrebrød lunch or hearty dinner. Evidence of the customers' affection lines the walls and shelves, from old Carlsberg and Tuborg caps worn by the deliverymen to ancient shop scales—all gifts from happy diners after they retired or closed down their businesses. The menu includes roasted salmon with spinach and boiled potatoes, and fried pork with parsley sauce. Round out the meal with a plate of fresh Fyn cheeses served with radishes and chives. In summer you can dine in the outdoor courtyard, surrounded by the neighborhood's yellow, half-timber houses. ⊠ *Nørreg. 6* ☎ *65/31–01–83* ⊟ *AE, DC, MC, V* ☉ *Closed Sun. Oct.–June.*

$–$$$ ✕ **Danehofkroen.** Outside Nyborg Slot, this family-run restaurant does a brisk lunch business, serving traditional Danish meals to tourists who enjoy a view of the castle and its tree-lined moat. The menu is basic meat and potatoes, with such dishes as *flæskesteg* (sliced pork served with the crisp rind). ⊠ *Slotspl.* ☎ *65/31–02–02* ⌕ *Reservations essential* ⊟ *V* ☉ *Closed Mon. and Oct.–May.*

$$$$ 🛏 **Hesselet.** A modern brick slab outside, this hotel is a refined Anglo-
Fodor'sChoice Asian sanctuary on the inside. Guest rooms have cushy, contemporary
★ furniture, most with a splendid view of the Storebæltsbro. ⊠ *Christianslundsvej 119, DK–5800* ☎ *65/31–30–29* 🖷 *65/31–29–58* ⊕ *www.hesselet.dk* 🛏 *43 rooms, 4 suites* ⌕ *Restaurant, indoor pool, bar, meeting room* ⊟ *AE, DC, MC, V.*

$$$ 🛏 **Nyborg Strand.** This large hotel complex, owned by the Best Western hotel chain, sprawls along the shoreline 1½ km (1 mi) east of Nyborg's city center. The Nyborg Strand caters to the conference crowd, with numerous meeting rooms and an antiseptic lobby that reverberates with the din of noisy groups. However, the seaside location can't be beat, and the summer rates, particularly for families, are surprisingly low, especially considering the hotel's lovely location. ⊠ *Østerøvej 2, DK–5800* ☎ *65/31–31–31* 🖷 *65/31–37–01* ⊕ *www.nyborgstrand.dk* 🛏 *228 rooms* ⌕ *Restaurant, indoor pool, bar, meeting rooms, some pets allowed (fee)* ⊟ *AE, DC, MC, V.*

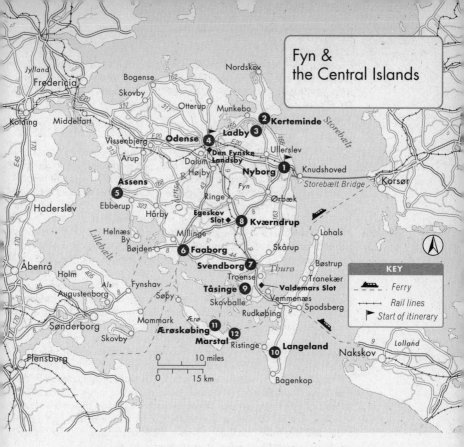

Nightlife & the Arts

★ Take on the Nyborg night at the popular **Café Anthon** (✉ Mellemg. 25 ☎ 65/31–16–64), a laid-back bar in the heart of town, with live jazz, blues, or rock on Friday and Saturday nights. The quirky decor includes an upright piano with a built-in aquarium and an old grandfather clock in the corner. The walls are hung with all sorts of instruments, from accordions to cellos to electric guitars, many of which were gifts from musicians who have played here.

Shopping

ANTIQUES Many of Fyn's manor houses and castles now double as antiques emporiums. The largest is **Hindemae** (✉ Hindemaevej 86, Ullerslev ☎ 65/35–32–60), which lies 12 km (7 mi) west of Nyborg. The site is only open to the public during auctions.

Kerteminde

❷ *21 km (13 mi) north of Nyborg, 20 km (13 mi) northeast of Odense.*

Kerteminde is an important fishing village and popular summer resort. The pastel paints and red roofs of the town's houses contrast with the cool blues of the nearby ocean, which supports recreational fishing, swimming, and other watersports in the summer. On Langegade, walk past the neat half-timber houses to Møllebakken and the **Johannes Larsen Museet**, dedicated to the work of the Danish painter (1867–1961). Across from a strawberry patch and a century-old windmill, the artist built a large country villa that has been perfectly preserved, right down to the teacups. In front is a sculpture of a woman done by Kai Nielsen. Local legend has it that one night, after a particularly wild party in Copenhagen, its legs were somehow broken off. An ambulance was called, and once it arrived, the enraged driver demanded that the artists pay a fine. A chagrined Larsen paid, and in return kept Nielsen's wounded sculpture. ☒ *Møllebakken 14* ☎ *65/32–11–77* ⊕ *www.kert-mus.dk* ☒ *Dkr 50* ☉ *June–Aug., daily 10–5; Mar.–May, Sept., and Oct., Tues.–Sun. 10–4; Nov.–Feb., Tues.–Sun. 11–4.*

Where to Eat

★ **$$$$** ✕ **Rudolf Mathis.** This busy harborside restaurant is topped by two chimneys, which are needed to ventilate the open grills where popular fish dishes are broiled. Favorites are catfish with butter, fennel, and Pernod sauce, and grilled turbot in green-pepper–and–lime sauce. ☒ *Dosseringen 13, 13 km (8 mi) northeast of Odense on Rte. 165* ☎ *65/32–32–33* ⊟ *AE, DC, MC, V* ☉ *Closed Mon. and Jan. and Feb.*

$$$–$$$$ ✕ **Gittes Fiskehus.** Dine to the gentle sounds of lapping water at this friendly fish restaurant that extends out over Kerteminde's small canal amid colorful, bobbing fishing boats. Dishes include shrimp smothered in garlic, cream, rum, and Pernod, or the "Hemingway steak," a plate of blue marlin, the fish protagonist of *The Old Man and the Sea.* An additional dining room is housed inside a permanently moored boat that sits alongside the restaurant. Come summer, diners spill out onto the deck to enjoy their seafood under the sun. ☒ *Hindsholmvej 5* ☎ *65/32–12–38* ⊟ *MC, V* ☉ *Closed Sun.–Tues. No lunch Sept.–May.*

$ ✕ **Tornøes Hotel.** Steps from Kerteminde's harbor is this comfortable hotel with basic rooms, many of which have partial views of the waterfront. The handsome restaurant has pale yellow walls and matching tablecloths, and serves contemporary Danish fare, including a set "Kerteminde menu" of fried sole as well as crepes with ice cream and strawberries for dessert. Cate Wenzel, a lively café-bar with light meals, has a pool table, and live music on the weekends. ☒ *Strandg. 2, DK–5300* ☎ *65/32–16–05* 🖷 *65/32–48–40* ⊕ *www.tornoeshotel.dk* ⬱ *30 rooms, 2 suites with bath* ♿ *Restaurant, bar, some pets allowed* ⊟ *AE, DC, MC, V.*

¢ 🏠 **Danhostel Kerteminde Vandrehjem.** South of Kerteminde, this well-maintained hostel is surrounded by a peaceful patch of woodland and is just a few minutes' walk from the beach. Families flock here in summer, drawn by the low prices and a plethora of outdoor activities that awaits just beyond the front door, from hiking to biking to swimming. The rooms are outfitted in typical Danish hostel style, with sturdy wooden bunks and basic showers. An industrial-size kitchen and cafeteria—built to feed the large school groups that come through—serves breakfast. Sheets and towels also cost extra. If you pay by credit card, you'll have to pay a surcharge. ☒ *Skovvej 46, DK–5300 Kerteminde* ☎ *65/32–39–29* 🖷 *65/32–39–24* ⊕ *www.danhostel.dk* ⬱ *30 rooms with shower* ⊟ *MC, V.*

Shopping

CERAMICS A few miles west of Kerteminde is **Bjørnholt Keramik** (☒ Risingevej 12, Munkebo ☎ 65/97–40–90), where you can watch ceramics being made.

off the beaten path

ROMSØ – The 250-acre, pristine island of Romsø, just a half-hour ferry ride from Kerteminde, attracts nature-lovers, hikers, and bird-watchers. A hardwood forest blankets half the island, making it something of a rarity among Denmark's islands, only a few of which have forests. More than 170 species of birds have been recorded here, and during their breeding season (March through June) part of the island is closed to visitors. Deer roam freely through the wooded areas, and hiking trails crisscross the island (bicycles are not allowed). Romsø's population peaked at 50 after World War I, but after the lighthouse closed in 1973, the population dwindled to just a handful of residents. Bring all supplies that you might need, as there are no accommodations or food on the island. Camping is not permitted. A high-speed **passenger boat** (☎ 65/32–13–77 for reservations with Leif Hansen) connects Kerteminde with Romsø. The cost is around Dkr 100 roundtrip. The boat operates only in the summer months, usually from June through August. Schedules change frequently so call ahead.

Ladby

❸ *4 km (2½ mi) south of Kerteminde, 16 km (10 mi) east of Odense.*

The village of Ladby is best known as the home of the 1,100-year-old remains of the *Ladbyskibet.* This ship belonging to a Viking chieftain was buried along with the hunting dogs and horses he would need for Valhalla—the afterlife. Today you can see a massive hull-shaped indentation in the ground where the excavation took place. All the wooden parts of the ship disintegrated centuries ago, but exhibited at the site are the ship's anchor, and also the remains of the horses and hunting dogs. A replica of the ship (in real size) was in the works until the project stalled because of practical and financial difficulties; if and when it's completed, it will be shown alongside the burial site. ⊠ *Vikingevej 123* ☎ *65/32–16–67* ⊕ *www.kert-mus.dk* ☎ *Dkr 25* ☉ *June–Aug., daily 10–5; Mar.–May, Sept., and Oct., Tues.–Sun. 10–4; Nov.–Feb., Wed.–Sun. 11–3.*

Odense

▶ ❹ *20 km (12 mi) southwest of Ladby on Rte. 165, 144 km (90 mi) west of Copenhagen.*

It's no coincidence that Odense, the capital of Fyn and third largest city in Denmark, is reminiscent of a storybook village—much of its charm is built upon the legend of its most famous son, author Hans Christian Andersen. The town is named after another famous Scandinavian, Odin, the king of the Nordic gods. When you're in town, first see the flourishing Kongens Have (King's Garden) and 18th-century Odense Castle, now a government building. If you walk east on Østre Stationsvej to Thomas B. Thriges Gade and Hans Jensens Stræde, you'll come to ★ the **Hans Christian Andersen Hus** (H. C. Andersen House), which sits amid half-timber houses and cobbled streets. Inside, the storyteller's life is chronicled through his photographs, drawings, letters, and personal belongings. The library has Andersen's works in more than 100 languages, and you can listen to fairy tales on tape. ⊠ *Hans Jensens Str. 37–45* ☎ *66/13–13–72 Ext. 4601* ⊕ *www.odmus.dk* ☎ *Dkr 35* ☉ *Mid-June–Aug., daily 9–7; Sept.–mid-June, Tues.–Sun. 10–4.*

☾ The **Børnekulturehuset Fyrtøjet** (Children's Culture House, The Tinderbox) museum includes walk-through fairy-tale exhibits as well as studios where children can draw and write their own tales and plays and then dress up and perform them. ⊠ *Hans Jensen Str. 21* ☎ *66/14–44–11* ⊕ *www.fyrtoejet.com* ☎ *Dkr 50* ☉ *Feb.–Dec., Tues.–Sat. 10–3.*

The sleek **Carl Nielsen Museum** creates multimedia exhibits of the life and work of Denmark's most famous composer (1865–1931) and of his wife, the sculptor Anne Marie Carl-Nielsen (yes, that's the way she took his name). ⊠ *Claus Bergs G. 11* ☎ *66/13–13–72 Ext. 4601* ⊕ *www. odmus.dk* ☎ *Dkr 25* ☉ *Nov.–Mar., Thurs.–Fri. 4–8, weekends noon–4; Apr.–May and Sept.–Oct., Thurs.–Sun. noon–4; June–Aug., Tues.–Sun. noon–4.*

Møntergården, Odense's city museum, occupies four 17th-century row houses adjacent to a shady, cobbled courtyard. Exhibits range from Middle Age interiors to coverage of Denmark's Nazi occupation to an extensive and impressive collection of ancient coins from all over the world. ⊠ *Overg. 48–50* 🕾 *66/13–13–72 Ext. 4601* ⊕ *www.odmus.dk* 🎫 *Dkr 25* ☉ *Tues.–Sun. 10–4.*

The stately **Skt. Knuds Kirke**, built from the 13th to the 15th century, is the only purely Gothic cathedral in Denmark. The intricate wooden altar covered with gold leaf was carved by German sculptor Claus Berg. Beneath the sepulchre are the bones of St. (King) Knud, killed during a farmers' uprising in 1086, and his brother. ⊠ *Toward the pedestrian zone of Skt. Knuds Kirkestræde, in front of Andersen Park.*

In the diminutive **Hans Christian Andersens Barndomshjem** (H. C. Andersen's Childhood Home), the young boy and his parents lived in three tiny rooms. The rooms are outfitted with rustic, period furnishings (chairs, lamps, a table) and little else, befitting a humble abode of the early 1800s. ⊠ *Munkemøllestr. 3–5* 🕾 *66/13–13–72 Ext. 4601* 🎫 *Dkr 15* ☉ *June–Aug., daily 10–4; Sept.–May, Tues.–Sun. 11–3.*

Near the center of town is the elegant **Fyns Kunstmuseum** (Funen Art Museum), which displays a large and varied collection of Danish art, from the 18th century to the present. Featured artists include Jens Juel, Vilhelm Hammershøj, P. S. Krøyer, and Robert Jacobsen. The museum's highlight is its comprehensive collection of Fyn artists, from Johannes Larsen to Peter Hansen. ⊠ *Jernbaneg. 13* 🕾 *66/13–13–72 Ext. 4601* ⊕ *www.odmus.dk* 🎫 *Dkr 30* ☉ *Tues.–Sun. 10–4.*

For something completely different, head just west of the center of town to the **Superbowl Odense**, an indoor entertainment center with bowling alleys, a restaurant, and a go-cart track. ⊠ *Grønøkken 3* 🕾 *66/ 19–16–40.*

Odense River Cruises (🕾 *65/95–79–96*) operates several boat trips on the Odense Å River from Filosofgangen. You can catch a boat (May through mid-August, daily on the hour 10–5, returning 35 minutes later) downriver to the Fruens Bøge (Lady's Beech Forest) and then walk down Erik Bøghs Sti (Erik Bøgh's Footpath) to **Den Fynske Landsby** (the Fyn Village). Among the country's largest open-air museums, it includes 25 farm buildings and workshops, a vicarage, a water mill, and a theater, which in summer stages adaptations of Andersen's tales. Afterward, cruise back to the town center or catch Bus 42, and walk down the boutique- and café-lined pedestrian street Vestergade (Kongensgade running perpendicular to the town hall), which in summer is abuzz with street performers, musicians, and brass bands. ⊠ *Sejerskovvej 20* 🕾 *66/13–13–72 Ext. 4601* ⊕ *www.odmus.dk* 🎫 *Dkr 35* ☉ *Apr.–mid-June and mid-Aug.–Oct., Tues.–Sun. 10–5; mid-June–mid-Aug., daily 9:30–7; Nov.–Mar., Sun. 11–3.*

Fodor'sChoice ★

Occupying a former textile factory, the four-story artist compound **Brandts Klædefabrik** houses the **Museet for Fotokunst** (Museum of Photographic Art), **Danmarks Grafiske Museum** (Danish Graphics Museum), **Dansk Presse Museum** (Danish Press Museum), and **Kunsthallen** (Art Gallery). National and international exhibits shown here vary widely, but the photography museum and the art gallery gravitate toward especially experimental work. The press museum chronicles the history of Denmark's printing trade, and houses lithography, bookbinding, and papermaking workshops. ⊠ *Brandts Passage 37 and 43, north of the river and parallel to Kongensgade* 🕾 *66/13–78–97* ⊕ *www.brandts.dk* 🎫 *Combined ticket Dkr 50; photography museum Dkr 25; graphics museum Dkr 25; press museum Dkr 25; art gallery Dkr 30* ☉ *July and Aug., daily 10–5; Sept.–June, Tues.–Sun. 10–5.*

off the beaten path

HOLLUFGÅRD – This 16th-century manor houses the city's archaeological department. The house has reopenened after a renovation and its grounds contain a completely renovated old barn and adjacent buildings showing special exhibits, including the archaeological find of the month and an ecology display. Nearby are a sculpture garden and a sculpture center, where you can see an artist at work. Take Bus 61 from the railway station on Østre Stationsvej 10 km (6 mi) south of Odense. ⊠ *Hestehaven 201* ☎ *66/13–13–72 Ext. 4601* 🖃 *Dkr 25* ⊙ *Apr.–Oct., Tues.–Sat. 10–4; Nov.–Apr., Sun. 10–4.*

Where to Eat

$$$$ ✕ **LPC** (La Petite Cuisine). This romantic little restaurant, tucked in the Brandts Passage, can accommodate about 40 diners. The southern French specialties change every day according to what can be purchased fresh at the market. Typical dishes include Asian-inspired marinated duck breast, grilled skewered salmon or catfish with vegetables, and white mocha parfait for dessert. Dishes can be combined in three- to five-course menus. ⊠ *Brandts Passage 13* ☎ *66/14–11–00* 🜲 *Reservations essential* 🖃 *DC, MC, V.*

$$$–$$$$ ✕ **Marie Louise.** Headed by the illustrious chef Michel Michaud, this is
FodorsChoice considered one of Fyn's—if not Denmark's—finest French restaurants.
★ The elegant whitewashed dining room glitters with crystal and silver. The French-Danish menu typically offers such specialties as scalloped salmon with bordelaise sauce and grilled veal with lobster cream sauce. Business and holiday diners are sometimes treated to gratis extras—such as quail's-egg appetizers or after-dinner drinks. ⊠ *Lottrups Gaard, Vesterg. 70–72* ☎ *66/17–92–95* 🖃 *AE, DC, MC, V* ⊙ *Closed Sun. and Mon.*

$$$–$$$$ ✕ **Restaurant Under Lindetræet.** The snug corner restaurant, situated in the same cozy, cobblestoned neighborhood as the Hans Christian Andersen House, serves homestyle Danish fare, including grilled redfish with boiled potatoes. Copper pots and Andersen-style paper cutouts hang on the wall, alongside a portrait of the great man himself. Old-fashioned lamps shed light onto the tables, which are set with gold-rim plates. Burgundy velvet drapes divide parts of the dining room, making dining an intimate experience. ⊠ *Ramsherred 2* ☎ *66/12–92–86* 🜲 *Reservations essential* 🖃 *MC, V* ⊙ *Closed Sun. and Mon.*

$$–$$$$ ✕ **Klitgaard.** Named after its young owner-chef, Jacob Klitgaard, this chic, cool-tone restaurant serves a changing menu of innovative French-Italian fusion fare. The season drives the menu; market-fresh produce graces every dish, from the young Fyn lamb with green asparagus to the lightly salted trout served with an herb mousse. Stuffed quail is seasoned with rosemary and accompanied by an endive salad; a fricassee of scallops and asparagus is enveloped in a tangy lemon sauce. The fresh cuisine is complemented by a soothing decor of tan walls, hardwood floors, and cane furniture that glow softly under recessed lights. ⊠ *Gravene 4* ☎ *66/13–14–55* 🜲 *Reservations essential* 🖃 *DC, MC, V* ⊙ *Closed Sun. and Mon.*

$$$ ✕ **Carlslund.** Ask most any Odense local where to find the best *æggekage* in town, and he'll probably point you in this direction. Cholesterol-watchers, beware: æggekage is a rich dish consisting of a fluffy, cream-whipped, parsley-speckled omelet topped with either bacon strips or pork rinds. Dab on some mustard and scoop it up with hunks of rye bread. It's traditionally washed down with shots of aquavit. The place also serves an extensive Danish menu of fish and meat dishes. Dating from 1860, the cozy, low-ceiling restaurant sits amid a wooded park on the outskirts of Odense. In summer, Carlslund sets up an outdoor stage and hosts live jazz on the weekends, drawing hundreds. ⊠ *Fruens Bøge Skov 7* ☎ *66/91–11–25* ⌕ *Reservations essential* ▭ *DC, MC, V.*

$–$$$ ✕ **Den Gamle Kro.** Built within the courtyards of several 17th-century homes, this popular restaurant has walls of ancient stone topped by a sliding glass roof. The French-Danish menu includes fillet of sole stuffed with salmon mousse and Châteaubriand with garlic potatoes, but there's also inexpensive smørrebrød. ⊠ *Overg. 23* ☎ *66/12–14–33* ▭ *DC, MC, V.*

$–$$$ ✕ **Franck A.** Overlooking the pedestrian street, this spacious, stylish café–restaurant–bar with exposed brick walls is Odense's answer to Copenhagen's trendy venues—minus the pretension. Hipsters and media types (it's a favorite with the folks from the local TV station) mingle over cocktails but, this being Odense, informality prevails. You're just as likely to sit next to families and older couples lingering over coffee. A rack of newspapers and Tintin comic books invites those who want to settle in for an afternoon read. Brunch is served all day; try the salmon–and–cherry-tomato omelet. The lunch and dinner menu of global cuisine runs the gamut from Thai chicken curry to hefty grilled burgers. Live music (usually Thursday through Saturday nights) draws a toe-tapping crowd. On Thursday, Franck A. often hosts a popular '80s music night, with lively cover bands. ⊠ *Jernbaneg. 4* ☎ *66/12–57–27* ▭ *MC, V.*

★ ¢–$ ✕ **Den Grimme Ælling.** The name of this chain restaurant means "the ugly duckling," but inside it's simply homey, with pine furnishings and a boisterous family ambience. It's extremely popular with tourists and locals alike, thanks to an all-you-can-eat buffet heaped with cold and warm dishes. ⊠ *Hans Jensens Str. 1* ☎ *65/91–70–30* ▭ *DC, MC.*

¢–$ ✕ **Målet.** A lively crowd calls this sports club its neighborhood bar. The schnitzel is served in a dozen creative ways from traditional schnitzel with sautéed potatoes and peas to Indian curry schnitzel with rice, chutney, and pineapple. After the steaming plates of food, watching and discussing soccer are the chief delights of the house. ⊠ *Jernbaneg. 17* ☎ *66/17–82–41* ⌕ *Reservations not accepted* ▭ *No credit cards.*

Where to Stay

$$$ ⊞ **Clarion Hotel Plaza.** A five-minute walk from the train station, this stately hotel dates from 1915 and overlooks Odense's leafy central park, Kongens Have. An old-fashioned wooden elevator takes you up to the ample, comfortable rooms outfitted in traditional dark-wood furniture. Adjoining the pale-green lobby is the glass-walled Restaurant Rosenhaven, which serves contemporary Danish fare, including wild rabbit wrapped in cabbage and topped with honey and berry preserves, and lemon-accented fillet of sole served in a puff pastry with a tarragon and saffron aspic. ⊠ *Østre Stationsvej 24, DK–5000* ☎ *66/11–77–45* 🖷 *66/ 14–41–45* ⊕ *www.hotel-plaza.dk* ⇴ *68 rooms* ⌕ *Restaurant, gym, sauna, bar, meeting rooms* ▭ *AE, DC, MC, V.*

$$$ ⊞ **Radisson SAS–Hans Christian Andersen Hotel.** Around the corner from the Hans Christian Andersen House, this blocky brick conference hotel has a plant-filled lobby and ample rooms done up in warm shades of red and yellow. In fall and winter, you have to battle your way through large conference groups to get to your room, but in summer it's half the normal price, and relatively quiet. ⊠ *Claus Bergs G. 7, DK–5000* ☎ *66/ 14–78–00 or 800/33–3333* 🖷 *66/14–78–90* ⊕ *www.radissonsas.com* ⇴ *145 rooms* ⌕ *Restaurant, sauna, bar, casino* ▭ *AE, DC, MC, V.*

$–$$$ ⊞ **First Hotel Grand Odense.** More than a century old, with renovated fin-de-siècle charm, this imposing four-story, brick-front hotel greets guests with old-fashioned luxury. The original stone floors and chandeliers lead to a wide staircase and upstairs guest rooms that are modern with plush furnishings and sleek marble bathrooms. ⊠ *Jernabaneg. 18, DK–5000* ☎ *66/11–71–71* 🖶 *66/14–11–71* ⊕ *www.firsthotels.com* ➦ *138 rooms with bath, 3 suites* ♿ *Restaurant, room service, sauna, bar, some pets allowed, no-smoking rooms* ⊟ *AE, DC, MC, V.*

¢ 🖼 **Hotel Ydes.** This well-kept, bright, and colorful hotel is a good bet
Fodor'sChoice for students and budget-conscious travelers tired of barracks-type ac-
★ commodations. The well-maintained rooms are spotless and comfort-
able. ⊠ *Hans Tausens G. 11, DK–5000* ☎ *66/12–11–31* 🖶 *66/12–14–13* ⊕ *www.ydes.dk* ➦ *25 rooms with bath* ♿ *Café* ⊟ *MC, V.*

Nightlife & the Arts

CAFÉS & BARS Odense's central arcade is an entertainment mall, with bars, restaurants, and live music ranging from corny sing-alongs to hard rock. For a quiet evening, stop by **Café Biografen** (⊠ Brandts Passage ☎ 66/13–16–16) for an espresso, beer, or light snack, or settle in to see one of the films screened here. The **Air Pub** (⊠ Kongsg. 41 ☎ 66/14–66–08) is a Danish pub that caters to a thirty- and fortysomething crowd, with meals and a small dance floor. At the **Boogie Dance Café** (⊠ Nørreg. 21 ☎ 66/14–00–39), a laid-back crowd grooves to pop, disco, and '60s music. In the heart of town is **Franck A** (⊠ Jernbaneg. 4 ☎ 66/12–57–27), a spirited café-restaurant with arched windows overlooking the pedestrian street. Live music on the weekends—from pop to jazz—draws a stylish crowd, as does the popular '80s night on Thursday. The specialty at **Klos Ands** (⊠ Vineg. 76 ☎ 66/13–56–00) is malt whiskey.

CASINO Fyn's sole casino is in the slick glass atrium of the **SAS Hans Christian Andersen Hotel** (⊠ Claus Bergs G. 7, Odense ☎ 66/14–78–00), where you can play blackjack, roulette, and baccarat.

JAZZ CLUBS **Dexter's** (⊠ Vinderg. 65 ☎ 66/13–68–88) has all kinds of jazz—from Dixieland to fusion—Friday and Saturday nights. **Grøntorvet Café and Bar** (⊠ Sortebrødre Torv 9 ☎ 66/14–34–37) presents live jazz at 5 PM Thursday and 2 PM Saturday.

THEATER **Den Fynske Landsby** stages Hans Christian Andersen plays from mid-July to mid-August. In summer the young members of the **Hans Christian Andersen Parade** present a pastiche of the bard's fairy tales in a couple of different languages at Lotzes Have, an herb garden behind the Hans Christian Andersen Museum.

Sports & the Outdoors

GOLF There are two major golf attractions and another smaller course near Odense for golf enthusiasts. Although the island appears to be flat, subtle hills provide excellent, challenging terrain for the golfer. Courses are well-groomed, with a number of natural water hazards. Golf has become an extremely popular sport in Denmark, so it would be wise to call ahead of time to inquire about starting times and the dates of tournaments. It's also very easy to find someone to play with—just ask in the clubhouse. **Odense Eventyr Golfklub** (⊠ Falen 227 ☎ 66/65–20–15), 4 km (2½ mi) southwest of Odense, has three 9-hole courses, one of which is entirely composed of challenging par-3s. The **Odense Golf Klub** (⊠ Hestehaven 200 ☎ 65/95–90–00), 6 km (4 mi) southeast of Odense, has 27 holes on relatively flat ground with some woods. **Blommenlyst** (⊠ Vejruplundvej 20 Blommenlyst ☎ 65/96–71–20) is a pleasant 9-hole course with a driving range and putting greens, 12 km (7 mi) west of Odense.

Shopping

Odense's compact city center is bustling with clothing, furniture, and shoe stores, and a Magasin department store. The main shopping strips are Vestergade and Kongensgade. Rosengårdcentret, one of Northern Europe's largest malls, is 5 km (3 mi) west of Odense. It has more than 125 shops and food outlets, including trendy clothing stores; jewelry, woodwork, and antique shops; a multiplex cinema; and a post office.

Denmark is well known for its paper mobiles and cutouts, inspired, in part, by Hans Christian Andersen. Using a small pair of scissors and white paper, he would create cutouts to illustrate his fairy tales. Today, replicas of Andersen's cutouts are sold at several Odense gift stores. Also popular are mobiles, often depicting Andersen-inspired themes, like swans and mermaids. Uniquely Danish—and light on the suitcase—they make great gifts to take home.

Jam-packed with mobiles, cutouts, and Danish flags and dolls, **Klods Hans** (⊠ Hans Jensens Str. 34 ☎ 66/11–09–40) opened just after World War II to cater to all the American soldiers on leave who wanted to bring back Danish gifts. For fine replicas of Scandinavian Viking jewelry, head to **Museums Kopi Smykker** (⊠ Klareg. 3 ☎ 66/12–06–96). Each piece, in either sterling silver or gold, comes with a printed leaflet explaining its Viking origins. Among the offerings are silver bracelets of various weights, once used by the Vikings as currency; pendants of the Nordic god "Odin," Odense's namesake; and a Viking "key to Valhalla." A modest selection of antiques is for sale at **Hønnerup Hovgård** (⊠ Hovgårdsvej 6, Hønnerup ☎ 64/49–13–00); take Exit 55 to Route 161 toward Middelfart; follow the signs to Hønnerup.

Assens

⑤ *30 km (21 mi) southwest of Odense.*

★ Near the quiet town of Assens is one of the most extraordinary private gardens in Denmark: Tove Sylvest's sprawling **De 7 Haver** (The Seven Gardens). A privately owned botanical United Nations, the gardens represent the flora of seven European countries, including many plants rare to Denmark. ⊠ Å Strandvej 33, Ebberup ☎ 64/74–12–85 ⊕ www.visit-vestfyn.dk ⌘ Dkr 45 ☉ Apr.–Oct., daily 10–6.

On the same street as Seven Gardens is the **Hviids Have,** a 1-acre Japanese garden complete with elegant ponds traversed by rough-plank walkways, as well as stone settings and modest amounts of greenery. ⊠ Å Strandvej 33, Ebberup ☎ 64/74–11–02 ⊕ www.visit-vestfyn.dk ⌘ Dkr 30 ☉ May–Oct., daily 10–6.

> **off the beaten path**
>
> **TERRARIET –** Children may appreciate this detour 18 km (11 mi) northeast to Fyn's Terrarium, where they can examine all kinds of slippery and slithery creatures, including snakes, iguanas, alligators, and the nearly extinct blue frog. ⊠ Kirkehelle 5, Vissenbjerg ☎ 64/47–18–50 ⊕ www.reptil-zoo.dk ⌘ Dkr 50 ☉ May–Aug., daily 10–6; Sept.–Apr., daily 10–4.

Faaborg

⑥ *30 km (18 mi) south of Odense (via Rte. 43).*

The beaches surrounding this lovely 13th-century town are invaded by sun-seeking Germans and Danes in summer. Four times a day you can hear the dulcet chiming of a carillon, the island's largest. In the town center is the controversial *Ymerbrønden* sculpture by Kai Nielsen, depicting a naked man drinking from an emaciated cow's udder while it licks a baby.

The 1725 **Den Gamle Gaard** (Old Merchant's House) chronicles the local history of Faaborg through furnished interiors and exhibits of glass and textiles. ⊠ *Holkeg. 1* ☎ *62/61–33–38* ⊕ *www.fkm.nu* ☎ *Dkr 30* ☉ *Mid-May–Aug., daily 10:30–4:30; Apr.–mid-May, Sept., and Oct., weekends 11–3.*

The **Faaborg Museum for Fynsk Malerkunst** (Fyn Painting Museum) has a good collection of turn-of-the-20th-century paintings and sculpture by the Fyn Painters, a school of artists whose work captures the dusky light of the Scandinavian sun. ⊠ *Grønneg. 75* ☎ *62/61–06–45* ⊕ *www. faaborgmuseum.dk* ☎ *Dkr 35* ☉ *Apr.–Oct., daily 10–4; Nov.–Mar., Tues.–Sun. 11–3.*

Where to Stay & Eat

$–$$$ ✕ **Vester Skerninge Kro.** Midway between Faaborg and Svendborg, this traditional inn is cluttered and comfortable. Pine tables are polished from years of serving hot stews and homemade *medister pølse* (mild grilled sausage) and æggekage. ⊠ *Krovej 9, Vester Skerninge* ☎ *62/24–10–04* ⊟ *AE, MC, V* ☉ *Closed Tues., Oct.–Mar.*

$$$$ ✕▦ **Falsled Kro.** Once a smuggler's hideaway, the 500-year-old Falsled
FodorsChoice Kro is one of Denmark's most elegant inns. A favorite among well-heeled
★ Europeans, it has appointed its cottages sumptuously with European antiques and stone fireplaces. The restaurant combines French and Danish cuisines, using ingredients from markets in Lyon and its own garden. ⊠ *Assensvej 513, DK–5642 Millinge, 13 km (8 mi) northwest of Faaborg on Millinge-Assens Hwy.* ☎ *62/68–11–11* 🖷 *62/68–11–62* ⊕ *www.falsledkro.dk* ⇗ *19 rooms, 8 suites* ⌂ *Restaurant, cafeteria, bar, some pets allowed* ⊟ *AE, DC, MC, V.*

$$–$$$$ ✕▦ **Steensgård Herregårdspension.** A long avenue of beeches leads to this 700-year-old moated manor house, 7 km (4½ mi) northwest of Faaborg. The rooms are elegant, with antiques, four-poster beds, and yards of silk damask. The fine restaurant serves Danish classics crafted from the wild game from the manor's own reserve. ⊠ *Steensgård 4, DK–5642 Millinge* ☎ *62/61–94–90* 🖷 *62/61–78–61* ⊕ *www. herregaardspension.dk* ⇗ *15 rooms, 13 with bath* ⌂ *Restaurant, tennis court, horseback riding* ⊟ *AE, DC, MC, V* ☉ *Closed Feb.*

¢–$ ✕▦ **Hotel Faaborg.** Rising over Faaborg's rustic main square, this small hotel is housed in a brick town house. The rooms are basic and simply furnished. The corner rooms overlook the central square. The Danish menu at the spacious restaurant includes baked cod smothered in a tomato ratatouille sauce with oregano, shallots, garlic, and anchovies. Veal is topped with honey-fried apple slices and served with seasonal vegetables. On weekdays, it serves a decently priced lunch buffet, which includes herring, smoked salmon in a mustard sauce, and chicken salad. ⊠ *Torvet 13–15, DK–5600 Faaborg* ☎ *62/61–02–45* 🖷 *62/61–08–45* ⊕ *www.hotelfaaborg.dk* ⇗ *10 rooms with bath* ⌂ *Restaurant, bar* ⊟ *AE, DC, MC, V.*

★ $ ▦ **Hotel Færgegaarden.** For well over 150 years this spot has been a favorite of budget-conscious tourists and traveling artists with its traditional, dusty yellow and red facade. Newly refurbished, Færgegaarden offers elegantly modern rooms right on the medieval-era harbor front. ⊠ *Christian IXs Vej 31, DK–5600 Faaborg* ☎ *62/61–11–15* 🖷 *62/ 61–11–95* ⊕ *www.hotelfg.dk* ⇗ *24 rooms with bath* ⌂ *Restaurant, some pets allowed* ⊟ *AE, DC, MC, V.*

Nightlife & the Arts

Near the waterfront is **Bar Heimdal** (⊠ Havneg. 12 ☎ No phone), where Faaborg's fishermen crowd into booths and knock back cold ones after hauling in their nets. An inexpensive menu of simple Danish fare includes fillet of sole with tartar sauce and smoked ham with asparagus. In summer, the sunny outdoor terrace draws a mixed crowd of tourists and locals. Just off Faaborg's main square is the homey **Oasen Bodega** (✉ Strandg. 2 ☎ 62/61–13–15), frequented by regulars who enjoy lingering while imbibing in the local brew. Most of the local residents sit by the wooden bar, and this can be a good place to strike up a conversation. **Tre Kroner** (✉ Strandg. 1 ☎ 62/61–01–50) is a traditional watering hole with varied clientele and the enchantment of an inn from the turn of the 20th century. Perhaps Faaborg's most *hyggelig* hangout is the historic **Schankstube** (tap house; ✉ Havneg. 12, ☎ 62/61–11–15), inside the harborside Hotel Færgegaarden. Housed in a former beer tap house, this small bar has worn wooden tables, yellow walls hung with richly colored paintings by Faaborg artists, and small windows with views of the harbor. The menu is traditional—*smørrebrød* and beer.

off the beaten path

LYØ, AVERNAKØ, AND BØRNØ – A string of verdant little islands speckles the sea off Fyn's southern coast. Three of these islands—Lyø, Avernakø, and Bjørnø—are easily accessible by ferry from Faaborg. Lyø, just 4 km (2½ mi) long, has a year-round population of 150 residents and a tangle of hiking and biking trails that lure Fyn families in summer. In the center of the island sits Lyø village, a rustic assortment of half-timber houses and a church with a unique circular churchyard. Eight-km-long (5-mi-long) Avernakø is the hilliest and largest of the three islands, with several farmhouses, a pleasant little village, and a few meandering hiking trails. Bjørnø, 3 km (1½ mi) south of Faaborg, is the smallest island, both in population and size. What it lacks in human residents, however, it makes up with avian. A rich birdlife draws binocular-toting bird-watchers, particularly during the summer breeding season. If you wish to stay overnight on the islands, contact the Faaborg tourist office for information on local families who offer accommodation. The **Avernakø–Lyø ferry** (☎ 62/61–23–07 ⊕ www.oe-faergen.dk) travels five to seven times daily in summer from the Faaborg harbor. Travel time is about 30 minutes to Avernakø, and then another 30 minutes to Lyø, though the ferry sometimes arrives at Lyø first. The round-trip cost is about Dkr 85. The **Bjørnø ferry** (☎ 20/29–80–50) departs from Faaborg three to five times daily; the trip takes 20 minutes, and costs about Dkr 45.

Svendborg

❼ *25 km (15 mi) east of Faaborg (via Rte. 44 east), 44 km (28 mi) south of Odense.*

Svendborg is Fyn's second-largest town, and one of the country's most important cruise harbors. It celebrates its eight-centuries-old maritime traditions every July, when old Danish wooden ships congregate in the harbor for the circular Fyn *rundt,* or regatta. Play your cards right, and you might hitch aboard and shuttle between towns. Contact the tourist board or any agreeable captain. With many charter-boat options and good marinas, Svendborg is an excellent base from which to explore the hundreds of islands of the South Fyn archipelago.

On Fruestræde near the market square at the center of town is the black-and-yellow **Anne Hvides Gård,** the oldest secular structure in Svendborg and one of the four branches of Svendborgs Omegns Museum (Svendborg County Museum). This evocative exhibit includes 18th- and 19th-century interiors and glass and silver collections. ✉ *Fruestr. 3* ☎ *62/21–76–45* ⊕ *www.svendborgmuseum.dk* ✄ *Dkr 25* ⊙ *Mid-June–Sept., Tues.–Sun. 10–5; Oct.–Dec., Wed.–Sun. 10–4.*

Bagergade (Baker's Street) is lined with some of Svendborg's oldest half-timber houses. At the corner of Grubbemøllevej and Svinget is the **Viebæltegård,** the headquarters of the Svendborg County Museum and a former poorhouse. You can wander through dining halls, washrooms, and the "tipsy clink," where, until 1974, inebriated citizens were left to sober up. ⊠ *Grubbemøllevej 13* ☎ *62/21–02–61* ⊕ *www.svendborgmuseum.dk* ⊡ *Dkr 40* ☉ *June–Sept., Tues.–Sun. 10–5; Oct.–May, Tues.–Sun. 10–4.*

Changing contemporary-art exhibits are showcased at the two-story **SAK Kunstbygningen** (SAK Art Exhibitions), a skylit gallery-museum just to the west of the city center. The museum's highlight is the small collection of sculptures by Svendborg native Kai Nielsen. One of Denmark's most popular sculptors, Nielsen is best known for his sensual figures of women in languid repose and chubby angelic babies playing together. Nielsen's sculptures are displayed in a sun-drenched octagonal gallery with views over a leafy garden. His works are exhibited all over Denmark, most famously in Copenhagen's Ny Carlsberg Glyptotek. Here, his "Water Mother" fountain sculpture depicts a voluptuous woman reclining atop a lily pond, while a half-dozen plump, adorable babies crawl out of the water and over her curves, suckling at her breasts and dozing between her thighs. ⊠ *Vesterg. 27–31* ☎ *62/22–44–70* ⊡ *Dkr 25* ☉ *Tues.–Sun. 11–4.*

need a break? In the heart of Svendborg, tucked behind the main street of Brogade, is a small, cobblestone courtyard surrounded by red half-timber houses. Dating from 1650, this charming square used to house Svendborg's general store. **Vintapperiet** (⊠ Brog. 37 ☎ 62/22–34–48), a snug, low-ceiling wine bar and shop, now occupies the square, and here you can taste your way—by the glass or by the bottle—through a range of top-notch French and Italian wines. Wine barrels line the entranceway; the small dining room, with less than a half dozen tables, overlooks the courtyard. They serve a light menu to complement the wines, including pâté and pungent cheese with hunks of bread, and olives. It is open for lunch only, and closed on Sunday; in winter it's also closed on Monday.

Where to Stay & Eat

$$$ ✕ **Svendborgsund.** In a harborside building dating from 1682, this warm, maritime-theme restaurant serves traditional Danish cuisine, including pork tenderloin heaped with grilled onions and mushrooms and served with potatoes and pickled cucumbers. The extensive smørrebrød lunch menu includes marinated herring topped with egg yolk and fried fillet of plaice with shrimp, caviar, and asparagus. The summertime terrace is an inviting spot to soak up sun, beer, and the waterfront views. ⊠ *Havnepl. 5* ☎ *62/21–07–19* ⊟ *AE, DC, MC, V* ☉ *Closed Sun. Oct.–Mar.*

¢–$$ ✕ **Hotel Ærø.** A hodgepodge of ship parts and nautical doodads, this dimly lighted restaurant and inn looks like it's always been here. Brusque waitresses take orders from serious local trenchermen. The menu is staunchly old-fashioned, featuring *frikadeller* (fried meatballs), fried *rødspætte* (plaice) with hollandaise sauce, and dozens of smørrebrød options. ⊠ *Brog. 1, Ærøfærgen, at the Ærø ferry, DK–5700* ☎ *62/21–07–60* 🖨 *62/21–06–78* ⊕ *www.hotel-aeroe.dk* ⊟ *DC, MC, V.*

★ **$** 🏨 **Missionshotellet Stella Marris.** Southwest of Svendborg, this lovely seaside villa dates from 1904. An old-fashioned English-style drawing room, complete with piano, stuffed chairs, and an elegant chandelier, overlooks the villa's spacious gardens; follow a path through the greenery and you can dive right off the private pier into the sea. Each of the rooms has its own color scheme; one room has flowery wallpaper and white lace curtains, while another has a simple tan-and-rose decor. Bathrooms are basic and include a shower only. The hotel is part of Missionhotel, a Christian hotel chain in operation since the early 1900s. The Stella Marris is one of the few Missionhotels that still maintains an alcohol- and smoke-free environment. ⊠ *Kogtvedvænget 3, DK–5700* ☎ *62/21–38–91* ᕦ *62/21–41–74* ⊕ *www.stellamaris.dk* ⟿ *25 rooms, 19 with bath* ⚲ *Dining room* ⊟ *AE, DC, MC, V.*

Nightlife & the Arts

BARS & LOUNGES A diverse crowd congregates at **Banjen** (⊠ Klosterpl. 7 ☎ 62/21–35–40) to hear live rock and blues. The popular blues shows, usually Friday and Saturday nights, attract all ages. Adjoining the bar is La Tumba nightclub, which throbs with dance music on the weekends. The beer flows freely at the cavernous pub **Børsen** (⊠ Gerritsg. 31 ☎ 62/22–41–41), in a building dating from 1620. A young rowdy crowd of tourists and locals packs the place nightly. If this isn't your scene, skip the evening and stop by in the quieter early afternoon instead, when you can better enjoy your beer amid the old-style pub atmosphere.

Chess (⊠ Vesterg. 7 ☎ 62/22–17–16) is popular with a young crowd that comes for the live bands. **Crazy Daisy** (⊠ Frederiksg. 6 ☎ 62/21–67–60) attracts a casual, over-21 crowd that dances to oldies and rock on Saturday night; a younger crowd pours in on Friday. The restaurant **Oranje** (⊠ Jessens Mole [Jessens Pier] ☎ 62/22–82–92), an old sailing ship moored in the harbor, sometimes has live jazz in summer. Tucked back from the street, **Barbella Nightclub** (⊠ Vesterg. 10A ☎ 62/22–47–83) is a dimly lit bar with dark-rose walls and long wooden tables. A casual vibe and friendly staff draws a mixed-age crowd that mingles over cocktails, cheap bar grub (open-face sandwiches and meatballs), and live music in the evenings—jazz on Thursday; rock, pop, or classical on Friday and Saturday nights. On the first Sunday of the month, the club has live jazz starting at around noon. (It's closed the other Sundays of the month.)

CAFÉS In the heart of town is the spacious **Under Uret Café** (⊠ Gerritsg. 50 ☎ 62/21–83–08), playfully decorated with oversize watches on the wall—"Under Uret" means "under watch." For prime people-watching, settle in at one of the outdoor tables. The café menu includes brunch, club sandwiches, burritos, and a range of salads, from Greek to Caesar. Come nightfall, there's live music ranging from soul to rock.

Shopping

Svendborg's **city center** is bustling with shops, particularly on Gerritsgade and Møllergade, which are peppered with clothing stores, gift shops, and jewelers. For colorful, hand-blown glassworks head to **Glas Blæseriet** (⊠ Brog. 37A ☎ 62/22–83–73), which shares a half-timber courtyard in the center of town with the wine restaurant Vintapperiet. Glassblower Bente Sonne's lovely nature-inspired creations—in pale greens, oranges, and blues—are decorated with seashells, starfish, lizards, fish, and lobsters. You can watch Sonne blowing glass weekdays 10–3:30. On Saturday the shop is open 10–3:30 with no glassblowing demonstration.

Kværndrup

❽ *15 km (9 mi) north of Svendborg, 28 km (18 mi) south of Odense.*

Fodor'sChoice The moated Renaissance **Egeskov Slot,** one of the best-preserved island-
★ castles in Europe, presides over this town. Peaked with copper spires

and surrounded by Renaissance, baroque, English, and peasant gardens, the castle is still a private home, though visitors can see a few of the rooms, including the great hall, the hunting room, and the Riborg Room, where the daughter of the house was locked up from 1599 to 1604 after giving birth to a son out of wedlock. The castle also has an antique vehicle museum. ⊠ *Kværndrup, 15 km (9 mi) north of Svendborg* ☎ *62/27–10–16* ⊕ *www.egeskov.com* ✆ *Castle and museum Dkr 135* ☉ *Castle May, June, Aug., and Sept., daily 10–5; July, daily 10–7; Museum June and Aug., daily 10–6; July, daily 10–8, Wed. open until 11 PM; May and Sept., daily 10–5.*

Tåsinge

❾ *3 km (2 mi) south of Svendborg (via the Svendborg Sound Bridge), 43 km (27 mi) south of Odense.*

Tåsinge Island is known for its local 19th-century drama involving Elvira Madigan and her married Swedish lover, Sixten Sparre. The drama is featured in the 1967 Swedish film *Elvira Madigan*. Preferring heavenly union to earthly separation, they shot themselves and are now buried in the island's central Landet churchyard. Brides throw their bouquets on the lovers' grave.

Fodor'sChoice
★

Troense is Tåsinge's main town, and one of the country's best-preserved maritime villages, with half-timber buildings and their hand-carved doors. South of town is **Valdemars Slot** (Valdemars Castle), dating from 1610, one of Denmark's oldest privately owned castles. You can wander through almost all of the sumptuously furnished rooms, libraries, and the candlelit church. There's also an X-rated 19th-century cigar box not to be missed. A yachting museum, with gleamingly restored yachts and skiffs, along with ship models and historical dioramas, explores Denmark's extensive yachting history. ⊠ *Slotsalleen 100, Troense* ☎ *62/22–61–06* ⊕ *www.valdemarsslot.dk* ✆ *DKr 55* ☉ *May–Aug., daily 10–5; Sept., Tues.–Sun. 10–5; Apr. and Oct., weekends 10–5. Call to confirm opening hours.*

Where to Stay & Eat

$$$$ ✕ **Lodskroen.** This whitewashed, thatch-roof restaurant opened its doors in 1774 to serve as an inn for passing sailors. For the past 30 years, it has been run by the husband-and-wife team of Hans and Kirsten Dahlgaard, who treat diners as if they were guests in their own home. In fact, diners are asked to not order more than two main dishes per table because, as a placard explains, "the cook, who is also the hostess, is always alone by the kitchen range and the food is never pre-prepared." The French-inspired Danish menu includes fillet of plaice stuffed with mushrooms, peppers, and herbs. For dessert, try the figs pickled in a sweet sherry and served with whipped cream. A surcharge is applied to credit cards. ⊠ *Troense Strandvej 80, Troense* ☎ *62/22–50–44* 🗏 *MC, V* ☉ *Closed Mon.–Thurs. Feb., Nov., and Dec.; closed Jan. No lunch weekdays.*

¢–$$ ✕ **Bregninge Mølle.** If you've ever wondered what the inside of a windmill looks like, this is your chance to find out. Within the Bregninge windmill, built in 1805, circular stairs lead to this restaurant's three levels, each with 360-degree views of the surrounding sea and Tåsinge countryside. On a clear day, you can see the southern tip of Jylland and the islands of Langeland and Thurø. The traditional Danish menu features *frikadeller* (fried meatballs) served with rice and peas, and æggekage. ⊠ *Kirkebakken 19, Bregninge* ☎ *62/22–52–55* 🗏 *MC, V* ☉ *Closed mid-Oct.–Mar.*

Fodor'sChoice
★

$ ✕⊡ **Hotel Troense.** Dating from 1908, this harborside hotel has bright, simply furnished rooms with fringed white bedcovers. One-third of the rooms look toward the harbor. The restaurant, with rose walls and a fireplace, serves a Danish menu with such dishes as salmon served with spinach topped with almonds. It also offers a couple of vegetarian dishes, including a pie stuffed with seasonal vegetables. The smørrebrød lunch menu includes open-face sandwiches of herring, salmon, eggs, liver pâté, or shrimp. The hotel often has discounted weekend deals that include breakfast and dinner. ⊠ *Strandg. 5, DK–5700 Troense* ☎ *62/ 22–54–12* 🖷 *62/22–78–12* ⊕ *www.hoteltroense.dk* ⊲⊃ *30 rooms with bath* ⌂ *Restaurant, bar* ⊟ *AE, DC, MC, V.*

$ ✕⊡ **Valdemars Slot.** The castle's guest rooms are not enormous, but they are nicely decorated in beige, ochre, light-green, and light-blue tones. Some have a view out to the north; others look out onto the adjacent yard and palace garden. Down below, a domed restaurant is ankle-deep in pink carpet and aglow with candlelight. Fresh French and German ingredients and wild game from the castle's reserve are the menu staples. Venison with cream sauce and duck breast *à l'orange* are typical of the French-inspired cuisine. A second eatery, Æblehaven, serves inexpensive sausages and upscale fast-food. ⊠ *Slotsalleen 100, DK–5700 Troense* ☎ *62/22–59–00* 🖷 *62/22–72–67* ⊕ *www.valdemarsslot.dk* ⊲⊃ *8 rooms, 1 suite* ⌂ *2 restaurants* ⊟ *MC, V.*

¢ ⊡ **Det Lille Hotel.** This red half-timber, thatch-roof family house–turned–small hotel has eight snug rooms (none with bath or shower) with pale green walls and flowery curtains. The well-tended back garden blooms brilliantly in summer. A breakfast of homemade bread and jam is included. You can rent a bike for around Dkr 50 per day. ⊠ *Badstuen 15, DK–5700 Troense* ☎ *62/22–53–41* 🖷 *62/22–25–41* ⊕ *www.detlillehotel.dk* ⊲⊃ *8 rooms, 3 with bath* ⌂ *Dining room* ⊟ *MC, V* ☉ *Closed Nov.–Mar.*

Shopping

For delicate hand-blown glass, visit **Glasmagerne** (⊠ Vemmenæsvej 10, Tåsinge ☎ 62/54–14–94).

Langeland

❿ *16 km (10 mi) southeast of Troense, 64 km (40 mi) southwest of Odense.*

Reached by a causeway bridge from Tåsinge, Langeland is the largest island of the southern archipelago, rich in relics, with smooth, tawny beaches. Bird-watching is excellent on the southern half of the island, where migratory flocks roost before setting off on their cross-Baltic journey. To the south are Ristinge and Bagenkop, two towns with good beaches; at Bagenkop you can catch the ferry to Kiel, Germany.

Sports & the Outdoors

FISHING   Langeland has particularly rich waters for fishing, with cod, salmon, flounder, and gar. For package tours, boat rentals, or fishing equipment, contact **Ole Dehn** (⊠ Sønderg. 22, Tranekær ☎ 62/55–17–00).

Ærøskøbing

★ **⓫** *30 km (19 mi) south of Svendborg, 74 km (46 mi) south of Odense, plus a one-hour ferry ride, either from Svendborg or Langeland.*

The island of Ærø, where country roads wind through fertile fields, is aptly called the Jewel of the Archipelago. About 27 km (16 mi) southeast of Søby on the island's north coast, the storybook town of Ærøskøbing is the port for ferries from Svendborg. Established as a market town in the 13th century, it did not flourish until it became a sailing center during the 1700s. Today, Ærøskøbing is a bewitching tangle of cobbled streets lined with immaculately preserved half-timber houses. Stop by the red 17th-century home at the corner of Vestergade and Smedegade, considered to be one of the town's finest examples of its provincial architecture. Ærøskøbing is a bastion of small-town Denmark: every morning, the whistling postman, in a red jacket and black-and-gold cap, strides the streets and delivers the mail; the friendly mayor pedals home for lunch and waves to everyone on the way.

As you wander through town, you'll notice that many of the homes display a pair of ceramic dogs on their windowsills. Traditionally, these were used by sailors' wives to signal to outsiders—and, as rumor has it, potential suitors—the whereabouts of their husbands. When the dogs were facing in, it meant that the man of the house was home, and when the dogs were facing out, that he was gone. Ironically, these ceramic dogs were brought home, usually from the Orient, by the sailors themselves, who had received them as "gifts" from prostitutes they had been with. The prostitutes gave these ceramic dogs as a cover-up, so that it appeared that they were selling souvenirs rather than sex.

Ferries provide the only access to Ærø. The ferry from Svendborg to Ærøskøbing takes 1 hour, 15 minutes. In addition, there's a one-hour ferry from Faaborg to Søby, a town on the northwest end of the island; and a shorter one from Rudkøbing—on the island of Langeland—to Marstal, on the eastern end of Ærø.

History is recorded in miniature at the **Flaskeskibssamlingen** (Bottle-Ship Collection), thanks to a former ship's cook known as Peter Bottle, who painstakingly built nearly 2,000 bottle ships in his day. The combination of his life's work and the enthusiastic letters he received from fans and disciples around the world makes for a surprisingly moving collection. ⊠ *Smedeg. 22, Ærøskøbing* ☎ *62/52–29–51* 🎫 *Dkr 30* ☻ *May–Oct., daily 10–4; Nov.–Apr., Tues.–Fri. 1–3, weekends 10–2.*

Ærø Museum houses numerous relics—including some from the Stone Age—culled from archaeological digs on the island. Also displayed are antique domestic furnishings from the homes of skippers on the island. Call ahead or check at the tourist office, because nonsummer hours can vary. ⊠ *Brog. 3–5, Ærøskøbing* ☎ *62/52–29–50* 🎫 *Dkr 20* ☻ *May–mid-Oct., weekdays 10–4, weekends 11–3; mid-Oct.–Apr., weekdays 10–3.*

The two-story half-timber **Hammerichs Hus** (Hammerich's House) was once the home of sculptor Gunnar Hammerich. Today it features reconstructed period interiors of ancient Ærø homes, including antique maritime paintings, furniture, and porcelain pieces. ⊠ *Gyden 22, Ærøskøbing* ☎ *65/52–29–50* 🎫 *Dkr 20* ☻ *Mid-June–mid-Sept., weekdays noon–4.*

Where to Stay & Eat

★ ¢-$$ ✕ **Hos Grethe.** In the heart of town is this amiable restaurant, run by long-time local Grethe. The dining room, with low white ceilings and a black-and-white checkered floor, is nicknamed the *kongelogen* (the royal box) because of the royal portraits, past and present, that line the walls. Grethe is famous for her steaks, thick-cut and juicy, which come with large salads. In summer, the outside terrace and beer garden overflow with day-trippers from the mainland. ⊠ *Vesterg. 39* ☎ *62/52–21–43* 🖃 *MC, V* ☻ *Closed Oct.–May. No lunch Apr.–mid-June and mid-Aug.–Sept.*

¢-$ ✕🏠 **Det Lille Hotel.** Six large, simply furnished rooms make up the second floor of this friendly *lille* (little) hotel. Flowery curtains frame small windows that overlook the garden below. Dating from 1865, the building once housed the offices of Ærø's farmer's journal. It later became a boarding house. On the bottom floor are a popular restaurant and bar, both of which draw a daily crowd of regulars (reservations are essential for the restaurant). Paintings of ships and schooners hang on the walls, and a collection of old porcelain coffee- and teapots lines the shelves. A brick-floor terrace opens up in summer, and from here you can catch glimpses of the sea through the trees. The Danish menu includes fried plaice topped with butter sauce and pork fillet with tomatoes, mushrooms, and a white-wine cream sauce. The snug bar is decorated with a ship wheel and lanterns. ⊠ *Smedeg. 33, DK–5970* 🕿🕿 *62/52–23–00* 🔊 *6 rooms without bath* ⛁ *Restaurant* ⊟ *MC, V.*

$$$ ⊡ **Ærøhus Marina.** A half-timber building with a steep red roof, the Ærøhus looks like a rustic cottage on the outside and an old, but overly renovated, aunt's house on the inside. Hanging pots and slanted walls characterize the public areas, and pine furniture and cheerful duvets keep the guest rooms simple and bright. The garden's five cottages have small terraces. ⊠ *Vesterg. 38, DK–5970* 🕿 *62/52–10–03* 🖷 *62/52–21–23* ⊕ *www.aeroehus-hotel.dk* 🔊 *67 rooms, 56 with bath* ⛁ *Restaurant, bar, some pets allowed* ⊟ *V.*

¢ ⊡ **Pension Vestergade 44.** Rising over Ærøskøbing's main street are two superbly maintained patrician homes. Standing side by side, they are mirror images of each other, built by two ship captains, brothers, who wanted to raise their families in identical surroundings. One of the homes has been converted into this small hotel that has been lovingly restored by its owners, a friendly British-German couple, to recapture all of the building's former charms. A clawfoot iron stove heats up the breakfast room that overlooks a sprawling back garden with clucking chickens who lay the eggs for breakfast. White lace curtains frame the windows and an antique wooden plate rack displays blue-and-white English porcelain dishes. The beautifully appointed rooms, each with their own color scheme, have naturally sloping floors and vintage wooden towel racks laden with fluffy, bright-white towels. If you want to pedal around town, they'll lend you a bike. ⊠ *Vesterg. 44, DK 5970* 🕿 *62/52–22–98* 🔊 *6 rooms without bath* ⛁ *Dining room.*

Nightlife & the Arts

Of Ærøskøbing's few bars, one of the most popular is **Arrebo** (⊠ Vesterg. 4 🕿 62/52–28–50), with yellow walls, wooden tables, and local art on the walls. On the weekends, it hosts live music, from blues to rock to jazz. A bell dangles at one end of the bar, and in the sailor tradition, whoever rings it must buy the whole bar a round of drinks.

Shopping

Ærøskøbing is sprinkled with a handful of craft and gift shops. Unfortunately, there are virtually no more bottle-ship makers on the island. Instead, the labor-intensive curiosities are made in Asia and modeled on original ærø bottle-ship designs. For souvenir bottle-ships, head to **Kolorit** (⊠ Torvet 1A 🕿 62/52–25–23), a small gift shop crammed with Danish mementos.

Marstal

★ ⓬   *10 km (6 mi) southeast of Ærøskøbing, 40 km (25 mi) south of Svendborg, 84 km (52 mi) south of Odense. From Svendborg, it's a one-hour ferry ride to Ærøskøbing; from Langeland it's a 45-min ferry ride to Marstal.*

Southeast of Ærøskøbing, past a lush landscape of green and yellow hills rolling toward the sea, is the sprightly shipping town of Marstal. From its early fishing days in the 1500s to its impressive rise into a formidable shipping port in the 1700s, Marstal's lifeblood has always been the surrounding sea. At its seafaring height, in the late 1800s, Marstal had a fleet of 300 ships. During this heady time, the Marstal government couldn't expand the harbor fast enough to accommodate the growing fleet, so Marstal's seamen took it upon themselves to extend their port. Working together in the winter season, they built the 1-km (½-mi) stone pier—still in use today—by rolling rocks from the fields, along the ice, and onto the harbor. They began in 1835 and completed the pier in 1841.

Today, Marstal is home port to 50 vessels, from tall-masted schooners to massive trawlers. Much of the town's activity—and its cobbled streets—radiates from the bustling port. A nautical school, first established in the 1800s, is still going strong, with more than 150 students. In a nod to its seafaring heritage, the Marstal harbor is one of the few places in the world still constructing wooden ships.

Marstal's winding streets are dotted with well-preserved skipper's homes. **Maren Minors Hjem** (Maren Minor's Home) was once the genteel abode of successful Marstal seaman Rasmus Minor, who eventually settled in the United States. The house has been carefully restored inside and out to look just as it did in the 1700s, including vintage art and furniture. Opening hours vary from year to year, so check with the tourist office. ⊠ *Teglg. 9* ☎ *62/53–24–25* ⊠ *Free* ⊙ *June–Aug., Tues.–Sun. 11–3.*

Spread out over three buildings, the sprawling **Marstal Søfartsmuseum** (Marstal Maritime Museum) offers a rich and fascinating account of Marstal's formidable shipping days. Thirty-five showrooms are jam-packed with maritime memorabilia, including more than 200 ship models, 100 bottle-ships, navigation instruments, and a collection of maritime paintings by artist Carl Rasmussen. He was born in Ærøskøbing and made his name painting Greenland sea- and landscapes. Wandering the museum is like exploring a massive ship: step aboard large-scale decks and hulls and command the gleaming ship wheels like a Marstal captain. Mind your head as you climb up and down the steep ship stairs that connect many of the rooms. "Back on land," you can duck into the low-ceiling parlors of a skipper's house, meticulously reproduced with period furnishings. Long-time museum director and Marstal historian Erik B. Kromann is a font of maritime information, and will enthusiastically take you on a tour of the museum if you ask. The museum shop is bursting with nifty gifts, including key chains made from maritime rope knots. ⊠ *Prinsensg. 1* ☎ *62/53–23–31* ⊕ *www.marmus.dk* ⊠ *Dkr 40* ⊙ *July, daily 9–8; June and Aug., daily 9–5; May and Sept., daily 10–4; Oct.–Apr., Tues.–Fri. 10–4, Sat. 11–3.*

Where to Stay & Eat

¢ ✕▦ **Marstal.** Mere paces from the waterfront is this homey locals' favorite, with wooden ceilings, dim lighting, and a ship's wheel on the wall. The homestyle Danish dishes include minced steak with peas, potatoes, and béarnaise sauce, and smoked salmon served with asparagus and scrambled eggs. Another favorite is mussels-and-bacon on toast. The cozy bar draws a friendly pre- and post-dinner crowd of dockworkers. Above the restaurant are eight very basic rooms, none with bath, and two with partial views of the harbor. ⊠ *Dronningestr. 1A, DK–5960* ☎ *62/53–13–52* ⊷ *8 rooms without bath* ⌂ *Restaurant, bar* ▤ *MC, V* ⊙ *Closed Sept.–May.*

$ ▦ **Ærø Strand.** On the outskirts of Marstal lies this holiday hotel that caters to the island's summer tourists. Blond-wood and dark-blue tones adorn the comfortable rooms. In the center of the hotel is a heart-shape pool and, for the after-hours crowd, a popular nightclub disco. ⊠ *Ege-*

hovedvej 4, DK–5960 ☎ *62/53–33–20* 🖷 *62/53–31–50* ⊕ *www.hotel-aeroestrand.dk* ➮ *100 rooms with bath, 20 suites* ⌂ *Restaurant, tennis court, indoor pool, gym, sauna, nightclub* ▤ *AE, DC, MC, V.*

Nightlife & the Arts

Marstal's night scene is sedate, but when locals want a beer they head to the informal **Café Victor** (⊠ Kirkestr. 15 ☎ 62/53–28–01), with its yellow walls and a brass-lined bar. Here you can also tuck into simple Danish dishes, such as fillet of sole with french fries.

Shopping

The maritime paintings of Marstal artist Rita Lund are popular throughout the island, gracing the walls of several restaurants and decorating the sunny sitting rooms of the ferries that shuttle between Svendborg and Ærø. For a further look, visit Rita Lund's **Galleri Humlehave** (⊠ Skoleg. 1 ☎ 62/53–21–73) which, appropriately enough, is near the Marstal harbor. Her extensive collection includes paintings of crashing waves, ships at sea, and Ærø during the four seasons.

Fyn & the Central Islands A to Z

BIKE TRAVEL

With their level terrain and short distances, Fyn and the Central Islands are perfect for cycling. A bike trip around the circumference of the main island, stopping at the series of delightful port towns that ring Fyn like a string of pearls, is a wonderful way of spending a few days. The Odense tourist office has a helpful map of cycle routes in and around Odense. You can rent bikes through City Cykler in Odense or at several hotels around the islands. Contact Fyntour for longer cycling tour packages that include bike rental, hotel accommodations, and a half-board (breakfast and one meal) meal plan.

🚲 **City Cykler** ⊠ Vesterbro 27, Odense ☎ 66/13–97–83 ⊕ www.citycykler.dk. **Fyntour** ⊠ Svendborgvej 83–85, DK-5260 Odense ☎ 66/13-13-37 🖷 66/13-13-38 ⊕ www.fyntour.dk.

BUS TRAVEL

Buses are one of the main public-transportation options in the area. Timetables are posted at all bus stops and central stations. Passengers buy tickets on board and pay according to the distance traveled. If you plan on traveling extensively by bus, ask at any bus station about a 24-hour bus pass, which cuts costs considerably. Contact Fynbus for more information about routes between cities. Odense Bytrafik runs the bus system within Odense.

🚌 **Fynbus** ⊠ Odense Bus Station ☎ 63/11-22-33 🖷 63/11-22-99. **Odense Bytrafik** (Odense City Transport) ☎ 65/51-29-29 🖷 66/19-40-27.

CAR TRAVEL

From Copenhagen, take the E20 west to Halsskov, near Korsør, and drive onto the Great Belt bridge, which costs about Dkr 250 per car. You'll arrive near Nyborg, which is 30 minutes from either Odense or Svendborg.

The highways of Fyn are excellent, and small roads meander beautifully on two lanes through the countryside. A trip around the circumference of the island can be done in a day, but stopping for a night or two at one of the enchanting port towns can be fun, and offers the chance to meet some of the locals. Traffic is light, except during the height of summer in highly populated beach areas.

EMERGENCIES

For fire, police, or ambulance anywhere in Denmark, dial 112. Lægevagten is the service for house calls, but will also dispatch an ambulance in case of emergencies. Trained phone personnel are generally able to judge whether a house call would be sufficient. The doctor's visits are made according to a priority list, with serious illnesses and sick children at the top of the list. Falck is the emergency road service, for towing vehicles in trouble or in case of accidents.

🚑 **Lægevagten** (Emergency Doctor) ☎ 65/90-60-10, 4 PM–7 AM. **Falck** ☎ 70/10-20-30 🌐 www.falck.dk. **Odense University Hospital** ✉ Søndre Blvd. 29, Odense ☎ 66/11-33-33. **Ørnen Apoteket** ✉ Vesterg. 80, Odense ☎ 66/12-29-70.

TOURS

Few towns offer organized tours, but check the local tourist offices for step-by-step walking brochures. The Hans Christian Andersen Tours are full-day tours to Odense that depart from Copenhagen's Rådhus Pladsen. (Six of 11 hours are spent in transit.) Call ahead because departure days and times may vary. The two-hour Odense tour departs from the local tourist office. Contact Fyntour or Odense Tourist Office for details about prices and times of tours. Most itineraries include the exteriors of the Hans Christian Andersen sites and the cathedral and the guides are generally more than willing to answer questions about the area or Denmark as a whole. Odense Tourist Office also offers one-hour tours of the Italian Gothic Odense City Hall. Inside is a long memorial wall commemorating famous Fyn citizens. The local calendar of events often presents interesting activities at the city's sites, so it would be wise to call one of the tourist offices to inquire about any events.

🚩 **Fyntour** ✉ Svendborgvej 83–85, Odense ☎ 66/13-13-37 🌐 www.fyntour.dk. **Odense Tourist Office** ✉ Vesterg. 2 Odense ☎ 66/12-75-20 🌐 www.odenseturist.dk.

TRAIN TRAVEL

Direct trains from Copenhagen's main station depart for the 90-minute trip to Odense's train station about hourly from 5 AM to 10:30 PM, every day. The Odense station is central, close to hotels and sites. Large towns in the region are served by intercity trains. The Nyborg–Odense–Middelfart and the Odense–Svendborg routes are among the two most important. You can take the train to Odense direct from Copenhagen Airport.

RESERVATIONS   A reservation, which is required during rush hour, costs an additional Dkr 15.

🚩 **DSB Train Booking and Information** ☎ 70/13-14-15 🌐 www.dsb.dk.

VISITOR INFORMATION

For central Odense, the Odense Eventyrpas (Adventure Pass), available at the tourism office and the train station, affords admission to sites and museums and free city bus and train transport. The cost for a 48-hour pass is Dkr 150; for a 24-hour pass, Dkr 110.

🚩 **Assens Touristbureau** ✉ Damg. 22, DK-5610 Assens ☎ 64/71-20-31 🖨 64/71-49-39 🌐 www.visit-vestfyn.dk. **Egeskov Touristbureau** ✉ Egeskov 1, DK-5772 Kværndrup ☎ 62/27-10-46 🖨 62/27-10-48. **Fyntour** ✉ Svendborgvej 83–85, DK-5260 Odense ☎ 66/13-13-37 🌐 www.fyntour.dk. **Faaborg Touristbureau** ✉ Banegårdspl. 2A, DK-5600 Faaborg ☎ 62/61-07-07 🖨 62/61-33-37 🌐 www.visitfaaborg.dk. **Kerteminde Touristbureau** ✉ Strandg. 1B, DK-5300 Kerteminde ☎ 65/32-11-21 🖨 65/32-18-17 🌐 www.kerteminde-turist.dk. **Langeland Touristforeningen** ✉ Torvet 5, DK-5900 Rundkøbing ☎ 62/51-35-05 🖨 62/51-43-35 🌐 www.langeland.dk. **Marstal Touristbureau** ✉ Havneg. 5, DK-5960 Marstal ☎ 62/52-13-00 🖨 62/53-25-17 🌐 www.arre.dk. **Nyborg Touristbureau** ✉ Torvet 9, DK-5800 Nyborg ☎ 65/31-02-80 🖨 65/31-03-80 🌐 www.nyborgturist.dk. **Odense Touristbureau** ✉ Vesterg. 2, DK-5000 Odense ☎ 66/12-75-20 🖨 66/12-75-86 🌐 www.odenseturist.dk. **Sydfyns Touristbureau**

✉ Centrumpl. 4, DK-5700 Svendborg ☎ 62/21-09-80 🖷 62/22-05-53 ⊕ www. visitsydfyn.dk. **Ærø Touristbureau** ✉ Vesterg. 13, DK-5970 Ærøskøbing ☎ 62/52-13-00 🖷 62/52-14-36 ⊕ www.arre.dk.

JYLLAND

Jylland (Jutland), Denmark's western peninsula, is the only part of the country naturally connected to mainland Europe; its southern boundary is the frontier with Germany. In contrast to the smooth, postcard-perfect land of Fyn and Sjælland, this Ice Age–chiseled peninsula is bisected at the north by the craggy Limfjord and spiked below by the Danish "mountains." Himmelbjerget, the zenith of this modest range, peaks at 438 feet. Farther south, the Yding Skovhøj plateau rises 568 feet—modest hills just about anywhere else.

Hunters first inhabited Denmark, in southern Jylland, some 250,000 years ago. You can see flint tools and artifacts from this period locked away in museums, but the land holds more-stirring relics from a later epoch: after 1,000 years, Viking burial mounds and stones still swell the land, some in protected areas, others lying in farmers' fields, tended by grazing sheep.

The windswept landscapes filmed in *Babette's Feast,* the movie version of the Karen Blixen (Isak Dinesen) novel, trace the west coast northward to Skagen, a luminous, dune-covered point. To the east, facing Fyn, Jylland is cut by deep fjords rimmed with forests. The center is dotted with castles, parklands, and the famed Legoland. Denmark's oldest and youngest towns, Ribe and Esbjerg, lie in southwest Jylland. In Ribe's medieval town center is the country's earliest church; modern Esbjerg, perched on the coast, is the departure point for ferries to nearby Fanø, an island of windswept beaches and traditional villages. Århus and Aalborg, respectively Denmark's second- and fourth-largest cities, face east and have nightlife and sights to rival Copenhagen's.

Nearly three times the size of the rest of Denmark, with long distances between towns, the peninsula of Jylland can easily take at least several days, even weeks, to explore. If you are pressed for time, concentrate on a single tour or a couple of cities. Delightful as they are, the islands are suitable only for those with plenty of time, as many require an overnight stay.

Kolding

❶ *71 km (44 mi) northwest of Odense (via the Little Belt Bridge), 190 km (119 mi) west of Copenhagen.*

Lying in Jylland's heartland, the lively town of Kolding is a pleasing blend of old and new, with a historical center of cobbled streets and brightly painted half-timber houses that give way to industrial suburbs.

The well-preserved **Koldinghus,** a massive stonework structure that was once a fortress, then a royal residence in the Middle Ages, is today a historical museum. In the winter of 1808, during the Napoleonic Wars, Spanish soldiers set fire to most of it while trying to stay warm. ✉ *Rådhusstr.* ☎ *76/33–81–00* ⊕ *www.koldinghus.dk* 🎟 *Dkr 50* ⊗ *Daily 10–5.*

FodorsChoice Just east of town is the **Trapholt Museum for Moderne Kunst** (Trapholt Museum of Modern Art), one of Denmark's largest—and most highly acclaimed—modern-art museums outside Copenhagen. Rising over the banks of the Kolding Fjord, this sprawling white complex has been artfully incorporated into its natural surroundings, affording lovely views

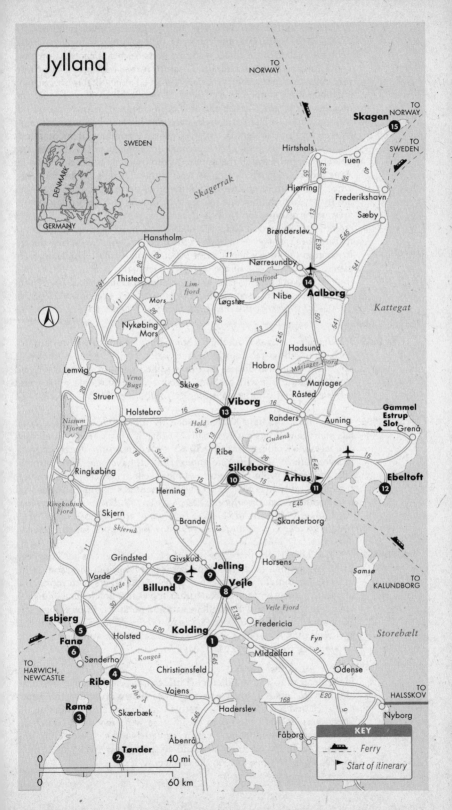

Jylland

SWEDEN
DENMARK
GERMANY

TO NORWAY

Skagerrak

TO NORWAY
TO SWEDEN

Skagen **15**

Hirtshals
Tuen

Hjørring
Frederikshavn

Sæby

Brønderslev

Hanstholm
Nørresundby
Limfjord
Nibe
Aalborg **14**

Thisted
Mors
Limfjord
Løgstør

Nykøbing
Mors
Hadsund
Hobro
Mariager Fjord
Mariager

Lemvig
Skive
Råsted

Struer
Viborg **13**
Randers
Auning

Holstebro
Hald
So
**Gammel
Estrup
Slot**
Grenå

Ribe
Gudenå
Kattegat

Ringkøbing
Silkeborg
10
Århus
11

Herning
Skanderborg

Skjern
Brande
Ebeltoft
12

Grindsted
Givskud
Jelling **9**
Horsens

Varde
7
Vejle
Billund
8

Esbjerg
5
Holsted
Kolding
1
Fredericia

Fanø
6
Middelfart
Fyn
Odense

Sønderho
Kongeå
Christiansfeld

Ribe **4**
Vojens
Haderslev

Rømø
3
Skærbæk

Åbenrå
Fåborg
Nyborg

Tønder **2**

TO HARWICH,
NEWCASTLE

Veno
Bugt

Nissum
Fjord

Ringkøbing
Fjord

Skjernå

Varde Å

Ribe Å

Samsø

TO KALUNDBORG

Storebælt

TO HALSSKOV

TO NORWAY

TO SWEDEN

0 ———— 40 mi
0 ———— 60 km

KEY

Ferry

Start of itinerary

of the fjord and parkland from its soaring floor-to-ceiling windows. An extensive collection of 20th-century Danish paintings is displayed in the light-filled galleries; it includes works by Anna Ancher, Richard Mortensen, Aksel Jørgensen, and Franciska Clausen. A true highlight is the furniture collection, housed in a specially designed annex that is accessed via a circular ramp topped by a skylight. The superbly displayed collection includes the largest assemblage of Danish-designed chairs in the world, offering a unique historical overview of the birth and popularization of Danish furniture design. Best of all, you can try out any of the hundreds of chairs for yourself thanks to the museum's philosophy that art should be experienced with all the senses, from visual to tactile. Sink into an Arne Jacobsen egg chair, or play with Nanna Ditzel's children's stools; when you're bored of sitting, turn the stool on its side, and it becomes a nifty toy that can be rolled along the ground. Also on display are numerous furnishings by prolific designer Hans J. Wegner, including a rounded, blond-wood chair entitled "The Chair." The museum keeps its furniture storage room open to the public, so you can peruse the entire collection even when it's not officially on display. The Danish ceramics collection, one of the largest in Denmark, is also well worth a look. Check out the one-of-a-kind ceramics by Danish artist Axel Salto, whose pieces often resemble living organisms. ⊠ *Æblehaven 23* ☎ *76/ 30–05–30* ⊕ *www.trapholt.dk* ⊠ *Dkr 50* ☉ *Daily 10–5.*

Where to Stay & Eat

★ **$$$$** ✕ **Admiralen.** Across from the harbor is this elegant seafood restaurant, with pale yellow tablecloths, white walls, and blue-suede chairs. It serves excellent fish dishes, including grilled salmon with spinach and steamed lemon sole with scallops. Pigeon with mushrooms, apples, and a basil gravy is another option. ⊠ *Toldbodeg. 14* ☎ *75/52–04–21* ⊟ *AE, DC, MC, V.*

$$$–$$$$ ✕▦ **Radisson SAS Hotel Koldingfjord.** This impressive neoclassical hotel has mahogany floors and pyramid skylights. It's five minutes from town and faces the Kolding Fjord and 50 acres of countryside. The rooms vary in size (with 39 in a separate annex), but all have pale-wood furnishings and bright prints. The motto of the excellent French-Danish restaurant is "good food is art"; expect well-presented seafood dishes, as well as intriguing vegetarian options. ⊠ *Fjordvej 154, DK–6000 Strandhuse* ☎ *75/51–00–00* ⊟ *75/51–00–51* ⊕ *www.koldingfjord.dk* ⊅ *134 rooms, 9 suites* ⅙ *Restaurant, tennis court, indoor pool, sauna, billiards, bar* ⊟ *AE, DC, MC, V.*

★ **$$–$$$** ✕▦ **Saxildhus Hotel.** Just steps from the train station, this has long been Kolding's premier hotel. Its rooms come in a range of styles, some with old-fashioned mahogany four-poster beds and others with more-contemporary furnishings. The restaurant serves top-notch Danish dishes, including fried plaice with parsley sauce and potatoes. ⊠ *Jernbaneg. 39, Banegårdspl., DK–6000* ☎ *75/52–12–00* ⊟ *75/53–53–10* ⊕ *www. saxildhus.dk* ⊅ *80 rooms, 7 suites* ⅙ *Restaurant, bar, some pets allowed, no-smoking rooms* ⊟ *AE, DC, MC, V.*

Nightlife & the Arts

In the heart of town, on Lilletorv (Little Square), is the stylish and amiable **Den Blå Café** (⊠ Slotsg. 4 ☎ 75/50–65–12), with British and American rock and blues music playing to a backdrop of film posters. In the afternoons, locals sidle up to the picture windows overlooking the square and enjoy coffee and warm baguette sandwiches or chips and guacamole. In the evening, beer and cocktails flow freely, and on the weekends, there's live jazz on the terrace.

Shopping

Kolding's town center is a jumble of walking streets dotted with clothing and jewelry stores and ice cream shops. The two-story **Bahne** (✉ Sønderg. 9 ☎ 75/50–56–22) sells all the big names in Danish design, from Stelton and Georg Jensen tableware to functional wooden furniture made by the Danish design firm Trip Trap.

Tønder

❷ *105 km (66 mi) southwest of Kolding, 195 km (122 mi) southwest of Århus.*

Just 4 km (2½ mi) north of the German border, the historical town of Tønder has long been closely allied with its southern neighbor. In 1864, Tønder was annexed by Germany. After Germany's defeat in World War I, plebiscites were held in the area, and Tønder chose to become reunited with Denmark. Nevertheless, Tønder is still home to a small but important German community, with a German kindergarten and library.

Tønder received its official municipal charter in 1243, making it one of Denmark's oldest towns. Amble back in time among the winding cobbled streets in the heart of town, where half-timber gabled houses, many with intricately carved doors, lean up against small old-fashioned shops.

The town is surrounded by low-lying marshes, and has been subject to major floods throughout its history. To combat the floods, a series of protective dikes was built in the 16th century. The result was double-edged: though Tønder was now safe from the sea, it also lost its natural harbor and waterways and, most importantly, its shipping industry. So, the town turned its sights inward, to the Tønder women's sewing rooms, and built itself up as the "lace capital of the world." In the 18th century, lace making became Tønder's most lucrative export, and at its height more than 12,000 women and girls were working as lace makers. Throughout town are the stately gated homes once owned by successful lace merchants.

Tønder comes vibrantly alive in the last week of August for the **Tønder Folk Music Festival** (☎ 74/72–46–10 ⊕ www.tf.dk), which has been drawing folk music–lovers from all over the world since 1974. Big names and local acts perform everything from blues, zydeco, and gospel to the more traditional Irish, Scottish, and American folk tunes. Reserve hotel rooms well in advance, as the town fills up to capacity during this time.

Founded in 1923, the **Tønder Museum** has amassed an impressive collection of South Jylland arts and crafts. The extensive lace exhibit includes delicate doilies and baptismal gowns. In another room, intricately etched silverware is displayed alongside antique furnishings. A highlight is the collection of hand-painted glazed Dutch tiles brought back by sailors during the 17th and 18th centuries. The tiles served as ballast for the ships, and were then used to decorate the home. Tønder's old water tower, connected to the museum via a glass corridor, houses the world's largest collection of chairs designed by Tønder native Hans J. Wegner, one of Denmark's best-known furniture designers. The 40-meter (130-foot) tower with eight sun-drenched decks is the ideal showroom for Wegner's chairs and furnishings, which range from a rope and ash-wood circle chair to his Y-chair, made of beech wood with a plaited paper yarn seat. The skylit top deck, above which sits the old water-tower lantern, displays a massive circular table, designed by Wegner's daughter. Around the table sit 25 of Wegner's most popular chair, a rounded blond-wood design that he called simply "The Chair," which brought Wegner worldwide recognition, particularly in the United States, after both Kennedy and Nixon each sat in one during a television interview. Settle into one and enjoy the 360-degree views of Tønder's red rooftops and surrounding green marshland that unfold to the sea. If you're in the market for some Tønder lace, you can buy some in the small museum store. ⊠ *Kongevej 51* ☎ *74/72–89–89* ⊕ *www.tonder-net.dk/museerne* ☒ *Dkr 35* ☉ *June–Aug., daily 10–5; Sept.–May, Tues.–Sun. 10–5.*

Lace-lovers will be richly rewarded at the **Drøhses Hus**, a well-preserved 1672 town house with exhibits of lace and lace making. In summer, lace makers often work their trade inside the house. ⊠ *Storeg. 14* ☎ *74/72–49–90* ☒ *Dkr 20* ☉ *Apr.–Dec., weekdays 10–5, Sat. 10–1.*

Where to Stay & Eat

$$$–$$$$
FodorsChoice
★

×⊞ **Schackenborg Slotskro.** This elegant hotel is the official royal inn of the nearby Schackenborg Castle, the residence of Prince Joachim and his wife Princess Alexandra. Stay at the inn, and you can say that while in Denmark, you were a guest of the Danish royal family (albeit a paying guest). Alexandra personally decorated the rooms in rich blues, greens, and reds; each has a large, sparkling bathroom and views of the castle. The castle and inn are 4 km (2½ mi) west of Tønder, in the small village of Møgeltønder. Though the castle is not open to the public, you can roam about the lush grounds that are surrounded by a moat. Møgeltønder's narrow cobbled main street, lined with lime trees, rose gardens, and lovely brick and half-timber houses, has been rightfully named "Denmark's most beautiful village street." The inn's highly acclaimed restaurant serves superb Danish-French cuisine, including beef tournedos with foie gras, cherry tomatoes, and potatoes topped with a truffle sauce. ⊠ *Slotsg. 42, DK–6270 Møgeltønder* ☎ *74/73–83–83* ☒ *74/73–83–11* ⊕ *www.slotskro.dk* ⌨ *25 rooms, 2 suites* ♨ *Restaurant, bar, some pets allowed, no-smoking rooms* ⊟ *AE, DC, MC, V.*

Sports & the Outdoors

Biking trails crisscross Tønder's lush and flat countryside. The tourist office has helpful cycling maps that detail the bike routes in the area. You can rent bikes at **Top Cycler** (⊠ Jernbaneg. 1C ☎ 74/72–18–81).

Shopping

Since 1671, **Det Gamle Apotek** (The Old Pharmacy; ⊠ Østerg. 1 ☎ 74/72–51–11) has dispensed medicine to Tønder's townspeople. In 1989 the pharmacy was converted into a Danish gift and crafts center, but the entire building, both inside and out, was left intact. The beautifully carved front entranceway opens onto a vintage interior lined with pharmaceutical artifacts and medicine jars. Craft items for sale include antique stationery and pens, and handmade candles, glassware, and ceramics. From March to September, the cellar bursts with Danish Christmas items, from tree decorations and festive paper cutouts to elves and angels.

Rømø

❸ *34 km (21 mi) northwest of Tønder, 30 km (19 mi) southwest of Ribe.*

The lush island of Rømø boasts one of Denmark's widest beaches, which unfurls along the island's sunny western coast. Rømø has just 850 permanent residents, but masses of vacationing German and Danish families increase this number tenfold in summer. A 10-km (6-mi) causeway crosses green fields and marshy wetlands to connect Rømø to the mainland. A varied birdlife lives here, feeding off the seaweed and shellfish washed up by the tides. Summer houses dot the island; most of Rømø's services and accommodations are in and around the village of Havneby,

8 km (5 mi) south of the causeway, and in the camping and shopping complex of Lakkolk, in the west.

The 18th century was a golden age in Rømø's seafaring history, when more than 50 local sailors were appointed captains of Dutch and German whaling expeditions to Greenland. Upon their return, the newly prosperous captains built lavish farmsteads, such as **Kommandørgård** (Captain's House), in Toftum, 2 km (1 mi) north of the causeway. Part of the Danish National Museum, this stately, thatch-roof–and–brick farmhouse, dating from 1874, has been meticulously restored, with opulent period furnishings including brass-lined chests and marble-top tables. Blue-and-white glazed Dutch tiles cover the walls, alongside hand-painted rococo panels and doors. ⊠ *Juvrevej 60, Toftum* ☎ *74/75–52–76* ⊕ *www.natmus.dk* ☑ *Dkr 20* ☉ *May–Sept., Tues.–Sun. 10–6; Oct., Tues.–Sat. 10–3.*

North of the Captain's House, in the tiny village of Juvre, is a **whale jawbone fence** built in 1772. Lacking wood and stone, villagers constructed this fence from the whalebones that Rømø captains brought back from Greenland.

Off the main road south of the causeway rises the whitewashed, 18th-century **Rømø Kirke** (Rømø Church), dedicated to St. Clemens, the patron saint of fisherman and sailors. Inside are several hand-painted ship models. The churchyard gravestones, brought back by Rømø captains, are made of Greenlandic stone and carved with depictions of ships. ⊠ *Havnebyvej 152* ☎ *No phone* ☉ *Tues.–Fri. 8–4.*

Where to Stay & Eat

$–$$ ✕🏠 **Hotel Færgegaarden.** In the costal village of Havneby, this holiday hotel has basic rooms with white bedspreads and flowery pillows. The cozy maritime-theme restaurant, with a brick fireplace, Dutch-tile walls, and model ships, serves simple Danish-French fare, including fried plaice with butter sauce. ⊠ *Vesterg. 1, DK–6792 Havneby* ☎ *74/75–54–32* 🖨 *74/75–58–59* ⊕ *www.faergegaarden.dk* ➷ *35 rooms* ⚒ *Restaurant, pool, bar* ⊟ *AE, DC, MC, V.*

Ribe

★ ❹ *60 km (36 mi) southwest of Kolding, 150 km (103 mi) southwest of Århus.*

In the southwestern corner of Jylland, the country's oldest town is well worth the detour for its medieval center preserved by the Danish National Trust. From May to mid-September, a night watchman circles the town, recalling its history and singing traditional songs. If you want to accompany him, gather at the main square at 10 PM.

The **Ribe Domkirke** (Ribe Cathedral) stands on the site of one of Denmark's earliest churches, built around AD 860. The present structure, which dates from the 12th century, is built of a volcanic tufa stone, transported by boats from quarries in Cologne, France. Note the Cat Head Door, said to be for the exclusive use of the devil. The 14th-century brick bell tower once clanged out flood and fire warnings to Ribe's citizens, and today affords sweeping views of the town's red slate rooftops and surrounding marshes. ⊠ *Torvet 15* ☎ *75/42–06–19* ☑ *Dkr 12* ☉ *May–Sept., Mon.–Sat. 10–5, Sun. noon–5; Oct. and Apr., Mon.–Sat. 11–4, Sun. noon–3; Nov.–Mar., Mon.–Sat. 11–3, Sun. noon–3. Call first to confirm hrs.*

The **Ribes Vikinger** (Ribe Viking Museum) chronicles Viking history with conventional exhibits of household goods, tools, and clothing.

There's a multimedia room with an interactive computer screen where you can search for more Viking information in the form of text, pictures, and videos. ⊠ *Odinspl.* ☎ *76/88–11–33* ⊕ *www.ribesvikinger. dk* ⊠ *Dkr 50* ⊘ *June–Aug., daily 10–6; Apr., May, Sept., and Oct., daily 10–4; Nov.–Mar., Tues.–Sun. 10–4.*

Take Bus 57 (confirm with the driver) from the railway station across the street from the Ribes Vikinger. The bus travels 2 km (1 mi) south and arrives at the **Viking Center,** an outdoor exhibit detailing how the Vikings lived day-to-day, with demonstrations about homes, food, and crafts. ⊠ *Lustrupvej 4, Lustrupholm* ☎ *75/41–16–11* ⊕ *www. ribevikingecenter.dk* ⊠ *Dkr 60* ⊘ *May, June, and Sept., weekdays 11–4; July and Aug., daily 11–4:30.*

Where to Stay & Eat

¢–$ ✕ **Sælhunden.** The 300-year-old canal-side "Seal Tavern" barely holds a dozen tables, but its coziness draws both wayfarers and locals. The only seal mementos left are a few skins and pictures, but you can still order a "seal's special" of cold shrimp, sautéed potatoes, and scrambled eggs or—an old Danish favorite—fat strips of pork served with cream gravy and boiled potatoes (only served on winter Wednesdays). Console yourself in summer with *rød grød med fløde* (red porridge with cream); the pronunciation of this dessert—which defies phonetic spelling—is so difficult that Danes get a kick out of making foreigners pronounce it. ⊠ *Skibbroen 13* ☎ *75/42–09–46* ▭ *DC, MC, V* ⊘ *Closed after 8:45 PM.*

$$–$$$ ✕▦ **Hotel Dagmar.** In Ribe's quaint center, this cozy half-timber hotel FodorśChoice encapsulates the charm of the 16th century—with stained-glass windows, ★ sloping wooden floors, and carved chairs. The lavish rooms have antique canopy beds, fat armchairs, and chaise longues. The fine Danish-French restaurant serves such specialties as fillet of salmon in sorrel cream sauce. For drinks and light meals, descend into the atmospheric cellar restaurant-bar, with beamed ceilings and colorfully tiled pillars. ⊠ *Torvet 1, DK–6760* ☎ *75/42–00–33* ▤ *75/42–36–52* ⊕ *www.hoteldagmar.dk* ◄ *48 rooms* ⚬ *Restaurant, bar, meeting room, some pets allowed* ▭ *AE, DC, MC, V.*

$–$$ ▦ **Den Gamle Arrest.** Spend the night in the clink at "The Old Jail," a FodorśChoice simple yet cozy hotel housed in what was Ribe's main jail from 1893 ★ to 1989. The artist-owner has done a brilliant job of modernizing the cells into comfortably habitable rooms, while preserving all the prison details. The cells, which used to house five prisoners, have been creatively refashioned into single and double rooms with lofts in which the bed can be stored during the day. The tiny windows, once covered with mesh-like gratings so that prisoners couldn't see outside, now offer glimpses of blue sky. The original prison gates, with iron bars and padlocks, still serve as the entrances into the hallways. The prison dungeons have been converted into a sprawling gift shop with handmade Danish crafts, from inventive candles and glassware to hundreds of Christmas decorations. The former guardroom, which opens onto the prison yard–turned–terrace, is now a clothing store with fashions by Danish designers. ⊠ *Torvet 11, DK–6760* ☎ *75/42–37–00* ▤ *75/42–37–22* ⊕ *www.dengamlearrest.dk* ◄ *11 rooms, 2 with bath* ⚬ *Café.*

¢ ▦ **Danhostel Ribe.** In the town center, this plain, redbrick hostelry has six- and four-bed family rooms arranged in clusters of two, each with its own private bath and toilet in a small hallway. There are also double rooms with private bath and eight four-bed rooms with completely private facilities. They are functional and childproof, with pine bunks and industrial carpeting. A kitchen is available. ⊠ *Ribehallen, Skt. Pedersg. 16, DK–6760* ☎ *75/42–06–20* ▤ *75/42–42–88* ⊕ *www.danhostel-*

ribe.dk ⤴*152 beds in 40 shared rooms, 38 with bath* ⚲ *Cafeteria* ⊟ *No credit cards* ⊗ *Closed Dec. and Jan.*

Shopping

Antikgaarden (⊠ Overdammen 5 ☎ 75/41–00–55) has a varied collection of Danish antiques, including old Royal Copenhagen plates. **Idé Butik Aps** (⊠ Overdammen 4 ☎ 75/42–14–14) sells Danish crafts ranging from paper cutouts and glassware to figurines of Danish *nisser* (elves). For amber jewelry, head to **Rav I Ribe** (⊠ Nedderdammen 32 ☎ 75/42–03–88), one of the largest amber purveyors in town.

Esbjerg

❺ *35 km (22 mi) northwest of Ribe, 145 km (90 mi) southwest of Århus.*

The thriving port town of Esbjerg is the capital of South Jylland and Denmark's fifth largest city. Esbjerg's nerve center is its formidable harbor, crowded with fishing trawlers, tankers, and ferries. Scandinavian Seaways operates ferries from here for the 20-hour journey to Harwich, England.

Founded in 1868, Esbjerg is Denmark's youngest town, with a pleasant mish-mash of architectural styles, including stately turn-of-the-20th-century brick government buildings. The fortified **water tower** (⊠ Havneg. 22 ☎ 75/12–78–11) was built in a medieval German design. Climb to the top (admission is Dkr 10) for splendid views of Esbjerg and the sea. Reigning over Esbjerg's central square is a statue of Christian IX, who was in power when Esbjerg was founded.

The highlight at the **Esbjerg Museum** is its amber collection, one of the largest in Denmark. The west coast of Jylland is well-known for being rich in amber. Detailed exhibits trace the history of amber along the Jylland coast over a whopping 10,000-year period. ⊠ *Torveg. 45* ☎ *75/ 12–78–11* ⊕ *www.esbjergmuseum.dk* ☒ *Dkr 30, free Wed.* ⊗ *June–Aug., daily 10–4; Sept.–May, Tues.–Sun. 10–4.*

The **Esbjerg Kunstmuseum** (Esbjerg Art Museum) showcases a fine collection of Danish contemporary art, including works by Richard Mortensen. Innovative temporary exhibits feature up-and-coming Danish artists, and have included a retrospective of Danish mobile art and avant-garde sculptures and installations. ⊠ *Havneg. 20* ☎ *75/13–02–11* ☒ *Dkr 30* ⊗ *June–Dec., daily 10–4.*

One of Esbjerg's most striking sights is the giant whitewashed sculpture by Danish artist Svend Wiig Hansen entitled **Menesket ved Havet** (*Man Meets Sea*), depicting four 19-foot-tall men staring solemnly out to sea.

Where to Stay & Eat

$$$ ✕ **Sand's Restauration.** Founded in 1907, this warm, dimly lit restaurant is one of Esbjerg's oldest. The creative Danish menu includes garlic-marinated ostrich steak with red-wine gravy and panfried haddock drizzled with a sweet-and-sour sauce. The original owners collected more than 50 works of art by West Jylland artists, which now cover the walls. ⊠ *Jyllandsg. 32* ☎ *75/12–02–07* ⊟ *MC, V* ⊗ *Closed Sun.*

¢–$ ▥ **Palads Cab Inn.** In the heart of Esbjerg is this budget hotel, affiliated with the popular Cab-Inn Copenhagen chain. The rooms have pale green walls and purple flowery bedspreads, and all are equipped with a TV and telephone. The smaller "cabin" rooms are also comfortable and clean. Breakfast, included in the price, is served in a colossal, high-ceiling dining room that once served as a ballroom. ⊠ *Skoleg. 14, DK–6700* ☎ *75/*

18–16–00 🖨 *75/18–16–24* ⊕ *www.cabinn.dk* ⮌ *107 rooms with bath*
☖ *Cafeteria, bar, no-smoking rooms* ⊟ *AE, DC, MC, V.*

Nightlife & the Arts

Pubs dot Esbjerg's main drag, Skolegade. In the center of town is the
friendly restaurant-bar **Dronning Louise** (⊠ Torvet 19 ☎ 75/13–13–44),
named after Queen Louise, the wife of Christian IX. The bar has red-
leather chairs and a wall lined with bookshelves. In the upstairs club, a
DJ spins dance tunes on Friday and Saturday nights. Esbjerg locals
flock to the live Saturday-afternoon jazz sessions that start at 1 PM. In
summer, the jazz is performed on a terrace that faces the main square.
The adjoining restaurant serves light lunches (burgers, club sandwiches,
and chicken wings) and a Danish dinner menu of meat and fish dishes.

Fanø

6 *30 km (19 mi) northwest of Ribe, plus 12-min ferry from Esbjerg, 153
km (96 mi) southwest of Århus, plus 12-min ferry from Esbjerg.*

During the 19th century, this tiny island had an enormous shipbuilding
industry and a fleet second only to Copenhagen's. The shipping industry deteriorated, but the proud maritime heritage remains. Today, Fanø
is a summer oasis for legions of Danes and other Northern Europeans.
Silky sand beaches unfold along the west coast, buffered by windswept
dunes and green reeds. Cars are allowed on the beach, and it's well worth
taking a ride along the flat sandy coast between the ferry port in Nordby,
Fanø's capital, and the traditional town of Sønderho, in the south. Spinning along the white sandy expanse is like crossing a desert; only the
dark blue sea off in the distance reminds you of your island whereabouts.
The beach is so level and wide that the military used to train here. In
the off season, when the summer visitors have packed up and returned
home, the Fanø shore becomes a tranquil retreat, hauntingly silent save
for the rustle of reeds and the far-off squawk of a bird.

The old-fashioned village of Sønderho, 13 km (8 mi) south of Nordby,
has tiny winding lanes and thatch-roof cottages decorated with ships'
relics, figureheads, painted doors, and brass lanterns. You may even see
people wearing the traditional costumes, especially on Sønderhodag, a
town festival held on the third Sunday in July.

Fanø's annual kite festival, held in mid-June, draws scores of aficionados who fill the sky with hundreds of their colorful, swooping kites.

Where to Stay & Eat

★ **$–$$** ✕ **Café Nanas Stue.** This half-timber farmhouse restaurant, dating from
1854, doubles as the **Fanø Flisemuseum** (Fanø Tile Museum). The walls
and old-fashioned wooden cupboards are lined with glazed Dutch tiles,
brought back by Danish sailors from the 17th to 19th centuries. The
handmade tiles, usually in blue and white, depict everything from bible
stories and ships at sea to frolicking children. After their introduction
to Denmark in the 1600s, the tiles became a characteristic part of most
Fanø homes. The restaurant is a favorite among locals, who gather around
the wooden tables to tuck into traditional Danish fare, including smørrebrød and pepper steak topped with a cognac sauce. Round out the
meal with a taste of their specialty drink, a potent aquavit flavored with
orange, vanilla, and coffee beans. In summer, local musicians perform
traditional Fanø folk music on the violin, guitar, bagpipe, and har-
monica. Inquire at the tourist office for a schedule. ⊠ *Sønderland 1* ☎ *75/
16–40–25* ⊟ *MC, V* ☉ *Closed Mon. Aug. and Sept.; closed Mon.–Thurs.
Oct.–May. No dinner Sun.*

★ **$$–$$$** ✕🖼 **Sønderho Kro.** In the heart of Sønderho, this 270-year-old thatch-roof inn is one of Jylland's finest, its charm preserved with painted doors and beamed ceilings. Rooms are jazzed up with four-poster beds, elegant tapestries, and gauzy curtains. The French-Danish restaurant serves excellent seafood. ⊠ *Kropl. 11, DK–6720 Sønderho* 🕾 *75/16–40–09* 🖷 *75/16–43–85* ⊕ *www.sonderhokro.dk* 🛏 *14 rooms with bath* ♨ *Restaurant, some pets allowed* ⊟ *AE, DC, MC, V* ♥ *Closed Feb. and weekdays Nov.–Jan.*

Billund

❼ *101 km (63 mi) southwest of Århus.*

℧ Billund's claim to fame is **Legoland,** an amusement park in which everyFodor'sChoice thing is constructed from 45 million plastic Lego bricks. Among its in-★ credible structures are scaled-down versions of cities and villages, working harbors and airports, the Statue of Liberty, a statue of Sitting Bull, Mt. Rushmore, a safari park, and Pirate Land. Grown-ups might marvel at toys from pre-Lego days, the most exquisite of which is Titania's Palace, a sumptuous dollhouse built in 1907 by Sir Neville Wilkinson for his daughter. The Lego empire is expanding: the company's goal is to open one park globally every three years, but Danes maintain that theirs, the original, will always be the best. The park also has a massive theme building–ride–restaurant extravaganza that's much better experienced than described. It all takes place within the massive Castleland, where guests arrive via a serpentine dragon ride. Most everything inside is made of the ubiquitous bricks, including the wizards and warlocks, dragons, and knights that inhabit it. At the Knight's Barbecue, waiters in Middle Ages garb hustle skewered haunches of beef, "loooong sausages," and typical fare of the period. ⊠ *Normarksvej 9* 🕾 *75/33–13–33* ⊕ *www.legoland.dk* 🎟 *Dkr 170* ♥ *Apr., May, Sept., and Oct., weekdays 10–6, weekends 10–8; June and late Aug., daily 10–8; July–mid-Aug., daily 10–9.*

Vejle

❽ *40 km (25 mi) east of Billund, 73 km (46 mi) southwest of Århus.*

Vejle is beautifully positioned on a fjord on the east coast, amid forest-clad hills. You can hear the time of day chiming on the old **Dominican monastery clock**; the clock remains, but the monastery long ago gave way to the town's imposing 19th-century city hall.

In the town center, at Kirke Torvet, is **Skt. Nikolai Kirke** (St. Nicholas Church). In the left arm of the cross-shape church, lying in a glass Empire-style coffin, is the body of a bog woman found preserved in a peat marsh in 1835; she dates to 500 BC. The church walls contain the skulls of 23 thieves executed in the 17th century. ⊠ *Kirke Torvet* 🕾 *75/82–41–39* ♥ *May–Sept., weekdays 9–5, Sat. 9–noon, Sun. 9–11:30.*

Where to Stay & Eat

$$$$ 🖼 **Munkebjerg Hotel.** Seven kilometers (4½ mi) southeast of town and surrounded by a thick beech forest and majestic views of the Vejle Fjord, this elegant hotel attracts guests who value their privacy. Beyond the rustic lobby, rooms furnished in blond pine and soft green overlook the forest. There are also two top-notch French-Danish restaurants and a swank casino. ⊠ *Munkebjergvej 125, DK–7100* 🕾 *75/42–85–00* 🖷 *75/72–08–86* ⊕ *www.munkebjerg.dk* 🛏 *149 rooms, 3 suites* ♨ *3 restaurants, cafeteria, tennis court, indoor pool, gym, sauna, bar, casino, meeting room, some pets allowed, no-smoking rooms* ⊟ *AE, DC, MC, V.*

$ 🏨 **Park Hotel.** Centrally located and offering very spacious rooms considering the small stature of this establishment, the pleasant service caps off an overall enjoyable experience and ensures return visits from its patrons. A bountiful breakfast is included in the price, and the restaurant is good though perhaps a bit thin on variety. ✉ *Orla Lehmannsg. 5, DK–7100* ☎ *75/82–24–66* 🖷 *75/72–05–39* 🌐 *www.park-hotel.dk* ⇱ *33 rooms with bath* ⚘ *Restaurant, bar, some pets allowed* 🖃 *AE, DC, MC, V.*

Nightlife

The casino at the **Munkebjerg Hotel** (✉ Munkebjergvej 125 ☎ 75/72–35–00) has blackjack, roulette, baccarat, and slot machines.

Jelling

❾ *10 km (6 mi) northwest of Vejle (via Rte. 18), 83 km (52 mi) southwest of Århus.*

In Jelling, two 10th-century burial mounds mark the seat of King Gorm and his wife, Thyra. Between the mounds are two **Runestener** (runic stones), one of which is Denmark's certificate of baptism, showing the oldest known figure of Christ in Scandinavia. The inscription explains that the stone was erected by Gorm's son, King Harald Bluetooth, who brought Christianity to the Danes in 960.

The most scenic way to get to Jelling is via the **vintage steam train** that runs from Vejle every Sunday in July and the first Sunday in August. Call the Jelling tourist office for schedules.

Silkeborg

❿ *60 km (38 mi) north of Jelling, 43 km (27 mi) west of Århus.*

At the banks of the River Gudenå begins Jylland's lake district. Stretching southeast from Silkeborg to Skanderborg, the area contains some of Denmark's loveliest scenery and most of its meager mountains, including the 438-foot **Himmelbjerget**, at Julsø (Lake Jul), 15 km (10 mi) southeast of Silkeborg. You can climb the narrow paths through the heather and trees to the top, where an 80-foot tower stands sentinel. It was placed there on Constitution Day in 1875 in memory of King Frederik VII.

In late June, jazz-lovers from all over Europe come to celebrate Silkeborg's **Riverboat Jazz Festival** (☎ 86/80–16–17 🌐 www.riverboat.dk), with live jazz performed on indoor and outdoor stages.

The best way to explore the lake district is by water, as the Gudenå winds its way some 160 km (100 mi) through lakes and wooded hillsides down to the sea. Take one of the excursion boats or the world's last coal-fired paddle steamer, *Hjejlen,* which departs in summer from Silkeborg Harbor. Since 1861 it has paddled its way through narrow stretches of fjord, where the treetops meet overhead, to the foot of the Himmelbjerget. ✉ *Havnen* ☎ *86/82–07–66* 🖃 *Dkr 90* 🕐 *Mid-June–Aug.*

The **Silkeborg Museum** houses the city's main attractions: the 2,200-year-old Tollund Man and Elling Girl, two bog people preserved by the chemicals in the soil and water. Discovered in 1950, the Tollund Man remains the best-preserved human face from the Iron Age. He was killed by strangulation—the noose remains around his neck—with a day's worth of stubble that can still be seen on his hauntingly serene face. ✉ *Hovedgårdsvej 7* ☎ *86/82–14–99* 🌐 *www.silkeborgmuseum.dk* 🖃 *Dkr 40* 🕐 *May–mid-Oct., daily 10–5; mid-Oct.–Apr., Wed. and weekends noon–4.*

Where to Eat

$$$–$$$$ ✕ **Aalekroen.** Also known as Onkel Peters Hus (Uncle Peter's Place), this spot is noted for its house specialties, fried eel and seafood. The grilled meat dishes are also an excellent choice. This old inn stands at the shore of a scenic lake, an aspect that adds to dining pleasure. ⊠ *Julsøvænget 5* ☎ *86/84–60–33* ▭ *AE, DC, MC, V* ☉ *Closed Mon.*

Århus

▶ ⑪ *40 km (24 mi) east of Silkeborg.*

Århus is Denmark's second-largest city, and, with its funky arts and college community, one of its most pleasant. Cutting through the center of town is a canal called the Århus Å (Århus Creek). It used to run underground, but was uncovered a few years ago. Since then, an amalgam of bars, cafés, and restaurants has sprouted along its banks, creating one of Denmark's most lively thoroughfares. At all hours of the day and night, this waterfront strip is abuzz with crowds that hang out on the outdoor terraces and steps down to the creek.

The tourist office has information about the **Århus Pass,** which includes passage on buses, free or discounted admission to museums and sites, and tours. A one-day pass is Dkr 97, a two-day pass is Dkr 121, and a seven-day pass is Dkr 171.

The town comes most alive during the first week of September, when the **Århus Festival** (☎ 89/40–91–91 ⊕ www.aarhusfestuge.dk) begins, combining concerts, theater, and art exhibitions with beer tents and sports. The **Århus International Jazz Festival** bills international and local greats in early or mid-July. In July, the **Viking Moot** draws aficionados to the beach below the Museum of Prehistory at Moesgård. Activities and exhibits include market booths, ancient defense techniques, and rides on Viking ships.

The **Rådhus** is probably the most unusual city hall in Denmark. Built in 1941 by noted architects Arne Jacobsen and Erik Møller, the pale Norwegian-marble block building is controversial but cuts a startling figure when illuminated in the evening. ⊠ *Park Allé* ☎ *89/40–67–00* ▤ *City hall Dkr 10, tower Dkr 5* ☉ *Guided tours, in Danish only, mid-June–early Sept., weekdays at 11; tower tours weekdays at noon and 2.*

Rising gracefully over the center of town, the **Århus Domkirke** (Århus Cathedral) was originally built in 1201 in a Romanesque style but was later expanded and redesigned into a Gothic cathedral in the 15th century. Its soaring, whitewashed nave is one of the longest in Denmark. The cathedral's highlights include its chalk frescoes, in shades of lavender, yellow, red, and black that grace the high arches and towering walls. Dating from the Middle Ages, the frescoes depict biblical scenes, including the valiant St. George slaying a dragon and saving a maiden princess in distress. Also illustrated is the poignant death of St. Clement who drowned from an anchor tied around his neck. Nonetheless, he became the patron saint of sailors. Climb the tower for bird's-eye views of the rooftops and thronged streets of Århus. ⊠ *Bispetorv* ☎ *86/20–54–00* ⊕ *www.aarhus-domkirke.dk* ▤ *Tower Dkr 10* ☉ *Jan.–Apr. and Oct.–Dec., Mon.–Sat. 10–3; May–Sept., Mon.–Sat. 9:30–4.*

★ Don't miss the town's open-air museum, known as **Den Gamle By** (Old Town). Its 70 half-timber houses, mill, and millstream were carefully moved from locations throughout Denmark and meticulously re-created, inside and out. ⊠ *Viborgvej* ☎ *86/12–31–88* ⊕ *www.dengamleby.dk*

Dkr 45–Dkr 75 depending on season and activities June–Aug.,
daily 9–6; Apr., May, Sept., and Oct., daily 10–5; Jan., daily 11–3; Feb.,
Mar., Nov., and Dec., daily 10–4. Grounds always open.

South of the city is **Marselisborg Slot** (Marselisborg Castle), the palatial
summer residence of the royal family. The changing of the guard takes
place daily at noon when the Queen is staying in the palace. When the
royal family is away (generally in the winter and spring), the palace
grounds, including a sumptuous rose garden, are open to the public.
 Kongevejen 100 *No phone* *Free.*

In a 250-acre forest south of Århus is the **Moesgård Forhistorisk Museum**
(Prehistoric Museum), with exhibits on ethnography and archaeology,
including the famed Grauballe Man, a 2,000-year-old corpse so well preserved in a bog that scientists could determine his last meal. In fact, when
the discoverers of the Grauballe Man stumbled upon him in 1952, they
thought he had recently been murdered and called the police. The
Forhistorisk vej (Prehistoric Trail) through the forest leads past Stone-
and Bronze Age displays to reconstructed houses from Viking times.
 Moesgård Allé, Bus 6 from the center of town *89/42–11–00*
 www.moesmus.dk *Dkr 45* *Apr.–Sept., daily 10–5; Oct.–Mar.,*
Tues.–Sun. 10–4.

If you are in Århus with children, visit its provincial **Tivoli**, with rides,
music, and lovely gardens. *Skovbrynet* *86/14–73–00* *Dkr 35*
 Late Apr.–mid-June, daily 2–10; mid-June–early Aug., daily 1–11.

Where to Stay & Eat

¢¢¢ ££££ ✕ **Restaurant Margueritten.** Tucked into a cobbled courtyard, this cheery
restaurant is housed in former stables, which accounts for the low
wood-beam ceiling. Well-worn wooden tables and tan walls round out
the warm atmosphere. Contemporary Danish fare includes guinea fowl
stuffed with tiger shrimp and marinated in tandoori and yogurt, and
chicken breast served with Italian ham. *Guldsmedg. 20* *86/
19–60–33* *AE, DC, MC, V.*

$$–$$$$ ✕ **Seafood.** Just south of town is Marselis Harbor, a bustling little sail-
Fodor'sChoice boat cove surrounded by waterfront restaurants and cafés that draw big
★ crowds on sunny summer weekends. Here you'll find Seafood, one of
the best seafood restaurants in Århus. Its signature dish, which draws
moans of delight from diners, is a seafood bouillabaisse heaped with
tiger prawns, squid, Norwegian lobster, and mussels, and served with
aioli on the side. Other dishes include oven-baked catfish with aspara-
gus and warm ginger butter. The restful interior has light-blue walls.
 Havnevej 44, Marselisborg *86/18–56–55* *AE, DC, MC, V*
 Closed Sun. Sept.–Apr.

$$$ ✕ **Prins Ferdinand.** Sitting on the edge of Old Town, this premier Dan-
ish-French restaurant is named after the colorful Århus-based Prince Fred-
erik (1792–1863), who was much loved despite his fondness for gambling
and carousing about town. Here, elegant crystal chandeliers hang over
large round tables with crisp linen tablecloths and ceramic plates created by a local artist. Vases of sunflowers brighten the front room.
Grilled turbot is topped with a cold salsa of radishes, cucumber, and
dill. Cabbage, foie gras, and new potatoes accompany a venison dish.
A daily vegetarian option is offered, and might include grilled asparagus with potatoes, olives, and herbs. *Viborgvej 2* *86/12–52–05*
 AE, DC, MC, V *Closed Sun. and Mon.*

¢–$$ ✕ **Bryggeriet Sct. Clemens.** At this popular pub, you can sit among cop-
Fodor'sChoice per kettles and quaff the local brew, which is unfiltered and without ad-
★ ditives, just like in the old days. Between the spareribs and Australian

steaks, you won't go hungry either. ⊠ *Kannikeg. 10–12* ☎ *86/13–80–00* ⊟ *AE, DC, MC, V.* ·

$$$ ✕⊡ **Philip.** Occupying a prime spot along the canal, this hotel offers an original—but pricey—concept in lodging. Eight former studio apartments have been converted into luxury suites, each outfitted in its own sumptuous style. Suites have original white wood-beam ceilings, elegant wooden furniture imported from France and Italy, huge gleaming bathrooms, and views of the canal. The plush restaurant, with dark hardwood floors and brass candleholders, serves a blend of cuisines that may include cannelloni stuffed with Serrano ham, Danish feta, and crayfish and served with truffles and new potatoes. ⊠ *Åboulevarden 28, DK–8000* ☎ *87/32–14–44* 🖶 *87/32–69–55* ⊕ *www.hotelphilip.dk* ⤴ *8 suites* ⚲ *Restaurant, bar* ⊟ *DC, MC, V.*

★ **$$$$** ⊡ **Royal Hotel.** In operation since 1838, Århus's grand hotel has welcomed such greats as musicians Arthur Rubinstein and Marian Anderson. Well-heeled guests enter through a stately lobby appointed with sofas, modern paintings, and a winding staircase. Plush rooms vary in style and decor, but all have velour and brocade furniture and marble bathrooms. ⊠ *Store Torv 4, DK–8100* ☎ *86/12–00–11* 🖶 *86/76–04–04* ⊕ *www.hotelroyal.dk* ⤴ *98 rooms, 7 suites* ⚲ *Restaurant, cafeteria, sauna, bar, casino, some pets allowed* ⊟ *AE, DC, MC, V.*

$ ⊡ **Hotel Guldsmeden.** Small and intimate, this hotel with a personal touch is housed in a renovated 19th-century town house. The soothing rooms are dressed in cool greens and yellows and have teak shelves. The sunny garden blooms with flowers in summer, and the outdoor terrace is just the spot to enjoy the organic breakfast of fruit, muesli, toast, and marmalade. ⊠ *Guldsmedg. 40, DK–8000* ☎ *86/13–45–50* 🖶 *86/ 13–76–76* ⊕ *www.hotelguldsmeden.dk* ⤴ *20 rooms, 14 with bath* ⚲ *Bar, some pets allowed* ⊟ *AE, DC, MC, V.*

¢ ⊡ **Danhostel Århus.** As in all Danish youth and family hostels, the rooms here are clean, bright, and functional. The secluded setting in the woods near the fjord is downright beautiful. Unfortunately, the hostel can get a bit noisy. Guests may use the kitchen. ⊠ *Marienlundsvej 10, DK–8100* ☎ *86/16–72–98* 🖶 *86/10–55–60* ⊕ *www.hostel-aarhus.dk* ⤴ *138 beds in 30 shared rooms, 11 with private shower* ⚲ *Dining room* ⊟ *AE, MC, V* ⊙ *Closed mid-Dec.–mid-Jan.*

Nightlife & the Arts

There's no better time to visit Århus than during the 10-day **Århus Festival Week** in early September, when jazz, classical, and rock concerts are nonstop, in addition to drama, theater, and dance.

BARS, LOUNGES & DISCOS
As in most other towns, the local discos come and go with remarkable frequency; stop by at a local café for the latest on what's happening. A prime spot to start—and perhaps end—your night is along the Århus Å, which is thronged with bars and cafés. **Carlton** (⊠ Rosensg. 23 ☎ 86/20–21–22) is a classy bar and restaurant, presided over by a carousel horse. Sip cocktails in the front bar–café, or dine on contemporary Danish fare in the dining room. The friendly **Café Jorden** (⊠ Badstueg. 3 ☎ 86/19–72–22) has a brass-and-wood bar and a heated outdoor terrace with a red awning. Students and young professionals mix with the chatty bar staff, who like to sing along to the pop and
★ rock classics. The **Café Under Masken** (Under the Mask Café; ⊠ Bispeg. 3 ☎ 86/18–22–66), next door to the Royal Hotel, is the personal creation of Århus artist Hans Krull, who also designed the unique iron sculptures that grace the entrance to the hotel. The surreal bar is crammed with every type of mask imaginable, from grinning Balinese wooden masks to black-and-yellow African visages. Pygmy statues

and stuffed tropical birds and fish line the shelves. Everything was collected by Krull and other bar patrons. The back wall is one long aquarium filled with exotic fish. As the bar manager puts it, "Everyone's welcome. This bar is a no-man's-land, a place for all the 'funny fish' of the world." If that's not enough of a draw, consider that the drink prices are the lowest in town, and more than 30 kinds of beer are on offer. The **Hotel Marselis** (✉ Strandvejen 25 ☎ 86/14–44–11) attracts a varied crowd to its two venues: the **Beach Club**, with danceable rock and disco, and the more elegant **Nautilus** piano bar. **Sidewalk** (✉ Åboulevarden 56–58 ☎ 86/18–18–66) has a large waterfront terrace that draws crowds on warm nights; in the equally lively interior you can sip cocktails at the long bar or graze on tapas and light meals, including hummus with olives and salad topped with soy-roasted chicken and spinach pasta.

CASINO   The **Royal Hotel** (✉ Store Torv 4 ☎ 86/12–00–11), the city's casino, offers blackjack, roulette, baccarat, and slot machines.

CONCERTS, DANCE & THEATER   The state-of-the-art **Musikhuset Århus** (Århus Concert Hall; ✉ Thomas Jensens Allé 2 ☎ 89/40–40–40) has a splendid glass foyer housing palm trees and a fine Danish-French restaurant. The concert hall showcases theater, opera, ballet, and concerts of all kinds, from classical music to rock. In summer it often hosts free musical and theater performances on its outdoor stages; ask at the tourist office for a schedule.

JAZZ CLUBS   For jazz, head to **Bent J's** (✉ Nørre Allé 66 ☎ 86/12–04–92), a small club with free-admission jam sessions three times a week and occasional big-name concerts. **Café Brasserie Svej** (✉ Åboulevarden 22 ☎ 86/12–30–31), on the canal, hosts live jazz acts on Sunday at 1 PM. **Lion's Pub** (✉ Rosensg. 21 ☎ 86/13–00–45) showcases live jazz on Friday night (mid-August through May) in its downstairs club, which is lined with black-and-white photos of jazz greats. A small stage faces several long tables that fill up with toe-tapping jazz aficionados.

Shopping

Stylish yet laid-back, Århus is a grand place to shop. Søndergade, the main pedestrian strip through town, is lined with clothing, jewelry, and home-furnishing stores. As befits a student town, Århus also has its "Latin Quarter," a jumble of cobbled streets around the cathedral, with boutiques, antiques shops, and glass and ceramic galleries. At the **Bülow Duus Glassworks** (✉ Studsg. 14 ☎ 86/12–72–86), you can browse among delicate and colorful glassworks from fishbowls to candleholders. **Folmer Hansen** (✉ Sønderg. 43 ☎ 86/12–49–00) is packed with Danish tableware and porcelain, from sleek Arne Jacobsen–designed cheese cutters, ice buckets, and coffeepots to Royal Copenhagen porcelain plates. For the best selection of Georg Jensen designs, head to the official **Georg Jensen** (✉ Sønderg. 1 ☎ 86/12–01–00) store. It stocks Jensen-designed and -inspired watches, jewelry, table settings, and art nouveau vases.

Ebeltoft

🕐 *45 km (28 mi) east of Århus.*

Danes refer to Ebeltoft—a town of crooked streets, sloping row houses, and crafts shops—as Jylland's nose. In the middle of the main square is Ebeltoft's half-timber **Det Gamle Rådhus** (Old Town Hall), said to be the smallest town hall in Denmark. Dating from 1789, it served as the town hall until 1840; today it is an annex of the Ebeltoft Museum, with historical exhibits displayed in its traditionally decorated rooms. The mayor still receives visitors here, and couples come from all over Denmark to be married in the quaint interior.

Near the town hall is the **Ebeltoft Museum,** which holds the Siamesisk Samling (Siamese Exhibit), a motley collection of Thai artifacts—from silks and stuffed lemurs to mounted tropical insects—brought back by explorer and Ebeltoft local Rasmus Havmøller. The museum also encompasses the nearby well-preserved dye-works factory, where the Ebeltoft peasants had their wool dyed until 1925. In summer, dyeing demonstrations are often held. ✉ *Juulsbakke 1* ☏ *86/34–55–99* 💰 *Dkr 25, includes the town hall* 🕐 *June–Aug., daily 10–5; Sept.–mid-Oct., Apr., and May, Sat.–Thurs. 11–3; mid-Oct.–Dec., Feb., and Mar., weekends 11–3.*

Danish efficiency is on display beside the ferry at the **Vindmølleparken,** one of the largest windmill parks in the world. Sixteen wind-powered mills on a curved spit of land generate electricity for 600 families. ✉ *Færgehaven* ☏ *86/34–12–44* 💰 *Free* 🕐 *Daily.*

You can't miss the *Frigate Jylland,* dry-docked on the town's main harbor. The renovation of the three-masted tall ship was financed by Danish shipping magnate Mærsk McKinney Møller, and it's a testament to Denmark's seafaring days of yore. You can wander through to examine the bridge, gun deck, galley, captain's room, and the 10½-ton pure copper and pewter screw. Don't miss the voluptuous Pomeranian pine figurehead. ✉ *Strandvejen 4* ☏ *86/34–10–99* ⊕ *www.fregatten-jylland. dk* 💰 *Dkr 60* 🕐 *Mid-June–Aug., daily 10–7; Apr.–mid-June, Sept., and Oct., daily 10–6; Nov.–Mar., daily 10–5.*

The small, light, and airy **Glasmuseum** is on the Ebeltoft harbor, a perfect setting for the collection, which ranges from the mysterious symbol-laden monoliths of Swedish glass sage Bertil Vallien to the luminous gold pavilions of Japanese artist Kyohei Fujita. Once a customs and excise house, the museum has a glass workshop where international students come to study. The shop sells functional pieces, art, and books. ✉ *Strandvejen 8* ☏ *86/34–17–99* ⊕ *www.glasmuseet.dk* 💰 *Dkr 40* 🕐 *Jan.–June and Aug.–Dec., daily 10–5; July, daily 10–7.*

Where to Stay & Eat

★ **$$$$** ✕🏨 **Molskroen.** Perched on the coast northwest of Ebeltoft, in a sunflower-yellow, half-timber manor house from 1923, is this swanky inn and restaurant. The ample rooms are tastefully decorated in cool tones with four-poster beds and Bang & Olufsen televisions. The large, gleaming bathrooms, done up with designer fixtures, could easily grace the pages of an interior-design magazine. Half the rooms overlook the water. Acclaimed young chef Jesper Koch heads the restaurant, which serves fine French fare with an imaginative twist. Roasted duck is stuffed with apricots, figs, and dates and drizzled in a sauce of rum and raisins. Marinated cod sashimi comes with mussels and dill salad. Four brightly colored, original Warhol prints of famous queens—including Queen Margrethe, of course, and Queen Nomi of Swaziland—lend a dazzling touch to the blond-wood floors and pale orange walls. Large picture windows overlook the lush garden, through which a path winds to the private beach. The adjoining sitting room is perfect for a post-dinner brandy and cigar in front of the fireplace. ✉ *Hovedg. 16, DK–8400* ☏ *86/ 36–22–00* 🖨 *86/36–23–00* ⊕ *www.molskroen.dk* 🛏 *18 rooms, 3 suites* 🍴 *Restaurant, beach, bar* 🟰 *AE, DC, MC, V* 🕐 *Restaurant closed Mon.–Tues. Oct.–Mar.*

Viborg

⑬ *22 km (36 mi) north of Silkeborg, 66 km (41 mi) northwest of Århus.*

Viborg dates back at least to the 8th century, when it was a trading post and a place of pagan sacrifice. Later it became a center of Christianity, with monasteries and an episcopal residence. The 1,000-year-old **Hærvejen**, the old military road that starts near here, was once Denmark's most important connection with the outside world; today it lives on as a bicycle path. Legend has it that in the 11th century, King Canute set out from Viborg to conquer England; he succeeded, of course, and ruled from 1016 to 1035. You can buy reproductions of a silver coin minted by the king, embossed with the inscription "Knud, Englands Kong" (Canute, King of England).

Built in 1130, Viborg's **Domkirke** (cathedral) was once the largest granite church in the world. Only the crypt remains of the original building, which was restored and reopened in 1876. The dazzling early-20th-century biblical frescoes are by Danish painter Joakim Skovgard. ⊠ *Sct. Mogensg. 4* ☎ *87/25–52–50* 🖼 *Free* ☉ *June–Aug., Mon.–Sat. 10–5, Sun. noon–5; Apr., May, and Sept. Mon.–Sat. 11–4, Sun. noon–4; Oct.–Mar., Mon.–Sat. 11–3, Sun. noon–3.*

Where to Stay & Eat

$$$ ✕ **Brygger Bauers Grotter.** A former brewery dating from 1832, this cozy, cavernous underground restaurant has arched wooden ceilings, old paintings depicting Viborg history, and beer barrels lining the back wall. The contemporary Danish menu includes a hearty beef stew served with rice, and chicken breast stuffed with Gorgonzola. ⊠ *Sct. Mathiasg. 61* ☎ *86/61–44–88* 🖃 *MC, V.*

$$$ 🏨 **Palads Hotel.** This large hotel near the center of town has ample, simply furnished rooms done up in a rose decor. A third of the rooms are designed for longer stays and have kitchenettes. ⊠ *Sct. Mathiasg. 5, DK–8800* ☎ *86/62–37–00* 🖷 *86/62–40–46* ⊕ *www.hotelpalads.dk* ⤳ *99 rooms, 19 suites* ⚭ *Bar, some kitchenettes, sauna, some pets allowed, no-smoking rooms* 🖃 *AE, DC, MC, V.*

Aalborg

⑭ *80 km (50 mi) northeast of Viborg, 112 km (70 mi) north of Århus.*

The gentle waters of the Limfjord cut off the top segment of Jylland completely. Perched on its narrowest point is Aalborg, Denmark's fourth-largest city. The town, founded in 692, is the gateway between north and mid-Jylland. The city is a charming combination of new and old; twisting lanes filled with medieval houses and, nearby, broad modern boulevards.

★ The local favorite site is the magnificent 17th-century **Jens Bang Stenhus** (Jens Bang's Stone House), built by a wealthy merchant. Chagrined he was never made a town council member, the cantankerous Bang avenged himself by caricaturing his political enemies in gargoyles all over the building and then adding his own face, its tongue sticking out at the town hall. The five-story 1624 building has a vaulted stone beer-and-wine cellar, Duus Vinkælder, one of the most atmospheric in the country. ⊠ *Østeråg. 9.*

The Baroque **Budolfi Kirke** (Budolfi Cathedral) is dedicated to the English St. Botolph. The stone church, originally made of wood, has been rebuilt several times in its 800-year history. It includes a copy of the original spire of the Rådhus in Copenhagen, which was taken down about a century ago. The money for the construction was donated to the church by a generous local merchant and his sister, both of whom, locals say, had no other family on which to lavish their wealth. ⊠ *Gammel Torv.*

Next to Budolfi Kirke is the 15th-century **Helligåndsklosteret** (Monastery of the Holy Ghost). One of Denmark's best-preserved monasteries—and perhaps the only one that admitted both nuns and monks—it is now a home for the elderly. During World War II the monastery was the meeting place for the Churchill Club, a group of Aalborg schoolboys who became world famous for their sabotage of the Nazis, even after the enemy thought they were locked up. ⊠ *C. W. Obels Pl., Gammel Torv* ☎ *98/ 12–02–05* ☉ *Guided tours mid-June–mid-Aug. at 1:30.*

In the center of the old town is **Jomfru Ane Gade,** named, as the story goes, for an aristocratic maiden accused of being a witch, then beheaded. Now the street's fame is second only to that of Copenhagen's Strøget. Despite the flashing neon and booming music of about 30 discos, bars, clubs, and eateries, the street attracts a thick stream of pedestrian traffic and appeals to all ages.

The only Fourth of July celebrations outside the United States annually blast off in nearby **Rebild Park,** a salute to the United States for welcoming some 300,000 Danish immigrants. The tradition dates back to 1912.

Just north of Aalborg at Nørresundby (still considered a part of greater Aalborg) is **Lindholm Høje,** a Viking and Iron Age burial ground where stones placed in the shape of a ship enclose many of the site's 682 graves. At its entrance there's a museum that chronicles Viking civilization. ⊠ *Vendilavej 11* ☎ *96/31–04–28* ☞ *Museum Dkr 30, burial ground free* ☉ *Easter–mid-Oct., daily 10–5; mid-Oct.–Easter, Tues.–Sun. 10–4.*

The blocky marble-and-glass structure of the **Nordjyllands Kunstmuseum,** (Museum of Contemporary Arts of North Jutland) was designed by architects Alvar and Elissa Aalto and Jacques Baruël; the building was completed in 1972. The gridded interior partition system allows the curators to tailor their space to each exhibition, many of which are drawn from the museum's permanent collection of 20th-century Danish and international art. On the grounds there is also a manicured sculpture park and an amphitheater that hosts occasional concerts. ⊠ *Kong Christians Allé 50* ☎ *98/13–80–88* ⊕ *www.nordjyllandskunstmuseum.dk* ☞ *Dkr 30* ☉ *Easter–mid-Oct., daily 10–5; mid-Oct.–Easter, Tues.–Sun. 10–4.*

The **Aalborg Historical Museum** contains the well-preserved underground ruins of a medieval Franciscan friary, including a walled cellar and the foundations of the chapel. Enter via the elevator outside the Salling department store. ⊠ *Alg. 19* ☎ *96/31–04–10* ⊕ *www.aahm.dk* ☞ *Dkr 30* ☉ *Weekdays 10–5.*

Where to Stay & Eat

$$$ ✕ **Benzon's.** Light and bright on an old cobble street, this is one of the most popular eateries in town. Downstairs is a French-style bistro, with marble-top tables, engraved mirrors, and windows overlooking Jomfru Ane Gade. The upstairs is elegant and quiet. The French menu includes lobster-and-cognac soup for two, sliced roast duck with Waldorf salad, and beef fillet. ⊠ *Jomfru Ane G. 8* ☎ *98/16–34–44* ▭ *AE, DC, MC, V.*

$–$$$ ✕ **Spisehuset Kniv og Gaffel.** In a 400-year-old building parallel to Jomfru Ane Gade, this busy restaurant is filled with oak tables, crazy slanting floors, and candlelight; the year-round courtyard is a veritable greenhouse. Young waitresses negotiate the mayhem to deliver inch-thick steaks, the house specialty. ⊠ *Maren Turisg. 10* ☎ *98/16–69–72* ▤ *DC, MC, V* ⊘ *Closed Sun.*

★ **¢–$$** ✕ **Duus Vinkjælder.** Most people come to this cellar—part alchemist's dungeon, part neighborhood bar—for a drink, but you can also get a light bite. In summer enjoy smørrebrød; in winter sup on grilled specialties such as frikadeller and *biksemad* (a meat-and-potato hash), and the restaurant's special liver pâté. ⊠ *Østeråg. 9* ☎ *98/12–50–56* ▤ *DC, V* ⊘ *Closed Sun.*

$$$ ▦ **Helnan Phønix.** In a central and sumptuous old mansion, this hotel is popular with vacationers as well as business travelers. The rooms are luxuriously furnished with plump chairs and polished, dark-wood furniture; in some the original wooden ceiling beams are still intact. The Brigadier restaurant serves excellent French and Danish food. ⊠ *Vesterbro 77, DK–9000* ☎ *98/12–00–11* ⊟ *98/10–10–20* ⊕ *www.helnan.dk* ⊸ *219 rooms, 2 suites* ⌂ *Restaurant, gym, bar, meeting room, some pets allowed, no-smoking rooms* ▤ *AE, DC, MC, V.*

Nightlife & the Arts

BEER & WINE CELLARS Consider a pub crawl along the famed **Jomfru Ane Gade,** wildly popular for its party atmosphere but also for its rock-bottom drink prices, which are much lower than anywhere else in Denmark. Opt for the house drink of the night (usually a Danish beer), and you'll often pay one-third of the normal cost. The street has become overrun by the pre-teen crowd, but increasingly the bars are enforcing age restrictions, with an eye to drawing more-mature crowds. Dimly lit and atmospheric, **Duus Vinkjælder** (⊠ Østeråg. 9 ☎ 98/12–50–56) is extremely popular, one of the most classic beer and wine cellars in all of Denmark. It's an obligatory stop for anyone who wants a taste of Aalborg's nightlife. **Rendez-Vous** (⊠ Jomfru Ane G. 5 ☎ 98/16–88–80) has a pleasant outdoor terrace with black and brown wicker chairs. Thursday through Saturday, it opens its upstairs dance floor, which attracts 18- to 25-year-olds with standard disco.

CASINO The city's sole casino is at the **Radisson SAS Limfjord Hotel** (⊠ Ved Stranden 14–16 ☎ 98/16–43–33).

MUSIC & DISCOS Aalborg doesn't have a regular jazz club, but local musicians get together at least once a week for jam sessions. Ask the tourist board for details.

Gaslight (⊠ Jomfru Ane G. 23 ☎ 98/10–17–50) plays rock and grinding dance music to a young crowd. If you're here in fall or winter, head to the harborside **Kompasset** (⊠ Vesterbådehavn ☎ 98/13–75–00), where live jazz is paired with a Saturday-afternoon lunch buffet. **Natsværmeren** (⊠ Ved Stranden 9 ☎ 98/11–60–22) is popular with a mature audience. **Vesterå 4** (⊠ Vesterå 4 ☎ 98/16–99–99), with pale gray walls and flickering orange candles, hosts live jazz performances several times a month.

Skagen

⑮ *88 km (55 mi) northeast of Aalborg, 212 km (132 mi) north of Århus.*

At the windswept northern tip of Jylland is Skagen (pronounced *skane*), a very popular summer beach area for well-heeled Danes. The long beaches and blue light, soft as silk and enhanced by reflections in the calm sea, have inspired painters and writers alike. The 19th-century Danish artist Holger Drachmann (1846–1908) and his friends, including the well-known P. S. Kroyer and Michael and Anna Ancher, founded the Skagen School of painting, which sought to capture the special quality of

★ light here. You can see their efforts on display in the **Skagen Museum.** The museum store offers the best selection in town of posters, postcards, and other souvenirs depicting the Skagen paintings. ⊠ *Brøndumsvej 4* ☎ *98/44–64–44* ⊕ *www.skagensmuseum.dk* ⊠ *Dkr 60* ☉ *June–Aug., daily 10–6; May and Sept., daily 10–5; Apr. and Oct., Tues.–Sun. 11–4; Nov.–Mar., Wed.–Fri. 1–4, Sat. 11–4, Sun. 11–3.*

Michael and Anna Ancher are Skagen's—if not Denmark's—most famous artist couple, and their meticulously restored 1820 home and studio, **Michael og Anna Ancher's Hus** (Michael and Anna Ancher's House), is now a museum. Old oil lamps and lace curtains decorate the parlor; the doors throughout the house were painted by Michael. Anna's studio, complete with easel, is awash in the famed Skagen light. More than 240 paintings by Michael, Anna, and their daughter, Helga, grace the walls. ⊠ *Markvej 2–4* ☎ *98/44–30–09* ⊕ *www.anchershus.dk* ⊠ *Dkr 40* ☉ *May–Sept., daily 10–5, until 6 late June–mid-Aug.; Apr. and Oct. daily 11–3; Nov.–Mar., weekends 11–3.*

Danes say that in Skagen you can stand with one foot on the Kattegat, the strait between Sweden and eastern Jylland, the other in the Skagerrak, the strait between western Denmark and Norway. The point is so **Fodor'sChoice** thrashed by storms and roiling waters that the 18th-century **Tilsandede** ★ **Kirke** (Sand-Buried Church), 2 km (1 mi) south of town, is completely covered by dunes.

Even more famed than the Buried Church is the west coast's dramatic **Råbjerg Mile**, a protected migrating dune that moves about 33 feet a year and is accessible on foot from the Kandestederne.

Where to Stay & Eat

$$–$$$ ✕🏠 **Strand Hotel.** In the old part of Skagen, this bright and romantic hotel is the perfect foil to the wild, windy sea- and sandscapes nearby. Filled with gently curved wicker furnishings, painted woods, and original art, the hotel's rooms are simple and restful; the staff is friendly and accommodating. Sømærket, the traditional Danish fish restaurant, is open only between April and October, but breakfast, which includes healthful and fortifying fresh breads and berries, is available year-round. ⊠ *Jeckelsvej 2, DK–9990* ☎ *98/44–34–99* ⧉ *98/44–59–19* ⊕ *www. strandhotellet.glskagen.dk* ➫ *21 rooms, 6-person house* ☼ *Restaurant, meeting room* ⊟ *AE, DC, MC, V.*

$ ✕🏠 **Brøndums Hotel.** A few minutes from the beach, this 150-year-old gabled inn is furnished with antiques and Skagen School paintings, and although it is charming, it is beginning to show its age. The very basic 21 guest rooms in the main building are old-fashioned and include wicker chairs, Oriental rugs, and pine four-poster beds. The 25 annex rooms are more modern. The fine French-Danish restaurant, where the Skagen School often gathered, has a lavish cold table. Brøndums Hotel became associated with the Skagen School early on: Anna Ancher was the daughter of Eric Brøndum, the hotel proprietor. ⊠ *Anchersvej 3, DK–9990* ☎ *98/44–15–55* ⧉ *98/45–15–20* ⊕ *www.broendums-hotel. dk* ➫ *47 rooms, 19 with bath, 3 suites* ☼ *Restaurant, bar, meeting room, some pets allowed* ⊟ *AE, DC, MC, V.*

Shopping

Skagen's artistic heritage and light-drenched landscapes continue to draw painters and craftspeople, making for excellent souvenir shopping opportunities. For colorful, innovative handblown glass, head for **Glaspusterblæser** (⊠ Sct. Laurentii Vej 33 ☎ 98/44–58–75), a large glass-blowing workshop housed in what was once Skagen's post office. The amber store and workshop **Ravsliberen I Skagen** (⊠ Sct. Laurentii Vej 6 ☎ 98/44–55–27) sells top-quality amber jewelry, including pieces with insects trapped inside. You can buy miniature replicas of figureheads,

ships' "guardian angels," at **Trip Trap** (✉ Sct. Laurentii Vej 17A ☎ 98/
44–63–22), a branch of the popular Danish home-decorating chain.

Jylland A to Z

AIRPORTS & TRANSFERS

Jylland has regional hubs in Aalborg, Århus, and Billund, which handle mainly domestic and some European traffic. Billund Airport, 2 km
(1 mi) southwest of downtown, is the largest and on the arrival end of
flights from major European, Scandinavian, and Danish airports.
🛫 **Airports Aalborg Airport** ☎ 98/17-11-44 ⊕ www.aal.dk **Århus Airport** ☎ 87/
75-70-00 ⊕ www.aar.dk. **Billund Airport** ☎ 76/50-50-50 ⊕ www.billund-airport.dk.

TRANSFERS Hourly buses run between the Århus airport and train station. The trip
takes around 45 minutes and costs Dkr 60. Bus 212 runs from Århus
airport to Randers (60 minutes) and Ebeltoft (20 minutes). A taxi ride
from the airport to central Århus takes 45 minutes and costs well over
Dkr 300.

From Billund airport there are buses to Århus (Radisson-Sas Hotel, Dkr
130), Esbjerg, Kolding, Vejle, Odense, and the Legoland Hotel near the
airport.

Taxi and bus routes connect Aalborg airport with the city. A taxi costs
around Dkr 175 and takes roughly 20 minutes. Nordjyllands Trafikselskab has buses connecting the airport to towns near Aalborg, and the
company Flybusnord runs routes to Sæby and Frederikshavn.
🛫 **Flybusnord** ☎ 98/43-30-00 ⊕ www.flybusnord.dk. **Nordjyllands Trafikselskab** ☎ 98/
11-11-11

BIKE TRAVEL

Jylland has scores of bike paths, and many auto routes also have cycle
lanes. Keep in mind that distances feel much longer here than elsewhere
in the country, and that even these humble hills are a challenge for children and novice cyclists. Consider prearranged package holidays, which
range from island day trips to eight-day excursions. Among the offices
that can help with bike tips are the visitor information offices in the different towns. Bike rentals are available in most towns from the tourism
board, which can also supply maps and brochures. Contact Visit Nord
for routes and tour packages in North Jylland.

In the west, the Vestkyst-stien (west-coast path) goes from Skagen in the
north to Bulbjerg in the south. In the east, the Vendsyssel-stien (winding path) goes from Frederikshavn to the mouth of the Limfjord. The
Østkyst-stien (east-coast path) follows and leads to the south of the Limfjord. In the south, much of the 1,000-year-old Hærvejen (Old Military
Road) has been converted into a network of scenic cycling lanes. It's
signposted for all 240 km (145 mi) through the center of Jylland, from
Padborg in the south to Viborg in the north.
🛫 **Visit Nord** ☎ 96/96-12-00 ⊕ www.visitnord.dk.

BOAT & FERRY TRAVEL

More than 20 ferry routes still connect the peninsula with the rest of
Denmark (including the Faroe Islands), as well as England, Norway, and
Sweden, with additional connections to Kiel and Puttgarden, Germany,
the Baltics, Poland, and Russia. For most ferries you can get general information and make reservations by calling FDM (Danish Motoring Association). Other major routes include those of Scandinavian Seaways,
which links England's Harwich to Esbjerg in the southwest. There are
ferries from Göteborg (3¼ hours), on Sweden's west coast and Oslo,

Norway (10 hours), to Frederikshavn in the northeast. Call Stena Line for both. For direct Sjælland to Jylland passage, you can take a car-ferry hydrofoil from Sjælland's Odden to Ebeltoft (45 minutes) or Århus (1 hour). You can also take the slower, but less expensive, car ferry from Kalundborg (on Sjælland) to Århus (2 hours 40 minutes). Both ferries travel five times daily on weekdays, and slightly less on the weekends. For ferry schedules and information, call Mols-Linien.

🚩 **FDM** ☎ 70/11-60-11. **Mols-Linien** ☎ 70/10-14-18 🖥 89/52-52-90 ⊕ www.molslinien.dk. **Scandinavian Seaways** ☎ 79/17-79-17 Esbjerg, 33/42-30-00 Copenhagen ⊕ www.dfdsseaways.dk. **Stena Line** ☎ 96/20-02-00 ⊕ www.stenaline.com.

BUS TRAVEL

Bus and train travel inside Denmark is made more convenient by way of "Bus/Tog Samarbejde," a comprehensive route and schedule information source. Bus tickets are usually sold onboard the buses immediately before departure. Ask about discounts for children, senior citizens and groups.

Intercity buses are punctual and slightly cheaper but slower than trains. You can buy tickets on the bus and pay according to destination. For schedules and fares, call the local tourist office, as a network of different bus companies covers the peninsula. Thinggaard Buses traverse Jylland from north to south, between Frederikshavn and Esbjerg, with stops in Aalborg and Viborg; a one-way ticket between Frederikshavn and Esbjerg costs around Dkr 245. Abildskou buses travel between Kastrup Airport on Sjælland to Ebeltoft and Århus. The trip lasts about 3 hours and 45 minutes, similar to the train; a one-way ticket is Dkr 230.

Schedules for most bus travel within towns are posted at all bus stops and fares are usually about Dkr 15.

🚩 **Abildskou** ✉ Graham Bellsvej 40, Århus ☎ 70/21-08-88 ⊕ www.abildskou.dk. **Bus/Tog Samarbejde** ⊕ www.rejseplan.dk. **Thinggaard Bus** ☎ 70/10-00-20 ⊕ www.thinggaard-bus.dk.

CAR TRAVEL

Although train and bus connections are excellent, sites and towns in Jylland are widely dispersed, and the peninsula is best explored by car. Whether you decide to take speedy, modern highways or winding old roads, traffic is virtually nonexistent.

Getting around Denmark these days is much easier than in the past thanks to bridges that connect the kingdom to both Sweden and the Continent; that said, it's best to confirm all passage with either a local tourist board or FDM before setting out, to avoid confusion caused by ferry mergers and discontinued routes. Although there are several ferry connections to other parts of Denmark and Europe, most travelers drive north from Germany, or arrive from the islands of Sjælland or Fyn. Ferry prices can get steep and vary according to the size of the vehicle and the number of passengers.

From Copenhagen or elsewhere on Sjælland, you can drive the approximately 110 km (69 mi) across the island, then cross the world's second-longest suspension bridge, the Storebæltsbro (Great Belt Bridge), to Knudshoved. You then drive the 85 km (53 mi) across Fyn and cross from Middelfart to Fredericia, Jylland, over the Lillebæltsbro (Little Belt Bridge). There are more choices, since two bridges link Middelfart to Fredericia. The older, lower bridge (2 km/1 mi) follows Route 161, whereas the newer suspension bridge (1 km/½ mi) on E20 is faster.

🚩 **FDM** ☎ 70/11-60-11.

EMERGENCIES

For ambulance, fire, or police anywhere in Denmark, dial 112. You can contact local pharmacies in Aalborg or Århus for information on emergency doctors.

🚹 **Aalborg** ⊠ Budolfi Apotek, Alg. 60 ☎ 98/12-06-77. **Århus** ⊠ Løve Apoteket, Store Torv 5 ☎ 86/12-00-22.

SPORTS & THE OUTDOORS

CANOEING Canoes can be rented (about Dkr 220 per day) in the lake district, Limfjord, and at almost all lakes and rivers. One- to three-day package tours are available throughout the region, with either camping or hostel accommodation. Local tourist boards can provide more information.

FISHING The lake district is a great place for fishing and angling. License requirements vary and package tours are also available; contact any local tourist office for details.

TOURS

Guided tours are few and far between, although some local tourism offices do provide them. Check with the individual city tourism offices—especially the one in Århus—for tips, reservations, and brochures that describe walking tours and scenic routes.

TRAIN TRAVEL

DSB makes hourly runs from Copenhagen to Frederikshavn, in northern Jylland, stopping in Fredericia (2½ hours), Århus (3½ hours), and Aalborg (4¾ hours) along the way. The trip includes train passage across the Storebæltsbro between Korsør, on west Sjælland, and Nyborg, on east Fyn. A one-way trip from Copenhagen to Frederikshavn is about Dkr 320. For long trips, the DSB trains are fast and efficient, with superb views of the countryside. Smaller towns do not have inter-city trains, so you have to switch to buses once you arrive.

🚹 **DSB** ☎ 70/13-14-15 ⊕ www.dsb.dk.

VISITOR INFORMATION

At the Århus tourist office, check out the Århus Pass, which includes bus travel, free or discounted admission to museums and sites, and tours.

🚹 **Aalborg** ⊠ Østeråg. 8 ☎ 98/12-60-22 🖶 98/16-69-22 ⊕ www.visitaalborg.com. **Århus** ⊠ Park Allé 2 ☎ 89/40-67-00 ⊕ www.visitaarhus.com. **Ebeltoft** ⊠ Strandvejen 2 ☎ 86/34-14-00 ⊕ www.visitdjursland.com. **Esbjerg** ⊠ Skoleg. 33 ☎ 75/12-55-99 🖶 75/12-27-67 ⊕ www.visitesbjerg.com. **Fanø** ⊠ Færgevej 1, Nordby ☎ 75/16-26-00 🖶 75/16-29-03 ⊕ www.fanoeturistbureau.dk. **Jelling** ⊠ Gormsg. 23 ☎ 75/87-13-01 🖶 75/82-10-11 ⊕ www.visitvejle.com. **Kolding** ⊠ Akseltorv 8 ☎ 76/33-21-00 🖶 76-33-21-20 ⊕ www.visitkolding.dk. **Mid-Jylland** ⊕ www.midtjylland.dk. **North Jylland Tourist Office** ⊕ www.visitnord.dk. **South and Southeast Jylland Tourist Information** ☎ 75/83-59-99 🖶 75/83-45-67 ⊕ www.visitsouth-eastjutland.com. **Ribe** ⊠ Torvet 3 ☎ 75/42-15-00 🖶 75/42-40-78 ⊕ www.ribetourist.dk. **Rømø** ⊠ Havnebyvej 30 ☎ 74/75-51-30 🖶 74/75-50-31 ⊕ www.romo.dk. **Silkeborg** ⊠ Åhavevej 2A ☎ 86/82-19-11 🖶 86/81-09-83 ⊕ www.silkeborg.com. **Skagen** ⊠ Sct. Laurentii Vej 22 ☎ 98/44-13-77 🖶 98/45-02-94 ⊕ www.skagen-tourist.dk. **Tønder** ⊠ Torvet 1 ☎ 74/72-12-20 🖶 74/72-09-00 ⊕ www.visittonder.dk. **Vejle** ⊠ Banegårdspl. 6 ☎ 75/82-19-55 🖶 75/82-10-11 ⊕ www.visitvejle.com. **Viborg** ⊠ Nytorv 9 ☎ 87/25-30-75 🖶 86/60-02-38 ⊕ www.viborg.dk/turisme.

BORNHOLM

Called the Pearl of the Baltic for its natural beauty and winsomely rustic towns, Bornholm, 177 km (110 mi) southeast of Sjælland, is geographically unlike the rest of Denmark. A temperate climate has made this 588-square-km (235-square-mi) jumble of granite bluffs, clay soil, and rift valleys an extravagance of nature. Rich plantations of fir bristle beside wide dunes and vast heather fields; lush gardens teem with fig, cherry, chestnut, mulberry, and blue-blooming Chinese Emperor trees; and meadows sprout 12 varieties of orchids. Denmark's third-largest forest, the Almindingen, crowns the center; the southern tip is ringed with some of Europe's whitest beaches.

During the Iron and Bronze ages, Bornholm was inhabited by seafaring and farming cultures that peppered the land with burial dolmens and engravings. From the Middle Ages to the 18th century, the Danes battled the Swedes for ownership of the island, protecting it with strongholds and fortified churches, many of which still loom over the landscape. Bornholm's unique round churches—whitewashed splendors topped with black conical roofs—are a sight to behold. Considered to be some of the finest examples of Scandinavian medieval architecture, the churches imbue the island landscape with a lovely, stylized simplicity.

Today Bornholmers continue to draw their livelihood from the land and sea—and increasingly from tourism. Chalk-white chimneys rise above the rooftops, harbors are abob with painted fishing boats, and in spring and summer fields blaze with amber mustard and grain.

Few people come to Bornholm to stay indoors. Long, silky beaches, gentle hills, and lush forests make this a summer haven for walking, hiking, and swimming—particularly for families, many of whom take their summer vacations by packing provisions and children onto bikes, and cycling throughout the island.

Bornholm is famous throughout Scandinavia for its craftspeople, especially glassblowers and ceramicists, whose work is often pricier in Copenhagen and Stockholm. In the center of each town (especially Gudhjem and Svaneke) you can find crafts shops and *værksteder* (workshops). When you're on the road, watch for KERAMIK signs, which direct you to artists selling from home.

Rønne

▶ ❶ *190 km (120 mi) southeast of Copenhagen (7 hrs by ferry from Køge or 3 hrs from Ystad, Sweden).*

Bornholm's capital, port, and largest town is Rønne, a good starting point for exploring northward or eastward. East of Nørrekås Harbor on Laksegade is an enchanting area of rose-clad 17th- and 18th-century houses, among them the tile-roof **Erichsens Gård** (Erichsen's Farm). The home of the wealthy Erichsen family, whose daughter married the Danish poet Holger Drachmann, it includes paintings by Danish artist Kristian Zahrtmann, period furnishings, and a lovely garden. ⊠ *Lakseg. 7* 🕾 *56/95–87–35* ⊕ *www.bornholmsmuseer.dk/erichs* 🎫 *Dkr 30.* ☾ *Mid-May–mid-Oct., Mon.–Sat. 10–5.*

Near Store Torv, the main square, is the **Bornholm Museum**, which puts on local geological and archaeological exhibits in addition to regular displays of more than 4,500 pieces of ceramics and glass. The museum also displays 25 18th-century Bornholmure (Bornholm Clocks), as characteristic of the island as smoked herring. In 1744 a Dutch ship was wrecked on Bornholm, and the English grandfather clocks it carried became the models for the island's clocks. ⊠ *Skt. Mortensg. 29* 🕾 *56/95–07–35* ⊕ *www.bornholmsmuseum.dk* 🎫 *Dkr 35* ☾ *Mid-Apr.–mid-Oct., Mon.–Sat. 10–5; mid-Oct.–mid-Apr., Mon.–Sat. 1–4.*

Bornholm

KEY

🚢 _Ferry_

▶ _Start of itinerary_

0   6 miles

0   ⅄ km

Bornholm has long been recognized for its beautiful ceramics. **Hjorths Fabrik** (Hjorth's Factory), founded in 1859 by ceramicist Lauritz Hjorth, is one of Bornholm's oldest ceramics factories, and is today a "working ceramics museum." Follow the "route of clay" through the old factory and workshops, from the mixer and the kiln to the painting and decorating rooms. Along the way you see the ceramicists at work, casting, glazing, decorating, and firing, and you can observe how a lump of raw clay slowly takes shape on the potter's wheel, blossoming into a lovely vase or bowl. (Note that the ceramicists take a lunch break from about noon to 1.) The museum displays ceramics made at Hjorths factory since 1859, from Greek Revival pieces of the mid-1800s to ceramic apothecary jars from 1930–50. Many of the ceramic pieces dating from the mid- to late 1900s were made by Ulla and Marie Hjorth, sisters of the factory's founder. The museum shop sells a wide range of Hjorth ceramics, from its distinctive stoneware to old-fashioned pharmacy jars. ⊠ _Krystalg. 5_ ☎ _56/95–01–60_ ⊕ _www.bornholmsmuseer.dk/hjorths_ 🎫 _May–Oct. Dkr 30, Nov.–Apr. Dkr 10_ ⊙ _May–Oct., Mon.–Sat. 10–5, factory closed Sat.; Nov.–Apr., weekdays 1–5, Sat. 10–1, exhibits and shops only._

Where to Stay & Eat

★ **$$$** ✕ **Fyrtøjet.** Overlooking the Strøget, this bright and spacious restaurant offers an ample dinner buffet with soup, salad, a selection of fish dishes (usually smoked salmon and cod), and beef. The lunchtime herring and fish buffet is a hit with summer crowds as is the restaurant's inviting interior of pale yellow walls, blue tablecloths, and wooden floors. The house specialty is _granitbøf_, a hefty slab of beef served on a heated Bornholm granite-and-iron tray. While the beef is cooking on the hot granite, it's flambéed with whiskey. You pour the accompanying cold sauce (usually béarnaise) over the meat when it's suitably done. The former owner patented this unique tray. ⊠ *Store Torveg. 22* ☎ *56/95–30–12* ▤ *AE, DC, MC, V* ⊘ *No lunch Jan.–Mar.*

★ ¢–$$$ ✕ **Strøgets Spisehûz.** When the hunger pangs hit, Rønne locals head for this friendly, family-owned restaurant at the end of Strøget. The hearty Danish fare includes beef with cognac sauce and potatoes, and smoked salmon sprinkled with lemon. The mood is casual, with hanging plants, little Danish flags, paper napkins, and pink and purple curtains. ⊠ *Store Torveg. 39* ☎ *56/95–81–69* ▤ *MC, V* ⊘ *Closed Mon.*

$$–$$ ✕ **Rådhuskroen.** With exposed timbers, comfortable armchairs, and close-set tables, this restaurant provides a softly lit change from Rønne's busy streets. The menu highlights substantial beef dishes such as pepper steak with wine and cream sauce, but you can also choose from a couple of local fish specialities—try the poached Baltic salmon or grilled fillet of sole, both served with lobster sauce. ⊠ *Nørreg. 2* ☎ *56/ 95–00–69* ▤ *AE, DC, MC, V.*

$$$ ▥ **Radisson SAS Fredensborg.** Along a curve of forest near a small beach, this hotel sets the island's standard for luxury. The glass-and-tile lobby is spare and sunny, the staff pleasant and eager. The dozen ample apartments have full kitchens, and guest rooms have modern furniture and balconies overlooking the sea. The rustic restaurant, De Fem Ståuerne, serves traditional French-Danish food. ⊠ *Strandvejen 116, DK–3700* ☎ *56/95–44–44* 🖷 *56/95–03–14* ⊕ *www.bornholmhotels.dk* ⇋ *72 rooms with bath, 4 suites, 12 apartments* ⌂ *Restaurant, room service, tennis court, hot tub, sauna, bar, meeting room, some pets allowed, nosmoking rooms* ▤ *AE, DC, MC, V.*

$$ ▥ **Hotel Griffen.** One of Bornholm's largest and most modern hotels is just off a busy street near the Rønne harbor. Three stories tall with plenty of windows, it has wonderful views—the sea on one side and Rønne on the other. Rooms have every modern convenience. ⊠ *Nordre Kystvej 34, DK–3700* ☎ *56/95–51–11* 🖷 *56/95–52–97* ⊕ *www.bornholmhotels. dk* ⇋ *142 rooms, 2 suites with bath* ⌂ *Restaurant, room service, cable TV, indoor pool, sauna, bar, dance club, meeting room, some pets allowed, no-smoking rooms* ▤ *AE, DC, MC, V.*

$ ▥ **Hotel Hoffmann.** This modern but somewhat institutional hotel has comfortable rooms, a third of which look out on the Rønne harbor. Highlights include a sunlit interior courtyard where you can enjoy a drink from the bar, and a full-service gym (popular with Rønne locals) with all the latest exercise equipment as well as a sauna and massage center. The gym fee for hotel guests is Dkr 40 (for nonguests, it's Dkr 50). ⊠ *Nordre Kyst 32, DK–3700* ☎ *56/95–03–86* 🖷 *56/95–25–15* ⊕ *www. bornholmhotels.dk* ⇋ *85 rooms with bath* ⌂ *Gym, sauna, bar, meeting room, some pets allowed, no-smoking rooms* ▤ *AE, DC, MC, V.*

¢ ▥ **Sverres Hotel.** Near the harbor in a building dating from 1850, this cheery hotel has simple, clean rooms. Enjoy a morning meal in the sunny breakfast room. Contented guests have covered the walls with artwork and drawings; the former owner, a jazz musician, sounded his own note by leaving behind his collection of jazz memorabilia. ⊠ *Snellemark 2, DK–3700* ☎ *56/95–03–03* 🖷 *56/95–03–92* ⊕ *www.sverres-hotel.dk* ⇋ *20 rooms, 10 with bath* ⌂ *Dining room* ▤ *AE, DC, MC, V.*

¢ ⌂ **Galløkken Camping.** This site is just a short walk from the Rønne center, near an old military museum. The open grounds are surrounded by a perimeter of trees. The shower and cooking facilities are good. ⊠ *Strandvejen 4, DK–3700 Rønne* ☎ *56/95–23–20* ⊕ *www.gallokken. dk* ⌂ *Flush toilets, laundry facilities, showers, drinking water, kitchen, general store, playground.*

Nightlife & the Arts

Bornholm's nightlife is limited to a handful of discos and clubs in Rønne, which open and close frequently as tastes change. For live jazz on the weekends, head for the atmospheric **Doctor Jazz** (⊠ Snellemark 26 ☎ No phone), outfitted with an ample stage surrounded by round tables and jazz instruments hanging on the walls. At the ever-popular **O'Malley Irish Pub** (⊠ Store Torveg. 2 ☎ 56/95–00–16), a friendly crowd of locals and tourists mingles with frothy pints in hand.

Shopping

Bornholm is famous for its quality ceramics, and Rønne, as the island's capital city, offers the widest variety. The island's history of ceramics starts in 1773 when ceramicist Michael Andersen established a factory in Rønne. Today, his legacy lives on at the large factory-turned-shop **Michael Andersen Bornholmsk Keramik** (⊠ Lille Torv 7 ☎ 56/95–00–01 ☉ Weekdays 10–5:30, Sat. 10–3) on a small square near the center of town. The shop's wide selection includes the distinctive *krakelering* ceramics, where the surface of the ceramics is covered with a web of tiny black lines that give the pieces a cracked look. Ceramicists still work in the back studio, and the store sells a range of ceramics.

The distinctive clocks, or Bornholmures, sold on the island are all handmade and hand painted with round (or sometimes rectangular) faces. The new-style clocks have a modern touch: on the hour they play classics such as Mozart or Verdi and some even sound the hour with Stephen Sondheim or Andrew Lloyd Webber. Antique versions are the costliest, with prices from Dkr 10,000 to Dkr 80,000 and up. A handmade custom clock costs Dkr 37,000 on average. Reproductions modeled on original clocks are custom-made by **Bornholmerure** (⊠ Torneværksvej 26 ☎ 56/95–31–08).

You can pick up unusual gifts and one-of-a-kind clothing made of handprinted textiles at **Bente Hammer** (⊠ Nyker Hovedg. 32 ☎ 56/96–33–35).

Hammershus

★ ❷ *8 km (5 mi) north of Jons Kapel, 30 km (19 mi) north of Rønne.*

The **fortress of Hammershus,** now in ruins, was once northern Europe's largest stronghold. The hulking fortress was begun in 1255 by the archbishop of Lund (Sweden), and became the object of centuries of struggle between Denmark and Sweden. In 1658 Danes under Jens Kofoed killed its Swedish governor, and the castle was given back to Denmark. Used until 1743, it was quarried for stone to fortify Christiansø and that island's buildings. The government finally intervened in 1822, and the site is now a mass of snaggle-toothed walls and towers atop a grassy knoll. Occasionally, concerts and other performances are held here. 🎫 *Free.*

Nightlife & the Arts

Special events don't happen nearly often enough, but check with the Bornholm's **Main Tourist Office** (☎ 56/95–95–00 ⊕ www.bornholminfo.dk) to see if any are planned at or near Hammershus. The ruins add a spectacular dimension to classical music and the performing arts.

Hammeren

❸ *5 km (3 mi) north of Hammershus, 36 km (23 mi) north of Rønne.*

This knuckle of land jutting from the island's northern tip is nearly separated from the island by a deep rift valley and the Hammer Sø (Hammer Lake). Despite constant Baltic winds, rare plants and trees grow on the warm, granite-scattered Hammeren (the Hammer), including radiant anemones. Look across the water south of the tip to the stone formation known as the Camel Heads.

en route A little more than 3 km (2 mi) southeast of Hammeren is **Madsebakke,** the largest collection of Bronze Age rock carvings in Denmark. They are presumed to be ceremonial carvings, which ancient fishermen and farmers hoped would bring good weather and bountiful crops. The most interesting of them depicts 11 ships, including one with a sun wheel, an ancient type of sun dial.

Allinge

4 *3 km (2 mi) east of Madsebakke, 21 km (13 mi) north of Rønne.*

In Allinge and its twin town Sandvig you'll find centuries-old neighborhoods and, particularly in Allinge, half-timber houses and herring smokehouses sprouting tall chimneys. Just south is a wood that the islanders call **Trolleskoven** (Trolls' Forest). Legend says that fog comes from the brew in the troll's kitchen and that when the trolls are brewing something they leave their little abodes under the cover of fog to wander the forest looking for trouble. The most mischievous is the littlest troll, Krølle Bølle, who has become a mascot of sorts for Bornholm. His likeness is everywhere—especially in souvenir shops.

Where to Stay

$–$$ **Strandhotellet.** Romantic charm is the draw at this venerable hotel on
Fodor'sChoice a corner across from the harbor. A white arched entry leads into a
★ stone-and-whitewashed lobby. Rooms are furnished in plain beech furniture with woolen covers and pastel colors. ⊠ *Strandpromenaden 7, Sandvig DK–3770* ☎ *56/48–03–14* 🖷 *56/48–02–09* 🌐 *www. strandhotellet.dk* 🛏 *52 rooms, 1 suite with bath* ♢ *Restaurant, bar* ▤ *MC, V.*

¢ **Sandvig Familie Camping.** Pleasantly close to the beach, most of the camping sites here have a view of the water. The large kitchen and bathing facilities are well maintained. ⊠ *Sandlinien 5, DK–3770* ☎ *56/48–04–47 or 56/48–00–01* ♢ *Showers, kitchen, playground* ⊗ *Closed Nov.–Mar.*

en route Eight kilometers (5 mi) southeast of Allinge along the coastal path are the grottoes and granite cliffs of the **Helligdomsklipperne** (Cliffs of Sanctuary), which contain a well-known rock formation best seen from the boats that sail the nearby waters in summer. In the Middle Ages, people used to visit these waters, believing that they had healing powers—hence the name. The **Helligdomsklipperne boat** (☎ 58/48–51–65) departs several times daily in the summer from the Gudhjem harbor. The round-trip costs Dkr 60. Just southeast of the Helligdomsklipperne, a pastoral coastal path leads to the tiny, preserved **Døndalen Forest.** Its fertile soil bears a surprising profusion of Mediterranean vegetation, including fig and cherry trees. During rainy periods look for a waterfall at the bottom of the dale.

Gudhjem

★ **5** *18 km (11 mi) east of Allinge, 33 km (21 mi) northeast of Rønne.*

At the height of summer, Gudhjem (God's Home) is perhaps the most tourist-packed town on Bornholm. Tiny half-timber houses and gift shops with lace curtains and clay roofs line steep stone streets that loop around the harbor. The island's first smokehouses still produce alder-smoked golden herring.

★ ⚲ Walk down Brøddegade, which turns into Melstedvej; here you'll find the **Landsbrugs Museum** (Agricultural Museum) and Melstedgård, a working farm. The farm includes the well-kept house and garden of a 19th-century family who lived here. Notice the surprisingly bright colors used on the interior of the house, and leave time to visit the old shop where you can buy locally produced woolen sweaters, wooden spoons, and even homemade mustard. ⊠ *Melstedvej 25* ☎ *56/48–55–98* ⊕ *www. bornholmsmuseer.dk/melstedg* ⊡ *Dkr 30* ☉ *Mid-May–mid-Oct., Tues.–Sun. 10–5.*

Up the hill from Gudhjem's waterfront is the **Oluf Høst Museet**, with a collection of paintings by Bornholm artist Oluf Høst, including his series of a whitewashed Bornholm farm called Bognemark, which he depicted with glowing splashes of oranges and reds from the setting sun. Høst and other modernist Bornholm artists are well known for their ability to capture Bornholm's natural light. The museum is in Høst's home, which he built in 1929 out of two fisherman's cottages and lived in until his death in 1966. It's easy to see why Høst found artistic inspiration here. At the top of the house's leafy, rock-strewn garden are lovely views over the colorful cottages of Gudhjem. ⊠ *Løkkeg. 35* ☎ *56/ 48–50–38* ⊕ *www.ohmus.dk* ⊡ *Dkr 40* ☉ *Mid-June–mid-Aug., daily 11–5; mid-Aug.–Sept., Tues.–Sun. 11–5; mid-Apr.–mid-June and early Oct., Tues.–Sun. 1–5.*

off the beaten path

BORNHOLMS KUNSTMUSEUM – If you follow the main road, Hellidomsvej, out of Gudhjem in the direction of Allinge/Sandvig, you'll come to Bornholm's art museum, an excellent example of the Danes' ability to integrate art, architecture, and natural surroundings. Built by the architectural firm of Fogh and Følner, the white-painted brick, granite, and sandstone building is centered by a thin stream of "holy" trickling water that exits the building and leads the visitor to a walkway and overlook above the Helligdomsklipperne. Throughout, the walls of the museum are punched with picture windows overlooking nearby grazing cows and the crashing Baltic: a natural accompaniment to the art. Most of the works are by Bornholmers, including a body of modernist work by Oluf Høst, Karl Esaksen, and Olaf Rude. The museum also displays some sculpture and glass, as well as a survey of more historical paintings. Check out the restaurant and shop. ⊠ *Hellidomsvej 95* ☎ *56/48–43–86* ⊕ *www.bornholms-kunstmuseum.dk* ⊡ *Dkr 35* ☉ *May, Sept., and Oct., Tues.–Sun. 10–5; June–Aug., daily 10–5; Nov.–Apr., Tues. and Thurs. 1–5, Sun. 10–5.*

CHRISTIANSØ – A 45-minute boat ride northeast from Gudhjem will bring you to the historic island of Christiansø. Though it was originally a bastion, the Storetårn (Big Tower) and Lilletårn (Little Tower) are all that remain of the fort, built in 1684 and dismantled in 1855. The barracks, street, and gardens, for which the earth was hauled here by boat, have hardly changed since that time. They remain under the jurisdiction of the defense ministry, making this a tiny tax-free haven for its 100 inhabitants. Nearby, the rocky, uninhabited island of **Græsholmen** is an inaccessible bird sanctuary—the only place in Denmark where the razorbill and guillemot breed.

Where to Stay & Eat

¢–$ ✕ **Café Klint.** Locals flock to this red, half-timber harborside restaurant, where the portions of good 'ole Danish fare are generous and the prices are low. Dishes include smoked salmon with spinach, fillet of sole with remoulade, or a plate heaped with different kinds of herring. In summer, tables are set out on the terrace. In winter the restaurant changes its name to Vinter Klint (Winter Klint), and you can't get cozier than sitting in the low-ceiling dining room, surrounded by pine-green walls, and perhaps warmed by a glass or two of the house wine. ⊠ *Ejnar Mikkelsensvej 20* ☎ *56/48–56–26* ▱ *MC, V.*

$–$$ ✕▦ **Jantzens Hotel.** Founded in 1872, this bright-yellow building with white shutters and wrought-iron balconies is Gudhjem's oldest hotel. The front windows face the sea, and the backyard gives way to a sunny, idyllic terrace and rose garden. Much of the hotel has been lovingly restored, with an eye to recapturing its turn-of-the-20th-century ambience. Rooms are outfitted with hardwood floors, pale green walls, and rattan furniture. The balconies have views over Gudhjem's yellow and red houses, clustered against a backdrop of the blue Baltic. The bathrooms are small and basic, but all rooms are equipped with a refrigerator. The hotel's interior is still a work in progress; so far half the rooms have been restored, so ask when booking. What was once a pavilion and tea terrace is now utilized by the restaurant, Andi's Kokken, which includes on its French-Danish menu such dishes as mussels in a mild curry sauce with capers, and venison with shallots and mushrooms. Dessert might be fresh blueberries, hand-picked by the chef from the nearby fields. The restaurant is closed Mondays and November through April. ⊠ *Brøddeg. 33, DK–3760* ☎ *56/48–50–17* ☎ *56/48–57–15* ⊕ *www.jantzenshotel.dk* ⇥ *18 rooms with bath* ⚭ *Restaurant, some pets allowed (fee)* ▱ *MC, V* ☉ *Closed Nov.–Apr.*

¢ ▦ **Danhostel Gudhjem.** In a half-timber 100-year-old former manor house, this hostel in the middle of Gudhjem offers single- to eight-bed rooms of standard Danish hostel style: pine bunks and industrial carpeting. There are six kitchens available for use. ⊠ *Løkkeg. 7, DK–3760* ☎ *56/48–50–35* ☎ *56/48–56–35* ⊕ *www.danhostel-gudhjem.dk* ⇥ *50 rooms without bath* ⚭ *Restaurant, laundry facilities* ▱ *MC, V.*

Shopping

Baltic Sea Glass (⊠ Melstedvej 47 ☎ 56/48–56–41), on the main road just on the outskirts of town, offers high-quality, bright, and imaginative decanters, glasses, candlesticks, and one-of-a-kind pieces, including an old-fashioned contraption to catch flies. In town, see the delicate porcelain bowls of **Per Rehfeldt** (⊠ Salenevej 1 ☎ 56/48–54–13). Unique, hand-thrown ceramic work is available from and by **Julia Manitius** (⊠ Holkavej 12 ☎ 56/48–55–99).

Rø Plantage

❻ *6 km (4 mi) southwest of Gudhjem, 24 km (15 mi) northeast of Rønne.*

Rø Plantation is dense forest that serves as a quiet foil to the hubbub of Gudhjem. A century ago it was a heather-covered grazing area, but after stone dikes were erected to keep the cattle out, spruce, pine, larch, and birch were cultivated. The cool refuge now consists largely of saplings and new growth—the result of devastating storms in the late '50s and '60s.

Rø Golfbane (⊠ Spellingevej 3 ☎ 56/48–40–50) has won various European and Scandinavian awards for its natural beauty—and challenges. Its 18 holes are set close to the coastal cliffs and have views of the sea. It has a pro shop and a restaurant.

Østerlars

❼ *5 km (3 mi) east of Rø Plantage, 22 km (14 mi) northeast of Rønne.*

Fodor'sChoice
★

The standout attraction here is the **Østerlars Kirke.** The largest of the island's four round churches, it was built in about 1150; extensions, including the buttresses, were added later. Constructed from boulders and slabs of limestone, the whitewashed church was part spiritual sanctuary, part fortification, affording protection from enemy armies and pirates. Inside is the island's only painted tympanum, with a faded image of a cross and decorative foliage. Several Gothic wall paintings—including depictions of the Annunciation and Nativity—have survived from the 1300s. ⊠ *Gudhjemsvej 28* ☎ *56/49–82–64* ☒ *Dkr 6* ☉ *May–mid-Oct., Mon.–Sat. 9–5.*

---

off the beaten path

KIRSTEN CLEMANN'S CERAMIC STUDIO – Bornholm, with its Baltic Sea location and wide-open skies, has been drawing artists to its shores for the past century. Kirsten Clemann has been here for several decades, creating her fanciful, one-of-a-kind ceramic designs in a clay-spattered studio adjoining her home, west of the small, blink-and-you'll-miss-it town of Østermarie, 5 km (3 mi) southeast of Østerlars. As Clemann tells it, it took awhile to be accepted into the island community, but now her pieces are proudly displayed in restaurants and craft shows across Bornholm—and across the globe. Clemann works out of her pleasantly chaotic studio, where she creates turtles; hens; birdbaths; and delicate, floating ceramic balls for ponds. She usually works with the colors of blue and rose. Clemann's large, unique reliefs are often snapped up by German buyers; the pieces may depict rows of dancing women twirling their umbrellas, or be covered with protruding glazed ceramic fish heads, inspired by a display at a fish market. Clemann's other passion is her garden, which is teeming with blooming bushes and flowers and is strewn with her ceramic creations. Call ahead. ⊠ *Almindingensvej 84, 2½ km (1½ mi) west of Østermarie* ☎ *56/47–27–05.*

Svaneke

❽ *21 km (13 mi) east of Østerlars, 49 km (31 mi) northeast of Rønne.*

The coastal town of Svaneke, Denmark's easternmost settlement, is an enchanting hamlet of 17th- and 18th-century houses, winding cobbled streets, and a harbor sliced from the rocky earth. Once a fishing village, it is now immaculately preserved and the site of a thriving artists' community.

Bornholm's smoked herring is famous throughout Scandinavia, and no visit to the island is complete without sampling it for yourself—preferably in the manner of the Danes, who eat it outside on a sunny terrace, with a cold Carlsberg in hand. For more than 35 years, Hjorth Hansen has been smoking herring at **Hjorths Røgeri** (Hjorth's Smokehouse), 2 km (1 mi) south of Svaneke. Every morning at 6 AM, Hjorth hauls in big baskets of elmwood, lights a fire, and begins smoking the fresh herring, tending to the fire with a long pole wrapped with rags at one end. Five hours later, he serves up plates of warm, smoked herring in the adjoining terrace. Hjorth works from late April to October. The best time to watch him in action is around 10 AM, in the last hour of the smoking process. ⊠ *Brugsebakken 18, Årsdale,* ☎ *56/49–61–10* ☉ *Late Apr.–Oct.*

Where to Stay & Eat

¢–$$ ✕ **Bryghuset.** Microbreweries are a new concept in the land of Carls-berg, but the idea is catching on, and Svaneke's Bryghuset (Brew House) is one of the first. All the beer is brewed on the premises, in a massive copper brew kettle linked by piping to the kitchen. The menu is based on the concept that food should compliment the beer. The house spe-cialty is Bryggerben ("Brewer's bone"), a messy, finger-licking plate of spareribs smothered in barbecue sauce, which can be enjoyed at one of the long wooden tables set under the beam ceilings or on the large sum-mer terrace. Also on offer is a platter of Christiansø herring served with egg, rye bread, and butter. At Easter and Christmas, try the stronger fes-tive brew. ✉ *Torvet 5* ☎ *56/49–73–21* ☰ *MC, V* ☉ *Closed Jan.*

$$ ✕▣ **Siemsens Gaard.** Built in a 270-year-old merchant house, this U-shape hotel with a gravel-courtyard café overlooks the harbor. The inside is cushy with sofas below severe black-and-white prints and antiques. The rooms differ, but all have stripped pine and soft colors. The bright, modern restaurant serves French-Danish food, with a menu of 75 dishes—from club sandwiches to smoked Baltic salmon to smørrebrød. The restaurant is closed from November to May. ✉ *Havnebryggen 9, DK–3740* ☎ *56/49–61–49* ☐ *56/49–61–03* ⊕ *www.siemsens.dk* ⬐ *51 rooms with bath* ⚘ *Restaurant, café, some pets allowed, no-smoking rooms* ☰ *AE, DC, MC, V.*

Shopping

Stroll through the boutiques in the central Glastorvet in Svaneke. Among them is the studio of **Pernille Bülow** (✉ Glastorvet, Brænderigænget 8 ☎ 56/49–66–72), one of Denmark's most famous glassblowers. Her work is sold in Copenhagen's best design shops. Even if you buy directly from her studio, don't expect bargains—though you may be lucky to find sec-onds—but do expect colorful, experimental work.

Neksø

9 *9 km (5½ mi) south of Svaneke, 48 km (30 mi) northeast of Rønne.*

Neksø (or Nexø) bustles with tourists and locals who shop and live around its busy harbor, lined with fishing boats from throughout the Baltics and Eastern Europe. It might seem like a typical 17th-century town, but it was rebuilt almost completely after World War II, when the Russians bombed it to dislodge stubborn German troops who refused to surren-der—three days after the rest of Denmark had been liberated. The Rus-sians lingered on the island until April 1946.

Wander down to the harbor to find the **Neksø Museum,** housed in a mus-tard-yellow building that was once the town's courthouse. The museum has a fine collection of fishing and local history exhibits and maritime memorabilia. ✉ *Havnen* ☎ *56/49–25–56* ⊕ *www.bornholmsmuseer. dk* ▨ *Dkr 15* ☉ *May–Oct., Tues.–Sun. 10–4.*

The **Andersen Nexøs Hus** contains photographs and mementos of Dan-ish author Martin Andersen Hansen (1909–55), who changed his last name to Nexø after his beloved town. A complicated man and vehe-ment socialist, he wrote, among other works, *Pelle the Conqueror,* set in Bornholm at the turn of the 20th century, when Swedish immigrants were exploited by Danish landowners. The story was turned into an Academy Award–winning film. ✉ *Ferskesøstr. 36* ☎ *56/49–45–42* ⊕ *www.bornholmsmuseer.dk/manexo* ▨ *Dkr 20* ☉ *Mid-May–Oct., weekdays 10–4, Sat. 10–2.*

Where to Eat

$$–$$$ ✕ **Tre Søstre.** Facing Nexø's bustling harbor, this spacious restaurant, housed in a converted storage warehouse, is named after a 19th-century Danish ship *The Three Sisters,* a model of which hangs on the wall. The creatively decorated interior (right down to the plates and the candlesticks) pays tribute to Bornholm's artists. The lavender, pale-orange, and sea-green vases of Svaneke glassblower Pernille Bülow grace the window sills, providing a bright and delicate contrast to the restaurant's rustic furnishings. Hanging from the ceiling is a playful, blue-and-green ceramic fish, created by long-time Bornholmer Kirsten Clemann. The Danish menu includes grilled salmon with spinach and hollandaise sauce, and fried scampi flavored with cognac, garlic, and curry. ⊠ *Havnen 5* ☎ *56/49–33–93* ⊟ *AE, DC, MC, V* ☾ *Closed Sept.–May.*

Shopping

For exquisite woodwork see **Bernard Romain** (⊠ Rønnevej 54 ☎ 56/48–86–66).

Almindingen

➓ *23 km (14 mi) west of Neksø, 27 km (17 mi) northeast of Rønne.*

The lush Almindingen, Denmark's third-largest forest, is filled with ponds, lakes, evergreens, and well-marked trails, and it blooms with lily of the valley in spring. Within it, the oak-lined ☾ **Ekkodalen** (Echo Valley)—where children love to hear their shouts resound—is networked by trails leading to smooth rock faces that soar 72 feet high. At the northern edge, near the road to Østermarie, once stood one of Bornholm's most famous sights: seven evergreens growing from a single trunk. The plant succumbed to old age in 1995, but you may still be able to see the remains of its curious trunk.

Sports & the Outdoors

HIKING   Check with the tourist board for a map showing three 4-km (2½-mi) hikes through the Almindingen Forest and several more through its Echo Valley. The *Bornholm Green Guide,* available in shops and tourism offices, offers walking and hiking routes.

Åkirkeby

⓫ *5 km (3 mi) south of Almindingen, 16 km (9 mi) east of Rønne.*

Åkirkeby is the oldest town on the island, with a municipal charter from 1346. The town's church, the **Åkirke,** is Bornholm's oldest and largest, dating from the mid-12th century. Though it is not one of the more typical round churches, its walls and tower were well suited for defense. The altarpiece and pulpit are Dutch Renaissance pieces from about 1600, but the carved sandstone font is as old as the church itself. ⊠ *Torvet* ☎ *56/97–41–03* ⊠ *Dkr 10* ☾ *Mon.–Sat. 10–4.*

Nylars

⓬ *8 km (5 mi) west of Åkirkeby, 9 km (6 mi) east of Rønne.*

Like the Østerlars church, the round **Nylars Kirke** dates from 1150. The chalk paintings from the Old Testament on its central pillar are the oldest on the island, possibly dating from 1250. Even older are the runic stones on the church's porch. Both are of Viking origin. ⊠ *Kirkevej* ☎ *56/97–20–13* ⊠ *Suggested donation Dkr 5* ☾ *Mid-May–mid-Sept., Mon.–Sat. 9–5.*

Bornholm A to Z

AIRPORTS

The Bornholms Lufthavn airport is 5 km (3 mi) south of Rønne at the island's southwestern tip.

🛪 **Bornholms Lufthavn** ☎ 56/95-26-26 ⊕ www.slv.dk/bornholm.

BIKE TRAVEL

Biking is eminently feasible and pleasant on Bornholm, thanks to a network of more than 200 km (125 mi) of cycle roads, including an old railway converted to a cross-island path. Rentals of sturdy two-speeds and tandems are available for about Dkr 50 a day at more than 20 different establishments all over the island—near the ferry; at the airport; and in Allinge, Gudhjem, Hasle, Pedersker (near Åkirkeby), Rønne, Svaneke, and most other towns.

🛪 Bike Rentals **Bornholms Cykeludlejning** ⊠ Nordre Kystvej 5, Rønne ☎ 56/95-13-59. **Cykel-Centret** ⊠ Sønderg. 7, Rønne ☎ 56/95-06-04.

BOAT & FERRY TRAVEL

The *Bornholmstrafikken* car ferry from Copenhagen's Kvæsthusbro Harbor (near Nyhavn) departs at 11:30 PM year-round; from late January to mid-March, it departs only on Wednesday, Friday, and Sunday. From late June to mid-August, there are also departures at 8 AM on Monday, Wednesday, Friday, and weekends. During the rest of the year, there is often one weekly 8:30 AM departure, usually on Tuesday or Friday. Call for details. The night trip takes seven hours, and the day trip takes six hours. To avoid delays, make reservations. Comfortable sleeping bunks in a massive hall are also available for an extra charge. At this writing, the public operators of the ferry line were discussing changes in overall service in conjunction with a privatization plan. The schedule above should be valid until 2005, but it would be wise to double check as the fate of the line may be determined in the interim.

With the opening of the Øresund Bridge between Copenhagen and Malmö, *Bornholmstrafikken* has increased its ferry departures from Ystad, which lies 57 km (36 mi) southeast of Malmö. There are two to four departures from Ystad to Rønne daily, on either the high-speed ferry (1 hr 20 min), or the conventional ferry (2½ hrs).

Nordbornholms Turistbureau (North Bornholm Tourist Board) is the agent for a summer ferry that links Neu Mukran and Fährhafen Sassnitz on the island of Rügen in Germany. Scandlines, a competing company, offers passage aboard the ferry to Fährhafen Sassnitz. Prices vary according to the number of people traveling and the size of the vehicle. There is also a boat between Swinoujscie, Poland and Rønne (7 hrs); call Polferries in Poland.

🛪 **Bornholmstrafikken** ☎ 56/95-18-66 ⊕ www.bornholmferries.dk. **Nordbornholms Turistbureau** ☎ 56/48-00-01 ⊕ www.bornholmsbookingcenter.dk. **Polferries** ⊠ Norgesvej 2 Rønne ☎ 56/95-10-69, 48/943-552-102 in Poland ⊕ www.polferries.com. **Scandlines** ☎ 33/15-15-15 ⊕ www.scandlines.dk.

BUS TRAVEL

The *Bornholmerbussen* (Bornholm Bus) No. 866 runs from Copenhagen's main station, travels across the Øresund Bridge to Malmö, in Sweden, and then continues to Ystad, where it connects with a ferry to Rønne. The trip takes around three hours. Buses depart two to four times daily, usually once in the morning and several times in the afternoon and evening. Call Bornholmerbussen for more details.

Though bus service is certainly not as frequent as in major cities, there are regular connections (with BAT, see below) between Bornholm towns. Schedules are posted at all stations, and you can usually pick one up on board. The fare is Dkr 8.50 per zone, or you can buy a klip kort (punch ticket) of 10 tickets for Dkr 68. A 24-hour bus pass costs Dkr 110.
🚍 **Bornholmerbussen** ☎ 44/68-44-00. **BAT** (Bornholm Municipality Traffic Company) ☎ 56/95-21-21 ⊕ www.bat.dk.

CAR RENTAL

Rønne's Hertz agency is near the ferry arrivals and departures area. The Avis branch is also nearby.
🚗 **Avis** ⊠ Snellemark 19, Rønne ☎ 56/95-22-08 **Hertz** ⊠ Munch Petersens Vej 1, Rønne ☎ 56/91-00-12.

CAR TRAVEL

There are excellent roads on the island, but be alert for cyclists and occasional leisurely paced cows.

EMERGENCIES

The general emergency number for ambulance, accident, or fire anywhere in Denmark is 112.
🚑 **Bornholm's Central Hospital** ⊠ Sygehusvej, Rønne ☎ 56/95-11-65. **Rønne Apotek** (Rønne Pharmacy) · ⊠ Store Torveg. 12, Rønne ☎ 56/95-01-30.

SPORTS & THE OUTDOORS

FISHING Cod, salmon, and herring fishing are excellent in season, though better from a boat than from shore. Licenses cost Dkr 25 per day, Dkr 75 per week, and Dkr 100 per year. Contact the tourist office for details and information on charter trips.

TOURS

Klippefly can arrange a 20- to 40-minute aerial tour in a Cessna or Piper plane that covers either the entire coast or the northern tip.

The BAT (Bornholm Municipality Traffic Company) offers some inventive summer tours. All are available Tuesday through Friday, from mid-July until early August. All begin at the red bus terminal at Snellemark 30 in Rønne at 10 AM and cost Dkr 110. (You can also buy a 24-hour bus card for Dkr 110, or a five- or seven-day card for Dkr 390, good for both the regional buses and the tours.) Tour prices do not include some Dkr 5–Dkr 10 admissions or lunch at a herring smokehouse. The five-hour tour aboard the Kunsthåndværkbussen (Arts and Crafts Bus) includes stops at glass, pottery, textile, and silver studios. In summer, different studios are visited each day. The Havebussen (Garden Bus) visits sights that illustrate the ways in which the island's exquisite flora and fauna are being preserved. The Veteranbussen (Veteran Bus), a circa World War II Bedford, connects some of Bornholm's oldest industries, including a clockmaker, water mill, and Denmark's last windmill used for making flour.

From mid-June to mid-September, boats to the Helligdomsklipperne (Sanctuary Cliffs) leave Gudhjem at 10:30, 1:30, and 2:30, with extra sailings from mid-June to mid-August. Call Thor Båd. Boats to Christiansø depart from Svaneke at 10 AM daily year-round; May to September daily at 10:20 from Gudhjem, and at 1 from Allinge; and between mid-June and August, an additional boat leaves Gudhjem weekdays at 9:40 and 12:15. Call Christiansø Farten for additional information.
🚌 **BAT** (Bornholm Municipality Traffic Company) ☎ 56/95-21-21 ⊕ www.bat.dk. **Christiansø Farten** ⊠ Ejnar Mikkelsensvej 25, Gudhjem ☎ 56/48-51-76 ⊕ www.christiansoefarten.dk. **Klippefly** ⊠ Søndre Landevej 2, Rønne ☎ 56/95-35-73 ⊕ www.bornholmerguiden.dk/klippefly. **Thor Båd** ⊠ Melstedvej 17, Gudhjem ☎ 56/48-51-65.

TRAIN TRAVEL

A DSB Intercity train travels two to five times a day from Copenhagen's main station, across the Øresund Bridge to Malmö, and then to Ystad, where it connects with a ferry to Rønne.

DSB ☎ 70/13-14-15 ⊕ www.dsb.dk.

VISITOR INFORMATION

The main tourist office in Rønne operates a Web site with area listings. **Bornholm Tourist Office** ✉ Nordre Kystvej 3, DK-3700 Rønne ☎ 56/95-95-00 🖶 56/95-95-68 ⊕ www.bornholminfo.dk. **Allinge-Nordbornholms Turistbureau** ✉ Kirkeg. 4, DK-3770 Allinge ☎ 56/48-00-01 🖶 56/48-00-20 ⊕ www.bornholmsbookingcenter. dk. **Åkirkeby** ✉ Torvet 2, DK-3720 Åkirkeby ☎ 56/97-45-20 🖶 56/97-58-90 ⊕ www. sydborn.dk. **Gudhjem** ✉ Åbog. 9 DK-3760 Gudhjem ☎ 56/48-52-10 🖶 56/48-52-74. **Hasle** ✉ Havneg. 1 DK-3790 Hasle ☎ 56/96-44-81 🖶 56/96-41-06 ⊕ www.hasle-turistbureau.dk. **Nexø** ✉ Søndre Hammer 2A DK-3730 Nexø ☎ 56/49-70-79 🖶 56/49-70-10 ⊕ www.nexoe-dueodde.dk. **Svaneke** ✉ Storeg. 24, DK-3740 Svaneke ☎ 56/49-70-79 🖶 56/49-70-10 ⊕ www.nexoe-dueodde.dk.

GREENLAND

When Eric the Red discovered Greenland (Kalaallit Nunaat in Greenlandic, Grønland in Danish) a thousand years ago, his Norsemen thought they had reached the edge of the world. After it, there was only Ginnungagap, the endless abyss.

Greenland still commands awe from the growing number of tourists who venture off the usual Scandinavian path to explore the world's largest island. Measuring more than 2.1 million square km (1.3 million square mi), it's larger than Italy, France, Great Britain, Germany, and Spain combined. The coastal regions are sparsely populated with about 7,500 Danes and 48,000 Inuit—the indigenous people, whose roots can be traced to the native inhabitants of Canada's Arctic, and further back to the people of Alaska. More than 80% of the land is perpetually frozen beneath an ice cap that, at its deepest, reaches a thickness of 3 km (2 mi). If it melted, sea levels around the world would rise about 21 feet.

Greenland's first inhabitants probably arrived some 5,000 years ago from what is today Canada, which is only around 26 km (16 mi) away at the closest point. Inuit peoples continued to migrate to and roam across the island. Greenland's recorded history began at about the same time, in AD 982, when Eric and his Norse settlers claimed the land, but after 400 years of colonization they mysteriously disappeared. During this period Denmark and Norway were joined under the Danish crown, a union that muddled ownership of Greenland until 1933, when the International High Court awarded Denmark complete sovereignty. (Until 1997 every town had both a Greenlandic and a Danish name; today the Greenlandic names are used on modern maps with the Danish included in brackets.) Geographically isolated and increasingly politically independent, Greenlanders are intent on redefining their ethnic identity in a modern world. They refer to themselves as Inuit, in solidarity with native peoples of Canada, Alaska, and the former Soviet Union, and speak their own language in addition to Danish.

In 1979 Denmark granted Greenland home rule, vesting its tiny Landsting (parliament) in the capital Nuuk/Godthåb with power over internal affairs. Though Denmark continues to devolve power, it still administers foreign policy and provides financial aid to an economy based on fishing, animal husbandry, construction, and tourism.

The number of visitors has been growing at an impressive rate, from just 3,000 in 1993 to 18,000 in 1997, and then well over 30,000 in 2001. The island also garnered national attention when Crown Prince Frederik of Denmark completed a highly publicized dogsled trip across northern Greenland in early 2001. Relatively speaking, though, with still few tourists (almost all on package tours), Greenland remains one of the world's least developed regions. By its nature, the region is far more difficult to explore than dwarfed mother Denmark. Travel is possible only by airplane, helicopter or coastal boat, because there are few roads and no railroads. However, the southern and western towns—trimmed with building-block red-and-green houses and well-used harbors—have adequate hotels, airfields, and helicopter pads, and regular summertime ferry service. Man-made luxuries are few, but the rewards of nature are savagely beautiful. Below the Arctic Circle, the attractions include Norse ruins, Ice Age–gouged mountains, and jagged fjords. Farther north, dogsleds whip over icy plains, and ferries glide past icebergs as big as city blocks.

The country remains a wilderness that offers unique opportunities for hunting, fishing, hiking, skiing, dogsledding, and camping. True, some of this can be done on your own, but there are state-certified outfitters who cater to every need and are familiar with the characteristics of the wilderness in their territories. Their expertise can make all the difference. They know where the big fish lurk, where the big game can be found, and the safest routes to sites—this is especially important in winter. An outfitter makes it possible to get the very best out of a visit to this breathtaking country.

Because most travelers follow preset routes, towns and sites are arranged south to north in geographic order and not necessarily in the order they would be visited. Perhaps only one major museum or site is noted per village, but there is much more to see in Greenland's mercurial natural landscape. Venture along the wooden stairs and boardwalks that connect most private homes and provide inner-village walking paths. Cruise beneath the expanse of an iceberg and listen to it moan. Take a hike, a bike ride, or a motor-vehicle excursion to the inland ice and marvel at its magnitude. Rise at 3 AM to take a stroll through the summer sunshine. There is no private property in Greenland—nature is free for all to enjoy, and in Greenlandic fashion, it is best savored slowly. Those who love this island do not move through it at a clip; it's more gratifying to let it move you.

Narsarsuaq

❶ *4 hrs, 50 min northwest of Copenhagen by plane.*

Narsarsuaq, meaning Great Plain in English, aptly describes the wide, smooth land harboring one of Greenland's largest civilian airports. The town is accessible from Copenhagen, Reykjavík, and Kangerlussuaq by plane only, and from Nuuk/Godthåb by plane and boat—though such boats are booked months in advance.

Not far from the edge of town, you can take a 10-km (6-mi) boat ride from the Narsarsuaq harbor to an area where icebergs have broken off from a nearby glacier. There you are invited to collect glacial ice for the cocktails served on board.

Near Narsarsuaq is the point locals call **Hospitalsdalen** (Hospital Valley), a controversial area named for an alleged American hospital where Korean War wounded were said to have been hidden away so as not to weaken morale back home. Though history books deny the story, many

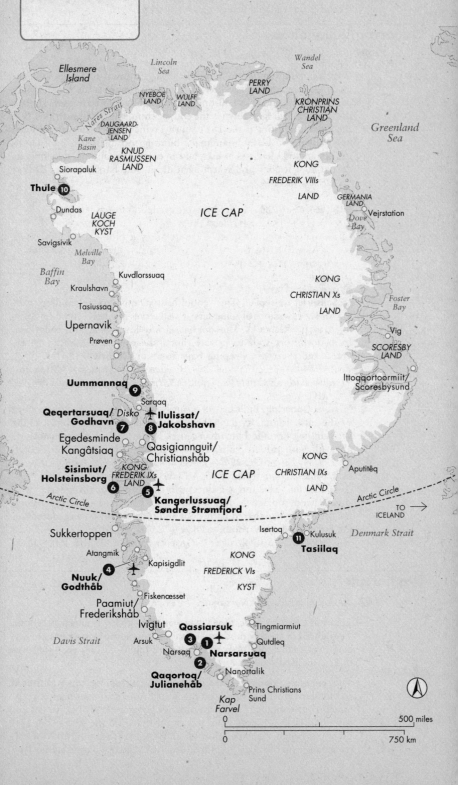

Greenland

Ellesmere Island

Lincoln Sea

Wandel Sea

PERRY LAND

NYEBOE LAND

WULFF LAND

KRONPRINS CHRISTIAN LAND

Greenland Sea

Nares Strait

DAUGAARD-JENSEN LAND

Kane Basin

KNUD RASMUSSEN LAND

KONG FREDERIK VIIIs LAND

GERMANIA LAND

Vejrstation

Siorapaluk

Thule **10**

ICE CAP

Dove Bay

Dundas

LAUGE KOCH KYST

Savigsivik

Melville Bay

Baffin Bay

Kuvdlorssuaq

KONG CHRISTIAN Xs LAND

Foster Bay

Kraulshavn

Tasiussaq

Upernavik

Prøven

Vig

SCORESBY LAND

Uummannaq **9**

Saqqaq

Ittoqqortoormiit/ Scoresbysund

Qeqertarsuaq/ Godhavn **7**

Disko

Ilulissat/ Jakobshavn **8**

Egedesminde

Kangâtsiaq

Qasigiannguit/ Christianshåb

Sisimiut/ Holsteinsborg

KONG FREDERIK IXs LAND

6

5

KONG CHRISTIAN IXs LAND

ICE CAP

Aputitêq

Arctic Circle

Kangerlussuaq/ Søndre Strømfjord

Arctic Circle

TO ICELAND →

Sukkertoppen

Isertoq

Kulusuk

Denmark Strait

Atangmik

Kapisigdlit

Tasiilaq **11**

KONG FREDERICK VIs KYST

Nuuk/ Godthåb **4**

Paamiut/ Frederikshåb

Fiskenœsset

Ivigtut

Qassiarsuk

Tingmiarmiut

Davis Strait

Arsuk

3

1

Qutdleq

Narsaq

2

Narsarsuaq

Qaqortoq/ Julianehåb

Nanortalik

Prins Christians Sund

Kap Farvel

0		500 miles
0		750 km

locals swear it's true. Nothing remains of the hospital, so proof of the legend is unavailable here.

Qaqortoq/Julianehåb

❷ *6 hrs south of Narsarsuaq by ferry.*

With a population of 3,600, this is the largest town in southern Greenland—and one of the loveliest. In the town square is the island's only fountain, surrounded by half-timber and brightly colored houses. Though the oldest building in town is the cooper shop, which dates from 1797, the most interesting is the 1871 smithy, which now houses the **Julianehåb Museum.** Inside are handmade hunting tools, kayaks, Inuit clothing, and a furnished sod house you can enter. A traditional dwelling, its design kept it cozy and warm even during the harsh winter. ☞ *Free* ⊙ *Weekdays 11–4.*

off the beaten path

HVALSEY CHURCH – A nice half-day excursion from Qaqortoq is the 14½-km (9-mi) sailboat ride to the well-preserved Hvalsey Church ruins, site of a well-attended Norse wedding in 1408—the community's last recorded activity before it mysteriously disappeared. As the church is close to a rocky beach, the hardy can opt for a frigid dip.

Where to Stay

$$$$ ⊡ **Sulisartut Højskoliat.** This school hosts Danish schoolchildren visiting for short sessions or semesters; it also serves as a hotel complex catering to all pocketbooks. The spot has various levels of accommodations, from dormitory-style to private, hotel-like rooms. Meals can be ordered and there are sleeping bags for rent. ⊠ *Box 132, DK–3920* ☎ *299/64–24–66* 🖷 *299/64–29–73* ⊕ *www.sulisartut.gl* ⋧ *70 rooms, 41 with bath* ⌂ *Cafeteria, laundry facilities, meeting rooms* ▤ *AE, DC, MC, V.*

$ ⊡ **Hotel Qaqortoq.** Built in 1987, this hotel is among the more modern on the entire island. Its glass-and-white facade atop a hill overlooks the surrounding fjord and the town center. Rooms are simple but comfortable, all with private bath, TV, and phone. ⊠ *Box 155, DK–3920* ☎ *299/64–22–82* 🖷 *299/64–12–34* ⋧ *50 rooms with bath* ⌂ *Restaurant, billiards, bar* ▤ *AE, DC, MC, V.*

¢ ⊡ **Siniffik Inn.** This inn is a dormitory-style spot for the traveler who simply needs a place to sleep and facilities for a bath. This fine option for the thrifty has shared bathroom and toilet facilities, a common living room, and a TV room. ⊠ *Box 172, DK–3920* ☎ *299/64–27–28* 🖷 *299/64–23–28* ⋧ *26 beds* ⌂ *Grocery* ▤ *AE, DC, MC, V* ⊙ *Closed Oct.–Apr.*

Qassiarsuk

❸ *30 min northwest of Narsarsuaq by boat.*

The main focus of the tiny village of Qassiarsuk is sheep breeding. Though there are few modern facilities in town, the **Norse ruins** are fascinating and include, for example, the **Brattahlíð**—1,000-year-old ruins of Eric the Red's farm.

The remains of **Tjodhilde Kirke** are especially intriguing: this was touted as the first Christian church on the North American continent (Greenland is considered part of North America geographically but part of Europe politically). It was from this point that Eric the Red's son, Leif Ericsson, began the expedition in AD 1000 that took him to Vinland, somewhere on the coast of North America. The first Greenlandic Ting (outdoor parliament), fashioned after those in Iceland, was also held here at about the same time.

Nuuk/Godthåb

❹ *1 hr, 25 min northwest of Narsarsuaq by small plane (15 hrs by ferry), 7 hrs east of Ottawa by plane.*

Nuuk/Godthåb, the capital of Greenland, is beautifully situated on a peninsula between two fjords. It was founded in 1728 by the Norwegian missionary Hans Egede; his harborside home is now the private residence of the island's home-rule premier. The university, the National Museum, and Greenland's only cultural center are also in town. The annual snow sculpture contest in March brings artists from near and far.

The centrally located **Landsmuseet** (National Museum) has a good permanent display of kayaks, costumes, and hunting weapons; an art exhibit; and the five 15th-century mummies of Qilakitsoq, one of Greenland's archaeological treasures. Among the most striking are a woman and child so well preserved that even their 500-year-old clothes are in pristine condition. ⊠ *Hans Egede Vej 8* ☎ *299/32–26–11* ⊕ *www.natmus.gl* ⊠ *Free* ⊗ *Tues.–Sun. 1–4.*

Where to Stay & Eat

$$$ ✕⬜ **Hotel Hans Egede.** This hotel is the largest in Greenland. The rooms are plain and functional but have such extras as minibars, TVs, VCRs, and phones. The sixth-floor Sky Top Restaurant, known for its lovely view of the fjords and its inventive nouveau Greenlandic menu, prepares local fish employing French methods. ⊠ *Box 289, DK–3900* ☎ *299/32–42–22* 🖨 *299/32–44–87* ⊕ *www.hhe.gl* 🛏 *108 rooms* ♨ *Restaurant, in-room VCRs, bar, dance club, meeting room* ⊟ *AE, DC, MC, V.*

$$ ⬜ **Sømandshjemmet Nuuk.** This is one of the oldest of the seaman's hotels that are found in many of Greenland's southern ports. It was at these establishments that the (mostly Danish) seamen spent their nights while their ships were being loaded or when the waters iced over. This particular example has been converted into a standard hotel, but it retains its atmosphere and history. ⊠ *Marinevej 3, Box 1021, DK–3900* ☎ *299/ 32–10–29* 🖨 *299/32–21–04* ⊕ *www.soemandshjem.gl* 🛏 *36 rooms with bath* ♨ *Cafeteria, meeting room* ⊟ *AE, DC, MC, V.*

Nightlife & the Arts

Katuaq (⊠ Skibshavnsvej ☎ 299/32–33–00) is the city's newest landmark and the country's only cultural center. A triangular-shape construction fronted by a wavy wall—inspired by the aurora borealis—contains spaces for concerts, exhibitions, theatrical performances, conventions, and cinema; it also has a café. Its residents include the Greenland Art School; the Nordic Institute on Greenland; and the Groenlandica Collection, a modern lending library with what is thought to be the largest collection of literature on the Arctic regions. The center is open weekdays 10–9:30 and on weekends 1:30–9:30. Performance schedules are available from the tourist office.

Shopping

Shopping is limited to native arts and these are sold in hotels, restaurants, and tourist offices all over Greenland. The arts and crafts are of very high quality and in the tradition of the Inuit. Probably the most popular souvenirs are the *tupilaks,* small distorted figures carved from animal tusks or teeth and meant to represent evil spirits. These amulets were worn primarily by hunters to keep away evil spirits. The idea was that if you already had an evil spirit, another one wouldn't come after you.

The Nuuk tourism office offers the 90-minute **Greenlandic Handicraft Shopping Tour** (✉ Box 199 ☎ 299/32–27–00), which stops at a few local artists' studios where you can purchase handicrafts.

Kangerlussuaq/Søndre Strømfjord

⑤ *1 hr northeast of Nuuk/Godthåb by plane; 4 hrs, 20 min northwest of Copenhagen by plane.*

Kangerlussuaq/Søndre Strømfjord is at the head of one of the longest and deepest fjords in the world. The airport, Greenland's most vital, lies just 25 km (15 mi) from the ice cap. Until World War II, nobody lived here permanently, but Greenlanders would come in spring to hunt reindeer. During the war, the U.S. Air Force chose its dry, stable climate for an air base, called Blue West Eight. The military moved out in the fall of 1992, selling the facilities to the local government for the sum of $1.

Where to Stay

$$$ ⌂ **Hotel Kangerlussuaq.** Just 10 minutes from the airport, this hotel is on the reclaimed U.S. Air Force base. The landing strip here serves as the town's airport and the former barracks have been converted to provide adequate rooms as well as conference facilities. The restaurant serves mainly European cuisine. The hotel also runs a hostel with considerably cheaper rooms (around Dkr 315 per person). ✉ *Box 1006, DK–3910* ☎ *299/84–13–00* 🖷 *299/ 84–14–43* 🛏 *88 rooms ↻ Restaurant, laundry service, meeting rooms* ▤ *AE, DC, MC, V.*

★ ¢ ⌂ **Hotel Igloo Village.** This peculiar hotel offers visitors the novel opportunity to sleep in igloos on beds made of ice. Though the hotel exists only during the sub-zero winter, the bedding, consisting of an expedition-class sleeping bag tucked into musk ox skins, is guaranteed to keep you warm inside the igloo. In the bar you can relax with a drink served in a glass made of ice and enjoy the ice sculptures and candlelight that fills the space. ✉ *Adjacent to the airport* ☎ *299/84–11–80* 🖷 *299/84–12–84* 🛏 *10 rooms ↻ Bar* ▤ *AE, DC, MC, V* ◷ *Closed Apr.–Nov.*

Sisimiut/Holsteinsborg

⑥ *20 min west of Kangerlussuaq/Søndre Strømfjord by airplane.*

On the Davis Strait, this hilltop town is full of Danish-style wooden houses—a local luxury, as all wood is imported. Sisimiut, the second-largest town in Greenland with about 3,600 inhabitants, has become a center for winter tourism and is adapting to accommodate a growing influx of visitors. The area gets more snowfall than nearby towns, making it perfect for winter sports.

Sisimiut also marks the southernmost boundary for walrus hunting; the walrus, though extremely rare, is a popular game animal because of its valuable tusks. Sisimiut, like all other Greenlandic towns, has a "table" where local hunters and fishermen bring their catch—including walrus, whale, and local fish—to market. In all, the market consists of no more than a few tables, but it displays many of the ingredients that are staples of the local cuisine.

The Greenlandic name Sisimiut means Burrow People. There are many explanations of the source of this name; some people believe it refers to hunters who, during severe weather, burrow down in the snow and spend the night there.

On the outskirts of town is the archaeological site of **Asummiut,** where Inuits have made their homes for more than 4,000 years. Remnants of various prehistoric villages as well as Danish and Greenlandic whaling settlements have been uncovered here. To visit the site, contact the Sisimiut Museum. ⊠ *Near the airport* ☎ *299/86–50–87.*

In a cluster of old buildings dating back to 19th-century colonial times, the tiny **Sisimiut Museum** is a delight. It displays the anthropological history of Greenland, telling of the development of the hunter and trapper societies that evolved in harmony with the natural surroundings. The site also has Danish-inspired local art, old original colonial homes, and a post-colonization Greenlandic dwelling. An added benefit is the enthusiasm of the helpful, informed staff. ⊠ *Jukkorsuup aqq. 9, Box 308* ☎ *299/86–50–87* ⊕ *www.museum.gl/sisimiut* ⊠ *Dkr 25* ☉ *June–Aug., Tues.–Sun. 2–5; Sept.–May, Wed., Thurs., and Sun. 2–5.*

Where to Stay & Eat

$$$ ✕🏨 **Hotel Sisimiut.** The hotel has received four-star status in Greenland and provides excellent accommodation. Refurbished to a high standard, the rooms have telephones, TVs, and data ports. The restaurant is very large and is often used for conferences and sometimes as a nightclub. ⊠ *Box 70, DK–3911* ☎ *299/86–48–40* 🖷 *299/86–56–15* ⊕ *www. hotelsisimiut.gl* ⇄ *39 rooms, 6 suites, 1 apartment with kitchen* ♻ *Restaurant, in-room data ports, meeting rooms* ▤ *AE, MC, V.*

$ 🏨 **Sømandshjemmet Sisimiut.** Situated on the harbor, The Seaman's Home provides basic lodging at a low price in a former sailors' boarding house. The cafeteria has simple, hearty fare at modest prices. ⊠ *Box 1015, DK–3911* ☎ *299/86–41–50* 🖷 *299/86–57–91* ⊕ *www.soemandshjem. gl* ⇄ *40 rooms* ♻ *Lounge, meeting rooms* ▤ *AE, MC, V.*

Shopping

Shopping is not high on the list of things to do in Greenland. However, Sisimiut has a bigger selection than anywhere else on the giant island. Here you can find souvenirs such as handmade jewelry or hand-stitched leather goods. **Mersortarfik Panigiit** (⊠ Jaakunnguup aqq. 19 ☎ 299/ 86–55–75) is primarily a leatherwork studio but also sells souvenirs. **Skindsystuen Natseq** (⊠ Paamaap Kuua 11 ☎ 299/86–43–55) is a coop of sorts, selling leatherwork such as clothes, bags, and mittens from its studio. Keep an eye out for the traditional hand-stitched items. Occupying a converted warehouse, the **Society of Artists' workshop** (⊠ At the harbor ☎ 299/86–59–51) is a great place to see artists at work in their studios. It has no set hours, but you can find most artists in residence on weekdays.

Sports & the Outdoors

In summer there are great opportunities for fishing in the fjords, or getting an outfitted excursion to fishing spots known only to local residents. In the warmer months, it's also possible to take a week-long hiking and camping trip to Kangerlussuaq. All activities can be arranged through the local tourist office.

DOGSLEDDING   You can take a dogsled ride for just a few hours or go off on an overnight adventure; tiny shedlike cabins dot the countryside and many are free for overnight stays. These sites run on a first-come, first-served basis and are mostly used by hunters and trappers. Check with the Sisimiut tourist office before you set out.

SKIING   Locals and visiting skiers make good use of the Solbakken ski lift ½ km (⅓ mi) outside of town. A snowmobile taxi shuttles back and forth between the town and the ski lift for a fee, but you could also walk or ski

there. The ski lift operates daily, but consult the tourist office just in case
before setting out. Cross-country skiing tracks exist in the areas surrounding the town, although you should confer with the tourist office
to find routes and be sure to inform your hotel where you plan to go
and when you expect to return.

Qeqertarsuaq/Godhavn

7 *1 hr, 20 min west of Ilulissat by helicopter (8 hrs, 30 min by coastal
boat; reserve far in advance).*

In the Disko Bugt (Disko Bay) sits the island of Qeqertarsuaq/Disko.
The main town here is Qeqertarsuaq/Godhavn. Until 1950 this was the
capital of northern Greenland; Nuuk/Godthåb served as the southern
capital. Accessible by helicopter and ship, Godhavn is often booked to
capacity by European tourists. It's the only area in Greenland with
summertime dogsledding. Contact the tourist office for recommendations of tour operators specializing in such trips.

Ilulissat/Jakobshavn

8 *45 min north of Kangerlussuaq/Søndre Strømfjord by plane.*

In the center of Disko Bay is Ilulissat/Jakobshavn, 300 km (185 mi)
north of the Arctic Circle. At the tip of its fjord is the Northern Hemi-
sphere's most productive glacier, calving 20 million tons of floes each
day—equivalent, according to the Greenland tourist board, to the
amount of water New York City uses in a year. For a humbling experience, take one of the helicopter tours encircling the glacier. A violent
landscape of floating ice giants and dazzling panoramas, it's been inhabited by the Inuit for as long as 4,000 years. The town was founded
in 1741 by a Danish merchant, Jakob Severin. Today the largest industry
is shrimping, though in the winter dogsledders also fish for halibut along
the fjord. From mid-May to mid-June, the sun doesn't set and the regular routine is ignored as people congregate at all hours to enjoy the
sunny nights.

Visit the **Knud Rasmussens Fødehjem** (boyhood home of Knud Rasmussen); this Danish-Greenlandic explorer (1879–1933) initiated the seven
Thule expeditions, which enhanced the knowledge of Arctic geography
and Inuit culture. At the museum you can follow his explorations
through photographs, equipment, and clothing. ⌨ *Dkr 20* ☉ *Daily 10–4.*

Where to Stay & Eat

$$$ ✕⌨ **Hotel Arctic.** This modern hotel, divided into two low-lying red build-
ings, is in the mountains on the edge of town and provides views of the
icy fjord. Rooms are simple, with bathroom, phone, radio, and TV. The
main dining room has panoramic views of the iceberg-filled harbor and
serves fine beef and fish dishes. ⌨ *Box 1501, DK–3952* ☎ *299/94–41–53*
🖷 *299/94–40–49* ⊕ *www.hotel-arctic.gl* 🛏 *40 rooms* ⌂ *Restaurant,
sauna, billiards, meeting room* ▭ *AE, DC, MC.*

$$$ ✕⌨ **Hotel Hvide Falk.** The compact rooms in this central, moderate-size,
two-story building are furnished with TVs and small desks, and have
magnificent views of the icebergs and the Disko Mountains. The restaurant, which specializes in seafood—especially herring, cod, and salmon—
looks out over the bay and its looming icebergs. The director of the hotel,
Lars Rasmussen, is explorer Knud Rasmussen's grandson. ⌨ *Box 20,
DK–3952* ☎ *299/94–33–43* 🖷 *299/94–35–08* ⊕ *www.greenland-guide.
gl/hvidefalk* 🛏 *27 rooms* ⌂ *Restaurant, bar* ▭ *DC.*

Uummannaq

❾ *55 min north of Ilulissat/Jakobshavn by helicopter.*

The inhabitants of the town of Uummannaq—on the island of the same name—maintain Greenlandic traditions in step with modern European life. Their professional fields range from hunting to linguistics and they are as apt to drive dogsleds as sport-utility vehicles. The town lies beneath the magnificent hues and double domes of the granite Uummannaq Mountain, 3,855 feet high. Because the village is also perched on uneven stone cliffs, housing largely consists of brightly painted, freestanding cottages rather than the ugly Danish barracks that line some of Greenland's larger towns. Every April (if the weather cooperates, Uummannaq hosts the Drambuie World Ice Golf Championships.

The **Uummannaq Museum** gives a good overview of life on the island, with photographs and costumes of local hunters and displays on the now-defunct mines of the area. Exhibits also detail the doomed 1930 expedition of German explorer and scientist Alfred Wegener, and there is a section on the Qilakitsoq mummies, found in a nearby cave in 1977 and now displayed in Nuuk/Godthåb. ✉ *Alfred Berthelsen-ip aqq. B9* ☎ *299/95–15–18* ✉ *Free* ⊙ *Weekdays 8–4.*

The **Uummannaq Church**, dating from 1937, is the only stone church in Greenland and is made from local granite. Next door are three sød huts, traditional Inuit dwellings that were occupied until just a few decades ago.

Where to Stay & Eat

$$$ ✕⊡ **Uummannaq Hotel.** This tidy harborside hotel and a nearby 10-room extension offer bright, compact rooms with white, Danish-design furniture. The fine restaurant serves local specialties, including polar bear, caribou, seal, and plenty of fish. ✉ *Box 202, DK–3961* ☎ *299/95–15–18* 🖨 *299/95–12–62* 📞 *32 rooms* ⚲ *Restaurant, bar* ▭ *AE, MC, V.*

Sports & the Outdoors

DOGSLEDDING Though there is plenty of **dogsledding** north of the Arctic Circle, the trips that set forth from Uummannaq are the most authentic, as local hunters do the mushing. The trips are also gentler, because the terrain here is especially smooth. Visitors sit comfortably in heavy, fur-lined sleighs that tear across the frozen fjord. Trips can be arranged at the Hotel Uummannaq and range from a few hours to several days of racing through the terrifying beauty of the landscape and sleeping in the shadows of towering icebergs.

Thule

❿ *2 hrs, 40 min north of Uummannaq by passenger-cargo plane; 1 hr, 45 min north of Kangerlussuaq/Søndre Strømfjord by plane.*

The northern reaches of Greenland are sparsely populated, with few accommodations in the scattered coastal outposts. The inhabitants of Thule were relocated to Qaanaaq when the U.S. Air Force established a base there. The extreme northern region is often called "the most original Greenland," as this is the cradle of the Inuit society of polar hunters. The surrounding landscape is simply breathtaking. The American **air base** at Thule, used for monitoring the Northern Hemisphere, is difficult but not impossible to visit. Check with the **Danish Ministry of Foreign Affairs** (✉ Asiatisk Pl. 2, DK–1448 Copenhagen ☎ 33/92–00–00). Also ask the **Royal Danish Embassy** (✉ 3200 Whitehaven St. NW, Washington, DC 20008-3683 ☎ 202/234–4300) about the feasibility of a visit.

Tasiilaq

⑪ *2 hrs west of Reykjavík by plane, connecting via helicopter from Kulusuk.*

Much of the east coast is empty. Most accessible are the town of Tasiilaq and, slightly farther northeast, the tiny village of Kulusuk. Both welcome day-trippers from Iceland, who are their most frequent visitors. Tours, arranged through Icelandair, are usually short and very well organized, offering an accurate (and relatively affordable) peek at Greenlandic culture and the natural splendor of the Arctic.

Where to Stay

$$$ 🏨 **Hotel Kulusuk.** On the coast close to the tiny town of Kulusuk, this hotel offers splendid views from each of its rooms. The accommodations and amenities here, like at most hotels in Greenland, are comparable to a decent North American motel room. ⊠ *Box 1500, DK–3915* ☎ *299/98–69–93* 🖷 *299/98–69–83* ⊕ *www.arcticwonder.com* ⬐ *34 rooms* ⚭ *Restaurant, bar* ⊟ *AE, DC, MC, V.*

$$ 🏨 **Hotel Angmagssalik.** Perched on a mountain, with a lovely view of the town and harbor, this hotel is decorated with a simple wood interior, both in the guest rooms and common areas. ⊠ *Box 117, DK–3900* ☎ *299/98–12–93* 🖷 *299/98–13–93* ⊕ *www.arcticwonder.com* ⬐ *30 rooms, 18 with shower* ⚭ *Restaurant, bar* ⊟ *AE, DC, MC, V.*

Greenland A to Z

AIR TRAVEL

Helicopters and small planes are the only way to connect small towns because inter-city roads are basically nonexistent and there are no railroads. Flying over Greenland is not merely a way to get around; the grandeur of the icebergs comes into full view only from the window of an airplane or helicopter. Because of Greenland's highly variable weather, delays are frequent. Air Greenland is the only airline licensed for domestic flights on the island. Its modest fleet of helicopters and small planes is booked year-round, so make reservations well in advance. Confirm all flights, connections, and details with your local travel agent or airline representative before you leave home.

The most common points of departure for Greenland are Denmark and Iceland. If you're going by way of Iceland, Icelandair has flights from New York, Baltimore, Fort Lauderdale, and Orlando to Keflavík, Iceland, daily in summer.

From Copenhagen, Air Greenland has service to Kangerlussuaq/Søndre Strømfjord on weekdays from June through August, and four times weekly from September through May. The Air Greenland flight to Narsarsuaq runs on a weekly basis in the off-season, increasing in frequency to three times a week during peak summer months. For connections from North America, contact the Great Canadian Travel Company about charter flights.

🛪 Carriers & Charters **Air Greenland** ☎ 299/34–34–34 in Greenland, 32/31–40–88 in Denmark ⊕ www.airgreenland.gl. **Great Canadian Travel Company** ⊠ 333 N. Michigan Ave., Suite 812, Chicago IL 60601 ☎ 204/949–0199 ⊕ www.greatcanadiantravel. com. **Icelandair** ☎ 354/505–0300 in Iceland, 0207/874–1000 in U.K., 800/223–5500 in North America, 33/70–22–00 in Denmark ⊕ www.icelandair.com.

AIRPORTS

The main international airport in Greenland is Kangerlussuaq/Søndre Strømfjord. Narsarsuaq has some international routes and hubs domestic service in the south. Kulusuk is the main airport for the east coast. Nuuk and Ilulissat also serve as domestic airports. Greenland also has ten heliports that service the coastal towns and islands in the southern half of the country; the pad at Aasiatt/Egedesminde provides access to Disko Bay. Air Greenland can provide a full roster of regular helicopter routes.

🛈 **Aasiatt/Egedesminde Heliport** ☎ 299/89-28-88 🖷 299/89-27-88. **Ilulissat Airport** ☎ 299/94-35-88 🖷 299/94-37-88. **Kangerlussuaq/Søndre Strømfjord Airport** ☎ 299/84-13-00 🖷 299/84-10-47. **Kulusuk Airport** ☎ 299/98-69-88 🖷 299/98-69-36. **Narsarsuaq Airport** ☎ 299/66-52-88 🖷 299/98-69-36. **Nuuk Airport** ☎ 299/34-34-34 🖷 299/32-72-88.

BOAT & FERRY TRAVEL

The most beautiful way to pass the distance between towns is by water. Local tourist offices offer various types of water excursions, for transportation or for sightseeing. Some cruise and coastal boats make frequent stops. You must reserve through a travel agency. Boat voyages, including luxury cruises, are also available from Canada's Frobisher Bay, Norway's Svalbard (archipelago), and Iceland. Contact Arctic Umiaq Line or Greenland Travel in Copenhagen.

🛈 **Arctic Umiaq Line** ✉ Box 608, DK-3900 Nuuk ☎ 299/32-52-11 🖷 299/32-32-11 ⊕ www.aul.gl. **Greenland Travel** ✉ Gammel Mønt 12, Copenhagen ☎ 33/13-10-11.

EMERGENCIES

Every community has its own fire, ambulance, and police numbers and dentist and doctor, all of which you may reach through your hotel. The best way to handle emergencies is to avoid danger in the first place. Don't take risks, ask for advice, and give your travel agent and hotel your itinerary so that they can reach you in case of emergencies—or if you don't show up when you're due. If you are taking medication, bring enough to last throughout your visit.

🛈 **Sana Dronning Ingrids Hospital** ✉ Nuuk ☎ 299/34-40-00.

TOURS

On-the-spot excursions are available in most towns and range from about Dkr 250 for a half day to Dkr 600 for a full day, more for dogsledding, boat, and helicopter trips.

Because transportation and accommodations are limited, you may want to have all details of your trip—connections, accommodations, sightseeing, and meals—arranged by an experienced travel agent, tour organizer, or airline. It's also prudent to bring a copy of your tour contract and all confirmations. Tour packages range from one- to four-day eastcoast excursions from Reykjavík by Icelandair to month-long excursions, which can include sailing, hiking, hunting, dogsledding (February to May), whale safaris, and iceberg-watching.

🛈 **United States Bennett of Scandinavia** ✉ 270 Madison Ave., New York, NY 10016 ☎ 800/221-2420. **Borton Overseas** ✉ 5412 Lyndale Ave. S., Minneapolis, MN 55419 ☎ 612/822-4640 🖷 612/843-0602 ⊕ www.bortonoverseas.com. **Eurocruises** ✉ 303 W. 13th St., New York, NY 10014 ☎ 800/688-3876. **Five Stars of Scandinavia** ✉ 13104 Thomas Rd., KPN, Gig Harbor, WA 98329 ☎ 253/857-4852 🖷 253/857-4978 ⊕ www.5stars-of-scandinavia.com. **Great Canadian Travel Company** ✉ 333 N. Michigan Ave., Suite 812, Chicago, IL 60601 ☎ 204/949-0199 ⊕ www.greatcanadiantravel.com. **Icelandair** ✉ Symphony Woods, 5950 Symphony Woods Rd., Columbia, MD 21044 ☎ 800/223-5500. **Katlin Travel Group** ✉ 15 Depot Sq., Lexington, MA 02173 ☎ 617/862-6229 🖷 781/674-2080 ⊕ www.katlintravel.com. **Quark Expeditions** ✉ 980 Post Rd., Darien, CT 06820 ☎ 203/656-0499. **ScanAm World Tours Inc.** ✉ 108 N. Main St., Cranbury, NJ 08512 ☎ 609/655-1600 🖷 609/555-1622 ⊕ www.scanamtours.com. **Scantours Inc.** ✉ 3439 Wade St., Los Angeles, CA 90006 ☎ 310/636-4656 🖷 310/390-0493 ⊕ www.scantours.com. **Taylor Travel** ✉ 818 North Tejom St., Colorado Springs,

CO 80903 ☎ 719/636-3871 ⎙ 719/636-3879. **Travcoa** ✉ 2350 S.E. Bristol St., Newport Beach, CA 92660 ☎ 949/476-2538 or 800/992-2003.

🇨🇦 Canada **Carlson Wagonlit Travel** ✉ Proctor & Gamble Bldg., 4711 Yonge St., Suite 701, North York, Ontario M2N 6K8 ☎ 416/730-0911 ⎙ 416/730-1986. **Great Canadian Travel Company Ltd.** ✉ 158 Fort St., Winnipeg, Manitoba R3C 1C9 ☎ 204/949-0199 ⎙ 204/949-0188 ⊕ www.greatcanadiantravel.com. **North Winds Arctic Adventures** ✉ Box 820, Iqaluit, NT X0A 0H0 ☎ 867/979-0551 ⎙ 868/979-0573 ⊕ www.northwinds-arctic.com. **Nunavut Tourism** ✉ Box 1450, Iqaluit, NT X0A 0H0 ☎ 819/979-6551 ⎙ 819/979-1261 ⊕ www.nunavuttourism.com. **Silami Voyages** ✉ 70 Dahlia St., Dorval, Quebec H9S 3N2 ☎ 514/633-0893 ⎙ 514/633-6415. **The Wilderness Adventure Company** ✉ R.R. #3 Parry Sound, Parry Sound, Ontario P2A 2W9 ☎ 705/746-1372 ⎙ 705/746-7048 ⊕ www.wildernessadventure.com.

🇩🇰 Denmark **Arctic Adventure** ✉ Reventlowsg. 30, Vesterbro, DK-1651 Copenhagen ☎ 33/25-32-21 ⎙ 33/25-63-08 ⊕ www.arctic-adventure.dk. **Greenland Travel** ✉ Gammel Mønt 12, Downtown, DK-1004 Copenhagen ☎ 33/13-10-11 ⎙ 33/13-85-92 ⊕ www.greenland-travel.dk.

VISITOR INFORMATION

Greenland Tourism, the national board, is able to provide extensive information about the country. Consider it imperative to contact the office well before departure. There is a tourism office in almost every town, but brochures, maps, and specific information may be limited. Call ahead for an exact street address (a 299 access code must be dialed before all phone numbers when calling from outside Greenland).

🔢 Tourist Information **Greenland Tourism** ✉ Box 1139, DK-1010 Copenhagen ☎ 45/33-69-32-00 ⎙ 45/33-93-38-83 ⊕ www.greenland.com or www.gt.gl. **Greenland Travel** ✉ Gammel Mønt 12, Downtown, DK-1004 Copenhagen ☎ 33/13-10-11 ⎙ 33/13-85-92 ⊕ www.greenland-travel.dk. **Ilulissat/Jakobshavn** ✉ Box 272, DK-3952 Ilulissat ☎ 299/94-43-22 ⎙ 299/94-39-33. **Kangerlussuaq/Søndre Strømfjord** ✉ Box 49, DK-3910 Kangerlussuaq ☎ 299/84-10-98 ⎙ 299/84-14-98 ⊕ www.kangerlussuaqtourism.gl. **Nuuk/Godthåb** ✉ Box 199, DK-3900 Nuuk ☎ 299/32-27-00 ⎙ 299/32-27-10 ⊕ www.nuuk-tourism.gl. **Qaanaaq/Thule** ✉ Box 70, DK-3971 Qaanaaq ☎ 299/97-14-73 ⎙ 299/97-14-74 ⊕ www.turistqaanaaq.gl. **Qaqortoq/Julianehåb** ✉ Box 183, DK-3920 Qaqortoq ☎ 299/64-29-13 ⎙ 299/64-29-87. **Qeqertarsuaq/Godhavn** ✉ Box 175, DK-3953 Qeqertarsuaq ☎ 299/92-11-96 ⎙ 299/92-11-98 ⊕ www.qeqertarsuaq.gl. **Sisimiut/Holsteinsborg** ✉ Box 65, DK-3911 Sisimiut ☎ 299/86-48-48 ⎙ 299/86-56-22. **Tasiilaq** ✉ Box 112, DK-3913 Tasiilaq ☎ 299/98-13-11 ⎙ 299/98-17-11. **Uummannaq** ✉ Atuarfimmut B821, Box 200, DK-3961 Uummannaq ☎ 299/95-17-05 ⎙ 299/95-14-75.

WHERE TO STAY

BED-AND-BREAKFASTS

In recent years the bed-and-breakfast has become popular in Greenland, especially in Nuuk/Godthåb. The system is centrally organized, and you should consult the Nuuk tourism office for information. The B&Bs generally have single or double rooms with access to a bathroom and kitchen. You can also expect to spend significantly less per night than in a standard hotel room.

Also contact the Nuuk tourism office about staying in turf cottages, which are (often reconstructed) relics of the way Greenlanders used to live. Nightly rates start at Dkr 625.

THE FAROE ISLANDS

The 18 Faroe Islands (Føroyar in Faroese; Færøerne in Danish) rise up out of the North Atlantic as the extended knuckle of a volcanic archipelago. All but one—Lítla Dímun—are inhabited by a population totaling 46,000 people and twice as many sheep. For obvious reasons,

Føroyar means "Islands of the Sheep." The native Faroese live by fishing, fish farming, and shepherding.

Situated 300 km (188 mi) northwest of Scotland, 430 km (270 mi) southeast of Iceland, and 1,300 km (812 mi) northwest of Denmark, the fjord-chiseled islands support little vegetation besides short grasses and moss. The climate is oceanic: humid, changeable, and stormy, with surprisingly mild temperatures—52°F in summer, 37°F in winter—and a heavy annual rainfall of 63 inches.

Of their 1,399 square km (540 square mi), only 6% is fertile, the rest rough pasture—an Eden for 70 breeding and 120 migratory species of birds, among them thousands of gannets, auks, and puffins. Beneath azure skies and rugged, mossy mountains, villages of colorful thatch-roof houses cling to hillsides while large trawlers and small fishing boats glide in and out of their harbors. Religious and proud, the Faroese have built churches in nearly every settlement.

Catholic monks from Ireland were the first to settle the islands in the middle of the 7th century, but they died out without leaving a trace and were replaced by Norwegian Vikings, who settled the land about AD 800. It was here that the Løgting (parliament) met for the first time in AD 900 in Tórshavn, where it still meets today. In 1035 the islands came under Norwegian rule and remained so until 1380 when Olaf III of Denmark became king of both Denmark and Norway. Under the Danish crown, the islands have had a home-rule government since 1948, with their own flag and language. The roots of the Faroese language are in Old West Norse. Most people speak English but a Danish dictionary can be helpful to the visitor. Danish is the second language.

It's difficult for visitors to understand the isolation or the practical relationship the Faroese have with the natural world. Dubious outsiders, for example, accuse locals of cruelty during the traditional pilot-whale harvests. An essential foodstuff, the sea mammals are killed in limited numbers to reduce the islands' dependence on imported meat. The profit factor is eliminated: whale meat is not sold—it's given away to the townspeople in equal portions on a per capita basis. The hunt is also an important social bond involving both the young and the old.

After having plunged into a severe depression at the beginning of the 1990s, the islands have recovered well and are enjoying a healthy economy again. The unemployment rate stands at 3%, tourism is increasing at an annual rate of 10%–15%, and international oil companies believe there is oil in the region. If they strike it rich, the Faroese, who currently receive Dkr 650,000 from Denmark each year, could become economically independent. However, many people fear that the black gold will irrevocably change the face of their islands. Oil or not, the autonomous government is committed to achieving independence from Denmark.

Tórshavn on the island of Streymoy is the largest city in the Faroes and makes for a good touring base; the town of Klaksvík on the island of Borðoy is also a pleasant place to overnight. Efficient bus and ferry service is the best way to travel between towns, but be prepared for service interruptions during inclement weather.

Because you can experience the full range of Faroese seasons in the span of just a few hours, a good rain jacket and sunglasses are necessities. If you intend to do any hiking, bring a sturdy pair of hiking boots.

Tórshavn

▶ ❶ *1,343 km (839 mi) northwest of Copenhagen, 2 hrs by plane.*

Most visitors begin their explorations on the largest and most traveled island of Streymoy, which, though carved by sheer cliffs and waterfalls, has good roads and tunnels. On the northern end of the island are bird sanctuaries and a NATO base. On its southeastern flank is one of the world's tiniest capitals, Tórshavn, named for the Viking god Thor. Centrally located, Tórshavn has a population of 16,000. St. Olaf's Day, July 29, is named for the Norwegian king who brought Christianity to the islands in the 14th century. Celebrations include rowing competitions and group dances in the form of a chain—a sort of North Atlantic ring dance.

The rugged **Tinganes** is a small peninsula between the east and west bays that was the site of both the old trading post and the meetings of the local parliament (*tinganes* means "assembly place"). Here you can see some of the town's oldest buildings, dating from the 17th and 18th centuries, and some old warehouses, which today house the government offices. At the end of the docks is **Skansin**, a fort built in 1580 by Magnus Heinason to protect the town against pirates; after many reconstructions, it assumed its present form in 1790. The British navy used this site as its Faroe headquarters during World War II, and two guns from that era remain.

Down from the Tinganes is Old Main Street, lined with small 19th-century houses and crossed by twisting streets. You'll come to the slate **Havnar Kirkju** (Tórshavn's Church), rebuilt many times in its 200-year history. Inside is a model of a ship salvaged from an 18th-century wreck, the ship's bell, and an altarpiece dating from 1647.

There are very few trees on the islands. **Viðalundin Park**, a walk up Hoydalsvegur, is the pride of the town—a rare cultivated oasis of green trees in a land where storms and strong winds flatten most tall vegetation.

Atop a hill in the center of town, **Kongaminnið** (King's Memorial) is an obelisk commemorating the visit King Christian IX paid to the island in 1874. Christian IX was the first representative of the still-reigning Glucksborger family to serve as Denmark's king. ⊠ *Norðrari Ringvegur, just off R. C. Effersøes gøta.*

★ **Listasavn Føroya** (National Art Gallery) has a permanent exhibition, which provides an overview of contemporary Faroese arts. Special attention is paid to the painter Mykines and also to Tróndur Patursson, known for his painted-glass sculptures. ⊠ *Gundadalsvegur 9* ☎ *298/31-35-79* ⊕ *www.art.fo* ☒ *Dkr 25* ☉ *June–Aug., weekdays 11–5, weekends 2–6; Sept.–mid-Dec. and mid-Jan.–May, Tues.–Fri. 2–5, weekends 2–6.*

The Museum of Natural History, **Føroya Náttúrugripasavn**, highlights the central role played by nature in Faroese history. It also portrays the islanders' point of view on the controversial issue of pilot-whale hunting. ⊠ *V. U. Hammershaimbsgøta 13* ☎ *298/31-23-00* ⊕ *www.ngs.fo* ☒ *Dkr 20* ☉ *June–Aug., weekdays 11–4, weekends 3–5; Sept.–May, Sun. 3–5.*

Where to Stay & Eat

★ **$$** ✕🏨 **Hotel Föroyar.** Five minutes by car from Tórshavn center, this Best Western hotel has a splendid view of the Old Town and the Isle of Nólsoy. Island specialties are to be found in the restaurant. All rooms have TVs and phones and some have access for the disabled. ⊠ *Við Oygg-*

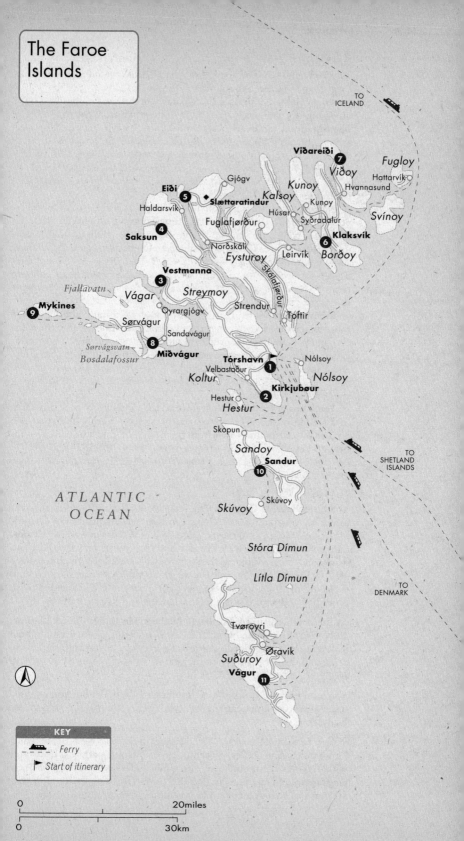

The Faroe Islands

TO
ICELAND

Viðareiði **7** Viðoy

Fugloy

Kunoy

Hattarvík

Gjógv

Kalsoy Hvannasund

Eiði **5**

◆ Slættaratindur

Svínoy

Haldarsvík

Kunoy

Húsar

Fuglafjørður

Syðradalur

Saksun 4

Klaksvík **6**

Norðskáli

Leirvík Borðoy

Eysturoy

Vestmanna

Fjallavatn

3

Streymoy

Vágar

Skálafjørður

Mykines

Strendur

9

Oyrargjógv

Tóftir

Sørvágur

Sandavágur

Sørvágsvatn

8

Tórshavn

Nólsoy

Bøsdalafossur

Miðvágur

Velbastaður

1

Koltur

Kirkjubøur

2

Nólsoy

Hestur

Hestur

Skopun

Sandoy

Sandur

TO
SHETLAND
ISLANDS

10

Skúvoy

ATLANTIC
OCEAN

Skúvoy

Stóra Dímun

Lítla Dímun

TO
DENMARK

Tvøroyri

Øravík

Suðuroy

Vágur

11

KEY

Ferry

Start of itinerary

0 _____ 20miles

0 _____ 30km

jarvegur, FO–110 ☎ *298/31–75–00* 🖨 *298/31–60–19* ⊕ *www.hotelforoyar.fo* 🛏 *108 rooms, 4 suites* ♨ *Restaurant, minibars, billiards, Ping-Pong, bar, meeting rooms* 🗎 *AE, DC, MC, V.*

$$ ✕🏠 **Hotel Hafnia.** In the middle of Tórshavn, this modern business hotel offers big-city ambience and a view of the town from the roof terrace. The restaurant serves Faroese, Danish, and French cuisine. All rooms are comfortably appointed with TVs, telephones, and desks. Some rooms are specifically suited for travelers with disabilities. ⊠ *Áarvegur 4–10, FO–110* ☎ *298/31–32–33* 🖨 *298/31–52–50* ⊕ *www.hafnia.fo* 🛏 *57 rooms, 4 suites* ♨ *Restaurant, minibars, hair salon, sauna, meeting rooms* 🗎 *AE, DC, MC, V.*

¢ 🏠 **Bládýpi.** Its central location makes this guest house–youth hostel especially appropriate if you want to enjoy Tórshavn's nightlife. The guest house has rooms sleeping up to four people; the youth hostel has dormitory rooms. Breakfast is not included, but guests may use the kitchen. ⊠ *Dr. Jakobsensgøta 14–16, FO–100* ☎ *298/31–19–51* 🖨 *298/31–94–51* ⊕ *www.farhostel.fo* 🛏 *12 rooms without bath* ♨ *Dining room* 🗎 *No credit cards* ⊘ *Closed for individuals Sept.–Apr. Open year-round for groups.*

¢ 🏠 **Skansin Guesthouse.** This is a warm and welcoming alternative for
Fodor'sChoice those who would like to experience Faroese hospitality within the mod-
★ esty and personality of a private home. The Restorffs, your hosts, offer expert advice and assistance in planning activities. All rooms have TVs and sinks. Guests may use the kitchen. ⊠ *Jekaragøta 8, FO–110* ☎ *298/31–22–42* 🖨 *298/31–06–57* 🛏 *11 rooms without bath* ♨ *Refrigerators* 🗎 *No credit cards.*

¢ 🏠 **Youth Hostel Tórshavn.** Next door to the Hotel Føroyar is this clean and simple hostel. The view over Tórshavn's harbor is expansive. Shuttle buses run into town from the hostel, or you can stroll 15 minutes to get there. ⊠ *Við Oyggjarvegin, FO–100* ☎ *298/31–89–00* 🖨 *298/34–59–50* ⊕ *www.farhostel.fo* 🛏 *22 rooms without bath* 🗎 *AE, DC, MC.*

Nightlife & the Arts

The little nightlife that exists in Tórshavn is concentrated in the very center of town and is at its height in summer. Frequented by friendly locals, **Café Natur** (⊠ Áarvegur 7 ☎ 298/31–26–25) has a rowdy Faroese atmosphere complete with live pop and rock music on weekends. Eat, drink, and sing karaoke at the youth-filled **Club 20** (⊠ Tinghúsvegur 8 ☎ 298/31–56–28). On summer weekends the club remains open until 4 AM. Adults flock to **Club Kaggin** (⊠ Dalavegur 1 ☎ 298/31–41–70) on Friday and Saturday nights for dancing and live rock music.

At the northern tip of Tórshavn, **Norðurlanda Húsið.** (Nordic House; ⊠ Norðari Ringvegur, FO–110 ☎ 298/31–79–00, ⊕ www.nlh.fo) built in 1983 to promote Nordic culture in the region, hosts exhibitions, concerts, and theater throughout the year.

Shopping

You won't knock yourself out shopping in Tórshavn but you can find original Faroese knitwear, Viking-style jewelry, stamps, and even stuffed birds.

Shop at **Føroyskt Heimavirki** (⊠ Kongabrúgvin ☎ 298/31–17–67) for hand-knit woolen items based on centuries-old Faroese patterns. Decorated with Tróndur Patursson's colorful stained-glass sculptures, **SMS Shopping Center** (⊠ Trapputrøðin ☎ 298/31–30–41) is a mall with more than 30 shops as well as a bank and post office.

Kirkjubøur

★ ❷ *13 km (8 mi) south of Tórshavn.*

From Tórshavn, a bus takes you to Kirkjubøur, a tiny town populated by about 60 people. The townsfolk live in black houses with red window frames and green grass roofs perched on hillsides around the tiny, often fog-shrouded harbor. At the southern tip of the island of Streymoy, Kirkjubøur was a spiritual and cultural center of the island in the Middle Ages.

A particularly ambitious priest, Bishop Erlendur, built a cathedral in the town in the 13th century—there is some controversy over whether or not it was ever completed—and the ruins of the Gothic **Magnus Cathedral** still stand. Inside the church is a large stone tablet engraved with an image of Christ on the cross, flanked by the Virgin Mary and Mary Magdalene, and an inscription to St. Magnus and St. Thorlak. During restoration work in 1905, the tablet was removed to reveal well-preserved relics of the saints. In 1538, after the Reformation, the episcopal see was dissolved and with it the town's power.

Just next door to the Magnus Cathedral is the restored **St. Olaf's Church,** which dates from 1111 and is now the only church from that time still in use. Most of its sculptures have been removed to Copenhagen, leaving little to see, but there's a hole in the north wall that once allowed lepers standing outside to watch the mass and receive the Eucharist. The altarpiece is the work of the most famous painter of the islands, Sámal Mykines. The interior of the cathedral is only open for the 11 AM service on Sunday.

Near the church is **Roykstovan**, a former farmhouse now in use as a museum. Legend has it that the lumber for the building came drifting to the town, neatly numbered and bundled, from the Sogne Fjord in Norway. Inside are the traditional Faroese one-main-room living quarters and a dozen other rooms. It's been in the same family for the last 16 generations, and it is here that foreign dignitaries are welcomed to the town. The large split-log building is said to be about 900 years old and is the oldest cabin in Europe. ☎ 298/32–80–89 ☉ *June–Aug., Fri.–Wed. 2–5; Sept.–May by appointment only.*

Vestmanna

★ ❸ *49 km (30 mi) northwest of Tórshavn.*

On the western coast of Streymoy, this town of 1,200 inhabitants is easily accessible from Tórshavn by bus. Once there, you can take a boat tour through narrow channels and see thousands of nesting birds, including puffins and kittiwakes. Although the bird life is the big draw, the sheep life is nearly as fascinating. In the spring sheep are hoisted with ropes 2,310 feet up to graze atop the sheer cliffs, and in the fall they are caught and brought back down.

Saksun

❹ *47 km (30 mi) northwest of Tórshavn.*

Among the fjords slicing the northern end of Streymoy is the tiny town of Saksun, one of the most popular excursions on the islands. The town and its scattered sod-and-thatch-roof houses are idyllically situated on a small bay sheltered on both sides by steep, imposing cliffs leading into a long, narrow fjord. Saksun swarms with great skuas, large brown seabirds prone to low dives. As you unwittingly near their nests, you will certainly notice their cantankerous presence. Not far from the village are two picturesque lakes, Pollur and Saksunarvatn, both perfect for trout and salmon fishing. The valley has gushing waterfalls and fantastic hiking.

Visit the **Dúvugarðar Museum** for a re-creation of Faroese living conditions in the 19th century and a portrait of the islands' history since the Middle Ages. ☎ 289/31–07–00 ☉ *June–Aug., Fri.–Wed. 2–5.*

Eiði

⑤ *52 km (32 mi) northwest of Tórshavn.*

The island of Eysturoy, just east of Streymoy, is connected to the latter by a bridge and bus service. The center of activity is the town of Eiði, which lies to the northwest amid a spectacular landscape. Looking northwest from town, you can see two 250-foot cliffs, a part of local mythology: one night an Icelandic giant and his wife came to carry the islands to Iceland to provide food for their land. They put the islands into a sack but she dropped them, giving the islands their cracked topography. Once the sun rose, the giants were petrified and transformed into the bluffs.

Due east of Eiði is the islands' highest point, the 2,910-foot **Slættaratindur** mountain. To the south, on the shores of the **Skálafjørður**, the longest fjord in the archipelago, the majority of the island's 10,500 people live.

Where to Stay

¢ ☒ **Hotel Eiði.** Perched on a hilltop in a village near the sea, this slightly dated hotel is small and clean, with a TV in every room. ⊠ *FO–470* ☎ *298/42–34–56* 🖷 *298/42–32–00* 🖈 *16 rooms, 12 with bath* ⚱ *Restaurant, cafeteria, minibars* 🖃 *AE, DC, MC, V* ☉ *Closed Sept.–Apr.*

¢ ☒ **Gjáargarður.** This youth hostel occupies a prime position on the north end of the island, with nearby access to the ocean and the mountains. Built in traditional Faroese style, the foundation is stone, the exterior wooden walls painted black, and the roof is thatch. Inside you'll find a combined kitchen and family room with a fireplace in the middle. Breakfast is not included, but guests have use of the Internet as well as the kitchen. Campsites are also available. ⊠ *FO–476 Gjógv* ☎ *298/ 42–31–71* 🖷 *298/42–35–05* 🌐 *www.gjaarhostel.dk* 🖈 *11 rooms, 10 with bath* ⚱ *Cafeteria, Ping-Pong, meeting room* 🖃 *No credit cards* ☉ *Closed mid-Aug.–mid-June.*

Klaksvík

⑥ *75 km (47 mi) northeast of Tórshavn, 2 hrs by bus and ferry.*

The six islands in the far northeast region of the Faroese archipelago are gathered under the name of Norðoyar (Northern Islands). Three of them, Borðoy, Viðoy, and Kunoy are connected by causeways, while Fugloy, Svinoy, and Kalsoy are accessible only by passenger boat or helicopter.

Borðoy is reached by boat from Leirvík on eastern Eysturoy. On its southwest coast, nearly divided by two fjords, Klaksvík is the Faroes' second-largest town and most important fishing harbor; its fleet of sophisticated boats harvests cod, haddock, herring, and other fish.

Within Klaksvík, the baptismal font in the **Christianskirkjan** (Christian's Church) is a piece of carved granite thought to have been used in pagan rituals in Denmark 4,000 years ago. Suspended from the church roof is a 24-foot boat used by a former vicar to visit nearby towns; the boat—common in Danish churches—is a symbol that God is watching over the village fishermen. ☎ 289/45–57–70 ⊙ May–Sept., Mon.–Sat. 11–noon and 2–3.

Where to Stay

$ 🏨 **Klaksvíkar Sjómansheim.** Sheep graze on the front lawn of this big hotel; the back overlooks the colorful harbor. The staff is cheery and helpful, and rooms—request one with a harbor view—offer no-frills comfort. Toilets are in the hallways but all rooms have sinks. The restaurant serves generous portions of the homemade special of the day but doesn't have a liquor license. ✉ Vikavegur 38, FO–700 ☎ 298/45–53–33 🖷 298/45–72–33 🛏 31 rooms, 11 with bath ♨ Restaurant, cafeteria, meeting rooms ➴ No credit cards.

¢ 🏨 **Ferðamannaheimið Íbúð.** Housed in a former hotel built in 1945, this youth hostel and guesthouse is near a ferry slip and is surrounded by hiking trails. ✉ Garðavegur 31, FO–700 ☎ 298/45–75–55 or 298/28–79–65 🖷 298/45–75–55 ⊕ www.farhostel.fo 🛏 12 rooms without bath ➴ No credit cards ⊙ Closed for individuals mid-Sept.–mid-May; for groups mid-Dec.–early Jan.

Viðareiði

★ ❼ 18 km (11 mi) north of Klaksvík.

The island of **Viðoy** is among the wildest and most beautiful of the islands, with mountains of 2,800 feet and sheer cliffs plunging into extremely rough, unnavigable waters. Amazingly, 600 people live here, many in the town of Viðareiði. Cape Enniberg, at its northernmost tip, reaches 2,460 feet; it's the world's highest cape rising directly from the sea. From the town of Viðareiði you can take a boat tour to see many seabirds nesting on cliff walls, including kittiwakes and puffins—endearing little black-and-white birds with enormous orange beaks. The Faroese have a remarkable relationship with the puffins, harvesting them by the thousands for food and yet remaining careful not to diminish their numbers.

Where to Stay

¢ 🏨 **Hotel Norð.** In the tiny town of Viðareiði on the northern end of the island, this simple business hotel has beautiful surroundings and great bird-watching nearby. ✉ FO–750 ☎ 298/45–12–44 🖷 298/45–12–45 🛏 15 rooms ♨ Restaurant, billiards, meeting room ➴ MC, V ⊙ Closed Sept.–May.

Miðvágur

❽ 18 km (11 mi) west of Tórshavn.

Vágar, the third-largest island in terms of area, takes its name from the three fjords that slice into it. There are also two major lakes on the island, Fjallavatn and Sørvágsvatn, the last of which is fed by the Bøsdalafossur, a 100-foot waterfall. The main town here is Miðvágur, an excellent perch for watching auks and gannets.

Where to Stay

$ 🏨 **Hotel Vágar.** Next to the airport, this hotel is small and standard. ✉ FO–380 Sørvágur ☎ 298/33–29–55 🖷 298/33–23–10 ⊕ www.hotelvagar.fo 🛏 26 rooms ♨ Restaurant, minibars, meeting room ➴ AE, DC, MC, V ❙❙❙ BP.

¢ 🏨 **Á Giljanesi.** This youth hostel is 10 minutes by bus from Vágar Airport. Guests have access to the kitchen, and meals are available on request. There is also camping. ✉ FO–360 Sandavágur ☎ 298/33–34–65 🖷 298/33–29–01 ⊕ www.farhostel.fo 🛏 11 rooms without bath ♨ Dining room ➴ No credit cards.

Mykines

❾ *48 km (30 mi) west of Miðvágur (1 hr, 15 min by boat, 15 min by helicopter).*

It's rough sailing to the tiny atoll of Mykines and only manageable when weather permits. In the town of the same name, population 19, the dwellings are roofed with sod. The town was placed here to be close to the **Mykineshólmur,** an islet swarming with thousands of puffins, which are harvested for food. You can get here by traversing the island northward on foot about 2 km (1 mi) from the boat landing in Sørvágur.

Where to Stay

¢ ⊡ **Kristianshús.** Stay at this small guest house with compact rooms to experience real Faroese home and native cuisine—fried puffin is available in the cafeteria. ⊠ *FO–388* ☎ *298/32–19–85* 🖨 *298/31–09–85* ➳ *11 rooms without bath* ♨ *Cafeteria* ▭ *No credit cards* ☉ *Closed Sept.–Apr.*

Sandur

❿ *25 km (16 mi) south of Tórshavn.*

Sandoy, the fifth-largest island, lies to the south. Relatively fertile, it's named for the sandy white beaches of the town of Sandur, on its bay. Sheep graze on green hills, and the lakes north and west of town swell with auks, purple sandpipers, and great skuas. Puffin colonies dwell in the island's cliffs. You can visit the island of Sandoy as a day trip from Tórshavn.

Vágur

⓫ *64 km (40 mi) south of Tórshavn.*

The southernmost island, Suðuroy, is milder than the others, with cultivated green fields at its center and mountains along the coast. Ferries from Tórshavn dock either in Vágur or the quieter village of Tvøroyri.

Where to Stay

¢ ⊡ **Hotel Tvøroyri.** In the middle of town, this old hotel has simple, clean rooms, and minimal service. ⊠ *FO–800 Tvøroyri* ☎ *298/37–11–71* 🖨 *298/37–21–71* ➳ *15 rooms, 2 with bath* ♨ *Cafeteria* ▭ *AE, V.*

¢ ⊡ **Vallaraheimið Áargarður.** Overlooking the fjord of Trongisvágsfjørður, this youth hostel is centrally located for exploring the island of Suðoroy. Access to the kitchen is provided, and campsites are available. ⊠ *FO–827 Øravík* ☎ *298/37–13–02* 🖨 *298/37–20–57* ⊕ *www.farhostel.fo* ➳ *15 rooms without bath* ♨ *Dining room, meeting room* ▭ *No credit cards.*

The Faroe Islands A to Z

AIR TRAVEL

There are daily flights from Copenhagen to Vágar airport in Sørvágur, on the western island of Vágar. Delays due to heavy fog are common. The flight from Copenhagen takes about two hours.

CARRIERS For reservations, call either Atlantic Airways or Mærsk Air in Copenhagen. Both fly year-round between Copenhagen and the Faroe Islands and also from Billund in Jylland in the summer season. There are also connections available from Reykjavík (Iceland), Stavanger (Norway), Aberdeen (Scotland), and London on Atlantic Airways. Two weekly flights are also available from Reykjavík on Icelandair. Helicopter service is available in Vágar.
🛫 **Atlantic Airways** ☎ 45/32-50-47-00 in Denmark, 298/34-10-10 in the Faroes ⊕ www.atlantic.fo. **Helicopter Service (Atlantic Airways)** ☎ 298/34-10-60 **Icelandair**

✆ 800/223-5500, Ext. 2 prompt 1, in North America, 354/50-50-100 in Iceland, 45/ 33-70-22-00 in Denmark ⊕ www.icelandair.com. **Mærsk Air** ✆ 45/70-10-74-74 in Denmark, 298/34-00-60 in the Faroes ⊕ www.maersk-air.com.

AIRPORTS
🛪 **Vágar Airport** ✉ FO-380 Sørvágur ✆ 298/33-22-28 🖷 298/33-29-98 ⊕ www. slv.dk/vagar.

TRANSFERS From Vágar Airport, count on another 1½ hours to get to Tórshavn by bus and ferry. The SL Visitor Travelcard is a good value for exploring the islands; it affords free passage on all SL (the local transportation company) buses and ferries. Be sure to buy the card at the airport (or from your travel agent) to pay for the trip to Tórshavn.

BIKE TRAVEL
It's hard work peddling up and down the steep hills. The islands' roads aren't designed for safe cycling; many roads aren't paved and those that are don't have real shoulders. Nevertheless, if you're determined, renting a bike is an option. For information about routes and rentals, call J. W. Thomsen.
🛪 **J. W. Thomsen** ✉ Nólsoyar Páls gøta, FO-700, Klaksvík ✆ 298/45-58-58.

BOAT & FERRY TRAVEL
Every Saturday night in summer, from mid-May to mid-September, car ferries ply the waters between Hanstholm in Jylland and Tórshavn (34 hours). The same service is available from mid-October to mid-May with a different timetable. There is usually no ferry service between mid-September and mid-October. Call Smyril Line for more information. For information on frequent ferry service to all islands in the Feroese, call Strandfaraskip Landsins. The most remote areas are linked by mailboat and helicopter.

The SL Visitor Travelcard, which includes ferry and bus travel throughout the Faroes, is available from Strandfaraskip Landsins and costs around Dkr 400 for 4 days, Dkr 650 for 7 days, and Dkr 1,000 for 14 days.
🛪 **Smyril Line** ✉ Jónas Broncksgøta 37 FO-110 Tórshavn ✆ 45/96-55-03-60 or 45/ 33-16-40-04 in Denmark, 298/34-59-00 in the Faroes ⊕ www.smyril-line.com. **Strandfaraskip Landsins (SL)** ✉ Eystara Bryggja, FO-100 Tórshavn ✆ 298/34-30-00 🖷 298/ 34-30-01 ⊕ www.ssl.fo.

BUS TRAVEL
In towns, and between islands that are connected by bridges, there is regular bus service, and the drivers tend to be friendly toward perplexed travelers. For schedules and reservations, call Strandfaraskip Landsins in Tórshavn.
🛪 **Strandfaraskip Landsins** ✆ 298/34-30-30 ⊕ www.ssl.fo.

CAR RENTAL
Car rentals are available in Tórshavn and at Vágar Airport. Although cars are the most convenient method of travel on the islands, they are quite expensive to rent (Dkr 600–Dkr 900 per day).
🛪 **Avis** ✆ 298/31-35-35 in Tórshavn, 298/34-88-00 at the airport. **Hertz** ✆ 298/ 34-00-0730 in Tórshavn, 298/34-00-60 at the airport.

CAR TRAVEL
A network of two-lane asphalt roads has been built between towns, using tunnels and bridges. The roads are best on the nine main islands, but once outside towns, beware of untethered animals. Driving laws are the same as in Denmark. Speed limits are 50 kph (30 mph) in urban areas, 80 kph (50 mph) outside.

EMERGENCIES

For ambulance, fire, or police dial 112.

🏥 Hospital **Landssjúkrahúsið** ✉ J. C. Svvaboes gøta, Tórshavn ☎ 298/31-35-40.
🏥 Pharmacies **Klaksví** ✉ Fornagarður ☎ 298/45-50-55. **Runavík** ✉ Heiðavegur
☎ 298/44-93-66. **Tórshavn** ✉ R. C. Effersøes gøta 31, by SMS shopping center ☎ 298/
31-11-00.

TOURS

In addition to the local tours offered by many hotels, there are four main
tour operators offering angling, city, hiking, and bird-watching tours:
Flogfelag Føroyar, Tora Tourist Traffic, Smyril-Line and MB-Tours.

Besides the four operators mentioned above, there are two others spe-
cializing in the spectacular bird-cliffs of Vestmanna: Skúvadal and Palli
Lamhauge. Other bird-watching tours are available on the islands of
Nólsoy (guided by Jens Kjeld Jensen) and Koltur (guided by Koltur).
Berg Hestar organizes horseback riding trips.

🏇 **Berg Hestar** ✉ Við Oyggjarvegin, FO-100, Tórshavn ☎ 298/31-68-96 or 298/
21-68-96. **Flogfelag Føroyar** ✉ Áarvegur 6, FO-110, Tórshavn ☎ 298/34-00-10
🌐 www.ff.fo. **Jens Kjeld Jensen** ✉ FO-270, Nólsoy ☎ 298/32-70-64 🖶 298/32-70-54.
Koltur ✉ Koltursgarður, FO-285, Koltur ☎ 298/29-92-70. **MB-Tours** ✉ Bryggjubakki
2, FO-100, Tórshavn ☎ 298/32-21-21 🌐 www.mb-tours.com. **Palli Lamhauge** ✉ FO-350,
Vestmanna ☎ 298/42-41-55 🌐 www.sightseeing.fo. **Skúvadal** ✉ FO-350, Vestmanna
☎ 298/42-43-05 🌐 www.puffin.fo/skuvadal. **Smyril-Line** ✉ Jonas Broncksgøta 37,
FO-110, Tórshavn ☎ 298/34-59-00, 96/55-03-60 in Denmark 🌐 www.smyril-line.fo.
Tora Tourist Traffic ✉ Niels Finsensgøta 21, Box 3012, FO-110, Tórshavn ☎ 298/
31-55-05 🖶 298/31-56-67 🌐 www.tora.fo.

VISITOR INFORMATION

The helpful brochure *Faroe Islands Tourist Guide* is published by the
Faroese Tourist Board.

🏛 **Faroe Islands Tourist Board** ✉ Undir Bryggjubakka 17, Box 118, FO-110, Tórshavn
☎ 298/31-60-55 🖶 298/31-08-58 ✉ Hovedvagtsg. 8, 2nd fl., DK-1103 Copenhagen
☎ 45/33-14-83-83 🌐 www.tourist.fo. **Streymoy Kunningarstovan** (Streymoy Tourist
Information) ✉ Niels Finsens gøta 13, FO-110, Tórshavn ☎ 298/31-57-88 🖶 298/
31-68-31 🌐 www.kunning.fo.

DENMARK A TO Z

*To research prices, get advice from other travelers, and book travel ar-
rangements, visit www.fodors.com.*

AIR TRAVEL

CARRIERS Nearly all international air service to Denmark flies into Copenhagen
Airport. SAS, the main carrier, makes nonstop flights to the capital
from Chicago, Newark, and Seattle. British Airways offers connecting
flights via London from Atlanta, Baltimore, Boston, Charlotte, Chicago,
Dallas, Denver, Detroit, Houston, Los Angeles, Miami, New York, Or-
lando, Philadelphia, Phoenix, Pittsburgh, San Diego, San Francisco,
Seattle, Tampa, and Washington, D.C. Icelandair makes connecting
flights to Copenhagen via Reykjavík from Baltimore, Fort Lauderdale,
New York, and Orlando. Finnair has service through Helsinki from
Miami, New York, and—from May to September—San Francisco.

British Airways flies nonstop to Copenhagen from London (Heathrow
and Gatwick), Birmingham, and Manchester. SAS Scandinavian Airlines
flies nonstop from London, Manchester, and Glasgow, and also from
London to Århus. Aer Lingus flies from Dublin, connecting in London;
the flights are operated by British Airways. Mærsk Air flies nonstop from
Gatwick to Billund and Copenhagen. Easyjet has cheap flights between

London's Stansted airport and Copenhagen. Virgin Airlines is also inexpensive and flies between London's Gatwick and Stansted airports via Brussels to Copenhagen. Air France also flies out of Copenhagen.

In Jylland, Billund Airport is Denmark's second-largest airport. Mærsk Air flies to Billund from Amsterdam, Bergen, Brussels, the Faroe Islands, Frankfurt, London, Manchester, Nice, Oslo, Stockholm, and Paris. Sunair serves Århus, Billund, Göteborg, Oslo, and Stockholm. Several domestic airports, including Aalborg, Århus, and Esbjerg, are served by Mærsk and SAS, both of which have good connections to Copenhagen. Cimber Air links Sønderborg, just north of the German border, with Copenhagen.

Cimber Air makes several daily flights to Bornholm from Copenhagen, and flies also from Berlin. Lufthansa flies to Bornholm from Berlin and Hamburg.

For service to the Faroe Islands and Greenland, see the relevant A to Z sections above.

Aer Lingus ☎ 800/474-7424 in North America, 0161/832-5771 in Ireland ⊕ www.aerlingus.com. **Air France** ☎ 800/237-2747 in North America, 82/33-27-01 in Denmark ⊕ www.airfrance.com/dk. **Air Greenland** ☎ 299/34-34-34 in Greenland, 32/31-40-88 in Denmark ⊕ www.airgreenland.gl. **British Airways** ☎ 0207/491-4989 in U.K., 800/247-9297 in North America, 80/20-80-22 in Denmark ⊕ www.britishairways.com. **Cimber Air** ☎ 74/42-22-77, 56/95-11-11 in Bornholm ⊕ www.cimber.dk. **Finnair** ☎ 800/950-5000 in North America, 32/50-45-10 in Denmark ⊕ www.finnair.fi. **Easyjet** ☎ 0870/6000-000 in U.K., 70/12-43-21 in Denmark ⊕ www.easyjet.com. **Icelandair** ☎ 354/505-0300 in Iceland, 0207/874-1000 in U.K., 800/223-5500 in North America, 33/70-22-00 in Denmark ⊕ www.icelandair.com. **Lufthansa** ☎ 33/37-73-33 ⊕ www.lufthansa.com. **Mærsk Air** ☎ 0207/333-0066 in U.K., 32/31-44-44 or 70/10-74-74 in Denmark ⊕ www.maersk-air.dk. **SAS Scandinavian Airlines** ☎ 0207/706-8832 in U.K., 800/221-2350 in North America, 32/32-00-00 in Denmark ⊕ www.scandinavian.net. **Sunair** ☎ 75/33-16-11. **Virgin Airlines** ☎ 01293/450-150 in U.K., 800/862-8621 in North America ⊕ www.virgin-atlantic.com.

CUTTING COSTS Intra-Scandinavian air travel is usually expensive. If you want to economize, look into the **SAS Visit Scandinavia/Europe Air Pass** offered by SAS. One coupon costs about $85; six about $510, but they vary greatly depending on routing and destination—generally, the cost rises the farther north the destination. The coupons are valid for destinations within Denmark, Norway, and Sweden, and also between Sweden and Finland. They are sold only in the United States and only to non-Scandinavians. Coupons can be used year-round for a maximum of three months and must be purchased in conjunction with transatlantic flights. SAS also provides family fares—children between 2 and 17 and a spouse can receive 50% off the full fare of business-class tickets with the purchase of one full-fare business-class ticket. Contact SAS for information.

The least expensive airfares to Scandinavia must usually be purchased in advance and are non-refundable. It's smart to call a number of airlines and check the Internet; when you are quoted a good price, book it on the spot—the same fare may not be available the next day, or even the next hour. Always check different routings and look into using alternate airports. Also, price off-peak flights, which may be significantly less expensive than others. Travel agents, especially low-fare specialists (⇨ Discounts and Deals), are helpful. Consolidators are another good source. They buy tickets for scheduled flights at reduced rates from the airlines, then sell them at prices that beat the best fare available directly from the airlines. Sometimes you can even get your money back if you need to return the ticket. Carefully read the fine print detailing penalties for changes and cancellations, purchase the ticket with a credit card, and confirm your consolidator reservation with the airline.

FLYING-TIMES   The flight from London to Copenhagen takes 1 hour, 55 minutes. From New York, flights to Copenhagen take 7 hours, 40 minutes. From Chicago, they take 9 hours, 30 minutes. From Seattle and Los Angeles the flight time is about 10 hours, 55 minutes. Flight times within the country are all less than one hour, except for longer routes from Copenhagen to Greenland (5 hours) and the Faroe Islands (2 hours, 15 minutes).

AIRPORTS

Kastrup International Airport (CPH) is the hub of Scandinavian and international air travel in Denmark, 10 km (6 mi) from the center of Copenhagen. Jylland has regional hubs in Aalborg (AAL), Århus (AAR), and Billund (BLL), which handle mainly domestic and some European traffic. Rønne (RNN) is the main airport in Bornholm.

Kastrup International Airport 🕿 32/31-32-31 ⊕ www.cph.dk.

BIKE TRAVEL

Biking is a way of life in Denmark, with more people biking to work than driving. Biking vacations in Denmark are popular and they are easy for all ages due to the flat landscape. Most towns have rentals, but check with local tourism offices for referrals. For more information, contact the Danish Cyclist Federation. The Danish Tourist Board publishes helpful bicycle maps and brochures.

DSB allows cyclists to check their bikes as luggage on most of their train routes, but only if there is room. S-trains that serve the suburbs of Copenhagen don't permit bikes during rush hour (7 AM–8:30 AM and 3:30 PM–5 PM). Bicycles can also be carried onto most trains and ferries; contact the DSB Travel Office for information; a bicycle ticket usually costs from Dkr 10 to Dkr 60, depending on the distance traveled. Taxis are required to take bikes and are equipped with racks, though they add a modest fee of Dkr 10.

From May to October, you'll also see bycykler (city bikes) parked at special bike stands placed around the center of Copenhagen and Århus. Deposit Dkr 20 and pedal away. The bikes are often dinged and dented, but they do function. Your deposit will be returned when you return the bike.

Danmarks Turistråd (Danish Tourist Board) ✉ Vesterbrog. 6D, Vesterbro, DK-1620 Copenhagen 🕿 33/11-14-15 🖷 33/93-14-16 ⊕ www.visitdenmark.com. **Dansk Cyklist Forbund** (Danish Cyclist Federation) ✉ Rømersg. 7, Downtown, DK-1362 Copenhagen 🕿 33/32-31-21 🖷 33/32-76-83 ⊕ www.dcf.dk. **DSB** 🕿 70/13-14-15 ⊕ www.dsb.dk.

BOAT & FERRY TRAVEL

Once upon a time, ferries were an indispensable mode of transport in and around the many islands of Denmark. This is changing as more people drive or take trains over new bridges spanning the waters. However, ferries are still a good way to explore Scandinavia, especially if you have a rail pass.

Scandinavian Seaways Ferries (DFDS) sail from Harwich in the United Kingdom to Esbjerg (20 hours) on Jylland's west coast. Schedules in both summer and winter are highly irregular. DFDS also connects Denmark with the Baltic States, Belgium, Germany, the Netherlands, Norway, Poland, Sweden, and the Faroe Islands. There are many discounts, including 20% for senior citizens and travelers with disabilities, and 50% for children between the ages of 4 and 16.

Molslinien links up Jylland and Sjælland, while Scandlines services the southern islands as well as Germany, Sweden, and the Baltic countries. The island of Bornholm, Denmark's furthest outpost to the East and a popular domestic tourist destination, is reachable with Bornholms Trafikken.

The ScanRail Pass, for travel anywhere within Scandinavia (Denmark, Sweden, Norway, and Finland), and the Interail and EurailPasses are valid on some ferry crossings. Call the DSB Travel Office for information.

CAR FERRIES Vehicle-bearing hydrofoils operate between Fyn's Ebeltoft or Århus to Odden on Sjælland; the trip takes about one hour. You can also take the slower (2 hours, 40 minutes), but less expensive, car ferry from Århus to Kalundborg on Sjælland. From there, Route 23 leads to Copenhagen. Make reservations for the ferry in advance through Mols-Linien. Scandlines services the southern islands. (*Note:* During the busy summer months, passengers without reservations for their vehicles can wait hours.)

Some well-known international vehicle and passenger ferries run between Helsingør, Denmark, and Helsingborg, Sweden, and between Copenhagen and Göteborg, Sweden. The Helsingør/Helsingborg ferry (Scandlines) takes only 20 minutes; taking a car costs between SKr 255 and SKr 275 (about $24–$26 or £16–£18.50) one-way. Round-trip fares are cheaper, and on weekends the Øresund Runt pass (for crossing between Copenhagen and Malmö one way and Helsingborg and Helsingør the other way) costs only SKr 475 (about $45 or £31).

FARES & SCHEDULES 🇩🇰 **Bornholms Trafikken** ✉ Havnen, DK–3700 Rønne ☎ 56/95–18–66 📠 56/91–07–66 🌐 www.bornholmstrafikken.dk. **DSB** ☎ 70/13–14–15 🌐 www.dsb.dk. **Mols-Linien** ☎ 70/10–14–18 📠 89/52–52–90 🌐 www. molslinien.dk. **Scandinavian Seaways Ferries (DFDS)** ✉ Skt. Annæ Pl. 30, DK–1295 Copenhagen ☎ 33/42–33–42 📠 33/42–33–41 🌐 www.dfds. com. **Scandlines** ☎ 33/15–15–15 📠 35/29–02–01 🌐 www.scandlines.dk.

BUSINESS HOURS

BANKS & OFFICES Banks in Copenhagen are open weekdays 9:30 to 4 and Thursdays until 6. Several *bureaux de change,* including the ones at Copenhagen's central station and airport, stay open until 10 PM. Outside Copenhagen, banking hours vary.

MUSEUMS & SIGHTS A number of Copenhagen's museums hold confounding hours, so always call first to confirm. As a rule, however, most museums are open 10 to 3 or 11 to 4 and are closed on Monday. In winter, opening hours are shorter, and some museums close for the season, especially on the smaller islands, including Bornholm, Ærø, and Fanø. Check the local papers or ask at tourist offices for current schedules.

SHOPS Though many Danish stores are expanding their hours, sometimes even staying open on Sunday, most shops still keep the traditional hours: weekdays 10 to 5:30, until 7 or 8 on Friday, and until 1 or 2 on Saturday—though the larger department stores stay open until 5. Everything except bakeries, kiosks, flower shops, and a handful of grocers are closed on Sunday. The first Saturday of every month is a Long Saturday, when even the smaller shops, especially in large cities, stay open until 4 or 5. Grocery stores stay open until 8 on weekdays, and kiosks until much later.

BUS TRAVEL

Although not particularly comfortable or fast, bus travel is inexpensive. Eurolines departs from London's Victoria Station on Saturday at 2:30 PM, crossing the North Sea on the Dover-Calais ferry, and arrives in Copenhagen about 22 hours later. With its many other routes, Eurolines links the principal Danish cities to a network of service that includes major European cities. Safflebussen is the other main bus company with international routes to Denmark. The company offers regular trips between Copenhagen and Berlin, Göteborg, Karlstad, Stockholm, and Oslo.

To encourage travelers to make full use of Denmark's domestic transportation services, private bus operat ors and Danish State Railways (DSB) have collaborated to create Bus/Tog Samarbejde. This useful resource consolidates schedule and route information for the country's trains and buses.

Domestic bus companies include Thinggaard, which has regular routes between Sjælland and Jutland, and Abildskou, which offers service from Århus to Copenhagen and Ebeltoft, as well as between Roskilde and the Copenhagen airport. Bus tickets are usually sold on board the buses immediately before departure. Ask about discounts for children, senior citizens, and groups.

🚌 Bus Information **Abildskou** ✉ Graham Bellsvej 40, DK-8200 Århus ☎ 70/21-08-88 🌐 www.abildskou.dk. **Bus/Tog Samarbejde** 🌐 www.rejseplan.dk. **Eurolines** ✉ 52 Grosvenor Gardens, SW1 London ☎ 0207/730-8235 ✉ Reventlowsg. 8, DK-1651 Copenhagen ☎ 70/10-00-30 🌐 www.eurolines.com. **Säfflebussen** ✉ Halmtorvet 5, DK-1700 Copenhagen ☎ 33/23-54-20 🌐 www.safflebussen.se. **Thinggaard Ekspres** ✉ Jyllandsg. 6, DK-9000 Aalborg ☎ 70/10-00-20 🌐 www.thinggaard-bus.dk.

CAR RENTAL

Rental rates in Copenhagen begin at Dkr 500 a day and Dkr 2,500 a week. This does not include an additional per-km fee and any insurance you choose to purchase; there is also a 25% tax on car rentals.

🚗 Major Agencies **Budget-Pitzner Auto** ✉ Copenhagen Airport ☎ 32/50-90-65. **Europcar** ✉ Copenhagen Airport ☎ 32/50-30-90.

CAR TRAVEL

The only part of Denmark that is connected to the European continent is Jylland, via the E45 highway from Germany. The E20 highway then leads to Middelfart on Fyn and east to Nyborg. The Storebæltsbro bridge connects Fyn and Sjælland via the E20 highway; the E20 then continues east, over the Lillebæltsbro bridge, to Copenhagen. The bridges have greatly reduced the driving time between the islands. You can reach many of the smaller islands via toll bridges. In some locations, car ferries are still in service; for ferry information, *see* Boat & Ferry Travel.

In Scandinavia your own driver's license is acceptable for a limited time; check with the Danish Tourist Board before you go. International driving permits (IDPs) are available from the American and Canadian automobile associations and, in the United Kingdom, from the Automobile Association and Royal Automobile Club. These international permits, valid only in conjunction with your regular driver's license, are universally recognized; having one may save you a problem with local authorities.

EMERGENCY SERVICES Members of organizations affiliated with Alliance International de Tourisme (AIT) can get technical and legal advice from the Danish Motoring Organization, open 10–4 weekdays. All highways have emergency phones, and you can call the rental company for help. If you cannot drive your car to a garage for repairs, the rescue corps Falck can help anywhere, anytime. In most cases they do charge for assistance. In the event of an emergency, call 112.

🚗 **Danish Motoring Organization** (FDM) ✉ Firskovvej 32, 2800 Lyngby ☎ 45/27-07-07. **Falck** ☎ 70/10-20-30.

🚗 **Falck** ✉ Polititorvet, DK-1780 Copenhagen ☎ 70/10-20-30 emergencies, 33/15-83-20 headquarters 🖷 33/91-00-26 🌐 www.falck.dk. **Forenede Danske Motore-**

jere (Danish Motoring Organization) ✉ Firskovvej 32, DK–2800 Lyngby ☎ 70/13–30–40
🖷 45/27–09–93 🌐 www.fdm.dk.

GASOLINE   Gasoline costs about Dkr 8 per liter (¼ gallon). Stations are mostly self-service and open from 6 or 7 AM to 9 PM or later.

PARKING   You can usually park on the right-hand side of the road, though not on main roads and highways. Signs reading PARKERING/STANDSNING FORBUNDT mean no parking or stopping, though you are allowed a three-minute grace period for loading and unloading. In town, parking disks are used where there are no automated ticket-vending machines. Get disks from gas stations, post offices, police stations, or tourist offices, and set them to show your time of arrival. For most downtown parking, you must buy a ticket from an automatic vending machine and display it on the dash. Parking costs about Dkr 10 or more per hour.

ROAD CONDITIONS   Roads in Denmark are in good condition and largely traffic-free (except for the manageable traffic around Copenhagen).

RULES OF THE ROAD   To drive in Denmark you need a valid adult driver's license, and if you're using your own car, it must have a certificate of registration and national plates. A triangular hazard-warning sign is compulsory in every car and is provided with rentals. No matter where you sit in a car, you must wear a seat belt, and cars must have low beams on at all times. Motorcyclists must wear helmets and use low-beam lights as well. Talking on the phone while operating a car, bicycle, or any other kind of vehicle is illegal.

Bicyclists have equal rights on the road, and a duty to signal moves and observe all traffic regulations. Be especially careful when making turns. Check for bicyclists, who have the right of way if they are going straight and a car is turning.

Drive on the right and give way to traffic—*especially to bicyclists*—on the right. A red-and-white YIELD sign or a line of white triangles across the road means you must yield to traffic on the road you are entering. Do not turn right on red unless there is a green arrow indicating that this is allowed. Speed limits are 50 kph (30 mph) in built-up areas; 100 kph (60 mph) on highways; and 80 kph (50 mph) on other roads. If you are towing a trailer, you must not exceed 70 kph (40 mph). Speeding and, especially, drinking and driving are punished severely, even if no damage is caused. The consumption of one or two beers might lead to a violation, and motorists traveling across the Øresund Bridge must remember that Sweden has an even lower legal limit for blood-alcohol levels. As such, it is possible to drive legally out of Denmark and illegally into Sweden. Americans and other foreign tourists must pay all fines on the spot.

CUSTOMS & DUTIES

If you are 16 or older, have purchased goods in a country that is a member of the European Union (EU), and pay that country's value-added tax (V.A.T.) on those goods, you may import duty-free 1½ liters of liquor and 300 cigarettes or 150 cigarillos or 75 cigars or 400 grams of tobacco. If you are entering Denmark from a non-EU country or if you have purchased your goods on a ferryboat or in an airport not taxed in the EU, you must pay Danish taxes on any amount of alcoholic beverages greater than 1 liter of liquor or 2 liters of strong wine, plus 2 liters of table wine. For tobacco, the limit is 200 cigarettes or 100 cigarillos or 50 cigars or 250 grams of tobacco. You are also allowed 50 grams of perfume. Other articles (including beer) are allowed up to a maximum of Dkr 1,350.

Non-EU citizens can save 20% (less a handling fee) off the purchase price if they shop in one of the hundreds of stores throughout Denmark displaying the TAX-FREE SHOPPING sign. The purchased merchandise must value more than Dkr 300 and the taxes will be refunded after submitting the application with customs authorities at their final destination before leaving the EU.

🔃 **Told og Skat** (Toll and Taxes) ✉ Tagensvej 135, DK-2200 Copenhagen ☎ 35/87-73-00 🖷 35/85-90-94 ⊕ www.toldskat.dk.

EMBASSIES

New Zealanders should contact the U.K. embassy for assistance.

🔃 **Australia** ✉ Dampfærgevej 26, 2nd. floor, Østerbro, DK-2100 Copenhagen ☎ 70/26-36-76 🖷 70/26-36-86 ⊕ www.denmark.embassy.gov.au.

🔃 **Canada** ✉ Kristen Bernikows G. 1, Downtown, DK-1105 Copenhagen ☎ 33/48-32-00 🖷 33/48-32-20 ⊕ www.canada.dk.

🔃 **Ireland** ✉ Østbaneg. 21, Østerbro, DK-2100 Copenhagen ☎ 35/42-32-33 🖷 35/43-18-58.

🔃 **South Africa** ✉ Gammel Vartov Vej 8, DK-2900 Hellerup ☎ 39/18-01-55 🖷 39/18-40-06 ⊕ www.southafrica.dk.

🔃 **United Kingdom** ✉ Kastelsvej 36-40, Østerbro, DK-2100 Copenhagen ☎ 35/44-52-00 🖷 35/44-52-93 ⊕ www.britishembassy.dk.

🔃 **United States** ✉ Dag Hammarskjölds Allé 24, Østerbro, DK-2100 Copenhagen ☎ 35/55-31-44 🖷 35/43-02-23 ⊕ www.usembassy.dk.

EMERGENCIES

The general 24-hour emergency number throughout Denmark is 112.

LANGUAGE

Danish is a difficult tongue for foreigners—except those from Norway and Sweden—to understand, let alone speak. Danes are good linguists, however, and almost everyone, except perhaps elderly people in rural areas, speaks English. In Sønderjylland, the southern region of Jylland, most people speak or understand German. If you are planning to visit the countryside or the small islands, it would be a good idea to bring a phrase book.

Difficult-to-pronounce Danish characters include the "ø," pronounced a bit like a very short "er," similar to the French "eu"; "æ," which sounds like the "a" in "ape" but with a glottal stop, or the "a" in "cat," depending on the region; and the "å" (also written "aa"), which sounds like "or." The important thing about these characters isn't that you pronounce them correctly—foreigners usually can't—but that you know to look for them in the phone book at the very end. Mr. Søren Åstrup, for example, will be found after "Z;" Æ and Ø follow.

LODGING

The lodgings we list are the cream of the crop in each price category. We always list the facilities that are available—but we don't specify whether they cost extra: When pricing accommodations, always ask what's included and what costs extra.

APARTMENT &
VILLA RENTALS
If you want a home base that's roomy enough for a family and comes with cooking facilities, consider a furnished rental. These can save you money, especially if you're traveling with a group. Home-exchange directories sometimes list rentals as well as exchanges.

Each year many Danes choose to rent out their summer homes in the verdant countryside and along the coast. Typically, a simple house accommodating four persons costs from Dkr 1,000 weekly up to 10 times that amount during summer. You should book well in advance. A group of Danes who regularly rent out their holiday houses have formed the Association of Danish Holiday House Letters (ADHHL). You can also contact DanCenter and Lejrskolebureauet for information. Homes for You lists fully furnished homes and apartments.

🛈 International Agents **Hideaways International** ✉ 767 Islington St., Portsmouth, NH 03801 ☎ 603/430-4433 or 800/843-4433 🖷 603/430-4444 ⊕ www.hideaways.com, membership $145.

🛈 Local Agents **DanCenter** ✉ Lyngbyvej 20, Østerbro, DK-2100 Copenhagen ☎ 70/13-16-16 🖷 70/13-70-73 ⊕ www.dancenter.com. **Feriehusudlejernes Brancheforeningen (ADHHL)** ✉ Obels Have 32, DK-9000 Aalborg ☎ 96/30-22-44 🖷 96/30-22-45 ⊕ www.fbnet.dk. **Homes for You** ✉ Vimmelskaftet 49, Downtown, DK-1161 Copenhagen ☎ 33/33-08-05 🖷 33/32-08-04 ⊕ www.hay4you.dk. **Lejrskolebureauet (LSB)** ✉ Nordlævej 13, DK-3250 Gilleleje ☎ 48/30-14-88 🖷 48/30-14-66.

B&BS Contact Dansk Bed & Breakfast to order their B&B catalog for the whole of Denmark. Faaborg Touristbureau maintains its own list for the Fyn and the Central Islands region.

🛈 Reservation Services **Dansk Bed & Breakfast** ✉ Bernstorffsvej 71a, DK-2900 Hellerup ☎ 39/61-04-05 🖷 39/61-05-25 ⊕ www.bedandbreakfast.dk. **Faaborg Touristbureau** ✉ Banegaardspl. 2A, DK-5600 Faaborg ☎ 62/61-07-07 🖷 62/61-33-37 ⊕ www.bed-breakfast-fyn.dk.

CAMPING If you plan to camp in one of Denmark's 500-plus approved campsites, you'll need an International Camping Carnet or Danish Camping Pass (available at any campsite and valid for one year). Call Campingrådet for information.

🛈 **Campingrådet** ✉ Mosedalsvej 15, DK-2500 Valby ☎ 39/27-88-44 🖷 39/27-80-44 ⊕ www.campingraadet.dk.

FARM VACATIONS & HOMESTAYS A farm vacation is perhaps the best way to experience the Danish countryside, sharing meals with your host family and perhaps helping with the chores. Bed-and-breakfast packages are about Dkr 200, whereas half board—an overnight with breakfast and one hot meal—runs around Dkr 280. Full board, including an overnight with three square meals, can also be arranged. The minimum stay is three nights. Contact Landboferie for details.

If you aren't necessarily looking for a pastoral experience but would still like to get an insider's view of Danish society, you might want to consider a homestay. Meet the Danes helps travelers find accommodation in Danish homes. The informative local hosts can give you invaluable tips regarding sightseeing, shopping, dining, and nightlife.

🛈 **Landboferie** (Holiday in the Country) ✉ Ceresvej 2, DK 8410 Rønde ☎ 86/37-39-00 🖷 86/37-35-50 ⊕ www.bondegaardsferie.dk. **Meet The Danes** ✉ Ravnsborgg. 2, 2nd fl., Nørrebro DK-2200 Copenhagen ☎ 33/46-46-46 🖷 33/46-46-47 ⊕ www.meetthedanes.dk.

HOME EXCHANGES If you would like to exchange your home for someone else's, join a home-exchange organization, which will send you its updated listings of available exchanges for a year and will include your own listing in at least one of them. It's up to you to make specific arrangements.

🛈 Exchange Clubs **HomeLink International** ✆ Box 47747, Tampa, FL 33647 ☎ 813/975-9825 or 800/638-3841 🖷 813/910-8144 ⊕ www.homelink.org; $110 yearly for a listing, online access, and catalog; $70 without catalog. **Intervac U.S.** ✉ 30 Corte San Fernando, Tiburon, CA 94920 ☎ 800/756-4663 🖷 415/435-7440 ⊕ www.intervacus.com; $105 yearly for a listing, online access, and a catalog; $50 without catalog.

HOSTELS No matter what your age, you can save on lodging costs by staying at hostels. In some 4,500 locations in more than 70 countries around the world, Hostelling International (HI), the umbrella group for a number of national youth-hostel associations, offers single-sex, dorm-style beds and, at many hostels, rooms for couples and family accommodations. Membership in any HI national hostel association, open to travelers of all ages, allows you to stay in HI-affiliated hostels at member rates; one-year membership is about $28 for adults (C$35 for a two-year minimum membership in Canada, £13.50 in the U.K., A$52 in Australia, and NZ$40 in New Zealand); hostels charge about $10–$30 per night. Members have priority if the hostel is full; they're also eligible for discounts around the world, even on rail and bus travel in some countries.

Youth hostels in Denmark are open to everyone regardless of age. If you have an International Youth Hostels Association card (it costs Dkr 160 to obtain in Denmark), the rate is roughly Dkr 115 for a single bed, Dkr 150–Dkr 575 for a private room accommodating up to 4 people. Without the card, there's a surcharge of about Dkr 30 per person. Prices don't include breakfast.

The hostels fill up quickly in summer, so make your reservations early. Most hostels are sympathetic to students and will usually find them at least a place on the floor. Bring your own linens or sleep sheet, though these can usually be rented at the hostel. Sleeping bags are not allowed. Contact Danhostel Danmarks Vandrehjem—the organization charges for information, but you can get a free brochure, *Camping/Youth and Family Hostels,* from the Danish Tourist Board.

🗂 Organizations **Danhostel Danmarks Vandrerhjem** ✉ Vesterbrog. 39, Vesterbro, DK-1620, Copenhagen ☎ 33/31-36-12 🖷 33/31-36-26 ⊕ www.danhostel.dk. **Hostelling International–USA** ✉ 8401 Colesville Rd., Suite 600, Silver Spring, MD 20910 ☎ 301/495-1240 🖷 301/495-6697 ⊕ www.hiayh.org. **Hostelling International–Canada** ✉ 205 Catherine St., Suite 400, Ottawa, Ontario K2P 1C3 ☎ 613/237-7884 or 800/663-5777 🖷 613/237-7868 ⊕ www.hihostels.ca. **YHA England and Wales** ✉ Trevelyan House, Dimple Rd., Matlock, Derbyshire DE4 3YH, U.K. ☎ 0870/870-8808, 0870/770-8868, or 0162/959-2700 🖷 0870/770-6127 ⊕ www.yha.org.uk. **YHA Australia** ✉ 422 Kent St., Sydney, NSW 2001 ☎ 02/9261-1111 🖷 02/9261-1969 ⊕ www.yha.com.au. **YHA New Zealand** ✉ Level 4, Torrens House, 195 Hereford St., Box 436, Christchurch ☎ 03/379-9970 or 0800/278-299 🖷 03/365-4476 ⊕ www.yha.org.nz.

HOTELS All hotels listed have private baths unless otherwise noted. Many Danes prefer a shower to a bath, so if you particularly want a bath, ask for it, but be prepared to pay more. Taxes are usually included in prices, but check when making a reservation. As time goes on, it appears that an increasing number of hotels are eliminating breakfast from their room rates; even if it is not included, breakfast is usually well worth its price. Many of Denmark's larger hotels, particularly those that cater to the conference crowd, offer discounted rates on the weekends, so inquire when booking. Try www.danishhotels.dk for listings not included in this book.

The Scandinavian countries offer Inn Checks, or prepaid hotel vouchers, for accommodations ranging from first-class hotels to country cottages. These vouchers, which must be purchased from travel agents or from the Scandinavian Tourist Board (⇨ Visitor Information) before departure, are sold individually and in packets for as many nights as needed and offer savings of up to 50%. Most countries also offer summer bargains for foreign tourists; winter bargains can be even greater. For further information about Scandinavian hotel vouchers, contact the Scandinavian Tourist Board.

ProSkandinavia checks can be used in 400 hotels across Scandinavia for savings up to 50%, for reservations made usually no earlier than 24 hours before arrival, although some hotels allow earlier bookings. One check costs about $40 U.S. Two checks will pay for a double room at a hotel, one check for a room in a cottage. The checks can be bought at many travel agencies in Scandinavia or directly from ProSkandinavia.

The old stagecoach *kroer* (inns) scattered throughout Denmark can be cheap yet charming alternatives to standard hotel rooms. You can cut your costs by contacting Danske Kroer & Hoteller to invest in a book of Inn Checks, valid at 83 participating inns and hotels throughout the country. Each check costs about Dkr 675 per couple and entitles you to an overnight stay in a double room including breakfast. Family checks for three (Dkr 775) and four (Dkr 875) are also available. Order a free catalog from Danske Kroer & Hoteller, but choose carefully; the organization includes a few chain hotels bereft of the charm you might be expecting. Some of the participating establishments tack on a Dkr 150 surcharge.

🚩 Reservation Services **Danske Kroer & Hoteller** ✉ Vejlevej 16, DK-8700 Horsens ☎ 75/64-87-00 🖷 75/64-87-20 ⊕ www.krohotel.dk. **ProSkandinavia** ✉ Akersgt. 11, N-0158 Oslo, Norway ☎ 47/22-41-13-13 ⊕ www.proskandinavia.com.

RESERVING A ROOM
Make your reservations well in advance, especially in resort areas near the coasts. Many places offer summer reductions to compensate for the slowdown in business travel and conferences. The very friendly staff at the hotel booking desk at Wonderful Copenhagen can help find rooms in hotels, hostels, and private homes, or even at campsites in advance of a trip. If you find yourself in Copenhagen without a reservation, head for the tourist office's hotel booking desk, which is open May through August, Monday to Saturday 9–8 and Sunday 10–8; September through April, weekdays 10–4:30 and Saturday 10–1:30. Note that hours of the hotel booking desk can be fickle, and change from year to year depending on staff availability; in the low season, they are often closed on the weekends. Young travelers looking for a room should head for Use It, the student and youth budget travel agency.

Reservations should be made two months in advance, but last-minute (as in same-day) hotel rooms booked at the tourist office can save you 50% off the normal price.

🚩 Local Reservation Services **Hotel booking desk** ✉ Bernstorffsg. 1, Vesterbro, DK-1577 Copenhagen ☎ 70/22-24-42 ⊕ www.woco.dk. **Use It** ✉ Rådhusstr. 13, Downtown, DK-1466 Copenhagen ☎ 33/73-06-20 🖷 33/73-06-49 ⊕ www.useit.dk.

MAIL & SHIPPING

POSTAL RATES
Airmail letters and postcards to non-EU countries cost Dkr 6.50 for 50 grams. Airmail letters and postcards within the EU cost Dkr 5.50. Length, width, and thickness all influence the postage price. Contact Copenhagen's main post office for more information. You can buy stamps at post offices or from shops selling postcards.

RECEIVING MAIL
You can arrange to have your mail sent general delivery, marked *poste restante,* to any post office, hotel, or inn. If no post office is specified, the letter or package is automatically sent to the main post office in Copenhagen.

🚩 **Copenhagen Main Post Office** ✉ Tietgensg. 37, Vesterbro DK-1566 Copenhagen ☎ 80/20-70-30 ⊕ www.postdanmark.dk.

MONEY MATTERS

Denmark's economy is stable, and inflation remains reasonably low. On the other hand, the Danish cost of living is quite high, even for Europe. In some areas prices are comparable to other European capitals, while other goods or services tend to be higher. As in all of Scandinavia, prices for alcoholic beverages and tobacco products are steep due to heavy taxation. Prices are highest in Copenhagen, lower elsewhere in the country. Some sample prices: cup of coffee, Dkr 15–Dkr 25; bottle of beer, Dkr 20–Dkr 30; soda, Dkr 20–Dkr 25; ham sandwich, Dkr 20–Dkr 40; 1½-km (1-mi) taxi ride, about Dkr 50.

ATMS   Automatic Teller Machines (ATMs) are located around most towns and cities. Look for the red signs for KONTANTEN/DANKORT AUTOMAT. You can use Visa, Plus, Mastercard/Eurocard, Eurochequecard, and sometimes JCB cards to withdraw cash. Many, but not all, machines are open 24 hours. Check with your bank about daily withdrawal limits before you go.

🛈 **ATM Locations Mastercard/Cirrus** ☎ 800/424-7787 ⊕ www.mastercard.com.

CREDIT CARDS   Most major credit cards are accepted in Denmark, though it's wise to inquire about American Express and Diners Club beforehand. Throughout this guide, the following abbreviations are used: **AE**, American Express; **DC**, Diners Club; **MC**, MasterCard; and **V**, Visa.

🛈 **Reporting Lost Cards American Express** ✉ Amagertorv 18, DK-1146 Copenhagen ☎ 33/11-50-05. **Diners Club** ✉ H. J. Holst Vej 5 DK-2605 Brøndby ☎ 36/73-73-73. **Master Card** ☎ 44/89-27-50. **Visa** ☎ 44/89-29-29.

CURRENCY   The monetary unit in Denmark is the krone (Dkr), divided into 100 øre. Even though Denmark has not adopted the euro, the Danish krone is firmly bound to it at about Dkr 7.5 to 1€ with only minimal fluctuations in exchange rates.

At this writing (winter 2003), the krone stood at 7.43 to the euro, 4.23 to the Australian dollar, 10.53 to the British pound, 4.67 to the Canadian dollar, 3.76 to the New Zealand dollar, 0.89 to the South African rand, and 6.56 to the U.S. dollar.

SPORTS & THE OUTDOORS

FISHING   Licenses are required for fishing along the coasts; requirements vary from one area to another for fishing in lakes, streams, and the ocean. Licenses cost about Dkr 100 for a year, Dkr 75 for a week, and Dkr 25 for a day, and you can buy them at any post office. Remember—it is illegal to fish within 1,650 feet of the mouth of a stream. Contact the Danish Tourist Board for more information.

🛈 **Danish Tourist Board** ✉ Vesterbrog. 6D, Vesterbro, DK-1620 Copenhagen ☎ 33/11-14-15 🖷 33/93-14-15 ⊕ www.visitdenmark.dk.

GOLF   Danish golf courses can be a real challenge, with plenty of water, roughs that live up to their name, and wind that is often a factor. Due to environmental controls, chemical fertilization is prohibited, so greens tend to be flatter with fewer breaks. Motorized riding carts are prohibited for general use, though most courses have one on hand for anyone with (documented) ambulatory problems.

Danish golf courses are open to any player who is a members of a certified golf club or has a valid handicap card. When entering a clubhouse to pay a greens fee, you will be asked to present documentation of membership in a club or a card stating your handicap. This can present a problem for Americans, many of whom are unfamiliar with this system and can produce no such evidence. The Danes are generally flexible when a golfer doesn't have a card, but it's wise to have some sort of documentation handy just in case.

🛈 **Dansk Golf Union** ✉ Brøndby Stadium 20, DK-2605 Brøndby ☎ 43/26-27-00 🖷 43/26-27-01 ⊕ www.dgu-golf.dk.

TAXES

All hotel, restaurant, and departure taxes and V.A.T. (what the Danes call *moms*) are automatically included in prices. V.A.T. is 25%; non-EU citizens can obtain an 18% refund. The more than 1,500 shops that participate in the tax-free scheme have a white TAX FREE sticker on their windows. Purchases must be at least Dkr 300 per store and must be sealed and unused in Denmark. At the shop, you'll be asked to fill out a form and show your passport. The form can then be turned in at any airport or ferry customs desk, where you can choose a cash or charge-card credit. Keep all your receipts and tags; occasionally, customs authorities do ask to see purchases, so pack them where they will be accessible.

TELEPHONES

Telephone exchanges throughout Denmark were changed over the past couple of years. If you hear a recorded message or three loud beeps, chances are the number you are trying to reach has been changed. Contact the main Danish operator, TDC, for current numbers.

Denmark, like most European countries, has a different cellular-phone switching system from the one used in North America. Newer phones can handle both technologies; check with the dealer where you purchased your phone to see if it can work on the European system. If all else fails, several companies rent cellular phones to tourists. Contact local tourist offices for details.

COUNTRY CODE The country code for Denmark is 45.

DIRECTORY & OPERATOR ASSISTANCE Most operators speak English. For national directory assistance, dial 118; for an international operator, dial 113; for a directory-assisted international call, dial 115. You can reach U.S. operators by dialing local access codes.

INTERNATIONAL CALLS Dial 00, then the country code (1 for the United States and Canada, 44 for Great Britain), the area code, and the number. It's very expensive to call or fax from hotels, although the regional phone companies offer a discount after 7:30 PM. You can save a lot on the price of calls by purchasing a country-specific telephone card from any post office or one of the many kiosks and groceries in Copenhagen's Vesterbro and Nørrebro neighborhoods.

LOCAL CALLS Phones accept 1-, 2-, 5-, 10-, and 20-kroner coins. Pick up the receiver, dial the number, always including the area code, and wait until the party answers; then deposit the coins. You have roughly a minute per krone; on some phones you can make another call on the same payment if your time has not run out. When it does, you will hear a beep and your call will be disconnected unless you deposit another coin. Coin-operated phones are becoming increasingly rare; it is cheaper and less frustrating to buy a local phone card from a kiosk.

Dial the eight-digit number for calls anywhere within the country. For calls to the Faroe Islands (298) and Greenland (299), dial 00, then the three-digit code, then the five-digit number.

LONG-DISTANCE SERVICES AT&T, MCI, and Sprint access codes make calling long-distance relatively convenient, but you may find the local access number blocked in many hotel rooms. First ask the hotel operator to connect you. If the hotel operator balks, ask for an international operator, or dial the international operator yourself. One way to improve your odds of getting connected to your long-distance carrier is to travel with more than one company's calling card (a hotel may block Sprint, for example, but not MCI). If all else fails, call from a pay phone.

🔲 Access Codes **AT&T USADirect** ☎ 800/10010 🌐 www.travel.att.com. **World Phone** ☎ 800/10022 🌐 www.mci.com. **Sprint Global One** ☎ 800/10877 🌐 www.sprint.com.

TIPPING

It has long been held that the egalitarian Danes do not expect to be tipped. This is often the case, but most people do tip and those who receive tips appreciate them. Service is included in hotel bills, but when paying at bars or restaurants a token tip is the general rule of thumb. The same holds true for taxis—if a bill comes to Dkr 58, most people will give the driver Dkr 60. If the driver is extremely friendly or helpful, tip more at your own discretion. Hotel porters expect about Dkr 5 per bag.

SIGHTSEEING TOURS

For information on tours, call the Danish Tourist Board, as well as Copenhagen Excursions.

🔁 Fees and Schedules **Copenhagen Excursions** ☎ 32/54-06-06.

BIKE TOURS Copenhagen-based BikeDenmark combines the flexibility of individual tours with the security of an organized outing. Choose from seven pre-planned 5- to 10-day tours, which include bikes, maps, two fine meals per day, hotel accommodations, and hotel-to-hotel baggage transfers. BikeDenmark tours can be booked directly by fax, via their Web site, or through any travel agency below. Many U.S. tour companies can arrange booking. Try Borton Oversees, Nordique Tours, ScanAm World Tours, or Gerhard's Bicycle Odysseys.

Bike and Sea also leads biking tours through southern Jylland, Fyn, and southern Sjælland.

🔁**Bike and Sea** ⊠ Svendborgvej 83-85, DK-5260 Odense ☎ 66/13-13-37 🖷 66/13-13-38 🌐 www.bikeandsea-denmark.com. **BikeDenmark** ⊠ Olaf Poulsens Allé 1A, DK-3480 Fredensborg ☎ 48/48-58-00 🖷 48/48-59-00 🌐 www.bikedenmark.com. **Borton Oversees** ⊠ 5412 Lyndale Ave. S, Minneapolis, MN 55419 ☎ 612/822-4640 or 800/843-0602 🖷 612/822-4755 🌐 www.bortonoverseas.com. **Gerhard's Bicycle Odysseys** ⊡ Box 757, Portland, OR 97207 ☎ 800/966-2402 🖷 503/223-5901 🌐 www.since1974.com. **Nordique Tours Norvista** ☎ 310/645-7527 or 800/995-7997 🖷 310/645-1071 🌐 www.nordiquetours.com. **ScanAm World Tours** ⊠ 108 N. Main St., Cranbury, NJ 08512 ☎ 800/545-2204 toll-free 🖷 609/655-1622 🌐 www.scandinaviantravel.com.

TRAIN TRAVEL

Trains within Europe are well connected to Denmark, with Copenhagen serving as the main hub; however, it's often not much cheaper than flying, especially if you make your arrangements from the United States. Scanrail Passes offer discounts on train, ferry, and car transportation in Denmark, Finland, Sweden, and Norway. EurailPasses, purchased only in the United States, are accepted by the Danish State Railways and on some ferries operated by DSB.

DSB and a few private companies cover the country with a dense network of services, supplemented by buses in remote areas. Hourly intercity trains connect the main towns in Jylland and Fyn with Copenhagen and Sjælland, using high-speed diesels, called IC-3s, on the most important stretches. All these trains make one-hour crossings of the Great Belt Bridge. You can reserve seats (for an extra Dkr 15) on intercity trains, and you *must* have a reservation if you plan to cross the Great Belt. Buy tickets at stations. From London, the transit takes 18 hours, including ferry. Call the British Rail European Travel Center or Wasteels for information.

CUTTING COSTS The ScanRail pass, which affords unlimited train travel throughout Denmark, Finland, Norway, and Sweden and restricted ferry passage in and beyond Scandinavia, comes in various denominations: five days of travel within 15 days ($249 first class, $187 second class); 10 days within a month ($400 first class, $301 second class); or 21 days unlimited use ($452 first class, $348 second class).

For car and train travel, consider the Scanrail 'n' Drive Pass: over 15 days you can get five days of unlimited train travel and two days of car rental (and a choice of three car categories) with unlimited mileage in Denmark, Norway, and Sweden. You can purchase extra car-rental days and choose from first- or second-class train travel. Individual rates for two adults traveling together (compact car $385 first-class/$308 second-class) are considerably lower (about 25%) than for single adults; the third or fourth person sharing the car only needs to purchase a Scanrail pass.

In the United States, call Rail Europe, Nordic Saga Tours, ScanAm Tours, Passage Tours, or DER Travel Services for rail passes. You can also buy the ScanRail Pass at the train stations in most major cities, including Copenhagen, Odense, and Århus. But no matter where you get it, various discounts are offered to holders of the pass by hotel chains and other organizations; ask DER, Rail Europe, or your travel agent for details. The ScanRail Pass and Interail and Eurail passes are also valid on all DSB trains. Compare prices at www.scanrail.com before you leave home.

Call Arriva for train travel in central and northern Jutland, or the DSB travel office for the rest of the country.

ℹ·Train Information Arriva ☎ 72/13-96-00 ⊕ www.arriva.dk. **DSB Information** ☎ 70/13-14-15 ⊕ www.dsb.dk.

ℹ Where to Buy Rail Passes Wasteels ✉ Skoubog. 6, Downtown, DK-1158 Copenhagen ☎ 33/14-46-33 🖶 33/14-08-65 ⊕ www.wasteels.dk.

VISITOR INFORMATION

ℹ Tourist Information Danish Tourist Board ✉ 655 3rd Ave., New York, NY 10017 ☎ 212/885-9700 🖶 212/885-9726 ✉ 55 Sloane St., London SW1X 9SY ☎ 44/20-7259-5959 🖶 44/20-7259-5955 ✉ Level 4, 81 York St. Sydney NSW 2000 ☎ 61/2-9262-5832 🖶 61/2-9290-1981 ⊕ www.visitdenmark.com. **Danmarks Turistråd** (Danish Tourist Board) ✉ Vesterbrog. 6D, Vesterbro, DK-1620 Copenhagen ☎ 33/11-14-15 🖶 33/93-14-16.

FINLAND

2

FODOR'S CHOICE

Cloudberry-picking, *August in Lapland*

Lusto Finnish Forest Museum, *Punkaharju*

Nykytaiteenmuseo (Kiasma), *museum in Helsinki*

Ortodoksinen Kirkkomuseo, *museum in Kuopio*

"Ruska," *the fall colors in Lapland*

Seurasaaren Ulkomuseo, *outdoor museum in Helsinki*

Taidekeskus Retretti, *modern art complex in Punkaharju*

Temppeliaukio Kirkko, *church in Helsinki*

Tuomiokirkko, *cathedral in Tampere*

Uspenskin Katedraali, *cathedral in Helsinki*

Many other great sights, restaurants, and hotels enliven this area. For other favorites, look for the stars as you read this chapter.

Updated by
Joan Lofgren

If you like majestic open spaces, fine architecture, and the Nordic quality of life, Finland is for you. Nature dictates life in this Nordic land, where winter brings perpetual darkness, and summer, perpetual light. Crystal-clear streams run through vast forests lit by the midnight sun, and reindeer roam free. Even the arts mimic nature: Witness the music of Jean Sibelius, Finland's most famous son, which can swing from a somber nocturne of midwinter darkness to the tremolo of sunlight slanting through pine and birch, or from the crescendo of a blazing sunset to the pianissimo of the next day's dawn. The architecture of Alvar Aalto and the Saarinens—Eliel and son Eero, visible in many U.S. cities, also bespeaks the Finnish affinity with nature, with soaring spaces evocative of Finland's moss-floored forests. Eliel and his family moved to the United States in 1923 and became United States citizens—but it was to a lonely Finnish seashore that Saarinen had his ashes returned.

Until 1917, Finland was under the domination of its nearest neighbors, Sweden and Russia, who fought over it for centuries. After more than 600 years under the Swedish crown and 100 under the Russian czars, the country inevitably bears many traces of the two cultures, including a small (just under 6%) but influential Swedish-speaking population and a scattering of Orthodox churches.

The Finns themselves are neither Scandinavian nor Slavic. They are descended from wandering tribes who probably migrated from the south and southwest to settle on the swampy shores of the Gulf of Finland before the Christian era. The Finnish tongue belongs to the Finno-Ugric language group; it is related to Estonian and, very distantly, Hungarian.

There is a tough, resilient quality to the Finns. Finland is one of the very few countries that shared a border with the Soviet Union in 1939 and retained its independence. Indeed, no country fought the Soviets to a standstill as the Finns did in the grueling 105-day Winter War of 1939–40. This resilience stems from the turbulence of the country's past and from the people's determination to work the land and survive the long, dark winters. Finns are stubborn, patriotic, and self-sufficient, yet not aggressively nationalistic. On the contrary, rather than boasting of past battles, Finns are proud of finding ways to live in peace with their neighbors.

As evidenced by the role of Finnish leaders in international diplomacy and Finland's contributions to peacekeeping and humanitarian aid worldwide, the country's neutrality has provided the basis for its steadfast role in the international political landscape. It has not shied away from other alliances, however, and plays an active role in EU affairs, particularly promoting eastern enlargement.

The country's role as a crossroads between East and West is vibrantly reflected in Helsinki, from which it has become increasingly convenient to arrange brief tours to Tallinn (the capital of Estonia), and St. Petersburg, Russia. The architectural echoes of St. Petersburg in Helsinki are particularly striking in the "white night" light of June. Tallinn, with its medieval Old Town and bargain shopping, is a popular trip that can be done in a day. Traveling there takes an hour and a half by hydrofoil, three and a half by ferry.

"The strength of a small nation lies in its culture," noted Finland's leading 19th-century statesman and philosopher, Johan Vilhelm Snellman. As though inspired by this thought, Finns—who are among the world's top readers—continue to nurture a rich cultural climate, as is illustrated by its 900 museums and the festivals throughout Finland that continue to attract the top performers, in jazz (Pori), big bands (Imatra), opera (Savonlinna), folk music (Kaustinen) and rock (Ruisrock in Turku).

The average Finn volunteers little information, but that's a result of reserve, not indifference. Make the first approach and you may have a friend for life. Finns like their silent spaces, though, and won't appreciate backslapping familiarity—least of all in the sauna, still regarded by many as a spiritual as well as a cleansing experience.

Exploring Finland

Finland's capital, Helsinki, commands the southern coast and shelters more than one-tenth of the country's population. Towns were first settled in the southwest, where the culture of the South Coast and the Åland Islands has a decidedly Swedish influence. Northern Finland—Finnish Lapland—straddles the Arctic Circle and is populated by few. Finland's central region is dominated by the Lakelands, the country's vacation belt.

Numbers in the text correspond to numbers in the margin and on the maps.

About the Restaurants

Finnish food emphasizes freshness rather than variety, although in keeping with larger European trends, restaurants are getting more and more innovative with their cooking, and expanding on classic Finnish ingredients—from forest, lake, and sea. If you get tired of fish or reindeer, then pizza, Tex-Mex, Chinese, and Thai food can also easily be found in larger cities.

That more coffee is consumed per capita in Finland than in any other country is evidenced by the staggering number of cafés throughout the country. Particularly in Helsinki, patrons of cafés downtown and around the waterfront spill outside onto the streets. In addition to coffee, Finnish cafés serve a large selection of baked goods: *munkki* (doughnuts), *pulla* (sweet bread), and other confections are consumed with vigor by both young and old. Coffee bars have come to most major cities—travelers need not go without espresso or latte while in northern Europe. Internet cafés are not as common as in other areas, mainly due to the high per capita use of the Internet in homes.

Prices of alcohol in Finland are steep, but beer-lovers should not miss the well-made Finnish brews. Jacket and tie are required in most of the restaurants in the $$$$ category.

About the Hotels

Every class of lodging exists in Finland, from luxurious urban hotels to rustic cabins on lake shores and in the forest. Cleanliness and modern comforts are standard. Expect private baths in rooms unless otherwise noted. Prices almost always include a generous breakfast and sauna privileges.

The price categories below are based on weekday rates. Greater discounts are available on weekends and in summer months, especially between *Juhannus* (Midsummer, the summer solstice holiday in late June) and July 31, when prices are usually 30% to 50% lower.

Keep in mind that Finland is a large country, and though train service between towns is quite good, some trips can take an entire day. To make the most of your time, take advantage of Finnair's efficient domestic air service between Helsinki and destinations farther afield, such as Savonlinna and Rovaniemi.

If you have 2 days

You'll have plenty of time to take in all the sites of **Helsinki** ①–㊳, but not enough to venture outside the capital city area. Since Helsinki is fairly small and its major attractions are within walking distance of one another, in one day you can see the architectural highlights and at least one important museum. On the second day, you might take a harbor tour and visit the island fortress **Suomenlinna** ㉚, or take a side trip to **Espoo, Porvoo,** or **Vantaa,** or to the **Gallen-Kallela Estate** in Tarvaspää. The museum in the former studio home of the architects Saarinen, Gesellius, and Lindgren at **Hvitträsk** is another must.

If you have 5 days

After spending one or two nights in **Helsinki** ①–㊳, head to the destination of your choice: **Lapland,** the **Southwestern Coast and the Åland Islands,** or the **Lakelands.** Another option is to spend four nights in Helsinki, venturing out for easy, fun day-trips to nearby towns: the cultural center **Turku** ㊷; **Tampere** ㊾, with its amusement park; and the castle town **Hämeenlinna** ㊿ all take two hours or less by train.

If you have 10 days

Ten days allows the tireless traveler time to explore much of Finland. If your goal is to see all of the regions, one option is to spend your first night in **Helsinki** ①–㊳, then take a train to **Turku** ㊷, on the southwest coast, the following day. Using Turku as a base, take a side trip to see the fancy homes and beaches of **Hanko** ㊶, the historic wooden town of **Rauma** ㊸, or the medieval pilgrimage village, **Naantali** ㊹. From Turku you can fly to **Rovaniemi** (51), the gateway to Finnish Lapland. From Rovaniemi, go as deep into the Lapland wilderness as you desire. Take a train or a plane back down south to **Savonlinna** ㊻ in eastern Finland, home of Finland's greatest castle. Take a scenic boat ride through the heart of Finland from Savonlinna to **Kuopio** ㊽, site of the Ortodoksinen Kirkkomuseo (Orthodox Church Museum) and within reach of Uusi Valamo (the New Valamo Monastery). From Kuopio, you can fly back to Helsinki.

WHAT IT COSTS In Euros

	$$$$	$$$	$$	$	¢
	MAIN CITIES				
RESTAURANTS	over €29	€23–€29	€17–€23	€10-€17	under €10
HOTELS	over €240	€190–€240	€140–€190	€80–€140	under €80
	ELSEWHERE				
RESTAURANTS	over €22	€18–€22	€14–€18	€10–€14	under €10
HOTELS	over €175	€140–€175	€105–€140	€70–€105	under €70

Restaurant prices are per person, for a main course at dinner, excluding tip. Hotel prices are for two people in a standard double room in high season, including service charge and taxes.

Timing

Finland's tourist season commences in June, when the growing daylight hours herald the opening of summer restaurants and outdoor museums, and the start of boat tours and cruises. Summer is by far the best time to visit Helsinki, the Lakelands, and the Southwestern Coast and Ålands, which come out of hibernation for the long, bright, but not overly hot, summer days. A special draw in the Lakelands is the Savonlinna Opera Festival, held in late July or early August.

Finland can also be exhilarating on clear, brisk winter days. For a real treat, visit Lapland—home of Santa Claus—in December. Operating on a different schedule altogether, the tourist season in the north focuses on winter events, when the snow is deep and the Northern Lights bright. Ski trips in Lapland in early spring are popular and many resorts offer tourist packages. Summer weather in Lapland offers a different repertoire to the traveler, when the snow and ice of the north give way to flowing rivers and greenery. The Midnight Sun Film Festival in Sodankylä offers round-the-clock screenings in tents.

You can expect warm (not hot) days in Helsinki from mid-May, and in Lapland from mid-June. The midnight sun can be seen from May to July, depending on the region. For a period in midwinter, the northern lights almost make up for the fact that the sun does not rise at all. Even in Helsinki, summer nights are brief and never really dark, whereas in midwinter daylight lasts only a few hours.

HELSINKI

A city of the sea, Helsinki was built along a series of odd-shape peninsulas and islands jutting into the Baltic coast along the Gulf of Finland. Streets and avenues curve around bays, bridges reach to nearby islands, and ferries ply among offshore islands.

Having grown dramatically since World War II, Helsinki now absorbs over one-tenth of the Finnish population and the metropolitan area covers a total of 764 square km (474 square mi) and 315 islands. Most sights, hotels, and restaurants cluster on one peninsula, forming a compact central hub. The greater Helsinki metropolitan area, which includes Espoo and Vantaa, has a total population not far short of a million.

Helsinki is a relatively young city compared with other European capitals. In the 16th century, King Gustav Vasa of Sweden decided to woo trade from the Estonian city of Tallinn and thus challenge the Hanseatic League's monopoly on Baltic trade. Accordingly, he commanded the people of four Finnish towns to pack up their belongings and relocate at the rapids on the River Vantaa. The new town, founded on June 12, 1550, was named Helsinki.

For three centuries, Helsinki (Helsingfors in Swedish) had its ups and downs as a trading town. Turku, to the west, remained Finland's capital and intellectual center. Ironically, Helsinki's fortunes improved when Finland fell under Russian rule as an autonomous grand duchy. Czar Alexander I wanted Finland's political center closer to Russia and, in 1812, selected Helsinki as the new capital. Shortly afterward, Turku suffered a disastrous fire, forcing the university to move to Helsinki. The town's future was secure.

Just before the czar's proclamation, a fire destroyed many of Helsinki's traditional wooden structures, precipitating the construction of new buildings suitable for a nation's capital. The German-born architect Carl Lud-

Boating Finns love all kinds of boating, and there are good facilities for guests' boats in most ports. Southwest Finland is a wonderful destination for sailors. The towns have colorful marinas that welcome visitors, and provide a full range of services. Hanko, the southernmost town in Finland, has the country's largest marina.

2

Fishing The fish-rich waters of the Baltic archipelago and innumerable inland lakes and streams assure you will never run out of places to go fishing. The waters of the Ålands are especially rich with pike, whitefish, salmon, and perch, and ice fishing makes this a year-round sport.

Saunas An authentic Finnish sauna is an obligatory experience, and not hard to find: there are 1.6 million saunas in this country of just over 5 million people—even the parliament has its own sauna. The traditional Finnish sauna—which involves relaxing on wooden benches, pouring water onto hot coals and swatting your neighbor's back with birch branches—is an integral part of cabin life and now city life, as apartments are outfitted with small saunas in their bathrooms. Almost every hotel has at least one sauna available free of charge, usually at standard times in the morning or evening for men and women to use separately. Larger hotels offer a private sauna in the higher-class rooms and suites. Public saunas (with swimsuits required) are becoming increasingly popular, even in winter, when saunagoers jump into the water through a large hole in the ice (called *avantouinti*). Public swimming pools are also equipped with saunas that can be used at no extra charge. For information, contact the Finnish Sauna Society.

Shopping Like some of its Nordic counterparts, Finland is known for its design. Helsinki has the widest selection of goods—from Arabia ceramics to littala glass to Marimekko clothing and textiles—and the highest prices. Handicrafts in birch and other woods are also distinctively Finnish. Furs, called *turkki* in Finnish, are a good buy. You might also want to take home some of the delicious smoked or marinated fish—available vacuum-packed at Helsinki Airport.

Wilderness Expeditions Opportunities to explore the forests and moors, rapids and waterfalls, mountains and gorges of Lapland abound. Intrepid explorers can probe the deepest areas of the national forests on skis or by snowmobile, take a photo safari to capture the unrivaled landscape, canoe down the clear rivers filled with salmon and trout, forage for mushrooms in the forest, or pick cloudberries and lingonberries in the bogs.

---

vig Engel was commissioned to rebuild the city, and as a result, Helsinki has some of the purest neoclassical architecture in the world. Add to this foundation the influence of Stockholm and St. Petersburg with the local inspiration of 20th-century Finnish design, and the result is a European capital city that is as architecturally eye-catching as it is distinct from other Scandinavian capitals. You are bound to discover endless delightful details—a grimacing gargoyle; a foursome of males supporting the weight of a balcony on their shoulders; a building painted in strik-

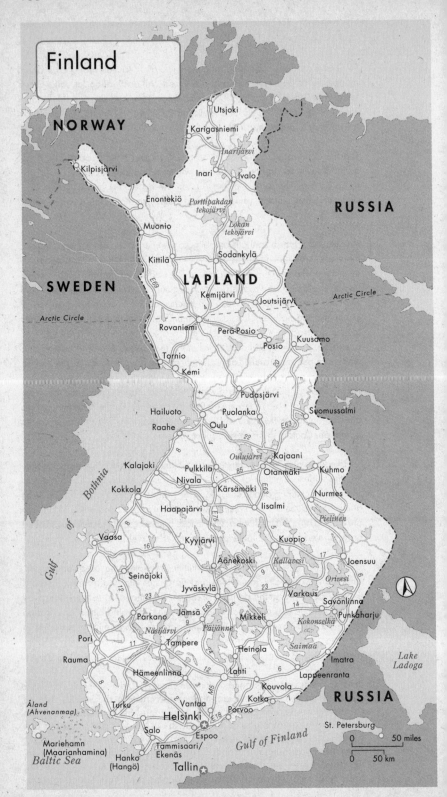

Finland

NORWAY

Utsjoki

Karigasniemi

Kilpisjärvi

Inarijärvi

Inari

Ivalo

Enontekiö

Porttipahdan tekojärvi

RUSSIA

Muonio

Lokan tekojärvi

Kittilä

Sodankylä

SWEDEN

LAPLAND

E69

Kemijärvi

Joutsijärvi

Arctic Circle

Arctic Circle

Rovaniemi

Perä-Posio

4

Posio

Kuusamo

Tornio

20

Kemi

4

Pudasjärvi

Hailuoto

Puolanka

Suomussalmi

Raahe

Oulu

E63

8

4

22

Oulujärvi

Kajaani

Kalajoki

Pulkkila

85

Otanmäki

Kuhmo

Nivala

Kärsämäki

E63

Nurmes

Kokkola

Haapajärvi

Iisalmi

Pielinen

E75

Gulf

Vaasa

16

Kyyjärvi

5

Kuopio

of

Äänekoski

Kallavesi

17

Joensuu

Seinäjoki

9

Orivesi

6

Bothnia

8

12

Jyväskylä

23

Varkaus

23

Parkano

Jämsä

E63

14

Savonlinna

Pori

Näsijärvi

9

Päijänne

Mikkeli

Kokonselkä

Punkaharju

11

Tampere

Saimaa

Rauma

Heinola

Imatra

Lake Ladoga

Hämeenlinna

12

Lahti

6

Lappeenranta

3

M5

Kouvola

Åland (Ahvenanmaa)

Turku

2

Vantaa

Kotka

1

RUSSIA

Helsinki

E18

Porvoo

St. Petersburg

Salo

Espoo

50 miles

Mariehamn (Maarianhamina)

Tammisaari/ Ekenäs

Gulf of Finland

50 km

Baltic Sea

Hanko (Hangö)

Tallin

ing colors, with contrasting flowers in the windows. The city's over 400 parks make it particularly inviting in summer.

Today, Helsinki is still a meeting point of eastern and western Europe, which is reflected in its cosmopolitan image, the influx of Russians and Estonians, and generally multilingual population. Outdoor summer bars ("terrassit" as the locals call them) and cafés in the otherwise bustling city center are perfect for people-watching on a summer afternoon.

Exploring Helsinki

The city center is densely packed and easily explored on foot, the main tourist sites grouped in several clusters; nearby islands are easily accessible by ferry. Just west of Katajanokka, Senaatintori and its Tuomiokirkko mark the beginning of the city center, which extends westward along Aleksanterinkatu.

Museums & Markets

The orange tents of the Kauppatori market brighten even the coldest snowy winter months with fresh flowers, fish, crafts, and produce. In warm weather, the bazaar fills with shoppers and browsers who stop for the ubiquitous coffee and munkki, the seaborne traffic in Eteläsatama, or South Harbor, a backdrop. From here you can take the local ferry service to Korkeasaari (Korkea Island), home of the zoo, or take a walk through the neighborhoods of Helsinki, encompassing the harbor; city center shopping district; tree-lined Bulevardi; and the indoor Hietalahden Tori, another marketplace.

a good walk

Begin your walk at the indoor redbrick market hall, **Vanha Kauppahalli** ❶ ▶, along the South Harbor. From here you can see the orange tents of the outdoor market, the **Kauppatori** ❷. If you are with children and want to take a jaunt, Helsinki's zoo, **Korkeasaari Eläintarha** ❸, is accessible by metro or daily ferry from the South Harbor, just east of the market.

Helsinki's oldest public monument, the Obeliski Keisarinnan kivi, stands in Kauppatori along Pohjoisesplanadi. The series of beautiful old buildings along Pohjoisesplanadi includes the pale-blue **Kaupungintalo** ❹ and, at the easternmost end of the street, the well-guarded **Presidentinlinna** ❺. Walk back west along Pohjoisesplanadi and cross the street to the square with the **Havis Amanda** ❻ statue and fountain. You can stop at the City Tourist Office at Pohjoisesplanadi 19. To your left is the Esplanadi, a tree-lined boulevard park that starts at the harbor.

A few yards west of the City Tourist Office, you'll see the art nouveau **Jugendsali** ❼. After walking past the Arabian ceramics and the Marimekko clothing stores, you'll see the elephantine Gröngvistin Talo, or Grönqvist's block, on your left across the park: designed by architect Theodor Höijer and built in 1903, this was Scandinavia's largest apartment building in its day. On your right as you pass an ornate block of buildings is the site of the luxurious Kämp Hotel, renowned in Scandinavia at the end of the 19th century and now beautifully restored. Before hitting Mannerheimintie, you'll pass Akateeminen Kirjakauppa and Stockmann's, respectively Finland's largest bookstore and department store. The bookstore was designed by Alvar Aalto, Finland's most famous architect.

At the intersection of Pohjoisesplanadi and Mannerheimintie, the distinctive round **Svenska Teatern** ❽ is sure to catch your eye. Turn left on Mannerheimintie, cross the street, and take a right onto broad, tree-shaded Bulevardi, passing Vanha Kirkkopuisto, or Old Church Park, usually called Ruttopuisto, or Plague Park, for the 18th-century plague

Helsinki

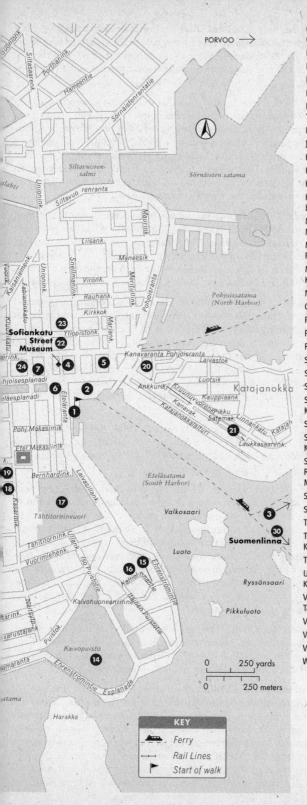

victims buried there. Continue southwest on Bulevardi until you reach the **Sinebrychoffin Taidemuseo** ⑨, a former mansion surrounded by a beautiful park. The **Hietalahden Tori** ⑩ is just across the street and slightly southeast of the museum, with an indoor food market and a flea market outside.

TIMING It will take about 45 minutes to walk this route from Kauppatori to Hietalahden Tori, stops not included. Head out early if you want to see both markets in action, as they close around 2 PM. In summer the Kauppatori by the South Harbor reopens at 3:30 PM, when the fruit and berry vendors do a brisk trade and local crafts stalls set up shop. Note that the Sinebrychoffin Taidemuseo is closed on Tuesday. For a side trip to the zoo, the ferry to Korkeasaari Island takes less than a half hour, but allow time to wait for the ferry coming and going.

WHAT TO SEE **Havis Amanda.** This fountain's brass centerpiece, a young woman perched
⑥ on rocks surrounded by dolphins, was commissioned by the city fathers to embody Helsinki. Sculptor Ville Vallgren completed her in 1908 using a Parisian girl as his model. Partying university students annually crown the Havis Amanda with their white caps on the eve of Vappu, the May 1 holiday. ⊠ *Eteläespl. and Eteläranta, Keskusta/Kauppatori.*

⑩ **Hietalahden Tori** (Hietalahti Market). The brick market hall is crammed with vendors selling fish, flowers, produce, and meat. A simultaneous outdoor flea market has tables piled with the detritus of countless Helsinki attics and cellars. Shoppers can stop amid the action for coffee, doughnuts, and meat pies. This market is especially popular with Helsinki's Russian community. ⊠ *Bulevardi and Hietalahdenk, Hietalahti* ☉ *Regular market weekdays 6:30–2, Sat. 6:30–3; flea market weekdays 8–2, Sat. 8–3; summer evening flea market weekdays 3:30–8, Sun. 10–4.*

❼ **Jugendsali.** Originally designed as a bank in 1906, this now serves as a cultural information office and a temporary exhibition hall for Finnish art. ⊠ *Pohjoisespl. 19, Keskusta* ☎ *09/169–02278* ☉ *Aug.–June, weekdays 9–5, Sun. 11–5; July, weekdays 9–4.*

❷ **Kauppatori** (Market Square). At this Helsinki institution, open year-round, wooden stands with orange and gold awnings bustle in the mornings when everyone—tourists and locals alike—comes to shop, browse, or sit and enjoy coffee and conversation. You can buy a freshly caught perch for the evening's dinner, a bouquet of bright flowers for a friend, or a fur pelt or hat. In summer the fruit and vegetable stalls are supplemented by an evening arts-and-crafts market. ⊠ *Eteläranta and Pohjoisespl., Keskusta/Kauppatori* ☉ *Sept.–May, weekdays 6:30–2, Sat. 6:30–3; June–Aug., weekdays 6:30–2 and 3:30–8, Sat. 6:30–3, Sun. 9–4.*

❹ **Kaupungintalo** (City Hall). The light blue building on Pohjoisplanadi (North Esplanade), the political center of Finland, is the home of city government offices. ⊠ *Pohjoisespl. 1 Keskusta/Kauppatori* ☎ *09/169–2598* ☉ *Guided tours on Thurs. by appointment.*

☾ ❸ **Korkeasaari Eläintarha** (Helsinki Zoo). Snow leopards and reindeer like the cold climate at one of the world's most northern zoos. The zoo is entirely within the limits of this small island, but the winding paths make the zoo seem much larger than it actually is. Children love the outdoor play equipment. May to September the ferry departs approximately every 30 minutes from the Market Square and the cost of the ferry ticket (€7) includes entrance to the zoo. The trip takes less than a half hour; arrival and departure times are posted at the harbor. Alternatively, you can take the metro to the Kulosaari stop, cross under the tracks, and follow the signs 20 minutes to the zoo. Bus connections are from Erottaja or Hertoniemi (weekends). ⊠ *Korkeasaari (Korkea Island), Korkeasaari* ☎ *09/169–5969* ⊕ *www.hel.fi/zoo* ⊠ *€5* ⊘ *Mar. and Apr., daily 10–6; May–Sept., daily 10–8; Oct.–Feb., daily 10–4.*

Obeliski Keisarinnan kivi (Czarina's Stone). This obelisk with a double-headed golden eagle, the symbol of Imperial Russia, was erected in 1835, toppled during the Russian Revolution in 1917, and fully restored in 1972. ⊠ *Kauppatori along Pohjoisespl., Keskusta/Kauppatori.*

❺ Presidentinlinna (President's Palace). The long history of this edifice mirrors the history of Finland itself: originally built in 1818 as a private residence for a German businessman, it was redesigned in 1843 as a palace for the czars; then it served as the official residence of Finland's presidents from 1919 to 1993. Today it houses the offices of Finland's first female president, Tarja Halonen, and is the venue for official receptions. The best part of the house is said to be its hall of mirrors. It is closed to the public except for prearranged group tours organized by Helsinki Expert, the Helsinki Tourist Association, on Wednesdays and Saturdays, from 11–4. ⊠ *Pohjoisespl. 1, Keskusta/Kauppatori* ☎ *09/2288–1222.*

❾ Sinebrychoffin Taidemuseo (Sinebrychoff Museum of Foreign Art). The wealthy Russian Sinebrychoffs owned a brewing company and lived in this splendid yellow-and-white 1840 neo-Renaissance mansion filled with wildly opulent furniture. The family's home and foreign art collection are now a public museum; you'll find a staid collection of Dutch and Swedish 17th- and 18th-century portraits, a lively collection of landscapes, miniatures, and porcelain, and the mansion's original decorative furniture. In summer, outdoor concerts are occasionally held in the once-private **Sinebrychoff Park**. ⊠ *Bulevardi 40, Hietalahti* ☎ *09/ 1733–6460* ⊕ *www.fng.fi* ⊠ *€4* ⊘ *Tues., Fri. 10–6, Wed. and Thurs. 10–8, weekends 11–5.*

❽ Svenska Teatern (Swedish Theater). Dating from 1827, the first wooden theater on this site was considered too vulnerable to fire and was replaced by a stone building in 1866. Ironically, the stone building was itself nearly destroyed by a fire. In 1936, a team of architects—Eero Saarinen and Jarl Eklundhe among them—renovated it. The whitewashed round theater today displays an attractive shape and dignified simplicity of design. The Swedish Theater's own company performs plays in Swedish year-round. ⊠ *Pohjoisespl. 2, Esplanadi/Erottaja* ☎ *09/ 6162–1411* ⊕ *www.svenskateatern.fi* ⊘ *Box office daily noon–performance time.*

need a break?   The **Aalto Café** (⊠ Pohjoisespl. 39, Esplanadi ☎ 09/121–4446) on the Academic Bookstore's mezzanine is pleasant for lunch or a snack.

▶ ❶ Vanha Kauppahalli (Old Market Hall). From piles of colorful fish roe to marinated Greek olives, the old brick market hall on the waterfront is a treasury of delicacies. The vendors set up permanent stalls with decorative carved woodwork. ⊠ *Eteläranta, along the South Harbor, Kauppatori* ⊘ *Weekdays 8–7, Sat. 8–4.*

Residential & Seaside Helsinki

Bordered by the sea, the south side of Helsinki is resplendent with elegant 20th-century residences and parks with winding paths. The waterfront Kaivopuisto leads into the upscale embassy neighborhood.

Begin at the sharp-spired **Mikael Agricolan Kirkko** ⓫ ☞ in the small park, Tehtaanpuisto. Cross Tehtaankatu and walk south down Laivurinkatu past Eiran Sairaala, or Eira Hospital, with its witch-hat towers and triangular garret windows. Continue south on Laivurinkatu, passing the art nouveau **Villa Johanna** ⓬ on your left. An open view of the Baltic will be just ahead. At the end of the street, turn right on Merikatu. After passing the beautiful **Villa Ensi** ⓭, you'll arrive at the eternal flame of the Merenkulkijoiden Muistomerkki, or Seafarers' Torch, commissioned by the city as a tribute to Finnish sailors and a symbol of hope for their safe return.

Turn east to walk along Merisatamaranta, the seaside promenade. Out at sea is a handful of the thousands of islands that make up the **Gulf of Finland Archipelago.** Turn away from the water and walk south on Iso Puistotie to the shady **Kaivopuisto** ⓮ bordered by opulent estates and embassies; plan on spending half an hour wandering along its pleasant paths. From the park, follow the eastward loop of Kalliolinnantie through the embassy district to the **Mannerheim Museo** ⓯. On the same street is the tiny **Cygnaeuksen Galleria** ⓰. Follow Itäinen Puistotie north to Tehtaankatu 1, where you'll see the enormous fenced-in Russian Embassy complex; then walk up Ullankatu to the park **Tähtitorninvuori** ⓱. For those seriously interested in architecture, the **Suomen Rakennustaiteen Museo** ⓲ is just west of the observatory; follow any of the small streets that go west, and turn right on Kasarmikatu. Just north is the **Designmuseo** ⓳.

TIMING It takes a little more than one hour to walk this route, not counting time to relax in the parks and see art collections. Although the Seafarers' Torch is best seen at night, you might choose to make the walk during the day to take in the subtle beauty of the elegant residences in the area. Note some of the sites below are closed Monday and Tuesday; Monday to Thursday the Mannerheim Museo requires an appointment; the Mikael Agricolan Kirkko is usually open for Sunday services but will close for renovation through 2004.

WHAT TO SEE **Cygnaeuksen Galleria** (Cygnaeus Gallery). This diminutive gallery, in a
⓰ cottage with a tower overlooking the harbor, is the perfect setting for works by various Finnish painters, sculptors, and folk artists. This was once the summer home of Fredrik Cygnaeus (1807–81), a poet and historian who generously left his cottage and all the art inside to the Finnish public. ✉ *Kalliolinnantie 8, Kaivopuisto* ☎ *09/4050–9628* 🎫 *€3* ⏰ *Tues. and Fri. 9–6, Wed. and Thurs. 9–8, weekends 11–5.*

⓳ **Designmuseo**(Finnish Museum of Art and Design). The best of Finnish design can be seen here in displays of furnishings, jewelry, ceramics, and more. ✉ *Korkeavuorenk. 23, Keskusta* ☎ *09/622–0540* 🌐 *www.designmuseum.fi* 🎫 *€7* ⏰ *Sept.–May, Tues. and Thurs.–Sun. 11–6, Wed. 11–8; June–Aug., daily 11–6.*

Gulf of Finland Archipelago. In winter Finns walk across the frozen sea to the nearby islands with dogs and even baby buggies. On the land side, the facades of the Eira and Kaivopuisto districts' grandest buildings form a parade of architectural splendor. One tradition that remains, even in this upscale neighborhood, is rug-washing in the sea—an incredibly arduous task. You may be astounded to see people leave their rugs to dry in the sea air without fear of theft. ✉ *South of Merisatamaranta, Merisatama.*

⓮ **Kaivopuisto** (Well Park). This large, shady, path-filled park was once the site of a popular spa that drew people from St. Petersburg, Tallinn, and all of Scandinavia until its popularity faded during the Crimean War.

All the spa structures were eventually destroyed except one, the **Kaivo-huone,** now a popular bar-restaurant. Across from the entrance of Kaivohuone, take Kaivohuoneenrinne through the park past a grand Empire-style villa built by Albert Edelfelt, father of the famous Finnish painter who bore the same name. Built in 1839, it is the oldest preserved villa in the park. ⊠ *South of Puistok. on water, Kaivopuisto.*

⑮ **Mannerheim Museo** (Mannerheim Museum). Marshal Karl Gustaf Mannerheim (1867–1951) was a complex character sporting a varied résumé: he served as a high-level official in the Russian czar's guard, was a trained anthropologist who explored Asia, and is revered as a great general who fought for Finland's freedom and later became the country's president. The Mannerheim Museo is inside the great Finnish military leader's well-preserved family home and exhibits his letters and personal effects. European furniture, Asian art, and military medals and weaponry are on display. ⊠ *Kalliolinnantie 14, Kaivopuisto* ☎ *09/635–443* ⊕ *www.mannerheim-museo.fi* ☏ *€7 includes guided tour* ☉ *Fri.–Sun. 11–4; Mon.–Thurs. by appointment.*

⑪ **Mikael Agricolan Kirkko** (Mikael Agricola Church). Built in 1935 by Lars Sonck, this church is named for the Finnish religious reformer considered to be the father of written Finnish. Mikael Agricola (circa 1510–57) wrote the first Finnish children's speller, the *Abckirja* (published around 1543), and translated the New Testament into Finnish (published in 1548). The church's sharp spire and tall brick steeple are visible amid **Tehtaanpuisto,** a small neighboring park. The inside of the church is quite bare, and no visitors are allowed except during Sunday services. ⊠ *Tehtaank. 23A, Eira* ☎ *09/709–2270* ☉ *Closed for renovations until 2005.*

⑱ **Suomen Rakennustaiteen Museo** (Museum of Finnish Architecture). Stop by to pick up a list of Helsinki buildings designed by Alvar Aalto, the most famous being Finlandiatalo in Töölö. The permanent exhibits of this museum are far from comprehensive, and specialists will want to visit the extensive library and bookstore. ⊠*Kasarmik. 24, Keskusta* ☎*09/8567–5100* ⊕ *www.mfa.fi* ☏ *€3.35–€5* ☉ *Tues. and Thurs.–Sun. 10–4, Wed. 10–8.*

⑰ **Tähtitorninvuori** (Observatory Tower Hill). Named for the astronomical observatory within its borders, this park has sculptures, winding walkways, and a great view of the South Harbor. The observatory belongs to the astronomy department of Helsinki University and is closed to the public. ⊠ *West of Laivasillank. and South Harbor, Kaivopuisto.*

need a break? **Café Ursula** (⊠ Ehrenströmintie. 3, Kaivopuisto ☎ 09/652–817) by the sea, with views across to Suomenlinna, is a favorite among locals for coffee, ice cream, pastries, and light lunches.

⑬ **Villa Ensi.** This pale ocher art nouveau villa, now a private apartment building, was designed by Selim A. Lindqvist and named after his daughter, Ensi. The two bronze statues in front—*Au Revoir* and *La Joie de la Maternité* by J. Sören-Ring—date from 1910. ⊠ *Merik. 23, Kaivopuisto* ☉ *Closed to the public.*

⑫ **Villa Johanna.** Although this stunning art nouveau villa (circa 1906) is now privately owned by a bank, which uses the villa for corporate dinners and events, it's still worth a visit for its facade. Look for the carved roaring serpent above the front door. ⊠ *Laivurink. 25, Eira* ☉ *Closed to the public.*

Katajanokka & Senaatintori

Katajanokka is separated from the mainland by a canal and begins just east of Kauppatori. A charming residential quarter as well as a cargo- and passenger-ship port, this area also has one of the city's main landmarks, the dazzling Orthodox Uspenskin Katedraali, one of the biggest cathedrals in Europe. Not far from Katajanokka is the elegant Lutheran Cathedral that dominates Senaatintori. The Valtion Taidemuseo is also nearby.

a good walk

The first sight on Katajanokka is the onion-dome **Uspenskin Katedraali** ⑳ on Kanavakatu. From the cathedral, walk down Kanavakatu, turn left on Ankkurikatu, and then right on Laukkasaarenkatu, where a sign will point out the **Wanha Satama** ㉑, a cleverly converted complex of brick warehouses now sheltering an exhibition center and restaurants. From there, head back southwest a short distance to the seafront and cross one of the two short bridges back over to Kauppatori.

From Kauppatori, walk along Sofiankatu (the Street Museum) and step through various periods of the city's history. The Kaupunginmuseo (Helsinki City Museum) is on the same street and has exhibits tracing Helsinki's growth from a rural village into the nation's capital. Nearby is **Senaatintori** ㉒. The north side of the square is dominated by the **Tuomiokirkko** ㉓; the Valtionneuvosto, or Council of State; and the main building of Helsingin Yliopisto, or Helsinki University, flank the east and west sides, respectively. The main university library is just north of the main building on Unioninkatu. At the south end of the square, old merchants' homes are currently occupied by stores, restaurants, and the Kiseleff Bazaar Hall.

Walk one block west to Fabianinkatu; just south is **Pörssitalo** ㉔, on the west side of the street. Head back north on Fabianinkatu 1½ blocks; then turn left on Yliopistonkatu. You'll run into the side of the **Valtion Taidemuseo** ㉕, the Finnish National Gallery at the Ateneum; to enter the museum, turn right on Mikonkatu and then immediately left on Kaivokatu. Just west on Kaivokatu is the **Rautatieasema** ㉖, and on the north side of Rautatientori (Railway Square) is the **Suomen Kansallisteatteri** ㉗, which stages Finnish theater. Walk west around the train station and up Postikatu; just past the main post office you'll see the **Nykytaiteenmuseo** ㉘ on your right, a controversial backdrop to the **Mannerheimin Patsas** ㉙, standing sentinel over Mannherheimintie.

TIMING Allow 45 minutes to an hour to walk this route. Be sure to check the opening hours of both cathedrals before you leave; both close on religious holidays, and the Uspenskin Katedraali is always closed Monday, and also Saturday off-season. The Pörssitalo closes weekends and the Valtion Taidemuseo closes Monday; plan accordingly.

WHAT TO SEE **Mannerheimin Patsas** (Statue of Marshal Karl Gustaf Mannerheim). The ㉙ equestrian gazes down Mannerheimintie, the major thoroughfare named in his honor. ✉ *Mannerheimintie, in front of the main post office and Museum of Contemporary Art, west of the station, Keskusta/Pääposti.*

off the beaten path

LINNANMÄKI – Helsinki's amusement park to the north of the city can be reached by Trams 3B and 3T from in front of the railway station. ✉ *Tivolikuja 1, Linnanmäki* ☎ *09/773–991* ⊕ *www.linnanmaki.fi* ✉ *Free entrance to the park, €4 for individual rides, day pass €22* ⊙ *May–late Aug., daily, hrs. vary, call ahead or visit the Web site.*

★ ㉘ **Nykytaiteenmuseo (Kiasma)** (Museum of Contemporary Art). Praised for the boldness of its curved steel shell but condemned for its encroachment on the territory of the Mannerheim statue, this striking museum displays a wealth of Finnish and foreign art from the 1960s to the present. Look for the "butterfly" windows, and don't miss the view of Töölönlahti from the café. ⊠ *Mannerheiminaukio 2, Keskusta/ Pääposti* ☎ *09/1733–6501* ⊕ *www.kiasma.fi* ✉ *€5.50* ⊙ *Tues. 9–5, Wed.–Sun. 10–10.*

㉔ **Pörssitalo** (Stock Exchange). Although the trading is fully automated, the beautiful interior of the Stock Exchange, with its bullet-shape chandeliers, is worth seeing. The Pörssitalo was designed by Lars Sonck and built in 1911. ⊠ *Fabianink. 14, Keskusta* ⊙ *Weekdays 8–5.*

㉖ **Rautatieasema** (train station). This outdoor square and the adjoining train station are the city's bustling commuter hub. The station's huge granite figures are by Emil Wikström; the solid building they adorn was designed by Eliel Saarinen, one of the founders of the early 20th-century National Romantic style. ⊠ *Kaivok., Rautatientori, Keskusta* ☎ *0307/20902 information in English; 0307/23702 international fares* ⊕ *www.vr.fi.*

★ ㉒ **Senaatintori** (Senate Square). You've hit the heart of neoclassical Helsinki. The harmony of the three buildings flanking Senaatintori exemplifies one of the purest styles of European architecture, as envisioned and designed by German architect Carl Ludvig Engel. On the square's west side is one of the main buildings of **Helsingin Yliopisto** (Helsinki University), and up the hill is the university library. On the east side is the pale yellow **Valtionneuvosto** (Council of State), completed in 1822 and once the seat of the Autonomous Grand Duchy of Finland's Imperial Senate. At the lower end of the square, stores and restaurants now occupy former merchants' homes. ⊠ *Bounded by Aleksanterink. to the south and Yliopistonk. to the north, Senaatintori.*

㉗ **Suomen Kansallisteatteri** (National Theater). Productions in the three theaters inside are in Finnish. The elegant granite facade overlooking the railway station square is decorated with quirky relief typical of the Finnish National Romantic style. In front is a statue of writer Aleksis Kivi. ⊠ *North side of Rautatientori, Keskusta/Rautatieasema* ☎ *09/ 1733–1331* ⊕ *www.nationaltheatre.fi.*

㉓ **Tuomiokirkko** (Lutheran Cathedral of Finland). The steep steps and green domes of the church dominate Senaatintori. Completed in 1852, it is the work of famous architect Carl Ludvig Engel, who also designed parts of Tallinn and St. Petersburg. Wander through the tasteful blue-gray interior, with its white moldings and the statues of German reformers Martin Luther and Philipp Melancthon, as well as the famous Finnish bishop Mikael Agricola. Concerts are frequently held inside the church. The crypt at the rear is the site of frequent historic and architectural exhibitions and bazaars. ⊠ *Yliopistonk. 7, Senaatintori* ☎ *09/709–2455* ⊙ *June–Aug., Mon.–Sat. 9–midnight, Sun. noon (or when worship service ends)–midnight, other times Mon.–Sat. 9–6, Sun. noon (or when worship service ends)–6.*

need a break? | **Café Engel** (⊠ Aleksanterink. 26, Senaatintori ☎ 09/652–776), named for the architect Carl Ludvig Engel, serves coffee and berry cheesecake right on Senaatintori.

★ ⑳ **Uspenskin Katedraali** (Uspenski Cathedral). Perched atop a small rocky cliff over the North Harbor in Katajanokka is the main cathedral of the

Orthodox church in Finland. Its brilliant gold onion domes are its hallmark, but its imposing redbrick edifice, decorated by 19th-century Russian artists, is no less distinctive. The cathedral was built and dedicated in 1868 in the Byzantine-Slavonic style and remains the biggest Orthodox church in Scandinavia. ✉ *Kanavak. 1, Katajanokka* ☎ *09/634–267* ◷ *May–Sept., Mon., Wed.–Fri. 9:30–4, Tues. 9:30–6, weekends 9:30–3; Oct.–Apr., Tues.–Fri. 9:30–4, weekends 9:30–3* ◷ *Closed for weddings and other special events.*

need a break? On the north flank of Katajanokka, near the end of Katajanokan Pohjoisranta, you'll see the **Katajanokan Casino** (✉ *Laivastok. 1, Katajanokka* ☎ *09/622–2772*). It was built in 1911 as a warehouse, later became a naval officers' casino, and today is a seaside restaurant. Set on its own headland, the casino has a summer terrace from which you can gaze across the North Harbor to the Kruunuhaka district while sipping a cold beer.

★ ㉕ **Valtion Taidemuseo** (Finnish National Gallery). The best traditional Finnish art is housed in this complex, which includes the splendid neoclassical **Ateneum,** one of three museums organized under the National Gallery umbrella. The gallery holds major European works, but the outstanding attraction is the Finnish art, particularly the works of Akseli Gallen-Kallela, inspired by the national epic *Kalevala*. The rustic portraits by Albert Edelfelt are enchanting, and many contemporary Finnish artists are well represented. The two other museums that make up the National Gallery are **Kiasma** and **Synebrychoff.** ✉ *Kaivok. 2–4, Keskusta* ☎ *09/1733–6401* ⊕ *www.fng.fi* ✉ *€5.50, additional charge for special exhibits* ◷ *Tues. and Fri. 9–6, Wed. and Thurs. 9–8, weekends 11–5.*

㉑ **Wanha Satama** (Old Harbor). Despite its old-brick-warehouse appearance, this is actually a small shopping center with several food stores, restaurants, and cafés. There's even an exhibition hall in the left-hand (north) wing. The "W" in Wanha is pronounced "V." ✉ *Kanavak. and Pikku Satamak, Katajanokka.*

Suomenlinna

㉚ **Fodor'sChoice** ★ A former island fortress, **Suomenlinna** (Finland's Castle) is a perennially popular collection of museums, parks, and gardens, which has been designated a UNESCO World Heritage Site. In 1748 the Finnish army helped build the impregnable fortress, long referred to as the Gibraltar of the North; since then it has expanded into a series of interlinked islands. Although Suomenlinna has never been taken by assault, its occupants surrendered once to the Russians in 1809 and came under fire from British ships in 1855 during the Crimean War. Today Suomenlinna makes a lovely excursion from Helsinki, particularly in early summer when the island is engulfed in a mauve-and-purple mist of lilacs, introduced from Versailles by the Finnish architect Ehrensvärd.

There are no street names on the island, so get a map for about €2 from the Helsinki City Tourist Office before you go, or buy one at the Tourist Information kiosk on the island. From June 1 to August 31, guided English-language tours leave daily at 11 AM and 2 PM from the **information kiosk** (✉ Suomenlinna ☎ 09/684–1880; 09/684–1850 tours ⊕ www.suomenlinna.fi); call to arrange tours at other times.

a good walk Suomenlinna is easily reached by public ferry (€2 one-way) or private boat (€3 one-way, €5 round-trip), both of which leave from Helsinki's Kauppatori. Although its fortification occupied six islands, its main attractions are now concentrated on two: Susisaari and Kustaanmiekka. When you land at Suomenlinna, go through the archway and proceed uphill to the **Suomenlinna Kirkko,** the local church-lighthouse. Walk past the church and the pastel-color private wooden homes to the **Ehrensvärd Museo,** a historical museum. Visit the Inventory Chambers Visitor Center, housing the Suomenlinna Experience multivision show, alongside Tykistölahti Bay. Walk along the eastern coast of Susisaari until you reach the submarine *Vesikko*. From there, walk south and cross over to Kustaanmiekka, where you can visit the **Rannikkotykistömuseo** and learn everything you ever wanted to know about arms and artillery.

TIMING The ferry ride from South Harbor to Suomenlinna takes about a half hour. Plan to spend an afternoon on the islands; you'll need about four hours to explore the fortress and museums. Note that days open and hours of sites are limited off-season.

WHAT TO SEE **Ehrensvärd Museo** (Ehrensvärd Museum). Augustin Ehrensvärd directed the fortification of the islands of Suomenlinna from 1748 until 1772, the year of his death. This historical museum named for the military architect exhibits a model-ship collection and officers' quarters dating from the 18th century. Ehrensvärd's tomb is also here. ⊠ *Susisaari, Suomenlinna* ☎ *09/684–1850* 🖾 *€3* ⊙ *March–late Apr., weekends 11–5; early May–Aug., daily 10–5; Sept., daily 11–5; Oct., weekends 11–5.*

Rannikkotykistömuseo (Coastal Guard Artillery Museum). Part of the Military Museum, Rannikkotykistömuseo displays arms from World Wars I and II in a vaulted arsenal. Jump aboard *Vesikko* submarine (⊙ Early May–Aug., daily 10–6; Sept., daily 11–3), which was built in Turku in 1931–33 and served in World War II. ⊠ *Kustaanmiekka, Suomenlinna* ☎ *09/181–5295* 🖾 *€ 2 for museum, € 3.50 for submarine, €5.50 for joint ticket* ⊙ *May–Aug., daily 10–6; Sept., daily 11–3.*

Suomenlinna Kirkko (Suomenlinna Church). This dual-function church-lighthouse was built in 1854 as an Orthodox church and has since become Lutheran. Call for opening hours and schedule of services. ☎ *09/ 709–2665.*

Töölö

Most of Helsinki's major cultural buildings—the opera house, concert hall, and national museum—are within a short distance of each other around the perimeter of the inlet from the sea called Töölönlahti. The inlet itself is lovely in all seasons, and the walking and biking paths are well trodden by locals. The winding streets just east of Mannerheimintie enfold the Temppeliaukio Kirkko (Temple Square Church), whose unexceptional facade gives way to an amazing cavernous interior. Also nearby, the Sibelius park cuts a large swath out of the neighborhood and borders the sea.

a good walk Begin in the lakeside area of Mannerheimintie by the equestrian statue of Gustaf Mannerheim, directly behind the main post office and next to the Museum of Contemporary Art (Kiasma). Walk northwest on Mannerheimintie, passing the red-granite **Eduskuntatalo** ③① ▶ on your way to the **Suomen Kansallismuseo** ③②, Finland's national museum, on the left. When you leave the museum, cross Mannerheimintie then follow the road a short distance north to the **Finlandiatalo** ③③, the Alvar Aalto–designed concert and congress hall. Behind the hall lies the inlet bay of Töölönlahti. If you walk along the well-used paths that follow the contour of the lake, you'll soon come to the **Suomen Kansallisooppera** ③④, Helsinki's opera house. From here, you can take the lengthy walk to the Seurasaaran Ulkomuseo.

From the opera house, walk southeast on Mannerheimintie until you see the white tower of the **Olympiastadion** ③⑤ on your left. Return to Mannerheimintie, crossing over to Cygnaeuksenkatu; take a left on Nervanderinkatu, where you'll reach the **Helsingin Taidehalli** ㊱, with its fine collection of Finnish art. Go a few steps farther and take the small street directly across from the art hall to the modern **Temppeliaukio Kirkko** ㊲, a church carved into rock outcrops. If you still have energy, cross Runeberginkatu and walk west on Simonkatu until you reach Mechelininkatu. Walk a ways north on Mechelininkatu, and **Sibeliusken Puisto** ㊳ will appear on your left. Here you'll find the reason you came: the magnificent Sibelius-Monumentti.

TIMING   Allow 45 minutes to follow this tour as far as the Temppeliaukio Kirkko, adding half an hour for each museum if you decide to venture inside; from the church, it's a 20-minute walk to the Sibelius Puisto. Be sure to check the Temppeliaukio Kirkko's hours, which are slightly irregular. Note the Suomen Kansallismuseo closes its doors Monday.

WHAT TO SEE   **Eduskuntatalo** (Parliament House). The imposing, colonnaded, red-
▶ ㉛   granite Eduskuntatalo stands near Mannerheim's statue on Mannerheimintie. The legislature has one of the world's highest proportions of women. ✉ *Mannerheimintie 30, Keskusta* ☎ *09/432–2027* ⊕ *www.eduskunta.fi.*

㉝   **Finlandiatalo** (Finlandia Hall). This white, winged concert hall was one of Alvar Aalto's last creations. It's especially impressive on foggy days or at night. If you can't make it to a concert here, try to take a guided tour. ✉ *Karamzininkatu 4, Keskusta* ☎ *09/402–4246* ⊕ *www.finlandia.hel.fi* ☉ *Concerts usually held Wed. and Thurs. nights.*

㊱   **Helsingin Taidehalli** (Helsinki Art Gallery). Here you'll see the best of contemporary Finnish art, including painting, sculpture, architecture, and industrial art and design. ✉ *Nervanderink. 3, Keskusta* ☎ *09/454–2060* ✉ *€ 7, can vary for special exhibitions* ☉ *Tues., Thurs. and Fri. 11–6, Wed. 11–8, weekends noon–5.*

㉟   **Olympiastadion** (Olympic Stadium). At this stadium built for the 1952 Games, take a lift to the top of the tower for sprawling city views. ✉ *East of Mannerheim, Olympiastadion* ⊕ *www.stadion.fi* ✉ *€2* ☉ *weekdays 9–8, weekends 9–6.*

off the beaten path   **SEURASAAREN ULKOMESEO** – On an island about 3 km (2 mi) northwest of city center, the Seurasaari Outdoor Museum was founded in 1909 to preserve rural Finnish architecture. The old farmhouses and barns that were brought to Seurasaari come from all over Finland. Many are rough-hewn log buildings dating from the 17th century, of primary inspiration to the late 19th-century architects of the national revivalist movement in Finland. All exhibits are marked by signposts along the trails; be sure not to miss the church boat and the gabled church. Seurasaari Island is connected to land by a pedestrian bridge and is a restful place for walking throughout the year, with its forest trails and ocean views. You can walk there in about 40 minutes from the opera house; follow Mannerheimintie northeast, then turn left onto Linnankoskenkatu and follow signs along the coast. Alternatively, take Bus 24 from city center, in front of the Swedish Theater at the west end of Pohjoisesplanadi; its last stop is by the bridge to the island. Plan on spending at least three hours exploring and getting to the museum. ✉ *Seurasaari* ☎ *09/4050–9660 in summer; 09/4050–9574 in winter* ⊕ *www.nba.fi* ✉ *€4.50. Guided tours daily at 11:30 and 3:30, starting at ticket kiosk.* ☉ *Mid-May–late May and early Sept.–mid-Sept., weekdays 9–3, weekends 11–5; June–Aug., Thurs.–Tues. 11–5, Wed. 11–7; mid-Sept.–late Nov., weekends 11–5.*

38 **Sibeliuksen Puisto.** The Sibelius-Monumentti (Sibelius Monument) itself is worth the walk to this lakeside park. What could be a better tribute to Finland's great composer than this soaring silver sculpture of organ pipes? ⊠ *West of Mechelinin, Töölö.*

32 **Suomen Kansallismuseo** (National Museum of Finland). Architect Eliel Saarinen and his partners combined the language of Finnish medieval church architecture with elements of art nouveau to create this vintage example of the National Romantic style. The museum's collection of archaeological, cultural, and ethnological artifacts gives you an insight into Finland's past. ⊠ *Mannerheimintie 34, Keskusta* ☎ *09/40501* ⊕ *www.nba.fi* ◻ *€5* ☾ *Tues. and Wed. 11–8, Thurs.–Sun. 11–6.*

34 **Suomen Kansallisooppera** (Finnish National Opera). Grand gilded operas, classical ballets, and booming concerts all take place in Helsinki's splendid opera house, a striking example of modern Scandinavian architecture. All events at the Opera House draw crowds, so buy your tickets early. ⊠ *Helsinginkatu 58, Keskusta* ☎ *09/4030–2210 house tours; 09/4030–2211 box office* ⊕ *www.operafin.fi* ☾ *Tues.–Fri. 10–5; house tours, in English, in summer Tues. and Thurs. at 3, also by appointment.*

★ **37** **Temppeliaukio Kirkko** (Temple Square Church). Topped with a copper dome, the church looks like a half-buried spaceship from the outside. In truth, it's really a modern Lutheran church carved into the rock outcrops below. The sun shines in from above, illuminating the stunning interior with its birch pews, modern pipe organ, and cavernous walls. Ecumenical and Lutheran services in various languages are held throughout the week. ⊠ *Lutherinkatu 3, Töölö* ☎ *09/494–698* ☾ *Weekdays 10–8, Sat. 10–6, Sun. noon–1:45 and 3:15–5:45* ☾ *Closed Tues. 1–2 and during weddings, concerts, and services.*

> off the beaten path

URHO KEKKONEN MUSEUM TAMMINIEMI – The grand house overlooking Seurasaari from the mainland is Tamminiemi, where the late Finnish president Urho Kekkonen lived from 1956 to 1986. Originally known as Villa Nissen, Tamminiemi was built in 1904. Inside are the scores of gifts presented to Finland's longest-serving president by leaders from around the world. His study is the most fascinating room, with its gift from the United States of a cupboard full of *National Geographic* maps of the world. To assure an English-speaking guide, call ahead. When you've seen the house, stop for pastries and Russian-style tea at **Tamminiemintien Kahvila** (⊠ Tamminiemintie 8, Seurasaari ☎ 09/481–003) or the nearby **Café Angelica** (⊠ Tamminiementie 3, Seurasaari ☎ 09/458–4081). To get here, follow directions to Seurasaaren Ulkomuseo; it's on the mainland before the footbridge. ⊠ *Seurasaarentie 15, Seurasaari* ☎ *09/4050–9650* ◻ *€4, includes guided tour in English, daily at 1:30* ☾ *Mid-May–mid-Aug., Mon and Tues., Thurs.–Sun., 11–5; Wed. 11–7; mid-Aug.–mid-May, Wed. 11–7, Thurs.–Sun. 11–5.*

Where to Eat

Helsinki has some of Finland's best eating establishments. Although Russian restaurants are the star attraction, try to seek out Finnish specialties such as game—pheasant, reindeer, hare, and grouse—accompanied by wild-berry compotes and exotic mushroom sauces.

Most restaurants close on major national holidays—only a few hotel restaurants stay open for Christmas. Many of the more expensive establishments close on weekends.

Around Kauppatori & Katajanokka

★ **$$$$**
Fodor'sChoice
★
✕ Alexander Nevski. Helsinki is reputed to have the best Russian restaurants in the Nordic region, and the Nevski is foremost among them. It sets high standards in the preparation of czarist-era dishes, with an emphasis on game specialties and roe-filled *blini* (thin pancakes). Among the more extraordinary offerings is roast bear in a pot, which must be ordered in advance. The dining room, too, is worthy of a Czar, with its heavy draperies, glistening samovars, potted palms, and crisp linen tablecloths. ☒ *Pohjoisesplanadi 17, Kauppatori* ☎ *09/686–9560* ☱ *AE, DC, MC, V.*

$$$$
✕ GW Sundmans. This elegant restaurant by the harbor was formerly the home of Captain G. W. Sundman. The building was designed by C. L. Engel, architect of the historical center of Helsinki under Czar Alexander I. The grand main restaurant, with molded ceilings and chandeliers, serves modern international cuisine: dishes such as quail stuffed with apples and fois gras and fried arctic char with frothy crayfish jus. Sundmans Krog on the ground floor has a nautical theme and vaulted ceilings, and has an excellent herring buffet. ☒ *Eteläranta 16, Kauppatori* ☎ *09/622–6410* ☱ *AE, DC, MC, V* ⊘ *Closed Sun. No lunch Sat. and July.*

$$$$
Fodor'sChoice
★
✕ Palace Gourmet. This outstanding hotel restaurant has a magnificent view of the South Harbor. Its specialties are French and Finnish fare, including such creations as baked whitefish with truffle mille-feuille and basil sauce, and carré of lamb with cashew nuts. ☒ *Palace Hotel, Eteläranta 10, Kauppatori* ☎ *09/1345–6715* ☱ *AE, DC, MC, V* ⊘ *Closed weekends. No lunch July.*

$$$$
Fodor'sChoice
★
✕ Savoy. With its airy, Alvar Aalto–designed, functionalist dining room overlooking the Esplanade Gardens, the Savoy is a frequent choice for business lunches and was also Finnish statesman Marshal Karl Gustaf Mannerheim's favorite; he is rumored to have introduced the *Vorschmack* (minced lamb and anchovies) recipe. Savoy's menu includes the ubiquitous reindeer fillet, as well as the unusual combination of whitefish baked with liver and cabbage. ☒ *Eteläespl. 14, Esplanadi* ☎ *09/684–4020* ⊘ *Closed weekends.*

★ **$$$–$$$$**
Fodor'sChoice
★
✕ Havis Amanda. Across the street from the Havis Amanda statue, its namesake restaurant specializes in fish dishes with central European accents, such as the herb-marinated salmon in a cabbage-truffle sauce or the smoked halibut with apple purée and garlic sauce. Several different fixed menus are also available. ☒ *Pohjoisesplanadi 17, Kauppatori* ☎ *09/6869–5660* ☱ *AE, DC, MC, V* ⊘ *Closed Sun. mid-Sept.–Apr.*

$$$–$$$$
✕ Sipuli. Sipuli stands at the foot of the Russian Orthodox Uspenski Cathedral and gets its name—meaning onion—from the church's golden onionlike cupolas. The restaurant is in a 19th-century warehouse building, with redbrick walls and dark-wood panels, and a skylight with a spectacular view of the cathedral. Classic French-Finnish combinations may include fennel soup with forest mushroom ravioli, smoked fillet of pike perch with salmon mousse, and noisettes of reindeer topped with game sauce. ☒ *Kanavaranta 3, Katajanokka* ☎ *09/622–9280* ☱ *AE, DC, MC, V* ⊘ *Closed weekends except for group dinners.*

$$–$$$
✕ Bellevue. The spare lines of Bellevue belie its real age—it has been around since 1917, serving dishes inspired by combinations of Russian and Finnish cuisine. Try the *shashlik* (cubed lamb kebab served with mushroom rice) or the ox fillet à la Novgorod. The plush interior of this elegant town house has many shining samovars, but only some of them are functional; each table has lighted candles. ☒ *Rahapajank. 3, Keskusta* ☎ *09/179–560* ☱ *AE, DC, MC, V* ⊘ *No lunch weekends and July.*

$$–$$$
✕ Nokka. In a historical building on the Katanajanokka quay and downstairs from the Helsinki Culinary Institute, this innovative restaurant spe-

cialize in seasonal fare with fresh Finnish ingredients. Try the spice roasted lamb fillet and trout with fried spinach polenta and crayfish broth. It was chosen the Helsinki Menu restaurant of the year in 2003. ⊠ *Kanavaranta 7, Katajanokka* ☎ *09/687-7330* ⊟ *AE, DC, MC, V* ⊙ *Closed Sun. No lunch Sat. and July and Aug.*

$-$$ ✕ **Papa Giovanni.** Don't let the whimsical interior with Venetian gondolas fool you. This cozy restaurant serves up sophisticated Italian fare, such as fillet of roebuck with goat cheese crostini, spinach and olive oil, grilled chicken with grape sauce and saffron rice, or smoked salmon and spinach lasagne. Wine suggestions are included on the menu and the service is excellent. ⊠ *Keskuskatu 7, Keskusta* ☎ *09/666-882* ⊟ *AE, DC, MC, V.*

$-$$ ✕ **Raffaello.** In the heart of Helsinki's financial district, this cozy Italian restaurant with redbrick walls, parquet floors, and decorative frescoes has a reputation for friendly service, reasonable prices, and tasty pasta, salad, and meat dishes. Try the steak gratinated wth gorgonzola, basil potatoes, ratatouille and red wine sauce or the grilled breast of pheasant with pesto duchesse potatoes. ⊠ *Aleksanterink. 46, Keskusta* ☎ *09/6844-0718* ⊟ *AE, DC, MC, V.*

¢-$$ ✕ **Zetor.** Known as the tractor restaurant, Zetor is a haven for the weary traveler in need of some homey high-cholesterol cooking—choose from meatballs, Karelian stew, sausage, or schnitzel, washed down with the house brew. Wooden tables, farm equipment and a witty menu make for an entertaining evening. ⊠ *Kaivopiha, Keskusta/Kaivopiha* ☎ *09/666-966* ⊟ *AE, DC, MC, V* ⊙ *No lunch Sun.–Fri.*

¢-$ ✕ **Namaskaar and Wok it.** Try generous portions of Thai, Indian, and Japanese food served in simple and elegant surroundings at this Nordic-Asian dining room. The mango and black bean salad and the salmon tikka are unusual but delicious. Seats on the balcony overlook the modern atrium of the Sanomatalo building. ⊠ *Sanomatalo, Postikuja 2, Rautatieasema* ☎ *09/6812-1450* ⊟ *AE, DC, MC, V* ⊙ *Closed Sun.*

West of Mannerheimintie

$$-$$$ ✕ **Babushka Ira.** The cozy interior and authentic Russian food here will make you think you're at Grandma Irina's. Red damask curtains and paintings brought from St. Petersburg form the perfect backdrop for the excellent *selyanka* (a hearty soup of meat, cabbage, and winter vegetables topped with sour cream), *pelmeny* (meat ravioli with sour cream), and blini—all prepared traditionally. ⊠ *Uudenmaankatu 28, Punavuori* ☎ *09/680-1405* ⊟ *DC, MC, V* ⊙ *Closed Sun. and Mon., lunch Sat. only.*

$-$$$ ✕ **Ravintola Torni.** A 1930s functional design interior provides the backdrop to the innovative contemporary cooking at this establishment, the main restaurant of the central Sokos Hotel Torni. Interesting combinations include salmon pastrami with grilled scampi and oyster sauce, fillet and osso bucco of reindeer with garlic sauce, and rhubarb pecan pie with peach ice cream. ⊠ *Hotel Torni, Kalevank. 5, Keskusta* ☎ *09/1311-3448* ⊟ *AE, DC, MC, V* ⊙ *Closed weekends.*
Fodor's Choice ★

¢-$$$ ✕ **Ravintola Lautanen.** This restaurant offers homey Finnish dishes such as traditional salmon soup, smoked reindeer and cheese soup and reindeer tournedos. Lighter dishes include spinach-chanterelle pasta. For dessert try the classic farmer's cheese with arctic cloudberry jam or the peppermint-chocolate parfait with strawberry sauce. ⊠ *Lönnrötinkatu13, Keskusta* ☎ *09/601-031* ⊟ *AE, DC, MC, V* ⊙ *Closed Sun.*

★ $-$$ ✕ **Kosmos.** Just a short walk from Stockmann's department store, this cozy restaurant has become a lunchtime favorite among businesspeople working nearby. Come evening, it's given over to artists and journalists. Its high ceilings and understated interior give it a Scandinavian
Fodor's Choice ★

Where to Stay
& Eat in Helisinki

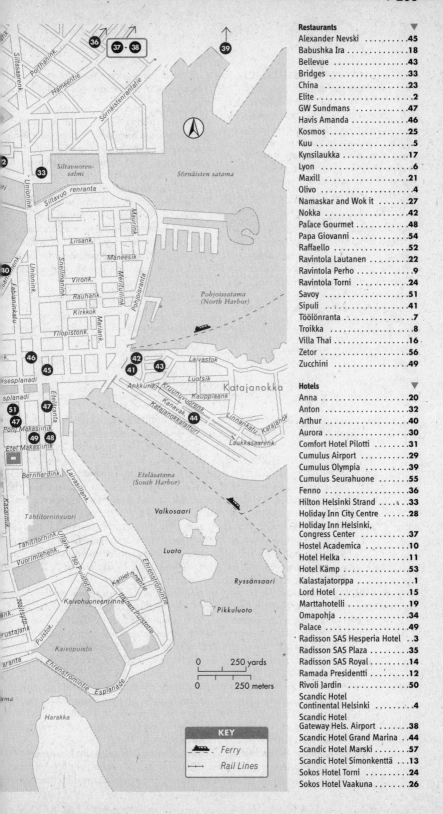

Restaurants ▼

Alexander Nevski 45
Babushka Ira 18
Bellevue 43
Bridges 33
China 23
Elite .2
GW Sundmans 47
Havis Amanda 46
Kosmos 25
Kuu 5
Kynsilaukka 17
Lyon .6
Maxill 21
Olivo .4
Namaskar and Wok it 27
Nokka 42
Palace Gourmet 48
Papa Giovanni 54
Raffaello 52
Ravintola Lautanen 22
Ravintola Perho 9
Ravintola Torni 24
Savoy 51
Sipuli 41
Töölönranta 7
Troikka 8
Villa Thai 16
Zetor 56
Zucchini 49

Hotels ▼

Anna 20
Anton 32
Arthur 40
Aurora 30
Comfort Hotel Pilotti 31
Cumulus Airport 29
Cumulus Olympia 39
Cumulus Seurahuone 55
Fenno 36
Hilton Helsinki Strand 33
Holiday Inn City Centre 28
Holiday Inn Helsinki,
Congress Center 37
Hostel Academica 10
Hotel Helka 11
Hotel Kämp 53
Kalastajatorppa 1
Lord Hotel 15
Marttahotelli 19
Omapohja 34
Palace 49
Radisson SAS Hesperia Hotel . .3
Radisson SAS Plaza 35
Radisson SAS Royal 14
Ramada Presidentti 12
Rivoli Jardin 50
Scandic Hotel
Continental Helsinki 4
Scandic Hotel
Gateway Hels. Airport 38
Scandic Hotel Grand Marina . .44
Scandic Hotel Marski 57
Scandic Hotel Simonkenttä . . .13
Sokos Hotel Torni 24
Sokos Hotel Vaakuna 26

CloseUp

DINING IN FINLAND

THE BETTER FINNISH RESTAURANTS offer some of the country's most stunning game—pheasant, reindeer, hare, and grouse—accompanied by wild-berry compotes and exotic mushroom sauces. The chanterelle grows wild in Finland, as do dozens of other edible mushrooms, the tasty morel among them. Fish wears many hats in Finland, and is especially savored smoked. Come July 21, crayfish season kicks in.

Other specialties are poronkäristys (sautéed reindeer), lihapullat (meatballs in sauce), uunijuusto (light, crispy baked cheese), and hiilillä paistetut silakat (charcoal-grilled Baltic herring). Seisova pöytä, the Finnish version of the smörgåsbord, is a cold and hot buffet available at breakfast, lunch, or dinner, and is particularly popular on cruise ships. To stretch a tight travel budget, eat a hearty breakfast in your hotel (always

included in the price unless stated otherwise) and grab a snack for lunch.

Local yogurt and dairy products are extremely good and ice cream is popular; an increasing number of places sell low-fat flavors or frozen yogurts, although the fat-free craze hasn't completely taken over. Finnish desserts and baked goods are renowned. Mämmi, a dessert made of wheat flour, malt, and orange zest and served with cream and sugar, is a treat during Easter. More filling are karjalan piirakka, thin, oval rye-bread pirogi filled with rice or mashed potatoes and served warm with munavoi, a mixture of egg and butter.

air of simplicity and efficiency. Menu highlights include reindeer fillet in a sauce of spruce shoots and rosemary served with roasted potatoes and vorschmack with duchesse potatoes, pickles, and beets. ⊠ *Kalevank. 3, Keskusta* 🕾 *09/647–255* ⊟ *AE, DC, MC, V* ⊘ *Closed weekends.*

$–$$ ✕ **Maxill.** Helsinki's café boom and an increasing demand for Continental-style bars have inspired this hybrid on a lively street just south of the city center. The trendy menu includes salad with goat cheese croutons. ⊠ *Korkeavuorenk. 4, Keskusta* 🕾 *09/638–873* ⊟ *AE, DC, MC, V.*

$–$$ ✕ **Villa Thai.** Near Helsinki's shopping district, this restaurant has authentic Thai food served in traditional surroundings. The prawn curry with coconut milk and pineapple is a house specialty. And yes, you can get salmon here too, Thai style. ⊠ *Bulevardi 28, Bulevardi* 🕾 *09/680–2778; 040/828-4456 reservations* ⊟ *AE, DC, MC, V.*

★ ¢–$$ ✕ **Kynsilaukka.** This cozy yet sophisticated restaurant appeals to the senses
Fodor's Choice with fresh, beautifully prepared food highlighting garlic. Stellar dishes
★ include the garlic cream soup and bouillabaise; for dessert try the classic crepes with cloudberry sauce. A generous four-course lunch menu and the fact it's open on holidays help make it a local favorite. All portions are served in two sizes. ⊠ *Fredrikink. 22, Keskusta* 🕾 *09/651–939* ⊟ *AE, DC, MC, V.*

$ ✕ **China.** One of the city's oldest Chinese restaurants, this place specializes in Cantonese fare. Apart from beef, pork, and chicken dishes, there's an unusual pike perch with sweet-and-sour sauce. The Peking duck is a specialty, and must be ordered two days in advance. ⊠ *Annank. 25, Keskusta* 🕾 *09/640–258* ⊟ *AE, DC, MC, V.*

¢–$ ✕ **Ravintola Perho.** Helsinki's catering school operates this brasserie-style restaurant decorated in pine. The emphasis is on Finnish food, particularly salmon and reindeer. Its reasonable prices, central location (just west of Mannherheimintie), and own microbrew make it a favorite. ✉ *Mechelinkatu 7, Töölö* ☎ *09/5807–8649* ▭ *AE, DC, MC, V.*

¢ ✕ **Zucchini.** For a vegetarian lunch or just coffee and dessert, Zucchini is a cozy hideaway with quiet music, magazines, and a few sidewalk tables. Pizzas, soups, and salads are all tasty here. ✉ *Fabianinkatu 4, Keskusta* ☎ *09/622–2907* ▭ *DC, MC, V* ⊗ *No dinner.*

North of City Center

$–$$ ✕ **Bridges.** This atrium restaurant in the Hilton Helsinki Strand serves
Fodor'sChoice international steak, burger and pasta dishes alongside Finnish classics
★ like slightly smoked Arctic char in a black currant butter sauce. ✉ *John Stenbergin ranta 4, Hakaniemi* ☎ *09/39351* ▭ *AE, DC, MC, V* ⊗ *No lunch.*

Keskusta & Töölö

$$$–$$$$ ✕ **Lyon.** As you might expect from its name, French cuisine is the specialty in this eatery across Mannerheimintie from the opera. Lyon is small and unpretentious but consistent in high quality and service. Menu highlights include lavaret (fish) with spring vegetables and dill potatoes; grilled Arctic char with asparagus sauce and truffle-seasoned pasta; and breast of pigeon with poultry sausage and cherry sauce. ✉ *Mannerheim. 56, Töölö* ☎ *09/408–131* ▭ *AE, DC, MC, V.*

★ $–$$$ ✕ **Elite.** A short distance from the town center, but a welcome oasis after excursions to the Temppeliaukio Kirkko and the Sibelius monument, Elite's simple art deco interior and spacious layout are popular with artists and writers. Traditional Finnish dishes to sample are fried Baltic herring, salmon soup with rye bread, and select game. If you want more contemporary dishes, try the cold-smoked salmon rolls with asparagus, or the reindeer roast with Madeira sauce and nettle-seasoned potato purée. The outdoor seating in summer is very popular. ✉ *Etelä Hesperiank. 22, Töölö* ☎ *09/434–2200* ▭ *AE, DC, MC.*

$–$$$ ✕ **Olivo.** This trendy restaurant in the Scandic Hotel Continental Helsinki serves creative Mediterranean dishes, including tuna fillet with gnocchi, chateaubriand and bacon risotto with Madeira sauce; for dessert, try the pistachio gelato. ✉ *Mannerheim. 46, Scandic Hotel Continental Helsinki, Töölö* ☎ *09/4737–2207* ▭ *AE, DC, MC, V* ⊗ *Closed weekends. No lunch.*

★ $–$$$ ✕ **Troikka.** The Troikka takes you back to czarist times with its samovars, icons, and portraits of Russian writers—as well as the exceptionally good Russian food and friendly service. Try the *zakusky,* an assortment of Russian appetizers including such delicacies as Baltic herring, homemade poultry pâté, wild mushrooms, and marinated garlic. ✉ *Caloniuksenk. 3, Keskusta* ☎ *09/445–229* ▭ *AE, DC, MC, V* ⊗ *Closed Sun. and weekends in July.*

★ $–$$ ✕ **Töölönranta.** The upscale Töölönranta packs in plenty of operagoers,
Fodor'sChoice since it's right behind the National Opera House overlooking the bay.
★ An innovative water-cooled wok on display in the wide-open kitchen turns out stir-fried specials. Other favorites include arctic char, wild duck, and lamb dishes. In summer, when the patio catches the evening sun, this is a superb place to savor a beer. ✉ *Helsinginkatu 56, Töölö* ☎ *09/454–2100* ▭ *AE, MC, V* ⊗ *Closed Sun. mid-Sept.–Apr.*

$ ✕ **Kuu.** If you thrive on getting to the true character of a city and enjoy local color, try looking in simple, friendly restaurants such as Kuu, literally Moon. The menu combines Finnish specialties such as fried Baltic herring with imaginative international fare. It's especially convenient for nights at the opera. ✉ *Töölönk. 27, Töölö* ☎ *09/2709–0973* ▭ *AE, DC, MC, V.*

Where to Stay

Helsinki's top hotels are notoriously expensive, generally have small rooms, and mostly cater to the business traveler. Standards are high, and the level of service usually corresponds to the price. Rates are almost always less expensive on weekends, and most include a generous breakfast and sauna privileges.

City Center

$$$$ 🏨 **Sokos Hotel Vaakuna.** The quirky 1950s architecture and interior design of the Vaakuna dates back to the 1952 Helsinki Olympics. Rooms are spacious, with simple but stylish furnishings. The rooftop terrace restaurants are traditionally the haunts of members of parliament. The hotel is at the top of the Sokos department store, opposite the train station. ⊠ *Asemaaukio 2, Rautatieasema 00100* ☎ *09/43370* 🖷 *09/4337–7100* ⊕ *www.sokoshotels.fi* 🛏 *265 rooms, 12 suites* ⌂ *2 restaurants, 3 saunas, nightclub, meeting room* ▤ *AE, DC, MC, V.*

$$$–$$$$ 🏨 **Cumulus Seurahuone.** Built in 1914, this Viennese-style town-house hotel across from the train station has a loyal clientele won over by its ageless charm and cosmopolitan interiors. A patina of well-worn elegance pervades all areas, from the grand main stairway and the chandeliered art nouveau café to the ornate, skylit pub. Rooms come in many styles, from traditionally furnished ones with brass beds and high ceilings in the old section, to the newer ones with a sleek, modern design. ⊠ *Kaivokatu 12, Rautatieasema 00100* ☎ *09/69141* 🖷 *09/691–4010* ⊕ *www.cumulus.fi* 🛏 *118 rooms* ⌂ *Restaurant, café, sauna, bar, pub, nightclub* ▤ *AE, DC, MC, V.*

$$ 🏨 **Holiday Inn Helsinki City Centre.** Adjacent to the railway station, this hotel is conveniently central with comfortable rooms. It is popular with business travelers. ⊠ *Elielinaukio 5, Keskusta 00100* ☎ *09/5425–5000* 🖷 *09/5425–5299* ⊕ *www.hi-helsinkicity.com* 🛏 *174 rooms, 12 suites* ⌂ *Restaurant, minibars, cable TV, gym, 2 saunas, bar, no-smoking rooms,* ▤ *AE, DC, MC, V.*

¢ 🏨 **Omapohja.** Dating from 1906, this inn, which occupies a mint-green Jugendstil building, used to be a base for actors performing at the state theater next door. The rooms, named after Finnish actors, are cozily old-fashioned, with wood-paneled walls and handwoven bedspreads; they also have tremendous windows. Extra beds cost only €20, making it a good buy for families or small groups. ⊠ *Itäinen Teatterikuja 3, Rautatieasema 00100* ☎ *09/666–211* 🖷 *09/6228–0053* 🛏 *15 rooms, 3 with shower* ▤ *MC, V.*

Around Kauppatori & Katajanokka

$$$$ 🏨 **Palace.** Built for the 1952 Olympic games, this clublike hotel is on the 9th and 10th floors of a waterfront commercial building with splendid views of the South Harbor. Its faithful clientele—largely British, Swedish, and from the United States—appreciates the personal service that comes with its small size, such as the daily afternoon tea. Guest rooms have wood paneling and plush carpets. The hotel's restaurants, especially the Palace Gourmet, are among Helsinki's best. ⊠ *Eteläranta 10, Kauppatori 00130* ☎ *09/134–561* 🖷 *09/654–786* ⊕ *www.palacehotel.fi* 🛏 *37 rooms, 2 suites* ⌂ *2 restaurants, café, room service, sauna, bar* ▤ *AE, DC, MC, V.*

★ $$$ 🏨 **Rivoli Jardin.** This high-class town house is tucked into the heart of
Fodor'sChoice Helsinki's shopping and business center. All rooms face the inner courtyard, and are free of traffic noise. They have simple yet elegant furnishings. ⊠ *Kasarmikatu 40, Keskusta 00130* ☎ *09/681–500* 🖷 *09/656–988* ⊕ *www.rivoli.fi* 🛏 *55 rooms* ⌂ *Sauna, bar* ▤ *AE, DC, MC, V.*

$$$ ⊞ **Scandic Hotel Grand Marina.** Housed inside an early-19th-century customs warehouse in the posh Katajanokka island neighborhood, the Grand Marina has one of the best convention centers in Finland, accommodating up to 1,000 people. Its good location, friendly service, ample modern facilities, and reasonable prices have made this hotel a favorite among tourists. Ask for a room with a view of South Harbor. ⊠ *Katajanokanlaituri 7, Katajanokka 00160* ☎ *09/16661* 📠 *09/664–764* ⊕ *www.scandic-hotels.com* 🛏 *462 rooms* ♨ *2 restaurants, sauna, 2 bars* ⊟ *AE, DC, MC, V.*

Near Mannerheimintie

$$$$ ⊞ **Hotel Kämp.** Opposite the Esplanade Park stands this splendid, luxurious, late-19th-century cultural landmark. In the past the hotel was the site of a theater and was the meeting point for Finland's most prominent politicians, artists, and celebrities, including Mannerheim, Saarinen, and former president Paasikivi, who became one of the hotel owners. Sibelius himself often visited the hotel and dedicated a song to it. Take the beautiful, sweeping staircase up to the grand ballroom, known as the mirror room. ⊠ *Pohjoisesplanadi 29, Keskusta 00100* ☎ *09/576–1111* 📠 *09/576–1122* ⊕ *www.luxurycollection.com* 🛏 *179 rooms* ♨ *2 restaurants* ⊟ *AE, DC, MC, V.*

★ $$$$ ⊞ **Radisson SAS Plaza Hotel Helsinki.** This Renaissance-style former office building in the heart of the city has been adapted into a first-class hotel by renowned Finnish architects Ilmo Valjakka and Pervin Imaditdin. Rooms and suites come in three styles: Nordic, with contemporary light wood furnishings; classic, with darker wood furnishings and carpeting; and Italian, with sunny bright colors and bold designs. The courtyard-like main restaurant, the Pääkonttori (headquarters), is brightened by a large skylight. The sophisticated Lasibaari bar has beautiful stained-glass windows. Rates drop considerably on weekends. ⊠ *Mikonkatu 23, Keskusta 00100* ☎ *09/77590* 📠 *09/7759–7100* ⊕ *www.radissonsas.com* 🛏 *195 rooms, 6 suites* ♨ *2 restaurants, in-room data ports, 4 saunas, 2 bars, nightclub, business services, meeting room* ⊟ *AE, DC, MC, V.*

Fodor'sChoice

$$$$ ⊞ **Radisson SAS Royal Hotel Helsinki.** This hotel was conceived and built to serve the business traveler. It's in a residential section of the central city, right on the metro line. Two floors are made up of business-class rooms, including several suites and conference areas. Rooms have different styles; some are elegant Scandinavian (light colors and wood), others Asian (warm colors and silk bedcovers), and some are Italian (modern with primary colors). If you want more space and privacy, try the art deco business-class rooms on the top floor. There's an SAS check-in counter and service center in the lobby. ⊠ *Runebergink. 2, Keskusta 00100* ☎ *09/69580* 📠 *09/6958–7100* ⊕ *www.radissonsas.com* 🛏 *256 rooms, 6 suites* ♨ *2 restaurants, room service, health club, sauna, bar, meeting room* ⊟ *AE, DC, MC, V.*

$$$$ ⊞ **Sokos Hotel Torni.** The original part of this hotel was built in 1903, and its towers and internal details still reflect some of the more fanciful touches of Helsinki's Jugendstil period, although a new functionalist-style section was added in 1931. The higher floors of the original section, especially the Atelier Bar, have striking views of Helsinki. Old-section rooms on the courtyard are best; some have high ceilings with original carved-wood details and wooden writing desks; many also have little alcoves and other pleasing design oddities. A conference room at the top of the tower has art exhibitions that change monthly. ⊠ *Yrjönkatu 26, Keskusta 00100* ☎ *09/131–131* 📠 *09/131–1361* ⊕ *www.sokoshotels.fi* 🛏 *144 rooms, 9 suites* ♨ *Restaurant, room service, 4 saunas, 4 bars, meeting room* ⊟ *AE, DC, MC, V.*

$$$–$$$$ 🏨 **Scandic Hotel Marski.** The Marski is favored for its absolutely central spot, on the main Mannerheimintie artery and dead opposite Stockmann's department store. The suites are the last word in modern luxury, and all rooms are soundproof, shutting out the traffic. The Marski Bar and Restaurant is easygoing, with good views of the heart of the city. ✉ *Mannerheim. 10, Keskusta 00100* ☎ *09/68061* 🖷 *09/642–377* ⊕ *www.scandic-hotels.com* ↪ *289 rooms, 6 suites* ♨ *Restaurant, coffee shop, health club, 3 saunas, 2 bars, business services, meeting room, free parking* ⊟ *AE, DC, MC, V.*

$$$–$$$$ 🏨 **Scandic Hotel Simonkenttä.** Located next to the bus station and the Forum shopping center, this hotel was specially designed to be environmentally friendly and to fulfill hypoallergenic standards. The rooms have blue, green, or red color schemes, wood floors, and cherry wood and leather furnishings. Rooms on the upper floors have good views of the city. ✉ *Simonkatu 9, Keskusta 00100* ☎ *09/683–80* 🖷 *09/683–8111* ⊕ *www.scandic-hotels.com* ↪ *360 rooms, 3 suites* ♨ *Restaurant, bar, 3 saunas, 8 meeting rooms* ⊟ *AE, DC, MC, V.*

$$$ 🏨 **Ramada Presidentti.** In the heart of Helsinki, this hotel is spacious and quiet, with well-lit rooms. The hotel has extensive facilities and services; these include a brasserie, a formal restaurant, and an international casino. ✉ *Eteläinen Rautatiek. 4, Keskusta 00100* ☎ *09/6911* 🖷 *09/694–7886* ⊕ *www.ramadahotels.com* ↪ *495 rooms, 5 suites* ♨ *2 restaurants, indoor pool, massage, 3 saunas, casino, nightclub, meeting room, no-smoking rooms* ⊟ *AE, DC, MC, V.*

$$ 🏨 **Anna.** Pleasantly situated in a central, residential neighborhood, the Anna is in a seven-story apartment building dating from the 1930s. Room fittings are modern, with light, comfortable furniture. The room price includes a buffet breakfast. ✉ *Annank. 1, Keskusta 00120* ☎ *09/616–621* 🖷 *09/602–664* ⊕ *www.hotelanna.fi* ↪ *61 rooms, 3 suites* ♨ *Sauna, parking (fee), no-smoking floors* ⊟ *AE, DC, MC, V* ⏇ *BP.*

★ **$$**   🏨 **Lord Hotel.** On a quiet side street, this small luxury hotel distinguishes
FodorśChoice itself with a rare combination of character, consistency, and service. The
★   front section is a handsome 1903 stone castle with wood-beam, medieval-style restaurants, lounges, conference rooms, a cavernous banquet hall, and more. A walkway across an inner court brings you to the modern building housing the guest rooms, which have comfortable, contemporary furnishings. ✉ *Lönnrotink. 29, Hietalahti 00180* ☎ *09/615–815* 🖷 *09/680–1315* ⊕ *www.lordhotel.fi* ↪ *46 rooms* ♨ *2 restaurants, some in-room hot tubs, sauna, bar, meeting room, free parking* ⊟ *AE, DC, MC, V.*

$ 🏨 **Hotel Helka.** Privately owned by the Finnish YWCA, this is a pleasant, affordable alternative to the higher-price chain hotels in Helsinki. Although in the heart of the city, the Helka is surprisingly quiet, thanks to double windows. Furnishings are in light wood and mixed pastels. The Aurinko restaurant has a bright interior and an open kitchen, where international dishes are prepared at reasonable prices; choose from the very good wine selection. ✉ *Pohjoinen Rautatiekatu 23A, Keskusta 00100* ☎ *09/613–580* 🖷 *09/441–087* ⊕ *www.helka.fi* ↪ *147 rooms, 3 suites* ♨ *Restaurant* ⊟ *AE, DC, MC, V.*

$ 🏨 **Marttahotelli.** Run by a century-old women's association, this convenient establishment is small and cozy, with simply decorated rooms. ✉ *Uudenmaank. 24, Keskusta 00120* ☎ *09/618–7400* 🖷 *09/618–7401* ⊕ *www.marttahotelli.fi* ↪ *44 rooms, 1 suite* ♨ *Sauna* ⊟ *AE, DC, MC, V* ⊘ *Closed last weekend in June.*

¢   🏨 **Hostel Academica.** This summer hostel is made up of what are, during the rest of the year, university students' apartments. You can choose between rooms in the old or new sections; the latter have higher rates. Each floor has a small lounge; the rooms are functional, modern, and have their own small kitchens. Family rooms and extra beds are also available, and there are special family rates. The central location is good for shopping and transport. ✉ *Hietaniemenk. 14, Hietaniemi 00100* ☎ *09/1311–4334* 🖷 *09/441–201* ⊕ *www.hostelacademica.fi* 🛏 *215 rooms* ⚒ *Kitchenettes, tennis court, pool, sauna, laundry facilities* 🖃 *AE, DC, MC, V* ⊙ *Closed Sept.–May.*

North of City Center

★ **$$$$**
Fodor's Choice
★
🏨 **Hilton Helsinki Strand.** From the tastefully furnished rooftop saunas and the large, crisply decorated rooms, to the bathrooms with heated floors and the car-wash service in the basement garage, this hotel pampers you for a price. The distinctive use of granite and Finnish marble in the central lobby is accentuated by a soaring atrium, where the Bridges restaurant is also located. The waterfront vistas are a pleasure. An entire floor is reserved for nonsmokers, and some of the suites have panoramic views of the sea. ✉ *John Stenbergin ranta 4, Hakaniemi 00530* ☎ *09/39351* 🖷 *09/393–5255* ⊕ *www.interconti.com* 🛏 *192 rooms, 8 suites* ⚒ *2 restaurants, room service, in-room data ports, indoor pool, sauna, bar, laundry service, business services, no-smoking rooms* 🖃 *AE, DC, MC, V.*

$$
🏨 **Comfort Hotel Pilotti.** In a quiet suburb, within a five-minute drive of the airport, the Pilotti is also about 5 km (3 mi) from Heureka, the Finnish Science Center. It is modern inside and out; each compact room has a large, round porthole-style window. ✉ *Veromäentie 1, 01510 Airport Vantaa* ☎ *09/3294–800* 🖷 *09/3294–8100* ⊕ *www.choicehotels.fi* 🛏 *109 rooms, 3 suites* ⚒ *Restaurant, sauna, pub, meeting room* 🖃 *AE, DC, MC, V.*

★ **$$**
🏨 **Cumulus Airport.** This fully equipped, modern accommodation satisfies Helsinki's need for an airport hotel that meets the highest international standards. Convenient for layovers, the hotel borders the airport commercial zone and has the best conference facilities in the area. A standard room includes a large sofa and usually a king-size bed and has such soft touches as paisley bedspreads and wicker furniture; all rooms are soundproof and air-conditioned. ✉ *Robert Huberintie 4, 01510 Airport Vantaa* ☎ *09/4157–7100* 🖷 *09/4157–7101* ⊕ *www.cumulus.fi* 🛏 *260 rooms, 4 suites* ⚒ *2 restaurants, minibars, indoor pool, 4 saunas, piano bar, convention center, no-smoking room* 🖃 *AE, DC, MC, V.*

$$
🏨 **Cumulus Olympia.** The elegant public areas of this hotel have stone floors, wood-panel walls, and sturdy furniture. By contrast, the rooms have a light touch, with white walls and blue-green textiles and upholstery. There's a gym around the corner from the hotel. ✉ *Läntinen Brahenk. 2, Kallio 00510* ☎ *09/69151* 🖷 *09/691–5219* ⊕ *www.cumulus.fi* 🛏 *96 rooms, 5 family rooms* ⚒ *2 restaurants, sauna, nightclub, no-smoking room* 🖃 *AE, DC, MC, V.*

$$
🏨 **Holiday Inn Helsinki, Congress Center.** This hotel caters mainly to people attending events at the Helsinki Fair and Congress Center, which lies just on its doorstep. Transport to downtown Helsinki, 3 km (2 mi) away, is by local train (the Pasila station is a three-minute walk away) or by tram. Select rooms are for the allergy-sensitive, and some for people with disabilities. There's even a ballroom for 2,000. ✉ *Messuaukio 1, Pasila 00520* ☎ *09/150–900; 0800/13113 reservations* 🖷 *09/150–901* ⊕ *www.holiday-inn.com* 🛏 *239 rooms, 5 suites* ⚒ *Sauna, bar, business services, meeting room* 🖃 *AE, DC, V.*

$$
🏨 **Scandic Hotel Gateway Helsinki Airport.** At the heart of the Helsinki-Vantaa Airport, this hotel is ideal for early morning regrouping or quick overnights before connecting flights. The clean, modern design is typical of newer Finnish hotels. Some rooms are "air-side," for transit passengers who have no need or wish to leave the airport. Personal computer connections are available and there's a 24-hour breakfast service.

✉ *Helsinki-Vantaa Airport, 01530 Airport Vantaa* ☎ *09/818–3600* 🖷 *09/818–3609* 🌐 *www.scandic-hotels.com* 🛏 *35 rooms* ♨ *Sauna, bar, meeting room* ▱ *AE, DC, MC, V.*

$ ⊞ **Anton.** The furnishings in this hotel's rooms are much like those you'd find in a typical Finnish home: simple, clean lines; a plethora of wood tones; and duvets in bright, primary colors. In a traditional Helsinki working-class neighborhood and near the center and Kauppatori, the Anton is also conveniently close to the airport bus stop and the Hakaniemi metro stop. Note that some rooms have shared bathrooms. ✉ *Paasivuorenk. 1, Hakaniemi 00530* ☎ *09/774–900* 🖷 *09/701–4527* 🌐 *www.hotelanton. fi* 🛏 *45 rooms* ♨ *No smoking* ▱ *AE, DC, MC, V.*

$ ⊞ **Arthur.** Owned by the Helsinki YMCA, the Arthur is centrally located, unpretentious, and comfortable. ✉ *Vuorikatu 19, Keskusta 00100* ☎ *09/173–441* 🖷 *09/626–880* 🌐 *www.hotelarthur.fi* 🛏 *144 rooms* ♨ *Restaurant, sauna* ▱ *AE, DC, MC, V.*

$ ⊞ **Aurora.** This redbrick hotel has small modern rooms decorated in pale blues, greens, and peach; larger rooms have brown wood paneling. A 10-minute bus ride from the city center, it's also just across from the Linnanmäki Amusement Park and is therefore popular with families. Some rooms have a kitchenette. ✉ *Helsinginkatu 50, Alppila 00530* ☎ *09/ 770–100* 🖷 *09/7701–0200* 🌐 *www.hotelaurorahelsinki.com* 🛏 *70 rooms* ♨ *Restaurant, pool, sauna, spa, squash* ▱ *AE, DC, MC, V.*

¢ ⊞ **Fenno.** Ten minutes from the city center by tram (3B), in the Kallio neighborhood, this apartment hotel has simple, reasonably priced rooms. You can opt to stay in a private studio apartment with kitchenette and bathroom; an even less expensive choice is an unpretentious, light-color economy room, which includes shared bath and kitchen facilities with other guests on the same floor. ✉ *Franzenink. 26, Kallio 00530* ☎ *09/ 774–980* 🖷 *09/701–6889* 🌐 *www.hotelfenno.fi* 🛏 *68 apartments for 1–2 persons, 32 economy single rooms with shared facilities* ♨ *Café, sauna, laundry facilities, parking (fee)* ▱ *AE, DC, MC, V.*

Töölö & Munkkiniemi

★ $$$–$$$$ ⊞ **Scandic Hotel Continental Helsinki.** One of the most popular hotels in
FodorsChoice Helsinki, this local institution is modern and central and particularly
★ popular with business travelers from the United States. It has hosted superpower summits and various diplomatic guests, and has a comprehensive range of business services. The hotel is close to Finlandia Hall and the Finnish National Opera. Olivo, the hotel's excellent restaurant, serves Mediterranean dishes and there's a separate wine bar. ✉ *Mannerheim. 46, Töölö 00260* ☎ *09/47371* 🖷 *09/4737–2211* 🌐 *www. scandic-hotels.com* 🛏 *500 rooms, 12 suites* ♨ *Restaurant, in-room data ports, pool, gym, hair salon, 3 saunas, bar, dry cleaning, laundry service, business services, meeting room* ▱ *AE, DC, MC, V.*

★ $$$ ⊞ **Kalastajatorppa.** In the plush western Munkkiniemi neighborhood a
FodorsChoice 15- to 25-minute taxi ride from city center, this hotel routinely hosts
★ statesmen and celebrities. The best rooms are in the seaside annex, but all are large and airy, done in fresh pastel colors with clear pine and birchwood paneling. Rooms in the main building may either be equipped with bath and terrace or with showers only; prices vary accordingly. ✉ *Kalastajatorpantie 1, Munkkiniemi 00330* ☎ *09/45811* 🖷 *09/458–1668* 🌐 *www.scandic-hotels.com* 🛏 *235 rooms, 8 suites* ♨ *Restaurant, indoor pool, sauna, beach, 2 bars, meeting room, no-smoking rooms* ▱ *AE, DC, MC, V.*

$$$ ⊞ **Radisson SAS Hesperia Hotel Helsinki.** On Helsinki's main avenue, facing Hesperia Park and across the street from the Opera House, this upscale property has relatively spacious rooms with a modern Finnish flair; business-class rooms and suites are also available. The light and

airy breakfast room has a large buffet. ✉ *Mannerheimintie. 50, Töölö 00260* 🕾 *09/43101* 🖨 *09/431–0995* ⊕ *www.radissonsas.com* ⇥ *379 rooms, 4 suites* ⚒ *Restaurant, room service, minibars, indoor pool, health club, hair salon, sauna, 2 bars, concierge, business services, helipad, no-smoking rooms* ☰ *AE, DC, MC, V.*

Nightlife & the Arts

Nightlife

Helsinki nightlife has perked up considerably in recent years, and your choice extends from noisy bars and late-night clubs to more intimate cafés. The relatively small size of the central area makes it possible to visit several places in one night, but after around 9 on weekends expect lines at the popular hangouts. Cover charges, when required, average €5 to €10.

The Helsinki City Tourist Office has a *Clubs and Music Bars* listing of music nights and cover charges for various venues.

BARS & LOUNGES **Angleterre** (✉ Fredrikinkatu 47, Keskusta 🕾 09/647–371) is a cozy English ale house run by a well-known Helsinki cellar master; it's frequented by an upwardly mobile, professional crowd. **Baker's Family** (✉ Mannerheim. 12, Keskusta 🕾 09/612–6330) is a popular central café, with a lively nightclub upstairs. **Cantina West** (✉ Kasarmikatu 23, Keskusta 🕾 09/622–0900) is a lively spot with imported country and country-rock music and Tex-Mex food. **Kappeli** (✉ Eteläespl. 1, Esplanadi 🕾 09/681–2440) was the first Finnish restaurant-café to brew its own beer. Its leaded windows offer an excellent view of the Havis Amanda statue. The **Lady Moon** (✉ Kaivok. 12, Keskusta 🕾 09/6843–7370) at the Seurahuone has its own DJ. **O'Malley's** (✉ Sokos Hotel Torni, Yrjönkatu 26, Keskusta 🕾 091311–3459) is the oldest Irish pub in Helsinki. **Molly Malone's** (✉ Kaisaniemenkatu 1C, Keskusta 🕾 09/171–272) is a popular Irish pub, with nightly live music.

Raffaello (✉ Aleksanterink. 46, Keskusta 🕾 09/6844–0718) attracts a young crowd of professionals from the Helsinki financial district. **Vanha Ylioppilastalo** (✉ Mannerheim. 3, Keskusta 🕾 09/1311–4368) has a large selection of beers and attracts students with live music, usually on weekends—blues, folk, and jazz. The **William K** (✉ Annankatu 3, Keskusta 🕾 09/680–2562 ✉ Mannerheim. 72, Töölö 🕾 09/409–484 ✉ Fleminginkatu 6, Töölö 🕾 09/821–816 ✉ Fredrikinkatu 65[Tennispalatsi], Keskusta 🕾 09/693–1427) bars offer an excellent selection of European ales.

CASINOS **Casino Ray** (✉ Eteläinen Rautatienkatu 4, Keskusta 🕾 09/680–800) has roulette, blackjack, and slot machines on the third floor of the Ramada Presidentti Hotel.

GAY & LESBIAN BARS For up-to-date details of the gay scene, contact the gay rights organization **SETA** (🕾 09/681–2580 ⊕ www.seta.fi). **Con Hombres** (✉ Eerikink. 14, Keskusta 🕾 09/608–826) is a popular gay bar. **dtm** (✉ Iso Roobertink. 28, Keskusta 🕾 09/676–314) is for men only. **Lost and Found** (✉ Annank. 6, Keskusta 🕾 09/680–1010) is a bar as well as full-scale restaurant and is known for being straight-friendly. **Mann's Street** (✉ Mannerheim. 12A, Keskusta 🕾 09/612–1103) is popular among older gay men and has dancing on weekends.

INTERNET CAFÉS **Mbar** (✉ Mannherheim. 22–24, Keskusta 🕾 09/6124–5420 ⊕ www.meteori.com/netcafe) is a small Internet café with 13 terminals, in the Lasipalatsi complex. You can purchase connections for 10 ¢ a minute, charged in 10-minute increments (€1 for 10 minutes). A full hour costs

€5. There is a minimum charge of €2. The café is open late. **NetCup** (⊠ Stockmann's Department Store Aleksanterinkatu 52, Keskusta ☎ 09/ 121–3759) offers a deal where you can get 15 minutes free with a purchase at the store.

JAZZ CLUBS Helsinki's most popular jazz club, **Storyville** (⊠ Museok. 8, Keskusta ☎ 09/408–007), has live jazz and dancing every night.

NIGHTCLUBS For a night of dancing, head downtown to **Fennia** (⊠ Mikonkatu 17, Keskusta ☎ 09/621–7170). The **Hesperia Nightclub** (Radisson SAS Hesperia Hotel ⊠ Mannerheimintie 50, Töölö ☎ 09/43101), Helsinki's largest and most famous club, occasionally hosts big-name acts. Famed hockey star Jari Kurri's hip sports-theme restaurant and nightclub, **Highlight Cafe** (⊠ Fredrikinkatu 42, Keskusta ☎ 09/734–5822), is inside a former church. **Kaivohuone** (⊠ Kaivohuone Kaivopuisto, Kaivopuisto ☎ 09/684–1530) is an old spa structure in beautiful Kaivopuisto; its dance floor is often packed weekends. **Tenth Floor** (⊠ Sokos Hotel Vaakuna, Asemaaukio 2, Keskusta ☎ 09/1311–8225) is one of Helsinki's main hot spots.

On weekends, late night at **Botnia Club** (⊠ Museok. 10, Töölö ☎ 09/ 446–940) is an extraordinary cocktail of elegant tango in the main hall and frenetic disco on the top floor. The university-owned **Tavastia Club** (⊠ Urho Kekkosenk. 4–6, Keskusta ☎ 09/694–3066) is one of the best rock clubs for top Finnish talent and some solid imports.

The Arts

For a list of events, pick up *Helsinki This Week,* available in hotels and tourist offices. For tickets, contact **Lippupalvelu** (⊠ Mannerheim. 5 [Kaivopiha], Keskusta ☎ 0600/10080, €1 per minute plus a local call charge ⊕ www.lippupalvelu.fi). Call **Tiketti** (⊠ Forum shopping mall, Kukontori, Keskusta ☎ 0600/11616, €.66 per minute plus a local call charge ⊕ www.tiketti.fi) for the goods on pop concerts, theaters, student and film clubs. There's also a service point on the seventh floor of Stockmann's department store.

In summer, plays and music are performed at many outdoor theaters, including Keskuspuisto, Suomenlinna, Mustikkamaa, and the Seurasaari Islands, and also at the Rowing Stadium. **Helsinki Festival** (☎ 09/ 6126–5100 for information ⊕ www.helsinkifestival.fi), a performance and visual-arts celebration that goes on around the city, including a specially erected tent near the City Theater, is held yearly in late August–early September. The Festival includes the **Night of the Arts,** during which much of the population is outdoors watching street performances, while galleries and theaters are open late and free of charge.

An important part of Helsinki's cultural and artistic life is the **Kaapeli Tehdas** (Cable Factory; ⊠ Tallbergink. 1, Ruoholahti ☎ 09/4763–8330 ⊕ www.kaapelitehdas.fi). This huge converted industrial building houses a restaurant, the Cable Gallery, which doubles as a vast theater as well as various small but worthy museums, including the **Suomen Valokuvataiteen Museo** (Finnish Museum of Photography). The complex also has radio stations and artists' studios. It's a short bus or metro ride (Ruoholahti station) to the west of the town center.

CONCERTS **Finlandiatalo** (Finlandia Hall; ⊠ Karamzinkatu 4, Keskusta ☎ 09/402– 4246 ⊕ www.finlandia.fi), the home of the Helsinki Philharmonic, hosts visiting world-class orchestras. Finland has produced numerous fine conductors, and because many of them are based abroad—Esa-Pekka Salonen, Jukka-Pekka Saraste, and Paavo Berglund, for example—their homecomings are lavishly fêted, as are performances by opera diva

Karita Mattila. The **Sibelius Academy** (⊠ Pohjois Rautatienkatu 9, Töölö ☎ 09/405–4662) hosts frequent performances, usually by students. The splendid **Suomen Kansallisooppera** (Finnish National Opera; ⊠ Helsinginkatu 58, Keskusta ☎ 09/4030–2211), is in a waterside park by Töölönlahti. Original Finnish opera is often performed here, in addition to international favorites. The rock-hewn **Temppeliaukio Kirkko** (⊠ Lutherinkatu 3, Töölö ☎ 09/494–698) is a favorite venue for choral and chamber music.

FILM   There are about 50 cinemas in Helsinki. Foreign films have Finnish and Swedish subtitles. You'll find movie listings in most daily papers the Tennis Palace cineplex is a short walk from the train station. Most cinemas have assigned seats, and tickets cost €7–€10, depending on the day and time; afternoon shows are generally cheaper. A series of ticket coupons (usually five) are useful for groups or for longer stays. The national reservation line is 0600/007–007.

THEATER   Private support of the arts in Finland continues to be strong—especially for the theaters, the best-known of which are the **National Theater, City Theater, Swedish Theater,** and **Lilla Teatern.** However, unless you are fluent in Finnish or Swedish, you'll have a difficult time understanding the performances. Check *Helsinki This Week* for a listing of the latest performances.

Sports & the Outdoors

Biking

Helsinki and environs make for excellent biking through a decent network of trails, many traversing the downtown area and running through parks, forests, and fields. The free area sporting map ("Ulkoilukartta") gives details of all trails; pick up a copy at the tourist office. Daily rentals, including mountain bikes, are available from **Green Bike** (⊠ Mannerheim. 13, 00100 Keskusta Helsinki ☎ 09/8502–2850). The city also has bikes with fluorescent wheels for free—drop a coin in the slot as a deposit, take a ride, and drop it off at any of 26 sites around the city.

Swimming

The best beaches in Helsinki are Pihlajasaari, Mustikkamaa, and Uunisaari. The beach at **Hietaniemi** is especially popular with young people. ⊠ *Hietaniemi.* Among Helsinki's indoor pools and saunas, the oldest and one of the most famous is **Yrjönkatu Uimahalli** (⊠ Yrjönk. 21B, Keskusta ☎ 09/3108–7400), which allows some swimming in the nude.

Tennis

There are some six tennis centers and 31 clubs in Helsinki. It's best to bring your own equipment, although rentals are available. For information and details about playing tennis in Helsinki, contact the **Finnish Tennis Association** (⊠ Myllypuro Tennis Center, Varikkotie 4, 00900 Myllypuro/Itäkeskus Helsinki ☎ 09/341–7151 ⊕ www.tennis.fi).

Shopping

Helsinki's shopping facilities are constantly improving. Although the signs in Finnish may be a mystery, most sales staff in the main shopping areas speak English and can help guide you. Smaller stores are generally open weekdays 9–6 and Saturday 9–1 and larger department stores are open 'til 9 weekdays and 'til 6 on Saturdays. Small grocery stores are often open on Sundays year-round; other stores are often open on Sundays from June through August and December. The Forum complex and Stockmann's department store are open weekdays 9–9, Saturday 9–6, and (in summer and Christmastime) Sunday noon–6. An ever-expanding network of pedestrian tunnels connects the Forum, Stockmann's, and the train-station tunnel.

Kiosks remain open late and on weekends; they sell such basics as milk, juice, camera film, and tissues. Stores in Asematunneli, the train-station tunnel, are open weekdays 10–10 and weekends noon–10.

Department Stores
Stockmann's (✉Aleksanterink. 52, Keskusta ☎09/1211 ⊕www.stockmann. fi) is Helsinki's premier department store. The 1950s showpiece landmark near the train station, **Sokos** (✉ Asema-aukio 2C, Rautatieasema ☎010/ 765–000) is a high-quality alternative to Stockmann's.

Shopping Districts
Pohjoisesplanadi, on the north side of the Esplanade, packs in most of Helsinki's trademark design stores. ✉ *Esplanadi.* The southern part of **Senaatintori** has a host of souvenir and crafts stores, with several antiques shops and secondhand bookstores on the adjoining streets. ✉ *Senaat-intori.* Next to Senaatintori is the **Kiseleff Bazaar Hall,** (✉ Aleksan-terinkatu 22–28, Senaatintori), an attractive shopping gallery.

You'll find many smaller boutiques in the streets **west of Mannerheim-intie,** Fredrikinkatu and Annankatu, for example. ✉ *Keskusta.* There is one pedestrian shopping street a few blocks south of the Esplanade, on **Iso Roobertinkatu**; stores here are conventional, they are more relaxed than around Mannerheimintie and the Esplanade. ✉ *Keskusta.*

Shopping Malls
All of Helsinki's shopping malls have a good mix of stores plus several cafés and restaurants. **Forum** (✉ Mannerheim. 20, Keskusta) is the largest shopping complex in Helsinki, with 120 stores. **Kaivopiha** (✉ Kaivok. 10, Keskusta) is across from the train station. **Kluuvi** (✉ Aleksanterink. 9–Kluuvik. 5, Keskusta) is a major shopping mall. The large **Itäkeskus** shopping complex in east Helsinki, perhaps the biggest indoor mall in Scandinavia, with 190 stores, restaurants, and other services, can be reached by metro. The **Kämp Galleria**, bounded by Kluuvikatu, Pohjoisesplanadi, Mikonkatu, and Aleksanterinkatu has 50 stores, including Finnish and international design shops. ✉ *Pohjoisesplanadi 33 Keskusta.*

Specialty Stores
ANTIQUES Many shops sell china, furniture, and art. Cut glass and old farm fur-niture are other popular products; the latter is harder to find. The **Kru-unuhaka** area north of Senaatintori is the best bet if you're shopping for antiques. ✉ *Kruunuhaka.* Try **Antik Oskar** (✉ Rauhank. 7, Kruunuhaka ☎ 09/135–7410) for a selection of furniture from the 19th century, sil-ver, glass, and some porcelain. **Antiikkiliike Karl Fredrik** (✉ Mariank. 13, Kruunuhaka ☎ 09/630–014) stocks high-class 19th-century antiques, ranging from furniture, chandeliers, and other light fixtures, to glass and paintings, as well as a good selection of Russian objects. **Punavuoren An-tiikki** (✉ Mariank. 14, Kruunuhaka ☎ 09/662–682) sells jewelry, lamps, dolls, and various machines and technical objects. Some date as far back as the 18th century. The **Punavuori district,** between Eerikinkatu and Tehtaankatu, has many shops that sell secondhand books (there's usu-ally a small selection in English). ✉ *Punavuori.*

CERAMICS & **Pentik** (✉Mannerheimintie 5, Keskusta ☎09/6124-0795 ✉Forum shop-
ACCESSORIES ping mall, Mannerheim. 20, Keskusta ☎ 09/694–9884) is known for its classy but homey style of ceramic dishes and other housewares. In-ventive gift items and cards are also on sale. **Aarikka** (✉ Pohjoises-planadi 27, Esplanadi ☎ 09/652–277 ✉ Eteläesplanadi 8, Esplanadi

✆ 09/175–462) sells wooden jewelry, toys, and gifts. The **Designor** store (✉ Pohjoisesplanadi 25, Esplanadi ✆ 0204/393–501 ✉ Hämeentie 135, Arabia ✆ 0204/393–507) has Arabia, Hackman, and Iittala and Rörstrand tableware, glassware, cutlery, and cookware.

CLOTHING At its four locations in central Helsinki, **Marimekko** (✉ Pohjoisespl. 2, Esplanadi ✆ 09/622–2317 ✉ Pohjoisespl. 31 [Kämp Galleria], Esplanadi ✆ 09/6860–2411 ✉ Eteläespl. 14, Esplanadi ✆ 09/170–704 ✉ Mannerheim. 20 [Forum shopping center], Keskusta ✆ 09/694–1498) sells bright, unusual clothes for men, women, and children in quality fabrics. Though the products are costly, they're worth a look even if you don't plan to buy.

JEWELRY **Kaunis Koru** (✉ Aleksanterink. 28, Keskusta ✆ 09/686–0400) produces avant-garde silver and gold designs. **Kalevala Koru** (✉ Unionink. 25, Keskusta ✆ 09/686–0400) bases its designs on traditional motifs dating back as far as the Iron Age. Its designs are also available at most jewelry shops around Finland at reasonable prices. **Union Design** (✉ Eteläranta 14, inner courtyard Kauppatori ✆ 09/6220–0333) is an atelier workshop of goldsmiths, silversmiths, and jewelers emphasizing limited series and unique pieces, displaying top-notch talent in Finnish design.

SAUNA SUPPLIES For genuine Finnish sauna supplies such as wooden buckets, bath brushes, and birch-scented soap, visit the **Sauna Shop** in the Kiseleff Bazaar (✉ Aleksanterink. 28, Keskusta). The fourth floor of **Stockmann's** (✉ Aleksanterink. 52, Keskusta ✆ 09/1211) stocks accessories and supplies for the sauna.

Street Markets

Helsinki's main street markets and market halls specialize in food, but all have some clothing (new and used) and household products. **Hakaniemi Street Market and Market Hall** (✉ North of town center, off Unionink., Hakaniemi ☉ Indoor Market Hall: Weekdays 8–6, Sat. 8–4; street market: weekdays 6:30–3) has everything from Eastern spices to used clothing and ceramics. Visit **Kauppatori** (⇨ Exploring Helsinki), Helsinki's popular Market Square, to browse among the colorful stalls or just relax with a coffee. ✉ *Kauppatori.* At the **Old Market Hall** (☉ Weekdays 8–7, Sat. 8–4), almost adjacent to Kauppatori, you can browse and shop for anything from flowers to vegetables, meat, and fish. ✉ *Kauppatori.* **Hietalahden Tori,** at Bulevardi and Hietalahdenkatu, is open weekdays 6:30–2 and Saturday 6:30–3 (with extended summer hours). At the outdoor flea market (open weekdays 8–2, Saturdays 8–3) you can get an ever-changing assortment of used items; the indoor market is brimming with food, flowers, fish, and more. ✉ *Hietalahti.*

Helsinki A to Z

AIR TRAVEL TO & FROM HELSINKI

CARRIERS Helsinki is served by most major European airlines, as well as several East European carriers. North American service is available with Finnair in cooperation with American Airlines. European airlines include SAS, Lufthansa, Swiss International Airlines, British Airways, and Air France. Check the Finnair Web site for its One World partners in order to maximize frequent flyer miles.

🛪 **Air France** ✉ Helsinki-Vantaa airport, Airport ✆ 09/856-80500 ⊕ www.airfrance.fi. **British Airways** ✆ 0800/177-877 ⊕ www.britishairways.fi. **Finnair** ✉ City Terminal, Elielin aukio 3, Rautatieasema ✆ 09/818-7750; 09/818-800 general reservations or 0203/140-160 in Finland only; 09/818-5980 airport. Note phone line schedules may be cut back in late June-early August to weekdays only. Check the Finnair Web site for

up-to-date information. ⊕ www.finnair.fi. **Lufthansa and SAS** ✉ Keskusk 7A, Keskusta
☎ 020/386-000 Lufthansa; 0106/8000 SAS ⊕ www.scandinavian.net, www.lufthansa.
com share an office. **Swiss International Air lines** ✉ Helsinki-Vantaa airport, Airport
☎ 09/6937-9034 ⊕ www.swiss.com.

AIRPORTS & TRANSFERS
All domestic and international flights to Helsinki use Helsinki-Vantaa
International Airport, 20 km (12 mi) north of the city center.
🛫 **Helsinki-Vantaa Airport** ☎ 0200/14636, costs €.57 per minute plus a local call charge
⊕ www.helsinki-vantaa.fi

AIRPORT
TRANSFERS
Two local buses, 615 and 617, run between the airport and the main
railway station downtown from 6 am to 1 pm. The fare is €3 and the
trip takes about 40 minutes. Finnair buses carry travelers to and from
the railway station (Finnair's City Terminal) two to four times an hour,
with a stop at the Scandic Hotel Continental Helsinki. Stops requested
along the route from the airport to the city are also made. Travel time
from the Scandic Hotel Continental to the airport is about 30 minutes,
35 minutes from the main railway station; the fare is €5.

A limousine ride into central Helsinki will cost about €92 for one to
two people, €97 for three to four; contact International Limousine System or its partner company, Limousine Service, if ordering from abroad.

There is a taxi stop at the arrivals building. A cab ride into central Helsinki
costs about €25. Driving time is 20 to 35 minutes, depending on the
time of day. Check to see if your hotel has a shuttle service, although
this is not common here. Airport Taxi costs €18 for one to four passengers, and operates shuttles between the city and the airport. You must
reserve by 7 PM the day before departure. The yellow line taxi stand at
the airport also offers fixed rate trips into the city.
🚖 **Airport Taxi** ☎ 0100/4800. **International Limousine System** ✉ Alkutie 32H, Pakila
00660 ☎ 09/724-4577 or 0400/421-801 🖨 09/724-4647. **Limousine Service** ✉ Kääpätie
4A Heikinlaakso 00760 Helsinki ☎ 09/2797-800 ⊕ www.limousineservice.fi.

BOAT & FERRY TRAVEL
A ferry to the Suomenlinna fortress island runs about twice an hour, depending on the time of day, and costs €2. Ten-trip tickets issued for city
public transport can be used on the ferry, too. From June to August,
private water buses run from Kauppatori to Suomenlinna, charging €3
one-way and €5 round-trip.
🚢 **Suomenlinna Ferry** ☎ 06/633-800.

BUSINESS HOURS
BANKS & OFFICES
Banks are open weekdays 9 or 9:15 to 4 or 5. Many offices and em-
bassies close at 3 June to August.

SHOPS
Stores are open weekdays 9 to 6 and Saturday 9 to 1 or 2 and are closed
on Sunday, but several of the larger stores stay open until 8 or 9 weekdays. Big stores in the town center are open Sunday, June to August,
December, and five other Sundays throughout the year from noon to 6
or 9. Some stores in malls stay open until 9 on weekdays and until 5 on
Saturday. In the Asematunneli (train station tunnel), stores are open weekdays 10 to 10 and weekends noon to 10.

CAR TRAVEL
Ring Roads One and Three are the two major highways that circle the
city. Mannerheimintie and Hämeentie are the major trunk roads out of
Helsinki. Mannerheimintie feeds into Highway E79, which travels west
and takes you to the Ring Roads. Hämeentie leads you to Highway E4

as well as Roads 4 and 7. From either route, you will find directions for Road 137 to the airport. For specific route information, contact The Automobile and Touring Club of Finland or the City Tourist Office.

🚗 **The Automobile and Touring Club of Finland** ✉ Autoliitto ry, Hämeentie 105 A, PL 35, 00550 Arabia Helsinki ☎ 09/7258-4400; 09/7747-6400 24-hour info service ⊕ www.autoliitto.fi. **Finnish Motor Insurers' Centre** ✉ Bulevardi 28 00120 Helsinki ☎ 09/680-401 ⊕ www.vakes.fi/lvk.

EMBASSIES

🚗 Australia ✉ Museokatu 25B, Keskusta 00100 ☎ 09/447-503.

🚗 Canada ✉ Pohjoisespl. 25B, Esplanadi 00100 ☎ 09/228-530.

🚗 New Zealand **Honorary Consul General of New Zealand, c/o KohdematkatKaleva** ✉ Ruoholahdenkatu 23, Ruoholahti 00180 ☎ 020/561-5328.

🚗 United Kingdom ✉ Itäinen Puistotie 17, Kaivopuisto 00140 ☎ 09/2286-5100.

🚗 United States ✉ Itäinen Puistotie 14A, Kaivopuisto 00140 ☎ 09/616-250.

EMERGENCIES

The general emergency number is 112; call it for any emergency situation. Coins are not needed to make this call on pay phones. If you summon an ambulance, specify whether the situation seems life-threatening so medical attendants can prepare for immediate treatment in the ambulance.

Töölön Sairaala is about 2 km (1 mi) from the city center, with a 24-hour emergency room and first-aid service. Mehiläinen is a private healthcare chain that offers 24-hour service in the Helsinki area. You can call their number or get a walk-in appointment at their medical center on Runeberginkatu. The company also has medical centers in Turku and Kuopio.

🚗 Emergency Services **General Emergency** ☎ 112. **Police** ✉ Central precinct: Pieni Roobertinkatu 1–3 ☎ 1022; 1891 for central precinct.

🚗 Doctors & Dentists **Doctor Referrals** ☎ 09/10023. **Emergency Dentist on Call** ☎ 09/612-2660. **Mehiläinen** ✉ Runeberginkatu 47A, 2nd fl. ☎ 010/414-4444.

🚗 Hospitals **Töölön Sairaala** ✉ Töölönk. 40, Töölö ☎ 09/4711. **Meilahden Sairaala** ✉ Haartmaninkatu 4, Meilahti ☎ 09/4711.

🚗 24-Hour Pharmacies **Yliopiston Apteekki** ✉ Mannerheim. 96, Töölö ☎ 0203/20200.

ENGLISH-LANGUAGE MEDIA

BOOKS Akateeminen Kirjakauppa (Academic Bookstore) is the largest English-language bookstore; it's also the most expensive. Like the Academic Bookstore, Suomalainen Kirjakauppa (The Finnish Bookstore) sells English-language books, newspapers, and magazines. English-language newspapers are also on sale at the kiosks in the main train station.

🚗 Bookstores **Akateeminen Kirjakauppa** ✉ Keskuskatu 1, Keskusta ☎ 09/12141. **Suomalainen Kirjakauppa** ✉ Aleksanterink. 23, Keskusta ☎ 09/696-2240.

TAXIS

There are numerous taxi stands; central stands are at Rautatientori at the station, the main bus station, Linja-autoasema, and in the Esplanade. Taxis can also be flagged, but this can be difficult, as many are on radio call and are often on their way to stands, where late-night lines may be very long. An average taxi ride in Helsinki can cost around €10; a taxi from the airport can cost €30 or more. All taxis in Helsinki go through the Taxi Center, or you can call Kovanen, a private company, for vans, luxury minibuses, and limousine services.

🚗 **Kovanen** ☎ 0200/6060, €.95 plus local charge, open 24 hours. **Taxi Center** ☎ 0100/06000, €.74 plus 8 cents per 10 seconds plus local charge; 0100/0700 for advance booking.

TOURS

BOAT TOURS · All boat tours depart from Kauppatori Market Square. The easiest way to choose one is to go to the square in the morning and read the information boards describing the tours. Most tours run in summer only. You can go as far afield as Porvoo or take a short jaunt to the Helsinki Zoo on Korkeasaari.

BUS TOURS · Bus tours are a good way to get oriented in Helsinki. The TourExpert (Helsinki Tourist Association) 1½-hour bus tour of central Helsinki sites comes free with the Helsinki Card; otherwise the cost is €19.50. Tours leave from Esplanade Park, and the Katajanoka and Olympia Terminals. For more information, contact TourExpert at the Helsinki City Tourist Office.

London Bus Transport gives two-hour tours on original London double-decker buses, from early July to late August at 11:00 AM. Pick up a brochure at the City Tourist Office to find out the departure point. The cost is €22 for adults and €15 for children. Purchase tickets aboard the bus 15 minutes before departure.

🚍 **London Bus Transport** ☎ 09/884-5490. **TourExpert** ☎ 0600/02288 ⊕ www. helsinkiexpert.fi.

WALKING TOURS · The Helsinki City Tourist Office employs Helsinki-Help guides, dressed in green and white. Daily, June to August, 8 to 8, they walk the streets in the city center and harbor area, freely answering questions and giving directions. Helsingin Matkailuyhdistys (Helsinki Tourist Association) is a guide booking center that will arrange personal tour guides. The City Tourist Office also has an excellent brochure, *See Helsinki on Foot*, with six walks covering most points of interest.

TRAIN TRAVEL

Helsinki's suburbs and most of the rest of southern, western, and central Finland are well served by trains. Travel on trains within the city limits costs the same as all public transport, €2 or less if you use the 10-trip tickets (*Kymmenen matkan lippu*). A single regional ticket costs €3 and is good for 80 minutes, including transfers. Regional tourist tickets are available for one day (€8), three days (€16), and five days (€24).

TRANSPORTATION AROUND HELSINKI

Helsinki center is compact and best explored on foot. The City Tourist Office provides a free Helsinki route map detailing all public transportation. The Helsinki Kortti (Helsinki Card) allows unlimited travel on city public transportation, free entry to many museums, a free sightseeing tour, and other discounts. It's available for one, two, or three days (€24, €34, or €42 respectively). You can buy it at more than 70 places, including the airport (information desks), ferry terminals, some hotels and travel agencies, Stockmann's department store, the Hotel Booking Centre, some R-kiosks in the city center, and the Helsinki City Tourist Office. Visit www.helsinkicard.com for more information.

The bus and tram networks are compact but extensive, and service is frequent, with more infrequent service nights and on Sunday. Be sure to pick up a route map at the tourist office—many stops do not have them. Tickets bought from the driver cost €3 for buses and €1.70 for trams. Get significant reductions by using a travel card, loaded with an amount or for a time period. Extensive information on routes, fares and timetables is available from the Helsinki City Transport Web site.

🚍 **Helsinki City Transport** ⊕ www.hel.fi/HKL.

TRAVEL AGENCIES

Try TourExpert for tour (or sightseeing) information. Suomen Matka-toimisto (Finland Travel Bureau), is the country's main travel agency.
▶ **Local Agent Referrals Suomen Matkatoimisto** ⊠ Kaivok. 10 A, PL 319, 00101 Keskusta Helsinki ☎ 09/18261. **TourExpert** ⊠ Helsinki City Tourist Office, Pohjoisespl. 19, Esplanadi ☎ 0600/02288, €.78 per minutes plus local charge.

VISITOR INFORMATION

The Helsinki City Tourist Office is open May to September, weekdays 9 to 8 and weekends 9 to 6; October to April, weekdays 9 to 6 and weekends 10 to 4. The Finnish Tourist Board's Information Office, covering all of Finland, is open May to September weekdays 9 to 5 and weekends 11–3; October to April, weekdays 9 to 5.
▶ **Tourist Information Finnish Tourist Board's Information Office** ⊠ Eteläespl. 4, 00130 Esplanadi Helsinki ☎ 09/4176-9211 or 09/4176-9300 ⊕ www.mek.fi. **Helsingin Matkailuyhdistys** Helsinki Tourist Association, a.k.a. Helsinki Expert ⊠ Lönnrotink. 7B, Keskusta 00120 ☎ 09/2288-1200 ⊕ www.helsinkiexpert.fi. **Helsinki City Tourist and Convention Bureau** ⊠ Pohjoisespl. 19, 00100 Esplanadi Helsinki ☎ 09/169-3757 ⊕ www.hel.fi/tourism.

SIDE TRIPS FROM HELSINKI

Helsinki's outskirts are full of attractions, most of them no more than a half-hour bus or train ride from the city center. From the idyllic former home of Finland's national artist to the utopian garden city of Tapiola in Espoo, options abound.

Gallen-Kallela Estate

10 km (6 mi) northwest of Helsinki.

Set at the edge of the sea and surrounded by towering, wind-bent pines, the turreted brick-and-stucco Gallen-Kallela Estate was the self-designed studio and home of the Finnish Romantic painter Akseli Gallen-Kallela. Gallen-Kallela (1865–1931) lived in the mansion on and off from its completion in 1913 until his death. Inside, the open rooms of the painter's former work spaces make the perfect exhibition hall for his paintings. Also displayed are some of his posters and sketches of the ceiling murals he made for the Paris Art Exhibition at the turn of the 20th century. To get to the estate, take Tram 4 from in front of the Sokos department store on Mannerheimintie. From the Munkkiniemi stop transfer to Bus 33, or walk the 2 km (1 mi) through the woods. ⊠ *Gallen-Kallelantie 27, Tarvaspää* ☎ *09/541-3388* ✍ *€8* ⊙ *Mid-May–Aug., daily 10–6; Sept.–mid-May, Tues.–Sat. 10–4, Sun. 10–5.*

Espoo

20 km (13 mi) west of Helsinki.

Tapiola Garden City, an architectural showpiece in its day, is in the city of Espoo, west of Helsinki. Designed by top Helsinki artists of the 1950s—Ervi, Blomstedt, and Rewell among them—the urban landscape of alternating high and low residential buildings, fountains, gardens, and swimming pools blends into the natural surroundings. Guides and sightseeing tours of Tapiola for architecture enthusiasts and professionals are available from the **Espoo Convention and Marketing** (⊠ Pohjantie 3, 02100 Espoo ☎ 09/8164-7230 🖷 09/8164-7238 ⊕ www.espootravel.fi). The Helsinki Area Ticket provides discount fares to Espoo.

Hvitträsk

40 km (25 mi) west of Helsinki.

On the northwest edge of the Espoo area is Hvitträsk, the studio home of architects Herman Gesellius, Armas Lindgren, and Eliel Saarinen. In an idyllic position at the top of a wooded slope, the property dates back to the turn of the 20th century, and is now a charming museum. The whimsical main house reveals the national art nouveau style, with its rustic detail and paintings by Akseli Gallen-Kallela; Saarinen lived here, and his grave is nearby. A café and restaurant are set up in one of the architects' houses. Hvitträsk can be reached in 45 minutes by Bus 166 (last stop) from Helsinki's main bus station, Linja-autoasema, platform 60. ✉ *Hvitträskintie 166, Luoma, Kirkkonummi, Hvitträsk* ☎ *09/4050–9630* ⊕ *www.nba.fi* ✉ *€4* ☉ *Museum June–Aug., daily 10–6; Sept. and Oct. and Apr. and May, daily 11–6; Nov.–Mar., Tues.–Sun. 11–5.*

Ainola

50 km (31 mi) north of Helsinki.

The former home of Finland's most famous son, composer Jean Sibelius, was designed by Lars Sonck in 1904 and takes its name from his wife, Aino. From late spring through summer, the intimate wooden house set in secluded woodland is open to the public as a museum. Take a bus from the Helsinki Linja-autoasema (bus station) or a local train first to the town of Järvenpää; Ainola is 2 km (1 mi) farther by bus or taxi. ✉ *04400 Järvenpää* ☎ *09/287–322* ⊕ *www.ainola.fi* ✉ *€5* ☉ *June–Aug., Tues.–Sun. 11–7; early May–Sept., Wed.–Sun. 11–7.*

Porvoo

50 km (31 mi) east of Helsinki.

Porvoo is a living record of the past, with its old stone streets and painted wooden houses lining the riverbank. Artisan boutiques around the old Town Hall Square invite exploration. Take a stroll into the Old Quarter to see the multicolor wooden houses. Visit the 15th-century stone-and-wood cathedral, **Porvoon Tuomiokirkko**, where the diet of the first duchy of Finland was held in the 1800s. The **Walter Runebergin Veistoskokoelma** (Walter Runeberg Sculpture Collection ✉ Aleksanterink. 5, ☎ 019/582–186) has some wonderful pieces and is well worth a visit. The **Porvoo Museo** (✉ Välik. 11 ☎ 019/574–7500 or 019/574–7589), inside the historic town hall built in 1764, captures the region's social and cultural history through exhibits on daily life and household objects. Next door to the Porvoo Museo, the **Edelfelt-Vallgren Museo** (✉ Välik. 11 ☎ 019/574–7500 or 019/574–7589) exhibits Edelfelt's art, as well as paintings, sculpture, glass, and ceramics by other artists.

Near Porvoo in Haikko, you can visit the **Albert Edelfeltin Atelje**, (☎ 019/577–414) the painter's studio of Albert Edelfelt. Contact the **Porvoo City Tourist Office** (✉ Rihkamakatu 4, 06100 Porvoo ☎ 019/520–2316 ⊕ www.porvoo.fi) for details about all local sights.

Part of the fun of visiting Porvoo is the journey you take to get there. On summer Saturdays (early June through the end of August, except Midsummer) there is a train connection along the historical museum rail between Helsinki and Porvoo, on board the old trains from the 1950s and 1960s. Prices are €11 one-way, €18 round-trip. Once in Porvoo, you can take a historic ride on a steam train to Hinthaara and back. Contact the **Porvoo Museum Railway Society** (☎ 0400/700–717

⊕ helsinkiww.net/pmr) for details. Far more regular than the historic train journey is the boat service. Mid-June to mid-August daily cruises depart from Helsinki's South Harbor: the *J. L. Runeberg* takes 3½ hours and the round-trip costs €28; the *King* takes 3 hours each way and costs €32 for a round-trip. You will be taken westward through dozens of islands before landing at Porvoo, which is small enough to be covered on foot. Contact **Porvoon Sataman Info** (Porvoo Harbor Information; ☎ 019/584–727; 019/524–3331 boat company ⊕ www. msjlruneberg.fi). There are also bus and road connections.

Vantaa

20 km (13 mi) north of Helsinki.

Though not remarkable, Vantaa—the municipality north of Helsinki proper and the home of the international airport—has a few notable attractions. A welcome surplus of open green space and trails for biking, hiking, and running create an oasis for outdoor enthusiasts. Don't miss the 15th-century **Helsingin Pitajan Kirkko** (Parish Church).

Consider using Vantaa as home base if your trip to Helsinki coincides with a convention and you can't find accommodations there: The airport is within the city's municipal boundaries and easily reached by public transport; you can use the Helsinki Area Ticket in Vantaa.

The **Heureka Suomalainen Tiedekeskus** (Heureka Finnish Science Center) has interactive exhibits on topics as diverse as energy, language, and papermaking. There is also a cafeteria, a park, and a planetarium with taped commentary in English as well as the Verne IMAX-type theater. ⊠ *Tiedepuisto 1, Tikkurila* ☎ *09/85799* ⊕ *www.heureka.fi* ☒ *€12.50 exhibitions only, €7 for the Verne theater only, €17 for both* ☉ *Mon., Wed., and Fri. 10–5; Thurs. 10–8; weekends 10–6.*

The peaceful **Viherpaja Japanese and Cactus gardens** in Vantaa include an exhibition of carnivorous plants. ⊠ *Meiramitie 1* ☎ *09/822–628* ⊕ *www.viherpaja.fi* ☒ *Japanese Garden and carnivorous plants €1, other gardens free* ☉ *June–Aug., weekdays 8–6, weekends 9–4; Sept.–May, weekdays 8–7, weekends 9–5.*

The **Suomen Ilmailumuseo** (Finnish Aviation Museum) has more than 60 military and civilian aircraft on display. ⊠ *Tietotie 3* ☎ *09/870–0870* ⊕ *www.suomenilmailumuseo.fi* ☒ *€5* ☉ *Daily 11–6.*

Contact the **Vantaa Travel Center** (⊠ Ratatie 7, Tikkurila, 01300 ☎ 09/ 8392–3134 🖷 09/8392–2371 ⊕ www.vantaa.fi) for more information.

SOUTHWESTERN COAST & THE ÅLAND ISLANDS

A magical world of islands stretches along Finland's coastline. In the Gulf of Finland and the Baltic, more than 30,000 islands form a magnificent archipelago. The rugged and fascinating Åland Islands group lies westward from Turku, forming an autonomous province of its own. Turku, the former capital, was the main gateway through which cultural influences reached Finland over the centuries.

A trip to Turku via Hanko and Tammisaari will give you a taste of Finland at its most historic and scenic. Many of Finland's oldest towns lie in this southwest region of the country, having been chartered by Swedish kings—hence the predominance of the Swedish language here.

The southwest is a region of flat, often mist-soaked rural farmlands, and villages peppered with traditional wooden houses. At other times pastoral and quiet, the region's culture comes alive in summer.

It's easy to explore this region by rail, bus, or car, then to hop on a ferry bound for the Ålands, halfway between Finland and Sweden. Drive along the southern coast toward Turku, the regional capital, stopping at the charming coastal towns along the way. Or take a train from Helsinki to Turku, catching buses from Turku to other parts of the region.

Snappertuna

▶ ❸❾ *124 km (77 mi) southeast of Turku, 75 km (47 mi) southwest of Helsinki.*

Snappertuna is a small farming town with a proud hilltop church, a charming homestead museum, and the handsome restored ruins of **Raaseporin Linna** (Raseborg Castle), set in a small dale. The castle is believed to date from the 14th century. One 16th-century siege left the castle damaged, but restorations have given it a new face. In summer, concerts and plays are staged here, and there are old-fashioned market fairs. Call for information on guided tours. ☎ *019/234–015* ☞ *€1* ⊙ *May and mid–late Aug., daily 10–5; June–mid-Aug., daily 10–8; Sept., weekends 10–5.*

Tammisaari

❹⓿ *16 km (10 mi) west of Snappertuna, 109 km (68 mi) southeast of Turku.*

Tammisaari (or Ekenäs) has a colorful Old Quarter, 18th- and 19th-century buildings, and a lively marina. The scenery is dazzling in summer, when the sun glints off the water and marine traffic is at its peak. The **Tammisaaren Museo** (Tammisaari Museum) is the provincial museum of western Uusimaa, providing a taste of the region's culture and history. ⊠ *Kustaa Vaasank. 11* ☎ *019/263–3161 or 019/263–2440* ⊕ *www. tammisaari.fi* ☞ *€2, guided tour €20 weekdays, €30 weekends* ⊙ *Mid-May–mid-Aug., daily 11–5; Sept.–May, Tues.–Thurs. 4–7, Fri.–Sun. noon–4.*

Where to Stay

$ 🏨 **Ekenäs Stadshotell.** This modern, airy hotel is in the heart of Tammisaari, amid fine lawns and gardens and near the sea and Old Quarter. Some of the rooms have their own balconies; all have wide picture windows and comfortable modern furnishings in pale and neutral colors. ⊠ *Pohjoinen Rantakatu 1, 10600 Tammisaari* ☎ *019/241–3131* 🖶 *019/ 246–1550* ⊕ *www.stadshotell.nu* ⇆ *18 rooms, 1 suite* ⌖ *Room service, indoor pool, 2 bars, nightclub* ⊟ *AE, DC, MC, V.*

Hanko

❹❶ *37 km (23 mi) southwest of Tammisaari, 141 km (88 mi) southeast of Turku.*

In the coastal town of Hanko (Hangö), you'll find long stretches of sandy beach—about 30 km (19 mi) of it—some sandy and some with sea-smoothed boulders. Sailing abounds here, thanks to Finland's largest guest harbor. A sampling of the grandest and most fanciful private homes in Finland dot the seacoast, their porches edged with gingerbread iron detail and woodwork, and crazy towers sprouting from their roofs. Favorite pastimes here are beachside strolls; bike rides along well-kept paths; and, best of all, long walks along the main avenue past the great wooden houses with their wraparound porches.

This customs port has a rich history. Fortified in the 18th century, Hanko defenses were destroyed by the Russians in 1854, during the

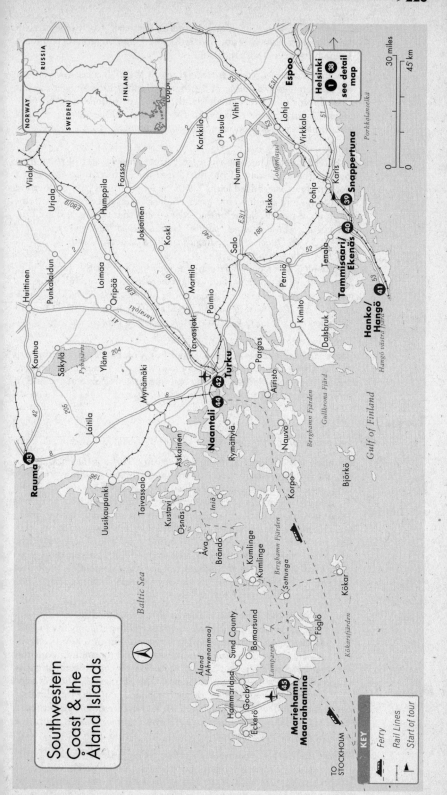

Crimean War. Later it became a popular spa town for Russians, then the port from which more than 300,000 Finns emigrated to North America between 1880 and 1930.

🕑 Through the telescope of **Vesitorni** (Hanko's Water Tower), you can follow the comings and goings of the town's marine traffic and get a grand view of some of the very small islands sprinkled around the peninsula's edges. ⊠ *Vartiovuori* ☎ *019/220–3411 tourist office* ☎ *€1* ☉ *Early June–mid-Aug., daily noon–6; mid–late Aug., daily 1–3.*

Where to Stay

$ 🏨 **Hotel Regatta.** This historic seaside hotel in the center of town near the eastern harbor dates from the turn of the 20th century, although a modern annex was added in the 1960s. Sea-view rooms have dark-wood furnishings and a yellow-and-green color scheme, and street-side rooms are done in pastels. Some of the older rooms share baths and are thus less costly. ⊠ *Merikatu 1, 10900 Hanko* ☎ *019/248–6491* 🖷 *019/ 248–5535* ⊕ *www.surfnet.fi/regatta* 🛏 *38 rooms, 1 suite* ⚲ *Sauna, beach, meeting room.*

$ ⚠ **Camping Silversand.** There are various facilities at this large campground near the water, including eight-person cabins and full hook-ups for trailers, as well as trailers and tents for rent. ⊠ *Hopeahietikko, 10960 Hanko* ☎ *019/248–5500; 09/6138–3210 off-season* 🖷 *019/248–6434* ⊕ *www.lomaliitto.fi* ⚲ *Cafeteria, sauna, shop* ☉ *Closed mid-Aug.–May.*

The Outdoors

BOATING　Boats can be rented at the guest harbor Info-Point in Hanko, or through the local tourist office. Young people and families race in and attend the annual **Hanko Regatta**, setting sail during a weekend at the end of June or beginning of July.

Turku

㊷ *140 km (87 mi) northwest of Hanko, 166 km (103 mi) west of Helsinki.*

Founded at the beginning of the 13th century, Turku is the nation's oldest and fifth-largest city and was the original capital of newborn Finland. Its early importance in the history of Finland has earned Turku the title of "the cradle of Finnish culture." Turku has a long history as a commercial and intellectual center (the city's name means trading post); once the site of the first Finnish university, it has two major universities, the Finnish University of Turku and the Swedish-speaking Åbo Akademi. Turku has a population of over 170,000, and a busy, year-round harbor. In summer the banks of the river come alive with boat and ship cafés and the city hosts various festivals, including Baltic Jazz and Medieval Turku festivals in July.

The 700-year-old **Turun Tuomiokirkko** (Turku Cathedral) remains the seat of the archbishop of Finland. It was partially gutted by fire in 1827 but has subsequently been completely restored. In the choir are R. W. Ekman's frescoes portraying Bishop Henry (an Englishman) baptizing the then-heathen Finns and Mikael Agricola offering the Finnish translation of the New Testament to Gustav Vasa of Sweden. The cathedral also houses a museum, which displays medieval church vestments, silver chalices, and wooden sculptures. ⊠ *Turun Tuomiokirkko, Keskusta* ☎ *02/251–7100* ⊕ *www.turunsrk.fi* ☉ *Mid-Apr.–mid-Sept., daily 9–8; mid-Sept.–mid-Apr., daily 9–7.*

Where the Aura flows into the sea stands **Turun Linna** (Turku Castle), one of the city's most important historical monuments. The oldest part of the fortress was built at the end of the 13th century, and the newer part dates from the 16th century. The castle was damaged by bombing in 1941, and its restoration was completed in 1961. Many of its seemingly infinite rooms hold rather incongruous exhibits: next to a display on medieval life (featuring a dead rat to illustrate the Black Death) is a roomful of 1920s flapper costumes. The vaulted chambers themselves give you a sense of the domestic lives of the Swedish royals. A good gift shop and a pleasant café are on the castle grounds. ⊠ *Linnank. 80, Keskusta* ☎ *02/262–0300* ✉ *€6.50 without a guide, €8 with a guide* ☉ *Mid-Apr.–mid-Sept., daily 10–6; mid-Sept.–mid-Apr., Tues.–Sun. 10–3.*

The **Luostarinmäki Handicrafts Museum** is an authentic collection of wooden houses and buildings that escaped fire in the 19th century, containing shops and workshops where traditional crafts are demonstrated and sold. Ask staff about the history of a particular workshop or call ahead for schedule of guided tours, offered several times daily in summer. ⊠ *Vartiovuorenk. 4, Keskusta* ☎ *02/262–0350* ⊕ *www.turku.fi* ✉ *€3.40 without a guide, €4.80 with a guide* ☉ *Mid-Apr.–mid-Sept., daily 10–6; mid-Sept.–mid-Apr., Tues.–Sun 10–3.*

The **Aboa Vetus/Ars Nova** museum displays a unique combination of history and art. Begun as a straightforward extension of the Villa von Rettig collection, the museum's concept changed when workers discovered archaeological remains, which were excavated and incorporated into the museum. Modern art in the old villa includes works by Auguste Herbin (1882–1960) and Max Ernst (1891–1976), as well as Picasso's *The Swordsman*. The preserved excavations in the Aboa Vetus section date to the 15th century. ⊠ *Itäinen Rantakatu 4–6, Keskusta* ☎ *02/250–0552* ⊕ *www.aboavetusarsnova.fi* ✉ *€9.50 combined ticket for villa and excavations, €7 each* ☉ *Jan.–mid-Apr., Thurs.–Sun. 11–7; mid-Apr.–late Sept., daily 11–7; late Sept.–Dec., Thurs.–Sun., 11–7; early–mid-Dec., weekends 11–7.*

The **Turun Taidemuseo** (Turku Art Museum) holds some of Finland's most famous paintings, including works by Akseli Gallen-Kallela, and a broad selection of turn-of-the-20th-century Finnish art and contemporary works. Due to renovation, exhibits are temporarily being held on the Vartiovuorenmäki hill, in the Old Observatory (Vartiovuorenmäen Tähtitorni) designed by Carl Ludvig Engel; the building itself is worth the visit, in addition to the view of the city. There are steps that go up the hill to the observatory, at Uudenmaankatu and Teininkuja. Alternatively you can take a taxi there. The museum is scheduled to reopen in spring 2004—check the Web site for updated information on the reopening. Call ahead for information on guided tours. ⊠ *Vartiovuori, Vartiovuori/Keskusta* ☎ *02/262–7100* ⊕ *www.turuntaidemuseo.fi* ✉ *€5.50–€7* ☉ *Old Observatory: Tues.–Thurs., 11–7; Fri.–Sun., 10–4.*

Where to Stay & Eat

$$–$$$$ ✕ **Suomalainen Pohja.** This classic Finnish restaurant is decorated in dark wood with large windows offering a splendid view of an adjacent park. Seafood, poultry, and game dishes have earned a good reputation here. Try the fillet of reindeer with sautéed potatoes or the cold smoked rainbow trout with asparagus. ⊠ *Aurak. 24, Keskusta* ☎ *02/251–2000* ▭ *AE, DC, MC, V* ☉ *Closed weekends and July.*

$–$$$$ ✕ **Brahen Kellari.** This cellar restaurant near the market square is named for one of Turku's most famous historical figures. It combines coziness with clean Scandinavian lines and contemporary cuisine. Classic Finnish ingredients are prepared with international accents, such as the grilled salmon in mango sauce or the whitefish with polenta and tomato sauce. Traditional game such as reindeer and pheasant are also specialties. Take a break from sightseeing with the generous lunch buffet in quiet sur-roundings. ⊠ *Puolankatu 1, Kauppatori* ☎ *02/232–5400* ⊟ *AE, DC, MC, V* ⊙ *Closed Sun.*

$$–$$$ ✕ **Calamare.** In the heart of the city at the Hotel Marina Palace, this restaurant has maintained a high standard for its fish dishes. Try the fried *kuha* (pike-perch) with beet terrine. Calamare has impressive views of the Aura River and Roman-style statues and palm trees that recall the Mediterranean. ⊠ *Linnankatu 32, Keskusta* ☎ *02/336–300* ⊟ *AE, DC, MC, V.*

$$$$ ⊡ **Sokos Hotel Hamburger Börs.** This is one of Turku's best-known and finest hotels. Guest rooms have TVs and modern amenities. The Ger-man-style tavern is great for drinks; the main restaurant serves Conti-nental cuisine and Finnish specialties such as fillet of reindeer with bacon. There's even a jazz club. ⊠ *Kauppiask. 6, 20100 Turku* ☎ *02/ 337–381* 🖨 *02/2231–1010* ⊕ *www.sokoshotels.fi* ⤳ *343 rooms, 3 suites* ⚴ *2 restaurants, café, indoor pool, sauna, bar, 2 nightclubs, park-ing (fee), no-smoking rooms* ⊟ *AE, DC, MC, V.*

$$$–$$$$ ⊡ **Park Hotel.** Built in 1904 in the art nouveau style for a British exec-utive who ran the local shipyard, the castlelike Park Hotel is one of Fin-land's most unusual lodgings. Rooms have high ceilings and antique furniture but offer all the comforts of a modern hotel. It's in the heart of Turku, two blocks from the main market square. ⊠ *Rauhank. 1, 20100 Turku* ☎ *273–2555* 🖨 *02/251–9696* ⊕ *www.parkhotelturku.fi* ⤳ *19 rooms* ⚴ *Restaurant, minibars, sauna* ⊟ *AE, DC, MC, V.*

Nightlife & the Arts

A lively artistic community thrives in Turku, and like most Finnish towns, it comes into its own in the summer. It is most active in July dur-ing the **Ruisrock Festival,** drawing international acts to the seaside park 5 km (3 mi) west of the city. August's **Turku Music Festival** features baroque and contemporary performances. The highlight of the festival is the well-attended, outdoor **Down by the Laituri,** with stages set up along the city's waterfront.

BARS & LOUNGES   Turku has several distinctive bars in historic buildings. The **Uusi Apteekki (New Pharmacy)** (⊠ Kaskenkatu 1, Keskusta ☎ 02/250–2595), has its own brew, served in an old apothecary. **Old Bank** (⊠ Aurakatu 3, Keskusta ☎ 02/274–5700), near the market square, is one of the most popular bars in Turku, housed in a former bank and offering 120 brands of beer from all over the world. **Koulu (School)** (⊠ Eerikinkatu 18, Keskusta ☎ 02/274–5757) is a brewery restaurant in what used to be a school for girls built in the 1880s. **Puutorin Vessa (Toilet)** (⊠ Pu-utori [Puu Square], Keskusta ☎ 02/233–8123) is decidedly Turku's most unusual pub, in a functionalist building once serving as a public rest room but now housing what the owners call a "nice-smelling bar" and restaurant.

Rauma

43 *92 km (57 mi) northwest of Turku, 238 km (148 mi) northwest of Helsinki.*

The third-oldest city in Finland, Rauma is renowned for its old wooden houses painted in original, distinctive 18th- and 19th-century colors. The colors are so extraordinary, in fact, that no house can be repainted until the Old Rauma Association approves the color. UNESCO has designated Rauma's Old Town a World Heritage Site. It's also widely known for its tradition of lace making and its annual **Lace Week,** held every year at the end of July. You can take a bus to Rauma from Turku in 1½ hours. For information and bus schedules, contact the local tourist office.

Naantali

44 *17 km (10½ mi) west of Turku.*

Built around a convent of the Order of Saint Birgitta in the 15th century, the coastal village of Naantali is an aging medieval town, former pilgrimage destination, artists' colony, and modern resort all rolled into one. Many of its buildings date from the 17th century, following a massive rebuilding after the Great Fire of 1628. You'll also see a number of 18th- and 19th-century buildings, which form the basis of the Old Town—a settlement by the water's edge. These shingled wooden buildings were originally built as private residences, and many remain so, although a few now house small galleries.

Naantali's extremely narrow cobblestone lanes gave rise to a very odd law. During periods when economic conditions were poor, Naantalians earned their keep by knitting socks and exporting them by the tens of thousands. Men, women, and children all knitted so feverishly that the town council forbade groups of more than six from meeting in narrow lanes with their knitting—and causing road obstructions.

A major attraction in the village is **Kultaranta,** the summer residence for Finland's presidents, with its more than 3,500 rosebushes. Guided tours for groups can be arranged through the Naantali tourist board year-round. ✉ *Luonnonmaasaari, Kultaranta* ☎ *02/435–9800* ⊕ *www. naantalinmatkailu.fi* ☉ *Guided tours late June–mid-Aug. daily; call Naantali tourist office or check Web site for times.*

The convent **Naantalin Luostarikirkko** (Naantali's Vallis Gratiae) was founded in 1443 and completed in 1462. It housed both monks and nuns, and operated under the aegis of the Catholic church until it was dissolved by the Reformation in the 16th century. Buildings fell into disrepair, then were restored from 1963 to 1965. The church is all that remains of the convent. ✉ *Nunnak, Keskusta* ☎ *02/437–5432; 02/437–5413 to check current schedules* ✑ *Free* ☉ *May, daily 10–6; June–Aug., daily 10–8; Sept.–Apr., Wed. noon–2, Sun. noon (or after worship service ends)–3.*

Near Naantali's marina, a footbridge leads to **Kailo Island,** in summer abuzz with theater, beach, sports, picnic facilities, and a snack bar. The **Moomin World** theme park brings to life all the famous characters of the beloved children's stories written by the Finnish woman Tove Jansson. The stories emphasize family, respect for the environment, and new adventures. ✉ *Kailo Island, PL 48, Kailo* ☎ *02/511–1111* ⊕ *www. muumimaailma.fi* ✑ *€13, €22 also including exploring on Väski Island* ☉ *Mid-June–mid-Aug., daily 10–8.*

Where to Stay

$$$ 🏨 **Naantali Kylpylä Spa.** The emphasis here is on pampering, with foot massages, shiatsu physical therapy, mud packs, spa-water, and algae baths. Activities include gymnastics and a special seven-day fasting program offered twice a year under medical supervision. All kinds of health packages can be arranged, including health-rehabilitation programs. It is set on a peninsula in a grandiose building that replaced the original spa on the site. ✉ *Matkailijantie 2, 21100* ☎ *02/44550* 🖷 *02/445–5621* ⊕ *www.naantalispa.fi* ✑ *325 rooms* ♨ *2 pools, hair salon, massage, Turkish bath* ▤ *AE, DC, MC, V.*

Nightlife & the Arts

The **Naantali Music Festival** (☎ *02/434–5363* ⊕ www. naantalinmusiikkijuhlat.fi) has chamber music performances and takes place at the beginning of June.

Shopping

Mannerheiminkatu near the beach is the main shopping drag in Naan-tali. Stop at **Ho-Qu's** (⊠ Mannerheimink. 5, Keskusta ☎ 044/522–3768), a handicrafts and gift shop that also houses a café and several guest apartments for rent.

Mariehamn & the Åland Islands

㊺ *155 km (93 mi) west of Turku.*

The Ålands are composed of more than 6,500 small rocky islands and skerries, inhabited in large part by families that fish or run small farms. Virtually all the more than 25,000 locals are Swedish speaking and very proud of their largely autonomous status, which includes having their own flag and stamps. Their connection with the sea is indelible, their seafaring traditions revered. Åland is demilitarized and has special privileges within the EU that allow duty-free sales on ferries between Finland and Sweden.

Mariehamn (Maariahamina), on the main island, is the capital (population more than 10,000) and hub of Åland life. At its important port, some of the greatest grain ships sailing the seas were built by the Gustav Eriksson family.

The **Museifartyget Pommern** (*Pommern* Museum Ship), in Mariehamn West Harbor at town center, is one of the last existing grain ships in the world. Once owned by the sailing fleet of the Mariehamn shipping magnate Gustaf Erikson, the ship carried wheat between Australia and England from 1923 to 1939. ☎ 018/531–421 ⊕ *www.pommern.aland. fi* ⛉ *€4.50* ⊙ *May–June and Aug., daily 9–5; July, daily 9–7; Sept. and Oct., daily 10–4.*

In prehistoric times the islands were, relatively speaking, heavily populated, as is shown by traces of no fewer than 10,000 ancient settlements, graves, and strongholds. A visit to **Sund County** will take you back to the earliest days of life on the islands, with its remains from prehistoric times and the Middle Ages. **Kastelholm** is a medieval castle built by the Swedes to strengthen their presence on Åland. ⊠ *Kastelholm* ☎ *018/ 432–150* ⛉ *€5* ⊙ *Guided tours May–June and early–mid-Aug., daily 10–5; July, daily 10–5:30, mid-Aug.–Oct. 10–4:30.*

Jan Karlsgården Friluftsmuseum (Jan Karlsgården Open-air Museum) is a popular open-air museum, with buildings and sheds from the 18th century that portray farming life on the island 200 years ago. ⊠ *Kastelholm* ☎ *018/432–150* ⛉ *€2* ⊙ *May–Sept., daily 10–5.*

About 8 km (5 mi) from the village of Kastelholm in Sund are the scattered ruins of **Bomarsund Fortress,** a huge naval fortress built by the Russians in the early 19th century. It was only half finished when it was destroyed by Anglo-French forces during the Crimean War. ☎ *018/44032* ⊙ *May and June, Tues.–Sun. 10–3; July–mid-Aug., Tues.–Sun. 10–5.*

Where to Stay & Eat

$$–$$$ ✕▥ **Arkipelag.** In the heart of Mariehamn, the bayside Arkipelag Hotel is known for its fine marina and lively disco-bar. Rooms are modern and comfortable, with huge picture windows and balconies. Ask for a seaside room. The restaurants, set in long, wood-panel rooms with wide windows overlooking an ocean inlet, serve fresh Åland seafood. Try the crayfish when it's in season. In the terrace restaurant, the fresh shrimp sandwiches with dill mayonnaise are a treat. ⊠ *Strandgatan 31, 22100 Mariehamn* ☎ *018/24020* ⊟ *018/24384* ⊕ *www.hotellarkipelag.*

com ⟿ 78 rooms, 8 suites ⚲ 2 restaurants, indoor-outdoor pool, sauna, bar, casino, nightclub, meeting room ▤ DC, MC, V.

$$ ▣ **Björklidens Stugby.** The cabins are small, but the draw here is really the outdoors. You can take out one of the free rowboats, or relax on the lawns and the tree swings. It is 25 km (16 mi) north of Mariehamn. There are outdoor grills and washing machines for guests to use. ⊠ 22240 Hammarland ☎ 018/37800 🖷 018/37801 ⊕ www.bjorkliden. aland.fi ⟿ 14 cabins, 5 apartments ⚲ Beach, fishing, playground ▤ No credit cards ⊘ Closed late Nov.–Mar.

The Outdoors

BIKING Most towns have bikes for rent from about €10 per day (€50 per week). The fine scenery and the terrain, alternately dead flat and gently rolling, make for ideal cycling. The roads are not busy once you leave the highway. **Suomen Retkeilymajajärjestö** (Finnish Youth Hostel Association; ⊠ Yrjönk. 38B, 00100 Helsinki ☎ 09/565–7150 🖷 09/565–7151 ⊕ www.srmnet.org) has reasonably priced bicycle rental–hostel packages for one to two weeks starting in Helsinki. For Åland bicycle routes and tour packages, contact **Ålandsresor Ab** (⊠ PB 62, 22101 Mariehamn ☎ 018/28040 🖷 018/28380 ⊕ www.alandsresor.fi). **Viking Line** (⊠ Storagatan 2, 22100 Mariehamn ☎ 018/26211 🖷 018/26116) is a bike-friendly outfit that also offers cottage rentals in Åland.

BOATING These are marvelous sailing waters for experienced mariners. Boats can be rented through the Åland tourist office.

FISHING Try **Ålandsresor** (⊠ Torggatan 2, 22100 Mariehamn ☎ 018/28040) for fishing packages in the Ålands. **Viking Line** (⊠ Storagatan 2, 22100 Mariehamn ☎ 018/26211) also offers packages for anglers.

Southwestern Coast & the Åland Islands A to Z

AIR TRAVEL
🇫 Finnair ☎ 018/634-500 🖷 018/634-506 ⊕ www.finnair.fi.

AIRPORTS
The region's airports are at Mariehamn and Turku. Both have connections to Helsinki and Stockholm, with service by Finnair.

BOAT & FERRY TRAVEL
Åland is most cheaply reached by boat from Turku and Naantali. Call Silja Line in Turku, Mariehamn, Tampere, or Helsinki. Or call Viking Line in Turku, Mariehamn, Tampere, or Helsinki. Tickets can also be purchased at the harbor.
🇫 Silja Line ☎ 02/335-6244 Turku; 018/16711 Mariehamn; 03/216-2000 Tampere; 09/18041 Helsinki ⊕ www.silja.fi. Viking Line ☎ 02/63311 Turku; 018/26011 Mariehamn; 03/249-0111 Tampere; 09/12351 in Helsinki ⊕ www.vikingline.fi.

BUS TRAVEL
Good bus service connects the capital to the southwest from Helsinki's long-distance bus station, west of the train station off Mannerheimintie. The Helsinki bus station is undergoing major construction that's due to last until 2006. Departure platforms for metropolitan area buses have been moved to the surrounding streets.
🇫 Matkahuolto ⊠ Lauttasaarentie 8 or Box 111, 00200 Helsinki ☎ 0200/4000, €1.15 per call plus local charge 🖷 09/6136-8426 ⊕ www.matkahuolto.com.

CAR TRAVEL
The Helsinki–Turku trip is 166 km (103 mi) on Route E1; signs on E1 will tell you where to turn off for the south-coast towns of Tammisaari

and Hanko. Most of southwestern Finland is well served by public transport, so a car is not necessary.

EMERGENCIES

A major medical center in the region is the Turun Yliopistollinen Keskusairaala (University of Turku Central Hospital). For a dentist, call the Turun Hammaslääkärikeskus (Turku Dental Center).

🚪 **Police, ambulance** ☎ 112. **Turun Hammaslääkärikeskus** ✉ Hämeenk. 2, Turku ☎ 02/269-0670. **Turun Yliopistollinen Keskusairaala** ✉ Kiinamyllynk. 4-8, Turku ☎ 02/313-1222.

TOURS

Turku TouRing is the main regional tourist organization, offering various theme trips and package tours. The Manor Tour is organized from late June to early August and lasts about six hours. The Alvar Aalto tour includes highlights of the famous architect–designer's works in the city and its surroundings and lasts about 8½ hours.

The Tammisaari tourist office has information on boat tours run by Archipelago Tours. You board a restaurant boat and visit the national park; costs range from €12–€24 per person depending on the length of the cruise. See the city tourism Web site, www.ekenas.fi/english or www.surfnet.fi/saaristoristeilyt. You can take a 3½- to 4-hour steamship cruise between Turku and Naantali, which includes a smörgåsbord lunch, or dinner, while drifting around the archipelago (€12–€17 not including meals); cruises run from mid-June to mid-August. Contact the Naantali tourist office or the Steamship Company SS *Ukkopekka*.

🚪 **Steamship Company SS** *Ukkopekka* ✉ Linnank. 38, 20100 Turku ☎ 02/515-3300 🌐 www.ukkopekka.fi. **Turku TouRing** ✉ Aurakatu 4, 20100 Turku ☎ 02/262-7444.

TRAIN TRAVEL

Trains leave Helsinki and other cities for Turku several times a day, and some go directly to the harbor within a short walk of the ferries. For most smaller towns, you must stop at stations along the Helsinki–Turku route and change to a local bus. Bus fares are usually a bit cheaper than train fares.

VISITOR INFORMATION

🚪 **Tourist Information Åland** ✉ Storagatan 8, 22100 Mariehamn ☎ 018/24000 🖨 018/24265 🌐 www.goaland.net. **Hanko** ✉ Raatihuoneentori 5, Box 14, 10901 ☎ 019/220-3411 🖨 019/220-3261 🌐 www.hanko.fi. **Naantali** ✉ Kaivotori 2, 21100 ☎ 02/435-9800 🖨 02/435-0852 🌐 www.naantali.fi. **Tammisaari** Ekenäs ✉ Raatihuoneentori, 10600 ☎ 019/263-2100 🖨 019/263-2212 🌐 www.tammisaari.fi. **Turku TouRing** ✉ Aurak. 4, 20100 Turku ☎ 02/262-7444 🖨 02/233-7673 🌐 www.turkutouring.fi.

THE LAKELANDS

Finland is perhaps best known for its lakes, numbering about 188,000, and you don't need to travel far in this region to appreciate their beauty, whether in winter or summer. Almost every lake, big or small, is fringed with tiny cabins. The lake cabin is a Finnish institution, and until the advent of cheap package tours abroad, nearly every Finnish family vacationed in the same way—in its cabin on a lake.

The towns in this region, while traditionally drawing fewer tourists, have much to offer, especially during summer music and theater festivals. Savonlinna stands out among the towns, not only for its stunning, waterbound views—it is hugged by gigantic Lake Saimaa—but for its cultural life. The month-long Savonlinna Opera Festival in July is one of Finland's—and Europe's—greatest. The quality of the opera, ballet, drama, and instrumental performance here during the annual festival weeks is world-class. Most events are staged at the 14th-century Olavinlinna Castle, splendidly positioned just offshore. To the west, the smaller Hämeenlinna has its own lakeside castle. North of Hämeenlinna, high-tech Tampere has the cultural variety of a city and is nestled between two large lakes. There are small medieval churches scattered through the Lakelands, the most famous of which is the stone church in Hattula, its interior a gallery of medieval painted scenes.

For centuries the lakeland region was a much-contested buffer zone between the warring empires of Sweden and Russia. After visiting the people of the Lakelands, you should have a basic understanding of the Finnish word *sisu* (guts), a quality that has kept Finns independent.

Savonlinna is the best-placed town in the Lakelands and can make a convenient base from which to begin exploring the region. Savonlinna, Tampere, and Hämeenlinna are only short train rides from Helsinki; all three make good day-long excursions from the capital city. The Land of a Thousand Lakes is also perfect for a long or short boat cruise. Travel from one town to the next by boat, take a lake cruise with dinner on board, or simply take a sightseeing cruise.

Canoeing

The Finlandia Canoe Relay takes place in mid-June. Stretching over a grueling seven days, the 400- to 500-km (250- to 310-mi) relay is a real test of endurance. For information on where the race will kick off, contact the Finnish Canoe Association.

Produce Markets

Traditional outdoor markets are held throughout the region, especially on Saturday, and also on weekdays in the summer. Most sell produce, and you'll find the wild mushrooms and berries that are so abundant in this region. The various preserves—jams, compotes, and sauces included—are all delicacies and make good gifts; Finns slather them on thin pancakes. In the autumn you'll find slightly larger markets when towns have their September fairs. These vestiges of harvest festivals are now mostly excuses to hold fun fairs and sip coffee and gobble up doughnuts.

Shopping

Many Lakelands towns have textile workshops or factories, called *Tekstiilitehdas* or *Tekstiilimyymälä*, featuring woven wall hangings and rya rugs (*ryijy* in Finnish). The Lakelands region is the birthplace of famous Finnish glassware, and you'll find the Iittala Glass Center near Hämeenlinna. The soil here yields a rich clay, and ceramics works selling dishes and pottery are ubiquitous.

Windsurfing

There are numerous windsurfing centers on the shores of Lakes Saimaa and Paijanne. For details, contact the Finnish Windsurfing Association.

Savonlinna

46 *335 km (208 mi) northeast of Helsinki.*

One of the larger Lakelands towns, Savonlinna is best known for having the finest castle in all of Finland. The town takes advantage of this stunning attraction by holding major events, such as the annual opera festival, in the castle courtyard. The islands that make up Savonlinna center are linked by bridges. First, stop in at the tourist office for information; then cross the bridge east to the open-air market that flourishes alongside the main passenger quay. From here you can catch the boat to Kuo-

The Lakelands

KEY
↦ Rail Lines

pio and Lappeenranta. In days when waterborne traffic was the major form of transportation, Savonlinna was the central hub of the passenger fleet serving Saimaa, the largest lake system in Europe. Now the lake traffic is dominated by cruise and sightseeing boats, but the quayside still bustles with arrivals and departures every summer morning and evening.

A 10-minute stroll from the quay to the southeast brings you to Savonlinna's most famous site, the castle **Olavinlinna.** First built in 1475 to protect Finland's eastern border, the castle retains its medieval character and is one of Scandinavia's best-preserved historic monuments. Still surrounded by water that once bolstered its defensive strength, the fortress rises majestically out of the lake. Every July the **Savonlinna Opera Festival** (✉ Olavinkatu 27, 57130 ☎ 015/476–750 🖷 015/476–7540 ⊕ www.operafestival.fi) is held in the castle's courtyard, which creates a spellbinding combination of music and surroundings. The festival is a showcase for Finnish opera but it also hosts foreign companies such as the Los Angeles Opera and the Royal Opera. You will need to make reservations well in advance for both tickets and hotel rooms (note higher hotel rates during the festival), as Savonlinna draws many music lovers. The festival also includes arts and crafts exhibits around town. ✉ *Olavinlinna, Olavinlinna* ☎ *015/531–164* ⊕ *www.nba.fi/castles/OLOF* 🖾 *€5 entrance to Olavinlinna* ☉ *June–mid-Aug., daily 10–5; mid-Aug.–May, daily 10–3* ☞ *Guided tours daily on the hr.*

For a glimpse into the history of lake traffic, including the fascinating floating timber trains still a common sight on Saimaa today, visit the **Savonlinnan maakunta museo** (Savonlinna Provincial Museum), to which belong the 19th-century steam schooners, the SS *Salama*, the SS *Mikko*, and the SS *Savonlinna*. ✉ *Riihisaari island, near Olavinlinna, Riihisaari*

☎ *015/571–4712* ⊕ *www.savonlinna.fi/museo* ⊠ €4 ⊘ *Sept.–June, Tues.–Sun. 11–5; July–mid-Aug., daily 11–6. Boats: mid-May–mid-Aug. during museum hrs.*

off the beaten path

VISULAHDEN MATKAILUKESKUS – In Mikkeli, 5 km (3 mi) from Savonlinna, the Visulahti Tourist Center includes a waxworks, an old car museum, and an amusement park.

Where to Stay & Eat

$–$$$ ✕ **Majakka.** The centrally located Majakka feels intimate due to its booths, two aquariums, and many plants. Some tables offer nice views of the adjacent park and the Haukivesi Lake harbor. Try the steak topped with a pepper-and-cream sauce. Reservations are essential during festival season. ⊠ *Satamak. 11, Keskusta* ☎ *015/531–456* ⊟ *AE, DC, MC, V.*

¢–$$$ ✕ **Paviljonki.** Just 1 km (½ mi) from the city center is Paviljonki, the restaurant of the Savonlinna restaurant school. The menu is short but sweet; try the fried vendace with herb-spiced potato salad or the classic pepper steak. The restaurant closes early (8 PM) and has a lunch buffet. ⊠ *Rajalahdenk. 4, Nojanmaa* ☎ *015/574–9303* ⊟ *DC, MC, V.*

$–$$$ 🛏 **Seurahuone.** This hotel in an old town house is near the market and passenger harbor. Rooms are small but comfortable and have modern fittings; be sure to ask for one that overlooks the picturesque harbor. ⊠ *Kauppatori 4–6, 57130* ☎ *015/5731* 🖷 *015/273–918* ⊕ *www.savonhotellit.fi* ⇌ *84 rooms* ♨ *Restaurant, sauna, bar, dance club, nightclub* ⊟ *AE, DC, MC, V.*

$$ 🛏 **Spa Hotel Casino.** A 1960s relic, the Spa Hotel Casino has a restful lakeside location on an island linked to the town by a pedestrian bridge. Rooms are basic with brown cork floors, white walls, and simple furnishings; all except one have a balcony. ⊠ *Kylpylaitoksentie, Kasinonsaari, 57130* ☎ *015/73950* 🖷 *015/272–524* ⇌ *80 rooms* ♨ *Restaurant, pool, sauna, spa, boating* ⊟ *AE, DC, MC, V.*

$–$$ 🛏 **Family Hotel Hospitz.** In the heart of Savonlinna overlooking Saimaa Lake, this YMCA hotel has small, unpretentious rooms. ⊠ *Linnank. 20, 57130* ☎ *015/515–661* 🖷 *015/515–120* ⊕ *www.hospitz.com* ⇌ *21 rooms* ♨ *Sauna* ⊟ *AE, DC, MC, V.*

$ 🛏 **Summer Hotel Vuorilinna.** The simple white rooms of this modern student dorm become hotel rooms in summer. Guests may use the facilities, including the restaurant, of the nearby Casino Spa hotel. ⊠ *Kasinonsaari, 57130* ☎ *015/739–5430 or 015/739–5431* 🖷 *015/272–524* ⇌ *220 rooms* ⊟ *AE, DC, MC, V* ⊘ *Closed Sept.–May.*

The Outdoors

BOATING **Saimaa Sailing Oy** (⊠ Maaherrankatu 21, 53100 Lappeenranta ☎ 05/411–8560) is the biggest boat-rental firm in the Lakeland region. Sailboats and motorboats can be rented on a weekly basis. The base is the handsome, historic coastal town of Lappeenranta, 155 km (96 mi) southeast of Savonlinna. For information on the Saimaa canal, visit the Finnish Maritime Administration's Web site, www.fma.fi.

off the beaten path

OLD MINE OF OUTUKUMPU – This child-friendly complex 187 km (116 mi) north of Savonlinna consists of an amusement park, mining museum, and mineral exhibition. ⊠ *Outokummun Matkailu OY, Kiisuk. 6* ☎ *013/554–794* ⊕ *www.outokummunkaupunki.fi* ⊘ *June–mid-Aug., daily 10–6; mid-Aug.–late Aug., daily 11–5.*

Punkaharju

47 *35 km (22 mi) east of Savonlinna.*

Rising out of the water and separating the Puruvesi and Pihlajavesi lakes, the 8-km (5-mi) ridge of Punkaharju is a geographic wonder that pre-dates the Ice Age. At times the pine-covered rocks narrow to only 25 feet, yet the ridge still manages to accommodate a road and train tracks.

★ Just south of Punkaharju is the **Taidekeskus Retretti** (Retretti Art Center). One of the most popular excursions from Savonlinna, Retretti is accessible via a two-hour boat ride or a 30-minute, 29-km (18-mi) bus trip. It consists of a modern art complex of unique design and has a cavern section built into the Punkaharju ridge. It's also a magnificent setting for concerts in summer and the site of more than 40 different indoor and outdoor scheduled summertime activities. ☎ *015/775–2200* ⊕ *www. retretti.fi* ☜ *€15* ☉ *June and Aug., daily 10–5; July, daily 10–6.*

★ Combine your trip to Retretti with a visit to the nearby **Lusto Finnish Forest Museum.** Every kind of forestry—from the industrial to the artistic—and every aspect of Finland's close relationship with its most abundant natural resource are examined here in imaginative and absorbing displays. ✉ *Lustontie 1, 58450 Punkaharju* ☎ *015/345–1030* ⊕ *www.lusto. fi* ☜ *€7* ☉ *Jan.–Apr., Tues.–Sun. 10–5; May and Sept., daily 10–5; June–Aug., daily 10–7; Oct.–Dec., Tues.–Sun. 10–5* ☉ *Closed last 2 wks in Jan.*

Where to Stay & Eat

$–$$ ✕ **Punkaharju Valtion Hotelli.** Near Retretti, the Punkaharju National Hotel was constructed as a gamekeeper's lodge for Czar Nicholas I in 1845. Enlarged and restored, it is now a restful spot for a meal or an overnight visit. The manor house with small rooms is decorated in the old Finnish country style. The restaurant serves simple local dishes such as fried vendace, the tiny, tasty fish abundant in the lakes. It's a half-hour drive from Savonlinna. ✉ *Punkaharju 2, 58450* ☎ *015/739–611* 🖶 *015/441–784* ⊕ *www.lomaliitto.fi/valtionhotelli* ⇖ *24 rooms* ☍ *Restaurant, 2 tennis courts, sauna, beach* ▭ *DC, MC, V.*

Kuopio

48 *220 km (137 mi) northwest of Punkaharju, 185 km (115 mi) northwest of Savonlinna.*

You'll get a deeper understanding of the meaning of Finland's proximity to Russia and the East in Kuopio, with its Russian Orthodox monastery and museum. The boat from Savonlinna arrives at Kuopio's passenger harbor, where a small evening market holds forth daily from 3 to 10.

Kuopio's tourist office is close to the **Tori** (marketplace). Coined *maailman napa*—the belly-button of the world—Kuopio's market square should be one of your first stops, for it is one of the most colorful outdoor markets in Finland. Try the famous *kalakukko pie* (fish and bacon in a rye crust). ☉ *May–Sept., weekdays 7–5, Sat. 7–3; Oct.–Apr., Mon.–Sat. 7–3.*

★ The **Ortodoksinen Kirkkomuseo** (Orthodox Church Museum) possesses one of the most interesting and unusual collections of its kind. When Karelia (the eastern province of Finland) was ceded to the Soviet Union after World War II, religious art was taken out of the monasteries and brought to Kuopio. The collection is eclectic, and includes one of the most beautiful icon collections in the world, as well as embroidered church textiles. ⊠ *Karjalank. 1, Kuopio* ☎ *017/287–2244* ☜ *€2.50* ☉ *May–June and Aug., Tues.–Sun. 10–4; July, Tues.–Sun. 11–5; Sept.–Apr., weekdays noon–3, weekends noon–5.*

If you were fascinated by the treasures in the Orthodox Church Museum, you'll want to visit the Orthodox convent of Lintula and the **Valamon Luostari** (Valamo Monastery) in Heinävesi, between Varkaus and Joensuu. As a major center for Russian Orthodox religious and cultural life in Finland, the monastery hosts daily services. Precious 18th-century icons and sacred objects are housed in the main church and in the icon conservation center. The Orthodox library is the most extensive in Finland and is open to visitors. A café-restaurant is on the grounds, and very modest hotel and hostel accommodations are available at the monastery. ⊠ *Uusi Valamo, Valamontie 42* ☎ *017/570–111; 017/570–1504 hotel reservations* ⊕ *www.valamo.fi* ☜ *€3.50* ☉ *Mar.–Sept., daily 7 AM–9 PM; Oct.–Feb., daily 8 AM–9 PM; guided tours daily June–Aug., other times by appointment.*

The **Lintulan Luostari** (Lintula Convent) can be reached by boat from Valamo, or you can visit both the convent and the monastery by boat on scenic day excursions from Kuopio. Boat tours from Kuopio are available mid-June to mid-August from Kuopio Roll Cruises Ltd. Tours depart from the bus station, and return by boat to the harbor (Valamo only). ☜ *Tours approximately €50 including boat and ground transportation* ☉ *Convent June 13–Aug.*

The slender **Puijon Näkötorni** (Puijo Tower), 3 km (2 mi) northwest of Kuopio, is best visited at sunset, when the lakes shimmer with reflected light. It has two observation decks and is crowned by a revolving restaurant with marvelous views. ☎ *017/255–5250* ☜ *€2.50* ☉ *May–Aug., Mon.–Sat. 9 AM–10 PM, Sun. noon–8.*

Where to Stay & Eat

$$–$$$ ✕ **Musta Lammas.** Near the passenger harbor, Musta Lammas is in the basement of a brewery founded in 1862. It has been attractively adapted from its beer-cellar days, retaining the original redbrick walls and beer barrels. The specialty here is the smoked *muikku* (vendace) with sour cream and mashed potatoes. ⊠ *Satamak. 4, Keskusta* ☎ *017/581–0458* ▭ *AE, DC, MC, V* ☉ *Closed Sun. No lunch.*

$–$$$ ✕ **Isä Camillo.** This popular restaurant is in a former Bank of Finland building and serves Finnish and international cuisine—steaks and pastas are particularly popular—at reasonable prices. Ask to eat in the bank vault. ⊠ *Kauppak. 25–27, Keskusta/Tori* ☎ *017/581–0450* ▭ *AE, DC, MC, V.*

¢–$$ ✕ **Restaurant Sampo.** In the town center, Sampo was founded in 1931, and its Scandinavian furniture dates from the 1950s. High ceilings and large chandeliers impart an elegant look. Try the muikku, which comes smoked, fried, grilled, or in a stew with pork, potatoes, and onions. ⊠ *Kauppak. 13, Keskusta/Tori* ☎ *017/261–4677* ▭ *AE, DC, MC, V.*

$$–$$$ ▥ **Scandic Hotel Kuopio.** This is the newest and most modern of the local hotels. Rooms are spacious by European standards, with large beds and generous towels. It's on the lakefront and also close to the town. ⊠ *Satamakatu 1, 70100* ☎ *017/195–111* ▤ *017/195–170* ⊕ *www.scandic-hotels.com* ⇆ *134 rooms* ⚇ *2 restaurants, coffee shop, pool, hot tub, sauna, boating, 2 bars, meeting room* ▭ *AE, DC, MC, V.*

$$ ▥ **Iso-Valkeinen Hotel.** On the lakeshore only 5 km (3 mi) from town center, this hotel has large, quiet rooms in four one-story buildings. Several rooms have balconies with views of the nearby lake. ⊠ *Päiväranta, 70420* ☎ *017/539–6100* ▤ *017/539–6555* ⊕ *www.travel.fi/int/ IsoValkeinen* ⇆ *100 rooms with shower* ⚇ *2 restaurants, miniature golf,* *tennis court, pool, sauna, beach, boating, fishing, nightclub* ⊟ *AE, DC, MC, V.*

$$ 🛏 **Spa Hotel Rauhalahti.** About 5 km (3 mi) from town center, Rauhalahti is set near the lakeshore and has no-frills rooms and cabins. A number of amenities cater to sports lovers and families. The hotel has three restaurants, and has live dance music three times a week. ✉ *Katiskaniementie 8, 70700* ☎ *017/473–473* 🖷 *017/473–470* ⊕ *www. rauhalahti.com* 🛏 *106 rooms, 20 apartments, 26 rooms in row houses* ♨ *3 restaurants, tennis court, pool, gym, hot tub, sauna, spa, boating, horseback riding, squash* ⊟ *AE, DC, MC, V.*

Tampere

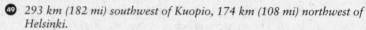

49   *293 km (182 mi) southwest of Kuopio, 174 km (108 mi) northwest of Helsinki.*

Tampere is an industrial center with a difference. From about the year 1000, this was a base from which traders and hunters set out on their expeditions to northern Finland; it was not until 1779 that a Swedish king, Gustav III, founded the city itself. In 1828 a Scotsman named James Finlayson came to the infant city and established a factory for spinning cotton. This was the beginning of "big business" in Finland. The Finlayson firm is today one of the country's major industrial enterprises, but its local factory complex has been converted to house software firms, restaurants, a museum, and a multiplex cinema. Although cotton and textile manufacturers put Tampere on the map as a traditional center of industry, the city is now known for its high-tech companies and large universities. The mobile-phone giant Nokia got its start in a small city of the same name nearby; don't be surprised to see many of the locals strolling down Tampere's compact main street, Hämeenkatu, with a *kännykkä* (cell phone) in use. Tampere's approximately 200,000 inhabitants also nurture an unusually sophisticated cultural environment, with the international festivals of short film (March) and theater (August) among the most popular offerings.

Artful siting is the secret of this factory town. An isthmus little more than a half-mile wide at its narrowest point separates the lakes Näsijärvi and Pyhäjärvi, and at one spot the **Tammerkoski Rapids** provide an outlet for the waters of one to cascade through to the other. Called the Mother of Tampere, these rapids once provided the electrical power on which the town's livelihood depended. Their natural beauty has been preserved in spite of the factories on either bank, and the well-designed public buildings grouped around them enhance their general effect. Don't be surprised to see people fishing for salmon off a bridge in the shadow of a pulp mill, a reminder of conscious efforts since the 1970s to keep the city's environment clean.

The old workers' wooden-housing area of **Pispala,** clustered around the steep slopes of the **Pyynikki Ridge,** is one of the most picturesque urban districts in Finland. The old **observation tower** at the top of the ridge has marvelous views across both lake systems to the north and south. The café at the foot of the tower serves excellent fresh doughnuts daily.

Adding to Tampere's natural beauty is the **Hämeensilta Bridge** in the heart of town, with its four statues by the well-known Finnish sculptor Wäinö Aaltonen. Close to the bridge, near the high-rise Sokos Hotel Ilves, are some old factory buildings that have been restored as shops and boutiques. At Verkatehtaankatu 2, the city **tourist office** offers helpful services such as walking and bus tours and free bicycle rentals. You can also buy a Traveler's Ticket for one or more days (€4 first day plus €3 each additional day), which allows unlimited travel on city buses.

A 1½-km (1-mi) walk west, then north from the heart of Tampere brings you to the **Särkänniemen Huvikeskus** (Särkänniemi Recreation Center), a major recreation complex for both children and adults. Its many attractions include an amusement park, a children's zoo, a planetarium, and a well-planned aquarium with a separate dolphinarium. Within Särkänniemi, the **Sara Hildénin Taidemuseo** (Sara Hildén Art Museum) is a striking example of Finnish architecture, with the works of modern Finnish and international artists, including Chagall, Klee, Miró, and Picasso. Särkänniemi's profile is punctuated by the 550-foot **Näsinneulan Näkötorni** (Näsinneula Observatory Tower), Finland's tallest observation tower and the dominant feature of the Tampere skyline. The top of the tower holds an observatory and a revolving restaurant. The views are magnificent, commanding the lake, forest, and town—the contrast between the industrial maze of Tampere at your feet and the serenity of the lakes stretching out to meet the horizon is unforgettable. ⊠ *Särkänniemi, Särkänniemi* ☎ *03/248–8111; 03/214–3134 museum* ⊕ *www.sarkanniemi.fi* ☒ *Admission (€4) includes the museum and the tower or children's zoo. Dolphinarium, aquarium, and planetarium €5 each, individual rides in the amusement park €3.50; 1-day Särkänniemi Key (pass to all sights and rides in the park) €27; 2 days €34* ☉ *Museum daily 11–6; children's zoo and tower: call for hrs.*

Among the most unusual structures in Tampere is the **Tampere pääkirjasto** (Tampere Central Library), nicknamed "Metso" (wood grouse) for its unusual shape. Designed by the famous Pietilä couple, it houses an exhibit celebrating the *Moomintroll* books of Finnish author Tove Jansson. ⊠ *Pirkankatu 2, Hämeenpuisto* ☎ *03/314–614* ⊕ *www.tampere. fi* ☉ *Sept.–May, weekdays 9:30–8, Sat. 9:30–3; June–Aug., weekdays 9:30–7, Sat. 9:30–3.*

While in western Tampere, be sure to visit one of the city's best museums, the **Amurin Työläiskorttelimuseo** (Amuri Museum of Workers' Housing), which consists of more than 30 apartments in a collection of wooden houses, plus a sauna, a bakery, a haberdashery, and more from the 1880s to the 1970s. Its cozy café has garden seating in summer and serves fresh bread baked on the premises. ⊠ *Makasiininkatu 12, Amuri* ☎ *03/3146–6690* ☒ *€4* ☉ *Mid-May–mid-Sept., Tues.–Sun. 10–6.*

Not far from Amuri Museum, in the old Tampella factory area, is the **Museokeskus Vapriikki** (Museum Center Vapriikki), which consolidates the collections of five separate museums (700,000 pieces) to illustrate the city's role in Finnish industrial history. Housed in a former textile and turbine factory complex that dates from the 1880s, the permanent exhibit focuses on local history, while other displays cover archaeological finds and modern art. The center also includes an excellent café and gift shop. ⊠ *Veturiaukio 4, Tampella* ☎ *03/3146–6966* ⊕ *www.tampere. fi/vapriikki* ☒ *€4* ☉ *Tues. and Thurs.–Sun. 10–6, Wed. 11–8.*

The **Lenin Museo** (Lenin Museum), the only one of its kind left in the world, occupies the hall where Lenin and Stalin first met; photos, memorabilia, and temporary exhibits document the life of Lenin and the Russian Revolution. ⊠ *Hämeenpuisto 28, 3rd fl., Hämeenpuisto* ☎ *03/276–8100* ⊕ *www.tampere.fi/culture/lenin* ☒ *€2* ☉ *Weekdays 9–6, weekends 11–4.*

At the foot of the Pyynikki ridge is the **Pyynikin Kesäteatteri** (Pyynikki Summer Theater ⊠ Joselininniemi, Pyynikki, Pyynikki ☎ 03/216–0300), with an outdoor revolving auditorium that can be moved, even with a full load of spectators, to face any one of the sets. It's open mid-June to mid-August. On the east side of town is the modern **Kalevan Kirkko** (Kaleva Church), a soaring monument to light and space designed by

Reima (1923–93) and Reili (b. 1926) Pietilä, the famous architect couple who also designed the Tampere city library, "Metso." ⊠ *Liisanpuisto 1, Kaleva* ☉ *May–Aug., daily 9–6; Sept.–Apr., daily 11–3.*

★ Most buildings in Tampere, including the cathedral, are comparatively modern. The **Tuomiokirkko** (Cathedral) was built in 1907 and houses some of the best-known masterpieces of Finnish art, including Magnus Encknell's fresco *The Resurrection* and Hugo Simberg's *Wounded Angel* and *Garden of Death.* ⊠ *Tuomiokirkonkatu 3, Keskusta* ☉ *May–Aug., daily 9–6; Sept.–Apr., daily 11–3.*

> **off the beaten path**
>
> **HAIHARAN NUKKE-JA PUKUMUSEO –** This unusual museum is housed in the Hatanpää Mansion overlooking Pyhäjärvi Lake, about 2 mi southwest of the city center. The Haihara Doll and Costume Museum exhibits from a collection of nearly 5,000 dolls from all over the world, dating from the 12th to the 20th centuries. The tiniest are Mexican fleas in festival attire. Costumes are mainly Finnish from the 19th century. ⊠ *Hatanpää kartano, Hatanpäänpuistokuja 1, Haihara* ☎ *03/222–6261* ⊕ *user.sgic.fi/~haihara* ⊠ *€5* ☉ *Mid-Feb.–Apr., Oct., and Nov., weekends 11–5; May–Sept., Tues.–Sun. 11–5.*

Where to Stay & Eat

$$–$$$$ ✕ **Astor.** Here you'll find a moderately priced brasserie menu and a more expensive selection on the main menu. Parquet floors, soft yellow and red walls, and candlelight lend a touch of elegance. In the restaurant, try the rosettes of salmon with a red wine–onion sauce, or the roast duck in a saffron-calvados-nut sauce. Brasserie favorites include smoked-reindeer quiche and mushroom-vegetable turnovers. ⊠ *Aleksis Kivenk. 26, Keskusta* ☎ *03/260–5700* ⚙ *Reservations essential* ▭ *DC, MC, V.*

$$–$$$$ ✕ **Tiiliholvi.** A romantic cellar in an art nouveau building with a colorful past, Tiiliholvi serves Finnish haute cuisine and the best wine selection in town. Try the wild mushroom soup and reindeer with a cranberry and bread-cheese sauce, then indulge in a crème brûlée. ⊠ *Kauppak. 10, Keskusta* ☎ *03/272–0231* ▭ *AE, DC, MC, V* ☉ *Closed Sun.*

$–$$$$ ✕ **Bodega Salud.** Salud mixes Spanish specialties with classics such as lamb chops and steaks and unconventional dishes such as kangaroo. A salad bar with cheese and fruit is a favorite. Try the tapas prix fixe lunch. ⊠ *Tuomiokirkonkatu 19, Keskusta* ☎ *03/366–4460* ⊕ *www. bodega-salud.fi* ⚙ *Reservations essential* ▭ *DC, MC, V.*

$–$$$ ✕ **Harald.** The Viking details and the hearty fare make this quirky restaurant in the heart of the city a nice change of pace. Choose from stews and soups of fish and game at sturdy wooden tables, along with beer served in earthenware mugs. ⊠ *Hämeenkatu 23, Keskusta* ☎ *03/ 213–8380* ▭ *AE, DC, MC, V.*

$–$$$ ✕ **Tillikka.** Long known as a hangout for leftist intellectuals, Tillikka now prepares hearty meals overlooking the rapids for a variety of political persuasions. The most famous dish is *pyttipannu,* a tasty hash of sausage, onion, and potatoes topped by an egg and served with pickled beets; it is best washed down with one of the local brews. The restaurant is housed in the same building as the city theater. ⊠ *Teatteritalo, Hämeenkatu 14 Keskusta* ☎ *03/254–4724* ▭ *AE, DC, MC, V.*

$–$$ ✕ **Laterna.** In a czarist-era hotel and once the haunt of artists and writers, Laterna specializes in Russian fare with a Finnish twist. Live music on the weekends can include the famous Finnish tango. Classic Russian dishes include vorschmack and mushroom-filled *pelmeny* (Russian ravioli). ⊠ *Puutarhakatu 11, Keskusta* ☎ *03/272–0241* ▭ *AE, DC, MC, V.*

$$$$ ▥ **Sokos Hotel Ilves.** Soaring above a gentrified area of old warehouses near city center, this 18-story hotel is Tampere's tallest building. All rooms above the sixth floor have spectacular views of the city and Pyhäjärvi and Näsijärvi lakes. ⊠ *Hatanpään valtatie 1, 33100* ☎ *03/262–6262* ☐*03/262–6264* ⊕*www.sokoshotels.fi* ⤴*325 rooms, 9 suites* ♨*4 restaurants, pool, gym, hot tub, 3 saunas, nightclub, no-smoking rooms* ☐ *AE, DC, MC, V.*

$$$–$$$$ ▥ **Sokos Hotel Tammer.** A beautiful historic hotel overlooking a park, the Hotel Tammer has a grand dining room. Guest rooms are individually decorated and have modern fittings. ⊠ *Satakunnankatu 13, 33100* ☎ *03/262–6265* ☐ *03/262–6266* ⤴ *87 rooms* ♨ *Restaurant, nightclub, no-smoking rooms* ☐ *AE, DC, V.*

$$$ ▥ **Scandic Hotel Tampere.** This Scandic property in the heart of the city center, opposite the train station, caters to business travelers and tourists. ⊠ *Hämeenkatu 1, 33100* ☎ *03/244–6111* ☐ *03/2446–2211* ⤴ *124 rooms, 3 suites* ♨ *2 restaurants, café, 3 saunas, bar, no-smoking rooms* ☐ *AE, DC, MC, V.*

¢ ▥ **Iltatähti Apartment Hotel.** This centrally located hotel has pleasant and unpretentious accommodations at budget rates. ⊠ *Tuomiokirkonkatu 19, 33100* ☎ *03/315–161* ☐ *03/3151–6262* ⊕ *www.hoteliltatahti.fi* ⤴ *90 rooms, 33 with bath* ♨ *No smoking* ☐ *AE, DC, MC, V.*

Nightlife & the Arts

Tampere has a lively pub and beer bar scene. Don't be surprised if you see a quiz competition going on in one of the local pubs, a popular Tampere pastime, particularly in the winter. The Irish theme is at its most popular in Tampere at **O'Connell's** (⊠ Ratatienkatu 24, Keskusta ☎ 03/222–7032) with occasional live music. Try the in-house brew at **Plevna** (⊠ Itäinenk. 8, Keskusta ☎ 03/260–1200), timing your visit to coincide with a performance by the German-style brass band. The English-style **Salhojankadun Pub** (⊠ Salhojank. 29, Keskusta ☎ 03/255–3376) is an old favorite. The converted post office is now the family-run **Wanha Posti** (⊠ Hämeenk. 13, Keskusta ☎ 03/223–3007), lauded for its own brews and other local brands.

For live jazz music, visit **Paapan Kapakka** (⊠ Koskikatu 9, Keskusta ☎ 03/211–0037). Stroll down from Koskikeskus to Kehräsaari island, with its old brick buildings converted to shops and restaurants, to **Fall's Cafe** (⊠ Kehräsaari, Keskusta ☎ 03/223–0061), in a cozy cellar, with central European beers on tap. Tampere's most unique bar, **Telakka** (⊠ Tullikamarin aukio 3, Keskusta ☎ 03/225–0700), is in an old granary. Founded by a cooperative of actors, who also serve tables, it has live music and a theater upstairs. There's a menu of pub food and a grill on the terrace in summer. The **Ilves Night Club** (⊠ Hotel Ilves, Hatanpään valtatie 1, Keskusta ☎ 03/262–6124) is one of the most popular night spots in Tampere, drawing a mixed crowd, professionals, and students, for dancing and drinks.

> **off the beaten path**
>
> **RUNOILIJAN TIE –** One of the most popular excursions from Tampere is the Poet's Way steam boat tour along Lake Näsijärvi. The Tarjanne, built in 1908, passes through the agricultural parish of Ruovesi, where J. L. Runeberg, Finland's national poet, once lived. Shortly before the boat docks at Virrat, you'll pass through the straits of Visuvesi, where many artists and writers spend their summers. ⊠ *Laukontori 10A 3, 33100 Tampere* ☎ *03/212–4804* ⊕ *www.finnishsilverline.com/ poetsway* ▨ *Same-day round-trip fare for boat–bus package €32 Tampere–Ruovesi* ⊙ *June–Aug. 17, Tues., Thurs., and Sat.*
>
> **ÄHTÄRI –** Not far north of Virrat is Ähtäri, where you will find Finland's first wildlife park in beautiful countryside; it has a "holiday village," a good hotel, and recreation facilities.

Hämeenlinna

50 *78 km (49 mi) southeast of Tampere, 98 km (61 mi) north of Helsinki (via Hwy. 12).*

The big castle and small museums of Hämeenlinna make this town a good place for a day trip. It's a good point from which to visit nearby gems such as the **Iittala Lasikeskus** (Iittala Glass Center), which offers museum tours and has a shop. Top designers produce the magnificent glass; the seconds in the factory shop are bargains you won't find elsewhere. ⊠ *14500 Iittala* ☎ *0204/396–230* ≊ *€2* ⊙ *Museum May–Aug., daily 10–6; Sept.–Apr., daily 10–5; shop May–Aug., daily 9–8; Sept.–Apr., daily 10–6.*

Hämeenlinna's secondary school has educated many famous Finns, among them composer Jean Sibelius (1865–1957). The only surviving timber house in the town center is the **Sibeliuksen syntymäkoti** (Sibelius birthplace), a modest dwelling built in 1834. The museum staff will play your favorite Sibelius CD as you tour the rooms, one of which contains the harmonium Sibelius played as a child. ⊠ *Hallitusk. 11, Keskusta* ☎ *03/621–2755* ≊ *€2.50* ⊙ *May–Aug., daily 10–4; Sept.–Apr., daily noon–4.*

Swedish crusaders began construction on **Hämeen Linna** (Häme Castle) in the 13th century to strengthen and defend the Swedish position in the region. What began as a fortified camp evolved over the centuries into a large castle of stone and brick. In modern times, the castle, one of Finland's oldest, has served as a granary and a prison, and it is now restored and open to the public for tours and exhibitions. The castle sits on the lakeshore, 1 km (½ mi) north of Hämeenlinna's town center. Tours in English take place every hour in the summer and are available every hour in winter by appointment only. ⊠ *Kustaa III:n k. 6, Hämeenlinna* ☎ *03/675–6820* ≊ *€5 includes guided tour* ⊙ *May–mid-Aug., daily 10–6; mid-Aug.–Apr., daily 10–4.*

The **Hämeenlinnan Taidemuseo** (Hämeenlinna Art Museum), housed partly in a 19th-century granary designed by Carl Ludvig Engel, exhibits Finnish art from the 19th and 20th centuries and foreign art from the 17th century; works evacuated from Vyborg in 1939 form the core of the collection. ⊠ *Viipurintie 2, Keskusta* ☎ *03/621–2669* ⊙ *Tues., Wed., and Fri.–Sun. noon–6, Thurs. noon–8.*

> **off the beaten path**

PYHÄN RISTIN KIRKKO – Six kilometers (3½ mi) north of Hämeenlinna is Hattula, whose Church of the Holy Cross is the most famous of Finland's medieval churches. Its interior is a fresco gallery of biblical scenes whose vicious little devils and soulful saints are as vivid and devious as when they were first painted around 1510. ⊠ *Hattula* ☎ *03/672–3383 during opening hrs; 03/631–1540 all other times* ≊ *€2.50* ⊙ *Mid-May–mid-Aug., daily 11–5; open at other times by appointment.*

Where to Stay & Eat

$$–$$$ ✕ **Huviretki.** In the heart of the city, Huviretki has specialties such as "vineyard lamb," a fillet of lamb with garlic potatoes, zucchini, mushrooms, tomatoes, and garlic cloves; and salmon and crayfish with a Gouda cheese sauce. There are many salads on the menu. ⊠ *Cumulus Hotel, Raatihuoneenk. 16–18, Keskusta* ☎ *03/648–8210* ▭ *AE, DC, MC, V.*

$–$$$ ✕ **Piiparkakkutalo.** In a renovated old-timber building, Piiparkakkutalo specializes in meat dishes; try the chateaubriand with cream cognac sauce and blue-cheese potatoes. ⊠ *Kirkkorinne 2, Keskusta* ☎ *03/648–040* ▭ *AE, DC, MC, V.*

★ **$$$**　　🔲 **Rantasipi Aulanko.** One of Finland's top hotels sits on the lakeshore
Fodor'sChoice　in a beautifully landscaped park 6½ km (4 mi) from town. All rooms
★　　have wall-to-wall carpeting and overlook the golf course, park, or lake.
　　✉ *13210 Hämeenlinna* ☎ *03/658–801* 🖨 *03/658–1922* ⊕ *www.*
rantasipi.fi ↪ *245 rooms* ⚒ *Restaurant, 18-hole golf course, tennis court,*
indoor pool, massage, sauna, boating, horseback riding, nightclub, no-
smoking rooms ▤ *AE, DC, MC, V.*

The Outdoors

SKIING　The **Finlandia Ski Race Office** (✉ Urheilukeskus, 15110 Lahti ☎ 03/816–
813 ⊕ www.finlandiahiihto.fi) has details on events. In February, you can
attend the **Finlandia-hiihto**, a 60-km (37-mi) ski race. The **Lahti Ski Games**
(☎ 03/816–810 ⊕ www.lahtiskigames.com) take place in March.

en route　If you're driving between Helsinki and Hämeenlinna along Highway
12, consider stopping at **Riihimäki**, home of the **Suomen Lasimuseo**
(Finnish Glass Museum); it's 35 km (22 mi) south of Hämeenlinna.
Here you can examine an outstanding display on the history of glass
from early Egyptian times to the present, artfully arranged in an old
glass factory. In a manor house in a park nearby, try **Lehmushovi**
(✉ Lehmustie 5 ☎ 019/738–946) for dependable Finnish and
international cuisine. ✉ *Tehtaankatu 23, Riihimäki* ☎ *019/741–*
7494 ⊕ *www.riihimaki.fi* 🎟 *€2.50* ◷ *May–Aug., daily 10–6;*
Sept.–Dec. and Feb.–Apr., Tues.–Sun. 10–6.

Lakelands A to Z

AIRPORTS
Airports in the Lakelands are at Tampere, Mikkeli, Jyväskylä, Varkaus,
Lappeenranta, Savonlinna, Kuopio, and Joensuu. Flight time to the
Savonlinna area from Helsinki is 40 minutes. All airports are served by
Finnair's domestic service.

BUS TRAVEL
Buses are the best form of public transport into the region, with frequent
connections to lake destinations from most major towns. It is a six-hour
ride from Helsinki to Savonlinna.

CAR TRAVEL
The region is vast, so the route you choose will depend on your desti-
nation. You can drive inland or follow the coast to the eastern lake re-
gion from the capital. A drive to Kuopio could take you either through
Tampere to Jyväskyla or to the east, close to the border with Russia.
Consult The Automobile and Touring Club of Finland or tourist boards
for route advice.

The Joensuu–Kuopio–Lahti–Tampere road belt will transport you
quickly from one major point to the next, but if you are going to be
taking a lake vacation you will usually finish your journey on small roads.
The last stretch to the *mökki* (cabin) may be unpaved. You will need a
detailed map to find most mökkis, which tend to be tucked away in well-
hidden spots.
🚗 **The Automobile and Touring Club of Finland** ✉ Hämeentie 105A, PL 35, 00551
Helsinki ☎ 09/7258–4400 ⊕ www.autoliitto.fi.

EMERGENCIES
The nationwide emergency number is ☎ 112; it can be used to call po-
lice and ambulance services. A major hospital is Tampere Keskussairaala
(Tampere Central Hospital). For dental care, call Hammaslääkäri

Päivystys. Tampereen Yliopistollinen Sairaala (TAYS) is the Tampere University hospital.

🔢 **Hammaslääkäri Päivystys** ☎ 0400/625–555. **Tampereen Yliopistollinen Sairaala (TAYS)** ✉ Teiskontie 35, Tampere ☎ 03/247–5111.

TOURS

Avid canoeists should contact the Finnish Canoe Federation. Almost all of its 67 clubs arrange guided tours; canoes are rented at about €30 per day. Lintusalon Melontakeskus gives numerous lakeland canoe tours; Ikaalinen Tourist Service runs white-water trips and canoe safaris in the region; Lieksan Matkailu Oy is another river-trip outfitter; and Mika's Canoeing Service designs tailor-made canoe tours.

A program of Friendly Finland Tours, available through travel agencies in Finland and abroad, offers escorted packages that include stops in the Lakelands. The three-day "Saimaa Lake Tour" and the seven-day "Scenic Tour" both start in Helsinki. Brochures are available from the Finland Travel Bureau in Helsinki.

There are dozens of boat-tour companies operating in the Lakelands; contact the Finnish Tourist Board or local tourist offices in the region for a complete list as well as details of routes. Kuopio Roll Cruises Ltd. offers tours to the Lintulan Luostari (Lintula Convent).

🔢 **Finland Travel Bureau** ✉ Kaivokatu 10A, Box 319, 00101 Helsinki ☎ 09/18261 ⊕ www.ftb.net. **Finnish Silverline and Poets' Way Tours** ✉ Laukontori 10A 3, 33200 Tampere ☎ 03/212–4804 ⊕ finnishsilverline.com. **Ikaalinen Tourist Service** ✆ Box 33, 39501 Ikaalinen ☎ 03/450–1221. **Kuopio Roll Cruises Ltd.** ✉ Matkustajasatama, 70100 Kuopio ☎ 017/266–2466 🖥 017/266–2464. **Lieksan Matkailu Oy** ✉ Pielisentie 7, 81700 Lieksa ☎ 013/689–4050 ⊕ www.lieksa.fi. **Wild Canoe** ✉ Visulahti Camping, 50180 Mikkeli ☎0500/840–362 ⊕www.wildcanoe.com. **Saimaa Lakeland** ✉Roll Cruises of Kuopio Ltd., Matkustajasatama, 70100 Kuopio ☎ 017/266–2466. **Western Lakeland and Lake Päijänne Tour** ✉ Lake Päijänne Cruises, Pellonpää, 40820 Haapaniemi ☎ 014/618–885 or 014/263–447.

TRAIN TRAVEL

Trains run from Helsinki to Lahti, Mikkeli, Imatra, Lappeenranta, Joensuu, and Jyväskylä. There is sleeping-car service to Joensuu and Kuopio and to Savonlinna. The trip from Helsinki to Savonlinna takes 5½ hours.

VISITOR INFORMATION

🔢 Tourist Information **Hämeenlinna** ✉ Raatihuoneenk. 11, 13100 ☎ 03/621–3373 ⊕ www.hameenmatkailu.fi. **Heinola** ✉ Matkailutoimisto Kauppakatu 12, 18100 ☎ 03/849–3615 ⊕ www.tournee.fi. **Imatra** ✉ Koskenparras 6, 55120 ☎ 05/681–2500 ⊕ www.travel.imatra.fi. **Joensuu** ✉ Karelia Expert Tourist Info, Koskik. 5, 80100 ☎ 013/267–5300. **Jyväskylä** ✉ Asemak. 6, 40100 ☎ 624–903 or 624–904 ⊕ www.jyvaskyla.fi. **Kuopio** ✉ Haapaniemenk. 17, 70110 ☎ 017/182–584 ⊕ www.kuopioinfo.fi. **Lahti** ✉ Aleksanterink. 13, 15110 ☎ 03/877–677 ⊕ www.lahtitravel.fi. **Lappeenranta** ✉ Marketplace, Lievarinkatu 1, PL 113, 53101 ☎ 05/667–788 ⊕ www.lappeenranta.fi. **Mikkeli** ✉ Porrassalmenkatu 15, 50100 ☎ 015/194–3900 ⊕ www.travel.fi/mikkeli. **Savonlinna** ✉Puistokatu 1, 57100 ☎015/517–510 ⊕www.savonlinnatravel.com. **Tampere** ✉Verkatehtaank. 2, PL 487, 33100 ☎ 03/3146–6800 ⊕ www.tampere.fi.

LAPLAND

Lapland is often called Europe's last wilderness, a region of endless forests, fells, and great silences. Settlers in Finnish Lapland walked gently and left the landscape almost unspoiled. Now easily accessible by plane, train, or bus, this Arctic outpost offers comfortable hotels and modern amenities, yet you won't have to go very far to find yourself in an almost primordial setting.

The oldest traces of human habitation in Finland have been found in Lapland, and hordes of Danish, English, and even Arabian coins indicate the existence of trade activities many centuries ago. Until the 1930s, Lapland was still largely unexploited, and any trip to the region was an expedition. Lapland's isolation ended when the Canadian-owned Petsamo Nickel Company completed the great road connecting Rovaniemi with the Arctic Sea, now known as the Arctic Highway. Building activities increased along this route, the land was turned and sown, and a few hotels were built to cater to an increasing number of visitors.

Only about 4,000 native Sámi (also sometimes known as Lapps) still live in Lapland; the remainder of the province's population of 203,000 is Finnish. The Sámi population makes up a small minority in the northern regions of Finland, Norway, Sweden, and Russia. Though modern influences have changed many aspects of their traditional way of life, there is still a thriving Sámi culture. Sámi crafts make use of natural resources, reflected in skilled woodwork, bonework, and items made of reindeer pelts. In March, on Maria's Day, a traditional church festival takes place in Hetta, a village near Enontekiö. It is particularly colorful, attended by many Sámi in their most brilliant dress, and usually has reindeer racing or lassoing competitions. Contact the Enontekiö tourist office for details.

Summer in Lapland has the blessing of round-the-clock daylight, and beautiful weather typically accompanies the nightless days. In early fall the colors are so fabulous that the Finns have a special word for it: *ruskaa*. If you can take the intense but dry cold, winter in Lapland is full of fascinating experiences, from the northern lights to reindeer roundups. Depending on how far north of the Arctic Circle you travel, the sun might not rise for several weeks around midwinter. But it is never pitch-black; light reflects from the invisible sun below the horizon even during midday, and there is luminosity from the ever-present snow.

Finns cherish the outdoors no matter what the light. Here it is the wilderness that's the draw. For although the cities have fine facilities and cultural events, it is the lonely moors with the occasional profile of a reindeer herd crossing, the clear forest streams, and the bright trail of the midnight sun reflected on a lake's blackest waters that leave the most indelible impressions.

While you're here sample such local foods as cloudberries; lingonberries; fresh salmon; and reindeer, served smoked and sautéed, roasted, and as steaks. Restaurants serve hearty soups, crusty rye bread, delicious baked Lappish cheese, and dark brewed coffee in wooden cups with meals—you won't leave hungry.

Crafts

You'll find unique souvenirs in Lapland, and you may learn to love the traditional Sámi crafts, both functional and attractive. Keep an eye out for the camping knives with beautifully carved bone or wooden handles, birch mugs, colorful weaving and embroidered mittens and gloves, felt shoes, and birch-bark baskets and rucksacks.

Summer Sports

In summer, canoeing is a popular pursuit; you can take canoe trips on Lake Inari, or, for the intrepid, forays over the rapids of the Ivalojoki River. Summer golf takes on such unusual guises as midnight-sun golf and Green Zone Tornio-Haparanda Golf—you'll play 9 holes in Finland and the other 9 in Sweden **Meri-Lapin Golfklubi** (✉ Narantie, 95400 Tornio ☎ 016/431–711 🖷 016/431–710 ⊕ www.golf.fi/mlgk). In the summer it is so light that you can play during the night. The course is famous for its one-hour putt.

Winter Sports

Winter sports reign here, from the quirky ice golfing to the traditional cross-country skiing. Ylläs, Levi, and Saariselkä are Lapland's leading centers for both downhill and cross-country skiing; Kiilopää is known for cross-country skiing. Other popular resorts include Pyhä, Luosto, Salla, Suomu, Pallas and Olos. In Western Lapland, the **Levi resort** (⊠ Levi Tourist Info, Levin Portti, 99130 Sirkka ☎ 016/639–3300 ⊕ www.levi.fi) has 45 slopes and 19 lifts in an extensive fell area. **Pyhä and Luosto** (⊠ Pyhä-Luosto Travel Ltd., Laukotie 1, 99555 Luosto ☎ 0207/303–020 ⊕ www.pyha-luostomatkailu.fi), in the Pyhätunturi National Park in southern Lapland, have cross-country and downhill skiing, and snowboarding possibilities. In the middle of the fells near Urho Kekkonen National Park, **Saariselkä** (⊠ Pohjois-Lapin Matkailu, Saariseläntie 1, 99830 Saariselkä ☎ 016/668–402 ⊕ www.saariselka. fi) is an international tourist center with a network of well-marked hiking, skiing, and biking trails. Downhill and cross-country skiing are popular at **Ruka** (⊠ Rukakeskus, 93825 Rukatunturi ☎ 08/860–0200 ⊕ www.ruka.fi), which is also one of the most unrestricted areas in the world for snowmobiling.

Rovaniemi

▶ ⑤ *832 km (516 mi) north of Helsinki.*

The best place to start your tour of Lapland is Rovaniemi, where the Ounas and Kemi rivers meet almost on the Arctic Circle. Often called the Gateway to Lapland, Rovaniemi is also the administrative hub and communications center of the province.

If you're expecting an Arctic shantytown, you're in for a surprise. After Rovaniemi was all but razed by the retreating German army in 1944, Alvar Aalto directed the rebuilding and devised an unusual street layout: from the air, the layout mimics the shape of reindeer antlers! During rebuilding, the population rose from 8,000 to its present-day size of around 35,500—so be prepared for a contemporary city, university town, and cultural center on the edge of the wilderness.

One of the town's architectural wonders is **Lappia-Talo** (Lappia House), the Aalto-designed concert and congress center that houses the world's northernmost professional theater. ⊠ *Hallitusk. 11, Keskusta* ☎ *016/ 322–2495 ticket office* ⊙ *Closed June–Aug.*

One of the best ways to tune in to the culture of Finland's far north is to visit the **Arktikum** (Arctic Research Center), 1 km (½ mi) north of Lappia-Talo. The Arktikum houses the Lapland Provincial Museum, whose riveting exhibit on Sámi life tells the full story of their survival. ⊠ *Pohjoisranta 4, Ratantaus* ☎ *016/317–840* ⊕ *www.arktikum.fi* 🗃 *€9* ⊙ *May–mid-June, daily 10–6; mid-June–mid-Aug., daily 9–7; mid-late Aug., daily 10–6; Sept.–Apr., Tues.–Sun. 10–6.*

Rovaniemi's real claim to fame is that Santa Claus lives in its suburbs, as reflected in the growing number of tourist attractions in the area. The **SantaPark** Christmas theme park is set deep inside a rocky cavern and offers a Magic Sleigh Ride, a Puppet Circus, and a Christmas Carrousel, among other attractions. Take the Santa Train from the Park to **Joulupukin Pajakylä** (Santa Claus Village) and stop along the way at the Reindeer Park to see Santa's sleigh team. Sámi in native dress and reindeer hauling sleighs enhance the authenticity of the village. (This is likely to be the only place where your children will be able to pet a reindeer—the ones you'll see in the wild are shy.) Here gifts can be bought in midsummer for shipping at any time of year, and postcards can be

mailed from the special Arctic Circle post office. There's also a complete souvenir shopping complex, plus the impressive mountains of mail that pour in from children all over the world. And yes, he does answer every letter. The village is closed when he is abroad, on December 25. ✉ *96930 Arctic Circle* ☎ *016/333–0000 park; 016/356–2157 village* ⊕ *www.santapark.com* ✉ *Park €20, family ticket (3–6 persons) €50, village free* ☉ *Call for hrs.*

off the beaten path

SALLA REINDEER PARK – In winter, visitors of all ages can obtain a reindeer driver's license and feed the animals at this farm 150 km (93 mi) east of Rovaniemi. ✉ *Hautajärventie 111 98900 Salla* ☎ *016/837–771* ⊕ *www.sallareindeerpark.fi* ✉ *License €10* ☉ *Daily 10–6.*

Where to Stay & Eat

$$$ ✕ **Ounasvaaran Pirtit.** This is one of Rovaniemi's best restaurants, focusing on traditional Finnish and Lapp food. Try the sautéed salmon with cream and boiled potatoes or sautéed reindeer with mashed potatoes. There is a buffet and a set menu only. ✉ *Antinmukka 4, Ounasvaara* ☎ *016/369–056* ⌕ *Reservations essential* ▭ *AE, DC, MC, V.*

$–$$$ ✕ **Fransmanni.** This restaurant, with a nice view of the Kemijoki River, specializes in different types of international, Finnish, and Lapp casserole dishes. Try the grilled veal fillet in mustard cream sauce. Service is friendly. ✉ *Vaakuna Hotel, Koskik. 4, Keskusta* ☎ *016/332–211* ▭ *AE, DC, MC, V.*

$$–$$$ ✕▭ **Sky Hotel Rovaniemi.** On a hilltop 3 km (2 mi) from the town, Sky Hotel is the top choice in Rovaniemi for views, hiking, and skiing—both slalom and cross-country—especially for those with a car. Some rooms have bathtubs, a rarity, and 47 rooms have saunas. Larger rooms with

kitchenettes are available for families. At the restaurant dine on roasted whitefish or arctic char with cranberry butter sauce, and try one of the desserts based on local fruits such as cloudberries. ✉ *96400 Rovaniemi* ☎ *016/335–3311* 📠 *016/318–789* ⊕ *www.laplandhotels.com* 🛏 *58 rooms, 11 apartments* ⚲ *Restaurant, sauna, hiking, cross-country skiing, 2 bars* 🖃 *AE, DC, MC, V.*

$$ 🏨 **Rantasipi Pohjanhovi.** Stretched along the shore of the Kemijoki River, this hotel combines modern amenities with quick access to the moors. Rooms are large, with low ceilings and big windows. Some are white-walled with autumn-tone upholstery and wood trim, while others have black walls with light upholstery—for those who have trouble sleeping during the days of the midnight sun. ✉ *Pohjanpuistikko 2, 96200* ☎ *016/33711* 📠 *016/313–997* ⊕ *www.rantasipi.fi* 🛏 *212 rooms, 4 suites* ⚲ *Restaurant, café, sauna, boating, fishing, squash, bar, casino, meeting room* 🖃 *AE, DC, MC, V.*

$$ 🏨 **Scandic Hotel Rovaniemi.** This modern hotel is in the heart of Rovaniemi, five minutes from the railway station. Guest rooms are simply furnished and comfortable. Nine rooms have individual saunas and eight have Jacuzzis. ✉ *Koskik. 23, 96200* ☎ *016/4606–000* 📠 *016/4606–666* ⊕ *www.scandic-hotels.com* 🛏 *167 rooms* ⚲ *2 restaurants, 3 saunas, bar, pub, nightclub, meeting room, no-smoking rooms* 🖃 *AE, DC, MC, V.*

$$ 🏨 **Sokos Hotel Vaakuna.** The Vaakuna has small but comfortable guest rooms painted in pastel shades. Some are no-smoking. The lobby is dotted with armchairs and has marble floors. There are two restaurants: Fransmanni and Rosso, the latter of which turns out pastas and pizzas. ✉ *Koskikatu 4, 96200 Rovaniemi* ☎ *016/332 211* 📠 *016/332–2199* ⊕ *www.sokoshotels.fi* 🛏 *157 rooms, 2 suites* ⚲ *2 restaurants, gym, 3 saunas, pub, nightclub* 🖃 *AE, DC, MC, V.*

$ 🏨 **Best Western Hotel Oppipoika.** Modern furnishings and central location are two of the attractions of this small hotel. Rooms have pressed birch paneling and are well lit. ✉ *Korkalonk. 33, 96200 Rovaniemi* ☎ *016/338–8111* 📠 *016/346–969* ⊕ *www.bestwestern.com* 🛏 *40 rooms, 1 suite* ⚲ *Restaurant, indoor pool, gym, sauna, meeting room, no-smoking rooms* 🖃 *AE, DC, MC, V.*

The Outdoors

HIKING **Genimap** (✉ PL 106, 01600 Vantaa ☎ 0201/34040 📠 0201/340449 ⊕ www.genimap.fi), provides maps of marked trails in Lapland.

Sodankylä & the Moors

🟡 *130 km (81 mi) north of Rovaniemi (via Rte. 4 or 5), 960 km (595 mi) north of Helsinki.*

The Sodankylä region is one of the oldest Sámi settlements, and today it is one of the most densely populated areas of Finnish Lapland. In the town of Sodankylä is a Northern Lights Observatory (for professionals only) and an ancient wooden church. The Midnight Sun Film Festival draws crowds during the height of summer, running films in tents throughout the night.

Lapland is dominated by great moorlike expanses. The modern tourist center of **Luosto**, 25 km (16 mi) south of Sodankylä, is in the heart of the moor district of southern Lapland—an area of superb hiking, mountain cycling, orienteering, and skiing. If you don't have a car, a daily bus makes the 60-km (37-mi) trip from Kemijärvi to Luosto. Kemijarvi is 87 km (54 mi) north of Rovaniemi and can be reached via local train.

Where to Stay

$$ ⊡ **Scandic Hotel Luosto.** Amid the plains southeast of Sodankylä, this small-scale hotel is modern and comfortable. It is built in a unique *kelo* (dead-wood) timber style. Each cabin has a fireplace, sauna, and kitchenette. If you get tired of cross-country skiing, visit the amethyst mine nearby. ✉ *99550 Luostotunturi* ☎ *016/624–400* 🖷 *016/624–410* ⊕ *www.scandichotels.com* ↝ *54 cabins, 5 rooms* ♨ *3 restaurants, kitchenettes, sauna, boating, cross-country skiing, snowmobiling, meeting room* ▭ *AE, DC, MC, V.*

Tankavaara

❺❸   *105 km (65 mi) north of Sodankylä, 130 km (81 mi) north of Luosto, 225 km (140 mi) north of Rovaniemi.*

🌀   The town of Tankavaara is the most accessible and the best-developed of several gold-panning areas. The **Kultamuseo** (Gold Museum) tells the century-old story of Lapland's hardy fortune seekers. Guides will show you how to pan for gold dust and tiny nuggets from the silt of an icy stream. ✉ *Kultakylä, 99695 Tankavaara* ☎ *016/626–158* ⊕ *www.tankavaara.fi* ✉ *Summer €10, includes gold panning, winter €7* ☉ *June–mid-Aug., daily 9–6; mid-Aug.–Sept., daily 9–5; Oct.–May, weekdays 10–4.*

Where to Stay & Eat

$–$$ ✕ **Wanha Waskoolimies.** In the tradition of the old gold prospectors, this rustic restaurant consists of three rooms hewn from logs. Daily specials such as traditional sautéed reindeer with mashed potatoes and lingonberry sauce will give you a taste of simple but high-quality Lapland fare. ✉ *Tankavaaran Kultakylän* ☎ *016/626–158* ▭ *DC, V.*

$ ⊡ **Hotel Korundi.** Just off the Arctic Highway, this hotel has quiet surroundings and cozy, contemporary rooms for two to five people; most have a fireplace. You can try your luck at panning for gold here. The restaurant is in a separate building. ✉ *99695 Tankavaara* ☎ *016/626–158* 🖷 *016/626–261* ↝ *8 rooms* ♨ *Restaurant, sauna, bicycles, hiking, cross-country skiing* ▭ *AE, DC, MC, V.*

Saariselkä

❺❹   *40 km (25 mi) north of Tankavaara, 135 km (84 mi) north of Sodankylä, 265 km (165 mi) north of Rovaniemi.*

You could hike and ski for days in this area without seeing another soul. Saariselkä has many hotels and is a good central base from which to set off on a trip into the true wilderness. Marked trails traverse forests and moors, where little has changed since the last Ice Age. More than 1,282 square km (560 square mi) of this magnificent area has been named the **Urhokekkosen Kansallispüisto** (Urho Kekkonen National Park). The park guide center is at Tankavaara.

Where to Stay

$$–$$$ ⊡ **Riekonlinna.** On the fringes of the wilderness fells, the pinewood fittings and blue textiles of this contemporary Lappish hotel go well with its natural surroundings. All the rooms have a balcony. The restaurant serves fresh local specialties, including reindeer, salmon, and snow grouse. The hotel is only 30 minutes from Ivalo airport, and its location provides excellent cross-country and downhill skiing; snowmobiling and reindeer safaris are also offered. There is a children's play room. ✉ *Saariseläntie, PL 5, 99831 Saariselkä* ☎ *016/679–4455* 🖷 *016/679–4456* ⊕ *www.riekkoparvi.fi* ↝ *122 rooms, 2 suites* ♨ *Restaurant,*

2 *tennis courts, 2 pools, massage, sauna, boating, squash, ski storage, meeting rooms* ⊟ *AE, DC, MC, V.*

$$–$$$ ⊞ **Saariselkä Spa.** This hotel is known for its luxurious spa center. The glass-dome swimming area is crammed with foliage, fountains, water slides, wave machines, and a hot tub. The solarium, saunas, and Turkish baths are adjacent. Guest rooms have blond and dark wood fittings and slate blue carpets. Moderately priced cabin accommodations are also available. Note that the breakfast and spa facilities are included in prices. Children 7 to 14 stay at half-price; children under 7 stay free. The bus stops at the hotel. ✉ *99830 Saariselkä* ☎ *016/6828* 🖷 *016/ 682–328* ⊕ *www.spa-saariselka.com* 🖙 *134 rooms, 5 suites* ♨ *Restaurant, miniature golf, tennis court, gym, hot tub, sauna, Turkish bath, badminton, paddle tennis, squash, volleyball, meeting rooms, no-smoking rooms* ⊟ *AE, DC, MC, V* ⴲ *BP.*

$–$$ ⊞ **Hotelli Riekonkieppi.** This twin to the Riekonlinna provides a more rustic alternative. The piney comfort of the rooms and the quiet countryside make this a good Lapland retreat. Eight wood buildings with 12 to 16 rooms each make it especially popular with families. The restaurant has a cozy fireplace, pine furniture, and a small exhibition of Sámi jewelry. Its regional and Continental menu is strong on reindeer and fish. ✉ *Raitopolku 2, PL 5, 99831 Saariselkä* ☎ *016/679–4455* 🖷 *016/679– 4456* ⊕ *www.riekkoparvi.fi* 🖙 *104 rooms* ♨ *Restaurant, 2 pools, sauna, squash* ⊟ *AE, DC, MC, V* ⴲ *Closed May and Oct.*

Sports

SWIMMING   Lapland's waters are exceptionally clean and good for swimming. Many hotels have pools, and **Saariselkä Spa** at Saariselkä has an indoor water world.

Ivalo

⑤⑤   *40 km (25 mi) north of Saariselkä, 193 km (116 mi) north of Rovaniemi.*

The village of Ivalo is the main center for northern Lapland. With its first-class hotel, airport, and many modern amenities, it offers little to the tourist in search of a wilderness experience, but on the huge island-studded expanses of **Inarijärvi** (Lake Inari), north of Ivalo, you can go boating, fishing, hiking, and hunting.

The Outdoors

⟳ **Tunturikeskus Kiilopää** (✉ 99830 Saariselkä ☎ 016/667–0700 ⊕ www. suomenlatu.fi/kiilopaa) has a multiactivity center for children, including snow-castle building, centrifuge sledding, ski tracks, and reindeer and dogsled trips; there are summer activities, too.

BOATING   A seven-hour trip up the Lemmenjoki River from Ivalo can be arranged by **Lemmenjoen Lomamajat Oy Ahkuntupa** (✉ 99885 Lemmenjoki ☎🖷 016/ 673–475 ⴲ Mar.–Sept.).

Where to Stay

$ ⊞ **Hotel Ivalo.** Modern and well equipped for business travelers and families, this hotel is 1 km (½ mi) from Ivalo, right on the Ivalojoki River. The lobby has marble floors, the lounge a brick fireplace. The rooms are spacious and modern, with burlap woven wallpaper, oatmeal carpets, and lots of blond birchwood trimming; ask for one by the river. The restaurant serves Continental fare, as well as delicious Lappi dishes. ✉ *Ivalontie 34, 99800 Ivalo* ☎ *016/688–111* 🖷 *016/661–905* ⊕ *www. hotelivalo.fi* 🖙 *94 rooms* ♨ *Restaurant, pool, 3 saunas, boating, bar, recreation room, baby-sitting* ⊟ *AE, DC, MC, V.*

$ ⊞ **Kultahippu.** In the heart of Ivalo, along the Ivalojoki River, Kultahippu claims to have the northernmost nightclub in Finland. Guest rooms are cozy, with simple birchwood furnishing; larger rooms with sauna are available for families. The restaurant serves traditional Lapp meals à la carte. ⊠ *Petsamontie 1, 99800 Ivalo* ☎ *016/661–825* 🖷 *016/ 662–510* ⊕ *www.kultahippuhotel.fi* ⟿ *27 rooms* ♨ *Restaurant, hot tub, sauna, beach* ▱ *AE, DC, MC, V.*

$ 🏠 **Tunturikeskus Kiilopää.** This "Fell Center" is in the midst of hiking and cross-country skiing territory in the Urho Kekkonen National Park district, 45 km (28 mi) south of Ivalo Airport. Accommodations are in beautifully crafted log cabins, apartments, or individual hotel rooms, all made of wood and stone. Apartments have picture windows and fireplaces. The restaurant serves reindeer and other game entrées. Check the Web site for rates. ⊠ *99830 Saariselkä* ☎ *016/670–0700* 🖷 *016/667–121* ⊕ *www.suomenlatu.fi/kiilopaa* ⟿ *8 cabins, 8 apartments, 34 rooms, 9 youth hostel rooms* ♨ *Restaurant, cross-country skiing, ski shop, no-smoking rooms* ▱ *AE, DC, MC, V.*

Inari

🔟 *40 km (24 mi) northwest of Ivalo, 333 km (207 mi) north of Rovaniemi.*

It is a stunning drive northwest from Ivalo along the lakeshore to Inari, home of the *Sámi Parlamenta* (Sámi Parliament). The **SIIDA Center,** on the village outskirts, hosts exhibits on the Sámi people and the northern seasons. The center houses the **Saamelaismuseo** (Sámi Museum) and the **Ylä-Lapin luontokeskus** (Northern Lapland Nature Center). The Nature Center includes the **Metsähallitus** (Forest and Park Service; ☎ 0205/ 647–740 🖷 0205/647–750), which can provide camping and fishing permits along with advice on exploring the wilderness. A 17-acre open-air museum complements the indoor exhibits at the center during the summer. ⊠ *Rte. 4 by Lake Inari, 99870 Inari* ☎ *016/665–212 or 0205/647– 740* 🖷 *016/665–156 or 0205/647–750* ⊕ *www.siida.fi* 🎫 *€7* ☉ *Saamelaismuseo: June–Sept., daily 9–8; Oct.–May, Tues.–Sun. 10–5.*

<table>
<tr><td>off the
beaten
path</td><td>**INARIN POROFARMI –** At this is a working reindeer farm 14 km (9 mi) southeast of Inari, you can drive a reindeer sled or be pulled on skis by the magical beasts. ⊠ *Kaksamajärvi, 99800 Ivalo* ☎ *016/ 673–912* 🖷 *016/673–922* ☉ *June–mid-Aug., daily 10–7, or by appointment.*</td></tr>
</table>

Where to Stay & Eat

$ ✕🏠 **Inarin Kultahovi.** This cozy inn is on the wooded banks of the swiftly flowing Juutuajoki Rapids. The no-frills double rooms are small, with handwoven rugs and birchwood furniture. In summer you'll need a reservation to get a table at Kultahovi's restaurant; the specialties are salmon and reindeer, but try the tasty whitefish caught from nearby Lake Inari. ⊠ *99870 Inari* ☎ *016/671–221* 🖷 *016/671–250* ⟿ *29 rooms* ♨ *Restaurant, sauna, bar* ▱ *DC, MC, V.*

The Outdoors

Many local travel agencies throughout Lapland offer different types of tours of the region. **Arctic Safaris** (⊠ Koskikatu 6, 96200 Rovaniemi ☎ 016/ 340–0400 🖷 016/340–0455 ⊕ www.arcticsafaris.fi), offers summer and winter tours including canoeing, hiking, and snowmobiling.

Lapland A to Z

AIR TRAVEL

There is service every day but Sunday between Rovaniemi and Ivalo. You can also fly between Oulu or Rovaniemi to Ivalo, Enontekiö, Kemi, and Sodankylä, all on Finnair domestic services. Finnair also has daily flights directly from Helsinki to Kuusamo. There are seasonal schedules.

AIRPORTS

The airports serving Lapland are at Enontekiö, Ivalo, Kemi, Kittilä, Kusamo, Oulu, Rovaniemi, and Sodankylä. Finnair serves all these airports with flights from Helsinki, though not all flights are nonstop. You can also fly to the north from most of southwestern Finland's larger cities and from the lakes region.

BUS TRAVEL

Bus service into the region revolves around Rovaniemi; from there you can switch to local buses.

CAR TRAVEL

If you are driving north, follow Arctic Highway No. 4 (national highway) to Kuopio–Oulu–Rovaniemi, or go via the west coast to Oulu, then to Rovaniemi. From Rovaniemi, the national highway continues straight up to Lake Inari via Ivalo. Roads are generally good, but some in the extreme north may be rough.

EMERGENCIES

Lapland's leading hospital is Lapin Keskussairaala (Lapland Central Hospital). Dentists can be reached at Hammashoitola Viisaudenhammas.
🚓 Police; emergency services ☎ 112. **Hammashoitola Viisaudenhammas** ⊠ Ukkoherrantie 15, Rovaniemi ☎ 016/334-0400. **Lapin Keskussairaala** ⊠ Ounasrinteentie 22, Rovaniemi ☎ 016/3281; 016/328-2100 evenings and weekends.

TOURS

Guided tours in towns are arranged through city tourist offices. Tours to Lapland can also be purchased in Helsinki through TourExpert. For adventure tours and other specialty tours that cater to both general and special interests, contact Finland Travel Bureau. For independent travelers, the Finnish Youth Hostel Association SRM) offers a hosteling and bicycling package that can be used in Lapland.

Lapland Travel Ltd. (Lapin Matkailu OY) and Lapland Safaris offer fly-fishing and combined canoe-and-fishing trips, in addition to reindeer and snowmobile safaris and ski treks. Lake Lines Inari offer Sámi tours that include a visit to SIIDA, the Sámi Museum in Inari, and a cruise on Lake Inari (operated by Lake Lines Inari).
🚩 **Finland Travel Bureau** ⊠ PL 319, Kaivokatu 10A, 00101 Helsinki ☎ 09/18261 ⊕ www. ftb.fi. **Finnish Youth Hostel Association** ⊠ Yrjönk. 38B, 00100 Helsinki ☎ 09/565-7150 🖷 09/5657-1510. **Lake Lines Inari** ⊠ Meska-Set Oy, Ruskatie 3, 99800 Inari ☎ 0400/391-017 🖷 016/663-582. **Lapland Safaris** ⊠ Koskikatu 1, 96200 Rovaniemi ☎ 016/331-1200 🖷 016/331-1222 ⊕ www.lapinsafarit.fi. **Lapland Travel Ltd. (Lapin Matkailu Oy)** ⊠ Koskikatu 1, 96200 Rovaniemi ☎ 016/332-3400 🖷 016/332-3411 ⊕ www.laplandtravel.fi. **Helsinki Expert Tour Shop** ⊠ Pohjoisesplanadi 19, 00100 Helsinki ☎ 0600/02288, €.78 per minute plus local call charge 🖷 09/2288-1599 ⊕ www. helsinkiexpert.fi.

TRAIN TRAVEL

Train service will get you to Rovaniemi and Kemijärvi. From there you must make connections with other forms of transport.

TRANSPORTATION AROUND LAPLAND

The best base for exploring is Rovaniemi, which connects with Helsinki and the south by road, rail, and air links; there is even a car-train from Helsinki.

The Arctic Highway will take you north from Rovaniemi at the Arctic Circle to Inari, just below the 69th parallel. If you'd rather not rent a car, however, all but the most remote towns are accessible by bus, train, or plane. Buses leave five times daily from Rovaniemi to Inari (five hours) and five times a day to Ivalo (four hours). You can take countryside taxis to your final destination; taxi stands are at most bus stations. Taxi drivers invariably use their meters, and specially negotiated fares—even for long distances—are unusual, but you can ask for an estimate before starting the trip.

VISITOR INFORMATION

⑦ Tourist Information **Enontekiö** ☎🖷 016/556-211 ⊕ www.enontekio.fi. **Inari** ✉ Northern Lapland Tourism Ltd., Saariseläntie 1, 99830 Saariselkä ☎ 016/668-402. **Kemijärvi** ✉ Kuumaniemenk. 2 A 98100 ☎ 016/878-394 ⊕ www.kemijarvi.fi. **Kuusamo** ✉ Torangintaival 2, 93600 ☎ 08/850-2910. **Rovaniemi** ✉ Koskikatu 1, 96200 ☎ 016/346-270. **Saariselkä** ✉ Saariseläntie, PL 22, 99831 ☎ 016/668-402. **Salla** ✉ C/o Salla Reindeer Park-Cooperative Jotos, Hautajärventie 111, 98900 Salla ☎ 016/837-771. **Sodankylä** ✉ Jäämerentie 7, 99600 ☎ 016/618-168.

FINLAND A TO Z

To research prices, get advice from other travelers, and book travel arrangements, visit www.fodors.com.

AIR TRAVEL

CARRIERS Finnair, British Airways, and some charter companies fly from London to Helsinki. Ask the Finnish Tourist Board for names of companies specializing in travel packages to Finland.

Finnair also runs an extensive domestic service. Domestic flights are relatively cheap, and as some planes have a set number of discount seats allotted, it's best to reserve early. There are also special fares available through the Finnair Web site.

American Airlines and British Airways are among Finnair's partners in the One World Alliance. Other European airlines include SAS, Lufthansa, Swiss International Airlines, and Air France.

⑦ British Airways ✉ Speedbird House, Heathrow Airport, London TW6 2JA ☎ 020/8759-1258; 0345/222-111 reservations ⊕ www.ba.com. **Finnair** ✉ 14 Clifford St., London W1X 1RD ☎ 020/7408-1222 ⊕ www.finnair.com. **Lufthansa** ☎ 800/645-3880. **SAS** ☎ 800/221-2350.

FLYING TIMES Flying time from New York to Helsinki is about eight hours, nine hours for the return trip. Flying time from London to Helsinki is two hours, 45 minutes.

AIRPORTS

All international flights arrive at Helsinki–Vantaa International Airport, 20 km (12 mi) north of city center. Finnair offers domestic and international flights, with daily direct service from New York in summer and almost daily service at other times. For 24-hour arrival and departure information, call the phone number for the airport listed below.

⑦ Helsinki-Vantaa International Airport ☎ 0200/14636 ⊕ www.helsinki-vantaa.fi.

BIKE TRAVEL

Finland is a wonderful place for biking, with its easy terrain, light traffic, and wide network of bicycle paths. You can get bike-route maps for most major cities. In Helsinki, cycling is a great way to see the main peninsula as well as some of the surrounding islands, linked by bridges. Rentals average about €7–€20 per day. Bicycles can be rented from Green Bike in Helsinki. Suomen Retkeilymajajärjestö (Finnish Youth Hostel Association) offers a hostelling by bicycle package for 7 or 14 days (regular bikes €249–€431, hybrid bikes €275–€462) that includes a rental bike from Helsinki and Finnish Hostel Cheques for accommodation in hostels. Route maps are available from local tourist offices and from the Finnish Youth Hostel Association. Order or download a copy of *Cycling Finland,* an informative brochure available from the Finnish Tourist Board

🔲 Bike Maps **Suomen Retkeilymajajärjestö** (Finnish Youth Hostel Association) ✉ Yrjönk. 38B, 00100 Helsinki ☎ 09/565-7150 🖨 09/5657-1510 🌐 www.srmnet.org.

🔲 Bike Rentals **Green Bike** ✉ Mannerheim. 13, 00100 Helsinki ☎ 09/8502-2850.

BOAT & FERRY TRAVEL

DFDS Scandinavian Seaways sails from Newcastle to Göteborg, Sweden, with overland (bus or train) transfer to Stockholm; from there, Silja and Viking Line ships cross to the Finnish Åland Islands, Turku, and Helsinki. Traveling time is about two days.

Finland is still a major shipbuilding nation, and the ferries that cruise the Baltic to the Finnish Åland Islands and Sweden seem more like luxury liners. The boat operators make so much money selling duty-free alcohol, perfume, and chocolate that they spare no expense on facilities, which include saunas, children's playrooms, casinos, a host of bars and cafés, and often superb restaurants. With both Finland and Sweden in the EU, all ferries between them now stop at Mariehamn in order to sell duty-free alcohol on board (Åland, with its special autonomous status within Finland, has special rights within the EU).

All classes of sleeping accommodations are available on board the journeys from Stockholm to Turku (about 11 hours) and from Stockholm to Helsinki (about 15 hours). Other connections are Vaasa–Umeå (Sweden), Helsinki or Hanko–Rostock, Travemünde, or Lübeck (Germany), and Helsinki–Tallinn (Estonia).

Since ferry travel is common for budget and family travelers in the region, porters are not readily available. If you need assistance with luggage, contact the information desk in the harbor and/or on the ship. There are storage boxes for luggage in the Helsinki and Stockholm terminals if you are planning a day of sightseeing in either city.

In Helsinki the Silja Line terminal for ships arriving from Stockholm is at Olympialaituri (Olympic Harbor), on the west side of the South Harbor. The Viking Line terminal for ships arriving from Stockholm is at Katajanokkanlaituri (Katajanokka Harbor), on the east side of the South Harbor. Both Silja and Viking have downtown agencies where brochures, information, and tickets are available. Ask about half-price fares for bus and train travel in conjunction with ferry trips.

🔲 **DFDS Scandinavian Seaways** ✉ Scandinavia House, Parkeston Quay, Harwich, Essex, England ☎ 0255/244-382. **Silja Line** ✉ Mannerheim. 2, Pl 880, Helsinki ☎ 09/18041 🌐 www.silja.com. **Viking Line** ✉ Mannerheim. 14, 00100 Helsinki ☎ 09/ 12351 🌐 www.vikingline.fi.

BUS TRAVEL

The Finnish bus network, Matkahuolto, is extensive and the fares reasonable. You can travel the network between Finland and Norway, Sweden, or Russia.

CUTTING COSTS For trips over 80 km (50 mi), full-time students get a discount of 50% and senior citizens 30%. Adults in groups of three or more are entitled to a 25% discount. A Bus Holiday Ticket (€65) is good for up to 1,000 km (621 mi) of travel for two weeks.

🔲 **Matkahuolto** ✉ Lauttasaarentie 8, PL 111, 00201 Helsinki ☎ 09/6136-8433 🌐 www. matkahuolto.fi.

CAR RENTAL

Car rental in Finland is not cheap, but a group rental might make it worthwhile. There are package rates for three- and seven-day trips. Be on the lookout also for weekend and summer discounts. It is cheaper to rent directly from the United States before coming to Finland; most agencies allow booking through their Web sites. Some Finnish service stations also offer car rentals at reduced rates.

Regular daily rates range from about €55 to €160, and unlimited mileage rates are the norm. Car rentals are normally cheaper on weekends. Insurance is sold by the rental agencies.

🚗 **Major Agencies Avis** ✉ Pohjoinen Rautatiek. 17, 00100 Helsinki ☎ 09/441-155; 09/822-833 airport office ⊕ www.avis.fi. **Budget** ✉ Malminkatu 24, 00100 Helsinki ☎ 0800/124-424; 09/870-0780 airport office ⊕ www.budget.fi. **Europcar** ✉ Hitsaajankatu 7C, 00810 Helsinki ☎ 09/7515-5300; 0800/12154 general reservation number; 09/7515-5700 airport office ⊕ www.europcar.fi. **Hertz** ✉ Mannerheimintie, 44, 00100 Helsinki ☎ 020/555-2300; 020/112-233 general reservation number ✉ Airport office ☎ 020/555-2100 ⊕ www.hertz.fi.

CAR TRAVEL

Driving is pleasant on Finland's relatively uncongested roads.

EMERGENCY SERVICES Foreigners involved in road accidents should immediately notify the Finnish Motor Insurers' Center as well as the police.

🚗 **Finnish Motor Insurers' Center** ✉ Liikennevakuutuskeskus, Bulevardi 28, 00120 Helsinki ☎ 09/680-401 ⊕ www.vakes.fi/lvk.

GASOLINE Gasoline costs about €1.20 per liter.

ROAD CONDITIONS Late autumn and spring are the most hazardous times to drive. Roads are often icy in autumn (*kelivaroitus* is the slippery road warning), and the spring thaw can make for *kelirikko* (heaves).

🚗 **The Automobile and Touring Club of Finland** ✉ Autoliitto ry, Hämeentie 105 A, 00550 Helsinki ☎ 09/7258-4400; 09/7747-6400 24-hour information service 🖨 09/7258-4460 ⊕ www.autoliitto.fi.

RULES OF THE ROAD Driving is on the right-hand side of the road. You must use headlights at all times and seat belts are compulsory for everyone. Yield to cars coming from the right at most intersections where roads are of equal size. There are strict drinking-and-driving laws in Finland, and remember to watch out for elk and reindeer signs, placed where they are known to cross the road.

Outside urban areas, speed limits vary between 60 kph and 100 kph (37 mph and 62 mph), with a general speed limit of about 80 kph (50 mph). In towns the limit is 40 kph to 60 kph (25 mph to 37 mph) and on motorways it's 100 kph to 120 kph (62 mph to 75 mph).

CUSTOMS & DUTIES

Spirits containing over 60% alcohol by volume may not be brought into Finland. Those under 19 may not bring in spirits. Visitors to Finland may not import goods for their own use from another European Union (EU) country duty-free. If the items were purchased in a duty-free shop at an airport or harbor, or on board an airplane or ship, visitors may bring in 1 liter of spirits, 2 liters of aperitifs or sparkling wines, 2 liters of table wine, and 16 liters of beer. For more information, consult the Finnish customs Web site ⊕ www.tulli.fi.

EMBASSIES & CONSULATES

🚗 **Australia** ✉ Museokatu 25B, 00100 Helsinki ☎ 09/447-233 ⊕ www.austemb.se.
🚗 **Canada** ✉ Pohjoisespl. 25B, 00100 Helsinki ☎ 09/228-530 ⊕ www.canada.fi.

United Kingdom ✉ Itäinen Puistotie 17, 00140 Helsinki ☎ 09/2286-5100 ⊕ www. ukembassy.fi.

United States ✉ Itäinen Puistotie 14A, 00140 Helsinki ☎ 09/171-931; 09/6162-5701 consular section inquiries weekdays 2-4 ⊕ www.usembassy.fi.

EMERGENCIES

The nationwide emergency number is 112.

Late-night pharmacies are only in large towns. Look under *Apteekki* in the phone book; listings include pharmacy hours.

LANGUAGE

Finnish, the principal language, is a Finno-Ugric tongue related to Estonian with distant links to Hungarian. The country's second official language is Swedish, although only about 6% of the population speaks it as their primary language. In the south, most towns have Finnish and Swedish names; if the Swedish name is listed first, it indicates more Swedish than Finnish speakers live in that area. A third language, Sámi, is actually a group of languages spoken by the Sámi, the original dwellers of Lapland in the north, and has semi-official status in certain northern areas. English is spoken in most cities and resorts.

LODGING

CAMPING Finland's wealth of open space promises prime camping territory. If you camp outside authorized areas and in a settled area, you must get the landowner's permission, and you cannot camp closer than 300 feet to anyone's house. Finncamping Cheque (€12) is a coupon system for campers. For more information, and to find out about the National Camping Card, contact the Finnish Travel Association. The annually updated list of campsites, including classifications and English-language summary, is sold at large bookstores and R-kiosks. A free brochure listing 200 campsites in Finland is available from city tourist offices.

Finnish Campingsite Association ✉ Mäntytie 7, 00270 Helsinki ☎ 09/4774-0740 🖷 09/4772-002 ⊕ www.camping.fi.

HOSTELS & DORMITORIES During the summer season (June–August) many university residence halls in Finland open their doors to visitors. Accommodation in dormitories is usually in double rooms with shared toilet, shower, and cooking facilities among two to three rooms. In addition, regular youth hostels are available to all travelers year-round regardless of age and have various types of accommodations, including single and double rooms. Prices can range from €10 to €30 per person. Meals are generally available in a coffee shop or cafeteria. Ask the Finnish Tourist Board for information on budget accommodations or contact the Finnish Youth Hostel Association.

Finnish Youth Hostel Association ✉ Yrjönk. 38B, 00100 Helsinki ☎ 09/565-7150 ⊕ www.srmnet.org.

HOTELS The Hotel Booking Centre, run by Helsinki Expert in the Helsinki railway station, can make reservations for you in several ways: when booked in person, the charge is €5 for rooms in Helsinki and in surrounding areas and €7 for all other areas. Requests for bookings via telephone, fax, e-mail and the Internet are free. Suomen Hotellivaraukset will make reservations anywhere in Finland at no cost by telephone, fax, and e-mail (no bookings in person). The largest hotel chains in Finland are Scandic, Sokos, Rantasipi, Cumulus, Radisson SAS, Best Western, and Ramada.

RESERVING A ROOM Lomarengas has lists of reasonably priced bed-and-breakfasts, holiday cottages, and farm accommodations available in Finland. It also arranges stays at different facilities, including mökki holidays.

MAIL & SHIPPING

Post offices are open weekdays 9–5 ('til 7, 8, or 9 and on weekends in some cities); stamps, express mail, registered mail, and insured mail service are available. There is no Saturday delivery.

POSTAL RATES Air mail letters and postcards to destinations within Finland (up to 50 grams), to other EU countries, and other parts of the world (up to 20 grams) cost about €.65. For more information, visit the Finnish post Web site: www.posti.fi.

RECEIVING MAIL You may receive letters care of poste restante anywhere in Finland; the poste restante in the capital is at the side of the rail station. It is open weekdays 7 AM–9 PM, weekends 10–6.
🖪 Post Restante ✉ Elielinaukio 1F, 00100 Helsinki

MONEY MATTERS

The strength of the euro may make Finland seem somewhat expensive to travelers from non-euro countries. Some sample prices include: cup of coffee, €1; glass of beer, starting from €3; soft drink, €2.50; ham sandwich, €3; two kilometer (one mile) taxi ride, €6–€9 (depending on time of day).

CURRENCY The sole unit of currency in Finland is the euro, abbreviated as EUR or the symbol €. Euro bills are divided into 5, 10, 20, 50, 100, 200, and 500. The euro is divided into 100 cents in denominations of 1-, 2-, 5-, 10-, 20-, and 50-cent coins as well as €1 and €2 coins. At this writing the exchange rate was €0.84 to the U.S. dollar, €1.41 to the pound sterling, and €0.64 to the Canadian dollar.

Finland is making advancements in the use of "smart" prepaid electronic cash cards that process even the smallest of anonymous cash transactions made at designated public pay phones, vending machines, and McDonald's—of all places. Disposable prepaid cards can be purchased at kiosks.

CURRENCY There are exchange bureaus in all bank branches and major hotels; Forex
EXCHANGE booths in major cities; and at Helsinki–Vantaa Airport. Some large harbor terminals also have exchange bureaus, and international ferries have exchange desks. The Forex offices give the best rates and charge a minimal commission. You can also change back any unused currency (no coins) at no fee with the original receipt. There is also an exchange cart moving through the trains to Russia.

SPORTS & THE OUTDOORS

For general information, contact the Finnish Sports Federation, the umbrella organization for the many specific sports associations, several of which are housed in the same building.
🖪 Finnish Sports Federation ✉ Radiok. 20, Helsinki, 00093 SLU ☎ 09/348-121
🌐 www.slu.fi.

FISHING A fishing license is not usually needed for basic angling with a hook and line, so it is possible to angle and ice fish for free in sea areas and virtually all lakes. For other types of fishing, a management fee of €15 per year or €5 per week can be paid into a state giro account. In addition to this general fishing license, a regional fishing permit must also be obtained. The Wild North travel service, operating within the Forestry and Parks Service, offers various packages including fishing. Order or download a copy of *Fishing Finland*, an informative booklet available from the Finnish Tourist Board. For more information also visit the Web site of the Federation of Finnish Fisheries Associations.
🖪 Finnish Fisheries Association ☎ 09/684-4590 🌐 www.ahven.net. Finnish Forest
and Parks Service ✉ Vernissakatu 4, PL 94, 01301 Vantaa ☎ 0205/64125 customer service; 0203/44122 Wild North, the nature travel agency of the service 🌐 www.metsa.fi.

GOLF   For information on Finland's golf courses, contact the Finnish Golf Union. **Finnish Golf Union** ⊠ Radiok. 20, 00240 SLU ☎ 09/3481-2244 ⊕ www.golf.fi.

HIKING   Order or download the informative *Hiking Finland* booklet from the Finnish Tourist Board Web site. If you want to hike on state-owned land in eastern and northern Finland, write to the Finnish Forest and Parks Service. For organized hiking tours for families with children, as well as beginners, contact Suomen Latu (Finnish Ski Track Association). Maps of marked trails throughout Finland can be ordered through Genimap Oy. Trekkers may also contact the Finnish Orienteering Federation. **Finnish Orienteering Federation** ⊠ Radiok. 20, 00093 SLU ☎ 09/348-121. **Genimap Oy** ⊠ PL 106, 01600 Vantaa ☎ 0201/34040 ☐ 0201/340-449 ⊕ www.genimap. fi. **Suomen Latu** (Finnish Ski Track Association) ⊠ Fabianinkatu 7, 00130 Helsinki ☎ 09/4159-1100 ⊕ www.suomenlatu.fi.

SAUNAS   **Finnish Sauna Society** ☎ 09/686-0560 ⊕ www.sauna.fi.

SKIING   Contact Suomen Latu (Finnish Ski Track Association) for information about ski centers and resorts nationwide. The Finnish Tourist Board also has information on its Web site. **Suomen Latu** (Finnish Ski Track Association) ⊠ Fabianink. 7, 00130 Helsinki ☎ 09/ 4159-1100 ⊕ www.suomenlatu.fi.

WATERSPORTS   Boating enthusiasts may contact the Finnish Yachting Association or the Finnish Boating Association. For paddling trips on Finnish waterways, contact the Finnish Canoe Federation. Some of Finland's most popular inland sailing races are the Hanko Regatta, the Helsinki Regatta, the Rauma Sea Race, and the Päijäinne Regatta. Contact the Finnish Yachting Association for further information. For windsurfing information, contact the Finnish Windsurfing Association. **Finnish Boating Association** ⊠ Radiok. 20, 00093 SLU ☎ 09/3481-2561. **Finnish Canoe Federation** ⊠ Olympiastadion, 00250 Helsinki ☎ 09/494-965. **Finnish Windsurfing Association** ⊠ C/o the Finnish Yachting Association, Radiok. 20, 00093 SLU ☎ 09/348-121. **Finnish Yachting Association** ⊠ Radiok. 20, 00093 SLU ☎ 09/348-121.

TAXES

VALUE-ADDED TAX (V.A.T.)   There is a 22% sales tax on most consumer goods. Residents of countries outside the EU can recover 12% to 16% by going through the "tax-free for tourists" procedure: when you ask for your tax rebate—and be sure to ask for it at the point of purchase—you'll get a tax-free voucher and your goods in a sealed bag. The minimum purchase required is €40. Present the voucher and unopened bag at tax-free cashiers when leaving Finland or when departing the EU. These are located at most major airports, at the departure terminals for most long-distance ferries, and at major overland crossings into Norway and Russia. For a high fee, the tax refund can also be sent to your home country.

TAXIS

Taxis travel everywhere in Finland. The meter starts at about €4 daytime and about €6 evenings and weekends. In cities people generally go to one of the numerous taxi stands and take the first available taxi. You can hail a cab, but most are on radio call. The taxi information number costs €.74 per call plus 8 cents per 10 seconds. Most taxi drivers take credit cards. Tipping is unnecessary; if you want to leave something, round up to the nearest euro. A receipt is a *kuitti*. **Helsinki Taxi Information** ☎ 0100-0700; 0100-0600 advance booking.

TELEPHONES

AREA & COUNTRY CODES The country code for Finland is 358.

DIRECTORY & OPERATOR ASSISTANCE Dial 118 for information in Helsinki and elsewhere in Finland; 020208 for international information (€3.49 per minute plus local charge).

INTERNATIONAL CALLS The front of the phone book has overseas calling directions and rates. You must begin all direct overseas calls with 990, 996, 999, or 00, plus country code (1 for the United States and Canada, 44 for Great Britain). Finnish operators can be reached by dialing ☎ 020–208 for overseas information or for placing collect calls. The long-distance services below will place collect calls at no charge.

LOCAL CALLS Remember that if you are dialing out of the immediate area you must dial 0 first; drop the 0 when calling Finland from abroad. To avoid exorbitant hotel surcharges on calls, use card or coin pay phones; note that coin phones are becoming a rarity.

LONG-DISTANCE SERVICES 🔢 Access Codes **AT&T** ☎ 9800/10010. **MCI Worldphone** ☎ 0800/110280. **Sprint and Global One** ☎ 0800/110284.

PHONE CARDS Major urban areas in Finland have moved to a phone-card system, and some phones only accept cards (no coins), which fortunately are usually available nearby at post offices, R-kiosks, and some grocery stores in increments such as €6, €10, €20, and €30. Public phones charge a minimum of about €.50. Kiosks often have phones nearby. Airport and hotel phones take credit cards. Ringing tones vary but are distinguishable from busy signals, which are always rapid. Most pay telephones have picture instructions illustrating how they operate. Note that regional phone companies have their own cards that don't work in telephones in other regions. The main companies include Sonera, Elisa (Helsinki), and Soon Communications (Tampere).

TIPPING

Tipping is not the norm in Finland, but it is not unheard of, so use your own discretion. Finns normally do not tip cab drivers, but if they do they round up to the nearest euro. Give one euro to train or hotel porters. Coat-check fees are usually posted, and tips above this amount are not expected.

TRAIN TRAVEL

Passenger trains leave Helsinki twice daily for St. Petersburg (eight hours) and once daily on an overnighter to Moscow (15 hours). Travel to Russia requires a visa. To get to northern Sweden or Norway, you must combine train–bus or train–boat travel.

The Finnish State Railways, or VR, serve southern Finland well, but connections in the central and northern sections are scarcer and are supplemented by buses. Helsinki is the main junction, with Riihimäki to the north a major hub. You can get as far north as Rovaniemi and Kemijärvi by rail, but to penetrate farther into Lapland, you'll need to rely on buses, domestic flights, or local taxis.

Note that all train travelers in Finland must have a reserved seat, but it is possible to buy a seat ticket on the train. Special fast trains (Intercity and the Helsinki-Turku Pendolino) are more expensive but also more comfortable. Inquiries on train travel can be made to the Finnish State Railways at the main railroad station in Helsinki or to the Information Service.

CLASSES First- and second-class seats are available on all express trains.

CUTTING COSTS Children ages 6–16 travel half-fare, and there is a 20% reduction when three or more people travel together. Senior citizens (over 65) can get 50% discounts on train fares.

The Finnrail Pass gives unlimited first- or second-class travel within a month's time for passengers living permanently outside Finland; the 3-day pass costs €118, the 5-day pass €158, and the 10-day pass €214 (€177, €237, or €321 for first-class, respectively). Children and teens under 17 pay half-fare. Passes can be bought in the United States and Canada by calling Rail Europe; in the United Kingdom from Norvista; and from the Finnish Railways, or VR. TourExpert at the Helsinki City Tourist Office also sells Finnrail passes.

The ScanRail Pass allows unlimited second-class train travel throughout Denmark, Finland, Norway, and Sweden, and comes in various denominations. It is valid for five days of travel within 15 days (€226) or 21 days consecutively (€350). When sold in Scandinavia the pass is good for up to three days in the country of purchase. Senior citizens 60 and over, and children under 25 get discounts. Free connections or discounts on certain ferries and buses are included. The Eurailpass is good for train travel throughout all of Europe. In the United States, call Rail Europe or DER.

🚆 DER ☎ 800/782-2424. **Finnish Railways** (VR) ☎ 0307/20902 ⊕ www.vr.fi. **Norvista** ☎ 0171/409-7334. **Rail Europe** ☎ 800/438-7245.

TRAVEL AGENCIES

Suomen Matkatoimisto (Finland Travel Bureau) is the country's main travel agency. The agency specializes in all kinds of travel arrangements, including special-interest tours throughout Finland, as well as Scandinavia, Russia, and the Baltic States.

The Finland Travel Bureau's affiliate in the United Kingdom is Norvista. Finnway Inc. is the U.S. affiliate of the Finland Travel Bureau.

🚆 **Local Agent Referrals Finnway Inc.** ✉ 228 E. 45th St., 14th fl., New York, NY 10017 ☎ 212/818-1198. **Norvista** ✉ 227 Regent St., W1R 8PD London ☎ 0171/409-7334. **Suomen Matkatoimisto** (Finland Travel Bureau) ✉ Kaivok. 10 A, PL 319, 00100 Helsinki ☎ 09/18261.

VISITOR INFORMATION

🚆 Tourist Information **Finnish Tourist Board** ✉ Suomen Matkailun edistämiskeskus, Eteläespl. 4, PL 249, 00101 Helsinki ☎ 09/4176-9300 ⊕ www.finland-tourism.com ✉ Box 4649 Grand Central Station, New York, NY 10163-4649 ☎ 212/885-9700 or 800/346-4636 ✉ Box 33123, London W6 8JX ☎ 020/7365-2512.

ICELAND

FODOR'S CHOICE

Árbæjarsafn, *outdoor village in Reykjavík*

Dómkirkjan, *cathedral in Reykjavík*

Hallgrímskirkja, *church in Reykjavík*

The northern lights

Þjóðleikhús, *National Theater in Reykjavík*

Many other great sights, restaurants, and hotels enliven this area.
For other favorites, look for the stars as you read this chapter.

Updated by
Michael J.
Kissane

ON THE HIGHWAY from Keflavík International Airport into Iceland's capital, Reykjavík, you're met by an eerie moonscape under a mystical sub-Arctic sky. The low terrain is barely covered by its thin scalp of luminescent green moss. Here and there columns of steam rise from hot spots in the lava fields. Although trees are few and far between, an occasional scrawny shrub clings to a rock outcropping. The air smells different—clean and crisp—and it's so clear that you can see for miles.

Welcome to Iceland, one of the most dramatic natural spectacles on this planet. It is a land of dazzling white glaciers and black sands, blue hot springs, rugged lava fields, and green, green valleys. This North Atlantic island offers insight into the ferocious powers of nature, ranging from the still-warm lava from the 1973 Vestmannaeyjar (Westman Islands) and the 2000 Mt. Hekla volcanic eruptions to the chilling splendor of the Vatnajökull Glacier. The country is mostly barren, with hardly a tree to be seen, but its few birches, wildflowers, and delicate vegetation are all the more lovely in contrast. Contrary to the country's forbidding name, the climate is surprisingly mild.

So far north—part of the country touches the Arctic Circle—Iceland has the usual Scandinavian long hours of darkness in winter. Maybe this is why Icelanders are such good chess players (Iceland played host to the memorable Fischer–Spassky match of 1972). Such long nights may also explain why, per capita, more books are written, printed, purchased, and read in Iceland than anywhere else in the world. It's no surprise that the birth rate is unusually high for Europe, too.

Another reason for Iceland's near-universal literacy might be its long tradition of participatory democracy, dating from AD 930, when the first parliament met at Þingvellir. Today it's a modern Nordic—most find the term "Scandinavian" too limited—society with a well-developed social-welfare system. Women have a unique measure of equality: they keep their surname on marriage. Children are given a surname created from their father's first name, so that Magnús, son of Svein, is Magnús Sveinsson; Guðrún, daughter of Pétur, is Guðrún Pétursdóttir. Guðrún keeps her maiden name even after she marries, as naturally enough she remains her father's daughter rather than becoming her father-in-law's son. Her children take a patronymic from their father's first name. Perhaps there is no connection, but it is interesting to note that in 1980 Iceland voted in as president the first woman head of state to take office in a democratic election anywhere in the world, Vigdís Finnbogadóttir. After four four-year terms in office, she did not seek reelection in 1996, and Ólafur Ragnar Grímsson was chosen as the new president.

More recently, Iceland has garnered worldwide attention for its use as something of a living laboratory, mapping the genes of its 300,000 inhabitants. In a move that has stirred much controversy, the Icelandic Parliament voted to allow a private company access to the country's unusually complete set of genealogical and public health records (it's estimated that 80% of all Icelandic people who ever lived can be traced genealogically on a computerized database). Citing right-to-privacy and other ethical concerns, opposition groups have convinced health officials to allow people to withdraw from the database by completing a simple form.

Iceland was settled by Vikings, with some Celtic elements, more than a thousand years ago (the first Norse settlers arrived in AD 874, but there is some evidence that Irish monks landed even earlier). Icelanders today speak a language remarkably similar to the ancient Viking tongue in which the sagas were recorded in the 13th century. The Norse settlers brought

With only a few days on your hands, you can experience a fair number of Iceland's major attractions. You can take organized day-trips from Reykjavík or explore the surrounding area yourself with a rental car. Ask travel agents or tour operators about special offers within Iceland that allow you to fly one way and take a bus the other. Theoretically, you can drive the Ring Road—the most scenic route, which skirts the entire Iceland coast—in two days, but that pace qualifies as rally-race driving, and you won't see much. You should plan on at least a week to travel the Ring Road, enjoying roadside sightseeing and relaxing in the tranquil environment along the way. Side jaunts add significant time, as secondary roads are often not paved. When traveling outside Reykjavík, always allow plenty of time to make it back for departing flights. (Note: In the following itineraries, only towns that have accommodations listings are preceded by the hotel icon.)

3

**If you have
4 days**

Start by taking a leisurely tour of 🏨 **Reykjavík ❶**–**㉓**. The mix of the old and new in the capital's midtown is seen in the 19th-century **Alþingishús** and the **Ráðhús**, barely a decade old. Colorful rooftops abound, and ornate gingerbread can be spotted on the well-kept older buildings. A family favorite is the pool at **Laugardalur Park,** where you'll find a botanical garden and farm-animal zoo. Those who prefer a wider, less urban scope should opt for the **Golden Circle** approach on their first day, and take in the spectacular **Gullfoss** waterfall, the **Geysir** hot springs area, and **Þingvellir National Park.**

On Day 2, check the weather report. Depending on conditions, you could take a flight for a day in the 🏨 **Westman Islands** and see how the islanders have turned the 1973 eruption of **Heimaey** to their advantage. A cruise around the island takes you to bird cliffs, and you may even spot seals or dolphins. The island's celebrity guest, Keiko, the Orca whale (a.k.a. Willy of *Free Willy* fame) surprised marine biologists in the summer of 2002 by leaving his escort boat and disappearing for six weeks, only to emerge in Norway. On your third day, spend a leisurely morning in Heimaey, and head back to Reykjavík to take in any missed sights.

If it's sunny in the west on your second day, another alternative is to head north to the **Snæfellsnes Peninsula** on Iceland's west coast. The **Hvalfjörður tunnel** cuts travel time dramatically and allows more flexibility than having to meet the former ferry schedule. On emerging from the tunnel, bypass the town of Akranes and drive north to 🏨 **Borgarnes.** Just north of it, turn west (left) on Route 54 out on the peninsula and head to the tiny village of **Arnarstapi.** If you left the capital before 9 AM, here is a good place to have lunch and take a stroll along the shore, watch small boats come and go, and marvel at the seabirds as they dive and soar. Afterward, enter Iceland's newest national park, Snæfellsjökull, and marvel at the mystical moods of this mountain as you circle north to Ólafsvík en route to 🏨 Stykkishólmur. If there's time, a cruise among the Breiðafjörður Islands taken either this day, or the morning of the next, will provide both a visual and gourmet treat.

On Day 3, depart Stykkishólmur and cross the Snæfellsnes arm, going south from here to close the loop. Return to Reykjavík via the tunnel, since the state is saving money by neglecting the once good road through the pretty countryside around **Hvalfjörður,** or Whale Fjord. On Day 4, be packed for your flight home, and stop at the surreal and supremely improved **Blue Lagoon,** not far from **Grindavík,** for a late morning–early afternoon dip that will leave you refreshed and only 20 minutes from the airport for an afternoon flight connection.

If you have 6 days

Complete the first three days of the four-day tour above, and on the morning of Day 4 fly northeast to ⊞ **Akureyri.** With a rental car visit the numerous historical houses here, such as **Matthíasarhús, Nonnahús, Laxdalshús,** and **Davíðshús.** After lunch, take some time at the **Lystigarðurinn.** Next drive east to the Lake Mývatn area, taking in **Goðafoss** and maybe even **Dettifoss** along the way. Spend a good part of Day 5 around ⊞ **Mývatn,** visiting **Dimmuborgir** lava formations, **Námaskarð** sulfur springs, and the shoreline birding areas. Return to Akureyri and stay the fifth night, possibly taking in a trio of fascinating churches at **Saurbær, Grund,** and **Möðruvellir.** On Day 6, leave the north on a morning flight back to Reykjavík, and if time permits, duck in for a quick dip in the **Blue Lagoon.**

If you have 10 days

Having first made reservations for you and your vehicle on the car ferry *Baldur* for Day 2, follow the Snæfellsnes Peninsula itinerary from the four-day tour above as far as ⊞ **Stykkishólmur** and spend the first night there, perhaps taking an evening cruise of the **Breiðafjörður Islands.** On Day 2 take the *Baldur* ferry to Brjánslækur, where you disembark and take a rather rough gravel road for nearly two hours west toward the village of ⊞ **Patreksfjörður** and the incredible bird cliffs at **Látrabjarg.** Overnight in Patreksfjörður and return back along the rugged Barðarstönd coast toward the inland area of **Hrútafjörður,** staying in ⊞ **Brú,** ⊞ **Glaumbær,** or ⊞ **Sauðárkrókur** for night 3.

Day 4 starts with the **Vatnsnes Circle,** where the peculiar, huge **Hvítserkur** stands offshore. Back on Route 1, turn north at **Varmahlíð** and visit the major classic farmstead **Glaumbæ,** and go through **Sauðárkrókur** to the ancient cathedral at **Hólar.** Once back on the Ring Road, end the day in ⊞ **Akureyri.**

After exploring Akureyri on the morning of Day 6, head east past **Goðafoss** and **Dettifoss** to the aviary crossroads at **Lake Mývatn.** By all means spend at least one night in ⊞ **Mývatn,** and on Day 7 visit the false craters, the eerie shapes at **Dimmuborgir,** and the bubbling sulfur muds of **Námaskarð.** Spend the night near the lake in ⊞ **Reykjahlíð.** Head three hours east to ⊞ **Egilsstaðir** for the eighth night. A nice outing from here is to the large forestry station at Hallormsstaðir and to the museum estate, **Skriðuklaustur,** depending on timing.

Rest well in Egilsstaðir, because Day 9 is a long haul around the entire southeast corner of Iceland. You'll see the southeastern fjords, the south end of Europe's largest glacier **Vatnajökull,** the town of **Höfn,** glacier lagoons, and **Skaftafell National Park.** The Ring Road takes you over wide lava flows and broad sandy plains to the town of ⊞ **Vík.** The sea arch of **Dyrhólaey,** with its beautiful black beach, is just east of town. Overnight in Vík and depart early the next morning, about 9 AM, for **Reykjavík** ❶–㉓, or earlier if your flight leaves in the afternoon from **Keflavík.** Along the way you'll pass the stunning waterfalls of **Skógafoss** and **Seljalandsfoss,** beneath the glacier Eyjafjallajökull (each is off a short spur road). If you have an afternoon departure from Keflavík on this same day, you'll have to keep pace and be satisfied with a Ring Road glimpse of **Mt. Hekla** to the north of **Hella**. After going through **Selfoss,** a good-size town on the Ölfusá river, you will come to **Hveragerði,** beyond which the road climbs up the plateau along the home stretch to the capital area.

---

to the island sturdy horses, robust cattle, and Celtic slaves. Perhaps Irish tales of the supernatural inspired Iceland's traditional lore of the *huldufólk,* or hidden people, said to reside in splendor in rocks, crags, caves, and lava tubes.

Iceland is the westernmost outpost of Europe, 800 km (500 mi) from the nearest European landfall, Scotland, and nearly 1,600 km (1,000 mi) from Copenhagen, the country's administrative capital during Danish rule from 1380 to 1918. Where the warm southern Gulf Stream confronts the icy Arctic currents from the north, Iceland straddles the mid-Atlantic ridge at the merger of the North American and European tectonic plates. Volcanic activity continues to form the island by slowly forcing the plates to separate. During the past few centuries, a volcanic eruption has occurred on average every five years. Mt. Hekla erupted in February 2000, and the cauldron that awoke under the Vatnajökull glacier in the fall of 1996 quickly melted through hundreds of feet of ice not far from Grímsvatn. Yet no one need wait for an eruption to be reminded of the fiery forces' presence, because they also heat the hot springs and geysers that gurgle, bubble, and spout in many parts of the country. The springs, in turn, provide hot water for public swimming pools and heating for most homes and buildings, helping to keep the air smog-free. Hydropower generated by harnessing some of the country's many turbulent rivers is another main energy source that helps to keep pollution and the expense of fossil fuels at a minimum.

More than 80% of the island's 103,000 square km (40,000 square mi) is uninhabited. Ice caps cover 11% of the country, more than 50% is barren, 6% consists of lakes and rivers, and less than 2% of the land is cultivated. Surrounded by the sea, the Icelanders have become great fishermen, and fish remains the cornerstone of the economy. Seafood exports pay for imported foodstuffs and other goods, all of which could not be produced economically in such a small society. Because of importation needs and high value-added taxes on most goods and services, prices tend toward the steep side. Hotels and restaurants are pricey, but with a little digging you can usually find inexpensive alternatives.

Start your visit in the capital, Reykjavík, before venturing out into the countryside, where rainbow-arched waterfalls cleave mountains with great spiked ridges and snowcapped peaks. You can climb mountains, ford rivers, watch birds, catch trout or salmon, even tend sheep and cattle at a typical Icelandic farm. The warmest months—June, July, and August—are the most popular with visitors, but a growing number has been coming in winter for the promise of skiing, snowmobiling, and snow-trekking vehicle tours. Although swimming in the perpetually frigid ocean isn't a possibility, inviting hot springs and naturally heated pools dimple the landscape. Icelanders from all walks of life—cabinet ministers on down—congregate for a soak or a swim any time of year.

Exploring Iceland

Iceland almost defies division into separate regions, thanks to its inlets and bays, thorough lacework of rivers, and complex coastline of fjords, all crowned by an unpopulated highland of glaciers and barrens. To divide the country into four compass directions is to oversimplify, but since the Icelandic national emblem (seen on the "tails" side of every local coin) depicts four legendary symbols—one for each corner of the country—the number is not totally arbitrary.

Reykjavík is the logical starting point for any visit to Iceland. The west is an expansive section of rugged fjords and lush valleys, starting just north of Reykjavík and extending all the way up to the extreme northwest. The north is a region of long, sometimes broad valleys and fingerlike peninsulas reaching toward the Arctic Circle. The east has fertile farmlands, the country's largest forest, and its share of smaller fjords. Iceland's south stretches from the lowest eastern fjords, essentially all the way west to the capital's outskirts. It encompasses rich piedmont farmland and wide, sandy coastal and glacial plains. Powerful rivers drain the area, carved with impressive waterfalls. The national parks of Skaftafell and Þingvellir are here, as well as the nation's highest peak, Hvannadalshnúkur.

About the Restaurants

Restaurants in Iceland are small and diverse. You can expect superb seafood and lamb, and the fresh fish is not to be missed—surely some of the best you'll ever have. Besides native cuisine, eateries offer everything from Asian and Indian to French and Italian. Pizzas, hamburgers, and a tasty local version of the hot dog, with fried onions, are widely available. Most restaurants—even the two McDonald's in Reykjavík—accept major credit cards.

Perhaps the best way to save substantially on meal costs (besides choosing from the specials of the day) is to forego alcohol, the price of which essentially doubles from liquor store (where it isn't cheap to begin with) to restaurant table.

About the Hotels

Hotels in Reykjavík and larger towns usually offer standard amenities: hair dryer, trouser press, telephone, and satellite TV. Unless otherwise noted, assume rooms listed have bath or shower. Breakfast is usually included in the hotel price, but inquire to be certain.

Many travelers find simple guest houses adequate, whereas others prefer a bed-and-breakfast in a private home. Icelandic farm holidays have been growing in popularity, even among Icelanders. On about 110 properties—half of them working farms—you can come in close contact with the country, its people, and the magnificent natural surroundings. Accommodations vary widely: you might stay in a separate cottage, in a bed in the farmhouse, or in a sleeping bag in an outbuilding. Some farms have cooking facilities; others serve full meals if requested. Make reservations well in advance.

WHAT IT COSTS In Iceland Króna					
	$$$$	**$$$**	**$$**	**$**	**¢**
RESTAURANTS	over 3,100	2,400–3,100	1,700–2,400	1,000–1,700	under 1,000
HOTELS	over 22,900	15,800–22,900	8,700–15,800	1,600–8,700	under 1,600

Restaurant prices are per person, for a main course at dinner. Hotel prices are for two people in a standard double room in high season.

3

Bird-Watching

Even in settled areas bird-watchers are likely to find a fascinating assortment of species, among them the golden plover, a harbinger of spring; arctic terns, streamlined circumpolar migrators; and the colorful puffins, with their broad bills, expressive eyes, and tuxedo plumage. Of several birds of prey, two earn special status because of their rarity: the regal gyrfalcon, the emblem for Iceland's Independence Party, and the majestic white-tailed eagle, whose grayish head and white tail are strikingly similar to the bald eagle's.

A summer walk along Reykjavík's Tjörnin Lake might be accompanied by duck species, swans, gulls, and the ever-present terns. Puffins can be spotted closest to Reykjavík at Lundey (Puffin Island, where else?). If you are a serious bird-watcher, by all means make a summer visit to Lake Mývatn, where you can find Europe's largest variety of ducks and water birds, from Barrow's goldeneye to the riotous harlequin duck. Grebes, mergansers, phalaropes, and even ever-elusive snipes further reward the sharp-eyed visitor.

Dining

Chefs in Iceland blend elements of classic French cuisine and the best in traditional Scandinavian cooking. And more and more of them are dreaming up innovative dishes employing exotic ingredients, imported and available year-round.

The distinctly wild taste of Icelandic lamb is cultivated by allowing the animals to roam free amid the grasslands of the interior, where they feed on highland herbs. Iceland also produces traditional *hangikjöt* (smoked lamb) and a more lightly flavored alternative, London lamb. Game such as duck, ptarmigan, and reindeer shows up on fancier restaurant menus. And you have not eaten in Iceland until you've tried the seafood: lobster, ocean perch, halibut, turbot, *tindabikkja* (starry ray), salmon, and trout pulled from clear mountain rivers. Herring is pickled and also marinated in wine, garlic, and other spices. Salmon is cut fresh from ample fillets, smoked with aromatic woods, or cured with dill to create gravlax.

Like other Nordic peoples, Icelanders appreciate ales and spirits, the most famous being their own *brennivín*, an 80-proof liquor similar to aquavit and affectionately referred to as the Black Death. Icelandic vodkas, such as Elduris and Icy, are also of high quality.

Fishing

The countryside abounds with rivers and lakes where you can catch salmon (April to mid-October), sea and brown trout (early June to September), and char. Permits can be bought at the closest farmstead, and sometimes at nearby gas stations and tackle shops. Fees range from about 900 krónas to several thousand per day. Guides and accommodations are provided at the more expensive salmon rivers.

Fishing at the most popular (and expensive) rivers, usually those with reliable, large, wild salmon, must be booked at least a year in advance in most cases; you pay the equivalent of IKr 58,000–IKr 150,000 per fishing rod per day, which typically includes comfortable lodge accommodations, some meals, a guide, and a cook–housekeeper. Usually there is no catch limit, though the "catch and release" philosophy has been gaining favor, and some rivers and sections have gone to fly-fishing only. In addition, the number of fishermen allowed on each section, or "beat," is limited.

Hiking

Much of Iceland's terrain, especially the highlands, offers breathtaking scenery and unparalleled solitude for hikers. Panoramas of vast, surreal volcanic mountains crowned by glaciers await at every turn. Wide vistas punctuated by steamy hot-spring plumes and laced with pristine streams and waterfalls are a photographer's dream. In late summer, you might find wild blueberries, crowberries, or bramble berries—a special bonus for your efforts.

Horseback Riding

The Icelandic horse is a purebred descendant of its ancestors from the Viking age, small but strong, exceptionally surefooted, intelligent, and easy to handle. This horse has a particularly interesting stepping style called the *tölt*, or "running walk," which yields an extraordinarily smooth ride. This gait is actually so smooth that a popular demonstration has the rider carrying a tray of drinks at full speed without spilling a drop! Horse lovers from around the world come to try these amazing five-speed steeds for themselves. A number of operators offers tours, from short 1-day trips to 12-day cross-country treks for more experienced riders.

Shopping

The classic gift to bring home is the Icelandic sweater; hand-knit in traditional designs, no two are alike. The natural lanolin and dual fiber layers—a long, sparse one to shed moisture and a short, denser one that acts as insulation—let the thick, soft Icelandic wool provide excellent protection from cold and damp. A good sweater costs about IKr 8,000 to IKr 9,000.

You may want to pick up a small jar of Icelandic lumpfish caviar or some *harðfiskur* (dried fish), best eaten in small bits (and some say privately with a clothespin on the nose).

For upward of IKr 1,000 you can bring home silver replicas of Viking brooches, rings, necklaces, and Old Norse religious symbols, such as the *Þórshamar* (Thor's hammer) and magical, pagan runic letters. A number of silversmiths also design beautiful modern jewelry with Icelandic stones—agate, jasper, and black obsidian.

Skiing

About 90 ski lifts whisk people up Iceland's mountains. The skiing season begins in January, when the days gradually become longer, and usually lasts through April. From late winter through summer you can ascend even higher on Jeep tours. The larger ski areas offer both alpine and cross-country trails. If you are less experienced on the slopes, you may take comfort in the fact that there's a scarcity of trees.

Snowmobiling

People ages 18 to 80 glide across Iceland's amazing white wonderland, within two hours of Reykjavík. Unlike elsewhere, this glacial grandeur occurs at just over 3,000 feet, so only the scenery and the rush leave you breathless, not the altitude. Supervised tours run from late winter through summer and include snowmobile instruction, mandatory helmets, and snowsuits.

Swimming

Almost every sizable community in Iceland has at least one public outdoor swimming pool, usually of freshwater that has been slightly chlorinated. Most are heated by thermal springs and enjoyed year-round. Groups of adults from all walks of life routinely start their day swimming laps, socializing, and soaking in hot tubs. Swimming is a required course in school and the nation's most popular sport. During the long days of summer, pools are open until 9:30 PM.

Timing

Don't let its name fool you—Iceland is a year-round destination. If you want to go fishing, ride Icelandic horses, or be enchanted by the midnight sun, May through August is the time to visit. From June through July, the sun barely sets. Unruly fall is beyond prediction: it can be a crisp time of berry picking and beautiful colors on the heaths, or of challenging gales, when lingering over a cup of coffee in a cozy café may be the most appealing activity. In December the sun shines for only three hours a day. Fall and winter bring a surprising assortment of cultural performances, both modern and classic. Nature provides its share of drama with the spellbinding Northern Lights, seen most often on cold, clear nights from September to March. First-time viewers are sure to be mesmerized by the magical iridescence of huge clouds and curtains of yellow-green to magenta, arching as if alive across the evening sky.

Iceland has a temperate ocean climate with cool summers and relatively mild winters. Most influential weather systems follow the Gulf Stream coming up from the southwest and the highlands temper some of the impact. So climate changes in the north are subtle with more Continental behavior, whereas the south is fickle and maritime. In general, Iceland's weather is more unpredictable than most: in June, July, and August, sunny days alternate with spells of rain showers, crisp breezes, and occasional driving winds. In winter it can be as high as 50°F (10°C) or as low as −14°F (−10°C)—and ironically, winter cloudiness is usually warmer than winter sun.

REYKJAVÍK

Sprawling Reykjavík, the nation's nerve center and government seat, is home to half the island's population. On a bay overlooked by proud Mt. Esja (pronounced AY shyuh), with its ever-changing hues, Reykjavík presents a colorful sight, its concrete houses painted in light colors and topped by vibrant red, blue, and green roofs. The predominant boxy architecture of modern structures results from the use of steel-reinforced concrete to meet building codes that require resistance to earthquakes of at least five on the Richter scale. In contrast to the almost treeless countryside, Reykjavík has many tall, native birches, rowans, and willows, as well as imported aspen, pines, and spruces.

Reykjavík's name comes from the Icelandic words for smoke, *reykur,* and bay; *vík.* In AD 874, Norseman Ingólfur Arnarson saw Iceland rising out of the misty sea and came ashore at a bay eerily shrouded with plumes of steam from nearby hot springs. Today most of the houses in Reykjavík are heated by near-boiling water from the hot springs. Natural heating avoids air pollution; there's no smoke around. You may notice, however, that the hot water brings a slight sulfur smell to the bathroom.

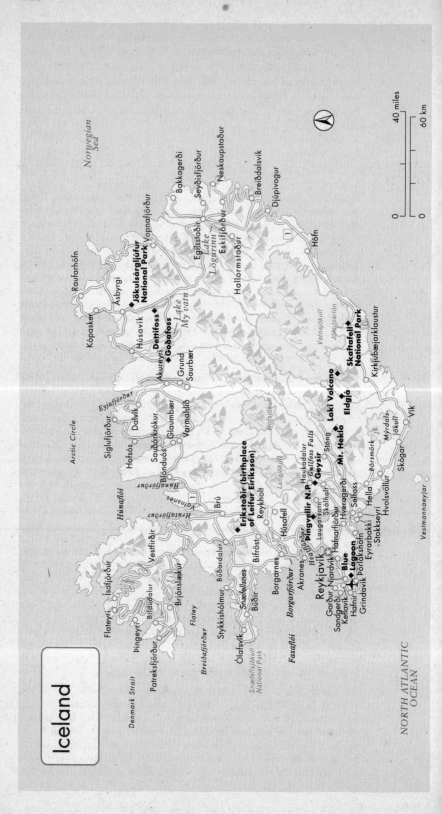

Prices are easily on a par with other major European cities. A practical option is to purchase a Reykjavík Tourist Card at the Tourist Information Center or at the Reykjavík Youth Hostel. This card permits unlimited bus usage and admission to any of the city's seven pools, the Family Park and Zoo, and city museums. The cards are valid for one (IKr 1,000), two (IKr 1,500), or three days (IKr 2,000), and they pay for themselves after three or four uses a day. Even lacking the Tourist Card, paying admission (IKr. 500 or IKr. 250 for seniors or handicapped) to one of the following city art museums gets you free same-day admission to the other two: Hafnarhús, Kjarvalsstaðir or Ásmundasafn.

Numbers in the text correspond to numbers in the margin and on the Reykjavík map.

Exploring Reykjavík

Any part of town can be reached by city bus, but take a walk around to get an idea of the present and past. In the Old Town, classic wooden buildings rub shoulders with modern timber and concrete structures.

Old Town

What better guiding presence on a tour of historic Reykjavík than the man who started it all, one of the first settlers of Iceland and Reykjavík's founder, Ingólfur Arnarson? Overlooking the old city center and harbor is a grassy knoll known as Arnarhóll, topped by the **Ingólfur Arnarson statue ❶ ▶**. From here there's a fine panorama of midtown Reykjavík.

Behind him on his left, on Hverfisgata, the classic white Landsbókasafnið (Old National Library) has been resurrected as the **Þjóðmenningarhúsið ❷**, or National Cultural House. Outside, its crests pay tribute to giants of Icelandic literature. Inside, it includes informative cultural exhibits. Next to it is the basalt-black **Þjóðleikhús ❸**, its interior reflecting the natural influence of polygonal lava columns. Across the street from the National Theater is **Alþjóðahús ❹**, the Intercultural Center where there are often art exhibitions and music shows—the lively café is a good place to stop for a coffee. Walk back from these buildings to Lækjargata, left of Hverfisgata, to the **Stjórnarráð ❺**, which contains the offices of the prime minister. Across Bankastræti, continuing along the hill above Lækjargata and the oversize pavement chessboard on the same side, stands the historic mid-19th-century Bernhöftstorfa—a row of distinct two-story wooden houses, two of which are now restaurants. The building across Amtmannsstígur and closer to the lake is **Menntaskólinn í Reykjavík ❻**.

Go south on Lækjargata to the corner of the Tjörnin Lake. Lækjargata, meaning "Brook Street," gets its name from an underground brook that connects the lake and the city harbor. This busy artery links the city center with main roads out to residential parts of town. Overlooking Tjörnin Lake from its northwest corner is the modern **Ráðhús ❼**, on the corner of Vonarstræti and Tjarnargata.

Sometimes referred to as the heart of the city, Austurvöllur, which lies between Tjörnin Lake and the harbor, was the first area developed in Reykjavík. From the lake, follow Templarasund a little more than a block north to **Austurvöllur Square ❽**, dominated by a statue of Jón Sigurðsson (1811–79), who led Iceland's fight for independence from Denmark. Sigurðsson looks approvingly at the 19th-century **Alþingishús ❾**, on Kirkjustræti. Next to the Parliament is the **Dómkirkjan ❿**, on the corner of Templarasund and Kirkjustræti. From the square toward the harbor runs Pósthússtræti, taking its name from the main post office, the large red building on the corner of **Austurstræti**. Lækjartorg Plaza is less than a minute away, and here you can end your tour at a nearby café.

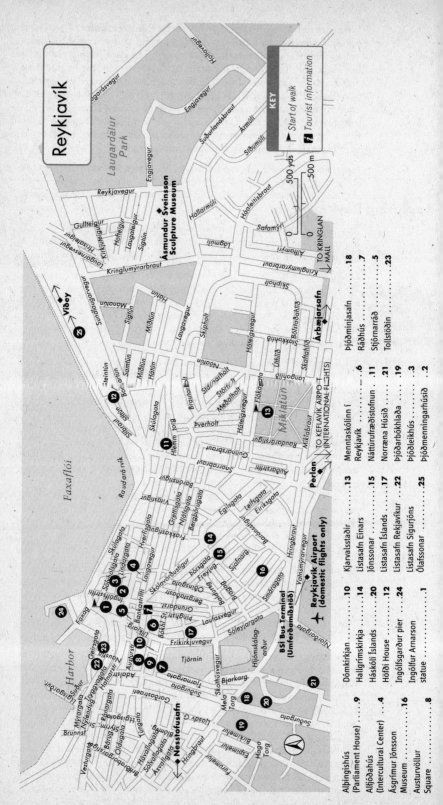

Reykjavík

Laugardalur Park

Ásmundur Sveinsson Sculpture Museum

Árbæjarsafn

TO KRINGLAN MALL

Perlan

TO KEFLAVIK AIRPO T (INTERNATIONAL FLIGHTS)

Reykjavík Airport (domestic flights only)

BSÍ Bus Terminal (Umferðamiðstöð)

Ingólfur Arnarson statue

Nesstofusafn

Harbor

Faxaflói

Viðey

500 yds

500 m

If you have some time left, the bus terminus at Lækjargata a few short blocks east is a good place to depart for the Perlan or the Árbæjarsafn, a re-created Icelandic village. On Tuesday and Thursday afternoons, you can take a bus ride to **Nesstofusafn**, a museum chronicling Iceland's medical history, in Seltjarnarnes, on the city's outskirts. If you don't want to leave the city proper, you can take a detour to the **Náttúrufræðistofnun** (Museum of Natural History) ⑪ and the **Höfði House** ⑫. The museum is near the bus station at Hlemmur, and the Höfði House is about a 15-minute walk northeast from the museum. Farther east is Laugardalur Park and the Ásmundur Sveinsson Sculpture Museum.

WHAT TO SEE

★ ❾ **Alþingishús** (Parliament House). Built in 1880–81, this structure is one of the country's oldest stone buildings. Iceland's Alþingi held its first session in AD 930 and therefore is the oldest continually functional representative parliament in the world. From October through May you can view the parliament proceedings from the visitors' gallery here. Depending on the urgency of the agenda, any number of Iceland's 63 parliament members, representing a spectrum of six political parties, may be present. Rarely are the current 11 ministers, who oversee 15 ministries, all gathered together. ⊠ *Austurvöllur Sq.* ☎ *563–0631* ⊕ *www.althingi.is.*

★ ❹ **Alþjóðahús** (Intercultural Centre). Look for the building with exotic gingerbreading, right across from (Þjóðleikhús (National Theater) and you've found this facility dedicated to multicultural society in Iceland. An in-house support group gives legal advice and counselling to immigrants and refugees. The events held here highlight cultures from around the globe— there are art shows, live music, and films. Caffé Kúlture is very likely the most eclectic hangout in town, where the menu is as varied as the culture. ⊠ *Hverfisgata 18* ☎ *530–9300* 🖷 *530–9301* ⊕ *www.ahus.is.*

Austurstræti. Sometimes closed to cars, this street starts at the junction of Lækjargata and Bankastræti (Bankastræti becomes Austurstræti). On those select weekends when the street is closed, an impromptu market with vendors selling anything from sweaters to foods and souvenirs occasionally gets under way.

off the beaten path

ÁRBÆJARSAFN – At the Open-Air Municipal Museum, 18th- and 19th-century houses furnished in old-fashioned style display authentic household utensils and tools for cottage industries. On summer weekends the museum hums with different educational events. You can see demonstrations of farm activities and taste piping-hot *lummur* (chewy pancakes) cooked over an old farmhouse stove. Take Bus 10 from Hlemmur station (or Bus 100 from Austurstræti) 20 minutes to get to the museum. ⊠ *Ártúnsblettur* ☎ *577–1111* ⊕ *www.arbaejarsafn.is* 🖅 *IKr 300* ☉ *June–Aug., Tues.–Sun. 10–6.*

off the beaten path

ÁSMUNDUR SVEINSSON SCULPTURE MUSEUM – Some originals by this sculptor, depicting ordinary working people, myths, and folk tale episodes, are exhibited in the museum's gallery and studio and in the surrounding garden. It's on the southwest edge of Laugardalur Park, opposite the traffic circle at its entrance. ⊠ *v/Sigtún (5-min ride from Hlemmur station on Bus 5)* ☎ *553–2155* ⊕ *www.listasafnreykjavikur.is* 🖅 *IKr 500, free Mon.* ☉ *June–Sept., daily 10–4; Oct.–May, daily 1–4.*

❽ **Austurvöllur Square.** East Field is a peculiar name for a west central square. The reason: it's just east of the presumed spot where first settler Ingólfur Arnarson built his farm, today near the corner of Aðalstræti.

★ ⑩ **Dómkirkjan** (Lutheran Cathedral). A place of worship has existed on this site since AD 1200. The small, charming church, built 1788–96, represents the state religion, Lutheranism. It was here that sovereignty and independence were first blessed and endorsed by the church. It's also where Iceland's national anthem, actually a hymn, was first sung in 1874. Since 1845, members and cabinet ministers of every Alþing parliament have gathered here for a service before the annual session. Among the treasured items inside is a baptismal font carved and donated by the famous 19th-century master sculptor Bertel Thorvaldsen, who was half Icelandic. ⊠ *Austurvöllur* ☏ *520–9700* ⊕ *www.domkirkjan.is/enska. html* ⊙ *Weekdays 10–5, unless in use for services.*

⑫ **Höfði House.** This historic building, solitary and unadorned, stands defiantly open to the sea on Borgartún. Some say this is where the cold war began to thaw when Mikhail Gorbachev and Ronald Reagan met at the Reykjavík Summit of 1986. The massive, impressive Höfði was built in 1909 as a residence for the French consul. Subsequent owners included the eccentric writer Einar Benediktsson and the British consul during the early part of World War II, who, legend has it, was driven out of the house by a ghostly presence. Eventually, the British sold the house and it became city property. It now serves as a venue for special city business and is decorated with some of the city's art holdings. You must register at Upplýsingur (information desk) in Ráðhús (City Hall) in order to visit the building, which is open on the first Sunday of the month or by prior arrangement. ⊠ *Near junction of Borgartún and Nóatún* ☏ *563–2000 to arrange visit* ⊕ *www.reykjavik.is* ⊙ *1st Sun. of every month.*

▶ ❶ **Ingólfur Arnarson statue.** If you look beyond Ingólfur, who faces you from his knoll, you can see the city's architectural mélange: 18th-century stone houses, 19th-century small wooden houses, office blocks from the '30s and '40s, and, to the north, the black, futuristic Seðlabanki (Central Bank). Take any of the crosstown buses that stop at Lækjartorg plaza. ⊠ *Arnarhóll.*

Lækjartorg (Brook Square). Now a focal point in Reykjavík's otherwise rambling city center, this square opens onto **Austurstræti**, a semi-pedestrian shopping street. A brook, now underground, drains Tjörnin Lake into the sea (hence the street's name). ⊠ *At Bankastræti and Lækjargata.*

(off the beaten path)

LAUGARDALAR PARK – This is actually made up of several parks in one large area. Besides a swimming pool, the recreational expanse has picnic and barbecuing facilities. The **Húsdýragarðurinn** (Farm Animal Park; ☏ 553–7700), has reindeer, goats, cows, horses, seals, and fish; it is open daily 10–6 from mid-May through August; the rest of the year it's open daily from 10–5. Admission is IKr 300. The **Fjölskyldugarðurinn** (Family Park; ☏ 575–7800 ⊕ www. husdyragardur.is) has rides and games, such as Crazy Bikes—a driving school complete with miniature traffic lights—and a scale model of a Viking ship. Joint admission to both the Farm Animal Park and Family Park is IKr 350 for those aged 6–12, and IKr 450 for those over 12. The free **Grasagarður** (Botanical Garden; ☏ 553–8870) has an extensive outdoor collection of native and exotic plants. Coffee and baked items are sold in summer at the cozy conservatory. To get to the park, you can take Bus 2 or 5 east. ⊠ *East of city center, bounded by Sundlaugarvegur to the north and Reykjavegur to the west* ☏ *Free.*

Laugavegur. Traditionally the city's main shopping street, Laugavegur now meets stiff competition from the Kringlan Mall uptown. You may have to go to Paris or Vienna to find as many eateries and coffeehouses packed into such a short stretch.

⑥ Menntaskólinn í Reykjavík (Reykjavík Grammar School). Many graduates from the country's oldest educational institution, established in 1846, have gone on to dominate political and social life in Iceland. Former president Vigdís Finnbogadóttir and numerous cabinet ministers, including Iceland's current prime minister, Davíð Oddsson, are graduates, as are film producer Hrafn Gunnlaugson and well-known author Þórarinn Eldjarn. ☒ *Corner of Amtmannsstígur and Lækjargata.*

⑪ Náttúrufræðistofnun (Museum of Natural History). One of the last great auks on display and several exhibits that focus on Icelandic natural history share space in the main terminus of the city's bus system. It's small as museums go. ☒ *Hverfisgata 116* ☎ *562–9822* ⊕ *www.ni.is* ☒ *Free* ☉ *May–Aug., Tues., Thurs., and weekends 1:30–5; Sept.–Apr., Tues., Thurs., and weekends 1:30–4.*

off the beaten path

NESSTOFA – What was originally the home of the nation's first chief doctor, Bjarni Pálsson, houses the Nesstofa Medical History Museum. A fine collection of instruments and exhibits explains the tough battle for public health services during the last two centuries. When the house was built in 1763, it was one of few stone structures in Iceland. Bus 3 takes you to Seltjarnarnes, a community on Reykjavík's west boundary, a couple of short blocks from the museum. ☒ *Seltjarnarnes* ☎ *561–1016* ☒ *IKr 300* ☉ *May 15–Sept. 14, Tues., Thurs., and weekends noon–4; also open for groups by appointment.*

PERLAN – On top of Öskjuhlíð, the hill overlooking Reykjavík Airport, Perlan (the Pearl) was built in 1991 as a monument to Iceland's invaluable geothermal water supplies. Among the indoor and outdoor spectacles are art exhibits, musical performances, a permanent Viking history exhibit, and fountains that spurt water like geysers. Above the six vast tanks, which held 800,000 cubic feet of hot water, the panoramic viewing platform offers telescopes and multilingual recorded commentaries, plus a coffee bar and ice-cream parlor. The crowning glory is a revolving restaurant under the glass dome; it's pricey, but the view is second to none. ☒ *Öskjuhlíð Hill* ☎ *562–0200* ☉ *Daily 11:30–10.*

★ ③ Þjóðleikhús (National Theater). Construction on architect Guðjón Samúelsson's basalt-black edifice began in 1928 but was interrupted during the Depression because of a lack of funds. British troops occupied it during World War II, and it officially opened in 1950. The concrete interior ceiling—an amazing architectural accomplishment in its day— mimics polygonal basalt columns occurring in Icelandic nature. From fall to spring, diverse cultural events are staged here; the biennial Reykjavík Arts Festival uses the venue for several events. Theatrical works are usually performed in Icelandic, but musicals and operettas are sometimes staged in their original languages. ☒ *Hverfisgata 19* ☎ *551–1200* ⊕ *www.leikhusid.is.*

② Þjóðmenningarhúsið (National Cultural House). Crests on the facade of the impressive former Landsbókasafnið (Old National Library) name significant Icelandic literary figures; the renovated building now houses interesting cultural exhibits, including a fixed exhibit of the precious vellum manuscripts of many of the sagas, a must-see for all interested in Norse or ancient literature. Erected between 1906 and 1908, it was a library for most of the century, but its book collection has been moved to the Þjóðarbókhlaðan at the University of Iceland. ⊠ *North side of Hverfisgata at old midtown* ☎ *545–1400* ⊕ *www.thjodmenning.is* 🎫 *IKr 300* ⊘ *Daily 11–5.*

❼ Ráðhús (City Hall). Modern architecture and nature converge at this building overlooking Tjörnin Lake. The architects deliberately planted moss on the northwest and east stone walls to further emphasize the scheme. Inside is a visitor information desk and coffee bar. A three-dimensional model of Iceland is usually on display in the gallery, which often hosts various temporary exhibitions. The natural pond attracts birds—and bird-lovers—year-round and is also popular among ice-skaters in winter. ⊠ *Bounded by Fríkirkjuvegur, Vonarstræti, and Tjarnargata* ☎ *563–2000* ⊕ *www.reykjavik.is* ⊘ *Weekdays 8:20–4:15; coffee bar weekdays 11–6, weekends noon–6.*

❺ Stjórnarráð (Government House). This low white building, constructed in the 18th century as a prison, today houses the office of the prime minister. ⊠ *Lækjatorg Plaza* ☎ *545–8000* ⊕ *www.stjr.is.*

Museums & the University

Art lovers can keep busy in what is still called Reykjavík's "eastern" quarter—even though it is now geographically in the west and center, as the city has been expanding to the east. This tour gives you a good look at some of Iceland's finest paintings and sculpture collections.

a good walk

Start at **Kjarvalsstaðir** ⓮ ▶, reached by Buses 6, 110, 111, and 112 from downtown. From here, set your sights on the 210-foot stair-stepped gray tower of **Hallgrímskirkja** ⓮, about a 10-minute walk from the art museum. From Flókagata, take a left at Snorrabraut and then the first right onto Egilsgata. The church tower offers Reykjavík's highest vantage point, with a fantastic panoramic view of the city. Exit the church and spend some time at the **Listasafn Einars Jónssonar** ⓯, which faces the church across Eiríksgata at the corner with Njarðargata. The monumental works in this gallery explore religious and mythical subjects. Walk four short blocks down Njarðargata and in summer take a left on Bergstaðastræti to the **Ásgrímur Jónsson Museum** ⓰ to see how a well-loved neo-impressionist painter responded to national inspiration. By all means, sign the visitor book, as this charming little museum–home has been sorely deprived of official funding.

Back on Njarðargata walk downhill toward the park to Sóleyjargata, turn right, and walk along Tjörnin Lake. As you pass the octagonal music practice room and a bridge dividing the lake, Sóleyjargata becomes Fríkirkjuvegur. At this intersection is Bertel Thorvaldsen's rendering of *Adonis,* guarding the corner of the grounds of the ornate Reykjavík Youth and Recreational Council, across Njarðargata from the president's offices.

Next to the Youth and Recreational Council is the **Listasafn Íslands** ⓱, where you can find Ásgrímur Jónsson's stunningly huge *Mt. Hekla*—perhaps the best painting of an Icelandic landscape. Exit past the pleasant, corrugated-iron-covered Fríkirkja; follow Fríkirkjuvegur over the bridge on Skothúsvegur, which divides the lake. At the end of Skothúsvegur, pass the old Reykjavík cemetery on your right and a traffic circle on your left.

On the south side is the concrete **Þjóðminjasafn** ⓲, the National Museum, which, due to extensive repairs, is scheduled to reopen in April 2004. It houses Viking artifacts, national costumes, weaving, and more. Just west, across Suðurgata, is the red **Þjóðarbókhlaða** ⓳; it serves as both university and national library. South of the museum is the main campus of the **Háskóli Íslands** ⑳, founded in 1911. Next to the museum's east side is the Félagsstofnun Stúdenta, the Student Union, with an excellent international bookshop. Continue south along a tree-lined walk to the main university building.

Once past the Lögberg Law Building you see Oddi, the Social Sciences Building, on your left; some works of the University Art Collection are displayed on Oddi's second and third floors. End your tour with a snack at the **Norræna Húsið** ㉑ cultural center on the eastern edge of campus.

WHAT TO SEE

Ásgrímur Jónsson Museum. Except for rotating exhibits of the artist's ex-
⑯ traordinary works in oils and watercolors, Ásgrímur Jónsson's house is left as it was when he died in 1958 at the age of 82. ⊠ *Bergstaðastræti 74* ☎ *551–3644* ⊕ *www.listasafn.is* ⊠ *Free* ☉ *June–Aug., Tues.–Sun. 1:30–4.*

★ ⑭ **Hallgrímskirkja** (Hallgrímur's Church). Completed in 1986 after more than 40 years of construction, the church is named for the 17th-century hymn writer Hallgrímur Pétursson. It has a stylized concrete facade recalling both organ pipes and the distinctive columnar basalt formations you can see around Iceland. You may luck into hearing a performance or practice on the church's huge pipe organ. In front of Hallgrímskirkja is a statue of Leifur Eiríksson, the Icelander who discovered America 500 years before Columbus. (Leif's father was Eric the Red, who discovered Greenland.) The statue, by American sculptor Alexander Stirling Calder, was presented to Iceland by the United States in 1930 to mark the millennium of the Alþing parliament. ⊠ *At the top of Skólavörðustígur* ☎ *551–0745* ⊠ *Tower IKr 200* ☉ *May–Sept., daily 9–6; Oct.–Apr., daily 10–6.*

⑳ **Háskóli Íslands** (University of Iceland). On the large crescent-shape lawn in front of the main university building is a statue of Sæmundur Fróði, a symbol of the value of book learning. Legend has it that after studying abroad, Sæmundur made a pact with the devil to get himself home, promising his soul if he arrived without getting wet. The devil changed into a seal to carry him home. Just as they arrived, Sæmundur hit the seal on the head with his Psalter, got his coattails wet, and escaped with soul intact. ⊠ *Across from Hringbraut and diagonally southwest from the park lake* ⊕ *www.hi.is.*

▶ ⑬ **Kjarvalsstaðir.** The Reykjavík Municipal Art Museum is named for Jóhannes Kjarval, the nation's best-known painter, and displays the artist's lava landscapes, portraits, and images of mystical beings. It also shows works by contemporary Icelandic artists and great masters, as well as visiting art collections. ⊠ *Flókagata* ☎ *552–6131* ⊕ *www. listasafnreykjavikur.is* ⊠ *IKr 500* ☉ *Daily 10–5.*

⑮ **Listasafn Einars Jónssonar** (National Gallery of Einar Jónsson). Cubic and fortresslike, this building was once the home and studio of Iceland's leading early-20th-century sculptor. His monumental works inside and in the sculpture garden explore profound symbolic and mystical subjects. The figure of Christ in Hallgrímskirkja is by Jónsson, and several of his unmistakable statues can be found around Reykjavík. ⊠ *Njarðargata* ☎ *551–3797* ⊕ *www.skulptur.is* ⊠ *IKr 400* ☉ *June–mid-Sept., Tues.–Sun. 2–5; mid-Sept.–Nov. and Feb.–May, weekends 2–5.*

⑰ **Listasafn Íslands** (National Gallery). Originally built as an icehouse, this was Reykjavík's hottest nightspot in the '60s. So hot, in fact, that it was gutted by fire in 1971. Now it has been adapted and extended as a temple to art. It holds an impressive collection of 20th-century Icelandic art, including works by old masters Kjarval and Gunnlaugur Scheving, as well as examples of 19th-century Danish art. In addition, the gallery stages international exhibitions, often from Nordic or Baltic countries, or from international collections of Icelandic paintings. The coffee shop with a view of the lake makes for a pleasant stop. ⊠ *Fríkirkjuvegur 7* ☎ *562–1000* ⊕ *www.natgall.is* ✉ *IKr 400, free Wed.* ☉ *Jan.–late Dec., Tues.–Sun. noon–6.*

㉑ **Norræna Húsið** (Nordic House). Designed by Finnish architect Alvar Aalto, this blue-and-white Scandinavian cultural center hosts exhibitions, lectures, and concerts, and has a coffee shop and library. University chamber concerts are held Wednesday at noon during the school year and other recitals are often held on the main level. On Sunday afternoon free children's film matinees are screened. Much of the nearby terrain is being returned to its former marshy condition to entice wetland birds that used to nest here. ⊠ *At Sturlugata and Sæmundargata* ☎ *551–7030* ⊕ *www. nordice.is* ☉ *Daily 2–7.*

⑲ **Þjóðarbókhlaða** (National and University Library). Clad in red aluminum, this structure is hard to miss. It houses the tome collection from the former Landsbókasafnið (Old National Library). ⊠ *Arngrímsgata, on the corner of Suðurgata and Hringbraut* ☎ *563–5600* ✉ *Free* ☉ *Weekdays 9–7, Sat. 10–5.*

⑱ **Þjóðminjasafn** (National Museum). Viking treasures and artifacts, silver work, wood carvings, and some unusual whalebone carvings are on display here, as well as maritime objects, historical textiles, jewelry, and crafts. There is also a coffee shop. The museum is scheduled to reopen, after extensive renovations, in April 2004; call ahead to make sure. ⊠ *Suðurgata 41* ☎ *552–8888* ⊕ *www.natmus.is* ✉ *IKr 200* ☉ *Mid-May–mid-Sept., Tues.–Sun. 11–5; mid-Sept.–mid-May, Tues., Thurs., and weekends noon–5.*

Harborfront

a good walk

Reykjavík's harborfront is an easy three-block stroll north from Lækjartorg Plaza. Ambling along Geirsgata you see on your right the pier at Ægisgarður, with colorful fishing and pleasure boats of all sizes coming and going. For a closer look, walk to the pier itself after taking a right on the obscure little street, Suðurbugt, which skirts the waterfront.

Backtracking on Suðurbugt to the light at Geirsgata, pick up Tryggvagata across the intersection, heading southeast back towards Lækjartorg Plaza. In the second block, at Tryggvagata17, is Hafnarhús, a former warehouse, now the **Listasafn Reykjavíkur** ▶ ㉒, the Reykjavík Art Museum. It's recognizable by its entrance under what looks like a wide gang-plank hinging from the wall overhead. After taking in the latest exhibition, continue on Tryggvagata to **Tollstöðin** ㉓ which is distinguished by Iceland's largest mosaic mural, a harbor scene by Gerður Helgadóttir.

Looping back to the waterfront and still curving southeast brings you to **Ingólfsgarður pier** ㉔, closest to Lækjatorg Plaza. Here you may spot Iceland's Coast Guard vessels docked for service. If you continue walking east along the shoreline, you'll pass the green, dual-pointed *Partnership* sculpture, a gift to Iceland from a former U.S. ambassador and his wife. Even more dramatic, a few hundred yards farther along the shore is *Sólfar,* a stunning modern tribute to Viking seafarers who first sailed into this harbor 1,100 years ago. It points proudly offshore toward Mt. Esja. The design for this brilliant stainless-steel sculpture won first prize in an art competition in conjunction with Reykjavík's 1986 bicentennial as a city.

If you continue to walk east along the water, you'll come to the **Listasafn Sigurjóns Ólafssonar** ㉕, a charming museum in what was the artist's studio. It's a wonderful retreat from the bustle of the city. In good weather take the Viðey ferry from its launch site at Klettavör, close to Sundahöfn harbor east of town, to the verdant nearby island of Viðey: don't miss *Áfangar,* Richard Serra's landscape art arrangement of basalt pillars on the island's northern side. From June to August the same ferry company also skirts the aptly-named neighbor islet, Puffin Island, which is closed to humans.

WHAT TO SEE

㉔ **Ingólfsgarður pier.** A berth for Coast Guard vessels, this pier has a distinctive yellow beacon pylon at its end. A handful of ships, which tenaciously stood up to the British Navy during the cod wars, still vigorously enforce offshore fishing limits. The Coast Guard is the closest thing Iceland has to a national military.

㉒ **Listasafn Reykjavíkur** (Reykjavík Art Museum). Also known as Hafnarhús, this former warehouse for the Port of Reykjavík now houses the city's art museum. The six galleries occupy two floors, and there's a courtyard and "multipurpose" space. The museum's permanent collection includes a large number of works donated by the Icelandic contemporary artist, Erró. There are also regular temporary exhibitions. ⊠ *Tryggvagata 17* ☎ *590–1200* ⊕ *www.listasafnreykjavikur.is* ⊠ *IKr 500, free Mon.* ☉ *Daily 10–5.*

㉕ **Listasafn Sigurjóns Ólafssonar.** (Sigurjón Ólafsson Museum). A simple but stylish museum on the seaside site of the late artist's studio workshop. Ólafsson was both a sensitive portrait sculptor and profound abstract artist working in steel, stone, wood, even concrete. The cafeteria is a delightful retreat from city bustle and the Tuesday evening concerts are among the joys of the Iceland summer. ⊠ *Laugarnestangi 70* ☎ *553–2906* ⊕ *www.iso.is* ⊠ *IKr 400* ☉ *June–Aug. 31., Tues.–Sun. 2–5; Sept.–Nov. and Feb.–May, weekends 2–5.*

㉓ **Tollstöðin.** A bureaucratic necessity, especially for an island nation, the Customs House is decorated with an impressive mosaic mural. ⊠ *Tryggvagata 19.*

off the beaten path

VI EY – This unspoiled island in Kollafjörður is great for a walk and a picnic. It's also a haven for nesting birds. Here you can also see a little church and the 18th-century governor's residence, Viðey House, which once hosted aviator Charles Lindbergh during a stopover flight in his heyday; now it's an upscale restaurant. Vehicles are not allowed on the island, which is accessible only by ferry from its own pier. You can take Buses 4 or 14 to the nearby Sundahöfn freight harbor. ☎ *892–0099 for ferry booking.*

Where to Eat

The dining scene in Reykjavík has been diversifying: traditional Icelandic restaurants now face competition from Asian, Italian, Mexican, Indian, and vegetarian places.

Old Town

$$$$ ✕ **Humarhúsið.** This restaurant in Bernhöftstorfa district specializes in lobster, as its name implies. You can try it in salad, soup, or as one of the many main courses. ⊠ *Amtmannsstíg 1* ☎ *561–3303* ⊟ *DC, MC, V.*

¢–$$$$ ✕ **Hornið.** This welcoming bistro is light and airy, with lots of natural wood, potted plants, and cast-iron bistro tables. The emphasis is on pizzas and pasta, but there's also a selection of meat and fish dishes. Try the lamb pepper steak with garlicky mushrooms or the seafood soup, a favorite for lunch. Their delicious cakes can be enjoyed with the obligatory espresso at any time of day. ⊠ *Hafnarstræti 15* ☎ *551–3340* ⊟ *AE, DC, MC, V.*

$$$ ✕ **Lækjabrekka.** Locals and visitors alike go to this established eatery for its excellent food at reasonable prices. On weekends, live background music emanates from a tight corner of this charming, classic restaurant. ⊠ *Bankastræti 2* ☎ *551–4430* ⊟ *AE, DC, MC, V.*

★ **$$$**   ✕ **Við Tjörnina.** Enter through a classic wooden doorway and go up a
FodorśChoice   flight of stairs and back in time in this early-20th-century house with a
★   hand-carved bar and chairs, embroidered tablecloths, and crocheted drapes. This is one of the best places in Iceland for delicious, innovative seafood dishes such as as plaice sautéed with blue cheese and bananas. The lunchtime dish of the day can be a bargain. ⊠ *Templarasund 3* ☎ *551–8666* ⊟ *AE, MC, V.*

$ ✕ **Pasta Basta.** You have four seating options at this small restaurant: an area with intimate booths on the lower level; a small, bright conservatory at ground level; a canvas-covered patio under the large silver rowan tree; and finally the *La Dolce Vita* bar upstairs. The food is mostly Italian, though some dishes branch out into the wider Mediterranean region. Crayons are provided for creative children. ⊠ *Klapparstíg 38* ☎ *561–3131* ⊟ *MC, V* ⊗ *No lunch.*

¢   ✕ **Bæjarins beztu.** Facing the harbor in a parking lot, this tiny but famous fast-food hut is famous for serving the original Icelandic hot dog; one person serves about a thousand hot dogs a day from the window. Ask for *ayn-ah-mud-lou* (pronounced quickly with stress on "mud"), which will get you "one with everything": mustard, tomato sauce, *rémoulade* (mayonnaise with finely chopped pickles), and chopped raw and fried onions. ⊠ *Tryggvagata and Pósthússtræti* ☎ *No phone* ⊟ *No credit cards.*

¢   ✕ **Ostabuðin.** Responding to popular demand, Ostabuðin, the Cheese Shop, has added some tables and chairs to allow customers to relax and enjoy fish dishes, fine imported and local cheeses, sandwiches, and desserts. ⊠ *Skólavörðustígur 8* ☎ *562–2772* ⊟ *MC, V.*

Museums, the University & Beyond

$$$$ ✕ **Grillið.** Atop the Saga Hotel near the university campus, this quiet, cozy restaurant has a spectacular view of the capital and the surrounding hinterlands. If you are really hungry, for only 100 krónur more than the price of a starter and main course, you can have a sumptuous four-course feast with starter, fish and meat entré and dessert. Specialties include grilled lobster tails with mushroom purée. ⊠ *Hagatorg* ☎ *552–5033* ⊟ *AE, DC, MC, V* ⊗ *No lunch.*

★ **$$$–$$$$**   ✕ **Gallery Restaurant.** Icelandic art covers the walls of this restaurant in
FodorśChoice   the Hótel Holt, within walking distance of downtown; the cocktail
★   lounge and bar showcase drawings by Jóhannes Kjarval. The Gallery has long been in the forefront of Icelandic restaurants, with impeccable service and mouthwatering wild-game and seafood dishes. The modestly priced semi-fixed lunch menu is quite a good value. Favorites include gravlax and reindeer. The Reading Room bar's whiskey selection is as diverse as any in Europe. ⊠ *Hótel Holt, Bergstaðastræti 37* ☎ *552–5700* ⊟ *AE, DC, MC, V.*

★ **$$$–$$$$**   ✕ **Hjá Sigga Hall á Oðinsvé.** There's an air of anticipation among the hun-
FodorśChoice   gry patrons waiting for their tables in the cozy greenhouse extension of
★   this glossy restaurant. The sylphlike waitstaff, all dressed in black, glides swiftly back and forth. Then, there he is, Iceland's celebrity chef Siggi Hall, a congenial figure who visits each table, chatting easily with ac-

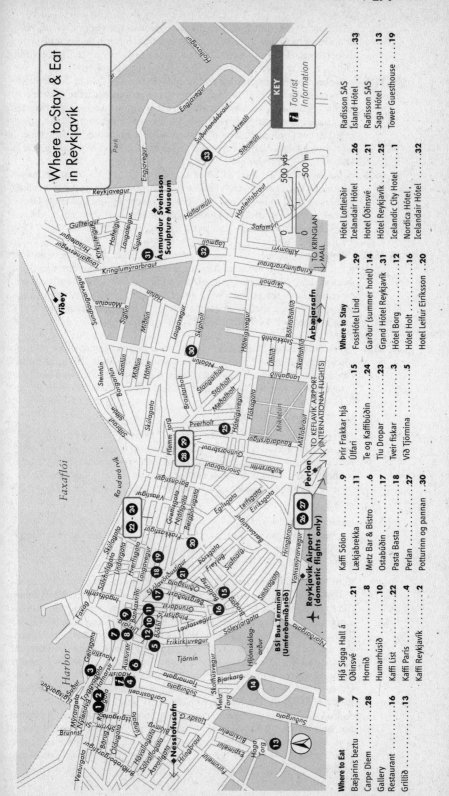

Where to Stay & Eat in Reykjavik

quaintances old and new. The regulars know what they're in for, and first-timers have heard about the chef's adventurous fish, lamb, and game dishes, meticulously prepared and beautifully presented. ⊠ *Hotel Óðinsvé, Oðinstorg* ☎ *552–5090* ⊟ *AE, DC, MC, V.*

$$$–$$$$ ✕ **Perlan.** This rotating restaurant, atop Reykjavík's hot-water distribution tanks on Öskjuhlíð Hill, is the city's most glamorous, with the most spectacular views in town (one revolution takes about two hours). The international menu emphasizes fresh, quality Icelandic ingredients, such as succulent lamb and seafood. Seafood dishes, prepared with the freshest fish available, change often. ⊠ *Öskjuhlíð Hill* ☎ *562–0203* ⊟ *AE, DC, MC, V* ⊙ *No lunch.*

$$–$$$$ ✕ **Carpe Diem.** Attached to FossHótel Lind, but under separate management, this restaurant has solid-wood parquet floors and a charming fireplace to add a glow in cool seasons. Lunch options include huge sandwiches or pasta with soup. Dinner entrées are equally hearty, and you can help yourself to the salad bar. ⊠ *Rauðarárstígur 18* ☎ *552–4555* ⊟ *AE, MC, V.*

$$–$$$$ ✕ **Potturinn og pannan.** The interior of this restaurant on the edge of downtown is bright and modern. Among entreés on the varied menu are Icelandic bacalao au gratin with olives, tomatoes, and Parmesan cheese; or grilled fresh tuna steak. Soup and salad bar are included with main course. There are special selections just for children, and a separate children's playroom. ⊠ *Brautarholt 22, entered from Nóatún* ☎ *551–1690* ⊟ *MC, V.*

$$–$$$$ ✕ **Þrír Frakkar hjá Úlfari.** In an unassuming building in an older part of town, this restaurant serves truly traditional Icelandic food, with an emphasis on seafood. Whale-meat sushi is one of the novelties here. The bright annex overlooks a tiny, tree-filled park. ⊠ *Baldursgata 14 at Nönnugata* ☎ *552–3939* ⊟ *MC, V.*

Harborfront

$$ ✕ **Tveir fiskar.** Although the name means "two fish" there's plenty more on the menu here. Try the delicious shellfish soup, lobster, or the restaurant's namesake fish duo, which changes according to what is freshest in the market. Carnivores can opt for lamb or chicken. For dessert, try the baked caramel apple. ⊠ *Geirsgata 9* ☎ *511–3474* ⊟ *MC, V.*

Cafés

Icelanders rival the Finns for the record for per capita caffeine consumption, so it should come as no surprise that coffee bars have replaced clothing boutiques as the most common enterprise in town. All cafés listed are in the Old Town or on Laugavegur.

Kaffi París (⊠ Austurstræti 14, ☎ 551–1020) is a popular spot; even Hillary Clinton dropped in, on a visit to Reykjavik. At artsy **Kaffi Sólon** (⊠ Bankastræti 7A ☎ 562–3232) you can see some modern art, maybe catch the Thursday evening jazz jam, eat a snack, and people-watch. Trendy **Kaffi List** (⊠ Laugavegiur 20A ☎ 562–5059) has an international flavor, with an emphasis on tapas. **Kaffi Reykjavík** (⊠ Vesturgata 2 ☎ 562–5530), in a picturesque 19th-century wooden building, has a veranda where you can sit outside in good weather. The man who started the Icelandic coffee revolution runs **Te og Kaffibúðin** (⊠ Laugavegur 27 ☎ 552–6260). The **Tíu Dropar** (⊠ Laugavegur 27 ☎ 551–9380) coffeehouse serves a tantalizing selection of homemade goodies. The **Metz Bar and Bistro** (⊠ Austurstræti 9 ☎ 561–3000) touts Oscar Wilde's witty comment, "Work is the curse of the drinking class." The wine prices here are hard to beat in Iceland. Check out the cellar disco if you want to dance.

Lodging

Lodgings range from modern, first-class Scandinavian-style hotels to inexpensive guest houses and B&Bs offering basic amenities at relatively low prices (contact the Tourist Information Center for a register). Iceland's climate makes air-conditioning unnecessary. Most hotel rooms have televisions, though not always cable TV. Lower-price hotels sometimes have a television lounge in lieu of TV in each room. Ask if your hotel offers complimentary admission tickets to the closest swimming pool. The **Reykjavík Youth Hostel** (⊠ Sundlaugavegur 34 ☎ 553–8110 🖨 588–9201 ⊕ www.hostel.is) has 108 beds for around IKr 1,250 (not including breakfast) per night.

Old Town & East

★ **$$$$**
FodorsChoice ★ 🏨 **Hótel Borg.** Some rooms in Reykjavík's oldest hotel, built in 1930 in the art deco style, may not seem spacious, but they are elegant and combine old-fashioned quality with modern comforts. All rooms have fluffy down comforters, tasteful prints (some antique), coffee machines, and CD players, as well as a fax machine on request. The hotel is in the heart of the city, overlooking Austurvöllur and close to Parliament House. Breakfast is a wonderful spread, with home-baked breads, cheeses, cold cuts, fruit, and more. ⊠ *Pósthússtræti 11 IS-101* ☎ *551–1440* 🖨 *551–1420* ⊕ *www.hotelborg.is* ➷ *51 rooms, 1 suite* ♦ *Restaurant, cable TV, in-room VCRs, bar* ▤ *AE, DC, MC, V.*

$$$–$$$$ 🏨 **Hótel Reykjavík.** Within a few blocks of both the Kjarvalsstaðir Municipal Art Museum and the Hlemmur bus station, this hotel has smart, Nordic-style furnishings and is operated by the same management as the Grand Hotel. The independently-run Rauðará steak house is in the same building. ⊠ *Rauðarárstígur 39 IS-101* ☎ *514–7000* 🖨 *514–7030* ⊕ *www.hotelreykjavik.is* ➷ *79 rooms, 7 suites* ♦ *2 restaurants, café, minibars, cable TV, bar, no-smoking rooms* ▤ *AE, DC, MC, V.*

$$$–$$$$ 🏨 **Nordica Hótel, Icelandair Hótel.** This luxury hotel is primarily geared toward business travelers, although families are given priority for available larger standard rooms. Business-class rooms are spacious and include breakfast and access to the lounge, with gorgeous views of the city, where you can read newspapers and help yourself to complementary wine, coffee, tea, and hors d'oeuvres. Executive rooms include free access to the health club. ⊠ *Suðurlandsbruat 2 IS 101* ☎ *444–5000* 🖨 *444–5001* ⊕ *www.icehotel.is* ➷ *284 rooms, 25 suites* ♦ *Restaurant, cable TV, health club, massage, sauna, spa, steam room, bar* ▤ *AE, DC, MC, V.*

$$$ 🏨 **Grand Hótel Reykjavík.** Relatively spacious rooms, free entry to Laugardalur Park and its pool, and complimentary shuttle service to town every morning are some of the pluses at the Grand. ⊠ *Sigtún 38 IS-101* ☎ *514–8000* 🖨 *514–8030* ➷ *100 rooms, 3 suites* ♦ *Restaurant, bar, lobby lounge, convention center* ▤ *AE, DC, MC, V.*

Museums, the University & Beyond

★ **$$$$**
FodorsChoice ★ 🏨 **Hótel Holt.** This quietly elegant member of the prestigious Relais & Chateau hotel group has impeccable service, an excellent restaurant, and computer links in every room, all of which make it a favorite among business travelers. Though the rooms are small by modern standards, all are decorated with works by leading Icelandic artists. It's in a pleasant neighborhood close to the town center. ⊠ *Bergstaðastræti 37 IS-101* ☎ *552–5700* 🖨 *562–3025* ⊕ *www.holt.is* ➷ *42 rooms, 12 suites* ♦ *Restaurant, bar, lobby lounge, meeting room* ▤ *AE, DC, MC, V.*

$$$$ 🏨 **Radisson SAS Saga Hótel.** Just off the university campus, this hotel is a 15-minute walk from most museums, shops, and restaurants. All rooms are above the fourth floor and have spectacular views. ⊠ *Haga-*

torg IS-107 ☎ *525–9900* 🖷 *562–3980* ⊕ *www.radisson.com* ⬮ *216 rooms, 8 suites* ♨ *Restaurant, grill, health club, hot tub, sauna, 6 bars, nightclub, meeting room, travel services, no-smoking room* ▭ *AE, DC, MC, V.*

$$$–$$$$ ⌂ **Hótel Loftleiðir Icelandair Hótel.** The advantage of this rather remote hotel is nearby Öskjuhlíð Hill, where you can take pleasant walks and stroll up to Perlan for ice cream. Rooms are modern, with Scandinavian pine furniture and pastel fabrics. To get here, take bus route 7. ✉ *Reykjavík Airport IS-101* ☎ *505–0900* 🖷 *505–0905* ⊕ *www. icehotels.is* ⬮ *220 rooms, 1 apartment suite* ♨ *Restaurant, pool, sauna, bar, convention center, travel services* ▭ *AE, DC, MC, V.*

$$$ ⌂ **FossHótel Lind.** This quiet, unpretentious hotel is uptown, a block south of the Hlemmur bus station. Rooms are decorated in shades of red and blue. The clientele is largely Icelanders from the country attending conferences or cultural events in Reykjavík. ✉ *Rauðarárstígur 18 IS-105* ☎ *562–3350* 🖷 *562–3351* ⊕ *www.fosshotel.is* ⬮ *56 rooms* ♨ *Restaurant, bar, meeting room* ▭ *DC, MC, V.*

$$$ ⌂ **Hotel Óðinsvé.** Three buildings in a calm corner in an older part of town make up this family-run hotel. No two rooms are alike, but all are cheery and efficient, some with nice views over colorful rooftops. Its many regular guests prefer its intimacy and convenience to Old Town. ✉ *Óðinstorg IS-101* ☎ *511–6200* 🖷 *511–6201* ⊕ *www. hotelodinsve.is* ⬮ *37 rooms* ♨ *Restaurant* ▭ *AE, DC, MC, V.*

$$$ ⌂ **Radisson SAS Ísland Hótel.** The chunky, postmodern, silver-and-blue hotel is close to the Laugardalur Park and recreation area. Its interior has elegant furnishings and bright, airy rooms with floral prints and dark woods in smooth, curved shapes. Some rooms have kitchenettes. ✉ *Armúli 9 IS-101* ☎ *595–7000* 🖷 *595–7001* ⊕ *www.radisson.com* ⬮ *119 rooms, 3 suites* ♨ *Restaurant, some kitchenettes, minibars, bar, nightclub* ▭ *AE, DC, MC, V.*

$$–$$$ ⌂ **Tower Guesthouse.** These brightly and stylishly decorated apartment units with kitchens are tucked a block off the shopping street, Laugavegur. You can have breakfast and unwind on your balcony, or take a dip in the jacuzzi, which is open to all guests. ✉ *Grettisgata 6 IS-101* ☎ *562–3350* 🖷 *552–5581* ⊕ *www.towerguesthouse.homestead.com* ⬮ *3 apartments* ▭ *MC, V.*

$$ ⌂ **Hotel Leifur Eiríksson.** Across the street from the hilltop church of Hallgrímskirkja, this hotel is a short walk from most of Reykjavík's major attractions and midtown shops. Some guest rooms have balconies. ✉ *Skólavörðustígur 45 IS-101* ☎ *562–0800* 🖷 *562–0804* ⊕ *www. hotelleifur.is* ⬮ *47 rooms* ♨ *Restaurant, bar* ▭ *MC, V.*

$$ ⌂ **Icelandic City Hotel.** This small hotel stands on a central but quiet residential street. Rooms have furnishings in pale wood, with navy blue fabrics. ✉ *Ránargata 4A IS-101* ☎ *511–1155* 🖷 *552–9040* ⊕ *www. icelandichotels.is* ⬮ *31 rooms* ▭ *AE, DC, MC, V.*

$ ⌂ **Garður.** This student residence is open as a hotel only in summer. Basic rooms are adequately comfortable and ideal for travelers on a tight budget. The property is convenient to downtown and other attractions, like the National Museum. Each floor has a shared bath and shower. City Hotel handles all bookings. ✉ *Hringbraut IS-107* ☎ *511–1155 City Hotel* 🖷 *552–9040* ⊕ *www.icelandhotels.is* ⬮ *44 rooms without bath* ▭ *AE, DC, MC, V.*

Nightlife & the Arts

Reykjavík has an active cultural life through most of the year, and is especially strong in the visual arts. The classical performing-arts scene tends to quiet down somewhat in summer; however, a growing number of rock and jazz concerts has been helping to fill in the lull. Beginning in 2004, the Reykjavík Arts Festival is to be an annual event held in late spring. Past festivals have drawn Luciano Pavarotti and David Bowie, among other stars. Consult the bimonthly *Around Reykjavík* and the biweekly *What's on in Reykjavík,* both of which can be found at most hotels.

Nightlife

Nightlife in Reykjavík essentially means two types of establishments: pubs and nightclubs with dancing and live music. Nightspots usually enforce some basic dress rules, so men should wear a jacket and tie and women should avoid wearing jeans. On weekends, unless you start before 9 PM, be prepared to wait in line, especially if summer weekend weather is good. Avoid downtown after midnight during the first weekends of summer, when excessive drinking can result in some raucous and aggressive behavior. Suffice it to say, Icelanders party en masse.

The fashionable place to see and be seen is **Astro** (⊠ Austurstræti 22 ☎ 552–9222), where live music of any modern genre goes on into the wee hours on weekends. **Broadway at Hótel Ísland** (⊠ Ármúli 9 ☎ 533–1100) is the largest restaurant and dance hall in Iceland and can hold more than 1,000 guests at a time. It has nightclub shows and music performances. Rub elbows with reclusive celebs at **Kaffibarinn** (⊠ Bergstaðastræti 1 ☎ 551–1588), which is part-owned by Damon Albarn of the band Blur. **Kaffi Reykjavík** (⊠ Vesturgata 2 ☎ 562–5530) is an ever-popular, spacious coffee bar–pub–restaurant. The bar and bistro **Metz** (⊠ Austurstræti 9 ☎ 561–3000) draws large crowds to its loud cellar space.

The Arts

FILM The seven movie houses around the capital have up to six screens each and usually show recent English-language films with Icelandic subtitles. For listings, see the movie ads toward the back of daily newspapers *Morgunblaðið* or *DV*. The **Háskólabíó** (University Cinema; ☎ 530–1919) is on Hagatorg, near the Radisson SAS Saga Hótel and university.

FOLKLORE You can go to **Light Nights** (⊠ Ioðnó 12, opposite City Hall,) to watch traditional folk performances in English, based on Icelandic sagas and folk tales; it takes place in July and August, and has been running for over 30 years.

MUSIC Visiting musicians play everything from classical to jazz, opera to rock. The Icelandic Opera, **Íslenska Óperan** (☎ 511–4200), a resident company, performs in winter at its home on Ingólfsstræti. The Iceland Symphony Orchestra **Sinfóníuhljómsveit Íslands** (☎ 545–2500 ⊕ www.sinfonia.is) has bloomed beautifully and won fine reviews for its tour performances at Carnegie Hall and the Kennedy Center. Regular performances are in winter and usually alternate Thursday and Saturday evenings at the University Cinemas. The Gerðuberg Cultural Center, **Menningarmiðstöðin Gerðuberg** (⊠ Gerðuberg 3–5 ☎ 575–7700 ⊕ www.gerduberg.is), is a suburban center in Breiðholt where chamber and solo music performances are often featured. The **Nordic House** (⊠ At Sturlugata & Sæmundargata ☎ 551–7030 ⊕ www.nordice.is) hosts chamber and other musical events, including a midday winter recital series on alternate Wednesdays.

Other less traditional concert venues can be found as well. The seaside **Sigurjón Ólafsson Sculpture Museum** (⊠ Laugarnestangi 70 ☎ 553–2906) hosts summer concerts every Tuesday evening at 8:30 in appropriately artistic surroundings. Liturgical and choral works are frequently performed in churches, including **Langholtskirkja** (⊠ Sólheimar 13 ☎ 520–1300). Pipe-organ, or other concerts at the large church **Hallgrímskirkja**

(⊠ Skólavörðurholt, at the top of Skólavörðurstígur ☎ 510–1000 ⊕ www.hallgrimskirkja.is) are memorable experiences, especially the trumpet and organ recital on New Year's Eve.

THEATER   In winter the City Theater, **Borgarleikhösið** (⊠ Listabraut 3 ☎ 568–8000) puts on modern and classic Icelandic plays, as well as local adaptations of well-known works. The **Þjóðleikhösið** (National Theater; ⊠ Hverfis-gata 19 ☎ 551–1200 ⊕ www.leikhusid.is) stages plays by Icelandic writers, such as Nobel Prize winner Halldór Laxness, as well as works by such diverse dramatists as Henrik Ibsen, Tennessee Williams, and Rodgers and Hammerstein.

Sports & the Outdoors

Fishing

The **Angling Club of Reykjavík** (⊠ Háaleitisbraut 68 ☎ 568–6050) can provide information on fishing in the area. The **Federation of Icelandic River Owners** (⊠ Bolholt 6 ☎ 553–1510) is another source for anglers. For tackle in Reykjavík, head to **Veiðihornið** (⊠ Hafnarstræti 5 ☎ 551–6760). **Útivist og Veiði** (⊠ Síðumúli 11 ☎ 588–6500) is a well-stocked tackle retailer.

Golf

At the southern tip of Seltjarnarnes, the westernmost part of the Reyk-javík area, **Golfklúbbur Ness** (⊠ Seltjarnarnes ☎ 561–1930) has a well-kept 9-hole course with a great view in all directions. **Golfklúbbur Reykjavíkur** (⊠ Korpúlfstöðum 112 Reykjavík ☎ 585–0200) is the grand-daddy of them all, a challenging 18-hole course just east of Reykjavik.

Handball

Team handball, a national obsession and a sport in which Iceland has finished as high as fourth in the Olympics, is a big draw in the winter. For information on the fast, furious, and exciting matches between Ice-land's leading teams, as well as thrilling confrontations with some of the world's best handball nations, contact the **Handball Federation** (☎ 568–5422).

Horseback Riding

Two stables in the Reykjavík area rent horses by the hour or by the day. **Íshestar** (Icelandic Riding Tours; ⊠ Sörlaskeiði 26, Hafnarfjörður ☎ 555–7000 ⊕ www.ishestar.is) offers two- to seven-hour rides for IKr 4,200–IKr 8,600, including guides and transportation from Reykjavík hotels. **Laxnes Horse Farm** (⊠ Mosfellsdalur ☎ 566–6179 ⊕ www. laxnes.is) offers three-hour riding tours for IKr 3,000, including guides and transportation to and from Reykjavík.

Ice Skating

The artificial skating rink Skautahöllin, in **Laugardalur Park** (☎ 588–9705) adjacent to the Botanical Gardens and Farmyard Animal Zoo, is open mid-September through the first week of May. If you have your own skates, admission is IKr 500. Otherwise, hockey or standard skates can be rented for IKr 300, and helmets are loaned free for the asking. If tem-peratures have been below freezing long enough and winds are relatively still, then **Tjörnin Lake** in the Old Town, is often groomed, and some-times even floodlit at night for skaters of all ages.

Running

In the crisp, clean air of the Reykjavík area, running is a pleasure on the wide sidewalks in the parks and along a growing network of paved bike-running paths. Favorite routes are around Tjörnin Lake (but re-member that the geese aren't potty-trained), in Laugardalur Park, Miklatún Park, and Öskjuhlíð. Distance runners from around the globe participate in the annual **Reykjavík Marathon** in August.

Skiing

In wintertime try the downhill and cross-country skiing at the **Bláfjöll** (☎ 561–8400), outside Reykjavík; **Skálafell** (☎ 570–7711) is a ski area within a 30-minute drive of the city. Both have ski lifts and can be reached by **Bifreiðastöð Íslands (BSÍ)**, (☎ 591–1000) the bus company.

Soccer

Catch an Icelandic soccer match in summer. Revved up by loyal followers, the national team has stunned better-known European teams and progressed further in competitions than most dared dream. A number of Icelandic soccer players are with professional soccer teams in Europe, but most have contract provisions to allow them to represent Iceland in international matches. The most important soccer matches are played at **Laugardalsvöllur Stadium** (✉ take Bus 2, 5, 10, 11, or 12 ☎ 510–2914). You can buy tickets at the box office just before the game, or inquire at downtown bookstores for advance sales.

Swimming

There are 11 swimming pools in the greater Reykjavík area, some with saunas. Rules of hygiene are strictly enforced—you must shower thoroughly, without a swimsuit, before entering the pool. There is a popular pool in **Vesturbær** at Hofsvallagata (via Bus 4). The pool at **Laugardalur Park** (Bus 5 goes closest; 10,11, or 12 stop within walking distance) is also a favorite summer spot, as is **Árbæjarrlaug** (Bus 10, 11, or 110 going east) with a water-linked indoor and outdoor pool and hot tubs of varying warmths. All are open seven days a week. A locker and access to the swimming pool cost IKr 220 for adults and IKr 100 for children ages 6–15; kids under 6 swim free. You can rent towels and swimsuits. Use of the sauna is extra. *Note:* Swimming pools are one of the few places in Iceland where you should be on guard against petty theft. If you are wearing snazzy running shoes, lock them up in a locker.

Shopping

Malls

The **Kringlan Mall** is on the east side of town at the intersection of Miklabraut and Kringlumýrarbraut; you can get to it by taking Bus 6, 110, 111 or 112 from Lækjartorg. Number 6 also leaves from the Hlemmur bus station, and Bus 17 from the Mjódd bus station also stops at Kringlan.

Iceland's second major shopping mall, **Smáralind** (pronounced *smow-ra-lind*), is in Kópavogur, a community neighboring Reykjavík to the south. Intent on rivaling Kringlan Mall, it is huge and houses, among other stores, British-based **Debenhams** as well as Iceland's own discount chain, **Hagkaup**. From Reykjavík you can take any of many buses that link to the Mjódd bus station (e.g., 3, 4, 6, 10, or from Hlemmur, No. 12) and from there take 114. Or take 140 to Hamraborg in Kópavogur and transfer to Bus 16 or 17, but a cab trip of a little over IKr 1,000 may save a lot of precious shopping time.

Shopping Streets

The main shopping downtown is on and around Austurstræti, Aðalstræti, Hafnarstræti, Bankastræti, Laugavegur, and Skólavörðustígur.

Specialty Stores

ART GALLERIES You can find crafts workshops and galleries all around town. **Gallery Fold** (✉ Laugavegur 118D, entrance from Raudarárstígur ☎ 551–0400) has a large selection of prints, drawings, paintings, and sculpture by contemporary Icelandic artists, as well as some older Icelandic art. **Listhús** (⊠ Engjateigur 17–19), opposite Nordica Hótel, is a complex of art stores and ateliers selling Icelandic arts and crafts.

COINS & STAMPS **Hjá Magna** (⊠ Laugavegur 15 ☎ 552–3011) offers a wide selection of mint coins and stamps. Due to the limited size of the issues involved, a number of Icelandic stamps and coins are considered valuable items. **Postphil** (⊠ Vesturgata 10A 101 Reykjavík) sees to collector sales and has a special philatelic service with subscription schemes for new issues; it is just a few minutes' walk from the Lækjatorg bus terminus.

CRAFTS Lava ceramics, sheepskin rugs, and Viking-inspired jewelry are popular souvenirs. An amble along **Skólavörðustígur** from Laugavegur to Hallgrímskirkja church takes you past many tempting woolen, jewelry, and crafts shops, as well as art galleries. The Handknitting Association of Iceland, **Handprjónasambandið** (⊠ Skólavörðurstígur 19 ☎ 552–1890), has its own outlet, selling, of course, only hand-knit items. **Hornstofan Handverkshús Arts and Crafts** (⊠ Laufásvegur 2 ☎ 551–7800), closed Thursday, is a summer showroom, working studio, and store run co-operatively by the Icelandic Handicrafts Association. **Islandia** (⊠ Kringlan Mall ☎ 568–9960) offers a range of woolens, giftware, and souvenirs.

Many hand- and machine-knitted woolen garments are sold at **Rammagerðin** (⊠ Hafnarstræti 19 ☎ 551–1122 ⊠ Hotel Loftleiðir ☎ 552–5460 ⊠ Nordica Hotel ☎ 444–5080).

Street Markets

In summertime **Lækjartorg** sometimes fills with the stands of outdoor merchants offering everything from woolens, records, and books to vegetables, fruit, and bread. During the weekend (and an occasional weekday), the lively and colorful **Kolaport flea market** (☎ 562–5030) is open in an old ground-floor warehouse by the harborside (look for the big banner).

Reykjavík A to Z

AIR TRAVEL TO & FROM REYKJAVÍK

CARRIERS For reservations and information in Reykjavík, contact Icelandair, SAS, or Iceland Express. For domestic reservations and information, contact either Icelandair or Íslandsflug.

✈ **Icelandair** ☎ 505-0300 ⊕ www.icelandair.com. **Iceland Express** ☎ 550-0600 ⊕ www.icelandexpress.is **Íslandsflug** ☎ 570-8090. **SAS** ☎ 577-6420 ⊕ www.scandinavian.net.

AIRPORTS & TRANSFERS

All international flights arrive and depart from Keflavík Airport, 50 km (31 mi) southwest of the capital. Reykjavík Airport is the central hub of domestic air travel in Iceland.

✈ **Keflavík Airport** ☎ 505-0500 ⊕ www.keflavikairport.com. **Reykjavík Airport** ☎ 570-3030.

AIRPORT TRANSFERS The Reykjavík FlyBus leaves Keflavík (from directly outside the terminal building) and arrives in Reykjavík at the Hótel Loftleiðir at Reykjavík Airport. From there you can take a taxi or municipal bus to your destination. FlyBuses are scheduled in connection with flight arrivals and departures. For departures you can catch the FlyBus at the Saga, Nordica, and Loftleiðir hotels and the Grand Hotel Reykjavík. The FlyBus also leaves the youth hostel in Laugardalur at 5 AM daily June through August. The fare is IKr 1,000 per person. The ride takes 40–50 minutes.

From Reykjavík Airport, the municipal (S) Bus 5 leaves from the Icelandair terminal on the western side of the airport. Other airlines operate from the east terminal (behind the Loftleiðir Hotel), which is served by Bus 1. A taxi from the Keflavík Airport to Reykjavík is a little faster than the FlyBus and costs IKr 8,000. If you share it with others, you can split the cost. From Reykjavík Airport a taxi to your hotel costs around IKr 700. T here are direct phones to taxi companies in the arrivals hall. Taxi companies from Keflavík include Aðalstöðin and Ökuleiðir. The taxi companies based in Reykjavík are Hreyfill and Bæjarleiðir, among others.

🚍 **Aðalstöðin** ☎ 421-1515 or 425-2525. **Bæjarleiðir** ☎ 553-3500. **Hreyfill** ☎ 588-5522. **Ökuleiðir** ☎ 421-4141. **Reykjavík FlyBus** ☎ 562-1011.

BUS TRAVEL WITHIN REYKJAVÍK

The municipal bus system has been consolidated with neighboring systems, so the greater Reykjavík area is now served by one carrier, with yellow buses bearing a large yellow 'S' logo on a red circular background, which abbreviates the system's affectionate nickname among Icelanders—Stræto (pronounced stry toe). Stræto is extensive, cheap, and reliable and now covers the suburb communities of Kópavogur (routes 16–18, 61, 62, 66, 114, 140, 112), Garðabær (routes 51, 114, 140, 150), and Hafnarfjörður (routes 41–46, 114, 150). Buses run from 7 AM to midnight or 1 AM. On most routes, buses run every 20 minutes during the day and every half hour evenings and weekends. Bus stops are either three-sided, modern plexiglass shelters, or are marked by signposts with the logo and have a posted list of routes to outlying communities in the greater Reykjavík area. Route booklets are available at the main terminals of Lækjatorg, Hlemmur, Mjódd, and Ártún.

The flat fare within the sprawling capital area is IKr 220, payable to the driver in exact change on boarding. You can buy strips of tickets at a lower price from the drivers or at the main terminals. The fare allows you to travel any distance in the metro area; depending on your destination, you may have to change buses. If so, ask for skiptimiða (skiff-teh-mee-tha), a transfer ticket that you give the second bus driver.

If you plan an extended stay in the Reykjavík area, it may be worthwhile to spend IKr 4,500 on a monthly ticket, the Green Card, valid on all routes. For shorter stays a practical investment is the Reykjavík Tourist Card, available from the Tourist Information Center. The card permits unlimited bus usage and admission to any of the capital city's seven pools, the Family Park and Zoo, and city museums.

🚍 **Stræto** ☎ 540-2700 🌐 www.bus.is/web/english.

BUSINESS HOURS

Most of the capital closes down early on weekdays, and many commercial and official establishments are closed Sunday.

GAS STATIONS Gas stations are usually open 7:30 AM–11 PM.

MUSEUMS & Museums and galleries are generally open Tuesday through Saturday
SIGHTS 11–4 and Sunday 2–6, and are usually closed Monday.

SHOPS Shops are open weekdays 9–6. A growing number of stores, especially food stores, are open on weekends with shorter hours. Many smaller food stores are open daily until 10 PM or 11 PM. Bakeries, souvenir shops, florists, and kiosks are open daily.

CAR RENTAL

Car-rental agencies in Reykjavík include Avis, Europcar, Geysir, and Hertz/Iceland. Both Avis and Hertz have offices in the Leifur Eiríksson Terminal at Keflavík Airport.

🚍 **Major Agencies Avis** ☎ 591-4000 🖨 591-4040. **Europcar** ☎ 591-4050 🖨 591-4060. **Hertz/Iceland** ☎ 505-0600 🖨 505-0650.
🚍 **Local Agencies Geysir** ☎ 568-8888 🖨 581-3102.

CAR TRAVEL

The excellent bus system and quick and reasonably priced taxis make automobiles unnecessary for getting around town, doubly so considering how expensive car rentals and gasoline are. Most gas stations have self-service pumps that accept IKr 500 and IKr 1,000 notes as well as credit cards.

EMBASSIES & CONSULATES

Canada ✉ Túngötu 14, IS-101 ☎ 533–5550.
United Kingdom ✉ Laufásvegur 31, IS-101 ☎ 550–5100.
United States ✉ Laufásvegur 21, IS-101 ☎ 562–9100.

EMERGENCIES

The city branch of the national university-affiliated hospital system, Landspítali Háskóli Sjúkrahús, Fossvogur, deals with serious emergencies at any time and can issue prescription medication when pharmacies are closed. Many of Reykjavík's pharmacies (apótek) are open into late evening. Lyf & heilsa and Lyfja apoteks each have a late evening location. Signs indicating other pharmacies with night hours (*næturvakt*) are posted in all pharmacies, and details are also published in newspapers.

Læknavakt (Duty Doctors) can provide general medical help during off-hours. During regular hours (8–5 weekdays), the Reykjavík Health Center, Heilsugæslan í Reykjavík, can refer you to officially appointed family doctors for general medical attention on short notice. Dentist referrals are available by calling ☎ 568–1041.

Doctors and Dentists **Dentist referrals** ☎ 568–1041. **Heilsugæslan í Reykjavík** (Reykjavík Health Center) ☎ 585–1300. **Læknavakt** (Duty Doctors) ☎ 1770.
Emergency Services **Ambulance, fire, police** ☎ 112.
Hospitals **Sjúkrahús Reykjavíkur, Fossvogur** (The City Hospital) ☎ 525–1000.
Late-Night Pharmacies **Lyf & heilsa apótek** ✉ Austerver, Háaleitisbraut 68 ☎ 581–2101 ✉ Domus Medica, Egilsgata 3 ☎ 563–1020. **Lyfja apótek** ✉ Lámúli 5 IS-108 ☎ 533–2300.

ENGLISH-LANGUAGE MEDIA

BOOKS Bóksala stúdenta (Students Union Building) stocks English-language books. Eymundsson-Penninn (on Austurstræti and opposite Hlemmur bus station, as well as at the Kringlan Mall) carries some English-language books, newspapers, and magazines, but some may be not current. Mál og menning, the largest bookstores in the city, have an extensive foreign section; the Laugavegur store has a congenial coffee bar.

Bookstores **Bóksala stúdenta** ✉ Hringbraut, next to Gamli Garður on the university campus, ☎ 570–0777. **Eymundsson-Penninn** ✉ Austurstræti 18 ☎ 551–1130. **Mál og menning** ✉ Laugavegur 18 ☎ 515–2500 ✉ Síðumúli 7–9 ☎ 510–2500.

MAIL & SHIPPING

Post offices are open weekdays 8:30–4:30. The main post office stays open until 6.

Main Post Office ✉ Pósthússtræti 5 IS-101 Reykjavík.

MONEY MATTERS

CURRENCY EXCHANGE **Exchange Services** **The Change Group** ✉ Aðalstræti 2 ☎ 552–3735.

TAXIS

Most cabs are new, fully equipped passenger sedans, including several Mercedes. They have small TAXI signs on top and can be hailed anywhere on the street; the LAUS sign indicates that the cab is available. There are taxi stands in a few locations around the city, but it is common to order a taxi by phone. Normally you have to wait only a few minutes. Some taxis accept major credit cards, but you must state that you want to pay with a credit card when requesting the taxi. Fares are regulated by meter; rides around Reykjavík run between IKr 700 and IKr 1,000. There is no tipping.

🔳 **Bæjarleiðir Taxi** ☎ 553-3500. **BSR Taxi** ☎ 561-0000. **Hreyfill Taxi** ☎ 588-5522.

TOURS

The Iceland Tour Guide Association can provide qualified guides who work in a variety of languages and have different specialties. The daily "Reykjavík City Sightseeing" tour of Reykjavík Excursions (with booking desks at hotels Loftleiðir, Nordica and Saga) includes museums and art galleries, shopping centers, and the like in 2½ hours. Ferjuleiðir runs short bird-watching excursions on the boat MS *Árnes*.

🔳 **Iceland Tour Guide Association** ✉ Mörkin 6 ☎ 588-8670. **Ferjuleiðir** ✉ Skipholt 25 ☎ 562-8000 🖶 562-2725. **Reykjavík Excursions** ✉ Hótel Loftleiðir ☎ 562-1011 or 505-0191 ✉ **Nordica Hótel** ✉ Suðurlandsbraut 2 ☎ 444-5000 ✉ **Radisson SAS Saga Hótel** ✉ Hagatorg ☎ 562-9500 ⊕ www.re.is.

TRANSPORTATION AROUND REYKJAVÍK

The best way to see Reykjavík is on foot. Many of the interesting sights are in the city center, within easy walking distance of one another. There is no subway system.

TRAVEL AGENCIES

🔳 **Local Agents Iceland Travel** ✉ Lágmúli 4 IS-128 Reykjavík ☎ 585-4300 🖶 585-4390 ⊕ www.icelandtravel.is.

VISITOR INFORMATION

The Reykjavík Tourist Information Center, in the classic Geysishús at Aðalstræti 2, is open daily June through August, 8:30–6. For the rest of the year it's open weekdays 9–5 and weekends 10–2. The Icelandic Tourist Board's headquarters upstairs is open June through August, weekdays 8–4; weekdays 9–5 during the other months.

🔳 Tourist Information **Icelandic Tourist Board** ✉ Gimli; Geysishús; Aðalstræti 2 ☎ 535-5500 🖶 535-5501. **Reykjavík Tourist Information Center** ✉ Geysishús; Aðalstræti 2 ☎ 562-3045 🖶 562-3057 ⊕ www.visitreykjavik.is.

SIDE TRIPS FROM REYKJAVÍK

Hafnarfjörður

10 km (6 mi) south of Reykjavík.

"Harbor fjord" had an important commercial port centuries before Reykjavík did, and today there's still healthy competition between the two. Iceland's **International Summer Solstice Viking Festival** is held here. Residents are not ashamed of their role as the butt of Icelanders' own odd ethnic humor, but they are serious about their respect for hidden folk said to live in local lava formations. As part of that respect, the local park, Hellisgerði has the world's northern-most bonsai garden. The **Tourist Information Center** (✉ Vesturgata 8 ☎ 565–0661) can give you a map of the town's sites and possible elfin homes. Next to the Tourist Information Center is the **Sjóminjasafn Íslands** (Maritime Museum) and a folk museum. Just off the harbor is the red-roof **Hafnarborg Art Center.** To get to the town, take AV (metro area) Bus 140 or 141 from Lækjatorg Plaza or Hlemmur station.

Where to Stay & Eat

$$–$$$$ ✕ **Fjörukráin Restaurant.** Immerse yourself in everything Viking—from the style of architecture to the menu. Excellent seafood and meat dishes

are served for those leery of traditional fare. It's next to the Viking Hotel. ⊠ *Strandgötu 55* ☎ *565–1213* ⊕ *www.fjorukrain.is* ▭ *MC, V.*

$–$$$ ✕ **A. Hansen.** In a classic building, this low-key restaurant serves up tasty nouvelle cuisine. If you'd rather enjoy wine without worrying about driving or transportation, you can order a package with dinner and round-trip stretch-limousine service. ⊠ *Vesturgötu 4* ☎ *565–1130* ▭ *MC, V.*

$–$$$ ✕ **Tilveran.** Ample portions and great prices on daily specials make this simple eatery a favorite of locals and visitors alike. Dinner specials offer a pre-course of either soup or salad, a choice of main course, ranging from arctic char or ocean fish, to lamb, chicken or beef. Save room for the homemade ice cream or coffee also included. Pasta, pizza and many à la carte dishes tempt those craving other options. ⊠ *Linnetstíg 1* ☎ *565–5250* ▭ *MC, V.*

¢ ✕ **Súfistinn.** At this modern coffee joint, you can choose from desserts and à la carte dishes, such as quiche or burritos. There are a couple of no-smoking rooms upstairs. Coffees, teas, and liqueurs—to blend, if you fancy—round out any meal. ⊠ *Strandgötu 9* ☎ *565–3740* ▭ *MC, V.*

$$ ▣ **Viking Hotel.** Look for the rooftop Viking dragonhead on this hotel. An old shipyard forge, with ornate Norse wood carvings, the building was converted into a hotel. Guest rooms have different themes based on the West-Nordic member countries of Greenland, Iceland, and the Faroe Islands. The West-Nordic Culture House is based in the lobby of the hotel. It hosts cultural exhibits, and you can buy quality crafts from Iceland and its little-known neighbors. ⊠ *Strandgata 50a Hafnarfjörður IS-220* ☎ *565–1213* ⊜ *565–1891* ⊕ *www.vikingvillage.is* ⇆ *29 rooms* ▭ *AE, DC, V* ⊚ *CP.*

The Outdoors

BIKING Biking tours are offered by **Blue Biking** (⊠ Stekkjarhvamur 60 ☎ 565–2089 or 894–1885 ⊕ www.simnet.is/bluebiking).

HORSEBACK You can ride horses at **Íshestar** (⊠ Sörlaskeiði 26 ☎ 555–7000 ⊕ www.
RIDING ishestar.is).

WHALE- The restored oak-hulled *Húni II* (☎ 555–2758 ⊕ www.islandia.is/~huni)
WATCHING has an impressive whale and dolphin sighting average of more than 90 percent and departs from the Hafnarfjöður harbor.

Reykjanes Peninsula

This boot-shape region south of Reykjavík is most often seen just superficially en route to or from the international airport. But closer examination reveals more to it than the Blue Lagoon or the modest landscape you see from a bus window. Reykjanesbæ—a bureaucratic union of the communities of Keflavík, Njardvík, and Hafnir—and Grindavík, Garður, and Sandgerði are busy fishing communities, each with its own character.

Garður has two lighthouses and a shoreline where you can spot birds and seals. Offshore, dolphins and whales sometimes reward keen-eyed visitors, and in good weather Snæfellsnes Peninsula can be seen gleaming on the horizon. **Hafnir,** at the arch of the peninsular foot, has a local aquarium containing most of Iceland's fish species. The neighbor to the north, **Sandgerði,** is the site of a nature center, which, in addition to having fine indoor exhibits, offers organized outdoor activities. Also near Sandgerði is Hvalsneskirkja, the church where Iceland's most famous hymnist, Hallgrímur Pétursson (1614–74), was once pastor. Most of his Passion Hymns were composed here.

Good-sized **Grindavík** has a center where fascinating exhibits and multimedia presentations explain the history and importance of the salt-fish industry, which has gone from the back-breaking toil of the early 1900s to being semi-automatic today. Close by are the Krísuvíkurberg bird cliffs; the unharnessed geothermal area Krísuvík; as well as the noted Blue Lagoon. In 1532 a fierce battle ensued in Grindavík when a group of Icelanders, Danes, and Hanseatic merchants drove English merchants away. A century later, invaders from Algiers ransacked the village. The large community of **Keflavík** (pronounced *Kep*-lah-veek) also has a history of trade and to reaffirm that, they purchased the handsome replica Viking ship, Íslendingur, saving it from debt-ridden exile in the U.S. It is now one of the town's most popular attractions. Many trails that run through the Reykjanes area originally were used by fishermen and traders; some of these are still marked by ancient rock cairns.

The Reykjanes Way Trail is a seven-part, 130-km (81-mi) trek through the region. It takes hikers past fascinating geologic formations, some due to volcanic activity, such as conical eruptions and fissure flows. The highest part of the area is a section of the Reykjanes Ridge, the tectonic seam where the North American and Eurasian plates meet. Now you can literally cross the Leif, or the "Lucky Bridge" linking the two. Locals mean it when they say a visit to Reykjanes expands your horizons, as these plates continue to drift apart.

Where to Stay

$$$–$$$$ 📺 **FlugHótel Keflavík, Icelandair Hótel.** This hotel with modern rooms is ideal if you don't want to get up at the crack of dawn to get from Reykjavík to catch a morning flight from Keflavík. ⊠ *Hafnagata 57 IS-230 Keflavík* ☎ *421–5222* 📠 *420–5223* ⊕ *www.icehotels.is* 🛏 *39 rooms, 3 suites* ♨ *Restaurant, bar* ▤ *AE, DC, MC, V.*

$$$ 📺 **Hótel Keflavík.** Light neutral tones prevail at this hotel, which is convenient to the airport. The rooms are modern and include whirlpool baths, so you can soak a bit more in Iceland's wonderful water. ⊠ *Vatnesvegur 12 IS-230 Keflavík* ☎ *420–7000* 📠 *420–7002* 🛏 *70 rooms* ♨ *Restaurant, minibars, bar, meeting room, no-smoking rooms* ▤ *AE, DC, MC, V.*

¢–$ 📺 **Youth Hostel Strönd.** Its name means "shore," and here you are literally a stone's throw from the water. This quiet spot in a small town 15 km (9 mi) from the Blue Lagoon puts you near many outdoor activities. Guests have access to a kitchen and washing machine. ⊠ *Njarðvíkurbraut 52-54, IS-260 Innri-Njarðvík* ☎📠 *421–6211* 🛏 *50 beds in 14 rooms* ♨ *Laundry facilities* ▤ *MC, V.*

The Outdoors

The Nature Center (⊠ Garðvegur 1, IS-245 Sandgerði ☎423–7551 ⊘Daily 1–5) organizes bird- and whale-watching and beachcombing outings.

HIKING   On the 130-km (81-mi) **Reykjanes Way Trail** (☎ 564–1788) system, you can take a seven-day self-guided hike, with the longest day covering about 20 km (13 mi). Iceland's longest trail is challenging for beginners—there's a little rugged climbing—but by no means insurmountable for the determined. Hikers need to bring food and be sure to have good hiking shoes, wet-weather gear, and a tent. The clearly marked trail (look for blue pegs) runs from the Reykjanesviti Lighthouse to Þingvellir National Park. If you need pampering, the second day ends near the Blue Lagoon, and though you're never far from civilization, in stretches you might think you're on the moon.

HORSEBACK   Through **Hestaleigan Vík** (⊠ Vesturbraut 15, IS-240 Grindavík
RIDING   ☎426–8303), you can have an easy, 90-minute introduction to the multigaited, good-natured Icelandic horse, plus a light lunch and a trip to the Blue Lagoon.

SWIMMING   Besides the famous Blue Lagoon, there are several pools in the area, including the **Keflavík Pool** (⊠ Sunnubraut, Keflavík ☎ 421–1500), the **Garður Pool** (⊠ Garðbraut, Garður ☎ 422–7300), the **Grindavík Pool** (⊠ Skólabraut, ☎ 426–7555), the **Njarðvík Pool** (⊠ Grundarvegur, Njarðvík ☎ 421–2744), and the **Sandgerði Pool** (⊠ Sandgerði ☎ 423–7736).

WHALE-
WATCHING   **Dolphin and Whale Spotting** (☎ 800–8777 or 896–5598 ⊕ www.dolphin.is) arranges trips aboard the *M. S. Moby Dick.*

Blue Lagoon

Fodor'sChoice   *15 km (9 mi) from Keflavík Airport and 50 km (31 mi) from Reykjavík*
★   *(turn off toward the village of Grindavík).*

This world-renowned therapeutic wonder is now in a sheltered site where man-made structures blend with geologic formations. A reception area includes food concessions and boutiques where you can buy health products made from the lagoon's mineral-rich ingredients. Bathing suits are available to rent, and futuristic bracelets keep track of your locker code, any other purchases, and the length of your visit (all of which no doubt make useful marketing statistics). Buses run from the BSÍ bus terminal in Reykjavík to the Blue Lagoon twice daily and three times a day in July and August. ⊠ *Bláalónið, Svartsengi power plant* ☎ *420–8800* ⊕ *www.bluelagoon.is* ☒ *IKr 490–IKr 980.*

GOLDEN CIRCLE

If you make only one foray outside Reykjavík, take this popular trip, offered by many tour operators, to the lakes, waterfalls, and hot springs just inland from the capital. If you take the trip after the spring thaw, it will begin at Þingvellir, the ancient seat of the world's oldest continually functioning parliament, before heading on to see the original Geysir hot spring (hence the term *geyser*) and the famed Gullfoss, the "Golden Waterfall."

Þingvellir

About 50 km (31 mi) northeast of Reykjavík. Take Ring Rd. about 9 km (5½ mi) just past the town of Mossfellsbær; turn right on Rte. 36.

After an hour-long drive from Reykjavík along Route 36 across the Mosfellsheiði heath, the broad lava plain of Þingvellir suddenly opens in front of you. This has been the nation's most hallowed place since AD 930, when the settler Grímur Geitskór chose it as the first site for what is today the world's oldest parliament, the Icelandic Alþingi (General Assembly). In July of each year delegates from all over the country camped at Þingvellir for two weeks, meeting to pass laws and render judicial sentences. Iceland remained a nation-state, ruled solely by the people without a central government, until 1262 when it came under the Norwegian crown; even then, the Alþingi continued to meet at Þingvellir until 1798, when it was banned from the site by Iceland's Danish rulers.

In AD 1000 the Alþingi decided that Iceland should become a Christian country, but the old heathen gods continued to be worshiped in private. These Viking gods remain part of everyday English: Týr (as in Tuesday), Óðinn (as in Wednesday), Þór (Thursday), and the goddess Frigg (Friday).

Þingvellir National Park, at the northern end of Þingvallavatn—Iceland's largest lake—is a potent symbol of Icelandic heritage. Many national celebrations are held here. Besides its historic interest, Þingvellir holds a special appeal for naturalists: it is the geologic meeting point of two continents. At Almannagjá, on the west side of the plain, is the easternmost edge of the North American tectonic plate, otherwise submerged in the Atlantic Ocean. Over on the plain's east side, at the Heiðargjá Gorge, you are at the westernmost edge of the Eurasian plate. In the 9,000 years since the Þingvellir lava field was formed, the tectonic plates have moved 231 feet apart. And they are still moving, at a rate of about half an inch per year.

You can drive straight to the central plain once you enter the park, or walk there after turning right along the short road at the sign for **Almannagjá** (Everyman's Gorge). At the rim, there is a fabulous view from the orientation marker.

A path down into Almannagjá from the top of the gorge overlooking Þingvellir leads straight to the high rock wall of **Lögberg** (Law Rock), where the person chosen as guardian of the laws would recite them from memory. At the far end of the gorge is the **Öxarárfoss** (Öxará Waterfall). Beautiful, peaceful picnic spots are a bit beyond it. Just below the waterfall in a deep stretch of the river lies the forbidding **Drekkingarhylur** pool, where it is said unfaithful wives were drowned.

Across the plain from Lögberg stand the church and **Þingvallabær**, the gabled manor house of Þingvellir, where the government of Iceland often hosts visiting heads of state. The **Nikulásargjá Gorge**, reached by a footbridge, is better known these days as Peningagjá (Money Gorge) because it's customary to fling a coin into the gorge's icy-cold water and make a wish. Don't even dream about climbing down to wade here— it might look shallow, but it's more than 30 feet deep.

Where to Stay

¢   **Þingvellir National Park Campground.** Camping in the National Park costs IKr 500 per adult and you pay at the park Service Center, Þjónustamiðstöð. Call before arriving as hours change throughout the year. ⊠ *Þingvellir National Park* ☎ *482–2660* ⊘ *Closed Dec. and Jan.*

The Outdoors

BOATING At Þingvellir you can rent boats for rowing on Þingvallavatn; the rental facility is on the lake by the Valhöll Hotel. Take extraordinary safety precautions: the shoreline drops off precipitously and the water is ice cold.

FISHING Trout and char are plentiful in Þingvallavatn, which is in fact the only lake in the world where you can catch four separate species of char. Fishing permits cost IKr 1,000 and are available at the park service center at Þingvallir, **Þjónustamiðstöð** (☎ 482–2660), which is open daily 8:30–5 in May and 8:30–8 (until 10 on weekends) June through August; weekends 8:30–5 September through November and February through April. It's closed December and January.

HORSEBACK RIDING The **Laxnes Pony Farm** (☎ 566–6179 🖷 566–6797 ⊕ www.laxnes.is), on Route 36 to Þingvallir, is one of a number of stables offering guided trail rides in the area.

en route Follow Route 36 for 7 km (4½ mi) east of the Þingvellir plain to Route 365, which climbs 16 km (10 mi) across the moor. Keep a close lookout halfway along this road: to the left under a high bluff is the large opening of a shallow cave in which a handful of people lived in the early 20th century.

Laugarvatn

About 20 km (12 mi) east of Þingvellir along Rtes. 36 and 365.

True to its name, Laugarvatn, or Warm Springs Lake, is warm enough for shoreline bathing. Its water is naturally heated by hot springs at the northern end of the lake. A cluster of buildings houses a school in winter and hotels in summer. Drive around them to a bathhouse at the lake's edge where you can rent towels and take showers year-round. The entrance fee also covers a natural steam bath in an adjoining hut, where you actually sit atop a hissing hot spring.

Where to Stay & Eat

$$ ✕▣ **Hótel Edda ÍKÍ Laugarvatn.** The comfortable, lakefront hotel–restaurant has rather plain, dorm-style accommodations (all with bath), but some of the double rooms have balconies with great lake views. Tasty, simply prepared meals include local lamb, fish, and vegetables. The large lounge is an inviting spot to relax and take in the scenery. ⊠ *840 Laugarvatni IS-840* ☎ *486–1279* ⊕ *www.hoteledda.is* ⇱ *28 rooms* ⚭ *Restaurant, bar* ▭ *MC, V* ☉ *Closed Sept.–mid-June.*

$$ ▣ **Hótel Edda, Menntaskóli á Laugarvatni.** This spot off the main drag has spartan yet tidy rooms with contemporary dorm-style furnishings. Rooms with communal baths are in three separate dorm buildings, and those with bath are on the second floor of the main building. It's within easy walking distance of the lake. ⊠ *IS-840* ☎ *486–1118* ⇱ *100 rooms, 13 with bath* ⚭ *Restaurant, bar* ▭ *MC, V* ☉ *Closed Sept.–mid-June.*

The Outdoors

BOATING Rowboats and sailboards can be rented on Laugarvatn Lake. At **Svína-vatn** (⊠ Grímsnes ☎ 486–4437) you can rent jet skis.

HORSEBACK **Efri-Brú horse rental** (☎ 482–2615) based in Grímsnes offers two-to-three-
RIDING hour tours with a guide, as well as other horseback riding excursions.

Haukadalur

About 35 km (22 mi) northeast of Laugarvatn via Rte. 37 and then Rte. 35.

The geothermal field in Haukadalur, home of the Geysir and Strokkur geysers, is one of Iceland's classic tourist spots.

The famous **Geysir** hot spring (the literal origin of the term, geyser) had been in a prolonged retirement until June 2000, when a pair of Richter 6 earthquakes jostled it from its nap. Now, modest eruptions occur almost daily, but they seldom reach the former splendor of 130- to 200-foot fountains. The more reliable **Strokkur** was drilled open in 1964 after a quiet period of 70 years; it spouts up boiling water as high as 100 feet at five-minute intervals. In the same area there are small natural vents from which steam rises, as well as beautiful, exotically colored pools. Don't crowd Strokkur, and always be careful when approaching hot springs or mud pots—the ground may be treacherous, suddenly giving way beneath you. Stay on formal paths or established tracks.

To get here from Laugarvatn, take Route 37 (from Lake Laugarvatn you can take the short spur, Route 364, southwest to Route 37) northeast for 25 km (16 mi) to the junction with Route 35. Take Route 35 about 10 km (6 mi) northeast to Hótel Geysir, which is next to the springs.

Where to Stay & Eat

$–$$$ ✕▣ **Hótel Geysir.** Exuberant Viking decorations, such as replica carved dragon heads, are crammed into this hotel next to the famous Geysir and Strokkur springs. Double rooms are in separate studio bungalows and also have cooking facilities; the singles are basic with shared bath. Various Icelandic specialties, such as salmon, rye bread baked in the heat of geothermal springs, and *skyr* (a delicious yogurtlike food made from skim milk) with cream, are served in the large ornate restaurant. ✉ *IS-801* ☎ *486–8915* 🖷 *486–8715* ⊕ *www.geysircenter.is* 🛏 *34 rooms, 28 with bath* ⚲ *Restaurant, pool, bar* ▭ *MC, V.*

Gullfoss

About 6 km (4 mi) east of Geysir along Rte. 35.

Measuring 105 feet high, thundering Gullfoss (Golden Falls) is a double cascade in the Hvítá River, turning at right angles in mid-drop. Gullfoss enters a dramatic chasm, which nonetheless has its gentle sides. On the western bank of the river—where the steep walls begin to slant more—is a beautiful hidden spot a short, steep climb from the road. Called **Pjaxi**, from the Latin *pax* (meaning "peace"), this nook of grassy knolls, natural springs, clear streams, and birch trees is ideal for a picnic. The modest visitor center is named in memory of Sigríður Tómasdóttir, who fought against flooding the falls for a hydro-electric reservoir scheme in the early 20th century. She is said to have threatened to throw herself into the falls; a trailside plaque further honors her.

Sports & the Outdoors

WHITE-WATER You can take a one-hour journey down the churning glacial Hvítá River
RAFTING below Gullfoss Falls; waterproof clothing and life jackets provided. For information, contact **Icelandic Adventure** (✉ Tangarhöfði 7, IS-108 Reykjavík ☎ 569–1000 ⊕ www.adventure.is).

Skálholt

From Gullfoss take Rte. 35 southbound for 36 km (22 mi); turn left onto Rte. 31 and go another 3½ km (2 mi) to the right-hand turnoff.

The seat of the southern bishopric, Skálholt was the main center of learning and religion in Iceland until the 18th century. On the way back from the Gullfoss falls to Reykjavík, stop at **Skálholt Cathedral**, a sanctuary established in 1056, soon after Iceland converted to Christianity. The current church, a wonderfully simple building, was consecrated in 1963 and is the 11th to be erected on this site. Beneath it lies an ancient crypt. A stone near the entry drive is believed to mark the spot where the last Catholic bishop, Jón Arason, and his son (celibacy was difficult to enforce so far from Rome) lost their heads when the Lutheran faith was ultimately enforced in 1550.

The modern memorial church at Skálholt houses historic relics and contemporary pieces. Works by two of Iceland's most important modern artists adorn the cathedral: a stunning mosaic altarpiece by Nína Tryggvadóttir and stained glass windows by Gerður Helgadóttir.

On summer weekends the cathedral hosts the free **Skálholt Music Festival**, which brings together splendid Icelandic and international musicians who perform baroque music on period instruments.

Where to Stay & Eat

$$–$$$ ✕🖷 **Hótel Flúðir Icelandair Hotel.** This hotel close to the scenic area near Skálholt has a classy restaurant–bar with excellent views over the river and beyond. Guest rooms reflect the multigabled architecture of old Icelandic farmsteads, but are fully modern with parquet floors, chic accessories, and contemporary Scandinavian furniture. To reach Flúðir from Skálholt, follow Route 31 southeast to Route 30 then head northeast

about 15 km (9 mi) to Flúðir. ⊠ *Vesturbrún 1, IS-845* ☎ *486–6630* 🖶 *486–6530* ⊕ *www.icehotel.is* ☞ *32 rooms with bath* ⚭ *Restaurant, gym, bar, meeting rooms* ▤ *MC, V.*

en route The return route from Skálholt to Reykjavík rolls through one of the most prosperous agricultural regions in Iceland. Drive 10 km (6 mi) from the cathedral along Route 31 and turn right, or from Flúðir, go south on Route 30; after 21 km (13 mi), Route 30 ends at the Ring Road (Route 1). Take a right onto it and head 73 km (44 mi) west to Reykjavík; if you have time, stop halfway in Hveragerði.

Hveragerði

40 km (25 mi) southeast of Reykjavík.

Hveragerði has a horticultural school, a large number of greenhouses heated by hot springs, and a fine swimming pool. The state's greenhouse research facility, where flowers and crops are grown with natural steam in large hothouses, is up the hill from the town's center. One of the country's most unabashed tourist spots, **Eden** awaits with an exotic display of tropical plants, souvenir items, and a snack bar.

Where to Stay & Eat

$$–$$$ ✕⊡ **Hótel Örk.** This white-concrete, blue-roof hotel is a few blocks away from Hveragerði's attractions. Rooms and public spaces have mahogany furniture, original Icelandic art, and plenty of potted plants. Specialties at the ground-floor restaurant ($$) might include lobster soup with a touch of champagne, leg of lamb roasted with Icelandic herbs, or fresh ocean fish from the nearby town of Þorlákshöfn. ⊠ *Breiðamörk 1* ☎ *483–4700* 🖶 *483–4775* ⊕ *www.icelandichotels.is* ☞ *85 rooms* ⚭ *Restaurant, 9-hole golf course, tennis court, pool, sauna, spa* ▤ *DC, MC, V.*

$ ⊡ **Ból & Ljósbrá Guesthouse.** Rooms in the standard youth hostel have up to five beds and shared kitchen facilities. The guest house has five doubles with bath. The staff is a helpful trove of information. ⊠ *Hveramörk 14, IS-810* ☎ *483–4198 hostel, 483–4588 guest house* 🖶 *483–4088* ⊕ *www.hostel.is* ☞ *20 beds* ▤ *MC, V* ⊘ *Closed mid-Sept.–mid-May.*

The Outdoors

SWIMMING The region has numerous swimming pools, located wherever there is an abundance of natural hot water. One of these is the **Hveragerði pool** (☎ 483–4113).

Golden Circle A to Z

BUS TRAVEL

It is possible to explore this area on your own by BSÍ bus, but you must allow plenty of time and perhaps stay overnight en route. BSÍ Travel serves Þingvellir twice daily (June to mid-September) and Gullfoss and Geysir twice daily (mid-June through August).

🚹 **BSÍ Bus Terminal** ☎ 591-1000 ⊕ www.bsi.is.

CAR RENTAL

Hertz rents several types of vehicles, including many with a CD player. A self-guided CD audio tour (IKr 1,500) is available in English, German, or French, and comes with a map, for those who'd like to do the Golden Circle themselves.

🚹 **Major Agencies Hertz** ☎ 505-0600 ⊕ www.hertz.com.

CAR TRAVEL

This circuit should take you seven or eight hours by car, if you make stops at the various sights. At the farthest point, Gullfoss, you're only 125 km (78 mi) from Reykjavík, and most of the drive is along paved main roads.

EMERGENCIES

Dial 112 for emergency assistance anywhere in Iceland.

🚹 **Emergencies** ☎ 112. **Police** ☎ 483-1154 in Hveragerði.

TOURS

Regardless of where you book a Golden Circle Tour, it's almost certainly going to be Reykjavík Excursions providing the eight-hour guided tour. The tours are run May through September daily at 9 AM (no Tuesday or Thursday tours October through April).

🚹 **Reykjavík Excursions** ☎ 562-1011 or 562-9500 🖷 444-5000 ⊕ www.re.is.

VISITOR INFORMATION

General information is available in Reykjavík at the Tourist Information Center and the Icelandic Tourist Board.

🚹 Tourist Information **South Iceland** ✉ Breiðumörk 2, Hveragerði ☎ 483-4601 🖷 483-4604 ⊕ www.sudurland.net/info.

THE WEST & THE VESTFIRÐIR

If you imagine the map of Iceland as the shape of a beast, two rugged western peninsulas—Snæfellsnes and Vestfirðir (West Fjords)—would make up the jaws of a peculiar dragonlike head, opening wide around the huge bay of Breiðafjörður. The North Atlantic, just off this coast, is one of the country's prime fishing grounds. Busy fishing villages abound in the Vestfirðir, but there are also tall mountains, remote cliffs thick with seabirds, and deep fjords carved out of basaltic rock. Inland in the extreme northwest corner, abandoned farmsteads and vestiges of ancient habitation speak of isolation and the forces of nature.

In the southern reaches, just north of the town of Borgarnes, the Ring Road northbound bends to the northeast, giving you a choice of routes. You can follow Route 54, which branches northwest, leading along the southern reaches of the Snæfellsnes Peninsula, which is crowned by the majestic Snæfellsjökull (Snæfells Glacier). Or you can choose to follow the Ring Road to the east. Here is a world rich in natural beauty and steeped in the history of the sagas. You should plan to give the east and west options a day each.

Borgarnes

74 km (43 mi) north of Reykjavík along the Ring Road, via the Hvalfjörður tunnel.

Borgarnes is the only coastal town of any size that does *not* rely on fishing for its livelihood; you're more likely to see modest industrial buildings than fishing boats. If you're coming from the south, take the tunnel under Hvalfjörður, which though only about 6 km (4 mi) long, is a major time-saver. Another time-saver is the long bridge, built in the late 1980s just outside of town, which shortens the Ring Road approach. Now you no longer need to make the circuitous drive around the fjord, Borgarfjörður.

Where to Stay

$$–$$$ 🏨 **Hótel Borgarnes.** Elegant leather sofas and light-grained wood tables fill the lobby area, which also has a bar serving drinks, coffee, and light

refreshments. Rooms are bright and decorated in neutral colors; a number of them face south, overlooking the fjord and nearby mountains. No-smoking rooms are available and an elevator makes upper level access convenient. ✉ *Egilsgata 14–16, IS-310 Borgarnes* ☎ 437–1119 ☎ 437–1443 ✍ *hotelbo@centrum.is* 🛏 *75 rooms with bath* ☒ *Restaurant, cafeteria, bar, no-smoking rooms* ⊟ *MC, V.*

$ 🏠 **Youth Hostel Hamar.** This friendly youth hostel, with 14 beds in 7 rooms, is in a renovated farmhouse that, in typical Icelandic style, has multiple gables with sleeping rooms in the lofts. It is also a golf lodge, and its location off the Ring Road makes it ideal for bikers. ✉ *Golfklúbbur, IS-310* ☎ 437–1663 or 692–4800 ☎ 437–2063 ⊕ *www.hostel.is* 🛏 *14 beds with shared bath* ⊟ *MC, V* ⊘ *Mid-May–mid-Sept.*

Sports & the Outdoors

HORSEBACK   If you'd like to explore the Borgarfjörður area on horseback, call **Guðrún**
RIDING   **Fjeldsted-Horse Rental** (✉ Ölvalsstaðir, IS-311 Brogarnes ☎ 437–1686).

SWIMMING   You can take a refreshing dip at the pool in **Borgarnes** (✉ Skallagríms-gata ☎ 437–1444).

en route   To explore the area inland from Borgarfjörður, drive northeast from Borgarnes on the Ring Road 11 km (7 mi) to Route 53 leading east. Turn right onto Route 53 and cross the one-lane bridge over the cloudy glacial Hvítá River. Take the first left turn onto Route 52 and in 10 minutes you'll arrive at the **Laxfoss** (Salmon Falls) on the Grímsá River, where salmon leap the rapids in summer. Continue across the Grímsá north on Route 50 a little more than 10 km (6 mi) to the **Kleppjárnsreykir** horticultural center, with its many greenhouses heated by thermal water from the region's hot springs.

Reykholt

Head northeast on Rte. 50 past Kleppjárnsreykir about 1 km (½ mi), turn east onto Rte. 518 and follow 8 km (5 mi).

Reykholt was the home of scholar–historian Snorri Sturluson (1178–1241). Author of the prose work *Edda*; a textbook of poetics; and the *Heimskringla*, a history of Norway's kings, Sturluson was also a wealthy chieftain and political schemer. He was murdered in Reykholt in 1241 on the orders of the Norwegian king. A hot bathing pool dating from Snorri's time can be seen here; an underground passage once led from Snorri's homestead to the pool. Every summer, the community hosts the **Festival in Reykholt** (⊕ www.reykholt.is), an impressive program of chamber and vocal music.

Where to Stay & Eat

$–$$ ✕🏠 **Hótel Reykholt.** The wings of this former dormitory make up a simple year-round hotel. The restaurant's à la carte menu ($$–$$$$) makes good use of the region's plentiful farm products—try the delicious lamb served with fresh greenhouse produce—and trout and salmon from nearby streams. ✉ *Reykholt IS-320* ☎ 435–1260 🛏 *67 rooms, 17 with bath* ☒ *Restaurant, bar* ⊟ *MC, V.*

en route   Continue for about 30 minutes on Route 518 to the colorful **Hraunfossar** (Lava Falls). A multitude of natural springs emerges from under a birch-covered lava field above the Hvítá River, creating a waterfall hundreds of feet wide, appearing seemingly out of nowhere across the bank from you. A little farther up the Hvíta, a 10-minute walk from Hraunfossar, is the **Barnafossar** (Children's

Falls), which has carved out strange figures from the rock. Tradition says that two children lost their lives when a natural stone bridge over the churning maelstrom gave way. Today a trusty footbridge gives safe access to the opposite bank.

⚠ **Húsafell Park** (☎ 435–1550) is about 4 km (2½ mi) up Route 518 eastward. This somewhat sheltered wooded area is a popular camping site, with birch trees and a swimming pool. Bring your own tent and you'll find a spot—unless it's the first weekend in either July or August, when crowds are at their peak. There's a gasoline station and a small snack counter open daily 10–10. Most services are limited to June through August.

Bifröst

From Húsafell, return west past Reykholt along Rtes. 518 and 523 some 50 km (31 mi) to the Ring Road; go north about 13 km (8 mi) to Bifröst.

About 1½ km (1 mi) north of Bifröst just off the Ring Road is the **Grábrók** volcanic cone, which you can easily scale for a panoramic view. Grábrók's lava field, covered with moss, grass, and birches, has many quiet spots for a picnic. Eight kilometers (5 mi) north is the distinctive cone-shape **Mt. Baula,** a pastel-color rhyolite mountain. In the 19th century, Icelanders delighted in telling gullible foreign travelers fantastic stories of the beautiful green meadows and forests populated by dwarfs shepherding herds of fat sheep at Baula's summit.

en route A few miles past Grábrók, along the Ring Road, take the left turn-off for Route 60 northwestward toward the village of Býðardalur. Follow it about 30 km (20 mi) to a right turn-off near Haukardalur, where you'll see the approach to the heritage site that is the **birthplace of Leifur Eiríksson** (contact Stefán Jónsson for info ☎ 434–1131 🖶 434–1212). Here you'll find both a precise replica of Eirístaðir (the farmstead of Eiríkur, Leifur's father) complete with Viking-age furnishings, tools, and utensils, as well as the archaeological dig where researchers are studying the birth site of Iceland's most famous son. The farm, which is remarkably small in size for such a famous character, puts on living history presentations in August. If you're lucky, this will include tasting fresh-baked flat-bread and dry-cured lamb, called hangikjout (hanged meat).

Where to Stay

$ 🖼 **FossHótel Bifröst.** This summer hotel sits beside the Ring Road in Borgarfjörður. It consists of a series of low white school buildings with red roofs. ✉ *Borgarfjordur 311, Bifröst* ☎ *435–3090* 🖶 *562–4001* 🌐 *www.fosshotel.is* ↩ *74 rooms, 56 with bath* ⚐ *Restaurant, horseback riding, bar* ▭ *MC, V.*

Snæfellsnes Peninsula

About 40 km (25 mi) northwest of Borgarnes to the peninsula's southern shore; about 30 km (18 mi) south of Bifröst to the turnoff onto the peninsula from the Ring Road.

Begin the journey north from the crossroads with Route 54. As you drive farther west on the peninsula, you'll pass through the Staðarsveit district, with its beautiful mountain range. Many small lakes abound with water flowers, and there are myriad sparkling springs. At **Lýsuhóll,** a few minutes north of Route 54, you can bathe in the warm water of a naturally carbonated spring. About 10 km (6 mi) farther west is the **Búðahraun** lava field, composed of rough lava. Its surface makes walking difficult, but it's more hospitable to vegetation than are most other Icelandic landscapes; flowers, shrubs, herbs, and berries grow abundantly here.

Búðir

102 km (61 mi) northwest of Borganes.

This tiny shoreline establishment on the Snæfellsnes Peninsula has ancient origins as an inlet mooring for fishermen in the days of sails and rowing. If you look carefully, you may find centuries-old relics of the fishermen's shelters. An unpretentious church from 1850—a successor to the first chapel on this site in 1703—has retained its looks. The lava surrounding this site fosters unique flora, including a rare subspecies of the buttercup, called Goldilocks, or *Ranunculus auricomus islandicus* among scholars. The area is protected as a registered nature preserve.

> **en route**   From Búðir, take a left turn onto coastal Route 574 for a 61-km (36-mi) drive circling the tip of the peninsula clockwise. On your right you'll see the focus of what is Iceland's newest national park, the majestic Snæfells Glacier, **Snæfellsjökull**, which, like that on Fujiyama in Japan, caps a volcano. The glacier had a cameo in Jules Verne's novel *Journey to the Center of the Earth* as the spot where the explorers enter the depths of the world.

The coastal drive takes you past many small, beautiful villages. One such is **Arnarstapi**, where the roof of a shore cave has fallen in, leaving a high arch for cliff birds to loop through to and from their nests. **Hellnar**—with its sea-level cave, Baðstofa, which radiates blue at high tide—is also quaint. About an hour's walk from the road at the western tip of the peninsula lie the **Svörtuloft Cliffs**, where multitudes of seabirds take refuge in nesting season May to August.

Where to Stay & Eat

$$$ ✕▥ **Hótel Búðir.** Risen like the Phoenix from the ashes, this hotel is again functioning after burning to the ground in 2002. Antique furnishings and art objects are part of the opulent re-birth. It has one of the best restaurants ($$$) in the area, with some tables facing the stunning Snæfellsjökull. Not surprisingly, all rooms are no-smoking, but you may smoke in common areas. It's quietest mid-week and mercifully, the nearby campground, which was quite noisy in the summer months, has moved to a location further away. ⊠ *Búðum, IS-355* ☎ *435–6700* 🖷 *435–6701* ⊕ *www.budir.is* 🛏 *29 rooms with bath* 🍴 *Restaurant, bar.* ▭ *MC, V.*

Ólafsvík

Either 61 km (36 mi) clockwise around the peninsula on Rte. 574 or 14 km (8½ mi) across the Fróðárheiði cutoff from Búðir.

Commerce has taken place since 1687 in this small village under the north shoulder of Snæfellsjökull.

Where to Stay & Eat

$$ ✕▥ **Hótel Ólafsvík.** This family-style harborside hotel has floors that are wheelchair accessible and a family suite with two double bedrooms, a sitting room, and a refrigerator. It has an attractive restaurant that serves fresh local fare such as monkfish, haddock, and halibut. ⊠ *Ólafs-*

braut 20, IS-355 ☎ *436–1650* 📠 *436–1651* 🛏 *18 rooms with bath* ♨ *Restaurant* 🚪 *AE, MC, V.*

Sports & the Outdoors

HIKING & SNOWMOBILING From here you can hike to the top of the glacier or arrange snowmobile tours through the **Tourist Information Center** (✉ Gamla þakkhúsið ☎ 436–1543).

SWIMMING The local Ólafsvík **pool** (✉ Ennisbraut 9 ☎ 436–1199) is open to the public.

Stykkishólmur

67 km (42 mi) east of Ólafsvík.

Stykkishólmur is an active fishing and port community on the peninsula's north coast with a charming, well-sheltered natural harbor. Around the harbor, classic timber houses from the 1800s, many of them beautifully restored, give glimpses of a distinguished past, when many of the now-abandoned islets of Breiðafjörður were settled. One, from 1828, bears the name of Árni Thorlacius, an early merchant who established the nation's oldest weather station in 1845. The large hospital near the water was built in 1936 by the Order of the Franciscans and has been staffed since by its sisters.

A ferry sails twice daily from here skirting the rugged islets of Breiðafjörður, which have no permanent habitation. The tiny island **Flatey,** where the ferry stops on the way to the West Fjords, is worth a visit. The now sleepy vacation village was an important commerce and learning hub in the 19th century; many delightful old houses, including Iceland's most miniscule library, still stand today, and the bird life is remarkable.

Where to Stay & Eat

$–$$ ✕ **Narfeyrarstofa.** A charming little eatery in an old-time timber building serves homemade quiches, coffee, light entrées, and delicious desserts from noon to midnight in summer. In winter it's purely a coffee and dessert spot where impromptu live music is likely to erupt almost anytime. From September through May it's open Thursday through Sunday only; otherwise it's open daily. ✉ *Aðalgata 3* ☎ *438–1119* 📠 *438–1630* ⊕ *www. narfeyrarstofa.is* 🚪 *MC, V.*

¢ ✕ **Sjávarpakkhúsið.** A masterfully restored building from around 1900 houses this cozy restaurant. The mainstays here are sandwiches and soups that are meals in themselves. If you're hungry, choose either the creamy seafood soup, which varies according to the day's catch, or spoon up the goulash with ample chucks of lamb. It's no-smoking inside, but not on the patio, a congenial place to watch the small boat traffic. ✉ *Hafnargata 2a* ☎ *438–1001* 🚪 *MC, V.*

$$ ✕🏨 **Hótel Stykkishólmur.** This well-kept spot has a great vantage point and is a good option for overnighting in the area. Rooms are done in a crisp Scandinavian style with clean lines and parquet floors. The restaurant ($$$) specializes in seafood dishes, including local shellfish, as well as delicious, tender lamb. There is also a sports bar, with a widescreen TV. ✉ *Borgarbraut 6, IS-340* ☎ *430–2100* 📠 *430–2101* ⊕ *www. fosshotel.is* 🛏 *33 rooms with bath* ♨ *Restaurant, 9-hole golf course, bar* 🚪 *DC, MC, V.*

¢ 🏨 **Youth Hostel.** Eleven bunk house–like rooms are tucked in this well-kept lakefront building, which is one of the oldest in town. Boat trips for bird-watching and fishing excursions can be arranged. ✉ *Höfðagata 1, IS-340* ☎ *438–1095* 📠 *438–1417* 🛏 *47 beds in 11 rooms without bath* 🚪 *MC, V* ⊙ *Closed Oct.–Apr.*

Sports & the Outdoors

BOAT TOURS Cruise the islands of Breiðarfjörður and sample fresh-caught seafood, or go whale-watching off Snæfellsnes peninsula with **Seatours** (✉ Smiðjustígur 3, IS-340 Stykkishólmur ☎ 43–1450 ⊕ www.islandia. is/~eyjaferdir/) Information on boat trips linking several coastal spots with Ísafjörður on the West Fjords can be obtained from **Vesturferðir** (☎ 456–5111 ⊟ 456–5185 ⊕ www.vesturferdir.is).

SWIMMING Parents can soak in the hot tubs or swim laps while the kids enjoy the spiral waterslide at the **Stykkishólmur pool** (☎ 438–1150).

Ísafjörður

From Stykkishólmur, follow Rte. 57 for 70 km (50 mi) to Rte. 60. Alternatively, from the Ring Road, pick up Rte. 60 about 10 km (6 mi) past Bifröst and drive 35 km (27 mi) to the intersection with Rte. 57. From there it's a long drive north—about 340 km (211 mi).

The uncrowned capital of the West Fjords, Ísafjörður is one of the most important fishing towns in Iceland. It hosts a renowned Easter-week ski meet as well as a summer music festival, Við Djúpið (www.viddjupid. is), with concerts and master classes, sponsored by the Reykjavík Arts Festival and others. From here it is convenient starting point on tours to Hornstrandir, the splendidly peaceful and desolate land north of the 66th parallel inhabited by millions of seabirds on the northernmost cliffs of Hornbjarg and Hælavíkurbjarg. Geologically the oldest part of Iceland, Vestfirðir offers spectacular views of mountains, fjords, and sheer cliffs. Anglers come here for trout fishing in the rivers and lakes, and hikers and mountaineers explore this unspoiled region with the help of guides.

Where to Stay & Eat

$ ✕⌷ **Hótel Ísafjörður.** This is a good family hotel in the heart of town. No two rooms are alike, but all have old-fashioned furnishings and floral fabrics. The restaurant ($$) serves tasty seafood dishes, including grilled scallops in pesto sauce. Sightseeing tours and boat trips are offered in summer. ✉ *Silfurtorgi 2, IS-400* ☎ *456–4111* ⊟ *456–4767* ⤙ *32 rooms with bath* ♦ *Restaurant* ⊟ *AE, MC, V.*

¢ ✕ **Faktorshús.** Hidden away from traffic noise, this restaurant is housed in a lovingly renovated building dating from 1788. For the first 200 years of its existence, the building was the home of the wealthiest merchants in town. Now you needn't be rich to enjoy the piping-hot coffee with crunchy biscotti, or satisfying home-style fish or lamb dishes. ✉ *Hæstikaupstaður* ☎ *456–3868* ⊟ *MC, V* ☉ *Closed winters.*

The Outdoors

BIKING Bikes can be rented from the **Hotel Ísafjörður** (☎ 456–4111).

BOAT TRIPS From mid-June to mid-August **Vesturferðir** (☎ 456–5111 ⊟ 456–5185 ⊕ www.vesturferdir.is) goes daily to the tiny, single farmstead isle of Vígur, where a fourth generation of farmers conducts the vanishing practice of eiderdown gathering, which does no harm to the birds whatsoever; in fact, they seek out these nesting sites, which are protected from predators. Vesturferðir can also book you in a charter or scheduled trip aboard either the *Bliki* or *Kiddy*, which stop at Hesteyri, an abandoned fishing village where descendants have now restored family homes as summer cottages. A jungle of 6-foot archangelica plants skirts the village.

SWIMMING You can take a dip at the local Ísafjörður **pool** (✉ Austurvegur 9 ☎ 456–3200).

Patreksfjörður

190 km (114 mi) southwest of Ísafjörður, or 345 km (207 mi) north- west of Borgarnes. From Borgarnes take the Ring Road north; follow Rte. 60 north to Vatnsfjörður, then take Rte. 62 west. Alternately, take the ferry from Stykkishólmur to Brjánslækur, then drive 54 km (32 mi) to Patreksfjörður.

One of the West Fjords' many curious fishing villages, this one is named for the patron saint of Ireland. Houses here seem to crowd every available flat spot, right up to the shoreline. The harbor, built in 1946, was formed by deepening and opening a brackish lake to the sea.

The region's largest bird colony—with millions of residents—is at **Látrabjarg,** 60 km (36 mi) from Patreksfjörður. The immense vertical cliff, more than 650 feet high, runs along the south shore of the West Fjords. In years past, egg collectors dangled over the edges to gather eggs, which were an essential source of protein. This is Iceland's, and indeed Europe's, westernmost tip, and the waters offshore are treacherous to sailors. The skill of egg collectors proved heroic in 1947 in what has to qualify as one of maritime history's most incredible rescues: with mind-boggling agility, local Icelanders rappelled down the perilous cliff and shot a lifeline out to the stranded trawler *Dhoon.* Then, using a single-seat harness, all 12 crew members of the ship were hauled ashore and up to safety on the top of the cliff—in the near-total darkness of December, no less.

Where to Stay

$ 🏠 **Guest House Stekkaból.** Accommodations in this little spot are clean and comfortable, and there's a sitting room looking out over the fjord. ✉ *Stekkar 19, IS-450 Patreksfjörður* ☎ *456–1675* 🖨 *456–1547* 🛏 *14 rooms without bath.*

The West & the Vestfirðir A to Z

AIR TRAVEL

Air travel is the best way to visit the West Fjords. You can fly to Ísafjörður on Air Iceland (Flugfélag Íslands), the domestic division of Icelandair.
🔹 Air Iceland (Ísafjörður) ☎456-3000 ⊕ www.icelandair.is ✉ Reykjavík ☎570-3030.

BOAT & FERRY TRAVEL

In summer, the *Baldur* car ferry, run by Seatours, links Stykkishólmur, on the Snæfellsnes Peninsula, with Brjánslækur, on the southern coast of the Western Fjords, calling at Flatey Island. *Baldur* leaves Stykkishólmur at 9 AM and 4:30 PM in summer. It is essential to book in advance.
🔹 *Baldur* ☎ 438-1450 for booking at Stykkishólmur, 456-2020 at Brjánslækur ⊕ www. saeferdir.is.

BUS TRAVEL

BSÍ Travel runs frequent daily service to most towns in the region. It's a 45-minute trip to Borgarnes, three hours to Stykkishólmur. Bus travel is not the most convenient way to visit the West Fjords; service to Ísafjörður runs a couple of days a week in summer only, and it's an 11-hour trip.
🔹 BSÍ Bus Terminal ☎ 591-1000 ⊕ www.bsi.is.

CAR TRAVEL

From Reykjavík and the north, you reach the west via the Ring Road (Route 1). The Hvalfjörður tunnel, penetrating about 6 km (about 4 mi) underwater from an entrance about 30 km (19 mi) north of Reykjavík, eases accessibility to the west from the capital. The IKr 1,000 car toll (each way) is less than what you'd pay on gas to drive around the fjord, and you'll save more than 40 minutes each way. Upon emerging from the tunnel's north end, you'll be just 10 km (6 mi) from either Akranes or Borgarnes. Heading north after Borgarnes, Route 54 branches off to the Snæfellsnes Peninsula; Routes 60 and 68 branch off to the West Fjords. If you intend to rent a car to drive to the West Fjords, try to secure a relatively large car as roads can be rough, requiring good ground clearance underneath.

EMERGENCIES

Dial 112 for emergency assistance anywhere in Iceland.
🚔 Police **Borgarnes** ☎ 437-1166. **Ísafjörður** ☎ 456-4222. **Stykkishólmur** ☎ 488-1008.

TOURS

Vesturferðir operates boat tours linking several coastal spots with Ísafjörður on the West Fjords and also runs hiking and mountaineering trips to the rugged parts of Strandasýsla.

Iceland Travel operates a 12-hour day trip from Reykjavík to the West Fjords, with a flight to Ísafjörður and then sightseeing by bus. The tour departs daily June through August.

You can take a guided snowmobile trip to the top of the Snæfellsjökull or go in groups of six, minimum, in a snowcat trailer from Snjófell at Arnarstapi. Snowmobiles rent at IKr 5,200 per person for two riders, or IKr 6,500 for solo. The snowcat ride is IKr 3,500 per person.

Sæferðir runs whale-watching and island nature tours from the village of Stykkishólmur on the Snæfellsnes peninsula.
🚩 Tour Operators **Seatours** ☎ 438-1450 at Stykkishólmur, 456-2020 at Brjánslækur ⊕ www.saeferdir.is. **Snjófell** ✉ IS-311, Arnarstapi ☎ 435-6795 🖷 435-6795 ⊕ www.snjofell.is. **Iceland Travel** ☎ 585-4300. **Vesturferðir** (West Tours) ✉ Aðalstræti 7, IS-400 Ísafjörður ☎ 456-5111 🖷 456-5185 ⊕ www.vesturferdir.is.

VISITOR INFORMATION

🚩 Tourist Information **Akranes** ✉ Safnaskálinn að Görðum, IS-300 ☎ 431-5566 🖷 431-5567 ⊕ www.museum.is. **Borgarnes** ✉ Brúartorg 4, IS-310 ☎ 437-2214 🖷 437-2314 ⊕ www.west.is. **Stykkishólmur** ✉ Íþróttamiðstöðina ☎ 438-1150 🖷 438-1780. **Ísafjörður** ✉ Aðalstræti 7, IS-400 ☎ 456-5121 🖷 456-5185 ⊕ www.vestfirdir.is. **Ólafsvík** ✉ Gamla Pakkhúsið, IS-355 ☎ 436-1543 ⊕ www.snb.is/pakkhus 🕐 June–Aug., daily 9–7.

THE NORTH

From the Hrútafjörður (Rams' Fjord), which gouges deeply into the western end of the coast, to Vopnafjörður in the east, Iceland's north is a land created by the interplay of fire and ice. Inland, you can find the largest lava fields on earth, some with plants and mosses, others barren. Yet valleys sheltered by the mountains are lush with vegetation and rich in color, and the deeply indented coast offers magnificent views north toward the Arctic, especially spectacular under the summer's midnight sun.

The commercial and cultural center of Akureyri is Iceland's fourth-largest town. From there it's a pleasant drive to Lake Mývatn, where bird-watchers can spot vast numbers of waterfowl and hikers can explore weird lava formations. The climate is unusually mild around Mývatn, making it a pleasant outdoor destination.

Brú

27 km (16 mi) west of Hvammstangi, the nearest town to the Ring Rd.

If you're driving the full Ring Road route, you'll enter the north at Brú, snuggled at the inland end of the long Hrútafjörður. It is a tiny settlement, bordering on two regional districts where a post and telegraph station was established in 1950. A local **folk museum** offers a glimpse into the area's past.

Where to Stay & Eat

$$ ✕⊡ **Staðarskáli í Hrútafirði.** Rooms at this modestly priced accommodation east of Brú have laminate furnishings, wall-to-wall carpeting, floral decorations, and coffee makers. The restaurant (¢) serves home-style cooking—from burgers to tasty grilled lamb. ⊠ *Hrútarfirði, IS-500 Staður* ☎ *451–1150* ⊟ *451–1107* ⟳ *18 rooms with bath* ♨ *Restaurant, meeting room* ⊟ *MC, V.*

$ ⊡ **Youth Hostel.** There are 30 beds here and a hot tub at this quiet seaside farmhouse. ⊠ *Sæberg Reykir, Staður IS-500 Staður* ☎ *451–0015* ⊟ *451–0034* ⊕ *www.hostel.is* ⟳ *30 beds in 9 rooms without bath* ♨ *Hot tub* ⊟ *MC, V.*

> **off the beaten path**
>
> **HÚNAFLÓI –** The name, Polar Bear Cub Bay, is believed to be based on legend, for you'll catch nary a glimpse of a bear or daredevil bather. From Staðarskáli, follow the Ring Road east. You will be taking what locals call the Vatnsnes Circle around the namesake peninsula. The loop itself totals about 83 km (50 mi) along rather rough Routes 72 and 711. As you get farther out on the peninsula's west side, keep a lookout for seals and shore birds, maybe even spouting whales. Eventually the road becomes Route 711, and you turn around the tip of the peninsula and head south. As you near the mainland, look to the east for Hvítserkur, a bizarre dinosaur-shaped rock formation offshore. It is as if an escapee from the Jurassic era became petrified as it drank from the sea.

Blönduós

85 km (53 mi) east of Brú and 145 km (91 mi) west of Akureyri on the Ring Rd.

The largest town on the west end of the north coast is nestled beneath gently-sloping hills at the mouth of the glacially chalky Blandá River. Local shrimp and shellfish processing plants aren't pretty, but from Blönduós it is an easy drive to neighboring picturesque valleys. By all means, drive carefully in the area because Blönduós police are the nation's best at nabbing speeders.

About 19 km (12 mi) south, across the Vatnsdalsá River, is the turnoff heading 6 km (4 mi) north to **Þingeyrarkirja** (Þingeyri's Church). The humble stony exterior belies an exquisite blue-dome interior, replete with carvings and beautiful religious ornamentation. To get in, contact the sexton at the farm Steinnes; look for the sign that reads reads *Kirkjuvör ur* on the right-hand side of the approach road—it's about 3 km (2 mi) after you turn north.

Varmahlíð

136 km (82 mi) east of Brú and 94 km (56 mi) west of Akureyri at the crossroads of the Ring Road and Rte. 75 north to Sauðárkrókur. If you're coming from Rte. 711, Rte. 75 meets the Ring Road again, and here you should turn left and head east toward Blönduós and Varmahlíð.

The inland village of Varmahlíð has its own local abundant geothermal heating sources. In addition to a bank, hotel, general store, and gas station, a small natural history museum is here.

South of town you'll come to Víðimýri. Here you can visit the restored turf-roof **Víðimýrarkirkja** church, built in 1834 and still serving the local parishioners to this day. The late president of Iceland, Kristján Eldjarn—a world authority of Nordic antiquities—once called it one of the most sublimely built and beautiful remnants of Icelandic architecture.

Glaumbær

Returning north, cross the Ring Rd. and head north on Rte. 75 about 10 km (6 mi) north of Varmahlíð.

The **Glaumbær Folk Museum,** occupying a turf-roof farmhouse, offers a glimpse of 18th- and 19th-century living conditions in rural Iceland. In the 11th century, Glaumbær was the home of Guðríður Þorbjarnardóttir and Þorfinnur Karlsefni, two of the Icelanders who attempted to settle in America after it was discovered by Leifur Eiríksson. Their son, Snorri, was believed to be the first European to be born in the New World. ☎ 453–6173 ⊡ IKr 400 ☉ June–Aug., daily 9–6.

Where to Stay

$$$ ⊡ **Hótel Varmahlíð.** This quirky hotel—keep calling if nobody answers—is in the namesake crossroads community. Golfing, fishing, and horseback riding can be arranged. ⊠ *Varmahlíð, IS-560* ☎ *453–8170 or 453–8190* ᴁ *453–8870* ⇨ *20 rooms, 15 with bath* ⌂ *Restaurant* ▤ *MC, V.*

off the beaten path

HOFSÓS – Head northeast to the eastern shore of Skagafjörður and the miniscule village of Hofsós. The harbor is a trip back in time to the Danish realm, with the classic tar-black warehouses just as they were more than a century ago. Most poignant, though, is the Icelandic Emigration Center, which chronicles early Icelanders' emigration from here by the thousands to the New World. Local conditions then must have been truly bleak, as a bitter poem in an exhibit attests. However, the author surely had second thoughts, as the same Matthías Jochumsson would later write the glorious hymn that became Iceland's national anthem. ⊠ *Hofsós* ☎ *453–7935* ☉ *June 10–Sept. 10, daily 11–6.*

Sauðárkrókur

17 km (11 mi) north on Rte. 75 from Glaumbær.

In summer, boat trips from the large coastal town of Sauðárkrókur to Drangey and the Málmey Islands offer striking views of the fjord and bird cliffs. On the eastern side of Skagafjörður, off Route 75, is the 18th-century stone cathedral at **Hólar,** which contains beautiful and priceless religious artifacts.

Where to Stay

$$–$$$ ⊡ **FossHótel Áning.** The decent-size rooms at this summer hotel are bright, but not particularly decorative, which makes sense since they are off-season dorm digs. But students would be lucky if the chef worked year-round—the food is quite varied and tasty. Hiking, horseback riding, and boat tours can be arranged from here. ⊠ *Sæmundarhlíð, IS-550* ☎ *453–6717 or 562–4000* ᴁ *562–4001* ⇨ *71 rooms* ⌂ *Restaurant, meeting room* ▤ *MC, V* ☉ *Closed late Aug.–May.*

Akureyri

95 km (57 mi) east along the Ring Rd. from the junction with Rte. 75 south of Sauðákrókur.

Though not as cosmopolitan as Reykjavík, Akureyri—called the Capital of the North—is a lively city. More than a century ago, the farmers in the prosperous agricultural area surrounding Akureyri established KEA, a cooperative enterprise, to combat the Danish businesses dominating the area's economic life. Today KEA is still influential in commerce and trade in Akureyri.

Hemmed by the 64-km- (40-mi-) long Eyjafjörður, Akureyri is sheltered from the ocean winds and embraced by mountains on three sides. Late 19th-century wooden houses impart a sense of history, and the twin spires of a modern Lutheran church—rising on a green hill near the waterfront—provide a focal point. The church is named for Akureyri native Matthías Jochumsson, the Lutheran minister and poet who wrote Iceland's national anthem in 1874.

From the church it's a short walk from the town center on Eyrarlandsvegur to the **Lystigarðurinn** (Arctic Botanical Gardens), planted with more than 400 species of flora, including rare Arctic and foreign plants. **Matthíasarhús** (⊠ Eyrarlandsvegur 3), the house where Matthías Jochumsson once lived, is now a museum, open weekdays in summer, 1:30–3:30, and by request during the rest of the year. Two other museums honor Icelandic writers. **Davíðshús** (⊠ Bjarkastígur 6), the home of poet Davíð Stefánsson, is open daily, except Sunday 4–5:30 in summer and on request in winter. In summer, **Nonnahús** (⊠ Aðalstræti 54B), the boyhood home of children's writer and Jesuit priest Jón Sveinsson, is open daily 10–5, but in winter it is by request.

The **Minjasafnið** (Folk Museum) has a large collection of local relics and works of art, old farm tools, and fishing equipment. ⊠ *Aðalgata 58, IS-600 Akureyri* ☎ *462–4162* ✉ *IKr 400* ☉ *Daily 11–5.*

Dating from the 18th century, the beautifully restored **Laxdalshús** (Laxdal House) is the oldest house in Akureyri. A Lutheran priest now resides here. You can explore the grounds and see the interior if staff is present. ⊠ *Hafnarstræti 11, IS-600 Akureyri* ☎ *461–1841.*

In June and July, make a point of taking an evening drive north from Akureyri along Route 82. The midnight sun creates breathtaking views along the coast of **Eyjafjörður**. Better still, take a cruise on the fjord: a ferry plies the waters of Eyjafjörður to and from the island of **Hrísey**, home of Galloway cattle, and out to **Grímsey Island**, 40 km (25 mi) offshore and straddling the Arctic Circle. Contact **Nonni Travel** (⊠ Brekkugata 5, IS-600 Akureyri ☎ 461–1841).

To the south of Akureyri is the pyramid-shape rhyolite mountain **Súlur**. Beyond it is **Kerling**, the highest peak in Eyjafjörður.

Where to Stay & Eat

$$–$$$$ ✕ **Fiðlarinn.** What better name for a rooftop restaurant than Fiddler? Dine with a fabulous view overlooking Akureyri Harbor and Eyjafjörður. The food is modern Icelandic, with French and Danish influences. Based on goose and reindeer, the dishes feature seasonal ingredients. ⊠ *Skipagata 14, IS-600* ☎ *462–7100* ⊕ *www.fidlarinn.is* ▭ *AE, DC, MC, V.*

$$$ ✕▨ **FossHótel KEA.** Mauve-and-maroon hues and dark-wood trim characterize this hotel, which is on par with many of the capital's better accommodations. An excellent ground-level restaurant, Rósagarðurinn ($$), serves exquisite haute cuisine. ⊠ *Hafnarstræti 87–89, IS-602 Akureyri*

☎ 462–2000 🖨 460–2060 ⇆ *73 rooms with bath, 1 suite* ⚫ *Restaurant, bar, lobby lounge, meeting room* ▤ *AE, DC, MC, V.*

$$$ ▨ **Hótel Norðurland.** All rooms here have floral prints, Danish modern furniture, and satellite TV. On the ground floor is the separately run Pizza 67 restaurant. ⊠ *Geislagata 7, IS-600 Akureyri* ☎ *462–2600* 🖨 *462–7962* ⇆ *34 rooms with bath* ⚫ *Restaurant, minibars, bar* ▤ *MC, V.*

$ ▨ **Hostelling in Akureyri.** Options here run from bunks for those with sleeping bags to rooms with beds and linens in the hostel, or two completely-equipped separate, year-round cottages that sleep six comfortably and have their own baths. The accommodations are close to the main shops. ⊠ *Stórholt 1, IS-600* ☎ *462–3657* 🖨 *461–2549* ⊕ *www.hostel.is* ⇆ *60 beds* ▤ *MC, V* ⊘ *Closed mid-Dec.–early Jan.*

Sports & the Outdoors

GOLF   Enjoy golf at perhaps the world's northernmost 18-hole course at the **Akureyri Golf Club** (☎ 462–2974) in Jaðar, on the outskirts of Akureyri. Golfers compete here well past midnight during the **Arctic Open Golf Tournament,** held each year around the longest day of the year (in the midnight sun, needless to say). For details, contact the Akureyri Golf Club or the **Ferðaskrifstofa Akureyrar** (⊠ Ráðhústorg 3, IS-600 ☎ 460–0600).

Golfing is also possible at the course in **Ólafsfjörður** (☎ 466–2611). You can also tee off in **Sauðárkrókur** (☎ 453–5075).

HIKING   For many different hiking choices, contact **Ferðafélag Akureyrar** (Touring Club of Akureyri; ⊠ Strandgata 23, IS-600 ☎ 462–2720 🖨 462 7210). **Nonni Travel** (⊠ Brekkugata 5, IS-600 ☎ 461–1841) runs mountain hiking tours from Akureyri. **Ferðaskrifstofa Akureyrar** (⊠ Ráðhústorg 3, IS-600 ☎ 460–0600) can also provide a walk on the wild side.

HORSEBACK   RIDING   For horseback trips from the Akureyri area—from hour-long to days-long—contact **Pólarhestar** (⊠ Grýtubakki II, IS-600 ☎ 463–3179 🖨 463–3144 ⊕ www.nett.is/polar). It operates mid-May to mid-October.

SWIMMING   Akureyri has an excellent open-air **pool** (⊠ Þingvallastræti 13 ☎ 461–4455).

Shopping

As Iceland's fourth-largest city, Akureyri offers better shopping than most other towns outside Reykjavík, with many temptations along the pedestrian street Hafnarstræti. The shop **Folda-Anna** (⊠ Hafnarstræti 5, IS-600 ☎ 461–4120 🖨 461–1167) sells woolens, knitting kits, sheepskin rugs, and other souvenirs.

> **off the beaten path**

SIGLUFJÖRUR – In the mid-1960s this town was prosperous due to the area's abundance of herring, the silver of the sea. When the Klondike era ended with the collapse of the herring stock in 1968, the fleet turned to other fish types and Siglufjörður settled down. Today, however, the herring era has been reborn with the recovery of the herring stock. Demonstrations on the pier show just how little time it takes to dress and salt herring and fill the barrels. The Herring Adventure, held the first weekend in August, turns the harbor into a festival of living history, followed by merrymaking with music and dancing. If you miss the action, there is the Síldarminnjasafn (Herring Years Memorabilia Museum), on Snorragata, with herring exhibits, pictures, and paraphernalia—including wooden barrel lids with various "brandings." Drive 192 km (115 mi) north of Akureyri on Route 82, and then follow Route 76.

Grund

15 km (9 mi) south along Rte. 821 from Akureyri.

Grund is an ancient farmstead and was once home to some of the clansmen of the bloody Sturlungar feuds of the 13th century. Don't miss the attractive turn-of-the-20th-century **church**, which has been on the historical registry since 1978. This impressive edifice was built in 1905 entirely at the personal expense of Magnús Sigurðsson, a farmer at Grund. It breaks tradition from the east–west orientation of most churches and is instead built on a north–south line. Behind the altar in its north end is a painting of the resurrection, dating from the 19th century.

Saurbær

13 km (8 mi) south on Rte. 821 from Grund.

Here you'll find a church built in the 1850s from wood and turf, typical of Icelandic dwellings through the centuries. Be prepared for, well, sheepish looks from locals if you ask what the name Saurbær means.

| en route |

From the Saurbær pullout, turn left back onto Route 821. After about 1½ km (1 mi), take a right over the Eyjafjarðará River to Route 829, which runs north parallel to Route 821. Within a few hundred yards you'll reach the historic **Möðruvellir farm.** The church at Möðruvellir has an English alabaster altarpiece dating from the 15th century. From here it is 25 km (16 mi) north to the Ring Road.

If you drive east from Akureyri on the Ring Road, passing farms left and right, you'll soon cross the **Vaðlaheiði** (Marsh Heath). You'll then enter the **Fnjóskadalur** (Tree-Stump Valley), formed by glaciers only a few thousand years ago. Go several hundred feet past Route 833, which leads south into the western part of the valley, and turn right onto the next road to the **Vaglaskógur** (Log Forest), one of the largest forests in this relatively treeless country. Its tallest birches reach some 40 feet.

Goðafoss

From the Saurbær pullout, turn left back onto Rte. 821 and travel 28 km (17 mi) north to the Ring Road. Proceed east about 22 km (13 mi). Directly from Akureyri, Goðafoss is about 50 km (30 mi) east.

The name Goðafoss—Waterfall of the Gods—derives from a historic event in AD 1000 when Þorgeir Ljósvetningagoði, ordered by the Icelandic Parliament to choose between paganism and Christianity, threw his pagan icons into the waterfall. Just before you reach Goðafoss, in the Skjálfandi River, you'll pass the **Ljósavatn church** on land where Þorgeir lived a millennium ago. Although the farm is long gone, you can visit the church, which houses, among other relics, some interesting runic stones.

Mývatn

About 100 km (62 mi) along the Ring Rd. east of Akureyri.

Spend at least a day exploring this superbly natural area influenced by active geology; a fissure eruption occurred here in 1984. The area's "false craters" were formed when hot lava of ancient eruptions ran over marshland, causing steam jets to spout up, forming small cones. **Lake Mývatn** is an aqueous gem amid mountains and lava fields. Fed by cold springs in the lake bottom and warm springs in the northeastern corner, the shallow lake—42 square km (15 square mi) in area yet only 3 feet to 13 feet deep—teems with fish, birds, and insects, including the swarming midges for which the lake is named. These tiny flies are essential in the bird food chain.

Waterfowl migrate long distances to breed at Mývatn, where the duck population numbers up to 150,000 in summer. Indeed, the lake has Europe's greatest variety of nesting ducks, including some—the Harlequin duck and Barrow's goldeneye—found nowhere else in Europe. Dozens of other kinds of waders, upland birds, and birds of prey also nest here. Be sure to stay on established trails and pathways, as nests can be anywhere. During summer you should wear a head net to protect yourself against the huge midge swarms.

Turning off the Ring Road at Route 848, you'll pass **Skútustaðir**, a village on the lake's southern shore. Proceed along the eastern shore to the 1,300-feet-high **Hverfjall** ash cone, several hundred feet from the road. Many paths lead to the top. The outer walls of this volcanic crater are steep, but the ascent is easy. The walk around the top of the crater is about 4,300 feet. Southwest of Hverfjall is the **Dimmuborgir** (Dark Castles) lava field, a labyrinth of tall formations where you can choose between short and longer signposted routes through the eerie landscape. Among its mysterious arches, gates, and caves, the best-known is the **Kirkja** (church), resembling a Gothic chapel (it's marked by a sign, lest you miss it). Don't wander off the paths, as Dimmuborgir is a highly fragile environment.

Proceeding a few kilometer south from Mývatn on the Ring Road, you'll pass a factory that processes diatomite—tiny skeletons of algae—sucked from the bottom of the lake, where they have been deposited through the centuries. Diatomite is used in filters and is an important local export. The diatomite factory at Mývatn is highly controversial; conservationists fear that it may endanger the ecosystem of the lake, yet it provides welcome employment for some of the local population. Research has indicated—and cabinet ministers have concurred—that the plant should be closed by the year 2010 to preserve the lake's unique natural ecosystem. But, contrary to this, plant operators are asking for an environmental impact study, in an attempt to postpone or eliminate this deadline and thus keep jobs in the area.

Where to Stay & Eat

$$$ ✕⌂ **Hótel Reynihlíð.** This popular hotel has pastel-color rooms and staff members who provide helpful general information about surrounding attractions. The restaurant ($$) serves entrées such as fresh trout from the lake, and rhubarb pie for dessert. Another on-site though separate eatery, Gamli Bærinn, changes from a friendly daytime café to a congenial pub at night. ✉ *Reykjahlíð, IS-660, Mývatnssveit* ☎ *464–4170* 🖶 *464–4371* ⊕ *www.reynihlid.is* ↩ *41 rooms* ♨ *Restaurant, bicycles, horseback riding, bar* ⊟ *AE, DC, MC, V.*

$$$ ⌂ **Hótel Gígur.** This modern hotel has a delightful dining area with large windows giving stunning, panoramic views of the lake and surrounding landscape. ✉ *Skútustaðir, IS-660* ☎ *464–4455* 🖶 *551–6031* ⊕ *www.hotelkea.is* ↩ *37 rooms* ♨ *Restaurant* ⊟ *MC, V* ☉ *Closed mid-Sept.–mid-May.*

$$ ⌂ **Hótel Reykjahlíð.** The small, family-run hotel has a prime lakeside location with great views. Bird-watchers can add to their lists by simply looking out their windows. ✉ *Reykjahlíð, IS-660 Mývatnssveit* ☎ *464–4142* 🖶 *464–4336* ↩ *9 rooms* ⊟ *MC, V.*

Sports & the Outdoors

BIKING The **Hótel Reynihlíð** (✉ IS-660 Mývatnssveit ☎ 464–4170) in Mývatn rents bicycles for exploring the area around the lake.

BOATING At Mývatn, **Eldá Travel** (✉ Reykjahlíð, IS-660, Mývatnssveit ☎ 464–4220) rents boats on Lake Mývatn.

FISHING **Eldá Travel** (✉ Reykjahlíð, IS-660 Mývatnssveit ☎ 464–4220) has information about fly-fishing June through August on the famous Laxá River. Trout-fishing permits for Laxá River can be obtained from **Hotel Reynihlíð** (✉ IS-660 Mývatnssveit ☎ 464–4170).

HORSEBACK
RIDING Near Hrútafjörður, **Arinbjörn Jóhannsson** (☎ 451–2938) in Brekkulækur organizes horseback rides. The helpful folks at **Hotel Reynihlíð** (✉ IS-660 Mývatnssveit ☎ 464–4170) in Mývatn offer pony treks around the lake.

en route In the **Námaskarð Mountain Ridge,** on the eastern side of the Ring Road, are bubbling mud and purple sulfur, boiling like a witch's cauldron in the strange red-and-yellow valleys. Hike around this fascinating area, but remember to step carefully. Though the sulfurous vapors smell like rotten eggs, the fumes are generally harmless.

Húsavík

From Akureyri, drive east 46 km (29 mi) to the north junction of Rte. 85 and take it 45 km (28 mi) north to Húsavík. Or it's a straight shot 46 km (29 mi) from Lake Mývatn, first on Rte. 87 as it branches northwest off the Ring Rd., then 8 km (5 mi) north on Rte. 85.

Húsavík is a charming, bustling port on the north coast; it has a timber church dating from 1907. Conveniently near the winter ski area, it is also a good base for summer hiking. Whale-watchers have had amazing success on tours aboard a restored oak ship.

The **Húsavík Whale Center & Museum** (✉ IS-640 Húsavík, Hafnarstétt ☎ 464–2520 ⊠ IKr 400 ☉ Mid-June–mid-Aug., 9–9) is small and locally run, but is Iceland's main museum dedicated to whales and whaling. It has exhibits on both utilization and preservation of whales, as well as the folklore and natural history of these giants of the deep. A subtle case is made for sensible utilization of whales, as Norway has done lately.

Where to Stay & Eat

$$$ ✕⌧ **FossHótel Húsavík.** This hotel has two restaurants ($). Salmon, halibut, and trout star on the à la carte menu. Tex-Mex fare feeds the Sports Bar crowd around the clock, and there's a lunch buffet, too. ✉ *Ketilsbraut 22, IS-640* ☎ *464–1220* 🖶 *464–2161* ⊕ *www.fosshotel.is* ⤢ *44 rooms* ♻ *Restaurant, café, bar* ⊟ *AE, DC, MC, V.*

en route From Húsavík take Route 85 north and east for 61 km (38 mi) first, along the coast to Tjörnes, ending up inland at the lush nature reserve of Ásbyrgi.

Ásbyrgi

The forest of **Ásbyrgi,** or Shelter of the Gods, is surrounded by steep cliffs on all sides except the north, making it a peaceful shelter from the wind. Legend says this horseshoe-shape canyon was formed by the giant hoof of Sleipnir, the eight-leg horse of Óðinn.

Contiguous with Ásbyrgi is the wild and magnificent **Jökulsárgljúfur National Park,** the rugged canyon of the glacial Jökulsá River. At the southernmost point of the park, on Route 864, see Europe's most powerful waterfall, **Dettifoss,** where 212 tons of water cascade each second over a 145-foot drop. Farther inland at **Kverkfjöll,** hot springs rise at the edge of the **Vatnajökull icecap,** creating spectacular ice caves that can collapse at any time, so resist entering. Tours operate from Húsavík.

The North A to Z

AIR TRAVEL
Air Iceland (Flugfélag Íslands) has hour-long flights from Reykjavík to Akureyri. Air Iceland also flies from Akureyri to Grímsey, Vopnafjörður and Þórshöfn, in Denmark's Faroe Islands. Íslandsflug flies four days a week to Sauðárkrókur. The Mýflug air charter company flies daily charters June–August, based at the Mývatn airfield.

🛈 **Air Iceland** ✉ Akureyri ☎ 460-7000 ⊕ www.flugfelag.is ✉ Reykjavík ☎ 570-3030. **Íslandsflug** ☎ 570-8030 ⊕ www.islandsflug.is. **Mýflug** ☎ 464-4400 🖷 464-4401 ⊕ www.myflug.is.

BUS TRAVEL
BSÍ Travel runs daily bus service from Reykjavík to the north. It's 4½ hours to Blönduós and 6½ hours to Akureyri. Bus service from Akureyri takes less than 1½ hours to Húsavík and two hours to Mývatn. The Akureyri bus terminal, Umferðamiðstöðin, handles nationwide coach service.

The Akureyri Bus Company operates scheduled trips around the region, including a tour by bus and ferry to Hrísey Island and to Grímsey Island on the Arctic Circle.

🛈 **BSÍ Travel** ☎ 552-2300. **Umferðamiðstöðin** ✉ Hafnarstræti 82, IS-600 Akureyri ☎ 462-4442.

CAR TRAVEL
It's a 432-km (268-mi) drive from Reykjavík to Akureyri along the Ring Road (Route 1), a full day of driving. Branch off on Route 75 to Sauðárkrókur, or on Route 85 to Húsavík.

EMERGENCIES
Dial ☎ 112 for emergency assistance anywhere in Iceland.

🛈 **Emergencies** ☎ 112. **Police** ☎ 462-3222 in Akureyri.

TOURS
Iceland Travel operates a 12-hour day trip from Reykjavík to Akureyri and Lake Mývatn; you take a plane to Akureyri and then a bus to Mývatn. The tour departs daily June through mid-September. Nonni Travel runs tours from Akureyri to Mývatn, historic sites, and the islands off the north coast. Norður Sigling conducts whale-watching tours on a classic oak ship. Whale-watching, tours of Dettifoss, Kverkfjöll, and Vatnajökull are operated from Húsavík by SBA–Norðurleið.

🛈 Tour-Operator Recommendations **SBA–Norðurleið** ✉ Héðinsbraut 6, IS-640 Húsavík ☎ 464-2200 🖷 464-2201. **Iceland Tourist Bureau-Úrval-Útsýn** ☎ 462-5000. **Nonni Travel** ✉ Brekkugata 5, IS-600 Akureyri ☎ 461-1841 🖷 461-1843 ⊕ www. nonnitravel.is. **Norður Sigling** ✉ Gamli Baukur, IS-640 Húsavík ☎ 464-2350. **Ferðaskrifstofa Akureyrar** ✉ Ráðhústorg 3, IS-600 Akureyri ☎ 460-0600).

VISITOR INFORMATION
🛈 Tourist Information **Akureyri** ✉ Coach Terminal, Hafnarstræti 82, IS-600 ☎ 462-7733 ☉ June–Aug., weekdays 8:30-7. **Húsavík** ✉ Garðarsbraut 5, IS-640 ☎ 464-4300 ☉ June–mid-Sept., 9-7).

THE EAST

In 1974, when the final bridge across the treacherous glacial rivers and shifting sands south of the Vatnajökull was completed, the eastern side of the island finally became readily accessible by car from Reykjavík. The journey by car is still long, but as you approach the area from the south, from certain vantage points, you can watch ice floes gliding toward the sea while great predatory skuas swoop across black volcanic beaches.

The east coast has a number of busy fishing towns and villages. Those whose names end with "fjörður" each have their own private fjord. Farming thrives in the major valleys, which enjoy almost Continental summers. The Ring Road ties the inland hub Egilsstaðir to the southeastern coastal villages, and secondary roads make outlying communities accessible.

Egilsstaðir

273 km (164 mi) southeast of Akureyri, 700 km (420 mi) northeast of Reykjavík.

This major eastern commercial hub straddles the Ring Road and lies at the northeastern end of the long, narrow **Lake Lögurinn,** legendary home of a wormlike serpent that guards a treasure chest. The **Minjasafn Austurlands** (East Iceland Heritage Museum; ⊠ Laufskógum 1, IS-700 ☎ 471–1412) displays fascinating artifacts found in the area. The most dramatic is a Viking chieftain's grave site and its lavish relics, believed to be nearly 1,000 years old.

★ One of Iceland's most accessible and beautiful nature areas, **Hallormsstaður Forestry Reserve** contains the country's largest forest; more than 40 varieties of trees grow here—mostly aspen, spruce, birch, and larch. It's an easy 25-km (15-mi) drive from town along the lake's southern shore, first on the Ring Road and then onto Route 931. The Atlavík campground is on the lake south of Hallormsstaðaskógur. Cross the valley bridge from the forest to visit **Skriðuklaustur** (☎ 471–2990), an unusual stone-covered mansion built by the writer Gunnar Gunnarsson and donated by him to the state for an agricultural research station and visiting artist's residence.

In the highlands west of Lögurinn you may be able to spot Icelandic reindeer. Though not indigenous to the island (they were brought from Norway in the 18th century), the reindeer have thrived to the point that they have damaged tree saplings and farm growth.

Where to Stay

$$$ 🏨 **FossHótel Hallormsstaður.** Part of the Foss hotel chain, this hotel is set in one of Iceland's largest forests. It's a beautifully located summer facility, with a pool and pleasant trails for hiking and horseback riding that lace through the woods. ⊠ IS-707 Hallormsstaður ☎ 471–1705 🖨 562–4001 ⊕ www.foshotel.is 🛏 35 rooms ⚸ Restaurant, pool ☰ MC, V.

$$ 🏨 **Hótel Hérað, Icelandair Hotel.** One of a growing number of consistently excellent year-round hotels, the Hérað has tastefully decorated rooms with smart Nordic teak, ultramodern furnishings, and parquet flooring. In a valley with views of the nearby countryside, it's convenient to Egilsstaðir's shopping center and pool. ⊠ Miðvangur 5–7, IS-701 ☎ 471–1500 🖨 471–1501 ⊕ www.icehotel.is 🛏 36 rooms with bath ⚸ Restaurant, bar, meeting room ☰ AE, MC, V.

¢ 🏨 **Youth Hostel Húsey.** This hostel, open mid-May through September, has 16 beds. ⊠ Norður hérað, IS-701 Egilsstaðir ☎ 471–3010 🖨 471–3009 🛏 16 beds ☰ MC, V ☺ Closed Oct.–mid-May.

Nightlife & the Arts

Egilsstaðir supports a lively amateur theater group and vigorous music scene; call the **Tourist Information Office** (☎ 471–2320) for details.

The Outdoors

BIKING   Bikes can be rented at the **campsite** (☎ 471–2320) in Egilsstaðir.

SWIMMING   There is a swimming **pool** (☎ 471–1467) in Egilsstaðir.

Seyðisfjörður

25 km (16 mi) east of Egilsstaðir.

When visiting this quaint seaside village today—with its Norwegian-style wooded houses and 18th-century buildings—you may find it hard to imagine the tall sailing frigates of yesteryear crowding the fjord. Yet in the 19th century Seyðisfjörður was one of Iceland's major trade ports. The ships plying the fjord nowadays include the *Norröna* ferry, dispatching tourists and their vehicles from Europe every summer.

Where to Stay & Eat

$ ✕⊞ **Hótel Seyðisfjörður.** Overlooking the dramatic fjord, this classic Norse-style wooden building has tidy, cozy, but humble rooms. A varied buffet is laid out on summer Wednesdays, accompanied by live music in the restaurant. ⊠ *Austurvegur 3, IS-710* ☎ *472–1460* 🖷 *472–1570* ⇆ *9 rooms* ♨ *Restaurant, fishing, horseback riding, bar* ⊟ *MC, V.*

$ ⊞ **Youth Hostel.** There are 28 beds at this year-round hostel. ⊠ *Ránargata 9, IS-710* ☎ *472–1410* 🖷 *472–1610* ⇆ *28 beds* ⊟ *MC, V.*

Bakkagerði

71 km (44 mi) northeast of Egilsstaðir; take Rte. 94.

Bakkagerði is by **Borgarfjörður** (not to be confused with its larger namesake in the west). The Borgarfjörður Road, though bumpy, is entirely safe, but don't be in a hurry. Savor the swooping descent from the Vatnsskarð mountain pass and the spectacular coast road along Njarðvíkurskriður. In a land of stunning mountain scenery, Borgarfjörður (east) is a natural masterpiece, where the changing tones in the landscape have to be seen to be believed. The painter Jóhannes Kjarval lived here, and as can be seen in his paintings, the countryside made a deep impression on him.

Neskaupstaður

71 km (43 mi) east of Egilsstaðir, driving south along Rte. 92, curving east through Eskifjörður; travel north over Iceland's highest pass, completing a U-shape path on Rte. 92.

In a tranquil position under rugged mountainsides, the east coast's largest town thrived during the '60s herring boom. The settlement started as a trading center in 1882; fishing and minor industrial concerns are the mainstays today. The natural history museum, **Náttúrugripasafnið í Neskaupstað,** is the main attraction.

Where to Stay & Eat

$ ✕⊞ **Hótel Egilsbúð.** An economic option for those who don't need a private bath, the Egilsbúð is also a popular local eatery ($$). ⊠ *Egilsbraut 1, IS-740* ☎ *477–1321* 🖷 *477–1322* ⇆ *5 rooms without bath* ⊟ *AE, DC, MC, V.*

Sports & the Outdoors

FISHING Angling permits for the Norðfjarðurá are available at **Tröllanaust** (✉ Melgata 11, IS-740 ☎ 477–1444).

SEA CRUISES Cruises on the **Norðfjörður** (☎ 477–1321 or 853–1718) with sea angling as an option are available.

SWIMMING The Neskaupstaður **pool** (✉ Miðstræti 15 ☎ 477–1243) is open to the public.

Eskifjörður

48 km (30 mi) southeast of Egilsstaðir; either backtrack 23 km (14 mi) from Neskaustaður on Rte. 92 over the breathtaking 2,300-foot pass at Oddskarð, or go 48 km (29 mi) from Egilsstaðir.

This charming fishing village has a fish-freezing plant with murals by Iceland's Catalan artist, Baltazar. Eskifjörður is on the beautiful Hólmanes Cape, noted for a large variety of flora and bird life; its southern part is now a protected area. The town's stunning landmark mountain—**Hólmatindur**—unfortunately shades the town from the sun from late September to April. The **East Iceland Maritime Museum** (✉ Strandgata 39B, IS-735 Eskifjörður ☎ 476–1605) is open June through August, daily 2–7, and by appointment the rest of the year.

Where to Stay

$ 🛏 **Hotel Askja.** This cozy, old-fashioned year-round hotel has rooms with a shared bathroom. The sitting room with its fireplace is a great place to unwind. The hotel is run by a keen golfer who provides shuttle service and lessons for guests. ✉ *Hólvegur 4, IS-735* ☎ *476–1102* 🖨 *476–1103* ⌨ *7 rooms without bath* ⌂ *Restaurant, bar* ▭ *MC, V.*

Sports & the Outdoors

FISHING Angling permits for the river **Eskifjarðará** (☎ 476–1170 town council) are available.

SWIMMING You can swim in Eskifjörður's local **pool** (✉ Lambeyrarbraut 14 ☎ 476–1238).

Breiðdalsvík

83 km (50 mi) south of Egilsstaðir along the Ring Rd. or, more circuitously, about 74 km (45 mi) along Rte. 96 from Reyðarfjörður.

Trade in this tiny village of a few hundred kindred souls dates from 1883. Hugging the shore on its own small inlet, the hamlet is gradually growing thanks to the development of a harbor deep enough for most ships.

Where to Stay & Eat

$$ ✕🛏 **Hótel Bláfell.** The small hotel has a rustic yet inviting exterior; the interior is bright, and there's a noted restaurant ($$$) that specializes in seafood, lamb, and beef dishes. Fishing permits are available for the area. ✉ *Sólvellir 14, IS-760* ☎ *475–6770* 🖨 *475–6668* ⊕ *www.travelnet.is/ blafells* ⌨ *23 rooms, 17 with bath* ⌂ *Restaurant, bar* ▭ *DC, MC, V.*

Djúpivogur

144 km (87 mi) south of Egilsstaðir on the Ring Rd.

A fishing village has existed on this site since about 1600, and some of the oldest buildings in town date from the days of Danish merchant control, 1788 to 1920. One, **Langabúð** (✉ on Búð—it's the second house inland from the boat pier ☎ 478–8220) is a local museum and coffee shop, and pays tribute to the late master wood carver and sculptor, Ríkarður Jónsson, whose breathtakingly ornate Rococo mirror-frame, done to complete his apprenticeship, would fit handsomely in any Tuscan palace. The nearby basaltic **Búlandstindur** mountain, rising to 6,130 feet, is legendary as a force of mystical energy, perhaps because of its pyramidal shape.

Where to Stay & Eat

$$ ✕🏠 **Hótel Framtíð.** Built of square-hewn Finnish timber, this is a warm and friendly hotel, right off the harbor. It has an enlarged dining area ($–$$$), where seafood reigns supreme. ⊠ *Vogalandi 4, IS-765* ☎ *478–8887* 🖶 *478–8187* ⊕ *www.simnet.is/framtid* ➴ *18 rooms* ♨ *Restaurant, sauna, bar* ▤ *MC, V.*

¢ 🏠 **Youth Hostel.** Open May through September, this seafront hostel retains the rustic charm of the quaint farmhouse it once was. In the main house, six bedrooms (some with bunk beds) share two baths, and all reflect cozy rural comforts with simple, yet classic furnishings. Three separate family apartments have kitchens and baths, and can easily accommodate five people. ⊠ *Berunes, Berufjörður, IS-765* ☎☎ *478–8988* ⊕ *www.simnet.is/berunes* ➴ *30 beds without bath* ▤ *MC, V* ☯ *Mid-May–mid Sept.*

en route
To continue along the Ring Road, drive south from Egilsstaðir 150 km (93 mi) to the rugged stretch of coast indented by the inlets of **Álftafjörður** (Swan Fjord) and **Hamarsfjörður.** Surrounded by majestic mountains, these shallow waters host myriad swans, ducks, and other birds that migrate here from Europe in the spring and summer.

Höfn

103 km (62 mi) south of Djúpivogur on the Ring Rd.

Höfn is slowly being closed off from the ocean by silt washed down by glacial rivers into the fjord. Spread out on a low-lying headland at the mouth of the fjord, Höfn offers a fine view of the awesome **Vatnajökull.** Not only is this gigantic glacier Iceland's largest but it is also equal in size to all the glaciers on the European mainland put together. You can arrange tours from Höfn.

The **Glacier Exhibition** (⊠ IS-780 Höfn ☎ 478–2665 ☯ June–Aug., daily 1–6 and 8–10) takes a thorough and fascinating look at glaciers, including their behavior, geology, and exploration—both past and present. Naturally, Vatnajökull plays a starring role, reigning as Europe's largest. An ancient homemade snowmobile, named Kári, stands as a tribute to Icelandic ingenuity and is worth a picture to any off-road traveler.

off the beaten path
JÖKULSÁRLÓN – At the Glacial River Lagoon, about 50 km (31 mi) west of Höfn, you can see large chunks of the glacier tumble and float around in a spectacular ice show. So spectacular is the scenery, it has been used as a location for scenes in some James Bond movies. Boat trips on the lagoon are operated throughout the summer; for details call Einar B. Einarsson (⊠ IS-780 Höfn ☎ 478–2122 ⊕ www.jokulsarlon.com). Light meals and refreshments are available at a small coffeehouse at the lagoon. On the **Breiðamerkur sands** west of the lagoon is the largest North Atlantic colony of skua, large predatory seabirds that unhesitatingly dive-bomb intruders in the nesting season.

Where to Stay & Eat

$$$ ✕⊡ **FossHótel Vatnajökull.** Spectacular views of the glacier are featured at this hotel, which has a nationwide reputation for quality accommodations and excellent food ($$–$$$), including fine meat and seafood dishes. ⊠ *Lindarbakka, Hornafjörður, IS-780* ☎ *478–2555* 🖷 *562–4001* ⊕ *www.fosshotel.is* 📭 *26 rooms with bath* ⚒ *Restaurant* ⊟ *AE, DC, MC, V* ⊙ *Closed late Sept.–Jan. 1.*

$$$ ✕⊡ **Hótel Höfn.** Emphasis here is on impeccable rooms as well as tasty dining. Light-wood furnishings, parquet floors, and cheerful pastel yellows fill the warm rooms. Back-facing rooms view Europe's largest glacier, and deluxe rooms come complete with guest robes and slippers for trips to the sauna. In the upper-level restaurant ($) you may feast on reindeer steak or lamb, or sumptuous buffets. In the ground-level bistro you can have lobster a million ways (give or take). ⊠ *Víkurbraut IS-780, Höfn, Hornafjörður* ☎ *478–1240* 🖷 *478–1996* 📭 *36 rooms, 32 with bath* ⚒ *2 restaurants, sauna, bar* ⊟ *MC, V.*

¢ ⊡ **Stafafell.** The 19th-century farmhouse has now been fully restored at this accommodation in the gorgeous rhyolite countryside near Höfn. Though the classic exterior has been preserved, the rooms inside are modern and comfortable. Three separate cottages, with six rooms in total, have shared baths. Buses stop on request. ⊠ *Stafafell, Lón, IS-781 Höfn* ☎ *478–1717* 🖷 *478–1785* ⊕ *ww.eldhorn.is/stafafell* 📭 *1 double room with bath, 56 beds without bath.* ⊟ *MC, V* ⊙ *Closed Oct.–Mar.*

¢ ⊡ **Youth Hostel Nýibær.** This hostel, open May through September, has 33 beds. ⊠ *Nýibær, Hafnarbraut 8, IS-780* ☎ *478–1736* 🖷 *478–1965* 📭 *33 beds without bath* ⊟ *MC, V* ⊙ *Closed Oct.–Apr.*

Sports & the Outdoors

SWIMMING The Höfn swimming **pool** (⊠ Hafnarbraut, IS-780 Hornafjörður ☎ 478–1157) is open to the public.

WHALE-WATCHING **Whale-watching trips** (☎ 478–1500) are available from Höfn.

The East A to Z

AIR TRAVEL

Air Iceland (Flugfélag Íslands), operates scheduled flights from Reykjavík to Egilsstaðir and Höfn í Hornafjörður. Íslandsflug also goes to Höfn three times a week.

⧉ Air Travel Information **Air Iceland** ⊠ Egilsstaðir ☎ 471-1210 ⊕ www.airiceland. is ⊠ Reykjavík ☎ 570-3030. **Íslandsflug** ⊠ Reykjavík ☎ 570-8030 ⊕ www.islandsflug. is ⊠; Höfn í Hornafjörður ☎ 478-1250

BOAT & FERRY TRAVEL

The luxury Norröna ferry carries almost 1,500 passengers and over 800 cars and runs summers from Norway or Denmark via the Faroe Islands to Seyðisfjörður. On-board facilities rival those of cruise ships, and include fitness center, sauna, and night club. Contact Austfar or Terra Nova Sól Travel.

⧉ **Austfar** ⊠ Fjarðargata 8, IS-710 Seyðisfjörður ☎ 472-1111 🖷 472-1105. **Terra Nova Sól Travel** ⊠ Stangarhyl 3, IS-110 Reykjavík ☎ 591-9000 🖷 591-9001 ⊕ www. terranova.is.

BUS TRAVEL

The east is so far from Reykjavík that bus travel is recommended only if you are making the entire Ring Road circuit. From Akureyri the six-hour trip to Egilsstaðir runs daily in summer, three times a week the rest of the year. From Egilsstaðir there's frequent service around the region;

it takes about five hours to get to Höfn from Reykjavík, along the south coast. Call Austurleið Coaches for information.

🚌 **Austurleið Coaches** ☎ 545-1717 ⊕ www.austurleid.is.

CAR TRAVEL

The region is accessible by car on the Ring Road (Route 1) but you'll encounter its last tough vestiges (120 km or 72 mi) of gravel. So, even at a brisk pace, give the drive from Reykjavík, along the south coast, to Egilsstaðir—about 700 km (434 mi)—at least two days. From Akureyri to Egilsstaðir is 273 km (170 mi) and can easily be done in a day.

EMERGENCIES

You can dial ☎ 112 for emergency assistance anywhere in Iceland.

🚓 **Police Bakkagerði** ☎ 473-1400. **Djúpivogur** ☎ 478-8817. **Egilsstaðir** ☎ 471-1223. **Eskifjörður** ☎ 476-1106. **Höfn** ☎ 478-1282. **Neskaupstaður** ☎ 477-1332. **Seyðisfjörður** ☎ 472-1334.

TOURS

Iceland Travel operates a day trip from Reykjavík to Höfn by plane, with a snowmobile tour of the Vatnajökull and a boat tour on the Jökulsárlón Glacier Lagoon. The tour runs daily mid-June–August. Fjarðaferðir of Neskaupstaður offers sea trips of Norðfjörður and neighboring Mjóifjörður.

Wilderness and glacier tours of Vatnajökull are operated from many different locations: from Höfn by Jöklaferðir and from Eskifjörður by Tanni.

Glacier Tours offers a nine-hour bus tour from Höfn in Hornafjörður, including a snowmobile or Sno-Cat ride and a visit to a glacier lagoon. The trip costs about IKr 10,000 per person or IKr 25,000 as a day trip with flight from Reykjavík.

🚍 **Tour Operators Fjarðaferðir** ☎ 477-1321 🖶 477-1322. **Glacier Tours** ✉ Box 66, IS-780 Hornafjörður ☎ 478-1000 🖶 478-1901. **Jöklaferðir** ☎ 478-1000 🖶 478-1901 ⊕ www.glaciertours.is. **Tanni Travel** ☎ 476-1399 🖶 476-1599. **Iceland Travel** ☎ 585-4300.

VISITOR INFORMATION

🛈 **Tourist Information Egilsstaðir** Tourist Information Office at campsite ✉ Hafnarbraut 52 ☎ 471-2320. **Höfn** Tourist Information Center at campsite ☎ 478-1500. **Seyðisfjörður** Austfar Travel Agency ✉ Fjarðargata 8, IS-710 ☎ 472-1111.

THE SOUTH

The power of volcanoes is all too evident on this final leg of the Ring Road tour. At Kirkjubæjarklaustur you can still see scars of the great Laki eruption of 1783. At Stöng you can visit excavated ruins of a farmstead buried by the 1104 eruption of Mt. Hekla, known throughout medieval Europe as the abode of the damned—and still mightily active. Off the coast, the Vestmannaeyjar (Westman Islands) are still being melded by volcanic activity—a 1973 eruption forced the evacuation of all inhabitants. Other regional natural wonders include Skaftafell National Park and Þórsmörk (Thor's Wood), a popular nature reserve.

Five years after Mt. Hekla's fiery 1991 eruption, the world was treated to more fierce volcanic glory as a separate cauldron erupted not far from subglacial Grímsvatn and quickly melted through the several-hundred-foot thickness of Vatnajökull glacier. Clues before the eruption gave the media and geologists time to observe this rare type of eruption. Powerful flooding resulted, destroying a minor bridge and taking out many sections of the long bridge over the river Skeiðará. This temporary disconnection of the Ring Road has been mended, and though the colossal, ever-changing ice sculptures, which resembled giant, rough diamonds, are a mere memory, the twisted, massive steel bridge girders have been piled like pasta, not far from the bridge, as a reminder of Nature's might. Then, just to keep its memory alive and close out the millennium with a bang, Mt. Hekla went off again in the year 2000. Fortunately, there was no damage to report. In fact, Icelandic seismologists, with their thorough instrumentation, have now actually accurately predicted epicenter location and timing of a major earthquake to within a day.

Skaftafell National Park

50 km (31 mi) west of Jökulsárlón.

Bordering Vatnajökull is Skaftafell National Park, the largest of Iceland's three national reserves. Glaciers branching off Vatnajökull shelter Skaftafell from winds, creating a verdant oasis. In the park, you can walk for days on beautiful trails through a rare combination of green forest, clear water, waterfalls, sands, mountains, and glaciers. Iceland's highest peak, **Hvannadalshnúkur,** reaching 6,950 feet, is just outside the park and provides a stunning backdrop. The famous **Svartifoss** (Black Falls) tumbles over a cliff whose sides resemble the pipes of a great organ. Do not miss **Sel,** a restored gabled farmhouse high up on the slope. Guided walks in the national park are organized daily.

Where to Stay

$$ 🏨 **Hótel Skaftafell.** Few hotels in Iceland have such a serendipitous setting—near breathtaking Skaftafell National Park. A roomy bar is upstairs over the expanded lobby of this family-run facility. A travel shop and gas station are also on the property. There are also rooms for sleeping bags with shared bath and kitchen facilities. ⊠ *Freysnes, Öræfi, IS-785* 🕾 *478–1945* 🖷 *478–1846* ⊕ *www.hotelskaftafell.is* 🛏 *53 rooms, 43 with bath* ⚿ *Restaurant, bar* ⊟ *AE, MC, V.*

The Outdoors

BIRD-WATCHING   For a fairly sedate adventure and close-up views of puffins, you can take a hay ride in a wagon across a tidal flat to nearby Ingólfshöfði for **bird-watching excursions** (⊠ Hofsnes, IS-785 Fagurhólsmýri 🕾 478–1682). It pays to sit in the back of the "bus" and let somebody else block the spray from the tractor.

MOUNTAIN   **Öræfaferðir** (⊠ Hofsnes-Öræfi, IS-785 Fagurhólsmýri 🕾 478–1682), a
CLIMBING   father-and-son outfit, puts together tours ranging from introductory ice-climbing to assaults on the summit of Iceland's highest mountain to bird-watching, or as they put it, "From Coast to Mountains."

Kirkjubæjarklaustur

272 km (163 mi) east of Reykjavík along the Ring Rd.

Aptly named Kirkjubæjarklaustur—or church farmstead cloister—this outpost was once the site of a medieval convent. Two waterfalls and the three-day August chamber music festival are among local attractions. North of here is the **Laki Volcano,** with more than 100 craters dotting the landscape. The great lava field was created by this volcano in a single eruption in 1783–84. The worst in Iceland's history, it wiped out about 70% of the country's livestock and a fifth of the population. Jón Steingrímsson, then the priest at Kirkjubæjarklaustur, is said to have stopped the advance of the lava by prayer. You need a four-wheel drive vehicle to get to Laki, because the 45-km- (28-mi-) long highland road leading north off the Ring Road, some 6 km (4 mi) west of Kirkjubæjarklaustur, fords icy rivers and is extremely primitive. About 30 km (19 mi) east of Kirkjubæjarklaustur on the Ring Road, don't miss the little chapel at **Núpsstaður,** one of a handful of extant turf churches. This well-preserved building has remained almost unchanged since the 17th century and has a dramatic backdrop of the notched massive cliffs of nearby Lómagnúpur.

Where to Stay

$$ 🏨 **Hótel Kirkjubæjarklaustur, Icelandair Hotel.** One of a growing number of year-round hotels, this property is in a modern building and within strolling distance to the the foot of the falls. Sleeping-bag accommodations ($) are also available. ⊠ *Klausturvegur 6, IS-880* ☎ *487–4799* 🖷 *487–4614* 🌐 *www.icehotel.is* ↩ *73 rooms, 57 with shower* ⚒ *Restaurant, pool* ▭ *MC, V.*

The Outdoors

BOATING   **Boats** (☎ 487–4620) can be rented for an outing on Lake Hæðargarðsvatn near Kirkjubæjarklaustur.

HIKING   **Hannes Jónsson** (⊠ Hvoll, IS-880 ☎ 487–4785 or 853–4133), a driver–guide, knows Núpsstaðarskógur like the back of his hand and takes visitors on the slopes of the Eystrafjall Mountain. Highlighting the nine-hour trip are large twin falls: the clear Núpsárfoss and the glacially milky Hvítárfoss, which plunge side-by-side into the same pool. A good bit of hiking is well rewarded; pack a good hearty lunch and of course wear hiking shoes.

en route   If you've rented a four-wheel drive vehicle you can travel 25 km (15 mi) west from Kirkjubæjarklaustur on Route 1, turn right onto Route 208, and continue for 20 km (12 mi) on the very rugged mountain road Route F22 to **Eldgjá,** a 32-km- (20-mi-) long volcanic rift. Historic records suggest that it erupted in AD 934 with a ferocity similar to that of the Laki eruption.

Vík

80 km (48 mi) west of Kirkjubæjarklaustur.

Proceeding west along the Ring Road from Kirkjubæjarklaustur, you'll cross the Mýrdalssandur Desert and arrive at the coastal village of Vík, with its vast population of migratory Arctic terns. Pay heed to the sandstorm warning signal en route. Foolhardy drivers have been stranded or emerged with their car's finish burnished down to bare metal. About 12 km (7 mi) past Vík, turn left toward the ocean to reach the southernmost point of the main island, the **Dyrhólaey Promontory,** with its lighthouse. The ocean has worn the black basalt here into an arch 394 feet high; boats can sail through it in calm weather. This headland is also a bird sanctuary, so expect it to be closed during the nesting period in early summer.

Where to Stay & Eat

$ ✕ **Brydebúð.** Café, pub, restaurant, and as if that weren't enough, it's also the town's local cultural and tourist information center. The old trading post's character has been carefully brought back to life, mak-

ing this a congenial spot off the main drag. ✉ *Víkurbraut 28* ☎ *487–1202*
⊕ *www.vik.is* 🖃 *MC, V.*

$$ 🏨 **Hótel Dyrhólaey.** This family-run hotel has fantastic vistas of the
mountains and the sea. Pleasant, contemporary rooms, all with bath,
are bright and quiet, but not opulent. The buildings stand uphill from
a turnoff 9 km (5½ mi) west of Vík. ✉ *Brekkur 1, IS-871* ☎ *487–1333*
🖨 *487–1507* ⊠ *37 rooms with bath* ⚭ *Restaurant* 🖃 *MC, V* ⊙ *Closed
Nov.–Feb., except for groups.*

$$ 🏨 **Hótel Vík.** This hotel, nestled beneath a town bluff, has good access
for those with disabilities. Although it is a summer hotel, five cozy du-
plex cottages are available year-round and offer 10 double units with
bath, at a savings. ✉ *Klettsvegur IS-871* ☎ *487–1480* 🖨 *487–1302* ⊠ *21
rooms, 10 doubles in 5 cottages* 🖃 *MC, V.*

¢–$ 🏨 **Norður-Vík Youth Hostel.** This site, with 36 beds in nine rooms, has a
great sea view; it's open mid-May through mid-September. ✉ *Suðurvíkurve-
gur 5, IS-870* ☎ *487–1106* 🖨 *487–1303* ✉ *nordur-vik@simnet.is* ⊠ *36
beds* 🖃 *No credit cards* ⊙ *Closed mid-Sept.–mid-May.*

Sports & the Outdoors

BIKING Bikes can be rented at the **Ársalir Guesthouse** (✉ Austuvegur 7,
☎ 487–1400).

SNOWMOBILING Snowmobiling is possible in summer on a glacial tongue of the Mýrdalsjökull Glacier, which looms over Vík, through **Arcanum** (✉ Sólheimaskála
IS-871 ☎ 487–1500 🖨 487–1496 ⊕ www.snow.is).

Shopping

Vikurprjón (✉ Austurvegur 20 ☎ 487–1250) is a factory outlet that sells
woolen goods.

Skógar

32 km (19 mi) west of Vík.

The tiny settlement of Skógar has one of Iceland's best folk museums,
Byggðarsafnið Skógar. The curator of these beautifully preserved old
houses and memorabilia is highly knowledgeable and has been com-
mended for his efforts with the Falcon Medal of Honor, Iceland's highest distinction. He may even serenade you on the antique harmonium.
Among the mementos of this region's past is a tiny, frail boat local fishermen once navigated along the treacherous coast. ✉ *100 yards east
of the Edda Hotel* ☎ *487–8845* ⊙ *May–mid-Sept., daily 9–noon and
1–6, or by appointment.*

Where to Stay

$ 🏨 **Hótel Edda, Skógar.** Close to the local waterfalls, Skógafoss, this hotel
also has views of the sea, mountains, and glaciers. The downside is shared
baths for all. Sleeping-bag accommodations are available. The restaurant serves a supper buffet. ✉ *Skógum IS-861 Hvollsvöllur,* ☎ *487–8870*
🖨 *487–8858* ⊠ *34 rooms without bath* ⚭ *Restaurant, indoor pool,
outdoor hot tub* 🖃 *AE, MC, V* ⊙ *Closed Sept.–May.*

en route Several hundred feet west of Skógar, just off the Ring Road, is the
impressive **Skógafoss,** a waterfall that's more than 197 feet high and
just the last in a series of huge cascades up the mountain. If you drive
30 km (19 mi) farther west along the Ring Road from Skógar, follow
the turnoff north to **Seljalandsfoss,** another waterfall on the right.
This graceful, ribbonlike waterfall drops from an overhanging lava
cliff as though it belongs in Hawaii. If you step carefully, you can
walk behind it, but be prepared to get wet.

Þórsmörk

30 km (19 mi) north of Skógar along the Ring Rd.

North of Skógar on the Ring Road you'll come to the powerful **Markarfljót River.** Route 249 on its east bank leads 15 km (9 mi) east across some treacherous streams into the **Þórsmörk** nature reserve, a popular vacation area bounded on its eastern and southern sides by the Eyjafjalla and Mýrdals glaciers. This route is passable only to four-wheel-drive vehicles, preferably traveling in groups. Þórsmörk, nestled in a valley surrounded by mountain peaks, enjoys exceptionally calm and often sunny weather, making it a veritable haven of birch trees and other Icelandic flora.

The road on the west bank of the Markarfljót leads 10 km (6 mi) north into saga country, to **Hlíðarendi,** the farm where Gunnar Hámundarson lived and died. He was one of the heroes of *Njáls Saga,* the single greatest classic work of Icelandic saga literature, written around the 12th century. Exiled by the Alþing parliament for murdering Þorgeir Oddkelsson, he refused to leave "these beautiful slopes."

In the lowlands to the southwest of the Markarfljót (turn off the Ring Road toward shore, and then onto Route 252 and drive 20 km [12 mi]) is another famous place from *Njáls Saga,* **Bergþórshvoll.** This is where Njál's enemies surrounded his farmhouse and burned it to the ground, killing everyone inside except for Kári, Njál's son-in-law. Kári survived by hiding in a barrel of creamy skyr and escaped under cover of smoke from the burning house.

The Outdoors

HIKING There are many excellent trekking routes, such as a day's trip over the **Fimmvörðuháls Mountain Pass** down to Skógar (bring a compass). Adventurers can take a three-day hike into the interior to visit **Landmannalaugar,** where hot and cold springs punctuate a landscape rich in yellow, brown, and red rhyolite hills carved by glacial rivers.

Hvolsvöllur

54 km (33 mi) west of Skógar along the Ring Rd.; 39 km (24 mi) from Þórsmörk Preserve.

This small community was settled in 1932. Hvolsvöllur is a busy service center for the fertile farm country surrounding it. A major meat-processing operation is also stationed here, and has brought jobs to the area. Hvolsvöllur is a good base if you are interested in *Njáls Saga* or the glacial scenery.

Where to Stay

$$ 🖼 **Hótel Hvolsvöllur.** Double rooms with bath are bright and large, with wall-to-wall carpeting and mahogany and teak furnishings. The peaceful side-street location, combined with fine service and a good restaurant, make this hotel one of the best in the region. Lower-price rooms with common bath are also available. ⊠ *Hlíðarvegur 7, IS-861* ☎ *487–8187* 📠 *487–8391* 🛏 *41 rooms, 28 with bath* ♨ *Restaurant, bar* ☰ *MC, V.*

$ 🖼 **Youth Hostel Fljótsdalur.** This is a rustic, traditional Icelandic turf-wall house with a gorgeous, secluded location. It's 18 mi from the nearest store, so you might want to bring your own food. ⊠ *Fljótsdalur, Fljótshlíð IS-861* ☎ *487–8498* 📠 *487–8497* 🛏 *15 beds* ☰ *MC, V* ☾ *Closed mid-Oct.–mid-Apr.*

The Outdoors

HIKING The **Ferðafélag Íslands** touring club (✉ Mörkin 6, IS-108 Reykjavík ☎ 568–2533 🖷 568–2535 ⊕ www.fi.is) conducts cabin and camping tours of the region. **Útivist** (✉ Laugavegur 178, IS-105 Reykjavík ☎ 562–1000 ⊕ www.utivist.is) is another option for hiking tours with both cabin and sleeping-bag accommodations. Both groups offer many long-distance hikes from Þórsmörk.

Hella

12 km (7 mi) west of Hvolsvöllur on the Ring Rd.; 51 km (31 mi) west of Þórsmörk; 93 km (58 mi) traveling west to Reykjavík.

About 10 km (6 mi) west of Hella, turn right onto Route 26 and drive 40 km (25 mi) or so until you see, on your right, the tallest peak in the region. **Mt. Hekla** is also an active volcano, rightfully infamous since the Middle Ages as it has erupted 21 times in recorded history and as recently as 2000. Some 25 km (16 mi) farther, Route 26 intersects Route 32; turn left and go 15 km (9 mi) to the right turn for **Stöng,** an ancient settlement on the west bank of the Þjórsá River, Iceland's longest. The original farm here dates back almost 900 years; it was buried by Hekla's eruption in 1104, but you can visit the excavated ruins. A complete replica has been built, using the same materials the settlers used, south of Stöng at Búrfell on Route 32.

Where to Stay

$ 🏨 **Guesthouse Leirubakki.** This property with 15 rooms has shared baths and is a well-placed ringside seat for fans of Mt. Hekla—all the beds were quickly booked the last time it erupted. ✉ *Leirubakki Landssveit, IS-851* ☎🖷 *487–6591* ⤶ *49 bunk beds in 15 rooms, without bath* ▭ *MC, V.*

Selfoss

36 km (22 mi) west of Hella on the Ring Rd.

This bustling town on the shores of the turbulent Ölfusá River is the largest town in southern Iceland. Selfoss came into being in the 1930s and is a major agricultural community with the country's largest and oldest intact cream and butter plant. It is the hub community in the rural district called Árborg, formed with Stokkseyri and Eyrarbakki. You can take a guided tour to the plant and other sites—including Þuríðabúð in Stokkseyri where a rugged woman ran a fishing operation herself for 25 years in the 1800s.

Where to Stay

$$$ 🏨 **Hótel Selfoss.** This quality hotel in Selfoss has an excellent restaurant and bar and is a perfect spot from which to base short trips inland or to the coast. A newer wing has 80 rooms. ✉ *Eyarvegur 2, IS-800* ☎ *482–2500* 🖷 *482–2524* ⊕ *www.icehotel.is* ⤶ *108 rooms* ♨ *Restaurant, bar* ▭ *AE, MC, V.*

Shopping

The **KÁ Verslanir** (✉ Austurvegur 3–5/Ring Rd. ☎ 482–1000) is the area's largest supermarket, and the department store has a wide selection of goods.

en route At Hveragerði, turn south onto Route 38 and drive 20 km (12 mi) to Þorlákshöfn—the gateway to Vestmannaeyjar (the Westman Islands) and one of three interesting coastal villages.

Eyrarbakki

12 km (7 mi) southwest of Selfoss along Rte. 34.

This close-knit village right on the shore of the North Atlantic was the largest community in the south less than a century ago. A few buildings remaining from that era have been restored. The pleasant **Árnes Folk Museum** (⊠ Húsið ☎ 483–1504), an older gentry house, has interesting exhibits. Its surrounding turf walls were the most effective means of shelter from stiff onshore breezes. Another attraction is the **Eyrarbakki Maritime Museum** (⊠ Túngata 10 ☎ 483–1165). Nearby tidal marshes are a birdwatcher's wonderland.

Where to Eat

$$–$$$$ ✕ **Rauða husið.** Seafood and vegetarian dishes, along with homemade desserts and great java, are served here. Artwork by local artists usually decorates the interior walls of this classic structure, which is only a few steps from the shore. ⊠ *Búðarstígur 12, IS-800* ☎ *483–3330* ▭ *MC, V.*

Stokkseyri

14 km (8 mi) southwest of Selfoss; take Rte. 34 and Rte. 33.

Third in a trio of neighboring shoreline villages, Stokkseyri lacks a good harbor, but fishing is nonetheless important to this tiny community. On the beach you can look for water birds and imagine how it must have been when Þuríður Einarsdóttir ran her fishing operation out of a sod-covered base some 150 years ago.

Where to Eat

$$–$$$ ✕ **Veitingastaðurinn Við Fjöruborðið.** Don't let its plain exterior and humble interior fool you—this place serves lobster tails so good that the interior ceases to matter. Pay a bit more for the side-order veggies with couscous and you're on your way to culinary delirium (a panful makes a hearty lunch). ⊠ *Eyrarbraut 3B* ☎ *483–1550* 🖷 *483–1545* ▭ *MC, V.*

The Outdoors

KAYAKING   Kajak tours at **Fjörborðl** (⊠ Heiðarbrún 24, IS-825 ☎ 896–5716 ⊕ www.kajak.is) runs summer tours by self-paddled kayaks through the area's calm marshes, canals, and offshore skerries. This is a quiet and tranquil way to get closer to waterfowl in their own territory.

Vestmannaeyjar

3¼ hours south from Þorlákshöfn on the passenger-car ferry Herjólfur; 1 hr by plane.

Hjörleifur, sworn brother of Reykjavík settler Ingólfur Arnarson, settled in Heimaey (the only inhabited island of the Westman archipelago) with five Irish slaves—called Westmen. The slaves soon murdered their master and fled to the offshore islands. Ingólfur avenged his brother by driving most of the slaves off the cliffs of the islands and killing them. This tiny cluster of 15 islands off the south coast was named in honor of the Irish slaves.

The Vestmannaeyjar (Westman Islands) were formed by volcanic eruptions only 5,000 to 10,000 years ago, and there is still much volcanic activity here. **Surtsey,** the latest addition, was formed in November 1963 with an eruption that lasted 3½ years. It is now totally restricted from public visitation and influence as a biological research area. In 1973 a five-month-long eruption on **Heimaey** wiped out part of the town. The island's entire population of about 5,000 was forced to flee in fishing boats, with only a few hours' notice. A few years later, however, the people of the Westman Islands had removed tons of black lava dust and cinder from their streets and rebuilt most of what was ruined. The lava, still hot, is used for heat by the resourceful islanders.

The main industry here is fishing, but another occupation—nowadays more a sport than a job—is more unusual: egg hunting. Enthusiasts dangle from ropes over the sheer black volcanic cliffs to collect eggs—a local delicacy—from the nests of seabirds. The islands are rich in birds, especially puffins, which number about a million; a few thousand puffins are used for food.

Heimaey has one of Iceland's best natural history museums, **Náttúrugripasafn Vestmannaeyja.** Its fine research aquarium contains peculiar creatures of the deep and played a role in attempting to return Keiko, the Orca whale of *Free Willy* fame, back to Icelandic waters. Marine biologists have been re-acclimating the islands' celebrity to the open waters he left more than 20 years ago. In the summer of 2002, Keiko went missing during a boat-escorted jaunt in the open ocean. Six weeks later he emerged in Norway, to the delight of children there.

On the first weekend of August, islanders celebrate the 1874 grant of Icelandic sovereignty with a huge festival in the town on Heimaey. The population moves into a tent city in the **Herjólfsdalur** (Herjolf's Valley), a short distance west of town, for an extended weekend of bonfires, dance, and song. The atmosphere is akin to Rio's Carnaval—don't say you weren't warned.

Where to Stay

$$ ⊞ **Gistihúsið Hamar.** The management of the Hótel Þórshamar operates this spot, which has slightly larger rooms more suited for families who won't mind slightly more spare facilities. Back-facing rooms on both levels have balconies, and breakfast can be had at the sister property, a three-minute walk away. ⊠ *Herjólfsgata 4, IS-900* ☎ *481-3400* 🖶 *481-1696* ⤺ *14 rooms* ⊟ *MC, V.*

$$ ⊞ **Hótel Þórshamar.** This property has tidy, good-size rooms, with modern teak and laminate furnishings, phones, and even minibars. The hotel is considered to be among the best accommodations on the island, and the restaurant serves fresh fish and other delicacies. ⊠ *Vestmannabraut 28, IS-900* ☎ *481-2900* 🖶 *481–1696* ⤺ *18 rooms* ⚐ *Restaurant* ⊟ *MC, V.*

¢ ⛺ **Herjólfsdalur.** Summer camping is possible here, except when locals take over the spot on the first weekend in August for their holiday. ⊠ *Dalvegur* ☎ *481–1471* ⊙ *Closed Sept.–May.*

The South A to Z

AIR TRAVEL

Air Iceland flies daily from Reykjavík Airport to Vestmannaeyjar. Flight time is about 30 minutes.

🛈 **Air Iceland** ☎ 481-3300 Flugfélag Íslands/Vestmannaeyjar, 570-3030 Reykjavík.

BOAT & FERRY TRAVEL

The passenger and car ferry Herjólfur sails daily to Vestmannaeyjar from Þorlákshöfn. There are immediate bus connections to Reykjavík from the Westman Islands ferry at Þorlákshöfn; the bus trip takes about 90 minutes while the ferry ride is two hours and 45 minutes.

🛈 **Herjólfur** ☎ 481-2800 or 483-3413 ⊕ www.herjolfur.is.

BUS TRAVEL

BSÍ has daily service from Reykjavík, stopping in Hella, Hvolsvöllur, Selfoss, Vík, and Þorlakshöfn. The journey to Vík takes less than four hours; to Þorlakshöfn or Selfoss, one hour.

🚌 **Bus Terminal** ✉ Fossnesti IS-800 Selfoss ☎ 482-1599.

CAR TRAVEL

Kirkjubæjarklaustur is 272 km (169 mi) east of Reykjavík on the Ring Road. West from Höfn, it is 201 km (125 mi) to Kirkjubæjarklaustur.

EMERGENCIES

Dial ☎ 112 for emergency assistance anywhere in Iceland.

🚓 **Police: Hvolsvöllur** ☎ 487-8434. **Kirkjubæjarklaustur** ☎ 487-4822. **Selfoss** ☎ 482-1111. **Vestmannaeyjar** Westman Islands ☎ 481-1666. **Vík** ☎ 487-1414.

TOURS

Hannes Jónsson runs driving–hiking tours of Núpsstaðarskógur on the sides of Eystrafjall mountain.

Iceland Travel operates a 10-hour day trip from Reykjavík to the Vestmannaeyjar by plane, running daily all year. Arrangements can also be made for a three-hour sightseeing flight over Heimaey.

Austurleið bus company operates tours to Þórsmörk, Skaftafell, the Eastern Fjords, and the interior.

Westman Islands Travel Service, in cooperation with PH Tours, offers informative, reasonably-priced sightseeing trips by bus and boat in the Vestmannaeyjar; if you call ahead, it can provide airport pick-up service.

🚐 **Tour-Operator Recommendations Austurleið** ✉ Austurvegi 1, IS-861 Hvolsvöllur ☎ 487-8197. **Hannes Jónsson** ✉ Hvoll, IS-880 Kirkjubæjarklaustur ☎ 487-4785 or 853-4133 🖶 487-4890. **Westman Islands Travel Service** ✉ Box 402, IS-900 Vestmannaeyjar ☎ 892-7652 🖶 481-2949.

VISITOR INFORMATION

🚩 Tourist Information **Kirkjubæjarklaustur** (Community Center) ✉ Klausturvegur 10, IS-880 ☎ 487-4620 ⏱ June-Aug. **Selfoss** ✉ Austurvegur 2, IS-800 ☎ 482-2422 ⊕ www.sudurland.inet/info **Vík** ✉ Campsite (Brydebud): Víkurbraut 28 ☎ 487-1395.

ICELAND A TO Z

To research prices, get advice from other travelers, and book travel arrangements, visit www.fodors.com.

AIRPORTS

Virtually all international flights originate from and arrive at Keflavík Airport 50 km (31 mi) south of Reykjavík. On arrival you may spot some military aircraft, for Keflavík is also a NATO military installation, manned by the U.S. Navy.

✈ **Keflavík Airport** ☎ 505-0500 ⊕ www.keflavikairport.com.

AIR TRAVEL

Because so much of Iceland's central region is uninhabited, domestic air transport has been well developed to link the coastal towns. It isn't particularly cheap—round-trip fares for open tickets range from IKr 21,000 to IKr 24,000—but discounts are available. The longest domestic flight takes just over an hour.

CARRIERS In summer, Air Iceland (Flugfélag Íslands) schedules daily or frequent flights from Reykjavík to most of the large areas, such as Akureyri, Egilsstaðir, Höfn, Ísafjörður, and Vestmannaeyjar. Bus connections between airports outside Reykjavík and nearby towns and villages are available.

Air Iceland serves the north from Akureyri. Íslandsflug flies five times a week from Reykjavík to Bíldudalur and four times weekly to Sauðárkrókur. APEX tickets are available on domestic flights if booked two days in advance. These offer savings of 50% on the full airfare.

From April to November, Icelandair operates regular direct flights—which take 5½ hours—five times a week from New York's JFK airport; service from Boston is daily, and from Baltimore, daily, except Saturday; service from Orlando runs twice a week in winter. You can also leave from Minneapolis, the newest city in Icelandair's network, daily except Tuesday.

Icelandair flies daily from London's Heathrow Airport, as well as from Paris, Frankfurt Stockholm, Copenhagen and Oslo to Keflavík Airport. There are four flights a week from Glasgow, and five a week from Amsterdam. The flight from London takes three hours.

Former competitors Icelandair and SAS now coordinate services between mainland Scandinavia and Iceland, and travelers on SAS who are members of Icelandair's frequent flyer club get SAS miles credited.

To & From Iceland Icelandair ☎ 45/33-70-22-00 Copenhagen, 46/8-690-98-76 Stockholm, 47/22-03-40-50 Oslo, 358/9-612-60-710 Helsinki ⊕ www.icelandair.com. **Icelandair Netklubbar** ⊕ www.icelandair.com. **SAS** ☎ 45/70-10-20-00 Copenhagen, 46/8-797-4000 Stockholm, 47/815-20-400 Oslo, 358/(0)20-386-000 Helsinki ⊕ www.scandinavian.net.

Around Iceland Air Iceland ☎ 570-3030 ⊕ www.airiceland.is. **Íslandsflug** ☎ 570-8030 ⊕ www.islandsflug.is. **Iceland Express** ⊕ www.icelandexpress.is.

CUTTING COSTS The Fly As You Please Holiday Ticket is valid for unlimited travel on all Air Iceland (Flugfélag Íslands) domestic routes for 12 days. It's sold exclusively in advance to Icelandair international passengers. The Four-Sector Air Iceland Pass is valid for a month and can be used on any four sectors flown by Icelandair and its domestic line, Air Iceland (Flugfélag Íslands); this pass must also be booked before arrival in Iceland. Several other types of air passes, covering different combinations of sectors, are also available. The Mini–Air Iceland Pass is valid on two sectors.

Internet promotions, such as those from Icelandair and upstart Iceland Express, which flies from London's Stansted Airport and Copenhagen, offer sharp discounts to those who can fly on short notice, sometimes with unusual departure times. Be warned that the flights have very basic services.

BOAT & FERRY TRAVEL

It is possible to sail to Iceland on the car-and-passenger ferry *Norröna*, operated by Smyril Line. The *Norröna* plies among the Faroes and Esbjerg in Denmark, Bergen in Norway, and Seyðisfjörður on the east coast of Iceland. Depending on your point of departure and your destination, the trip may involve a stopover of some days in the Faroes. Special offers for accommodations may be available through Smyril Line, and special fly-cruise arrangements are available through Smyril Line and Icelandair.

The *Baldur* car ferry sails twice daily in summer from Stykkishólmur, on the Snæfellsnes Peninsula, across Breiðafjörður Bay to Brjánslækur. Ferries run daily between Þorlákshöfn and Vestmannaeyjar on the ferry *Herjólfur*.

Baldur ☎ 438-1450 for booking at Stykkishólmur, 456-2020 at Brjánslækur ⊕ www.saeferdir.is. **Herjólfur** ☎ 483-3413 or 481-2800 🖨 551-2991. **Smyril Line** ✉ Passenger Dept., Box 370, FR–110 Tórshavn, Faroe Islands ☎ 298-315-950 🖷 298-315-707 ⊕ www.smyril-line.fo ⊠ via Engelgarden ⊠ Nye Bryggen, N-5023 Bergen, Norway ☎ 47/55-59-65-20 ⊠ via Terra Nova-Sól ⊠ Stangarhyl 3, IS-110 Reykjavík Iceland ☎ 591-9000 🖷 591-9001 ⊠ From Hanstholm, Denmark ☎ 45-33-16-4004.

BUSINESS HOURS

BANKS & OFFICES   All banks in Iceland are open weekdays 9:15–4. In addition, ATMs have sprouted up like mushrooms, almost wherever there is a sizable store.

SHOPS   Even outside Reykjavík, most food stores are generally open daily until at least 5, but the ones known by Icelanders as the "clock" stores—because their hours are in their name (like "10–10" and "10–11")—stay open later.

BUS TRAVEL

An extensive network of buses serves most parts of Iceland. Services are intermittent in the winter season, and some routes are operated only in summer. Fares from Reykjavík range from IKr 1,400 for a round-trip in summer to Þingvellir, to IKr 8,300 for a summer round-trip, Reykjavík to Akureyri. The bus network is operated by Bifreiðastöð Íslands; its terminal is on the northern rim of Reykjavík Airport.

🚌 **Bifreiðastöð Íslands (BSÍ)** ⊠ Vatnsmýrarvegur 10, IS-101 ☎ 591-1000 🖷 591-1050 ⊕ www.bsi.is.

CUTTING COSTS   Holders of BSÍ Passport tickets are entitled to discounts on ferries, BSÍ-rented mountain bikes, stays at campsites and Edda hotels, and other travel needs.

If you want to explore the island extensively, it's a good idea to buy the Omnibus Passport, which covers travel on all scheduled bus routes with unlimited stopovers. The Full Circle Passport is valid for a circular trip on the Ring Road mid-July to mid-September; you can take as long as you like to complete the journey but you have to keep heading in the same direction on the circuit (detours into the interior must be paid for separately). The Air/Bus Rover ticket offered by Air Iceland (Flugfélag Íslands) and BSÍ allows you to fly one-way to any domestic Air Iceland destination and travel by bus back, so you can save some time and still have a chance to explore the countryside.

CAR RENTAL

Renting a car in Iceland is relatively expensive; it may well be worth arranging a car in advance over the Internet or through your travel agent, who may be able to offer a better deal. A typical price for a compact car without insurance is around IKr 7,000 per day, with 100 km (62 mi) free, plus about IKr 50 per km, or about IKr 11,000 for a compact with unlimited mileage and all insurance. A four-wheel-drive vehicle for rougher roads will cost about IKr 12,500 per day, with Collision Damage Waiver (CDW) and 100 km (62 mi) included plus IKr 100 per km. There are many car-rental agencies in Iceland, so it is worth shopping around for the best buy. If you plan to explore the interior, make sure you rent a four-wheel-drive vehicle.

Avis and Hertz/Icelandair operate offices in the Leifur Eiríksson Terminal at Keflavík Airport. Greiði. Hasso Car Rental is also a competitive car rental option.

🚗 **Major Agencies Avis** ☎ 591-4000. **Hertz/Icelandair** ☎ 505-0600.
🚗 **Local Agencies Geysir Car Rental** ⊠ Dugguvogi 10, IS-104 Reykjavík ☎ 568-8888 ⊕ www.geysir.is. **Hasso Car Rental** ⊠ Álfaskeið 115, IS-220 Hafnarfjörður ☎ 555-3330 🖷 565-5500 ⊕ www.hasso.co.is.

CAR TRAVEL

The Ring Road, which generally hugs the coastline, runs for 1,400 km (900 mi) around Iceland. Although 90% of the road is paved, a stretch across the Möðrudalsöræfi highlands and stretches in the east are still gravel. Much of Iceland's secondary road system is unpaved. Take great care on these roads, as driving on loose gravel surface takes some getting used to and is not for the timid motorist. Be careful of livestock that may stray onto roadways.

Caution pays off when driving in Iceland's interior, too. The terrain can be treacherous, and many roads can be traversed only in four-wheel-drive vehicles; always drive in the company of at least one other car. Unbridged rivers that must be forded constitute a real hazard and should never be crossed without the advice of an experienced Iceland highland driver. Most mountain roads are closed by snow in winter and do not open again until mid-June or early July, when the road surface has dried out after the spring thaw.

When parking in windy weather it's best to turn the car's nose into the wind: though this makes for tougher exits, it's better than having a car door blown back on its hinges. Use extra caution when approaching single-lane bridges or blind hills (blindhæð). Before driving any distance in rural Iceland, be sure to pick up the brochure *Driving in Iceland* from any Tourist Information Center, if your rental agency hasn't already given you one. It has informative tips and advice about driving the country's back roads.

EMERGENCY SERVICES The general emergency number, available 24 hours throughout Iceland, is ☎ 112.

GASOLINE Gas prices are high, about IKr 95 to IKr 97 per liter (¼ gallon) depending on octane rating. Service stations are spaced no more than half a day's drive apart, on both main roads and most side roads. Service stations in the Reykjavík area are open Monday through Saturday 7:30 AM–8 PM; opening hours outside Reykjavík vary, but gas stations are often open until 11:30 PM; the cheaper, unmanned ÓB stations are open later and have multilingual creditcard machines. For information on the availability of gas off the beaten track, call Vegagerð Ríkisins (Public Roads Administration).

📘 **Vegagerð Ríkisins** (Public Roads Administration) ✉ Borgartún 5–7, IS-105, Reykjavík ☎ 522-1112 for 24-hr road status in English 🌐 www.vegag.is/faerd/indexe.html.

ROAD MAPS It is essential to have a good map when traveling in rural Iceland.

Don't be fooled into thinking all site names on some maps are settlements where services can be had. Many of these sites (Icelanders call them "Örnefni") are landmarks or farm sites, possibly even abandoned. They may have historic significance, but in general lack service stations or food stores.

RULES OF THE ROAD Traffic outside Reykjavík is generally light, but roads have only one lane going in each direction; stay within the speed limit: 90 kph (55 mph) in rural areas on the Ring Road, 70 kph (42 mph) on secondary open roads, and 30 kph–50 kph (about 20 mph–30 mph) in urban areas; the slower speed limits also apply near schools or in denser neighborhoods. Drivers are required by law to use headlights at all times. Seat belts are required for the driver and all passengers; child seats are mandatory.

CUSTOMS & DUTIES

Tourists can bring to Iceland 200 cigarettes and one of the following: 6 liters of beer; 1 liter of liquor with up to 60% alcohol; 3 liters of wine containing up to 21% alcohol; or 1 liter each of strong spirits and wine.

EMBASSIES

Canada ⊠ Túngötu 14, IS-101 Reykjavík 533-5550.
United Kingdom ⊠ Laufásvegur 31, IS-108 Reykjavík 550-5100.
United States ⊠ Laufásvegur 21, IS-101 Reykjavík 562-9100.

EMERGENCIES

Dial 112 in an emergency; it is a nationwide number.

LANGUAGE

The official language is Icelandic, a highly inflected Germanic tongue brought to the country by the early Viking settlers. Since it has only changed slightly over the centuries, modern Icelanders can read the ancient manuscripts of the sagas without difficulty. Icelandic is kept pure by an official committee that invents new words for modern usage. Nouns may either be masculine, feminine, or neutral. English and Danish are widely spoken and understood; many Icelanders also speak other Scandinavian languages or German, and some speak French.

The Icelandic alphabet contains two unique letters—þ, called 'thorn' and pronounced like the *th* in thin, and ð, called 'eth' and pronounced like the *th* in leather. The Scandinavian ligature, æ, is pronounced, as it is called in everyday Icelandic, as a long "i" as in "bike." Otherwise, the "j" is pronounced as "y" and whenever you see a vowel accented, it becomes long.

LODGING

In Reykjavík, you can rent a studio apartment on a short-term basis. Those near the Tjörnin Lake and the National Gallery of Iceland are called Castle House Luxury Apartments, others are offered through Tower Guesthouse.

Renting a summer house or cottage or staying on a farm are pleasant, economical alternatives for those seeking more independence. Icelandic Farm Holidays has a listing of places around the country, including farms and cottages; write for a booklet describing all the properties and their facilities; it can also be ordered on the Internet. Many offer fishing, touring with a guide, and horseback riding. They can also arrange a self-driven tour with nights at various farms along the way. A double room on a farm with breakfast costs IKr 2,500–IKr 5,000 per night; sleeping-bag accommodations without breakfast cost IKr 1,400–IKr 2,000 per night.

Summer cottages can be rented by the week, with rates varying according to number of beds, location and conveniences. For example, a six-bed cottage may run about IKr 35,000–IKr 42,000 during peak season. A number of cottages are available nationwide from Viator, with a minimum of three or four nights' rental. Contact the local Tourist Information Center for other cottage options. You can stay at any of more than 30 mountain huts (or sæluhús–pronounced sigh-lu-hoos) throughout the country that are owned by Ferðafélag Íslands, the Touring Association of Iceland. In summer it is necessary to book space in these in advance. Depending on location, huts accommodate from 12 to 120 campers and are rated in two categories: A-class huts have running water and gas for cooking during summers, in addition to bunk beds and mattresses; B-class huts are basic shelters with bunk beds and mattresses. Rental fees are discounted to Touring Association Members. A-class huts are IKr 1,700 per person per night for nonmembers, IKr 1,200 for members; B-class huts are IKr 1,600 per person per night for nonmembers, IKr 1,100 for members.

Organized campgrounds are available throughout the country. Some are on private property, others are owned and operated by local communities, and still others are in protected areas supervised by the Nature Conservation Council. For a comprehensive listing of campgrounds, write or call the Association of Leisure Site Owners (c/o Tourist Information Center; ⇨ Visitor Information). On the road, look for signs reading TJALD-STÆÐI (camping allowed), or TJALDSTÆÐI BÖNNUÐ (camping prohibited), or a simple tent symbol. Most campgrounds charge about IKr 500 per person per night, plus IKr 200 for the tent. Campsites in national parks tend to be more expensive.

It is forbidden to use scrubwood for fuel; bring kerosene or gas stoves and buy fuel locally for cooking. Camping equipment can be rented in Reykjavík from Útilíf sporting goods.

In summer, 15 boarding schools around the country open up as Edda hotels, now privately operated under the umbrella of Icelandair and offering both accommodations with made-up beds and more basic sleeping-bag facilities. A double room without bath costs IKr 6,200, a single IKr4,900, and doubles with bath, where available, are IKr10,400. You can sleep on a mattress in your sleeping bag for IKr 1,500 to IKr 2,000 per night depending on facilities. Most Edda hotels have restaurants offering good home-style cooking. Two former Edda hotels have been upgraded to bear the additional formal title Icelandair Hótels and are open year-round: at Flúðir, toward the interior and in Kirkjubæjarklaustur, somewhat inland in the central south. Now, staying at these, or any other Icelandair hotel, gives frequent flier points in the Icelandair Frequent Flier System. For information and bookings, call the Icelandair Hótel Booking Office.

At Iceland's 31 youth hostels, accommodations are predictably inexpensive: about IKr 1,900 per night, or IKr 1,550 for members of the Youth Hostel Association. You get a bed, pillow, and blanket and access to a kitchen and bathroom. Breakfast costs about IKr 700. Some hostels are crowded during the summer, so call ahead. Hostels outside Reykjavík permit you to use your own sleeping bag. For information, write to Farfugladeild Reykjavíkur.

🎇 **Castle House Luxury Apartments** ✉ Skálholtsstígur 2A, IS-101 Reykjavík ☎ 511-2166 ⊕ www.thewinner.is/apartment. **Ferðafélag Íslands** ✉ Mörkin 6, IS-108 Reykjavík ☎ 568-2533 🖨 568-2535 ⊕ www.fi.is. **Icelandic Farm Holidays** ✉ Síðumúli 13, IS-108 Reykjavík ☎ 570-2700 🖨 570-2799 ⊕ www.farmholidays.is. **Viator Service Center** ✉ Njarðarbraut 11a, IS-260 Njarðvík ☎ 544-8990 ⊕ www.viator.is/index.en.php. **Útili[ac:f** ✉ Glæsibæ Álfheimum 74, IS-104 Reykjavík ☎ 545-1500 🖨 545-1515. **Tower Guesthouse** ✉ Grettisgata 6, IS-101 ☎ 562-3350 🖨 552-5581 ⊕ www.towerguesthouse. homestead.com.

🎇 Hostel Organizations **Farfugladeild Reykjavíkur** ✉ Sundlaugavegi 34, IS-105 Reykjavík ☎ 553-8110 🖨 567-9201 ⊕ www.hostel.is.

HOTELS Both Icelandair and Radisson SAS have affiliate hotels offering points in their frequent flier associations. In addition to the Icelandair-operated Edda summer hotels, there are two other local hotel chains: the year-round FossHótels and the Icelandic Hotels. In summer, hotels and even youth hostels may be fully booked, so make reservations well in advance.

🎇 **FossHótels** ✉ Skipholt 50C, Reykjavík ☎ 562-4000 🖨 562-4001 ⊕ www.fosshotel. is. **Icelandair Hotels** ✉ Reykjavíkurflugvelli, IS-101 Reykjavík ☎ 505-0910 🖨 505-0915 ⊕ www.icehotels.is. **Icelandic** (Icelandic Hotels) ✉ Pósthússtræti 13, IS-101 Reykjavík ☎ 511-2700 🖨 511-1179 ⊕ www.icelandichotels.is.

MAIL & SHIPPING

Post offices in most towns are open weekdays only from 8:30 or 9 to 4:30 or 5.

POSTAL RATES Within Europe, postcards and airmail letters both need IKr 60 postage. Letter and postcard postage to the United States is IKr 85.

RECEIVING MAIL Mail to Iceland from northern Europe and Scandinavia usually takes two to three days; other services are slower. All post offices have fax machines.

MONEY MATTERS

Iceland is an expensive destination. However, some luxury items are actually cheaper than in other large international cities, especially after tax refunds.

Some sample prices are: a cup of coffee, IKr 290; imported German beer or Icelandic brew, IKr 600; can of soda, IKr 150; film, IKr 1,200 for 36 exposures; short taxi ride within Reykjavík, IKr 800.

CURRENCY The unit of currency in Iceland is the króna; plural krónur (IKr). Icelandic notes come in denominations of IKr 500, 1,000, 2,000, and 5,000. Coins are IKr 1, 5, 10, 50, and 100. The króna was divided into 100 aurar, which are no longer in circulation, but are sometimes still used in unit calculations, such as gasoline pricing and phone utility rates. In winter 2003, the rate of exchange was IKr 73 to the U.S. dollar, IKr 54 to the Canadian dollar, IKr 122 to the pound sterling, IKr to the euro, IKr 47 to the Australian dollar, IKr 42 to the New Zealand dollar, and IKr 10 to the South African rand. No limitations apply to the import and export of currency.

CURRENCY
EXCHANGE Don't bother trying to exchange currency before you depart, because Icelandic money is usually unavailable at foreign banks, and sometimes when it is, you'll get old banknotes, no longer accepted in Iceland. It is also highly unlikely that Icelandic money will be exchangeable back home, so exchange any last krónur at the departure terminal in Keflavík Airport.

SPORTS & THE OUTDOORS

FISHING Fishing-rod rentals can often be arranged through fishing agents for salmon and trout streams. Upon arrival, anglers bringing their own equipment will be asked by an inspector to show it, and if it is not obviously new, or if a certificate verifying that it is disinfected is not provided, it will be sterilized at modest cost by authorities at Keflavík Airport.

Sea angling is a popular leisure sport in Iceland, with several town clubs forming Iceland's membership in the European Federation of Sea Anglers. Fishing cruises can be organized from many of the country's fishing towns and villages and are often combined with whale-watching trips. Several weekend deep-sea fishing competitions are held each year; a few follow: a competition is held at Whitsun in Vestmannaeyjar. In June, one is held in Reykjavík. One in July is at Ísafjörður. In August, anglers head to Akureyri. For further information, contact the Tourist Information Center.

🎣 **Akureyri Fishing Competition** Pétur Sigurðsson ☎ 466-1954. **Ísafjörður Fishing Competition** Þórir Sveinsson ☎ 456-3298. **Reykjavík Fishing Competition** Lárus Einarsson ☎ 566-6374. **Vestmannaeyjar Fishing Competition** Elínborg Bernódusdóttir ☎ 481-1118.

GOLF Iceland has 56 golf courses. Most are primitive 9-hole courses, but there are six good 18-hole courses. The Arctic Open, played at the Akureyri Golf course during the midnight sun in June, is one of the world's most unusual tournaments. Greens fees range from IKr 2,000 for nine-hole courses to IKr 4,000 for 18-hole minimums. For information on golfing opportunities in Iceland, contact the Golf Federation.

🏷 **Golf Federation of Iceland** ☎ 514-4050 ⊕ www.golf.is.

HANDBALL During Icelandic winters, team handball is a national obsession with a huge following; not surprising considering the national team has twice reached Olympic finals. Contact the Handball Federation to find out about competitions.

🏷 **Handball Federation** ☎ 568-5422.

HIKING Many organized tours from Reykjavík and other towns include some days of hiking. Contact Ferðafélag Íslands (Iceland Touring Association) or Útivist (Útivist Travel Association).

For serious exploring or hiking, you can obtain good up-to-date Icelandic Geodetic Survey maps from Bókabúð Eymundsson or Mál og menning bookstores, or the outdoor-lover's shop Nanoq.

Many hikers consider Iceland to be Europe's best bet for a true wilderness experience—away from noise and machinery. Note that trails marked with short pegs or less can be rather rugged, especially in areas of jagged lava. Footing can be tricky, as moss layers often hide uneven terrain. Avoid crowding too close to hot springs and sulfur springs, as the ground surrounding them may suddenly give way, leaving you standing in boiling water or mud. It always pays to research territory in advance and, particularly if venturing into remote highland areas, a detailed map is essential. Compass orientation is more reliable than the sun, because in summer at this latitude it seems never to set, and technically it's not due west. When admiring the delicate flora, soft mosses, and lichen, remember that in preserves and national parks it is illegal to pick flowers or take rock samples. Remember, too, that at sub-Arctic latitudes, it takes centuries for even the most common flowers to become established on this terrain. Dress in layers, with a windproof outer shell, and have sturdy broken-in hiking shoes. When you are camping, tents should be firmly anchored against possible winds. Finally, always let someone know of your hiking plans. Avoid hiking alone, but if you do, a portable GSM-compatible phone would be a wise accessory, as might a GPS (Global Positioning System) unit.

🏷 **Bókabúð Eymundsson** ✉ Kringlan Mall, South Wing, Kringlan 4–6, IS-103 Reykjavík ☎ 533-1130. **Ferðafélag Íslands** ✉ Mörkin 6, IS-108 Reykjavík ☎ 568-2533 📠 568-2535 ⊕ www.fi.is. **Mál og menning** ✉ Laugavegur 18, IS-101 Reykjavík ☎ 515-2500. **Nanoq** ✉ Kringlan 4–12 at the Kringlan Mall, IS-103 Reykjavík ☎ 575-5100 📠 575-5110 ⊕ www.nanoq.is. **Útivist** ✉ Laugavegur 178, IS-105 Reykjavík ☎ 562-1000 📠 562-1001 ⊕ www.utivist.is.

HORSEBACK Many equestrian events are held around the country during the summer months, from
RIDING local races and contests to major regional championships. Contact Landssamband Hestamannafélaga (Equestrian Federation) for details of upcoming horse events. There is even the international association FEIF for those in 20 countries who own or admire the Icelandic horse. An English version of the magazine *Eiðfaxi* is published five times a year for fanciers of the Icelandic horse.

🏷 **Landssamband Hestamannafélaga** ✉ Íþróttamiðstöðinni, Engjavegi 6, IS-104 Reykjavík ☎ 514-4030 ⊕ www.lhhestar.is/enska. **Eiðfaxi** ✉ Dugguvogi 10, IS-104 Reykjavík ☎ 588-2525 ⊕ www.eidfaxi.is.

SKIING In summer, the Kerlingarfjöll Ski School west of the Hofsjökull Glacier runs five- to six-day courses; you can also get lift tickets without taking lessons, and there are accommodations and food at the school. Contact Úrval-Útsýn Travel Agency.

🏷 **Iceland Travel** ✉ Lágmúli 4, IS-128 Reykjavík ☎ 585-4300 ⊕ www.icelandtravel.is.

Having both Europe's largest glacier, Vatnajökull, and it's longest—so named, Langjökull—it's not surprising Iceland offers numerous options to enjoy the thrill of glacier trips. Iceland's only dogsledding trips (believe it or not) are offered by Dog Steam Tours and are on Langjökull.

Arcanum also runs a popular excursion to the glacial tongue, Sólheimajökull, part of the larger Mýrdalsjökull glacier in the south.

🎿 **Arcanum** ⊠ Sólheimaskála, IS-871 Vík ☎ 487-1500 🖷 487-1496 ⊕ www.snow.is. **Destination Iceland** ⊠ Vatnsmýrarvegur 10, IS-101 Reykjavík ☎ 591-1000 ⊕ www.dice. is. **Dog Steam Tours** ⊠ IS-851 Hella ☎ 487-7747 ⊕ www.dogsledding.is.

SUPPLIES Should you need outdoor or camping gear, touring maps, or spares for broken or lost equipment, you may well find what you need in Reykjavík at the outdoor suppliers, Nanoq. Also try Everest. If you prefer to rent a tent, your best bet is Útilíf.

🎿 **Nanoq** ⊠ Kringlan 4-12, inside Kringlan Mall, IS-103 Reykjavík ☎ 575-5100 🖷 575-5110 ⊕ www.nanoq.is. **Everest** ⊠ Skeifunni 67, IS-108 Reykjavík ☎ 533-4450. **Útilíf** ⊠ Glæsibæ Álfheimum 74, IS-104 Reykjavík ☎ 545-1500.

SWIMMING Almost every sizable community in Iceland has at least one public outdoor swimming pool. Since most are generally heated by thermal springs, they can be enjoyed year-round. Inquire at the tourist office or a local hotel for the nearest pool.

PACKING

It may seem odd to suggest a bathing suit as the first item to pack for visiting a country named Iceland, but the wonderful pools and hot spring baths are a joy to experience. Layering is the secret to comfort in Iceland, so bring a waterproof, wind-tight jacket or shell, regardless of season. In winter, bring a good, heavy coat. Durable, broken-in walking or hiking boots with good ankle support are needed for hiking (forget tennis shoes for this), and a telescoping walking staff might also prove handy. If you'll be going to the highlands to ski or snowmobile, be sure to bring good gloves. Likewise sunscreen and sunglasses are a must to protect against the low, lingering sun of spring and fall, which can be a real bother to drivers. Sweaters are useful—perhaps why Icelanders are so good at making them. If you're a sports enthusiast, note that all fishing tackle, riding tack, and riding garments should be certified sterile by a veterinarian or doctor unless it is obviously new and unused. If not, gear will be cleaned at your expense upon arrival, or impounded.

TAXES

VALUE-ADDED
TAX (V.A.T.) A 24.5% *virðisaukaskattur* (value-added tax, or V.A.T.), commonly called VSK, applies to most goods and services. Usually the V.A.T. is included in a price; if not, that fact must be stated explicitly. Foreign visitors can claim a partial refund on the V.A.T., which accounts for 19.68% of the purchase price of most goods and services. Fifteen percent of the purchase price for goods is refunded, provided you buy a minimum of IKr 5,000 at one time. Souvenir stores issue "tax-free checks" that allow foreign visitors to collect the V.A.T. rebates directly in the duty-free store when departing from Keflavík Airport. To qualify, keep your purchases in tax-free packages (except woolens), and show them to customs officers at the departure gate along with a passport and the tax-free check. If you depart the country from somewhere other than Keflavík, have customs authorities stamp your tax-free check, then mail the stamped check within three months to **Iceland Tax-Free Shopping** (✉ Box 1200, 235 Keflavík, Iceland). You will be reimbursed in U.S. dollars at the current exchange rate.

TELEPHONES

Iceland's telephone system is entirely digital, which, along with widespread introduction of the ITT phone–modem jack, greatly facilitates computer transmissions. The country is part of the Nordic Automatic Mobile Telephone System (NMT) and the GSM global mobile phone network. Coverage for phones with NMT capability includes all but the highest remote glacial areas of Iceland; the GSM system has expanded tremendously and nearly matches the NMT range. Iceland has one of the world's highest per-capita mobile phone distributions.

AREA & COUNTRY CODES
Iceland's country code is 354.

DIRECTORY & OPERATOR ASSISTANCE
Iceland has no area codes; within the country, simply dial the seven-digit number. Those starting with 4 are generally billed as long distance, being mostly outside the capital area. A number of companies and institutes have so-called "green" 800 numbers for which the rate is the same regardless of where the call is placed in Iceland. Non-800 numbers starting with 8 often indicate cellular phones. For domestic directory assistance dial ☎ 118. Dial ☎ 115 for operator assistance with overseas calls, including directory assistance.

INTERNATIONAL CALLS
You can dial direct, starting with 00 then following with the country code and local number. An international calling card is a convenient mode of payment. Avoid charging overseas calls to your hotel bills, as the surcharge can double the cost of the call.

You can dial local access codes to reach U.S. operators AT&T and Sprint.

LOCAL CALLS
Phone listings are now split into two separate telephone books—one for the capital area (Höfuðborgarsvæði) and one for the rest of the country (Landsbyggðin). Names are listed alphabetically in the telephone book by first name as a result of the patronymic system (for a last name, men add -*son* to their father's first name, women add -*dóttir*). Jobs or professions are often listed together with names and addresses.

Pay phones are usually indoors in post offices, hotels, or at transportation terminals. They accept IKr 5-, IKr 10-, or IKr 50-coins, which are placed in the slot before dialing. The dial tone is continuous. A 10-minute call between regions costs between IKr 50 and IKr 75. Card phones are becoming more common: 100-unit phone cards (IKr 500) can be purchased at all post offices and some other outlets, such as supermarkets, gas stations, and kiosks.

LONG-DISTANCE SERVICES
☎ Access Codes **AT&T** ☎ 001/800–9001. **Sprint** ☎ 001/800–9003. **MCI** ☎ 001/800–9002.

TIPPING

Tipping is not conventional in Iceland and might even be frowned upon. Service charges of 15% to 20% are included in restaurant prices, but may not be itemized on the final bill.

TOURS

Inclusive guided tours are offered by a number of travel agencies in Iceland, the largest of which are listed below. Most operators offer tours by bus; some itineraries include air travel. Many agencies also combine Icelandic vacations with Greenland tours.

For the fit and active, hiking, biking, or horseback-riding tours are also available. In these cases, accommodations will usually be in tents, guest houses, or mountain huts. Guided hiking tours of the interior are organized by Ferðafélag Íslands (Iceland Touring Association). The Útivist Travel

Association is another group with assorted tours of varying lengths. Smaller travel agencies also offer tours, some of them quite specialized. The Icelandic Tourist Board also has information on other agencies.

🎟 Tour Operators **Ferðafélag Íslands** ✉ Mörkin 6, IS-108 Reykjavík ☎ 568-2533 🖨 568-2535. **Guðmundur Jónasson Travel** ✉ Borgartún 34, IS-105 Reykjavík ☎ 511-1515 🖨 511-1511 🌐 www.gjtravel.is. **Reykjavík Excursions** ✉ Vesturvör 6, IS-200 Kópavogur 🌐 www.re.is ✉ Sales desks ✉ Hótel Loftleiðir ☎ 562-1011 ✉ Nordica Hótel ☎ 568-8922 ✉ Bankastræti 2 ☎ 562-4422. **Útivist** ✉ Laugavegur 178, IS-105 Reykjavík ☎ 562-1000 🖨 562-1001 🌐 www.utivist.is.

TRAVEL AGENCIES

🎟 Local Agencies **Iceland Travel** ✉ Lágmúli 4, IS-128 Reykjavík ☎ 585-4300 🖨 585-4390 🌐 www.icelandtravel.is.

VISITOR INFORMATION

🎟 Tourist Information **Icelandic Travel Industry Association** ✉ Borgatún 35, IS-105 Reykjavík ☎ 511-8000 🖨 511-8008 🌐 www.saf.is. **Icelandic Tourist Board** ✉ 655 3rd Ave., New York, NY 10017 ☎ 212/885-9700 🖨 212/885-9710 🌐 www.IcelandTouristboard. com ✉ Geysishús, Aðalstræti 2, IS-101 Reykjavík ☎ 535-5500 🖨 535-5501 🌐 www. icetourist.is. **Icelandair** ✉ 172 Tottenham Court Rd., 3rd fl., London W1T 7LY ☎ 0870/ 787-4020 🌐 www.icelandair.co.uk.

NORWAY

FODOR'S CHOICE

Akershus Slott og Festning, *fortress and castle in Oslo*

Bergen's seven mountains

Det Kongelige Slottet, *palace in Oslo*

Hardangervidda, *Europe's largest mountain plateau*

Ishavskatedralen, *cathedral in Tromsø*

Jostedalsbreen, *Europe's largest glacier*

The midnight sun, *the Nordkapp (North Cape)*

Munchmuseet, *museum in Oslo*

Nidaros Cathedral, *Trondheim*

Norsk Fjellmuseum, *museum in Lom*

Norsk Folkemuseum, *open-air museum in Bygdøy, Oslo*

Norsk Oljemuseum, *museum in Stavanger*

Stave churches, *around Norway*

Troldhaugen, *house outside Bergen*

Vikingskiphuset, *museum in Oslo*

Many other great sights, restaurants, and hotels enliven this area.
For other favorites, look for the stars as you read this chapter.

Updated by
Sonya
Procenko and
Lars Ursin

NORWEGIANS HAVE A STRONG ATTACHMENT to the natural beauty of their mountainous homeland. Whether in the verdant dales of the interior, the broodin mountains of the north, or the fjords and archipelagoes of the coast, Norwegians' *hytter* (mountain cabins) dot even the harshest landscapes.

In almost any kind of weather, blasting or balmy, large numbers of Norwegians are outdoors, fishing, biking, skiing, hiking, or playing soccer. Everybody—from cherubic children to hardy, knapsack-toting senior citizens—bundles up for just one more ski trip or hike in the mountains. In one recent research poll, 70% of Norwegian respondents said that they wanted to spend even more time in nature. Although Norway is a modern, highly industrialized nation, vast areas of the country (up to 95%) remain forested or fallow. When discussing the size of their country, Norwegians like to say that if Oslo remained fixed and the northern part of the country were swung south, it would reach all the way to Rome. Perched at the very top of the globe, this northern land is long and rangy, 2,750 km (1,705 mi) in length, with only 4.5 million people scattered over it—making it the least densely populated country in Europe, after Iceland.

Westerly winds carry moisture from the Gulf Stream, leaving the coastal regions with high precipitation, cool summers, and mild winters. The interior and east have a blend of clearer skies, hotter summers, and colder winters.

Norwegians are justifiably proud of their ability to survive the elements. The first people to appear on the land were reindeer hunters and fisherfolk who migrated north, following the path of the retreating ice. By the Bronze Age, settlements began to appear, and, as rock carvings show, Norwegians first began to ski—purely as a form of locomotion—some 4,000 years ago.

The Viking Age has perhaps left the most indelible mark on the country. The Vikings' travels and conquests took them west to Iceland, England, Ireland (they founded Dublin in the 840s), and North America, and east to Kiev and as far as the Black Sea. Though they were famed as plunderers, their craftsmanship, fearlessness, and ingenuity have always been respected by Norwegians.

Harald I, better known as Harald the Fairhaired, swore he would not cut his hair until he united Norway, and in the 9th century he succeeded in doing both. But a millennium passed between that great era and Norwegian independence. Between the Middle Ages and 1905, Norway remained under the rule of either Denmark or Sweden, even after the constitution was written in 1814.

The 19th century saw the establishment of the Norwegian identity and a blossoming of culture. This Romantic period produced some of the nation's most famous individuals, among them composer Edvard Grieg, dramatist Henrik Ibsen, expressionist painter Edvard Munch, polar explorer Roald Amundsen, and explorer-humanitarian Fridtjof Nansen. Vestiges of nationalist lyricism, including Viking dragonheads and scrollwork, spangle the buildings of the era, symbolizing the rebirth of the Viking spirit.

Faithful to their democratic nature, Norwegians held a referendum to choose a king in 1905, when independence from Sweden became reality. Prince Carl of Denmark became King Haakon VII. His baby's name was changed from Alexander to Olav, and he, and later his son, presided over the kingdom for more than 85 years. When King Olav V died in

If you have 5 days

Oslo, Norway's capital, makes a good starting point since most flights to Norway arrive here. Spend your first two days exploring ▦ **Oslo.** Take it easy on the first day by exploring the downtown area—meander on Karl Johans Gate, see Akershus Castle and the Kvadraturen, and walk through Vigelands (Frogner) Park. On Day 2, head out to Bygdøy and visit the area's museums—the Folkemuseum is a must. On the third day, depart for Bergen by train; service between Oslo and Bergen is convenient and regular, and passes through Hardangervidda. This six-hour trip across Norway's interior allows you to see some of the country's spectacular scenery, including **Hardangervidda.** When you get to ▦ **Bergen,** check into your hotel and head to Bryggen for dinner. Here along Bergen's wharf are some of the city's oldest and best-preserved buildings. Spend your fourth day exploring Bergen. If you have time, visit Troldhaugen, which was composer Edvard Grieg's house for 22 years; it's a half-day trip from Bergen's center. Spend the last night in Bergen, and on the fifth day, fly back to Oslo.

4

If you have 10 days

Spend your first four days following the tour above. On your fifth day, take the day-trip Norway in a Nutshell, which is a bus-train-boat tour that takes you through some of the western fjord country. Spend your fifth night in Bergen, and on your sixth day, fly to **Tromsø,** which is north of the Arctic Circle. Spend the rest of the day touring Tromsø. Overnight here, and on your seventh day, rent a car and head for **Alta.** If you arrive early enough, visit the Alta Museum. Spend the night in Alta, and on the eighth day, continue your voyage, driving farther on to **Hammerfest,** the world's northernmost town. Overnight in Hammerfest, and the next day, take an excursion up the treeless tundra of the **Nordkapp** (North Cape). Return to Hammerfest, and on your last day, fly back to Oslo via Alta.

There are frequent ferries that run between towns in fjord country on the west coast of Norway; by land, you can take buses and trains, which run regularly between the towns and villages. As you get toward the North Cape, it's most convenient to travel by car.

January 1991, normally reserved Norwegians stood in line for hours to write in the condolence book at the Royal Palace. Rather than simply sign their names, they wrote personal letters of devotion to the man they called "the people's king."

Harald V, Olav's son, is now king, with continuity assured by his popular son, Crown Prince Haakon Magnus, who married in August 2001. Norwegians continue to salute the royal family with flag-waving and parades on May 17, Constitution Day, a spirited holiday of independence that transforms Oslo's main boulevard, Karl Johans Gate, into a massive street party.

The 1968 discovery of oil in the North Sea dramatically changed Norway from an outpost for fishing, subsistence farming, and shipping to a highly developed industrial nation. Norway has emerged as a wealthy country, with a per capita income, standard of living, and life expectancy that are among the world's highest.

Domestically, great emphasis has been placed on social welfare programs. Internationally, Norway is known for the annual awarding of the Nobel Peace Prize and participating in peace talks about the Middle East and other areas.

Unlike its Nordic siblings, Norway has resisted the temptation to join the European Union (EU). In a referendum in November 1994, Norwegians rejected EU membership for the second time. However, Norwegians are warming to the EU as it expands its membership across Europe.

Exploring Norway

Norway is long and narrow, bordered by Sweden to the east and with jagged coastline to the west. The west coast is carved by deep, dramatic fjords and small coastal villages dot the shores in between. Bergen, the country's second largest city, is touted as the capital of the West Coast.

Norway's official capital, Oslo, is in the east, only a few hours from the Swedish border. The coast, from Oslo around the southern tip of the country up to Stavanger, is filled with wide beaches and seaside communities. North of here, in Norway's central interior, the country is blanketed with mountains that sculpt the landscape, creating dramatic valleys and plateaus. Moving north, the land becomes wild and untouched. Outside the north's two main cities, Trondheim and Tromsø, the land stretches for miles into the Arctic Circle and up to the Russian border. We describe each of these regions in its own section below.

About the Restaurants

Major cities such as Oslo, Bergen, and Stavanger, offer a full range of dining choices, from traditional to international restaurants. Restaurants in Norway are expensive, but eating out is popular among Norwegians all the same, especially in cosmopolitan centers like Bergen, Stavanger, and Oslo. In these large cities, the restaurant scenes are vibrant and constantly evolving. Until the late 1990s, fine Norwegian restaurants were invariably inspired by French cuisine and based their menus around meat entrées. Today, traditional Norwegian restaurants still serve the classic, national dishes. But there are many more restaurants specializing in crossover dishes or Asian, African, Latin American, and Mediterranean cuisine.

For centuries, Norwegians regarded food as fuel, and their dining habits still bear traces of this. *Frokost* (breakfast) is a fairly big meal, usually with a selection of crusty bread, jams, herring, cold meat, and cheese. Norway's famous brown goat cheese, *Geitost* (a sweet, caramel-flavor whey cheese made from goat and cow milk) and *Norvegia* (a Norwegian Gouda-like cheese) are on virtually every table. They are eaten in thin slices, cut with a cheese plane or slicer—a Norwegian invention—on buttered wheat or rye bread.

Lunsj (lunch) is simple and usually consists of *smørbrød* (open-face sandwiches). Most businesses have only a 30-minute lunch break, so unless there's a company cafeteria, people bring their lunch from home.

Middag (dinner), the only hot meal of the day, is early—from 1 to 4 in the country, 3 to 7 in the city—so many cafeterias serving home-style food close by 6 or 7. In Oslo it's possible to get dinner as late as midnight, especially in summer. Most restaurants in Oslo stop serving dinner around 10.

Beaches

Every summer, Norwegians flock to the beaches of southern Norway, or the "Southern Riviera." The beaches around Mandal in the south, and Jaeren's Ogna, Brusand, and Bore beaches, near Stavanger, are the country's best, with fine white sand. The beaches along the Oslo Fjord are also popular. The western fjords have warmer and calmer shores than the open beaches of the south, although they are rocky beaches, without the fine white sand found in the south. Inland freshwater lakes are chillier than the fjords warmed by the Gulf Stream. Topless bathing is common, and there are nude beaches all along the coast.

4

Mountain Hiking

One of the most common expressions in the Norwegian language is *gå på tur,* or "go for a walk." Naturally, in the country's mountainous landscape, Norwegians have been *fjellfolk* (mountain people) for thousands of years. Today, it's never far to the mountain trails where many Norwegians spend their *fritid* (free time) hiking and strolling. Much of Norway's 19,000 km (12,000 mi) of trails have been marked by *Den Norske Turistforening* (Norwegian Mountain Touring Association)—look for red "T"s—and DNT cabins are available for hikers to rest, eat, and even spend the night. Established in 1868, DNT (⊕ www.turistforening. no) is Norway's biggest outdoor leisure organization, counting 200,000 members in chapters all across the country. Members mark the routes and operate the network of mountain cabins so hikers can safely and economically enjoy the scenery.

Orienteering

One of Norway's most popular mass-participation sports is based on running or hiking over territory with a map and compass, to find control points marked on a map. Special cards can be purchased at sports shops, which you can then punch at control points found during an orienteering season.

Shopping

Almost no visitor leaves Norway without buying a hand-knit sweater. Although the prices for these sweaters may seem high, the quality is outstanding and they're much more expensive outside the country. While the classic knitting designs, with snowflakes and reindeer, are still best-sellers at *husfliden* (homecraft) outlets, gift stores tend to sell more contemporary, fashionable designs by Oleana and Dale.

Norway's handicrafts include embroidered cloth; pewter and wrought-iron candlesticks; candles; glass; and wood bowls, spoons, and platters made of birch roots, decorated with rosemaling (intricate painted or carved floral folk-art designs). Other, more offbeat, items include *ostehøvler* (cheese slicers) and *kransekakeformer,* graduated forms for making almond ring cakes. Silver is a good buy in Norway, especially with the value-added tax refund. Norwegian silver companies produce a wide range of distinctive patterns. Though Norwegian traditional antiques may not be exported, you can get good replicas of old Norwegian farm furniture.

Skiing

Norwegians are "born with skis on their feet" goes the popular saying. Skiing dates back thousands of years in Norway, where it was first used as a mode of transportation. Cross-country or Nordic skiing is a perfect way to experience Norway's nature, either on pristine prepared trails through forests, or off-trail. Among the popular cross country skiing areas are Rondane, Peer Gynt Ski Region, Lillehammer, Beitostolen, Midt-Valdres, Hallingdal and Dovrefjell. Downhill or alpine skiing and snowboarding is offered at more than 500 ski centers, including Hafjell, Trysil, Hemsedal, and Kvitfjell. In addition to cross-country and downhill, there's traditional Telemark skiing and newer hybrid sports such as kite-skiing and ski-sailing. Norway's ski season lasts from November to Easter, after which there is summer skiing on select glaciers through August.

The restaurants we list (all of which are indicated by a ✕) are the cream of the crop in each price category. Properties indicated by a ✕▦ are lodging establishments whose restaurants warrant a special trip.

About the Hotels

Norwegian hotels have high standards in cleanliness and comfort and prices to match. Even the simplest youth hostels provide good mattresses with fluffy down comforters and clean showers or baths. Breakfast, usually served buffet style, is almost always included in the room price at hotels, whereas hostels often charge extra for the morning meal. Travelers can reduce accommodation expenses with summer and weekend specials and discount passes and programs.

Several hotel chains operate in Norway, including Radisson SAS, Scandic, Best Western, Choice, and Quality Hotels. In recent years, Rica Hotels (⊕ www.rica.no) has been the most interesting chain, with newer designs like Rica Seilet in Molde (which resembles Dubai's Meridien) and Stavanger's eclipse-shape Rica Forum. The chain Det virkelig gode liv (⊕ www.dvgl.no) has a few properties known for first-class service, fine food and wine, and traditional style.

The Farmer's Association operates simple hotels in most towns and cities. These reasonably priced accommodations usually have *heimen* as part of the name, such as Bondeheimen in Oslo. The same organization also runs cafeterias serving traditional Norwegian food, usually called Kaffistova. All of these hotels and restaurants are alcohol-free. Rustic cabins and campsites are also available all over the countryside, as are independent hotels.

In the Lofoten and Vesterålen islands, *rorbuer,* (fishermen's cabins) are the most popular form of accommodation. These rustic quayside cabins, with mini-kitchens, bunk beds, living rooms, and showers, are reasonably priced and listed through the local tourist office.

Norwegian youth hostels are considered among the best in the world, squeaky clean, and with excellent facilities. If you prefer camping, there are more than 500 inspected and classified campsites in the country, many with showers, bathrooms, and hook-ups for electricity. Most also have cabins or chalets to rent by the night or longer.

WHAT IT COSTS In Norwegian Kroner				
$$$$	**$$$**	**$$**	**$**	**¢**
OSLO AND BERGEN				
RESTAURANTS over 270	230–270	180–230	110–180	under 110
HOTELS over 2,000	1,600–2,000	1,200–1,600	800–1,200	under 800
OTHER AREAS				
RESTAURANTS over 230	190–230	150–190	90–150	under 90
HOTELS over 1,500	1,000–1,500	800–1,000	400–800	under 400

Restaurant prices are for a main course at dinner, excluding tip. Hotel prices are for two people in a standard double room in high season.

Timing

The tourist season peaks in June, July, and August, when daytime temperatures are often in the 70s (21°C to 26°C) and sometimes rise into the 80s (27°C to 32°C). In general, the weather is not overly warm, and a brisk breeze and brief rainstorms are possible anytime. Nights can be chilly, even in summer.

Visit in summer if you want to experience the endless days of the midnight sun; the best time to visit is mid-May to late July. Hotels, museums, and sights have longer opening hours and the modes of transportation run on more frequent schedules. If you decide to travel in May, try to be in the country on the 17th, or *Syttende Mai*, Norway's Constitution Day, when flag-waving Norwegians bedecked in national costumes, or *bunader*, fill the streets. Fall, spring, and even winter are pleasant, despite the Nordic reputation for gloom. The days become shorter quickly, but the sun casts a golden light not seen farther south. On dark days, fires and candlelight will warm you indoors.

The Gulf Stream warms the western coast of Norway, making winters there similar to those in London. Even the harbor of Narvik, far to the north, remains ice-free year-round. Away from the protection of the Gulf Stream, however, northern Norway has cold, clear weather that attracts skiers.

Winter Norway is a wonderland of snow-covered mountains glowing under the northern lights, and few tourists are around to get in your way (although many tourist attractions are also closed). The days may seem perpetually dark, and November through February can be especially dreary. If it's skiing you're interested in, plan your trip for March or April, as there's usually still plenty of snow left. Take note that during Easter Week, many Norwegians head for the mountains, so it's hard to get accommodations—cities are virtually shut down, and even grocery stores close.

OSLO

What sets Oslo apart from other European cities is not so much its cultural traditions or its internationally renowned museums as its simply stunning natural beauty. What other world capital has subway service to the forest, or lakes and hiking trails within city limits? But Norwegians will be quick to remind you that Oslo—with thriving theaters, vibrant nightlife, and more—is as cosmopolitan as any world capital. And like other major metropolises, Oslo also has modern architectural monstrosities, traffic problems, and even a bit of urban sprawl.

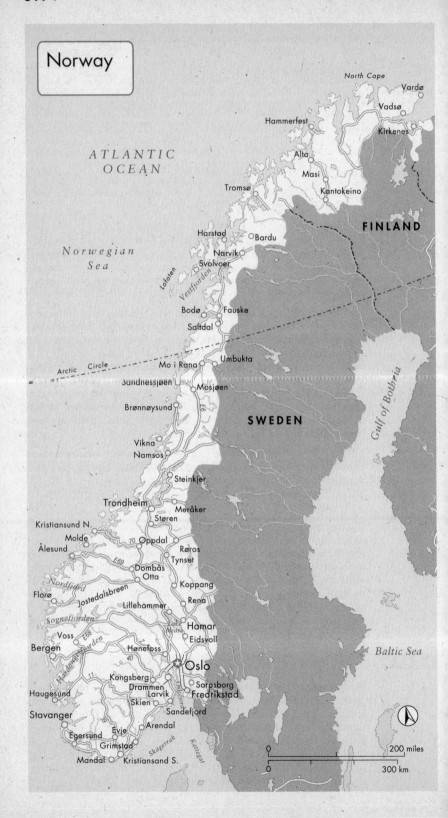

Norway

North Cape

ATLANTIC
OCEAN

Vardø

Vadsø

Hammerfest

Kirkenes

Alta

Masi

FINLAND

Tromsø

Kantokeino

Norwegian
Sea

Harstad

Bardu

Narvik

Svolvoer

Lofoten

Vestfjorden

Bodø

Fauske

Saltdal

Arctic Circle

Mo i Rana

Umbukta

Sandnessjøen

Mosjøen

Brønnøysund

E6

SWEDEN

Gulf of Bothnia

Vikna

Namsos

Steinkjer

Trondheim

Meråker

Kristiansund N.

Støren

Molde

70 Oppdal

Ålesund

Røros

E69

Tynset

Nordfjord

Dombås

Otta

Florø

Jostedalsbreen

Koppang

Lillehammer

Rena

Sognefjorden

Lake Mjøsa

Voss

E68

Hamar

Baltic Sea

Bergen

Hønefoss

Eidsvoll

Hardangerfjorden

40

Haugesund

Kongsberg

Oslo

Drammen

Larvik

Sarpsborg

Skien

Fredrikstad

Stavanger

Sandefjord

Egersund

Evje

Arendal

Grimstad

Glomma

Skagerrak

Kattegat

Mandal

Kristiansand S.

| 0 | | 200 miles |

| 0 | | 300 km |

As recently as the 1980s, Oslo had a reputation for being provincial and less sophisticated than its big-city peers of Stockholm and Copenhagen. Times have changed. Now a world-class city, Oslo has a cosmopolitan character and prosperity fueled through a strong Norwegian economy. It's one more change for this town of 500,000—a place that has become good at survival and rebirth throughout its nearly 1,000-year history. In 1348 plague wiped out half the city's population. In 1624 a fire burned almost the whole of Oslo to the ground. It was redesigned and renamed Christiania by Denmark's royal builder, King Christian IV. After that it slowly gained prominence as the largest and most economically significant city in Norway.

During the mid-19th century, Norway and Sweden were ruled as one kingdom, under Karl Johan. It was then that the grand main street that's his namesake was built, and Karl Johans Gate has been at the center of city life ever since. In 1925 an act of Parliament finally changed the city's name back to Oslo, its original, Viking name. Today, Oslo is Norway's political, economic, industrial, and cultural capital. The Norwegian royal family lives in Oslo, and it's where the Nobel Peace Prize is awarded.

Open-minded and outgoing, Oslo has increasingly embraced global and European trends. There are many exclusive shops and trendy boutiques, fancy golf courses, and restaurants with eclectic menus. This hip city caters to many tastes and tempos: for urban souls there are cultural attractions, nightclubs, and cafés, and for sports and outdoors enthusiasts there is hiking, sailing, and skiing within the vast expanse of parks, forests, and fjords that make up greater Oslo.

Exploring Oslo

Karl Johans Gate, starting at Oslo Sentralstasjon (Oslo Central Station, also called Oslo S Station) and ending at the Royal Palace, forms the backbone of downtown Oslo. Many of Oslo's major museums and historic buildings lie between the parallel streets of Grensen and Rådhusgata. To the southeast of the center of town is Gamlebyen, a historic district with a medieval church. West of downtown are Frogner and Majorstuen, residential areas known for their fine restaurants, shopping, cafés, galleries, and the Vigeland sculpture park. Farther west is the Bygdøy Peninsula, with a castle and five interesting museums that honor aspects of Norway's taste for exploration. Northwest of town is Holmenkollen, with its stunning bird's-eye view of the city and the surrounding fjords, a world-famous ski jump and museum, and three historic restaurants. On the more multicultural east side, where a diverse immigrant population lives alongside native Norwegians, are the Munch Museum and the Botanisk Hage og Museum (Botanical Gardens and Museum). The trendy neighborhood of Grünerløkka, with lots of cafés and shops, is also on the east side.

Numbers in the text correspond to numbers in the margin and on the Oslo map.

Downtown: The Royal Palace to City Hall

Although the entire city region is huge (454 square km [175 square mi]), downtown Oslo is compact, with shops, museums, historic sights, restaurants, and clubs concentrated in a small, walkable center that's brightly illuminated at night.

a good walk

Oslo's main promenade, Karl Johans Gate, runs from **Det Kongelige Slottet** ❶ ▶ through town. Before venturing down Karl Johans Gate, walk across the street from the palace to **Ibsen-Museet** to see the playwright Henrik Ibsen's final apartment as well as a museum devoted to his life. Walk down Drammensveien to Munkedamsveien and the **Stenersen-**

museet, to see its latest temporary exhibition or works by Edvard Munch and other Norwegian artists. From the gallery, walk back to Karl Johans Gate. Just beyond the castle to your left are three yellow buildings, which were part of the old **Universitet** ❷—today they are used only by the law school. Murals painted by Munch decorate the interior walls of these buildings. Around the corner from the university on Universitetsgata is the **Nasjonalgalleriet** ❸, which contains hundreds of Norwegian, Scandinavian, and other European works. Back-to-back with the National Gallery, across a parking lot, is a big cream-brick art nouveau–style building housing the **Historisk Museum** ❹. There's an impressive collection of Viking artifacts on display. Continue along Frederiksgate back to the university and cross Karl Johans Gate to Studenterlunden Park and the **Nationaltheatret** ❺. This impressive building is not only the national theater, but a popular meeting place—many buses stop out front, and the T-bane (short for *tunnelbane,* which is an underground railway, or subway) is right beside it.

Walk farther down Karl Johans Gate to see **Stortinget** ❻, the Norwegian Parliament, facing the castle. Then go back to Stortingsgata, one of the streets bordering Studenterlunden Park. Head back in the direction of the Nationaltheatret and then turn left on Universitetsgata. Walk toward the water to reach the redbrick **Rådhuset** ❼, its two block towers a familiar landmark. After visiting Rådhuset, end your tour with an *øl* (beer) at one of the many outdoor cafés at Aker Brygge.

TIMING   The walk alone should take no more than two hours. If you happen to be at the Royal Palace midday, you might catch the changing of the guard, which happens every day at 1:30. Note that many museums are closed on Monday.

WHAT TO SEE   **Det Kongelige Slottet** (The Royal Palace). At one end of Karl Johans Gate,
▶ ❶   the vanilla- and cream-color neoclassical palace was completed in 1848.
Fodor'sChoice   Although generally closed to the public, the palace is sometimes open for
★   special guided tours in summer. An equestrian statue of Karl Johan, King of Sweden and Norway from 1818 to 1844, stands in the square in front of the palace. ✉ *Drammensvn. 1, Sentrum* ☎ *22/04–89–52* ⊕ *www. kongehuset.no* ✉ *NKr 90* ⊙ *Late-June–mid-Aug., guided tours only.*

❹ **Historisk Museum** (Historical Museum). In partnership with the Vikingskiphuset (in Bygdøy), this forms the University Museum of Cultural Heritage, which concentrates on national antiquities as well as ethnographic and numismatic collections. See the intricately carved *stavkirke* (wood church) portals and exhibitions on subjects ranging from the Arctic to Asia. You can also gain a deeper understanding of Norway's Viking heritage through artifacts on display here. ✉ *Frederiksgt. 2, Sentrum* ☎ *22/ 85–99–12* ⊕ *www.ukm.uio.no* ✉ *NKr 40* ⊙ *Mid-May–mid-Sept., Tues.–Sun. 10–4; mid-Sept.–mid-May, Tues.–Sun. 11–4.*

Ibsen-museet. Famed Norwegian dramatist Henrik Ibsen, known for *A Doll's House, Hedda Gabler,* and *Peer Gynt* among other classic plays, spent his final years here, in the apartment on the second floor, until his death in 1906. Every morning, Ibsen's wife, Suzannah, would encourage the short literary legend to write before allowing him to head off to the Grand Café for his brandy and foreign newspapers. His study gives striking glimpses into his psyche. Huge, intense portraits of Ibsen and his archrival, August Strindberg, face each other. On his desk still sits his "devil's orchestra," a playful collection of frog and troll-like figurines that inspired him. Take a guided tour by well-versed and entertaining Ibsen scholars. Afterward, visit the museum's exhibition of Ibsen's drawings and paintings and first magazine writings. ✉ *Arbiensgt. 1, Sen-*

trum ☎ *22/55–20–09* ⊕ *www.norskfolke.museum.no* ✉ *NKr 50* ☉ *Tues.–Sun., guided tours at noon, 1, and 2.*

★ ❸ **Nasjonalgalleriet.** The National Gallery houses Norway's largest collection of art created before 1945. The deep-red Edvard Munch room holds such major paintings as *The Dance of Life* and several self-portraits. Classic fjord and country landscapes by Hans Gude and Adolph Tidemand—including *Bridal Voyage on the Hardangerfjord*—share space in other galleries with other works by major Norwegian artists. The museum has works by Monet, Renoir, Van Gogh, and Gauguin. ⊠ *Universitetsgt. 13, Sentrum* ☎ *22/20–04–04* ⊕ *www.nasjonalgalleriet.no* ✉ *Free* ☉ *Mon., Wed., Fri. 10–6, Thurs. 10–8, Sat. 10–4, Sun. 11–4.*

❺ **Nationaltheatret** (National Theater). In front of this neoclassical theater, built in 1899, are statues of Norway's great playwrights, Bjørnstjerne Bjørnson, who also composed the national anthem, and Henrik Ibsen. Most performances are in Norwegian, so you may just want to take a guided tour of the interior, which can be arranged by appointment. ⊠ *Stortingsgt. 15, Sentrum* ☎ *22/00–14–00* ⊕ *www.nationaltheatret.no.*

❼ **Rådhuset** (City Hall). This redbrick building is best known today for the awarding of the Nobel Peace Prize that takes place here every December. In 1915, the mayor of Oslo made plans for a new City Hall, and ordered the clearing of slums that stood on the site. The building was finally completed in 1950. Inside, many museum-quality masterpieces are on the walls. After viewing the frescoes in the Main Hall, walk upstairs to the Banquet Hall to see the royal portraits. In the East Gallery, Per Krohg's mosaic of a pastoral scene covers all four walls, making you feel like you're part of the painting. On festive occasions, the Central Hall is illuminated from outside by 60 large spotlights that simulate daylight. ⊠ *Rådhuspl., Sentrum* ☎ *23/46–16–00* ✉ *NKr 40* ☉ *May–Aug., Mon.–Sat. 9–5, Sun. noon–5; Sept.–Apr., Mon.–Sat. 9–4, Sun. noon–4.*

Fodor'sChoice
★

Stenersen-museet. Named for art collector Rolf E. Stenersen, this city-owned museum often has highly regarded and sometimes provocative temporary exhibitions. Opened in 1994, its permanent collection consists of works from Stenersen's collection—including art by Edvard Munch—and paintings donated by such artists as Amaldus Neilsen and Ludvig Ravensberg. ⊠ *Munkesdamsvn. 15, Sentrum* ☎ *23/49–36–00* ⊕ *www.stenersen.museum.no* ✉ *NKr 40* ☉ *Tues., Thurs. 11–7; Wed., Fri., Sat., Sun. 11–5.*

❻ **Stortinget** (Norwegian Parliament). Informative guided tours of this classic 1866 building are conducted daily throughout the summer, and on Saturday during the rest of the year. In front of the Parliament building, the park benches of Eidsvolls Plass are a popular meeting and gathering place. ⊠ *Karl Johans gt. 22, Sentrum* ☎ *23/31–35–96* ⊕ *www.stortinget.no* ✉ *Free* ☉ *Guided tours July–mid-Aug., weekdays at 10, 11:30, and 1; mid-Aug.–June, Sat. at 10, 11:30, and 1.*

❷ **Universitetet** (The University). The great hall in the middle building (there are three in all) is decorated with murals by Edvard Munch. Look for *The Sun*, which shows penetrating rays falling over a fjord. This building was the site of the Nobel Peace Prize award ceremony until 1989, when it was moved to the City Hall. ⊠ *Aulaen, Karl Johans gt. 47, Sentrum* ☎ *22/85–97–11* ✉ *Free* ☉ *July, weekdays 10–2.*

Kvadraturen & Akershus Castle

The Kvadraturen is the oldest part of Oslo still standing. In 1624, after the town of Oslo burned down for the 14th time, King Christian IV renamed the city Christiania and moved it from the area that is south-

Oslo

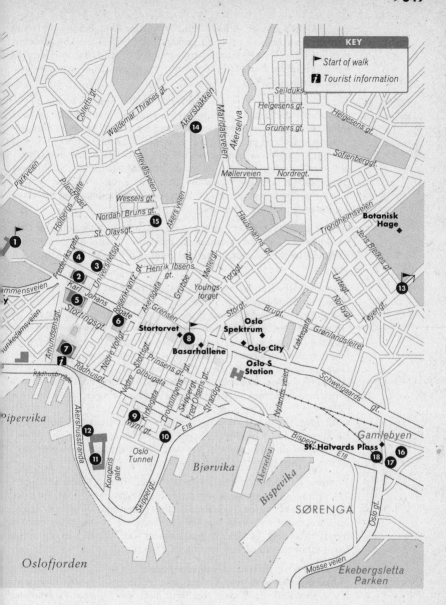

east of Oslo S Station, called Gamlebyen, rebuilding it adjacent to the Akershus fortress. In order to prevent future fires, the king decreed that houses were to be built of stone or brick instead of wood. He also built a stone wall around the rebuilt city to protect it from his enemies, the Swedes.

The Kvadraturen area, which includes Akershus Slott, is bound on the east side of the fortress by Skippergata and on the north side by Karl Johans Gate between Oslo Domkirke and Stortorvet. The boundary follows Øvre Vollgata around to the other side of the fortress. Kvadraturen translates roughly as "square township," which refers to the area's geometrically ordered streets. Be aware that the streets around Skippergata and Myntgata are seedy and known as a mini–red-light district. Avoid theft by keeping a close eye on your surroundings and by securing purses and other valuables.

Start at Stortorvet, Oslo's main square. To the east of the square is **Oslo Domkirke** ⑧ ▶, the city's landmark cathedral. Artists have been contributing to the cathedral's richly decorated interior since the 18th century.

From the cathedral, follow Kirkegata left past Karl Johans Gate to the **Museet for Samtidskunst** ⑨, inside the 1906 Bank of Norway building. Spend time wandering through the museum's halls to admire both its art nouveau architecture and contemporary art. From the museum, take the side street Revierstredet to Dronningensgate, where there's a building that does not seem to fit in with its 17th-century neighbors. Designed and built in the early 1990s, this brick-and-steel office building houses the **Astrup Fearnley Museet for Moderne Kunst** ⑩. The museum's permanent and temporary exhibitions emphasize modern art. Make a right onto Dronningensgate and head up to Rådhusgata. Take a left and walk down the street. Keep an eye out for the 17th-century building at Rådhusgata 11. It houses the Statholdergården restaurant, in a building that was once the home of the *statholder,* the official representative from Copenhagen when Norway was under Danish rule.

Continue on Rådhusgata until you reach the corner of Nedre Slottsgate. The yellow building you see was originally the city hall (1641), but since the 1800s has been the Det Gamle Rådhus restaurant. Diagonally across Rådhusgata in two 17th-century buildings are an art gallery and a trendy, artsy café. The building that houses Kafé Celsius was one of the first buildings erected in Christian IV's town.

Turn left on Akersgata and walk alongside the grassy hill to the entrance of **Akershus Slott og Festning** ⑪, the center of Christian IV's Kvadraturen. It's a worthwhile stroll to the top for its incredible Oslo harborfront and fjord views, especially at sunset. The castle became the German headquarters during the occupation of Norway in World War II, and many members of the Resistance were executed on the castle grounds. In a building next to the castle, at the top of the hill, is the **Norges Hjemmefront Museum** ⑫, which tells the gripping story of German occupation and Norwegian resistance.

Walk back to Rådhusgata to see another interesting building, Skogbrand Insurance, at Rådhusgt. 23B. Architects Jan Digerud and Jon Lundberg have won awards for their innovative 1985 vertical addition to this 1917 building. Take a break from history and architecture and head to the **Emanuel Vigelands Museet,** a collection of artistic erotica created by the brother of the celebrated sculptor Gustav Vigeland. To get here, turn right on any of the streets along Rådhusgata back to Karl Johans Gate and take the T-bane line 1 from Nationaltheatret Station, in the direction of Frognerseteren, and get off at Slemdal, one of Oslo's hillside residential neighborhoods.

TIMING   The walk alone will take at least three hours. Combined with museum visits and breaks, the itinerary could take more than half a day. Akershus Slott will take at least half an hour. Try to do this tour during daylight hours, catching late-afternoon sun from atop the Akershus grounds. Also note that the T-bane ride to the Emanuel Vigeland Museet in Slemdal takes about 15 minutes and that the museum is open only on Sunday afternoon.

WHAT TO SEE   **Akershus Slott og Festning** (Akershus Castle and Fortress). Dating to
★ ⑪   1299, this stone medieval castle and royal residence was developed into a fortress armed with cannons by 1592. After that time, it withstood a number of sieges and then fell into decay. It was finally restored in 1899. Summer tours take you through its magnificent halls, the Castle church, the royal mausoleum, reception rooms, and banqueting halls. ✉ *Akershus Slott, Festningspl., Sentrum* ☎ *22/41–25–21* ✆ *Grounds and concerts free; castle NKr 30* ☉ *Grounds daily 6 AM–9 PM; castle May–mid-Sept., Mon.–Sat. 10–4, Sun. 12:30–4; mid-Sept.–Oct., Mon.–Sat. 10–4, Sun. 12:30–4. Guided tours May–Sept., daily at 11, 1, and 3.*

⑩   **Astrup Fearnley Museet for Moderne Kunst** (Astrup Fearnley Museum for Modern Art). This privately funded museum opened in 1993 and earned an international reputation for its collections of postwar Norwegian and international art. In its smaller gallery, British artist Damien Hirst's controversial installation *Mother and Child Divided* is on display. Selections from the museum's permanent collection, which includes works by post-war Britons as well as such Norwegians as Odd Nerdrum and Olav Christopher Jenssen, are exhibited every summer. There's also a glassed-in sculpture garden with Niki de St. Phalle's sparrow and several other oversize 20th-century figures. ✉ *Dronningensgt. 4, Sentrum* ☎ *22/93–60–60* ⊕ *www.af-moma.no* ✆ *NKr 50, Tuesday free* ☉ *Tues., Wed., and Fri. 11–5, Thurs. 11–7, weekends noon–5. Guided tours weekends at 1.*

off the beaten path   **EMANUEL VIGELANDS MUSEET** – Although he never gained the fame of his older brother Gustav, the creator of Vigeland Park, Emanuel is an artist of some notoriety. His alternately saucy, natural, and downright erotic frescoes make even the sexually liberated Norwegians blush. ✉ *Grimelundsvn. 8, Slemdal* ☎ *22/14–93–42* ⊕ *www.emanuelvigeland.museum.no* ✆ *Free* ☉ *Sun. noon–4.*

⑨   **Museet for Samtidskunst** (National Museum of Contemporary Art). A stunning granite and marble example of art nouveau architecture, this 1906 former bank building is the largest museum of postwar Norwegian and international art. Its ornate gilded interior contrasts with the modern and contemporary art shown in its permanent and temporary exhibitions. The permanent collection of 4,300 works spans the genres of graphic art, drawing, photography, sculpture, decorative arts, installations, and video. Take time to ponder the two fascinating permanent installations: Ilya Kabakov's "The Man Who Never Threw Anything Away" and Per Inge Bjørlo's "Inner Room V." ✉ *Bankpl. 4, Sentrum* ☎ *22/86–22–10* ⊕ *www.museumsnett.no/mfs* ✆ *NKr 40, Thurs. free* ☉ *Tues.–Wed. and Fri. 10–5, Thurs. 10–8, Sat. 11–4, Sun. 11–5. Guided tours by appointment only.*

⑫   **Norges Hjemmefront Museum** (Norwegian Resistance Museum). Striped prison uniforms, underground newssheets, and homemade weapons tell the history of the resistance movement that arose before and during Norway's occupation by Nazi Germany. A gray, winding path leads to two underground stone vaults in which models, pictures, writings, and recordings trace the times between Germany's first attack in 1940 to Norway's liberation on May 8, 1945. Every year, on the anniversaries of these dates, Norwegian resistance veterans gather here to commemorate Norway's dark days and honor those who lost their lives. The former ammunitions depot and the memorial lie at the exact spot where Norwegian patriots were executed by the Germans. ⊠ *Akershus Slott, Sentrum* ☎ *23/09–31–38* ⊕ *www.mil.no/felles/nhm* ☎ *NKr 30* ☉ *Mid-Apr.–mid-June, Mon.–Sat. 10–4, Sun. 11–4; mid-June–Aug., Mon., Wed., Fri., Sat. 10–5, Tues., Thurs. 10–6, Sun. 11–5; Sept., Mon.–Sat. 10–4, Sun. 11–4; Oct.–mid-Apr,, weekdays 10–3, weekends 11–4.*

▶ ❽ **Oslo Domkirke** (Oslo Cathedral). Consecrated in 1697, this dark-brown brick structure has been Oslo's main church ever since. The original pulpit, altarpiece, and organ front with acanthus carvings still stand. Take a look at the endless ceiling murals made between 1936 to 1950 and stained-glass windows by Emanuel Vigeland. In the 19th century the fire department operated a lookout from the bell tower, which you can visit. ⊠ *Stortorget 1, Sentrum* ☎ *23/31–46–00* ☎ *Free* ☉ *Daily 10–4.*

need a break? Pascal Konditori (⊠ Tollbugt. 11, Sentrum ☎ 22/42–11–19), a trendy, Parisian-style patisserie inside an old-fashioned Norwegian *konditori* (café), is known for its enormous croissants, pastries, and French coffee. It's a place to see and be seen.

East, North & South of Downtown: Munch Museum, Damstredet & Gamlebyen

The Munch Museum is east of the city center in Tøyen, an area in which Edvard Munch spent many of his years in Oslo. The Tøyen district has a much different feel than Oslo's cushy west side—it's ethnic and more industrial. West of Tøyen, north of the city center near Vår Frelsers Gravlund, is the quiet, old-fashioned district of Damstredet, its streets lined with artisans' shops. If you're an ever curious history buff, you'll probably enjoy the last half of this tour through Gamlebyen. However, if this is your first trip to Oslo and you have a limited amount of time, you may want to end your tour at the Kunstindustrimuseet. Gamlebyen is somewhat off the beaten track, and although the area is interesting, some of the ruins are barely discernible.

a good walk Start by taking any T-bane from the city center (Sentrum) to Tøyen, where **Munchmuseet** ⑬ sits on a hill near the Botanisk Hage, a quiet oasis of plants and flowers. After visiting the museum, head back to town center. Take the T-bane and get off at Stortinget.

Head down Karl Johans Gate and take a left onto Akersgata. Follow it past the offices of *Aftenposten,* Norway's leading daily paper. As you head up the hill, you can see a huge rotund building, Deichmanske Bibliotek, the city's library. When you reach St. Olavs Church, veer gently to the right on Akersveien. You may want to take a detour down Damstredet when you come to it—it's one of the city's oldest streets, with well-preserved houses from the 19th century. Afterward, continue back along Akersveien. On your left is Vår Frelsers Gravlund (Our Savior's Graveyard), where you can seek out the gravestones of many famous Norwegians, including Ibsen and Munch. At the graveyard's northeastern corner is **Gamle Aker Kirke** ⑭, the city's only remaining medieval church.

After visiting the church, walk along the north side of the cemetery and then take a left onto Ullevålsveien. Take the road down the hill to the corner of St. Olavs Gate and Akersgata, where you'll find the **Kunstindustrimuseet** ⓯, one of Europe's oldest museums of decorative arts and design.

If you've got a yen for history and archaeology, visit **Gamlebyen** ⓰, the old town, to the southeast of Oslo S Station. Nearby on Oslo Gate is St. Halvards Plass. During the 13th century, the area was the city's ecclesiastical center. Also here are the intact foundations of **St. Halvards Kirke** ⓱, which dates from the early 12th century. Other ruins, including Korskirke and Olavs Kloster, lie in **Minneparken**. Nearby on Bispegata is **Oslo Ladegård** ⓲, a restored baroque-style mansion that sits on foundations of a 13th-century bishop's palace.

The oldest traces of human habitation in Oslo are the 5,000-year-old carvings on the runic stones near Ekebergsletta Park. They are across the road from the park on Karlsborgveien and are marked by a sign reading FORTIDSMINNE. To reach the park, walk south on Oslo Gate until it becomes Mosseveien. The stones will be on your right. The park is a good spot to rest your feet and end your tour.

TIMING   The Munch Museum will take up most of the morning, especially if you take a guided tour. The second half of the tour, from Gamlebyen to Ekebergsletta, is a perfect way to spend a summer Sunday afternoon. Things are quiet, and locals tend to stroll around this area when the weather is nice.

WHAT TO SEE   **Gamle Aker Kirke** (Old Aker Church). Dating to 1100, this medieval stone
★ ⓮   basilica is Oslo's oldest church—it's still in use as a parish church. Inside, the acoustics are outstanding, so inquire about upcoming concerts. ⊠ *Akersbakken 26, Bislett* ☎ *22/69–35–82* ⊕ *www.orgnett.no/kor/gak* ⊠ *Free* ☉ *Mon.–Sat. noon–2, Sun. 9 AM–11 AM.*

★ ⓰   **Gamlebyen** (The Old City). Sometimes referred to as the "Pompeii of Scandinavia," this area contains the last remains of medieval Oslo. It's one of the largest homogeneous archaeological sites found in any capital city in Scandinavia. To get here, take *trikk* (as the Norwegians fondly call the streetcars) 18, marked "Ljabru," from Stortorvet to St. Halvards Plass (you can also take trikk 19 from Nationaltheatret). Contact **Oslo Byantikvar** (☎ 23/46–02–50), the Antiquities Department of Oslo, for information on guided tours of the area. The department and the tourist office have a self-guided-tour brochure for the area.

⓯   **Kunstindustrimuseet** (Museum of Decorative Arts and Design). Rich Baldishol tapestries from 1100, Norwegian dragon-style furniture, and royal apparel (including Queen Sonja's wedding gown from 1968) make this a must-see museum. Founded in 1876, it also has exquisite collections of Norwegian 18th-century silver, glass, and faience. A contemporary Scandinavian section follows the history of design and crafts in the region. ⊠ *St. Olavs gt. 1, Sentrum* ☎ *22/03–65–40* ⊠ *NKr 25, special exhibits NKr 65* ☉ *Tues., Wed., Fri. 11–4, Thurs. 11–7, weekends noon–4.*

Minneparken. Oslo was founded by Harald Hardråde ("Hard Ruler") in 1048, and the earliest settlements were near what is now Bispegata, a few blocks behind Oslo S Station. Ruins are all that's left of the city's former religious center: the **Korskirke** (Cross Church; ⊠ Egedesgt. 2, Gamlebyen), a small stone church dating from the end of the 13th century; and **Olavs Kloster** (Olav's Cloister; ⊠ St. Halvards pl. 3, Gamlebyen), built around 1240 by Dominican monks. ✉ *Entrance at Oslogt. and Bispegt, Gamlebyen* ✆ *Sun. noon–2.*

► **⑬ Munchmuseet** (The Munch Museum). Edvard Munch, Norway's most
Fodor'sChoice famous artist, bequeathed his enormous collection of works (about
★ 1,800 paintings, 4,500 drawings, and 18,000 graphic works) to the city when he died in 1944. The museum is a monument to his artistic genius, housing the largest collection of his works and changing exhibitions. His most popular painting, *The Scream,* now a 20th-century icon, is not always on exhibition. While most of the Munch legend focuses on the artist as a troubled, angst-ridden man, he moved away from that pessimistic and dark approach to more optimistic themes later in his career. ✉ *Tøyengt. 53, Tøyen* ☎ *23/24–14–00* ⊕ *www.munch. museum.no* ✉ *NKr 60* ✆ *June–mid-Sept., daily 10–6; mid-Sept.–May, Tues.–Sat. 10–4, Sun. 11–5.*

⑱ Oslo Ladegård. The original building, the 13th-century Bispegård (Bishop's Palace), burned down in the famous 1624 fire, but its vaulted cellar survived. The present mansion was restored and rebuilt in 1725; it now belongs to the city council and contains scale models of 16th- to 18th-century Oslo. ✉ *St. Halvards pl., Oslogt. 13, Gamlebyen* ☎ *22/ 19–44–68* ✉ *NKr 40* ✆ *Late May–mid-Sept., Tues., Thurs., Fri. 2–4, Wed. 2–6; guided tours Sun. at 4.*

⑰ St. Halvards Kirke (St. Halvard's Church). This medieval church, named for the patron saint of Oslo, remained the city's cathedral until 1660. ✉ *Minneparken, entrance at Oslogt. and Bispegt, Gamlebyen.*

Frogner, Majorstuen & Holmenkollen

Among the city's most stylish neighborhoods, Frogner and Majorstuen combine classic Scandinavian elegance with contemporary European chic. Incredibly hip boutiques and galleries coexist with embassies and ambassadors' residences on the streets near and around Bygdøy Allé. Holmenkollen, the hill past Frogner Park, has the famous ski jump and miles of ski trails.

a good walk

Catch the No. 15 Majorstuen trikk from Nationaltheatret on the Drammensveien side of the Royal Palace grounds. You can also take the No. 15 from Aker Brygge.

Opposite the southwest end of the palace grounds is the triangular U.S. Embassy, designed by Finnish-American architect Eero Saarinen and built in 1959. Look to the right at the corner of Drammensveien and Parkveien for a glimpse of the venerable Nobel Institute. Since 1905 these stately yellow buildings have been the secluded setting where the five-member Norwegian Nobel Committee decides who will win the Nobel Peace Prize. The library is open to the public.

Stay on the trikk and ride to Frogner Park or walk the seven blocks. To walk, get off at Balders Gate and follow the road to Arno Bergs Plass, with its central fountain. Turn left on Gyldenløves Gate until you reach Kirkeveien. Turn right past the Dutch Embassy, and cross the street at the light. Frogner Park, also called Vigelandsparken, is ahead.

Walk through the front gates of the park and toward the monolith ahead: you are entering **Vigelandsparken ⑲** ►. This stunning sculpture garden was designed by one of Norway's greatest artists, Gustav Vigeland. Spend a few minutes and walk over to Frogner Stadion (Stadium) and **Skøytemuseet**, which highlights Norway's contribution to the sport of ice skating. Across from the park, you can study the method to Vigeland's madness at **Vigelandsmuseet ⑳**. Cross the street to the **Oslo Bymuseum ㉑**, a cultural and historical look at the city and its development.

After you leave the museum, take a left onto Kirkeveien and continue to the Majorstuen underground station, near the intersection of Bogstadveien. Here you have two options: you can walk down Bogstadveien, look at the shops, explore the Majorstuen area, and then take the Holmenkollen line of the T-bane to Frognerseteren; or you can skip the stroll down Bogstadveien and head right up to Holmenkollen. The train ride up the mountain passes some stunning scenery. If your party includes children, you may want to make a detour at the first T-bane stop, Frøen, and visit the **Barnekunstmuseet** 22.

Continue on the T-bane to the end of the line. This is Frognerseteren—a popular destination on winter weekends. The view of the city here is spectacular. The **Tryvannstårnet** 23 has an even better panoramic view of Oslo. Downhill is **Holmenkollbakken** 24, where Norway's most intrepid skiers prove themselves every March during the Holmenkollen Ski Festival.

TIMING   This is a good tour for Monday, since the museums mentioned are open, unlike most others in Oslo. You will need a whole day for Frogner and Majorstuen since there is some travel time involved. The trikk ride from the city center to Frogner Park takes about 15 minutes; the T-bane to Frognerseteren takes about 20. You're no longer in the compact city center, so distances between sights are greater. The walk from Frognerseteren to Frogner Park is about 15 minutes and is indicated with signposts. Try to save Holmenkollen, with its magnificent views, for a clear day.

WHAT TO SEE   **Barnekunstmuseet** (Children's Art Museum). A brainchild of Rafael
22   Goldin, a Russian immigrant, the museum showcases her collection of children's drawings from more than 150 countries. You can see the world though the eyes of a child in its exhibitions of textiles; drawings; paintings; sculptures; and children's music, dancing, and other activities. ✉ *Lille Frøens vei 4, Blindern* ☎ *22/46–85–73* ⊕ *www.barnekunst.no* 🎫 *NKr 50* ☾ *Late-June–early Aug., Tues.–Thurs. and Sun. 11–4; mid-Sept.–mid-Dec., late Jan.–late June, Tues.–Thurs. 9:30–2, Sun. 11–4.*

24   **Holmenkollbakken** (Holmenkollen Ski Museum and Ski Jump). A distinctive
Fodor'sChoice   part of the city's skyline, Oslo's ski jump holds a special place in the
★   hearts of Norwegians. Originally built in 1892, it was reconstructed for the 1952 Winter Olympics, and is still a popular site for international competitions; it also attracts a million visitors every year. Take the elevator and walk to the top for the view that skiers have in the moment before they take off. Back down at the base of the jump, turn right, past the statue of King Olav V on skis, to enter the oldest ski museum in the world. A hands-on exhibition awaits you, with alpine and cross-country skis, poles, and bindings that have been used through the ages. See the earliest skis, from AD 600, explorer Fridtjof Nansen's wooden skis from his 1888 Greenland crossing, and the autographed specimens used by retired champion Bjørn Daehlie. Then, head to the ski simulator outside for the thrilling sensation of a ski jump and downhill race. ✉ *Kongevn. 5, Holmenkollen* ☎ *22/92–32–00* ⊕ *www.skiforeningen.no* 🎫 *NKr 50* ☾ *Jan.–Apr. and Oct.–Dec., daily 10–4; May and Sept., daily 10–5; June–Aug., daily 9–8.*

21   **Oslo Bymuseum** (Oslo City Museum). One of the world's largest cities, Oslo has changed and evolved greatly over its thousand years. A two-floor, meandering exhibition covers Oslo's prominence in 1050, the Black Death that came in 1349, the great fire of 1624 and subsequent rebuilding, and the urban development of the 20th century. Among the more interesting relics are the red coats that the first Oslo police, the watch-

men, wore in 1700, and the first fire wagon in town, which appeared in 1765. Plan to visit the museum near the beginning of your stay for a more informed understanding of the Norwegian capital. ⊠ *Frognervn. 67, Frogner* ☎ *23/28–41–70* ⊕ *oslobymuseum.no* ⊠ *NKr 40* ⊘ *Wed.–Sun. noon–4, Tues. 10–7.*

Skøytemuseet (The Ice Skating Museum). Tucked away in Frogner Stadium, this is Norway's only museum devoted to ice skates and ice skaters. Gleaming trophies, Olympic medals, and skates, skates, and more skates serve to celebrate the sport. Photographs of skating legends such as Johan Olav Koss, Hjalmar Andersen, and Oscar Mathisen line the walls. Take a look at ways that skates have evolved—compare the bone skates from 2,000 BC to the wooden skates that came later. ⊠ *Frogner Park, Middelthunsgt. 26, Majorstuen* ☎ *22/43–49–20* ⊠ *NKr 20* ⊘ *Tues. and Thurs. 10–2, Sun. 11–2.*

★ ㉓ **Tryvannstårnet** (Tryvann's Tower). The view from Oslo's TV tower encompasses 36,000 square foot of hills, forests, cities, and several bodies of water. You can see as far as the Swedish border to the east and nearly as far as Moss to the south. ⊠ *Voksenkollen, Holmenkollen* ☎ *22/ 14–67–11* ⊠ *NKr 40* ⊘ *May and Sept., daily 10–5; June–Aug., daily 10–7; Oct.–Apr., daily 10–4.*

㉒ **Vigelandsmuseet.** "I am anchored to my work so that I cannot move. If I walk down the street one day a thousand hands from work hold on to me. I am tied to the studio and the road is never long," said Gustav Vigeland in 1912. This museum was the Norwegian sculptor's studio and residence. It houses models of almost all his works as well as sculptures, drawings, woodcuts, and the original molds and plans for Vigeland Park. Wander through this intense world of enormous, snowy-white plaster, clustered nudes, and busts of such famous Norwegians as Henrik Ibsen and Edvard Grieg. ⊠ *Nobelsgt. 32, Frogner* ☎ *22/54–25–30* ⊕ *www.vigeland.museum.no* ⊠ *NKr 30* ⊘ *Oct.–Apr., Tues.–Sun. noon–4; May–Sept., Tues.–Sat. 10–6, Sun. noon–6.*

⌐ ★ ⑲ **Vigelandsparken** (Vigeland's Park). Also known as Frogner Park, Vigelandsparken has 212 bronze, granite, and wrought-iron sculptures by Gustav Vigeland (1869–1943). Most of the stunning park sculptures are placed on a nearly 1-km-long (½ mi-long) axis and depict the stages of life: birth to death, one generation to the next. See the park's 56-foot-high granite *Monolith Plateau,* a column of 121 upward-striving nude figures surrounded by 36 groups on circular stairs. The most beloved sculpture is a bronze of an enraged baby boy stamping his foot and scrunching his face in fury. Known as *Sinnataggen* (The Angry Boy), this famous statue has been filmed, parodied, painted red, and even stolen from the park. It is based on a 1901 sketch Vigeland made of a little boy in London.

Bygdøy

Several of Oslo's best-known historic sights are concentrated on the Bygdøy Peninsula, as are several beaches, jogging paths, and the royal family's summer residence.

a good walk

The most pleasant way to get to Bygdøy—available from May to September—is to catch ferry 91 from the Rådhuset. Times vary, so check with Trafikanten for schedules. Another alternative is to take Bus 30, marked "Bygdøy," from Stortingsgata at Nationaltheatret along Drammensveien to Bygdøy Allé, a wide avenue lined with chestnut trees. The bus passes Frogner Church and several embassies on its way to Olav Kyrres Plass, where it turns left, and soon left again, onto the peninsula. The royal family's summer residence, actually just a big white frame house, is on the right. Get off at the next stop, Norsk Folkemuseum. The pink castle nestled in the trees is **Oscarshall Slott** ㉕ ⌐, once a royal summer palace.

The **Norsk Folkemuseum** ㉖ consists of an open-air museum as well as some indoor exhibits of folk art. Around the corner from the museum, to the right, is the **Vikingskiphuset** ㉗, one of Norway's most popular attractions; it houses some of the best-preserved Viking-era remains yet discovered.

Follow signs on the road to the **Fram-Museet** ㉘, a pyramid-shape structure resembling a Viking boathouse. After viewing the exhibitions, you can watch a panoramic movie about Norway's maritime past at the Norsk Sjøfartsmuseum. Across the parking lot is the older **Kon-Tiki Museum** ㉙, with Thor Heyerdahl's famous raft, along with the papyrus boat *Ra II*. You can get a ferry back to the City Hall docks from the dock in front of the Fram-Museet. If your children are squirming to break out of the museum circuit, entertain the thought of a trip to Tusenfryd, an amusement park packed with rides.

TIMING   Block out a day for Bygdøy. You could spend at least half a day at the Folkemuseum alone. Note that the museums on Bygdøy tend to be open daily, but close early. The tour bus company HMK conducts an afternoon trip to Tusenfryd, so count on spending half a day. It takes between 10 and 20 minutes to reach the park from downtown Oslo by bus. If you decide to go on your own from Oslo S Station, you might want to spend a leisurely day in the area.

WHAT TO SEE   **Fram-Museet.** Once known as the strongest vessel in the world, the enor-
★ ☾ ㉘   mous, legendary Norwegian polar ship *Fram,* has advanced farther north and south than any other surface vessel. Built in 1892, it made three arctic voyages conducted by Fridtjof Nansen (1893–96), Otto Sverdrup (1898–1902) and Roald Amundsen (1910–12). Climb onboard and peer inside the captain's quarters, which has explorers' sealskin jackets and other relics on display. Surrounding the ship are many expedition artifacts. ⊠ *Bygdøynes, Bygdøy* ☎ *23/28–29–50* ⊕ *www. fram.museum.no* ⊠ *NKr 30* ☾ *Nov.–Feb., weekdays 11–2:45, weekends 11–3:45; Mar. and Apr., daily 11–3:45; early May and Sept., daily 10–4:45; mid-May–mid-June, daily 9–5:45; mid-June–Aug., daily 9–6:45; Oct., daily 10–3:45.*

★ ☾ ㉙   **Kon-Tiki Museum.** The museum celebrates Norway's most famous 20th-century explorer. Thor Heyerdahl made a voyage in 1947 from Peru to Polynesia on the *Kon-Tiki,* a balsa raft, to lend weight to his theory that the first Polynesians came from the Americas. The *Ra II* sailed from Morocco to the Caribbean in 1970. ⊠ *Bygdøynesvn. 36, Bygdøy* ☎ *22/ 43–80–50* ⊕ *www.kon-tiki.no* ⊠ *NKr 35* ☾ *Apr. and May and Sept., daily 10:30–5; June–Aug., daily 9:30–5:45; Oct.–Mar., daily 10:30–4.*

☾ ㉖   **Norsk Folkemuseum** (Norwegian Folk Museum). One of the largest open-
Fodor'sChoice   air museums in Europe, this is a perfect way to see Norway in a day.
★   From the stoic stave church to farmers' houses made of sod, the old buildings here span Norway's history throughout the ages and regions. Indoors, there's a fascinating display of folk costumes. The displays of richly embroidered, colorful *bunader* (national costumes) from every region includes one set at a Telemark country wedding. The museum also has stunning dragon-style wood carvings from 1550 and some beautiful rose-maling. The traditional costumes of the Sámi (Lapp) people of northern Norway are exhibited around one of their tents. If you're visiting in summer, inquire about Norwegian Evening, a summer program of folk dancing, guided tours, and food tastings. During Sundays in De-

cember, the museum holds Oslo's largest Christmas market. ⊠ *Museumsvn. 10, Bygdøy* ☎ *22/12–37–00* ⊕ *www.norskfolke.museum.no* ⌨ *NKr 75* ☉ *Mid-Sept.–mid-May, weekdays 11–3, weekends 11–4; mid-May–mid-Sept., daily 10–6.*

Ⓒ **Norsk Sjøfartsmuseum** (Norwegian Maritime Museum). Norwegian fishing boats, paintings of fishermen braving rough seas, and intricate ship models are all on display here. The Arctic vessel *Gjøa* is docked outside. The breathtaking, panoramic movie *The Ocean: A Way of Life* delves into Norway's unique coastal and maritime past. ⊠ *Bygdøynesvn. 37, Bygdøy* ☎ *22/43–82–40* ⊕ *www.norsk-sjofartsmuseum.no* ⌨ *NKr 40* ☉ *Mid-May–Sept., daily 10–6; Oct.–mid-May, Mon.–Wed., Fri.–Sun. 10:30–4, Thurs. 10:30–6.*

▶ ㉕ **Oscarshall Slott.** This small country palace was built (1847–52) in eccentric English Gothic style for King Oscar I. There's a park, pavilion, fountain, and stage on the grounds. The original interior has works by the Norwegian artists Adolph Tidemand and Hans Gude. ⊠ *Oscarshallvn., Bygdøy* ☎ *22/56–15–39* ⌨ *NKr 20* ☉ *Late May–mid-Sept., Tues., Thurs., and Sun. noon–4.*

off the beaten path

Ⓒ **TUSENFRYD** – At Norway's foremost amusement park, the thrills are many. In May 2001 ThunderCoaster, a huge wooden roller coaster with the steepest drop in Europe, opened here. The tour bus company H.M. Kristiansen Automobilbyrå (HMK) provides an afternoon bus excursion from the Norway Information Center. There's also a shuttle bus that departs from Oslo Bussterminalen Galleriet, the city's main train station, which is right by Oslo S Station. ⊠ *Vinterbro* ☎ *64/97–64–00* ⊕ *www.tusenfryd.no* ⌨ *NKr 215* ☉ *Early June–mid-Aug., daily 10:30–7; May and late Aug., weekends 10:30–7.*

★ ㉗ **Vikingskiphuset** (Viking Ship Museum). The Viking legacy in all its glory lives on at this classic Oslo museum. Chances are you'll come away fascinated by the three blackened wooden Viking ships *Gokstad, Oseberg,* and *Tune,* which date to AD 800. Discovered in Viking tombs around the Oslo fjords between 1860 and 1904, the ships have been exhibited since the museum's 1957 opening. In Viking times, it was customary to bury the dead with food, drink, useful and decorative objects, and even their horses and dogs. Many of the well-preserved tapestries, household utensils, dragon-style wood carvings, and sledges were found aboard ships. The museum's rounded white walls give the feeling of a burial mound. Avoid summertime crowds by visiting at lunchtime. ⊠ *Huk Aveny 35, Bygdøy* ☎ *22/13–52–80* ⊕ *www.ukm.uio.no* ⌨ *NKr 40* ☉ *May–Sept., daily 9–6; Oct.–Apr., daily 11–4.*

Where to Eat

The culinary revolution that has swept Europe since the early 1990s has also been witnessed in Oslo's restaurants. In keeping with the capital's increasingly cosmopolitan image, the city's chefs have incorporated Mediterranean and Asian flavors into traditional dishes, often with outstanding results. Inspired by international experiences and travels, and by the availability of foreign ingredients, chefs such as Magma's Sonja Lee are bringing new energy and expertise to their kitchens. Fusion and crossover cooking have come to stay, even in fast-food restaurants. Sushi bars are immensely popular, and trendy bistros and cafés abound.

Take time to taste the exciting variations on traditional cooking, for a taste of modern Norway. Menus are still based on traditional Norwegian fare—seafood, farm-fresh produce, and game, especially reindeer—but you'll find unusual sauces and accompaniments. If you're a purist and your taste doesn't run to fusion cooking, don't worry; Oslo's traditional restaurants are alive and well, and as sophisticated as ever.

Spend at least one sunny summer afternoon harborside at Aker Brygge eating shrimp and watching the world go by. Floating restaurants serve shrimp in bowls with baguettes and mayonnaise. Or better still, buy steamed shrimp off the nearby docked fishing boats and plan a picnic in the Oslo fjords or Vigeland or another of the city's parks. Note that most restaurants close through the Christmas holiday season and the often week-long Easter break.

Downtown: Royal Palace to the Parliament

$$$$ ✕ **Restaurant Eik.** This is Norway's first smoke-free restaurant, although cigar smoke would not be out of place here, among the plush chairs, deep-red sofa, somber artwork, and soft music. The food, in contrast, is thoroughly up to date. Choose between three- and five-course menus that change daily. ⊠ *Universitetsgt. 11, Sentrum* ☎ *23/35–42–00* ▭ *AE, DC, MC, V* ☉ *Closed Sun. and Mon.*

$$$–$$$$ ✕ **Oro.** Celebrity chef Terje Ness opened this Mediterranean restaurant, whose name means "gold" in Spanish, in September 2000. Now the city's

Fodor'sChoice hottest restaurant, it requires reservations months ahead. In the restaurant's open kitchen, you can see Ness and his personable staff at work.

★ The dining room is hip and airy. Ness recommends the grilled scallops with eggplant and orange, the turbot with lentils, capers, and truffles, and the Taste of Oro (a 7- or 12-course dinner). For dessert, savor the delicious Chocolate Oro—chocolate mousse with passion fruit, topped with gold leaf. ⊠ *Tordenskjolds gt. 6, Sentrum* ☎ *23/01–02–40* ▭ *AE, DC, MC, V* ⌕ *Reservations essential* ☉ *Closed Sun. No lunch.*

$$–$$$ ✕ **Terra Bar & Restaurant.** Spanish pottery and earth tones hint at the Mediterranean-inspired dishes served here. Across the street from the parliament building, it attracts its share of politicians. Half the menu is fish—you may wish to sample the baked halibut, or the chargrilled tuna with melon and pernod sauce. A special treat is the Tired of Everything dessert: homemade strawberry ice cream served with a balsamic syrup. ⊠ *Stortingst. 2, Sentrum* ☎ *22/40–55–20* ▭ *AE, DC, MC, V* ☉ *No lunch July–mid-Aug.*

$$–$$$ ✕ **A Touch of France.** As its name suggests, this wine bar near the Parliament building is straight out of Paris. The waiters' long, white aprons; the art nouveau interior; old French posters; and closely packed tables all add to the illusion. The tempting menu includes a delicious, steaming-hot bouillabaisse. ⊠ *Øvre Slottsgt. 16, Sentrum* ☎ *23/10–01–65* ▭ *AE, DC, MC, V.*

$$ ✕ **Babette's Gjestehus.** Near City Hall, this restaurant's dark-blue walls and lace curtains make it resemble an old-fashioned Norwegian living room. French chef Dominique Choquet serves Scandinavian and international dishes with flair. Try the reindeer fillet in port sauce, lamb with apricots, or monkfish. The staff is friendly and welcoming. ⊠ *Rådhuspassasjen, Roald Amundsensgt. 3, Sentrum* ☎ *22/41–64–64* ▭ *AE, DC, MC, V* ☉ *Closed Sun. No lunch.*

★ **$** ✕ **Dinner.** The bland name belies the fact that this is one of the best places in Oslo for Chinese food, as well as dishes that combine Norwegian and Cantonese styles. Peking Duck is a speciality here, or, for a lighter meal, try the delectable platter of seafood in chili-pepper sauce. ⊠ *Stortingst. 22, Sentrum* ☎ *23/10–04–66* ▭ *AE, DC, MC, V* ☉ *No lunch.*

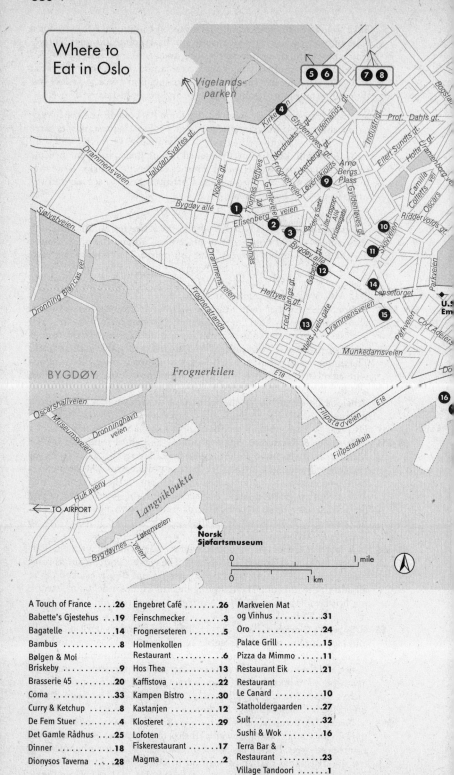

Where to Eat in Oslo

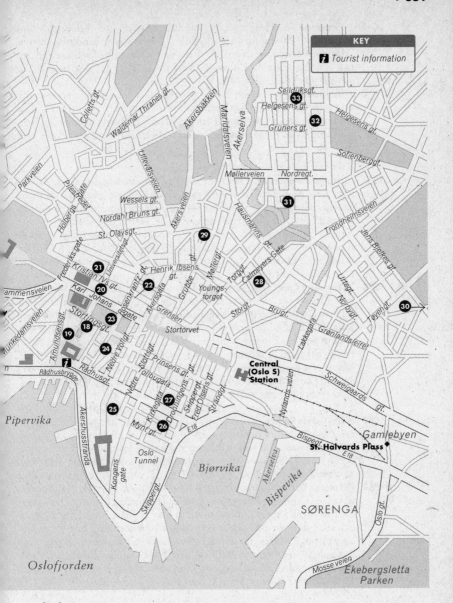

KEY

🛈 *Tourist information*

¢–$ ╳ **Brasserie 45.** This romantic, candlelit brasserie on the second floor overlooks the fountain on Karl Johans Gate. It has a Scandinavian-style interior to match the cuisine. Fish dishes such as grilled salmon and catfish are the signatures here. ⊠ *Karl Johans Gt. 45, Sentrum* ☎ *22/41–34–00* ▤ *AE, DC, MC, V.*

¢ ╳ **Kaffistova.** Norwegian home cooking is served cafeteria-style at this downtown restaurant. Daily specials come in generous portions and include soup and a selection of entrées. There is always at least one vegetarian dish. ⊠ *Rosenkrantz gt. 8, Sentrum* ☎ *22/42–99–74* ▤ *AE, DC, MC, V.*

Kvadraturen & Aker Brygge

$$$$ ╳ **Statholdergaarden.** Chef Bent Stiansen's Asian-inspired French dishes have long been popular with locals. The six-course gastronomic menu changes daily; you can also order from the à la carte menu. Try his sesame-roasted breast of duck with ginger sauce, or the pan-fried perch with tomato cannelloni. More than 400 years old, the rococo dining room is one of Norway's largest, and seats 75 people. ⊠ *Rådhusgt. 11, Sentrum* ☎ *22/41–88–00* ⌂ *Reservations essential* ⌂ *Jacket and tie* ▤ *AE, DC, MC, V* ⊘ *Closed Sun. and 3 wks in July.*

$$$–$$$$ ╳ **Engebret Café.** This somber, old-fashioned restaurant at Bankplassen was a haunt for bohemian literati at the turn of the 20th century. The formal, French-tinged Norwegian dinner menu includes traditional seasonal fare around *Juletide* (Christmastime), including lutefisk and *pinnekjøtt* (sticks of meat), which is lamb steamed over branches of birch. For a real taste of Norway, try the *smalahove* (a whole sheep's head). Many Norwegian families consider it a treat to visit the restaurant around Christmas, so book early if that's your plan, too. During the rest of the year, try the reindeer in cream sauce or the poached catfish. ⊠ *Bankpl. 1, Sentrum* ☎ *22/82–25–25* ▤ *AE, DC, MC, V.*

$$$ ╳ **Det Gamle Rådhus.** Inside Oslo's City Hall, this is the city's oldest restaurant. Its reputation is based mostly on traditional fish and game dishes. An absolute must, if you're lucky enough to be visiting at the right time, is the house specialty, the pre-Christmas lutefisk platter. ⊠ *Nedre Slottsgt. 1, Sentrum* ☎ *22/42–01–07* ▤ *AE, DC, MC, V* ⊘ *Closed Sun.*

★ $$$ ╳ **Lofoten Fiskerestaurant.** Named for the Lofoten Islands off the northwest coast, this Aker Brygge restaurant is considered one of Oslo's best for fish, from salmon to cod to monkfish. It has a bright, fresh, minimalistic interior with harbor views and a summertime patio. From January through March, try the cod served with its own liver and roe; April through September, the shellfish; and from October through December, the lutefisk. Call ahead, since sometimes only large groups are served. ⊠ *Stranden 75, Aker Brygge, Sentrum* ☎ *22/83–08–08* ▤ *AE, DC, MC, V.*

$–$$ **Sushi & Wok.** The sushi bar trend took a while to get to Oslo, but it's now firmly entrenched. This minimalist restaurant is one of a chain. Traditional nigiri-sushi and makimono garner rave reviews from aficionados. Try the Sushi Moriawase, which includes 10 assorted sushi and six maki. You can drop by for "Sushi Happy Hour" between 3 and 7 for three specially-priced meals. ⊠ *Bryggetorget 7, Aker Brygge, Sentrum* ☎ *22/83–63–51* ▤ *AE, DC, MC, V.*

East of Downtown

$$$ ╳ **Klosteret.** A popular east-side eatery, its name means "the cloisters." Its not-very-medieval, informal dining room is in a spacious, candlelit, rounded brick cellar. Pictures of saints and other religious figures adorn the walls, and Gregorian chants play in the background. The handwoven menus, bound to look like hymnals, contain a list of appealing meat and fish dishes, plus a daily vegetarian option. Consider the fried salmon

NORWAY: ON THE MENU

FOOD AND THE RITUALS of mealtimes are central to Norwegian culture. The Norwegians pride themselves on gracious entertaining and lavish dinner parties, for which they using their finest silver and glassware. Dining out in Norway is expensive, so many weekend nights are spent at the houses of friends and family, savoring long, candlelit dinners.

Chefs such as Terje Ness have been winning international cooking competitions and earning celebrity status back home. They're traveling and cooking widely, often inspired by their international colleagues and by stints abroad. Increasingly, they're taking pride in traditions, cooking Norwegian ingredients like lamb and wild game, and serving them with sauces made from the wild berries that make up the animals' diet.

Desserts, too, often feature fruit and berries. Norwegian strawberries and raspberries ripen in the long, early summer days and are sweeter and more intense than those grown farther south. Red and black currants are also widely used in desserts. Two berries native to Norway are tyttebær (lingonberries), which taste similar to cranberries but are much smaller; and molter (cloudberries), which look like orange raspberries but whose taste has been compared to that of a mango or peach. Molter are often served as moltekrem (in whipped cream) as a dessert, whereas tyttebær preserves often accompany traditional meat dishes.

Traditional, home-style Norwegian food is stick-to-the-ribs fare, served in generous portions and smothered in gravy. One of the most popular dishes is kjøttkaker (meat cakes), which resemble small Salisbury steaks and are served with boiled potatoes, stewed cabbage, and brown gravy. Almost as popular are medisterkaker (mild pork sausage patties), served with brown gravy and caraway-seasoned sauerkraut, and reinsdyrkaker (reindeer meatballs), served with cream sauce and lingonberry jam. Other typical meat dishes include fårikål, a great-tasting lamb and cabbage stew, and steik (roast meat), always served well done. Fish dishes include poached torsk (cod) or laks (salmon), served with creamy sauce; seibiff, (pollack) fried with onions; and fiskegrateng, a fish soufflé, usually served with carrot slaw.

There are also regional specialties such as smalahove (sheep's head), common on the west coast, and klippfisk (also known as bacalao). This dried and salted fish is exported to Portugal, Italy, Spain, South America, and the Caribbean. Pinnekjøtt, (salted lamb ribs), and lutefisk (fish that's been soaked in lye and then simmered) are popular around Christmas.

Traditional desserts include karamellpudding (crème caramel), rømmegrøt (sour-cream porridge served with cinnamon sugar), and saft (drinks made from concentrated berry juices.). Rømmegrøt—a typical farm dish—tastes very much like warm cheesecake batter. It's often served with fenalår (dried leg of mutton) and lefser—a thin, tortillalike pancake made with sour cream and potatoes that's buttered and coated with sugar. Christmastime brings a delectable array of light, sweet, and buttery pastries. Bløtkake (layered cream cake with custard, fruit, and marzipan) is a favorite dessert for Christmas and special occasions, but can be purchased in bakeries year-round.

The Norwegians take their kaffe (coffee) black and bitter, and they typically drink it several times a day. The tradition of locally brewed øl (beer) dates back to the Viking Ages, and most major cities have their signature brew. Wine is imported since Norway is too far north to cultivate wine grapes. A special Norwegian liquor, however, is its akevitt or aquavit, which in this rendition is distilled from potatoes and usually flavored with caraway.

with lemon-baked fennel, and the delicious chocolate fondant. ✉ *Fredensborgvn. 13, Sentrum* ☎ *23/35–49–00* ▭ *AE, DC, MC, V* ☻ *Closed Sun. and July.*

$$ ✕ **Coma.** This eccentric but very hip restaurant has white, blue, green, and purple ceiling lights, striped walls, and comfy pillows to create a dreamy mood. Tongue-in-cheek signs over the door are there to let you know when you are entering and when you are leaving the coma. Try one of the fish dishes on the French-inspired menu. ✉ *Helgesensgt. 16, Grünerløkka* ☎ *22/35–32–22* ▭ *AE, DC, MC, V.*

$$ ✕ **Markveien Mat og Vinhus.** This restaurant in the heart of the Grünerløkka district serves fresh French-inspired cuisine. It's a relaxed, artsy place with a bohemian clientele. Paintings cover the yellow walls, and the tables are laid with white linen. For a special treat, try the homemade cheesecake. ✉ *Torvbakkgt. 12, entrance on Markvn. 57, Grünerløkka* ☎ *22/37–22–97* ▭ *AE, DC, MC, V* ☻ *Closed Sun.*

$$ **Sult.** Trendy, Norwegian, bohemian informality is the essence of this small restaurant, whose name means "hunger." Large windows, small square tables, and a simple homemade look attracts students and writers. Try one of the fish or pasta specials. Next door, the bar–lounge, appropriately named *Tørst* (thirst), has it own unique blended drinks, including Raspberry Parade, a blend of raspberry juice, champagne, and vodka. ✉ *Thorvald Meyers gt. 26, Grünerløkka* ☎ *22/87–04–67* ▭ *AE, DC, MC, V.*

★ $ ✕ **Dionysos Taverna.** Owner Charalambos Eracleous imports fresh fish, wine, and ouzo from Greece to serve at his cobalt blue and whitewashed restaurant. The *tzatziki* (yogurt and cucumber salad), souvlakia, and moussaka are authentically prepared, as are the more unusual casseroles, such as *exohiko* (lamb baked with red wine, tomatoes, and onions). For a taste of everything, order *mezes*, Greek-style tapas. A bouzouki trio accompanies your dining experience on Thursday, Friday, and Saturday nights. ✉ *Calmeyersgt. 11, Sentrum* ☎ *22/60–78–64* ▭ *MC, V* ☻ *No lunch.*

$ **Kampen Bistro.** On the first floor of the community house in this traditionally working-class area, Kampen Bistro offers simple but tasty Mediterranean-inspired dishes in a relaxed setting. The friendly staff, reasonable prices, and slightly corny interior have made this neighborhood café a hit with locals. Menus change daily, but the three-course special is always a feast. ✉ *Bøgata 21, Kampen* ☎ *22/19–77–08* ▭ *MC, V.*

Frogner & Majorstuen

$$$$ ✕ **Bagatelle.** Chef and owner Eyvind Hellstrøm's has established an international reputation for his modern Norwegian cuisine and superb service. Bagatelle attracts the who's who of Oslo society, and is widely recognized as one of the city's best restaurants. Paintings by contemporary Norwegian artists accent the understated, elegant dining room. The three-, five-, and seven-course menus change daily. The lobster is always a standout. ✉ *Bygdøy Allé 3, Frogner* ☎ *22/44–63–97* ▭ *AE, DC, MC, V* ☻ *Closed Sun., mid-July–mid-Aug. No lunch.*

Fodor'sChoice ★

$$$$ ✕ **Restaurant Le Canard.** Behind the Royal Castle, this elegant restaurant is in what looks like a brick manor house. Inside are such antique furnishings as a stained-glass window by Maria Vigeland, the wife of Emanuel. Chef Trond Andresen shows off his simple, French-inspired compositions in a menu that changes weekly. The wine cellar of 30,000 bottles includes rare champagne from 1928. In summer you can dine in special style on Le Canard's stunning garden terrace. ✉ *Pres. Harbitz gt. 4, Frogner* ☎ *22/54–34–00* ⌨ *Reservations essential* ▭ *AE, DC, MC, V* ☻ *Closed Sun. No lunch.*

$$$–$$$$
Fodor'sChoice
★
✕ **Bølgen & Moi Briskeby.** Restaurateurs Toralf Bølgen and Trond Moi have a winner in this minimalistic restaurant. If you're tired of eating breakfast in your hotel, rise and shine here instead. Housed in a redesigned industrial building, the restaurant incorporates the past with an eye-catching, long cement dining table. Well-known Norwegian artists such as photographer Knut Bry showcase their work in the restaurant's bar, brasserie, and formal dining room. Try the oversized Thorenfeldt burger, or the three-course set menu, which changes daily. Most dishes are cooked in the wood-burning oven in the corner. ⊠ *Løvenskioldsgt. 26, Frogner* ☎ *24/11–53–53* ▤ *AE, DC, MC, V* ☉ *Closed Sun. and Mon.*

$$$–$$$$
✕ **Feinschmecker.** The name is German, but the food is international and Scandinavian. Modern and stylish, the dining room's warm, earthy tones give it a cozy look. Owners Lars Erik Underthun, one of Oslo's foremost chefs, and Bengt Wilson, a leading food stylist, make sure the food looks as good as it tastes. Feinschmecker is a haven for vegetarians, with a three-course menu that changes according to season. ⊠ *Balchensgt. 5, Frogner* ☎ *22/44–17–77* ⌔ *Reservations essential* ▤ *AE, DC, MC, V* ☉ *Closed Sun. and last 3 wks of July. No lunch.*

$$$–$$$$
Fodor'sChoice
★
✕ **Magma.** Vibrant, warm, and intense, the orange- and yellow-splashed interior captures the character of this Mediterranean restaurant–bar and its celebrity chef, Sonja Lee. Fresh from successes in London and Provence, Lee and partner Laurent Surville (also a chef) opened Magma in April 2000. It has become one of the city's hottest restaurants, attracting everyone from businesspeople to artists. The changing menu is based on seasonal ingredients and follows the owners' philosophy of rough-hewn simplicity. Consider the ricotta ravioli and the spit-roasted veal with macaroni gratin. ⊠ *Bygdøy Allé 53, Frogner* ☎ *23/08–58–10* ▤ *AE, DC, MC, V.*

$$–$$$
✕ **Palace Grill & Palace Reserva.** A tiny, eight-table restaurant near the Royal Palace, the Palace Grill is one of the most fashionable spots on the Oslo dining scene. Don't let the "grill" part fool you: it may be relaxed, but its French-inspired cuisine is certainly not fast food. The original Palace Grill doesn't take reservations and is usually full, so try to get here before 5 PM for a table. Alternatively, reserve a table at its new sister restaurant, the more spacious and slightly less expensive Palace Reserva. ⊠ *Solligt. 2, off Drammensvn., Frogner* ☎ *23/13–11–40* ▤ *AE, DC, MC, V* ☉ *Closed Sun.*

★ $$
✕ **Hos Thea.** An intimate yet lively dining experience awaits in this white-and-blue restaurant with a fleur-de-lis motif. From the open kitchen, owner Sergio Barcilon and the other chefs often serve the French and Spanish food themselves. The small menu lists four or five choices for each course, but every dish is superbly prepared. Noise and smoke levels can be high late at night. ⊠ *Gabelsgt. 11, entrance on Drammensvn., Skillebekk* ☎ *22/44–68–74* ⌔ *Reservations essential* ▤ *AE, DC, MC, V* ☉ *No lunch.*

★ $$
✕ **Kastanjen.** This rustic, laid-back Frogner bistro, named after the chestnut trees that line the street, is the kind every neighborhood needs. Try the aged sirloin with baked shallots, or the skate wings with fennel, from the all-French menu. The warmly lit downstairs lounge serves drinks and light snacks. ⊠ *Bygdøy Allé 18, Frogner* ☎ *22/43–44–67* ▤ *AE, DC, MC, V* ☉ *Closed Sun. and July.*

$
Bambus. Vietnamese owner Heidi NGuyen and her friendly staff have all lived and cooked throughout Asia, and "Bamboo" reflects this: the menu has delicious and authentic Thai, Japanese, Vietnamese, and Chinese dishes. The Banh Tom Ho Tay (Vietnamese shrimp and sweet-potato pancakes) and Kaeng Phets (Thai duck, shrimp or lamb in coconut milk and vegetables) are both good. The yellow, orange, and pink in-

terior has a bamboo floor and Andy Warhol–type prints on an Asian theme. ⊠ *Kirkevn. 57, Majorstuen* ☎ *22/85–07–00* ▤ *AE, DC, MC, V* ☉ *No lunch.*

$	**Village Tandoori.** Walking through this restaurant feels like a nighttime wander through an Indian or Pakistani village, about a hundred years ago. Pakistani owner Mobashar Hussain has collected antique rugs, including vibrant silk ones with embroidery and beadwork. The chicken and lamb curries and tandooris are delicious. ⊠ *Bygdøy Allé 65, Frogner* ☎ *22/56–10–25* ▤ *AE, DC, MC, V* ☉ *No lunch.*

¢–$	**Curry & Ketchup.** Just down the road from the elegant, pan-Asian Bambus, this popular, boisterous Indian restaurant is cozy and homely, with tiny tables that seem almost stacked on top of each other, and plates, glasses and cutlery that rarely match. The menu holds few surprises, but the basic north-Indian fare, from *rogan josh* (Kashmiri lamb curry) to *palak paneer* (spinach-and-cheese curry), comes in generous portions, and is reasonably priced. That's probably why the clientele is generally more cheerful than the notoriously grumpy but efficient staff. ⊠ *Kirkevn. 51, Majorstuen* ☎ *22/69–05–22* ▤ *MC, V.*

¢–$	**Pizza da Mimmo.** Named for owner Domenico Giardina, a.k.a. Mimmo,
Fodor'sChoice	this is Oslo's best pizzeria. In 1993, Mimmo, who's originally from Cal-
★	abria, was the first to bring thin-crusted Italian pizza to the city. Taste his perennially popular panna and prosciutto pizza, and the Pizza Calabrigella. The restaurant is casual, and earthy colors and hanging rugs give it a cavelike appearance. ⊠ *Behrensgt. 2, Frogner* ☎ *22/44–40–20* ⌂ *Reservations essential* ▤ *AE, DC, MC, V.*

Holmenkollen

$$$$	✕ **De Fem Stuer.** Near the famous Holmenkollen ski jump, in the his-
Fodor'sChoice	toric Holmenkollen Park Hotel, this restaurant has first-rate views and
★	food. Chef Jørn Dahl's modern Norwegian dishes have strong classic roots. The fish dishes, particularly those made with salmon, cod, and wolffish, are his specialty. ⊠ *Holmenkollen Park Hotel, Kongevn. 26, Holmenkollen* ☎ *22/92–27–34* ⌂ *Jacket and tie* ▤ *AE, DC, MC, V.*

$$	✕ **Holmenkollen Restaurant.** An old-fashioned, luxury mountain cabin café, restaurant, and banquet hall, this Oslo institution dates to 1892. The spacious café is perfect for an afternoon coffee and cake after walking or skiing. In the smaller, formal restaurant, dishes come from the hands of well-known chef Harald Osa. The menu focuses on Norwegian fish and game dishes served with innovative sauces. ⊠ *Holmenkollvn. 119, Holmenkollen* ☎ *22/13–92–00* ▤ *AE, DC, MC, V.*

$–$$	✕ **Frognerseteren.** Just above the Holmenkollen ski jump and therefore with sweeping mountain views, this is possibly Oslo's most famous restaurant. Popular with locals and travelers, it specializes in fish and game. The scrumptious apple cake is legendary, and perfect for dessert or for an afternoon treat with coffee. Take the Holmenkollbanen to the end station and then follow the signs downhill to the restaurant. ⊠ *Holmenkollvn. 200, Holmenkollen* ☎ *22/92–40–40* ▤ *DC, MC, V.*

Where to Stay

"Comfort and convenience at a cost" is a perfect characterization of Oslo hotels. Most lodgings, from the elegant Radisson SAS classics to the no-frills Rainbows, are central, just a short walk from Karl Johans Gate. Many are between the Royal Palace and Oslo S Station, with the newer ones closer to the station. For a quiet stay, choose a hotel in either Frogner or Majorstuen, elegant residential neighborhoods just minutes from downtown.

Special summer and weekend rates may save you money. Consider cutting costs by buying an Oslo Package combined with an Oslo Card in advance. Inquire at hotel chains about their discount programs. Through the Rainbow and Norlandia Hotels, you can purchase their money-saving Scan+ Hotel Pass. The pass entitles you to receive up to a 50% discount and a fifth night free at 200 of their hotels in Scandinavia.

Downtown: Royal Palace to the Parliament

★ **$$$–$$$$**
Fodor's Choice
★
Hotel Continental. An elegant turn-of-the-20th-century facade has put the Continental on Norway's historic-preservation list. Near Nationaltheatret, and close to many cafés, clubs, and movie theaters, the hotel is ideal for leisure as well as business travelers. The hotel's Theatercafeen restaurant is an Oslo landmark, and the newest addition, Lipp, a restaurant, which is also a café, bar, and nightclub, is a trendy hangout. Dagligstuen (The Sitting Room) is a popular meeting place for drinks and quiet conversation. ⊠ *Stortingsgt. 24–26, Sentrum 0161* ☎ *22/82–40–00* 🖷 *22/42–96–89* ⊕ *www.hotel-continental.no* 🛏 *159 rooms, 23 suites* ♢ *3 restaurants, in-room data ports, 2 bars* 🖃 *AE, DC, MC, V.*

★ **$$$–$$$$**
Grand Hotel. In the center of town on Karl Johans Gate, the Grand opened in 1874. Ibsen used to drink brandy at the Grand Café in the company of journalists. Munch was also a regular guest; you can see him with his contemporaries in Per Krohg's painting on the café's far wall. Norwegians book several years in advance for Constitution Day, May 17, in order to have a room overlooking the parades below. ⊠ *Karl Johans gt. 31, Sentrum 0101* ☎ *23/21–20–00* 🖷 *22/42–12–25* ⊕ *www. rica.no* 🛏 *289 rooms, 51 suites* ♢ *2 restaurants, indoor pool, health club, sauna, bar, meeting room* 🖃 *AE, DC, MC, V.*

$$–$$$
Hotel Bristol. The Bristol has a dignity and class all its own. Rooms are elegant and understated. The lounge and bar were decorated in the 1920s with an intricate Moorish theme and recall Fez more than Scandinavia. Josephine Baker performed in the piano bar in the 1920s. Today, the library and bar, with their red, burnished leather sofas, are among Oslo's places to see and be seen. ⊠ *Kristian IVs gt. 7, Sentrum 0130* ☎ *22/82–60–00* 🖷 *22/82–60–01* ⊕ *www.bristol.no* 🛏 *252 rooms, 10 suites* ♢ *3 restaurants, health club, sauna, 3 bars, nightclub, convention center* 🖃 *AE, DC, MC, V.*

$$–$$$
Radisson SAS Scandinavia Hotel. Popular with business travelers, this 1974 hotel has a winning combination of service and classic style. Simple, elegant rooms come in different designs: art deco, Italian, Asian, Continental, Scandinavian, and—predictably, for a hotel run by an airline—69 high-tech business-class rooms. The Summit 21 Bar has a stunning, panoramic view of Oslo—it's a great place for an evening cocktail. ⊠ *Holbergsgt. 30, Sentrum 0166* ☎ *23/29–30–00* 🖷 *23/29–30–01* ⊕ *www.radissonsas.com* 🛏 *488 rooms, 3 suites* ♢ *2 restaurants, pool, health club, 2 bars, business services* 🖃 *AE, DC, MC, V.*

$$
Rainbow Hotel Stefan. A home away from home, this hotel tries hard to make guests feel well looked-after. Hot drinks are served to late arrivals, and breakfast tables come with juice boxes and plastic bags for packing a lunch (request this service in advance). The top-floor lounge has magazines in English. The restaurant serves one of the best buffet lunches in town. ⊠ *Rosenkrantz gt. 1, Sentrum 0159* ☎ *23/31–55–00* 🖷 *23/31–55–55* ⊕ *www.rainbow-hotels.no* 🛏 *139 rooms* ♢ *Restaurant, lounge, library, meeting room* 🖃 *AE, DC, MC, V.*

$–$$
Norlandia Karl Johan Hotel. The late-19th-century Karl Johan Hotel, once known as the Nobel, is elegant, with stained-glass windows that line the circular staircase, bringing to mind 19th-century Paris. Every room is decorated with Norwegian antique pieces, giving the place an

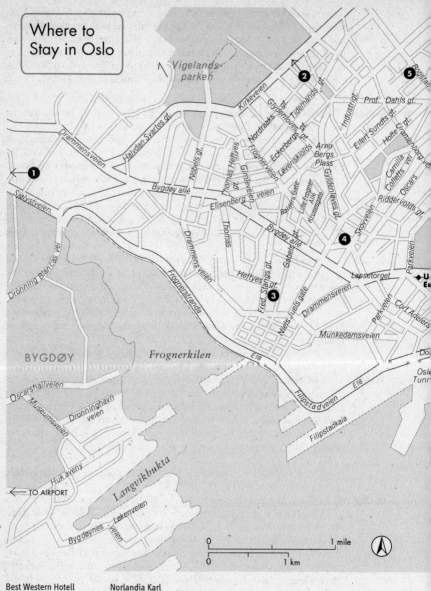

Where to Stay in Oslo

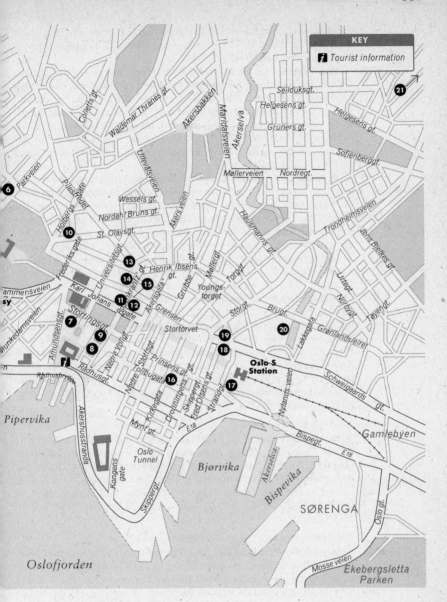

air of sophisticated luxury. ⊠ *Karl Johans gt. 33, Sentrum 0162* ☎ *23/16–17–00* 🖷 *22/42–05–19* ⊕ *www.norlandia.no* 📞 *111 rooms, 1 suite* ♨ *Restaurant, bar* ⊟ *AE, DC, MC, V.*

$–$$ 🏨 **Rica Victoria.** This modern business hotel occupies one of the city center's taller buildings, giving some top-floor rooms views of Oslo's rooftops. The rooms, built around a center atrium, are elegant and stylish: they're furnished with Biedermeier reproductions, brass lamps, and paisley fabrics in bold reds and dark blues. ⊠ *Rosenkrantz gt. 13, Sentrum 0121* ☎ *24/14–70–00* 🖷 *24/14–70–01* ⊕ *www.rica.no* 📞 *199 rooms, 5 suites* ♨ *Restaurant, bar, convention center, meeting rooms* ⊟ *AE, DC, MC, V.*

$ 🏨 **Rainbow Cecil.** A short walk from Parliament, this modern hotel is a relatively inexpensive option in the center of town. Although the rooms are basic, they are perfectly suited to the active, on-the-go traveler. The second floor opens onto a plant-filled atrium, the hotel's "activity center." In the morning it's a breakfast room, but in the afternoon it becomes a lounge, serving coffee, juice, and fresh fruit, with newspapers available in many languages. ⊠ *Stortingsgt. 8, Sentrum 0130* ☎ *23/31–48–00* 🖷 *23/31–48–50* ⊕ *www.rainbow-hotels.no* 📞 *112 rooms, 2 suites* ♨ *Lounge, no-smoking rooms* ⊟ *AE, DC, MC, V.*

FodorsChoice
★

¢–$ 🏨 **Best Western Hotell Bondeheimen.** Founded in 1913 for country folk visiting the city, Bondeheimen, which means "farmers' home," still gives discounts to members of Norwegian agricultural associations. Rooms have a minimalistic look, in dark greens and earthy reds. This is a good choice for families, but if you are looking for quiet, ask for a room in back. The Kaffistova restaurant is in the same building. ⊠ *Rosenkrantz gt. 8, entrance on Kristian IVs gt., Sentrum 0159* ☎ *23/21 41 00* 🖷 *23/21–41–01* ⊕ *www.bondeheimen.com* 📞 *127 rooms, 5 suites* ♨ *Cafeteria, shop, meeting rooms* ⊟ *AE, DC, MC, V.*

East of Downtown

¢ 🏨 **Haraldsheim.** Named for King Harald, Oslo's hilltop hostel is Europe's largest. Opened in 1954, it has maintained an old-fashioned Scandinavian style. Most of the large rooms have full bathrooms, and have four beds. Bring your own sheets or rent them here. A supermarket is close by and local public transport is easily accessible. ⊠ *Haraldsheimvn. 4, 0409* ☎ *22/22–29–65* 🖷 *22/22–10–25* 📞 *71 rooms, 40 with bath* ⊟ *MC, V.*

Frogner, Majorstuen & Holmenkollen

$$–$$$$ 🏨 **Holmenkollen Park Hotel Rica.** This distinguished hotel towers over Oslo, to the northwest of the city center. Dating to 1894, it has a peaceful mountaintop setting with unparalleled views of the city below. Guest rooms have earth tones and dark wood furniture. Next to the Holmenkollen Ski Arena, the property provides the perfect base for outdoor pursuits such as cycling, skiing, and running. It's worth a visit even if you don't stay here, perhaps to dine at De Fem Stuer, the wonderful restaurant. ⊠ *Kongevn. 26, Holmenkollen 0787* ☎ *22/92–20–00* 🖷 *22/14–61–92* ⊕ *www.rica.no* 📞 *221 rooms* ♨ *2 restaurants, pool, gym, sauna, spa, cross-country skiing, bar, convention center* ⊟ *AE, DC, MC, V.*

$–$$$ 🏨 **Gabelshus.** With only a discreet sign above the door, this ivy-cover brick house in a posh residential area is one of Oslo's most intimate hotels. The lounges are filled with antiques, some in the National Romantic style, but the rooms are plain. ⊠ *Gabelsgt. 16, Frogner 0272* ☎ *22/55–22–60* 🖷 *23/27–65–60* ⊕ *www.gabelshus.no* 📞 *43 rooms* ♨ *Lounge, meeting room* ⊟ *AE, DC, MC, V.*

$–$$ 🏨 **Frogner House.** In the heart of Oslo's West End, this charming, small hotel is popular with business travelers. The five-story redbrick and stone

structure was built in 1890 as an apartment house and now sits incon-
spicuously amid rows of other turn-of-the-20th-century town houses.
It has a reputation for quiet rooms, which are equipped with WebTVs
(with Internet and e-mail access). ⊠ *Skovvn. 8, Frogner 0257* ☎ *22/
56–00–56* 🖷 *22/56–05–00* ⊕ *www.frogner-house.com* 🛏 *60 rooms,
8 suites* ♢ *Internet, meeting room* ⊟ *AE, DC, MC, V.*

★ ¢–$ 🖼 **Rainbow Hotel Gyldenløve.** Nestled among the many shops and cafés
on Bogstadveien, this hotel is very good value for its location. Rooms
are light and airy and have stylish Scandinavian furniture. It is within
walking distance of Vigeland Park, and the trikk stops just outside the
door. ⊠ *Bogstadvn. 20, 0355* ☎ *22/60–10–90* 🖷 *22/60–33–90* ⊕ *www.
rainbow-hotels.no* 🛏 *168 rooms* ♢ *Coffee shop* ⊟ *AE, DC, MC, V.*

¢ 🖼 **Cochs pensjonat.** A stone's throw from the Royal Palace, this no-frills
guesthouse has reasonably priced, comfortable, but rather spartan
rooms. All have TVs, but there are no phones. Most of the 88 rooms
have private bathrooms, but check when you make your booking; some
also have kitchenettes. No meals are served. ⊠ *Parkvn. 25, 0350* ☎ *23/
33–24–00* 🖷 *23/33–24–10* ⊕ *www.virtualoslo.com/cochs_pensjonat/*
🛏 *88 rooms* ♢ *No room phones, no TV in some rooms* ⊟ *MC, V.*

Near Oslo Airport & Oslo S Station

★ $$–$$$$ 🖼 **Clarion Royal Christiania Hotel.** What was once bare-bones housing
for 1952 Olympians is now a luxury hotel. Although the original plain
exterior has been retained, the interior is more recent, designed using
feng shui principles. Rooms have white walls that contrast with the ma-
hogany furniture. ⊠ *Biskop Gunnerus gt. 3, 0106* ☎ *23/10–80–00*
🖷 *23/10–80–80* ⊕ *www.royalchristiania.no* 🛏 *505 rooms, 91 suites*
♢ *Restaurant, indoor pool, health club, bar, convention center* ⊟ *AE,
DC, MC, V.*

$$–$$$ 🖼 **Radisson SAS Airport Hotel.** Steps away from Oslo Airport, this is a
real beauty of a business hotel. The interiors make use of stone and metal
and have a color scheme that emphasizes burnt orange and deep pur-
ple. There are three room styles: Asian, Scandinavian, and maritime. Both
the restaurant, Toot's International Bar and Grill, and the lobby bar are
relaxing and inviting. The spacious sports center is larger than most.
There are spinning classes, a trainer on call, and massage services.
⊠ *Hotellvegen, Box 163, 2061, Gardermoen* ☎ *63/93–30–00* 🖷 *63/
93–30–30* ⊕ *www.radissonsas.com* 🛏 *350 rooms, 88 suites* ♢ *2 restau-
rants, health club, massage, sauna, bar, business services, meeting room*
⊟ *AE, DC, MC, V.*

★ $–$$$ 🖼 **Radisson SAS Plaza Hotel.** Standing out from other buildings on the
city's skyline, Northern Europe's largest hotel is the jewel of the Radis-
son SAS chain. The understated, elegant rooms have gilded fixtures and
marble, and many have spectacular views. The Panorama Bar on the
top floor, the fit-for-a-king breakfast buffets, and luxuriously grand bath-
tubs all make a stay in this 37-floor glass extravaganza particularly memorable. Since it's next to Oslo S Station, buses and other local transit
are convenient. ⊠ *Sonja Henies pl. 3, 0134* ☎ *22/05–80–00* 🖷 *22/
05–80–10* ⊕ *www.radissonsas.com* 🛏 *673 rooms, 20 suites* ♢ *2
restaurants, indoor pool, health club, bar, convention center* ⊟ *AE, DC,
MC, V.*

$–$$ 🖼 **Rainbow Hotel Opera.** Named after the opera building under con-
struction next door and scheduled to open in 2007, this is arguably Oslo's
most conveniently located hotel. It's just 100 meters from Karl Johans
gate, and a stone's throw from the Oslo S railway station. Rooms are
elegant and well-equipped, although slightly plain. Views from most of
the rooms aren't special, but the two grand suites, the gym, and the terrace bar offer sweeping views of the Oslo Fjord. ⊠ *Christian Frederiks*

plass 5, 0103 🕿 *24/10–30–00* 🖷 *24/10–30–10* ⊕ *www.rainbow-hotels. no* 🖘 *434 rooms, 2 suites* ♿ *Restaurant, gym, sauna, bar, convention center* 🖃 *AE, DC, MC, V.*

$–$$ Rica Oslo Hotel. Close to Oslo S station, this former office building calls itself an art hotel. There are paintings by Norwegian artists throughout, and many prints of works that are in the National Gallery. Rooms are painted yellow and have redwood furnishings. The Rica is popular with business travelers because it's central and has a convention center on the premises. ⊠ *Europarådetspl. 1, 0105* 🕿 *23/10–42–00* 🖷 *23/ 10–42–10* ⊕ *www.rica.no* 🖘 *174 rooms, 2 suites* ♿ *Restaurant, gym, sauna, bar, convention center* 🖃 *AE, DC, MC, V.*

¢–$ First Hotel Millennium. This boutique hotel is comfortable, with an understated, downtown chic. Guest rooms are simple, with a dark blue, green, and yellow color theme; all have bathtubs. Several rooms are geared toward women and come with a bathrobe, skin products, and women's magazines. The main-floor lounge has games, a music room, Internet access, and a library. The restaurant–bar, Primo, serves an impressive, international menu, which includes quail and swordfish. ⊠ *Tollbugt. 25, 0157* 🕿 *21/02–28–00* 🖷 *21/02–28–30* ⊕ *www.firsthotels.com* 🖘 *112 rooms with bath, 10 suites* ♿ *Restaurant, cable TV, bar, lounge* 🖃 *AE, DC, MC, V.*

Nightlife & the Arts

Nightlife

More than ever, the Oslo nightlife scene is vibrant and varied. Cafés, restaurant bars, and jazz clubs all offer a laid-back, chill atmosphere. But if you're ready to party, there are many pulsating, live-rock and dance clubs to choose from. Day or night, people are usually out on Karl Johans Gate, and many clubs and restaurants in the central area stay open until the early hours. Drinking out is very expensive, though, starting around NKr 50 for a beer or a mixed drink. Many Norwegians save money by going first to friends' houses before heading out on the town. For special nightlife listings, pick up a copy of the free monthly paper *Natt og Dag.*

BARS & LOUNGES   **Bar Boca** (⊠ Thorvald Meyers gt. 30, Grünerløkka 🕿 22/04–10–80) is a Fifties-inspired, intimate bar. It serves almost every drink under the sun. The trendiest of the postcollegiate crowd drink the night away at **Beach Club** (⊠ Aker Brygge, Sentrum 🕿 22/83–83–82), a kitschy hamburger joint with tables and booths that wouldn't look out of place in an American diner. If you're more partial to lounging than drinking, try **The Bristol,** an English-style pub (⊠ Kristian IVs gt. 7, Sentrum 🕿 22/ 82–60–00). With its 1970s theme, **Café Con Bar** (⊠ Brugt. 11, Sentrum 🕿 22/05–02–00), is another of Oslo's trendy crowd pleasers. For a change of pace, get an outdoor table at **Lorry** (⊠ Parkvn. 12, Sentrum 🕿 22/ 69–69–04), across from the Royal Palace. Filled with a cast of grizzled old artists, the place advertises 204 brews, but don't be surprised if not all of them are in stock. Serious beer drinkers may find **Oslo Mikrobryggeriet** (⊠ Bogstadvn. 6, Majorstuen 🕿 22/56–97–76) worth a stop. Eight different beers are brewed on the premises, including the increasingly popular Oslo Pils. Head to the **Tea Lounge** (⊠ Thorvald Meyers gt. 33B, Grünerløkka 🕿 22/37–07–07) for alcoholic and nonalcoholic tea drinks. It's very stylish, with mellow music, a mosaic tile bar, picture windows, and high-backed plush red sofas, and attracts a trendy crowd.

CAFÉS   As a mark of Oslo's growing cosmopolitanism, the city now has a Continental café culture, with bohemian coffee houses and chic cafés dotting the sidewalks. The Frogner neighborhood especially has lots of cafés to suit every taste; they're great for people-watching and whiling away warm summer afternoons.

Café Bacchus (✉ Dronningensgt. 27, Sentrum ☎ 22/33–34–30), in the old railroad offices by Oslo Domkirke, is tiny but serves a mean brownie. Background music is classical during the day, jazz at the night. **Clodion Art Café** (✉ Bygdøy Allé 63, Frogner ☎ 22/44–97–26) has a childlike charm that makes it popular with locals. **Glazed & Amused** (✉ Vestheimgt. 4B, Frogner ☎ 22/56–25–18) offers a twist on a normal coffee shop, since you can paint your own ceramic mug here. A cup of coffee to go takes on new meaning. For a slightly bohemian experience, head to **Fru Hagen** (✉ Thorvald Meyers gt. 40, Grünerløkka ☎ 22/35–68–71), where the walls are bright and funky and there's a picture-perfect window seat. Hip, little **Java Espresso Bar** (✉ Ullevålsvn. 45B, Bislett ☎ 22/59–46–37) has what may be the world's best cup of coffee. **Kaffebrenneriet** (✉ Storgt. 2, Sentrum) is Oslo's answer to Starbucks, with good coffee and shops throughout town.

GAY BARS For information about gay and lesbian clubs and bars in Oslo, you can read *Blikk,* the gay newsletter; check out www.gaysir.no; or call **LLH** (Landsforening for Lesbisk og Homofil Frigjøring; ☎ 22/36–19–48), the national gay and lesbian liberation association. A popular spot is **Soho** (✉ Kirkegt. 34, Sentrum ☎ 22/42–91–00), a large venue with nightclub, lounge, and bar areas, and a separate stage with live shows or DJs spinning the decks. A fixture on Oslo's gay scene since the 1970s, **London Pub** (✉ C. J. Hambros pl. 5, Sentrum ☎ 22/70–87–00) has a piano bar on the top floor and Sunday theme parties. **Potpurriet** (✉ Øvre Vollgt. 13, Sentrum ☎ 22/41–14–40) organizes well-attended women's dance nights on the last Friday of each month.

JAZZ CLUBS Norwegians take their jazz seriously. Every August, the **Oslo Jazz Festival** (✉ Tollbugt. 28, Sentrum ☎ 22/42–91–20) brings in major international artists and attracts big crowds. **Blå** (✉ Brennerivn. 9C, Grünerløkka ☎ 22/20–91–81), considered the leading club for jazz and related sounds in the Nordic countries, has a popular summer riverside patio. At **Herr Nilsen** (✉ C. J. Hambros pl. 5, Sentrum ☎ 22/33–54–05), some of Norway's most celebrated jazz artists perform in a stylish space. There's live music three nights a week and jazz on Saturday afternoon. **Stortorvets Gjæstgiveri** (✉ Grensen 1, Sentrum ☎ 23/35–63–60) often presents New Orleans–style jazz on Thursday and Saturday nights.

MUSIC CLUBS At Oslo's numerous rock clubs, the cover charges are low, the crowds young and boisterous, and the music loud. The lineup at **Rockefeller/John Dee** (✉ Torggt. 16, Sentrum ☎ 22/20–32–32) includes alternative acts, including Nick Cave. **Oslo Spektrum** (✉ Sonia Henies pl. 2, Sentrum ☎ 22/05–29–00), one of Norway's largest live-music venues, is just behind the Oslo City shopping center. Past acts have included big names such as Radiohead and Britney Spears. The popular outdoor music festival **Norwegian Wood** (☎ 67/10–34–50 ⊕ www.norwegianwood.no) is held at the Frognerbadet (Frogner Swimming Pool) in June. Begun in the early '90s, the festival hosts performers such as Iggy Pop and Bob Dylan as well as fledgling Norwegian bands.

NIGHTCLUBS Most dance clubs open late, so the beat doesn't really start until midnight. Many establishments have a minimum age for entry, which can be as high as 25. There's also usually a cover of around NKr 50. Oslo's beautiful people congregate at the elegant **Barock** (✉ Universitetsgt. 26, Sentrum ☎ 23/35–63–10). **Cosmopolite** (✉ Møllergt. 26, Sentrum ☎ 22/20–78–76) has a big dance floor and plays music from all over the world, especially Latin America. **Galleriet** (✉ Kristian IVs gt. 12, Sentrum ☎ 22/42–29–46), a hot spot in town, has a live jazz club, a disco, and a bar spread over its four art-bedecked floors. **Lipp** (✉ Olav Vs gt. 2, Sentrum ☎ 22/82–40–60) is an extremely popular restaurant, nightclub, and bar. Most of the big hotels have discos that appeal to the over-30 crowd. **Smuget** (✉ Rosenkrantz gt. 22, Sentrum ☎ 22/42–52–62) is an institution: it hosts live rock and blues bands every nightexcept Sunday, when crowds flock to the in-house discotheque.

The Arts

The monthly tourist information brochure *What's on in Oslo* lists cultural events in Norwegian, as does *Aftenposten,* Oslo's (and Norway's) leading newspaper, in its evening Oslopuls section. The Friday edition of *Dagbladet,* Oslo's daily liberal tabloid, also gives an exhaustive preview of the week's events. Tickets to virtually all performances in Norway, from classical or rock concerts to hockey games, can be purchased at any post office.

FILM   Filmgoing is a favorite pastime for many Norwegians. A number of festivals, including the Oslo Internasjonale Filmfestival, usually held in November, celebrate the medium. Films are usually subtitled in Norwegian and shown in their original language, though children's films are dubbed. Tickets cost NKr 60 or more and are discounted on some days in summer.

Near the Studenterlunden park, there is a six-screen cinema called **Saga** (✉ Stortingsgt. 28, Sentrum ☎ 82/03–00–01). Across the street from Saga, the four-screen **Klingenberg** (✉ Olav Vs gt. 4, Sentrum ☎ 82/03–00–01) plays the latest box office hits. If you like alternative or classic films and film festivals, try **Cinemateket** (✉ Dronningensgt. 16, Sentrum ☎ 22/47–45–05), the city's only independent cinema.

MUSIC   The **Oslo Philharmonic Orchestra** is one of Europe's leading ensembles. Its home, **Konserthuset** (✉ Munkedamsvn. 14, Sentrum ☎ 23/11–31–00), was built in 1977 in marble, metal, and rosewood. In summer folk dancing is performed here twice a week. **Den Norske Opera** (✉ Storgt. 23, Sentrum ☎ 23/31–50–00 information, 815/44–488 tickets) and the ballet perform at Youngstorvet. The opulent **Gamle Logen** (✉ Grev Wedels pl. 2, Sentrum ☎ 22/33–44–70), Norway's oldest concert hall, often sponsors classical music series, especially piano music.

THEATER   **Nationaltheatret** (✉ Stortingsgt. 15, Sentrum ☎ 22/00–14–00) performances are in Norwegian: bring along a copy of the play in translation, and you're all set. The biennial Ibsen Festival, during which plays by the great dramatist are performed in both Norwegian and English, takes place in the summer of even-numbered years. **Det Norske Teatret** (✉ Kristian IVs gt. 8, Sentrum ☎ 22/47–38–00) is a showcase for pieces in Nynorsk (a language compiled from rural Norwegian dialects).

Sports & the Outdoors

Oslo's natural surroundings and climate make it ideally suited to outdoor pursuits. The Oslo Fjord and its islands; the forested woodlands called the *marka*; a mild year-round temperature; and as many as 18 hours of daylight in the summer, all make the Norwegian capital an irresistable place for outdoor activities. Just 15 minutes north of the city center by tram is the **Oslomarka**, where locals ski in winter and hike in summer. The area contains 27 small *hytter* (cabins), which are often available free of charge for backpackers on foot or on skis. These can be reserved through the **Den Norske Turistforening** (✉ Storgt. 3, Sentrum ☎ 22/82–28–00), which has maps of the marka surrounding Oslo as well as equipment for rent, and other information; it also organizes events. The **Villmarkshuset** (✉ Chr. Krohgs gt. 16, Sentrum ☎ 22/05–05–22) is an equipment, activities, and excursion center specializing in hiking, climbing, hunting, fishing, cycling, and canoeing. There's also an indoor climbing wall, a pistol range, and a diving center and swimming pool. Books and maps are also availabel here. The **Oslo Archipelago** is a favorite destination for sunbathing urbanites, who hop ferries to their favorite isles.

Beaches

Beaches are scattered throughout the archipelago. Sun-loving Scandinavians pack every patch of sand during the long summer days to make up for lack of light in winter. The most popular beach is Paradisbukta at Huk (on the Bygdøy peninsula), one portion of which is for nude bathing. To get to the beach, follow signs along Huk Aveny from the Folk and Viking Ship museums. You can also take Bus 30A, marked "Bygdøy," to its final stop.

Biking

Oslo is a great biking city. One scenic ride starts at Aker Brygge and takes you along the harbor to the Bygdøy peninsula, where you can visit the museums or cut across the fields next to the royal family's summer house.

Glåmdal Cycledepot (✉ Vestbanepl. 2, Sentrum ☎ 22/83–52–08), a few doors down from the Norway Information Center, rents bikes and equipment, including helmets. The store also offers five different sight-seeing tours and has maps of the area for those braving it on their own. If you feel like roughing the terrain of the Holmenkollen marka, you can rent mountain bikes from **Tomm Murstad** (✉ Tryvannsvn. 2, Holmenkollen ☎ 22/13–95–00) in summer. Take T-bane 1 to Frogner-seteren and get off at the Voksenkollen station. **Syklistenes Landsforening** (National Organization of Cyclists; ✉ Stortingsgt. 23C, Sentrum ☎ 22/41–50–80) sells books and maps for cycling holidays in Norway and abroad and gives friendly, free advice.

Fishing

A national fishing license and a local fee are required to fish in the Oslo Fjord and the surrounding lakes. For information on fishing areas and on where to buy a license, contact **Oslomarkas Fiskeadministrasjon** (✉ Kongevn. 5, Holmenkollen ☎ 22/49–90–04). You can also fish throughout the Nordmarka woods area in a canoe rented from **Tomm Murstad** (✉ Tryvannsvn. 2, Holmenkollen ☎ 22/13–95–00). Ice fishing is popular in winter, but finding an ice drill could prove difficult—you may want to bring one from home.

Golf

More and more Norwegians are taking up golf. Oslo's international-level golf course, **Oslo Golfklubb** (✉ Bogstad, 0740 Oslo 7 ☎ 22/51–05–60) is private and heavily booked. However, it admits members of other golf clubs weekdays before 2 and weekends after 2 if space is available. Visitors must have a handicap certificate of 20 or lower for men, 28 or lower for women. Fees range from NKr 250 to NKr 500.

Health Clubs

If you need a fitness fix, whether aerobics, weight training, spinning, or climbing, try one of the health clubs that use the "klippekort" system. In this method, you pay a charge that entitles you to a certain number of workout sessions, which are marked as "klips" on your card. **Friskis & Svettis** (✉ Munkesdamsvn. 19, Sentrum ☎ 22/83–94–40) offers free aerobics classes on the green of Frogner Park from mid-May to mid-August. Class types and times vary, so call for the summer schedule. **SATS** (✉ Filipstadbrygge 2, Sentrum ☎ 22/04–80–80) has some of the better equipped and more attractive clubs around the city and throughout Norway.

Hiking & Running

Head for the woods surrounding Oslo, the marka, for jogging or walking; there's an abundance of trails, and many are lit. Frogner Park has many paths, and you can jog or hike along the Aker River, but take extra care late at night or early in the morning. Or you can take the Sognsvann trikk to the end of the line and walk or jog along Sognsvann lake.

Grete Waitz and Ingrid Kristiansen put Norway on marathon runners' maps two decades ago. Every May, a women's minimarathon is held in Grete Waitz's name; hundreds of women flock to Oslo to enjoy a nice day—and usually night—out. In September, the Oslo Marathon attracts runners from around the world. **Norges Friidretts Forbund** (✉ Sognsvn. 75, 0855 Oslo ☎ 21/02–90–00) has information about local clubs and competitions.

Sailing

Spend a sunny summer afternoon at Oslo's harbor, Aker Brygge, admiring the docked boats; or venture out into the fjords on a charter or tour. Sky-high masts and billowing white sails give the **Christian Radich** (☎ 22/47–82–70) a majestic, old-fashioned style. This tall ship makes nine different sailing trips, varying from a three-day voyage to an autumn sail across the Atlantic. Although you aren't required to have prior sailing experience, do expect rough seas, high waves, lots of rain, and being asked to participate in crew-members' tasks.

Skiing

Cross-country, downhill, telemarking, and snowboarding—whatever your snow-sport pleasure, Oslo has miles of easily accessible outdoor areas minutes from the center of town. Nine alpine ski areas have activities until late at night. More than 2,600 km (1,600 mi) of prepared cross-country ski trails run deep into the forest, of which 90 km (50 mi) are lit for special evening tours.

The **Skiforeningen** (✉ Kongevn. 5, 0787 Oslo ☎ 22/92–32–00) provides national snow-condition reports and can give tips on cross-country trails. They also offer cross-country classes for young children (3- to 7-year-olds), downhill classes for older children (7- to 12-year-olds), and both kinds of classes, as well as instruction in telemark-style racing and snowboarding techniques, for adults.

Among the **floodlit trails in the Oslomarka** are the **Bogstad** (3½ km [2 mi]), marked for the disabled and blind; the **Lillomarka** (25 km [15½ mi]); and the **Østmarka** (33 km [20½ mi]).

The downhill skiing season usually lasts from mid-December to March. There are 15 city slopes, or you can take organized trips to several outside slopes, including **Norefjell** (☎ 32/15–01–00), 100 km (66 mi) north of the city.

You can rent downhill and cross-country skis from **Tomm Murstad Skiservice** (✉ Tryvannsvn. 2, Holmenkollen ☎ 22/13–95–00) at the Tryvann T-bane station. This is a good starting point for skiing; although there are few downhill slopes in this area, a plethora of cross-country trails exist for every level of skill.

Swimming

If you don't want to head to the beach, there are several public swimming pools in the city. All pools cost NKr 40 but are free with the Oslo

Card. **Besserudtjernet** (⊠ Holmenkollen) is a small, summer lake at the foot of the Holmenkollen ski jump. The south-facing terraces are ideal for sunbathing. Swimming here is a novelty, with fantastic views of Oslo spread out before you. Lifeguards aren't posted, so swim here at your own risk. **Tøyenbadet** (Tøyen Swimming Pool; ⊠ Helgesensgt. 90, Tøyen ☎ 23/30–44–70) is next to the Munch Museum and Botanical Gardens. The facilities include one indoor and three outdoor swimming pools for all ages, a sauna, a solarium, a water slide, and an exercise area. **Frogner-badet** (Frogner Swimming Pool; ⊠ Vigeland Park, Majorstuen ☎ 23/27–54–50) has four large outdoor swimming pools for all ages and a water slide. The pools are open from mid-May through late August, depending on the weather (weekdays 7 AM–7:30 PM, weekends 10–5:30). In June, you can hear performances from the nearby Norwegian Wood music festival.

Tennis

There are several tennis clubs throughout the city to consider for a game, set, or match. **Frognerpark** has municipal tennis courts, open in the summer. **Holmenkollen Tennisklubb** (⊠ Bjørnvn. 74, Holmenkollen ☎ 22/13–60–00) has 11 outdoor courts, a minicourt, and four winter courts inside bubbles that protect them from the elements. **Oslo Tennisklubb** (⊠ Hyllvn. 5, Frogner ☎ 22/55–69–81) is the biggest outdoor tennis club in Norway. It has 10 clay courts, two hard courts, and four indoor courts for winter play. Near Vigelandspark, the easily accessible club has a casual dress code, rents racquets, and charges roughly NKr 150 per hour for court time.

Shopping

Oslo is the best place in the country for buying anything Norwegian. Popular Norwegian souvenirs and specialties include knitware, boxes with rosemaling, trolls, wooden spoons, gold and silver jewelry, smoked salmon, and caviar. Established Norwegian brands include Porsgrund porcelain, Hadeland and Magnor glass, David Andersen jewelry, and Husfliden handicrafts. You may also want to look for popular, classical, or folk music CDs; English translations of Norwegian books; or clothing by a Norwegian designer.

Prices are generally much higher than in other European countries. Prices of handmade articles, such as knitwear, are controlled, making comparison shopping useless. Otherwise, shops have both sales and specials—look for the words *salg* and *tilbud*. In addition, if you are a resident of a country other than Norway, Sweden, Finland, or Denmark, you can have the Norwegian Value Added Tax (moms) refunded at the airport when you leave the country. When you make a purchase, you must clearly state your country of residence in order to have the necessary export document filled in by store staff.

Department Stores

GlasMagasinet (⊠Stortorvet 8, Sentrum ☎22/90–89–00) is more accurately an amalgam of shops under one roof rather than a true department store. Traditionally, families visit GlasMagasinet at Christmastime, so the store is usually open on Sunday in December. **Steen & Strøm** (⊠ Kongensgt. 23, Sentrum ☎ 22/00–40–01), one of Oslo's first department stores, sells the usual: cosmetics, clothing, books, and accessories. It also has a well-stocked floor of accoutrements for outdoor activities.

Shopping Centers

Aker Brygge, Norway's first major shopping center, is right on the water across from the Tourist Information Center at Vestbanen. Shops are open until 8 most days, and some open on Sunday. **Oslo City** (⊠ Stenersgt. 1, Sentrum ☎ 81/54–40–33), at the other end of downtown, with access to the street from Oslo S Station, is the city's largest indoor mall, but the shops are run-of-the-mill, and the restaurants mostly serve fast food. The elegant **Paleet** (⊠ Karl Johans gt. 39–41, between Universitetsgt. and Rosenkrantz gt., Sentrum ☎ 22/03–38–88) opens up into a grand, marbled atrium and has many clothing, accessories, and food stores, including a basement food court.

Shopping Neighborhoods

Basarhallene, the arcade behind the cathedral, is worth a browse for glass and crystal and handicrafts made in Norway. From the city center, you can wander up the tree-lined Bygdøy Allé and browse the fashionable **Frogner** area, which is brimming with modern and antique furniture stores, interior design shops, food shops, art galleries, haute couture, and Oslo's beautiful people. The streets downtown around **Karl Johans Gate,** draw many of Oslo's shoppers. The concentration of department stores is especially high in this part of town. **Majorstuen** starts at the T-bane station with the same name and proceeds down Bogstadveien to the Royal Palace. There's a flower market on Stortorget in front of the Oslo Cathedral, and a fruit and vegetable market at Youngstorget. Every Saturday, a flea market is open at Vestkanttorget near Frognerpark. Throughout spring and summer, many local schools arrange fund-raising flea markets.

Specialty Stores

ANTIQUES Norwegian rustic antiques (those objects considered of high artistic and historic value) cannot be taken out of the country, but just about anything else can with no problem. The Frogner district has many antiques shops, especially on Skovveien and Thomas Heftyes Gate between Bygdøy Allé and Frogner Plass. Deeper in the heart of Majorstuen, Industrigate is famous for its good selection of shops. **Blomqvist Kunsthandel** (⊠ Tordenskiolds gt. 5, Sentrum ☎ 22/70–87–70) has a good selection of small items and paintings, with auctions six times a year. The rare volumes at **Damms Antiqvariat** (⊠ Tollbugt. 25, Sentrum ☎ 22/41–04–02) will catch the eye of any antiquarian book buff, with volumes in English as well as Norwegian. **Esaias Solberg** (⊠ Kirkeristen, Sentrum ☎ 22/86–24–80), behind Oslo Cathedral, has exceptional small antiques. **Kaare Berntsen** (⊠ Universitetsgt. 12, Sentrum ☎ 22/20–34–29) sells paintings, furniture, and small antique items. **Marsjandisen** (⊠ Fridtjof Nansens plass 2, Sentrum ☎ 22/42–71–68), specializes in Hadeland glass, silver, cups, and mugs. **West Sølv og Mynt** (⊠ Niels Juels gt. 27, Frogner ☎ 22/55–75–83) has the largest selection of antique silver in town.

ART GALLERIES **Kunstnernes Hus** (The Artists' House; ⊠ Wergelandsvn. 17, Sentrum ☎ 22/85–34–10 ☐ 22/85–34–11 ⊕ www.kunstnerneshus.no) exhibits contemporary art, and hosts an art show every fall.

BOOKS In Oslo bookshops, you can always find some English language books. You may want to pick up some classic works by Henrik Ibsen and Knut Hamsun in translation, as well as some by contemporary writers such as Jostein Gaarder, Linn Ullmann, and Nikolaj Frobenius.

ARK Qvist (⊠ Drammensvn. 16, Sentrum ☎ 22/54–26–00), considered Oslo's "English bookshop," specializes in fiction, crime, and Norwegian–Scandinavian translations. **Avalon** (⊠ Paleet, Karl Johans gt. 39–41, Sentrum ☎ 22/41–43–36) has Norway's largest selection of science fiction and fantasy (all in English) as well as board, computer, and card games and comics. **Bjørn Ringstrøms Antikvariat** (⊠ Ullevålsvn. 1, Sentrum ☎ 22/20–78–05), across the street from the Museum of Applied Art, carries a wide selection of used books and records.

Bokkilden Interbok (✉ Akersgt. 34, Sentrum ☎ 23/31–77–00) stocks an amazing 6,000 maps as well as two walls of travel books. Head to **Nomaden** (✉ Uranienborgvn. 4, Frogner ☎ 22/56–25–30) for travel-related books and guidebooks as well as photography books and equipment. **Norli** (✉ Universitetsgt. 24, Sentrum ☎ 22/00–43–00) keeps a substantial number of Scandinavian-language fiction and travel books on hand. **Tanum** (✉ Karl Johans gt. 43, Sentrum ☎ 22/41–11–00) is strong in the arts, health and healing, and travel.

Clothing

Norway is famous for its handknit, colorful wool sweaters, and even mass-produced (machine-knit) models are of top quality. Prices are regulated and they are always lower than buying a Norwegian sweater abroad.

Stylish men's, women's, and children's fashions are available at several chains. For designer clothing, Oslo has an increasing number of exclusive boutiques carrying Norwegian and international labels. Look out for clothes designed by established Norwegian design stars such as Pia Myrvold.

KNITWEAR **Maurtua Husflid** (✉ Akershusstranda, Sentrum ☎ 22/41–31–64), on the waterfront beneath Akershus Castle, has a large selection of sweaters and blanket coats. The designer at **Oleana** (✉ Stortingsgt. 8, Sentrum ☎ 22/33–31–63), Solveig Hisdahl, takes traditional women's sweater patterns and updates them in elegant ways. **Oslo Sweater Shop** (✉ SAS Scandinavia Hotel, Tullinsgt. 5, Sentrum ☎ 22/11–29–22) is known for having one of the widest selections in the city. **Rein og Rose** (✉ Ruseløkkvn. 3, Sentrum ☎ 22/83–21–39), in the Vika shopping district, has friendly salespeople and a good selection of knitwear, yarn, and textiles. **William Schmidt** (✉ Fridtjof Nansens pl. 9, Sentrum ☎ 22/42–02–88), founded in 1853, is Oslo's oldest shop. The firm specializes in sweaters and souvenirs.

EMBROIDERY **Husfliden** (✉ Møllergt. 4, Sentrum ☎ 24/14–12–80) sells embroidery kits, including do-it-yourself bunader, the national costumes of Norway.

FASHION & **H & M** (Hennes & Mauritz; ✉ Oslo City and other locations, Sentrum
SPORTSWEAR ☎ 22/17–13–90) carries fresh, up-to-date looks at reasonable prices. **Kamikaze** (✉ Hegdehaugsvn. 24, Majorstuen ☎ 22/60–20–25) and the nearby **Kamikaze Donna** (✉ Hegdehaugsvn. 27, Majorstuen ☎ 22/59–38–45) specialize in men's and women's designer fashions, mainly from France and Italy. **Soul** (✉ Vognhallene, Karenlyst Alle 18, Skøyen ☎ 22/55–00–13) carries Norwegian and international labels from major London, Milan, and Paris fashion houses; shoes and accessories; and home products. **MA** (✉ Hegdehaugsvn. 27, Majorstuen ☎ 22/60–72–90) puts the spotlight on Norwegian designers.

Norwegian sportswear chain stores are easy to spot in the city's malls and on Karl Johans Gate, but also consider checking out some specialty shops. **Skandinavisk Høyfjellutstyr** (✉ Bogstadsvn. 1, Majorstuen ☎ 23/33–43–80) has a great selection of traditional mountain sportswear. **Peak Performance** (✉ Bogstadsvn. 13, Majorstuen ☎ 22/96–00–91) is a top choice for fashionable sportswear.

FUR **Hansson** (✉ Kirkevn. 54, Majorstuen ☎ 22/69–64–20), near Majorstuen, has an excellent selection of furs. **Studio H. Olesen** (✉ Karl Johans gt. 31, enter at Rosenkrantz gt., Sentrum ☎ 22/33–37–50) stocks exclusive furs.

FOOD Throughout Oslo, there are bakeries, delis, fishmongers, and gourmet food shops to tempt all tastes. **Åpent Bakeri** (⊠ Inkognito Terrasse 1, Frogner ☎ 22/44–94–70) bakes the city's best tasting bread for devoted locals and top restaurants. **Fjelberg Fisk og Vilt** (⊠ Bygdøy Allé 56, Frogner ☎ 22/44–60–41) has a reputation for its high-quality fish and seafood, including salmon (smoked, tartar, fresh, and cured), lobster, shrimp, and fish soup. **Hotel Havana** (⊠ Thorvald Meyers gt. 36, Grünerløkka ☎ 23/23–03–23) is a hip delicatessen with cheeses, Cuban coffee and cigars, tapas plates, and fresh fish. **Skafferiet** (⊠ Elisenbergvn. 7, Frogner ☎ 22/44–52–96), open daily from 10 to 10, is popular with sophisticated Oslo residents for its high-quality foods and fresh flowers. **Solbærtorvet** (⊠ Hammerstadsgt. 23, Majorstuen ☎ 22/60–00–63) carries a delectable selection of foods, including cheeses, oils, spices, and fresh produce.

FURNITURE Several Oslo furniture shops highlight Scandinavian and international designers. **Expo Nova Møbelgalleri** (⊠ Bygdøy Allé 58B, Frogner ☎ 22/13–13–40) is an established Oslo shop that showcases many Scandinavian designers. **Rom for Idé** (⊠ Jacob Aalls gt. 54, Majorstuen ☎ 22/59–81–17) stocks international and Norwegian designs by established and up-and-coming names. **Tannum** (⊠ Stortingsgt. 28, Sentrum ☎ 23/11–53–90) is a perfect starting point for classic and contemporary designs.

GLASS, CHINA, **Abelson** (⊠ Skovvn. 27, Frogner ☎ 22/55–55–94), behind the Royal
CERAMICS & Palace, is crammed with contemporary glassware and china. The shops
PEWTER at **Basarhallene,** behind the cathedral, sell glass and ceramics. **Gastronaut** (⊠ Bygdøy Allé 56, Frogner ☎ 22/44–60–90) sells top-quality china, cutlery, linen, and glass, as well as spices and condiments from Spain and Italy.

If there's no time to visit a glass factory outside of town, department stores are the best option: **GlasMagasinet** (⊠ Stortorvet 9, Sentrum ☎ 22/90–89–00) stocks both European and Norwegian designs. **Norway Designs** (⊠ Stortingsgt. 28, Sentrum ☎ 23/11–45–10) showcases Scandinavian art glass, kitchenware, ceramics, silver, and other household items.

HANDICRAFTS **Basarhallene,** the arcade behind the cathedral, is worth a browse for handicrafts made in Norway. **Format Kunsthandverk** (⊠ Brynjulf Bulls pl. 2, Sentrum ☎ 22/01–55–70) has beautiful, colorful pieces. **Heimen Husflid A/S** (⊠ Rosenkrantz gt. 8, enter at Christian IVs gt., Sentrum ☎ 23/21–42–00) has small souvenir items and a department dedicated to traditional Norwegian costumes. **Husfliden** (⊠ Møllergt. 4, Sentrum ☎ 22/14–12–80), one of the finest stores for handmade goods in the country, has an even larger selection than that at Heimen Husflid. You can find pewter, ceramics, knits, and Norwegian hand-made textiles, furniture, felt boots and slippers, loafers, sweaters, traditional costumes, wrought-iron accessories, Christmas ornaments, and wooden kitchen accessories.

JEWELRY Gold and precious stones are no bargain, but silver and enamel jewelry and Viking period productions can be. Some silver pieces are made with Norwegian stones, particularly pink thulite. **David-Andersen** (⊠ Karl Johans gt. 20, Sentrum ☎ 24/14–88–00) is Norway's best-known goldsmith. He makes stunning silver and gold designs. The **ExpoArte** (⊠ Drammensvn. 40, Frogner ☎ 22/55–93–90) gallery specializes in custom pieces and displays the work of avant-garde Scandinavian jewelers. **Heyerdahl** (⊠ Roald Amundsensgt. 6, Sentrum ☎ 22/41–59–18), near City Hall, is a good, dependable jeweler.

MUSIC More and more Norwegian artists are making names for themselves internationally, often crossing over to singing in English. Some of the bigger Norwegian music names include Sissel and Lene Marlin for pop music, Leif Ove Andsnes for classical music, Silje Nergaard for jazz, and Kari Bremnes for folk singing. Ask informed record store staff to recommend other Norwegian–Scandinavian artists. **Platekompaniet** (⊠ Oslo City, Sentrum ☎ 22/42–77–35) has the most reasonable prices and best overall selection of mainstream music as well as alternative rock, house, and techno. Run by one of Norway's most celebrated jazz sax players, Bodil Niska, **Barejazz** (⊠ Grensen 8, Sentrum ☎ 22/33–20–80) is a specialist store for jazz lovers. **Musikk-huset** (⊠ Karl Johans gt. 45, Sentrum ☎ 22/42–72–84) is the last store in Norway dedicated to classical music. Eccentric, eclectic **Los Lobos** (⊠ Thorvald Meyers gt. 30, Grünerløkka ☎ 22/38–24–40) carries rockabilly, surf-guitar, salsa and mambo, and blues music. They also sell vintage Hawaiian shirts and leather jackets from the '50s.

PERFUME **Gimle Parfymeri** (⊠ Bygdøy Allé 39, Frogner ☎ 22/44–61–42) is a tiny, traditional Oslo perfume institution. Hip perfumery **Gimle Speiz** (⊠ Bygdøy Allé 51B, Frogner ☎ 23/27–11–05) carries the latest in fragrances, skin care, jewelry, bags, and accessories from all over.

WATCHES Swiss watches are much cheaper in Norway than in many other countries. **Urmaker Bjerke** (⊠ Karl Johans gt. 31, Sentrum ☎ 23/01–02–10 ⊠ Prinsensgt. 21, Sentrum ☎ 22/42–60–50) has established a reputation for quality and selection. **Thune Gullsmed & Urmaker** (⊠ Rådhuspassasjen, Olav Vs gt. 6, Sentrum ☎ 22/42–99–66) has a good selection of watches by the top Swiss manuacturers.

Oslo A to Z

AIR TRAVEL TO & FROM OSLO

CARRIERS SAS Scandinavian Airlines is the main carrier, with both international and domestic flights. The main domestic carriers are Norwegian Air Shuttle, Braathens ASA, and Widerøe. Other major airlines serving Oslo Airport include British Airways, Air France, Aeroflot, Finnair, KLM, and Lufthansa.

🔃 **Aeroflot** ☎ 22/33–38-88. **Air France** ☎ 23/50–20–01. **Braathens** ☎ 815–20–000. **British Airways** ☎ 800–33–142. **Crossair** ☎ 810–00–021. **Finnair** ☎ 810–01–100. **Flyservice a/s (Air Lithuania, Avianca, China Airlines, TWA)** ☎ 24/14–87–50. **KLM Royal Dutch Airlines and Northwest Airlines** ☎ 820–02–002. **LOT Polish Airlines** ☎ 810–00–023. **Lufthansa** ☎ 23/35–54–00. **Norwegian Air Shuttle** ☎ 67/59–30–00. **Sabena** ☎ 23/16–25–68. **SAS** ☎ 815–20–400. **Swissair** ☎ 810–00–012. **Tap Air Portugal** ☎ 810–00–015. **Widerøe** ☎ 810–01–200.

AIRPORTS & TRANSFERS

Oslo Airport is 37 km (23 mi) north of the city. The spacious airport has huge windows that give excellent views of the landscape and the Nordic light. State-of-the-art weather systems have decreased the number of delayed flights, but always check with your airline regarding the status of your flight.

🔃 **Oslo Airport** ☎ 64/81–20–00, 815–50–250 flight information ⊕ www.osl.no.

AIRPORT Oslo Airport is a 50-minute car ride via the E6 from Oslo's city center.
TRANSFERS From Oslo S Station, it's a 19-minute ride by Flytoget (express train, NKr 150 one-way), with trains scheduled every 10 minutes (4:40 AM–1:16 AM).

Flybussen buses depart from Oslo Bussterminalen Galleriet every 20 minutes and reach Oslo Airport approximately 45 minutes later (NKr 100 one-way, NKr 150 round-trip; to Oslo weekdays and Sun. 7:30 AM–11:30 PM, Sat. 7:30 AM–11 PM; to Oslo Airport weekdays 6 AM–9:40 PM, Sat. 6 AM–7:40 PM, Sun. 6 AM–9:50 PM). Another bus departs from the SAS

Scandinavia Hotel. Buses also stop at the central train station, as well as at Stortinget, Nationalteatret, and near Aker Brygge on the way.

There is a taxi line at the front of the airport. By taxi the trip into town takes about 50 minutes and is extremely expensive—upward of 600 NKr—so try to catch the Flytoget. All taxi reservations should be made through the Oslo Airport Taxi no later than 20 minutes before pickup time.
🚹 **Flybussen** ☎ 81/50-01-76. **Flytoget** ☎ 815-00-777. **Oslo Airport Taxi** ☎ 23/23-23-23, dial 1 for direct reservation.

BOAT & FERRY TRAVEL
Several ferry lines connect Oslo with the United Kingdom, Denmark, Sweden, and Germany. Color Line sails to Kiel, Germany, and to Hirtshals, Denmark; DFDS Scandinavian Seaways to Copenhagen via Helsingborg, Sweden; and Stena Line to Frederikshavn, Denmark.

A ferry to Hovedøya and other islands in the harbor basin leaves from Aker Brygge (take Bus 60 from Jernbanetorget). These are great spots for picnics and short hikes. From April through September, ferries run between Rådhusbrygge 3, in front of City Hall, and Bygdøy, the western peninsula, where many of Oslo's major museums are located. There is also ferry service from Aker Brygge to the town of Nesodden, as well as to popular summer beach towns along the fjord's coast, including Drøbak.
🚹 **Bygdøfergene Skibs A/S** ☎ 23/35-68-90. **Color Line** ☎ 810-00-811. **DFDS Scandinavian Seaways** ☎ 66/81-66-00 ⊕ www.scansea.com. **Nesodden Bunnefjord Dampskibsselskap** ☎ 22/83-30-70. **Stena Line** ☎ 23/17-91-00.

BUS TRAVEL TO & FROM OSLO
The main bus station, Oslo Bussterminalen, is across from the Oslo S Station. You can buy local bus tickets at the terminal or on the bus. Tickets for long-distance routes on Nor-Way Bussekspress can be purchased here or at travel agencies. Trafikanten provides transit information.
🚹 **Nor-Way Bussekspress** ⊠ Oslo Bussterminalen Galleriet, Sentrum ☎ 815/44-444 🖨 22/17-59-22 ⊕ www.nor-way.no. **Oslo Bussterminalen** ☎ 23/00-24-00. **Trafikanten** ☎ 815-00-176 or 177 within Oslo ⊕ www.trafikanten.no.

BUS TRAVEL WITHIN OSLO
About 50 bus lines, including 16 night buses on weekends, serve the city. Most stop at Jernbanetorget opposite Oslo S Station. Tickets can be purchased from the driver.

CAR RENTAL
🚹 Major Agencies in Oslo **Avis** ☎ 64/81-06-60 at Oslo Airport, 815-69-044 downtown. **Hertz** ☎ 64/81-05-50 at Oslo Airport, 22/21-00-00 downtown. **Sixt** ⊠ Oslo Airport ☎ 64/81-05-80.

CAR TRAVEL
The E18 connects Oslo with Göteborg, Sweden (by ferry between Sandefjord and Strömstad, Sweden); Copenhagen, Denmark (by ferry between Kristiansand and Hirtshals, Denmark); and Stockholm directly overland. The land route from Oslo to Göteborg is the E6. All streets and roads leading into Oslo have toll booths a certain distance from the city center, forming an "electronic ring." The toll is NKr 15 and was implemented to finance road development in and around Oslo. If you have the correct amount in change, drive through one of the lanes marked "Mynt." If you don't, or if you need a receipt, use the "Manuell" lane. Car rentals can be made directly at Oslo Airport or downtown.

If you plan to do any amount of driving in Oslo, buy a copy of the *Stor Oslo* map, available at bookstores and gasoline stations. It may be a small city, but one-way streets and few exit ramps on the expressway make it very easy to get lost.

EMERGENCY SERVICES **NAF Car Rescue** (Norwegian Automobile Association) ☎ 810-00-505. **Falken** ☎ 02222.

PARKING Oslo Card holders can park for free in city-run street spots or at reduced rates in lots run by the city (P-lots), but pay careful attention to time limits and be sure to ask at the information office exactly where the card is valid. Parking is very difficult in the city—many spaces have one-hour limits and can cost over NKr 25 per hour. Instead of individual parking meters in P-lots, a machine dispenses validated parking tickets to display in your car windshield. Travelers with disabilities with valid parking permits from their home country are allowed to park free and with no time limit in specially reserved spaces.

EMBASSIES & CONSULATES

Australia ✉ Jerbanetorget 2, Sentrum ☎ 22/47-91-70.

Canada ✉ Wergelandsvn. 7, Sentrum ☎ 22/99-53-00.

New Zealand ✉ Billengstadsletta 19, Billingstad ☎ 66/77-53-30.

United Kingdom ✉ Thomas Heftyes gt. 8, Frogner ☎ 23/13-27-00 ⊕ www. britain.no.

United States ✉ Drammensvn. 18, Sentrum ☎ 22/44-85-50 ⊕ www.usa.no.

EMERGENCIES

Norway's largest private clinic, Volvat Medisinske Senter, is near the Borgen and Majorstuen Norway's largest private clinic, Volvat Medisinske Senter, is near the Borgen and Majorstuen T-bane stations, not far from Frogner Park. It is open weekdays from 8 AM to 10 PM, weekends from 10 to 10. Oslo Akutten is an emergency clinic downtown, near Stortinget. Centrum Legesenter is a small, friendly clinic across from City Hall.

For dental emergencies, Oslo Kommunale Tannlegevakt at Tøyen Senter is open evenings and weekends. Oslo Private Tannlegevakt, near the American Embassy, is a private dental clinic open seven days a week.

Oslo Kommunale Legevakt, the city's public and thus less expensive, but slower, hospital, is near the Oslo S Station and is open 24 hours. Volvat Medisinske Senter operates an emergency clinic from 8 AM to 10 PM weekdays and 10 to 10 on weekends. Jernbanetorgets Apotek, across from Oslo S Station, is open 24 hours. Sfinxen Apotek, near Frogner Park, is open weekdays from 8:30 AM to 9 PM, Saturday from 8:30 AM to 8 PM, and Sunday from 5 PM to 8 PM.

Doctors & Dentists Oslo Akutten ✉ Nedre Vollgt. 8, Sentrum ☎ 22/00-81-60. **Oslo Kommunale Tannlegevakt** ✉ Kolstadgt. 18, Tøyen ☎ 22/67-30-00. **Oslo Private Tannlegevakt** ✉ Hansteensgt. 3, Frogner ☎ 815-00-345. **Volvat Medisinske Senter** ✉ Borgenvn. 2A, Majorstuen ☎ 22/95-75-00.

Emergency Services Ambulance ☎ 113. **Fire** ☎ 110. **Police** ☎ 112.

Hospitals Centrum Legesenter ✉ Fritjof Nansens pl., Sentrum ☎ 22/41-41-20. **Oslo Kommunale Legevakt** ✉ Storgt. 40, Sentrum ☎ 22/93-22-93.

Late-Night Pharmacies Jernbanetorgets Apotek ✉ Jernbanetorget 4B, Sentrum ☎ 22/41-24-82. **Sfinxen Apotek** ✉ Bogstadvn. 51, Majorstuen ☎ 22/46-34-44.

Lost & Found Police ☎ 22/66-98-65. **NSB (Norwegian State Railway)** ✉ Oslo S Station, Sentrum ☎ 23/15-40-47. **Oslo Sporveier (trams, buses, subway)** ☎ 22/08-53-61.

INTERNET SERVICE

Coffee & Juice Internett Cafe ✉ Nedre Slottsgt. 12, Sentrum ☎ 22/41-21-90. **Studenten Nett-Café** ✉ Karl Johans gt. 45, Sentrum ☎ 22/42-56-80.

LAUNDRY

Self-service laundry facilities are available in several Oslo neighborhoods. ▮ **A-Vask Selvbetjening** ⊠ Thorvald Meyers gt. 18, Grünerløkka ☎ 22/37-57-70 ⊙ 10-8. **Majorstua Myntvaskeri** ⊠ Vibesgt. 15, Majorstuen ☎ 22/69-43-17 ⊙ Weekdays 8-8, weekends 8-5.

LODGING

The tourist office at Oslo S Station (⇨ Visitor Information) can book you in anything from a luxury hotel to a room in a private home for a fee of NKr 45. Usually there are last-minute discount rooms.

If you want to rent an apartment, contact Oslo Apartments. Most of their 80 properties are reasonably close to downtown Oslo, but there are also a few in Bærum, 15 minutes away. There are also some in Skøyen, a grassy suburban area that's closer to both the airport and city center. All are within a 10-minute walk from public transport. ▮ **Oslo Apartments** ⊠ St. Edmundsv. 37, Skøyen ☎ 22/51-02-50 ⊠ 22/51-02-59 ⊙ Weekdays 8:15 AM-11 PM.

MONEY MATTERS

CURRENCY EXCHANGE Foreign currencies can be exchanged at a variety of places throughout the city. At most post offices, hours are limited to weekdays from 8 to 5 and Saturday from 9 to 1. The Tourist Information Center at Vestbanen (⇨ Visitor Information) also exchanges currency.

At most banks, the hours are weekdays from 8:15 to 3, with many open until 5 on Thursday. The express Flytoget terminal at Oslo S has automatic currency exchange machines available 24 hours. The K Bank Bureau de Change at Oslo S station is open weekdays from 7 to 7, weekends 8 to 5. At Oslo Airport, there are 16 automatic currency machines as well as a Bureau de Change in the Departure and the Arrival Halls. ▮ **American Express** ⊠ Fr. Nansens pl. 6, Sentrum ☎ 22/98-37-35. **Oslo Central Post Office** ⊠ Dronningensgt. 15, Sentrum ☎ 23/14-90-00.

SUBWAY TRAVEL

Oslo has seven T-bane (subway) lines, which converge at Stortinget station. The four eastern lines all stop at Tøyen before branching off, whereas the four western lines run through Majorstuen before emerging aboveground for the rest of their routes to the northwestern suburbs. Tickets can be purchased at the stations. ▮ **Trafikanten** (public transportation information) ⊠ Jerbanetorget, Sentrum ☎ 815-00-176 or 177 within Oslo ⊙ Weekdays 7 AM-8 PM, weekends 8-6 ⊕ www.trafikanten.no.

TAXIS

Taxis are radio-dispatched from a central office, and it can take up to 30 minutes to get one during peak hours. Cabs can be ordered from 20 minutes to 24 hours in advance. (If you leave a cab waiting after you've sent for one, there is an additional fee added to your fare.) Special transport, including vans and cabs equipped for people with disabilities, can be ordered. Taxi stands are located all over town, usually near Narvesen newsstands and kiosks.

It is possible to hail a cab on the street, but cabs are not allowed to pick up passengers within 100 yards of a stand. It is not unheard of to wait for more than an hour at a taxi stand in the wee hours of the morning, after everyone has left the bars. Never take pirate taxis; all registered taxis should have their roof lights on when they're available. Rates start at NKr 30 for hailed or rank cabs, and NKr 49 for ordered taxis, depending on the time of day. ▮ **Oslo Taxi** ☎ 02323. **Norgestaxi** ☎ 08000. **Taxi 2** ☎ 02202.

TOURS

Tickets for all tours are available from either tourist office (⇨ Visitor Information). Tickets for bus tours can be purchased on the buses. All tours, except HMK's Oslo Highlights tour, operate in summer only. Starting at noon and continuing at 45-minute intervals until 10 PM, the Oslo Train, which looks like a chain of dune buggies, leaves Aker Brygge for a 30-minute ride around the town center. The train runs every day in summer. Contact a tourist center for departure times.

BOAT TOURS   Taking a boat tour in and around the Oslo fjords is a memorable way to see the capital. The Norway Yacht Charter arranges lunch or evening tours or dinner cruises for anywhere from 12 to 600 passengers. Viking Cruise offers chartered tours on sailing yachts or replica Viking ships that serve traditional viking fare. Cruise-Båtene organizes fjord excursions for all occasions on modern luxury or older restored vessels.

📍**Cruise-Båtene** ✉ Rosenkrantz gt. 22, Sentrum ☎ 22/42-36-98. **Norway Yacht Charter** ✉ Rådhusbrygge 3, Sentrum ☎ 23/35-68-90. **Viking Cruise** ✉ Skogfaret 20 b, Ullern ☎ 22/83-19-18.

BUS TOURS   HMK Sightseeing offers several bus tours in and around Oslo. Tours leave from the Norway Information Center at Vestbanen; combination boat–bus tours depart from Rådhusbrygge 3, the wharf in front of City Hall. Båtservice Sightseeing has a bus tour, five cruises, and one combination tour.

📍**Båtservice Sightseeing** ✉ Rådhusbryggen 3, Sentrum ☎ 23/35-68-90. **HMK Sightseeing** ✉ Hegdehaugsvn. 4, Majorstuen ☎ 23/15-73-00.

HELICOPTER TOURS   For a bird's-eye view of Oslo, take a helicopter tour with the Pegasus company.

📍**Pegasus Helicopter** ✉ Gardermoen Vest ☎ 64/81-92-00.

PRIVATE GUIDES   A guest agency or the Tourist Information Centre (⇨ Visitors' Information) can provide an authorized city guide. OsloTaxi also gives private car tours.

📍**Guideservice** ✉ Akershusstranda 35, Sentrum ☎ 22/42-70-20. **Oslo Guidebureau** ✉ Nedre Slottsgt. 13, Sentrum ☎ 22/42-28-18. **OsloTaxi** ☎ 02323.

SPECIAL-INTEREST TOURS   For an exhilarating experience, tour the forests surrounding Oslo (the marka) by dogsled. Both lunch and evening winter tours are available through Norske Sledehundturer. The Tourist Information Center (⇨ Visitor Information) can arrange four- to eight-hour motor safaris through the marka, and in the winter Vangen Skistue can arrange an old-fashioned sleigh ride—in summer, they switch to carriages).

📍**Norske Sledehundturer** ✉ Einar Kristen Aas, 1514 Moss ☎ 69/27-56-40 🖶 69/27-37-86. **Vangen Skistue** ✉ Laila and Jon Hamre, Fjell, 1404 Siggerud ☎ 64/86-54-81.

WALKING TOURS   Organized walking tours are available through Oslo City and Nature Walks. Authorized city guides with acting experience lead you on themed walks, including a ghost walk through the old Kvadraturen area, exploring the creepier parts of Oslo's history.

📍**Oslo City and Nature Walks** ✉ Elgefaret 70b, 1362 Hosle ☎ 41/31-87-40 ⊕ www.oslowalks.no.

TRAIN TRAVEL

Norway's state railway, NSB (Norges Statsbaner), has two train stations downtown—Oslo Sentralstasjon (Oslo S), and a station at Nationaltheatret. Long-distance domestic and international trains arrive at and leave from Oslo S Station. Suburban commuter trains use one or the other station. Commuter cars reserved for monthly passholders are marked with a large black "M" on a yellow circle. Trains marked "C," or InterCity, offer such upgraded services as breakfast and office cars—with phones and power outlets—for an added fee.

🔂 NSB Customer Service ☎ 81/50-08-88.

TRANSPORTATION AROUND OSLO

The subways and most buses and trikken start running at 5:30 AM, with the last run after midnight. On weekends, there's night service on certain routes. Trips on all public transportation within Oslo cost NKr 20, with a one-hour free transfer; tickets that cross municipal boundaries have different rates. It often pays to buy a pass or multiple-travel card, which includes transfers. A day card (*dagskort*) costs NKr 60 and a seven-day pass costs NKr 160.

A NKr 140 *flexikort*, available at Narvesen newsstands and 7-Eleven stores, tourist information offices, T-bane stations, and on some routes, is valid for eight trips by subway, bus, or trikk. The **Oslo Pass** offers unlimited travel on all public transport in greater Oslo. A one-day Oslo Pass costs NKr 190, a two-day pass NKr 280, and a three-day pass NKr 370. Children's cards cost NKr 60, NKr 80, and NKr 110 and a family pass costs NKr 395. The passes can be purchased at tourist information offices and hotels. The Oslo Pass also includes free admission to museums and sightseeing attractions; free parking in certain public spaces; a miniboat cruise; admission to public swimming pools; discounts on car, ski and skate rentals; and discounts at specified restaurants and theaters.

TRAVEL AGENCIES

The city's travel agencies cater to different markets and different age groups. Ving is a popular overall choice among Norwegians because of the package tours they offer. Bennett BTI Nordic is an international, business travel agency. Kilroy Travels Norway and STA Travel cater to the youth and university market, distributing ISIC cards for students and GO cards for people younger than 25.

🔂 Local Agent Referrals **American Express** ✉ Mariboesgt. 13, Sentrum ☎ 22/98-37-00. **Bennett BTI Nordic** ✉ Kristian Krohgs gt. 32, Sentrum ☎ 22/59-78-00. **Kilroy Travels Norway** ✉ Universitetssenteret, Blindern ☎ 02633 ✉ Nedre Slottsgt. 23, Sentrum ☎ 02633. **Scantours UK** ☎ 0207-839-2927 in London 🖷 0207-839-5891. **STA Travel** ✉ Karl Johans gt. 8, Sentrum ☎ 815-59-905. **Ving** ✉ Karl Johans gt. 18, Sentrum ☎ 08888.

VISITOR INFORMATION

🔂 In Oslo **Oslo Sentralstasjonen (Oslo S Station)** ✉ Jernbanetorget, Sentrum ☎ No phone ⏲ Daily 8 AM–11 PM. **Tourist Information Center in Oslo** ✉ Fridtjof Nansens pl. 5, Sentrum, entrance from Roald Amundsens gate ☎ 23/11-78-80 🖷 22/83-81-50 🌐 www.visitoslo.com ⏲ Weekdays 9-4.

SIDE TRIPS FROM OSLO

The lush, green, and hilly suburbs and towns northwest of Oslo are a pleasure to visit in themselves, but they also contain many historic monuments, museums, and manor houses that give you a glimpse into the region's past. Day trips to this area are easily manageable from the capital, by bus or T-bane, and are great for catching a glimpse of the countryside even if you're on a purely urban trip.

Numbers in the text correspond to numbers in the margin and on the Oslo Fjord map.

Byrud Gård

This town at the southern end of Lake Mjøsa is best known for its **Smaragdgruvene ved Minnesund** (Emerald Mines at Minnesund), the only such mines in northern Europe. Ask for a guided tour or go on a treasure hunt: in one section, emerald finders are emerald keepers. Handmade emerald and stone items are available at the gift shop. ⊠ *Rte. 33, off E6, Byrud Gård* ☎ *63/96–86–11* ⊠ *NKr 70* ⊙ *Mid-Apr.–Oct., daily 8–6.*

Gardermoen

The Military Plane Collection, **Forsvarets Flysamling Gardermoen,** at the Sør-Gardermoen Culture and Business Center at Oslo Airport, contains aircraft from the early days of flying, rare World War II planes, and Norwegian air force jets from the Cold War era. By car, take E6 in the direction of Rv 174 to Nannestad. Turn onto Road 4 and go about 3 km (1½ mi) before turning right and heading toward the airplane collection. ⊠ *Sør-Gardermoen culture and business center, Gardermoen* ☎ *63/92–86–60* ⊠ *NKr 60* ⊙ *Tues.–Sun. 11–5.*

Eidsvoll

Norway's constitution was written and passed in 1814 at **Eidsvoll,** a manor house about 80 km (50 mi) north of Oslo. May 17, National Day, commemorates that occasion. Portraits of all the members of the 1814 Norwegian parliament hang here. Trains for Eidsvoll depart from Oslo S Station. ⊠ *Carsten Ankers v.* ☎ *63/92–22–10* ⊕ *www.eidsvoll1814. museum.no* ⊠ *NKr 40* ⊙ *Mid-May–mid-Aug., daily 10–5; mid-Aug.–mid-Sept., Mon.–Sat. 10–3; mid-Sept.–mid-May, weekends noon–4.*

Skibladner, the world's oldest paddle steamer, makes a stop at Eidsvoll, as well as at Hamar, Gjøvik, Lillehammer, and elsewhere. While aboard, dine in the first class lounge on boiled salmon and fresh strawberries. Schedules for the steamer (and for the corresponding train stops) are available at Oslo S Station. ⊠ *Torggt. 1* ☎ *61/14–40–80* ⊠ *NKr 150–NKr 300* ⊙ *Sailings late June–mid-Aug., Wed., Fri., and Sun.*

Årnes

The **Gamle Hvam Museum,** inside a former manor house that dates from 1728, looks back at Norwegian country life. In the main building, learn how women lived in 1900 and how farming has changed since 1950. Take a walk outdoors and visit agriculture and handicraft exhibits, rose gardens, and beds of other flowers. To get here, take the train to Årnes. On weekdays you can also take Bus 835. ⊠ *Årnes* ☎ *63/90–96–09* ⊕ *www.gamlehvam.museum.no* ⊠ *NKr 40* ⊙ *Late May–Aug., weekdays 11–4, weekends noon–5; early Sept., Sun. noon–4.*

Bærum

One of Oslo's fashionable suburbs, Bærum is about 20 minutes from the city. The area is mostly residential, but along the banks of the Lomma River is the charming **Bærums Verk.** In the 1960s, the owners of the Bærums Verk iron foundry fixed up their old industrial town and made it into a historical site. Today, the stores, workshops, and exhibitions among the idyllic surroundings attract many visitors to its grounds. As you explore the beautifully restored village, notice the cramped wooden cottages lining **Verksgata,** where the workers once lived. Notice that the doors are in the back of the buildings; this was in case

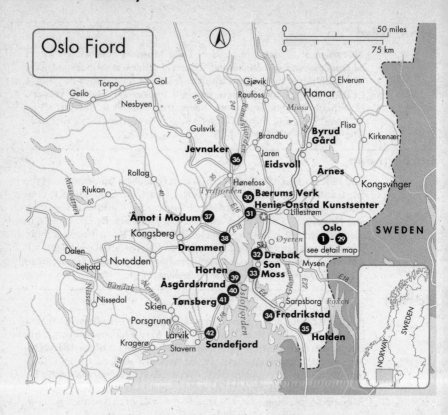

Oslo Fjord

a fire from the works spread through the main street. The Museum Bærums Verk has an extensive collection of iron ovens as well as temporary exhibitions. Take Bus 143 or 153 from Grønland or Universitetsplassen. ⊠ *Bærums Verk* ☎ *67/13–00–18* ⊕ *www.baerumsverk. no* 🖾 *Museum NKr 20* ☉ *Museum: mid-June–mid-Aug., daily noon–4; mid-Aug.–mid-June, weekends noon–4; Verksgata: weekdays 10–5, Sat. 10–4, Sun. noon–4.*

Where to Eat

$$ ✕ **Værtshuset Bærums Verk.** Norway's oldest restaurant, this spot is a must
Fodor'sChoice on any itinerary that includes the neighboring iron works. The inn
★ opened in 1640 and was a frequent stop on the King's Road road from Oslo to Bergen. It is now one of the country's finest restaurants, specializing in Norwegian cuisine. Low ceilings, pastel-painted wood floors, and shiny pewter tableware make you feel as though you've stepped into 19th-century Norway. The fresh mountain trout and the fillet of reindeer in cream sauce are particularly good. ⊠ *Vertshusvn. 10, Bærums Verk* ☎ *67/80–02–00* 🖴 *AE, DC, MC, V.*

Høvikodden

③ The **Henie-Onstad Kunstsenter** (Henie-Onstad Art Center) is just outside Oslo, about 12 km (7 mi) southwest on E18. It houses Norway's largest collection of international modern art. After skater Sonja Henie married shipping magnate Niels Onstad, they began to put together a fine collection of early-20th-century art, with important works by Munch, Picasso, Bonnard, and Matisse. Henie died in 1969, but she still skates her way through many a late-night movie. The three-time Olympic gold-medal winner was the first to realize the potential of the ice show, and her technical assistant, Frank Zamboni, achieved immortality through the worldwide use of the eponymous ice-finishing machine he developed for her. The temporary exhibitions here are often thought-provoking and memorable. Restaurateurs Toralf Bølgen and Trond Moi run the restaurant on the premises. Buses 151, 152, and 251 from Oslo S Station stop near the grounds. ⊠ *1311 Høvikodden* ☎ *67/80–48–80* ⊕ *www.henieonstad. no* ✉ *NKr 75* ⊙ *Tues.–Thurs. 11–7, Fri.–Mon. 11–6.*

EAST OF THE OSLO FJORD

The eastern side of the Oslo Fjord is summer-vacation country for many Norwegians, who retreat to cabins by the water during July. Many towns along the fjord offer history and culture as well as a place to swim. Viking ruins and inscriptions, fortified towns, and bohemian 19th-century artists' colonies provide a glimpse into the region's rich heritage.

Some of the towns mentioned can easily be visited as day trips from Oslo. Roads can be winding, though, adding to the driving time, so you might want to devote several days to exploring the area. Note that ferries shuttle cars and people back and forth between the archipelago islands and between either side of the fjord, so it is possible to combine this tour with a trip to the West of the Oslo Fjord and make a complete circle without backtracking.

Drøbak

③② *35 km (21 mi) south of Oslo.*

Mention the summer resort town of Drøbak to many Norwegians, and strangely enough, they'll start talking about Father Christmas. Although there is some question as to where the *Julenisse* (Christmas elf) came from, Norwegians claim that at least his adopted home is in Drøbak.

The inviting **Tregaardens Julehus** (Christmas House) dominates the town's central square. Just around the corner from the post office, this 1876 building was once a mission for seafarers unable to reach Oslo because the fjord was frozen over. Now it's a retail store that sells Christmas wares and gifts such as wooden dolls and mice made of cloth—all handmade by Eva Johansen, the store's creator and owner. ⊠ *1440 Drøbak* ☎ *64/93–41–78.*

> **need a break?** Back on the main square, stop in **Det Gamle Bageri Ost & Vinstue** (The Old Bakery Wine and Cheese Room; ☎ 64/93–21–05) for salads, pies, and hearty fare such as salmon in a mouthwatering sweet-mustard sauce. The timber interior is around 250 years old, and the wine list is extensive.

🐄 **Jegstad Gård farm**, a traditional Norwegian dairy, has animals to visit and horse carriages to ride. Wander along the nature trail or visit the stable, farm museum, and Viking burial mounds. You can play sports or relax on the large lawn. The farm is between Drøbak and Vestby, to the south. ⊠ *Rte. E6, Vestby* ☎ *64/95–00–58* ✉ *NKr 50* ⊙ *Apr.–Aug., Sun. noon–4; by special arrangement rest of the year.*

Shopping
Take time to stroll the downtown and browse through the charming small shops. **Nautilus** (⊠ Niels Carlsens gt. 5 ☎ 64/93–44–55) specializes in blue and maritime-theme gifts. Artists and craftspeople exhibit and sell their work at such local galleries as **Galleri Havstad** (⊠ Storgt. 15 ☎ 64/ 93–46–55).

Where to Stay

$$ ⊞ **Reenskaug Hotel.** Old-fashioned, wooden, and whitewashed, this early-20th-century hotel is on Drøbak's main road. With its traditional Norwegian country style interior, it is a very Scandinavian place to stay. Ask for Room 213; in 1904, Norway's Nobel Prize for Literature winner Knut Hamsun wrote here. ⊠ *Storgt. 32, 1440 Drøbak* ☎ *64/93–33–60* 🖷 *64/93–36–66* 📠 *27 rooms* 🍴 *Restaurant, bar, nightclub, meeting room* ☰ *AE, DC MC, V.*

Son

25 km (15 mi) south of Drøbak.

You can swim, sail, or sun on the banks of Son (pronounced *soon*), just south of Drøbak. An old fishing and boating village, this resort town has traditionally attracted artists and writers. Artists still flock here, as do city folk in summer.

In the summer season, you can count on **Klubben Soon** (☎ 64/95–70–42) for a good mix of disco, jazz, and other concerts.

Moss

③③ *10 km (6 mi) south of Son.*

Although the area has been inhabited since Viking times, Moss gained borough status in the 18th century and is one of the area's main commercial and shipping centers.

> off the beaten path

GALLERI F15 – A 5-km (3 mi) ride from Moss, on the island of Jeløy, is an art center set in an old farm. Exhibits displayed here range from photography to Scandinavian crafts. ⊠ *Alby Gård* ☎ *69/27–10–33* ☉ *June–Aug., Tues.–Sun. 11–7; Sept.–May, Tues.–Sun. 11–5.*

Where to Stay & Eat

★ $$–$$$ ⊠⊞ **Refsnes Gods.** This historic hotel has one of Norway's best kitchens and a fine wine cellar. The French–Norwegian food is especially good; the emphasis is on seafood, meat, and game dishes. Try the breast of duck, and the champagne from 1975. While dining, take a look at one of the four Munch paintings in the dining room, including *Blue Lady.* The main building dates from 1767, and used to be part of a family estate. The Victorian-style, blue-and-beige rooms are airy and pretty. ⊠ *Godset 5, 1502 Moss* ☎ *69/27–83–00* 🖷 *69/27–83–01* ⊕ *www.refsnesgods.no* 📠 *61 rooms, 4 suites* 🍴 *Restaurant, pool, gym, sauna, beach, boating, meeting room* ☰ *AE, DC, MC, V.*

Fredrikstad

③④ *34 km (20 mi) south of Moss.*

Norway's oldest fortified city lies peacefully at the mouth of the Glomma, the country's longest river. Its bastions and moat date from the 1600s. After spending time in town browsing the shops and museum, venture outside the city to Hvaler, a popular vacation spot.

Fodor'sChoice ★ **Gamlebyen** (Old Town) has been preserved and has museums, art galleries, cafés, artisans' workshops, antiques shops, and old bookstores.

The **Fredrikstad Museum** documents the town's history in two separate exhibitions. The first focuses on the town's maritime and shipping heritage and has period commercial vessels and sailing boats. The second tells the story of the development of the town and city from 1860 to

1960 through objects related to its industrial, commercial, hospital, and day-to-day life. ☎ 69/30–68–75 🖼 *NKr 40* ⊙ *June–Sept., daily noon–5.*

★ In the center of town is **Fredrikstad Domkirke** (Fredrikstad Cathedral). Built in 1860 in a flamboyant neo-Gothic style, it contains decorations by leading Norwegian artists of the time. ☎ *69/30–02–80* 🖼 *Free* ⊙ *Tues.–Fri. 11–3.*

Where to Stay

$–$$ 🏨 **Hotel City.** This comfortable, stylish hotel is in the center of downtown, but is still quiet and peaceful. The restaurant serves a mixture of Norwegian and Italian dishes. ⊠ *Nygaardsgt. 44–46, 1607 Fredrikstad* ☎ *69/38–56–00* 🖨 *69/38–56–01* 🖥 *110 rooms* ⌂ *Restaurant, sauna, dance club, nightclub, convention center, meeting rooms* 🖃 *MC, V.*

Shopping

Glashytte (⊠ Torsnesvn. 1 ☎ 69/32–28–12) is a well-known glassblowing studio and shop; its glassware is exhibited and sold in galleries throughout Norway. You can watch glassblowers perform their magic, creating everything from schnapps glasses to vases in primary colors. If you're in the area, you can place a special order and go see your glass object blown. You can pick it up a few days later after it's been cooled slowly in a kiln, which makes it less fragile.

Halden

③ *30 km (18 mi) south of Fredrikstad.*

This idyllic little town has several historical attractions well worth a visit. Since it's close to the Swedish border, it once needed fortifications in order to fend off attacks—Norwegians and Swedes had ongoing border disputes. The most famous skirmish at Fredriksten fortress resulted in the death of King Karl XII in 1718.

★ Built in the late 1600s in the shape of a star, the complex of buildings that make up the **Fredriksten Festning** (Fredriksten Fort) (☎ 69/19–09–80) are at the city's highest point. The exhibit in the former prison describes Halden war history from the 17th century to World War II. An old pharmacy in the residence illustrates the history of pharmacology with bird claws used in folk medicine. At the far end of the inner courtyard, the bakery and brewery could bake enough bread to feed 5,000 men and brew 3,000 liters of beer. The exhibition *Byen brenner* (The Burning City), documents the many fires that attacked Halden's (primarily wood) buildings. Inside the fort itself is **Fredriksten Kro**, an old-fashioned pub with outdoor seating. ☎ *69/17–52–32* 🖼 *NKr 40* ⊙ *Mid-May–Aug., daily 10–5.*

Fodor'sChoice **Rød Herregård** is one of the finest and best preserved 18th-century
★ manors in Norway. A restored building houses period furniture, artwork, and hunting trophies. The house, open only for tours, has a unique weapons collection. ⊠ *1771 Halden* ☎ *69/18–54–11* 🖼 *NKr 40* ⊙ *Sun. tours at noon, 1, and 2.*

Where to Eat

¢–$$ ✕ **Rekekafeen.** Near dockside sheds on a floating pier in the marina, Rekekafeen has a reputation for fresh fish and seafood. Taste their smoked fish and shrimp. You can also have eel, choosing yours from those swimming in a nearby tank. At a separate fish counter, fishing equipment and bait are sold, and there are changing exhibitions of local arts and crafts. On weekends, musicians perform. ⊠ *Waterfront* ☎ *69/ 18–29–06.*

East of the Oslo Fjord A to Z

BOAT & FERRY TRAVEL

A ferry links Drøbak, on the east side of the fjord, with Hurum, on the west side, just north of Horten. Contact Drøbak Turistinformasjon for schedule information.

BUS TRAVEL

Bus 541 from outside Oslo S Station to Drøbak affords great glimpses of the fjord (and its bathers). The trip takes an hour, and buses depart hourly at 10 minutes past the hour during the week, with reduced service on weekends. Bus 100 (E6 Ekspress) departs every three hours during the day, stopping at Svindsen, where you can catch a local bus to Halden. Contact Nor-Way Bussekspress for schedules.

⑦ Nor-Way Bussekspress ☎ 815/44-444 ⊕ www.nor-way.no.

CAR TRAVEL

Follow Route E18 southeast from Oslo to Route E6. Follow signs to Drøbak and Son. Continue through Moss, following signs to Halden, farther south on E6. The road then takes you north to Sarpsborg, where you can turn left to Fredrikstad.

TRAIN TRAVEL

Trains for Halden leave from Oslo S Station and take two hours to make the 136-km (85-mi) trip, with stops in Moss, Fredrikstad, and Sarpsborg.

VISITOR INFORMATION

⑦ Tourist Information Drøbak Drøbak Turistinformasjon ☎ 64/93-50-87. **Fredrikstad** Fredrikstad Turistkontor ✉ Turistsentret vøstre Brohode ✉ 1632 Gamle Fredrikstad ☎ 69/30-60-00. **Halden** Halden Turist Kontor ✉ Storgt. 6, Box 167, 1751 Halden ☎ 69/19-09-80. **Moss** Moss Turistkontor ✉ Fleischersgt. 17, 1531 Moss ☎ 69/24-15-20. **Son** Son Kystkultursenter ✉ 1555 Son ☎ 64/95-82-13.

WEST OF THE OSLO FJORD

Towns lining the western side of the fjord are more industrial on the whole than their neighbors on the eastern side. Still, the western towns have traditionally been some of Norway's oldest and wealthiest, their fortunes derived from whaling and lumbering. An increasing number of restaurants and museums have made the region more attractive to travelers.

Jevnaker

㊱ *Follow E16 toward Hønefoss, then follow Route 241 to Jevnaker, which is about 70 km (42 mi) northwest of Oslo; it's about a 2-hr drive.*

A day trip to Jevnaker combines a drive along the Tyrifjord, where you can see some of the best fjord views in eastern Norway, with a visit to Norway's oldest glassworks, in operation since 1762.

Ⓒ At **Hadeland Glassverk** you can watch artisans blowing glass, or, if you get there early enough, you can blow your own for NKr 75. Both practical table crystal and one-of-a-kind art glass are produced here, and you can buy first quality pieces as well as seconds at the gift shop. Learn the history of glass at the Glass Museum. For children, there's a Honey House of bees and a Children's House that celebrates Christmas every weekend from April through December. ✉ *Rte. 241, Postboks 85* ☎ *61/31-66-00* ⊕ *www.hadeland-glassverk.no* ✉ *Glass museum NKr 30* ☉ *Weekdays 10-5, Sat. 10-4, Sun. 11-5.*

Åmot i Modum

③⑦ *If you're coming from Jevnaker, take Route 35 south, along the Tyrifjord. If you're coming from the E18, take Route 11 west to Hokksund, and Route 35 to Åmot. Then turn onto Route 287 to Sigdal. Åmot i Modum is 70 km (42 mi) west of Oslo.*

The small village of Åmot is famous for its cobalt mines. The blue mineral was used to make dyes for glass and porcelain industries around the world.

The **Blaafarveværket** (Cobalt Works) was founded in 1773 to extract cobalt from the Modum mines. Today the complex is a museum and a national park. A permanent collection displays old cobalt-blue glass and porcelain. For children there's a petting farm, and the restaurant serves Norwegian country fare. Up the hill from the art complex is Haugfossen, the highest waterfall in eastern Norway. Also nearby are Nymoen Nr. 9, a museum of social history, as well as the Th. Kittelsen Museet, which has Norway's largest collection of the haunting, mysterious works of this artist. ⌧ *Rte. 507* ☎ *32/78–67–00* ⊕ *www.blaa.no* ⌐ *Special exhibitions NKr 50; cobalt works free. Guided tours in English* ☉ *Mid-May–mid-June, daily 10–5; mid-June–mid-Aug., daily 10–6; mid-Aug.–mid-Sept., Tues.–Sun. 10–5.*

Drammen

③⑧ *40 km (25 mi) from Oslo, 45 km (27 mi) south of Åmot i Modum.*

Drammen, a timber town and port for 500 years, is an industrial city of 55,000 on the Drammen River. Called the River City, it was the harbor for exported silver from the Kongsberg mines. These days many cars are imported into Norway here. The river divides the city into two: Bragernes (historically more prosperous) and Strømsø. Being a port and having lower costs than places like Oslo, the city has a more diverse population than other Norwegian cities its size. Around the Bragernes Torget (town square) there has been a flowering of shops, cafés, and restaurants. The Gothic Bragernes Church is at the square's head. The city's mountainous hills are ideal spots for fishing, hiking, skiing, and other outdoor activities.

The **Drammen Museum of Art and Cultural History** actually comprises several smaller museums scattered around the city. Marienlyst Manor (1750) has Nøstetangen glass and rustic folk and church art. The Art Department's permanent gallery has many great works of 19th and 20th century Norwegian masters, including Hans Heyerdahl's *The Champagne Girl*. At Spiraltoppen, the Open Air Museum chronicles 300 years of area architecture. ⌧ *Konnerudgt. 7* ☎ *32/20–09–30* ⌐ *NKr 30* ☉ *Tues.–Sat. 11–3, except Thurs. 11–8, Sun. 11–5.*

Spiralen is the name of the spiraled, more than 1¼-mi-long tunnel cut through Bragernesåsen (Bragernes Hill). **Spiraltoppen,** the area around the tunnel entrance, has a marvelous view of Drammen, the river, and the fjord. In summer, Drammens Museum runs a small, open air heritage museum here that's free of charge. Spiraltoppen is also the starting point for many downhill and cross-country skiing trails. Several footpaths make up a 2 km (1 mi) nature trail. ⌧ *Spiraltoppen* ☎ *32/20–09–30.*

Where to Stay & Eat

★ **$–$$$** ✕ **Skutebrygga.** Right on the riverbank and just off the square, this popular meeting place has miniature boats, anchors, and old maps inside, an echo of the maritime life outside its windows. Candlelight, an open fireplace, and a summer patio make this a warm, welcoming place. The seafood dishes, such as grilled monkfish in bacon and curry sauce, are delicious. ⊠ *Nedre Strandgt. 2* ☎ *32/83–33–30* ▭ *AE, DC, MC, V.*

$$ ✕ **Åspavilongen.** This hillside restaurant and bar is known for its panoramic view of the entire valley and fjord. Dating back to the turn of the 20th century, its walls are covered with historic photographs. Try the beef steak and onions on the hearty menu. ⊠ *Bragerenesåsen* ☎ *32/83–37–47* ▭ *AE, DC, MC, V* ☾ *Closed early Sept. and Nov.–Apr.*

$–$$ ▦ **Rica Park.** As with all Rica hotels, the Park is relaxed. The rooms are comfortable, light, and airy. The hotel's dining and entertainment options include a nightclub that attracts an over-30 crowd. Take a walk in the nearby woods, and then have coffee and cake at the Spiraltoppen Café, which has great views. ⊠ *Gamle Kirkepl. 3, 3019* ☎ *32/26–36–00* 🖷 *32/26–37–77* ⊕ *www.rica.no* ↩ *100 rooms, 6 suites* ♦ *2 restaurants, 2 bars, pub, dance club, nightclub* ▭ *AE, DC, MC, V.*

¢–$$ ▦ **First Hotel Ambassadeur.** One of the better places to stay in Drammen, this hotel is especially popular with business travelers who like its stylish, comfortable guest rooms. The convention center has 30 meeting rooms. It's close to both the railway station and the bus terminal. ⊠ *Strømsø Torg 7, 3044* ☎ *31/01–21–00* 🖷 *31/01–21–11* ⊕ *www.first-hotels.no* ↩ *230 rooms, 12 suites* ♦ *Restaurant, gym, sauna, 2 bars, convention center, meeting rooms* ▭ *AE, DC, MC, V.*

Nightlife

If you want to have a drink, hear live music, or go dancing, try the city's hotels, or head downtown to check out Drammen's bars, pubs, and clubs. **Rock på Union Scene** (⊠ Gronland 68 ☎ 32/83–77–88) books new bands for concerts every Friday night. The **Riggen Pub** (⊠ Amtmann Blomsgt. ☎ 32/83–67–00) has blues performances on Friday and Saturday nights. **Pavarotti** (⊠ Nedre Torggt. 9 ☎ 32/83–55–74) is known for its live jazz on Wednesday night and on Saturday starting at 3 PM.

Shopping

The city's main shopping mall, **Steen & Strom Magasinet** (⊠ Nedre Storgt. 6 ☎ 32/21–39–90) has 65 shops and restaurants.

About 8 km (5 mi) from Drammen, on Route 135 toward Hokksund, is **Buskerud Storsenter** (☎ 32/23–15–45), the region's largest shopping mall, with more than 80 shops and restaurants.

Sports & the Outdoors

Drammen is known throughout Norway for its wealth of outdoor activities, which include fishing, skiing, cycling, boating, and hiking. Four cycling trails are outlined on maps available from the Tourist office. Wherever you are, you are never more than a few minutes from footpaths, nature trails, miles of forest land, lakes, grassy hills, and scenic countryside.

BOATING **MS *Drammen* Charter and Turistbåt** (⊠ Bragernes Torg 13 ☎ 32/83–50–45) organizes river excursions, fjord tours, fishing trips, and river safaris. A boat with catering and crew is available for hire.

FISHING The fjord and the river have great fishing, particularly at Hokksund and Hellefossen. Salmon and trout are most prized; it's not uncommon to catch salmon weighing 22 to 44 pounds. Forty other fish breeds can also be caught in the river. The fishing season runs from mid-May through

September. Contact the **Drammens Sportfiskere** (☎ 32/82–09–31) for information on national and local fishing licenses as well as regulations and events.

HORSE RACING The **Drammen Racecourse** is one of 10 permanent betting courses in Norway. Tuesday is racing day, beginning at 6 PM; there are also five special Saturday races. The horses can be seen at close range, making the race that much more immediate and exciting. ✉ *Buskerudvn. 200* ☎ *32/21–87–00.*

SKIING Cross-country skiers have 100 km of trails available outside the city, including 42 km of well-maintained tracks that are lit up at night. Downhill skiers can head to Haukåsløypa on the Strømsø side or Aronsløypa on the Bragernes side.

SWIMMING Make a splash poolside at one of Drammen's indoor and outdoor swimming complexes. **Marienlystbadet** (☎ 32/83–34–05 ☉ Late June–mid-Aug.) has an Olympic-size pool, diving pool, and children's pool all heated to nearly 80° F (26° C). The complex also has a water slide, water toys, beach-volleyball courts, a sauna, and places to sunbathe. **Sentralbadet** (☎ 32/83–65–86 ☉ Mid-Aug.–May) has an indoor 25-meter swimming pool and a warm pool that's heated to 93°F (34 °C). There's also a Jacuzzi, water slide, solarium, sauna, Nautilus exercise room, and a lounge.

Horten

③ *35 km (17 mi) south of Drammen.*

Off the main route, E18, going south, the coastal village of Horten has several distinctive museums worth an afternoon's visit. The town was once an important Norwegian Royal Navy station and still retains the cadet school.

The **Marinemuseet** (Royal Norwegian Navy Museum), built in 1853 as a munitions warehouse, displays 16th- and 17th-century Danish and Norwegian naval relics. Outside is the world's first torpedo boat, from 1873, and some one-person submarines. ✉ *Karl Johans Vern* ☎ *33/03–35–46* 🎫 *Free* ☉ *May–Sept., daily noon–4; Oct.–Apr., Sun. noon–4.*

The **Norsk Museum for Fotografi: Preus Fotomuseum** (Norwegian Museum for Photography: Preus Photography Museum) houses the fascinating private collection of Leif Preus. Opened in 1994, it was later sold, and re-opened in May 2001 on the fourth and fifth floors of the huge naval warehouse. The extensive collection has between 4,500 and 5,000 cameras, including a rare 1840s camera obscura. All kinds of photographs—documentary, press, portraits, scientific, fine art—are here, including the work of August Sander and Tom Sandberg. The museum has one of the world's largest libraries of photography books. Look for the photographer's studio of a hundred years ago, as well as the tiny camera used for early aerial photographs: it was strapped to a pigeon. ✉ *Karl Johans Vern* ☎ *33/03–16–30* ⊕ *www.foto.museum.no* 🎫 *NKr 35* ☉ *June–Aug., daily noon–6; Sept.–May, Thurs. and Fri. noon–4, weekends noon–6.*

The **Horten Bil Museum** traces the development of motor vehicles from 1900 to 1970 through exhibits of 35 cars and motorcycles. Everything from the earliest autos to modern Porsches is on view. ✉ *Sollistrandvn. 12* ☎ *33/02–08–50* 🎫 *NKr 35* ☉ *Mid-June–mid-Aug., daily noon–3; mid-Aug.–mid-June, Sun. noon–3.*

Åsgårdstrand

④ *10 km (6 mi) south of Horten.*

Since 1920, the coastal town of Åsgårdstrand has been a popular vacation and bathing spot. A couple decades before that, it was known as an artists' colony for outdoor painting, attracting Edvard Munch, Fritz Thaulow, and others. The local tourist office can arrange guided historic tours of the area given by well-versed guides.

Fodor'sChoice **Munchs lille hus** (Munch's Little House) was the summer house and studio in which the artist spent seven summers. Now a museum, it was here that he painted *Girls on the Bridge* and earned a reputation as a ladies' man. ⊠ *Munchsgt.* ☎ *33/08–21–31* ⌨ *NKr 40* ◷ *May and Sept., weekends 11–7; June–Aug., Tues.–Sun. 11–7.*

Where to Stay

$$ **Åsgårdstrand Hotell.** Steps away from the harbor, the Åsgårdstrand has large, airy rooms with spectacular ocean views. Perfect for those who want to be part of the town's active sailing culture, it even has a harbor that guests can use. ⊠ *Havnengt. 6, 3167* ☎ *33/08–10–40* 🖨 *33/ 08–10–77* ⊕ *www.asgardstrand-hotell.no* ⇌ *70 rooms, 3 suites* ⚐ *Restaurant, bar* ▤ *AE, DC, MC, V.*

> **en route** Travel south from Åsgårdstrand toward Tønsberg and you'll pass **Slagen,** where the *Oseberg* Viking ship, dating from around 800, was found. (It's now on display at Vikingskiphuset in Oslo.) Look for the mound where it was buried as you pass Slagen's church.

Tønsberg

④ *11 km (6½ mi) south of Åsgårdstrand.*

According to the Sagas, Tønsberg is Norway's oldest non-Sámi settlement, founded in 871. Little remains of Tønsberg's early structures, although the ruins at **Slottsfjellet** (Castle Hill), by the train station, include parts of the city wall, the remains of a church built around 1150, and a 13th-century brick citadel, the **Tønsberghus.** Other medieval remains are below the cathedral and near Storgata 17.

North of the railroad station, the **Vestfold Fylkesmuseum** (Vestfold County Museum) houses a small Viking ship, several whale skeletons, and some inventions. See the whale-factory ships where whales were processed onboard. The open-air museum focuses on farming life. ⊠ *Farmannsvn. 30* ☎ *33/31–24–18* ⌨ *NKr 40* ◷ *Mid-May–mid-Sept., Mon.–Sat. 10–5, Sun. noon–5; mid-Sept.–mid-May, weekdays 10–2.*

The intriguing art in **Haugar Vestfold Kunstmuseum** is mostly done by regional and other Norwegian artists. One of Norway's best known artists, Odd Nerdrum, has his own wing in the museum. The dark, rich, evocative character of Nerdrum's paintings (including the *Storyteller*) has been compared to that of Rembrandt's. ⊠ *Gråbrødragt. 17* ☎ *33/ 30–76–70* ⊕ *www.haugar.com* ⌨ *NKr 45* ◷ *Sept.–May, Tues.–Fri. 11–4, weekends noon–5; June–Aug., weekdays 11–5, weekends noon–5.*

Where to Stay

$–$$ **Best Western Grand Hotel.** This art deco hotel first opened its doors in 1931. The hotel's Grand Restaurant serves consistently good international cuisine, including a special seafood platter. The MS *Christina,* a boat owned by the hotel, is available for rent or charter. ⊠ *Øvre Langgt. 5, Tøns-*

berg ☎ *33/35–35–00* 🖷 *33/35–35–01* ⊕ *www.bestwestern.no* ⬦ *64 rooms, 3 suites* ♨ *2 restaurants, bar, nightclub* ▤ *AE, DC, MC, V.*

Sandefjord

㊷ *125 km (78 mi) south of Oslo, 25 km (15 mi) south of Tønsberg.*

Back in 1400, the Vikings had settlements and grave sites in Sandefjord. A natural harbor, the city was once the whaling capital of the world. Around 1900, it was possibly Norway's wealthiest city. Now that the whales are gone, all that remains of its commercial importance is a monument to it. With many beaches, 116 islands, and an archipelago, Sandefjord earns its nickname of *Badebyen,* or "Bathing City." In summer, boating and tourism thrive. From the Sandefjord Gjestehavn (guest, or public, harbor), take a short walk to the city's restaurants, shopping, and attractions.

Kommandør Christensens Hvalfangstmuseum (Commander Christensen's Whaling Museum) is perhaps best known for the suspended life-size model of a blue whale. The museum traces the development of the industry from small, primitive boats to huge floating factories. An especially intriguing display chronicles whaling in the Antarctic. ⊠ *Museumsgt. 39* ☎ *33/ 48–46–50* ⬛ *NKr 25* ⊙ *May–Sept., daily 11–5; Oct.–Apr., daily 11–3.*

Take a break from the beach to see the fascinating **Sandefjords Sjøfartsmuseum** (Sandefjord's Maritime Museum), which chronicles man's life at sea. Discover maritime history at exhibits about the sailing ships of the 19th century as well as more modern vessels. ⊠ *Prinsensgt. 18* ☎ *33/48–46–50* ⬛ *NKr 25* ⊙ *Early May–late June and mid-Aug.–late Sept., Sun. noon–4; late June–mid-Aug., daily noon–4.*

Where to Stay & Eat

★ **$$–$$$** ✕ **Ludls Gourmet Odd Ivar Solvold.** Celebrity chef Odd Ivar Solvold works his culinary magic here. In a place famous for its seafood, Solvold's grilled crayfish, turbot, catfish, scallops, and mussels are all highly recommended. For dessert, there's a wonderfully decadent chocolate truffle cake. ⊠ *Rådhusgt. 7* ☎ *33/46–27–41* ▤ *AE, DC, MC, V.*

¢–**$$** 🏨 **Comfort Home Hotel Atlantic.** The Atlantic Home was built in 1914, when Sandefjord was a whaling center. The history of whaling is traced in exhibits in glass cases and in pictures throughout the hotel. There's no restaurant, but the room rate includes *aften,* a supper consisting of bread and cold cuts, and hot soup and light beer. ⊠ *Jernbanealleen 33, 3201* ☎ *33/42–80–00* 🖷 *33/42–80–20* ⬦ *109 rooms* ♨ *Sauna, lobby lounge, library* ▤ *AE, DC, MC, V.*

¢–**$$** 🏨 **Rica Park Hotel.** The interior looks much the same as it did when the hotel was built in 1958. Ask for one of the 50 redecorated rooms, which are more spacious than the standard rooms. ⊠ *Strandpromenaden 9, 3200* ☎ *33/44–74–00* 🖷 *33/44–75–00* ⊕ *www.rica.no* ⬦ *233 rooms, 8 suites* ♨ *2 restaurants, indoor pool, health club, bar, nightclub, convention center* ▤ *AE, DC, MC, V.*

Cafés

Like many other Norwegian cities, Sandefjord has several trendy little spots that serve a great cup of coffee. **Iwonas Kaffebar** (⊠ Kongensgt. 26 ☎ 33/45–86–10) has the city's best coffee, from cappucinos to mochas. The popular café and bar **første etage** (⊠ Torvet 5 ☎ 33/ 46–27–80) also serves lunch and dinner. If you need to go on-line, head to **cafe 4u.no** (⊠ Storgt. 14 ☎ 33/42–94–98), an Internet café that serves coffees and breakfast, lunch, and dinner. The name's a play on Norway's top-level domain name, "no."

Sports & the Outdoors

Sandefjord is probably best known for its beaches and bathing. The tourist office has information on the multitude of sports played by locals, including soccer, handball, badminton, and tennis.

SWIMMING & DIVING Sandefjord has a beautiful, 146 km (90 mi) coastline brimming with wonderful beaches, especially those at the following islands and locations:

Vesterøya: Asnes, Sjøbakken, Langeby, Grubesand, Vøra og Fruvika. **Østerøya:** Flautangen, Skjellvika, Truber, and Yxnøy. **Along Highway 303 toward Larvik:** Granholmen. **Along Highway 303 toward Tønsberg:** Solløkka.

Neptun Dykkersenter (⊠ Bjerggt. 7, Sandefjord ☎ 33/46–14–90) is a diving center that teaches classes and sells and rents diving and water-sports equipment.

West of the Oslo Fjord A to Z

BOAT & FERRY TRAVEL

The most luxurious and scenic way to see the region is by boat. There are guest marinas at just about every port. The Drammen tourist office can provide information on boat rentals.

BUS TRAVEL

Because train service to towns south of Drammen is infrequent, bus travel is the best alternative to cars. Check with Nor-Way Bussekspress for schedules.

🚍 Bus Information Nor-Way Bussekspress ☎ 815-44-444 ⊕ www.nor-way.no.

CAR TRAVEL

Route E18 south from Oslo follows the coast to this region's towns.

TRAIN TRAVEL

Take a suburban train from Nationaltheatret or trains from Oslo S Station to reach Horten, Tønsberg, and Sandefjord.

VISITOR INFORMATION

🚍 Tourist Information Blaafarveværket ☎ 32/78-49-00. **Drammen** Drammen Kommunale Turistinformasjonskontor ⊠ Bragernes Torg 6, 3008 Drammen ☎ 32/80-62-10. **Hadeland** ☎ 61/31-66-00. **Horten and Åsgårdstrand** Horten Turist Kontor ⊠ Tollbugt. 1A, 3187 Horten ☎ 33/03-17-08. **Sandefjord** Sandefjord Reiselivsforening ⊠ Torvet, 3201 Sandefjord ☎ 33/46-05-90. **Tønsberg** Tønsberg og Omland Reiselivslag ⊠ Nedre Langgt. 36B, 3110 Tønsberg ☎ 33/31-02-20.

TELEMARK & THE SETESDAL VALLEY

In a landscape of wide-open vistas and deep forests, Telemark and the Setesdal Valley lie near the famed beaches and fjords of the coast. The region is veined with swift-flowing streams and scattered with peaceful lakes. Forested hills and deeply etched valleys stretch across the serene countryside. Here are natural surroundings so powerful and silent that, a few generations ago, trolls were the only reasonable explanation for what lurked in, or plodded through, the shadows.

Telemark was the birthplace of skiing as well as the birthplace of many Norwegian-Americans: the poor farmers of the region were among the first Norwegians to emigrate to the United States in the 19th century.

Numbers in the margin correspond to points of interest on the Telemark and Sørlandet map.

Kongsberg

▶ ❶ *84 km (52 mi) southwest of Oslo.*

Kongsberg, with 23,000 people today, was Norway's silver town for about 200 years. In 1623 two local children discovered a large ox butting a cliff in the area with his horns, revealing a silver vein in the hillside. News of the silver find reached King Christian IV in Copenhagen. He saw the area's natural potential and sent experts to investigate. A year later, the king himself came and founded the mining town of "Konningsberg." Norway's first industrial town was prominent until the mine closed in 1805.

Kongsberg Kirke (Kongsberg Church), finished in 1761, was built during the heyday of the silver mines. Along one wall is an impressive gilded Baroque altar, organ, and pulpit. The famous large glass chandeliers were made at **Nøstetangen glassworks** (☎ 32/73–19–02).

The Arts
In the last week of July, music fans descend on Kongsberg for its annual **jazz festival** (☎ 32/73–31–66 ⊕ www.kongsberg-jazzfestival.no).

Where to Stay & Eat
$$ ✕**Gamle Kongsberg Kro.** This café, next to the waterfall at Nybrofossen, has a reputation for traditional, hearty Norwegian dishes at reasonable prices. Try the broiled salmon with horseradish sauce or the pepper steak. ✉ *Thornesvn. 4* ☎ *32/73–16–33* ▭ *DC, MC, V.*

$$–$$$ 🏨**Quality Grand Hotel.** A statue of Kongsberg's favorite son, Olympic ski jumper Birger Ruud, stands in the park in front of this modern, centrally located hotel. The rooms are in a minimalistic style of white walls contrasting with dark furniture. ✉ *Christian Augusts gt. 2, 3600* ☎ *32/ 77–28–00* 📠 *32/73–41–29* ⊕ *www.quality-grand.no* ⇄ *99 rooms, 2 suites* ⚬ *Restaurant, indoor pool, 2 bars, nightclub, meeting room* ▭ *AE, DC, MC, V.*

Skien

❷ *88 km (55 mi) south of Kongsberg on Routes 32 and 36.*

Best known as the birthplace of playwright Henrik Ibsen, Skien, with a population of 50,000, is the capital of the Telemark region. Skien celebrates its favorite son every summer with the **Ibsen-Kultur-festival** (☎ 35/ 90–55–20), which includes concerts as well as plays.

The Telemark Museum at **Brekkeparken,** housed in a 1780 manor house, has a collection of Ibsen memorabilia that includes the interiors of his study and bedroom, and the "blue salon" from his Oslo flat (other interiors are at Ibsenmuseet in Oslo). The Telemark collection of folk art is from the 18th and 19th centuries. Brekkeparken is Northern Europe's largest tulip park. The exhibit "From Runes to E-mail" chronicles human communication over the course of the last millennium. ✉ *Øvregt. 41* ☎ *35/52–35–94* ⊕ *www.telemark.museum.no* 🎫 *NKr 40* ☉ *Mid-May–Aug., daily 10–6.*

Now the Henrik Ibsen Museum, **Venstøp** looks just as it did when the Ibsen family lived here from 1835 to 1843. The dark attic was the inspiration for the *Wild Duck.* This house, part of Skien's County Museum, is 5 km (3 mi) northwest of the city. ☎ *35/52–57–49* 🎫 *NKr 40* ☉ *Mid-May–Aug., daily 10–6; Sept., Sun. 10–6.*

Telemark & Sørlandet

KEY

▶ *Start of itinerary*

off the beaten path

BØ SOMMARLAND – Norway's largest water park has wave pools, slides, and Las Bøgas, a *tivoli* (amusement park). Always a sure-fire hit with families, it has more than 100 activities each year on the land and in the water here, including live concerts. The park is 50 km (30 mi) from Skien and 25 km (15 mi) from Notodden. ⊠ *3800 Bø* ☎ *35/95–16–99* ⊕ *www.sommarland.no* 🗝 *NKr 220, off-season discounts available.*

Where to Stay & Eat

★ **$$$$** ✕ **Boden Spiseri.** The consistently excellent kitchen here serves French-influenced Norwegian dishes. The fillet of reindeer is rich and delicious. For dessert, try the strawberry ice cream or the passionfruit cake. ⊠ *Landbrygga 5* ☎ *35/52–61–70* ▭ *AE, DC, MC, V* ⊗ *No lunch.*

$$ ⊡ **Rainbow Høyers Hotell.** This venerable hotel in the center of town has style and sophistication. The exterior, with its cornices and pedimented windows, is reflected in the hotel's lobby, in an incongruous mixture of old and new. The large rooms are bright, thanks to big windows, and have modern furnishings. ⊠ *Kongensgt. 6, 3700* ☎ *35/90–58–00* 🖷 *35/90–58–05* ⊕ *www.rainbow-hotels.no/hoyers* ⟿ *73 rooms, 8 suites* ⟁ *Restaurant, bar, meeting room* ▭ *AE, DC, MC, V.*

Sports & the Outdoors

BIKING The Coastal Route goes along the Telemark coastline and is part of the North Sea Cycle Route, which passes through six other countries. There's also a 115 km (71 mi) path along the Telemark Canal from Ulefoss to Dalen. **Telemark Reiser** (⊠ Skien ☎ 35/90–00–30) has cycling maps, and bicycle package trips that include accommodation and transport.

GOLF About 7 km (4½ mi) north of Skien is **Jønnevald** (☎ 35/59–07–03), an 18-hole championship golf course.

en route Running 105 km (65 mi) from Skien to Dalen with a detour to Notodden, **Telemarkskanalen** (Telemark Canal; ☎ 35/90–00–30 ⊕ www.telemarkskanalen.com) was carved into the mountains more than 100 years ago. It took 500 men five years to blast through the mountains to create 28 locks. The canal became "the fast route" between east and west Norway and upper and lower Telemark. Telemarkskanalen still has its original stone walls, locks, and closing mechanism.

Notodden

❸ *68 km (42 mi) northwest of Skien and 35 km (21 mi) west of Kongsberg.*

Notodden today is not much more than a small industrial town. It's believed that the area was prosperous in the Middle Ages, though, because of the size of the town's *stavkirke* (stave church), which is 85 foot high and 65 foot long. Notodden is known for its **summer blues festival** (⊕ www.bluesfest.no), which lasts four days in August and brings in Norwegian and American artists; past acts have included the Robert Cray Band.

★ **Heddal Stave Church** is Norway's largest church that's still in use. Dating back to the 12th century, the structure is resplendent with rosemaling (decorative flower painting from the 17th century), a bishop's chair, and incense vessels from the Middle Ages. Look out for the stylized animal ornamentation and the grotesque human heads on the portals. ☎ 35/02–08–40 ⊠ NKr 30 ☼ *Mid-May–mid-June and mid-Aug.–mid-Sept., daily 10–5; mid-June–mid-Aug., daily 9–7.*

Rjukan

❹ *96 km (59 mi) northwest of Notodden.*

The town of Rjukan may not ring a bell, but mention "heavy water," and those who lived through World War II or saw the film the *Heroes of Telemark* with Kirk Douglas, will recall the sabotage of the heavy water factory here, which thwarted German efforts to develop an atomic bomb. Rjukan became a town in the decade between 1907 and 1916, when its population grew from a few hundred to 10,000 because of a different kind of water, hydroelectric power.

Heavy water (used in nuclear reactors) was produced as a by-product in the manufacture of fertilizer at Vemork, 6 km (4 mi) west of Rjukan along Route 37, where a museum, **Industriarbeidermuseet Vemork** (The Norwegian Industrial Workers Museum) has been built. Vemork was the world's largest power station in 1911. In the machine hall, you can see a demonstration of a miniature power plant. Exhibitions document the development of hydroelectric power and the events that took place in Rjukan during World War II. ☎ 35/09–51–53 ⊠ NKr 55 ☼ *May–mid-June and mid-Aug.–Sept., daily 10–4; mid-June–mid-Aug., daily 10–6; Oct., weekends 11–4; Apr., Sat. 11–4.*

Rjukan is the site of northern Europe's first cable car, **Krossobanen** (Krosso Cable Car), built in 1928 by Hydro (the hydroelectric company) as a gift to the Rjukan inhabitants, so they could escape the shadowed valley and see Hardanger Mountain Plateau and Mount Gausta. ☎ 35/09–12–90 ⊠ NKr 35 ☼ *Times vary; call Rjukan tourist information for details.*

Where to Stay

$$$ ⊞ **Gaustablikk Høyfjellshotell.** At the foot of Mount Gausta, the highest mountain in southern Norway, this wooden cabin is a popular ski resort. There are nine downhill slopes and 80 km (50 mi) of cross-country trails. In summer these marked trails are ideal for walks and hikes. ✉ *3660* ☎ *35/09–14–22* 🖷 *35/09–19–75* ⊕ *www.gaustablikk.no* ↩ *98 rooms, 6 suites* ⌂ *Restaurant, indoor pool, gym, sauna, bar* ⊟ *AE, DC, MC, V.*

$–$$ 🖵 **Park Hotell.** This small tourist hotel in the center of town has a traditional Scandinavian look, and is family-friendly. Rooms are cheerful and painted with light colors. The restaurant is named Ammonia for the Norwegian ship of that name that sank during World War II. The menu is typically Norwegian—try the delicious pepper steak. ✉ *Sam Eydes gt. 67, 3660* ☎ *35/08–21–88* 🖷 *35/08–21–89* ↩ *39 rooms* ⌂ *Restaurant, bar, pub, nightclub* ⊟ *AE, DC, MC, V.*

Sports & the Outdoors

CYCLING Rjukan's local tourist office rents bikes weekdays 9–7 and weekends 10–6.

FISHING Telemark has more than 1,000 good fishing lakes. Contact the tourist office to find out about maps, licenses, and guides.

HORSEBACK Take the reins of an Icelandic horse on a riding trip organized by **Kalhovd**
RIDING **Turisthytte** (✉ Atrå ☎ 35/09–05–10) on Hardangervidda. Contact the tourist office for more information.

MOUNTAINEERING Whether you're an experienced mountain climber or a beginner, **Telemark Opplevelser** (☎ 99/51–31–40) can show you the ropes. They teach all levels of climbing courses and organize wilderness climbing and camping trips.

Seljord

❺ *50 km south of Rjukan.*

A serpent adorns the coat of arms of this otherwise peaceful town. The reason for its inclusion in the town's crest can be found in the depths of the nearby lake, Seljordsvatnet, where a giant sea serpent, reminiscent of the Loch Ness monster, and known affectionately by the locals as Selma, is supposed to live. She's thought to have occasionally broken through the lake's surface on warm summer days, or even to have crawled ashore. The serpent is quite an obsession for the people of Seljord (even the mayor claims to have proof of her existence), and serpent souvenirs aren't hard to come by. If scanning the lake for monsters gets tedious, you could always have a look at the beautiful 12th century stone church, or stroll through the town and have a bite to eat.

Everything you have ever wanted to know about Selma the serpent can be found at **Sjørmsenteret**, including eyewitness accounts and artists' impressions of the beast. ✉ *By E134 near the town center* ☎ *35/05–03–55* 🖼 *NKr 50* ⊙ *July, daily noon–6.*

Morgedal

❻ *77 km (46 mi) southwest of Rjukan via Åmot.*

In the heart of Telemark is Morgedal, the birthplace of modern skiing, thanks to the persistent Sondre Norheim, who in the 19th century perfected his skis and bindings, and practiced jumping from his roof. His innovations included bindings that close behind the heel and skis that narrow in the middle to facilitate turning. In 1868 he took off for a 185-km (115-mi) trek to Oslo just to prove it could be done. A hundred years ago, skiers used one long pole, held diagonally, much like high-wire artists. Eventually the use of two short poles became widespread, although purists still feel that the one-pole method is the "authentic" way to ski.

★ ℃ The **Norsk Skieventyr** (Norwegian Skiing Adventure Center) in Morgedal guides you through the 4,000-year history of the winter sport with life-size exhibits of typical ski cottages and authentic skis and costumes. Displays include the inside of Norway's original and last ski-wax factory, where specialists melted a variety of secret ingredients, including cheese, to make uphill and downhill slides smoother. Visit Norheim's cottage, Øvrebø, above the edge of the forest, where the Olympic flame was lit. Several action-packed 3-D skiing films can be seen here. ✉ *On Rte. 11 between Brunkeberg and Høydalsmo* ☎ *35/05–42–50* 🖾 *NKr 50* ☺ *Late May–mid-June, daily 11–5; mid-June–mid-Aug., daily 9–7; mid-Aug.–late Aug., daily 11–5; Sept.–mid-Dec. and mid-Jan–late May, Sat. 11–4.*

Dalen

❼ *60 km (37 mi) southwest of Morgedal.*

The area around Dalen is the place to hike, bike, and be outdoors. From Skien you can take boat tours on the Telemark waterways, a combination of canals and natural lakes between Skien, Dalen, and Notodden.

The trip to Dalen takes you through Ulefoss, where you can visit the neoclassical **Ulefoss Manor** (✉ Hovedgård ☎ 35/94–56–10), which dates from 1807. It's open weekdays June through September from 2 to 4 and Sunday from noon to 3.

At Eidsborg, just north of Dalen, **Vest-Telemark museum Eidsborg** (☎ 35/ 07–73–31 🖾 Nkr 30 ☺ June–Aug., daily 11–6) is an open-air museum consisting of more than 30 sod buildings, set in lush, green surroundings. The centerpiece is the small but beautiful **Eidsborg Stavkirke** (🖾 NKr 30; NKr 50 includes admission to the rest of the museum), known for its prime examples of rosemaling.

The historic **Dalen Hotel** is worth a peek, whether or not you stay there. A number of royal families have been guests, and locals are said to think ghosts haunt its creaky wooden walls. For trips to Dalen, contact the **Telemarkreiser tourist organization** (☎ 35/90–00–20 ⊕ www. telemarkreiser.no).

Where to Stay

$$$ ✕🏠 **Dalen Hotel.** At one end of the Telemark Canal, this opulent, Victorian "Swiss-style" hotel has retained its original decorations. Look for the dragonhead carvings and stained-glass windows on the balcony overlooking the stunning entrance hall. When the weather's fine, you can go rowing, or play croquet in the garden. ✉ *3880* ☎ *35/07–70–00* 🖨 *35/07–70–11* ⊕ *www.dalenhotel.no* 🛏 *38 rooms* ♿ *Breakfast room, lobby lounge, meeting room* ▭ *AE, V* ☺ *Closed Christmas–Easter.*

Valle

❽ *The Setesdal road, Rte. 9, follows the Otra River downstream and then runs alongside the Byglandsfjord; Valle is 56 km (35 mi) southwest of Dalen.*

Near Valle sits **Sylvartun,** a clump of grass-roof cottages that house a silversmith's workshop, a jewelry shop, and an art gallery. It's also a cultural center that hosts concerts and displays local crafts, including many Hardanger fiddles. Every summer during the "Setesdal Evenings," professional musicians and folk dancers perform while a traditional Norwegian dinner is served. ✉ *Rte. 19, Nomeland, near Valle* ☎ *37/ 93–63–06* ☺ *Silversmith's shop: May–Oct., Mon.–Sat. 10–6, Sun. 11–6. Call for program schedules.*

off the
beaten
path

SETESDAL MINERAL PARK – About 97 km (57 mi) south of Valle, just south of Evje, in Hornnes, is an interesting park where rock formations from Norway and elsewhere are displayed inside a mountain. ⊠ *Rte. 39, 4737 Evje* ☎ *37/93–13–10* 🗐 *NKr 60* ☉ *Mid-June–Aug., daily 10–5.*

Telemark & the Setesdal Valley A to Z

BUS TRAVEL

The many bus lines that serve the region are coordinated through Nor-Way Bussekspress in Oslo. Buses in the region rarely run more than twice a day, so get a comprehensive schedule from the tourist office or the bus company's office in Oslo.

🚹 Bus Information **Nor-Way Bussekspress** ⊠ Oslo Bussterminalen Galleriet ☎ 815/44-444 🖶 22/17-59-22.

CAR TRAVEL

On Route E18 from Oslo, the drive southwest to Kongsberg takes a little more than an hour. If you arrive by way of the Kristiansand ferry, the drive up Route 9 to Evje takes about the same time.

Roads in the southern part of the interior region are open and flat, but others are curvy and mountainous. Route E134 passes through Heddal and Morgedal, and connects with Routes 37/38, which go north to Rjukan and south toward Dalen. E134 also connects with Route 9, the main Setesdal road, which goes through Valle and Evje proceeding all the way to Kristiansand.

TRAIN TRAVEL

The train from Oslo S Station to Kongsberg takes 1 hour and 25 minutes; bus connections to Telemark are available. The only train service in the southern part of the region is the Oslo–Stavanger line (via Kristiansand).

VISITOR INFORMATION

🚹 Tourist Information **Kongsberg** ⊠ Karschesgt. 3 ☎ 32/29-90-50. **Notodden** ⊠ Teatergt. 3 ☎ 35/01-50-00. **Rjukan** ⊠ Torget 2 ☎ 35/09-12-90. **Setesdal** ⊠ 4735 Evje ☎ 37/93-14-00. **Skien** ⊠ Reiselivets Hus, N. Hjellegt. 18 ☎ 35/90-55-20. **Telemarkreiser** (Telemark Canal tourist organization) ⊠ Nedre Hjellegt. 18, 3702 Skien ☎ 35/90-00-20 🖶 35/90-00-21 ⊕ www.telemarkreiser.no.

SØRLANDET TO STAVANGER: THE NORTH SEA ROAD

In summer, Oslo's residents migrate to the southern coast to soak up some sunshine. Southern Norway is an ideal area for those who want to get close to nature, with a mild summer climate and terrain varying from coastal flatland to inland mountains and forests.

Many splendid points mark the route of the North Sea Road. Beginning in the relaxed resort town of Kristiansand, the road winds west along the major section of Norway's southern coast, Sørlandet. Wide, sun-kissed, inviting beaches have their blue waters warmed by the Gulf Stream. Sandy terrain turns to coastal flatlands, inland mountain peaks and green forests ideal for cycling, hiking, and mountaineering. Freshwater lakes and rivers, and this section of the ocean, are some of the best places to go salmon fishing—they're also superb for canoeing, kayaking, and rafting. The region is the perfect habitat for such wildlife as beavers, deer, foxes, and many birds.

When the North Sea Road reaches its final destination, it's in a landscape of fjords, islands, mountains, and valleys. Stavanger, Norway's oil capital, is here; a cosmopolitan city yet with small-town charm, it has some of the country's best restaurants, hotels, and cultural life.

Numbers in the margin correspond to points of interest on the Telemark and Sørlandet map.

Arendal

▶ ❾ *260 km (418 mi) south of Oslo.*

In Arendal's Tyholmen, the old town, there are many painted houses bearing window boxes filled with pink-and-red flowers. A popular speedboat race attracts international competitors to Arendal each summer.

An unusual gallery space, the restored **Bomuldsfabriken** (Cotton Factory) operated from 1898 to 1960 producing jeans, shirts, and cotton flannel clothing. Today, it has changing art exhibitions and a permanent collection of 35 works by some of Norway's foremost painters. ⊠ *Oddenvn. 5* ☎ *37/02–65–19* ⊠ *NKr 20* ⊕ *www.bomuldsfabriken.com* ⊙ *Tues.–Sun. noon–4.*

Established in 1832, the **Aust-Agder Museet** displays fascinating coastal artifacts and relics, from toys to farm tools. Find out about the 1767 slave ship *Fredensborg,* and learn more about the region's folk art and geology. ⊠ *Langsæ gård, Arendal* ☎ *37/07–35–00* ⊕ *www.aust-agder. museum.no* ⊙ *Late June–late Aug., weekdays 10–5, Sat. 9–1, Sun. noon–5; early Aug.–early June, weekdays 9–3, Sat. 9–1, Sun. noon–5.*

off the beaten path

MERDØGAARD MUSEUM – On the island of Merdøy, a 30-minute boat ride from Arendal's Langbrygga (long wharf), is an early 18th-century sea captain's home, now a museum exploring life in the region. After visiting, enjoy a swim on the beach or a walk around the island. ⊠ *Merdøy* ☎ *37/07–35–00* ⊠ *NKr 20* ⊙ *Late June–mid-Aug., daily noon–5.*

Where to Stay

$$–$$$ ⊞ **Clarion Tyholmen Hotel.** This maritime hotel has the sea at close quarters and a magnificent view of the fjord. The interior is modern and makes good use of blue paint and wood furniture. The hotel's outdoor restaurant, Bryggekanten, serves fish and steak dishes. It's a popular summer spot. ⊠ *Teaterpl. 2, Tyholmen 4801* ☎ *37/02–68–00* ☒ *37/02–68–01* ⇱ *60 rooms* ♨ *2 restaurants, sauna, bar* ⊟ *AE, DC, MC, V.*

Grimstad

❿ *15 km (9 mi) south of Arendal.*

Grimstad's glory was in the days of sailing ships—about the same time the teenage Henrik Ibsen worked as an apprentice at the local apothecary shop from 1844 to 1850.

★ Grimstad Apotek is now a part of **Ibsenhuset–Grimstad Bymuseum** (the Ibsen House) and has been preserved with its 1837 interior intact. Ibsen wrote his first play, *Catlina,* here. Every summer Grimstad holds an Ibsen festival celebrating the famous playwright. The museum also has a maritime department and section honoring Terje Vigen, a folk hero who was the subject of a poem by Ibsen. He is credited with riding to Denmark to bring back food for the starving Norwegians. ⊠ *Henrik Ibsens gt. 14, 4890* ☎ *37/04–04–90* ⊕ *www.ibsen.net* ⊠ *NKr 35* ⊙ *May–Sept. 11–5.*

Lillesand

❶ *20 km (12 mi) south of Grimstad.*

An idyllic summer vacation town, Lillesand has one of Norway's best guest (public) harbors, which is usually bustling. In town, you will see many of the white wooden houses that are typical of the region.

In an 1827 Empire-style building, the **Lillesand By og Sjøfartsmuseum** (Lillesand City and Maritime Museum) reconstructs maritime-related workplaces. You can see how sail makers worked and also see the city's first fire pump. ⊠ *Carl Knudsen gården* ☎ *37/27–04–30* 🖆 *NKr 15* ⊙ *Mid-June–Aug., weekdays 11–3, Sat. 11–2.*

Dating to AD 1,000, the 33 foot-long stone **Høvåg Kirke** was lengthened and restored in 1768 and 1828. Construction wasn't completed until 1966. ☎ *37/27–43–31* ⊙ *May–Sept., daily 9–4.*

Where to Stay

$$–$$$ 🛏 **Lillesand Hotel Norge.** Right on the harbor, this old hotel certainly has rooms with views. The sea-inspired guest rooms are classic yet modern. The restaurant serves delicious seafood dishes. ⊠ *Strandgt. 3, 4790* ☎ *37/27–01–44* 🖶 *37/27–30–70* ⊕ *www.hotelnorge.no* ⟋ *25 rooms* ⚭ *Restaurant, bar* ⊟ *AE, DC, MC, V.*

Kristiansand

❷ *55 km (34 mi) south of Grimstad on E18.*

Nicknamed *Sommerbyen* ("the Summer City"), Norway's fifth-largest city has 73,000 inhabitants. Kristiansand has good national and international travel connections. Norwegians come here for its sun-soaked beaches and beautiful harbor. Kristiansand has also become known internationally for the **Quart Festival** (☎ *38/14–69–69* ⊕ www.quart.no), which hosts local and international rock bands every July.

According to legend, in 1641 King Christian IV marked the four corners of Kristiansand with his walking stick, and within that framework the grid of wide streets was laid down. The center of town, called the **Kvadraturen**, still retains the grid, even after numerous fires. In the northeast corner is **Posebyen**, one of northern Europe's largest collections of low, connected wooden house settlements. Kristiansand's **Fisketorvet** (fish market) is near the south corner of the town's grid, right on the sea. **Christiansholm Festning** (⊙ Mid-May–Aug., daily 9–9) is a fortress on a promontory opposite Festningsgata. Completed in 1672, the circular building with 15-foot-thick walls has played more a decorative role than a defensive one; it was used once, in 1807, to defend the city against British invasion. Now it contains art exhibits.

The Gothic Revival **Kristiansand Domkirke** (Kristiansand Cathedral) from 1885 is the third-largest church in Norway. It often hosts summer concerts in addition to the weeklong **International Church Music Festival** (☎ *38/12–09–40*) in mid-May. Organ, chamber, and gospel music are on the bill. ⊠ *Kirkegt., 4610* ☎ *38/02–11–88* ⊕ *www.kirkefestspill.no* 🖆 *Free* ⊙ *June–Aug., daily 9–2.*

A wealthy merchant–shipowner built **Gimle Gård** (Gimle Manor) around 1800 in the Empire style. Inside are furnishings from that period, including paintings, silver, and hand-blocked wallpaper. To get there from the city center, head north across the Otra River on Bus 22 or drive to Route E18 and cross the bridge over the Otra to Parkveien. Turn left onto Ryttergangen and drive to Gimleveien; take a right. ⊠ *Gimlevn.*

23, 4630 ☎ 38/09–02–28 💳 NKr 45 ⊙ *Mid-June–mid-Aug., weekdays noon–4, Sun. noon–6; May–mid-June and mid-Aug.–early Jan., Sun. noon–5.*

The **Agder naturmuseum og botaniske hage** (Agder Nature Museum and Botanical Gardens) takes on Sørlandet's natural history from the Ice Age to the present, examining the coast and moving on to the high mountains. There's a rainbow of minerals on display, as well as a rose garden with varieties from 1850. There's even the country's largest collection of cacti. ✉ *Gimlevn. 23, 4630* ☎ *38/09–23–88* ⊕ *www.museumsnett. no/naturmuseum* 💳 *NKr 45* ⊙ *Mid-June–mid-Aug., Tues.–Fri. 10–6, Sat.–Mon. noon–6; mid-Aug.–mid-June, Tues.–Fri. 10–3, Sun. noon–5.*

The striking runestone in the cemetery of **Oddernes Kirke** (Oddernes Church) tells that Øyvind, godson of Saint Olav, built this church in 1040 on property he inherited from his father. One of the oldest churches in Norway, it is dedicated to Saint Olav. ✉ *Oddernesvn., 6430* ☎ *38/ 09–01–87* 💳 *Free* ⊙ *May–Aug., Sun.–Fri. 9–2.*

At the **Kristiansand Kanonmuseum** (Cannon Museum) you can see the cannon that the occupying Germans rigged up during World War II. With calibers of 15 inches, the cannon was said to be capable of shooting a projectile halfway to Denmark. In the bunkers, related military materials are on display. ✉ *Møvik* ☎ *38/08–50–90* 💳 *NKr 50* ⊙ *May–Sept., daily 11–6; prebooked tours available all year.*

☏ **Vest-Agder Fylkesmuseum** (County Museum), the region's largest cultural museum, has more than 40 old buildings on display. The structures, transported from other locations in the area, include two *tun*—farm buildings traditionally set in clusters around a common area—which suited the extended families. If you have children with you, check out the old-fashioned toys, which can still be played with. The museum is 4 km (2½ mi) east of Kristiansand on Route E18. ✉ *Kongsgård* ☎ *38/09–02–28* ⊕ *www.museumsnett.no/vafymuseum* 💳 *NKr 30* ⊙ *Mid-June–mid-Aug., Tues.–Fri. 10–6, Sat.–Mon. noon–6; mid-Aug.–mid-June, Sun. noon–5.*

FodorśChoice ★ A favorite with hikers and strolling nannies, **Ravnedalen** (Raven Valley) is a lush park that's filled with flowers in springtime. Wear comfortable shoes to hike the narrow, winding paths up the hills and climb the 200 steps up to a 304-foot lookout. ✉ *Northwest of Kristiansand.*

★ ☏ One of Norway's most popular attractions, **Kristiansand Dyreparken** is actually five separate parks, including a water park (bring bathing suits and towels); a forested park; an entertainment park; a theme park; and a zoo, which contains an enclosure for Scandinavian animals such as wolves and elk, and a large breeding ground for Bactrian camels. The theme park, **Kardemomme By** (Cardamom Town), is named for a book by Norwegian illustrator and writer Thorbjørn Egner. In the zoo, the "My Africa" exhibition allows you to move along a bridge observing native savanna animals such as giraffe and zebras. The park is 11 km (6 mi) east of town. ✉ *Kristiansand Dyreparken, Kardemomme By* ☎ *38/ 04–97–25* ⊕ *www.dyreparken.no* 💳 *NKr 225, includes admission to all parks and rides; discounts offered off-season* ⊙ *June–Aug., daily 10–7; Sept.–May, weekdays 10–3, weekends 10–5.*

Where to Stay & Eat

$$–$$$$ ✕**Bølgen&Moi.** Toralf Bølgen and Trond Moi, Norway's most celebrated restaurateurs, opened this, the southernmost addition to their chain of high-profile restaurants. Near the old fishing pier, the scene is more chic than rustic, with artwork and even dinnerware designed by local artist Kjell Nupen. ✉ *Sjølystvn. 1A* ☎ *38/17–83–00* 🖃 *AE, DC, MC, V.*

$$–$$$$ ✕ **Luihn.** In the center of town, Luihn is an elegant, intimate restaurant, perfect for a quiet dinner. Fish dishes are a specialty, and the menu varies according to season. Don't hesitate to call in advance if you have any special cravings—providing they can get hold of it, the chefs can prepare just about anything for you. The wine selection is impressive. ✉ *Rådhusgt. 15* ☎ *38/10–66–50* ⊟ *AE, DC, MC, V.*

★ **$$$** ✕ **Sjøhuset Restaurant.** Considered one of the city's best restaurants, Sjøhuset was built in 1892 as a salt warehouse—a white-trimmed red building. The specialty is seafood. Take a seat on the sunny patio and dine on fresh lobster. ✉ *Østre Strandgt. 12A* ☎ *38/02–62–60* ⊟ *AE, DC, MC, V.*

$$–$$$ 🏨 **Clarion Ernst Park Hotel.** Convenience is the main reason to stay at this rather traditional city hotel. It is central, and close to the city beach and main shopping street, Markens. You can stay connected on-line at the Internet café, an uncommon sight in Norway. A small tourist office makes it easy to inquire about local attractions and buy tickets to Dyreparken. ✉ *Rådhusgt. 2, 4601* ☎ *38/12–86–03* 🖷 *38/02–03–07* ⊕ *www.ernst.no* ⇥ *112 rooms, 4 suites* ♨ *Restaurant, 2 bars, nightclub, meeting rooms* ⊟ *AE, DC, MC, V.*

$$–$$$ 🏨 **Quality Hotel Kristiansand.** Nicknamed "the children's hotel," this chain hotel is perfect for young families on the go. Inside, there's a huge playroom, activity leaders, childcare, and a children's buffet. Even more toys are outdoors. Rooms are comfortable, with cheerful pastel walls and wood furniture. ✉ *Sørlandsparken, 4696* ☎ *38/17–77–77* 🖷 *38/17–77–80* ⊕ *www.quality-kristiansand.no* ⇥ *210 rooms* ♨ *Restaurant, indoor pool, baby-sitting, children's programs, nursery, playground* ⊟ *AE, DC, MC, V.*

$$–$$$ 🏨 **Rica Dyreparken Hotel.** Built like Noah's Ark, this modern hotel is designed to appeal to children of all ages. Inspired by the Kristiansand Dyreparken, many of the rooms go a little wild, with tiger-stripe chairs and paw prints on walls. Children have their own playroom and cinema on board this ark. ✉ *Dyreparken, Kristiansand 4609* ☎ *38/14–64–00* 🖷 *38/14–64–01* ⊕ *www.rica.no* ⇥ *160 rooms* ♨ *Restaurant, bar, children's programs.*

Nightlife & the Arts

Markens gate, the city's main street, is the place for clubbing, pubbing, and live music.

Dr. Fjeld (✉ Rådhusgt. 2 ☎ 38/12–86–03) at Clarion Ernst Park Hotel is a popular place to dance the night away. Party types in their late twenties and thirties head to **Lobbybaren** (✉ Vestre Strandgt. 7 ☎ 38/11–21–00) at Radisson SAS Caledonien Hotel. A younger crowd flocks to **Club Etcetera** (✉ Vestre Strandgt. 23 ☎ 38/02–96–66) for up-to-date beats. Every summer, **Agder Teater** (✉ Kongensgt. 2A ☎ 38/02–43–00) moves its performances outdoors to Fjøreheia near Grimstad. **Musikkens Hus** (✉ Kongensgt. 54 ☎ 38/14–87–30) schedules musical concerts throughout the year. The **Kristiansand Symfoniorkester** (Kristiansand Symphony Orchestra; ✉ Kongensgt. 6 ☎ 38/02–24–40) performs year-round.

Sports & the Outdoors

Troll Mountain (✉ Setesdal Rafting og Aktivitetssenter, Rte. 9, Evje ☎ 37/93–11–77), about one hour's drive from Kristiansand, organizes many activities. Be it mountain climbing, sailing, biking, rafting, paintball, or even beaver or deer safaris, this is the place for outdoorsy types.

BIKING Kristiansand has 70 km (42 mi) of bike trails around the city. The tourist office can recommend routes and rentals. **Kristiansand Sykkelsenter** (✉ Grim Torv ☎ 38/02–68–35) rents bicycles and off-road vehicles.

CLIMBING Whether you're an experienced pro or just a gung-ho beginner, you can rent climbing equipment or learn more about the sport from **Klatrehuset på Samsen** (⊠ Vestervn. 2 ☎ 38/00–64–15).

FISHING North of Kristiansand there's excellent trout, perch, and eel fishing at Lillesand's **Vestre Grimevann** lake. You can get a permit at any sports store or at the tourist office.

GOLF Enjoy Kristiansand's sunny weather and a round of golf at **Kristiansand Golfklubb** (☎ 38/14–85–60), which has a 9-hole course, equipment rentals, instruction, and a café. On rainy days, there's always **Kristiansand Golfsenter** (⊠ Barstølv 28B ☎ 38/09–80–08), which has a modern simulator, courses, driving range, and billiards.

HIKING In addition to the gardens and steep hills of Ravnedalen, the **Baneheia Skog** (Baneheia Forest) is full of evergreens, small lakes, and paths that are ideal for a lazy walk or a challenging run. It's just a 15-minute walk north from the city center.

RIDING If you're at home in the saddle, then head to **Islandshestsenteret** (The Icelandic Horse Center; ⊠ Søgne ☎ 38/16–98–82). Specializing in the Icelandic horse breed, this center offers courses, trips, and camping for children and adults.

WATER SPORTS **Kuholmen Marina** (⊠ Roligheden Camping ☎ 38/09–67–22) rents boats, water skis, and water scooters. **Dykkeren** (⊠ Kongsgårds Allé 53 ☎ 38/05–86–20) has everything related to diving, including organized trips, classes, and equipment.

Combining history with sailing, the magnificent square-rigger **Sørlandet** (⊠ Gravene 2, Kristiansand ☎ 38/02–98–90), built in 1927, takes passengers for two weeks trips, usually stopping for several days in a northern European port. The price is about NKr 750 per day.

Shopping

There are many shops next to Dyreparken in Kristiansand. **Sørlands Senteret** (☎ 38/04–91–00) is one of the region's larger shopping centers, with 96 stores, a pharmacy, and a post office. **Kvadraturen** (☎ 38/02–44–11) has 300 stores and eating spots.

Vennesla

🔟 *15 km (9 mi) north of Kristiansand. Follow Rte. 39 from Kristiansand to Mosby, veer right onto 405, and continue to Grovane.*

Untouched forests and excellent salmon fishing in the Otra River have made Vennesla a popular outdoor destination.

Setesdalsbanen (Setesdal Railway), a 7-km-long (4½ mi) stretch of narrow-gauge track, has a steam locomotive from 1896 and carriages from the early 1900s that are available for round-trip rides. The railway remained in normal use until 1962. An exhibition at Grovane Station explains the history of the locomotive. ⊠ *Vennesla Stasjon* ☎ *38/15–64–82* ⊕ *www.setesdalsbanen.no* ⊠ *NKr 80 round-trip* ⊙ *Mid-June–Aug., Sun. 11:30, 1 and 2:30; additional departures in July: Tues.–Fri. 6, Thurs. noon.*

Mandal

🔟 *42 km (28 mi) southwest of Kristiansand and 82 km (51 mi) from Evje.*

Mandal is Norway's southernmost town, famous for its historic core of well-preserved wooden houses and its beautiful long beach, Sjøsanden.

Mandal Kirke, built in 1821, is Norway's largest Empire-style wooden church. ☎ 38/26–35–77 ⏱ *Tues.–Thurs. 11–2.*

Lindesnes Fyr, Norway's first lighthouse, was lit in the Lindesnes municipality in February 1656, at the southernmost point in Norway. It was closed the same year by the Danish king and didn't reopen for 69 years. Many lighting methods have been used since, including coal in the early 1800s. An exhibition in the museum traces the changing methods. ✉ *Mandal* ☎ 38/26–19–02 ⏱ *Open during daylight hrs.*

Ogna

⓯ *93 km (57 mi) from Flekkefjord on Rte. 42.*

Ogna has a stretch of sandy beach that inspired many Norwegian artists, among them Kitty Kielland (1843–1914), who was best known for her Impressionist landscape paintings.

The complex making up **Hå Gamle Prestegaard** (Old Parsonage) was built in 1637 to face the ocean. It now houses a gallery of changing art and cultural exhibitions that are often worth visiting. ✉ *Ogna* ☎ *51/79–16–60* 🎫 *NKr 40* ⏱ *Mid-May–mid-Sept., Tues.–Fri. 11–6, Sat. noon–5, Sun. noon–6; mid-Sept.–mid-Apr., weekends noon–5.*

The ancient **Hå gravesite** lies below the Hå parsonage near the Obrestad lighthouse. The roughly 60 mounds, including two shaped like stars and one shaped like a boat, date from around AD 500. To get here take coastal Route 44.

The Outdoors

FISHING Three of the 10 best fishing rivers in Norway, the Ognaelva, Håelva, and Figgjo, are in Jæren, just south of Stavanger. Fishing licenses, sold in grocery stores and gas stations, are required at all of them.

Sandnes

⓰ *25 km (16 mi) south of Stavanger, 52 km (32 mi) north of Orre.*

For good reason, this city of 53,000 is called Bicycle Town. Local company Øglend DBS, founded in 1898, has manufactured nearly 2 million bicycles here. Sandnes has 200 free city bicycles, miles of bicycle paths, a bicycle museum, the Bicycle Blues Festival, a bicycle library, and an active racing club. Besides bicycles, brickworks, pottery, and textiles have been the traditional industries. Eleven factory outlets and art galleries sell historical and modern Sandnes crafts and products at reduced prices.

Even oatmeal gets its own museum in Norway. **Krossens Havremølle Museum** (Krossen's Oatmeal Museum) shows the significance oats have played in the region and the country. National, industrial, and cultural artifacts are on display, as is an authentic model of a mill showing how oats are processed. ✉ *Storgt. 26* ☎ *51/67–06–96* ⊕ *www.havre.museum.no* 🎫 *NKr 30* ⏱ *Mid-June–mid-Aug., daily noon–5; mid-Aug.–mid-June, Sun. noon–3.*

Where to Stay & Eat

$ ✕🏠 **Hotel GamlaVærket Gjæstgiveri og Tracteringsted.** A former brick-and-pottery works, this intimate hotel has a warm, old-fashioned charm. Simple white-wall rooms have slanted ceilings and dark wood furniture. The well-regarded restaurant has a menu that ranges from sandwiches to delicious seven-course meals. ✉ *St. Olavs gt. 38, 4306* ☎ *51/68–51–70* 🖷 *51/68–51–71* ⊕ *www.gamlavaerket.no* ⇥ *27 rooms* ⚐ *Restaurant* ▭ *AE, DC, MC, V.*

Sports & the Outdoors

BICYCLING Can you actually visit Norway's bicycle town and not spin a few wheels yourself? If the cycling mood strikes, borrow one of the 200 that are available for free downtown. You can rent one at **Spinn Sykkelshop** (☎ 51/68–62–65) or **Naboen** (☎ 51/57–07–10). The tourist office has bicycle maps of the area. **Scan One Tours** (☎ 51/89–39–00) organizes and sells packaged bicycle trips.

WATER SPORTS Scandinavia's largest indoor swimming facility, **Havanna Badeland** holds a total of 264,000 gallons (1 million liters) of water. A 300-foot water slide, playhouse, reading corner, whirlpool baths, saunas, and a Turkish bath entertain children and adults. The Havanna Lekeland next door has a ball pool, play equipment, climbing labyrinths, and five slides. ✉ *Hanavn. 17, Sandnes* ☎ *51/60–89–50* ⊕ *www.havanna.no* 💷 *NKr 115 for playland and water park* ☉ *Daily 10–8.*

Shopping

OUTLET STORES Sandnes has a tempting selection of factory outlets offering as much as 70% off regular-priced goods. Several times a year, the local tourist board organizes free bus trips to these. The region's most visited factory outlet, **Byrkjedalstunet** (✉ Rte. 45, Dirdal ☎ 51/61–29–00) has a candle-maker, children's activities, and a mountain farm as well as stores selling handicrafts and souvenirs. For fine porcelain, go to **Figgjo** (☎ 51/68–35–70), in the nearby town of the same name. It's the largest supplier to professional kitchens in Norway. **Skjæveland** (✉ Ålgård ☎ 51/61–24–19) carries high-quality knit sweaters and jackets for men and women.

Stavanger

 256 km (123 mi) from Kristiansand, 4½ hrs from Bergen by car and ferry, 8–9 hrs from Oslo.

Stavanger has always prospered from the riches of the sea. During the 19th century, huge harvests of brisling and herring established it as the sardine capital of the world. Some people claim the locals are called Siddis, from S (tavanger) plus *iddis,* which means "sardine label," although linguists argue it's actually a mispronunciation of the English word "citizen."

During the past three decades, a different product from the sea has been Stavanger's lifeblood—oil. Since its discovery in the late 1960s, North Sea oil hasn't just transformed the economy, Stavanger has emerged as cosmopolitan and vibrant, more bustling than other cities with a population of only 110,000. Norway's most international city, it has attracted residents from more than 90 nations. Roam its cobblestone streets or wander the harborfront and you're likely to see many cafés, fine restaurants, and lively pubs. For many visitors, Stavanger is a place to be entertained.

Fodor'sChoice The charm of the city's past is on view in **Old Stavanger,** Northern Eu-
★ rope's largest and best preserved wooden house settlement. The 150 houses here were built in the late 1700s and early 1800s. Wind down the narrow, cobblestone streets past small, white houses and craft shops with many-paned windows and terra-cotta roof tiles.

Legend has it that Bishop Reinald of Winchester ordered the construction of the **Stavanger Domkirke** (Stavanger Cathedral) in 1125, so that the king could marry his third wife there, after his divorce from Queen Malmfrid. The church was built in an Anglo–Norman style, probably with the aid of English craftsmen. Patron saint St. Svithun's arm is believed to be among the original relics. Largely destroyed by fire in 1272, the church was rebuilt to include a Gothic chancel. The result: its once elegant lines are now festooned with macabre death symbols and airborne putti. Next to the cathedral is **Kongsgård,** formerly a residence of bishops and kings but now a school and not open to visitors. ✉ *Near Target* ✆ *Free* ☉ *Mid-May–mid-Sept., Mon. and Tues. 11–6, Wed.–Sat. 10–6, Sun. 11–6; mid-Sept.–mid-May, Wed.–Sat. 10–3.*

Designed to help children learn about the prehistoric past, the **Arkeologisk Museum** (Museum of Archaeology) has changing exhibitions, instructive models, open archives, and movies designed to make learning history fun. Children can research their ancestors in computer games, treasure hunts, and other activities. In summer, children can look through stones in search of fossils and other signs of life. There are also old-fashioned games and toys, which have become popular attractions. ✉ *Peder Klowsgt. 30A* ✆ *51/84–60–00* ✉ *NKr 20* ☉ *June–Aug., Tues.–Sun. 11–5; Sept.–May, Tues. 11–8, Wed.–Sat. 11–3, Sun. 11–4.*

Four local museums—the Stavanger Sjøfartsmuseum, Norsk Hermetikkmuseum, Ledaal, and Breidablikk—make up the **Stavanger Museum.** In the zoological department in the main building, you'll find a collection of preserved birds and animals from around the world. In the Department of Cultural History there are re-enactments of church and school life, and artisans at work. It traces Stavanger's growth from its 12th-century beginnings to the oil city it is today. Buy a ticket to one of the museums and you get free admission to the other three on the same day.

✉ *Musėgt. 16* ✆ *51/84–27–00* ⊕ *www.stavanger.museum.no* ✉ *NKr 40* ☉ *Mid-June–mid-Aug., daily 11–4; early June and late Aug., Mon.–Thurs. 11–3, Sun. 11–4; Sept.–May, Sun. 11–4 or by appointment. Closed Dec.*

★ **Breidablikk** manor house has a perfectly preserved interior and exterior and feels as if the owner has only momentarily slipped away. The building is an outstanding example of what the Norwegians call "Swiss-style" architecture, and also has some elements of the Norwegian National Romantic style. It was built in 1882 by the Norwegian merchant and ship owner, Lars Berentsen. ✉ *Eiganesvn. 40A* ✆ *51/84–27–00* ⊕ *www. stavanger.museum.no* ✉ *NKr 40* ☉ *Mid-June–mid-Aug., daily 11–4; mid-Aug.–mid-June, Sun. 11–4 or by appointment.*

Ledaal, the royal family's Stavanger residence, is a mansion museum and is used for receptions by the Stavanger Council. It was built for shipping magnate Gabriel Schanche Kielland, and completed in 1803. The building is a prime example of the Norwegian neoclassical style, and it's decorated with rococo furnishings and details, as well as pieces in the Empire, and Biedermeier styles. The second-floor library is dedicated to writer Alexander Kielland, a social critic and satirist. ✉ *Eiganesvn. 45* ✆ *51/ 84–27–00* ⊕ *www.stavanger.museum.no* ✉ *NKr 40* ☉ *Mid-June–mid-Aug., daily 11–4; mid-Aug.–mid-June, Sun. 11–4 or by appointment.*

The fascinating **Norsk Hermetikkmuseum** (Norwegian Canning Museum) is in a former canning factory. From the 1890s to the 1960s, canning fish products like brisling, fish balls, and sardines was Stavanger's main industry. On special activity days, the public can take part in the production process, sometimes tasting newly smoked brisling—on the first Sunday of every month and Tuesdays and Thursdays in summer, the ovens used for smoking fish are stoked up once again. ✉ *Øvre Strandgt. 88A* ✆ *51/84–27–00* ⊕ *www.stavanger.museum.no* ✉ *NKr 40* ☉ *Mid-*

June–mid-Aug., daily 11–4; early June and late Aug., Mon.–Thurs. 11–3, Sun. 11–4; Sept.–May, Sun. 11–4 or by appointment.

Along Strandkaien, warehouses face the wharf; the shops, offices, and apartments face the street on the other side. Housed in the only two shipping merchants' houses that remain completely intact is the **Sjøfartsmuseet** (Stavanger Maritime Museum). Built between 1770 and 1840, the restored buildings trace the past 200 years of trade, sea-traffic, and shipbuilding. Visit a turn-of-the-20th-century general store, an early 1900s merchant's apartment, and a sail maker's loft. A reconstruction of a shipowner's office and a memorial are here, as are two 19th-century ships: *Anna af Sand* and *Wyvern.* ⊠ *Nedre Strandgt. 17–19* ☎ *51/84–27–00* ⊕ *www.stavanger.museum.no* ⊠ *NKr 40* ☉ *Mid-June–mid-Aug., daily 11–4; early June–mid-June and mid–late Aug., Mon.–Thurs. 11–3, Sun. 11–4; Sept.–May, Sun. 11–4 or by appointment* ☉ *Closed Dec.*

Fodor'sChoice
★ Resembling a shiny offshore oil platform, the dynamic **Norsk Oljemuseum** (Norwegian Petroleum Museum) is an absolute must-see. In 1969, oil was discovered off the coast of Norway. The museum explains how oil forms, how it's found and produced, its many uses, and its impact on Norway. Interactive multimedia exhibits accompany original artifacts, models, and films. A reconstructed offshore platform includes oil workers' living quarters—as well as the sound of drilling and the smell of oil. The highly recommended museum café, by restaurateurs Bølgen & Moi, serves dinners as well as lighter fare. ⊠ *Kjeringholmen, Stavanger Havn* ☎ *51/93–93–00* ⊕ *www.norskolje.museum.no* ⊠ *NKr 75* ☉ *Sept.–May, Mon.–Sat. 10–4, Sun. 10–6; June–Aug., daily 10–7.*

If you have a Norwegian branch on your family tree, trace your roots at **Det Norske Utvandresenteret,** in a harborside wharf house from the early 1700s. The Norwegian Emigration Center has passenger lists, parish registers, census records, and a comprehensive collection of books on Norway's rural past. Bring along any information you have, especially the dates and places from which your ancestors left Norway. The center organizes the annual Norwegian Emigration Festival, with exhibitions, concerts, and excursions to historical sites. ⊠ *Strandkaien 31* ☎ *51/53–88–60* 🖷 *51/53–88–63* ⊕ *www.emigrationcenter.com* ⊠ *NKr 35* ☉ *Mon. and Wed.–Fri. 9–3, Tues. 9–7.*

Rogaland Kunstmuseum (Rogaland Museum of Fine Arts) has the country's largest collection of works by Lars Hertervig (1830–1902), the greatest Romantic painter of Norwegian landscapes. With Norwegian paintings, drawings, and sculptures, the museum's permanent collection covers the early 19th century to the present. The Halvdan Haftsten Collection has paintings and drawings done between the world wars. There's also a collection of works by Kitty Kielland. The museum is near Mosvannet (Mos Lake), which is just off highway E18 at the northern end of downtown. ⊠ *Tjensvoll 6, Mosvannsparken* ☎ *51/53–05–20* ⊠ *NKr 50* ☉ *Tues.–Sun. 11–4.*

off the beaten path

UTSTEIN KLOSTER – Originally the palace of Norway's first king, Harald Hårfagre, and later the residence of King Magnus VI, Utstein was used as a monastery from 1265 until 1537, when it reverted to the royal family. Buses depart for Utstein from Stavanger weekdays at 12:15, returning from the monastery at 4:05. By bus or by car it's about a half-hour trip, which takes you north on coastal Highway 1, through the world's second-longest undersea car tunnel. There's a toll of NKr 75 for the tunnel passage.

As Stavanger began to become an important town in the Middle Ages, watchmen were hired to look out for fires, crime, and anything else out of the ordinary. The **Vektermuseet i Valbergtårnet** (Watchman's Museum in the Valberg Tower) examines the role the watchmen played in keeping the town safe. The Valbergtårnet was built in the 1850s to give a panoramic view of the town below. With so many wooden houses, an early warning was essential. The view remains as incredible as ever. ⊠ *Valbergtårnet* ☎ *51/89–55–01* ⊕ *www.stavanger.kommune.no/solverg* 🖾 *NKr 10* ⊗ *Mon.–Wed. and Fri. 10–4, Thurs. 10–6, Sat. 10–2.*

The **Norsk Barnemuseum** (Norwegian Children's Museum) has Norway's largest collection of children's toys. Storytelling, dramatic performances, and other activities focus on the country's culture and history. ⊠ *Sølvberget (Stavanger Culture Center)* ☎ *51/91–23–90* ⊕ *www.norskbarne. museum.no* 🖾 *NKr 65* ⊗ *Wed.–Fri. 1–7, Sat. noon–5, Sun. 1–5.*

Take a scented stroll in Stavanger's wild rose garden. At the **Botanisk Hage** (Botanical Gardens), you can find leaved and flowered earthly delights. Some 2,000 varieties of herbs and perennials are grown here. ⊠ *Rektor Natvig Pedersensv. 40* ☎ *51/50–78–61* 🖾 *Free* ⊗ *Apr.–Sept., weekdays 7 AM–8 PM, weekends 10–8; Oct.–Mar., weekdays 7–5, weekends 10–5.*

Although it's a reconstruction, the **Jernaldergarden** late Iron Age farm complex from the Migration Period (AD 350–550) feels like the real thing. The reconstructed historical buildings have been positioned on original foundations. Relics such as a Bronze Age gravestone have been discovered here. Research is still underway. Taste some mead, the Vikings' favorite drink, or have breakfast or lunch on wooden benches before fireplaces. ⊠ *Ullandhaugen.* ☎ *51/81 60 00* 🖾 *NKr 30* ⊗ *Mid June–mid-Aug., daily 11–4; May–mid-Oct., Sun. noon–6; mid-Aug.–mid-June, by appointment.*

The site where Norway was founded has been memorialized by the **Sverd i fjell** (Three Swords Monument). The three huge bronze swords were unveiled by King Olav in 1983 and done by artist Fritz Røed. The memorial is dedicated to King Harald Hårfagre (Harald the Fairhaired), who through an 872 battle at Hafrsfjord managed to unite Norway into one kingdom. The Viking swords' sheaths were modeled on ones found throughout the country; the crowns atop the swords represent the different Norwegian districts that took part in the battle. ⊠ *Hafrsfjord, on Grannesveien to Sola, 6 km (4 mi) south of Stavanger.*

More than 35 military and civilian planes make up the collection at the **Flyhistorisk Museum Sola** (History of Flying Museum, Sola municipality), which emphasizes aviation history from World War II on. Besides checking out changing exhibitions, you can sit in a passenger seat of a 1950s Metropolitan plane and see the changing designs through the years of the Norwegian Air Force's jet fighters. ⊠ *Sjøflyhaven, Stavanger Lufthavn* ☎ *51/65–56–57* 🖾 *NKr 40* ⊗ *Late June–mid-Aug., daily noon–4; May–late June and late Aug.–Nov., Sun. noon–4.*

Kongeparken amusement park has go-carts, radio cars, bumper boats, Norway's longest bobsled run, and its largest merry-go-round. In the Chocolate Factory, children can make their own Freia-brand milk chocolate. ⊠ *4330 Ålgård* ☎ *51/61–71–11* ⊕ *www.kongeparken.no* 🖾 *NKr 125* ⊗ *May–Sept., daily 10–6.*

off the beaten path

PREIKESTOLEN – The Pulpit Rock, a huge cube with a vertical drop of 2,000 feet, is not a good destination if you suffer from vertigo—it has a heart-stopping view. The clifflike rock sits on the banks of the finger-shape Lysefjord. You can join a tour to get to the region's best-known attraction, or you can do it on your own from early June to early September by taking the bus—it costs NKr 45 one-way from the town of Tau to the Pulpit Rock. The buses are paired with morning ferry departures from Stavanger at 8:20 and 9:15. Then you can either hike the two-hour walk on a marked trail or ride horseback. (The ferry and bus take a total of about 40 minutes from Stavanger.)

LYSEFJORDSENTERET – Lysefjord Center has a shape that mimics the mountains. A multimedia simulation, *Saga of the Fjord*, shows how a trickling brook created this sliver of a fjord. You'll also learn about the geology and culture of Lysefjord. A ferry to the bottom of Pulpit Rock drops off passengers midway; for more information, call **Rogaland Traffik** (☎ 51/86–87–00) or **Clipper Fjord Sightseeing** (☎ 51/89–52–70). The center is free but the multimedia simulation costs NKr 20. ✉ *Oanes, Forsand* ☎ *51/70–31–23* ⊙ *May–Aug., weekdays noon–6, Sat. noon–7, Sun. noon–8.*

Where to Eat

Stavanger has established a reputation for culinary excellence. In fact, the city has the distinction of having the most bars and restaurants per capita in Norway. Many restaurant menus burst with sumptuous international dishes. The city is home to the Culinary Institute of Norway, and hosts many food and wine festivals every year, icluding the Gladmat Festival, Garlic Week, Stavanger Wine Festival, Chili Festival, and Creole Week.

$$$$ ✗ **Cartellet Restaurant.** The elegant dining room reflects the timelessness of this classic restaurant that goes founded in 1890. It has gold accents, stone walls hung with richly colored paintings, a dark wood interior, and leather furniture. Based on fresh, seasonal ingredients from Norway's fjords and mountains, the menu changes every day. ✉ *Øvre Holmegt. 8* ☎ *51/89–60–22* ⌿ *Reservations essential* ▭ *AE, DC, MC, V.*

$$$–$$$$ ✗ **Craigs Kjøkken & Bar.** Oklahoman Craig Whitson's café–restaurant is a great place for wining as well as dining. Stylish glass cabinets house the collection of more than 600 bottles of wine, with a focus on Italy, and the Rhone and Alsace regions of France. The food is seasonal, experimental, and eclectic, its influences ranging from Mediterranean to Asian. Try the popular spring lamb burger, or the huge, juicy Babe burger. The café hosts annual events such as the chili and wine festivals. Whitson's offbeat sense of humor comes through in the "12 disciples" that sit against one wall—a dozen smoked, salted, and dried pigs' heads. ✉ *Breitorget* ☎ *51/93–95–90* ▭ *AE, DC, MC, V.*

$$$–$$$$ ✗ **Straen Fiskerestaurant.** Right on the quay, this esteemed fish restaurant claims it's "world famous throughout Norway." The nostalgic interior filled with memorabilia, and the white-clothed tables, make the restaurant comforting and homely. If you're traveling with a group, reserve the bookshelf-lined library dining room. Try the famous fish soup of salmon and cream of shellfish, or the grilled monkfish, or lutefisk. The three-course meal of the day is always the best value. The aquavit bar carries more than 30 varieties. ✉ *Nedre Strandgt. 15* ☎ *51/84–37–00* ▭ *AE, DC, MC, V.*

$$$ ✗ **Vertshuset Mat & Vin.** The style of this restaurant matches the traditional Norwegian dishes served up by the kitchen. Amid wood walls, white lace curtains, and traditional paintings, you can enjoy popular dishes such as monkfish with saffron and *komler* (dumplings) with salted meats. ✉ *Skagen 10* ☎ *51/89–51–12* ▭ *AE, DC, MC, V.*

$$–$$$ ✕ **Gaffel & Karaffel.** Framed shiny forks playfully line the red walls of this hip restaurant, whose name means "fork and carafe." Called a tapas restaurant, its international menu delights with items such as cheese-filled salmon rolls, beefsteak sukiyaki, and herb-marinated catfish. ⊠ *Øvre Holmegt. 20* ☎ *51/86–41–58* ▤ *AE, DC, MC, V.*

$$–$$$ ✕ **Harry Pepper.** Norway's first Tex-Mex restaurant is still considered one of the country's best. Earthtones, cacti, and tacky souvenirs combine to make the joint light-hearted and playful. Try the sizzling fajitas or the lime-grilled fish kebab served with triple pesto. Have a tequila shot or two at the lively bar. ⊠ *Øvre Holmegt. 15* ☎ *51/89–39–93* ▤ *AE, DC, V.*

$$–$$$ ✕ **Saken er Biff.** A Norwegian country-style steakhouse, this restaurant has a whole lot more than beef on its menu. Be daring and try venison, reindeer, or moose, prepared rare, medium, or well-done. ⊠ *Skagenkaien 28* ☎ *51/89–60–80* ▤ *AE, DC, MC, V.*

$$–$$$ ✕ **Sjøhuset Skagen.** A sort of museum, this 18th-century former boathouse is filled with wooden beams, ship models, lobster traps, and other sea relics. The Norwegian and international menu has such dishes as chicken confit and the Hunter's Dream—grilled medallions of reindeer, potatoes, and vegetables—which is highly recommended. ⊠ *Skagenkaien 16* ☎ *51/89–51–80* ▤ *AE, DC, MC, V.*

$$–$$$ ✕ **Timbuktu Bar and Restaurant.** This is one of the Stavanger's trendiest restaurants. Within its airy interior of blonde wood and yellow and black, enthusiastic chefs serve Asian-inspired cuisine with African ingredients such as tuna fish from Madagascar. Known for its NKr 350 three-course dinners and its sushi, the restaurant often has visiting celebrity chefs, and hosts special events such as salsa parties and nights of Spanish tapas. ⊠ *Nedre Strandgt. 15* ☎ *51/84–37–40* ▤ *AE, DC, MC, V.*

$–$$$ ✕ **N. B. Sørensen's Dampskibsexpedition.** Norwegian emigrants waited
Fodor'sChoice here before boarding steamships crossing the Atlantic to North Amer-
★ ica 150 years ago. Restored in 1990, the historic wharfhouse is now a popular waterfront restaurant and bar. Emigrants' tickets, weathered wood, nautical ropes, old maps, photographs, and gaslights may make you feel that you're at sea as well. The Norwegian and international menu has popular dishes such as barbecued spareribs. Delicious grilled entrecôte with garlic is served in the understated, elegant dining room upstairs. ⊠ *Skagen 26* ☎ *51/84–38–20* ▤ *AE, DC, MC, V.*

Where to Stay

$$–$$$ 🏨 **Radisson SAS Atlantic Hotel Stavanger.** In the heart of downtown, the Atlantic overlooks Breiavatnet pond. All rooms are elegantly decorated in understated yellow, beiges, and reds, with plush furniture. The King Oscar lobby bar, Alexander Pub, and Café Ajax are popular with Stavanger's residents. ⊠ *Olav Vs gt. 3, 4001 Stavanger* ☎ *51/52–75–20* 🖷 *51/53–48–69* ⊕ *www.radisson.com* ⇆ *350 rooms, 5 suites* ⟁ *Restaurant, café, sauna, bar, lounge, pub, dance club, nightclub, meeting rooms* ▤ *AE, DC, MC, V.*

$$–$$$ 🏨 **Rica Park Hotel.** Understandably popular among business travelers, this hotel has been designed for people who need space and facilities to work. Several rooms are equipped with a computer and a fax machine. One room is wheelchair accessible. Stylish and comfortable, the rooms have subtle colors and patterns, dark wood furniture, and sea-theme paintings. ⊠ *Kannikgt. 7, 4000 Stavanger* ☎ *51/50–05–00* 🖷 *51/50–04–00* ⊕ *www.rica.no* ⇆ *59 rooms* ⟁ *Restaurant, sauna, bar, meeting rooms* ▤ *AE, DC, MC, V.*

★ $$–$$$ 🏨 **Skagen Brygge Hotell.** A symbol of Stavanger, this classic hotel's white wooden wharfhouses are common subjects for city postcards and photographs. It has a well-deserved reputation for superb service. The blue-accented, wood-beam rooms tend to have somewhat irregular shapes. Request a room facing the harbor and watch the world dock outside your window. Have a coffee anytime at the fourth floor's relaxing Kaffekroken lounge. On weekends Hovemesteren Bar is a popular nightspot. The hotel has an arrangement with 14 area restaurants whereby when you dine at any of them, you can arrange for the tab to be added to your hotel bill. ⊠ *Skagenkaien 30, Postboks 793, 4004* ☎ *51/85–00–00* 🖷 *51/85–00–01* ⊕ *www.skagenbryggehotell.no* ⇨ *110 rooms, 2 suites* ♨ *Restaurant, health club, sauna, Turkish baths, bar, convention center* ⊟ *AE, DC, MC, V.*

$$–$$$ 🖫 **Victoria Hotel.** Stavanger's oldest hotel was built at the turn of the 20th century and retains a clubby, Victorian style, with elegant carved furniture and floral patterns. Ask for a room overlooking the harbor. Stavanger's museums, Gamle Stavanger, and shopping are all within short walking distances. ⊠ *Skansegt. 1, Postboks 279, 4001 Stavanger* ☎ *51/ 86–70–00* 🖷 *51/86–70–10* ⊕ *www.victoria-hotel.no* ⇨ *107 rooms, 3 suites* ♨ *Restaurant,bar, meeting rooms* ⊟ *AE, DC, MC, V.*

$–$$$ 🖫 **Clarion Hotel Stavanger.** This downtown business hotel has an up-to-the-minute design. Famed local artist Kjell Pahr Iversen's vibrant paintings hang on the hotel's walls. The light, simple interior is punctuated by the clean lines of Phillipe Starck lamps and Erik Jørgensen chairs. The rooms are also bright and simply furnished. ⊠ *Ny Olavskleiv 8, 4008 Stavanger* ☎ *51/91–00–00* 🖷 *51/91–00–10* ⊕ *www.clhs.no* ⇨ *251 rooms, 22 suites* ♨ *Restaurant, café, bar, meeting rooms* ⊟ *AE, DC, MC, V.*

Festivals

Stavanger has earned the title *festivalbyen*, (festival city) for its year-round celebrations. More than 20 official festivals are held throughout the year—comedy, garlic, chili, food, chamber music, jazz, literature, beach volleyball, wine, belly dancing, vintage boats, emigrants, immigrants. There are probably just as many unofficial events, since locals love any reason to have a party. Contact **Destination Stavanger** (☎ *51/85–92–00* ⊕ www.visitstavanger.com) for a listing.

Nightlife & the Arts

CAFÉS Stavanger has its share of cozy and hip locations to have a drink, read the papers, listen to live music, or just hang out. News junkies head to Norway's first news café, **Newsman** (⊠ Skagen 14 ☎ 51/84–38–80), for CNN on the TV and for Norwegian and foreign periodicals. **Café Sting** (⊠ Valberget 3 ☎ 51/89–38–78), a combination restaurant, nightclub, art gallery, and performance venue, is an institution. **Amys Coffeebar** (⊠ Salvågergt. 7 ☎ 51/86–07–65) is a sweet little spot for an afternoon coffee or takeaway lunch. At **Café Italia** (⊠ Skagen 8 ☎ 51/ 85–92–90), there's an Italian coffee bar, a restaurant, and even a boutique selling Italy's top fashion names. **Stavanger Sportscafé** (⊠ Skagenkaien 14A ☎ 51/89–17–41) is a big hit with sports fans. For a quick snack or a glass of freshly squeezed fruit juice, stop by **Sitrus Sandwichbar** (⊠ Bakkegt. 7, entrance from Salvågergt. ☎ 51/81–15–90); the smoothies are delicious.

CLUBS & PUBS Stavanger clubs and pubs can show you a good time year-round. Walk along **Skagenkaien** and **Strandkaien** streets for a choice of pubs and nightclubs. In summer, harborside places with patios don't usually close until dawn. Sun-kissed **Hansen Hjørnet** (⊠ Skagenkaien 18 ☎ 51/ 89–52–80 ⊙ Mid-May–mid-Sept.) is a bar and restaurant that always attracts a crowd. Dance the night away to pulsating sounds at the lively **Taket Nattklubb** (⊠ Nedre Strandgt. 15 ☎ 51/84–37–20), popular with those in their 20s and 30s. **Checkpoint Charlie** (⊠ Lars Hertevigs gt. 5

51/53–22–45) is popular with the twentysomethings, and sometimes doubles as a concert venue. College kids hang out at **Folken** (✉ Ny Olavskleiv 16 ☎ 51/56–44–44), an independent student club that frequently holds rock concerts. With its open fireplace and stone walls, **Nåloyet** (✉ Nedre Strandgt. 13 ☎ 51/84–37–60) is Stavanger's answer to the London pub. Step into the stylish wine cellar **Flaskehalsen** (✉ Øvre Holmegt. 20 ☎ 51/86–41–58) if you're seeking quiet, romantic moments.

THE ARTS **Stavanger Konserthus** (✉ Concert Hall, Bjergsted ☎ 51/53–70–00) often hosts local artists, and there are free summertime concerts in the foyer. **Stavanger Symphony Orchestra** (☎ 51/50–88–30) performs throughout the year. **Stavangeren Kultur & Revyscene** (✉ Vaisenhusgt. 37 ☎ 51/84–38–50) is a popular meeting place and venue for cultural activities and events. In the heart of the city, **Sølvberget** (Stavanger Culture House; ✉ Sølvberggt. 2 ☎ 51/50–71–70) has exhibitions, cultural events, a library, Internet access, and movie theaters.

Built on an island in the archipelago in the Middle Ages and once a palace as well as a monastery, **Utstein Kloster** (✉ Mosterøy ☎ 51/72–01–00 ⊕ www.herlige-stavanger.no) has superior acoustics—classical and jazz music concerts are performed here from June to August. **Rogaland Theatre** (☎ 51/91–90–90) performs plays throughout the region. **Rogaland Kunstsenter** (Rogaland Art Center; ✉ Nytorget ☎ 51/59–97–60) has a respected gallery and art shop. Every May, Norwegian and international jazz artists play at the **MaiJazz** (☎ 51/84–66–67) festival. If chamber music's more your style, attend the **International Chamber Music Festival** (☎ 51/84–66–70), held every August. For literary types, there's **Chapter 01** (☎ 51/50–72–57), the "International Festival of Literature and Freedom of Expression."

Sports & the Outdoors

FISHING Angling for saltwater fish doesn't require a license or a fee of any kind. The local tourist office can help you get the permits required for other types of fishing.

North of Stavanger is the longest salmon river in western Norway, the Suldalslågen, made popular 100 years ago by a Scottish aristocrat who built a fishing lodge there. **Lindum** (✉ Lakseslottet Lindum, 4240 Suldalsosen ☎ 52/79–91–61) still has cabins and camping facilities, as well as a dining room. The main salmon season is July through September. Wear diving gear and you can go on a **Salmon Safari** (✉ Mo Laksegard ☎ 52/79–76–90), floating in the river 2 km (1 mi) to study wild salmon in their natural environment.

On the island of Kvitsøy, in the archipelago just west of Stavanger, you can rent an apartment, complete with fish-smoking and -freezing facilities, and arrange to use a small sailboat or motorboat. **Kvitsøy Kurs & Konferanse** (✉ Box 35, 4090 Kvitsøy ☎ 51/73–51–88) can help with arrangments.

GOLF Golf enthusiasts can work on their game at several local courses. The **Stavanger Golf Klubb** (✉ Longebakken 45, Hafrsfjord ☎ 51/55–50–06) has a lush park and forest near its 18-hole, international-championship course.

The **Sola Golf Klubb** (✉ Åsenveien, Sola ☎ 51/70–91–70) has an 18-hole course set amid a forest. If you'd like to golf next to the sea, head to **Sandnes og Sola Golfklubb** (✉ Solastranden Golfbane ☎ 51/69–68–90) 20 km (12 mi) from Stavanger.

HIKING Specialized books and maps are available through **Stavanger Turistforening** (✉ Postboks 239, 4001 Stavanger ☎ 51/84–02–00 ⊕ www.

stavanger-turistforening.no). The office can help you plan a hike through the area, particularly in the rolling Setesdalsheiene and the thousands of islands and skerries of the Ryfylke Archipelago. The tourist board oversees 33 cabins for members (you can join on the spot) for overnighting along the way.

HORSEBACK RIDING **Fossanmoen** (☎ 51/70–37–61 ⊕ www.fossanmoen.no) organizes riding camps and trips on Iceland ponies that go through scenic surroundings. They can last anywhere from an hour to all day.

ICE SKATING **Stavanger Ishall** (⊠ Siddishallen ☎ 51/53–74–50) has ice skating from mid-September to mid-April. From November through March, you can skate outdoors at **Kunstisbanen** (⊠ Åsen, Sørmarka ☎ 51/58–06–44).

SKIING Skiing in the Sirdal area, 2½ hours from Stavanger, is possible from January to April. Special ski buses leave Stavanger on the weekends at 8:30 AM during the season. Especially recommended is **Sinnes** (☎ 38/37–12–65) for its non–hair-raising cross-country terrain. Downhill skiing is available at **Ålsheia**, which is on the same bus route. Other places to ski include **Gullingen skisenter, Suldal** (☎ 52/79–99–01), **Stavtjørn alpinsenter** (☎ 51/45–17–17), and **Sandalen skisenter, Sauda** (☎ 52/78–56–56). Contact **Connex Vest** (⊠ Treskevn. 5, Hafrsfjord, Stavanger ☎ 51/59–90–00) for transportation information.

WATER SPORTS Diving is excellent all along the coast—although Norwegian law requires all foreigners to dive with a Norwegian as a way of ensuring that wrecks are left undisturbed. If you just want to take a swim, plan a trip to **local beaches** such as **Møllebukta** and **Madia**, which are both deep inside the Hafrsfjord. **Solastranden** has 2⅓ km (1½ mi) of sandy beach ideal for windsurfing and beach volleyball. Other prime beach spots are Vaulen badeplass, Godalen badeplass, Viste Stranden, and Sande Stranden.

The local swimming pool is **Stavanger Svømmehall** (☎ 51/50–74–51). **Gamlingen Friluftsbad** (⊠ Tjodolfsgt. 53 ☎ 51/52–74–49) is an outdoor heated swimming pool that's open year-round.

Shopping

Stavanger Storsenter Steen & Strøm (⊠ Domkirkepl. 2) is a centrally located shopping center. **Kvadrat Kjøpesenter** (⊠ Lura, between Stavanger and Sandnes ☎ 51/96–00–00) is the area's best shopping center, with 155 shops, restaurants, a pharmacy, post office, a state wine store, and a tourist information office. In an early-17th-century wharfhouse, **Straen Handel** (⊠ Strandkaien 31 ☎ 51/52–52–02) has an impressive collection of knitted items, rosemaling, Norwegian dolls, trolls, books, and postcards. Bookworms might find literary treasures in the aptly titled **Odd Book Shop** (⊠ Kirkegt. 30 ☎ 51/89–47–66). Reindeer hides, sheepskin, and other souvenirs are sold at **Olaf Pettersen & Co.** (⊠ Kirkegt. 31 ☎ 51/89–48–04). If jewelry's your passion, head to the city's best shop: **Sølvsmeden på Sølvberget** (⊠ Sølvberggt. 5 ☎ 51/89–42–24).

Sørlandet to Stavanger A to Z

AIR TRAVEL

CARRIERS Kristiansand is served by Braathens, with nonstop flights from Oslo, Bergen, and Stavanger; and SAS, with nonstop flights from Copenhagen. MUK Air serves Aalborg, Denmark; Agder Fly serves Göteborg, Sweden, and Billund, Denmark. Tickets on the last two airlines can be booked through Braathens or SAS.

Braathens flies to Stavanger from Oslo, Kristiansand, Bergen, Trondheim, and Newcastle. SAS has nonstop flights to Stavanger from Bergen, Oslo, Copenhagen, Aberdeen, Göteborg, London, and Newcastle. The low-cost carrier Norwegian has flights from Oslo to Stavanger. Widerøe flyveselskap specializes in flights within Norway.

🛫 **Braathens** ☎ 81/52-00-00. **Norwegian Air Shuttle** ☎ 81/52-18-15. **SAS** ☎ 81/52-04-00. **Widerøe** ☎ 81/00-12-00.

AIRPORTS

Kristiansand's Kjevik Airport is about 16 km (10 mi) outside town. The airport bus departs from the Braathens office approximately one hour before every departure and proceeds to Kjevik, stopping at downtown hotels along the way. A similar bus makes the return trip from the airport.

In Stavanger, Sola Airport is 17 km (11 mi) from downtown. The Flybussen (airport bus) leaves the airport every 20 minutes. It stops at hotels and outside the railroad station in Stavanger. It then heads back to the airport.

🛫 **Stavanger Airport Bus** ☎ 91/63-51-65.

BOAT & FERRY TRAVEL

Color Line has four ships weekly on the Stavanger–Newcastle route. High-speed boats to Bergen are operated by Flaggruten. Fjord Line offers car ferries that go from Stavanger to Newcastle, England, and from Egersund to Hanstholm, in Northern Denmark. Another line connects Larvik to Frederikshavn, on Denmark's west coast. For information about this crossing, contact DSB in Denmark, or Color Line or DFDS Scandinavian Seaways in Norway.

🚢 **Color Line A/S** ✉ Nygt. 13, 4006 Stavanger ☎ 810-00-811 ⊕ www.colorline.no. **DSB** ☎ 33/14-17-01, 42/52-92-22 in Denmark ⊕ www.dsb.dk. **DFDS Scandinavian Seaways** 🖷 38/17-17-60 ⊕ www.seaeurope.com. **Fjord Line** ☎ 81/53-35-00 ⊕ www.fjordline.com. **Flaggruten** ☎ 51/86-87-80.

BUS TRAVEL

Aust-Agder Trafikkselskap, based in Arendal, has one departure daily in each direction for the 5½- to 6-hour journey between Oslo and Kristiansand. Sørlandsruta, based in Mandal, has two departures in each direction for the 4½-hour trip from Kristiansand bus terminal to Stavanger. The main bus terminal is outside the train station.

Bus connections in Sørlandet are infrequent; the tourist office can provide a comprehensive schedule. HAGA Reiser operates buses between Stavanger and Hamburg.

🚌 **Aust-Agder Trafikkselskap** ☎ 37/02-65-00. **HAGA Reiser** ☎ 51/67-65-00 or 38/12-33-12. **Kristiansand Bus Information** ✉ Strandgt. 33 ☎ 38/00-28-00. **Sørlandsruta** ☎ 38/03-83-00. **Ruteservice Stavanger, Norway Busekspress** ☎ 51/53-96-00.

CAR TRAVEL

From Oslo, it is 320 km (199 mi) to Kristiansand and 452 km (281 mi) to Stavanger. Route E18 parallels the coastline but stays slightly inland on the eastern side of the country and farther inland in the western part. Although seldom wider than two lanes, it is easy driving because it is so flat.

Sørlandet is also flat, so it's easy driving throughout. The area around the Kulturhus in the Stavanger city center is closed to car traffic, and one-way traffic is the norm in the rest of the downtown area.

CAR RENTALS 🚗 **Major Agencies Avis Bilutleie** ☎ 51/93-93-60 Stavanger, 38/07-00-90 Kristiansand. **Budget** ☎ 51/52-21-33 Stavanger, 38/06-37-97 Kristiansand. **Hertz Bilutleie** ☎ 51/52-00-00 Stavanger, 38/02-22-88 Kristiansand.

EMERGENCIES

For emergency medical care in Kristiansand, go to Kristiansand Legevekt, open daily from 4 PM to 8 AM. For an emergency in Stavanger, you can call Rogaland Sentralsykehusgo or go to Forus Akutten medical center, open 8 AM–8 PM weekdays.

In Kristiansand, Elefantapoteket (Elefant Pharmacy) is open weekdays from 8:30 to 8, Saturday from 8:30 to 6, and Sunday from 3 to 6. In Stavanger, Løveapoteket is open daily from 9 AM to 11 PM except for Christmas, New Year's Day, and Easter Sunday, when it closes at 8 PM.

Ambulance ☎ 113. **Egil Undem, Stavanger dentist** ✉ Kannikbakken 6 ☎ 51/52-84-52. **Elefantapoteket** (Elefant Pharmacy) ✉ Gyldenløvesgt. 13, 4611, Kristiansand ☎ 38/12-58-80. **Emergency Doctor, Stavanger** ☎ 51/51-02-02. **Fire** ☎ 110. **Forus Akutten medical center, Stavanger** ✉ Egsvn. 102 ☎ 38/07-69-00. **Løveapoteket** (Løve Pharmacy) ✉ Olav Vs gt. 11, 4005, Stavanger ☎ 51/91-08-80. **Police** ☎ 112. **Rogaland Sentralsykehus** ☎ 51/51-80-00.

TAXIS

All Kristiansand and Stavanger taxis are connected with a central dispatching office. Journeys within Stavanger are charged by the meter, elsewhere strictly by distance.

Norgestaxi Stavanger ☎ 08000. **Taxi Sør** ☎ 38/02-80-00 Kristiansand. **Stavanger Taxisentral** ☎ 51/90-90-90.

TOURS

Tours of Kristiansand are offered only in summer. The City Train is a 15-minute tour of the center part of town. The MS *Maarten* gives two-hour tours of the eastern archipelago and a three-hour tour of the western archipelago daily at 10 AM, from early June until August 8.

In Stavanger, a two-hour bus tour leaves from the marina at Vågen daily at 1 between June and August. Rødne Clipper Fjord Sightseeing offers three different tours. FjordTours operates sightseeing and charter tours by boat.

City Train ✉ Nedre Torv ☎ 38/03-05-24. **FjordTours** ☎ 51/53-73-40. **MS *Maarten*** ✉ Pier 6 by Fiskebrygga ☎ 38/12-13-14. **Rødne Clipper Fjord Sightseeing** ✉ Skagenkaien 18, 4006 ☎ 51/89-52-70.

TRAIN TRAVEL

The Sørlandsbanen leaves Oslo S Station four times daily for the five-hour journey to Kristiansand and five times daily for the 8½- to nine-hour journey to Stavanger. Two more trains travel the 3½-hour Kristiansand–Stavanger route. Kristiansand's train station is at Vestre Strandgata. For information on trains from Stavanger, call Stavanger Jernbanestasjon.

Kristiansand Train Station ☎ 38/07-75-32. **NSB** (Norwegian State Railways) ☎ 815-00-888. **Stavanger Jernbanestasjon** (Stavanger Train Station) ☎ 51/56-96-10.

VISITOR INFORMATION

Tourist Information Arendal SørlandsInfo ✉ Arendal Næringsråd, Friholmsgt. 1, 4800 ☎ 37/00-55-44. **Destinajon Sørlandet: Kristiansand** ✉ Vestre Torv, Vestre Strandgt. 32, Box 592, 4665 ☎ 38/12-13-14. **Destinasjon Sørlandet: Lillesand** ✉ Strandgt. 14, 4790 ☎ 37/26-16-80. **Destinasjon Sørlandet: Vennesla** ✉ Vennesla stasjon, 4700 ☎ 38/13-72-00. **Destinasjon Stavanger** ✉ Rosenkildetorget ☎ 51/85-92-00. **Hå Tourist Information** ✉ Hå Folkebiblioteket ☎ 51/43-40-11. **Mandal** Mandal og Lindesnes Turistkontor ✉ Bryggegt., 4500 ☎ 38/27-83-00. **Sandnes Tourist Board** ✉ Våsgt. 22 ☎ 51-97-55-55.

BERGEN

Many fall in love at first sight with Bergen, Norway's second largest city. Seven rounded, lush mountains, pastel-color wooden houses, historic Bryggen, winding cobblestone streets, and Hanseatic relics all make it a place of enchantment. Its many epithets include *Trebyen* ("Wooden City"; it has many wooden houses), *Regnbyen* ("Rainy City," due to its 200 days of rain a year), and *Fjordbyen* (gateway to the fjords). Surrounded by forested mountains and fjords, it's only natural that most Bergensers feel at home either on the mountains (skiing, hiking, walking, or at their cabins) or at sea (fishing and boating). As for the rainy weather, most residents quickly learn the necessity of rain jackets and umbrellas. Bergen is even the site of the world's first umbrella vending machine.

Residents take legendary pride in their city and its luminaries. The composer Edvard Grieg, the violinist Ole Bull, and Ludvig Holberg, Scandinavia's answer to Molière, all made great contributions to Norwegian culture. Today, their legacy lives on in nationally acclaimed theater, music, film, dance, and art. The singer Sissel Kyrkjebø, pianist Leif Ove Andsnes, choreographer Jo Strømgren, and author Gunnar Staalesen all live in Bergen. Every year, a host of lively festivals attracts national and international artists.

This harbor city has played a vital role in the Norwegian economy. Before the discovery of North Sea oil, and Bergen's subsequent rise as the capital of Norway's oil industry, the city was long a major center of fishing and shipping. In fact, Bergen was founded in 1070 by Olav Kyrre as a commercial center. During the 14th century, Hanseatic merchants settled in Bergen and made it one of their four major overseas trading centers. The surviving Hanseatic, wooden buildings on *Bryggen* (the quay) are topped with triangular cookie-cutter roofs and painted in red, blue, yellow, and green. Monuments in themselves (they are on the UNESCO World Heritage List), the buildings tempt travelers and locals to the shops, restaurants, and museums inside. In the evenings, when the Bryggen is illuminated, these modest buildings, together with the stocky Rosenkrantz Tower, the Fløyen, and the yachts lining the pier, are reflected in the waters of the habor—and provide one of the loveliest cityscapes in northern Europe.

Exploring Bergen

The heart of Bergen is at Torgalmenningen, the city's central square, which runs from Ole Bulls Plass to Fisketorget on the harbor, facing Bryggen. From here, the rest of Bergen spreads up the sides of the seven mountains that surround it, with some sights concentrated near the university and others near a small lake called Lille Lungegårdsvann. Fløyen, the mountain to the east of the harbor, is the most accessible for daytrippers. Before you begin your walking tour, you can take the funicular (cable car) up to the top of it for a particularly fabulous overview of the city.

Numbers in the text correspond to numbers in the margin and on the Bergen map.

Historic Bergen: Bryggen to Fløyen

Start your tour in the center of town at Torget, also called **Fisketorget ①** ▶ or the Fish Market, where fishermen and farmers deal their goods. Next, walk over to **Bryggen ②**, the wharf on the northeast side of Bergen's harbor. The gabled wood warehouses lining the docks mark the site of the city's original settlement. Take time to walk the narrow

a good walk

passageways between buildings; shops and galleries are hidden among the wooden facades. Follow the pier to the **Hanseatisk Museum** ❸ at Finnegårdsgaten and have a look inside. Afterward, continue your walk down the wharf, past the historic buildings, to the end of the Holmen promontory and to **Bergenhus Festning** ❹ (Bergenhus Fort), which dates from the 13th century; the nearby Rosenkrantztårnet is a 16th-century tower residence. After you've spent some time out here, retrace your steps back to the Radisson SAS Royal Hotel. Beside the hotel is **Bryggens Museum** ❺, which houses magnificent archaeological finds. Behind the museum is the 12th-century church called **Mariakirken** ❻. Around the back of the church up the small hill is Øvregaten, a street that's the back boundary of Bryggen. Walk down Øvregaten four blocks to **Fløibanen** ❼, the funicular that runs up and down Fløyen, one of the city's most popular hiking mountains. Don't miss a trip to the top, whether you hike or take the funicular—the view is like no other. When you've returned, walk south on Øvregaten to the **Domkirke** ❽ (Bergen Cathedral). It's on your left, at the intersection with Kong Oscars Gate. Finally, head back to Torgalmenningen in the center of town for a late afternoon snack at one of the square's cafés.

TIMING This tour will take a good portion of a day. Be sure to get to the Fisketorget early in the morning, as many days it may close as early as 1 or 2. Also, try to plan your trip up Fløyen for a sunny day. It may be difficult, as Bergen is renowned for rain, but you may want to wait a day or two and see if the skies clear up.

WHAT TO SEE

off the beaten path

AKVARIET – Here you will see one of the largest collections of North Sea fish and invertebrates in Europe, as well as tropical saltwater and fresh water fish. The aquarium has 70 tanks and three outdoor pools of seals, carp, and penguins. On a realistic nesting cliff, adorable penguins rest, waddle by, and stare back curiously at onlookers. Watch Lina, the first harbor seal born in captivity in Norway, or her companions as they zoom by like swimming torpedoes. Inside, there are schools of brilliant Amazon rainforest fish as well as common eels, which tend to wrap around each other. *The Aquarium: Bergen and the Local Coastline* is a 360° video directed by one of Norway's most beloved animators, the late Ivo Caprino. The aquarium is on Nordnes Peninsula, a 20-minute walk from the fish market. You can also get to it by taking Bus 11 or the ferry from the Fisketorget (Fish Market). ⊠ *Nordnesbakken 4, Nordnes* ☎ *55/55–71–71* ⊕ *www. akvariet.com* ⌚ *NKr 80* ☉ *May–Oct., daily 9–8; Oct.–May, daily 10–6. Feeding times: noon and 3.*

❹ **Bergenhus Festning.** (Bergenhus Fortress). The buildings here date from the mid-13th century. **Håkonshallen,** a royal ceremonial hall erected during the reign of Håkon Håkonsson between 1247 and 1261, was badly damaged by the explosion of a German ammunition ship in 1944 but was restored by 1961. Erected in the 1560s by the governor of Bergen Castle (Bergenhus), Erik Rosenkrantz, **Rosenkrantztårnet** (Rosenkrantz Tower) served as a combined residence and fortified tower. ⊠ *Bergenhus, Bryggen* ☎ *55/31–60–67* ⊕ *www.hd.uib.no/haakon.htm* ⌚ *NKr 20* ☉ *Mid-May–mid-Aug., daily 10–4; Sept.–mid-May, Sun. noon–3. Closed during Bergen International Music Festival.*

❷ **Bryggen** (The Wharf). A trip to Bergen is incomplete without a trip to Bryggen. A row of mostly reconstructed 14th-century wooden buildings that face the harbor makes this one of the most charming walkways in Europe, especially on a sunny day. The originals were built by Hansa

FodorśChoice
★

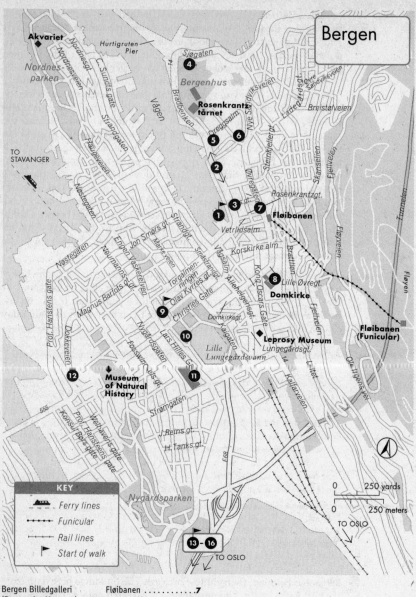

Bergen

Akvariet

Nordnes-
parken

Hurtigruten
Pier

Sjøgaten

Bergenhus

Rosenkrantz
tårnet

TO
STAVANGER

Fløibanen

Fløibanen
(Funicular)

Vetrlidsalm

Korskirke alm

Lille Øvregt.

Domkirke

Leprosy Museum

Domkirkegt.

Lille
Lungegårdsvann

Museum
of Natural
History

Strømgaten

J. Reins gt.

H. Tanks.gt.

Nygårdsparken

KEY

- Ferry lines
- Funicular
- Rail lines
- Start of walk

0   250 yards
0   250 meters

TO OSLO

13 – 16

TO OSLO

merchants, while the oldest reconstruction dates from 1702. Several fires, the latest in 1955, destroyed the original structures.

⑤ Bryggens Museum. This museum contains archaeological finds from the Middle Ages. An exhibit on Bergen circa 1300 shows the town at the zenith of its importance, and has reconstructed living quarters as well as artifacts such as old tools and shoes. Back then, Bergen was the largest town in Norway, a cosmopolitan trading center and the national capital. ⊠ *Dreggsalmenning 3* ☎ *55/58–80–10* ⊕ *www.uib.no/bmu* ▧ *NKr 30* ☉ *May–Sept., daily 10–5; Sept.–May, weekdays 11–3, Sat. noon–3, Sun. noon–4.*

⑧ Domkirke (The Bergen Cathedral). The cathedral's long, turbulent history has shaped the eclectic architecture of the current structure. The Gothic-style choir and the lower towers are oldest, dating from the 13th century. Note the cannonball lodged in the tower wall—it dates from a battle between English and Dutch ships in Bergen harbor in 1665. From June to September, a Sunday service is held in English at 9:30 AM in the Chapter House, an organ recital is held Thursdays at noon, and there is also music played on Sunday evenings at 7:30. ⊠ *Kong Oscars gt. and Domkirke gt.* ☎ *55/31–58–75* ☉ *Late May–Aug., Mon.–Sat. 11–5, Sun. 10–1; Sept.–late May, Tues.–Fri. 11–2, Sat. 11–3, Sun. 10–1.*

▶ **❶ Fisketorget** (Fish Market). Turn-of-the-20th-century photographs of this pungent square show fishermen in Wellington boots and mackintoshes and women in long aprons. Now, the fishmongers wear bright-orange rubber overalls as they look over the catches of the day. In summer, the selection is mostly limited to shrimp, salmon, and monkfish. There is much greater variety and more locals shopping during the rest of the year. There are also fruit, vegetable, and flower stalls, and some handicrafts and souvenir vendors at this lively market. You'll also find the world's first umbrella vending machine. Have a classic lunch of smoked shrimp or salmon on a baguette with mayonnaise and cucumber. ⊠ *Zachariasbryggen* ☎ *55/31–56–17* ⊕ *www.torgetibergen.no* ☉ *June–Aug., weekdays 7–5, Sat. 7–4; Sept.–May, Mon.–Sat. 7–4.*

★ **❼ Fløibanen** (Fløyen Funicular). A magnificent view of Bergen and its suburbs can be taken in from the top of **Mount Fløyen,** the most popular of the city's seven mountains. The eight-minute ride on the funicular takes you to the top, 1,050 feet above the sea. A car departs every half hour. Take a break at the restaurant and café (open daily in summer and weekends the rest of the year), the gift shop, or the children's playground. There are summer concerts every evening from mid-June to mid-August. Stroll down the walking path back to downtown or explore the mountains that lead to Ulriken, the highest mountain surrounding Bergen. ⊠ *Vetrlidsallmenning 21, Bryggen* ☎ *55/33–68–00* ⊕ *www.floibanen. no* ▧ *NKr 50* ☉ *Sept.–Apr., weekdays 7:30 AM–11 PM, Sat. 8 AM–11 PM, Sun. 9 AM–11 PM; May–Aug., same start times, runs until midnight.*

★ **❸ Hanseatisk Museum.** One of the best-preserved buildings in Bergen, the Hanseatic Museum was the 16th-century office and home of an affluent German merchant. The apprentices lived upstairs, in boxed-in beds with windows cut into the wall. Although claustrophobic, the snug rooms had the benefit of being relatively warm—a blessing in the unheated building. ⊠ *Bryggen* ☎ *55/31–41–89* ⊕ *www.hanseatisk. museum.no* ▧ *NKr 40, off-season NKr 25* ☉ *June–Sept., daily 9–5; Sept.–May, daily 11–2.*

❻ Mariakirken (St. Mary's Church). Considered one of the most outstanding Romanesque churches in Norway, this is the oldest building in Bergen used for its original purpose. It began as a church in the 12th century but gained a Gothic choir, richly decorated portals, and a splendid Baroque pulpit, much of it added by the Hanseatic merchants who owned it from 1408 to 1766. See the gilded triptych at the high altar that dates from the late Middle Ages. Organ recitals are held every Tuesday at 7:30 PM from June 24 through August. ⊠ *Dreggen, Bryggen* ☎ *55/31–59–60* 🖰 *NKr 10 in summer* ☉ *May 22–Sept., weekdays 11–4; Oct.–May 21, Tues.–Fri. noon–1:30.*

Rasmus Meyers Allé & Grieghallen

a good walk

From Torgalmenningen, walk to Nordahl Bruns Gate and turn left for the **Vestlandske Kunstindustrimuseum** ❾ ▶, the West Norway Museum of Decorative Art. After you've had your fill of the museum's elaborately crafted works, head out for Christies Gate. Follow it along the park and turn left on Rasmus Meyers Allé, which runs along the small lake, Lille Lungegårdsvann, to reach the **Bergen Billedgalleri** (Bergen Art Museum) ❿, which encompasses the **City Art Collection**, the **Stenersen Collection**, and the **Rasmus Meyer Collection**, all housed next to each other. Near these galleries, right on Lars Hilles Gate, is **Grieghallen** ⓫, Bergen's famous music hall.

Behind the hall, on Nygårdsgaten, walk up Herman Foss Gate to Muséplass to the **Bergen Museum** ⓬. Heading back into the center of the city, walk down Nygårdsgaten to Strømgaten to Kong Oscars Gate to the **Leprosy Museum.**

TIMING The museums on this tour are quite small and near each other, so you will be able to view most of them on a single outing if you want to, and you probably won't need more than half a day to go around them.

WHAT TO SEE

❿ **Bergen Billedgalleri** (Bergen Art Museum). This important Bergen institution, and one of the largest museums in Norway, is made up of the City Art, Rasmus Meyer, and Stenersen collections. The collections are housed in buildings along the Lille Lungegårdsvann Lake. The City Art Collection focuses on contemporary art. Standouts include Bjørn Carlsen's "Mother, I don't want to die in Disneyland" mixed-media piece, Tom Sandberg's photography, and poetry and installations by Yoko Ono. ⊠ *Bergen Art Museum, Rasmus Meyers allé 3 and 7, Lars Hilles gt. 10, City Center* ☎ *55/56–80–00* ⊕ *www.bergenartmuseum.no* 🖰 *NKr 50* ☉ *Mid-May–mid-Sept., daily 11–5; mid-Sept.–mid-May, Tues.–Sun. 11–5.*

⓬ **Bergen Museum.** Part of the University of Bergen, this museum has two collections. The **Cultural History Department** has a fascinating collection of archaeological artifacts and furniture and folk art from western Norway. Some of the titles of the displays are Inherited from Europe, Viking Times, Village Life in the Solomon Islands, and Ibsen in Bergen; the latter focuses on the famous playwright's six years in Bergen working with the local theater. The **Natural History Department** is perfect for lovers of the outdoors, since it includes botanical gardens. Exhibitions range from the Ice Age, Oil Geology, Fossils, Mineral Collections to the Evolution of Man. ⊠ *Haakon Sheteligs pl. 10 and Musépl. 3, City center* ☎ *55/58–31–40 or 55/58–29–20* ⊕ *www.museum.uib.no* 🖰 *NKr 30* ☉ *Mid-May–Sept., Tues.–Sat. 10–3, Sun. 11–4; Sept.–mid-May, Tues.–Sat. 11–2, Sun. 11–3.*

off the beaten path

GAMLE BERGEN MUSEUM (OLD BERGEN MUSEUM) – This family-friendly open-air museum transports you to 18th- and 19th-century Bergen. Streets and narrow alleys with 40 period wooden houses show town life as it used to be. A baker, dentist, photographer, jeweler, shopkeeper, and sailor are represented. Local artists often hold exhibitions here. The grounds and park are open free of charge year-round. ✉ *Elseros, Sandviken, Sandvika* ☎ *55/39–43–04* 💲 *NKr 25, NKr 50 with guided tour* ⊙ *May 11–Sept.; guided tours every hr, 10–5.*

⑪ **Grieghallen.** Home of the Bergen Philharmonic Orchestra and stage for the annual International Festival, this music hall is a conspicuous slab of glass and concrete. The acoustics are marvelous. Built in 1978, the hall was named for the city's famous son, composer Edvard Grieg (1843–1907). From September to May, every Thursday and some Fridays and Saturdays at 7:30 PM, the orchestra gives concerts. Throughout the year, the hall is a popular venue for cultural events. ✉ *Lars Hills gt. 3A* ☎ *55/21–61–50.*

Leprosy Museum. St. George's Hospital houses the Bergen Collection of the History of Medicine, which includes this museum. Although the current buildings date from the early 1700s, St. George's was a hospital for lepers for more than 500 years. This unusual museum profiles Norway's contribution to leprosy research. Many Norwegian doctors have been recognized for their efforts against leprosy, particularly Armauer Hansen, after whom "Hansen's disease" is named. ✉ *St. George's Hospital, Kong Oscars gt. 59* ⊕ *www.lepra.no* 💲 *NKr 30* ⊙ *Mid-June–Sept., daily 11–3.*

off the beaten path

NORWEGIAN MUSEUM OF FISHERIES – The sea and its resources, territorial waters, management and research, boats and equipment, whaling and sealing, and fish farming are all covered in the exhibits here. There are also substantial book, video, and photography collections. ✉ *Bontelabo 2* ☎ *55/32–12–49* 💲 *NKr 20* ⊙ *June–Aug., weekdays 10–6, weekends noon–4; Sept.–May, weekdays 10–4, weekends noon–4.*

⑩ **Rasmus Meyer Collection.** When the businessman Rasmus Meyer (1858–1916) was assembling his superb collection of works by what would become world-famous artists, most of them were unknowns. On display are the best Edvard Munch paintings outside Oslo, as well as major works by J. C. Dahl, Adolph Tidemand, Hans Gude, Harriet Backer, and Per Krohg. Head to the Blumenthal Room to see a fine 18th-century interior and some incredible frescoes. ✉ *Bergen Art Museum, Rasmus Meyers allé 3 and 7, Lars Hilles gt. 10, City Center* ☎ *55/56–80–00* ⊕ *www.bergenartmuseum.no* 💲 *NKr 50* ⊙ *Mid-May–mid-Sept., daily 11–5; mid-Sept.–mid-May, Tues.–Sun. 11–5.*

Fodor's Choice ★

★ ⑩ **Stenersen Collection.** This is an extremely impressive collection of modern art for a town the size of Bergen. Modern artists represented include Max Ernst, Paul Klee, Vassily Kandinsky, Pablo Picasso, and Joan Miró, as well as Edvard Munch. There's also a large focus here on Norwegian art since the mid-18th century. ✉ *Bergen Art Museum, Rasmus Meyers allé 3 and 7, Lars Hilles gt. 10, City Center* ☎ *55/56–80–00* ⊕ *www.bergenartmuseum.no* 💲 *NKr 50* ⊙ *Mid-May–mid-Sept., daily 11–5; mid-Sept.–mid-May, Tues.–Sun. 11–5.*

▶ ⑨ **Vestlandske Kunstindustrimuseum** (West Norway Museum of Decorative Art). One of Norway's best museums, this eclectic collection contains many exquisite art and design pieces. Its permanent "People and Possessions" exhibit spans 500 years and has everything from Bergen silverware to Ole Bull's violin, which was made in 1562 by the Italian master Saló. Bull's violin has a head of an angel on it, carved by Benvenuto Cellini. A fine collection traces the history of chair design. "The Art of China," the other permanent exhibition, presents one of Europe's largest collections of Buddhist marble sculptures alongside porcelain, jade, bronzes, textiles, and paintings. The silk robes embroidered with dragons and other ceremonial garments are stunning. Changing exhibitions focus on painting, decorative art, and design. ⊠ *Permanenten, Nordahl Bruns gt. 9, City Center* ☎ *55/33–66–33* ⊕ *www.vk.museum.no* ⊡ *NKr 40* ⊗ *Mid-May–mid-Sept., Tues.–Sun. 11–4; mid-Sept.–mid-May, Tues.–Sun. noon–4.*

Troldhaugen, Fantoft, Lysøen & Ulriken

a good drive

Once you've gotten your fill of Bergen's city life, you can head out to the countryside to tour some of the area's interesting, and lesser known, low-key attractions. Follow Route 1 (Nesttun/Voss) out of town about 5 km (3 mi) to **Edvard Grieg Museum, Troldhaugen** ⑬ ▶, the villa where Grieg lived for 22 years. After you've wandered the grounds, head for **Lysøen Island and Ole Bull's Villa** ⑭, the Victorian dream castle of Norwegian violinist Ole Bull. Getting here is a 30-minute trek by car and ferry, but it's well worth the effort. From Troldhaugen, get back on Route 1 or Route 586 to Fana, over Fanafjell to Sørestraumen. Follow signs to Buena Kai. From here, take the ferry to Lysøen. On your way back to Bergen, you can see the **Fantoft Stavkirke** ⑮, which was badly damaged in a fire in 1992 but has been completely rebuilt. End your day with a hike up **Ulriken Mountain** ⑯, the tallest of Bergen's seven mountains. If you're worn out from your sightseeing, but still want take in the view from the top, you can take the Ulriken cable car up the mountain.

About 12 km (7 mi) from Bergen city center, following Route 553 to the airport, is **Siljustøl**, the home of composer Harald S(ae)verud.

TIMING Driving and visiting time (or bus time) will consume at least a day or several depending on your pace and interest. Visiting these sights is a pleasant way to explore Bergen's environs.

WHAT TO SEE
⑮
Fodor'sChoice
★

Fantoft Stavkirke (Fantoft Stave Church). During the Middle Ages, when European cathedrals were built in stone, Norway used wood to create unique stave churches. These cultural symbols stand out for their dragon heads, carved doorways, and walls of staves (vertical planks). Though as many as 750 stave churches may have once existed, only 30 remain standing. The original stave church here, built in Fortun in Sogn in 1150 and moved to Fantoft in 1883, burned down in 1992. Since then, the church has been reconstructed to resemble the original structure. From *sentral bystasjonen* (the main bus station next to the railway station), take any bus leaving from Platform 19, 20, or 21. ⊠ *Paradis* ☎ *55/28–07–10* ⊡ *NKr 30* ⊗ *Mid-May–mid-Sept., daily 10:30–2 and 2:30–6.*

⑭ **Lysøen Island and Ole Bull's Villa.** The beautiful villa of Norwegian violin virtuoso Ole Bull (1810–80) is on Lysøen, which means "island of light." Bull was a musician and patron of great vision. In 1850, after failing to establish a "New Norwegian Theater" in America, he founded the National Theater in Norway. He then chose the young, unknown playwright Henrik Ibsen to write full time for the theater, and later encouraged and promoted another neophyte—15-year-old Edvard Grieg.

Built in 1873, this villa, with an onion dome, gingerbread gables, curved staircase, and cutwork trim just about everywhere, has to be seen to be believed. Stroll along the 13 km (8 mi) of pathways Bull created, picnic or swim in secluded spots, or rent a rowboat. Throughout the summer (the only season that Bull lived here), concerts are performed in the villa.

To get here by bus (Monday–Saturday), take the Lysefjordruta bus from Platform 19 or 20 at the main bus station to Buena Kai, where the *Ole Bull* ferry will take you across the fjord to the island. By car, it's a 25 km (15 mi) trip from Bergen to the ferry. Take road E39 south out of the city. Fork right onto Route 553, signposted FANA; continue straight over Fana Mountain to Sørestraumen and follow signs to Buena Kai from there. ☎ 56/30–90–77 ✉ NKr 25 ⊗ May 18–Aug., Mon.–Sat. noon–4, Sun. 11–5; Sept., Sun. noon–4.

off the beaten path

SILJUSTØL – Norway's most important composer of the last century, Harald Sæverud (1897–1992), called this unusual house home. He built it in 1939 of wood and stone and followed old Norwegian construction methods. Every Sunday in July, concerts are held here at 2 PM (admission NKr 200). Take Bus 30 from the Bergen bus station, Platform 20. By car, drive 12 km (7 mi) from Bergen center to Route 553 heading toward the airport. ✉ *Rådal* ☎ 55/92–29–92 ⊕ *www. siljustol.no* ✉ *NKr 50* ⊗ *June 19–Aug. 4, Wed.–Fri. and Sun. 11–4; Aug. 11–Nov. 3, Sun. noon–4; April 21–June 16, Sun. noon–4.*

➊ Edvard Grieg Museum, Troldhaugen (The Hill of the Trolls). Built in 1885, this was the home of Norway's most famous composer, Edvard Grieg. In the little garden hut by the shore of Lake Nordås, he composed many of his best known works. In 1867 he married his cousin Nina, a Danish soprano. They lived in the white clapboard house with green gingerbread trim for 22 years beginning in about 1885. A salon and gathering place for many Scandinavian artists then, it now houses mementos—a piano, paintings, prints—of the composer's life. Its 1907 interior shows it the way that Grieg knew it. At Troldsalen, a concert hall seating 200, chamber music is performed. Summer concerts are held on Wednesdays and weekends, and daily during the Bergen International Festival. To get here, catch a bus from Platform 19, 20, or 21 at the bus station, and get off at Hopsbroen. Turn right, walk 200 yards, turn left on Troldhaugsveien, and follow the signs for roughly 2 km (1 mi). ✉ *Troldhaugv. 65* ☎ *55/92–29–92* ⊕ *www.troldhaugen.com* ✉ *NKr 50* ⊗ *May–Sept., daily 9–6; Oct.–Dec. and Apr., weekdays 10–2, weekends noon–4; mid-Jan.–Mar. weekdays 10–2.*

➏ Ulriken Mountain. There are great views of the city, fjords, islands, and coast from the top of the highest of the seven Bergen mountains. The famous Ulriken cable car, running every seven minutes, transports you here. Bring a lunch and hike on well-marked trails in unspoiled mountain wilderness. Or take a break at Ulriken Restaurant and Bar. To get here from downtown, take the Bergen in a Nutshell sightseeing bus along the harbor and Bryggen, through the town center. The same bus returns you to town afterward. ✉ *Ulriken 1, 5009 Bergen* ⊕ *www.ulriken.no* ☎ *55/20–20–20* ✉ *Round-trip cost, including bus and cable car, is NKr 120* ⊗ *Daily 9 AM–10 PM; winter 10 AM–5 PM.*

Where to Eat

"Bergen is the city with the ocean and sea completely in its stomach," someone once said. Bergensers love their seafood dishes: *Fiskepudding* (fish pudding), *fiskekaker* (fish cakes), *fiskeboller* (fish balls), and *Bergensk fiskesuppe* (Bergen fish soup)—delicious renditions of such classic dishes show up on local menus with great regularity.

Any Bergen dining experience should start at *Fisketorget,* the fish market. Rain or shine, fresh catches go on sale here in shiny, stainless-steel stalls. The fishmongers dole out shrimp, salmon, monkfish, and friendly advice. Usually, they have steamed *rekker* (shrimp), or smoked *laks* (salmon), served on a baguette with mayonnaise and cucumber—a perfect quick lunch. As for desserts, *skillingsbolle,* a big cinnamon roll that often has a custard center, is popular. *Lefse* is a round flat cake of oatmeal or barley that has a sugar or cream filling. Like other major Norwegian cities, Bergen has international cuisines from Tex-Mex, tapas, and Mediterranean to Japanese sushi restaurants. Some Oslo celebrity chefs—for example Bølgen & Moi—have also opened restaurants here.

$$$$ ✕ **Fiskekrogen.** Right at the fish market, the Fishhook is a quintessential fish restaurant. The market's last original fish tank from 1888 holds the fresh lobster, codfish, and crab on offer here. The blue-and-white interior and open kitchen make the place feel rustic, as does the stuffed brown bear that still growls. Although Fiskekrogen also serves game, stick to seafood dishes such as the grilled monkfish in a goat cheese sauce or the mixture of catfish, salmon, shellfish, and mussels with vegetables. ✉ *Zachariasbryggen* ☎ 55/55–96–55 ⚓ *Reservations essential* ▭ *AE, DC, MC, V.*

$$$$ ✕ **Lucullus.** Although the eclectic interior—modern art matched with lace doilies and boardroom chairs—seems a bit out of kilter with the classic French menu here, don't be alarmed; the food is consistently good. The four-course meal is a particularly indulgent splurge. ✉ *Hotel Neptun, Walckendorfsgt. 8* ☎ 55/30–68–00 ⋔ *Jacket and tie* ▭ *DC, MC, V* ☾ *Closed Sun. No lunch.*

$$$–$$$$ ✕ **Bryggeloftet & Stuene.** Dining here on lutefisk in fall and at Christmastime is a time-honored tradition for many Bergensers. Also consider the *pinnkjøtt* (lumpfish) or the reindeer fillets. The hearty Norwegian country fare suits the somber, wooden dining room, with its fireplace and old oil paintings on the walls. ✉ *Bryggen 11* ☎ 55/31–06–30 ▭ *AE, DC, MC, V.*

$$$–$$$$
FodorsChoice
★ ✕ **Kafé Kristall.** This small, intimate restaurant is one of the most fashionable in town. The chef combines his own eclectic contemporary style with traditional Norwegian ingredients. Try the chili grilled angler with tomato, or the fish soup with grilled scampi. ✉ *Kong Oscars gt. 16* ☎ 55/ 32–10–84 ▭ *AE, DC, MC, V* ☾ *Closed Sun. No lunch.*

★ $$$ ✕ **Finnegaardstuene.** This classic Norwegian restaurant near Bryggen has four snug rooms. Some of the timber interior dates from the 18th century. The seven-course menu emphasizes seafood, although the venison and reindeer are excellent. Traditional Norwegian desserts, such as cloudberries and cream, are irresistible. ✉ *Rosenkrantzgt. 6* ☎ 55/ 55–03–00 ▭ *AE, DC, MC, V* ☾ *Closed Sun.*

$$$ ✕⬚ **von der Lippe.** Elegant and regal, this restaurant is in the catacombs of Kjøttbasaren, a restored meat market. Chef Knut Tau Hatlestad keeps the mainly poultry and seafood dishes simple. The lobster and the scallops stand out. If you're traveling in a group, reserve one of the two private rooms, which are like wine cellars. ✉ *Vetrlidsalmenningen 2* ☎ 55/55–22–22 ⋔ *Jacket and tie* ⚓ *Reservations essential* ▭ *AE, DC, MC, V.*

$$–$$$ ✕ **Baltazar.** In the cellar of a historic meat market, Kjøttbasaren, this candlelit restaurant with exposed brick walls is warm and romantic. Underneath the floor there's the keel of a wooden ship from 1300 that was discovered during the restoration of the building. The international menu emphasizes Norwegian ingredients. Try the fried ocean catfish served on a bed of spinach greens. The restaurant's chef, Knut Tau Hatlestad, is also behind several of the city's other successful restaurants, including von Lippe and Pasta Basta. ✉ *Vetrlidsalmenning 2* ☎ 55/55–22–00 ⚓ *Reservations essential* ▭ *AE, DC, MC, V.*

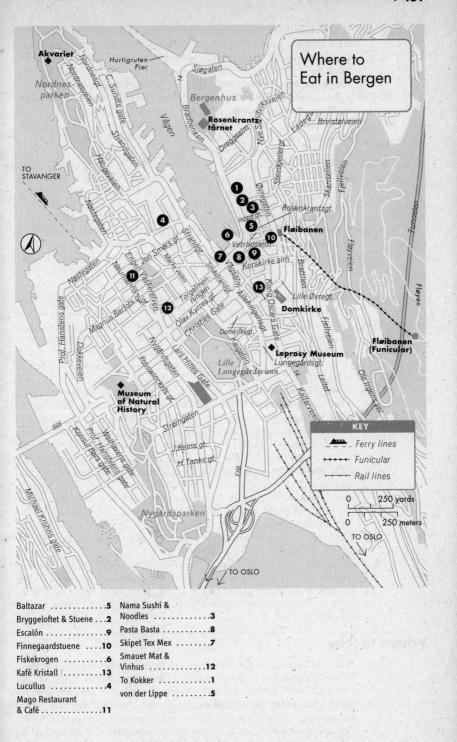

Where to Eat in Bergen

KEY

- ━━ *Ferry lines*
- •••••• *Funicular*
- ┼┼┼┼┼ *Rail lines*

0   250 yards
0   250 meters

★ **$$–$$$** ✕ **To Kokker.** Ranked among Bergen's best restaurants by many, Kokker is on Bryggen wharf. The 300-year-old building has crooked floors and slanted moldings. The seafood and game are excellent—especially the lobster and crayfish. ⊠ *Enhjørningsgården* ☎ *55/32–28–16* ⚔ *Reservations essential* ▤ *AE, DC, MC, V* ☉ *Closed Sun. No lunch.*

$$–$$$ ✕ **Smauet Mat & Vinhus.** Inside a cozy blue cottage is one of Bergen's least expensive fine restaurants. Chef Per Trygve Bolstad has a reputation for being innovative with Mediterranean and Norwegian cuisine. Try the ostrich or one of the seafood dishes. ⊠ *Vaskerelvssmauet 13* ☎ *55/ 21–07–00* ⚔ *Reservations essential* ▤ *AE, DC, MC, V.*

$–$$$ ✕ **Skipet Tex Mex.** One of Norway's best bets for Tex-Mex, Skipet is shaped like a sailboat. Since it overlooks the harbor, ask for a window table and take in the special view day or night. Try the fajitas, made from beef, chicken, jumbo prawns, or lamb, or the Beef El Paso, in Mexican pepper sauce. ⊠ *Zachariasbryggen* ☎ *55/55–96–55* ▤ *AE, DC, MC, V.*

$$ ✕ **Nama Sushi & Noodles.** The city's best sushi bar ("nama" means "fresh and raw" in Japanese) has garnered good reviews for its minimalistic, aquatic-inspired interior, and half-sushi, half-noodles menu. Their fish comes fresh from the market nearby, and there are daily Happy Hour sushi specials. The sashimi *moriawase* (assortment), the breast of duck, and the banana mousse dessert are delicious. The café–bar is perfect for an afternoon coffee break. ⊠ *Lodin Leppes gt. 2* ☎ *55/32–20–10* ▤ *AE, DC, MC, V.*

¢–$$ ✕ **Pasta Basta.** Renovated to resemble a Mediterranean vineyard, this small restaurant serves the city's finest Italian food at reasonable prices. The penne con pollo (grilled breast of chicken with penne served with lime and cilantro sauce and sautéed peppers) is popular. ⊠ *Zachariasbryggen* ☎ *55/55–22–22* ▤ *AE, DC, MC, V.*

¢–$ ✕ **Mago Restaurant & Café.** A magical health kick of a restaurant, Mago creates sumptuous yet healthful dishes based on organic ingredients. The menu lists a meticulous breakdown of proteins, carbohydrates, fiber, calories, vitamins and minerals for each dish. At Mago ("magician" in Italian), every dish is named after a song by the band Steely Dan, like the unforgettable dessert Rikki Don't Lose That Number (whole wheat, soy milk, and sunflower oil pancakes filled with seasonal berries, peaches and apricots). Popular main courses includePretzel Logic, which is a free-range chicken breast stuffed with avocado and Parma ham, then oven-roasted with sweet mango and chili sauce. And Mago has a juice bar serving up drinks like Speedy Gonzales (orange and kiwi) and Relax (banana, coconut milk and cinnamon). ⊠ *Neumanns Gate 5* ☎ *55/ 96–29–80* ▤ *AE, DC, MC, V.*

★ **¢** ✕ **Escalón.** Near the Fløibanen, this tiny tapas restaurant and bar is a trendy place to go for a bite or a drink. Taste the *gambas al ajillo* (scampi in wine and garlic) or the *albódigas en salsa de tomate* (meatballs in tomato sauce). ⊠ *Vetrlidsalmenningen 21* ☎ *55/32–90–99* ▤ *AE, DC, MC, V.*

Where to Stay

From the elegance of the Radisson SAS Hotels to the no-frills Crowded House, Bergen has a good selection of accommodation options for every traveler's budget and style. Most Bergen hotels are within walking distance of the city's shopping, restaurants, entertainment, and other attractions. Many hotels offer favourable summer and weekend rates depending on vacancies. Last-minute summer rates may be booked 48 hours prior to arrival June 16–August 31. Off-season (September–May), there are often weekend specials. Bergen Tourist Information will assist you in booking your accomodations for a fee of NKr 30, make a reservation for NKr 50, and process a cancellation for NKr 50.

$$$–$$$$ 🖼 **Radisson SAS Hotel Norge.** A Bergen classic, this luxury hotel attracts important people, from prime ministers to musicians. The architecture is modern, with large salmon-color, dark-wood rooms that blend contemporary Scandinavian comfort with traditional warmth. The restaurant Hereford Beefstouw specializes in beef, and T. G. I. Fridays has American-style fare. The second-floor American Bar and Library Bar are popular with locals and visitors alike. The Metro nightclub is packed on weekends. The hotel's fresh smörgåsbord breakfast is the perfect way to start your day. Ask for a room facing Lille Lungegårdsvann for a scenic view. Rooms facing Ole Bull Square can be noisy at night. ⊠ *Ole Bulls pl. 4, 5012* 🕾 *55/57–30–00* 🖷 *55/57–30–01* ⊕ *www.radissonsas.com* ↩ *347 rooms, 12 suites* ♨ *2 restaurants, cable TV, indoor pool, health club, 2 bars, nightclub, meeting room* ⊟ *AE, DC, MC, V.*

★ **$$–$$$** 🖼 **Clarion Hotel Admiral.** Known as "the hotel with the sea on three sides," the Clarion has stunning views of Bryggen, Fish Market, and Mount Fløien. The hotel staff is friendly and accommodating. Rooms are decorated in a classic, comfortable style. Emily and Sjøtonnen, the two à la carte restaurants, specialize in seafood. The cognac and cigar lounge with its burnished red leather sofas is popular. ⊠ *C. Sundts gt. 9–13* 🕾 *55/23–64–00* 🖷 *55/23–64–64* ⊕ *www.admiral.no* ↩ *210 rooms* ♨ *2 restaurants, lounge* ⊟ *AE, DC, MC, V.*

$$–$$$ 🖼 **Radisson SAS Royal Hotel.** Behind Bryggen, this hotel stands where old warehouses used to be. Ravaged by nine fires since 1170, the warehouses were repeatedly rebuilt in the same style, which has been carried over into Radisson's façade. The small but comfortable rooms have light gold walls and wood accents. Under a glass ceiling, the Café Royal Restaurant serves Scandinavian and international dishes as well as light snacks. The Madam Felle pub and bar on the waterfront is known for its live jazz and blues, as well as its whiskeys. Engelen nightclub keeps people dancing until the early hours. ⊠ *Bryggen, 5003* 🕾 *55/54–30–00* 🖷 *55/ 32–48–08* ⊕ *www.radissonsas.com* ↩ *273 rooms, 10 suites* ♨ *3 restaurants, cable TV, indoor pool, health club, sauna, bar, pub, dance club, nightclub, convention center* ⊟ *AE, DC, MC, V.*

$$ ✕ **Best Western Hotel Hordaheimen.** Dating to 1913, one of the city's oldest and most distinctive hotels is on a quiet, central street. The lobby has a memorable collection of painted Norwegian furniture by Lars Kinsarvik. The hotel's café–restaurant, Hordastova, is well known for its traditional fare, especially klippfisk, fried mackerel, and smoked cod. Rooms are small, but ideal for active travelers intending only to sleep at the hotel. ⊠ *C. Sundtsgt. 18, 5004* 🕾 *55/33–50–00* 🖷 *55/ 23–49–50* ⊕ *www.hordaheimen.no* ↩ *64 rooms* ♨ *Restaurant* ⊟ *AE, DC, MC, V.*

$–$$ ✕ **First Hotel Marin.** On the harborside near Bryggen, this business hotel is within walking distance of the city's buses, ferries, and trains. Every room has a bathtub and is decorated in yellows and blues, with oak furniture and wood floors. The penthouse suites have magnificent views of Bergen. ⊠ *Rosenkrantzgt. 8, 5003* 🕾 *53/05–15–00* 🖷 *53/05–15–01* ⊕ *www.firsthotels.com* ↩ *122 rooms, 28 suites* ♨ *2 restaurants, café, cable TV, gym, sauna, Turkish bath* ⊟ *AE, DC, MC, V.*

$–$$ ✕ **Scandic Hotel Bergen City.** This business hotel runs Bergen Congress Center, the city's largest convention center, and has warm, stylish, comfortable rooms. Take a seat in a wicker chair in the spacious lobby bar to meet people or relax. Right beside Bergen Kino, it's a short walk to Den Nationale Scene theater, Grieghallen, and restaurants. ⊠ *Håkonsgt. 2, 5015* 🕾 *55/30–90–90* 🖷 *55/23–49–20* ⊕ *www.scandic-hotels. com* ↩ *171 rooms, 4 suites* ♨ *Restaurant, bar, convention center* ⊟ *AE, DC, MC, V.*

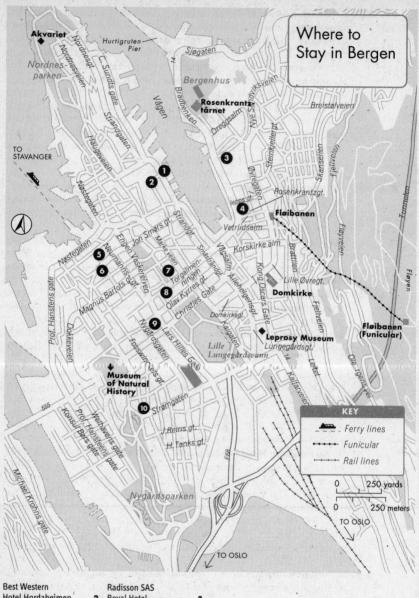

Where to Stay in Bergen

KEY

⚓ *Ferry lines*
•◆•◆• *Funicular*
┼┼┼┼ *Rail lines*

0   250 yards
0   250 meters

Best Western Hotel Hordaheimen **2**	Radisson SAS Royal Hotel **3**
Clarion Hotel Admiral . . .**1**	Rainbow Hotel Bristol . . .**7**
Crowded House **6**	Rica Travel Hotel **9**
First Hotel Marin **4**	Scandic Hotel Bergen City **5**
Hotel Park Pension **10**	
Radisson SAS Hotel Norge **8**	

¢–$$ ✕ **Rainbow Hotel Bristol.** The Bristol is minutes away from many popu-
FodorsChoice lar attractions. Built in the 1930s, its rooms are small but comfortable.
★ Several are wheelchair-accessible and allergen-free. ⊠ *Torgalmenningen,*
5014 ☎ *55/23–23–44* ⊟ *55/23–23–19* ⊕ *www.rainbow-hotels.no*
↩ *128 rooms, 1 suite* ⌂ *Restaurant, bar* ⊟ *AE, DC, MC, V.*

$ **Rica Travel Hotel.** Popular with business travelers, this hotel is steps away
from Torgalmenningen. The rooms are stylish and the location is ideal,
but there are few facilities. A public swimming pool and a popular fit-
ness center are nearby. ⊠ *Christiesgt. 5–7, 5808* ☎ *55/31–54–00* ⊟ *55/*
31–32–50 ⊕ *www.rica.no* ↩ *144 rooms* ⌂ *Restaurant, bar, meeting*
rooms, parking (fee) ⊟ *AE, DC, MC, V.*

★ ¢–$ ▦ **Hotel Park Pension.** Near the university, this intimate family-run hotel,
one of Norway's historic hotels, is in a well-kept Victorian structure built
in the 1890s. Both the public rooms and the guest rooms are furnished
with antiques. It's a short distance to Grieghallen, downtown, and the
bus and railway stations. ⊠ *Harald Hårfagres gt. 35, 5007* ☎ *55/*
54–44–00 ⊟ *55/54–44–44* ↩ *21 rooms* ⌂ *Dining room* ⊟ *AE, DC,*
MC, V.

¢ ▦ **Crowded House.** Named after an Australian band that was popular
in the 1980s, this no-frills lodge is perfect for students and budget trav-
elers. It's a short walk from shopping, restaurants, entertainment, and
other attractions, as well as train, bus, and ferry connections. Most of
the spartan rooms have good beds, telephones, and wash basins. Show-
ers and toilets are in the corridor. ⊠ *Håkonsgt. 27, 5015* ☎ *55/23–13–10*
⊟ *55/23–13–30* ⊕ *www.crowded-house.com* ↩ *34 rooms without*
bath ⌂ *Café* ⊟ *AE, DC, MC, V.*

Nightlife & the Arts

Nightlife

BARS & CLUBS Most nightclubs and bars in Bergen are in the city and Bryggen harbor
area. **Banco Rotto Puben** (⊠ Vågsalmenning 16 ☎ 55/55–49–60) has
pulsating music that attracts those in their twenties and thirties. **Dick-
ens** (⊠ Kong Olavs pl. 4 ☎ 55/36–31–30), across from the Hotel Norge,
is a relaxed place good for an afternoon or evening drink. Several Irish
style pubs, including **Finnegans** (⊠ Veiten 3 ☎ 55/55–31–31), attract na-
tive English speakers, both expats and visitors. The **Hotel Norge** (⊠ Ole
Bulls pl. 4 ☎ 55/57–30–00) piano bar and disco are low-key, with an
older crowd. The three-story **Rick's Café & Salonger** (⊠ Veiten 3 ☎ 55/
55–31–31) has a disco, an Irish pub, and Bergen's longest bar; it's
straight out of *Casablanca.* **Wesselstuen** (⊠ øvre Ole Bulls pl. 6 ☎ 55/
55–49–49) is a cozy gathering place for local students and academics.
Zachariasbryggen is a restaurant and entertainment complex right on
the water.

Bergen has an active gay community. Call Wednesday from 7 to 9 PM
or check the Web site of **Landsforeningen for Lesbisk og Homofil Frigjøring**
(⊠ Nygårdsgt. 2A ☎ 55/32–13–16 ⊕ home.powertech.no/llhbg), the
National Association for Lesbian and Gay Liberation, to ask about events
in the city. In the same building as the Landsforeningen, there's the pop-
ular gay bar **Fincken** (⊠ Nygårdsgt. 2A ☎ 55/32–13–16), which is open
daily until 1 AM.

CAFÉS **Café Opera** (⊠ 24 Engen ☎ 55/23–03–15) is a classic, both sumptuous
and stylish. It's often crowded on Friday and Saturday nights. Next to
the Mr. Bean Bar & Coffee Shop, there's **Dr. Livingstone's Traveller's
Café,** (⊠ Kong Oscars gt. 12 ☎ 55/56–03–12), where the walls are
covered with photographs, maps, and memorabilia from world travels.
If you're traveling by train, stop for a coffee at **Kaffehuset Friele** (⊠ Rail-

way Station). **Kafe Klippers** (⊠ Georgernes Verft 12 ☎ 55/31–00–60), Bergen's largest outdoor café, has a spectacular view of the water at sunset and cozy wool blankets. **På Folkemunne** (⊠ Ole Bulls pl. 9–11 ☎ 55/30–71–37) is a trendy, candelit café with clever quotes on its walls. Lunch and dinner are served. **Vågen Fetevare** (⊠ Kong Oscars gt. 10 ☎ 55/31–65–13) is a homey and bohemian coffeehouse. Books are sold and readings are held here.

LIVE MUSIC Bergensers love jazz. The **Bergen Jazz Forum** (⊠ Kulturhuset USF Georgernes Verft 3 ☎ 55/30–72–50 ⊕ www.usf.no) is *the* place to find it—there are concerts every Friday from September to May. The international **Nattjazz** festival offers more than 60 concerts in late May and early June. For live pop and rock, see local listings for concerts at **Den Stundesløse** (⊠ Ole Bulls pl. 9–11 ☎ 55/30–71–36), **Det Akademiske Kvarter** (⊠ Olav Kyrres gt. 49–53 ☎ 55/30–28–00), and **Club Maxime** (⊠ Ole Bulls pl. 9–11 ☎ 55/55–49–60).

The Arts

Bergen is known for its **Festspillene** (International Music Festival), held each year during the last week of May and the beginning of June. Famous names in classical music, jazz, ballet, the arts, and theater perform. Tickets are available from the festival office at Grieghallen (⊠ Lars Hilles gt. 3, 5015 ☎ 55/21–61–50 ⊕ www.festspillene.no). **Bergen Music Fest** (☎ 55/21–50–60 ⊕ www.oleblues.net), formerly known as Ole Blues, runs from late April to early May.

CLASSICAL MUSIC Recitals are held at **Troldhaugen** (☎ 55/92–29–92 ⊕ www.troldhaugen. com), home of composer Edvard Grieg, all summer. Tickets are sold at the tourist office and at the door. Performances are given from late June through August, Wednesday and Sunday at 7:30, and Saturday at 2; and from September through November, Sunday at 2.

The **Bergen International Chamber Music Festival** (☎ 55/99–07–55) takes place every August at Fløien Restaurant atop Fløyen. The **Bergen Filharmoniske Orkester** (Bergen Philharmonic Orchestra; ⊠ Grieghallen, Lars Hilles gt. 3, 5015 ☎ 55/21–61–50) performs from September to May.

FOLK MUSIC Twice a week in summer the **Bergen Folklore Dance Group** performs a one-hour program of traditional dances and music from rural Norway at the Bryggens Museum. Tickets are sold by the tourist office and at the door. ⊠ *Bryggen* ☎ 55/31–95–50 ⊠ *NKr 95.*

The extensive **Fana Folklore** program is an evening of traditional wedding food, dances, and folk music, plus a concert—at the 800-year-old Fana Church. ⊠ *A/S Kunst (Art Association), Torgalmenning 9, Fana* ☎ *55/91–52–40* ⊠ *NKr 270, includes dinner and return bus transportation* ⊙ *June–Sept., Thurs. and Fri. at 7 PM. Catch the bus from the center of Bergen and return by 10:30 PM.*

FILM If you're in the mood for a movie, all foreign films are shown in their original languages, with subtitles in Norwegian. Only children's films are dubbed in Norwegian. **Bergen Kino** (⊠ Konsertpaleet, Neumannsgt. 3 ☎ 55/56–90–50) is a complex of several theaters. The **Forum** (⊠ Danmarkspl.) is the town's big, old cinema.

REVUES & CABARETS There are a number of locations that host revues and cabaret shows in the city center, including **Logen Teater** (⊠ Ole Bulls pl. ☎ 55/23–20–15 ⊕ www.logen-teater.no), **Rick's** (⊠ Veiten 3 ☎ 55/55–31–31 ⊕ www. ricks.no), and **Ole Bull Teater** (⊠ Ole Bulls pl. 9–11 ☎ 55/30–71–35). **Radisson SAS Hotel Norge,** (⊠ Ole Bulls pl. 4 ☎ 55/57–30–00) stages performances in July and August.

THEATER Although theater is generally performed in Norwegian, check listings for occasional English performances in the city center. **Den Nationale Scene** (✉ Engen ☎ 55/54–97–10 ⊕ www.dns.no) has performances on three stages. It's closed in July and most of August. **Bergen International Theater (BIT)** (✉ Nøstegt. 54 ☎ 55/23–22–35 ⊕ www.bit-teatergarasjen.no) has Norwegian and international theatrical and modern dance performances. **Nye Carte Blanche** (✉ Danseteatret, Sigurdsgt. 6 ☎ 55/30–86–80) stages ballet and modern dance performances.

Sports & the Outdoors

Fishing

The **Bergen Angling Association** (✉ Fosswinckelsgt. 37 ☎ 55/32–11–64 ⊕ www.bergen.sportsfiskere.no) has information and fishing permits. Among the many charters in the area, the *Rjfylke* **Fjord Tour** (☎ 911/59–048 or 946/09–548) offers two-hour journeys from Bergen twice daily along the coast. Anglers can catch coalfish, cod, mackerel, and haddock.

Golf

North of Bergen at Fløksand, the **Meland Golf Club** (✉ Frekhaug ☎ 56/17–46–00 ⊕ www.melandgolf.no) has an 18-hole championship course with high-quality golf clubs and carts for rent.

Hiking

Mountainous and forest-filled Bergen and the surrounding region make it ideal for long walks and hikes in fresh, mountain air amid lush, green surroundings. Take the funicular up **Mount Fløyen,** and minutes later you'll be in the midst of a forest. **Mount Ulriken** is popular with walkers. Maps of the many self-guided walking tours around Bergen are available from bookstores and from **Bergens Turlag** (✉ Tverrgt. 2–4, 5017 Bergen ☎ 55/33–58–10 ⊕ www.turistforeningen.no/bergen), a touring club that arranges hikes and maintains cabins for hikers.

Racket Sports

Take your favorite racket and head to a couple of sports facilities outside downtown Bergen. **Bergen Racquet Center** (✉ Fjellsdalen 9, Bønes ☎ 55/12–32–30) has tennis, badminton, squash, soccer, and handball. The well-equipped **Paradis Sports Senter** (☎ 55/91–12–60) has five indoor tennis courts, four squash courts, and badminton courts. There's also spinning, aerobics, and sunbeds.

Swimming

The most exciting place to swim in Bergen is **Vannkanten** (✉ Off Rv 555 ☎ 55/50–77–77 ⊕ www.vannkanten.no), a water complex of several pools, which also has a coffee bar and restaurants. To get there, take buses 411 to 439 from the main bus station. **Sentralbadet** (✉ Teatergt.) is the city's main swimming pool, in the center of town. **Nordnes sjøbad** (✉ Near the Akvariet/Bergen Aquarium) is a popular recreational facility that has a heated outdoor swimming pool.

Shopping

Shopping Centers

Bergen has several cobblestoned pedestrian shopping streets, including Gamle Strandgaten, (Gågaten), Torgallmenningen, Hollendergaten and Marken. Most Bergen shops are open Monday, Tuesday, Wednesday, and Friday from 9 to 4:30; Thursday from 9 to 7; and Saturday from 9 to 3. Bergen's shopping centers—Galleriet, Kløverhuset, and Bergen Storsenter—are open weekdays from 9 to 8 and Saturday from 9 to 6.

Sundt (✉ Torgalmenningen 14) is the closest thing Norway has to a traditional department store, with everything from fashion to interior furnishings. But you can get better value for your kroner if you shop around for souvenirs and sweaters. **Kløverhuset** (✉ Strandkaien 10), between Strandgaten and the fish market, has 40 shops under one roof, including outlets for the ever-so-popular Dale knitwear, souvenirs, leathers, and fur. **Galleriet**, on Torgalmenningen, is the best of the downtown shopping malls. Here you will find **Glasmagasinet** and more exclusive small shops along with all the chains, including **H & M (Hennes & Mauritz)**. **Bergen Storsenter,** by the bus terminal near the train station, is a newer shopping center near the train station.

Specialty Stores

ANTIQUES   There are many antiques shops on **Øvregaten,** especially around Fløibanen.

BOOKS   **Melvær** (✉ Galleriet and other locations downtown ☎ 55/96–28–10) has a wide selection of maps, postcards, books about Norway, dictionaries, travel guides, novels, children's books, and books in English.

CLOTHING   **Oleana** (✉ Strandkaien 2A, Bryggen ☎ 55/31–05–20) sells Norwegian wool sweaters, silk scarves from Tyrihans and Norwegian silver.

FISHING   **Campelen** (✉ Strandkaien 2A and 18 ☎ 55/32–34–72 or 55/23–07–30
SUPPLIES   ⊕ www.campelen.no) has fishing equipment. Its staff also arranges fishing trips that leave from Bergen Harbor.

FOOD   **Kjøttbasaren** (✉ Vetrlidsalmenning 2 ☎ 55/55–22–23) is in a restored 1877 meat market. The Meat Bazaar sells everything from venison to sweets. Famous all over Norway, **Søstrene Hagelin** (✉ Olav Kyrres gt. 33 ☎ 55/32–69–49) sells traditional fish balls, fish pudding, and other seafood products made following its secret recipes.

GLASS,   **Tilbords, Bergens Glasmagasin** (✉ Olav Kyrres gt. 9 ☎ 55/31–69–67) claims
CERAMICS,   to have the town's largest selection of glass and china, in both Scandi-
PEWTER   navian and European designs. **Hjertholm** (✉ Olav Kyrres gt. 7 ☎ 55/31–70–27) is the ideal shop for gifts; most everything is of Scandinavian design. The pottery and glassware are of the highest quality—much of it made by local artisans.

HANDICRAFTS   **Husfliden** (✉ Vågsalmenning 3 ☎ 55/54–47–70) caters to all your handicrafts needs, including a department for Norwegian national costumes. This is one of the best places to pick up handmade Norwegian goods, especially handwoven textiles and hand-carved wood items. **Berle Bryggen** (✉ Bryggen 5 ☎ 55/10–95–00) has the complete Dale of Norway collection in stock and other traditional knitwear and souvenir items—don't miss the troll cave. **Amerie** (✉ Finnegårdsgt. 6 ☎ 55/31–18–20) has traditional and modern knitwear, jewelry, souvenirs, leather goods, china, and crystal.

INTERIOR DESIGN   Norwegian designers recommend the **Black & White Studio** (✉ Kong Oscard gt. 4 ☎ 55/90–35–40) for Scandinavian furniture and lamps.

JEWELRY   **Theodor Olsens** (✉ Ole Bulls pl. 7 ☎ 55/55–14–80) stocks silver jewelry of distinctive Norwegian and Scandinavian design. **Juhls' Silver Gallery** (✉ Bryggen ☎ 55/32–47–40) has its own exclusive jewelry called "Tundra," which is inspired by the Norwegian north.

TOYS   Take a stroll through **Troll** (✉ Audhild Viken, Bryggen ☎ 55/21–51–00) for adorable, mean-looking trolls of all shapes and sizes. The same complex that holds Troll also has an all-year **Julehuset** (✉ Audhild Viken, Bryggen ☎ 55/21–51–00 ⊕ www.goshopNorway.com), or Christmas House, full of cheery Norwegian *Nisser* (elves).

Bergen A to Z

AIR TRAVEL TO & FROM BERGEN

CARRIERS SAS, Braathens, KLM, Norwegian, Widerøe and Sterling are the major airlines flying into Bergen.

🛂 **Braathens** ☎ 815/20-000 ⊕ www.braathens.no. **KLM** ☎ 820/02-002 ⊕ www. norwayklm.com. **Norwegian** ☎ 815/21-815 ⊕ www.norwegian.no. **Scandinavian Airlines (SAS)** ☎ 815/20-400 ⊕ www.sas.no. **Sterling** ☎ 815/58-810 ⊕ www.sterlingticket. com. **Widerøe** ☎ 810/20-400 ⊕ www.wideroe.no.

AIRPORT TRANSFERS Flesland is a 30-minute bus ride from the center of Bergen at off-peak hours. The Flybussen (Airport Bus) departs three times per hour (less frequently on weekends) from the SAS Royal Hotel, the Braathens office at the Hotel Norge, and from the bus station.

Driving from Flesland to Bergen is simple, and the road is well marked. Bergen has an electronic toll ring surrounding it, so any vehicle entering the city weekdays between 6 AM and 10 PM has to pay NKr 5. There is no toll in the other direction.

A taxi stand is outside the Arrivals exit. The trip into the city costs about NKr 250.

🛂 **Bergen Taxi** ☎ 07000 or 55/99-70-60.

BOAT & FERRY TRAVEL

Boats have always been Bergen's lifeline to the world. Fjord Line serves North Norway, Stavanger and Haugesund, and Hardangerfjord and Sunnhordland. There's also service to Sognefjord, Nordfjord, and Sunnfjord.

The Smyril Line has a ferry that departs once a week in summer to the Shetland Islands, the Faroe Islands, and Iceland. Smyril also has service between Bergen and Scotland.

Hurtigruten (the Coastal Steamer) departs daily from Frielenes Quay, Dock H, for the 11-day round-trip to Kirkenes in the far north.

HSD express boats (to Hardangerfjord, Sunnhordland, Stavanger, and Haugesund) and Fylkesbaatane express boats (to Sognefjord, Nordfjord, and Sunnfjord) depart from Strandkai Terminalen.

International ferries depart from Skoltegrunnskaien.

🛂 **Fjord Line** ☎ 815/33-500 ⊕ www.fjordline.com. **Fylkesbaatane** ☎ 55/90-70-70 ⊕ www.fylkesbaatane.no. **HSD** ☎ 55/23-87-80 ⊕ www.hsd.no. *Hurtigruten* ✉ Coastal Express, Veiten 2B, 5012 ⊕ www.hurtigruten.com. **Smyril Line** ☎ 55/59-65-20 ⊕ www. smyril-line.com. **Strandkai Terminalen** ☎ 55/23-87-80.

BUS TRAVEL TO & FROM BERGEN

The summer-only bus from Oslo to Bergen, Geiteryggekspressen (literally, "Goat-Back Express," referring to the tunnel through Geiteryggen Mountain, which looks like a goat's back, between Hol and Aurland) leaves the Nor-Way bus terminal at 8 AM and arrives in Bergen 12½ hours later. Buses also connect Bergen with Trondheim and Ålesund. Western Norway is served by several bus companies, which use the station at Strømgaten 8.

🛂 **Central Bus Station** ✉ Strøgt. 8 ☎ 177.

CAR TRAVEL

Bergen is 478 km (290 mi) from Oslo. Route 7 is good almost as far as Eidfjord at the eastern edge of the Hardangerfjord, but then it deteriorates considerably. The ferry along the way, crossing the Hardanger Fjord from Brimnes to Bruravik, runs from 5 AM to midnight and takes 10 minutes. At Granvin, 12 km (7 mi) farther north, Route 7 joins Route E68, which is an alternate route from Oslo, crossing the Sognefjorden from Refsnes to Gudvangen. From Granvin to Bergen, Route E68 hugs the fjord part of the way, making for spectacular scenery.

Driving from Stavanger to Bergen involves two to four ferries and a long journey packed with stunning scenery. The Stavanger tourist information office can help plan the trip and reserve ferry space.

Downtown Bergen is enclosed by an inner ring road. The area within is divided into three zones, which are separated by ONE WAY and DO NOT ENTER signs. To get from one zone to another, return to the ring road and drive to an entry point for the desired zone. It's best to leave your car at a parking garage (the Birkebeiner Senter is on Rosenkrantz Gate, and there's a parking lot near the train station) and walk. You pay a NKr 5 toll every time you drive into the city—but driving out is free.

🚗 Car Emergencies **Vehicle Breakdown Service** ✉ Inndalsvn. 22 ☎ 55/59-40-70 operates 24 hours a day.

🚗 Car Rental Agencies **Avis** ✉ Lars Hilles gt. 20B ☎ 55/55-39-55 or 815/33-044. **Budget** ✉ Lodin Lepps gt. 1 ☎ 55/27-39-90. **Hertz** ✉ Nygårdsgt. 91 ☎ 55/96-40-70.

EMERGENCIES

The dental emergency center at Vestre Strømkai 19 is open weekdays from 6 PM to 8:30 PM and weekends from 3:30 PM to 8:30 PM. An emergency room at the outpatient center at the same location is open 24 hours. Apoteket Nordstjernen, Bergen Storsenter (55/21-83-84), is open Monday through Saturday from 8 AM to midnight, and Sunday from 9:30 AM to midnight.

🏥 Doctors & Dentists **Emergency Dental Care** ✉ Vestre Strømkai 19 ☎ 55/56-87-17.

🏥 Hospitals **Emergency Room** ✉ Vestre Strømkai 19 ☎ 55/32-11-20.

🏥 Late-Night Pharmacies **Apoteket Nordstjernen** ✉ Central Bus Station, Strømgt. 8, ☎ 55/21-83-84.

INTERNET SERVICE

💻 **Allezzo, Galleriet** ✉ Torgallm. ☎ 55/31-11-60. **Cyberhouse** ✉ Vetrlidsallm. 13 ☎ 55/36-66-16.

LAUNDRY

🧺 **Jarlens Vaskoteque** ✉ Lille Øvregt. 17 ☎ 55/32-55-04.

MONEY MATTERS

Most Bergen banks in downtown are open Monday, Tuesday, Wednesday, and Friday from 8:15 to 3:30, and Thursday from 8:15 to 6. Some are open on Saturday from 10 to 1. From mid-May through September, most close a half hour earlier. The 24-hour **Bergen Card,** which costs NKr 165 (NKr 245 for 48 hours), gives admission to most museums, as well as Fantoft Stave Church, St. Mary's Church, Banco Rotto, and Bergen Trotting Park; unlimited bus travel in central Bergen; parking at public meters and outdoor automatic ticket machines; unlimited funicular rides; and discounts at Bergen Aquarium, Troldhaugen, Vannkanten, and selected restaurants, and on car rentals, concerts, theatre, and selected souvenirs. The card is available at the tourist office and in most hotels.

CURRENCY EXCHANGE The Tourist Information Office in Bergen exchanges money outside banking hours.

TAXIS

Taxi stands are in strategic locations downtown. Taxis are dispatched by the Bergen Taxi central office and can be booked in advance.

🚕 Taxi Companies **Bergen Taxi** ☎ 07000 or 55/99-70-10 or 60 🌐 www.bergentaxi.no.

TOURS

Bergen is the guided-tour capital of Norway because it is the starting point for most fjord tours. Tickets for all tours are available from the tourist office.

Check with the tourist office (⇨ Visitor Information) for additional recommendations. The ambitious all-day Norway-in-a-Nutshell bus-train-boat tour (you can book through the tourist office) goes through Voss, Flåm, Myrdal, and Gudvangen—truly a breathtaking trip—and is the best way to see a lot of the area in a short amount of time.

BOAT TOURS   Traveling by boat is an advantage because the contrasts between the fjords and mountains are greatest at water level. The vessels are comfortable and stable (the water is practically still), so seasickness is rare. Stops are frequent, and all sights are explained. Bergen Fjord Sightseeing offers several local fjord tours. Fylkesbaatane (County Boats) i Sogn og Fjordane has several combination tours. Tickets are sold at the tourist office and at the quay.

Norway's largest and oldest tall sailing ship, *Statsraad Lehmkuhl,* (☎ 55/30–17–00 ⊕ www.lehmkuhl.no) is the pride of Bergen. Sailing cruises, short skerry cruises, and charters are available. The *TMSY Weller* (☎ 55/19–13–03 or 408/25–828 ⊕ www.weller.no) can be booked for charter and fishing tours.

🚢 **Bergen Fjord Sightseeing** ☎ 55/25–90–00.

BUS & WALKING   Bergen Guide Service has about a hundred authorized guides who give
TOURS   different city walking tours like the Unknown Bergen and Bergen Past and Present. Bergens-Expressen, a "train on tires," leaves from Torgalmenningen for a one-hour ride around the center of town (summer only).
🚢 **Bergens-Expressen** ☎ 55/53-11-50. **Bergen Guide Service** ☎ 55/32-77-00
⊕ www.bergenguideservice.no.

TRAIN TRAVEL

The Bergensbanen has several departures daily in both directions on the Oslo–Bergen route; it's widely acknowledged as one of the most beautiful train rides in the world. Trains leave from Oslo S Station for the 7½- to 8½-hour journey.
🚢 **Bergen Train Information** ☎ 55/96-69-00 or 815-00-888.

VISITOR INFORMATION

Bergen's Tourist Information Office is in the Fresco Hall in Vågsallmenning Square opposite the fish market. The office's staff sells the Bergen Card, brochures, and maps, arranges accommodations and sightseeing, and exchanges currency.
🚢 Tourist Information **Tourist Information** ✉ Vågsallmenningen 1 ☎ 55/55-20-00
⊕ www.visitBergen.com.

CENTRAL NORWAY: THE HALLINGDAL VALLEY TO HARDANGERFJORD

The mountain country between Hallingdal Valley and Hardangerfjord is a feast for the eyes—here are Europe's tallest peaks and the continent's highest plateau, the Hardangervidda, which also serves as Norway's largest national park. In summer the landscape provides a spectacular backdrop for hikers and for bikers on the Eventyrvegen (Adventure Road): crystal-clear streams ramble down mountainsides, sheep graze in pastures, and snowcapped summits glisten in the distance. In winter this area—especially Geilo, Gol, and Hemsedal—teems with skiers, both cross-country and downhill.

Rest your muscles between activities at a mountain farm where you can milk goats, or explore medieval stave churches or relics-filled folk museums. This chapter begins with the Hallingdal Valley at Flå and moves on to the heart of the valley at Nesbyn, then following the towns along the Hemsil River, which branches west in the direction of Geilo. Most towns in this region are small places which often have only one main road, the highway running through them.

Numbers in the margin correspond to points of interest on the Central and Interior Norway map.

Hallingdal Valley

Route 7 and the Bromma River wind through the historic Hallingdal Valley, which begins in the port town of Drammen. The valley is lined with small fishing villages and ski resort towns and is known for its wooden log buildings.

Between the Hallingdal and Valdres valleys lies Vassfaret, a forested, 30-km-long (18-mi-long) valley of large lakes, rivers and streams, steep rocky areas, mountain farms, and abandoned settlements. Many brown bears and *elg* (moose) make their homes here. The elg, often two meters in height, are known in Norway as "King of the Forest."

After the Black Death swept through the valley in the Middle Ages, it remained uninhabited until the 1740s. Land was cleared and permanent settlements established, which lasted until 1921. In 1985, Vassfaret was declared a preserved nature area.

Flå

❶ *87 km (54 mi) northwest of Oslo, on Rte. 7.*

Five brown bears (Rugg, Berte, Birgjit, Frigg, and Frøya) and two bear cubs make their home within the 10-acre **Vassfaret Bjørnepark** (Vassfaret Bear Park). There's also a separate moose enclosure for an adult male and female and a calf. Children can visit rabbits and chickens in the hen village and pet lambs, goats, pigs, and other farm animals. Take a seat in a Sámi tent, where you can picnic on grilled meats. The store Seterbua sells local handicrafts. In summer the park organizes special events, such as tours and horseback riding. ⊠ *3539, Flå* ☎ *32/05–35–10* ⊕ *www. vassfaret-bjornepark.no* 🎫 *NKr 90* ☉ *Early May–mid-June and mid-Aug.–mid-Sept., weekends and public holidays except May 17 11–6; mid-June–June 29, Aug. 5–18, daily 11–6; June 30–Aug. 4, daily 11–7.*

Nesbyen

❷ *33 km (20 mi) northwest of Flå.*

This small town in the heart of Hallingdal Valley has some memorable attractions. Overlooking the mountains and fjords between Hallingdal and Numedal is the family-owned **E.K.T. Langedrag Villmarkspark/Fjellgård og Leirskole** (Langedrag Wildlife Park and Mountain Farm). Caretakers of more than 250 animals representing 25 species, the Thorson family is well known in Scandinavia thanks to a nature series on television. Mountain farm life is emphasized—you can milk one of the farm's 40 goats, or just learn about the making of goat cheese. Pony-like fjord horses are available for rides, riding lessons, and carriage trips. In the surrounding countryside, moose, deer, wild reindeer, wolves, cougars, polar foxes, and wild pigs can be spotted. Fishing and theme activities are organized year-round. ⊠ *Tunhovd 3540 Nesbyen* ☎ *32/74–25–50* ⊕ *www. langedrag.no* 🎫 *NKr 100* ☉ *Daily 10–6.*

One of the oldest open-air museums in Norway, **Hallingdal Folkemuseum** was founded in 1899 next to Rukkedøla River. Twenty-five century-old timber–sod houses have an extensive collection of regional clothes, weapons, and art. In summer, handicrafts are demonstrated every Wednesday. An emigrant center shows changing exhibitions and has a genealogical archive. Between 1839 and 1915, 750,000 Norwegians— many of them born in this valley—emigrated to America. The museum maintains close ties with the Hallingdal League of America. The paths and waterfalls nearby were traversed by famous Norwegian painter and farmer Hans Gude (1825–1903). ⊠ *Møllevn. 18, Nesbyen* ☎ *32/ 07–14–85* ⊕ *www.museumsnett.no/hallingdal* ⊠ *NKr 50* ⊙ *Early June and late Aug., daily 11–3; mid-June–mid-Aug., daily 10–5; Sept.–May, Sat. 11–3.*

Gol

❸ *21 km (13 mi) northwest of Nesbyen.*

This small town is popular with summer campers and winter skiers, who throng the mountains north and east. The original 12th-century **Gol stavkyrkje** (Gol Stave Church) still stands, but nowadays in Oslo's Norsk Folkemuseum. This replica has an exhibition highlighting the principles of stave church architecture. A service is held every Wednesday at 9 pm in summer. ⊠ *Storeøyni* ☎ *32/07–54–11* ⊠ *Nkr 60* ⊙ *Daily 9–4.*

You can try your hand at blowing crystal glass every weekday from 10:30 to 3 for NKr 135 at **Halling Glass.** The store also sells the beautiful objects made here by its artisans. ⊠ *Sentrumsvn. 18* ☎ *32/07–53–11* ⊕ *www.hallinglass.no* ⊙ *Demonstrations weekdays 9–3. Store weekdays 9–4, Sat. 10–2.*

off the beaten path

EVENTYRGÅRDEN HUSO – This is a popular *støl,* or summer mountain farm. To get here, take Route 52 north from Gol to Robru; then take Øvrevegen to Huso. A country courtyard has 12 log houses from the 17th century, and several exhibition halls and presentations on the area's culture and business life. Don't miss the re-created house of a Viking chief and the Iron Age assembly hall. Sheep, goats, rabbits, chickens, and ducks inhabit the pasture. You can venture into the valley on a horseback tour, and go canoeing or fishing in the river. ⊠ *Huso* ☎ *32/07–54–11* ⊕ *www.pers.no* ⊠ *NKr 60* ⊙ *Mid-June–mid-Aug., daily 9–6; mid-Sept.–mid-May, daily 9–4.*

Sports
Fjell og Fjord Ferie A/S(⊠ Sentrumsvegen 93 ☎ 32/07–61–35) rents bikes.

Hemsedal

❹ *35 km (21½ mi) from Gol.*

The mountains in the area are nicknamed the Scandinavian Alps, and Hemsedal has some of Norway's most stunning high mountain scenery: you can see mountains and glaciers, numerous lakes, four rivers, as well as fjords and cascading waterfalls. It's the country's most popular skiing town, where Norway's top skiers and snowboarders live and train. The Maifestivalen (May Festival), which takes place on the first weekend of May, marks the end of the ski season; it's a well-attended event. In the summer months you can hike, play golf, and go fishing.

Where to Stay & Eat
★ $ ✕ **Hemsedal Café.** This hip café is a place to see and be seen, or you can just come for the simple dishes like burgers, Thai chicken, or the filling

skier's breakfast. Internet usage at the several computers is free. ⊠ *Brustabygge* ☎ *32/05–54–00* ▤ *MC, V.*

★ **$$$–$$$$** 🔲 **Harahorn.** Part of the "Good Life" chain, Harahorn offers high standards and service. On a mountaintop 1,000 meters (3,280 feet) above Hemsedal's center, Harahorn is comprised of 10 mountain cabins clustered around the main house. Decorated in deep blues and earthy shades, the luxurious *bonderomantikk* (country romantic) cabins are filled with antiques and art. You can visit the hotel just to dine at the main house's café and restaurant, or opt to stay here. There are many outdoor sports and activities available, such as skiing, dogsledding, mountain climbing, and moose safaris. ⊠ *Hemsedal 3580* ☎ *32/06–23–80* 🖶 *32/06–23–81* ⊕ *www.harahorn.no* ↝ *22 rooms* ⚭ *Restaurant, café, skiing, lounge* ▤ *AE, DC, MC, V.*

$$$–$$$$ ✕🔲 **Skarsnuten Hotell.** Perched like an eagle's nest, this mountainside **Fodor'sChoice** hotel is part of the village Skarsnuten Landsby. The minimalist interior ★ is shaped like a mountain itself, and dominated by *skifer*—Norwegian stone—gray brushed wool, and wood. Framed mountain-sports photographs line the white walls. Rooms have spectacular views and names like Little Matterhorn. Kids are thoroughly entertained at their own disco and an Internet café. Take the hotel's ski-lift down to its resort, Hemsedal Skisenteret. The hotel's restaurant is well-regarded for its French-inspired menu based on seasonal Norwegian ingredients. ⊠ *Skarsnuten Landsby Hemsedal 3560* ☎ *32/05–95–05* 🖶 *32/06–06–53* ⊕ *www.skarsnuten. no* ↝ *37 rooms, 2 suites* ⚭ *Restaurant, bar, lounge, Internet, laundry facilities; no smoking* ▤ *AE, DC, MC, V.*

Sports & the Outdoors

GOLF **Golf Hemsedal** (☎ 32/06–23–77 ⊕ www.golfhemsedal.com) is really a country club of sorts with a 9-hole driving range and putting green. You can also play tennis and go horseback riding here.

HORSEBACK **Elvestad Fjellridning** (☎ 97/63–99–70 ⊕ www.hemsedal.com) offers half-
RIDING day riding trips in the forest and mountains for all levels of riders. From late June through August, rides start at 9:30, last 3 to 3½ hours, and cost NKr 320.

MOUNTAIN Experienced guides at **HeimVegen** (⊠ Aalstveit, Hemsedal ☎☎ 32/
HIKING, 06–06–20 ⊕ www.heimvegen.no) offer mountain touring courses
CLIMBING year-round.

PARAGLIDING Paraglide in tandem with an experienced instructor. **Oslo Paragliding Klubb** (☎ 22/15–08–18 ⊕ www.opk.no) has its main base in Hemsedal.

SKIING **Hemsedal Skisenteret** (☎ 32/05–53–90 ⊕ www.skihemsedal.no) has 34 km (21 mi) of alpine slopes, 175 km (108 mi) of cross-country trails, and 17 ski lifts. The Ski School has superbly run courses for children to adults.

Torpo

⑤ *52 km (32 mi) from Hemsedal.*

While there are seven stave churches in the valley, this tiny village's medieval church is the oldest and best preserved. **Torpo stave church** is the only 12th-century church left in Hallingdal. Its decorative ceiling, which depicts the legend of Saint Margaret, dates the decorative ceiling dating back 700 years is considered the equal of any European church of its day. ☎ *32/08–31–37* ✉ *NKr 30* ☉ *June–Aug., daily 8:30–6.*

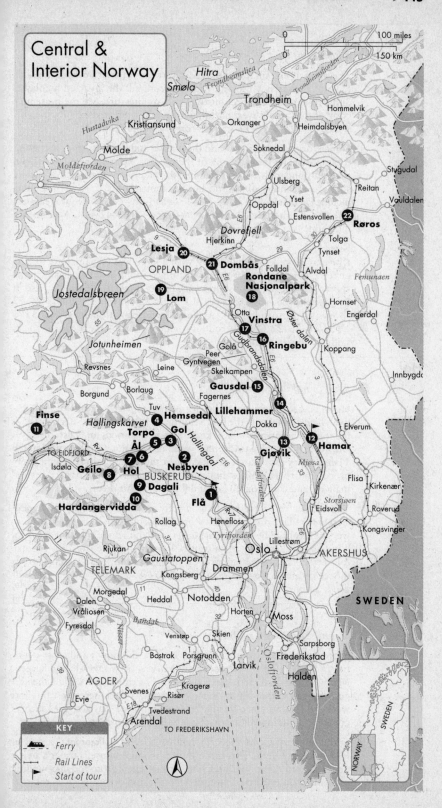

Central & Interior Norway

Hitra

Smøla

Trondheimsfjorden

Trondheim

Hommelvik

Hustadvika

Kristiansund

Orkanger

Heimdalsbyen

Molde

Soknedal

Ulsberg

Stugudal

Moldefjorden

Oppdal

Yset

Reitan

Vauldalen

Estensvollen

22 Røros

Dovrefjell

Hjerkinn

Tolga

Lesja **20**

21 Dombås

Tynset

Alvdal

Femunaen

OPPLAND

Folldal

Rondane Nasjonalpark

19 Lom

18

Hornset

Engerdal

Jostedalsbreen

Otta

Vinstra

Øster dalen

17

Jotunheimen

Golå

16 Ringebu

Koppang

Revsnes

Leine

Peer Gyntvegen

Skeikampen

Innbygda

Borlaug

Gudbrandsdalen

Gausdal **15**

Fagernes

Borgund

Tuv

14

Finse

Hemsedal

Lillehammer

Elverum

11

4

Dokka

12 Hamar

Hallingskarvet

Torpo

Gol

Hallingdal

13

TO EIDFJORD

Ål **5** **3**

Gjøvik

Mjøsa

Isdøla

7 **6**

2

Flisa

Geilo **8** Hol

Nesbyen

Kirkenær

BUSKERUD

Randsfjorden

Roverud

9 Dagali

Storsjøen

Hardangervidda **10**

Flå **1**

Eidsvoll

Kongsvinger

Rollag

Hønefloss

Tyrifjorden

Lillestrøm

Gaustatoppen

Oslo

AKERSHUS

TELEMARK

Drammen

Rjukan

Kongsberg

Morgedal

Heddal

Notodden

Dalen

Vråliosen

Bandak

Horten

SWEDEN

Fyresdal

Nisser

Venstøp

Skien

Moss

Bostrak

Porsgrunn

Sarpsborg

Larvik

Frederikstad

AGDER

Oslofjorden

Halden

Evje

Svenes

Kragerø

Tvedestrand

Risør

Arendal

TO FREDERIKSHAVN

KEY

⛴ Ferry

├─┤ Rail Lines

▶ Start of tour

SWEDEN

NORWAY

SWEDEN

0   100 miles

0   150 km

Ål

❻ *5 km (3 mi) west of Torpo.*

The small mountain town, Ål is best known for the **Ål Stavkyrkjemuseum** (Ål Stave Church Museum). Richly decorated, the museum highlights and explains stave church history and architecture. See the museum's copy of the famous west portal, which no longer exists. ✉ *Prestegard-slåven* ☎ *32/08–10–11* ⊙ *Year-round by appointment.*

Some Norwegian farmers send their cattle and sheep to graze at the traditional **summer farms.** Many of these farms welcome visitors between early July and mid-August to sample their dairy products such as cheese, sour cream, and *rømmegraut.* Local summer farms, open to the public, include **Fagerdalen** (☎ 32/08–98–06 or 911–09–779 ⊕ www.fagerdalen. no) and **Tormodset** (☎ 91/58–86–02 or 32/08–42–30). You should telephone in advance for an appointment to visit.

Sports

Kite-skiing or ski-sailing (skiing with a large kite or parachute to harness the wind), is one of the newest innovations in skiing and extreme sports. Norwegian kite-skiing enthusiasts have established a base at **Bergsjøstølen Mountain Lodge** (✉ Ål 3570 ☎ 32/08–46–18 🖷 32/08–46–72 ⊕ www.bergsjostolen.no). At **Rødungst øl Høyfjellshotel** (✉ Ål 3570 ☎ 32/08–46–22 ⊕ www.rodungstol.no) you can take a course on ski sailing and rent equipment.

Hol

❼ *5 km (3 mi) west of Ål.*

Hol is best-known in the valley for its **Holsdagen** (☎ 32/09–59–00) festival, held annually on the first Saturday in July or August. Back in 1957, the festival began as a way of keeping local traditions and customs alive. During the festival, a traditional wedding ceremony is performed in the 11th-century Hol Gamle Kyrkje. Then the bridal pair rides in a lively procession to Hol Bygdemuseum, where folk music, dance, performances, and traditional Hallingdal dishes await them.

You can see reconstructed buildings from the 1700s at the **Hol bygdemuseum** (Village museum). Costumed museum staff reenact early Norwegian farm life in its 17 sod houses, which include a tenant farmer's house, a barn, stables, and a smithy. Rosemaling, the late 18th-century folk art of decorative painting on furniture, and local costumes from the region are on view. ✉ *Hagafoss* ☎ *32/08–81–40* ⊙ *Late June–mid-Aug., daily 11–5.*

Geilo

❽ *35 km (21 mi) west of Torpo.*

More than a million visitors a year head to the slopes and cross-country trails of this *alpeby* (alpine town) halfway between Oslo and Bergen. Many people ski directly from their hotel or cabin doors. Plan ahead if you want to visit at Easter, since Norwegians flock here for a final ski weekend. The summer season, beginning in June, has activities such as guided mountain walks, horseback riding, and fishing.

In the center of Geilo, the 17th-century farm of **Geilojordet** is a part of Hol bygdemuseum. The cattle house, storage house, farmer's living quarters, and other buildings were brought here from the surrounding area and then restored. Cultural activities and events, such as rosemaling, wood carving, and folk music performances, take place here. A café serves coffee, waffles, *rømmebrød* (sour-cream cookies), *lefse* (flat cakes filled with sugar or cream), and other traditional sweets. ⊠ *Hagafoss* ☎ *32/08–81–40* ⊙ *Late June–mid-Aug., daily 11–5.*

Where to Stay & Eat

Norway's most popular resort town has many hotels, mountain lodges, traditional cabins, apartments, and camping sites. Rooms are booked early for high season: you can contact **Geilo Booking** (☎ 32/09–59–40 ⊕ www.geilo.no) for advice on accommodations.

$$–$$$ ✕ **Halling-stuene.** The region's best known chef, Frode Aga, has become a celebrity through his cookbooks and television appearances. His downtown restaurant has an elegant bonderomantikk style. His modern Norwegian cuisine features fish and game, with an international influence. Try classic Aga dishes like reindeer fillet with fresh vegetables and mushrooms, or the *bacalao tomat* (dried salt cod with tomato, onion, and paprika). ⊠ *Geilovn. 56* ☎ *32/09–12–50* ▭ *AE, DC, MC, V* ⊙ *Closed May.*

★ **$$–$$$$** ✕▭ **Dr. Holms Hotel.** Built in 1909 as a sanitorium for asthma sufferers, the building is now a well-established resort hotel. Resembling a luxury mountain cabin, the hotel has elegantly decorated rooms and has panoramic views of the surrounding mountains. Its Galleriet restaurant serves Continental–Norwegian dishes. Have drinks by the fire in the classy Ski bar, one of Norway's most popular après-ski bars, or in the cognac bar, Avec. You can read in the peaceful library with its 2,000 volumes, or watch stand-up comedy at the Recepten pub. Be pampered in the Japanese-style Dr. Holms Spa Klinikk. Make hotel reservations well in advance. ⊠ *Timrehaugvn., 2 3580* ☎ *32/09–57–00* ▭ *32/09–16–20* ⊕ *www.drholms.com* ⇌ *127 rooms* ⚭ *Restaurant, 2 indoor pools, gym, spa, 3 bars, lounge, pub, library, meeting rooms* ▭ *AE, DC, MC, V.*

Sports & the Outdoors

BIKING Ask for bike maps at Geilo Tourist information. Besides Rallarvegen, the Adventure Road, and Numedalsruta, there's excellent cycling in the countryside around Geilo on "summer" mountain roads. Bike rentals are available through **Intersport Geilo** (☎ 32/09–09–70 ⊕ www.intersport-geilo.no). They cost NKr 100–NKr 200 per day.

FISHING Geilo's 90 mountain lakes and river stretches are open to the public from June to September. Inquire about the Walks and Recreation maps for Geilo and Hallingskarvet at the tourist office. Fishing licenses, which are mandatory, are valid for one year and cost NKr 45 at any post office or tourist office. Fishing permits, needed for fishing in certain areas, are available at local shops and the Geilo tourist office for NKr 40 per day. Fishing tackle and boat rentals can be organized through **Geilo Camping** (☎ 32/09–07–33) for NKr 120 a day, while rowboats cost NKr 90 for three hours.

HORSEBACK RIDING Many Geilo businesses offer horseback riding and riding lessons and lead mountain trips, which can last from several hours to a week. **Eivindsplass Fjellgard** (☎ 32/09–48–45 ⊙ July). **Geilo Hestesenter** (☎ 32/09–01–81 ⊙ June–Oct.). **Hakkesetstølen** (☎ 32/09–09–20 ⊙ Mid-June–late Sept.). **Hallingskarvet Høyfjellshotell** (☎ 32/08–85–25 ⊙ June–Aug.). **Prestholtseter** (☎ 92/03–75–14 ⊙ July and Aug.). **Ustaoset Hesteridning** (☎ 94/49–39–59 ⊙ July–mid-Aug.).

MOUNTAIN HIKES & WALKS For independent walking, **Den Norske Turistforening (DNT)** (Norwegian Mountain Touring Association) has marked trails across the Hardangervidda plain and in the countryside around Hallingskarvet. Inquire at the tourist office about DNT routes and the use of their cabins.

Experienced guide Turid Linseth of **Hardangervidda Mountain Guiding** (☎ 975/41–860 ⊕ www.fjellguiding.no) has designed guided mountain walks and ski trips for all levels and interests.

SKIING   Geilo has 33 pistes and 18 lifts on both sides of the valley. You can purchase a downhill ski pass that allows you to use all the lifts. A free shuttle bus goes between the five ski centers. For cross-country skiers, there are 220 km of groomed and marked cross-country trails through woodland, Hardangervidda's hills and moors, and around Hallingskarvet, which is 1,933 m (6,341 feet) above sea level. Snow rafting is the latest winter thrill: participants slide down snowy slopes on rubber rafts.

Geilo Skiheiser (☎ 32/09–59–20) has 24 km (15 mi) of alpine slopes, 130 km (81 mi) of cross-country trails, 18 lifts, and a ski-board tunnel. **Havsdalsenteret** (☎ 32/09–17–77) attracts a young crowd to its long alpine slopes. **Vestlia** (☎ 32/09–55–10), west of the Ustedalsfjord, is a good choice for families. **Halstensgård** (☎ 32/09–10–20) and **Slaatta** (☎ 32/09–02–02) have a range of alpine and cross-country trails.

Dagali

❾ *25 km (15.5 mi) southeast of Geilo, off Rte. 40, on the border of Numedal and Hallingdal.*

The small village Dagali borders the Hardangervidda National Park and makes a good launching point for mountain-hiking, skiing, fishing, and white-water rafting. To replenish expended calories, savor the traditional Norwegian dishes at Dagali Hotell.

The **Dagali Museum** is in the heart of town, in the birchwood below the Fagerlund farm. Teacher Gunnar Stensen lived at Fagerlund from 1870 to 1970. He dedicated his life to the preservation of Norwegian and local culture. The museum houses his collections of agricultural equipment, furniture, and curiosities in 10 houses, an old schoolhouse, and an exhibition hall. ⊠ *Dagali center* ☉ *Mid-June–mid-Aug., daily.*

Where to Stay & Eat

$$–$$$ ✕⌂ **Dagali Hotell.** Ole and Kirsten Halland will make you feel at home
Fodor'sChoice   in their charming chalet-style hotel, 2,870 feet above sea level and over-
★   looking Dagali. The hotel was originally on one of the oldest farms in Dagali—it dates to the 1700s. Rooms are decorated in keeping with the Norwegian bonderomantikk style of this period. The restaurant is popular with locals for its traditional, and seasonal Norwegian dishes. Try Kirsten's mountain trout, which she catches herself in the local lake. During the Christmas season, sample *rakfisk*, a special fish dish, and *lefse* (traditional Norwegian pastry). A short distance away, the Dagali ski center offers downhill skiing and snowboarding and on the property are 2.5 km of well-lit cross country ski trails. In the summer, Kirsten or Ole will give you a tour of the family's private village museum. ⊠ *Dagali 3580 Geilo* ☎ *32/09–37–00* 🖷 *32/09–38–10* ⊕ *www.dagali.no* ⟟ *43 rooms* ⚐ *Restaurant, 3 bars, lounge, pub, library, cross-country skiing* ▱ *AE, DC, MC, V.*

Sports & the Outdoors

Eivind Erik Scharffenberg and his international guides at **Dagali Rafting** (☎ 32/09–38–20 or 90/94–36–12 ⊕ www.dagalirafting.no) lead white-water trips on the Numedal River.

Hardangervidda

❿ *90 km (56 mi) from Geilo to Eidfjord on Rte. 7, the main road that crosses Hardangervidda.*

Norwegians take great pride in their largest national park, which is also Europe's largest mountain plateau—10,000 square km (3,861 square mi). Hardangervidda is home to the largest wild reindeer herds in Europe and is the southernmost outpost of the Arctic fox, snowy owl, and other arctic animals and plants. A plateau with a thousand lakes, it has gently rolling hills and wide stretches of level ground. In the west, the mountains become more dramatic, the plant life richer, the climate wetter, and temperatures more moderate. In the east, the small amount of snow means that it's an almost barren, windswept moorland.

Some 250 Stone Age sites have been found in Hardangervidda. The earliest date from 6,300 BC, which proves that man reached the plateau at the same time as the reindeer. When touring the plateau, either on horseback or on foot, you can find a trail for any level of ability. Den Norske Turistforening (DNT; The Norwegian Mountain Touring Association) has built cabins along the trails. The asssociation organizes tours and activities. All plant and animal life is protected by law. Respect the area to make sure it remains a thing of beauty.

At the foot of Vøringfossen Waterfall and Måbødalen Valley, the **Hardangervidda Natursenter Eidfjord** (Hardangervidda Nature Center at Eidfjord) focuses on the area's geology, biology, and archaeology. More than half a billion years ago, Norway was south of the equator. Twenty-five million years ago, glaciers began their descent over Norway. An interactive program explains how glaciers form, grow, and recede. ⊠ *Øvre Eidfjord* ☎ *53/66–59–00* ⊕ *www.hardangervidda.org* ✉ *NKr 70* ⊙ *June–Aug., daily 9–8; Sept.–Oct. and Apr.–May, daily 10–6; Nov.–Mar., by arrangement.*

About an hour's drive north of Geilo is Hardangervidda's highest peak, **Hardangerjøkulen** (Hardanger Glacier), at 6,200 feet (1,891 m). In summer you can join guided glacier walks led by **Jøklagutane** (☎ 90/ 84–15–99 ⊕ www.finsehytta.no). Near Hardangerjøkulen you can take a guided hike to the archaeological digs of 8,000-year-old Stone Age settlements. Turid Linseth at **Hardangervidda Mountain Guiding** (☎ 975/ 41–860 ⊕ www.fjellguiding.no) leads guided walks explaining Hardangervidda's history, flora, and fauna.

Finse

⓫ *On the railway line from Oslo to Bergen, in the Hardangervidda plateau.*

The only way to get to car-free Finse is by train, cycling, hiking, or skiing, making a visit there a unique and very remote Norwegian mountain experience, 4,008 feet above sea level. On the Oslo to Bergen line, the railway station here is northern Europe's highest. Glistening glaciers, white plateaus, and extreme temperatures and conditions have made Finse a legendary place of pilgrimage for adventurers and outdoor lovers. Some of the oldest traces of Norwegian civilization were found here: the remains of reindeer-hunting settlements dating back 7,000 years. Finse is not a town; its year-round population is fewer than 10 people, and besides the train station, there is only a hotel and a few other buildings.

In the 1870s and 1880s, urban-dwelling Norwegian artists and university professors began to hike in the mountains here, and foreign tourists, particularly from Great Britain, started to visit the near-Arctic clime. By the early 1900s, polar explorers Fridtjof Nansen, Robert F. Scott, and Sir Ernest Shackleton tested their equipment here before setting off on their respective expeditions. In 1979, battle scenes of the second Star Wars film *The Empire Strikes Back* were filmed here.

Long cross-country ski trips, telemarking, ski sailing, glacier walking on Hardangerjøkulen, dogsledding, hiking, and cycling are still common pastimes. On the last Saturday in April, the traditional end to the ski season, Norwegian skiers gather here for the Skarverennet race.

Rallarmuseet Finse (Railroaders Museum Finse) recalls the legendary turn-of-the-20th-century construction of the Bergen Railway. One exhibition shows how the railway's high mountain section was built, between 1871 and 1909. Another exhibition, *Kampen mot snøen,* (The Fight Against the Snow), chronicles man's struggle against fierce winter forces. ⊠ *Østre lokomotivstall, Finse stasjon* ☎ *56/52–69–66* ⊕ *www.rallarmuseet.no* ⊠ *NKr 30* ☉ *Early July–Sept., daily 10–10; early Feb.–early June, weekdays 9–3.*

Galleri Finse is a small gallery run by Norwegian artist Rannveig Barstad in cooperation with the Bryggen Kunstskole (art school). Changing exhibitions feature Barstad's and regional artists' works. ☎ *56/52–63–57 or 97/56–47–97* ☉ *Daily 10–8.*

Every first weekend in February, the **Finse Jazz festival** (⊕ www. bergenjazzforum.no) is arranged by Bergen Jazzforum, presenting musicians from all over the world.

Where to Stay & Eat

$$–$$$ ✕⊡ **Finse 1222.** Named for Finse's position 1,222 meters (4,008 feet) above sea level, this 1909 hotel originally served travelers on the Bergen Railway who became snowed-in. Despite its remote location, this *villmarkshotell* (wilderness hotel) quickly became a gathering place for Europe's rich and famous. Murals and photographs throughout depict ski scenes and past guests. Guest rooms are spartan, with no televisions, radios, or telephones. The kitchen serves first-class Norwegian fare ($$), including warm smoked salmon, and leg of wild lamb. The pub and disco Boggin has authentic railway seating. Summer and winter activities, tours, courses, and ski and bike rentals are available. Make reservations as early as possible, especially for weekends. ⊠ *Next to Finse train station, 5719 Finse* ☎ *56/52–71–00* 🖳 *56/52–67–17* ⊕ *www.finse1222. no* ⊅ *44 rooms* ⌂ *Restaurant, skiing, bar, pub, dance club, library* ▱ *AE, DC, MC, V* ☉ *Closed late Oct.–mid-Jan.*

Sports & the Outdoors

BIKING The most popular bike trek in Norway is the 80-km (50-mi) **Rallarvegen,** which follows the Bergen Railway, westbound over the Hardangervidda, from Haugastøl to Flåm. The route was originally a construction and transportation track used during the building of the railway. (*Rallar* was the Norwegian word for the railway workmen.) The bikeway was established in 1974, and attracts 20,000 cyclists each year. You can rent a bicycle at Finse and return it at Flåm. Bike rental is available through **Haugastøl Tourist Center** (☎ 32/08–75–64) or at the Finse 1222 hotel.

HIKING, GLACIER WALKING Finse is an important connection for mountain trips, whether in summer or winter. Several hotels, including Finse 1222 and **Jøklagutane** (☎ 90/84–15–99) have programs and expert guides for mountain hikes and glacier walks.

DNT (☎ 56/52–67–32) arranges mountain trips; maintains well-marked trails south and north of Finse; and operates Finsehytta, a mountain cabin.

SKIING, SKI **Finse Skilag** (☎ 55/31–79–56) arranges skiing trips as well as summer
SAILING mountain activities. **Parmann AS Skiseiling** (☎ 66/91–37–01) offers ski-
sailing courses and sells sails.

Central Norway A to Z

BY AIR

Coast Air operates flight routes between Stavanger on the southern coast
and Dagali several times weekly.
Coast Air ⊠ Geilo Lufthavn Dagali ☎ 32/09–51–00 ⊕ www.coastair.no

BY BUS

Several bus companies operate in the region. Nor-Way Bussekspress can
you give an overview of regional, express and national routes and connections. Contact the local tourist office regarding special seasonal ski buses
Hallingdal Billag ☎ 177 or 81/50–01–83 ⊕ www.hallingdalbillag.no. **Sogn Billag**
☎ 32/05–51–55 ⊕ www.sognbillag.no. **Nettbuss** ☎ 32/20–30–90 or 177. **Nor-Way
Bussekspress** ☎ 81/54–44–44.

BY CAR

Follow Route 7 between Oslo–Hønefoss and Bergen. The roads through
central Norway are generally very well-maintained but note that your
trip will probably involve some mountain driving. In summer, road
conditions are good, but in winter there can be avalanches and other
obstacles.

BY TRAIN

This region is served by the Oslo–Bergen line of the Norwegian State
Railway (the whole run takes nearly seven hours). Between late June
and mid-September, a bicycle train, which stops at Finse, runs between
Oslo and Voss.
NSB (Norwegian State Railway) ☎ 81/50–08–88 ⊕ www.nsb.no.

LODGING

For information on the region's top ski resorts, check out Scandinavia's
online ski booking Web site, **Skistar** (⊕ www.skistar.com).

TOUR OPERATORS

Fjell og Fjord Ferie AS ⊠ Skysstasjonen, Sentrumsvegen 93 Gol ☎ 32/07–61–35
⊕ www.eventyrveien.com.

VISITOR INFORMATION

The main tourist offices of the region are in Ål, Geilo, Hemsedal, Gol,
and Hallingdal (Nesbyen).
Tourist Information Ål ☎ 32/08–10–60 ⊕ www.aal.as. **Geilo** ☎ 32/09–59–00
⊕ www.geilo.no. **Gol** ☎ 32/02–97–00 ⊕ www.golinfo.no. **Hallingdal (Nesbyen)** ☎ 32/
07–01–70 ⊕ www.nesbyen.no. **Hemsedal** ☎ 32/05–50–30 ⊕ www.hemsedal.com.

INTERIOR NORWAY:
LILLEHAMMER TO RØROS

The land turns to rolling hills and green forests as you travel northward
in Norway's inner midsection. The main town of Lillehammer draws
skiers from around the world to its slopes and trails. As you travel north,
you'll enter Gubrandsdalen (*dal* means valley), one of the longest and
most beautiful valleys in the country. Gudbrandsdalen extends from Lake
Mjøsa, north of Oslo, diagonally across the country to Åndalsnes. At
the base of the lake is Eidsvoll, where Norway's constitution was signed
on May 17, 1814.

Venture still farther north to reach the copper-mining town of Røros, which is listed on UNESCO's World Heritage List. This bucolic little town seems to have stood still for the past 100 years. The triangle between Oppland and Hedmark counties, heading south to Lillehammer, is called Troll Park.

Numbers in the margin correspond to points of interest on the Central and Interior Norway map.

Hamar

▶ ⑫ *134 km (83 mi) north of Oslo, 66 km (41 mi) north of Eidsvoll.*

On a northeast fork of Lake Mjøsa, Hamar was the seat of a bishopric during the Middle Ages. Four Romanesque arches, which are part of the cathedral wall, remain; they are today the symbol of the city. Ruins of the 13th-century monastery now form the backbone of a glassed-in exhibition of regional artifacts, some of which are from the Iron Age.

The four Romanesque arches that formed part of the wall of the medieval cathedral that stood here, form the centerpiece of the **Hedmarksmuseet and Domkirkeodden** (Hedemark Museum and Cathedral Point). Also on the grounds of the museum sit 50 or so idyllic grass-roof houses from the region that show the cultural and social life of Hamar when it was a flourishing town. There is an organic garden that has 375 different types of herbs. The museum is about a mile west of the city center. ✉ *Strandveien 100* ☎ *62/54–27–00* ⊕ *www.hedmarksmuseet.museum.no* ✉ *NKr 60* ☉ *Late-May–mid-June and mid-Aug.–Sept., daily 10–4; mid-June–mid-Aug., daily 10–6.*

The **Hamar Olympiahall** hosted the speed- and figure-skating events of the Lillehammer Winter Olympics in 1994, which helped rejuvenate the town's economy and gave it a new stadium. The multipurpose stadium is now used for exhibitions, conferences, fairs, concerts, and sports events. Shaped like an upside-down Viking ship, Olympiahall was voted most magnificent structure of the 20th century by the national Norwegian newspaper *Dagbladet.* ✉ *Åkersvikaveien Hamar* ☎ *62/55–01–00* ⊕ *www.noa.no.*

One of Europe's first railway museums, opened in 1896, the **Jernbanemuseet** documents the development of Norway's railways. Exhibits with train memorabilia are inside, while locomotives and carriages are on narrow-gauge tracks outside and in sheds. You can take a short ride on Ter-tittoget, the last steam locomotive built by Norway's state railway, from mid-May to mid-August. ✉ *Strandvn. 132* ☎ *62/51–31–60* ⊕ *www.jernbaneverket.no* ✉ *NKr 30* ☉ *Late May–June and Aug.–early Sept. daily 10–4; July, daily 10–6.*

The world's oldest paddle steamer still in operation, DS **Skibladner,** also called the "White Swan of the Mjøsa," was first launched in 1856. She departs daily from Hamar, connecting towns along the lake. The steamer creeps up to Lillehammer three days a week. The other days it stops at Eidsvoll. The Gentlemen's Saloon and Ladies Saloon have been restored. A traditional dinner, consisting of poached salmon and potatoes, with strawberries and cream for dessert, is available for an extra charge. ✉ *Torggt. 1* ☎ *62/52–70–85* ⊕ *www.skibladner.no* ☉ *Mid-May–mid-Sept.*

Gjøvik

⑬ *45 km (27 mi) west of Hamar.*

The DS *Skibladner* stops several times a week at this quiet, hillside town, which claims to be home to the world's largest underground auditorium. The **Gjøvik Olympiske Fjellhall** (Olympic Mountain Hall) is buried 400 feet below the mountain in the middle of town. ⊠ *Town Center* ☎ *61/ 13–82–00* 🖾 *NKr 20.*

Lillehammer

⑭ *40 km (25 mi) from Gjøvik, 60 km (37 mi) from Hamar, 180 km (111 mi) from Oslo.*

Many Norwegians have great affection for Lillehammer, the winter-sports resort town that hosted the 1994 Winter Olympics. In preparation for the games, the small town built a ski-jumping arena, an ice-hockey arena, a cross-country skiing stadium, and a bobsled and luge track. The "Winter City" is known for the slopes on the mountains Nordseter and Sjusjøen; *Vinterspillene,* its Winter Arts Festival, held in February; and its many old wooden buildings. Lillehammer is a cultural center as well. Sigrid Undset, who won the Nobel Prize in literature in 1928, lived in the town for 30 years.

The **Olympiaparken** has a range of winter as well as summer activities. You can visit the ski jump tower, take the chairlift, or step inside the bobsled simulator at the **Lysgårdsbakkene Ski Jump Arena,** where the Winter Olympics' opening and closing ceremonies were held. Also in the park are **Håkons Hall,** the main hockey arena, which now holds sporting events including an indoor golf event. The **Birkebeineren Ski Stadium** holds cross-country and biathlon events. You can go tobagganing at the **Kanthaugen Freestyle Arena.** ⊠ *Elvegt. 19* ☎ *61/25–11–40* ⊕ *www.olympiaparken. no* 🖾 *Arena NKr 20, fee varies for athletic events.*

The **Norges Olympiske Museum** (Norwegian Olympic Museum) covers the history of the games from their start in ancient Greece in 776 BC. Multimedia presentations and artifacts like sailboats and skis illustrate Norwegian sporting history in the **Gallery of Honor.** Some of the exhibition captions are in English. ⊠ *Håkons Hall, Olympic Park* ☎ *61/25–21–00* ⊕ *www.ol.museum.no* 🖾 *NKr 60* ☉ *June–Sept., Tues.–Sun. 10–6.*

★ ♻ Norway's oldest open-air museum, **Maihaugen–Sandvigsche Sammlungen,** was founded in 1887. The massive collection of the artifacts of folk life was begun by Anders Sandvik, an itinerant dentist who accepted odds and ends—and eventually entire buildings—from the people of Gudbrandsdalen in exchange for his services. Eventually Sandvik turned the collection over to the city of Lillehammer, which provided land for the museum. The exhibit "We Won the Land" is an inventive meander through Norway's history. It begins in 10,000 BC. After walking past life-size, blue-hued mannequins representing periods like the Black Death and the 400 years of Danish rule, you get to unsettling exhibits about the 20th century. ⊠ *Maihaugvn. 1* ☎ *61/28–89–00* ⊕ *www.maihaugen.no* 🖾 *NKr 75, includes guided tour* ☉ *Oct.–mid-May, daily 11–4.*

Fodor'sChoice ★ One of the most important art collections in Norway is housed at the **Lillehammer Kunstmuseum** (Lillehammer Museum of Art), which opened in 1927. The 1,000 works include pieces by Edvard Munch and Odd Nerdrum. The original 1963 building has been remodeled and joined by a new building designed by Snøhetta. Sculptor Bård Breivik created a sculpture garden using stone and water between the two buildings. ⊠ *Stortorgt. 2* ☎ *61/05–44–60* ⊕ *www.lillehammerartmuseum. com* 🖾 *NKr 60* ☉ *Late Aug.–June, Tues.–Sun. 11–4; July–late Aug., daily 11–5.*

Right on the pedestrian street, the tiny café **One Hand Clapping** (⊠ Storgata) serves some of the best international coffees to be found between Oslo and Trondheim.

HUNDERFOSSEN PARK – The world's biggest troll sits atop a cave in this tiny amusement park. The glittering gold Eventyrslottet, or fairy tale castle, is a must-see. There's a petting zoo for small children; plenty of rides; plus an energy center, with Epcotlike exhibits about oil and gas; and a five-screen theater. At the **The Bobsleigh and Luge Track** you can bobsleigh on ice. Bob rafting involves a rubber bobsleigh with wooden runners that seats five passengers and can travel as fast as 80 km/h. The park is 13 km (8 mi) north of Lillehammer. ⊠ *Fåberg* ☎ *61/27–72–22* ⊕ *www.hunderfossen.no* 🎟 *NKr 160* ☉ *Late May–early Sept., daily.*

Where to Stay & Eat

$–$$$ ✕ **Blåmann Restaurant & Bar.** Named after a Norwegian folktale about a buck called Blueman, this popular restaurant has a completely blue interior; it's spread over two floors. Try the Mexican tacos, or a reindeer or ostrich steak. ⊠ *Lilletorvet 1* ☎ *61/26–22–03* ⚓ *Reservations essential* ⊟ *AE, DC, MC, V.*

¢–$ ✕ **Nikkers, Svare & Berg.** Nikkers has a rustic, mountain-cabin style, with the predictable moose head. Svare & Berg has a roaring fireplace and caricatures of famous authors hanging on the walls. Next door to each other, these restaurant–bars share the same owner and international cuisine, ranging from nachos to pastas. ⊠ *Elvegt. 18* ☎ *61/24–74–30* ⊟ *AE, DC, MC, V.*

$$–$$$ ✕🏨 **Rica Victoria Hotel.** Red burnished leather chairs dot the English library–style lobby at this central hotel. Guest rooms are furnished in styles ranging from pure rural romanticism to more classic styles. The hotel has eight "ladies rooms," each with bed alcove and rocking chair. Victoria Stuené and Krambua, the hotel's two restaurants, face the town's pedestrian street. Terrassen, the hotel's summer restaurant, is a hot spot on summer nights and is popular for its barbecue dishes. ⊠ *Storgt. 84B, 2600* ☎ *61/25–00–49* 📠 *61/25–24–74* ⊕ *www.rica.no* ➲ *109 rooms, 17 suites* ⚒ *3 restaurants, café, lobby lounge, pub, nightclub, meeting room* ⊟ *AE, DC, MC, V.*

★ $$ 🏨 **Mølla Hotell.** In this converted 1863 mill, the small reception area gives the feeling of a private home. The yellow rooms in the former grain silo have rustic pine furniture. At the top of the silo, the Toppen Bar gives you a panoramic view of the Olympic ski jump and Lake Mjøsa. The Egon Restaurant is a beautiful outdoor retreat along the Mesna River. ⊠ *Elvegt. 12, 2600* ☎ *61/26–92–94* 📠 *61/26–92–95* ⊕ *www.mollahotell. no* ➲ *58 rooms* ⚒ *Restaurant, gym, sauna, bar* ⊟ *AE, DC, MC, V.*

$–$$ 🏨 **Birkebeineren Hotel/Motel & Apartments.** Ski trails and hiking terrain are steps away from this hotel's doors. The cream-color rooms are understated and country-style. Black-and-white photographs of skiers decorate the walls. ⊠ *Birkebeineren 24, Olympiaparken 2618* ☎ *61/ 26–47–00* 📠 *61/26–47–50* ⊕ *www.birkebeineren.no* ➲ *52 hotel rooms, 35 motel rooms, 40 apartments* ⚒ *Dining room, sauna, meeting rooms* ⊟ *AE, DC, MC, V.*

Sports & the Outdoors

A highlight of Lillehammer's ski year is the **Birkebeineren cross-country ski race.** The Birkebeiners were a faction in Norway's 13th-century civil war, who got their name because they wrapped their legs in birchbark (hence *birkebeiner*—birch legs). Birch bark was commonly used as footwear by people who couldn't afford wool or leather leggings. The ski race commemorates the trek of two Birkebeiner warriors who carried the heir to the throne, Prince Haakon, to safety from the rival Bagler faction who were pursuing him. The backpack carried by participants during the race is meant to symbolize the young prince being brought to safety through harsh weather conditions.

FISHING Within Troll Park, the **Gudbrandsdalåen** is touted as one of the best-stocked rivers in the country, and the size and weight of Mjøsa trout (locals claim it's 25 pounds) is legendary. Contact the local tourist board for information about fishing seasons, how to get the required national and local licenses, and other useful tips.

HIKING & The Nordseter and Sjusjøen tourist centers are good starting points for
BICYCLING mountain-biking and -hiking excursions. From **Nordseter Aktivitetssenter** (✉ Lillehammer ☎ 61/26–40–37) about 15 km from the city center, you can hike to Mount Neverfjell, at 3,573 feet. There you can see the Jotunheimen and Rondane mountain ranges. The center rents mountain bikes, canoes, and other boats. Mount Lunkefjell (3,320 feet) is a popular hiking destination accessible from **Sjusjøen Sport & Aktiviteter** (✉ Sjøen ☎ 62/36–35–82). Regular bicycles and mountain bikes can be rented. The center also organizes walks, bicycle and fishing trips, and canoeing.

RAFTING & The **Sjoa River,** close to Lillehammer, offers some of the most challeng-
CANOEING ing rapids in the country. Contact **Heidal Rafting** (☎ 61/23–60–37).

SKIING Lillehammer–Sjusjøen and Nordseter and the four other nearby skiing destinations—Hafjell, Skeikampen, Kvitfjell and Gålå—are collectively called **Lillehammer Ski Resorts** (⊕ www.lsr.no). Together, they have 35 lifts, 79 pistes, and more than 1,300 km (930 mi) of cross-country trails. Each destination has its particular charm. A Lillehammer Ski Resorts Pass admits you to all five.

With both high mountain and forest terrain, **Hafjell** (✉ 10 km [6 mi] north of Lillehammer ☎ 61/27–47–00) is the largest Alpine facility. Snow conditions are generally stable here. The Trollclub snowboard park is popular. There's also a childcare center, a ski school, and several après-ski spots.

Gålå (✉ 70 km [40 mi] from Lillehammer ☎ 61/29–85–28) is an all-around ski facility, with spectacular high mountain terrain and views of Jotunheimen and Rondane national parks. It has cross-country trails and organized activities that include ice fishing, snow rafting, sledding, winter riding, and sleigh riding.

Shopping
Most of Lillehammer's 250-odd shops are on or near Storgata Street. From Lilletorget, you can walk to the old industrial area of Mesna Brug, where there's the Mesnasenter (Mesna Center) group of clothing and craft shops. **Husfliden** (✉ Sigrid Undset pl. ☎ 61/26–70–70 ⊕ www.husfliden.no), one of the biggest and oldest home crafts stores in Europe, specializes in hand-knit sweaters and traditional and handmade goods from the Gudbrandsdalen area. Glassblowing is demonstrated at **Lillehammer Kunst Glass** (✉ Elvegt. 17 ☎ 61/25–79–80); you can also buy special glass souvenirs here.

Gausdal

🚇 *18 km (11 mi) northwest of Lillehammer.*

The composer of Norway's national anthem and the 1903 Nobel Prize winner in literature, Bjørnstjerne Bjørnson, lived at **Aulestad,** in Gausdal, from 1875 until he died in 1910. After his wife died in 1934, their house was opened as a museum. ✉ *Follebu* ☎ *61/22–41–10* 💶 *NKr 50* 🕐 *Mid-May and Sept., daily 11–2:30; June and Aug., daily 10–3:30; July daily 10–5:30.*

The scenic, well-marked **Peer Gynt Vegen** (Peer Gynt Road) begins in Gausdal. It's named for the real-life man behind Ibsen's character. Just 3 km (2 mi) longer than the main route, the road gives you splendid views of the mountains of Rondane, Dovrefjell, and Jotunheimen as you travel past old farmhouses. It passes two major resorts, **Skeikampen/Gausdal** and **Gålå/Wadahl**, before rejoining E6 at Vinstra.

Ringebu

⑯ *50 km (31 mi) north of Lillehammer, 30 km (20 mi) northeast of Gausdal.*

Ringebu is home to former Winter Olympic site Kvitfjell, now one of the World Cup Alpine Skiing venues. Although it has the challenging downhill course used in the 1994 Olympic Games, **Kvitfjell** (☎ 61/28–36–00 ⊕ www.kvitfjell.no) also has easier courses, including a family-friendly 2-km (1-mi) slope with a drop of 1,150 feet. There's also a snowboard park and more than 200 km (124 mi) of prepared cross-country trails.

Weidemannsamlingen-Ringebu Prestegard shows paintings by late Norwegian painter Jacob Weidemann. ☎ 61/28–27–00.

The stave church **Ringebu Stavkirke** (☎ 61/28–03–74) dates from the 13th century and is open for guided summer tours.

Where to Stay & Eat

$$ ✕▣ **Venabu Fjellhotell.** The Tvete family has been welcoming regulars
Fodor'sChoice to its mountain retreat in the village of Venabygd for many years. Guests
★ can join their unforgettable guided ski and mountain trips. Horseback riding, sleigh and wagon rides, canoeing, mountain biking, and snowshoeing are among other activities. Although the guest rooms are basic, without televisions, most guests spend their time outdoors and socializing in the lounges. Every meal is served buffet style, and the Wednesday night traditional Norwegian buffet is delicious, cooked with fresh local ingredients. ✉ 2632 Venabygd ☎ 61/28–40–55 📠 61/28–41–21 ⊕ www.venabu.no ☝ 42 rooms ⚲ Restaurant, cross-country skiing, hiking, Internet; no room TVs ⊟ AE, DC, MC, V.

Vinstra

⑰ *18 km (11 mi) north of Gausdal.*

Vinstra is the administrative, service, trade, and education center of the district. It is best known for the Peer Gynt Festival, named after the Ibsen play, which was based upon Per, a resident of Sødorp near Vinstra. The festival is held every summer for one week in July or August. A wooden 1743 farmhouse where the historical Per lived, the **Peer Gynt Stugu** (Peer Gynt's house) has an exhibition based on the play and the man who inspired it. Photographs, posters, programs, costumes, and books have been gathered from *Peer Gynt* theatrical productions around the world. ✉ Hågå, Sødorp ☎ 61/29–20–04 ☉ Mid-June–mid-Aug., daily 10–5.

> **off the beaten path**
>
> **SOLBRÅ MOUNTAIN FARM MUSEUM** – In Gålå you'll find one of Norway's most famous mountain farms. Solbrå is where Gudbrandsdalen, the brown Norwegian cheese, was first made, in 1863. Dairymaid Anne Hov first used only cow milk in the cheese; later, goat milk was added. The old cheese house is now a museum. ✉ Gålå ☎ 61/29–70–48 ☉ Early July–late Aug., Wed. and Sat. 11–3.

Where to Stay & Eat

★ $$ ✕▣ **Fefor Høifjellshotell og Hytter.** Norway's oldest winter sports hotel dates to 1903. The mountain lodge's lobby has an open fireplace, stuffed trophy heads, and rustic wooden furniture; black-and-white photographs recount the hotel's heyday, when royal family and explorers Fridtjof Nansen and Sir Robert Scott numbered among the guests. Every room is simple yet comfortable, some affording stunning views. Nearby is the trail up to Fefor Kampen, from which you can see many of the country's highest mountains. Guests come to cross-country or downhill ski, or canoe and fish in peaceful surroundings. Traditional Norwegian dishes based on seasonal ingredients are served in the restaurant. ✉ *13 km off Rte. E6 from Vinstra 2640 Vinstra-Gudbrandsdalen* ☎ *61/ 29–00–99* 🖷 *61/29–17–60* 🌐 *www.fefor.com* ⟿ *120 rooms, 6 suites, 20 cabins* ⚭ *Restaurant, pool, cross-country skiing, downhill skiing* ▭ *AE, DC, MC, V.*

★ **$–$$** ✕▥ **Gålå Høgfjellshotell og Hytter.** North of Vinstra, this is one of Norway's finest high mountain hotels, known for more than a century for its excellent service. Elegant navy blue rooms are furnished in *bonderomantikk* (country romantic) style. In the intimate hotel restaurant Mor Aases Kjøkken, freshly caught trout from Gålå Lake, wild game, fresh berries, and herbs are prepared in traditional Norwegian style. Plan to dine here on Wednesday night for the superb fish buffet. Downstairs, in Anitras, you can have coffee or browse the library of bestsellers available in several languages. High-standard *hytter* (mountain cabins) are also available for rent. The hotel is close to the summer festival stage. ✉ *2646 Gålå* ☎ *61/29–81–09* 🖷 *61/29–85–40* 🌐 *www. gala-resort.com* ⟿ *42 rooms* ⚭ *Restaurant, pool, cross-country skiing, downhill skiing, library, children's programs, meeting room* ▭ *AE, DC, MC.*

The Arts

Norwegian violinist Øystein Rudi and his wife Nina live on a cozy 17th-century farm, **Rudi Gard** (✉ East on Rte. E6 from Vinstra ☎ 61/ 29–86–60 or 913–85–388 🌐 www.rudigard.no). They've renovated the barn into a theater venue, gallery, and café. In summer Rudi Gard has performances by some of Norway's top folk musicians and actors, plus a sheep-shearing competition and other events. Overnight accommodation is available.

Sports & the Outdoors

BOATING Guided canoe safaris or independent trips are possible on four mountain lakes along the Peer Gynt Road. Contact **Gålå Sommer Arena** (☎ 61/ 29–85–28 🌐 www.gala.no) and **Fefor Høifjellshotell** (☎ 61/29–00–99 🌐 www.fefor.com) are connected to hotels in Vinstra.

CYCLING Area hotels rent mountain bikes. Contact **Norske Bygdeopplevelser** (☎ 61/ 28–99–70 🌐 www.norske-bygdeopplevelser.no) for cycling tours, guided or independent, for four to seven days. Overnight accommodation will be arranged at hotels and mountain lodges.

HIKING A network of marked trails and footpaths such as those kept by **DNT-The Norwegian Mountain Touring Association, The Peer Gynt Trail,** and **The Pilgrims' Track** offer varied challenges. You can pick up maps at **Vinstra Skysstasjon** (Vinstra Tourist and Transport Centre).

HORSEBACK RIDING **Sulseter Rideleir** (☎ 61/29–13–21) offers week-long and weekend treks in Rondane National Park.

SKIING Considered one of the best resorts for cross-country skiing (there are 630 km [391 mi] of trails), the **Peer Gynt Ski Region** (🌐 www. peergyntskiregion.com) includes the destinations Espedalen, Fefor and Gålå. For downhill skiers, there are pistes for all levels in Snowboard, Telemark and Alpine.

Rondane National Park

⑱ *19 km (12 mi) north of Vinstra. off Rte. E6.*

Rounded, harmonious mountains distinguish Rondane National Park, as you travel north from Vinstra on Route E6. A good point of entry to the park is the resort of Høvringen, off Route E6. For thousands of years, the area has given hunters their livelihood and they've left their mark in the form of reindeer traps and burial mounds. Today, Rondane is a popular recreation area, attracting hikers and skiers. Ten of the peaks rise more than 6,500 feet. Norwegian artist Harald Sohlberg (1869–1935) immortalized the Rondane mountains in his painting *Vinternatt,* which was declared Norway's national painting in 1995 and hangs in the National Gallery in Oslo.

Where to Stay & Eat

★ **$$–$$$$** ✕⊞ **Rondablikk Hotell.** Nestled in the mountains, near Kvam, Rondablikk has spectacular views of Rondane National Park and several lakes. Rooms are simply furnished and comfortable. Many guests spend their days cross-country skiing or mountain hiking. You can opt to order *halvpensjon* (half board), which includes the traditional Norwegian buffets at breakfast, lunch, and dinner. Rondablikk shares a lunch exchange program with Rondane SPA Hotel and Rondeslottet. Every summer, Norway's best musicians play on the hotel's outdoor stage as part of The Peer Gynt Festival. ⊠ *Route E6, 2642 Kvam* ☎ *61/29–49–40* 🖷 *61/29–49–50* ⊕ *www.rondablikk.com* ⤿ *72 rooms* ⚥ *Restaurant, pool, exercise room, sauna, cross-country skiing, bar, lounge* ⊟ *AE, DC, MC, V.*

★ **$$–$$$** ✕⊞ **Rondane SPA Hotel.** This hotel is high in the mountains south of Otta. The bright, simply furnished rooms have a country charm. A full range of services, from massage to baths, is on offer at the spa. Chef Kjell Eirk Lind-Hanssen changes the menu of international dishes based on Norwegian fish and game daily. To get to the hotel, turn right off Route E6 before the exit for Otto, and follow signs to Mysuseter and Rondane Spa. ⊠ *Mysuseter, off E6 2670 Otta* ☎ *61/23–39–33* 🖷 *61/23–39–52* ⊕ *www.spa.no* ⤿ *52 rooms* ⚥ *Restaurant, pool, massage, sauna, spa* ⊟ *AE, DC, MC, V.*

Lom

⑲ *62 km (38 mi) west of Otta, via Rte. 15.*

Glaciers, lakes, fertile valleys, and mountains make up **Jotunheimen National Park,** of which 90% lies in the muncipality of Lom. One of the park's well-known landmarks is **Galdhøpiggen,** the country's highest mountain, at 8,098 feet. Established in 1980, the park covers an area of 1,150 square km, and contains 27 of Norway's highest peaks. The rural town of Lom is distinguished by its dark-brown painted log-cabins and a stave church from 1170.

One of Norway's oldest and most beautiful stave churches, **Lom Stavkyrkje** (Lom Stave Church), dates to the 12th century and still is the principal church in Lom. Its oldest section is Romanesque; the church was enlarged in 1634. Wood carver Jakop S(ae)terdalen created the choir stalls and the pulpit. The church's Baroque painting collection is one of Norway's largest. ☎ *61/21–29–90* ✉ *NKr 40* ⊙ *Mid-May–mid-June and mid-Aug.–mid-Sept., daily 10–4; mid-June–mid-Aug., daily 9–9.*

A woolly mammoth looms at the entrance to **Norsk Fjellmuseum** (Norwegian Mountain Museum). The museum focuses on people's relationship with the Norwegian mountain landscape, from the primitive hunters and gatherers who lived here, to modern Norwegian society, with its belief in leisure time and outdoor recreational activities. Among the most interesting of the exhibitions is one dealing with early mountaineering and mountain road building. You can read the late 19th-century journals of W.C. Slingsby, the British father of Norwegian mountaineering, and see a reconstructed campsite. ⊠ *Town Center* ☎ *61/21–16–00* ⊕ *www.fjell.museum.no* ⊠ *NKr 60* ☉ *May and Sept. daily 9–4, weekends 10–5; early June, late Aug, weekdays 9–6, weekends 10–5; mid-June–mid-Aug. 9–9, weekends 10–8; late Sept.–Apr., weekdays 9–4, weekends by appointment.*

At **Lom Bygdamuseum Presthaugen** (Lom Open Air Museum), well-preserved 19th-century farm, you can see **Olavsstugu,** where Saint Olav is said to have spent the night; there are also exhibitions, including one about watering techniques and grain in Storstabburet. ⊠ *Town Center* ☎ *61/21–73–00* ⊠ *NKr 20* ☉ *July, daily 1–4, guided tours noon–4.*

Torgeir Garmo shares his passion for geology in his geological museum and jewelry gallery in the **Fossheim Steinsenter** (Fossheim Stone Center). His collection is the largest exhibition of Norwegian minerals and precious stones in the country. In the sales galleries, you can buy jewelry, minerals, and fossils. The Collector Mania museum shows rare objects that people have collected through the ages. The Fossheim Kulturpark offers an 18th-century–style landscape with nature trails. ☎ *61/21–14–60* ⊠ *Free* ☉ *June–Aug., daily 9–9.*

Where to Stay & Eat

★ **$$** ✕⊡ **Fossheim Turisthotell.** Svein Garmo and his family have run this mountain hotel since it began as a staging post in 1897. Solid-timber walls and antique furnishings give it a cozy look. Celebrity chef Arne Brimi and his dishes based on local ingredients have made the restaurant popular. Among the best known dishes is the succulent fillet of reindeer. Take a seat in the aromatic outdoor café Urtehagen, surrounded by herbs and flowers. ⊠ *2686 Lom* ☎ *61/21–95–00* 🖷 *61/21–95–01* ⊕ *www.fossheimhotel.no* ➳ *54 rooms* ♨ *Restaurant, café, bar* ⊟ *AE, DC, MC, V.*

Sports & the Outdoors

FISHING **Lom Fiskeguiding DA** (☎ 61/21–10–24) rents fishing boats and organizes fishing trips.

HIKING & Go glacier walking and climb Galdhøpiggen or other mountains. Call
GLACIER **Juvasshytta** (☎ 61/21–15–50) or **Natur Opplevingar** (☎ 61/21–11–55
WALKING ⊕ www.naturopplevingar.no).

HORSEBACK **Jotunheimen Hestesenter** (Jotunheimen Equestrian Center)
RIDING (⊠ Raubergstulen ☎ 61/21–18–00) has mountain riding tours for all ages, beginner to advanced, on Icelandic horses.

RAFTING Several local outfitters cater to your Sjoa River rafting needs, including **Lom Rafting** (☎ 90/52–57–03 ⊕ www.lomrafting.no), and **Villmarken** (☎ 61/23–39–57).

SUMMER SKIING You can go summer skiing at **Galdhøpiggen Sommerskisenter** (⊠ Lom ☎ 61/21–17–50) on a glacier 6,068 feet above sea level.

Lesja

⑳ *159 km (99 mi) north of Lom.*

As you follow Route E6 from Otta toward Lesja, the broad, fertile valleys and snow-capped mountains of the Upper Gudbrandsdal surround you. The area around Lesja is trout-fishing country; Lesjaskogvatnet, the lake, has a mouth at either end, so the current changes in the middle.

> **off the beaten path**

JØRUNDGARD MIDDELALDER SENTER – Anyone who read Sigrid Undset's 1928 Nobel prize–winning trilogy, *Kristin Lavransdatter,* will remember that the tale's heroine grew up on a farm of the same name as this one. The medieval-style farm, built for the 1995 Liv Ullmann movie, now houses the Jorundgård Medieval Center, a historical and cultural museum. ⊠ *Sel* ☎ *61/23–37–00* ⊕ *www. jorundgard.no* ☞ *NKr 55* ⊙ *June–mid-Sept., daily 10–6; guided tours every ½ hr.*

Dombås

㉑ *80 km (50 mi) east of Lesja on Rte. E136.*

From Dombås, you can follow Route E6 up to **Dovrefjell,** one of the last virtually intact high-mountain ecosystems in Europe. Wild reindeer, wolverines, wild musk ox, arctic fox, and rare plant species make their home here. Snøhetta, the highest peak in the park at 7,500 ft, is a popular hiking destination. There are many restrictions regarding hiking in the area, so contact the tourist office before setting out.

From 1932 to 1953, musk ox were transported from Greenland to the Dovrefjell, where about 60 still roam—bring binoculars to see them. For information on tours, call the Dombås Tourist Office. **Dovrefjell Aktivitetsenter** (☎ 61/24–15–55) organizes family rafting, moose safaris, mountain trips, and climbing and overnight wilderness camps. **Dovre Eventyr** (☎ 61/24–01–59) has guides that lead tours of the local flora and fauna. They also offer musk-oxen safaris and mountain climbing courses.

Where to Stay & Eat

★ **$$$** ✕⬚ **Norlandia Dovrefjell Hotell.** This quiet, peaceful mountain hotel is part of the Norlandia hotel chain, but it was built as a German hospital during World War II. Rustic Norwegian *bonderomantikk*(country style) dominates the lounges and dining rooms. The guest rooms are plainer. Take time to enjoy the outdoors in Dovrefjell, whether on mountain hikes, fishing trips, or musk ox safaris. ⊠ *2659 Dombås* ☎ *61/ 24–10–05* 🖷 *61/24–15–05* ⊕ *www.norlandia.no/dovrefjell* ☞ *89 rooms* ⌂ *Restaurant, bar, pool, sauna* ▤ *AE, DC, MC, V.*

Røros

㉒ *317 km (197 mi) from Lesja, 157 km (97 mi) from Trondheim.*

At the northern end of the Østerdal, the long valley to the east of Gudbrandsdalen, lies Røros, one of Norway's great mining towns. For more than 300 years practically everyone who lived in this one-company town was connected with the copper mines. In 1980, Røros was named a UNESCO World Heritage Site. Norwegian artist Harald Sohlberg's paintings of Røros made the town famous. His statue now stands in Harald Sohlberg's Plass, looking down the stretch of road that he immortalized.

★ Røros's main attraction is the **Old Town,** with its 250-year-old workers' cottages, slag dumps, and managers' houses, one of which is now City Hall. Descendants of the man who discovered copper ore in Røros live in the oldest of the nearly 100 protected heritage buildings. A 75-minute tour starts at the information office and ends at the church. ⊠ *Peder Hiorts gt. 2* ☎ *72/41–00–50* ☞ *NKr 50* ⊙ *Tours June and late Aug.–mid-Sept., Mon.–Sat. at 11; July–mid-Aug., Mon.–Sat. at 10, noon, 1, 2, and 3, Sun. at 1; mid-Sept.–May, Sat. at 11.*

The **Bergstadens Ziir** (Røros Church) towers over the wooden houses of the town. The eight-sided stone structure dates from 1784. On the tower, you can see the symbol of the mines. Called "the mountain's cathedral", it can seat 1,600, quite surprising in a town with a population of only about 3,500. The pulpit looms above the center of the altar, and seats encircle the top perimeter. ☎ 72/41–00–50 ☒ NKr 25 ☉ Mid–late June, weekends 11–1; July–mid-Aug., Mon.–Sat. 10–5, Sun. 2–4; late Aug.–mid-Sept., Mon.–Sat. 11–1; late-Sept.–mid-June, Sat. 11–1.

Røros Museum is in an old smelting plant, opened in 1646. In 1953, a fire destroyed the smelting works in Røros; the plant was closed and the machines were moved to Sweden. "Smelthytta," the smelting house, has been reconstructed using drawings of the workshop from 1888. Exhibitions show models of waterwheels, lift mechanisms, horse-driven capstans, and mine galleries and 19th-century clothing. ☒ Off Rte. 30 ☎ 72/41–05–00 ☒ NKr 60 ☉ Late July–mid-Aug., weekdays 10:30–6, weekends 10:30–4; mid-Aug.–late July, weekdays 11–3, weekends 11–2.

<table>
<tr><td>off the
beaten
path</td><td>

OLAVSGRUVA MINE – This is the only Norwegian copper mine that was saved for posterity (in 1977, the copper works went bankrupt). Known as Olavsgruva, it consists of Nyberget (1650) and Crown Prince Olav's Mine (1936). A museum has been built over the mine shaft. Visitors can walk 50 meters underground and approximately 500 meters into the Miners' Hall, complete with sound and light effects. Bring warm clothing and good shoes, as the temperature below ground is about 41°F. ☒ Near Rte. 31 ☎ 72/40–61–70 ☒ NKr 60 ☉ Guided tours early June and late Aug.–early Sept., Mon.–Sat. at 1 and 3, Sun. at noon; late June–mid-Aug., daily at 10:30, noon, 1:30, 3, 4:30, and 6; early Sept.–May, Sat. at 3.

</td></tr>
</table>

Where to Stay & Eat

If you want to explore the green, pastured mountains just south of Røros, more than a dozen farmhouses take overnight visitors. Some are *hytter* (cabins), but others, such as the **Vingelsgaard Gjestgiveri** (☎ 62/49–45–43), have entire wings devoted to guest rooms. Rates at Vingelsgaard are around 460 NKr per person. Contact **Vingelen Turistinformasjon** (☎ 62/49–46–65 or 62/49–46–83 ⊕ www.vingelen.com) for more information.

$$–$$$ ✕☒ **Bergstadens Hotel.** An elegant, country-style hotel, this is a Røros landmark. The staff is warm and friendly, creating a personal and intimate mood. The restaurant (ce) has a changing menu of traditional Norwegian fare. ☒ Oslovn. 2, 7361 ☎ 72/40–60–80 ☎ 72/41–60–81 ⊕ www.bergstaden.no ⤫ 88 rooms, 4 suites ☖ 2 restaurants, pool, sauna, 2 bars, pub, nightclub, meeting room ☰ AE, DC, MC, V.

Sports & the Outdoors

BOATING Femunden and Hodal lakes make great starting points for day trips or longer tours. A canoeing trip on your own or accompanied by a guide can be memorable. **Hodalen Fjellstue** (☎ 62/49–60–72) has boat and fish net rentals and fishing permits.

CYCLING Easy terrain in the Røros region make it ideal for cyclists. Røros Tourist Office offers bicycling package tours, which include maps and accommodation. Contact **Heimly Huskies Adventure** (☎ 72/41–47–93 ⊕ www.heimly-huskies.com) for mountain bike tours of 3 to 4 hours (600 NKr) or 7 to 8 hours (980 NKr).

FISHING Fishing is possible in the Gaula, one of Norway's finest salmon rivers, or in the Glåma, Norway's longest river, recommended for grayling and trout. An angling guidebook and fishing licenses are sold at the tourist office, in shops and petrol stations, and at the rangers' office in Holtålen. Skilled guides can show you the area and advise you on where and how to fish, preserving and cooking your catch. Contact **Ålen Fjellstyre**(72/ 41–55–77).

SKIING At the northern end of the Gudbrandsdalen region, west of Røros, is **Oppdal** (45 km [28 mi] of alpine pistes, 186 km [116 mi] of cross-country trails; 10 ski lifts), a World Cup venue. Like most other areas, it has lighted trails and snow-making equipment.

Interior Norway A to Z

CAR TRAVEL
The wide, two-lane Route E6 north from Oslo passes through Hamar and Lillehammer. Route 3 follows Østerdalen (the eastern valley) from Oslo. Route 30 at Tynset leads to Røros and E6 on to Trondheim, 156 km (97 mi) farther north.

Roads in the north become increasingly hilly and twisty as the terrain roughens into the central mountains. The northern end of the region is threaded by E16, E6, and Routes 51 and 3. High-tech markers at the roadside, particularly prevalent in the area of Vinstra and Otta, are cameras. Exceed the speed limit, and you may receive a ticket in the mail.

TRAIN & BUS TRAVEL
There are good bus and train connections between Oslo and the major interior towns to the north. The region is served by the Oslo–Trondheim railway line and two other lines.

VISITOR INFORMATION
🚩 Tourist Information **Dovre/Dovrefjell/Rondane Tourist Office** ☎ 61/24-14-44 ⊕ www.dovrenett.no. **Gjøvik** ✉ Jernbanegt. 2 ☎ 61/14-67-10. **Hamar** ✉ Vikingskipet, Olympia Hall ☎ 62/52-12-17. **Lillehammer** ✉ Skysstasjon ☎ 61/25-92-99 ⊕ www. lillehammerturist.no. **Lom/Jotunheimen Reiseliv** ☎ 61/21-29-90 ⊕ www.visitlom. com. **Otta** ☎ 61/23-66-50 ⊕ www.sel-rondane.no. **Øyer-Hafjell/Hunderfossen** ☎ 61/ 27-70-00. **Røros** ☎ 72/41-00-50 ⊕ www.rorosinfo.com. **Vågå/Jotunheimen** ✉ Vågå 37 ☎ 61/23-78-80. **Vinstra (Peer Gynts Rike)** ✉ Vinstra Skysstasjon ☎ 61/29-47-70 ⊕ www.peergynt.no.

THE WEST COAST: FJORD COUNTRY

The intricate outline of the fjords makes Norway's coastline of 21,347 km (13,264 mi) longer than the distance between the North and South poles. Majestic and magical, the fjords can take any traveler's breath away in a moment. Among the world's most spectacular geological formations, a typical fjord consists of a long, narrow, and deep inlet of the sea, with steep mountainsides stretching into mountain massifs. Fjords were created by glacier erosion during the Ice Ages. In spectacular inlets like Sognefjord and Geirangerfjord, walls of water shoot up the montainsides, jagged snowcapped peaks blot out the sky, and water tumbles down the mountains in an endless variety of colors. Lush green farmlands edge up the rounded mountainsides and the chiseled, cragged, steep peaks of the Jotunheimen mountains, Norway's tallest, seem to touch the blue skies.

The farther north you travel, the more rugged and wild the landscape. The still, peaceful Sognefjord is the longest inlet, snaking 190 km (110 mi) inland. At the top of Sogn og Fjordane county is a group of fjords referred to as Nordfjord, with the massive Jostedalsbreen, mainland Europe's largest glacier, to the south. In the county of Møre og Romsdal, you'll see mountains that would seem more natural on the moon—all gray rock—as well as cliffs hanging over the water below. Geirangerfjord is Norway's best known fjord. In the south, the Hardangerfjord, Norway's fruit basket, is best seen in summer when it's in full blossom.

Numbers in the margin correspond to points of interest on the West Coast map.

Åndalsnes

▶ ❶ *495 km (307 mi) north of Bergen, 354 km (219 mi) south of Trondheim.*

Åndalsnes is an industrial alpine village of 3,000 people that is best known for three things: its position as the last stop on the railway, making it a gateway to fjord country; the Trollstigveien (Troll Path); and the Trollveggen (Troll Wall). The tourist office has special maps and guides outlining the popular trails and paths. The tourist office can also make arrangements for you to join a fishing trip to the fjords. Trips last four hours, and leave three times a day; the cost is NKr 250. Six or seven species of mostly white fish, such as cod, live in the waters.

★ From **Horgheimseidet,** which used to have a hotel for elegant tourists— often European royalty—you can view **Trollveggen** (Troll Wall), Europe's highest vertical rock face at 3,300 feet. The birthplace of mountain-climbing sports in Scandinavia, this rock face draws elite climbers from all over.

Fodor'sChoice **Trollstigveien,** Norway's most popular tourist road, starts in Åndalsnes.
★ The road took 100 men 20 summers (1916–36) to build, in a constant struggle against the forces of rock and water. Often described as a masterpiece of construction, the road snakes its way through 11 hairpin bends up the mountain to the peaks named **Bispen** (the Bishop), **Kongen** (the King), and **Dronningen** (the Queen), which are 2,800 feet above sea level. The roads Trollstigveien and Ørneveien (at the Geiranger end) zigzag over the mountains separating two fjords. Roads are open only in summer. Halfway up, the road crosses a bridge over the waterfall **Stigfossen** (Path Falls), which has a vertical fall of nearly 600 feet. Walk to the lookout point, Stigrøra, by taking the 15-minute return path to the plateau. Signs show the way.

One of Norway's most famous mountaineers, Arne Randers Heen (1905–91), and his wife, Bodil Roland, founded the **Norsk Tindemuseum** (Norwegian Mountain Museum), which is dedicated to mountain climbing. Displays of Heen's equipment and photography follow the development of the sport and Heen's many feats. The mountain nearest to his heart was Romsdalshorn, 1,555 m (5,101 feet) high. He climbed that mountain 233 times, the last time when he was 85. He was the first to climb several mountains, especially those in northern Norway. ⊠ *2 km [1 mi] south of Åndalsnes center, along E139* ☎ *71/22–12–74* ☉ *Mid-June–mid-Aug., daily 1–5.*

Where to Stay

$$ 🏨 **Grand Hotel Bellevue.** Travelers often begin their exploration of the region at this hotel. All the rooms are done in bright yellow, with old prints of the fjord on the walls. The hotel's restaurant, Trollstua, has delicious seafood dishes, based on fresh, local catches. ⊠ *Åndalsgt. 5, 6301* ☎ *71/22–75–00* 🖶 *71/22–60–38* ⊕ *www.grandhotel.no* 🛏 *86 rooms* ♿ *Restaurant, bar, meeting room* ▭ *AE, DC, MC, V.*

Ålesund

❷ *240 km (150 mi) west of Åndalsnes.*

On three islands and between two bright-blue fjords is Ålesund, home to 38,000 inhabitants and one of Norway's largest harbors for exporting dried and fresh fish. About two-thirds of its 1,040 wooden houses were destroyed by a fire in 1904. In the rush to shelter the 10,000 homeless victims, Germany's Kaiser Wilhelm II, who often vacationed here, led a swift rebuilding that married German art nouveau (*Jugendstil*) with Viking flourishes. Winding streets are crammed with buildings topped with turrets, spires, gables, dragonheads, and curlicues. Today, it's considered one of the few art nouveau cities in the world. Inquire at the tourism office for one of the insightful walking tours.

Fodor'sChoice
★ A little gem, the **Ålesunds Museum** highlights the city's past, including the escape route that the Norwegian Resistance established in World War II—its goal was the Shetland Islands. Handicrafts on display are done in the folk-art–style of the area. You can also see the art nouveau room and learn more about the town's unique architecture. ⊠ *R. Rønnebergsgt. 16* ☎ *70/12–31–70* ✒ *NKr 30* ⊘ *Mid-June–Sept., Wed.–Sat. noon–5, Sun. noon–4.*

You can drive or take a bus up nearby Aksla Mountain to a vantage point, **Kniven** (the knife), for a splendid view of the city—which absolutely glitters at night. ☎ *70/12–41–70 for bus information.*

☏ **Atlanterhavsparken** (Atlantic Sea Park). Teeming with aquatic life, this is one of Scandinavia's largest aquariums. Right on the ocean, 3 km (2 mi) west of town, the park emphasizes aquatic animals of the North Atlantic, including anglers, octopus, and lobster. Nemo, the park's adorable seal mascot, waddles freely throughout the complex. See the daily diving show at which the fish are fed. The divers actually enter a feeding frenzy of huge, and sometimes aggressive, halibut and wolffish. After your visit, have a picnic, hike, or take a refreshing swim at the adjoining Tueneset Park. Bus 18, which leaves from St. Olavs Plass, makes the 15-minute journey to the park once every hour during the day, Monday through Saturday. ⊠ *Tueneset* ☎ *70/10–70–60* ⊕ *www. atlanterhavsparken.no* ✒ *NKr 85* ⊘ *Mid-June–mid-Aug., weekdays 10–7, Sat. 10–5; mid-Aug.–mid-June, Mon.–Sat. 11–4, Sun. noon–5.*

off the beaten path
RUNDE – Norway's southernmost major bird rock—one of the largest in Europe—is the breeding ground for some 240 species, including puffins, gannets, and cormorants. The region's wildlife managers maintain many observation posts here. During summer, straying into the bird's nesting areas is strictly forbidden. A catamaran leaves from Skateflua quay in Ålesund for the 25-minute trip to Hareid, where it connects with a bus for the 50-km (31-mi) trip to Runde. A path leads from the bus stop to the nature reserve. Call the Runde tourist office for more information.

Where to Stay & Eat

$ ✕ **Fjellstua.** This mountaintop restaurant has tremendous views over the
Fodor'sChoice surrounding peaks, islands, and fjords. The old-fashioned brick build-
★ ing has a stone and marine-blue interior, with picture windows. On the menu, try the Norwegian bacalao, salmon, and lamb. ⊠ *Top of Aksla Mountain* ☎ *70/10–74–00* ⊟ *AE, DC, MC, V* ⊘ *Closed Jan.*

★ **$$** ⊞ **Quality Hotel Scandinavea Hotel.** Part of the Quality chain, this hotel has impressive towers and arches and dates back to 1905. The modern rooms are beautifully decorated, especially those done in an art nou-

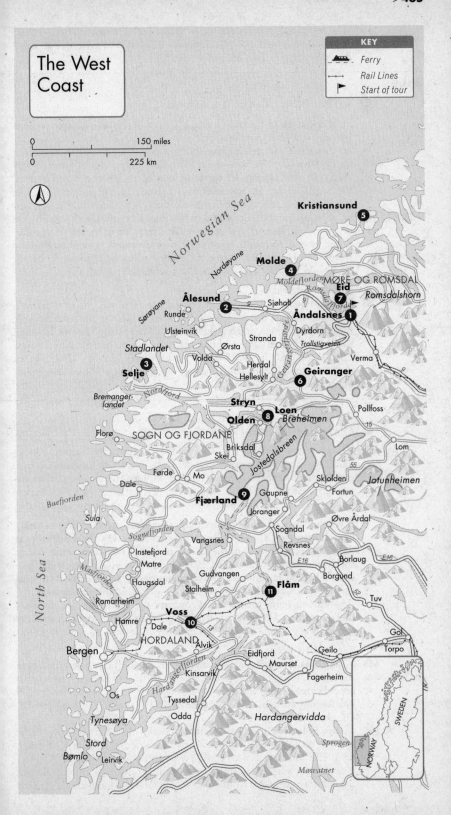

veau style. ⊠ *Løvenvoldgt. 8, 6002* ☎ *70/15–78–00* 🖨 *70/15–78–05*
⊕ *www.choicehotels.no* 🛏 *65 rooms* ⌂ *Restaurant, pizzeria, bar, meeting room* 🍽 *AE, DC, MC, V.*

Selje

❸ *135 km (85 mi) southwest of Ålesund.*

From the town of the same name, the ruins of the **Selje Cloister,** on Selje Island, are a 15-minute boat ride away. Dedicated to St. Sunniva, western Norway's patron saint, the cloister was built by the Benedictine order in the 10th century. Legend has it that on this island St. Sunniva was martyred after fleeing her native Ireland when it was overrun by heathens. She died in St. Sunniva Cave, a large mountainside cavern. The island also has ruins of the first parish church, St. Sunniva Church; and St. Albanus Church, dedicated to the English saint. On the south side of the island, several Viking graves and remains of an Iron Age longhouse have been found. In summer, a' boat departs several times daily from Selje Harbor for two-hour guided tours of the island. ☎ *57/85–66–06* 🎟 *NKr 110* ⊙ *Late May–Sept., daily 10–5.*

Where to Stay

$$ 🏨 **Selje Hotel.** Set on an idyllic coastal beach, this is one of Norway's most popular spa hotels. The modern spa is based on Thalasso therapy, focused on massage, and has skin, and body treatments. Rooms are comfortable, although some of the furnishings are a bit dated. ⊠ *6740, Selje* ☎ *57/85–88–80* 🖨 *57/85–88–81* ⊕ *www.seljehotel.no* 🛏 *49 rooms* ⌂ *Restaurant, indoor pool, hot tub, spa, bar, lounge, dance club, meeting rooms* 🍽 *AE, DC, MC, V.*

Molde

❹ *69 km (43 mi) north of Ålesund on Rte. 668.*

Known as the "City of Roses," Molde has kept its 19th-century nickname even though the only reminder today is the city hall rooftop rose garden that blooms in July and August. Molde is best known for its annual jazz festival, which includes art exhibitions, street festivals, and jazz films as well as performances by international and Norwegian artists.

If you like to walk, take the footpath that leads uphill to the charming **Romsdalsmuseet** (Romsdal Open-Air Museum). On the way, stop at Reknes Park for a view of the 222 mountain peaks on the other side of the Romdalsfjord. Costumed tour guides lead you through the museum's 40 sod farmhouses and churches dating back to the 14th century. See the collection of children's toys. During the jazz festival, the museum is a venue for the larger concerts. Inquire about the museum's other attraction, Hjertøya, a fish museum 3 km (2 mi) from the city. ⊠ *Per Amdams veg 4* ☎ *71/20–24–60* ⊙ *Early June–mid-Aug., daily 11–6.*

Where to Stay & Eat

$$$ ✕ **Lubbenes.** In a Swiss-style chalet, this is one of the best restaurants in
Fodor'sChoice the region. The grilled monkfish, steak, catfish, and bacalao (salted cod)
★ are delicious—Lubbenes excels at serving updated versions of traditional Norwegian cuisine. ⊠ *Sanestrandsvn. 117* ☎ *71/21–12–86* 🍽 *AE, DC, MC, V.*

★ $$$ 🏨 **Rica Seilet Hotel.** Shaped like its namesake, the 15-floor "Sail" is the western coast's high-design hotel, by Norwegian architect Kjell Mosberg. The hotel has its own seaside wharves and terraces. A sky bar, traditional Norwegian restaurant, and sauna and fitness club round out the features. Ask for a front room so you'll have a fantastic view of the mountains between Molde and Ålesund. ⊠ *Gideonvegen 2* ☎ *71/ 11–40–00* 🖷 *71/11–40–01* ⊕ *www.rica.no* ↪ *169 rooms* ⌂ *Restaurant, gym, sauna, 2 bars, meeting rooms* ☰ *AE, DC, MC, V.*

Kristiansund

❺ *68 km (42 mi) north of Molde on Rte. 64.*

By the 19th century, timber and klipfish had made Kristiansund one of Norway's biggest export ports. Today, Kristiansund is the offshore petroleum capital of central Norway: the Draugen and Åsgård oil fields are nearby. The city's lively harbor, Vågen, has the world's oldest collection of small boats. During World War II, almost everything in town was destroyed except for Vågen, where some well-preserved buildings remain.

A warehouse from the 18th-century houses the **Norwegian Coastal Cultural Center,** right on the harbor. Inside are museums and shops, including **Woldbrygga** (⊞ NKr 20 ⊗ Sun. 1–4), a cooper's workshop in use from 1875 to 1965. The equipment is still in working order. **Milnbrygge,** the Klippfisk Museum, pays tribute to the process and the history of the town's klippfisk industry—fishy smells and all. At the **Patrick Volkmar Roastery,** you can have a cup of coffee as well as browse through the wooden handicrafts, metal toys, and offbeat gifts available for sale. ⊠ *Harbor* ☎ *71/67–15–78* ⊞ *NKr 30* ⊗ *Mid-June–mid-Aug., Mon.–Sat. noon–5, Sun. 1–4.*

> **off the beaten path**
>
> **GRIP –** This group of 80 islands lies 15 km (9 mi) out in the open sea, a 2½-hour boat ride away. See the little stave church that was built around 1400 on the Grip's highest point, just 25 feet above sea level. Few people live year-round on the historic islands now, and most of those who come stay in summerhouses. ☎ *71/58–54–54* ⊗ *Mid-May–Aug., daily boats at 10:30 AM and 1:30 PM.*

Where to Stay & Eat

$$–$$$ ✗ **Smia Fiskerestaurant.** The antiques, exposed brick, and fireplace inside this 1787 house are in keeping with the food served. The dishes are based on *nordmørske mattradisjoner,* northern food traditions that emphasize fish. Try the famous fish soup; fish balls; or bacalao, the popular Mediterranean salt cod that's also a part of local culture. ⊠ *Fosnagt. 30B* ☎ *71/67–11–70* ☰ *AE, DC, MC, V.*

$$–$$$ ⊡ **Rica Hotel Kristiansund.** This popular business hotel opened a conference center in 2001. The art-filled rooms are calm and fairly standard. The Sky Bar, on the 10th floor, has a wonderful view of the harbor. ⊠ *Storgt. 41, 6508* ☎ *71/67–64–11* 🖷 *71/67–79–12* ⊕ *www. rica.no* ↪ *102 rooms* ⌂ *Restaurant, minibars, gym, sauna, 2 bars, nightclub, convention center, meeting rooms* ☰ *AE, DC, MC, V.*

Geiranger

★ ❻ *85 km (52½ mi) southwest of Åndalsnes, 413 km (256 mi) from Bergen.*

Geiranger is Norway's most spectacular and perhaps best known fjord. The 16-km-long (10-mi-long), 960-foot-deep Geirangerfjord's best-known attractions are its roaring waterfalls—the Seven Sisters, the Bridal Veil, and the Suitor. Perched on mountain ledges along the fjord, deserted farms at Skageflå and Knivsflå are being restored and maintained by local enthusiasts.

The village of Geiranger, at the end of the fjord, is home to only 300 year-round residents, but in spring and summer its population swells to

5,000 due to visitors traveling from Hellesylt to the east. In winter, snow on the mountain roads means that the village is often isolated.

The most scenic route to Geiranger is the two-hour drive along Route 63 over Trollstigveien from Åndalsnes. Once you are here, the Ørneveien (Eagles' Road) road to Geiranger, which has 11 hairpin turns and was completed in 1952, leads directly to the fjord.

Where to Stay

$$–$$$ ⚞ **Union Hotel.** One of the biggest hotels in the region, the Union is famous for its location near the fjords. Decked out in rosemaled wood furniture, the lobby has a country feel, although the rooms are modern. Ask for one of the rooms with good fjord views. ⊠ *6216 Geiranger* ☎ *70/ 26–30–00* 🖷 *70/26–31–61* ⊕ *www.union-hotel.no* ⇆ *168 rooms, 13 suites* ⚫ *Restaurant, miniature golf, 2 pools, sauna, Turkish bath, bar, nightclub, playground* ▤ *AE, DC, MC, V* ☉ *Closed Jan. and Feb.*

Sports & the Outdoors

HIKING   Trekking through fjord country can occupy a few hours or several days. Trails and paths are marked by signs or cairns with a red T on them. Area tourist offices and bookshops have maps, and of course you can always ask residents for directions or destinations.

Eid

❼ *Along E39, near Hornindals Vatnet Lake.*

A small agricultural community of about 6,000, Eid offers such fjord-village attractions as mountain walks, dairy and farm visits, and skiing. It is also near Hornindals Vatnet, Northern Europe's deepest lake. The town is best known for the *Fjordhest* (Fjord Horse), which even appears on the official town shield. This historic Norwegian horse breed was bred for farmwork and played a big role in helping western Norway develop. Every May the community hosts the **State Stallion Show,** which attracts horse enthusiasts from Norway and beyond.

The **Norsk Fjordhestsenter** is the official center for the breeding and use of the Fjord horse. Open year-round, the center's summer tourist program includes riding camps; riding and horsedrawn carriage trips; cabin rentals; and mountain horseback riding trips. ⊠ *Myroldhaug* ☎ *57/ 86–48–00* ⊕ *www.norsk-fjordhestsenter.no.*

Stryn, Loen & Olden

❽ *From Geiranger to Stryn, take the ferry across the Geiranger Fjord to Hellesylt, a 55-min ride. It's about 50 km (30 mi) from Hellesylt to Stryn on Rte. 60.*

Stryn, Loen, and Olden, at the eastern end of Nordfjord, were among the first tourist destinations in the region. English salmon fishermen became the first tourists in the 1860s. By the end of the 19th century, more hotels had been built, and cruise ships added the area to their routes. Tourism grew into an important industry. The most famous attraction in Stryn is the Briksdal Glacier, which lies between cascading waterfalls and high mountaintops. It's one arm of the Jostedal Glacier.

Covering the mountains between the Sognefjord and Nordfjord, **Jostedal Glacier** is the largest in Europe. Nearly ⅓ mi wide in parts, it has grown in recent years due to increased snowfall. There are about a hundred known routes for crossing Jostedal Glacier: if you want to hike it, you must have a qualified guide. Contact the Jostedalsbreen National Park Center or another tourist office. Such hikes should only be attempted in summer; mountain boots and windproof clothing are both essential.

Many of Jostedal's arms are tourist attractions in their own right. The best known arm, **Briksdal Glacier,** lies at the end of Oldedal Valley, about 20 km (12 mi) south of Olden. It can be visited by bicycle, car, or foot from April to October.

Right outside Stryn, **Jostedalsbreen Nasjonalparksenter** (Jostedal Glacier National Park Center; ☎ 57/87–72–00 ⊕ www.jostedalsbre.no) covers the glacier and the surrounding region in detail. Landscape models, mineral and photograph collections, films and dioramas get across the region's unique geography, flora, and fauna. There's also a garden of 325 types of wildflowers.

Where to Stay & Eat

$–$$ ✕**Kjenndalstova Kafé and Restaurant.** Perhaps western Norway's best kept secret, this café and restaurant serves up delicious traditional dishes. Close to Kjendal's glacier, towering mountains, cascading waterfalls, and a pristine lake, the scenery from the restaurant alone is well worth a visit. Try the fried fresh, the fish stew, and the dessert cakes. ✉ *Prestestegen 15, Loen* ☎ *945–38–385* ⊟ *AE, DC, MC, V* ✆ *Closed Oct.–Apr.*

¢–$ ✕ **Briksdalsbre Fjellstove** (Briksdal Glacier Mountain Lodge). The cafeteria at this lodge has a no-frills menu of fresh, hearty country fare. The trout, the fillet of reindeer, and the deep-fried cod's jaws are all worth a try. Accommodation is also available, and as you'd expect from its location, a large gift shop is nearby. ✉ *Briksdalbre* ☎ *57/87–68–00* ⊟ *AE, DC, MC, V.*

$$ ✕▣ **Visnes Hotel.** Dating to 1850, this small hotel is done in a Swiss style. The hotel is five minutes from Stryn's center. Specialities in the restaurant include smoked salmon and venison. The Norwegian dragon-style Villa Visnes, a restored 1898 conference center and apartment nearby, is operated by the same owners. ✉ *Prestestegen 1, 6781 Stryn* ☎ *57/ 87–10–87* 🖷 *57–87–20–75* ⊕ *www.visnes.no* ⇴ *15 rooms with bath* ⌂ *Restaurant, convention center* ⊟ *AE, DC, MC, V.*

★ $–$$ ✕▣ **Olden Fjordhotel.** Close to the fjord and cruise terminal, this hotel has simple, comfortable rooms, most with a balcony overlooking the fjord. Allergen-free rooms and larger rooms for families are also available. ✉ *6788, Olden* ☎ *57/87–34–00* 🖷 *57/87–33–81* ⊕ *www.olden- hotel.no* ⇴ *60 rooms* ⌂ *Restaurant, cable TV, bar, nightclub, library* ⊟ *AE, DC, MC, V.*

★ $–$$ ▣ **Alexandra.** This hotel was built in 1884 but has been entirely refurbished with stone and oak in a modern style. It remains one of the most luxurious hotels in the region. ✉ *6789 Loen* ☎ *57/87–50–00* 🖷 *57/ 87–50–51* ⊕ *www.alexandra.no* ⇴ *191 rooms, 9 suites* ⌂ *2 restaurants, tennis court, indoor pool, gym, 3 bars, nightclub, convention center* ⊟ *AE, DC, MC, V.*

Sports

In addition to taking a guided walk on the glaciers, you can follow the many other trails in this area. Ask at the Stryn tourist office for a walking map and hiking suggestions.

SKIING The **Stryn Sommerskisenter** (Summer Ski Center) has earned a reputation as Northern Europe's best summer-skiing resort. Its seasons last from May through June and from August through September. The trails run over Tystig Glacier. The center has a ski school, a snowboard park, and a children's June and July tow. ✉ *Rte. 258, near Videseter* ☎ *57/ 87–40–40* 🖷 *57/87–40–41* ⊕ *www.stryn-sommerski.no* ✆ *May–June and Aug.–Sept., daily 10–4.*

SOGNEFJORDEN

Sognefjorden, Europe's longest fjord, stretches 200 km (124 mi) into the country and meets Jotunheimen National Park, with some of the country's highest and wildest mountains, and Jostedalsbreen National Park with Europe's largest glacier at 500 square km (310 sq. mi). Along the glacier's wide banks are some of Norway's best fruit farms, with fertile soil and lush vegetation (the blossoms in May are spectacular). In summer this area draws mountain sport enthusiasts, who climb, hike, and glacier-walk. Ferries are the lifeline of the region.

Fjærland

❾ *From Olden it's 62 km (37 mi) south to Skei, at the base of Lake Jøl-ster, where Rte. E5 goes under the glacier for more than 6 km (4 mi) of the journey to Fjærland.*

Breheimsenteret (The Glacier Center; ☎ 57/68–32–50 ⊕ www.jostedal. com) is Jostedalbreen National Park's visitor center, with fascinating exhibitions on, for instance, glacier walking on Nigardsbreen, one of the arms of the glacier.

At **Norsk Bremuseum** (Norwegian Glacier Museum), one of Norway's most innovative museums, you can study glaciers up close by conducting experiments with thousand-year-old glacial ice. Exhibitions show glacier finds. Take time to watch Ivo Caprino's unforgettable panoramic film of Jostedal Glacier. ⊠ *Fjærland* ☎ *57/69–32–88* ⊕ *www.bre. museum.net* ☎ *NKr 75* ⊙ *June–Aug., daily 9–7; Apn and May and Sept. and Oct., daily 10–4.*

off the
beaten
path

ASTRUPTUNET – Halfway across the southern shore of Lake Jølster (about a 10-minute detour from the road to Fjærland) is Astruptunet, the farm of one of Norway's best-known artists, Nicolai Astrup (1880–1928). Astrup is known for his landscape paintings of western Norway. Set on a steep hill, this cluster of small sod houses was Astrup's home and studio until he died. His paintings and sketches are on view. The entertaining guides explain much about him and his family. The cozy café serves waffles and *rømmegrot* (sour-cream porridge). ⊠ *Sandal i Jølster* ☎ *57/72–67–82 or 57/72–61–45* ⊕ *www.astruptunet.com* ☎ *NKr 50* ⊙ *July, daily 10–6; late May–June and Aug., daily 10–5; or by appointment.*

Where to Stay & Eat

★ $$–$$$$ ⊡ **Kvikne's Hotel.** This 1913 hotel is best-known for its unforgettable views of Sognefjord. Kings, presidents, movie stars, and famous artists have stayed here. While the inside of the Swiss-chalet–style hotel has been modernized, old-fashioned touches like a verandah and dragon-style furniture have been retained. The area is ideal if you're interested in swimming, hiking, rowing, and fishing. ⊠ *Balholm, 6898 Balestrand* ☎ *57/69–42–00* 🖶 *57/69–42–01* ⊕ *www.kviknes.no* 🛏 *210 rooms* 🍴 *2 restaurants, gym, fishing* 🟰 *AE, DC, MC, V.*

★ ¢–$$$ ⊡ **Turtagrø Hotel.** Owner Ole Berge Drægni and his family have dedicated their lives to the mountains and mountain people. Turtagrø is called the cradle of mountain sports in Norway. The original hotel opened in 1888, burned down in 2001, and was rebuilt in the shape of a mountain, with brick, stone, and wood. Its interior is a blend of Scandinavian and Zen design in white and heavy oak furniture. Historic photographs show early-20th-century mountain sports, and rooms have very comfortable beds for you to sink into after a hiking trip. The hotel hosts the Nordic Mountain Film and Mountain Book Festivals. The original Swiss villa section of the hotel has simpler rooms with bunk beds. ⊠ *6877 Fortun* ☎ *57/68–08–00* 🖷 *57/68–08–01* ⊕ *www.turtagro.no* 🛏 *74 rooms* ♨ *Restaurant, lounge, library* ⊟ *AE, DC, MC, V.*

$$ ✕🖫 **Hotel Mundal.** Artists, mountaineers, and tourists first began coming to the Mundal in the late 1800s, via boat. This wooden yellow-and-white hotel has an eclectic style, mixing antiques from Norwegian *bonderomantikk* with contemporary furnishings. Descendants of the original owners run the hotel and have retained its country look. The small restaurant ($$) serves sumptuous traditional Norwegian fare. The café is popular in the evenings among locals and guests. ⊠ *Town Center, 6848 Fjærland* ☎ *57/69–31–01* 🖷 *57/69–31–79* ⊕ *www.fjordinfo.no/mundal* 🛏 *35 rooms* ♨ *Restaurant, café, billiards, bar, lounge, library, meeting rooms* ⊟ *DC, MC, V* ☯ *Closed mid-Sept.–mid-May.*

Shopping

Even if you can't read Norwegian, you may still be fascinated by Hotel Mundal's **Den norske bokbyen** (⊠ Town Center ☎57/69–31–01 ⊕ www. bokbyen.no). From June through August, "Norwegian Book Town" has 150,000 used books, cartoons, magazines, and records for sale in buildings around town.

Voss

⑩ *120 km south of Fjærland, 80 km (50 mi) south of Vangsnes; 80 km (50 mi) north (1-hr by train) from Bergen.*

Set between the Hardanger and Sognefjords, Voss is in a handy place to begin an exploration of Fjord Norway. Once considered a stopover, Voss now attracts visitors drawn by its concerts, festivals, farms, and other attractions. Norwegians know Voss best for its skiing and Vossajazz, its annual jazz festival. People come from all over Norway for the sheeps' heads festival, a celebration of the culinary delicacy of this area.

Dating to 1277, the enchanting **Voss Kyrkje–Vangskyrkja** (Voss Church) holds services every Sunday. Take a walk through to see the stained glass within. Concerts are occasionally held here. ☎ *56/51–22–78* 🖾 *Free* ☯ *Mid-June–mid-Sept., daily 10–4.*

Perched on the hillside overlooking Voss, **Mølstertunet** is an open-air museum. The 16 farm buildings here were built between 1600 and 1870. Along with handcrafted tools and other items, they reveal much about area farmers' lives and struggles. Along with Nesheimstunet Museum and the Old Vicarage at Oppheim, it makes up the Voss Folkemuseum. ⊠ *Mølstervn. 143* ☎ *56/51–15–11* 🖾 *NKr 35* ☯ *May–Sept., daily 10–5; Oct.–Apr., weekdays 10–3, Sun. noon–3.*

Galleri Voss shows the works of Norwegian artists in a bright, airy space. ⊠ *Stallgt. 6–8* ☎ *56/51–90–18* ☯ *Wed.–Sat. 10–4, Sun. noon–3.*

Where to Stay & Eat

$$$ ✕🖫 **Fleischer's Hotel.** One of Norway's historic wooden and dragon-style hotels, Fleischer's seats you in the lap of luxury with its elegant decor and first-class service. The restaurant Magdalene serves traditional renditions of sheep's head, grilled deer, fresh mountain trout, and salmon dishes. It's steps away from the railway tracks leading to Bergen. ⊠ *Evangervegen 13, 5700 Voss* ☎ *56/52–05–00* 🖷 *56/52–05–01* ⊕ *www. fleischers.no* 🛏 *90 rooms* ♨ *Restaurant, pool, sauna, bar, nightclub, children's programs, laundry, meeting rooms* ⊟ *AE, DC, MC, V.*

Sports & the Outdoors

FISHING The Tourist Information Office in Voss sells fishing licenses and has a Voss fishing guide to the nearly 500 lakes and rivers in the area where fishing is allowed. Fishing licenses (one-day for NKr 50) are also sold at campsites and the post office.

HIKING Walks and hikes are especially rewarding in this region, with spectacular mountain and water views everywhere. Be prepared for abrupt weather changes in spring and fall. Voss is a starting point for mountain hikes in Slølsheimen, Vikafjell, and the surrounding mountains. Contact the Voss Tourist Board for tips.

PARACHUTING At **Bømoen Airstrip** (☎ 92/05–45–56), 5 km (3 mi) from downtown, there's an active parachuting club. Jumps can be booked daily from mid-June to late August.

PARAGLIDING One of the best places to paraglide in Norway, Voss has easily accessed starting points and constant thermals. The tandem season runs roughly from June to August. To take a **tandem paraglider flight** (in which an instructor goes with you), you must weigh between 30–110 kg (70 to 240 pounds). The flight lasts an hour and costs NKr 650. Contact the **Voss Adventure Senter** (☎ 56/51–36–30).

RIVER SPORTS Rivers around Voss are ideal for river paddling, kayaking, and other water sports. **Voss Ski & Surf** (☎ 56/51–30–43) offers one- to three-day courses in river kayaking for both beginners and experienced kayakers. They also book tandem kayak trips with instructors. **Voss Rafting Senter** (☎ 56/51–05–25) offers rafting, river-boarding, and canyoning at prices beginning around NKr 500. **Nordic Ventures** (☎ 56/51 35 83) runs guided sea kayak tours through the waterfalls and mountains of Sognefjord from April to October; prices start at NKr 390.

SKIING Voss and its varied mountain terrain are ideal for winter sports. An important alpine skiing center in Norway, it has 40 km of alpine slopes; one cable car; eight ski lifts; eight illuminated and two marked cross-country trails; a snowboard park; and the Voss School of Skiing. Call the Voss Tourist Board for details.

Flåm

⑪ *131 km (81 mi) northeast of Voss.*

One of the most scenic train routes in Europe zooms from Myrdal, high into the mountains and down to the town of Flåm. After the day-trippers have departed, it's a wonderful place to extend your tour and spend the night.

The **train ride to Myrdal** is only 20 km (12 mi) long, but it takes 40 minutes to travel the 2,850 feet up a steep mountain gorge and 53 minutes to go down. The line includes 20 tunnels. From Flåm it's also an easy drive back to Oslo on E16 along the Lærdal River, one of Norway's most famous salmon streams—it was King Harald's favorite.

Shopping

Saga Souvenirs (✉ Flåm train station ☎ 57/63–22–44 ⊕ www.sagasouvenir.no) is one of the largest gift shops in Norway. The selection of traditional items includes knitwear, trolls, and jewelry.

Where to Stay

$$–$$$ 🏨 **Fretheim Hotell.** One of western Norway's most beautiful hotels, the Fretheim has a classic, timeless look. Staying true to the Fretheim's 1866 roots, the rooms are furnished simply. From the bar there's a spectacular view of the fjord. ✉ 5742 Flåm ☎ 57/63–63–00 🖷 57/63–64–00

⊕ *www.fretheim-hotel.no* ⊅ *121 rooms* ⚭ *2 restaurants, fishing, bar* 🖃 *AE, MC, V.*

Hardangerfjord

150 km (93 mi) south of Flåm, 50 km (31 mi) south of Voss.

Hardanger Fjord, known as the "Garden of Fjord Norway", is a place that Norwegians identify with blossoms and fruit. The mild climate and clear, light summer nights are ideal for fruits like apples and cherries. Composer Edvard Greig got inspiration for some of his masterpieces here. Springtime is the most enchanting season to visit the fjord: fruit trees bloom against the backdrop of the blue fjord, snow-topped mountains, and foaming waterfalls. Beginning in early May, the cherry and plum blossoms can be seen, and later in the month, pink apple flowers. Cherries ripen in July and early August, followed by plums, pears, and apples from mid-August to late October. Farmers sell fresh fruit at farm shops and storehouses, and many open their farms for sightseeing and refreshments. Every July, the Morello Festival in Ullensvang celebrates the cherry of the same name, brought here in 1146 by traveling Yorkshire monks. The main event is the Norwegian Championship in Morello Pit Spitting.

Where to Stay

★ **$$** 🏨 **Utne Hotel.** In the heart of Hardanger, at Utne, on the coastal highway 550, this hotel was built in 1722, and is considered Norway's oldest hotel. The white, wooden building has a wood-paneled, hand-painted dining room decorated with copper pans, old china, and paintings. ✉ *5797 Utne* ☎ *53/66–10–88* 🖷 *53/66–69–50* ⊅ *24 rooms* ⚭ *Restaurant* 🖃 *AE, DC, MC, V.*

The West Coast A to Z

AIR TRAVEL

CARRIERS Braathens has nonstop flights to Ålesund from Oslo, Bergen, Trondheim, and Bodø. SAS flies between Ålesund and Oslo.

🔳 Airlines & Contacts **Braathens** ☎ 70/11-48-00. **SAS** ☎ 70/10-49-00 in Ålesund.

AIRPORTS

Ålesund's Vigra Airport is 15 km (9 mi) from the center of town. It's a 25-minute ride from Vigra to town via Flybussen. Tickets cost NKr 50. Buses are scheduled according to flights—they leave the airport about 10 minutes after all arrivals and leave town about 60 or 70 minutes before each departure.

🔳 Airport Information **Vigra** ✉ ☎ 70/11-48-00.

BOAT & FERRY TRAVEL

Car ferries are a way of life in western Norway, but they are often crowded and don't run as frequently as they should in summer, which causes delays. Considerable hassle can be eliminated by reserving ahead, as cars with reservations board first. Call the tourist office of the area to which you're heading for ferry information. HSD operates fjord express boats from Bergen to Hardangerfjord and Sunnhordland. Fylkesbaatane fjord express boats operates on routes between Bergen and Sognefjord, Nordfjord and Sunnfjord.

The *Hurtigruten* (coastal steamer) stops at Skansekaia in Ålesund, at noon. It then heads northward at 3. It returns at midnight and heads southward at 1 AM.

A catamaran runs between Ålesund and Molde at least twice daily. In addition to regular ferries to nearby islands, boats connect Ålesund with other points along the coast. Excursions by boat can be booked through the tourist office.

🚩 **Fylkesbaatane i Sogn og Fjordane** ☎ 55/90-70-70 ⊕ www.fylkesbaatane.no. **HSD** ☎ 55/23-87-80 ⊕ www.hsd.no. **Hurtigruten** ☎ 81/03-00-00 ⊕ www.hurtigruten.com.

BUS TRAVEL

In Western Norway the bus routes are fairly extensive: there are north–south routes, like Bergen to Ålesund, and east–west routes like Trondheim to Oslo. HSD Buss operates routes in the Bergen–Hardangerfjord region. Nordfjord & Sunnmøre Billag services the Nordfjord region, and has glacier buses that run between Stryn and Briksdal.

NOR-WAY Bussekspress has a Nordfjordekspressen (Måøly–Oslo) route and a Bergen–Trondheim route.

🚩 **HSD Buss** ☎ 56/32-35-00 ⊕ www.hsd.no. **Nordfjord & Sunnmøre Billage** ☎ 57/87-46-00 ⊕ www.ruteinfo.net. **NOR-WAY Bussekspress** ☎ 815/44-444 ⊕ www.nor-way.no.

CAR TRAVEL

From Oslo, it's 450 km (295 mi) on Route E6 to Dombås and then Route 9 through Åndalsnes to Ålesund. Route 9 is a well-maintained two-lane road.

EMERGENCY 🚩 **Car Rescue** ☎ 70/14-18-33.
SERVICES

ROAD The 380-km (235-mi) drive from Bergen to Ålesund covers some of the
CONDITIONS most breathtaking scenery in the world. Roads are narrow two-lane ventures much of the time; passing is difficult, and in summer traffic can be heavy.

DISCOUNTS & DEALS

Fjord Pass, which costs NKr 100 for two adults and children under 15, is one of Norway's best hotel discount cards. The pass offers substantial discounts on accommodation at approximately 200 hotels, inns, cottages, and apartments all over Norway. Prices can be as low as NKr 225 per person per night.

🚩 **Fjord Pass** ☎ 55/55-76 ⊕ www.fjordpass.no.

EMERGENCIES

Nordstjernen, a pharmacy in Ålesund, is open weekdays 9–5, Saturday 9–2, and Sunday 6 PM–8 PM.

🚩 **Emergency: Hospital** ☎ 70/10-50-00; **Doctor** ☎ 70/14-31-13. **Nordstjernen** ✉ Korsegt. 8, Ålesund ☎ 70/12-59-45.

TOURS

A 1½-hour guided stroll through Ålesund, concentrating mostly on the art nouveau buildings, departs from the tourist information center (Rådhuset) Saturday, Tuesday, and Thursday at 1 PM from mid-June to mid-August. Aak Fjellsportsenter in Åndalsnes specializes in walking tours of the area.

From Easter through September, Jostedalen Breførlag conducts glacier tours, from an easy 1½-hour family trip on the Nigard branch (equipment is provided) to advanced glacier courses with rock and ice climbing. Besides ice climbing, Olden Aktiv Briksdalsbreen's offerings include a Blue Ice Excursion of three to four hours, and an easy glacier walk. The Stryn Fjell og Breførarlag leads five- to six-hour walks on Bødalsbreen from May to September.

From June through August, the MS *Geirangerfjord* offers 90-minute guided cruises on the Geirangerfjord. Tickets are sold at the dock in Geiranger.

Firdafly, based in Sandane, conducts plane tours over Jostedalsbreen. "Norway in a nutshell," Sognefjord & Flåmsbana railway, and other package tours are available through Fjord Tours AS. Kystopplevelser AS operates several Fjord Explorer tours.

🛈 Fees & Schedules **Aak Fjellsportsenter** ✉ Øran Vest, 6300 Åndalsnes ☎ 71/22-71-00 ⊕ www.aak.no. **Olden Aktiv Briksdalsbreen** ✉ 6792 Briksdalsbre ☎ 57/87-38-88 ⊕ www.briksdalsbreen.com. **Firdafly** ☎ 57/86-54-19. **Fjord Explorer** ☎ 55/31-59-10 **Fjord Tours** ☎ 55/55-20-00 ⊕ www.fjordtours.no. **Jostedalen Breførlag** ✉ 5828 Gjerde ☎ 57/68-31-11. **MS *Geirangerfjord*** ✉ Geiranger ☎ 70/26-30-07. **Stryn Fjell- og Breførarlag** (Glacier Guiding Association) ✉ 6792 Briksdalsbre ☎ 57/87-68-00 ⊕ www.strynglaciertours.no.

TRAIN TRAVEL
The *Dovrebanen* and *Raumabanen* between Oslo S Station and Åndalsnes via Dombås run three times daily in each direction. It's a 6½-hour ride. At Åndalsnes, buses wait outside the station to pick up passengers heading to points not served by the train. The 124-km (76-mi) trip to Ålesund takes close to two hours.

VISITOR INFORMATION
Fjord Norway in Bergen is a clearinghouse for information on western Norway. Its Web site and holiday guide are excellent resources for fjord travel planning.

🛈 Tourist Information **Ålesund** ✉ Rådhuset ☎ 70/12-58-04. **Åndalsnes** ✉ Corner Nesgt. and Romsdalsvn. ☎ 71/22-16-22. **Fjord Norway** ☎ 55/55-07-30 ⊕ www.fjordnorway.no. **Flåm** ✉ Railroad station ☎ 57/63-21-06 ⊕ www.visitflam.com. **Geiranger** ✉ Dockside ☎ 70/26-30-99. **Hardangerfjord** ☎ 56/55-38-70 ⊕ www.hardangerfjord.com. **Molde** ✉ Rådhuset ☎ 71/25-71-33. **Sognefjorden** ☎ 57/67-23-26 ⊕ www.sfr.no. **Stryn & Nordfjord** ✉ Stryn ☎ 57/87-40-40 ⊕ www.nordfjord.no. **Voss** ☎ 56/52-08-00 ⊕ www.voss-promotion.no.

TRONDHEIM TO THE NORTH CAPE

A narrow but immensely long strip of land stretches between Trondheim and Kirkenes in northern Norway. In this vast territory, you'll encounter the sawtooth, glacier-carved peaks of the Lofoten Islands, and the world's strongest tidal current, in Bodø. Thousands of islands and skerries hug the coast of northern Norway, and the provinces of Nordland, Troms, and Finnmark, up to the North Cape. Along this wild, unpredictable coast, the weather is as dramatic as the scenery: in summer you can see the Midnight Sun, and in winter experience Aurora Borealis, the Northern Lights.

Northern Norwegians still make their living in the fishing villages of the Lofoten Islands, in small, provincial towns, and modern cities like Tromsø. Tourism plays an important role in the region, especially with those seeking wild landscapes, outdoor activities, and adventure, whether it's mountaineering, dogsledding, skiing, caving, or wreck-diving. Basking in the Midnight Sun is one of Norway's most popular attractions; every year, thousands of people flock to Nordkapp (the North Cape) for it. To cater to the large number of visitors, northern Norway has well-run tourist offices which stock excellent maps and travel literature on the area.

Numbers in the margin correspond to points of interest on the Trondheim and the North map.

Trondheim

▶ ❶ *494 km (307 mi) north of Oslo, 657 km (408 mi) northeast of Bergen.*

One of Scandinavia's oldest cities, Trondheim is Norway's third largest, with a population of 150,000. Founded in 997 by Viking King Olav Tryggvasson, it was first named Nidaros (still the name of the cathedral), a composite word referring to the city's location at the mouth of the Nid River. Today, Trondheim is a university town as well as a center for maritime and medical research, but the wide streets of the historic city center are still lined with brightly painted wood houses and striking warehouses.

King Olav formulated a Christian religious code for Norway in 1024, during his reign. It was on his grave that **Nidaros Domkirke** (Nidaros Cathedral) was built. The town became a pilgrimage site for the Christians of northern Europe, and Olav was canonized in 1164.

Although construction began in 1070, the oldest existing parts of the cathedral date from around 1150. It has been ravaged on several occasions by fire and rebuilt each time, generally in a Gothic style. Since the Middle Ages, Norway's kings have been crowned and blessed in the cathedral. The crown jewels are on display here. Guided tours are offered in English from late June to late August, weekdays at 11, 2, and 4. ⊠ *Kongsgårdsgt. 2* ☎ *73/53–91–60* ⊕ *www.nidarosdomen.no* ✉ *NKr 35. Ticket also permits entry to Erkebispegården* ⊙ *Call for hrs.*

The **Erkebispegården** (Archbishop's Palace) is the oldest secular building in Scandinavia, dating from around 1160. It was the residence of the archbishop until the Reformation in 1537; after that it was a residence for Danish governors, and later a military headquarters. The oldest parts of the palace, which face the cathedral, are used for government functions. The **Archbishop's Palace Museum** (⊠ Kongsgårdsgt. ☎ 73/53–91–60 ✉ NKr 35 ⊙ Late June–late Aug., weekdays 10–5, Sat. 10–3, Sun. noon–5; late Aug.–late June, Mon.–Sat. 11–3, Sun. noon–4) has original sculptures from Nidaros Cathedral and archaeological pieces from throughout its history.

Within the Erkebispegården's inner palace is the **Rustkammeret/Resistance Museum** (Army Museum/Resistance Museum; ☎ 73/99–52–80 ⊙ June–Sept., weekdays 9–3, weekends 11–4; guided tours by appointment), which traces the development of the army from Viking times to the present through displays of uniforms, swords, and daggers. The Resistance Museum deals with events in Central Norway during World War II and its memorial hall remembers those who lost their lives. ⊠ *Kongsgårdsgt.* ☎ *73/53–91–60* ⊕ *www.nidarosdomen.no* ✉ *NKr 35. Ticket also permits entry to Nidaros Cathedral* ⊙ *Call for hrs.*

Built after the great fire of 1681, the **Kristiansten Festning** (Kristiansten Fort) saved the city from conquest by Sweden in 1718. During Norway's occupation by Germany, from 1940 to 1945, members of the Norwegian Resistance were executed here; there's a plaque in their honor. The fort has a spectacular view of the city, the fjord, and the mountains. ☎ *73/99–52–80* ⊙ *June–Aug., weekdays 10–3, weekends 11–4.*

★ The Tiffany windows are magnificent at the **Nordenfjeldske Kunstindustrimuseum** (National Museum of Decorative Arts), which houses an impressive collection of furniture, silver, and textiles. The Scandinavian Design section features a room interior designed by the Danish architect Finn Juhl in 1952. The 1690 bridal crown by Adrian Bogarth is also memorable. "Three Women–Three Artists" features tapestries by Hannah Ryggen and Synnøve Anker Aurdal, and glass creations by Benny

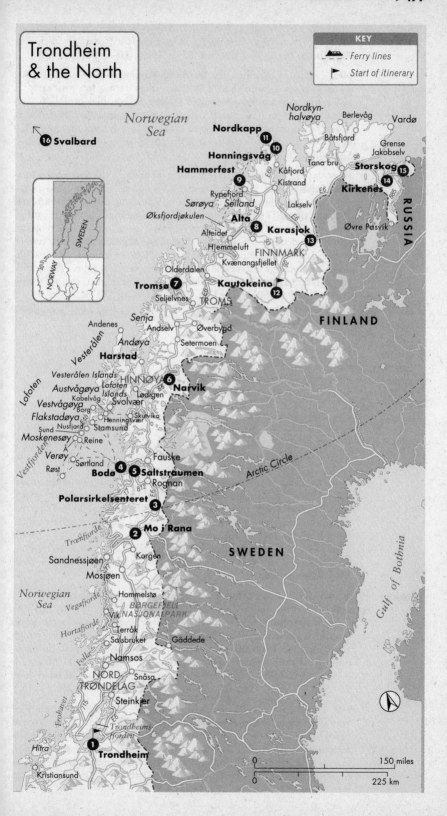

Trondheim & the North

KEY
🚢 Ferry lines
🚩 Start of itinerary

Norwegian Sea

16 Svalbard

Nordkyn-halvøya
Berlevåg
Vardø
Nordkapp
11
10
Båtsfjord
Grense Jakobselv
Honningsvåg
Tana bru
98
Storskog 15
Hammerfest
Kåfjord
9
Kistrand
E6
14
Kirkenes
Rypefjord
Lakselv
Sørøya *Seiland*
Øksfjordjøkulen
Alta
Øvre Pasvik
Alteidet
8
Karasjok
Hjemmeluft
13
FINNMARK
Kvænangsfjellet
Olderdalen
Kautokeino
Tromsø 7
12
Seljelvnes
TROMS
FINLAND

Andenes
Senja
Andselv
Øverbygd
Vesterålen
Andøya
Setermoen
Harstad
Vesterålen Islands
HINNØYA
6
Lofoten Islands
Narvik
Austvågøya
Kabelvåg
Lødingen
Vestvågøya
Svolvær
Borg
Henningsvær
Skutvika
Flakstadøya
Nusfjord
Stamsund
Sund
Moskenesøy
Reine
Fauske
Verøy
Å
Sørtland
Bodø 4
5 **Saltstraumen**
Røst
Rognan
812
E6
Polarsirkelsenteret
3
Arctic Circle
2 **Mo i Rana**
Trænfjorde
SWEDEN
Sandnessjøen
Korgen
Mosjøen
Norwegian Sea
Vegafjorde
Hommelstø
BØRGEFJELL
Hortafjorde
NASJONALPARK
Vik
Terråk
Gäddede
Salsbruket
Folla
Namsos
NORD-
Snåsa
TRØNDELAG
Trohavet
Steinkjer
115
E6
Trondheims-fjorden
1
Hitra
Trondheim
Kristiansund

0 _____ 150 miles
0 _____ 225 km

Norway *Sweden*

RUSSIA

Gulf of Bothnia

Motzfeldt. ⊠ *Munkegt. 5* ☎ *73/80–89–50* ⊕ *www.nkim.museum.no* ⊡ *NKr 30* ⊙ *June–late Aug., Tues.–Fri. 10–5, Sun. noon–5; late Aug.–June, Tues.–Wed. and Fri. 10–3, Thurs. 10–5, Sun. noon–4.*

Near Nidaros Cathedral, the **Trondheim Kunstmuseum** (Trondheim Art Gallery) houses more than 2,700 paintings dating from as early as 1800. Regional artists represented include Håkon Bleken, Jakob Weidemann, Adolph Tidemand, Christian Krohg, and Harald Solberg. There's a permanent exhibition of graphics by Edvard Munch. ⊠ *Bispegt. 7B* ☎ *73/53–81–80* ⊡ *NKr 40* ⊙ *June–Aug., daily 10–5; Sept.–June, Tues.–Sat. 11–5.*

Near the ruins of King Sverre's medieval castle is the **Sverreborg Trøndelag Folkemuseum,** which has re-creations of coastal, inland, and mountain village buildings that depict life in Trøndelag during the 18th and 19th centuries. The Haltdalen stave church, built in 1170, is the northernmost preserved stave church in Norway. In the "Old Town" you can visit a 1900 dentist's office and an old-fashioned grocery that sells sweets. A special exhibit examines how the stages of life—childhood, youth, adulthood, and old age—have changed over the past 150 years. The audiovisual **Trønderbua** depicts traditional regional wedding ceremonies with artifacts and a 360-degree film. ⊠ *Sverresborg allé* ☎ *73/89–01–00* ⊕ *www.sverresborg.no* ⊡ *NKr 75* ⊙ *June–Sept., daily 11–6; Sept.–June, weekdays 11–3, weekends noon–4.*

off the beaten path

MUNKHOLMEN (The Monks' Island) – Now a swimming and recreation area, Monk's Island was Trondheim's execution grounds in ancient times. In the 11th century, Benedictine monks built a monastery on the island, likely one of the first monasteries in Scandinavia. In 1658 the monastery was converted into a prison and fort and, later, a customs house. There is a display of handicrafts in what was once the caretaker's house. Boats to the island depart from the fish market. ☎ *73/80–63–00* ⊕ *www.lilletorget.no* ⊡ *NKr 45* ⊙ *Mid-May–late Sept., boats depart daily on the hr 10–6.*

Norway's oldest institution of science, the **NTNU Vitenskapsmuseet** (NTNU Science Museum) covers flora and fauna, minerals and rocks, church history, southern Sámi culture, and archaeological finds. The eclectic exhibits have relics from the Bronze Age as well as ecclesiastical articles from the 13th to 18th centuries. ⊠ *Erling Skakkes gt. 47* ☎ *73/59–21–45* ⊕ *www.ntnu.no/vmuseet* ⊡ *NKr 25* ⊙ *May–mid-Sept., weekdays 9–4, weekends 11–4; mid-Sept.–mid-Apr., Tues.–Fri. 9–2, weekends noon–4.*

Fodor'sChoice ★

Scandinavia's largest wooden palace, **Stiftsgården,** was built between 1774 and 1778 as the home of a prominent widow. Sold to the state in 1800, it's now the official royal residence in Trondheim. The architecture and interior is late baroque and highly representative of 18th-century high society's taste. Tours offer insight into the festivities marking the coronations of the kings in Nidaros Domkirke. ⊠ *Munkegt. 23* ☎ *73/84–28–80* ⊡ *NKr 50* ⊙ *June 1–19, Mon.–Sat. 10–3, Sun. noon–5; June 20–Aug. 20, Mon.–Sat. 10–5, Sun. noon–5. Tours on the hr.*

Off Munkegate near the water, you can see an immense variety of seafood at **Ravnklohallen Fiskehall** (Fish Market; ☎73/52–55–21 ⊕www.ravnkloa.no). A former 1725 prison now houses the little **Trondhjems Sjøfartsmuseum** (Maritime Museum). Models of sailing ships, figureheads, marine instruments, and photographs of local ships make up the exhibits. Standouts include a harpoon gun from a whaler and recovered cargo from *The Pearl*, a frigate that was wrecked in 1781. ⊠ *Fjordgt. 6A* ☎ *73/ 89–01–00* ☒ *NKr 25* ☽ *June–Sept., daily 10–4.*

The **Modern Art Gallery** (⊠ Olav Tryggvasonsgt. 33 ☎ 73/87–36–80) shows contemporary art, including watercolors, lithographs, and art posters from Norway and abroad.

off the beaten path

RINGVE MUSEUM – Norway's national museum of music and musical instruments is on a country estate outside Trondheim. The **Museum in the Manor House**, the oldest section, focuses on instruments in the European musical tradition—guides demonstrate their usage. **The Museum in the Barn** features modern sound and light technology as well as Norwegian folk instruments. ⊠ *Lade Allé 60.* ☎ *73/92–24–11* ⊕ *www.ringve.com* ☒ *NKr 70* ☽ *Jan.–mid-May and mid-Sept.–mid-Dec., Sun. 11–4; mid-May–mid-June and early Aug.–mid-Sept., daily 11–3; mid-June–early Aug., daily 11–5.*

Where to Stay & Eat

Trondheim is known for the traditional dish *surlaks* (marinated salmon served with sour cream). A sweet specialty is *tekake* (tea cake), which looks like a thick-crust pizza topped with a lattice pattern of cinnamon and sugar. The city's restaurant scene is vibrant and evolving, with more and more international restaurants serving Continental food, and bars and cafés where the city's considerable student population gathers.

★ $$$$ ✕ **Bryggen Restaurant.** One of the city's most popular restaurants is on the banks of the Nid River. The 250-year-old warehouse exudes elegant country style, with blond woods and earthy tones. Most diners choose one of the prix-fixe menus, which are often based on traditional Norwegian ingredients such as fish and reindeer. The wine list is extensive, with many French and Italian choices. ⊠ *Øvre Bakklandet 66* ☎ *73/ 87–42–42* ☖ *Reservations essential* ▤ *AE, DC, MC, V* ☽ *Closed Sun. No lunch.*

$$$ ✕ **Havfruen Fiskerestaurant.** "The Mermaid" is Trondheim's foremost and most stylish fish restaurant. Taking its cues from France, the restaurant excels at bouillabaisse as well as many other fish dishes, which change seasonally. The warm decor uses orange, greens, and reds accented by wood. The wine list includes a wide range of whites, highlighting dry French varieties. ⊠ *Kjøpmannsgt. 7* ☎ *73/87–40–70* ▤ *AE, DC, MC, V* ☽ *Closed Sun. No lunch.*

$$ ✕ **Grønn Pepper.** Tex-Mex is extremely popular throughout Norway, and this Trondheim restaurant serves a good rendition. Striped, vibrant Mexican blankets brighten up the hardwood floors and dark wood furniture. Mexican beer and tequila go well with the fiery food on offer, which includes some Cajun and creole dishes. ⊠ *Søndregt. 17 and Fjordgt. 7* ☎ *73/51–66–44* ▤ *AE, DC, MC, V.*

$$ ✕ **Sushi bar.** Trondheim's only sushi bar also serves other Japanese dishes in a bright and elegant space. Besides an excellent wine list, Japanese beer and sake are on the beverage menu. Come between 4 and 7 for less expensive happy hour sushi prices. ⊠ *Munkegt. 39* ☎ *73/ 52–10–20* ▤ *AE, DC, MC, V.*

$$ ✕ **Vertshuset Tavern.** Housed in what was once a 1739 tavern in downtown Trondheim, this restaurant is now part of the Trøndelag Folk Museum. The traditional menu includes homemade fish cakes; *rømmegrøt* (sour-cream porridge); *spekemat* (cured meat); and *Trøndelag klubb*, the local variation on potato dumplings. ⊠ *Sverresborg Allé 7* ☎ *73/ 52–09–32* ▤ *AE, DC, MC, V.*

$$–$$$$ ✕▨ **Britannia Hotel.** One of the Rica hotels, this classic in the heart of Trondheim opened in 1897. Luxurious rooms have regal yellow walls,

gold accents, and dark wood furniture. The elegant Palmehaven Restaurant ($$$) is popular for special occasions and serves breakfast, lunch, and dinner. You can dance here in the evenings. The Jonathan Restaurant is more rustic and laid back, and the Hjørnet Bar& Brasserie is ideal for steak tartare or a quick cup of coffee. ⊠ *Dronningensgt. 5, 7401* ☎ *73/800–800* 🖷 *73/800–801* ⊕ *www.britannia.no* ➶ *247 rooms* ♨ *3 restaurants, 2 bars, pub, meeting room* ⊟ *AE, DC, MC, V.*

★ **$$–$$$$** ✕⌂ **Radisson SAS Royal Garden Hotel.** This extravaganza of glass on the Nid River is Trondheim's largest hotel. Superb service and beautiful decor make a stay here memorable. The marble-accented atrium is full of thriving plants. Sun-kissed yellow rooms are subtly accented with deep blues and reds. Prins Olav Grill ($$$) is the hotel's main restaurant. The breakfast room Bakkus Mat & Vin is also ideal for lunch or a casual dinner overlooking the river. The Galleriet Bar is a popular meeting place for drinks. Musicians perform several nights a week in the jazz and blues club Blue Garden. ⊠ *Kjøpmannsgt. 73, 7410* ☎ *73/ 80–30–00* 🖷 *73/80–30–50* ⊕ *www.radissonsas.com* ➶ *298 rooms, 9 suites* ♨ *Restaurant, café, grill, indoor pool, gym, sauna, bar, nightclub* ⊟ *AE, DC, MC, V.*

$$–$$$ ⌂ **Clarion Hotel Grand Olav.** This reasonably priced hotel is in the same building as Trondheim's large concert hall. The interior is decorated with vibrant paintings and rich, bold colors. On Friday and Saturday nights, the lobby turns into a popular piano bar. ⊠ *Kjøpmannsgt. 48, 7010* ☎ *73/ 80–80–80* 🖷 *73/80–80–81* ⊕ *www.choicehotels.no* ➶ *112 rooms* ♨ *Restaurant, gym, bar, pub* ⊟ *AE, DC, MC, V.*

Nightlife

Olavskvartalet is the center of much of the city's nightlife, with dance clubs, live music, bars, and cafés. **Monte Cristo** (⊠ Prinsensgt. 38–40 ☎ 73/ 52–18–80) has a restaurant, bar, and dance club. Young people in search of cheap drinks, music, and dancing gravitate toward **Strossa** (⊠ Elgesetergt. 1 ☎ 73/89–95–10). **Café Remis** (⊠ Kjøpmannsgt. 12 ☎ 73/ 52–05–52) is one of the most popular gay clubs in Trondheim.

The bustling **Kontoret Bar & Spiseri** (⊠ Nordregt. 24 ☎ 73/53–40-4–0) has 40 varieties of malt whiskey and excellent cognacs in all price ranges. Downtown, in the area known as Solsiden (The Sunny Side), are several bars and clubs. **Blæst, Bar muda, and Luna Lounge** (⊠ TMV-Kaia 5, Nedre Elvehavn ☎ 73/60–06–10), are especially popular summer spots, partly because of their outdoor terraces. **Choco Boco** (☎ 73/ 600–300) is a chocolate-obsessed café.

The Arts

Trondheim Symphony Orchestra (⊠ Olavskvartalet, Kjøpmannsgt. 46 ☎ 73/99–40–50 ⊕ www.tso.no) performs weekly concerts with internationally acclaimed soloists and conductors. In late July, the annual **St. Olav Festival in Trondheim** (⊠ Dronningensgt. 1B ☎ 73/84–14–50 ⊕ www.olavsfestdagene.no) features a program of indoor and outdoor concerts, opera, and organ concerts at Nidaros Cathedral. Exhibits and children's activities are also staged.

Sports & the Outdoors

CYCLING Some 300 **Trondheim Bysykkel City Bikes** can be borrowed in the city center. Parked in easy-to-see stands at central locations, the distinctive green bikes have shopping baskets. You'll need a 20-kroner piece to release the bike (your money's refunded when you return the bike to a parking rack).

The Trampe elevator ascends the steep Brubakken Hill near Gamle Bybro and takes cyclists nearly to Kristiansten Festning (Kristiansten Fort).

Contact the tourist office to get the card you need in order to use the Trampe.

FISHING The river Nid is one of Norway's best salmon and trout rivers, famous for its large salmon (the record is 70 pounds). You can fish right in the city, but you need a license. For further information and fishing licenses, contact **TOFA (Trondheim og Omland Jakt- og Fiskeadministrasjon)** (✉ Leirfossvn. 76 ☎ 73/96–55–80 ⊕ www.tofa.org).

HIKING–WALKING **Bymarka,** a wooded area on Trondheim's outskirts, has a varied and well-developed network of trails—60 km (37 mi) of gravel paths, 80 km (50 mi) of ordinary paths, 250 km (155 mi) of ski tracks. The **Ladestien** (Lade Trail) is a 14-km (9-mi) trail that goes along the edge of the Lade Peninsula and offers great views of Trondheimsfjord. **The Nidelvstien Trail** runs along the river from Tempe to the Leirfossene waterfalls.

SKIING **Bymarka** and **Estenstadmarka,** wooded areas on the periphery of Trondheim, are popular with cross-country skiers. Bymarka's Skistua (ski lodge) also has downhill runs.

Vassfjellet Skisenter (☎ 72/83–02–00 ⊕ www.vassfjellet.com), 8 km (5 mi) south of Trondheim's city limits, has 5 tow lifts and 10 runs. There are facilities for downhill and Telemark skiing as well as snowboarding and tobogganing. In season (roughly mid-October through Easter), the center is open daily, and ski buses run every evening and weekend.

SWIMMING The Trondheimsfjord and inland lakes are both options for swimming. **Trondheim Pirbadet** (✉ Havnegt. 12 ☎ 73/83–18–00 ⊕ www.pirbadet. no) is Norway's largest indoor swimming center. There's a wave pool, a sauna, and a Jacuzzi as well as a gym here.

Shopping

Trondheim's **Mercur Centre** (✉ Nordregt. ⊕ www.mercursenteret.no) and **Trondheim Torg** shopping centers have helpful staffs and interesting shops.

For knitted sweaters by such makers as Oleana and Oda, try **Jens Hoff Garn & Ide** (✉ Olav Tryggvasongt. 20 ☎ 73/53–15-37). **Arne Ronning** (✉ Nordregt. 10 ☎ 73/53–13–30) carries fine sweaters by Dale of Norway. Founded in 1770 and Norway's oldest extant goldsmith, **Møllers Gullsmedforretning** (✉ Munkegt. 3) sells versions of the Trondheim Rose, the city symbol since the 1700s. Trondheim has a branch of the handicraft store **Husfliden** (✉ Olav Tryggvasongt. 18 ☎ 73/83–32–30).

Mo i Rana

❷ *450 km (280 mi) north of Trondheim.*

Mo i Rana, meaning "Mo on the Ranafjord," is known as the Arctic Circle city because the Arctic Circle crosses the municipal area from east to west. The city has long been a center for iron and steel smelted from the ore supplied by nearby mines. Starting in Mo i Rana, in Helgeland—the Arctic Circle region—you can discover thrilling coastline, high mountains, and glaciers. Year-round activities include fishing, crabbing, mountain rambling, mountaineering, island-hopping, glacier-trekking, caving, canoeing, rowing, sailing, rafting, and skiing.

The **Grønligrotta** (Grønli Cave) is one of almost 200 caves 26 km (16 mi) northwest of Mo i Rana. With 7,920 feet of charted underground paths, many narrow passages, natural chimneys, and an underground river, it's the only illuminated Scandinavian show cave. For almost 100 years, tourists have been visiting the "grotta." A 20-minute tour takes you several hundred feet inside. There's an underground waterfall, naturally formed potholes, and a rock formation carved by glacial flow over thousands of years. ⊠ *Grønli* ☎ *75/13–25–86* ⊠ *NKr 80* ⊙ *June 20–Aug. 30, daily 10–7.*

> **off the beaten path**

SVARTISEN GLACIER – Glacier fans can hike on the Svartisen, which means "black ice." The second-largest glacier in Norway covers 370 square km (230 square mi); the Arctic Circle crosses the glacier inside the Saltfjellet–Svartisen Nasjonale Park. Several entrances to the park are accessible from Mo i Rana.

The easiest way to get to the glacier from Mo i Rana is to head north 32 km (20 mi) by car to Svartisvannet Lake. The boat *Svartisbåten* crosses the lake to within 2½ km (1½ mi) of the Østerdal arm of the glacier. From there it's a 3 km (2 mi) hike up to Austerdalsvatnet Lake and the glacier. Glacier walking is extremely hazardous and should never be attempted without a professional guide. Contact the **Svartisen Tourist Center** (⊠ Holandsfjord Halsa ☎ 75/75–00–11) for referrals. Four-hour guided tours of the Engenbreen glacial arm are offered by **Svartisen bre-og turlag** (☎ 918–68–564 ⊕ www.svartisen.no). No previous experience is necessary.

Polarsirkelsenteret

❸ *80 km (50 mi) north of Mo i Rana.*

★ A bleak stretch of treeless countryside marks the beginning of the Arctic Circle. The **Polarsirkelsenteret** (Arctic Circle Center) is right on the line in the Saltfjellet Mountains. Here you can build a small cairn as evidence you passed the circle. You can also get an Arctic Circle certificate to show the folks back home. ⊠ *Rte. E6, Rognan* ☎ *75/12–96–96 or 75/12–96–95* ⊕ *www.polarsirkelsenteret.no* ⊠ *NKr 50* ⊙ *May–mid-Sept.*

Bodø

❹ *174 km (108 mi) north of the Polarsirkelsenteret.*

Bodø, a modern city of about 42,000 just above the Arctic Circle, is best known as the terminus of the Nordlandsbanen railroad and the *Hurtigruten* (a coastal boat)—it's also the gateway to the Lofoten Islands and the north of Norway. The midnight sun is visible from June 2 to July 10 and the polar night descends from December 15 to December 29. Like many coastal towns, Bodø began as a small fishing community, but today it is a commercial and administrative center.

Bodø is the best base for boat excursions to the coastal bird colonies on the Væren Islands. Sea eagles soar high above town and perch on the rocks on nearby islands. The friendly city offers above-standard lodgings, entertainment, shopping, and outdoor activities.In August there's the **Nordland Festival of Music** (☎ 75/54–90–40 ⊕ www.nordland-musikkfestuke.no).

The **Nordland County Museum,** in one of the city's oldest buildings (1903), covers regional history, including the fishing industry and the changes that the 20th century brought about. An exhibit on Sámi culture features a 350-year-old wooden box with inscribed runes. There's also silver treasure that dates back 1,000 years to the Rønvik era): these English and Arabic coins and jewelry were discovered in 1919. The Byen vårres (Our City) exhibition shows the history of Bodø. The museum's open-air section at Bodøsjøen has 14 historical buildings and a boat collection, which includes *Anna Karoline af Hopen,* the sole surviving Nordland cargo vessel, or *jekt.* ✉ *Prinsengt. 116* ☎ *75/52–16–40* ⊕ *www. museumsnett.no/nordlandsmuseet* ✉ *NKr 30* ☉ *Tues.–Fri. 9–3; weekends noon–3.*

☺ Down the road from Bodø's airport and 15 minutes from the town's center, the jumbo **Norwegian Aviation Museum** is housed in a building shaped like a propeller. The high-ceilinged and spacious exhibition hall Rotunda illustrates "Man's primeval dream of flight." On either side are exhibition halls, one for civilian aviation and the other for military aviation. Among the collection are a Junkers Ju-52, a U-2, and a Thunderwing Spitfire from 1993. Climb the control tower for an unforgettable view of the wild northern Norwegian landscape. Finally, take a turn on the flight simulators for a glimpse inside the controls of an F-16 or a Harrier. ✉ *Olav V gt.* ☎ *75/50–78–50* ⊕ *www.aviation-museum.no* ✉ *NKr 75* ☉ *Mid-June–Aug., weekdays 10–7, Sat. 10–5, Sun. 10–7; mid-Aug.–mid-June, weekdays 10–4, weekends 11–5.*

Set amid narrow fjords edging the peninsula, the **Old Kjerringøy Trading Post** has 15 well-preserved 19th-century buildings where Erasmus Zahl once made handsome profits buying and selling fish. Take a guided tour of the manor—many its original furnishings are intact. ✉ *Hwy. RV 834, 40 km north of Bodø, then 10-min ferry ride* ☎ *75/51–12–57* ⊕ *www. museumsnett.no/nordlandsmuseet* ✉ *NKr 40.*

Zahl's Barn, Kjerringøy. Author Knut Hamsun visited Kjerringøy in 1879 and found inspiration for his writing here. Several movies based on his novels were filmed here, including *Rosa and Benoni, The Telegraphist* (based on the book *Dreamers*), and *Pan.* An exhibition about the filming of Hamsun's literature includes clips from more than 20 films made since 1921. There is also locally produced art for sale here, and a boat-builder's workshop. For opening times, contact Destinasjon Bodø. ✉ *Branch road RV 834, 40 km (25 mi) north of Bodø* ☎ *75/55–77–40.*

☺ North Norway's major private collection of art and artifacts, **Atelier 88–Galleri Bodøgaard** is known for its ethnographic collections. The history of Bodø and northern Norway is shown through exhibits on hunting and fishing, handicrafts, and agriculture, as well as the Russian prisoner-of-war camp Bodøgård. There are pictures and handicrafts for sale. ✉ *Skeidalen 2, 2.5 km from Bodø city center* ☎ *75/56–32–41* ⊕ *www.bodogaard.no* ✉ *NKr 50.*

---

off the beaten path

ARTSCAPE NORDLAND – If you're an art lover, you can plan encounters with Artscape Nordland (⊕ skulpturlandskap.no), an international art project involving artists from 18 countries. The Nordland county does not have an art museum and people have to travel long distances to study modern art in museums and galleries. The idea behind the project, begun in 1992 and completed in 1998, was to collect modern art, and place one sculpture in every municipality, with the landscape as the backdrop to the art. Today, sculptures like English artist Antony Gormley's *Havmann* (Ocean Man) are located in beautiful, varied and often brutal landscapes along the coast of the Atlantic, in 33 Nordland municipalities.

Where to Stay & Eat

$–$$$
Fodor's Choice
★

✕🏨 **Landego Fyr.** Braving Vestfjord's pounding waves on Fyrholmen lighthouse rock is this red-and-white cast-iron lighthouse that dates from 1902. You can stay in the former lighthouse keepers' sky-blue and forest-green quarters, which maintain their original, wood-paneled, nautical style. Soak in the seawater-filled outdoor hot tub. Sea eagles, cormorants, and other sea birds keep you company, constantly circling overhead. Chef and manager Sindre Laksmark's fish dishes, especially the soups, are delicious. From the lighthouse's lookout, you can see as far as the Lofoten Islands on a clear day. Mainly available to groups, the lighthouse also accepts reservations from individuals, especially between July and early August. ⊠ *Eggsløysa, Bodø* ☎☎ *75/58–46–44 or 75/52–24–00* ⊕ *www. skagen-hotel.no* ↝ *13 rooms* ♨ *Restaurant, café, bar, meeting rooms* ⊟ *AE, DC, MC, V.*

$$–$$$ ⚏ **Suleitjema Hotel.** In remote, former mining country, surrounded by Northern Norway's highest mountains, Suleitjema Hotel, 100 km east of Bodø, is perfect for year-round wilderness adventures. In the Suleitjelma wilderness area you can ski, snowmobile, hike, fish, and more. The cozy rooms have modern furniture and are decorated in warm shades. The spa has massage, aromatherapy, skincare, and other treatments. In late June, the Mons Petter Festival celebrates the area's mining history with concerts, exhibitions, entertainment, athletic competitions, and mine tours. ⊠ *Nyholmsgata 11, 8005 Bodø* ☎ *75/64–04–01* ☎ *75/ 64–06–54* ⊕ *www.skagen-hotel.no* ↝ *60 rooms* ♨ *Restaurant, indoor pool, hot tub, sauna, spa, bar* ⊟ *AE, DC, MC, V.*

★ **$$** ⚏ **Skagen Hotel.** Skagen is a real gem of a hotel, known for its first-class, personal service. It has many regulars, so be sure to book early. The cherry-wood rooms have different personalities, from artsy and crowded to elegant and understated. There are complimentary waffles and coffee in the afternoon, in the English-style Library Bar. A complimentary cold evening buffet is served between 7 and 10. Skagen is hooked up to WiFi, a special wireless Internet service. ⊠ *Nyholmsgata 11* ☎ *75/52–24–00* ☎ *75/52–59–30* ⊕ *www.skagen-hotel.no* ↝ *72 rooms* ♨ *Restaurant, bar, library, Internet* ⊟ *AE, DC, MC, V.*

Cafés & Bars

The café **En Kopp** (⊠ Storgt.2–Radisson SAS Hotel ☎ 75/52–46–40) serves up freshly roasted coffee and light meals; lounge music plays in the background, and there are Internet terminals, board games, and regular cultural events. The **Kafé Kafka** (⊠ Sandgt. 5B ☎ 75/52–35–50) pays homage to its namesake author with a lovely painting of a Prague street scene. Come for the many desserts. The bohemian **Min Plass** (⊠ Sjøgt. 12 ☎ 75/52–26–88) is an easy place to lose an entire day, having a coffee or a drink, and dining on an international menu that offers everything from jambalaya to bruschettas. Trendy **Metz** (⊠ Glasshuset ☎ 75/ 54–00–99) has an aquarium, is a coffee bar by day, and popular pub by night. Red-leather sofas and a library theme set the scene at **Bonsak** (⊠ Sjøgat. 17 ☎ 75/52–29–90), a piano bar and nightclub named after former bishop Mathias Bonsak Krogh. If you're after a panoramic view of Bodø and the surrounding islands, head to **Top 13** (⊠ Storgt.2–Radisson SAS Hotel ☎ 75/51–90–26). The American-style **Rock Café** (⊠ Tollbugt. 13b ☎ 75/50–46–30) attracts a younger crowd with its concerts, DJs, comedians, rock and pop, and big-screen TV showing sports events. Popular Italian restaurant **Da Carlo** (⊠ Glasshuset ☎ 75/50–46–12) also has an informal café, and a terrace café and bar, TopHat.

Sports & the Outdoors

BIRD-WATCHING   Bodø is known as the sea eagle capital, because nowhere else are there more of these majestic birds. In July and early August sea eagle safaris are led by **Landego Lighthouse** (⊠ Eggsløysa ☎ 75/52–24–00 ⊕ www. skagen-hotel.no).

BOATING   Boats for fishing and other activities can be rented at several places in town. **Kjerringøy Rorbu Center** (☎ 75/58–50–07 ⊕ www.kjerringgoy-rorbusenter.no) has 14- to 17-foot boats with outboard motors and facilities for overnight accommodation. They also provide information on deep-sea fishing. **Aurora Borealis** (☎ 75/52–17–75 ⊕ www.gox.no) offers sailing trips on S/Y *Goxsheim,* one of north Norway's biggest sailing vessels.

CYCLING   Heading out on bicycle, especially on the Coastal Highway and Vestfjord route, is an excellent way to explore Bodø and the surrounding countryside. **Destinasjon Bodø** rents bicycles; rates range from NKr 60 to NKr 150 per day; there are also special weekly rates. Contact the tourist office for more information.

DIVING   **Polardykk** (☎ 75/52–52–93 or 91/64–23–30 ⊕ www.polardykk.no) offers diving excursions to shipwrecks and the world's strongest maelstrom, They conduct courses, and have equipment rental.

FISHING   Local rivers and lakes are home to trout, char, and salmon. **Destinasjon Bodø** (✉ Sjøgt. 3 ☎ 75/54–80–00 ⊕ www.visitbodo.com) has a list of outfitters that sell fishing licenses. **Salmon Islands** (☎ 75/75–99–99 ⊕ www.salmon-islands.no) offers salmon fishing, deep sea fishing, and rafting expeditions.

HIKING–WALKING   **Bodø og Omegn Turistforening- BOT** (Bodø Mountain Touring Association; ✉ Storgata 17 ☉ Tues., Wed., and Fri. noon–3, Thurs. 11–5 ☎ 75/52–14–13), the local chapter of the Norwegian Mountain Touring Association, owns and operates 23 cabins at 15 sites. It also services the 600-km (373 mi) stretch from the Saltenfjord in the north to the Arctic Circle in the south. The association has youth, glacier, cave-exploring, and rock-climbing groups.

Saltstraumen

❺ *33 km (20 mi) southeast of Bodø on Rte. 80–17.*

Saltstraumen is a 3-km-long (2-mi-long) and 500-foot-wide section of water between the outer fjord, which joins with the sea, and the inner fjord basin. During high tide, the volume of water rushing through the strait and into the basin is so great that whirlpools form. In fact, every six hours, 400 million cubic meters (500 million cubic yards) of water rushes through the narrow sound. This is the legendary maelstrom (*malstrøm* in Norwegian)—and the strongest one in the world. The rush of water brings an abundance of fish, including cod, saithe, wolffish and halibut, making the maelstrom a popular fishing spot.

On the shores of the maelstrom, you can visit **Saltstraumen Opplevelsesenter** (Saltstraumen Adventure Center). The center looks at 10,000 years of regional history, from the Ice Age, when humans first came here, through the Iron and Viking Ages, and on to the present day. There's also an aquarium holding indigenous fish and an outdoor seal pond. ✉ *Saltstraumen, Hwy. RV 17* ☎ *75/56–06–55* ⊕ *www.skagen-hotel.no* 💰 *NKr 60* ☉ *June–late Aug., daily 11–6.*

Every summer, the **World Saithe Fishing Championships** (☎ 75/54–8000 ⊕ www.visitbodo.com) attract anglers from near and far to compete in catching saithe, also known as pollack or coalfish. There are different categories, such as fishing from land or from a boat, as well as overall awards for the largest saithe caught. The world record for saithe caught with a fishing pole was set here by a 22.7-kg catch.

off the beaten path   **BLODVEIMUSEET** (Blood Road Museum) – Ninety minutes southeast of Bodø, in Rognan, the Blood Road Museum re-creates the sinister atmosphere of an icy north Norway Nazi prison camp, where Russian, Serb, and Polish prisoners of war were incarcerated by the Germans between 1942 and 1945. **Saltdal Bygdetun,** a collection of historic houses, is a few yards away. The stretch of road between Saltnes and Saksenvik was called "Blood Road" by the prisoners of war who worked on it; this later became its official name, in 1995. War memorials exist at Stamnes, Sundby, Røkland, Storjord, and on the Arctic Circle. ✉ *Bygetunet, Saltnes, Rognan* ☎ *75/68–22–90 or 75/68–23–00* ⊕ *www.museumsnett.no/saltdalmuseum* ✆ *NKr 50* ⊘ *Mid-June–mid-Aug., weekdays 9:30–4, Sat. 1–4, Sun. 1–6.*

Where to Stay & Eat

$$ ╳▦ **Saltstraumen Hotel.** Although it's rather plain, the hotel's position— it's practically on top of the maelstrom—makes it a memorable place to stay. The restaurant ($$) serves delicious steamed halibut in butter sauce. The Saltstraumen Gallery has regional paintings and other graphic art on display. ✉ *8056 Saltstraumen* ☎ *75/58–76–85* ⊕ *www. saltstraumen-hotel.no* ↳ *28 rooms, 7 cabins* ╰ *Restaurant, meeting room* ▭ *AE, DC, MC, V.*

Narvik

➏ *336 km (210 mi) north of Saltstraumen.*

Narvik was established as an ice-free port for exporting iron ore mined around the Swedish town of Kiruna.

From mid-June to September you can take a seven-minute trip on the **Narvik Mountain Lift**, a cable car that offers a view of the Ofotenfjord, the mountains, the midnight sun, and the city below. A restaurant is at the summit. Mount Fagernesfjellet and its marked trails are popular for hikes and hang gliding. A downhill mountain bike trail begins near the lift as well. ☎ *76/96–04–94* ⊘ *Mid-June–Aug. 1, daily noon–1 AM; Aug. 2–Aug. 31, daily 1–9.*

In April and May 1940, the Battle of Narvik and the fight for ore left the city razed and began five years of Nazi occupation. The **Nordland Red Cross War Memorial Museum** recounts this dark period in Narvik's history through an exhibition of photographs, models, and World War II equipment. ✉ *Torget–Narvik City Sq.* ☎ *76/94–44–26* ✆ *NKr 40* ⊘ *Mar.–June 2, daily 10–4; June 3–Aug. 19, daily 10–10; Aug. 20–Sept. 30, daily 10–4.*

Narvik has ancient rock carvings in the city center. At **Brennholtet** a rock carving estimated at 3,000 years old shows a Norwegian forefather's hope for good hunting. ✉ *City center.*

At the turn of the 19th century, this fishing and agriculture-based community was transformed by the building of the Ofotbanen railway and the development of the ore shipment port. The **Ofoten Museum**, in the center of town, traces these developments through permanent and changing exhibitions. ✉ *Administrasjonsveien 3* ☎ *76/96–00–50* ⊕ *www.ofoten.museum.no* ✆ *NKr 25* ⊘ *Aug.–June, weekdays 10:30–3:30; July, daily 10:30–3:30.*

> **off the beaten path**

RALLARVEIEN (Navvies' Road) – Here you can walk in the footsteps of the railway workers (navvies). This dirt track was vital to the building of Ofotbanen railway from Kiruna to Narvik. Some 5,000 men were employed in the construction of the ore shipment railway, which was completed in 1902. The road has been reopened as a site of cultural history and a cycling trail. It runs through a mountain realm between Sweden's Abisko and Rombaksbotn. Every summer, participants in the Svarta-Bjørn Walk (Black Bear Walk) take a train up to Katterat, wander down into Rombaksbotn, and take a boat back to Narvik. The lodge **Katterat Fjellstue** (☎ 908–544–84) offers guided tours and gold panning.

Where to Stay & Eat

$$ ✕⌷ **Radisson SAS Grand Royal Hotel.** Narvik's best hotel, this Radisson property has an elegant style and top-notch service. The Royal Blue restaurant ($$) has a menu based on first-rate ingredients from the north of Norway. Both the fresh char and meal of the day are highly recommended. The nightclub and traditional pub are popular with travelers and locals. ⊠ *Kongensgt. 64, 8501* ☎ 76/97–70–00 🖷 76/97–70–07 ⊕ *www. grandroyal.no* 🖅 *107 rooms* ⚬ *2 restaurants, sauna, 2 bars, nightclub, convention center* ⊟ *AE, DC, MC, V.*

Sports & the Outdoors

CAVING   Around Narvik, there are innumerable caves to explore on guided tours or guided adventures. Contact the Narvik Tourist Information office for schedules.

DIVING   During World War II, about 50 planes were shot down and 46 ships sank in the Narvik area. Three of the 11 German battleships that were sunk are still under water. There are several licensed dive shops, with experienced instructors who specialize in wreck exploration. Contact **Narvik Wreck Diving** (☎90/72–11–05 ⊕home.c2i.net/narvikwreckdiving).

FISHING   You can take fjord- and sea-fishing trips year-round on the *Delphin Senior,* a 46-foot fishing boat. Contact Narvik Tourist Information.

HIKING–WALKING   In the area stretching from Troms in the north to Hellemofjorden/ Tysfjord, **Narvik & Omegn Turistforening (NOT)** (☎ 76/94–60–33 ⊕ www. narvikjell.no) owns and operates 22 mountain cabins at 11 sites. The mountainous terrain varies in height from 1,312 feet to 3,280 feet above sea level. NOT arranges various mountain hikes, some of which are designed for families. Contact the tourist information office for details.

MOUNTAINEERING   Deep fjords and mountains up to 6,230 feet high make Narvik's landscape perfect for the walks and tours led by **North Norwegian School of Mountaineering** (☎ 76/95–13–53 ⊕ www.nord-norskklatreskole.no). **Nordland Adventures** (☎ 75/58–43–58 ⊕ www.nordlandturselskap.no) leads tours of the region's mountains, forests, and caves.

SKIING   Set amid fjords and mountains, the **Narvik Ski Center** (☎ 76/96–04–94 ⊕ www.narvikinfo.no ☉ Nov.–May) has challenging trails and off-piste skiing, making it an ideal stop for experienced skiers.

Lofoten & the Islands of the North

Extending out into the ocean north of Bodø are the Lofoten Islands, a 190-km (118-mi) chain of jagged peaks. In summer the farms, fjords, and fishing villages draw caravans of visitors, whereas in winter the coast facing the Arctic Ocean is one of Europe's stormiest. The midnight sun is visible here from May 25 to July 17. If you are lucky enough to be visiting on a clear midnight, drive over to the western side, where the spear-shape mountains give way to flat, sandy beaches that look oddly fluorescent in the hush of night. It is a spectacular sight.

Until the 1950s, fishing was the area's only industry. As many as 6,000 boats with 30,000 anglers would mobilize between January and March for *Lofotfisket,* the world's largest cod-fishing event. They fished in open boats, and took shelter during stormy nights in *rorbuer,* simple cabins built right on the water. Today, income from tourism helps supplement that from the still-thriving fisheries, and many rorbuer have been converted into tourist lodgings. Lofotfisket, however, is still an annual tradition.

The principal islands of Lofoten are Austvågøy, Gimsøy, Vestvågøy, Flakstadøy, Moskenesøy, Værøy and Røst. The best way to visit Lofoten is by car. On Austvågøy is **Svolvær**, the main town and administrative center for the villages on the islands. It's connected with the other islands by express boat and ferry, and with Bodø by coastal steamers and airplanes. The oldest part of Svolvær, about ½ mi from the town center, is Svinøya; this is where, in 1828, the first fish trading company in Lofoten was established. It faces Svolværgeita, the town's famous goatshape mountain, and is an idyllic place full of fishermen's cabins and art galleries.

You can chat with artists at the **North Norwegian Artists' Center,** and browse at the shop, which sells paintings, handicrafts, books, posters, and postcards. ⊠ *Svinøya Svolvær* ☎ *76/06–67–70* ⊠ *NKr 30* ☉ *Mid-June–Aug., daily 10–6; Sept.–mid-June, Mon. 11–3.*

Gunnar Berg (1863–93), Lofoten's most famous artist, was born and raised on Svinøya. The **Gunnar Berg Gallery** houses the largest collection of his works, including *The Battle of Trollfjord.* ⊠ *Svinøya Svolvær* ☎ *76/06–99–30* ⊠ *NKr 50* ☉ *June 15–Aug. 25, daily 10–6; Aug. 26–June 14, Tues.–Sun. 11–3.*

The **Lofoten War Memorial Museum** commemorates World War II events in Lofoten and northern Norway through an exhibition of uniforms and other objects. ⊠ *Svolvær town center, near Coastal Voyage docks* ☎ *91/ 73–03–28* ⊕ *www.lofotenkrigmus.no* ⊠ *NKr 50* ☉ *June–mid-Sept., weekdays 10–4.*

The **Lofoten Temagalleri** (Lofoten Theme Gallery) focuses on whaling and Lofoten. See the short film "Islands in the Sea" by Bjørn Kenneth Hansen. ⊠ *5-min walk from Svolvær town square* ☎ *76/07–03–36* ⊠ *NKr 50* ⊕ *www.svolver-sjohuscamp.no* ☉ *Daily 10–3:30; also open summer evenings 6–10.*

Just south of Svolvær, the hamlet of **Kabelvåg,** on the site of an old fishing settlement, provides the perfect introduction to the string of Lofoten islands, their history, and their inhabitants. There is a cluster of museums less than a mile from the quiet village center. Restored fishing cabins displayed at the **Lofotmuseet** (Lofoten Museum; ☎ 76/07–82–23) depict the rigorous life of a fishing community on the grassy edge of a fjord inlet. Next door, the **Galleri Espolin** (☎ 76/07–84–05) exhibits dark, haunting paintings and lithographs depicting fishermen in stormy weather by nationally renowned artist Kaare Espolin Johnsen, who died in 1994. The **Lofot-Akvariet** (Lofoten Aquarium; ⊠ Storvågan ☎ 76/ 07–86–65 ⊕ www.lofotakvariet.no ⊠ NKr 70) includes a salmon farm exhibit, an aquarium, and seal and otter ponds.

Southwest of Kabelvåg is **Henningsvær.** This village is home to **Lofoten House Gallery,** which exhibits Lofoten-inspired paintings by well-known Norwegian artists, including Karl Erik Harr. You can also view a slide show by Frank A. Jenssen, and photos of white-tailed eagles. ⊠ *Henningsv(ae)r* ☎ *76/07–15–73* ⊠ *NKr 60* ☉ *Mar. 7–Apr. 13, daily noon–3; Apr. 14–May 22, by appointment; May 23–June 9, daily 10–6; June 10–Aug. 10, daily 9–7; Aug. 11–31, daily 10–6.*

Viking enthusiasts might want to veer northwest to Borg, where archaeologists unearthed a long, low chieftain's house—the largest Viking building ever discovered. For the Vikings, the banquet hall was a sacred place where religious and political rituals occurred. Rebuilt exactly as it was, **Lofotr–The Viking Museum of Borg** houses the 1,000-year-old artifacts that were discovered here, including gold foil fertility figures, Frankish pottery, and Rhineland glass. The objects reveal contact with Germany, France, and England. ⊠ *Prestergårdsvn. 59* ☎ *76/08–49–00* ⊕ *www. lofotr.no* ✉ *NKr 90* ☉ *Mid-May–Aug., daily 10–7; Sept.–mid-May, Fri. 1–3 or by appointment.*

Other scenic stops include tucked-away **Nusfjord,** a 19th-century fishing village on an official European conservation list; **Sund,** with its smithy and small fisheries museum; and festive **Reine.**

need a break?

The traditional **Gammelbua** (⊠ Reine ☎ 76/09–22–22) serves excellent salmon mousse and chilled Norwegian beer. Locals and tourists flock here to eat, drink, and gossip.

A drive to the outer tip of Lofoten (130 km [80 mi] from Svolvær)— gets you to a town with the enigmatic name of Å. Here you can visit the **Norwegian Fishing Village Museum,** comprised of fishing houses dating back to the mid-19th century. Exhibitions include Life in the Fishing Village, the Lofoten Fishery, Stockfish, and Cod-Liver Oil. You can take home a souvenir bottle of cod-liver oil or a cod-liver oil lamp. ⊠ *Å, Hwy. E10, 10 km (6 mi) from Reine* ☎ *76/09–14–88* ⊕ *www.lofoten-info.no/nfmuseum* ✉ *NKr 45* ☉ *Aug. 1–June 19, weekdays 11–3; June 20–Aug. 20, daily 10–6.*

Off the tip of Moskenesøy, the last island on the Lofoten chain with a bridge, is **Moskenesstraumen,** a maelstrom that's not as dramatic as Saltstraumen.

North of the Lofotens are the **Vesterålen Islands,** with similar, stunning coastal landscapes, as well as fishing villages and rorbuer. There are fewer tourists in Vesterålen than on the Lofoten Islands, which means lower prices and more whale sightings.

Andenes island is the site of the islands' biggest attraction, Whale Safari. Andøya Island has many cultural monuments—medieval farms, Iron Age remnants, and northern Norway's best preserved Iron Age farm.

Just off Nordmela, a nature reserve reachable by boat, is the largest colony of common seals in Norway. The island of Bleiksøya is a haven for seabirds, including 70,000 pairs of puffins. Sortland, the region's communication and service center, is known as Blå Byen (Blue City) because the city's artists have been painting the buildings blue. Stokmarknes, known for its lively market place, is the home of the new Coastal Steamer Museum.

East of the Vesterålen Islands, on Hinnøya, Norway's largest island, is **Harstad,** where the year-round population of 23,000 swells to 42,000 during the annual June cultural festival (the lineup includes concerts, theater, and dance) and the July deep-sea-fishing festival.

Where to Stay & Eat

Staying in a *rorbu* (fisherman's cabin) is essential to the Lofoten experience. Rorbu is a combination of the Norwegian words "bu" for "dwelling" and "ro" for "rowing." The original, red-painted rorbuer were usually comprised of two rooms, one for living quarters and the other for the storage of nets, bait, and supplies. Rorbuer vary greatly in standards; some date back to the last century and others are brand new. If you do stay in a rorbu, it is completely self-service, so expect to shop for food to stock the refrigerator. Most villages have grocery stores. You can bring linens, or rent them for about NKr 100.

$$$ ✕ **Fiskekrogen Restaurant.** This quayside restaurant in a former fish factory is family-run. Specialties of chef and owner Otto Asheim include cod fish tongue, fried catfish, bacalao, "homemade" caviar directly from the sea, and the Krogen seafood plate—a selection of seasonal fare. ⊠ *Henningsvær* ☎ 76/07–46–52 ☰ *AE, DC, MC, V.*

★ $$–$$$ 🏠 **Henningsvær Bryggehotell.** Right on the quay of the island's largest fishing village, this member of Det Virkelig Gode Liv chain is one of Lofoten's finest hotels. Bright colors, stylish furniture, and modern art distinguish the hotel, which emphasizes high standards in facilities and service. Take a fishing trip on the *Symra* and the restaurant will prepare your cod catch for you. Henningsvær also offers sea-rafting, salmon fishing, eagle watching, mountain climbs and hikes, and visits to fish receiving stations and fish oil factories. ⊠ *8312 Henningsvær* ☎ *76/07–47–50* 🖷 *76/07–47–30* ⊕ *www.dvgl.no* ⇋ *32 rooms* ⚭ *Restaurant, sauna, bar, lounge, conference room* ☰ *V.*

$–$$$ 🏠 **Lofoten Rorbuferie.** In the quiet fishing village of Kabelvåg, these basic red rorbuer bear names like the Seagull and Sea Eagle. They are adequate, if basic, accommodations while you're on a fishing trip. Reserve far in advance, as the cabins get booked up quickly. ⊠ *8310 Kabelvåg* ☎ *76/07–84–44* 🖷 *76/07–84–53* ⊕ *www.lofoten-rorbuferie.no* ⇋ *15 rorbus* ☰ *AE, DC, MC, V.*

$$ 🏠 **Edvardas Hus.** Named after a character in Knut Hamsun's book, Edvardas Hus pays homage to Norway's most famous author. On Tranøy, intimate Edvardas Hus is a favorite vacation spot for many Norwegians visiting Hamarøy island. ⊠ *8297 Tranøy* ☎ *75/77–21–82* 🖷 *75/77–22–21* ⊕ *www.edvardashus.no* ⇋ *9 rooms* ☰ *AE, DC, MC, V.*

$$ 🏠 **Svinøya Rorbuer.** Svinøya is the oldest and most memorable part of Svolvær island. Many of the original, wooden rorbuer here have been converted into tourist accommodations. Step outside and you'll see cod drying on fish racks and screaming seagulls. The reception area has a museum of curiosities like fishermen's wooden-soled rubber boots. The former fish landing station, built in 1828, is now Borsen Spiseri restaurant. It's known for fish dishes like *boknafisk* (half-dried cod). Explore the island's artistic side at the Northern Norwegian Artist Center, Studio Lofoten, and Gallery Gunnar Berg. ⊠ *Gunnar Bergs vei 2 Svinøya 8300 Svolvær* ☎ *76/06–99–30* 🖷 *76/07–48–98* ⊕ *www.svinoya.no* ⇋ *30 rorbus* ⚭ *Restaurant, bar* ☰ *AE, DC, MC, V.*

$–$$ 🏠 **Nusfjord Rorbuanlegg.** These secluded cabins are extremely attractive for families—many stay for weeks. There's plenty to do—hiking, fishing, boating—in the surrounding area. For a glimpse at the midnight sun, drive to Flakstad, at the other side of the island. Rowboats are included in the price of a rorbu, and you can rent fishing gear and motorboats. ⊠ *8380 Ramberg* ☎ *76/09–30–20* 🖷 *76/09–33–78* ⇋ *34 1- or 2-bedroom rorbuer* ⚭ *Restaurant, pub, laundry* ☰ *AE, DC, MC, V.*

$–$$ 🏠 **Nyvågar Rorbuhotell.** Within the fishing village of Kabelvåg, Nyvågar is a rorbu and recreation complex, part of Det Virkelig Gode Liv hotel chain. Its red wooden rorbuer are well-maintained and decorated in earthy colors. The Lorchstua restaurant serves seasonal, country-style dishes. Activities are well organized, with fishing-boat tours, eagle safaris, and deep-sea rafting, as well as evening entertainment. Nyvågar is a two-minute walk from Storvågan's museums. ⊠ *Storvåganveien 22, Kabelvåg Storvågan 8310* ☎ *76/06–97–00* 🖷 *76/06–97–01* ⊕ *www. dvgl.no* ⇋ *30 rorbus* ⚭ *Restaurant, meeting room* ☰ *AE, DC, MC, V.*

$–$$ 🏠 **Rica Hotel Svolvær.** Withred, rustic rorbu style, this hotel blends right into the Lofoten setting. The rooms are small yet comfortable. The lobby and Bauen restaurant are inside an unusual boat-shaped building with panoramic harbor views. Try chef Henning Østlund's salmon or grilled dried fish. ✉ *Lamholmen, 8301 Svolvær* ☎ *76/07–22–22* 🖷 *76/07–20–01* ⊕ *www.rica.no* 🛏 *147 rooms* 🍴 *Restaurant, bar, convention center* 🖃 *AE, DC, MC, V.*

Sports & the Outdoors

BIRD-WATCHING A high-pitched hum emanates from some of northern Norway's arctic island cliffs, which pulsate with thousands of birds. From Moskenes, just north of Å, or from Bodø, you can take a ferry to the bird sanctuaries of **Værøy** and **Røst**. Many types of seabirds inhabit the cliffs, particularly *eider* (sea ducks). From Røst you can take boat trips to the cliffside seabird colonies and to Skomvær Lighthouse; from Reine, boats visit the seabird colonies of rocky Værøy, where puffins and cormorants live. Contact **Eventyr Rafting** (☎ 76/09–64–11).

COASTAL CAVES There are coastal caves, some 100 meters deep and 50 meters tall, at the tip of Lofotodden headland. Red, Stone-Age cave drawings were found in the caves. **Eventyr Rafting Lofoten** (☎ 76/09–20–00 ⊕ www.lofoten-info.no/rafting) organizes daily guided tours to the Refsvikhula cave. They depart from Reine on a giant rubber dinghy.

CYCLING In Lofoten, many accommodations have bicycles available for rent. Or you can contact the tourist offices in Moskenes and Leknes for information about hiring bicycles.

DIVING & UNDERWATER SAFARIS **Lofotfykk** (☎ 76/07–82–11 ⊕ www.lofotdykk.no) organizes dives, overnight accommodation, tank refills, and equipment rental. Consider donning a drysuit, diver's mask, and snorkel for an underwater safari with **Lofoten Opplevelser** (☎ 76/07–50–01 ⊕ www.lofoten-opplevelser.no)

MOUNTAINEERING The **North Norwegian School of Mountaineering** (☎ 76/07–49–11 ⊕ www.nordnorskklatreskole.no) is based in Henningsvær. The school offers week- or day-long mountaineering courses and guided mountain tours, and has a shop that sells mountaineering equipment. Climbs of famous Svolværgeita Peak take place daily in summer. The school's café, Den Siste Viking, is often described as a combination of English pub, Nepalese tea house, and Everest base camp.

WATER SPORTS **Jann's Adventure Lofoten** (☎ 76/07–89–10 ⊕ www.lofoten-aktiv.no) offers lessons in sea kayaking and rents kayaks. They also can arrange hiking, mountain walks, cycling, and fishing trips, and ski rentals. **Coastal Odyssey** (☎ 951/18062 ⊕ www.seakayaklofoten.com) gives guided tours, rents kayaks, and plans expeditions and tours.

WHALE-WATCHING The island of Andenes, part of the Vesterålen Islands, is the northernmost place in the world where sperm whales can be watched. The season runs from late May to mid-September. Since 1988 **Whale Safari** (☎ 76/11–56–00 ⊕ www.whalesafari.no) has organized whale watches. They have qualified researcher guides, and a whale-sighting guarantee. Brush up on your knowledge of the sea mammal at the island's **Whale Centre** (☎ 76/11–56–00), where you can see an exhibition on whales and whale research and a slide show. **Whale Tours A/S** (✉ Stø ☎ 76/13–44–99 ⊕ www.whaletours.no) scours the sea for minke, sperm, and killer whales, seal, and seabirds.

Tromsø

❼ *318 km (197 mi) northeast of Harstad.*

Tromsø surprised visitors in the 1800s: they thought it very sophisticated and cultured for being so close to the North Pole. It looks the way a polar town should—with ice-capped mountain ridges and jagged architecture that is an echo of the peaks. The midnight sun shines from

May 21 to July 21, and the city's total area—2,558 square km (987 square mi)—is the most expansive in Norway. Tromsø is about the same size as Luxembourg, but home to only 58,000 people. The city's center sits on a small, hilly island connected to the mainland by a slender bridge. The 13,000 students at the world's northernmost university are one reason the nightlife here is uncommonly lively for a northern city.

The **Ishavskatedralen** (Arctic Cathedral) is the city's signature structure. Designed by Jan Inge Hovig, it's meant to evoke the shape of a Sámi tent as well as the iciness of a glacier. Opened in 1964, it represents northern Norwegian nature, culture, and faith. The immense stained-glass window depicts the Second Coming. ⊠ *Tromsdalen* ☎ *77/63–76–11* ⊠ *NKr 22* ⊘ *Oct.–Apr. 14, daily 4–6; Apr. 15–May, daily 3–6; June–Aug. 15, Mon.–Sat. 10–8, Sun. 1–8; Aug. 16–Sept., daily 3–6.*

☾ The **Tromsø Museum, Universitetsmuseet,** North Norway's largest museum, is dedicated to the nature and culture of the region. Learn about the northern lights, wildlife, fossils and dinosaurs, minerals and rocks, and church art from 1300 to 1800. Outdoors you can visit a Sámi *gamme* (turf hut), and a replica of a Viking longhouse. ⊠ *Universitetet, Lars Thørings v. 10* ☎ *77/64–50–00* ⊕ *www.imv.uit.no* ⊠ *NKr 30* ⊘ *Sept. 15–May 14, weekdays 9–3:30, weekends 11–5; May 15–June 14, daily 9–6; June 15–Aug. 14, daily 9–8; Aug. 15–Sept. 14, daily 9–6.*

In an 1830s former customs warehouse, the **Polarmuseet i Tromsø** (Polar Museum) documents the history of the polar region, focusing on Norway's explorers and hunters. ⊠ *Søndre Tollbugt. 11B* ☎ *77/68–43–73* ⊕ *www.polarmuseum.no* ⊠ *NKr 43* ⊘ *Aug. 16–Sept. 15, daily 11–5; Sept. 16–May 15, daily 11–3; May 16–June 15, daily 11–5; June 16–Aug. 15, daily 10–7.*

Ludvik Mack founded **Macks Ølbryggeri** (Mack's Brewery) in 1877 and it is still family-owned. You can take a guided tour at the end of which you're given a beer stein, pin, and a pint of your choice in the Ølhallen pub. Call ahead to reserve a place on the tour. ⊠ *Storgt. 5–13* ☎ *77/ 62–45–00* ⊕ *www.mack.no* ⊠ *NKr 100* ⊘ *Guided tours Mon.–Thurs. noon–4.*

The adventure center **Polaria** examines life in and around the Polar and Barents regions with exhibits on polar travel and Arctic research, and a panoramic film from Svalbard. The aquarium has sea mammals, including seals. ⊠ *Hjarmar Johansens gt. 12* ☎ *77/75–01–00* ⊕ *www. polaria.no* ⊠ *NKr 75* ⊘ *Mid-May–mid-Aug., daily 10–7; mid-Aug.–mid-May, daily noon–5.*

★ **Tromsø Botaniske Hage** (Tromsø Botanic Garden) has plants from the Antarctic and Arctic as well as mountain plants from all over the world. Encompassing four acres, the garden has been designed as a natural landscape, with terraces, slopes, a stream, and a pond. Guides are available by advance arrangement. ⊠ *Tromsø University, Breivika* ☎ *77/64–50–78* ⊕ *www.imv.uit.no/botanisk* ⊠ *Free* ⊘ *Daily, 24 hrs.*

☾ To get a sense of Tromsø's immensity and solitude, take the **Fjellheisen** (cable car) from behind the cathedral up to the mountains, a few minutes out of the city center. **Storsteinen** (Big Rock), 1,386 feet above sea level, has a great city view. ⊠ *Sollivn. 12* ☎ *77/63–87–37* ⊠ *NKr 65* ⊘ *Mar., weekends 10–5; Apr.–Oct., daily 10–5; Oct.–Mar., by appointment.*

Where to Stay & Eat

$$ ✕ **Vertshuset Skarven.** Whitewashing recalls the Greek Islands at this landmark restaurant known for its fish. Sample the fish soup, beef stew, or seal lasagna. The Skarvens Biffhus and Sjømatrestauranten Arctandria

restaurants are in the same building. ⊠ *Strandtorget 1* ☎ *77/60–07–20* ♲ *Reservations essential* ⊟ *AE, DC, MC, V.*

$$–$$$ ⛱ **Comfort Home Hotel With.** This comfortable hotel on the waterfront has a great location. Breakfast and dinner are included in the room price. The ever-popular top floor lounge has skylights. ⊠ *Sjøgt. 35–37, 9257* ☎ *77/68–70–00* ⎙ *77/68–96–16* ⊕ *www.with.no* ➷ *76 rooms* ♺ *Dining room, sauna, Turkish bath, lounge, meeting room* ⊟ *AE, DC, MC, V* ⎮⊙⎮ *MAP.*

$–$$$ ⛱ **Radisson SAS Hotel Tromsø.** You can see splendid views over the Tromsø shoreline at this modern hotel. Rooms are tiny but stylish, and the service is professional and efficient. ⊠ *Sjøgt. 7, 9008* ☎ *77/60–00–00* ⎙ *77/68–54–74* ⊕ *www.radissonsas.com* ➷ *195 rooms, 2 suites* ♺ *Restaurant, pizzeria, sauna, 2 bars, nightclub* ⊟ *AE, DC, MC, V.*

★ **$–$$$** ⛱ **Rica Ishavshotel.** Shaped like a ship, Tromsø's snazziest hotel is right at the harbor and stretches over the sound toward Ishavskatedralen. Inside, polished wood furnishings with brass trim evoke the life of the sea. The breakfast buffet is one of the best in Norway, and even includes vitamins. Guests represent a mixture of business executives, tourists, and those attending scientific conferences. ⊠ *Fr. Langes gt. 2, Box 196, 9252* ☎ *77/66–64–00* ⎙ *77/66–64–44* ⊕ *www.rica.no* ➷ *180 rooms* ♺ *2 restaurants, 2 bars, convention center, meeting rooms* ⊟ *AE, DC, MC, V.*

$–$$ ⛱ **Comfort Hotel Saga.** Centrally located on a pretty town square, this hotel has basic rooms that are loaded with blond wood and warm colors. The restaurant serves affordable, hearty meals. ⊠ *Richard Withs pl. 2* ☎ *77/68–11–80* ⎙ *77/68–33–80* ⊕ *www.sagahotel.com* ➷ *67 rooms* ♺ *Restaurant, cafeteria* ⊟ *AE, DC, MC, V.*

Nightlife

At **Rica Ishavshotel** (⊠ Fr. Langesgt. 2 ☎ 77/66–64–00) you can see some of the best views in the city from the fifth-floor Skibsbroen Bar. Since 1928, polar explorers, Arctic skippers, hunters, whalers, and sealers have been meeting at Mack Brewery's **Ølhallen** (⊠ Storgt. 5 ☎ 77/62–45–80). Rock music and the city's largest selection of beer are at the **Blå Rock Café** (⊠ Strandgt. 14–16 ☎ 77/61–00–20), which has live concerts and DJs on weekends.

One of the city's largest cafés, **Meieriet Café & Storpub** (⊠ Grønnegt. 37/39 ☎ 77/61–36–39) has soups and wok dishes, billiards, backgammon, newspapers, and DJs on weekends. **Victoria Fun Pub/Subsirkus/Amtmandens Datter** (⊠ Grønnegt. 81 ☎ 77/68–49–06), a lively evening entertainment complex, has something for everyone. Subsirkus has bands and attracts a young crowd, while a broader range of ages is found at the English-style Victoria. The smoky Amtmandens Dattar is a mellow Continental café. The University's café and cultural center **DRIV** (⊠ Søndre Tollbod gt. 3 ☎ 77/60–07–76) is in a 1902 quayside building. Concerts, theater, and other cultural events are staged here.

Sports & the Outdoors

DIVING **Dykkersenteret** (⊠ Stakkevollveien 72 ☎ 77/69–66–00 ⊕ www.dykkersenteret.no), the world's northernmost five-star PADI center, sells and rents equipment and gives guided diving tours.

DOGSLEDDING Some 20 km (12 mi) outside the city, **Tromsø Villmarkssenter** (☎ 77/69–60–02 ⊕ www.villmarkssenter.no) organizes winter dogsledding trips, glacier walking, kayaking, summit tours, and Sámi-style dinners, which take place around a campfire inside a *lavvu* (a Sámi tent).

HIKING & WALKING Tromsø has more than 100 km (62 mi) of walking and hiking trails in the mountains above the city. They're reachable by funicular. **TROMSO Troms Turlag -DNT** (☎ 77/68–51–75 ⊕ www.turistforeningen.no) organizes tours and courses and has overnight cabins. For guided mountain and glacier walking, contact **Bo-med-oss** (☎ 77/71–06-92 ⊕ www.bo-med-oss.no) or **Svensby Tursenter** (☎ 77/71–22–25).

HORSEBACK **Holmeslet Gård** (☎ 77/61–9974) has horseback riding, carriage tours, RIDING and sleigh rides.

SKIING Eight minutes away by funicular, **Tromsø Alpine Ski Center** (☎ 77/60–66–80) is a convenient place for downhill skiing. There are also 70 km (43 mi) of cross-country trails, 33 of which are floodlit.

---

en route | The drive from Tromsø to Alta is mostly along the coast. At one point you'll drive along the **Kvænangsfjellet Ridge,** where Kautokeino Sámi spend the summer in turf huts—you might see a few of their reindeer along the way. Thirteen kilometers (8 mi) west of Alteidet you'll pass by **Øksfjordjøkelen,** the only glacier in Norway that calves (separates or breaks) into the sea.

Alta

❽ *409 km (253 mi) north of Tromsø, 217 km (134 mi) from the North Cape.*

Alta, population 17, 020, has three centers—Bossekop, which keeps old trading and market traditions; Elvebakken, in the east, with the airport and harbor; and the city center itself. The borough encompasses the mineral-rich island of Stjernøya, Langfjorden, and fishing villages on the banks of the Altafjord. Alta serves as the transportation, service, trade, research, and education center for the regions of West Finnmark and North Troms. Most travelers spend the night here before ascending to the North Cape.

Northern Europe's biggest canyon is the **Sautso–Alta Canyon,** on the Alta River, where you can go hiking and take riverboat trips and bus tours. At the **Alta Hydro-electric Power Station** you can view the reservoir and concrete dam through a panoramic window. Contact the Destination Alta tourist office (☎ 78/45–77–77) for information.

---

off the beaten path | **ALTA MUSEUM –** It's worth a trek to Hjemmeluft, southwest of the city, to see four groupings of 2,500- to 6,200-year-old prehistoric rock carvings, the largest groupings in northern Europe. The pictographs were discovered in 1973 and form part of the museum, which is a UNESCO's World Heritage Site. Exhibits cover prehistoric Finnmark and local history. The museum café has a stunning view of Altafjord, a souvenir shop, and playground. ⊠ *Altaveien 19* ☎ *78/45–63–30* ⊕ *www.alta.museum.no* 🖾 *NKr 70* ⊙ *May and Sept., daily 9–6; early-June–mid-June and mid-Aug.–late Aug., daily 8–8; mid-June–mid-Aug., daily 8 AM–11 PM; Oct.–May, weekdays 9–3, weekends 11–4.*

Where to Stay

$$–$$$ 🏨 **Rica Hotel Alta.** The decor here is light and airy, from the reflectors on the ceilings of public rooms to the white furniture in the guest rooms. ⊠ *Lokkevn. 1, 9501* ☎ *78/48–27–00* 🖷 *78/48–27–77* ⊕ *www.rica.no* 🛏 *154 rooms* ♨ *2 restaurants, cable TV, sauna, 2 bars, lobby lounge, nightclub, meeting room* ⊟ *AE, DC, MC, V.*

Sports & the Outdoors

On the banks of Alta River, **Alta Friluftspark AS Leisure Park** (☎ 78/43–33–78 ⊕ www.alta-friluftspark.no) has snowmobile safaris, riverboat trips, fishing, reindeer racing, dog-sled rides, and Sámi lavvu for overnight stays. It also has a hotel, the Alta Igloo.

DOGSLEDDING Whether half-, full-day, or longer excursions, sled dog tours are a classic winter activity on Finnmarksvidda. Contact **Canyon Huskies** (☎ 78/43–33–06 ⊕ www.canyonhuskies.no), **HolmenHundesenter** (☎ 78/43–66–45 ⊕ www.holmenhundesenter.no), or **Parken Gård Husky** (☎ 78/48–23–13 ⊕ hjem.sol.no/arnekar).

FARM VISITS One of the first Finnmark farms, **Altafjord Camping** is now a regional farm museum that was occupied by German soldiers during World War II. The battleship *Sharnehorst* was anchored nearby. Sámi reindeer herders, who have their summer settlements in Langfjordbotn, have frequent contact with the farm. ⊠ *Hwy. E6, 80 km (50 mi) west of Alta, 3 km (2 mi) from Troms county border* ☎ *78/43–28–24* ⊙ *June–Sept., daily. Call for hrs.*

FISHING **AKU Finnmark** (☎ 78/43–48–40 ⊕ www.aku-finnmark.no) leads deep-sea, salmon, and other types of fishing trips. You can go on a fishing trip on the famed river *Bubbelen* (The Bubble), which is actually an underground spring; contact **Altafjord Adventures and Camping** (☎ 78/43–28–24 ⊕ www.altafjord-camping.no) to organize an expedition. They also offer outings for deep-sea fishing below glaciers. You can also rent boats and fishing tackle here.

Hammerfest

❾ *145 km (90 mi) north of Alta.*

The world's northernmost town is one of the most widely visited and oldest places in northern Norway. "Hammerfest" means "mooring place" and refers to the natural harbor formed by the crags in the mountain. In 1891 the residents of Hammerfest, tired of the months-long night that winter always brought, decided to brighten the situation. They purchased a generator from Thomas Edison, and Hammerfest thus became the first city in Europe to have electric street lamps.

The Royal and Ancient Polar Bear Society was founded by two businessmen whose goal was to share the town's history as a center for hunting and commerce. Exhibits depict aspects of Arctic hunts. ⊠ *Town Hall basement* ☎ *78/41–31–00* ⊕ *www.hammerfest-turist.no/polarbear/* ⊠ *NKr 20* ⊙ *Call for hrs.*

Although it covers Finnmark's history since the Stone Age, the **Museum of Post-War Reconstruction** mainly focuses on World War II, when Finnmark's population was forced by the German army to evacuate, and the county was burnt to the ground as part of a "scorched earth" policy. Through photographs, videos and sound effects, the museum recounts the residents' struggle to rebuild their lives. The exhibition includes authentic rooms that were built in caves after the evacuation, as well as huts and postwar homes. ⊠ *Kirkegt. 21* ☎ *78/42–26–30* ⊕ *www. museumsnett.no/gjenreisningsmuseet* ⊙ *Jan.–June 15, daily 11–2; June 16–Aug. 24, daily 9–5; Aug. 25–Dec. 31, daily 11–2.*

On Mount Salen, **Mikkelgammen** (☎ 78/41–21–85 ⊕ www. mikkelgammen.no) is a traditional turf hut where you can learn about Sámi culture and traditions. Gather around a campfire for a meal of *bidos,* a Sámi reindeer dish. *Joik,* a kind of singing–chanting, is performed, and stories are told. You can also participate in reindeer herding in winter. Contact the tourist office for information on both programs.

Where to Stay & Eat

$$ ✕🔲 **Rica Hotel Hammerfest.** Guest rooms here are basic and small, but fairly comfortable. The restaurant serves hearty local dishes. ⊠ *Sørøygt. 15* ☎ *78/41–13–33* 🖶 *78/41–13–11* ⊕ *www.rica.no* ➴ *48 rooms* ⌂ *Restaurant, pizzeria, sauna, bar, convention center* 🖃 *AE, DC, MC, V.*

Honningsvåg

⑩ *130 km (80 mi) east of Hammerfest.*

Honningsvåg was completely destroyed at the end of World War II, when the Germans burned everything as they retreated. The town's location and infrastructure have since made it one of the most important harbors in northern Norway.

The **Nordkappmuseet** (North Cape Museum), on the third floor of Nordkapphuset (North Cape House), documents the history of the fishing industry in the region as well as the history of tourism at the North Cape. You can learn how the trail of humanity stretches back 10,000 years and about the development of society and culture in this region. ⊠ *Fiskerivn. 4* ☎ *78/47–28–33* ⊕ *www.museumsnett.no/ nordkappmuseet* 🎟 *NKr 20* ☉ *Call for hrs.*

Many people make an 18-km (11 mi) round-trip hike to **Knivskjelodden** (Crooked Knife), Europe's northernmost point. It has a spectacular view toward the North Cape Plateau. You can write your name in the hiking association's minute book and buy a diploma attesting to your visit.

Where to Stay & Eat

$$ ✕🔲 **Rica Hotel Honningsvå.** Right on the harbor, the town's best hotel has reasonably priced rooms. They're bright and cheerful, decorated in yellow and light woods. Bryggen Restaurant ($$) is a good choice for traditional food. ⊠ *Vågen 1, 9750* ☎ *78/47–23–33* 🖶 *78/47–33–79* ⊕ *www.rica.no* ➴ *42 rooms, 4 suites* ⌂ *Restaurant, bar* 🖃 *AE, DC, MC, V.*

Nordkapp

⑪ *34 km (21 mi) from Honningsvåg.*

On your journey to the Nordkapp (North Cape), you'll see an incredible treeless tundra, with crumbling mountains and sparse dwarf plants. The sub-Arctic environment is very vulnerable, so don't disturb the plants. Walk only on marked trails and don't remove stones, leave car marks, make campfires, or remove stones. Because the roads are closed in winter, the only access is from the tiny fishing village of Skarsvåg via Sno-Cat, a thump-and-bump ride that's as unforgettable as the desolate view.

The contrast between this near-barren territory and **Nordkapphallen** (North Cape Hall), the tourist center, is striking. Blasted into the interior of the plateau, the building is housed in a cave and includes an ecumenical chapel, a souvenir shop, and a post office. Exhibits trace the history of the cape, from Richard Chancellor, an Englishman who drifted around it and named it in 1533, to Oscar II, king of Norway and Sweden, who climbed to the top of the plateau in 1873. Celebrate your pilgrimage to the Nordkapp at Café Kompasset, Restaurant Kompasset, or at the Grotten Bar coffee shop. ⊠ *Nordkapplatået* ☎ *78/ 47–68–60* 🎟 *Entrance to the hall NKr 175* ⊕ *www.visitnorthcape.no* ☉ *Call for hrs.*

Sports & the Outdoors

BIRD SAFARIS **Gjesvær Turistsenter** (☎ 78/47–57–73 ⊕ www.birdsafari.com) organizes bird safaris and deep-sea fishing. **Nordkapp Reiseliv** (☎ 78/47–70–30 ⊕ www.northcape.no) books adventures and activities including bird safaris, deep-sea fishing, boat excursions, and winter expeditions.

DIVING Scuba-dive at the top of Europe with **North Cape Adventures** (☎ 78/ 47–22–22 ⊕ www.northcapeadventures.com), which also provides deep-sea rafting, kayaking, ski and guided tours, and bike rentals.

RAFTING Deep-sea rafting is as exhilarating as it is beautiful. Among the tours offered is a three-hour trip to the North Cape. Call **Nordkapp Safari** (☎ 78/ 47–52–33).

Trondheim & the North Cape A to Z

AIR TRAVEL

CARRIERS SAS, Norwegian, Widerøe, Arctic Air, Finnair, and Braathens are the major carriers offering extensive connections throughout northern Norway. Widerøe flies to 19 destinations in the region, including Honningsvåg, the airport closest to the North Cape.
🖪 **Arctic Air** ☎ 78/98-77-01 ⊕ www.arctic.no. **Braathens** ☎ 67/59-70-00 ⊕ www. braathens.no. **Finnair** ☎ 81/00-11-00 in Oslo ⊕ www.finnair.com. **Norwegian** ☎ 815-21-815. **SAS** ☎ 815/20-400. **Widerøe** ☎ 810/01-200.

AIRPORTS

Trondheim's Værnes Airport is 32 km (21 mi) northeast of the city. With the exception of Harstad, all cities in northern Norway are served by airports less than 5 km (3 mi) from the center of town. Tromsø is a crossroads for air traffic between northern and southern Norway and is served by Braathens, SAS, and Widerøe. Honningsvåg is served by Widerøe.
🖪 **Honningsvåg** ☎ 78/47-29-92. **Tromsø Airport** ☎ 77/64-84-00. **Trondheim Værnes Airport** ☎ 74/84-30-00.

BOAT & FERRY TRAVEL

Hurtigruten (the coastal express boat, which goes to 35 ports from Bergen to Kirkenes) stops at Trondheim, southbound at St. Olav's Pier, Quay 16, northbound at Pier 1, Quay 7. Other stops between Trondheim and the North Cape include Bodø, Stamsund and Svolvær (Lofotens), Sortland (Vesterålen), Harstad, Tromsø, Hammerfest, and Honningsvåg.

For travel on the *Hurtigruten* between any harbors, it is possible to buy tickets on the boats. OVDS, Ofotens og Vesterålens Dampskibsselskap, in partnership with TFDS (Troms Fylkes Dampskibsselskap), operates the Coastal Express ferries and express boats that serve many towns in the region.

Getting to the Lofoten Islands is easiest and most enjoyable by taking the *Hurtigruten* from Bodø or another coastal port of call.
🖪 **Hurtigruten-local ferry information** ☎ 77/64-82-00 ⊕ www.hurtigruten.com. **OVDS** ☎ 75/54-80-30. **TFDS** ✉ Tromsø ☎ 77/64-81-00 ✉ Trondheim ☎ 73/51-51-20.

BUS TRAVEL

Bus 135 (Østerdalsekspress) runs overnight from Oslo to Trondheim via Røros. Buses also connect Bergen, Molde, and Ålesund with Trondheim.

Nor-Way Bussekspress can help you put together a bus journey to destinations in the North. The Ekspress 2000 travels regularly among Oslo, Kautokeino, Alta, Nordkapp, and Hammerfest.

All local Trondheim buses stop at the Munkegata–Dronningens Gate intersection. Some routes end at the bus terminal at Trondheim Sentralstasjon.

North of Bodø and Narvik (a five-hour bus ride from Bodø), buses go virtually everywhere, but they don't go often. Get a comprehensive bus schedule from a tourist office or travel agent before making plans. Local bus companies include Saltens Bilruter, Ofotens Bilruter, Tromsbuss, Midttuns Busser, Finnmark Fylkesrederi og Ruteselskap and Ekspress 2000. ⓘ **Ekspress 2000** ✉ Alta ☎ 78/44-40-90. **Finnmark Fylkesrederi og Ruteselskap** ☎ 78/40-70-00 ⊕ www.ffr.no. **Lofoten (Nordtraffik)** ☎ 76/11-11-11. **Midttuns Busser** Tromsø ☎ 77/67-27-87. **Nor-Way Bussekspress** ☎ 815/44-444. **Ofotens Bilruter** ✉ Narvik ☎ 76/92-35-00. **Tromsbuss** Tromsø ☎ 77/67-75-00 ⊕ www.tromsbuss.no. **Trondheim Sentralstasjon** ☎ 72/57-20-20. **Saltens Bilruter** ✉ Bodø ☎ 75/55-22-10 ⊕ www.saltensbil.no.

CAR RENTALS

Book a rental car as far in advance as possible. There's no better way to see the Lofoten and Vesterålen islands than by car. Nordkapp (take the plane to Honningsvåg) is another excursion best made by car. ⓘ **Local Agencies Avis Bilutleie** ☎ 77/61-58-50. **Budget Bilutleie** ☎ 73/94-10-25.

CAR TRAVEL

Trondheim is about 500 km (310 mi) from Oslo: a seven- to eight-hour drive. Speed limits are 80 kph (50 mph) much of the way. The two alternatives are E6 through Gudbrandsdalen or Route 3 through Østerdalen. It's 727 km (450 mi) from Trondheim to Bodø on Route E6, which goes all the way to Kirkenes. There's an NKr 30 toll on E6 just east of Trondheim. The motorway toll also covers the NKr 11 toll (6 AM–10 PM) for cars entering the downtown area. Anyone who makes it to the North Cape sans tour bus will be congratulated with a NKr 150 toll.

The best way to see the Lofoten islands is by car, since bus service is often limited and there is much to see. The main tourist office in Svolvær can point you to local rental agencies, whose rates tend to be quite high. If you plan to stay in one village for a few days, you can rent a bicycle to visit the neighboring villages that are short distances from your base.

ROAD
CONDITIONS

Most roads in northern Norway are quite good, although there are always narrow and winding stretches, especially along fjords. Distances are formidable. Route 17—the *Kystriksvegen* (Coastal Highway) from Namsos to Bodø—is an excellent alternative to E6. Getting to Tromsø and the North Cape involves additional driving on narrower roads off E6. In winter, near-blizzard conditions and icy roads sometimes make it necessary to drive in a convoy.

EMERGENCIES

In Tromsø, Svaneapoteket pharmacy is open daily from 8:30 to 4:30 and from 6 to 9. In Trondheim, Svaneapoteket pharmacy is open weekdays from 8:30 to 3 and Saturday from 9 to 3. ⓘ **Svaneapoteket** ✉ Kongensgt. 14b Tromsø ☎ 73/52-23-01. **Svaneapoteket** ✉ Fr. Langesgt. 9 Trondheim ☎ 77-60-14-80.

TAXIS

ⓘ **Bodø Taxi** ☎ 75/60-18-99. **Nordland Taxi, Narvik** ☎ 76/94-65-00. **Tromsø** ☎ 77/60-30-00. **Trøndertaxi** ✉ Trondheim ☎ 73/90-90-73.

TRAIN TRAVEL

The Dovrebanen has frequent departures daily on the Oslo–Trondheim route. Trains leave from Oslo S Station for the seven- to eight-hour journey. Trondheim is the gateway to the north, and two trains run daily in each direction on the 11-hour Trondheim–Bodø route. The Nordlandsbanen has three departures daily in each direction on the Bodø–Trondheim route, an 11-hour journey. The *Ofotbanen* has two departures daily in each direction on the Stockholm–Narvik route, a 21-hour journey.

VISITOR INFORMATION

Bodø-based Nordland Reiseliv publishes a helpful holiday guide and a guide to interesting tours of the region. Their "Footprints in the North" pamphlet is a cultural history of North Norway and Namdalen, listing 103 sites. Finnmark Reiseliv publishes a detailed annual guide to Finnmark.

Tourist Information Alta (Destinasjon Alta) ☎ 78/45-77-77 ⊕ www.destinasjonalta. no. **Bodø (Destinasjon Bodø)** ✉ Sjøgt. 3, 8001 ☎ 75/54-80-00 ⊕ www.visitbodo.com. **Finnmark Reiseliv** ☎ 78/44-00-20 ⊕ www.visitnorthcape.com. **Hamarøy (Kingdom of Hamsun)** ☎ 75/77-18-90 ⊕ www.hamsuns-rike.no. **Hammerfest** ✉ 9600 ☎ 78/41-21-85 ⊕ www.hammerfest-turist.no. **Harstad** ☎ 77/01-89-89 ⊕ www. destinasjonharstad.no. **Lofoten (Destination Lofoten)** ✉ 8301 Svolvær ☎ 76/06-98-00 ⊕ www.lofoten.info. **Mo i Rana (Polarsirkelen Reiseliv** ✉ 8601 Mo ☎ 75/13-92-00 ⊕ www.arctic-circle.no. **Narvik (Narvik Aktiv)** ☎ 76/94-33-09 ⊕ www.narvikinfo.no. **Nordkapp** ✉ Fiskerivn. 4 Honningsvåg ☎ 78/47-70-30 ⊕ www.northcape.no. **Nordland Reiseliv** ☎ 75/54-52-00 ⊕ www.visitnordland.no. **Tromsø** ✉ Storgt. 61-63, 9253 ☎ 77/61-00-00 ⊕ www.destinasjontromso.no. **Trondheim** ✉ Munkegt. 19, Torget 7001 ☎ 73/80-76-60 ⊕ www.visittrondheim.com. **Vesterålen** ✉ Kjøpmannsgata 2 8401 Sortland ☎ 76/11-14-80 ⊕ www.visitvesteralen.com.

SÁMILAND TO SVALBARD & THE FINNISH-RUSSIAN CONNECTION

Europe's only ancient indigenous people, the Sámi, live on the rooftop of the Continent, atop the vast, windswept Finnmarksvidda. They recognize no national boundaries, and Sámiland, formerly called Lapland, stretches from the Kola Peninsula in Russia through Finland, Sweden, and Norway. The majority of Sámi, some 50,000, live in Norway. Norwegian Sámiland is centered around the communities of Karasjok and Kautokeino, in the Finnmark region.

The traditional symbol of the Sámi is the reindeer herder, and about a third still live this way. Many also earn their living from fishing. Most Sámi still live in traditional tents and dress in colorful costumes, although the most visible evidence of their lifestyle is roadside souvenir stands and tourist exhibits. As you'd expect, the Sámi have their own language, music, art, and handicrafts. The desolate expanses and treeless tundra make an inspiring trekking destination—you're almost guaranteed an encounter with reindeer. Take time to experience this traditional culture, whether it's expressed through the Sámis' *lavvus* (tents made of reindeer skin), their distinctive songs, or their cuisine, rich in reindeer and wild salmon dishes.

Numbers in the margin correspond to points of interest on the Trondheim and the North map.

Kautokeino–Guovdageaidnu

▶ ⑫ *129 km (80 mi) southeast of Alta.*

Kautokeino, with 3,000 inhabitants, is in the heart of Finnmarksvidda (the Finnmark mountain plateau). Because of such institutions as the Nordic Sámi Institute, Sámi Theater, and Sámi College, it has become the center for Sámi culture, research, and education.

MÁZE ZION – A mountain church stood here from 1721 to 1768, but only ruins remain. Headstones in the cemetery have names written in an old form of Sámi, in which special characters are used for each name. ✉ *Hwy. 93, en route to Alta from Kautokeino.*

PIKEFOSSEN FALLS – These beautiful falls on the Alta River between Kautokeino and Máze were named after a girl ("pike" means girl) who mysteriously drowned here. If you stay in the area overnight in a Sámi tent, legend has it that you may hear the girl's screams in the falls.

Where to Stay

$–$$ 🏨 **Norlandia Kautokeino Hotel.** This standard hotel has comfortable rooms. The restaurant serves Sámi dishes, Norwegian home fare, and international dishes. ✉ *9520 Kautokeino* ☎ *78/48–62–05* 🖷 *78/48–67–01* ⊕ *www.norlandia.no* ⤶ *50 rooms* ⚡ *Restaurant, sauna, bar* ⊟ *AE, DC, MC, V* ⊘ *Closed mid-Dec.–Mar.*

Nightlife & the Arts

Traditional Sámi culture is celebrated at Kautokeino's longstanding annual **Easter Festival** (☎ 78/48–71–00 ⊕ www.saami-easterfestival.org), which has craft exhibits as well as *joik*, a haunting kind of a cappella solo. Joik are usually songs of praise for nature. The festival also includes more recent cultural developments, including large Sámi weddings, reindeer races, concerts, theatrical performances, skiing, fishing competitions, and snowmobile rallies.

Shopping

Inside what was once a secret military facility, **Juhls' Silver Gallery** (☎ 78/48–61–89), home of Finnmark's first silversmith, carries the best selection of contemporary Sámi art—everything from paintings and posters to sculpture. Part Frank Lloyd Wright and part Buddhist temple, the interiors have been designed and decorated by the Danish-German Frank and Regine Juhls. Don't miss the ornamental ceiling in the Afghan room. It was made to honor the Sámis.

Sports & the Outdoors

FISHING Kautokeino has an abundance of lakes available for year-round fishing. Contact the **Kautokeino Environmental Office** (☎ 78/48–71–00).

HIKES & OUTINGS The plains and forests around Kautokeino make it excellent terrain for hiking year-round. In fact, it has one of the largest areas of untouched nature in northern Europe. The **Nordkalott Route,** an 800-km (500-mi) trail with ends in Kvikkjokk, Sweden, and Sulitjelma, Norway, cuts through Kautokeino.

DNT, the Norwegian Mountain Touring Association, organizes special activities in the region. Contact the **Kautokeino Environmental Office** (☎ 78/48–71–00). The **Suohpatjávri Nature and Cultural Trail,** 7 km (4½ mi) south of Kautokeino, is popular. Along the 4½-km (2¾-mi) marked trail, there's a picnic area, a *jordgamme* (earth-and-turf hut), and a *siedi,* (sacrificial stone), which is a protected cultural monument.

Karasjok–Kárásjoga

🔞 *178 km (110 mi) northeast of Kautokeino.*

A Sámiland crossroads as well as the Sámi capital, Karasjok has 2,900 residents and is 18 km (11 mi) from the Finnish border. Many of the most significant Sámi institutions are here, including Sámetinget, the Sámi parliament; De Sámiske Samlinger, the Sámi Collections; and the Sámi

Kunstnersenter, Sámi Artists' Center. If you're heading to the North Cape, Karasjok is a natural place to stop and take in the stunning scenery.

★ The **Sámiid Vuorká Dávvirat–De sámiske sáminger** (Sámi Collections) is an indoor and open-air museum dedicated to Sámi culture and history. It emphasizes the arts, reindeer herding, and the status of women in the Sámi community. There are also examples of the hunting pits used to catch wild reindeer. ⊠ *Museumsgt. 17* ☎ *78/46–99–50* ✆ *NKr 25* ☉ *Early June–mid-Aug., Mon.–Sat. 9–6, Sun. 10–6; mid-Aug.–Oct. and Apr.–early June, weekdays 9–3, weekends 10–3; Nov.–Mar., weekdays 9–3, weekends noon–3.*

Karasjok Opplevelser A/S (☎ 78/46–88–10) organizes Sámiland adventures. These may include dining in a lavvu, visiting a Sámi camp, listening to Sámi songs, and heading to Basevuovdi (Helligskogen, or the Sacred Forest) for gold panning. From late fall to early spring you can go **reindeer sledding**. A guide takes you out on a wooden sled tied to a couple of unwieldy reindeer, and you clop through the barren, snow-covered scenery of Finnmark.

The **Sámi Artists' Center** holds 10 temporary exhibitions of contemporary and traditional Sámi visual art. Guided tours must be arranged in advance. ⊠ *Jeagilvármádii 54* ☎ *78/46–90–02* ✆ *Free* ☉ *Mid-June–mid-Aug., daily 10–5; mid-Aug.–mid-June, weekdays 10–3, Sun. noon–5.*

The **Sápmi** theme park showcases the everyday life, mythology, food traditions, and art and crafts of the Sámi. Experience first-hand the *Siida*, which are the Sámi settlements. You can also enjoy a Sámi meal and take home a handmade silver souvenir. ⊠ *Porsangervn. 1* ☎ *78/ 46–88–00* ⊕ *www.sapmi.no* ☉ *Mon.–Wed., Fri. 10–6, Thurs. 10–8, Sat. noon–9, Sun. noon–5.*

Opened in 2000, the stunning **Sametinget** (Sámi Parliament; ☎ 78/ 74–00–00) building blends ancient Sámi forms with Scandinavian modernism. Inside, the walls are covered with Sámi art.

Where to Stay

★ **$$–$$$** ✕🏨 **Rica Hotel Karasjok.** Looking like a cozy ski chalet, this hotel has bright, warm rooms accented with blond woods, and blues and reds. The highly regarded Sámi restaurant, Storgammen, is in a *gamme* (turf hut). The kitchen produces centuries-old Sámi dishes, including reindeer in lingonberry sauce, cooked over an open fire. ⊠ *Porsangervn. 1, 9730 Karasjok* ☎ *78/46–74–00* 🖷 *78/46–68–02* ⊕ *www.rica.no* ⇙ *56 rooms* ⇘ *2 restaurants, gym, sauna, bar, nightclub, meeting rooms* 🖃 *AE, DC, MC, V.*

Sports & the Outdoors

DOGSLEDDING
Sven Engholm leads dogsledding tours in winter. You can lead your own dog sled, accompany one on skis, or just go along for the ride. Engholm also organizes gold panning, fishing trips, and wilderness tours. Dine in a gamme (turf hut), or rent a cabin. In summer you can hike with the huskies. Contact **Engholms Husky** (☎ 78/46–71–66 ⊕ www.engholm.no) for information.

HIKING &
FISHING
Finnmarksvidda, the plateau between Alta and Karasjok, has marked trails with places to stay overnight in lodges, cabins, lavvu, and tents. Fishing and canoe trips can be organized with a guide during July and August. Rather than hike to the fishing lakes, you can take an airplane or a helicopter: contact **Nils Rolf Johnsen** (⊠ Svenskebakken 35, 9730 Karasjok ☎ 78/46–63–02), who handles fishing trips and wilderness adventures on the Finnmarksvidda Plains, or **Karasjok Opplevelser A/S** (☎ 78/46–88–10).

Shopping

Sámi crafts, particularly handmade knives, are a specialty in this area. **Samelandssenteret** (☎ 78/46–71–55), a shopping center, has lots of stores selling northern crafts. See how an authentic Sámi knife is made at **Knivsmed Strømeng A/S** (☎ 78/46–71–05).

Kirkenes

14 *320 km (200 mi) northeast of Karasjok.*

At its very top, Norway hooks over Finland and touches Russia for 122 km (75 mi). The towns in east Finnmark have a more heterogeneous population than those in the rest of the country. A century ago, during hard times in Finland, many industrious Finns settled in this region, and their descendants keep the language alive.

A good way to visit here is to fly to Kirkenes and then explore the region by car. Kirkenes itself has 7,000 residents. The town was built up around Sydvaranger, an iron ore mining company that operated until 1996. Today, the town's industries include tourism and ship repair.

During World War II, Kirkenes was bombed more than 300 times—only Malta was bombed more—and virtually all buildings had to be rebuilt. Many residents sought cover in subterranean tunnels dug for use as bomb shelters. One of them, **Andersgrotta,** is open to the public every summer for tours (special arrangements can be made the rest of the year). The tour includes a film covering the use of the shelter during the war. ⊠ *Tellef Dahls gt.* ☎ *78/99–25–44* ☜ *NKr 60* ⏱ *Call for opening hrs.*

Dedicated to the works of the Sámi artist John Andras Savio (1902–38), the **Savio Museum** showcases his woodcutting, watercolors, and oils. Savio is best known for depicting Sámi life. The museum also has changing exhibits of contemporary Sámi art. ⊠ *Førstevannslia* ☎ *78/99–48–83.*

Wedged between Russia and Finland, **Pasvikdalen** is a valley known for its flora and fauna: Norway's largest bear population shares the valley with species of plants and birds that can't be found anywhere else in the country.

off the beaten path

ST. GEORGS KAPELL (St. Georg's Chapel) – The only Russian Orthodox chapel in Norway lies 45 km (28 mi) west of Kirkenes. This tiny building is where the Orthodox Skolt-sámi had their summer encampment. An annual outdoor mass is held the last Sunday in August, weather permitting.

Where to Stay

$$–$$$ ⌂ **Rica Arctic Hotel.** In the center of Kirkenes, this hotel is the perfect choice for outdoor sports enthusiasts. It's at the edge of the world's largest forest, stretching all the way from Pasvikdalen to the Bering Strait. The spacious rooms are pleasant, with white-painted furniture and floral and light-color fabrics. ⊠ *Kongensgt. 1–3, 9900* ☎ *78/99–29–29* ☒ *78/99–11–59* ⊕ *www.rica.no* ☞ *80 rooms* ⚒ *Restaurant, pool, gym, sauna, bar, convention center* ☰ *AE, DC, MC, V.*

Storskog

15 *About 15 km (9 mi) east of Kirkenes.*

Just east of Kirkenes is Storskog, for many years the only official land crossing between Norway and Russia. The tiny village of **Grense Jakobselv,** 50 km (30 mi) east of Kirkenes along the Russian border, is where King Oscar II built a chapel in 1869 as a protest against constant Russian encroachment in the area. Salmon river fishing is good and several beaches are popular.

off the beaten path

ØVRE PASVIK NATIONAL PARK – The southernmost part of Finnmark, about 118 km (73 mi) south of Kirkenes, is Øvre Pasvik national park, a narrow tongue of land tucked between Finland and Russia. This subarctic evergreen forest is the western end of Siberia's taiga and supports many unique varieties of flora.

Svalbard

🔟 *640 km (400 mi) north of the North Cape.*

The islands of the Svalbard archipelago, the largest of which is Spitsbergen, have only officially been part of Norway since 1920. This wild, fragile area lies halfway between the North Pole and the mainland. Icelandic texts from 1194 contain the first known mention of Svalbard. After the Dutch navigator Willem Barents visited Svalbard in 1596, whaling and winter-long hunting and trapping were virtually the only human activities here for the next 300 years.

In 1906 John M. Longyear established the first coal mine and named the area Longyear City. Now called Longyearbyen, Svalbard's capital has a population of 1,200. Surprisingly, it's a diverse community with excellent accommodations and restaurants. There's an abundance of organized exotic wilderness activities and tours such as dogsledding, snowmobiling, skiing, ice caving, igloo camping, and fossil hunting.

Svalbard has its share of sports and cultural events, too. Famous musicians and artists visit Svalbard for exhibitions and concerts. The Polar Jazz Festival takes place at the end of January, followed by the lively Sunfestival in early March. The Svalbard Ski Marathon is held late in April and early May, and the Spitsbergen Marathon in early June.

Sixty percent of Svalbard is covered by glaciers; plants and other vegetation cover only 6%; the rest of the surface is just rocks. Remote and isolated, the only way to fly in is from Tromsø. Only a few cruise ships and other boats land here, and no roads connect the communities on Svalbard—people travel between them with snowmobiles.

The archipelago's climate is surprisingly mild, with periods of summer fog. The small amount of precipitation makes Svalbard a sort of Arctic desert. Permafrost covers all of Svalbard, which means only the top meter of earth thaws in summer. Because it's so far north, it has four months of the midnight sun (as well as four months of polar night).

Although they spend most of their time on ice floes, polar bears can be encountered anywhere on Svalbard because they give birth to their cubs on land. They are a genuine threat, so don't travel outside the settlements without an experienced guide.

Once a pig farm, the **Svalbard Museum** profiles the early trapper period, various Svalbard expeditions, the war years, and the biology of the islands. Learn about the history of mining on the first floor, where you can change into a miner's outfit and crawl into a copy of a mine tunnel. ✉ *Longyearbyen* ☎ *79/02–13–84* ⏲ *Call for hrs.*

Mine No. 3, the last mine in Svalbard where coal was extracted using traditional methods, ended production in 1996. Guided visits can be arranged throughout the year. The mine is just outside of Longyearbyen. Contact **Svalbard Wildlife Service** (☎ 79/02–56–60).

Where to Stay & Eat

$$$–$$$$ ✕ **Huset.** Considered one of Longyearbyen's best restaurants, Huset serves fine Norwegian food in an elegant but relaxed dining room. A wintery Kåre Tveter painting of Svalbard graces one wall. Dramatically covering another wall is the snowy skin of a polar bear that wandered into Longyearbyen in 1983 and was shot. Try tartare of arctic char, grouse, or reindeer dishes. Popular with locals as well as visitors, the restaurant is often fully booked. ✉ *Longyearbyen* ☎ *79/02–25–00* ⌖ *Reservations essential* 🖃 *AE, DC, MC, V.*

$$–$$$$ ✕🖎 **Spitsbergen Funken Hotell.** This distinguished hotel is known for the relics that fill it as well as for the luxury and high level of service its staff provides. Each room is tastefully and elegantly decorated in dark woods and richly colored textiles. You can relax on a red burnished-leather couch by the library's roaring fireplace. At the Funktionærmessen Restaurant, dine on interpretations of local cuisine that include reindeer spring rolls. In cooperation with Spitsbergen Travel, the hotel offers such activities as snowmobiling, dog sledding, glacier walking, hiking, and boat trips. ✉ *9171, Longyearbyen* ☎ *79/02–62–00* 🖷 *79/02–62–01* ⊕ *www.spitra.no* ⟿ *88 rooms* ⌖ *Restaurant, sauna, bar, meeting rooms* 🖃 *AE, DC, MC, V.*

$$$ 🖎 **Radisson SAS Polar Hotel, Spitsbergen.** The world's northernmost Radisson SAS hotel excels in warm service and style. Every room is understated and elegant, with light walls, warm colors, and blond and dark woods. An enormous window in the dining and bar area provides a view of Mount Hjorthavnfjellet across the waters of the Icefjord. In summer you can watch the sun cross from one side of the mountain at dusk to the other at dawn. The Restaurant Nansen's menu includes seal and white grouse. Svalbard Polar Travel at the hotel can arrange tours and activities around the area. ✉ *Box 544, 9171 Longyearbyen* ☎ *79/02–34–50* 🖷 *79/02–34–51* ⊕ *www.radissonsas.com* ⟿ *99 rooms, 5 suites* ⌖ *Restaurant, sauna, bar, meeting rooms* 🖃 *AE, DC, MC, V.*

Arts

To get a sense of frosty Svalbard during other times of the year, head to **Gallery Svalbard.** One of Norway's most admired artists, Kåe Tveter, donated 40 illustrations to the gallery. The "Arctic Light Over Svalbard" slide show is an eye-opening presentation of what makes this area special. Centuries-old Arctic maps and books fill an adjacent exhibition room. ☎ *79/02–23–40.*

Shopping

For such a remote and small town, Longyearbyen has a surprising number of spots for souvenir shopping, including the **Lompensenteret** (79/02–36–53) shopping center. **Svalbardbutikken** (79/02–25–20) is a group of stores selling groceries, wine and liquor, cameras, clothes, souvenirs, and other things you may need. Head to **Skandinavisk Høyfjellsutstyr** (☎79/02–32–90) for sportswear and clothes for the outdoors.

Sámiland to Svalbard A to Z

AIR TRAVEL

Braathens and SAS service the Longyearbyen Airport.
🛪 **Braathens** (79/02–45–00). **Longyearbyen Airport** ☎ 79/02–38–00. **SAS** (79/02–16–50).

CAR TRAVEL

Most roads in northern Norway are quite good, although there are always narrow and winding stretches, especially along fjords. Distances between towns are often very big. Route E6 is the main highway that winds all the way to the north of the country, although getting to Tromsø and the North Cape involves additional driving on narrower roads off E6. In winter, near-blizzard conditions and icy roads sometimes make it necessary to drive in a convoy.

CRUISE TRAVEL

Hurtigruten, the coastal express boat, now cruises from Tromsø to Svalbard, dipping down to the North Cape afterward. Contact Bergen Line for information.

⚑ Bergen Line Travel Agents ✉ 405 Park Ave., New York, NY 10022 ☎ 212/319-1300.

TOURS

BOAT TOURS **Cavzo Safari** is a riverboat excursion from Máze to Alta Dam that includes guided tours, listening to joik in a lavvu, and traditional dishes such as *bidos,* which is made with reindeer meat.

⚑ Cavzo Safari ☎ 78/48-75-88.

TOURS IN & AROUND KIRKENES Several regional companies offer specialized tours in and around Kirkenes. Grenseland–Sovjetreiser focuses on the Barents Region, with nature, culture, and adventure tours in northwest Russia. Kirkenes Opplevelser's salmon and crab fishing boat expeditions span the region from the Kirkenes fjord to the Arctic Ocean. Bugøynes Opplevelser A/S visits a fishing community on the Arctic Ocean, where Kamchatka crab is served. Their tours include trying out an Arctic sauna. Neiden Fjellstue plans deep-sea, ice fishing, and snowmobile trips; staying in mountain cabins; and dining and entertainment in a lavvu.

⚑ Bugøynes Opplevelser A/S ☎ 78/99-03-75. **Destination Kirkenes** ☎ 78/99-80-69. **Grenseland–Sovjetreiser** ☎ 78/99-25-01. **Kirkenes Opplevelser** ☎ 91/53-62-31. **Neiden Fjellstue** ☎ 78/99-61-41.

TOURS IN SVALBARD Svalbard's environment is fragile, and polar bears are dangerous as well as numerous (there are 2,000 to 3,000 in and around Svalbard). For these reasons, heading into the wilderness should only be done on an organized tour with an experienced guide.

Spitsbergen Travel (SPITRA) organizes exciting activities and tours including glacier walks, horseback riding, dogsledding, and arctic barbecues. Svalbard Polar Travel (SPOT) handles skiing, dogsledding, and snowmobile tours in winter and spring cruises around Spitsbergen and the northwest coast in spring and summer.

For winter camping trips, Basecamp Spitsbergen sets you up with your very own Alaskan husky dogsledding team—or a snowmobile. In summer, the company operates hikes, trips with packdogs or packhorses, charter boat tours, and camping excursions. Svalbard Wildlife Service organizes tours into the Arctic wilderness and day trips in the Longyearbyen area. The day trips may include mine visits, glacier walks, and boating.

⚑ Basecamp Spitsbergen ☎ 79/02-46-00. **Spitsbergen Travel (SPITRA)** ☎ 79/02-61-00. **Svalbard Polar Travel (SPOT)** ☎ 79/02-34-00. **Svalbard Wildlife Service** ☎ 79/02-56-60.

VISITOR INFORMATION

⚑ Tourist Information Karasjok ✉ 9730 Karasjok ☎ 78/46-88-10. **Kautokeino** ✉ 9520 Kautokeino ☎ 78/48-65-00. **Kirkenes** ✉ 9915 Kirkenes ☎ 78/99-25-01. **Info-Svalbard** ✉ 9171 Longyearbyen ☎ 79/02-55-50 🌐 www.svalbard.com.

NORWAY A TO Z

To research prices, get advice from other travelers, and book travel arrangements, visit www.fodors.com.

AIR TRAVEL

CARRIERS
From North America, Scandinavian Airlines (SAS) has daily flights to Oslo (via Copenhagen, Stockholm, Frankfurt, Reykjavik, or London) from Newark, Baltimore, Boston, Chicago, Dallas, Denver, Miami, Montréal, Los Angeles, San Francisco, Seattle, Toronto, Vancouver, and Washington, D.C. Connecting flights depart from more than 45 cities in the U.S. and Canada at least twice a week. From the United Kingdom and Ireland, SAS flies from Heathrow to Oslo, Stavanger, and Bergen, and from Aberdeen and Newcastle to Stavanger. Braathens operates daily flights from London Gatwick and flies six days a week to Oslo, Bergen, Stavanger, and Trondheim. SAS flies to Oslo daily from Sydney and Melbourne via Bangkok and Copenhagen or Stockholm.

Coast Air, an SAS subsidiary, operates scheduled flights on weekdays from Aberdeen to Haugesund and to Bergen. Ryan Air offers twice-daily bargain-price flights from London's Stansted to Oslo's Torp airport, near Sandefjord to the south. British Airways offers five flights a day from Heathrow to Oslo. British Midland Airways flies once a day on the same route. Finnair has service to Oslo.

Within Norway, SAS serves most major cities, including Svalbard. SAS and Braathens are the major domestic airlines, serving cities throughout the country and along the coast as far north as Tromsø and Longyearbyen (on Svalbard). Braathens also has international routes from Oslo to Billund, Denmark; Malmö, Sweden; and Newcastle, England. A new low-cost carrier, Norwegian Air shuttle, serves most major cities in Norway. Widerøe serves smaller airports (with smaller planes), mostly along the coast and in northern Norway. Coast Air is a commuter airline linking both small and large airports.

Icelandair and American Airlines have direct flights from North America to Reykjavik or Stockholm, where you can connect with an Oslo-bound flight.

All flights within Norway are no-smoking, as are all airports.

🛫 Major Airlines **American** ☎ 800/433-7300 ⊕ www.aa.com. **Braathens** ☎ 0191/214-0991 in U.K., 81/52-00-00 in Norway. **British Airways** ☎ 0845/773377. **British Midland Airways** ☎ 0870/6070555. **Coast Air** ☎ 01224-725058. **Finnair** ☎ 800/950-5000 ⊕ www.finnair.com. **Icelandair** ☎ 800/223-5500 ⊕ www.icelandair.com. **Norwegian Air Shuttle** ☎ 67/59-30-00 ⊕ www.norwegian.no. **Ryan Air** ☎ 870/1569569. **SAS** ☎ 800/221-2350 in U.S. and Canada, 0845/607-2772 in U.K., 810/03-300 in Norway ⊕ www.scandinavian.net. **Widerøe** ☎ 810/01-200.

CUTTING COSTS
A number of special airfares are available within Norway year-round, including air passes, family tickets, weekend excursions, youth (up to the age of 25), student (up to the age of 33), and senior (older than 67) discounts. Youth fares are cheapest when purchased from the automatic ticket machines at the airport on the day of departure.

One or two stopovers can often be purchased more cheaply along with an international ticket. Icelandair, which connects Oslo with North America, gives the option to extend a layover in Reykjavik for up to three days at no extra charge; Icelandair also arranges Fly and Drive specials, which offer discounts on car rental and hotel fees if booking a flight to Oslo.

All Norwegian routes have reduced rates from July through the middle of August, and tickets can be purchased on the spot. Braathens sells a Visit Norway pass, which includes the Scandinavian BonusPass. Widerøe offers a special Summer Pass.

FLYING TIMES   A flight from New York to Oslo takes about 8 hours. From London, a nonstop flight gets to Oslo in 1¾ hours; it's about 1½ hours to Stavanger. From Sydney and major cities in New Zealand, the flight to Oslo will be over 20 hours, and will require at least one transfer.

AIRPORTS

Gardermoen Airport, about 53 km (33 mi) northeast of Oslo, is the major entry point for most visitors to Norway. Other international airports are in Bergen, Kristiansand, Sandefjord, Stavanger, and Trondheim. 📶 **Gardermoen Airport** ☎ 47/815-50-250 or 47/64-81-20-00 ⊕ www.osl.no/english. **Oslo Torp** ✉ Sandefjord ☎ 33/42-70-00.

BOAT & FERRY TRAVEL

Taking a ferry isn't only fun, it's often necessary in Norway. Many companies arrange package trips, some offering a rental car and hotel accommodations as part of the deal. The word "ferry" can be deceptive; generally, the ferries are more like small-scale cruise ships, with several dining rooms, sleeping quarters, shopping, pool and sauna, and entertainment.

Ferry crossings often last overnight. The trip between Copenhagen and Oslo, for example, takes approximately 16 hours; most lines leave at about 5 PM and arrive about 9 the next morning. Two ferry lines serve Norway from the United Kingdom. Fjord Line sails from Newcastle to Stavanger, Haugesund, and Bergen. Crossings take about 22 hours.

Smyril Line operates Bergen, Torshavn (Faroe Islands), and Lerwick (Shetland) on Mondays from mid-May to mid-September. DFDS Seaways has a number of crossings, including one from Newcastle to Kristiansand (southern Norway) that continues on to Göteborg (Sweden), and one between Copenhagen and Oslo.

Ferries remain important means of transportation within Norway. Along the west coast, the fjords make car ferries a necessity. More specialized boat service includes hydrofoil (catamaran) trips between Stavanger, Haugesund, and Bergen. There are also fjord cruises out of these cities and others in the north. 📶 **Color Line** ✉ Hjortneskaia, Box 1422 Vika, N-0115 Oslo ☎ 47/22-94-44-00 📠 47/22-83-04-30. **DFDS Seaways** ✉ Travel Centre, 28 Queensway Quay, W2 3RX London ☎ 020/7616-1400 ⊕ www.seaeurope.com. **Fjord Line** ✉ Norway House, Royal Quays, near Newcastle NE29 6EG North Shields ☎ 0191/296-1313 ⊕ www.fjordline.com. **Smyril Line** ✉ P & O Scottish Ferries, POB 5, Jamieson's Quay, AB9 8DL, Aberdeen ☎ 0122/457-2615 ⊕ www.smyril-line.com.

BUS TRAVEL

Bus tours can be effective for smaller regions within Norway, but the train system is excellent and offers much greater coverage in less time. Buses do, however, tend to be less expensive.

Every end station of the railroad is supported by a number of bus routes, some of which are operated by the Norwegian State Railway (NSB), others by local companies. Long-distance buses usually take longer than the railroad, and fares are only slightly lower. Virtually every settlement on the mainland is served by bus, and for anyone with a desire to get off the beaten track, a pay-as-you-go open-ended bus trip is the best way to see Norway.

Most long-distance buses leave from Bussterminalen close to Oslo Central Station. Nor-Way Bussekspress has more than 40 different bus services, covering 10,000 km (6,200 mi) and 500 destinations, and can arrange any journey.

CUTTING COSTS   Eurolines offers 15-, 30-, and 60-day passes for unlimited travel between Stockholm, Copenhagen, and Oslo, and more than 20 destinations throughout Europe.

🚹 **Ruteinformasjonen** ☎ 177 timetables and fares for the area you are situated in (except Finnmark and Svalbard). **Bussterminalen** ✉ Galleriet Oslo, Schweigaardsgt. 10 ☎ 23/00-24-00 bus information. **Nor-Way Bussekspress** ✉ Bussterminalen ☎ 820-21-300.

BUSINESS HOURS

BANKS & OFFICES   Standard bank opening hours are weekdays 8:15–4. On Thursday many banks stay open until 5. Offices are generally open from 9–4, but normally close 1 hour earlier in Summer.

SHOPS   Most shops are open from 9 or 10 to 5 weekdays, Thursday until 7, Saturday from 9 to 2 or 4, and are closed Sunday. In some areas, especially in larger cities, stores stay open later on weekdays. Large shopping centers, for example, are usually open until 8 weekdays and 6 on Saturday. Supermarkets are open until 9 or 10 weekdays and until 6 on Saturday. In summer, and especially in rural areas, most shops close weekdays at 4 and at 1 on Saturday.

CAR TRAVEL

Excellent, well-marked roads make driving a great way to explore Norway, but it can be an expensive choice. Ferry costs can be steep, and reservations are vital. Tolls on some major roads add to the expense, as do the high fees for city parking; tickets for illegal parking are painfully costly.

If you're planning to motor around Norway, call or check the Web site of Vegmeldingsentralen, an information center for the Statens Vegvesen (Public Roads Administration). The center monitors and provides information about roads and road conditions, distances, and ferry timetables. Phones are open 24 hours a day.

The southern part of Norway is fairly compact—all major cities are about a day's drive from each other. The distances are felt on the way north, where Norway becomes narrower as it inches up to and beyond the Arctic Circle and hooks over Sweden and Finland to touch Russia. It's virtually impossible to visit the entire country from one base.

In a few remote areas, especially in northern Norway, road conditions can be unpredictable, so plan carefully for safety's sake. Should your road trip take you over the mountains in autumn, winter, or spring, make sure that the mountain pass you're heading to is actually open. Some high mountain roads are closed as early as October due to snow, and do not open again until June. When driving in remote areas, especially in winter, let someone know your travel plans, **use a four-wheel-drive vehicle, and travel with at least one other car.**

🚹 **Vegmeldingsentralen (Road Information Center)** ☎ 175 in Norway, 81/54-89-91 from abroad ⊕ www.vegvesen.no.

EMERGENCY   Norsk Automobil-Forbund (NAF) offers roadside assistance. They patrol major roads and mountain passes from mid-June to mid-August. Another roadside assistance agency is Falken.

🚹 **Norsk Automobil-Forbund (NAF)** (Norwegian Automobile Association) ✉ Storgt. 2, Box 494, Sentrum, 0155 Oslo ☎ 22/34-14-00, 810/00-505 for 24-hour service ⊕ www.

naf.no. **Falken** ✉ Maridalsv. 300, 0872 Oslo ☎ 02468 02222 for 24-hour service ⊕ www.falken.no.

GASOLINE Gas stations are plentiful, and *blyfri bensin* (unleaded gasoline) and diesel fuel are sold everywhere from self-service pumps. Those marked *kort* are 24-hour pumps, which take oil-company credit cards or bank cards, either of which is inserted directly into the pump. Gas costs approximately NKr 10 (US$1.13) per liter (that's NKr 38, or US$4.29, per gallon). Don't wait until your tank is empty before looking for a gas station; hours vary greatly, especially outside the major cities.

INSURANCE All vehicles registered abroad are required to carry international liability insurance and an international accident report form, which can be obtained from automobile clubs. Collision insurance is recommended.

ROAD CONDITIONS Four-lane highways are the exception and are found only around major cities. Outside of main routes, roads tend to be narrow and twisting, with only token guardrails, and in summer roads are always crowded. Along the west coast, waits for ferries and passage through tunnels can be significant. Don't expect to cover more than 240 km (150 mi) in a day, especially in fjord country.

Norwegian roads are well marked with directional, distance, and informational signs. Some roads, particularly those over mountains, can close for all or part of the winter. If you drive outside major roads in winter, make sure the car is equipped with proper snow tires. Roads are generally not salted but are left with a hard-packed layer of snow on top of the asphalt. If you're renting, choose a small car with front-wheel drive. Bring an ice scraper, snow brush, small shovel, and heavy clothes for emergencies. In remote areas, or when roads are icy or steep, consider bringing along a set of tire chains. Although the weather along the coast is sunny, a few hours inland temperatures may be about 15°F colder, and snowfall is the rule rather than the exception.

RULES OF THE ROAD Driving is on the right. Yield to vehicles approaching from the right. Make sure you have an up-to-date map before you venture out, because some highway numbers have changed in the past few years, particularly routes beginning with "E."

The maximum speed limit is 90 kph (55 mph) on major motorways. On other highways, the limit is 80 kph (50 mph) or 70 kph (43 mph). The speed limit in cities and towns is 50 kph (30 mph), and 30 kph (18 mph) in residential areas.

Keep your headlights on at all times; this is required by law. By Norwegian law, everyone, including infants, must **wear seat belts.** Children under four years of age must ride in a car seat, and children over four years must ride in the back. All cars must carry red reflecting warning triangles, to be placed a safe distance from a disabled vehicle.

Norway has strict drinking-and-driving laws, and there are routine roadside checks. The legal limit is a blood-alcohol level of 0.02%, which effectively means that you should not drink any amount of alcohol before driving. If you are stopped, you may be required to take a breath test. If it is positive, you must submit to a blood test. No exceptions are made for foreigners, who can lose their licenses on the spot. Other penalties include fines and imprisonment. An accident involving a driver with an illegal blood-alcohol level usually voids all insurance agreements, so the driver becomes responsible for his own medical bills and damage to the cars.

Speeding is also punished severely. Most roads are monitored by radar and cameras in gray metal boxes. Signs warning of *Automatisk Trafikkontroll* (Automatic Traffic Monitoring) are posted periodically along many roads.

CRUISE TRAVEL

Norway's most renowned boat is *Hurtigruten,* which literally means "Rapid Route." Also known as the Coastal Steamer, the boat departs from Bergen and stops at 36 ports along the coast in six days, ending with Kirkenes, near the Russian border, before turning back. Tickets can be purchased for the entire journey or for individual legs. Tickets are available through Bergen Line travel agents or from Hurtigruten Coastal Express Bookings. Alternatively, you can contact one of the companies that run the service: FFR in Hammerfest, OVDS in Narvik, Hurtigruten in Bergen, and TFDS in Tromsø.

To learn how to plan, choose, and book a cruise-ship voyage, consult *Fodor's FYI: Plan & Enjoy Your Cruise* (available in bookstores everywhere). **Cruise Lines Bergen Line Travel Agents** ⊠405 Park Ave., New York, NY 10022 ☎212/319-1300. **FFR** ⊠ POB 308, 9615 Hammerfest ☎ 78/40-70-51 ⊕ www.ffr.no. *Hurtigruten* ⊠ Coastal Express, Veiten 2B, 5012 Bergen ☎ 810-30-300. **Hurtigruten Coastal Express Bookings** ☎810/30-000, 78/54-17-41 timetables ⊕ www.hurtigruten. no. **OVDS** ⊠POB 43, 8501 Narvik ☎76/96-76-00 ⊕www.ovds.no. **TFDS** ⊠9291 Tromsø ☎ 77/64-82-00.

CUSTOMS & DUTIES

IN NORWAY Custom regulations have the following duty-free limits: 2 liters of beer, 1 liter of liquor (up to 60% alcohol), 1 liter of wine (up to 22%) or 2 liters of wine or 2 liters of beer if no liquor, 200 cigarettes or 250 grams of tobacco and 200 cigarette papers. You must be over 20 to take in liquor and over 18 years for wine, beer, and tobacco products. You may not bring any vegetables, fruits, dairy products, or other uncooked foods into Norway. Dried and canned foodstuffs are allowed.

EMBASSIES

Australia ⊠ Jerbanetorget 2, Oslo ☎ 22/47-91-70.
Canada ⊠ Wergeslandsvn. 7, Oslo ☎ 22/99-53-00.
New Zealand ⊠ Billengstadsletta 19, Oslo ☎ 66/77-53-30.
United Kingdom ⊠ Thomas Heftyes gt. 8, Oslo ☎ 23/13-27-00.
United States ⊠ Drammensvn. 18, Oslo ☎ 22/44-85-50.

EMERGENCIES

Ambulance, fire, and police assistance is available 24 hours.
Ambulance ☎ 113. **Fire** ☎ 110. **Police** ☎ 112.

LANGUAGE

Despite the fact that Norwegian is in the Germanic family of languages, it is a myth that someone who speaks German can understand it. Fortunately, English is widely spoken. German is the most common third language. English becomes rarer outside major cities, and it's a good idea to **take along a dictionary or phrase book.** Even here, however, anyone under the age of 50 is likely to have studied English in school. Fluent Swedish speakers can generally understand Norwegian.

Norwegian has three additional vowels: æ, ø, and å. Æ is pronounced as a short "a." The ø, sometimes printed as *oe,* is the same as ö in German and Swedish, pronounced very much like a short "u." The å is a contraction of the archaic "aa" and sounds like long "o." These three letters appear at the end of alphabetical listings such as those in the phone book.

There are two officially sanctioned Norwegian languages, Bokmål and Nynorsk. Bokmål is used by 84% of the population and is the main written form of Norwegian and the language of books, as the first half of its name indicates. Nynorsk, which translates as "new Norwegian," is actually a compilation of older dialect forms from rural Norway. Every Norwegian also receives at least seven years of English instruction, starting in the second grade. The Sámi (or Lapps), who inhabit the northernmost parts of Norway, have their own language, which is distantly related to Finnish.

LODGING

APARTMENT & VILLA RENTALS If you want a home base that's roomy enough for a family and comes with cooking facilities, **consider a furnished rental.** These can save you money, especially if you're traveling with a group. Home-exchange directories sometimes list rentals as well as exchanges.

🛈 **International Agents Drawbridge to Europe** ✉ 98 Granite St., Ashland, OR 97520 ☎ 541/482-7778 or 888/268-1148 🖷 541/482-7779 ⊕ www.drawbridgetoeurope.com.

CABINS & CAMPING Norway has more than 1,000 campsites, all of which are given anywhere from one to five stars based on the standard facilities and activities available. Fees vary but generally each site costs NKr 80–160 per day. For camping information and a list of sites, contact local tourist offices. Open fires are illegal in forests or open land between April 15th and September 15th.

Many of Norway's campsites also have cabins available. These are also rated on a five-star system. Most have electricity and heat, but you may have to bring your own bedding. Cost per night is around NKr 250–NKr 750. The DNT hiking organization runs hundreds of cabins and lodges, especially in the south.

The Norsk Campingkort (Norwegian Camping Card) entitles you to faster check-in service and discounts on cabins and campsites. The card costs NKr 60 for a year and can be ordered before traveling through the Reiselivsbedriftenes Landsforening (RBL).

🛈 **Den Norske Turistforening (DNT)** (The Norwegian Mountain Touring Association) ✉ Box 7 Sentrum, 0101 Oslo 1 ☎ 22/82-28-00 🖷 22/82-28-01 ⊕ www.turistforeningen.no. **Reiselivsbedriftenes Landsforening (RBL)** (Norwegian Hospitality Association) ✑ Box 5465, Majorstua, 0305 Oslo ☎ 23/08-86-20 🖷 23/08-86-21 ⊕ www.camping.no.

FARM & COTTAGE HOLIDAYS The old-fashioned farm or countryside holiday, long a staple for Norwegian city dwellers, is becoming increasingly available to tourists. In most cases, you can choose to stay on the farm itself, and even participate in daily activities, or you can opt to rent a private cottage, which can include housekeeping. Seaside fisherman's cabins (or *rorbuer*) are also available, particularly in the Lofoten Islands. Contact local tourist boards for details.

HOME EXCHANGES If you would like to exchange your home for someone else's, **join a home-exchange organization,** which will send you its updated listings of available exchanges for a year and will include your own listing in at least one of them. It's up to you to make specific arrangements.

🛈 **Exchange Clubs HomeLink International** ✉ Box 47747, Tampa, FL 33647 ☎ 813/975-9825 or 800/638-3841 🖷 813/910-8144 ⊕ www.homelink.org 💳 $106 per year. **Intervac U.S.** ✉ Box 590504, San Francisco, CA 94159 ☎ 800/756-4663 🖷 415/435-7440 ⊕ www.intervacus.com 💳 $93 yearly fee includes one catalog and online access.

HOSTELS Norway has more than 100 youth hostels, part of Hostelling International Norway (Norske Vandrerhjem). Norwegian hostels are considered among the best in the world, squeaky clean, and with excellent facilities. The majority of rooms sleep two to four, but there are also family rooms and dormitories. You don't have to be a member, but members get discounts, so it's worth joining. Membership can be arranged at any *vandrerhjem* (youth hostel) and after six Norwegian youth hostel stamps, nonmembers can become international members. Duvets and pillows are always provided, but linens are usually rented by the night. You're welcome to bring your own—if you haven't, you can buy a *lakenpose* (sheet sleeping bag) at many department stores and at most youth hostels as well. Advanced booking is recommended, especially in summer. No two Norwegian hostels are alike; they range from modern buildings to old wooden houses and fisherman's cabins. Prices per night range from NKr 80 to NKr 225 in dormitories, NKr195 to NKr 740 in double rooms, and NKr 300 to NKr 600 for family rooms. Guests aged 3 to 15 in the same room as adults are eligible for 50% discounts and children under three not sleeping in beds stay for free. The largest Norwegian hostels are open year-round; smaller ones are often open only for the summer season.

🏠 **Norske Vandrerhjem** (Hostelling International Norway) ✉ Dronningensgt. 26, 0154 Oslo ☎ 23/13-93-00 🖨 23/13-93-50 🌐 www.vandrerhjem.no.

HOTEL PASSES All hotels listed have private baths unless otherwise noted.

Inn Checks—prepaid hotel vouchers—offer discounts of up to 50% for accommodations ranging from first-class hotels to country cottages. The vouchers must be purchased from travel agents or from the Scandinavian Tourist Board (⇨ Visitor Information) before departure and are sold individually and in packets for as many nights as needed. Winter bargains are often better than those in summer.

A *Fjord Pass,* which costs NKr 85, is valid for two adults and any number of children under the age of 15. Valid May through September, the discount card can make it possible to stay at a hotel for NKr 215 per person per day at 225 hotels, guest houses, apartments, and holiday cottages. You can get the Pass from travel agents and at tourist information offices, Fjord Pass hotels, some post offices, and railway stations.

ProSkandinavia checks can be used in 400 hotels across Scandinavia for savings up to 50%, for reservations made usually no earlier than 24 hours before arrival, although some hotels allow earlier bookings. One check costs about $35. Two checks will pay for a double room at a hotel, one check for a room in a cottage. The checks can be bought at many travel agencies in Scandinavia or ordered directly from ProSkandinavia.

🏠 **Best Western Hotels Norway** ☎ 0800/393-130 🌐 www.bestwestern.com. **Norway Fjord Pass** ☎ 55/55-76-60 🌐 www.fjordpass.com. **ProSkandinavia** ✉ Akersgt. 11, N-0158 Oslo ☎ 47/22-41-13-13 🌐 www.proskandinavia.com. **Scan+ Hotel Pass** ☎ 23/08-02-80 🌐 www.norlandia.no. **Scandic Club Card** ☎ 46/85-17-51-700 🌐 www.scandic.hotels.com. **Nordic Hotel Pass** ☎ 22/40-13-00 🌐 www.choice.no.

MAIL & SHIPPING
Most post offices are open weekdays 8 to 4 or 5, Saturday 9 to 1. In small towns, post offices are often closed on Saturday. In recent years, supermarkets or convenience stores have replaced post offices in certain rural areas.

POSTAL RATES The letter rate for Norway is NKr 5.50, NKr 7 for the other Nordic countries, NKr 9 for Europe, and NKr 10 for outside Europe for a letter weighing up to 20 grams (¾ ounce).

MONEY MATTERS
Prices throughout this guide are given for adults. Substantially reduced fees are almost always available for children, students, and senior citizens.

Costs are high in Norway. Here are some sample prices: cup of coffee, from NKr 14 in a cafeteria to NKr 25 or more in a restaurant; a 20-pack of cigarettes, NKr 60; a half-liter of beer, NKr 40–NKr 50; the smallest hot dog (with bun plus *lompe*—a flat Norwegian potato bread—mustard, ketchup, and fried onions) at a convenience store, NKr 20; cheapest bottle of wine from a government store, NKr 60; the same bottle at a restaurant, NKr 120–NKr 200; urban transit fare in Oslo, NKr 20; soft drink, from NKr 20 in a cafeteria to NKr 35 in a better restaurant; sandwich at a cafeteria, NKr 40–NKr 50; 1½-km (1-mi) taxi ride, NKr 40–NKr 60 depending on time of day.

Be aware that sales taxes can be very high, but foreigners can get some refunds by shopping at tax-free stores (⇨ Taxes). City cards can save you transportation and entrance fees in larger cities.

Liquor and strong beer (over 3% alcohol) can be purchased only in state-owned shops, at very high prices, during weekday business hours, usually 9:30 to 6 and in some areas on Saturday until mid-afternoon. (When you visit friends or relatives in Norway, a bottle of liquor or fine wine bought duty-free on the trip over is often much appreciated.) Weaker beers and ciders are usually available in grocery stores, except in certain rural areas, especially along the coast of Western Norway.

CURRENCY Norway is a non-EU country, and has opted to keep its currency while its neighbors convert to the Euro. The Norwegian *krone* (plural: *kroner*) translates as "crown," written officially as NOK. Price tags are seldom marked this way, but instead read "Kr" followed by the amount, such as Kr 10. (In this book, the Norwegian krone is abbreviated NKr.) One krone is divided into 100 *øre,* and coins of 50 øre and 1, 5, 10, and 20 kroner are in circulation. Bills are issued in denominations of 50, 100, 200, 500, and 1,000 kroner. At this writing (winter 2003), the rate of exchange was NKr 7 to the U.S. dollar, NKr 5 to the Canadian dollar, NKr 11 to the pound sterling, NKr 10 to the Irish punt, NKr 4 to the Australian dollar, NKr 4 to the New Zealand dollar, and NKr 1 to the South African rand. Exchange rates fluctuate, so be sure to check them when planning a trip.

No limitations apply to the import and export of currency.

SPORTS & THE OUTDOORS

Norway's wilderness and natural beauty, including 18 national parks, affords many special experiences. Whatever your sport or pursuit, the Norwegian Tourist Board advises travelers to use common sense: respect nature, know your physical limitations, take necessary precautions, use proper equipment and dress appropriately, pay attention to local weather forecasts, and take part in group outings if you have little outdoor experience.

Close to 100 recreational and competitive sports are recognized in Norway, each with its own national association. Contact the local tourist office or the Norwegian Tourist Board for more details.

BIKING Norway has many cycling paths, some of them old roads that are in the mountains and along the western fjords. The Rallarvegen, from Haugastøl in the Hardangervidda National Park to Flåm, is very popular among cyclists. The southern counties of Vestfold and Rogaland have a well-developed network of cycling paths.

Most routes outside large cities are hilly and can be physically demanding. **Wear protective helmets and use lights at night.**

Many counties have produced brochures that have touring suggestions and maps. Syklistenes Landsforening has maps and general information, as well as the latest weather conditions. Several companies, including Lillehammer's Trollcycling, organize cycling tours. Den Norske Turistforening (DNT; ⇨ Lodging) provides inexpensive lodging for cyclists planning overnight trips.

If you want to travel with your bike on an NSB long-distance train, you must make a reservation and pay an additional NKr 90. On local or InterCity trains, bikes are transported if space is available.

▸ Resources **Syklistenes Landsforening** ⊠Storgt. 23C, 0028 Oslo ☎ 22/47-30-30 🖷 22/47-30-31.

▸ **Cycling Tour Companies erik & reidar** ⊠ Kirkegt. 34A, 0153 Oslo ☎ 22/41-23-80 🖷 22/41-23-90. **PedalNor** ⊠ Kløvervn. 10, 4326 Sandnes ☎ 51/66-40-60 or 51/66-48-70. **Trollcycling** ⊠ Box 373, 2601 Lillehammer ☎ 61/28-99-70 🖷 61/26-92-50.

BIRD-WATCHING Northern Norway has some of northern Europe's largest bird sanctuaries. The area teems with fantastic numbers of seabirds, including sea eagles. Another popular spot is the island of Runde, just off Ålesund on the west coast. A half million birds nest there.

CANOEING & RAFTING There are plenty of lakes and streams for canoeing and kayaking in Norway. Popular spots include Aust-Agder, in the Sørlandet; Telemark; and suburban Oslo. Norges Padlerforbund (Norwegian Canoe Association) maintains a list of rental companies and regional canoeing centers.

Rafting excursions are offered throughout Norway. For more information, contact Norwegian Wildlife and Rafting, which operates guided two-day expeditions with accommodation and transport provided. The minimum age for white-water rafting is 18 (15 with parental guidance).

▸ Resources **Norges Padlerforbund** ⊠ Service Boks 1, Ullevaal Stadion, 0840 Oslo ☎ 21/02-98-35 ⊕ www.padling.no. **Norwegian Wildlife and Rafting** ⊠ 2680 Våg ☎ 61/23-87-27.

DIVING The Norwegian coast has many diving opportunities. There are centers with excellent facilities on the west coast, particularly in Møre og Romsdal county.

There are a few restrictions regarding sites. Special permission is required to dive in a harbor, and diving near army installations is restricted. Contact Norges Dykkeforbund or the local tourist office for a list of diving centers and clubs.

▸ **Norges Dykkeforbund** ⊠ Sognsvn. 75L, 0855 Oslo ☎ 21/02-97-42 ⊕ www.ndf.no.

FISHING Norway's fjords, lakes, and rivers make it a fisherman's paradise. Check with fly shops or the local tourist office to see what licenses you may need.

Using live fish as bait is prohibited, and imported tackle must be disinfected before use. Infectious parasites that are harmless to humans have decimated salmon populations in certain rivers in Norway. To avoid spreading parasites, make sure you dry and clean your gear before moving to another river.

GLACIER WALKING Glacier walking is an exhilarating way to experience the mountains of Norway. This sport requires the right equipment and training: only try it when accompanied by an experienced local guide. Since glaciers are always moving over new land, the ice and snow may just be a thin covering for a deep crevice. Glacier centers or local tourist offices can recommend guides and tours.

▸ Resources **Jostedalsbreen Nasjonalparksenter** ⊠ Rte. 15, 6781 Oppstryn ☎ 57/87-72-00 ⊕ www.museumsnett.no/jostedalsbreen. **Norsk Bremuseum** (Norwegian Glacier Museum) ⊠ Rte. 5, 6848 Fjærland ☎ 57/69-32-88 ⊕ www.bre.museum.no.

Breheimsenteret ✉ Jostedalen National Park Visitor's Center, Rte. 604, 6871 Jostedale ☎ 57/68-32-50.

GOLF   The many golf courses spread out across the country welcome nonmember guests for fees ranging from NKr 150 to NKr 350. Local tourist offices and the Norges Golfforbund can provide a list of golf clubs.

📋 Resources **Norges Golfforbund** (Norwegian Gold Association) ✉ Box 163, Lilleaker, 0216 Oslo ☎ 22/73-66-20 ⊕ ngf.golf.no.

HANG GLIDING   The mountains and hills of Norway provide excellent take-off spots. However, winds and weather conspire to make conditions unpredictable. For details on local clubs, regulations, and equipment rental, contact Norsk Aeroklubb.

📋 Resources **Norsk Aeroklubb** ✉ Rådhusgt. 5b, 0162 Oslo ☎ 23/01-04-50 ⊕ www.nak.no.

HIKING & MOUNTAINEERING   Naturally, hiking and mountaineering are popular pastimes in a land of mountain ranges and high plains. Well-known hiking areas include the Jotunheim Mountain Range; the Rondane and Dovrefjell mountains; the Hardangervidda (Hardanger Plateau), the Trollheimen District; and Finnmarksvidda. For multiday hikes, you can stay in hostels, camp out in your own tent, or head to one the DNT's cabins. Throughout the country, DNT organizes guided hiking tours as well as mountaineering courses year round.

📋 Resources **Den Norske Turistforening** (DNT; The Norwegian Mountain Touring Association) ✉ Box 7 Sentrum, 0101 Oslo 1 ☎ 22/82-28-22 🖷 22/82-28-23.

SAILING   Norway's rugged coastline can make for an ideal sailing vacation. Be sure to sail with up-to-date sea charts, since the water around Norway is filled with skerries and underwater rocks. Contact Norges Seilforbund about facilities around the country.

📋 Resources **Norges Seilforbund** (Norwegian Sailing Association) ✉ Box Ullevåls Stadion, 0840 Oslo ☎ 21/02-90-00.

SNOW SPORTS   The Skiforeningen provides national snow-condition reports; tips on trails; and information on courses for cross-country and downhill skiing, Telemarking, and snowboarding. If you can't make it to Norway in winter, Stryn Sommerskisenter, in the west, has a summer ski season that runs June–September.

📋 Resources **Skiforeningen** ✉ Kongevn. 5, 0390 Oslo 3 ☎ 22/92-32-00. **Stryn Sommerskisenter** ✉ 6782 Stryn ☎ 57/87-40-40.

SPORTS FOR PEOPLE WITH DISABILITIES   Norway encouraged active participation in sports for people with disabilities long before it became popular elsewhere and has many Special Olympics medal winners. Beitostølen Helsesportsenter has sports facilities for people with disabilities as well as training programs for instructors. Sports offered include skiing, hiking, running, and horseback riding. For more information call Norges Funksjonshemmede Idrettsforbund.

📋 Resources **Beitostølen Helsesportsenter** ✉ 2953 Beitostølen ☎ 61/34-11-07. **Norges Funksjonshemmede Idrettsforbund** (Norwegian Sports Organization for the Disabled) ✉ Ullevåll Stadion ☎ 21/02-94-81 ⊕ www.nfif.no.

SWIMMING   Swimming in the Norwegian outdoors is most enjoyable along the southern coast, where air temperatures can reach 68°F (20°C). In northern Norway, inland temperatures are generally cooler.

TAXES

VALUE-ADDED TAX   Value-added tax, V.A.T. for short but called *moms* all over Scandinavia, is a hefty 24% on all purchases except books; it is included in the prices of goods. All purchases of consumer goods totaling more than NKr 308 for export by nonresidents are eligible for V.A.T. refunds. Carry your passport when shopping to prove you are a nonresident.

Global Refund is a V.A.T. refund service that makes getting your money back hassle-free. Some 3,000 Norwegian shops subscribe to the service, called "Norway Tax-Free Shopping."

In participating stores, **ask for the Global Refund form** (called a Shopping Cheque). Have it stamped like any customs form by customs officials when you leave the country (be ready to show customs officials what you've bought). Then take the form to one of the more than 700 Global Refund counters—conveniently located at every major airport and border crossing—and 11%–18% of the tax will be refunded on the spot in the form of cash, check, or a refund to your credit-card account (minus a small percentage for processing).

Shops that do not subscribe to this program have slightly more detailed forms, which must be presented to the Norwegian Customs Office along with the goods to obtain a refund by mail. This refund is closer to the actual amount of the tax.

It's essential to have both the forms and the goods available for inspection upon departure. Make sure the appropriate stamps are on the voucher or other forms before leaving the country.

One way to beat high prices is to **take advantage of tax-free shopping.** You can make major purchases free of tax if you have a foreign passport. Ask about tax-free shopping when you make a purchase for $50 (about £32) or more. When your purchases exceed a specified limit (which varies from country to country), you receive a special export receipt. Keep the parcels intact and take them out of the country within 30 days of purchase.

Global Refund ✉ 99 Main St., Suite 307, Nyack, NY 10960 ☎ 800/566-9828 🖷 845/348-1549 ⊕ www.globalrefund.com. **Global Refund Norge** ☎ 67/15-60-10. **Directorate of Customs and Excise** ✉ POB 8122, 0032 Oslo ☎ 22/86-03-00 ⊕ www.toll.no.

TAXIS

Even the smallest villages have some form of taxi service. Towns on the railroad normally have taxi stands just outside the station. All city taxis are connected with a central dispatching office, so there is only one main telephone number for calling a cab. Look in the telephone book under "Taxi" or "Drosje."

Never use an unmarked, or pirate, taxi, since their drivers are unlicensed and in some cases may be dangerous.

TELEPHONES

The telephone system in Norway is modern and efficient; international direct service is available throughout the country. Phone numbers consist of eight digits.

AREA & COUNTRY CODES
The country code for Norway is 47. There are no area codes—you must dial all eight digits of any phone number wherever you are. Telephone numbers that start with a 9 or 4 are usually mobile phones, and considerably more expensive to call. Telephone numbers starting with the prefix 82 cost extra. Toll-free numbers begin with 800 or 810. In this book, area codes precede telephone numbers.

DIRECTORY & OPERATOR ASSISTANCE
Dial 1881 for information in Norway, 1882 for international telephone numbers. To place a collect or an operator-assisted call to a number in Norway, dial 115. Dial 117 for collect or operator-assisted calls outside of Norway.

INTERNATIONAL CALLS AT&T, MCI, and Sprint access codes make calling long distance relatively convenient, but you may find the local access number blocked in many hotel rooms. Ask the hotel operator to connect you. If the hotel operator balks, ask for an international operator, or dial the international operator yourself. One way to improve your odds of getting connected to your long-distance carrier is to travel with more than one company's calling card (a hotel may block Sprint, for example, but not MCI). If all else fails, call from a pay phone.

If you are able to dial directly, dial the international access code, 00, then the country code and the number. All telephone books list country code numbers, including those for the United States and Canada (1), Great Britain (44), Australia (61), and New Zealand (64). All international operators speak English.

🔢 **Access Codes AT&T Direct** ☎ 800/19011. **MCI WorldPhone** ☎ 800/19912. **Sprint International Access** ☎ 800/19877.

MOBILE PHONES Scandinavia has been one of the world leaders in mobile phone development; almost 90% of the population owns a mobile phone. Although standard North American cellular phones will not work in Norway, some companies rent cellular phones to visitors. Contact the Norwegian Tourist Office for details.

PHONE CARDS You can purchase Tellerskritt (phone cards) at Narvesen and Norsk Tipping shops and kiosks. Cards cost NKr 40 to NKr 140 and can be used in the 8,000 green card telephones. About half of these public phones also take major credit cards.

PUBLIC PHONES Public telephones are of two types. Push-button phones—which accept NKr 1, 5, and 10 coins (some also accept NKr 20 coins)—are easy to use: lift the receiver, listen for the dial tone, insert the coins, dial the number, and wait for a connection. The digital screen at the top of the box indicates the amount of money in your "account." Green card telephones only accept phone cards or credit cards.

Local calls cost NKr 3 or NKr 5 from a pay phone. If you hear a short tone, it means that your purchased time is almost up.

TIPPING

Tipping is kept to a minimum in Norway because service charges are added to most bills. It is, however, handy to have a supply of NKr 5 or NKr 10 coins for less formal service. Tip only in local currency.

Room service usually includes a service charge in the bill, so tipping is discretionary. Round up a taxi fare to the next round digit, or tip anywhere from NKr 5 to NKr 10, a little more if the driver has been helpful. All restaurants include a service charge, ranging from 12% to 15%, in the bill. It is customary to add up to 10% for exceptional service, but it is not obligatory. Maître d's are not tipped, and coat checks have flat rates, usually NKr 10 per person.

TOURS & PACKAGES

Because everything is prearranged on a prepackaged tour or independent vacation, you spend less time planning—and often get it all at a good price.

🔢 **Tour-Operator Recommendations American Society of Travel Agents** (⇨ Travel Agencies). **National Tour Association (NTA)** ✉ 546 E. Main St., Lexington, KY 40508 ☎ 859/226-4444 or 800/682-8886 ⊕ www.ntaonline.com. **Scantours** ☎ 800/223-7226 or 310/636-4656 in U.S. ⊕ www.scantours.com ✉ 47 Whitcomb St., WC2H 7DH London ☎ 020/7839-2927. **ScanMeridian** ✉ 28B Hampstead High St., NW3 1QA London

☎ 0207/431-5393. **United States Tour Operators Association (USTOA)** ✉ 342 Madison Ave., Suite 1522, New York, NY 10173 ☎ 212/599-6599 or 800/468-7862 ⎙ 212/599-6744 ⊕ www.ustoa.com.

TRAIN TRAVEL

NSB, the Norwegian State Railway System, has five main lines originating from the Oslo S Station. Its 2,500 miles of track connect all main cities. Train tickets can be purchased in railway stations or from travel agencies. NSB has its own travel agency in Oslo.

Norway's longest rail route runs north to Trondheim, then extends onward as far as Fauske and Bodø. The southern line hugs the coast to Stavanger, while the stunning western line crosses Hardangervidda, the scenic plateau that lies between Oslo and Bergen. An eastern line to Stockholm links Norway with Sweden, while another southern line through Göteborg, Sweden, is the main connection with Continental Europe. Narvik, north of Bodø, is the last stop on Sweden's Ofot line, the world's northernmost rail system, which runs from Stockholm via Kiruna.

If you are traveling from south to north in Norway, flying is often a necessity: Stavanger is as close to Rome as it is to the northern tip of Norway.

NSB trains are clean, comfortable, and punctual. Most have special compartments for travelers with disabilities and for families with children younger than age two. First- and second-class tickets are available.

Seat reservations are required on some European trains, particularly high-speed trains, and are a good idea on trains that may be crowded. In summer reserve your seats at least five days ahead; during major holidays, for Friday and Sunday trains reserve several weeks or a month ahead. You will also need a reservation if you purchase sleeping accommodations.

Many travelers assume that rail passes guarantee them seats on the trains they wish to ride. Not so. You need to book seats ahead even if you are using a rail pass.

FROM BRITAIN   Traveling from Britain to Norway by train is not difficult and takes 20 to 24 hours. The best connection leaves London's Victoria Station, connecting at Dover with a boat to Oostende, Belgium. From Oostende there are overnight connections to Copenhagen, where there are express and overnight connections to Oslo. Call Rail Europe for further information. ⨍**NSB** ✉ Skolen Tomtekaia 21, 0048 Oslo ☎ 81/50-08-88. **ScanAm World Tours** ✉ N. Main St. 108, Cranberry, NJ 08512 ☎ 800/545-2204. **Victoria Station** ✉ Terminus Pl., London ☎ 0845/748-4950 in U.K.

CUTTING COSTS   A number of special discount passes are available, including the Inter-Rail Pass, which is available for European residents of all ages, and the EurailPass, sold in the United States only. Norway participates in the following rail programs: EurailPass (and its flexipass variations), Scan-Rail Pass, Scanrail 'n Drive, InterRail, and Nordturist Card. A Norway Rail Pass is available for three, four, and five days of unlimited rail travel for nonresidents within Norway. The ticket is sold in the United States through ScanAm. First-class rail passes are about 30% higher.

Low-season prices are offered from October through April. Rail passes do not guarantee that you will get seats on the trains you want to ride, and seat reservations are sometimes required, particularly on express trains. You also need reservations for overnight sleeping accommodations.

Discounted fares also include family, student, senior-citizen (including their not-yet-senior spouses), and off-peak "mini" fares, which must be purchased a day in advance. NSB gives student discounts only to foreigners studying at Norwegian institutions.

Whichever pass you choose, remember that you must **purchase your pass before you leave** for Europe.

Rail passes may help you save money, but be aware that if you don't plan to cover many miles you may come out ahead by buying individual tickets.

⊞ CIT Tours Corp. ⊠ 342 Madison Ave., Suite 207, New York, NY 10173 ☎ 212/697-2100 or 800/248-8687, 800/248-7245 in western U.S. ⊕ www.cit-tours.com. **DER Travel Services** ⊠ Box 1606, Des Plaines, IL 60017 ☎ 800/782-2424 🖷 800/282-7474 ⊕ www.dertravel.com. **Rail Europe** ⊠ 226-230 Westchester Ave., White Plains, NY 10604 ☎ 800/438-7245, 914/682-5172, or 416/602-4195 ⊠ 2087 Dundas E, Suite 105, Mississauga, Ontario L4X 1M2 ☎ 800/438-7245, 914/682-5172, or 416/602-4195 ⊕ www.raileurope.com.

VISITOR INFORMATION

For U.S. Government travel advisories by mail, send a request letter to the U.S. Department of State that includes a self-addressed, stamped, business-size envelope.

⊞ Tourist Information Norwegian Tourist Board ⊠ Charles House, 5 [Lower] Regent St., London SW1Y 4LR, U.K. ☎ 44/207-839-6255 🖷 44/207-839-6014 ⊠ Box 2893, Drammensvn. 40, Solli 0230, Oslo, Norway ☎ 47/2414-4600 🖷 47/2414-4601 ⊕ www.visitnorway.com. **Scandinavian Tourist Board** ⊠ 655 3rd Ave., New York, NY 10017 ☎ 212/885-9700 🖷 212/855-9710 ⊕ www.goscandinavia.com. **U.S. Department of State** ⊠ Overseas Citizens Services Office, Room 4811 N.S., 2201 C St. NW, Washington, DC 20520 ☎ 202/647-5225 ⊕ travel.state.gov/travel/html.

SWEDEN

FODOR'S CHOICE

Carl Larsson Gården, *cottage in Sundborn*

Dogsledding in Norrland

Drottningholms Slott, *palace in Stockholm*

Hiking in Ørland

Kalmar Slott, *castle in Småland*

Kungliga Slottet, *castle in Stockholm*

Marinmuseum, *museum in Karlskrona*

Midsummer celebrations around Lake Siljan

Motala Motormuseum

Nationalmuseum, *Stockholm*

Skansen, *museum in Stockholm*

Stadshuset, *Stockholm*

Stockholm archipelago

Tjolöholms Slott, *castle in Tjolöholm, Swedish Riviera*

Vasamuseet, *museum in Stockholm*

Zorn Museet, *museum in Mora*

Many other great sights, restaurants, and hotels enliven this area.
For other favorites, look for the stars as you read this chapter.

Updated by
Rob Hincks
and Karin
Palmquist

SWEDEN REQUIRES THE VISITOR to travel far, in both distance and attitude. Approximately the size of California, Sweden reaches as far north as the Arctic fringes of Europe, where glacier-top mountains and thousands of acres of pine, spruce, and birch forests are broken here and there by wild rivers, countless pristine lakes, and desolate moorland. In the more populous south, roads meander through mile after mile of softly undulating countryside, skirting lakes and passing small villages with sharp-pointed church spires. Here the lush forests that dominate Sweden's northern landscape have largely fallen to the plow.

Once the dominant power of the region, Sweden has traditionally looked mostly inward, seeking to find its own Nordic solutions. During the cold war it tried with considerable success to steer its famous "middle way" between the two superpowers, both economically and politically. Its citizens were in effect subjected to a giant social experiment aimed at creating a perfectly just society, one that adopted the best aspects of both socialism and capitalism.

In the late 1980s, as it slipped into the worst economic recession since the 1930s, Sweden made adjustments that lessened the role of its all-embracing welfare state in the lives of its citizens. Although fragile, the conservative coalition, which defeated the long-incumbent Social Democrats in the fall of 1991, attempted to make further cutbacks in welfare spending as the country faced one of the largest budget deficits in Europe. In a kind of nostalgic backlash, the populace voted the Social Democrats back into power in 1994, hoping to recapture the party's policy of cradle-to-grave protection. The world economy didn't exactly cooperate; although Sweden appeared to be crawling toward stability in the mid-1990s, the struggle to balance the budget intensified again by the end of the decade. The Social Democrats won a further victory in 2002, but the social safety net once so heavily relied upon by the Swedes remains somewhat incomplete; a reflection perhaps of modern economics rather than any temporary budgetary hiccup.

Sweden took off with the rest of the globe with the explosion of the Internet and new technology and watched with it as the bubble burst at the start of the new millennium. It continues to be one of the world's dominant players in the information-based economy. Although many start-up companies (and well-established giants such as Ericsson) have taken their share of economic bumps and bruises, as a whole there remains a lively entrepreneurial spirit and an intense interest in the business possibilities of the Internet and wireless communications. During the past few years Sweden has received substantial international press coverage for its innovative technological solutions, new management philosophies, and unique Web design.

New technology is widely used and accepted throughout Sweden. The country has the highest Internet penetration in the world, and more than 50% of the population uses cell phones. If there's an expensive new gadget out on the market, chances are you'll see a stylish Stockholmer using it.

On the social front, an influx of immigrants, particularly from countries outside Europe, is reshaping what was once a homogeneous society. Sweden continues to face political and social difficulties in the areas of immigration and integration, although the tension appears to be fading slightly as more and more artists, musicians, actors, directors, and writers with immigrant backgrounds are receiving national recognition for their work. As considerable public debate about these issues sweeps the country, a society known for its blue-eyed blondes is considering what it means to be a Swede.

Another sign that Swedes seem more willing than ever to refashion their image was Sweden's decision to join the European Union (EU) in January 1995, a move that represented a radical break with its traditional independent stance on international issues. Thus far, the domestic benefits of membership are still debated heavily, but the country's exporting industries have made considerable gains. During its relatively short membership Sweden has held the presidency of the Union and hosted the first ever visit by a sitting U.S. president, when George W. Bush visited Göteborg for a meeting with EU member states. Despite these landmark moments and perhaps partly because of the lack of concrete results in being part of the EU, the first years of the millennium have seen citizens undecided about the value of membership and politicians struggling to demonstrate its importance.

The country possesses stunning natural assets. In the forests, moose, deer, bears, and lynx roam, coexisting with the whine of power saws and the rumble of automatic logging machines. Logging remains the country's economic backbone. Environmental awareness, however, is high. Fish abound in sparkling lakes and tumbling rivers, and sea eagles and ospreys soar over myriad pine-clad islands in the archipelagoes off the east and west coasts.

The country is Europe's fourth largest, 449,963 square km (173,731 square mi) in area, and its population of 8.8 million is thinly spread. If, like Greta Garbo—one of its most famous exports—you enjoy being alone, you've come to the right place. A law called Allemansrätt guarantees public access to the countryside; NO TRESPASSING signs are seldom seen.

Sweden stretches 1,563 km (977 mi) from the barren Arctic north to the fertile plains of the south. Contrasts abound, but they are neatly tied together by a superbly efficient infrastructure, embracing air, road, and rail. You can catch salmon in the far north and, thanks to the excellent domestic air network, have it cooked by the chef of your luxury hotel in Stockholm later the same day.

The seasons contrast savagely: Sweden is usually warm and exceedingly light in summer, then cold and dark in winter, when the sea may freeze and northern iron railway lines may snap. Spring and fall tend to make brief appearances, if any.

Sweden is also an arresting mixture of ancient and modern. The countryside is dotted with runic stones recalling its Viking past: trade beginning in the 8th century went as far east as Kiev and as far south as Constantinople and the Mediterranean, expanded to the British Isles in the 9th through 11th centuries, and settled in Normandy in the 10th century. Small timbered farmhouses and maypoles—around which villagers still dance at Midsummer in their traditional costumes—evoke both their pagan early history and more recent agrarian culture.

Many of the country's cities are sci-fi modern, their shop windows filled with the latest in consumer goods and fashions, but Swedes are reluctant urbanites: their hearts and souls are in the forests and the archipelagoes, and to there they faithfully retreat in the summer and on weekends to take their holidays, pick berries, or just listen to the silence. The skills of the wood-carver, the weaver, the leather worker, and the glassblower are highly prized. Similarly, Swedish humor is earthy and slapstick. Despite the praise lavished abroad on introspective dramatic artists such as August Strindberg and Ingmar Bergman, it is the simple trouser-dropping farce that will fill Stockholm's theaters, the scatological joke that will get the most laughs.

Sweden is made up of 21 counties. In the southeast is Stockholm county, which includes the capital of the same name. The industrial seaport city of Göteborg and the neighboring west-coastal counties of Bohuslän and Halland (the so-called Swedish Riviera) form another region, along with Värmland and Dalsland, on the Norwegian border. The southernmost part of Sweden, a lovely mix of farmland, forests, and châteaus, includes Skåne, Småland (the Kingdom of Glass), Blekinge, Västergötland, Östergötland, and the island of Öland. Dalarna, the country's heartland, is centered on Lake Siljan and the town of Mora; this is where Swedish folklore and traditions are most visible. To the north of Stockholm is the Bothnian Coast, a land of dramatic cliffs, fjords, and port towns that appear timeless. The northern half of Sweden, called Norrland and including the counties of Lappland and Norrbotten, is a great expanse consisting mostly of mountains and wilderness; here the hardy Sámi (also known as Lapps) herd reindeer. Many hardy visitors come to see the midnight sun.

5

Sampling all of Sweden's far-flung variety is best suited to a traveler with either no time constraints or an exceedingly generous purse. The few representative stops below, however, can make even a short visit worthwhile.

Numbers in the text correspond to numbers in the margin and black bullets on the maps. We list at least one hotel for each of the towns on the itinerary.

If you have 3 days

Spend two days in the capital city, **Stockholm**; one of these days may be spent on a boat trip in the archipelago or on Lake Mälaren. A night at the opera will set the scene, or, for the more budget-conscious traveler, some people-watching over a beer or two downtown. On the third day either visit **Göteborg**—a port town since the Viking era, marked with attractive boulevards, canals, and important museums—by high-speed train, or fly to **Mora**, in the heart of Sweden's folklore country, Dalarna. A summertime dip in Lake Siljan will bring freshness and clarity to your travel-worn senses. You could also fly to **Gotland** for a quick island adventure. The warm climate, golden, cliff-lined beaches, and delicious local lamb specialties make it difficult to leave.

If you have 5 days

Start with two days in **Stockholm**; add a third day if you want to make a side trip to **Uppsala**, Sweden's principal university town, along the banks of the Fyris River. You can take a long boat journey out into the archipelago, sleeping in a small waterside cabin. On Day 4 fly to **Mora** and rent a car for a drive around Lake Siljan, or fly to **Skellefteå** for a glimpse of northern Sweden's devout religious past and its musically innovative present. On Day 5 fly to **Göteborg**.

If you have 10 days

You can tackle this itinerary using public transportation. Start with three days in **Stockholm**, which will allow you to really get to know the city. Urban bustle, cultural highlights, and pastoral calm can all be absorbed in this time. On Day 4 take the high-speed train to **Göteborg** and stay two nights and perhaps take the chance to sail out in the west-coast archipelago. It's not as big as Stockholm's archipelago, but the locals will tell you it is much more beautiful. On Day 6 take the train to **Kalmar**, with Sweden's best-preserved Renaissance castle, via **Växjö**, the starting place for many of Sweden's 1 million immigrants to America in the 19th century, now the finishing place for many family-tree-tracing pilgrimages. From Kalmar catch the ferry to **Gotland**. On Day 8 return to Stockholm. Spend Day 9 flying to either **Mora** or **Kiruna**, the northernmost city in Sweden. Alternatively, from **Gotland** you could spend a couple of days taking the train up the **Bothnian Coast** to experience wild seas, pine-clad islands, tiny fishing villages, and grand towns built on 19th-century industrial fortunes. Stay in **Gävle, Sundsvall,** or **Umeå.** Return to Stockholm on Day 10.

Although it isn't unusual to see gray-haired men in pastel sweaters playing saxophones on TV, or to warp back to the 1950s in modern concert halls and discos, Sweden's cultural tenor also incorporates a host of global trends. Most radio stations play a mix of Swedish, American, and British hits, and a number of Swedish television programs track international music, art, and culture. Films from all over the world can be seen at the box office, although it's Hollywood that dominates. And when it comes to fashion and design, Stockholm is certainly among the trendiest cities in the world. Glossy magazines like *Wallpaper* seem to be in constant discussion about "cool Stockholm" and the like.

Despite the much-publicized sexual liberation of Swedes, the joys of hearth and home are most prized in what remains in many ways a conservative society. Conformity, not liberty, is the real key to the Swedish character; however, the good of the collective is slowly being replaced by that of the individual as socialism begins to lose its past appeal.

At the same time, Swedes remain devoted royalists and patriots, avidly following the fortunes of King Carl XVI Gustaf, Queen Silvia, and their children in the media and raising the blue-and-yellow national flag each morning on the flagpoles of their country cottages. Few nations, in fact, make as much of an effort to preserve and defend their natural heritage.

It is sometimes difficult in cities such as Stockholm, Göteborg, or Malmö to realize that you are in an urban area. Right in the center of Stockholm, you can fish for salmon or go for a swim. In Göteborg's busy harbor you can sit aboard a ship bound for the archipelago and watch fish jump out of the water; in Malmö hares hop around in the downtown parks. It is this pristine quality of life that can make a visit to Sweden a step out of time, a relaxing break from the modern world.

Exploring Sweden

Sweden consists of 21 counties. In the southeast is Stockholm county, which includes the capital of the same name. The industrial seaport city of Göteborg and the neighboring west coastal counties of Bohuslän and Halland (the so-called Swedish Riviera) form another region, along with Värmland and Dalsland on the Norwegian border. The southernmost part of Sweden, a lovely mix of farmland, forests, and châteaus, includes Skåne, Småland ("The Kingdom of Glass"), Blekinge, Västergötland, Östergötland, and the island of Öland. Dalarna, the country's heartland, is centered on Lake Siljan and the town of Mora; this is where Swedish folklore and traditions are most visible. To the north of Stockholm is the Bothnian Coast, a land of dramatic cliffs, fjords, and port towns that appear timeless. The northern half of Sweden, called Norrland and including the counties of Lappland and Norrbotten, is a great expanse consisting mostly of mountains and wilderness; here the hardy Sámi (also known as Lapps) herd reindeer. Many hardy visitors come to see the midnight sun.

Numbers in the text correspond to numbers in the margin and black bullets on the maps.

About the Restaurants

Sweden's major cities offer a full range of dining choices, from traditional to international restaurants. Outside the cities, restaurants are usually more local in influence, but most use good, fresh ingredients. Investments in training and successes in international competitions have spurred restaurant quality to fantastic heights in Sweden, and it easily competes among other major European countries in the gourmet stakes. It is worth remembering, though, that for many years eating out was prohibitively expensive for many Swedes, giving rise to a home socializing culture that still exists today. For this reason many smaller towns and rural areas are bereft of anything approaching a varied restaurant scene. The restaurants we list are the cream of the crop in each price category. Properties indicated by an ✕▥ are lodging establishments whose restaurant warrants a special trip.

Restaurant meals are big-ticket items throughout Scandinavia, but there are ways to keep the cost of eating down. Take full advantage of the large buffet breakfast often included in the cost of a hotel room. At lunch look for a "menu" that offers a set two- or three-course meal for a set price, often including bread and salad, or limit yourself to a hearty appetizer. Some restaurants now include a trip to the salad bar in the dinner price. At dinner pay careful attention to the price of wine and drinks, since the high tax on alcohol raises these costs considerably.

About the Hotels

Sweden offers a variety of accommodations, from simple bed-and-breakfasts, campsites, and hostels to hotels of the highest international standard. In the larger cities lodging ranges from first-class business hotels run by SAS, Sheraton, and Scandic to good-quality tourist-class hotels, such as RESO, Best Western, Scandic Budget, and Sweden Hotels, to a wide variety of single-entrepreneur hotels. In the countryside look for independently run inns and motels, known as guesthouses. In addition, farm holidays increasingly have become available to tourists, and Sweden has organizations that can help plan stays in the countryside.

Before you leave home, ask your travel agent about discounts, including summer hotel checks for Best Western, Scandic, and Inter Nor hotels, and enormous year-round rebates at SAS hotels for travelers over 65. All EuroClass (business-class) passengers can get discounts of at least 10% at SAS hotels when they book through SAS.

Two things about hotels usually surprise North Americans: the relatively limited dimensions of Scandinavian beds and the generous size of Scandinavian breakfasts. Scandinavian double beds are often about 60 inches wide or slightly less, close in size to the U.S. queen size. King-size beds (72 inches wide) are difficult to find and, if available, require special reservations.

Older hotels may have some rooms described as "double" that in fact have one double bed plus one foldout sofa big enough for two people. This arrangement is occasionally called a combi-room but is being phased out. Many older hotels, particularly the country inns and independently run smaller hotels in the cities, do not have private bathrooms. Inquire about this ahead of time if this is important to you.

Scandinavian breakfasts resemble what many people would call lunch, usually including breads, cheeses, marmalade, hams, lunch meats, eggs, juice, cereal, milk, and coffee. Generally, the farther north you go, the larger the breakfasts become. Breakfast is usually included in hotel rates.

Make reservations whenever possible. Even countryside inns, which usually have space, are sometimes packed with vacationing Europeans.

If you are visiting a city in Sweden it is worth looking at accommodation outside the city limits. This is where you will find the best budget lodging and good transport links and the relatively small Swedish cities means a trip downtown never takes too long.

WHAT IT COSTS In Swedish Kronor				
	$$$$	$$$	$$	$	¢
RESTAURANTS	over 420	250–420	150–250	100–150	under 100
HOTELS	above 2,900	2,300–2,900	1,500–2,300	1,000–1,500	under 1,000

Restaurant prices are for a main course at dinner. Hotel prices are for two people in a standard double room in high season.

Timing

The official tourist season—when hotel rates generally go down and museum and castle doors open—runs from mid-May through mid-September. This is Sweden's balmiest time of year; summer days are sunny and warm, nights refreshingly cool. (Summer is also mosquito season, especially in the north, but also as far south as Stockholm.) The whole country goes mad for Midsummer Day, in the middle of June. Many attractions close in late August, when the schools reopen at the end of the Swedish vacation season. The colors of autumn fade out as early as September, when the rainy season begins. The weather can be bright and fresh in the spring and fall (although spring can bring lots of rain), and many visitors prefer sightseeing when there are fewer people around. Winter comes in November and stays through March, sometimes longer. In Sweden this season is an Alpine affair, with subzero temperatures. The days can be magnificent when the snow is fresh, the sky a brilliant Nordic blue, and the air crystal fresh. Although many of the more traditional attractions are closed, there is skiing, skating, ice fishing, sleigh riding, and myriad other winter activities on offer throughout the country.

STOCKHOLM

Positioned where the waters of Lake Mälaren rush into the Baltic, Stockholm is one of Europe's most beautiful capitals. Nearly 1.6 million people live in the greater Stockholm area, yet it remains a quiet, almost pastoral city.

Built on 14 small islands joined by bridges crossing open bays and narrow channels, Stockholm is a handsome, civilized city filled with parks, squares, and airy boulevards, yet it is also a bustling modern metropolis. Glass-and-steel skyscrapers abound, but you are never more than a short walk from twisting medieval streets and waterside walkways.

The first written mention of Stockholm dates from 1252, when a powerful regent named Birger Jarl (d. 1266) built a fortified castle and township here. King Gustav Vasa (1496–1560) took it over in 1523, and King Gustavus Adolphus (1594–1632) made it the heart of an empire a century later.

5

Beaches

Beaches in Sweden range from wide and sandy strands, on the western side of the country, to steep and rocky shores, on the eastern side, from oceanfront to lakefront, from resorts to remote nature preserves. The area most favored for the standard sunbathing and wave-frolicking vacation is known as the Swedish Riviera, on the coast south of Göteborg. Wherever you go, a dip in the east's brackish Baltic or the west's wild Atlantic is a bracing experience that will set your pulse racing.

Dining

The nation's standard home-cooked meal is basically peasant fare—sausages, potatoes, wild game, fish, and other hearty foods to ward off the winter cold. Yet Sweden has also produced the *smörgåsbord,* a generous and artfully arranged buffet featuring both hot and cold dishes. Fish—fresh, smoked, or pickled—is a Swedish specialty; herring and salmon both come in myriad preparations.

Recently, restaurants in the larger cities have begun offering innovative dishes that combine the ingredients and simplicity of traditional Swedish cuisine with Mediterranean, Asian, and Caribbean influences, a fusion trend that dovetails with an increase in the number of foreign restaurants popping up throughout Sweden. Despite the popularity of such culinary endeavors, it's still easy to find *Husmanskost* (home-cooking) recipes, which are often served in restaurants as a *dagens rätt* (daily special) at lunch. Examples are *pyttipanna* (literally, "bits in the pan"—beef and potato hash topped with a fried egg); pea soup with pancakes, a traditional meal on Thursday; and, of course, *kötbullar,* Swedish meatballs, served with lingonberry jam, a creamy brown sauce, and mashed potatoes.

Look for *kräftor* (crayfish), boiled with dill, salt, and sugar, then cooled overnight; they are most popular in August. Swedes eat kräftor with hot buttered toast, caraway seeds, and schnapps or beer. Autumn heralds an exotic assortment of mushrooms and wild berries. Trout and salmon are common, as are various cuts of elk and reindeer. To the foreign palate, the best of Norrland's culinary specialties is undoubtedly *löjrom,* pinkish caviar from a species of Baltic herring, eaten with chopped onions and sour cream, and the various desserts made from the bittersweet cloudberries that thrive here.

Ice-Skating

Sweden produces some of the best hockey players in the world. Just look at Peter Forsberg and Mats Sudin, both stars of the National Hockey League. But there's another, slightly more unusual type of ice-skating that is also big in Sweden. In *långfärdsskridsåkning* (long-distance skating), extra-long skate blades are strapped onto mountaineering boots. This allows the skaters to travel great distances in long, smooth strides. It's especially popular in the Stockholm archipelago when the water between islands is frozen.

Lodging

Service in a Swedish hotel, no matter the price category, is always unfailingly courteous and efficient. Accommodations on the expensive side offer great charm and beauty, but the advantages of location held by less luxurious establishments shouldn't be overlooked. The woodland setting of a camper's *stuga* (small wooden cottage) may be just as desirable and memorable as the gilded antiques of a downtown hotel.

In summer many discounts, special passes, and summer packages are available. Some offer discounts approaching 50%. Weekend rates are also considerably cheaper. Sweden Hotel's ScanPlus Hotel pass costs SKr 90 and gives discounts of 15%–50%, depending on the hotel. Also, if you stay four nights in a row, you get your fifth night free.

Vandrarhem (hostels), also scrupulously clean and well run, are more expensive than elsewhere in Europe. The Swedish Touring Club (STF ⊕ www. stfturist.se) has 315 hostels and 40 mountain cabins nationwide, most with four- to six-bed family rooms, around 100 with running hot and cold water. They are open to anyone regardless of age. Prices are about SKr 100 per night for members of STF or organizations affiliated with Hostelling International. Nonmembers are charged an additional SKr 35 per night. STF publishes an annual hostel handbook. The Swedish Hostel Association also has a Web site with information in English (⊕ www.svif.se).

Sailing

Deep at heart, modern Swedes are still seafaring Vikings. Sweden's cultural dependence on boats runs so deep that a popular gift at Christmas is candles containing creosote, providing the comforting scent of dock and hull for when sailors can't be on their boats—which is most of the year. In summer thousands of craft jostle among the islands of the archipelago and clog the lakes and rivers. Statistics claim there are more than 250,000 boats in the Stockholm archipelago alone. Boating opportunities are plentiful, from hourly rentals to chartered cruises in anything from kayaks to motor launches to huge luxury ferry liners.

Skiing

Sweden is a skiing nation, with plenty of major mountains for downhill skiing and snowboarding and endless trials for Nordic skiing. The best areas are in the north, with Åre offering the most challenging terrain and Sälen better for families. One of Sweden's legendary sports heroes is Ingemar Stenmark, the champion downhill skier who dominated the sport in the 1970s. Today Pernilla Wiberg is the queen of the slopes.

Tennis

When Björn Borg began to win Wimbledon with almost monotonous regularity, Sweden became a force in world tennis. As such, the country is filled with indoor and outdoor courts, and major competitions—notably the Stockholm Open—take place regularly. One of the most unusual is the annual Donald Duck Cup, in Båstad, for children ages 11–15; ever since the young Björn won a Donald Duck trophy, the tournament has attracted thousands of youngsters who hope to imitate his success.

During the Thirty Years' War (1618–48), Sweden gained importance as a Baltic trading state, and Stockholm grew commensurately. But by the beginning of the 18th century, Swedish influence had begun to wane and Stockholm's development had slowed. It did not revive until the industrial revolution, when the hub of the city moved north from Gamla Stan.

Nowadays most Stockholmers live in high-rise suburbs that branch out to the pine forests and lakesides around the capital. They are linked by a highly efficient infrastructure of roads, railways, and a subway system that is one of the safest in the world. Air pollution is minimal, and the city streets are relatively clean and safe.

Exploring Stockholm

Although Stockholm is built on a group of islands adjoining the mainland, the waterways between them are so narrow and the bridges so smoothly integrated that the city really does feel more or less continuous. The island of Gamla Stan and its smaller neighbors, Riddarholmen and Helgeandsholmen, form what can be called the town center. South of Gamla Stan, Södermalm spreads over a wide area, its many art galleries and bars attracting a slightly bohemian crowd. North of Gamla Stan is Norrmalm, the financial and business heart of the city. West of Norrmalm is the island of Kungsholmen, site of the Stadshuset (city hall) and most of the city government offices. East of Norrmalm is Östermalm, an old residential neighborhood where many of the embassies and consulates are found. Finally, between Östermalm and Södermalm lies the island of Djurgården, once a royal game preserve, now the site of lovely parks and museums such as Skansen, the open-air cultural heritage park.

Modern Stockholm

The area bounded by Stadshuset, Hötorget, Stureplan, and the Kungliga Dramatiska Teatern (nicknamed Dramaten) is essentially Stockholm's downtown, where the city comes closest to feeling like a bustling metropolis. Shopping, nightlife, business, traffic, dining, festivals—all are at their most intense in this part of town.

a good walk

Start at the redbrick **Stadshuset** ❶ ⌐, a powerful symbol of Stockholm. Cross the bridge to Klara Mälarstrand and follow the waterfront to Drottninggatan. Take a left and continue along this popular shop-lined pedestrian street north to the hub of the city, **Sergels Torg** ❷. The **Kulturhuset** ❸ is in the imposing glass building on the southern side of Sergels Torg. Farther north on Drottninggatan is the market-filled **Hötorget** ❹. The intersection of Kungsgatan and Sveavägen, where the Konserthuset (Concert Hall) stands, is one of the busiest pedestrian crossroads in town.

Head north up Sveavägen for a brief detour to see the spot where Prime Minister Olof Palme was assassinated in 1986. A plaque has been laid on the right-hand side of the street, just before the intersection with Olof Palmes Gata; his grave is in Adolf Fredrik's Kyrkogård, a few blocks farther on. Continue north along Sveavägen until you reach the large intersection of Odengatan and Sveavägen. On your left will be **Stockholms Stadsbiblioteket** ❺. Go back down Sveavägen and turn right up Tegnérgatan to find **Strindbergsmuseet Blå Tornet** ❻, where playwright August Strindberg lived from 1908 to 1912. Return to Hötorget by way of Drottninggatan.

Next, walk east along Kungsgatan, one of Stockholm's main shopping streets, to Stureplan. On this street is Sturegallerian, an elegant mall. Head southeast along Birger Jarlsgatan—named for the nobleman generally credited with founding Stockholm around 1252—where there are still more interesting shops and restaurants. When you reach Nybroplan, take a look at the grand **Kungliga Dramatiska Teatern** ❼.

Heading west up Hamngatan, stop in at **Hallwylska Museet** ❽ for a tour of the private collection of Countess von Hallwyl's treasures. Continue along Hamngatan to **Kungsträdgården** ❾, a park since 1562. Outdoor cafés and restaurants are clustered by this leafy spot, a summer venue for public concerts and events. At the northwest corner of the park is Sverigehuset, or Sweden House, the tourist center; on the opposite side of Hamngatan is the NK department store.

Sweden

Riksgränsen
Kiruna

Arctic Circle

Norwegian Sea

Gällivare
Jokkmokk

Luleälven

400

Tärnaby
Arjeplog
Töre
Tårneå

E79
Arvidsjaur
Kalix

Sorsele
Luleå

Storuman
Piteå
95

342
Lycksele
Skellefteå

Åsele
Umeälven
99

Strömsund
Umeå

90

Åre

Östersund

E75

Tännäs
Ljungan
Sundsvall

84

FINLAND

Idre
Hudiksvall
Gulf of Bothnia

70
Bollnäs

Mora
Söderhamn

62
Falun
Gävle
80

Klarälven
Borlänge
Avesta

Fagersta

Karlstad
Västerås
Åland

E18
Uppsala
E4

Mellerud
Mälaren
Stockholm

Strömstad
Vänern
Örebro
Gulf of Finland

Uddevalla
Norrköping
ESTONIA

Trollhättan
Gotska Sandön

Göteborg
(Gothenburg)
Vättern
Linköping
Baltic Sea

40
Jönköping
Gulf of Riga

Borås
Visby

Falkenberg
Nässjö
E66

E6
Värnamo
Oskarshamn
Gotland

Halmstad
Växjö

23
Kalmar
Öland
LATVIA

Helsingborg
Karlskrona

Malmö
Kristianstad
LITHUANIA

DENMARK

Trelleborg
Ystad

NORWAY

0   50 miles

0   75 km

TIMING Allow about 4½ hours for the walk, plus an hour each for guided tours of Stadshuset and Hallwylska Museet (September–June, Sunday only). The Strindbergsmuseet Blå Tornet is closed Monday.

WHAT TO SEE **Hallwylska Museet** (Hallwyl Museum). This private late-19th-century palace with imposing wood-panel rooms houses a collection of furniture, paintings, and musical instruments in a bewildering mélange of styles assembled by Countess von Hallwyl, who left it to the state upon her death. ✉ *Hamng. 4, Normalm* ☎ *08/51955599* ⊕ *www.hallwylskamuseet.se* 🎫 *SKr 65* ☉ *Guided tours only. Tours in English July and Aug., daily at 1; Sept.–June, Sun. at 1.*

★ ❹ **Hötorget** (Hay Market). Once the city's hay market, this is now a popular gathering place with an excellent outdoor fruit-and-vegetable market. Also lining the square are the Konserthuset (Concert Hall), the PUB department store, and a multiscreen cinema Filmstaden Sergel. ✉ *Just west of Sveaväg, Normalm.*

> **need a break?**
> Stop at the food hall **Kungshallen** (✉ Hötorget opposite Filmstaden Sergel, Normalm ☎ 08/218005) and choose from Swedish and international goodies. Or get a window table at the café inside Filmstaden Sergel.

🖐 ❸ **Kulturhuset** (Culture House). Since it opened in 1974, architect Peter Celsing's cultural center, a glass-and-stone monolith on the south side of Sergels Torg, has become a symbol of Stockholm and of the growth of modernism in Sweden. Stockholmers are divided on the aesthetics of this building—most either love it or hate it. Here there are exhibitions for children and adults, a library, a theater, a youth center, an exhibition center, and a restaurant. Head to Café Panorama, on the top floor, to savor traditional Swedish cuisine and a great view of Sergels Torg down below. ✉ *Sergels Torg 3, City* ☎ *08/50831508* ⊕ *www. kulturhuset.stockholm.se.*

❼ **Kungliga Dramatiska Teatern** (Royal Dramatic Theater). Locally known as Dramaten, the national theater stages works by the likes of Strindberg and other playwrights of international stature in a grand appealing building whose facade and gilded statuary look out over the city harbor. The theater gave its first performance in 1788, when it was located at Bollhuset on Slottsbacken, next to the Royal Palace. It later moved to Kungsträdgården, spent some time in the Opera House, and ended up at its present location in 1908. Performances are in Swedish. ✉ *Nybroplan, Östermalm* ☎ *08/6670680* ⊕ *www.dramaten.se.*

🖐 ❾ **Kungsträdgården** (King's Garden). This is one of Stockholm's smallest yet most central parks. Once the royal kitchen garden, it now hosts a large number of festivals and events each season. The park has numerous cafés and restaurants, a playground, and, in winter, an ice-skating rink. ✛ *Between Hamng. and the Operan.*

❷ **Sergels Torg.** Named after Johan Tobias Sergel (1740–1814), one of Sweden's greatest sculptors, this busy junction in Stockholm's center is dominated by modern, functional buildings and a sunken pedestrian square with subterranean connections to the rest of the neighborhood.

▶ ❶ **Stadshuset** (City Hall). The architect Ragnar Östberg, one of the founders FodorśChoice of the National Romantic movement, completed Stockholm's city hall ★ in 1923. Headquarters of the city council, the building is functional but ornate: its immense **Blå Hallen** (Blue Hall) is the venue for the annual Nobel Prize dinner, Stockholm's principal social event. A trip to the top of the 348-foot tower, most of which can be achieved by elevator, is re-

Stockholm

ÖSTERMALM

Kommendörsgatan

Karlaplan

Karlavägen

Linnégatan

LADUGÅRDSGÄRDET

Artillerigatan
Skeppargatan
Grevgatan
Styrmangatan
Storgatan

Riddargatan

Linnégatan

Narvavägen

Bandegatan

Oxenstiernsgatan

Gärdesgatan
Skarpögatan

33

37 36

Strandvägen

Strandvägen

Djurgårdsbron

Djurgårdsbrunnsviken

26

27

25

31

Rosendalsvägen

32

DJURGÅRDEN

Sirishovsvägen

22

23

SKEPPSHOLMEN

Svensksundsvägen

Alkärret
Djurgårdsvägen
Falkenbergsg.

29

28

Djurgårds Slätten

Sollidsbacken

Singelbacken

30

24

Allmänna Gränd

KASTELL-
HOLMEN

BECKHOLMEN

Baltic →

Saltsjön

KEY

🚢 Ferry
⊢ Rail Lines
▶ Start of walk
🛈 Tourist information

0   500 yards
0   500 meters

warded by a breathtaking panorama of the city and Riddarfjärden. ✉ *Hantverkarg. 1, Kungsholmen* ☎ *08/50829000* ⊕ *www.stockholm. se* ✆ *SKr 45, tower SKr 20* ⊙ *Guided tours only. Tours in English, June–Aug., daily 10, 11, noon, and 2; Sept., daily 10, noon, and 2; Oct.–May, daily 10 and noon.*

> **need a break?**
>
> After climbing the Stadshuset tower, relax on the fine grass terraces that lead down to the bay and overlook Lake Mälaren. Or have lunch in **Stadshuskällaren** (City Hall Cellar; ☎ 08/6505454), where the annual Nobel Prize banquet is held. You can also head a few blocks down Hantverkargatan to find several good small restaurants.

❺ **Stockholms Stadsbiblioteket** (Stockholm City Library). Libraries aren't always a top sightseeing priority, but the Stockholm City Library is among the most captivating buildings in town. Designed by the famous Swedish architect E. G. Asplund and completed in 1928, the building's cylindrical, galleried main hall gives it the appearance of a large birthday cake. Inside is an excellent "information technology" center with free Internet access—and lots of books, too. ✉ *Sveav. 73, Vasastan* ☎ *08/50831100* ⊕ *www.ssb.stockholm.se* ⊙ *Mon.–Thurs. 10–7, Fri. 10–6, Sat. noon–4.*

★ ❻ **Strindbergsmuseet Blå Tornet** (Strindberg Museum, Blue Tower). Hidden away over a grocery store, this museum is dedicated to Sweden's most important author and dramatist, August Strindberg (1849–1912), who resided here from 1908 until his death four years later. The interior has been expertly reconstructed with authentic furnishings and other objects, including one of his pens. The museum also houses a library, printing press, and picture archives, and it is the site of literary, musical, and theatrical events. ✉ *Drottningg. 85, Norrmalm* ☎ *08/4115354* ⊕ *www. strindbergsmuseet.se* ✆ *SKr 40* ⊙ *Sept.–May, Tues. noon–7, Wed.–Sun. noon–4, June–Aug., Tues.–Fri. 11–4, weekends noon–4.*

Gamla Stan & Skeppsholmen

Gamla Stan (Old Town) sits between two of Stockholm's main islands and is the site of the medieval city. East of Gamla Stan is the island of Skeppsholmen, whose narrow, twisting cobble streets are lined with superbly preserved old buildings.

> **a good walk**

Start at the waterfront edge of Kungsträdgården and walk across Strömsbron to **Kungliga Slottet** ❿ ↳, where you can see the changing of the guard at noon every day. Walk up the sloping cobblestone drive called Slottsbacken and bear right past the Obelisk to find the main entrance to the palace. Stockholm's 15th-century Gothic cathedral, **Storkyrkan** ⓫, stands at the top of Slottsbacken, but its entrance is at the other end, on Trångsund.

Following Källargränd from the Obelisk or Trångsund from Storkyrkan, you will reach the small square called **Stortorget** ⓬, marvelously atmospheric amid magnificent old merchants' houses. Stockholm's Börshuset (Stock Exchange), which currently houses the **Nobelmuseet** ⓭, fronts the square.

Walk past Svartmangatan's many ancient buildings, including the Tyska Kyrkan, or German Church, with its resplendent oxidized copper spire and airy interior. Continue along Svartmangatan and take a right on Tyska Stallplan to Prästgatan, and just to your left will be Mårten Trotzigs Gränd; this lamplighted alley stairway leads downhill to Järntorget. From here take Västerlånggatan back north across Gamla Stan, checking out the pricey fashion boutiques, galleries, and souvenir shops along the way.

STOCKHOLM'S ARCHITECTURAL PROCESSION

AS IN MANY OTHER SWEDISH CITIES, a single afternoon walk in Stockholm offers a journey through centuries of architectural change and innovation. There are, of course, the classics. Take Kungliga Slottet (Royal Palace) on Gamla Stan. Designed by Nicodemus Tessin the Younger and built between 1690 and 1704, it's a rather austere palace—no domes, no great towers—and yet it commands a certain respect sitting so regally over the water. Nearby, on Riddarholmen, observe the gorgeous, medieval Riddarholmskyrkan (Riddarholm Church), with its lattice spire pointed toward the heavens. And let's not forget Drottningholm, a 17th-century châteauesque structure—designed by Tessin the Elder and finished by his son— that has been the home of the royal family since 1981. Also at Drottningholm is the Court Theater (1766), which, remarkably, still contains its original interior and fully functional stage machinery.

Stadshuset (city hall) is also a must-see on any architectural walking tour. Completed in 1923, the building contains more than 8 million bricks and 19 million gilded mosaic tiles. Each year the Nobel Prize ceremony is held in the building's Blå Hallen (Blue Hall). Built a few years later is Stadsbiblioteket (City Library), designed by Eric Gunnar Asplund—one of Sweden's most renowned architects. The library's eye-pleasing yet simple design foreshadows the funkis (functionalist) movement that Gunnar helped spearhead in the 1920s and '30s.

Skattehuset (Tax House), also known as Skatteskrapan (a play on the word skyscraper), is hard to miss, looming mercilessly as it does over Södermalm. Completed in the early 1950s as part of an attempt to consolidate the nation's tax offices, the singularly dull, gray, 25-story building is often criticized for having ruined the southern skyline of Stockholm. Except for the annual siege of thousands of Stockholmers flooding it with last-minute tax declarations every May, the building sees few visitors.

Farther south, another architectural oddity plagues—or enhances, depending on whom you ask—the skyline. Globen (the Globe), the world's largest spherical building, looks something like a colossal golf ball or a futuristic space-station still awaiting its launch into orbit. Unveiled in 1988, it's the main arena in Stockholm for indoor sporting events (especially hockey) and rock concerts. Despite debates concerning its aesthetics (or lack thereof), a look at the cables and beams inside reveals Globen's architecture marvel.

Another much debated architectural undertaking is Hötorgscity, across from the highly influential Kulturhuset at Sergels Torg. This postwar compound of five 18-story buildings was constructed in the mid-'50s and shares the oppressive style of its near-contemporary, the Skatteskrapan. Hötorgscity was built to house retail stores and offices and thus bring more commerce to downtown Stockholm. The project failed. A significant chunk of historic Stockholm was lost. Vandalized by ne'er-do-wells and ignored by prospective tenants, the buildings were shut down in the '70s, although today there is a renewed interest in the top floors of the buildings, especially among young business owners.

What is most striking about the buildings that make up Stockholm's architectural portfolio is their collective diversity. You'll glean a particularly remarkable sense of this if you in one day you visit buildings that collectively encompass all the architectural styles. Centuries of history involving both failures and successes are reflected in the styles these structures represent. Every building in Stockholm, new or old, tells a story.

Cut down Storkyrkobrinken to the 17th-century Dutch baroque **Riddarhuset** ⑭. A short walk takes you over Riddarholmsbron to Riddarholmen—Island of Knights—on which stands **Riddarholmskyrkan** ⑮. Also on Riddarholmen is the white 17th-century palace that houses the **Svea Hovrätt** ⑯. Returning across Riddarholmsbron, take Myntgatan back toward Kungliga Slottet and turn left onto Stallbron and cross the bridge. You'll then pass through the refurbished stone **Riksdagshuset** ⑰ on Helgeandsholmen, Holy Ghost Island. Another short bridge returns you to Drottninggatan; take a right onto Fredsgatan and walk until you reach **Medelhavsmuseet** ⑱, on the left, just before Gustav Adolfs Torg. Right there on the square is the **Dansmuseet** ⑲.

The **Operan** ⑳ occupies the waterfront between Gustav Adolfs Torg and Karl XII's Torg (part of Kungsträdgården). A little farther along, on Södra Blasieholmshamn, a host of tour boats docks in front of the stately Grand Hotel. Pass the Grand and visit the **Nationalmuseum** ㉑. Cross the footbridge to the idyllic island of Skeppsholmen, the location of the **Östasiatiska Museet** ㉒, with a fine collection of Buddhist art. Also on Skeppsholmen is the **Moderna Museet** ㉓, which is in the same complex that houses the **Arkitekturmuseet.** To the southwest is **Svensk Form** ㉔, a design museum. The adjoining island, Kastellholmen, is a pleasant place for a stroll, especially on a summer evening, with views of the Baltic harbor and Djurgården's lighted parks.

TIMING Allow three hours for the walk, double that if you want to tour the various parts of the palace. The Nationalmuseum and Östasiatiska Museet will take up to an hour each to view. Note that Kungliga Slottet is closed Monday off-season, and Stockholms Leksaksmuseum, Moderna Museet, Nationalmuseum, and Östasiatiska Museet are always closed Monday. The Riddarhuset is open weekdays only; off-season, hit the Riddarholmskyrkan on a Wednesday or weekend.

WHAT TO SEE **Arkitekturmuseet.** The Museum of Architecture uses models, photos, and drawings to tell the long and interesting story of Swedish architecture. Certain buildings shed light on specific periods, including the Stockholm Town Hall, Vadstena Castle, and the Helsingborg Concert House. The museum also hosts lectures, debates, and architectural tours of the city. ⊠ *Skeppsholmen* ☎ *08/58727000* ⊕ *www.arkitekturmuseet. se* ⊠ *Free* ☉ *Tues. and Thurs. 11–8, Fri.–Sun. 11–6.*

⑲ **Dansmuseet** (Museum of Dance). Close to the Royal Opera House, the Museum of Dance has a permanent collection that examines dance, theater, and art from Asia, Africa, and Europe. Such artists as Fernand Léger, Francis Picabia, Giorgio de Chirico, and Jean Cocteau are represented in the exhibitions. The Rolf de Maré Study Centre has a vast collection of dance reference materials, including about 4,000 books and 3,000 videos. ⊠ *Gustav Adolfs torg 22–24, City* ☎ *08/4417650* ⊕ *www. dansmuseet.nu* ⊠ *SKr 50* ☉ *Weekdays 11–4, weekends noon–4.*

Järntorget (Iron Square). Named after its original use as an iron and copper marketplace, this square was also the venue for public executions. ⊠ *Intersection of Västerlångg and Österlångg, Gamla Stan.*

⑩ **Kungliga Slottet** (Royal Palace). Designed by Nicodemus Tessin, the Royal
Fodor'sChoice Palace was completed in 1760 and replaced the previous palace that had
★ burned here in 1697. Just three weeks later, Tessin—who had also designed the previous incarnation, submitted his drawings for the new palace to the Swedish government. The rebuilding was finally completed, exactly according to Tessin's designs, 60 years later. The four facades of the palace each have a distinct style: the west is the king's, the east the queen's, the south belongs to the nation, and the north represents roy-

alty in general. Watch the changing of the guard in the curved terrace entrance, and view the palace's fine furnishings and Gobelin tapestries on a tour of the **Representationsvän** (State Apartments). To survey the crown jewels, which are no longer used in this self-consciously egalitarian country, head to the **Skattkammaren** (Treasury). The **Livrustkammaren** (Royal Armory) has an outstanding collection of weaponry, coaches, and royal regalia. Entrances to the Treasury and Armory are on the Slottsbacken side of the palace. ⊠ *Gamla Stan* ☎ *08/4026130* ⊕ *www. royalcourt.se* ⊠ *State Apartments SKr 70, Treasury SKr 70, Royal Armory SKr 70 combined ticket for all areas SKr 110* ☉ *State Apartments and Treasury May–Aug., daily 10–4; Sept.–Apr., Tues.–Sun. noon–3. Armory May–Aug., daily 11–4; Sept.–May, Tues.–Sun. 11–4.*

⑱ Medelhavsmuseet (Mediterranean Museum). During the 1700s this building housed the Royal Courts. Then, in the early 1900s, the vast interior of the building was redesigned to resemble the Palazzo Bevilaqua i Bologna, Italy. The collection has a good selection of art from Asia as well as from ancient Egypt, Greece, and Rome. In the Gold Room you can see fine gold, silver, and bronze jewelry from the Far East, Greece, and Rome. ⊠ *Fredsg. 2, City* ☎ *08/51955380* ⊕ *www.medelhavsmuseet. se* ⊠ *SKr 50* ☉ *Tues. 11–8, Wed.–Fri. 11–4, weekends noon–5.*

★ ㉓ Moderna Museet (Museum of Modern Art). Reopened in its original venue on Skeppsholmen, the museum's excellent collection includes works by Picasso, Kandinsky, Dalí, Brancusi, and other international artists. You can also view examples of significant Swedish painters and sculptors and an extensive section on photography. The building itself is striking. Designed by the well-regarded Spanish architect Rafael Moneo, it has seemingly endless hallways of blond wood and walls of glass. ⊠ *Skeppsholmen, City* ☎ *08/51955200* ⊕ *www.modernamuseet.se* ⊠ *Free* ☉ *Tues.–Thurs. 11–8, Fri.–Sun. 11–6.*

㉑ Nationalmuseum. The museum's collection of paintings and sculptures is made up of about 12,500 works. The emphasis is on Swedish and Nordic art, but other areas are well represented. Look especially for some fine works by Rembrandt. The print and drawing department is also impressive, with a nearly complete collection of Edouard Manet prints. ⊠ *Södra Blasieholmshamnen, City* ☎ *08/51954300* ⊕ *www. nationalmuseum.se* ⊠ *SKr 75* ☉ *Jan.–Aug., Tues. 11–8, Wed.–Sun. 11–5; Sept.–Dec., Tues. and Thurs. 11–8, Wed., Fri., and weekends 11–5.*

Fodor'sChoice ★

⑬ Nobelmuseet. The Swedish Academy meets at Börshuset (the Stock Exchange) every year to decide the winner of the Nobel Prize for literature. The building is also the home of the Nobel Museum. Along with exhibits on creativity's many forms, the museum displays scientific models, shows films, and has a full explanation of the process of choosing prizewinners. The museum does a good job covering the controversial selections made over the years. It's a must for Nobel Prize hopefuls and others. ⊠ *Börshuset, Stortorget, Gamla Stan* ☎ *08/232506* ⊕ *www. nobelprize.org/nobelmuseum* ☉ *Wed.–Mon. 10–6, Tues. 10–8.*

⑳ Operan (Opera House). Stockholm's baroque Opera House is almost more famous for its restaurants and bars than for its opera and ballet productions, but that doesn't mean an evening performance should be missed. There's not a bad seat in the house. For just SKr 35 you can even get a listening-only seat (with no view). Still, its food and drink status can't be denied. It has been one of Stockholm's artistic and literary watering holes since the first Operakällaren restaurant opened on the site in 1787. ⊠ *Gustav Adolfs Torg, City* ☎ *08/248240* ⊕ *www. operan.se.*

㉒ **Östasiatiska Museet** (Museum of Far Eastern Antiquities). If you have an affinity for Asian art and culture, don't miss this impressive collection of Chinese and Japanese Buddhist sculptures and artifacts. Although some exhibits are displayed with little creativity, the pieces themselves are always worthwhile. The more than 100,000 pieces that make up the holdings here include many from China's Neolithic and Bronze ages. ⊠ *Skeppsholmen, City* ☎ *08/51955750* ⊕ *www.mfea.se* ⊡ *Free* ⊙ *Tues. noon–8, Wed.–Sun. noon–5.*

⑮ **Riddarholmskyrkan** (Riddarholm Church). Dating from 1270, the Grey Friars monastery is the second-oldest structure in Stockholm and has been the burial place for Swedish kings for more than 400 years. The redbrick structure, distinguished by its delicate iron-fretwork spire, is rarely used for services: it's more like a museum now. The most famous figures interred within are King Gustavus Adolphus, hero of the Thirty Years' War, and the warrior King Karl XII, renowned for his daring invasion of Russia, who died in Norway in 1718. The most recent of the 17 Swedish kings to be put to rest here was Gustav V, in 1950. The different rulers' sarcophagi, usually embellished with their monograms, are visible in the small chapels dedicated to the various dynasties. ⊠ *Riddarholmen* ☎ *08/4026130* ⊡ *SKr 20* ⊙ *May–Aug., daily 10–4; Sept., weekends noon–3.*

⑭ **Riddarhuset.** Completed in 1674, the House of Nobles was used for parliamentary assemblies and administration during the four-estate parliamentary period that lasted until 1866. Since then Swedish nobility has continued to meet here every three years for administrative meetings. Hanging from its walls are 2,325 escutcheons, representing all the former noble families of Sweden. The building has excellent acoustic properties and is often used for concerts. ⊠ *Riddarhustorget 10, Gamla Stan* ☎ *08/7233990* ⊕ *www.riddarhuset.se* ⊡ *SKr 40* ⊙ *Weekdays 11:30–12:30.*

⑰ **Riksdagshuset** (Parliament Building). When in session, the Swedish Parliament meets in this 1904 building. Above the entrance, the architect placed sculptures of a peasant, a burgher, a clergyman, and a nobleman. Take a tour of the building not only to learn about Swedish government but also to see the art within. In the former First Chamber are murals by Otte Sköld illustrating different periods in the history of Stockholm, and in the current First Chamber a massive tapestry by Elisabet Hasselberg Olsson, *Memory of a Landscape,* hangs above the podium. ⊠ *Riksg. 3A, Gamla Stan* ☎ *08/7864000* ⊕ *www.riksdagen.se* ⊡ *Free* ⊙ *Tours in English late June–late Aug., weekdays 12:30 and 2; late Aug.–late June, weekends 1:30. Call ahead for reservations.*

off the beaten path

STOCKHOLMS LEKSAKSMUSEUM – In Södermalm, Stockholm's Toy Museum has a collection of toys and dolls from all over the world, as well as a children's theater with clowns, magicians, storytellers, and puppet shows. The museum is near the Mariatorget subway station, two stops south of Gamla Stan. ⊠ *Mariatorget 1, Södermalm* ☎ *08/64044492* ⊡ *SKr 40* ⊙ *Tues.–Fri. 10–4, weekends noon–4.*

⑪ **Storkyrkan.** Swedish kings were crowned in the 15th-century Great Church as late as 1907. Today its main attractions are a dramatic wooden statue of St. George slaying the dragon, carved by Bernt Notke of Lübeck in 1489, and the *Parhelion* (1520), the oldest-known painting of Stockholm. ⊠ *Trångsund 1, Gamla Stan* ☎ *08/7233016* ⊙ *Sept.–Apr., daily 9–4; May–Aug., daily 9–6.*

⑫ Stortorget (Great Square). Here in 1520 the Danish king Christian II ordered a massacre of Swedish noblemen. The slaughter paved the way for a national revolt against foreign rule and the founding of Sweden as a sovereign state under King Gustav Vasa, who ruled from 1523 to 1560. One legend holds that if it rains heavily enough on the anniversary of the massacre, the old stones still run red. ✉ *Near Kungliga Slottet, Gamla Stan.*

need a break? As you stroll along the busy shopping street of Västerlånggatan, you may suddenly notice the strong smell of waffles. That would be the fresh waffle-cones being made at **Café Kåkbrinken** (✉ Västerlång. 41, on corner of Kåkbrinken near Stortorget, Gamla Stan), which serves the best (and biggest) ice-cream cones in the Old Town.

⑯ Svea Hovrätt (Swedish High Court). The Swedish High Court commands a prime site on the island of Riddarholmen, on a quiet and restful quayside. Sit on the water's edge and watch the boats on Riddarfjärden (Bay of Knights) and, beyond it, Lake Mälaren. From here you can see the lake, the stately arches of Västerbron (West Bridge) in the distance, the southern heights, and above all, the imposing profile of the city hall, which appears almost to be floating on the water. At the quay you may see one of the Göta Canal ships. ✉ *Riddarholmen* ☉ *Not open to public.*

㉔ Svensk Form (Swedish Form). This museum emphasizes the importance of Swedish form and design, although international works and trends are also covered. Exhibits include everything from chairs to light fixtures to cups, bowls, and silverware. Find out why Sweden is considered a world leader in industrial design. Every year the museum gives out a prestigious and highly coveted design award called Utmärkt Svenskt Form (Outstanding Swedish Design). The winning objects are then exhibited in the fall. ✉ *Skeppsholmen Holmamiralens väg 2, Skeppsholmen, City* ☎ *08/6443303* ⊕ *www.svenskform.se* ☉ *Tues. and Thurs. noon–7, Fri.–Sun. noon–5.*

Djurgården & Skansen

Djurgården is Stockholm's pleasure island: on it are the outdoor museum Skansen, the Gröna Lund amusement park, and the *Vasa*, a 17th-century warship raised from the harbor bed in 1961, as well as other delights.

a good walk You can approach Djurgården from the water aboard the small ferries that leave from Slussen at the southern end of Gamla Stan. In summer ferries also leave from Nybrokajen, or New Bridge Quay, in front of the Kungliga Dramatiska Teatern. Alternatively, starting at the theater, stroll down the Strandvägen quayside—taking in the magnificent old sailing ships and the fine views over the harbor—and cross Djurgårdsbron, or Djurgården Bridge, to the island. Your first port of call should be the **Vasamuseet** ㉕ ▶, with its dramatic display of splendid 17th-century warships. If you have children in tow, be sure to visit **Junibacken** ㉖, off Djurgårdsbron. Return to Djurgårdsvägen to find the entrance to the **Nordiska Museet** ㉗, worth a visit for insight into Swedish folklore.

Continue on Djurgårdsvägen to the amusement park **Gröna Lund Tivoli** ㉘, where Stockholmers of all ages come to play. Beyond the park, cross Djurgårdsvägen to **Skansen** ㉙.

From Skansen continue on Djurgårdsvägen to Prins Eugens Väg and follow the signs to the beautiful late-19th-century **Waldemarsudde** ㉚. On the way back to Djurgårdsbron, take the small street called Hazeliusbacken around to the charmingly archaic **Biologiska Museet** ③. From the museum walk toward Djurgårdsbron and then take a right on Rosendalsvägen. Signs on this street lead to **Rosendals Trädgårder** ㉜, which has beautiful gardens and a delightful café. From here you can stroll back along the water toward the city.

TIMING   Allow half a day for this tour, unless you're planning to turn it into a full-day event with lengthy visits to Skansen, Junibacken, and Gröna Lund Tivoli. The Vasamuseet warrants two hours, and the Nordiska and Biologiska museums need an hour each. Waldemarsudde requires another half hour. Gröna Lund Tivoli is closed from mid-September to late April. The Nordiska Museet closes Monday, and the Biologiska Museet and Waldemarsudde are closed Monday off-season.

WHAT TO SEE   **Biologiska Museet** (Biological Museum). The Biological Museum, in the
☉ ③   shadow of Skansen, exhibits preserved animals in various simulated environments. The museum itself, unchanged since its 19th-century opening, is a delightful look into the past. ✉ *Hazeliusporten, Djurgården* ☎ *08/4428215* ⊕ *www.skansen.se* 💰 *SKr 30* ☉ *Apr.–Sept., daily 10–4; Oct.–Mar., Tues.–Sun. 10–3.*

☉ ㉘   **Gröna Lund Tivoli.** Smaller than Copenhagen's Tivoli or Göteborg's Liseberg, this amusement park is a clean, well-organized pleasure garden with rides, attractions, and restaurants. If you're feeling especially daring, try the Power Tower. At 350 feet (80 meters), it's Europe's tallest free-fall amusement-park ride. Concerts are held here all summer long, drawing top performers from Sweden and around the world. ✉ *Allmänna Gränd 9, Djurgården* ☎ *08/58750100* ⊕ *www.tivoli.se* 💰 *SKr 60, not including tickets or passes for rides* ☉ *Late Apr.–mid-Sept., daily. Hrs vary but are generally noon–11 PM. Call ahead for specific information.*

★ ☉ ㉖   **Junibacken.** In this storybook house you travel in small carriages through the world of children's book writer Astrid Lindgren, creator of the irrepressible character Pippi Longstocking. Lindgren's tales come alive as various scenes are revealed. It's perfect for children ages 5 and up. ✉ *Galärvarsv., Djurgården* ☎ *08/58723000* ⊕ *www.junibacken.se* 💰 *SKr95* ☉ *June–Aug., daily 9–6; Sept.–May, Wed.–Sun. 10–5.*

☉ ㉗   **Nordiska Museet** (Nordic Museum). An imposing late-Victorian structure housing peasant costumes from every region of the country and exhibits on the Sámi (pronounced *sah*-mee)—Lapps, the formerly seminomadic reindeer herders who inhabit the far north and many other aspects of Swedish life. Families with children should visit the delightful "village life" play area on the ground floor. ✉ *Djurgårdsv. 6–16, Djurgården* ☎ *08/51956000* ⊕ *www.nordm.se* 💰 *SKr 60* ☉ *Tues. and Thurs. 10–8, Wed. and Fri.–Sun. 10–5.*

㉜   **Rosendals Trädgärder** (Rosendal's Garden). This gorgeous slice of green-
Fodor'sChoice   ery is a perfect place to spend a few hours on a late summer afternoon.
★   When the weather's nice, people flock to the garden café, which is in one of the greenhouses, to enjoy tasty pastries and salads made from the locally grown vegetables. Pick your own flowers from the vast flower beds (paying by weight) or take away produce from the farm shop. ✉ *Rosendalsterrassen 12, Djurgården* ☎ *08/6622814* 💰 *Free* ☉ *May–Sept., daily 11–6; Oct.–Apr., call ahead for hrs.*

★ ☉ ㉙   **Skansen.** The world's first open-air museum, Skansen was founded in 1891 by philologist and ethnographer Artur Hazelius, who is buried here. He preserved examples of traditional Swedish architecture brought from all parts of the country, including farmhouses, windmills, barns, a working glassblower's hut, and churches. Not only is Skansen a delightful trip out of time in the center of a modern city, but it also provides insight into the life and culture of Sweden's various regions. In addition, the park has a zoo, carnival area, aquarium, theater, and cafés. ⊠ *Djurgårdsslätten 4951, Djurgården* ☎ *08/4428000* ⊕ *www.skansen. se* ⌨ *Park and zoo costs vary according to day of wk, but are approximately SKr 30 Sept.–Apr. and SKr 60 May–Aug., aquarium SKr 60* ⊙ *Oct.–Apr., daily 10–4; May, daily 10–8; June–Aug., daily 10–10; Sept., daily 10–5.*

need a break?

The **Cirkus Theater** (⊠ Djurgårdsslätten, Djurgården ☎ 08/ 58798750), on Hazeliusbacken right near the entrance to Skansen, has a lovely terrace café. If you want something a bit more hearty, head to **Hasselbacken Hotel** (⊠ Hazeliusbacken 20, Djurgården ☎ 08/51734300) and dine on its terrace.

▶ ★ ㉕ **Vasamuseet** (Vasa Museum). The warship *Vasa* sank 10 minutes into its maiden voyage in 1628, consigned to a watery grave until it was raised from the seabed in 1961. Its hull was preserved by the Baltic mud, free of the worms that can eat through ships' timbers. Now largely restored to her former glory (however short-lived it may have been), the man-of-war resides in a handsome museum. Daily tours are available year-round. ⊠ *Galärvarvsv., Djurgården* ☎ *08/51954800* ⊕ *www.vasamuseet. se* ⌨ *SKr 70* ⊙ *Thurs.–Tues. 10–5, Wed. 10–8.*

㉚ **Waldemarsudde.** This estate, Djurgården's gem, was bequeathed to the Swedish people by Prince Eugen upon his death, in 1947. It maintains an important collection of Nordic paintings from 1880 to 1940, in addition to the prince's own works. ⊠ *Prins Eugens väg 6, Djurgården* ☎ *08/54583700* ⊕ *www.waldemarsudde.com* ⌨ *SKr 75* ⊙ *May–Aug., Tues.–Wed. and Fri.–Sun. 11–5, Thurs. 11–8; Sept.–Apr., Tues.–Wed. and Fri. 11–4, Thurs. 11–8, weekends 11–4.*

Östermalm & Kaknästornet

Marked by waterfront rows of Renaissance buildings with palatial rooftops and ornamentation, Östermalm is a quiet residential section of central Stockholm, its elegant streets lined with museums and fine shopping. On Strandvägen, or Beach Way, the boulevard that follows the harbor's edge from the busy downtown area to the staid diplomatic quarter, you can choose one of three routes. The waterside walk, with its splendid views of the city harbor, bustles with tour boats and sailboats. Parallel to the walk (away from the water) is a tree-shaded walking and bike path. Walk, rollerblade, or ride a bike down the middle, and you just might meet the occasional horseback rider, properly attired in helmet, jacket, and high polished boots. Take the route farthest from the water, and you will walk past upscale shops and expensive restaurants.

a good walk

Walk east from the Kungliga Dramatiska Teatern, in Nybroplan, along Strandvägen until you get to Djurgårdsbron, an ornate little bridge that leads to the island of Djurgården. Resist going to the park, and instead turn left up Narvavägen and walk along the right-hand side until you reach Oscars Kyrka. Cross the street and continue up the left side until you reach the **Historiska Museet** ㉝ ▶. From here it's only a short walk farther up Narvavägen to Karlaplan, a pleasant circular park with a fountain. Go across or around the park to find Karlavägen. Heading northwest along this long boulevard, you'll pass by many small shops and galleries. At Nybrogatan turn left (this intersection is beyond the limits of the Stockholm map). Be sure to take some time to check out the exclusive furniture stores on your way down to **Östermalmstorg** ㉞, where there's an excellent indoor food market. Cut across the square and take a right down Sibyllegatan to the **Musik Museet** ㉟, installed in the city's oldest industrial building. Within the same block is the **Armémuseum**. Then go back to Nybroplan, where you can catch Bus 69 going east to **Kaknästornet** ㊱ for a spectacular view of Stockholm from the tallest tower in Scandinavia. From here walk back toward town along Djurgårds-brunnsvägen until you reach **Tekniska Museet** ㊲.

TIMING This tour requires a little more than a half day. You'll want to spend about an hour in each of the museums. The bus ride from Nybroplan to Kaknästornet takes about 15 minutes, and the tower merits another half hour. The Historiska and Musik museums are closed Monday, and the Millesgården is closed Monday off-season.

WHAT TO SEE **Armémuseum.** The large Military Museum covers everything from Sweden's early might as a kingdom to its unique, neutral military position during the 20th century. The castle guards and military band marches from this square every day on its walk to the Royal Palace on Gamla Stan. ⊠ *Riddarg. 13, Östermalm* ☎ *08/7889560* ⊕ *www.armemuseum. org* ⊠ *SKr 60* ⊙ *Tues. 11–8, Wed.–Sun. 11–4.*

> **need a break?** For some of the best baguettes and croissants outside Paris, stop by **Riddarbageriet** (⊠ Riddarg. 15, Östermalm) near the Armémuseum. Bread in Stockholm doesn't get any better than this: they deliver to the king and queen and many of the city's best restaurants. You can also get great coffee, sandwiches, and pastries. The bakery is closed in July.

㉝ **Historiska Museet** (Museum of National Antiquities). Viking treasures and the Gold Room are the main draw, but well-presented temporary exhibitions also cover various periods of Swedish history. The gift shop here is excellent. ⊠ *Narvav. 13–17, Östermalm* ☎ *08/51955000* ⊕ *www. historiska.se* ⊠ *SKr 50* ⊙ *Tues.–Wed. and Fri.–Sun. 11–5, Thurs. 11–8.*

㊱ **Kaknästornet** (Kaknäs TV Tower). The 511-foot-high Kaknäs radio and television tower, completed in 1967, is the tallest building in Scandinavia. Surrounded by satellite dishes, it is also used as a linkup station for a number of Swedish satellite TV channels and radio stations. Eat a meal in a restaurant 426 feet above the ground and enjoy panoramic views of the city and the archipelago. ⊠ *Mörkakroken off Djurgårdsbrunnsv., Djurgården* ☎ *08/6672180* ⊠ *SKr 30* ⊙ *June–Aug., daily 9 AM–10 PM; Sept.–May, daily 10–9.*

> **off the beaten path** **MILLESGÅRDEN –** This gallery and sculpture garden north of the city is dedicated to the property's former owner, American-Swedish sculptor Carl Milles (1875–1955). On display throughout the property are Milles's own unique works, and inside the main building, once his house, is his private collection. On the terrace is the beautiful Anne's House, designed by famous Austrian designer Josef Frank, where Milles spent the final years of his life. The setting is exquisite: sculptures top columns on terraces in a magical garden high above the harbor and the city. Millesgården can be easily reached via subway to Ropsten, where you catch the Lidingö train and get off at Herserud, the second stop. The trip takes about 30 minutes. ⊠ *Carl Milles väg 2, Lidingö* ☎ *08/4467580* ⊕ *www. millesgarden.se* ⊠ *SKr 75* ⊙ *May–Sept., daily 10–5; Oct.–Apr., Tues.–Fri. noon–4, weekends 11–5.*

㉟ **Musik Museet.** Inside what was the military's bread bakery from the 17th century to the mid-1900s, the Music Museum has more than 6,000 instruments in its collection, with the focus on items from 1600 to 1850. Its 18th-century woodwind collection is internationally renowned. The museum also holds jazz, folk, and world music concerts. Children are invited to touch and play some of the instruments, and the motion-sensitive "Sound Room" lets you produce musical effects simply by gesturing and moving around. ⊠ *Sibylleg. 2, Östermalm* 🕿 *08/51955490* ⊕ *www.musikmuseet.se* 🖃 *SKr 50* 🕑 *Tues.–Sun. 11–4.*

❸❹ Östermalmstorg. The market square and its neighboring streets represent old, established Stockholm. **Saluhall** is more a collection of boutiques than an indoor food market; the fish displays can be especially intriguing. At the other end of the square, **Hedvig Eleonora Kyrka**, a church with characteristically Swedish faux-marble painting throughout its wooden interior, is the site of frequent lunchtime concerts in spring and summer. ⊠ *Nybrog. at Humlegårdsg., Östermalm.*

need a break? | The little restaurants inside the **Saluhall** (⊠ Östermalmstorg, Östermalm) offer everything from takeout coffee to sit-down meals.

🖑 ❸❼ Tekniska Museet. Only a 10-minute bus ride from the city, the Museum of Science and Technology has a huge Machinery Hall displaying cars, bicycles, and even airplanes. There are also exhibits on technology in the home and the history of the printed word in Sweden (the first book dates from 1483). Teknorama, the museum's science center, encourages children and young adults to learn more about the natural sciences and technology. There are also a café and gift shop. ⊠ *Museiv. 7, Djurgårdsbrunnsv., Djurgården* 🕿 *08/4505600* ⊕ *www.tekniskamuseet.se* 🖃 *SKr 60, free Wed. night* 🕑 *Mon.–Tues. and Thurs.–Fri. 10–5, Wed. 10–8, weekends 11–5.*

Outside the City

There are a number of excellent sites only a short bus or subway ride from the city center, many of which can be combined. Trips to nearly all these places could be done in a morning or afternoon and even added on to the other walks.

WHAT TO SEE
Fodor'sChoice
★

Bergianska Trädgården. The beautiful Bergianska Botanical Gardens, on a peninsula extending out into the small bay of Brunnsvik, can provide a wonderful break from the city. They are only a short subway ride away. Paths weave along the water in the open park area. Visit Edvard Anderson's modern Växthus (Greenhouse) for its impressive Mediterranean and tropical environments. The century-old Victoriahuset (Victoria House) contains tropical plants as well and has one of the best collections of water plants in the world. ⊠ *Frescativ., near the university, Universitet* 🕿 *08/156545* ⊕ *www.bergianska.se* 🖃 *Park is free, Greenhouse SKr 40, Victoria House SKr 10* 🕑 *Park daily yr-round; Victoria House May–Sept., daily 11–4, weekends 11–5; Greenhouse daily 11–5.*

Fjärilshuset (Butterfly and Bird House). After a short bus ride and a nice walk through the magnificent Haga Park, you could be in a room filled with hundreds of tropical butterflies. In the bird room, hundreds of birds of 40 species fly freely. The Haga Park itself is impressive and worth a lengthy stroll, but be sure to combine it with a trip to this feather-filled oasis. ⊠ *Take Bus 515 from the Odenplan subway stop, Haga* 🕿 *08/7303981* ⊕ *www.fjarilshuset.se* 🖃 *SKr 70* 🕑 *Apr.–Sept., Tues.–Fri. 10–4, weekends 11–5:30; Oct.–Mar., Tues.–Fri. 10–3, weekends 11–4.*

🖑 Naturhistoriska Riksmuseet and Cosmonova (Museum of Natural History). Founded in 1739 by the famous Swedish botanist Linnaeus and his colleagues at the Science Academy, the museum has been in its present location near the university since 1916. The last decade has brought much rebuilding and other improvements. Exhibits include "Life in Water," "Marvels of the Human Body," and "Space Adventure." Cosmonova shows science and nature films in Sweden's only IMAX theater. The subway ride to the Universitet stop takes less than 10 minutes from the city center. ⊠ *Frescativ. 40, Universitet* ☎ *08/51954040* ⊕ *www.nrm.se* ✉ *SKr 65* ⊙ *Fri.–Wed. 10–7, Thurs. 10–8; Cosmonova mid-May–end of May and Aug.–Sept., Tues.–Sun.; June and July, daily 10–7.*

Tyresö Slottet (Tyresö Castle). After a quick, 20-minute bus ride from southern Stockholm, you'll find yourself in the gorgeous Romantic gardens that surround this castle, built in the 1660s. The Nordic Museum led the renovations that restored the grounds to their late-1800s glory. The main building is filled with elaborate salons, libraries, and studies, and the west wing has a nice café and restaurant. Be sure to leave time for both the castle and gardens. ⊠ *Take Bus 805 from Gullmarsplan to Tyresö Slott, Tyresö* ☎ *08/7700178* ⊕ *www.nordm.se/slott* ✉ *SKr 70* ⊙ *Sept.–Oct., daily 11–3; June 22–Aug. 19, Tues.–Sun. 11–4. Tours at noon, 1, and 2.*

Ulriksdals Slott (Ulriksdals Castle). Construction on the castle began in 1640, but it was during the first half of the 1700s that the castle took on the look that it has today. Built in the Renaissance style, the castle is most closely associated with King Gustav Adolf and Queen Louise, who in 1923 added a famous living room designed by Carl Malmsten. The Dutch Renaissance chapel from the mid-1800s is still used for masses, weddings, and concerts. ⊠ *Take Bus 503 from Bergshamra subway stop, on the Red Line, Ulriksdal* ☎ *08/4026130* ⊕ *www.royalcourt. se/ulriksdal* ✉ *SKr 50* ⊙ *Mid-May–Aug., Tues.–Sun. noon–4; Sept., weekends noon–4.*

Where to Eat

Stockholm's restaurant scene rivals that of any major European capital, with upscale restaurants offering creative menus at trendy modern locations. The best bring foreign innovations to bear on Sweden's high-quality raw ingredients. The city's top restaurants will charge accordingly, but you aren't likely to leave disappointed. Of course, there are also plenty of less expensive restaurants with traditional Swedish cooking. Among Swedish dishes, the best bets are wild game and fish, particularly salmon, and the smörgåsbord buffet, which usually offers a good variety at an inexpensive price. Reservations are often necessary on weekends.

Downtown Stockholm & Beyond

★ **$$$–$$$$**
Fodor's Choice
★

✕ **Edsbacka Krog.** In 1626 Edsbacka, just outside town, became Stockholm's first licensed inn. Its exposed rough-hewn beams, plaster walls, and open fireplaces still give it the feel of a resting post for the gentry, and careful modernization has created all the comforts you would expect at this end of the restaurant scale. Chef Christer Lindström interprets Swedish cuisine creatively. Ease into the meal with seared lobster served with a compote of root crops, followed by roasted breast and liver of wild duck with pear sauce. ⊠ *Sollentunav. 220, Sollentuna* ☎ *08/963300* ▬ *AE, DC, MC, V* ⊙ *Closed Sun. and Mon.*

★ **$$$–$$$$**
Fodor's Choice
★

✕ **Wedholms Fisk.** Noted for its fresh seafood dishes, Wedholms Fisk is appropriately set by a bay in Stockholm center. High ceilings, large windows, and tasteful modern paintings from the owner's personal collection create a spacious, sophisticated space. The traditional Swedish cuisine, which consists almost exclusively of seafood, is simple but outstanding. Try the poached sole in basil sauce or the scallops gratinéed with leeks. ⊠ *Nybrokajen 17, City* ☎ *08/6117874* ⊟ *AE, DC, MC, V* ⊘ *Closed Sun. and July.*

$$–$$$$ ✕**Operakällaren.** Open since 1787, the haughty grande dame of Stockholm is more a Swedish institution than a seat of gastronomic distinction. Thick carpeting, shiny polished brass, and handsome carved-wood chairs and tables fill the room. The crystal chandeliers are said to be Sweden's finest, and the high windows on the south side have magnificent views of the Royal Palace. The restaurant is famed for its seasonal smörgåsbord, offered from early June through Christmas. Coveted selections include pickled herring, *rollmops* (rolled herring), reindeer and elk (in season), and ice cream with cloudberry sauce. In summer the veranda opens as the Operabryggan Café, facing Kungsträdgården and the waterfront. Around the corner in the same building is the restaurant's *backficka,* a pleasantly active bar/restaurant with a less expensive menu. ⊠ *Operahuset, Jakobs Torg 2, City* ☎ *08/6765800* ⌂ *Reservations essential* ☖ *Jacket and tie* ⊟ *AE, DC, MC, V* ⊘ *Main dining room closed in July.*

$$–$$$$ ✕**Restaurangen.** This restaurant gained its fine reputation in large part due to its flavor-based menu. Diners build three-, five-, or seven-course meals from 20 flavors, 15 of which are salty and five of which are sweet. Thus, chili, coriander, and vanilla would result in a chicken spring roll with mint dipping sauce, seafood and tofu with lemongrass juice, and vanilla ice cream with a waffle and fresh strawberries. Each flavor has a letter next to it that corresponds to the wine-list offerings that are recommended to best complement the flavor. The restaurant, with its blond wood, beige and brown fabrics, and red- and cream-color walls, was created by three students from Stockholm's prestigious Beckman's School of Design. ⊠ *Oxtorgsg. 14, City* ☎ *08/220952* ⊟ *AE, DC, MC, V* ⊘ *Closed Sun.*

$$$ ✕**Bon Lloc.** With an elegant and spacious dining area and a creative
Fodor'sChoice Mediterranean-influence menu, Bon Lloc has established itself as one
★ of the hottest restaurants in town. The menu uses common ingredients like ham and cod to create dishes that recall Catalonia as much as Sweden. The extensive wine list offers an excellent selection of European wines. The interior's light-brown wood and mosaic tiles allude to Mediterranean styles while still evoking Swedish simplicity, much as the food does. ⊠ *Regeringsg. 111, Norrmalm* ☎ *08/6606060* ⌂ *Reservations essential* ⊟ *AE, DC, MC, V* ⊘ *Closed Sun.*

$$$ ✕**Fredsgatan 12.** The government crowd files into this funky restaurant
Fodor'sChoice at lunch; a more casual yet stylish crowd is there at night. All come here
★ to enjoy what is probably some of the best food in town. The young chef Melker Andersson works his magic here, creating Swedish-, Asian-, and European-inspired dishes that defy convention and positively demand enjoyment. The menu offers creative combinations, such as rabbit *taquitos* (filled tortillas rolled up and deep-fried) or asparagus Caesar salad with scallops and tiger prawns. When ordering a cocktail, choose a flavor such as mint and sugar or lemon-cherry and then an alcohol of your choice with which to mix it. From the bar you can get a nice view into the kitchen of this popular restaurant—always a good sign of a place that values its food. ⊠ *Fredsg. 12, City* ☎ *08/248052* ⊟ *AE, DC, MC, V* ⊘ *Closed Sun.*

★ **$$$** ✕**Ulriksdals Wärdshus.** The lunchtime smörgåsbord at this country inn can't be beat. Built in the park of an 18th-century palace in 1868, the traditionally decorated inn overlooks orchards and a peaceful lake. It's an expensive restaurant, but the impeccable service and outstanding cuisine make a splurge here worthwhile. Menu highlights include monkfish with a ragout of gnocchi, samphire, and lovage and seared sweetbread served with veal-shank ravioli, endive, and foie gras. The restaurant's cellar is listed in Guinness world records as the most complete in the world. There are more than 500 bottles of the top five Bordeaux chateaux from the 20th century, nearly one for every year for every wine. ⊠ *Ulriksdals Slottspark, Solna* ☎ *08/850815* ⌂ *Reservations essential* ⌂ *Jacket required* ⊟ *AE, DC, MC, V* ⊘ *No dinner Sun.*

$$–$$$ ✕ **Riche.** This Stockholm establishment was for many years an exclusive club. Today the elegance and style remain, but the diners are from a much broader pool. Eat in the casual glassed-in veranda on wicker chairs, or move inside to the main dining room for more formal dining. For the ultimate in posh tradition, book a table at the Teatergrillen, in the back: members of the Swedish royal family are fans, too. All three sections serve Swedish and French cuisine. Upstairs is a chill-out space where DJs play late night and you can buy simple smørrebrød (open-face sandwiches) until 2 AM. ⊠ *Birger Jarlsg. 4, Östermalm* ☎ *08/54503560* ⊟ *AE, DC, MC, V* ⊘ *Closed Sun.*

$$–$$$ ✕ **Stallmästaregården.** A historic old inn with an attractive courtyard and garden, Stallmästaregården is in Haga Park, just north of Norrtull, about 15 minutes by car or bus from the city center. Fine summer meals are served on a tented terrace overlooking the waters of Brunnsviken. Specialties include poached fillet of Dover sole with black *tagliolini* and lobster sauce. ⊠ *Norrtull near Haga; take Bus 52 to Stallmästaregården, Haga* ☎ *08/6101300* ⊟ *AE, DC, MC, V* ⊘ *Closed Sun.*

$–$$$ ✕ **Storstad.** A lighter and less expensive menu is served in the bar area of this popular hangout, which looks out on the street through wide arching windows. In the sparse but inviting dining room in the back you might try the sweet-corn soup with truffle pasta and Parmesan cheese before moving on to meat specialties such as fried duck breast with honey-baked beets, mushroom spring rolls, and port syrup. The wine list is excellent and especially strong on French and Californian wines. ⊠ *Odeng. 41, Vasastan* ☎ *08/6733800* ⌂ *Reservations essential* ⊟ *AE, DC, MC, V* ⊘ *Closed Sun. No lunch.*

¢–$$$ ✕ **Tranan.** There's something about Tranan that makes you want to go
Fodor's Choice back. The food is Swedish with a touch of French and is consistently
★ very good. The stark walls covered with old movie posters and the red-and-white-checked tablecloths are reminders of the days when it was a workingman's beer parlor. Try the *biff rydberg*—fillet of beef, fried potatoes, horseradish, and egg yolk—it's a Swedish classic. The bar downstairs has DJs and live music and gets packed to bursting on weekends. ⊠ *Karlbergsv. 14, Vasastan* ☎ *08/52728100* ⊟ *AE, DC, MC, V* ⊘ *No lunch weekends.*

★ **$$** ✕ **Prinsen.** Still in the same location as when it opened in 1897, the Prince serves both traditional and modern Swedish cuisine. The interior is rich with mellow, warm lighting; dark wood paneling; and leather chairs and booths. The staff is as delightfully starched as the white aprons they wear. On the walls are black-and-white oil paintings of famous people done by one of the long-serving staff members, as well as paintings by local artists that came into the restaurant's possession when they were used as payment to settle tabs. The restaurant is known for its scampi salad and wild-game dishes. Downstairs are a bar and a space for larger parties. ⊠ *Mäster Samuelsg. 4, City* ☎ *08/6111331* ⊟ *AE, DC, MC, V* ⊘ *No lunch weekends.*

$$ ✕ **Rolfs Kök.** Small and modern, Rolfs is a casual restaurant serving excellent Swedish-French cuisine to an eclectic mix of businesspeople and theater and arts folks. The chairs and the salt and pepper shakers hang on hooks on the wall above each table. Go for the lingonberry-glazed reindeer fillet with cauliflower; root vegetables and smoked chili pepper; or a feta cheese salad with lime, soy, and chili-fried chicken.

✉ *Tegnérg. 41, Norrmalm* ☎ *08/101696* 🖃 *AE, DC, MC, V* ☺ *No lunch weekends.*

$$ ✗ **Stockholms Matvarufabriken.** Although it's a bit hard to find, tucked away as it is on a side street, Stockholm's Food Factory is well worth seeking out. The popular bistro restaurant, serving French, Italian, and Swedish cuisine, is packed full on the weekends as young and old come to enjoy the exposed-brick, candlelighted dining room and varied menu: here omelets are taken to new levels with ingredients such as truffles and asparagus. Brown-paper tablecloths and kitchen cloths used as napkins set the informal tone. ✉ *Idung. 12, Vasastan* ☎ *08/320704* 🖃 *AE, DC, MC, V.*

$$ ✗ **Sturehof.** This massive complex of a restaurant with two huge bars is a complete social, architectural, and dining experience amid wood paneling, leather chairs and sofas, and distinctive lighting fixtures. There's a bar directly facing Stureplan where you can sit on a summer night and watch Stockholmers gather at the nearby Svampen, a mushroomlike concrete structure that has doubled as the city's meeting point for years. In the elegant dining room fine Swedish cuisine is offered. Upstairs is the O-Bar, a dark and smoky lounge filled well into the night with young people and loud music. ✉ *Stureplan 2, City* ☎ *08/4405730* 🖃 *AE, DC, MC, V.*

$$ ✗ **Undici.** First Tomas Brolin was a hero to the Swedish people on the soccer field; now he's a hero on the Stockholm restaurant scene. Undici is one of the city's most popular places, both to eat and hang out. A small seating area in the front is good for finalizing that business deal, while curved leather banquettes along the wall are better for festive groups of six or seven. The dining room in back is decked out in fine dark woods and white linens and serves a combination of northern Swedish and northern Italian cuisine. Dishes have included such standouts as lamb fillet with cannelloni and *rimmat lammlägg* (salt-cured lamb) with goat cheese, spinach, and spicy merguez sausage. ✉ *Stureg. 22, Norrmalm* ☎ *08/6616617* 🖃 *AE, DC, MC, V* ☺ *Closed Sun. No lunch Sat.*

$$ ✗ **Wasahof.** Across the street from Vasaparken, and just a short walk from Odenplan, Wasahof feels like an authentic bistro, but the cooking actually mixes Swedish, French, and Italian recipes. The pleasantly rustic space and good food have attracted all kinds of culturati—actors, writers, journalists—for some time. Seafood is a specialty here—this is the place in Stockholm to get oysters. ✉ *Dalag. 46, Vasastan* ☎ *08/323440* 🖃 *AE, DC, MC, V* ☺ *Closed Sun.*

$-$$ ✗ **Dramatenrestaurangen Frippe.** Connected to Lillascenen, the smaller stage that's behind the Royal National Theater, this is the perfect place to grab a bite before a performance. One wall is covered in black-and-white photos of the theater's most famous actors, and posters of major productions line the bar, behind which is the open kitchen. Bar stools along the window allow for great people-watching. The food is a modern take on *husmanskost,* traditional Swedish cooking. Try the classic Isterband sausage with creamy parsley potatoes. ✉ *Nybrog./Almlöfsg., City* ☎ *08/6656142* 🖃 *AE, DC, MC, V* ☺ *No lunch weekends.*

$-$$ ✗ **East.** Just off Stureplan, East is one of the city's culinary hot spots, offering enticing contemporary pan-Asian fare from Thailand, Japan, Korea, and Vietnam. Order a selection of appetizers to get a sampling of this cross-cultural cooking. East is a perfect spot to have dinner before a night on the town. Try the Luxor: chicken, tiger shrimp, and egg noodles with peanuts, mint leaves, and coconut sauce. The bar area at this vibrant restaurant turns into a miniclub at night, with soul and hip-hop on the turntables. ✉ *Stureplan 13, Norrmalm* ☎ *08/6114959* 🖃 *AE, DC, MC, V.*

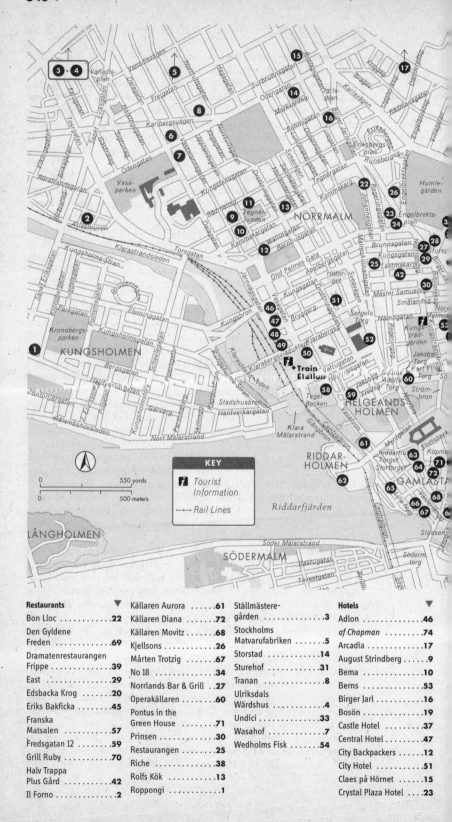

KEY

i Tourist Information

⟶ Rail Lines

550 yards

500 meters

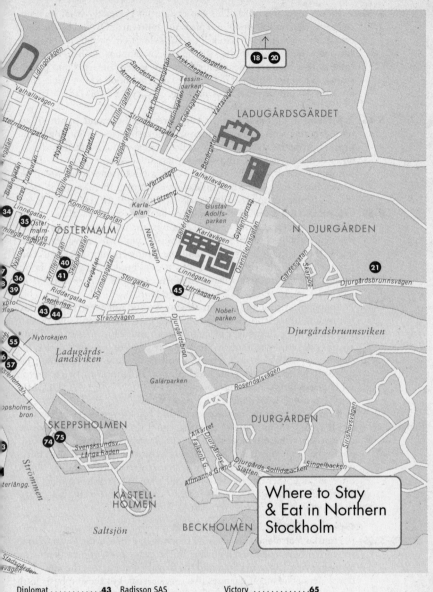

Where to Stay
& Eat in Northern
Stockholm

$–$$ ✕ **Halv trappa plus gård.** This hip restaurant is exactly what its name suggests: two half floors plus a pleasant courtyard. Owned by the same two guys who run Halv Grek Plus Turk (Half Greek plus a Turk), the retro vibe harks back to the '70s. The menu emphasizes fish, most of it done with a Mediterranean flair. The staff is good-hearted and professional. When possible, eat in the courtyard, but book a table, since there are only 10 out there. ⊠ *Lästmakarg. 3, City* ☎ *08/6110277* ▤ *AE, DC, MC, V* ⊘ *Closed Sun. No lunch.*

$–$$ ✕ **Kjellsons.** Kjellsons is a bar first and a restaurant second, but this doesn't mean the menu is short on high-caliber dishes (to say nothing of fine drinks). Appetizers include an excellent pea soup (a Swedish tradition) and a delicious avocado-and-smoked ham salad—most of the fare is traditional Swedish. And be sure to ask for a basket of cracker bread—it comes with a tube of the famous caviar. In summer there's outdoor seating. ⊠ *Birger Jarlsg. 36, City* ☎ *08/6110045* ▤ *AE, DC, MC, V.*

$–$$ ✕ **Norrlands Bar & Grill.** If it's people you like, then this is the place. Downstairs is a restaurant and cocktail bar, upstairs a bar and terrace. Both floors are always busy. The food is Swedish with Mediterranean influences, the cocktails are superb, and the dining room is sleek and contemporary. Norrlands has produced a cookbook and a drink book, both of which are best-sellers. ⊠ *Norrlandsg. 24, Norrmalm* ☎ *08/ 6118810* ▤ *AE, DC, MC, V* ⊘ *Closed Sun.*

¢–$$ ✕ **Roppongi.** Although far from downtown and not exactly in the most happening area, Roppongi's adventurous, creative menu and quality fish make it the best sushi place in Stockholm. This means it's almost always packed, so be ready to share the stripped-down space with other sushi lovers. The shrimp tempura rolls will leave you drooling for more and the *tamaki* cones are plump and bursting with flavor. ⊠ *Hantverkarg. 76, Kungsholmen* ☎ *08/6501772* ▤ *AE, DC, MC, V* ⊘ *No lunch weekends.*

¢–$ ✕ **Il Forno.** You might not expect to find brick-oven pizza in Sweden,

Fodor'sChoice but Il Forno serves some of the best you'll find north of the Mediter-
★ ranean. Choose from more than 25 combinations, all of which use only the freshest ingredients and a tasty, crunchy crust. The kitchen also churns out a number of pasta dishes and sells many varieties of Italian olives, olive oil, and other fine foods. As much Italian as Swedish is spoken here. Sit outside when possible—the interior can feel a bit stuffy. ⊠ *Atlasg. 9, Vasastan* ☎ *08/319049* ▤ *AE, DC, MC, V.*

Gamla Stan & Skeppsholmen

★ $$$–$$$$ ✕ **Franska Matsalen.** This classic French restaurant in the Grand Hotel serves the best true French cuisine in the city—plus, you can enjoy an inspiring view of Gamla Stan and the Royal Palace across the inner harbor waters. The menu changes five times a year, but the emphasis is always on Swedish ingredients. They're used to create such dishes as pike perch with oxtail and truffles. The lofty measure of opulence here is commensurate with the bill. ⊠ *Grand Hotel, Södra Blasieholmsh. 8, City* ☎ *08/6793584* ⌖ *Reservations essential* ⌂ *Jacket required* ▤ *AE, DC, MC, V* ⊘ *Closed weekends.*

★ $$$–$$$$ ✕ **Pontus in the Green House.** After working for some time under the guidance of the famous chef Erik Lallerstedt—who owned this exquisite restaurant when it was called Eriks—Pontus has taken over operations. You can still count on traditional fare of the haute variety, with a concentration on meat and fish dishes. The menu has both traditional Swedish and contemporary international cuisines. Everything is delicious, and expensive. For a calmer dining experience, choose a corner table upstairs; the ground floor always bustles. You'll be dining among Sweden's rich and famous. For a cheaper menu of traditional Swedish dishes, and slightly less fanfare, sit at the bar downstairs. ⊠ *Österlångg. 17, Gamla Stan* ☎ *08/238500* ▤ *AE, DC, MC, V* ◷ *Closed Sun. No lunch Sat.*

$$$ ✕ **Den Gyldene Freden.** Sweden's most famous old tavern has been open for business since 1722. Every Thursday the Swedish Academy meets here in a private room on the second floor. The haunt of bards and barristers, artists and adpeople, Freden could probably serve sawdust and still be popular, but the food and staff are worthy of the restaurant's hallowed reputation. The cuisine has a Swedish orientation, but Continental influences spice up the menu. Season permitting, try the oven-baked fillets of turbot served with chanterelles and crêpes; the gray hen fried with spruce twigs and dried fruit is another good selection. ⊠ *Österlångg. 51, Gamla Stan* ☎ *08/248760* ▤ *AE, DC, MC, V* ◷ *Closed Sun. No lunch.*

$$–$$$ ✕ **Källaren Diana.** This atmospheric Gamla Stan cellar dates from the Middle Ages. During the first part of the 18th century the building was used as a warehouse and owned by Jonas Alströmer, the scientist who introduced the potato to Sweden—by stealing two bags from England. Today the warehouse is a restaurant that uses the best indigenous ingredients from the Swedish forests and shores. Try the oven-roasted pheasant with calvados and grapes or the grilled fillet of reindeer with pepper sauce and honey-glazed salsify. ⊠ *Brunnsgränd 2–4, Gamla Stan* ☎ *08/ 107310* ▤ *AE, DC, MC, V* ◷ *Closed Sun.*

$–$$$ ✕ **Eriks Bakficka.** A favorite among Östermalm locals, Erik's Bakficka is a block from the elegant waterside, a few steps down from street level. Owned by the well-known Swedish chef Erik Lallerstedt (who also owns Gondolen), the restaurant serves Swedish dishes, including a delicious baked fillet of char with spring onions and green pea sauce. No smoking is allowed in the main dining room (a policy that's rare in Stockholm). A lower-priced menu is served in the pub section, where smoking is still allowed. ⊠ *Fredrikshovsg. 4, Östermalm* ☎ *08/6601599* ▤ *AE, DC, MC, V* ◷ *Closed in July.*

$–$$$ ✕ **Mårten Trotzig.** This contemporary functional space is both a dining room and a bar. The short menu demonstrates the chef's imagination, blending multicultural recipes in intriguing ways. Try the yellow- and red-tomato salad with arugula pesto, and then move on to the flounder fillet with artichoke hearts, asparagus, and a light grapefruit sauce. In a beautiful plant-lined courtyard, less expensive lunch specials are served. The staff is young, the service professional. ⊠ *Västerlångg. 79, Gamla Stan* ☎ *08/4422530* ▤ *AE, DC, MC, V* ◷ *Closed Sun.*

★ **¢–$$$** ✕ **Koh Phangan.** Creative food is served until midnight at this lively Thai restaurant, where you'll be seated in individual "huts," each with a special name and style. The entire restaurant is decked out in colored lights, fake palm fronds, and trinkets from Thailand. Recorded jungle sounds play in the background. Sign up for a table on the chalkboard next to the bar when you arrive. Although you can expect at least an hour-long wait on weekends, the food is well worth it. Grilled fish and seafood with extravagant, spicy sauces are the specialty. ⊠ *Skåneg. 57, Södermalm* ☎ *08/6425040* ⌦ *Reservations not accepted* ▤ *AE, DC, MC, V.*

$$ ✕ **Källaren Aurora.** Elegant, if a little stuffy, this Gamla Stan cellar restaurant is set in a beautiful 17th-century house. Its largely foreign clientele—most often busloads of tourists dropped off for a meal—enjoys top-quality Swedish and international cuisines served in small rooms. Charcoal-grilled spiced salmon, veal Parmesan, and orange-basted halibut fillet are all good. ⊠ *Munkbron 11, Gamla Stan* ☎ *08/ 219359* ▤ *AE, DC, MC, V* ◷ *Closed in July. No lunch.*

$–$$ ✕ **Grill Ruby.** This American-style barbecue joint (at least as American as it is possible to be in Gamla Stan) is just a cobblestone's throw away

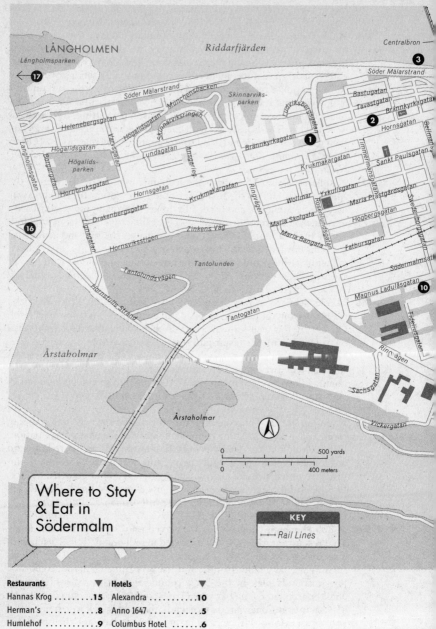

LÅNGHOLMEN   Riddarfjärden   Centralbron

Långholmsparken

← **17**

3

Söder Mälarstrand

Söder Mälarstrand   Münchensbacken   Skinnarviks-parken

Bastugatan

Tavastgatan   Brännkyrkagatan

Helenebergsgatan   Högalidsgatan   Skinnarviksringen

2   Hornsgatan

Varvsgatan   Brännkyrkagatan   **1**

Högalidsgatan   Lundagatan   Ansgarieg

Högalids-parken   Krukmakargatan   Sankt Paulsgatan

Hornbruksgatan   Wollmar   Yxkullsgatan   Maria Prästgårdsgatan

Borgargatan   Hornsgatan   Krukmakargatan   Rosenlundsgatan   Högbergsgatan

Drakenbergsgatan   Maria Skolgata   Fatbursgatan

16   Ringvägen   Maria Bangata

Lumagatan   Zinkens Väg   Södermalmsatl

Hornsviksstigen   Södermalmstg

Tantolunden   Magnus Ladulåsgatan   **10**

Hornstulls Strand   Tantolundsvägen

Årstaholmar   Tantogatan

Ringvägen

Sachsgatan

Vickergatan

Årstaholmar

0 ——————————— 500 yards
0 ——————————— 400 meters

Where to Stay & Eat in Södermalm

| KEY |
| ⊢—— Rail Lines |

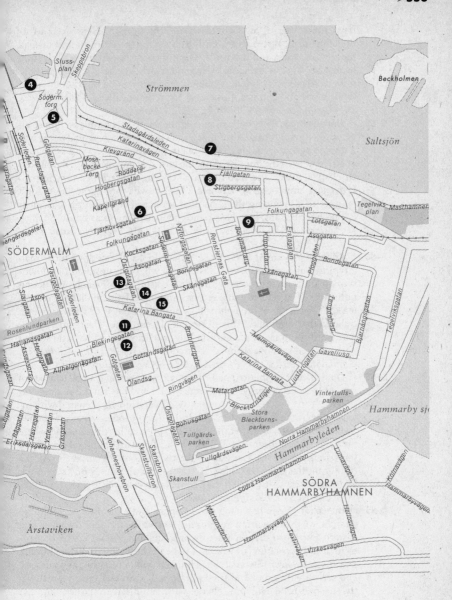

from the statue of St. George slaying the dragon. Next door to its French cousin, Bistro Ruby, Grill Ruby skips the escargot and instead focuses on steaks and fish grills. The grilled steak with french fries and béarnaise sauce is delicious. On Sunday an American-style brunch is served, where you can enjoy huevos rancheros and a big Bloody Mary while blues and country music drift from the speakers. ⊠ *Österlångg. 14, Gamla Stan* ☎ *08/206015* ▭ *AE, DC, MC, V.*

$–$$ ✕ **Hannas Krog.** This bohemian neighborhood restaurant is almost always filled with locals. Although it may not be as supertrendy as it was a decade ago, it remains a Södermalm hot spot. Diners are serenaded at 10 minutes to the hour by a mooing cow that emerges from the cuckoo clock just inside the door. The dishes—from Caribbean shrimp to Provençal lamb—are all flavorful. The crowds that gather here don't manage to slow down the consistent service. The bar in the basement is loud but pleasant. Local live bands play there on occasion. ⊠ *Skåneg. 80, Södermalm* ☎ *08/6438225* ▭ *AE, DC, MC, V* ⊘ *No lunch weekends and July.*

$–$$ ✕ **Källaren Movitz.** At first glance Movitz looks like nothing more than a typical European pub, which is exactly what it is upstairs. But downstairs it's a restaurant serving Swedish cuisine with French and Italian influences. The refined table settings and abundant candlelight reflecting off the curves of the light yellow walls of what used to be a potato cellar in the 1600s make this an elegant place to dine. The reindeer steak with mushroom sauce and currant jelly is delicious, as is the pasta stuffed with smoked salmon, shrimp, and ricotta cheese. ⊠ *Tyska Brinken 34, Gamla Stan* ☎ *08/209979* ▭ *AE, DC, MC, V* ⊘ *Closed Sun.*

$–$$ ✕ **Opus.** Don't let the stripped-down, albeit charming, small space fool you—Opus's food packs a big-time punch and has earned it a reputation as a top French restaurant in town. Everything is prepared with intense care by the French-born and -trained cook and is served attentively by his Polish wife. Together they own this popular little restaurant, where the sauces are unbeatable. Try the pork fillet with chanterelle sauce or the perch fillet with avocado sauce to find out for yourself. As the restaurant has only 10 tables, be sure to call ahead. ⊠ *Blekingeg. 63, Södermalm* ☎ *08/6446080* ⟁ *Reservations essential* ▭ *AE, DC, MC, V* ⊘ *Closed Sun. No dinner Mon.*

¢–$$ ✕ **Humlehof.** If you're feeling extra hungry and a bit tight on funds, go straight to this Bavarian restaurant serving traditional Swedish and eastern European dishes. Start by ordering an ice-cold Czech or Austrian draft beer, a bowl of what has to be the best goulash in Stockholm, and the *schweizer* (Swiss-style) schnitzel, which is as big as your face and served with salad and fried potatoes. If schnitzel's not your thing, try the pan-fried Haloumi cheese with sun-dried tomatoes, summer salad, and garlic bread. A TV in the corner above the bar means a sports-bar crowd gathers when a game is on, but it's never out of control and only adds to the restaurant's cheeriness. ⊠ *Folkungag. 128, Södermalm* ☎ *08/6410302* ▭ *AE, DC, MC, V.*

¢–$$ ✕ **no18.** Despite being a high-profile bar and restaurant, no18 remains casual and informal. Walk in, and to your left are tables and low leather chairs across from a bar that curves to a set of stairs. Go up to the colorful dining room, which extends farther into a lush courtyard open in summer. In the basement are a large bar and an open area for dancing. A less expensive menu has club sandwiches, burgers, and Caesar salad, but if you want to go all the way, try the good ol' entrecôte with béarnaise sauce and fries or a chicken fillet with olive-and-basil risotto. ⊠ *Linnég. 18, Östermalm* ☎ *08/6621018* ▭ *AE, DC, MC, V* ⊘ *Closed Sun.*

¢–$$ ✕ **Pelican.** Beer, beer, and more beer is the order of the day at Pelican,
Fodor'sChoice a traditional working-class drinking hall, a relic of the days when Sö-
★ dermalm was the dwelling place of the city's blue-collar brigade. Today's
more bohemian residents find it just as enticing, with the unvarnished
wood-panel walls, faded murals, and glass globe lights fulfilling all
their down-at-the-heel pretensions. The food here is some of the best
traditional Swedish fare in the city. The meatballs and the knuckle of
ham with three mustards are legendary. ✉ *Blekingeg. 40, Södermalm*
☎ *08/55609090* ⚏ *Reservations not accepted* ▤ *AE, DC, MC, V*
✪ *Closed Sun.*

$ ✕ **Restaurang Ho's.** Walk into this hidden gem of a Chinese restaurant
and something about it just feels right. Nothing fancy—Ho's lets its au-
thentic, intensely flavored food speak for itself. With more than 100
choices, the menu is never-ending and includes Chinese takes on duck,
squid, scallops, pork, chicken, beef, and tofu. The stir-fried squid with
green and red peppers in black-bean sauce packs a serious punch. Fin-
ish with a classic fried banana and ice cream. ✉ *Hornsg. 151, Söder-
malm* ☎ *08/844420* ▤ *AE, DC, MC, V* ✪ *Closed Mon.*

¢–$ ✕ **Herman's.** Herman's is a haven for vegetarians out to get the most
Fodor'sChoice bang for their kronor. The glassed-in back deck and open garden both
★ provide spectacular views of the water and Gamla Stan. The food is
always served buffet style and includes various vegetable and pasta sal-
ads, warm casseroles, and such entrées as Indonesian stew with peanut
sauce and vegetarian lasagna. The fruit pies and chocolate cakes and
cookies are delicious. ✉ *Fjällg. 23A, Södermalm* ☎ *08/6439480*
▤ *MC, V.*

¢–$ ✕ **Indira.** This busy Indian restaurant about a block off Götgatanhas has
an overwhelming 60 meal choices. The food is cheap and delicious and
the service fast. Order as soon as you enter and find a seat at one of the
mosaic-coated tables. There are a number of tables in the basement as
well, so don't leave right away if it looks packed on the first floor. The
chicken korma, with raisins and cashews, is fantastic, and the honey-
saffron ice cream is a perfect end to a meal. ✉ *Bondeg. 3B, Södermalm*
☎ *08/6414046* ▤ *AE, DC, MC, V.*

¢ ✕ **Jerusalem Grill House.** Enter this wild grill, and it may be hard to be-
lieve you're still in Stockholm. The men behind the counter sing along
to the music blaring from the sound system, and the menu is in both
Swedish and Arabic. On the walls are surreal landscape paintings, odd
sculptures, and loads of hookahs—in fact, there are five or six pipes that
the regulars use to smoke their tobacco. Falafel, chicken kebabs, gyros,
mixed fried-vegetable plates, lamb fillets—they've got it all, as well as
authentic Arabic tea and coffee. Late on weekend nights it's packed with
hungry partygoers. ✉ *Hornsg. 92, Södermalm* ☎ *08/6684131* ▤ *No
credit cards.*

Where to Stay

Although Stockholm has a reputation for prohibitively expensive ho-
tels, great deals can be found during the summer, when prices are sub-
stantially lower and numerous discounts are available. More than 50
hotels offer the "Stockholm Package," which includes accommodations
for one night, breakfast, and the *Stockholmskortet*, or Stockholm Card,
which entitles the cardholder to free admission to museums and travel
on public transport. Details are available from travel agents, tourist bu-
reaus, and the **Stockholm Information Service** (✉ Box 7542, 103 93 Stock-
holm ☎ 08/7892400 🖷 08/7892450). Also try **Hotellcentralen**
(✉ Centralstation, 111 20 Stockholm ☎ 08/7892425 🖷 08/7918666);
the service is free if you go in person, but a fee applies if you call.

All rooms in the hotels reviewed below are equipped with shower or bath unless otherwise noted. Some hotels close during the winter holidays; call ahead if you expect to travel during that time.

Downtown Stockholm & Beyond

$$$$ ▦ **Royal Viking (Radisson SAS).** For the weary traveler, the Royal Viking's location right next to the central station is a gift; fall off the airport train and into the comfortable beds. When you awake, enjoy the attractive natural textiles and artwork, sturdy writing desks, separate seating areas, and plush robes in the large bathrooms. Triple-glazed windows and plenty of insulation keep traffic noise to a minimum. The large atrium lobby and split-level lounge, extensively renovated in 2002, take the edge off what was previously another faceless international business hotel. But if it's business you want, there is a business-class SAS check-in counter in the lobby. ⊠ *Vasag. 1 City, 101 24* ☎ *08/50654000* 🖷 *08/50654001* ⊕ *www.radissonsas.com* ➳ *319 rooms* ♨ *Restaurant, bar, minibars, indoor pool, sauna, convention center, no-smoking rooms* ⊟ *AE, MC, V.*

$$$$ ▦ **Sheraton Hotel and Towers.** Popular with business executives, the Sheraton is also an ideal hotel for the tourist on a generous budget looking for comfort and luxury. English is the main language at the restaurant and bar, which fill up at night once the piano player arrives. The lobby is vast and modern. There's a gift shop selling Swedish crystal and international newspapers. Rooms have hardwood floors, leather chairs, thick rugs, and sturdy, fine wood furniture. The big buffet breakfast is not included in room rates. ⊠ *Tegelbackan 6 City, 101 23* ☎ *08/4123400* 🖷 *08/4123409* ⊕ *www.sheratonstockholm.com* ➳ *449 rooms* ♨ *? restaurants, gym, sauna, piano bar, casino* ⊟ *AE, DC, MC, V.*

★ $$$–$$$$
Fodor'sChoice
★   ▦ **Berns Hotel.** This cozy yet subtly ultramodern hotel was a hot spot when it opened its doors in the late 19th century and retains that status today. You can breakfast in the Red Room, immortalized by August Strindberg's novel of the same name; the hotel was one of his haunts. The restaurant and bar is a joint venture with restaurant entrepreneur and designer Terence Conran. Rates include the use of a nearby fitness center with a pool. ⊠ *Näckströmsg. 8 City, 111 47* ☎ *08/56632000* 🖷 *08/56632201* ⊕ *www.berns.se* ➳ *65 rooms, 3 suites* ♨ *Restaurant, bar, meeting room, no-smoking rooms* ⊟ *AE, DC, MC, V.*

$$–$$$$ ▦ **Scandic Hotel Anglais.** This '60s hotel, directly across from the Royal Library and the tree-filled Humlegården, is popular among North American business travelers and tourists. It's in the center of almost everything—shopping, sightseeing, and major businesses. The clean, pleasant rooms have wall-to-wall carpeting and furniture. An agreement with Sturebadet, Stockholm's most exclusive bathhouse, gives hotel guests access to their excellent facilities, which include tile pools from the turn of the 20th century. At night in Scandic's piano bar you'll hear more English than anything else. ⊠ *Humlegårdsg. 23* ☎ *08/51734000* 🖷 *08/51734011* ⊕ *www.scandichotels.se* ➳ *212 rooms* ♨ *2 restaurants, piano bar, meeting rooms* ⊟ *AE, DC, MC, V.*

$$$ ▦ **Nordic Hotel.** Next to the central station, this modern center for the business traveler is actually two hotels—Nordic Light and Nordic Sea—in one. The first focuses on simplicity. Rooms are a mix of dark wood, gray flannel, and black-and-white tile, with adjustable spotlights in the ceiling. Nordic Sea uses lighter wood with lots of blue fabric and mosaic tiles to create a Mediterranean touch. A huge aquarium in the lobby holds exotic fish, and you can chill out in Stockholm's only ice bar, where the temperature never rises above freezing. Both hotels are clean and bright and provide excellent service. ⊠ *Vasaplan City 101 37*

☎ 08/50563000 🖷 08/50563060 ⊕ *www.nordichotels.se* 🛏 *542 rooms* ♨ *2 bars, 2 lounges, meeting rooms* ▭ *AE, DC, MC, V.*

$$$ 🏨 **Radisson SAS SkyCity Hotel.** Right in the center of Arlanda Airport's SkyCity complex, this hotel is equipped and tastefully furnished. If your room faces the runway, you can watch the planes take off and land (the extensive soundproofing makes them seem to do so quietly). If you're flying out very early in the morning or are stuck with a layover in Stockholm, this is the ideal airport hotel. ✉ *Arlanda Airport, 190 45* ☎ *08/50674000* 🖷 *08/50674001* ⊕ *www.radissonsas.com* 🛏 *230 rooms* ♨ *Restaurant, gym, bar, meeting room, no-smoking rooms* ▭ *AE, DC, MC, V.*

$$$ 🏨 **Sergel Plaza.** The lobby in this stainless-steel-panel hotel is welcoming, with cane chairs set up in a pleasant, skylighted seating area. The bright rooms are practical but tend to lack the luxury that the price tag may lead you to expect. In fact, the run-of-the-mill furnishings and a tad too much gray make it a bit dull. But its central location on the main pedestrian mall makes it a great base if you're not going to spend much time at the hotel. For breakfast there is an international buffet or a Japanese breakfast; the Anna Rella Restaurant serves innovative Swedish and international dishes. At night the piano bar behind the lobby fills with guests. ✉ *Brunkebergstorg 9, 103 27* ☎ *08/51726300* 🖷 *08/51726311* ⊕ *www.scandic-hotels.se* 🛏 *405 rooms* ♨ *Restaurant, sauna, bar, casino, shops, convention center, no-smoking rooms* ▭ *AE, DC, MC, V.*

$$–$$$ 🏨 **Birger Jarl.** At this high-design hotel the lobby doubles as a modern-art gallery, with frequently changing exhibitions. Some rooms have been individually designed by several of the country's top designers: it costs extra to stay in these. Most rooms are not large, but all are well furnished and have nice touches, such as heated towel racks in the bathrooms; all double rooms have bathtubs. Four family-style rooms have extra floor space and sofa beds. You can choose your breakfast from an extensive buffet just off the lobby, but room service is also available. ✉ *Tuleg. 8, 104 32* ☎ *08/6741800* 🖷 *08/6737366* ⊕ *www.birgerjarl. se* 🛏 *225 rooms* ♨ *Coffee shop, sauna, meeting room, no-smoking rooms* ▭ *AE, DC, MC, V.*

$$–$$$ 🏨 **Crystal Plaza Hotel.** Housed in one of Stockholm's oldest hotel buildings (1895), the Crystal Plaza, with a circular tower and peach walls, is sure to catch the eye of anyone walking down Birger Jarlsgatan. Most rooms have a mix of birch-wood furniture, hardwood floors with small rugs, and the requisite hotel artwork on the walls. Rooms facing the inner courtyard can be a bit quieter than those on the street. If you want only the best, throw down a little extra money for one of the circular tower rooms, two of which have balconies. The hotel's location, just a stone's throw from the hip bars of Stureplan and downtown shopping, makes it an ideal place for folks looking to have quick access to a good time in the city. ✉ *Birger Jarlsg. 35, 111 45* ☎ *08/4068800* 🖷 *08/241511* ⊕ *www.crystalplaza.aos.se* 🛏 *112 rooms* ♨ *Restaurant, bar, breakfast room* ▭ *AE, DC, MC, V.*

★ $$–$$$ 🏨 **Lydmar Hotel.** Only a 10-minute walk from the downtown hub of Sergels Torg and a stone's throw from Stureplan, the epicenter of Stockholm's nightlife, the Lydmar is more than just a hotel—it's also one of the trendiest bars in town. Even if you don't stay here, be sure to take a ride in the elevator, in which you can choose from eight kinds of elevator music, all of (believe it or not) quality. The lobby lounge is alive on weekends with jazz and with DJs spinning the latest club music. The hotel reception is hidden away at the back of the bar, much to the amusement of the locals, who can sit for ages watching the bemused tourists wander aimlessly among the cool cocktail drinkers. ⊠ *Stureg. 10, 114 36* ☎*08/56611300* 🖷*08/56611301* ⊕*www.lydmar.se* ↝*61 rooms, 5 suites* ⊟ *AE, DC, MC, V.*

$$–$$$ 🛏 **Scandic Hotel Continental.** In city center across from the train station, the Continental is a reliable hotel that's especially popular with Americans. Rooms have a minibar, trouser press, and satellite television. An extravagant Scandinavian buffet is served in the Gustavian breakfast rooms. ⊠*Klara Vattugränd 4, 101 22* ☎*08/51734200* 🖷*08/517342311* ⊕ *www.scandic-hotels.com* ↝ *268 rooms* ⚷ *Restaurant, sauna, bar, meeting room, no-smoking rooms* ⊟ *AE, DC, MC, V.*

$–$$$ ✗🛏 **Villa Källhagen.** The changing seasons are on display in this beau-
FodorsChoice   tiful country hotel, reflected through the huge windows, glass walls, and
★   bedroom skylights. Originally an inn, dating to 1810, an extension was added in 1994, with natural light the main focus. Rooms are spacious and furnished in light woods and natural fabrics. It's only a few minutes from the city center, but its woodland surroundings can put you a million miles away. The restaurant also relies heavily on the seasons, serving a delicious blend of fresh Swedish ingredients cooked with a French influence. ⊠ *Djurgårdsbrunnsv. 10, 115 27* ☎ *08/6650300* 🖷 *08/ 6650399* ⊕ *www.kallhagen.se* ↝ *20 rooms* ⚷ *Restaurant, brasserie, bar, meeting room, no-smoking rooms* ⊟ *AE, DC, MC, V.*

$$ 🛏 **Adlon.** Although in a building dating from 1884, the Adlon considers itself a high-tech business hotel. All rooms, which are rather undistinguished, offer Internet connections. The hotel's proximity to downtown Stockholm and the central station make it ideal for the business traveler hoping to find some time to explore while in town. Despite traffic, rooms on the street remain quiet. Rates are cheaper if rooms are booked via the Web. ⊠ *Vasag. 42, 111 20* ☎ *08/4026500* 🖷 *08/208610* ⊕ *www.adlon.se* ↝ *78 rooms* ⚷ *Breakfast room, meeting rooms, no-smoking rooms* ⊟ *AE, DC, MC, V.*

$$ 🛏 **Central Hotel.** Less than 300 yards from the central station, this practical hotel is a good option for both business and pleasure travelers. The rooms are fairly small, but all face a pleasant, quiet courtyard. And thanks to extra sound insulation, the chaos of Vasagatan remains outside the room. Bathrooms have showers only. ⊠ *Vasag. 38, 101 20* ☎ *08/ 56620800* 🖷*08/247573* ⊕*www.centralhotel.se* ↝*93 rooms* ⚷ *In-room data ports, meeting room, no-smoking rooms* ⊟ *AE, DC, MC, V.*

$$ 🛏 **City.** This large modern-style hotel is near the city center and Hötorget Market, making it ideal for shopping and sightseeing (or movie watching, since it's also close to a movie complex). Rooms are filled with modern, no-frills furniture. Some have hardwood floors. Breakfast is served in the atrium Winter Garden restaurant. ⊠ *Slöjdg. 7, 111 81* ☎ *08/ 7237200* 🖷 *08/7237209* ⊕ *www.rica.cityhotels.se* ↝ *293 rooms* ⚷ *Restaurant, sauna, meeting room, no-smoking rooms* ⊟ *AE, DC, MC, V* ⦿ *BP.*

★ **$$**   ✗🛏 **Claes på Hörnet.** This may be the most exclusive—and smallest— hotel in town, with only 10 rooms in a former 1739 inn. The rooms, comfortably furnished with period antiques, go quickly (book three or so months in advance, especially around Christmas). The restaurant ($$) is worth visiting even if you don't spend the night: its old-fashioned dining room serves Swedish and Continental dishes such as outstanding *strömming* (Baltic herring) and cloudberry mousse cake. Reservations are essential. Note that the restaurant is closed in July. ⊠ *Surbrunnsg. 20, 113 48* ☎ *08/165130* 🖷 *08/6125315* ↝ *10 rooms* ⚷ *Restaurant* ⊟ *AE, DC, MC, V.*

$$ ✗🛏 **Stockholm Plaza Hotel.** On one of Stockholm's foremost streets for shopping and entertainment, and only a short walk from the city's nightlife and business center, this hotel is ideal if you want to be in a central location. The building was built in 1884, and the Elite hotel chain took over in 1984. Rooms are furnished in an elegant, traditional manner and are reasonably sized. The restaurant, Vassa Egen, is one of the best in the city, a bright, elegant domed dining room serving exquisite modern Scandinavian cuisine. ⊠ *Birger Jarlsg. 29, Downtown 103 95* ☎ *08/56622000* 🖷 *08/56622020* ⊕ *www.elite.se* 🛏 *151 rooms* ⚹ *Restaurant, bar, meeting rooms* ⊟ *AE, DC, MC, V.*

$$ 🏨 **Tegnérlunden.** A quiet city park fronts this modern hotel, a 10-minute walk along shop-lined Sveavägen from the downtown hub of Sergels Torg. Although the rooms are small and sparsely furnished, they are clean and well maintained. The lobby is bright with marble, brass, and greenery, as is the sunny rooftop breakfast room. ⊠ *Tegnérlunden 8, 113 59* ☎ *08/54545550* 🖷 *08/54545551* ⊕ *www.swedenhotels.se* 🛏 *103 rooms* ⚹ *Breakfast room, sauna, meeting room, no-smoking rooms* ⊟ *AE, DC, MC, V.*

$ 🏨 **Arcadia.** On a hilltop near a large waterfront nature preserve, this converted dormitory is within 15 minutes of downtown by bus or subway or 30 minutes on foot along pleasant shopping streets. Rooms are furnished in a spare, neutral style, with plenty of natural light. The adjoining restaurant serves meals on the terrace in summer. To get here, take Bus 43 to Körsbärsvägen. ⊠ *Körsbärsv. 1, 114 89* ☎ *08/56621500* 🖷 *08/56621501* ⊕ *www.arcadia.elite.se* 🛏 *82 rooms* ⚹ *Restaurant* ⊟ *AE, DC, MC, V.*

$ 🏨 **August Strindberg.** A narrow frescoed corridor leads from the street to the flagstone courtyard, into which the hotel's restaurant expands in summer. Parquet flooring and high ceilings distinguish the rooms, which are otherwise plainly furnished. Kitchenettes are available; some rooms can be combined into family apartments. The four floors have no elevator. ⊠ *Tegnérg. 38, 113 59* ☎ *08/325006* 🖷 *08/209085* 🛏 *19 rooms* ⚹ *Restaurant, some kitchenettes* ⊟ *AE, DC, MC, V.*

$ 🏨 **Hotel Gustav Wasa.** The Gustav Wasa, named after the first king of
Fodor'sChoice Sweden, is right next to Odenplan Square. The hotel is in a 19th-century residential building and has fairly large, bright rooms with her-
★ ringbone hardwood floors, original trim and details along the ceilings, and a funky blend of antiques and furniture that's more modern. Ask for a room with a window out to the street in order to get a direct view of the grand Gustav Wasa Church and the Odenplan. The other available view, of the inner courtyard, is much less exciting. The downtown location and lower prices make this an excellent place for budget travelers who prefer a friendly hotel. ⊠ *Västmannag. 61, 113 25* ☎ *08/343801* 🖷 *08/307372* ⊕ *www.hotel.wineasy.se/gustav.vasa* 🛏 *33 rooms* ⊟ *AE, DC, MC, V.*

¢ 🏨 **Bema.** This small hotel is relatively central, on the ground floor of an apartment block near Tegnérlunden park. Room have a modern Swedish style, with beech-wood furniture. One four-bed family room is available. Breakfast is served in your room. Given the price, it's difficult to beat. ⊠ *Upplandsg. 13, 111 23* ☎ *08/232675* 🖷 *08/205338* 🛏 *12 rooms* ⊟ *AE, DC, MC, V.*

Gamla Stan & Skeppsholmen

$$$$ 🏨 **Grand Hotel.** The city's showpiece hotel is an 1874 landmark on the
Fodor'sChoice quayside at Blasieholmen, across the water from the Royal Palace.
★ Visiting political dignitaries, Nobel Prize winners, and movie stars come to enjoy its gracious charm, which extends from the grand public rooms to the comfortable, luxurious bedrooms. One of the hotel's most alluring features is a glassed-in veranda overlooking the harbor, where an excellent smörgåsbord buffet is served. Guests have access to the high-class Sturebadet Health Spa nearby, and there is a small gym

area in the hotel. Franska Matsalen, the hotel's main restaurant, serves French cuisine and is ranked as one of the best in Sweden. ⊠ *Södra Blasieholmshamnen 8, Box 16424, City 103 27* ☎ *08/6793500* 🖷 *08/ 6118686* ⊕ *www.grandhotel.se* ➭ *310 rooms, 21 suites* ♤ *2 restaurants, sauna, fitness center, bar, shops, meeting room, no-smoking rooms* ☰ *AE, DC, MC, V.*

$$–$$$$ 🖾 **Radisson SAS Strand Hotel.** An art nouveau monolith, built in 1912 for the Stockholm Olympics, this hotel has been completely and tastefully modernized. It's on the water across from the Royal Dramatic Theater, directly in front of the quay, where many of the boats leave for the archipelago. It's also only a short walk from the Old Town and the museums on Skeppsholmen. No two rooms are alike, but all are furnished with simple and elegant furniture, offset by white woodwork and hues of moss green and cocoa brown. The Piazza restaurant has an outdoor feel to it: Italian cuisine is the specialty, and the wine list is superb. An SAS check-in counter for business-class travelers adjoins the main reception area. ⊠ *Nybrokajen 9, Box 16396, City 103 27* ☎ *08/50664000* 🖷 *08/6112436* ⊕ *www.radissonsas.com* ➭ *152 rooms* ♤ *Restaurant, sauna, meeting room, no-smoking rooms* ☰ *AE, DC, MC, V.*

$$–$$$ 🖾 **Lady Hamilton.** As charming as its namesake, Lord Nelson's mistress, the Lady Hamilton is a modern hotel inside a 15th-century building. Swedish antiques fill the guest rooms and common areas. Romney's *Bacchae* portrait of Lady Hamilton hangs in the foyer, where she also supports the ceiling in the form of a large smiling figurehead from an old ship. The breakfast room, furnished with captain's chairs, looks out onto the lively cobblestone street, and the subterranean sauna rooms, in whitewashed stone, provide a secluded fireplace and a change to take a dip in the building's original, medieval well. ⊠ *Storkyrkobrinken 5, Gamla Stan 111 28* ☎ *08/50640100* 🖷 *08/50640110* ⊕ *www.lady-hamilton.se* ➭ *34 rooms* ♤ *Bar, breakfast room, sauna, meeting room, no-smoking rooms* ☰ *AE, DC, MC, V.*

★ **$$–$$$** 🖾 **Reisen.** On the waterfront in Gamla Stan, this hotel opened in 1819. The rooms looking out over the water are fantastic, and for a small supplement you can get a room with a private sauna and Jacuzzi. There is a fine Italian restaurant with a grill, tea and coffee service in the library, and what is reputed to be the best piano bar in town. A small swimming pool, dominated by businessmen cooling off after the sauna, is built under the medieval arches of the foundations. ⊠ *Skeppsbron 12–14, Gamla Stan 111 30* ☎ *08/223260* 🖷 *08/201559* ⊕ *www.firsthotels.com* ➭ *144 rooms* ♤ *Restaurant, indoor pool, sauna, piano bar, meeting room, no-smoking floor* ☰ *AE, DC, MC, V.*

$$ 🖾 **Gamla Stan.** The feel of historical Stockholm living is rarely more prevalent than in this quiet hotel tucked away on a narrow street in one of the Gamla Stan's 17th-century houses. All rooms are decorated in the Gustavian style, with hardwood floors, Oriental rugs, and antique furniture. A short walk from the Gamla Stan metro stop, it's a perfect home base for later exploring. ⊠ *Lilla Nyg. 25, Gamla Stan* ☎ *08/7237250* 🖷 *08/7237259* ⊕ *www.rica.cityhotels.se* ➭ *51 rooms* ♤ *Meeting room, no-smoking floor* ☰ *AE, DC, MC, V.*

$$ 🖾 **Lord Nelson.** The owners of the Lady Hamilton and the Victory run this small hotel with a nautical theme right in the middle of Gamla Stan. Rooms are only a touch larger than cabins—but service is excellent. Noise from traffic in the pedestrian street outside can be a problem during the summer. ⊠ *Västerlångg. 22, Gamla Stan 111 29* ☎ *08/50640120* 🖷 *08/ 50640130* ⊕ *www.lord-nelson.se* ➭ *31 rooms* ♤ *Café, sauna, meeting room, no-smoking room* ☰ *AE, DC, MC, V.*

$$ 🖾 **Victory.** Slightly larger than its brother and sister hotels, the Lord Nelson and Lady Hamilton, this extremely atmospheric Gamla Stan building dates from 1640. The theme is nautical, with items from the HMS *Victory* and Swedish antiques. Each room is named after a 19th-century sea captain. The noted Lejontornet restaurant keeps an extensive wine cellar. ⊠ *Lilla Nyg. 5, Gamla Stan 111 28* ☎ *08/50640000* 🖷 *08/50640010* ⊕ *www.victory-hotel.se* 🛏 *48 rooms* ♨ *Restaurant, saunas, bar, meeting room, no-smoking floor* ⊟ *AE, DC, MC, V.*

$–$$ 🏨 **Mälardrottningen.** One of the more unusual establishments in Stockholm, Mälardrottningen, a Sweden Hotels property, was once Barbara Hutton's yacht. Since 1982 it has been a quaint and pleasant hotel, with a crew as service conscious as any in Stockholm. Tied up on the freshwater side of Gamla Stan, it is minutes from everything. The small suites are suitably decorated in a navy-blue-and-maroon nautical theme. Some of the below-deck cabins are a bit stuffy, but in summer you can take your meals out on deck. The ship's chief assets are novelty and absence of traffic noise. ⊠ *Riddarholmen 4, Riddarholmen 111 28* ☎ *08/54518780* 🖷 *08/243676* 🛏 *59 cabins* ♨ *Restaurant, grill, sauna, bar, meeting room, no-smoking rooms* ⊟ *AE, DC, MC, V.*

Östermalm

$$$–$$$$ 🏨 **Diplomat.** Within easy walking distance of Djurgården, this elegant
Fodor's Choice   hotel is less flashy than most in its price range but oozes a certain Eu-
★   ropean chic, evident in its subtle, tasteful designs and efficient staff. The building is a turn-of-the-20th-century town house that housed foreign embassies in the 1930s and was converted into a hotel in 1966. Rooms are all individual but have fresh colors, clean lines, and subtle hints of floral prints in common, and those in the front, facing the water, have magnificent views over Stockholm Harbor. The T-Bar, formerly a rather staid tearoom and restaurant, is now one of the trendiest bars among the city's upper crust. The second-floor bar is ideal for a break from sightseeing. ⊠ *Strandv. 7C, Östermalm 104 40* ☎ *08/4596800* 🖷 *08/4596820* ⊕ *www.diplomathotel.com.* 🛏 *128 rooms* ♨ *Restaurant, sauna, bar, meeting room, no-smoking room* ⊟ *AE, DC, MC, V.*

$$$ 🏨 **Hotel Esplanade.** Right on the water and only a few buildings down from Stockholm's Royal Dramatic Theater, Hotel Esplanade is a beautiful hotel with a real touch of old Stockholm. Originally a guest house operated by an elderly woman, the inn now has owners who have sought to maintain its hominess—you'll probably be offered a glass of fine brandy in the lounge when you check in. Rooms are individually decorated with antiques, and some offer water views. Breakfast is served in the original art nouveau–style breakfast room. Be sure to call well ahead to book a room, since many regulars return every year. ⊠ *Strandv. 7A, Östermalm 114 56* ☎ *08/6630740* 🖷 *08/6625992* ⊕ *www.hotelesplanade.se* 🛏 *34 rooms* ♨ *Breakfast room, sauna, lobby lounge* ⊟ *AE, DC, MC, V.*

$$–$$$ 🏨 **Castle Hotel.** On a backstreet just off Birgar Jarlsgatan, this centrally located hotel has been in operation since the 1930s. The owners are great jazz enthusiasts, and the hotel has hosted such jazz greats as Dizzy Gillespie, Chet Baker, and Benny Carter. Rooms are done with art deco furnishings but are on the diminutive side. Showing the spirit of the jazz theme along with a propensity for a good pun are the names of the two suites: Suite Georgia Brown and Suite Lorraine. ⊠ *Riddarg. 14, Östermalm 114 35* ☎ *08/6795700* 🖷 *08/6112022* ⊕ *www.castle-hotel.se* 🛏 *50 rooms, 2 suites* ♨ *Restaurant, meeting room* ⊟ *AE, DC, MC, V.*

$$–$$$ 🏨 **Mornington.** Off the main square of Östermalm, the Mornington is close to both the nightlife of Stureplan and the downtown business district. The lobby, bar, and restaurant area are hip places to hang out, and there's a lovely little library of more than 4,000 books (mostly in Swedish) spread throughout the lobby; you can borrow them during your stay. All rooms have hardwood floors and elegant furniture, but ask for a renovated room on the sixth or seventh floor—the older rooms are a bit worn out. ⊠ *Nybrog. 53, Östermalm 102 44* ☎ *08/50733000* 🖷 *08/50733039* ⊕ *www.mornington.se* ⇋ *140 rooms* ⟂ *Restaurant, sauna, steam room, solarium, bar, meeting room, no-smoking rooms* ▭ *AE, DC, MC, V.*

★ $$ 🖵 **Wellington.** From the outside the building resembles the Industrihuset (Industry House) across the street, but inside is a delightful hotel with polite, professional staff and quality service. It's in a quiet residential area in Östermalm near the Hedvig Eleonora Church and cemetery, a calm home base from which to enjoy the city. Rooms are modern and fresh with hardwood floors. Rooms facing the inner courtyard have balconies. Ask for a room on the top floor for a great view of the neighborhood's rooftops. The breakfast buffet is top-notch, serving all the Swedish classics, including pickled herring. ⊠ *Storg. 6, Östermalm 114 51* ☎ *08/6670910* 🖷 *08/6671254* ⊕ *www.wellington.se* ⇋ *60 rooms* ⟂ *breakfast room, in-room data ports, sauna, bar, meeting rooms* ▭ *AE, MC, V.*

★ $–$$ 🖵 **Örnsköld.** Right in the heart of the city, this hidden gem feels like an old private club, from its brass-and-leather lobby to the Victorian-style furniture in the moderately spacious, high-ceiling rooms. Rooms overlooking the courtyard are quieter, but those facing the street—not a particularly busy one—are sunnier. The hotel is frequented by actors appearing at the Royal Theater next door. ⊠ *Nybrog. 6, Östermalm 114 34* ☎ *08/6670285* 🖷 *08/6676991* ⇋ *30 rooms* ▭ *AE, MC, V.*

$ 🖵 **Pärlan.** The name of this hotel means the "Pearl" and that's exactly **Fodor's Choice** what it is. On the second floor of an early-19th century building on a ★ quiet street, the Pärlan is a friendly alternative to the city's bigger hotels. Furniture throughout is a mix of fine antiques and flea market bargains, making it quirky and homey. A balcony looking out over the inner courtyard is a perfect spot for eating breakfast, which is served buffet style in the kitchen every morning. Be sure to admire the ultra-Swedish tile oven in the corner of the dining room. If you want to get a feel for what it's like to really live in this neighborhood, this is your best bet. Book far in advance because the rooms are almost always full. ⊠ *Skepperg. 27, Östermalm 114 52* ☎ *08/6635070* 🖷 *08/6677145* ⇋ *9 rooms* ▭ *AE, MC, V.*

Södermalm

$$$ 🖵 **Hilton Hotel Slussen.** Working with what appears to be a dubious location (atop a tunnel above a six-lane highway), the Hilton has pulled a rabbit out of a hat. Built on special noise- and shock-absorbing cushions, the hotel almost lets you forget about the highway. The intriguing labyrinth of levels, separate buildings, and corridors is filled with such unique details as a rounded stairway lighted from between the steps. The guest rooms are exquisitely designed and modern, with plenty of stainless steel and polished-wood inlay to accent the maroon color scheme. The Eken restaurant and bar serves food indoors and out. If you eat or drink too much, there's a gym with excellent facilities. The hotel is at Slussen, easily accessible from downtown. ⊠ *Guldgränd 8, Södermalm 104 65* ☎ *08/51735300* 🖷 *08/51735311* ⊕ *www.scandic.se* ⇋ *264 rooms* ⟂ *2 restaurants, indoor pool, gym, hair salon, sauna, piano bar, meeting room, no-smoking rooms* ▭ *AE, DC, MC, V.*

★ $$ 🖵 **Anno 1647.** Named for the date the building was erected, this small, pleasant hotel is a piece of Stockholm history. Rooms vary in shape, but all have original, well-worn pine floors with 17th-century-style appointments. There's no elevator in this four-story building. The bar and café are a popular local hangout. The menu is international. Guest DJs control the sound waves. ⊠ *Mariagränd 3, Södermalm 116 41* ☎ *08/*

4421680 🖷 *08/4421647* 🖴 *42 rooms, 30 with bath* ☓ *Snack bar* 🚫 *AE, DC, MC, V.*

$–$$ 🏨 **Alexandra.** This economy hotel to the south of Gamla Stan is a five-minute walk from the subway and only a few stops from the city center. Rooms are fairly big but have a definite late-1980s look. There are a number of cheaper rooms, adjacent to the parking garage and without windows. ✉ *Magnus Ladulåsg. 42, Södermalm 118 27* 🖷 *08/840320* 🖷 *08/7205353* 🖴 *68 rooms, 5 2-room suites* ☓ *Breakfast room, sauna, no-smoking rooms* 🚫 *AE, DC, MC, V.*

¢–$$ 🏨 **Columbus Hotel.** Just a few blocks from busy Götgatan, the Columbus is an oasis of calm in the busy urban streets of Södermalm. Built in 1780, it was originally a brewery, then a jail, then a hospital, then a temporary housing area. Since 1976 the beautiful building, with its large, tranquil inner courtyard, has been a hotel. Rooms have wide beams, polished hardwood floors, antique furniture, and bright wallpaper and fabrics. Many look out over the courtyard, others on the nearby church. In summer breakfast is served outside. The peace and quiet this hotel provides, even though it's close to all the action, makes it ideal for a vacation. ✉ *Tjärhovsg. 11, Södermalm 116 21* 🖷 *08/6441717* 🖷 *08/7020764* 🌐 *www.columbus.se* 🖴 *64 rooms, 36 with bath* ☓ *Café, bar* 🚫 *AE, MC, V.*

FodorśChoice ★

¢–$ 🏨 **Pensionat Oden, Söder.** Clean, inexpensive, and centrally located, this bed-and-breakfast is on the second floor of a 19th-century building. Hornsgatan, the street it's on, is Södermalm's busiest and filled with pubs, restaurants, and shops. Rooms have hardwood floors, Oriental rugs, and an odd blend of new and old furniture. A kitchen is available for use. The hotel is popular with parents visiting their children in college, academics traveling on a budget, and backpackers. Book rooms well in advance, especially during the holidays. ✉ *Hornsg. 66B, Södermalm* 🖷 *08/6124349* 🖷 *08/6124501* 🌐 *www.pensionat.nu* 🖴 *35 rooms, 8 with bath* ☓ *No-smoking rooms* 🚫 *AE, MC, V.*

Youth Hostels

Don't be put off by the "youth" bit: there's actually no age limit. The standards of cleanliness, comfort, and facilities offered are usually extremely high.

¢–$ 🏨 ***Den Röda Båten Mälaren*** (The Red Boat). Built in 1914, the *Mälaren* originally traveled the waters of the Göta Canal under the name of *Sätra*. Today she has to settle for sitting still in Stockholm as a youth hostel. The hostel cabins are small but clean and have bunk beds. There are also four "hotel" rooms, which have private baths and nicer furniture and details. In the summer the restaurant offers great views of Stockholm along with basic, traditional Swedish food. Breakfast costs an additional 55 SKr, but sheets are included in your rate. ✉ *Södermälarstrand kajplats 6, 117 20* 🖷 *08/6444385* 🖷 *08/6413733* 🌐 *www.rodabaten. nu* 🖴 *35 rooms, 4 with bath* 🚫 *MC, V.*

¢ 🏨 ***af Chapman.*** This circa-1888 sailing ship, permanently moored in Stockholm Harbor just across from the Royal Palace, is a landmark in its own right. Book early—the place is so popular in summer that finding a bed may prove difficult. Breakfast (SKr 45) is not included in the room rate; there are no kitchen facilities. ✉ *Flaggmansv. 8, Skeppsholmen Skeppsholmen 111 49* 🖷 *08/4632266* 🖷 *08/6117155* 🌐 *www.stfchapman. com* 🖴 *293 beds, 2- to 6-bed cabins* ☓ *Café* 🚫 *DC, MC, V* ⊙ *Closed mid-Dec.–mid-Jan.*

¢ 🏨 **Bosön.** Out of the way on the island of Lidingö, this hostel is part of the Bosön Sports Institute, a national training center pleasantly close to the water. You can rent canoes on the grounds and go out for a paddle. Breakfast is included in the room rate. There are laundry facilities and a kitchen you can use. All rooms are clean and fresh. ⊠ *Bosön, 181 47 Lidingö* ☎ *08/6056600* 🖷 *08/7671644* 🖘 *70 beds* ⚲ *Cafeteria, sauna, boating, coin laundry* ⊟ *MC, V* ⎅ *BP.*

¢ 🖽 **City Backpackers.** You won't find cheaper accommodations closer to central station than City Backpackers, which has 65 beds. The 19th-century building typifies the European youth hostel, and this one is well run. Guests have access to a common kitchen, a lounge with cable TV, showers, and a courtyard. The seven-person apartment, with its own kitchen and bathroom, is ideal for a group of young backpackers or an adventurous large family. ⊠ *Upplandsg. 2A, Vasastan* ☎ *08/206920* 🖷 *08/100464* ⊕ *www.citybackpackers.se* 🖘 *15 rooms* ⊟ *MC, V.*

¢ 🖽 *Gustav af Klint.* A "hotel ship" moored at Stadsgården quay, near the Slussen subway station, the *Gustav af Klint* harbors 120 beds in its two sections: a hotel and a hostel. The hostel section has 18 four-bunk cabins and 10 two-bunk cabins; a 14-bunk dormitory is also available from May through mid-September. The hotel section has four single-bunk and three two-bunk cabins with bedsheets and breakfast included. The hostel rates are SKr 120 per person in a four-bunk room and SKr 140 per person in a two-bunk room; these prices do not include bedsheets or breakfast, which are available at an extra charge. All guests share common bathrooms and showers. There are a cafeteria and a restaurant, and you can dine on deck in summer. ⊠ *Stadsgårdskajen 153, 116 45* ☎ *08/ 6404077* 🖷 *08/6406416* 🖘 *7 hotel cabins, 28 hostel cabins, 28 dormitory beds, all without bath* ⚲ *Restaurant, cafeteria* ⊟ *AE, MC, V.*

¢ 🖽 **Långholmen.** This former prison, built in 1724, was converted into a combined hotel and hostel in 1989. The hotel rooms are made available as additional hostel rooms in the summer. Rooms are small, and windows are nearly nonexistent—you *are* in a prison, after all—but that hasn't stopped travelers from flocking here. Each room has 2–5 beds, and all but 10 have bathrooms with shower. The hostel is on the island of Långholmen, which has popular bathing beaches and the Prison Museum. The Inn, next door, serves Swedish home cooking, the Jail Pub offers light snacks, and a garden restaurant operates in the summer. ⊠ *Långholmen, Box 9116, 102 72* ☎ *08/6680500* 🖷 *08/7208575* ⊕ *www.langholmen. com* 🖘 *254 beds June–Sept., 26 beds Sept.–May* ⚲ *Restaurant, cafeteria, sauna, beach, coin laundry* ⊟ *AE, DC, MC, V.*

¢ 🖽 **Skeppsholmen.** This former craftsman's workshop in a pleasant and quiet part of the island was converted into a hostel for the overflow from the *af Chapman,* another hostel an anchor's throw away. Breakfast costs an additional SKr 45. ⊠ *Skeppsholmen, 111 49* ☎ *08/4632266* 🖷 *08/6117155* 🖘 *155 beds, 2- to 6-bed rooms* ⚲ *Café, coin laundry* ⊟ *DC, MC, V.*

Camping

You can camp in the Stockholm area for SKr 80–SKr 130 per night. **Bredäng Camping** (⊠ 127 31 Skärholmen ☎ 08/977071) has camping and a youth hostel. Its facilities are excellent and include a restaurant and bar. Fifteen kilometers (9 mi) from Stockholm, in Huddinge, is **Stockholm SweCamp Flottsbro** (⊠ 141 25 Huddinge ☎ 08/4499580), where you can camp, play golf, rent canoes and bikes, and hang out on a beach. At **Rösjöbaden Camping** (⊠ 192 56 Sollentuna ☎ 08/ 962184), a short drive north of town, you can fish, swim, and play minigolf and volleyball.

Nightlife & the Arts

Stockholm's nightlife can be broken up into two general groups based on their geography. First, there's Birger Jarlsgatan, Stureplan, and the city end of Kungsträdgården, which are more upscale and trendy, and thus more expensive. At the bars and clubs in this area, it's not unusual to wait in line with people who look like they just stepped off the pages of a glossy magazine. To the south, in Södermalm, things are a bit looser and wilder, but that doesn't mean the bars are any less hip. At night Söder can get pretty crazy—it's louder and more bohemian, and partygoers walk the streets.

In general, on weekends clubs and bars are often packed with tourists and locals, and you might have to wait in line. It's also sometimes hard to distinguish between a bar and nightclub, since many bars turn into clubs late at night. Many establishments will post and enforce a minimum age requirement, which could be anywhere from 18 to 30, depending on the clientele they wish to serve, and they may frown on jeans and sneakers. Your safest bet is to wear dark clothes. Most places are open until around 3 AM.

The tourist guide *What's On* (⊕ www.stockholmtown.com) is available free of charge at most hotels, tourist centers, and some restaurants. It lists the month's events in both English and Swedish. The Thursday editions of the daily newspapers *Dagens Nyheter* (⊕ www.dn.se) and *Svenska Dagbladet* (⊕ www.svd.se) carry current listings of events, films, restaurants, and museums in Swedish. There's also a monthly guide called *Nöjesguiden* (the Entertainment Guide; ⊕ www.nojesguiden.se), which has listings and reviews in Swedish.

Nightlife

BARS & NIGHTCLUBS Go to Stureplan (at one end of Birger Jarlsgatan) on any given weekend night, and you'll see crowds of people gathering around *Svampen* (the Mushroom), a concrete structure that's a roof over pay phones. It's *the* meeting place for people getting ready to go out in this area.

★ Glamour is on the menu at **Brasserie Godot** (⊠ Grev Tureg. 36, Östermalm ☎ 08/6600614), a toned-down chic bar and restaurant known
★ for its excellent cocktail list and hip crowd. **Berns Salonger** (⊠ Berns Hotel, Berzelii Park, City ☎ 08/56632000) has three bars—one in 19th-century style and two modern rooms—plus a huge veranda that's spectacular in the summer. Music here gets so thumping you can hear it down the street. **Folkhemmet** (⊠ Renstiernas Gata 30, Södermalm ☎ 08/6405595), marked by a blue F imitating the T for the subway, is a long-time favorite of the artsy locals. It's friendly and inviting, but be prepared for lots of smoke and a crowded bar. Close to the Mushroom is the casually hip **Lydmar Bar** (⊠ Stureg. 10, Östermalm ☎ 08/56611300), with black-leather couches and chairs and a small stage for bands and DJs. Many people who frequent the bar are in the music business. **Mosebacke Etablissement** (⊠ Mosebacke Torg 3, Södermalm ☎ 08/6419020) is a combined indoor theater, comedy club, and outdoor café with a spectacular view of the city. The crowd here leans toward over-30 hipsters. The **O-bar** (⊠ Stureplan 2, Östermalm ☎ 08/4405730), located upstairs through the restaurant Sturehof, is where the downtown crowd gathers for late-night drinks and music ranging from bass-heavy hip-hop to hard rock. The **Sturehof** itself is a prime location for evening people-watching. The outdoor tables are smack dab in the middle of Stureplan. For what has to be Stockholm's biggest rum collection (more than 64 varieties), slide into **Sjögräs** (Sea Grass; ⊠ Timmermansg. 24, Södermalm ☎ 08/841200), where the drinks go down smoothly to the sounds of reggae. Wander along Götagatan with its lively bars and head for **Snaps/Rangus Tangus** (⊠ Medborgarplatsen, Södermalm ☎ 08/6402868), an India-inspired eatery and cellar lounge–bar in a 300-year-old building. There is live music, and the latest DJs spin here as well. **Sophie's Bar** (⊠ Biblioteksg. 5, City ☎ 08/6118408) is one of Stockholm's

major celebrity hangouts. It can be a bit elitist and uptight, probably the reason Madonna checked it out when she was in town. From Sophie's Bar it's a short walk to **Spy Bar** (✉ Birger Jarlsg. 20, City ☎ 08/6118408), one of Stockholm's most exclusive clubs. It's often filled with local celebrities and lots of glitz and glamour. **Tiger** (✉ Kungsg. 18, City ☎ 08/244700) is a multilevel club and restaurant with a Latin touch. On the first floor it's all about salsa and *mojitos* (Cuban cocktails made with rum and mint). On the huge second floor the music is anything from hip-hop to house music. Always expect a line and two tough doormen. At Odenplan the basement bar of **Tranan** (✉ Karlbergsv. 14, Vasastan ☎ 08/52728100) is a fun place to party in semidarkness to anything from ambient music to hard rock. Lots of candles, magazines, and art are inside. A trendy youngish crowd props up the long bar at **WC** (✉ Skåneg. 51, Södermalm ☎ 08/7022963), with ladies' drink specials on Sunday. Luckily, the only things that'll remind you of the name (which stands for "water closet," or bathroom) are the holes in the middle of the bar stools.

Stockholm can also appease your need for pub-style intimacy. Guinness, ale, and cider enthusiasts rally in the tartan-clad **Bagpiper's Inn** (✉ Rörstrandsg. 21, Vasastan ☎ 08/311855), where you can get a large selection of bar food. **The Dubliner** (✉ Smålandsg. 8, City ☎ 08/6797707), probably Stockholm's most popular Irish pub, serves up pub food and hosts live folk music on stage. It's not unusual to see people dancing on the tables. As green as a four-leaf clover, **Limerick** (✉ Tegnérg. 10, Norrmalm ☎ 08/6731902) is a popular Hibernian watering hole. The very British **Tudor Arms** (✉ Grevg. 31, Östermalm ☎ 08/6602712) is just as popular as when it opened in 1969. Brits who are missing home cooking will be relieved when they see the menu. **Wirströms Pub** (✉ Stora Nyg. 13, Gamla Stan ☎ 08/212874) is in labyrinthine 17th-century cellars. Expect lots of smoke, live acoustic music, mostly anglophone patrons, and lots of beer. There are also 130 whiskeys available.

CABARET **Börsen** (✉ Jakobsg. 6, City ☎ 08/7878500) offers high-quality international cabaret shows. Tucked behind the Radisson SAS near Nybroplan is **Wallmans Salonger** (✉ Teaterg. 3, City ☎ 08/6116622), where singing and dancing waitstaff and talented stage performers entertain until midnight.

CASINOS Many hotels and bars have a roulette table and sometimes blackjack; games operate according to Swedish rules, which are designed to limit the amount you can lose. **Cosmopol Casino** (✉ Kungsg. 65, City ☎ 08/7818800) is Stockholm's only international casino; it was opened in 2003 after a relaxation in Sweden's gambling laws. Glitz and glamour abound in the huge chandelier-strung former theater, where games are plentiful and winnings are unlimited; as are losses.

DANCE CLUBS **Café Opera** (✉ Operahuset, City ☎ 08/6765807), at the waterfront end of Kungsträdgården, is a popular meeting place for young and old alike. It has the longest bar in town, fantastic 19th-century ceilings and details, plus dining and roulette, and major dancing after midnight. The kitchen offers a night menu until 2:30 AM. **Daily News Café** (✉ Kungsträdgården, City ☎ 08/215655), a glitzy nightclub near Sweden House, is returning to its 1980s popular glory. The crowd here varies depending on the night, with lots of late-night stragglers looking for fun before going home. Down on Stureplan is **Sturecompagniet** (✉ Stureg. 4, Östermalm ☎ 08/6117800), a galleried, multifloored club where the crowd is young, the dance music is loud, and the lines are long. **Mälarsalen** (✉ Torkel Knutssonsg. 2 ☎ 08/6581300) caters to the nondrinking jitterbug and fox-trot crowd in Södermalm. **Residence** (✉ Birger Jarlsg. 29, Norrmalm

08/201411) is a soft-disco nightclub specifically for a thirty- and fortysomething crowd.

GAY BARS **Patricia** (✉ Stadsgården, Berth 25, Södermalm ☎ 08/7430570) is a floating restaurant, disco, and bar right next to Slussen. And don't worry—the boat doesn't rock enough to make you sick. All are welcome at **TipTop** (✉ Sveav. 57, Norrmalm ☎ 08/329800), but most of the clientele is gay. Men and women dance nightly to '70s disco and modern techno. Hidden down behind the statue of St. George and the dragon on Gamla Stan, **Mandus Bar och Kök** (✉ Österlångg. 7, Gamla Stan ☎ 08/206055) is a warm and friendly restaurant and bar perfect for drinking and talking late into the night.

JAZZ CLUBS The best and most popular jazz venue is **Fasching** (✉ Kungsg. 63, City ☎ 08/216267), where international and local bands play year-round. The classic club **Nalens** (✉ Regeringsg. 74, City ☎ 08/4533434), which was popular back in the '50s and '60s, is back on the scene with major performances throughout the year; it has three stages. **Stampen** (✉ Stora Nyg. 5, Gamla Stan ☎ 08/205793) is an overpriced but atmospheric club in Gamla Stan with traditional jazz nightly. Get there early for a seat.

PIANO BARS Piano bars are part of Stockholm's nightlife. The **Anglais Bar** (✉ Humlegårdsg. 23, City ☎ 08/51734000), at the Hotel Anglais, is popular on weekends. Most people there are English-speaking international travelers staying at the hotel. The **Clipper Club** (✉ Skeppsbron 1214, Gamla Stan ☎ 08/223260), at the Hotel Reisen, is a pleasant, dark-wood, dimly lighted bar on Gamla Stan.

ROCK CLUBS **Pub Anchor** (✉ Sveav. 90, Norrmalm ☎ 08/152000), on Sveavägen's main drag, is the city's downtown hard-rock bar. **Krogen Tre Backar** (✉ Tegnérg. 1214, Norrmalm ☎ 08/6734400) is as popular among hard-rock fans as the Pub Anchor is. It's just off Sveavägen. International rock acts often play at **Klubben** (✉ Hammarby Frabriksv. 13, Södermalm ☎ 08/4622200), a small bar and club in the Fryshuset community center south of town.

The Arts
Stockholm's theater and opera season runs from September through May. Both *Dramaten* (the National Theater) and *Operan* (the Royal Opera) shut down in the summer months. When it comes to popular music, big-name acts such as Neil Young, U2, and Eminem frequently come to Stockholm during the summer months while on their European tours. Artists of this type always play at Globen sports arena. For a list of events pick up the free booklet *What's On*, available from hotels and tourist information offices. For tickets to theaters and shows try **Biljettdirekt** (☎ 077/1707070), at Sweden House (✉ Hamng. 27, City), or any post office.

CLASSICAL MUSIC International orchestras perform at **Konserthuset** (✉ Hötorget 8, City ☎ 08/102110), the main concert hall. The **Music at the Palace series** (☎ 08/102247) runs June through August. Off-season there are weekly concerts by Sweden's Radio Symphony Orchestra at **Berwaldhallen** (Berwald Concert Hall; ✉ Strandv. 69, Östermalm ☎ 08/7845000). After Konserthuset, the best place for classical music is **Nybrokajen 11** (✉ Nybrokajen 11, City ☎ 08/071700), where top international musicians perform in relatively small listening halls.

DANCE When it comes to high-quality international dance in Stockholm, there's really only one place to go. **Dansenshus** (✉ Barnhusg. 12–14, Vasastan ☎ 08/50899090) hosts the best Swedish and international acts, with shows

ranging from traditional Japanese dance to street dance and modern ballet. You can also see ballet at the Royal Opera house.

FILM   Stockholm has an abundance of cinemas, all listed in the *Yellow Pages*
under "Biografer." Current billings are listed in evening papers, normally
with Swedish titles; call ahead if you're unsure. Foreign movies are subtitled not dubbed. Most, if not all, movie theaters take reservations over
the phone: popular showings can sell out ahead of time. Cinemas are
either part of the SF chain or of **SandrewMetronome.** Listings for each
can be found on the wall at the theater or in the back of the culture pages
of the daily newspapers. **Filmstaden Sergel** (⊠ Hötorget, City ☏ 08/
56260000) is a 14-screen complex at one end of Hötorget. **Biopalatset
and Filmstaden Söder** (⊠ Medborgarplatsen, Södermalm ☏ 08/6443100
or 08/56260000) are on the south side of town and have many films
from which to choose. If you are interested in smaller theaters with character, try the **Grand** (⊠ Sveav. 45, Norrmalm ☏ 08/4112400), a nice
little theater with two small screens and not a bad seat in the house. **Röda
Kvarn** (⊠ Biblioteksg. 5, City ☏ 08/7896073) is a beautiful, old movie
theater right near Stureplan. **Zita** (⊠ Birger Jarlsg. 37, Norrmalm ☏ 08/
232020) is a one-screen theater that shows foreign films. A small restaurant is in the back.

OPERA   It is said that Queen Lovisa Ulrika began introducing opera to her subjects in 1755. Since then Sweden has become an opera center of standing, a launchpad for such names as Jenny Lind, Jussi Björling, and
★   Birgit Nilsson. **Operan** (Royal Opera House; ⊠ Jakobs Torg 2, City ☏ 08/
248240), dating from 1898, is now the de facto home of Sweden's op-
eratic tradition. **Folkoperan** (⊠ Hornsg. 72, Södermalm ☏ 08/6160750)
is a modern company with its headquarters in Södermalm. Casting traditional presentation and interpretation of the classics to the wind, the
company stages productions that are refreshingly new.

THEATER **Kungliga Dramatiska Teatern** (Royal Dramatic Theater, called Dramaten;
⊠ Nybroplan, City ☏ 08/6670680) sometimes stages productions of
international interest, in Swedish, of course. The exquisite **Drottningholms
Slottsteater** (Drottningholm Court Theater; ⊠ Drottningholm, Drottningholm ☏ 08/6608225) presents opera, ballet, and orchestral music
from May to early September; the original 18th-century stage machinery is still used in these productions. Drottningholm, the royal residence,
is reached by subway and bus or by a special theater-bus (which leaves
from the Grand Hotel or opposite the central train station). Boat tours
run here in summer.

Sports & the Outdoors

Like all Swedes, Stockholmers love the outdoors and spend a great deal
of time doing outdoor sports and activities. Because the city is spread
out on a number of islands, you are almost always close to the water.
The many large parks, including Djurgården and Haga Park, allow
people to quickly escape the hustle and bustle of downtown.

The most popular summertime activities in Stockholm are golf, biking,
rollerblading, tennis, and sailing. In the winter people like to ski and
ice skate.

Beaches
The best bathing places in central Stockholm are on the island of
Långholmen and at Rålambshov, at the end of Norr Mälarstrand. Both
are grassy or rocky lakeside hideaways. Topless sunbathing is virtually
de rigueur.

Biking & Rollerblading

Stockholm is laced with bike paths, and bicycles can be taken on the commuter trains (except during peak traveling times) for excursions to the suburbs. The bike paths are also ideal for rollerblading. You can rent a bike for between SKr 150 and SKr 250 per day. Rollerblades cost between Skr 80 and SKr 120. Most places require a deposit of a couple thousand kronor. **Cykelfrämjandet** (✉ Thuleg. 43, 113 53 ☎ 08/54591030 ⊕ www.cykelframjandet.a.se), a local bicyclists' association, publishes an English-language guide to cycling trips. City and mountain bikes can be rented from **Cykel & Mopeduthyrning** (✉ Strandv. at Kajplats 24, City ☎ 08/6607959) for SKr 170. Also try **Skepp & Hoj** (✉ Galärvarvsv. 2, Djurgården ☎ 08/6605757), pronounced "ship ahoy," which has nice city cruisers for SKr 250 per day.

Boating

Boating in Stockholm's archipelago is an exquisite summertime activity. From May to September sailboats large and small and gorgeous restored wooden boats cruise from island to island. Both types of boats are available for rental. Walk along the water on Strandvägen, where many large power yachts and sailboats (available for charter) are docked. Sea kayaking has also become increasingly popular and is a delightful way to explore the islands.

Contact **Svenska Seglarförbundet** (Swedish Sailing Association; ✉ Af Pontins väg 6, 115 21 ☎ 08/4590990 ⊕ www.ssf.se) for information on sailing. **Svenska Kanotförbundet** (Swedish Canoeing Association; ✉ Idrotts Hus, 123 87 Farsta ☎ 08/6056565 ⊕ www.svenskidrott.se/kanot) has information on canoeing and kayaking. **Capella Skärgårdscatering** (✉ Zirocco, Strandv. Kajplats 20, City ☎ 08/7326850) has a large power yacht available for afternoon and overnight charters for groups of up to 40 people. At the end of Strandvägen, before the bridge to Djurgården, is **Tvillingarnas Båtuthyrning** (✉ Djurgårdsbron, Djurgården ☎ 08/6633739), which has large and small motorboats and small sailboats. **Point 65 N** (✉ Styrmansg. 23, Östermalm), a short walk up from Strandvägen, has high-quality sea kayaks for rent. Its staff will help you get them down and back from the water if it's a two- or three-day rental.

Fitness Centers

Health and fitness is a Swedish obsession. The **Sports Club Stockholm** (✉ City Sports Club, Birger Jarlsg. 6C, City ☎ 08/6798310 ✉ Atlanta Sports Club St. Eriksg. 34, Vasastan ☎ 08/6506625) chain has women's and mixed gym facilities for SKr 90 a day. For a relatively inexpensive massage, try the **Axelsons Gymnastiska Institut** (✉ Gästrikeg. 1012, Vasastan ☎ 08/54545900). **Friskis & Svettis** (✉ St. Eriksg. 54, Vasastan ☎ 08/4297000) is a local chain of indoor and, in summer, outdoor gyms specializing in aerobics; branches are scattered throughout the Stockholm area. Monday through Thursday at 6 PM, from the end of May into late August, it hosts free aerobic sessions in Rålambshovs Park.

Golf

There are numerous golf courses around Stockholm. Greens fees run from about SKr 450 to SKr 650, depending on the club. Contact **Sveriges Golfförbund** (✉ Kevingestrand 20, Box 84, 182 11 Danderyd ☎ 08/7315370 ⊕ sfg.golf.se), which is just outside Stockholm, for information. **Stockholms Golfklubb**, which has a midlevel 18-hole course, is there as well. **Lidingö Golfklubb** (✉ Kyttingev. 2, Lidingö ☎ 08/7317900) has an 18-hole forest-and-park course. It's about a 20-minute drive from the city center. **Ingarö Golfklubb** (✉ Fogelvik, Ingarö ☎ 08/57028244), which has two 18-hole courses—one midlevel, one difficult—is also about 20 minutes away.

Running

Numerous parks with footpaths dot the central city area, among them **Haga Park** (which also has canoe rentals), **Djurgården,** and the wooded **Liljans Skogen.** A very pleasant public path follows the waterfront across from Djurgården, going east from Djurgårdsbron past some of Stockholm's finest old mansions and the wide-open spaces of Ladugårdsgärdet, a park that's great for a picnic or flying a kite.

Skiing

The **Excursion Shop** (✉ Sweden House, Kungsträdgården, Stockholm ☎ 08/7892415) has information on skiing as well as other sport and leisure activities and will advise on necessary equipment.

Spectator Sports

The ultramodern, 281-ft **Globen** (✉ Box 10055, 121 27, Globentorget 2 ☎ 08/7251000), the world's tallest spherical building, hosts such sports as ice hockey and equestrian events. It has its own subway station. Inside the same sports complex as Globen is **Söderstadion** (✉ Box 10055, 121 27, Globentorget 2 ☎ 08/7251000), the open-air stadium where the Hammarby soccer team plays professional soccer. North of the city is **Råsunda Stadion** (✉ Box 1216, Solnav. 51, 171 23 Solna ☎ 08/7350935), Stockholm's largest soccer stadium and host to the biggest games between the city's teams.

Swimming

In the town center, **Centralbadet** (✉ Drottningg. 88, City ☎ 08/54521313) has an extra-large indoor pool, whirlpool, steam bath, and sauna. **Eriksdalsbadet** (✉ Hammarby slussv. 20, Södermalm ☎ 08/50840250) is the city's largest swimming complex. At Stureplan the exclusive **Sturebadet** (✉ Sturegallerian, Östermalm ☎ 08/54501500) has a swimming pool, aquatic aerobics, and a sauna.

Shopping

If you like to shop 'til you drop, then charge on down to any one of the three main department stores in the central city area, all of which carry top-name brands from Sweden and abroad for both men and women. For souvenirs and crafts peruse the boutiques and galleries in Västerlånggatan, the main street of Gamla Stan. For jewelry, crafts, and fine art, hit the shops that line the raised sidewalk at the start of Hornsgatan on Södermalm. Drottninggatan, Birger Jarlsgatan, Biblioteksgatan, Götgatan, and Hamngatan also offer some of the city's best shopping.

★ Department Stores & Malls

Sweden's leading department store is **NK** (✉ Hamng. 18–20, across the street from Kungsträdgården, City ☎ 08/7628000); the initials, pronounced enn-*koh,* stand for *Nordiska Kompaniet.* You pay for the high quality here. **Åhléns City** (✉ Klarabergsg. 50, City ☎ 08/6766000) has a selection similar to NK, with slightly better prices. Before becoming a famous actress, Greta Garbo used to work at **PUB** (✉ Drottningg. 63 and Hötorget, City ☎ 08/4021611), which has 42 independent boutiques. Garbo fans will appreciate the small exhibit on level H2—a collection of photographs begins with her employee I.D. card.

Gallerian (✉ Hamng. 37, City ☎ 08/7912445), in the city center just down the road from Sergels Torg, is a large indoor mall closely resembling those found in the United States. Toys, shoes, music, a hardware store, designer clothes, and food are among the wares. **Sturegallerian**

(✉ Grev Tureg. 9, Östermalm ☎ 08/6114606) is a midsize mall on Sture-plan that mostly carries exclusive clothes, bags, and accessories.

Markets

At **Hötorget** there's a lively daily outdoor market where you can buy fresh fruit and vegetables at prices well below those found in grocery stores. It's open from 9 to 6. For a good indoor market hit **Hötorgshallen** (✉ Hötorget, City), directly under Filmstaden. The market is filled with butcher shops, coffee and tea shops, and fresh-fish markets. It closes at 6 PM. If you're interested in high-quality Swedish food, try the classic European indoor market **Östermalms Saluhall** (✉ Östermalmstorg, Östermalm).

Specialty Stores

AUCTION HOUSES Perhaps the finest auction house in town is **Lilla Bukowski** (✉ Strandv. 7, Östermalm ☎ 08/6140800), whose elegant quarters are on the waterfront. **Auktions Kompaniet** (✉ Regeringsg. 47, City ☎ 08/235700) is downtown next to NK. **Stockholms Auktionsverk** (✉ Jakobsg. 10, City ☎ 08/4536700) is under the Gallerian shopping center.

BOOKS **Akademibokhandeln** (✉ Mäster Samuelsg. 32, City ☎ 08/6136100 ⊕ www.akademibokhandeln.se) has a large selection of books in English.

If you don't find what you need at Akademibokhandeln, **Hedengrens** (✉ Stureplan 4. Sturegallerian, Östermalm ☎ 08/6115132) is also well stocked, especially with fiction and poetry. **Hemlins** (✉ Västerlångg. 6, Gamla Stan, Gamla Stan ☎ 08/106180) carries foreign titles and antique books.

GIFTS Swedish pottery, jewelry, kitchen items, wooden toys, linens, and cookbooks from all over the country are available at **Svensk Hemslöjd** (✉ Sveav. 44, City ☎ 08/232115). Though prices are high at **Vistra** (✉ Kungsg. 55, City ☎ 08/214726), so is the quality of gift items and souvenirs.

GLASS Kosta Boda and Orrefors produce the most popular and well-regarded lines of glassware. The **Crystal Art Center** (✉ Tegelbacken 4, City ☎ 08/217169), near the central station, has a great selection of smaller glass items. **Duka** (✉ Sveav. 24–26, City ☎ 08/104530) specializes in crystal and porcelain at reasonable prices. **NK** carries a wide representative line of Swedish glasswork in its Swedish Shop, downstairs. **Nordiska Kristall** (✉ Kungsg. 9, City ☎ 08/104372), near Sturegallerian, has a small gallery of one-of-a-kind art-glass sculptures as well as plates, vases, glasses, bowls, ashtrays, and decanters. **Svenskt Glas** (✉ Birger Jarlsg. 8, City ☎ 08/7684024), near the Royal Dramatic Theater, carries a decent selection of quality Swedish glass, including bowls from Orrefors.

INTERIOR DESIGN Sweden is recognized globally for its unique design sense and has contributed significantly to what is commonly referred to as Scandinavian design. All of this makes Stockholm one of the best cities in the world for shopping for furniture and home and office accessories.

On the corner of Östermalmstorg, in the same building as the marketplace, is **Bruka** (✉ Humlegårdsg. 1, Östermalm ☎ 08/6601480), which has a wide selection of creative kitchen items as well as wicker baskets and chairs. In Söder **CBI/Klara** (✉ Nytorgsg. 36, Södermalm ☎ 08/6949240) sells furniture, kitchen items, and other funky things for the home—all made by Swedish and international designers. **David Design** (✉ Nybrog. 7, Östermalm ☎ 08/6119855) sells fine furniture, rugs, mirrors, and decorative items for the house. **DIS** (✉ Humlegårdsg. 19, Östermalm ☎ 08/6112907) sells heavy dark-wood furniture that has an Asian flair. The rugs and pillowcases are also stunning.

For high-minded, trendy furniture that blends dark woods, stainless steel, and colorfully dyed wools, head to **House** (⊠ Humlegårdsg. 14, Östermalm ☎ 08/6611100). There's also a nice assortment of vases and glassware. If you're after the *best* of Scandinavian design (and the most expensive), try **Nordiska Galleriet** (⊠ Nybrog. 11, Östermalm ☎ 08/4428360). It has everything from couches and chairs to tables and vases. Slightly out of the way, in the Fridhemsplan neighborhood in west-

★ ern Stockholm, **R.O.O.M.** (⊠ Alströmerg. 20, Kungsholmen ☎ 08/6925000) has an impressive assortment of Swedish and international tables, chairs, rugs, pillows, beds—the list goes on. It also has a great book selection, lots of nice ceramic bowls and plates, and many deco-rations and utensils for the kitchen and bathroom. For elegant home furnishings, affluent Stockholmers tend to favor **Svenskt Tenn** (⊠ Strandv. 5A, Östermalm ☎ 08/6701600), best known for its selection of designer Josef Franck's furniture and fabrics.

MEN'S CLOTHING **Brothers** (⊠ Drottningg. 53, City ☎ 08/4111201) sells relatively inex-pensive Swedish clothes that are often inspired by the more expensive international brands. For suits and evening suits for both sale and rental, **Hans Allde** (⊠ Birger Jarlsg. 58, City ☎ 08/207191) provides good old-fashioned service. For the latest line of fine men's clothing, go to the **Hugo Boss Shop** (⊠ Birger Jarlsg. 6, City ☎ 08/6110750). **J. Lindeberg** (⊠ Grev Tureg. 9, Östermalm ☎ 08/6786165) has brightly colored clothes in many styles. The golf line has been made famous by Swedish golfer Jesper Parnevik. A great spot for trendy Swedish designs is **Mr. Walker** (⊠ Regeringsg. 42, City ☎ 08/7966096). The threads here are fabulous, but be prepared to part with some serious crowns—it's hard to walk out empty-handed. Top men's fashions can be found on the sec-ond floor of **NK** (⊠ Hamng. 18–20, City ☎ 08/7628000), which stocks everything from outdoor gear and evening wear to swimsuits and work-out clothes. The Swedish label **Tiger** (☎ 08/7628772), with a section in-side NK, sells fine suits, shoes, and casual wear.

PAPER PRODUCTS For unique Swedish stationery and office supplies in fun colors and styles, **Fodor's**Choice go to **Ordning & Reda** (⊠ NK, Hamng. 18–20, City ☎ 08/7628462).
★

WOMEN'S Swedish designer **Anna Holtblad** (⊠ Grev Tureg. 13, Östermalm ☎ 08/
CLOTHING 54502220) sells her elegant designs at her own boutique. She special-izes in knitted clothes. **Champaigne** (⊠ Biblioteksg. 2, City ☎ 08/6118803) has European and Swedish designs that are often discounted. **Filippa K** (⊠ Grev Tureg. 18, Östermalm ☎ 08/54588888) has quickly become one of Sweden's hottest designers. Her stores are filled with young women grabbing the latest fashions. The clothes at **Indiska** (⊠ Drottningg. 53 and elsewhere, City ☎ 08/109193) are inspired by the bright colors

★ of India. **Kookai** (⊠ Biblioteksg. 5, City ☎ 08/6119730) carries trendy, colorful European designs for young women. For lingerie and fashion-able clothing at a decent price go to **Twilfit** (⊠ Nybrog. 11, Östermalm ☎ 08/6637505 ⊠ Sturegallerian 16, Östermalm ☎ 08/6110455

Fodor's Choice ⊠ Gamla Brog. 3638, Norrmalm ☎ 08/201954). **Hennes & Mauritz** (H
★ & M; ⊠ Hamng. 22, City ⊠ Drottningg. 53 and 56, City ⊠ Sergelg. 1 and 22, City ⊠ Sergels Torg 12, City ☎ 08/7965500) is one of the few Swedish-owned clothing stores to have achieved international suc-cess. Here you can find updated designs at rock-bottom prices. **Polarn & Pyret** (⊠ Hamng. 10, Gallerian, Drottningg. 29, City ☎ 08/6709500) carries high-quality Swedish children's and women's clothing. For the modern rebel look, go to **Replay** (⊠ Kungsg. 6, City ☎ 08/231416), where the collection covers everything from jeans to underwear. One depart-ment store with almost every style and type of clothing and apparel is **NK** (⊠ Hamng. 18–20, City ☎ 08/7628000).

Stockholm A to Z

AIRPORTS & TRANSFERS

Initially opened in 1960 solely for international flights, Stockholm's Arlanda International Airport now also contains a domestic terminal. The airport is 42 km (26 mi) from the city center; a freeway links the city and airport. The airport is run by Luftfartsverket, a state-owned company.
🛈 **Arlanda International Airport** ✉ 190 45 Stockholm-Arlanda ☎ 08/7976000 🖷 08/7978600 ⊕ www.arlanda.lfv.se.

AIRPORT
TRANSFERS

Travel between Arlanda International Airport and Stockholm has been greatly improved with the completion of the Arlanda Express, a high-speed train service. The yellow-nose train leaves every 15 minutes, travels at a speed of 200 kph (125 mph), and completes the trip from the airport to Stockholm's central station in just 20 minutes; single tickets cost 150 SKr.

Flygbussarna (flight buses) leave both the international and domestic terminals every 10–15 minutes from 6:30 AM to 11 PM and make a number of stops on the way to their final destination at the Cityterminalen at Klarabergsviadukten, next to the central railway station. The trip costs SKr 80 and takes about 35 minutes.

A bus-taxi combination package is available. The bus lets you off by the taxi stand at Haga Forum, Jarva Krog, or Cityterminalen and you present your receipt to the taxi driver, who takes you to your final destination. A trip will cost between SKr 180 and SKr 240, depending on your destination.

For taxis be sure to ask about a *fast pris* (fixed price) between Arlanda and the city. It should be between SKr 350 and SKr 435, depending on the final destination. The best bets for cabs are Taxi Stockholm, Taxi 020, and Taxikurir. All major taxi companies accept credit cards. Watch out for unregistered cabs, which charge high rates and won't provide the same service.
🛈 **Arlanda Express** ✉ Vasag. 11 Box 130, City ☎ 020/222224 ⊕ www.arlandaexpress.com. **Flygbussarna** ☎ 08/6001000 ⊕ www.flygbussarna.com. **Taxi 020** ☎ 020/939393. **Taxikurir** ☎ 08/300000. **Taxi Stockholm** ☎ 08/150000.

BIKE TRAVEL

One of the best ways to explore Stockholm is by bike. There are bike paths and special bike lanes throughout the city, making it safe and enjoyable. Bike rentals will be about SKr 110 per day. One of the best places to ride is on Djurgården. Cykel & Mopeduthyrning and Skepp & Hoj both service that area.
🛈 **Cyke & Mopeduthyrning** (Bike and Moped Rentals) ✉ Standv. kajplats 24, City ☎ 08/6607959. **Skepp & Hoj, Djurgårdsbron** (bike rentals) ✉ Galärvarvsv. 2, Djurgården ☎ 08/6605757.

BOAT & FERRY TRAVEL

Waxholmsbolaget (Waxholm Ferries) offers the *Båtluffarkortet* (Inter-Skerries Card), a discount pass for its extensive commuter network of archipelago boats; the price is SKr 385 for 16 days of unlimited travel. The Strömma Kanalbolaget operates a fleet of archipelago boats that provide excellent sightseeing tours and excursions.
🛈 **Strömma Kanalbolaget** ☎ 08/58714000. **Waxholmsbolaget** ☎ 08/6795830.

BUS TRAVEL TO & FROM STOCKHOLM

All the major bus services, including Flygbussarna, Swebus Express, Svenska Buss, and Interbus, arrive at Cityterminalen (City Terminal), next to the central railway station. Reservations to destinations all over Sweden can be made by calling Swebus.

🚐**Cityterminalen** ✉Karabergsviadukten 72, City ☎08/4408570. **Interbus** ☎08/7279000 🌐 www.interbus.se. **Swebus Express** ☎ 0200/218218 🌐 www.express.swebus.se. **Svenska Buss** ☎ 0771/676767 🌐 www.svenskabuss.se.

BUS TRAVEL WITHIN STOCKHOLM

Late-night bus service connects certain stations when trains stop running. The comprehensive bus network serves out-of-town points of interest, such as Waxholm and Gustavsberg.

CAR RENTAL

Rental cars are readily available in Sweden and are relatively inexpensive. Because of the availability and efficiency of public transport, there is little point in using a car within the city limits. If you are traveling elsewhere in Sweden, you'll find that roads are uncongested and well marked but that gasoline is expensive (about SKr 10 per liter, which is equivalent to SKr 40 per gallon). All major car-rental firms are represented, including Avis, Budget, Hertz, and National. Statoil gas stations also rent out cars, as do local Swedish companies such as Berras and Auto, which can sometimes have better prices than the major companies.

🚗 **Major Agencies Auto** ✉ Östgötg. 75, Södermalm ☎ 08/6428040. **Avis** ✉ Ringv. 90, Södermalm ☎ 08/6449980. **Berras** ✉ Skepparg. 74, City ☎ 08/6611919. **Budget** ✉ Klarabergsviadukten 92, City ☎ 020/787787. **Hertz** ✉ Vasag. 26, City ☎ 08/240720. **National** ✉ Klarabergsg. 33, City ☎ 08/202659. **Statoil** ☎ 020/252525 throughout Sweden ✉ Vasag. 16, City ☎ 08/202064, ✉ Birger Jarlsg. 68, Norrmalm ☎ 08/211593.

CAR TRAVEL

Approach the city by either the E20 or E18 highway from the west, or the E4 from the north or south. The roads are clearly marked and well sanded and plowed during winter. Signs for downtown read ENTRUM.

Driving in Stockholm is often deliberately frustrated by city planners, who have imposed many restrictions to keep traffic down. Keep an eye out for bus lanes, marked with BUSS on the pavement. Driving in that lane can result in a ticket. Get a good city map, called a Trafikkarta, available at most service stations for around SKr 75.

EMBASSIES

🏛 **Australia** ✉ Sergels Torg 12, City ☎ 08/6132900 🌐 www.austemb.se.
🏛 **Canada** ✉ Tegelbacken 4 ☎ 08/4533000 🌐 www.canadaemb.se.
🏛 **New Zealand Consulate-General** ✉ Nybrog. 34, Östermalm ☎ 08/6118090.
🏛 **United Kingdom** ✉ Skarpög. 68, Östermalm ☎ 08/6713000 🌐 www.britishembassy.se.
🏛 **United States** ✉ Strandv. 101, Östermalm ☎ 08/7835300 🌐 www.usis.usemb.se.

EMERGENCIES

Dial 112 for emergencies—this covers police, fire, ambulance, and medical help, as well as sea and air rescue services. Private care is available via CityAkuten. A hospital is called a *sjukhus*, which is Swedish for "sick house," and regular doctors' offices are called *Läkerhuset*. Dentists are listed under under *tandläkare*, or *tandvård*. There is a 24-hour national health service via the emergency number listed below.

🏥 **Doctors & Dentists Folktandvården** (national dental service) ☎ 020/6875500. **Läkerhuset Hörtorgscity** ✉ Sveav. 13-15, City ☎ 08/243800. **Läkerhuset Riddargatan 12** ✉ Riddarg. 12, Östermalm ☎ 08/6797900.

▣ Emergency Services **CityAkuten** (Emergency Medical Care) ✉ Apelbergsg. 48, City ☎ 08/4122961. **CityAkuten Tandvården** (Emergency Dental Care) ✉ Olof Palmesg. 13A, Norrmalm ☎ 08/4122900.

▣ Hospitals **Ersta sjukhus** ✉ Fjällg. 44, Södermalm ☎ 08/7146100. **Karolinska Sjukhuset** ✉ Solna (just north of Stockholm), Solna ☎ 08/51770000. **Södersjukhuset** ✉ Ringv. 52, Södermalm ☎ 08/6161000. **St. Görans Sjukhus** ✉ Sankt Göransplan 1, Kungsholmen ☎ 08/58701000.

▣ Police **Polisen** (Stockholm Police Headquarters) ✉ Norra Agneg. 33–37, Kungsholmen ☎ 08/4010000.

▣ 24-Hour Pharmacies **C. W. Scheele** ✉ Klarabergsg. 64, City ☎ 08/4548130.

ENGLISH-LANGUAGE MEDIA

BOOKS Many bookshops stock English-language books. Akademibokhandeln has a wide selection of English books, with an emphasis on reference titles. Hedengren's has the best and most extensive selection of English- and other foreign-language books, from fiction to nonfiction, from photography to architecture. NK has a large bookstore with an extensive English-language section.

▣ Bookstores **Akademibokhandeln** ✉ Mäster Samuelsg. 32, near the city center, City ☎ 08/6136100. **Hedengrens** ✉ Stureplan 4, Sturegallerian shopping complex, Östermalm ☎ 08/6115132. **NK** ✉ Hamng. 18–20, City ☎ 08/7628000.

RADIO There are two major radio stations with English-language programming in Stockholm. Radio Sweden, part of the state-owned radio company, has news about Sweden in English, daily and weekly English programs, as well as many shows from National Public Radio in the United States and from the BBC in the United Kingdom. You can pick up Radio Sweden at 89.6 FM.

SUBWAY TRAVEL

The subway system, known as T-banan (*Tunnelbanan,* with stations marked by a blue-on-white T), is the easiest and fastest way to get around. Servicing more than 100 stations and covering more than 96 km (60 mi) of track, trains run frequently between 5 AM and 3 AM.

TAXIS

Stockholm's taxi service is efficient but overpriced. If you call a cab, ask the dispatcher to quote you a *fast pris* (fixed price), which is usually lower than the metered fare. Reputable cab companies are Taxi 020, Taxi Stockholm, and Taxikurir. Taxi Stockholm has an immediate charge of SKr 25 whether you hail a cab or order one by telephone. A trip of 10 km (6 mi) should cost about SKr 97 between 6 AM and 7 PM, SKr 107 at night, and SKr 114 on weekends.

▣ Taxi 020 ☎ 020/939393. **Taxikurir** ☎ 08/300000. **Taxi Stockholm** ☎ 08/150000.

TOURS

BOAT TOURS Strömma Kanalbolaget runs sightseeing tours of Stockholm. Boats leave from the quays outside the Royal Dramatic Theater, Grand Hotel, and City Hall. Stockholm Sightseeing, which leaves from Skeppsbron in front of the Grand, has four tours, including the "Under the Bridges" and "Historical Canal" tours. Trips last from one to four hours and cost from SKr 100 to SKr 280.

▣ City Hall late May–early Sept. ✉ Hantverkarg. 1, Kungsholmen ☎ 08/50829000. **Stockholm Sightseeing** ✉ Skeppsbron 22, Gamla Stan ☎ 08/57814020 ⊕ www.stockholmsightseeing.com. **Strömma Kanalbolaget** ✉ Skeppsbron 22, Gamla Stan ☎ 08/58714070.

BUS TOURS Open Top Tours offers a narrated bus tour available in a choice of eight languages via individual headphones. The tour, which covers all the main points of interest, leaves each day at 9:20 from the tourist center at Sweden House. More comprehensive tours, taking in museums, Gamla Stan, and city hall, are available through City Sightseeing.

🏢 **City Sightseeing** ✉ Skeppsbron 11, Gamla Stan ☎ 08/58714030 or 08/4117023 🌐 www.citysightseeing.com. **Open Top Tours** ✉ Hamng. 27, City ☎ 08/6860612. **Sweden House** ✉ Hamng. 27, Box 7542, 103 93 Stockholm ☎ 08/7892490.

PRIVATE GUIDES You can hire your own guide from Stockholm Information Service's Guide Centralen. In summer be sure to book guides well in advance.

🏢 **Guide Centralen** ✉ Sweden House, Hamng. 27, Box 7542, City ☎ 08/7892490 🖶 08/7892491.

WALKING TOURS City Sightseeing runs several tours, including the "Romantic Stockholm" tour of the cathedral and city hall; the "Royal Stockholm" tour, which includes visits to the Royal Palace and the Treasury; and the "Old Town Walkabout," which strolls through Gamla Stan in just over one hour.

🏢 **City Sightseeing** ☎ 08/4117023 🌐 www.citysightseeing.com.

TRAIN TRAVEL

Both long-distance and commuter trains arrive at the central station in Stockholm on Vasagatan, a main boulevard in the heart of the city. For train information and ticket reservations 6 AM–11 PM, call the SJ number below. There is a ticket and information office at the station where you can make reservations. Automated ticket-vending machines are also available.

🏢 **Central Station** ✉ Vasag., City ☎ 08/7622000. **Citypendeln** (Commuter Train) ☎ 08/6001000 🌐 www.citypendeln.se. **SJ** (State Railway Company) ✉ Central station, City ☎ 0771/757575 🌐 www.sj.se.

TRANSPORTATION AROUND STOCKHOLM

The cheapest way to travel around the city by public transport is to purchase the Stockholmskortet (Stockholm Card). In addition to unlimited transportation on city subway, bus, and rail services, it offers free admission to more than 60 museums and several sightseeing trips. The card costs SKr 220 for 24 hours, SKr 380 for two days, and SKr 540 for three days; you can purchase the card from the tourist center at Sweden House on Hamngatan, from the Hotellcentralen accommodations bureau at the central station, and from the tourist center at Kaknäs Tower.

Stockholm has an excellent bus system, which is operated by SL, the state train company. In 2000 the subway system was bought from SL by Connex, the same company that runs the subways in Paris and London. Tickets for Stockholm subways and buses are interchangeable. Maps and timetables for all city transportation networks are available from the SL information desks at Sergels Torg, the central station, Slussen, and online.

Bus and subway fares are based on zones. All trips in downtown will be SKr 20. As you travel farther out of downtown, zones are added to the fare in increments of SKr 10. Each ticket is good for one hour on both the bus system and the subway. Single tickets are available at station ticket counters and on buses, but it's cheaper to buy an SL Tourist Card from one of the many Pressbyrån newsstands. There's also a pass called a Rabattkupong, valid for both subway and buses; it costs SKr 110 and is good for 10 trips downtown (fewer if you travel in more zones) within the greater Stockholm area. There is no time limit within which the 10 trips must be used. If you plan to travel within the greater Stockholm area extensively during a 24-hour period, you can purchase a 24-hour pass for SKr 80 and a 72-hour pass for SKr 150. The 24-hour pass includes transportation on the ferries between Djurgården, Nybroplan, and Slussen. The 72-hour pass also entitles you to admission to Skansen, Gröna Lund Tivoli, and Kaknäs Tower. Those under 18 or over 65 pay SKr 40 for a one-day pass and SKr 75 for a two-day pass.

🖪 Connex 🕾 08/60010000 ⊕ www.connex.nu. **SL** 🕾 08/6001000 ⊕ www.sl.se.

TRAVEL AGENCIES

For a complete listing of travel agencies, check in the *Yellow Pages* under "Resor-Resebyråer," or contact American Express. For air travel contact SAS. SJ, the state railway company, has its main ticket office at central station.

🖪 Local Agent Referrals American Express ✉ Birger Jarlsg. 1, City 🕾 08/6795200, 020/793211 toll free. **SAS** ✉ Klarabergsviadukten 72, accessible from central station, City 🕾 0710/727727. **SJ** (Statens Järnvägar) ✉ Vasag. 1, City 🕾 0771/757575.

VISITOR INFORMATION

🖪 Tourist Information City Hall June–Aug. ✉ Hantverkarg. 1, Kungsholmen 🕾 08/50829000. **Fjäderholmarna** 🕾 08/7180100. **Kaknästornet** Kaknäs TV Tower ✉ Ladugårdsgärdet, Gädet 🕾 08/7892435 ⊕ www.stockholmtown.com. **Stockholm Central Station** ✉ Vasag., City 🕾 0771/757575. **Stockholm Information Service** Sweden House ✉ Hamng. 27, Box 7542, 103 93 Stockholm 🕾 08/7892490. **Swedish Travel and Tourism Council** ✉ Box 3030, Kungsg. 36, 103 61 Stockholm 🕾 08/7255500 🗐 08/7255531 ⊕ www. visit-sweden.com.

SIDE TRIPS FROM STOCKHOLM

Surrounding Stockholm is a latticework of small historic islands, most of them crowned with castles straight out of a storybook world. Set aside a day for a trip to any of these; half the pleasure of an island outing is the leisurely boat trip to get there. (Note that the castles can all be reached by alternative overland routes if you prefer the bus or train.) Farther afield is the island of Gotland, whose medieval festival, Viking remains, and wilderness preserves will take you back in time. The university town of Uppsala is another popular day-trip destination; it's a quiet, peaceful place with a wonderful Gothic cathedral that provides an edifying contrast to Stockholm's more energetic character.

Drottningholm

▶ ★ ❶ *1 km (½ mi) west of Stockholm.*

Occupying an island in Mälaren (Sweden's third-largest lake) some 45 minutes from Stockholm's center, **Drottningholms Slott** (Queen's Island Castle) is a miniature Versailles dating from the 17th century. The royal family once used this property only as a summer residence, but, tiring of the Royal Palace back in town, they moved permanently to one wing of Drottningholm in the 1980s. Designed and built by the same father-and-son team of architects that built Stockholm's Royal Palace, the castle began to be constructed in 1662 on the orders of King Karl X's widow, Eleonora. Today it remains one of the most delightful of European palaces, reflecting the sense of style practiced by mid-18th-century royalty. The interiors, dating from the 17th, 18th, and 19th centuries, are a rococo riot of decoration with much gilding and trompe l'oeil. Most sections are open to the public. ✉ *Drottningholm* 🕾 *08/4026280* ⊕*www.royalcourt.se* 🖾*SKr 50* ☉ *May–Aug., daily 10–4:30; Sept., daily noon–3:30; guided tours in summer only.*

The lakeside gardens of Drottningholms Slott are its most beautiful asset, containing **Drottningholms Slottsteater,** the only complete theater to survive from the 18th century anywhere in the world. Built by Queen Lovisa Ulrika in 1766 as a wedding present for her son Gustav III, the Court

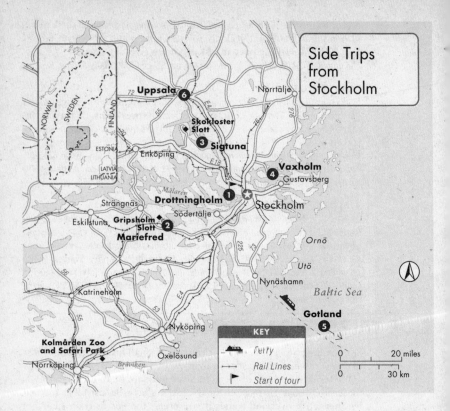

Side Trips
from
Stockholm

Theater fell into disuse after his assassination at a masked ball in 1792 (dramatized in Verdi's opera *Un Ballo in Maschera*). In 1922 the theater was rediscovered; there is now a small theater museum here as well, where you can sign up for a backstage tour and see the original backdrops and stage machinery and some amazing 18th-century tools used to produce such special effects as wind and thunder. To get performance tickets, book well in advance at the box office; the season runs from late May to early September. A word of caution: the seats are extremely hard—take a cushion. ⊠ *Drottningholm* ☎ *08/7590406, 08/6608225 box office* ⊕ *www.drottningholmsslottsteater.dtm.se* ☑ *SKr 50* ☉ *May–June and mid-July–Aug., daily noon–4:30; Sept., daily 1–3:30. Guided tours in English at 12:30, 1:30, 2:30, 3:30, and 4:30.*

Arriving & Departing

Boats bound for Drottningholms Slott leave from Klara Mälarstrand, a quay close to Stadshuset (City Hall). Call **Strömma Kanalbolaget** (⊠ Skeppsbron 22 111 30 ☎ 08/58714000 ⊕ www.strommakanalbolaget.com) for schedules and fares. Alternatively, you can take the T-bana (subway) to Brommaplan, and any of Buses 177, 301–323, or 336 from there. Call **Stockholms Lokal Trafik** (☎ 08/6001000) for details.

Mariefred

② *63 km (39 mi) southwest of Stockholm.*

The most delightful way to experience the true vastness of Mälaren is the trip to Mariefred—an idyllic little town of mostly timber houses—aboard the coal-fired steamer of the same name, built in 1903 and still going strong. The town's winding narrow streets, ancient squares, and wooded lakeside paths are all perfect for walking. The **Mariefred Tourist Office** has maps and information about tours.

Mariefred's principal attraction is **Gripsholm Slott.** Built in the 1530s by Bo Johansson Grip, the Swedish high chancellor, the castle contains fine Renaissance interiors, a superbly atmospheric theater commissioned in 1781 by the ill-fated Gustav III, and Sweden's royal portrait collection. ☎ *0159/10194* 🎫 *SKr 60* ⏲ *May–Aug., daily 10–4; Sept., Tues.–Sun. 10–3; Oct.–Apr., weekends noon–3; guided tours only.*

An old converted barn across from Gripsholm Slott houses **Grafikens Hus** (Graphic House), a center for contemporary graphic art. Visitors can view exhibitions or take part in workshops covering all aspects of graphic art. There are also a good coffee shop and a gift shop that sells artwork. ✉ *Mariefred, 647 21* ☎ *0159/23160* 🌐 *www.grafikenshus.se* 🎫 *SKr 50* ⏲ *May–Aug., daily 11–5; Sept.–Apr., Tues. 11–8, Wed.–Sun. 11–5.*

The **S.S. *Mariefred*** departs from Klara Mälarstrand, near Stadshuset, Stockholm's city hall. The journey takes 3½ hours each way, and there is a restaurant on board. ☎ *08/6698850* 🎫 *SKr 180 round-trip* ⏲ *Departures at 10: May, weekends; mid-June–late Aug., Tues.–Sun. Return trip departs from Mariefred at 4:30.*

You can also travel by narrow-gauge steam railway from Mariefred to a junction on the main line to Stockholm, returning to the capital by ordinary train. Contact the **Mariefred Tourist Office** for details.

Where to Stay & Eat

★ $$ ✕🏨 **Gripsholms Värdshus & Hotel.** At the oldest inn in Sweden (and the only one in Mariefred), guests get a sense of the real Sweden. Lovingly restored and luxuriously appointed, this yellow-wood hotel stands on the site of an old monastery. Rooms are large and airy, with wooden floors and highlights of bright yellow and sky blue. The whole hotel is full of art and artifacts, including some old Swedish-tile fireplaces. In an elegant wood-panel dining room, the restaurant serves local dishes with an international twist, including basil-and-coriander-marinated monkfish with wasabi cream and breast of guinea fowl with caramelized turnips and a lemon and Szechuan pepper gravy. ✉ *Kykog. 1, 647 23* ☎ *0159/34750* 📠 *0159/34777* 🌐 *www.gripsholms-vardshus.se* ⇨ *45 rooms, 44 with bath, 10 suites* ♁ *Restaurant, sauna, bar, no-smoking rooms* 💳 *AE, DC, MC, V* 🍽 *BP.*

Visitor Information

The **Mariefred Tourist Office** (☎ 0159/29790 🌐 www.strangnas.se) is open only in the summer; the rest of the year, call **Mälarturism** (☎ 0152/29690) for information for all of Lake Mälaren.

Sigtuna

❸ *48 km (30 mi) northwest of Stockholm.*

An idyllic town on a northern arm of Lake Mälaren, Sigtuna was the principal trading post of the Svea, the tribe that settled Sweden after the last Ice Age; its Viking history is still apparent in the many runic stones preserved all over town. Founded in 980, Sigtuna is Sweden's oldest town, and as such it's not surprising that it has Sweden's oldest street, Stora Gatan. After it was ransacked by Estonian pirates, its merchants went on to found Stockholm sometime in the 13th century. Little remains of Sigtuna's former glory, beyond parts of the principal church. The town hall dates to the 18th century, and the main part of the town dates from the early 1800s. There are two houses said to date to the 15th century.

About 20 km (12 mi) northeast of Sigtuna and accessible by the same ferryboat from Stockholm is **Skokloster Slott,** an exquisite Baroque castle. Commissioned in 1654 by a celebrated Swedish soldier, Field Marshal Carl Gustav Wrangel, the castle is furnished with the spoils of Wrangel's successful campaigns. ⊠ *Bålsta* ☎ *018/386077* ⊕ *www. skokloster.se* ⊠ *SKr 60* ☉ *Daily noon–6.*

Where to Stay & Eat

$ ✕⊡ **Sigtuna Stadshotell.** Near the lake shore, this beautifully restored hotel was built in 1909 and soon after became a central gathering place among locals—despite at the time being considered one of the ugliest buildings in all of Sigtuna. In its early days the hotel had Sigtuna's first cinema, and in the cellar the state liquor store operated an inn. Today's hotel rooms have hardwood floors, high ceilings, and interesting little nooks and angles. The restaurant ($–$$) offers a great view of the water. The traditional Swedish menu emphasizes herring dishes. Bread and ice cream are both made on the premises. ⊠ *Stora Nyg. 3, 193 30* ☎ *08/59250100* ☎ *08/59251587* ⊕ *www.sigtunastadshotell.se* ⟲ *24 rooms* �&ṣ *Restaurant, minibars, cable TV, meeting rooms, no-smoking rooms* ⊟ *AE, DC, MC, V* �| *BP.*

Arriving & Departing

From June to mid-August Sigtuna can be reached by boat from the quay near Stockholm's city hall (Strömma Kanalbolaget, ☎ 08/58714000); round-trip fare is SKr 150. Another option is to take a commuter train from Stockholm's central station to Märsta, where you change to Bus 570 or 575.

Vaxholm & the Archipelago

❹ *32 km (20 mi) northeast of Stockholm.*

Skärgården (the archipelago) is Stockholm's greatest natural asset: more than 25,000 islands and skerries, many uninhabited, spread across an almost tideless sea of clean, clear water. The islands closer to Stockholm are larger and more lush, with pine tree–covered rock faces and forests. There are also more year-round residents on these islands. As you move away from the mainland, the islands become smaller and more remote, turning into rugged, rocky islets. To sail lazily among these islands aboard an old steamboat on a summer's night is a timeless delight, and all throughout the warmer months Swedes flee the chaos of the city for quiet weekends on the waters.

For the tourist with limited time, one of the simplest ways to get a taste of the archipelago is the one-hour ferry trip to Vaxholm, an extremely pleasant, though sometimes crowded, mainland seaside town of small, red-painted wooden houses. Guarding what was formerly the main sea route into Stockholm, Vaxholm's fortress now houses the small **Vaxholms Fästnings Museum** (Vaxholm Fortress Museum), which documents the defense of Stockholm over the centuries. The museum contains military memorabilia and tells how the imposing stone castle helped defend against the Danes and Russians in the 17th and 18th centuries. You can reach the fortress by taking a small boat from the town landing, which is in front of the tourist office; a discounted combination ticket includes the boat fare and entrance to the museum. ☎ *08/54172157* ⊠ *SKr 30* ☉ *Mid-May–Aug., daily noon–4. Group admission at other times by appointment.*

An even quicker trip into the archipelago is the 20-minute ferry ride to ☙ **Fjäderholmarna** (the Feather Islands), a group of four secluded islands. In the 19th-century the islands were the last chance for a refreshment stop for archipelago residents rowing into Stockholm to sell their produce. After 50 years as a military zone, the islands were opened to the public in the early 1980s. Today they are crammed with arts-and-crafts studios, shops, an aquarium, a small petting farm, a boat museum, a large cafeteria, an ingenious "shipwreck" playground, and even a smoked-fish shop.

Although it's on the mainland, **Saltsjöbaden** is far enough out into the wilds to be considered the archipelago. Construction of the seaside town started in 1891. Designed from the beginning to be a community for the affluent, Saltsjöbaden was based partly on the suburban communities springing up at the same time in the United States. By 1893 the railway had been extended to Saltsjöbaden, and the town was one of the first in Sweden to have electric street lights. The town has some of Europe's grandest 19th-century buildings, which were designed by the leading architects of the time. The best way to reach the town is by train. SJ runs a regular service from central Stockholm.

If you are interested in a longer voyage out into the islands, there are several possibilities. Contact the Sweden House and ask for the "Destination Stockholm Archipelago" catalog, which lists more than 350 holiday homes for rent. For booking accommodations, contact **Hotellcentralen** (☎ 08/7892425). The representatives at Sweden House can also help you plan a customized trip.

One of the most popular excursions is to **Sandhamn,** the main town on the island of Sandön—south of Stockholm and home to about 100 permanent residents. The journey takes about three hours by steamship, but there are faster boats available. The Royal Swedish Yacht Club was founded here at the turn of the 20th century, and sailing continues to be a popular sport. Its fine-sand beaches also make it an ideal spot for swimming. Another option is to try scuba diving—introductory lessons are available; ask at the Sweden House for details. Explore the village of Sandhamn and its narrow alleys and wooden houses, or stroll out to the graveyard outside the village, where tombstones bear the names of sailors from around the world.

The island of **Utö,** which contains Sweden's oldest iron mine (ca. AD 1100–1200), is another popular spot. A number of the miners' homes from the 18th century have been restored. About 200 people live year-round on the island, which has cafés, camping sites, and swimming areas. You can also rent bicycles from a shop near the ferry landing. The boat trip to the island takes about three hours. Utö is particularly known for its bread. *Utö limpa,* a slightly sweetened and spiced sandwich bread, is to be found only on the island and is considered a high delicacy. Many of the thousands of people who go sailing in the archipelago every year make a special detour to stock up on the bread, partly because of its exquisite taste and partly because of its long-keeping properties.

A little bit closer to Stockholm is the island of **Grinda,** long a popular recreation spot among Stockholmers. Rental cabins from the '40s have been restored to their original condition; there are about 30 of these available through **Din Skärgård** (☎08/54249072). The **Grinda Wärdshus** (☎08/54249491), a still-functioning inn from the turn of the 20th century, is one of the largest stone buildings in the archipelago. Since a number of walking paths cut through the woods and open fields, it takes just 15 minutes to walk from one end of Grinda to the other, and exploring is easy. The trip to the island takes about two hours.

At the far southern tip of Stockholm's archipelago lies **Trosa,** a town full of wooden houses that's right on the Baltic Sea. The tiny river that runs through the middle of the town is flanked by beautiful villas painted white, red, yellow, and mint green—a reflection of Trosa's heritage as a seaside retreat for stressed, wealthy Stockholmers. Around the small, cobbled town square are arts-and-crafts shops and market stalls selling fish, fruit, and vegetables.

★ Five kilometers (3 mi) to the north of Trosa is the impressive **Tullgarns Slott.** Built in the early 1700s, the palace was turned into a playful summer retreat in 1772 by King Gustaf's younger brother, Fredrik Adolf. The grounds include sculptured parks and gardens, an orangery, and a theater. The palace's interiors are full of ornate plasterwork, paintings of royals and landscapes, and much of the original French-influenced furnishings. ⊠ *Trosa* ☎ *08/55172011* ⌨ *SKr 50* ☉ *May–Sept., daily 11–4.*

If you'd prefer to stay on board a boat and simply cruise around the islands, seek out the **Blidösund.** A coal-fired steamboat built in 1911 that has remained in almost continuous service, the *Blidösund* is now run by a small group of enthusiasts who take parties of around 250 on evening music-and-dinner cruises. The cruises depart from a berth close to the Royal Palace in Stockholm. ⊠ *Skeppsbron, Stockholm* ☎ *08/4117113* ⌨ *SKr 140* ☉ *Departures early May–late Sept., Mon.–Thurs. 7 PM; returns at 10:45 PM.*

Among the finest of the archipelago steamboats is the **Saltsjön,** which leaves from Nybrokajen, close to the Strand Hotel. Tuesday through Thursday evenings you can take a jazz-and-dinner cruise for SKr 150 weekends from late June to late August. To go to Utö, an attractive island known for its bike paths, bakery, and restaurant, will cost you SKr 190. In December there are three daily Julbord cruises, all of which serve a Christmas smörgåsbord. ⊠ *Strömma Kanalbolaget, Skeppsbron 22, Stockholm* ☎ *08/58714000* ☉ *Departures July–early Aug. and Dec.*

Where to Eat

$$$ ✗ **Sandhamns Värdshus.** Built in 1672 as a guest house and restaurant for tired sailors, the bright-yellow Sandhamn Inn is a delightful place to stop for meal. A terrace provides a view over the colorful seaside town below, and in the summer there's outdoor seating on a large veranda. The menu is rooted in Swedish traditions with a focus on local seafood. Try the seafood stew spiced with saffron and served with freshly baked bread and aioli. The grilled calf's liver with fried sage and apple chips is also a worthy choice. ⊠ *Sandhamn* ☎ *08/57153051* ⊟ *AE, DC, MC, V.*

★ **$$–$$$** ✗ **Fjäderholmarnas Krog.** A crackling fire on the hearth in the bar area welcomes the sailors who frequent this laid-back restaurant. In case you don't travel with your own sailboat, you can time your dinner to end before the last ferry returns to the mainland. The food here is self-consciously Swedish: fresh, light, and beautifully presented. The service is professional; it's a great choice for a special night out. ⊠ *Fjäderholmarna* ☎ *08/7183355* ⊟ *AE, DC, MC, V* ☉ *Closed Oct.–Apr.*

$$ ✗ **Dykarbaren.** The idea for this old wooden harborside restaurant came from similar cafés in Brittany, France. Simple local dishes, mostly of fish, are served up in an informal wooden-tabled dining area. Originally just catering to local divers, Dykarbaren now serves everyone. ⊠ *Strandpromenaden, Sandhamn* ☎ *08/57153554* ⊟ *AE, DC, MC, V.*

¢–$ ✗ **Gröna Caféet.** A grassy garden terrace and an appealing selection of fresh open sandwiches on hearty brown bread make this small, old-fashioned café a hit. It's on Rådhusgatan, by the town square. ⊠ *Rådhusg. 26, Vaxholm* ☎ *08/5413151* ⊟ *No credit cards.*

¢ ✕ **Tre Små Rum.** The old mint-green, red-roofed house that contains "Three
Fodor's Choice Small Rooms" is a fitting place for simple light lunches. The sand-
★ wiches (made from freshly baked bread) are delicious at this lunch-only
café. There are also delicious cakes and pastries—at least 40 types daily.
If you don't want to sit inside in one of the rooms, there is a small outside seating area. ⊠ *Östra Långg., Trosa* ☎ *0156/12151* ⊟ *MC, V*
⊘ *Closed dinner.*

Where to Stay

Lodging options in the archipelago vary from island to island. The
larger, more inhabited islands often have at least one decent hotel, if not
a few, whereas some of the smaller, more deserted islands have only an
inn or two or camping facilities. Hostels are available at low cost on
some islands, and some private homes rent out rooms and offer B&B
accommodations. It's also possible to rent small cabins. Details are
available from the Sweden House.

$$$$ ✕ **Radisson SAS Grand Hotel.** Many say that this is the only reason to
Fodor's Choice come to the beautiful but quiet town of Saltsjöbaden. Next to the sea
★ and the surrounding countryside, the hotel is one of the most breathtaking in the whole archipelago. Built in 1893, it's a castlelike concoc-
tion of white stone, arched windows, and towers. The huge rooms are
filled with colorful period furniture that is set off perfectly against the
plain stone fireplaces and pastel walls. The restaurant ($$$) is a grand
gilt, pillared, and mirrored affair with crisp linens, fine crystal, and a
classic French menu. ⊠ *113 83 Saltsjöbaden* ☎ *08/50617000* 🖷 *08/*
50617025 ⊕ *www.radisson.com* ⇔ *105 rooms, 85 with bath, 10 suites*
⟁ *Restaurant, room service, cable TV, minibars, miniature golf, 2 ten-*
nis courts, saltwater pool, sauna, spa, jogging, ice-skating, bar, no-
smoking rooms ⊟ *AE, DC, MC, V* ⟊ *BP.*

$$ **Sandhamn Hotel and Conference.** Built in the "archipelago" style, the
Sandhamn overlooks the local harbor. Rooms have light-wood accents
with pale white-and-blue furnishings. The curtains are linen. The recreational area has an indoor and outdoor pool as well as a gym. Live music
is often played on the grounds in summer. The hotel adjoins the Seglar-
restaurangen, also looking out over the water, which serves traditional
Swedish cuisine with a French influence. ⊠ *130 30 Sandhamn* ☎ *08/*
57153170 🖷 *08/57450450* ⊕ *www.sandhamn.com* ⇔ *81 rooms, 3 suites*
⟁ *Restaurant, indoor-outdoor pool, gym, sauna, bar, meeting room*
⊟ *AE, DC, MC, V.*

$–$$ **Waxholms Hotell.** Perched directly on Vaxholm's harbor, Waxholms
is a stone's throw from where the ferries land. Rooms in this excellent
little hotel are bright and elegant, and most have a view of the water
and the fortress that sits in the harbor. The restaurant and bar are the
best in town, and the wraparound dining room provides great views of
the boats on the water. The varied menu concentrates on local fish and
Swedish specialties. ⊠ *Hamng. 2, 185 21* ☎ *08/54130150* 🖷 *08/*
54131376 ⊕ *www.waxholmshotell.se* ⇔ *32 rooms* ⟁ *Restaurant, bar,*
meeting room, no-smoking rooms ⊟ *AE, DC, MC, V.*

★ $ **Bomans.** Right on the water and brimming with history, this family-
run hotel dates from the early 20th century. The bedrooms are stuffed
with floral patterns, iron bedsteads, feather quilts, lace, and linen.
Downstairs there is a small bar and a very good restaurant. Lace tablecloths, chandeliers, and tangerine linens and fabrics help create a warm
mood in the restaurant ($$), where you can also dine outside in the sum-
mer months. The menu is unashamedly Swedish, with high-quality ver-
sions of such classic dishes as meatballs, salmon, and elk with
lingonberries. ⊠ *619 30 Trosa* ☎ *0156/52500* 🖷 *0156/52510* ⊕ *www.*

bomans.se ➵ *31 rooms, 2 with bath, 2 suites* ⚷ *Restaurant, bar, meeting rooms, no-smoking rooms* 🗖 *AE, DC, MC, V* ¶◯╎ *BP.*

$ 🗖 **Grinda Wärdshus.** Housed in one of the archipelago's largest stone buildings, this 19th-century villa has homey rooms and bright, comfortable public areas. Since the hotel is right on the water, you may wish to take a refreshing dip in the sea before tackling the sumptuous breakfast buffet of Scandinavian classics. ✉ *Södra Bryggan, 100 05 Grinda* ☎ *08/54249491* 🖷 *08/54249497* ⊕ *www.grindawardshus.se* ➵ *34 rooms without bath* ⚷ *Restaurant, in-room VCRs* 🗖 *AE, DC, MC, V* ¶◯╎ *BP.*

¢–$ 🗖 **Utö Värdshus.** The rooms are large and well furnished here, with traditional furniture resembling that found in a Swedish farmhouse. Choose between a room in the sprawling white main hotel or 1 of the 30 that are in a cabin on the grounds. The restaurant ($$) has a grand wooden ceiling lighted with chandeliers. The food is eclectic, ranging from salmon with dill to Cajun chicken. ✉ *Gruvbryggan, 130 56 Utö* ☎ *08/50420300* 🖷 *08/50420301* ⊕ *www.uto-vardshus.se* ➵ *75 rooms without bath* ⚷ *Restaurant, sauna, bar, no-smoking rooms* 🗖 *AE, DC, MC, V* ¶◯╎ *BP.*

¢ 🗖 **Rum i Backen.** This pretty, early-20th-century wooden house on Vaxholm's main street is a charming B&B. It's run by a family that is more than happy to help you with anything you need. There's just one room, but as it's in an annex to the house, it's a sort of self-contained apartment, with a shower, kitchen, and small veranda. The breakfast, which you make yourself, is included. ✉ *Kungsg. 14, 185 34 Vaxholm* ☎ *08/314021* 🖷 *08/54133315* ➵ *1 room* 🗖 *No credit cards* ¶◯╎ *CP.*

Fodor'sChoice
★

Sports & the Outdoors

A visit to the islands is one of the best opportunities in Sweden you'll get to take a bracing swim in the fresh, clean waters of the Baltic sea. Sometimes surprisingly warm, mostly heart-racingly chilly, but always memorable, a quick dip in these waters will set you up for the day. There are literally thousands of great swimming spots, but Sandhamn and Utö have the sandy beaches and rocky outcrops that keep them among the best.

Vaxholm & the Archipelago A to Z

BOAT & FERRY TRAVEL
Regular ferry services to the archipelago depart from Strömkajen, the quayside in front of Stockholm's Grand Hotel. Boat cruises leave from the harbor in front of the Royal Palace or from Nybrokajen, across the road from the Royal Dramatic Theater. Ferries to the Feather Islands run almost constantly all day long in the summer (Apr. 29–Sept. 17), from Slussen, Strömkajen, and Nybroplan. Contact Strömma Kanalbolaget, Waxholmsbolaget, or Fjäderholmarna.

An excellent way to see the archipelago is to purchase an **Inter Skerries Card,** which costs 250 SKr and allows unlimited boat travel throughout the islands for 16 days. Use the card for day trips from Stockholm, or go out for longer excursions and bounce around from island to island. You can also purchase the **See Sea Card,** which costs 440 SKr and allows unlimited travel in Stockholm, Åland, and the Åbo (Finland) archipelago. Both cards are available at the tourist center at the Stockholm Information Service.

🛈 **Fjäderholmarna** ☎ 08/7180100. **Stockholm Information Service** ✉ Sweden House, Hamng. 27, Box 7542, 103 93 Stockholm ☎ 08/7892490. **Strömma Kanalbolaget** ☎ 08/58714000. **Waxholmsbolaget** ☎ 08/6795830.

TOURS
A great way to discover the remote, less visited parts of the archipelago is to go out with Sandhamnsguiderna, a tour group that operates out of Sandhamn. Experienced guides will take you on tailor-made excursions, in small or large groups, to explore the outer reaches of the de-

serted archipelago. A tour price depends on how many people go and for how long.

🛈 **Sandhamnsguiderna** ☎ 08/6408040.

TRAIN TRAVEL There are regular train services to Saltsjöbaden from Stockholm. The journey takes about 20 minutes. To get to Trosa, take a 1-hour train ride from Stockholm to Vagnhärad, where there is a bus waiting to take the 10-minute trip to Trosa.

🛈 Train information **SJ** ☎ 0771/757575 ⊕ www.sj.se.

VISITOR INFORMATION The Vaxholms Turistbyrå (Vaxholm Tourist Office) is in a large kiosk at the bus terminal, adjacent to the marina and ferry landing. Hours are daily 10–5. Sandhamn Turistbyrå (Sandhamn Tourist Office) is in the town center at Sandhamns Hamnservices. The Utö Turistbyrå (Utö Tourist Bureau) is near the ferry landing. More information on Grinda is available from the Sweden House.

🛈 Tourist Information **Sandhamn Turistbyrå** ☎ 08/57153000 ⊕ www.varmdo.se. **Sweden House** ✉ Hamng. 27, Box 7542, 103 93 Stockholm ☎ 08/7892490. **Trosa Turistbyrå** ☎ 0156/52222 ⊕ www.trosa.com. **Utö Turistbyrå** ☎ 08/50157410. **Vaxholms Turistbyrå** ✉ Söderhamnen, 185 83 Vaxholm ☎ 08/54131480 ⊕ www.visitvaxholm.se.

Gotland

⑤ *85 km (53 mi) southwest of Stockholm.*

Gotland is Sweden's main holiday island, a place of wide sandy beaches and wild cliff formations called *raukar*. Measuring 125 km (78 mi) long and 52 km (32 mi) at its widest point, Gotland is where Swedish sheep farming has its home. In its charming glades, 35 varieties of wild orchids thrive, attracting botanists from all over the world.

The first record of people living on Gotland dates from around 5000 BC. By the Iron Age it had become a leading Baltic trading center. When the German marauders arrived in the 13th century, they built most of its churches and established close trading ties with the Hanseatic League in Lübeck. They were followed by the Danes, and Gotland finally became part of Sweden in 1645.

Gotland's capital, **Visby**, is a delightful hilly town of about 20,000 people. Medieval houses, ruined fortifications, churches, and cottage-lined cobbled lanes make Visby look like a fairy-tale place. Thanks to a very gentle climate, the roses that grow along many of the town's facades bloom even in November.

In its heyday Visby was protected by a wall, of which 3 km (2 mi) survive today, along with 44 towers and numerous gateways. It is considered the best-preserved medieval city wall in Europe after that of Carcassonne, in southern France. Take a stroll to the north gate for an unsurpassed view of the wall.

Visby's cathedral, **St. Maria Kyrka,** is the only one of the town's 13 medieval churches that is still intact and in use. Built between 1190 and 1225 as a place of worship for the town's German parishioners, the church has few of its original fittings because of the extensive and sometimes clumsy restoration work done over the years. That said, the sandstone font and the unusually ugly angels decorating the pulpit are both original features worth a look.

Burmeisterska Huset, the home of the *Burmeister*—or principal German merchant—organizes exhibitions displaying the works of artists from the island and the rest of Sweden. Call the tourist office in Visby to arrange for viewing. ✉ *Strandg. 9* ☎ *No phone* 🎫 *Free.*

The **Fornsalen** (Fornsal Museum) contains examples of medieval artwork, prehistoric gravestones and skeletons, and silver hoards from Viking times. Be sure to also check out the ornate "picture stones" from AD 400–600, which depict ships, people, houses, and animals. ⊠ *Mellang. 19* ☎ *0498/ 292700* ✆ *SKr 30* ☾ *Mid-May–Sept., daily 11–6; Oct.–mid-May, Tues.–Sun. noon–4.*

The **Visby Art Museum** has some innovative exhibitions of contemporary painting and sculpture. On the first floor is the permanent display, which is mostly uninspiring, save for a beautiful 1917 watercolor by local artist Axel Lindman showing Visby from the beach in all its splendid medieval glory. ⊠ *St. Hansg. 21* ✆ *SKr 30* ☾ *May–Sept., daily 10–5.*

Medieval activities are re-created at **Kapitelhusgården.** Families can watch and take part in metal and woodworking skills, coin making, dressmaking, archery, and hunting. ⊠ *Drottensg. 8* ☎ *0498/292700* ✆ *SKr 40* ☾ *June–Aug., daily noon–6.*

The 4 km (2½ mi) of stalactite caves at **Lummelunda,** about 18 km (11 mi) north of Visby on the coastal road, are unique in this part of the world and are worth visiting. The largest was discovered in 1950 by three boys out playing. ⊠ *Lummelunds Bruk* ☎ *0498/273050* ✆ *SKr 65* ☾ *May–Sept., daily 9–5.*

A pleasant stop along the way to Lummelunda is the **Krusmyntagården** (☎ *0498/296900)*, a garden with more than 200 herbs, 8 km (5 mi) north of Visby.

The island has about 100 old churches dating from Gotland's great commercial era still in use. **Barlingbo,** from the 13th century, has vaulted paintings, stained-glass windows, and a remarkable 12th-century font. The exquisite **Dalhem** was constructed about 1200. **Gothem,** built during the 13th century, has a notable series of paintings of that period. **Grötlingbo** is a 14th-century church with stone sculptures and stained glass (note the 12th-century reliefs on the facade). **Öja,** a medieval church decorated with paintings, houses a famous holy rood from the late 13th century. The massive ruins of a Cistercian monastery founded in 1164 are now called the **Roma Kloster Kyrka** (Roma Cloister Church). **Tingstäde** is a mix of six buildings dating from 1169 to 1300.

Curious rock formations dot the coasts of Gotland, remnants of reefs formed more than 400 million years ago, and two **bird sanctuaries,** Stora and **Lilla Karlsö,** stand off the coast south of Visby. The bird population consists mainly of guillemots, which look like penguins. Visits to these sanctuaries are permitted only in the company of a recognized guide. ☎ *0498/241139* ✆ *SKr 180 for guided tour of both sanctuaries* ☾ *May–Aug., daily.*

Where to Eat

$$ ✕ **Gutekällaren.** Despite the name, the Gotlander Cellar is aboveground in a 12th-century building. Mediterranean dishes, including fish and shellfish stew with coconut and lemongrass and fillet of lamb with a salad of red beets, asparagus, and Parmesan, are the draw. The striking interior includes primary-color leather chairs and coffee-color walls. ⊠ *Stora Torget 3* ☎ *0498/210043* ⊟ *DC, MC.*

$–$$ ✕ **Björklunda Värdshuset.** This small restaurant in an old stone farmhouse is run by a husband-and-wife team. You can have an aperitif in the apple orchard before tucking into the menu of local salmon, lamb, and pork dishes, all of which come in ample proportions. ⊠ *Björklunda, Burgsvik* ☎ *0498/497190* ⊟ *AE, DC, MC, V.*

$–$$ ✕ **Clematis.** This campy restaurant is one of the most popular in Visby—guests are thrown back a few centuries to the Middle Ages for an authentic night of food, song, and dance. You get a flat slab of bread instead of a plate, and your only utensil is a knife. The staff dons period attire and is known to break into a tune while delivering food to tables. Traditional Swedish fare is served, with a focus on meats and island ingredients. Drinks are served in stone goblets. ⊠ *Strandg. 20* ☎ *0498/ 299690* ⊟ *AE, DC, MC, V* ☯ *No lunch.*

★ **$–$$** ✕ **Donners Brunn.** In a beautiful orange-brick house on a small square in Visby, the chef proprietor of this restaurant, Bo Nilsson, was once chef at the renowned Operakällaren in Stockholm. The menu uses excellent local ingredients to make French-influenced dishes that are reasonably priced, given their quality. The house specialty of Gotland lamb with fresh asparagus and hollandaise sauce is delicious. ⊠ *Donners Plats 3* ☎ *0498/271090* ⌕ *Reservations essential* ⊟ *AE, DC, MC, V.*

$–$$ ✕ **Krusmyntagården.** This marvelous little garden-café opened in the late '70s and has been passed down through several owners. The garden now has more than 200 herbs and other plants, all of them grown organically. Most are used in such traditional Gotland dishes as tender grilled lamb (served on Tuesday and Thursday nights). ⊠ *Brissund* ☎ *0498/296900* ⊟ *AE, DC, MC, V.*

¢–$$ ✕ **Konstnärsgården.** Hans and Birgitta Belin run a wonderful establishment in the tiny village of Ala. He is an artist, she a chef. As you eat your lovingly prepared food in this old manor-house restaurant, you can view and buy works by Hans and other artists. The venison that's often on the menu comes from deer raised on the premises, and in the summer months whole lambs are spit-roasted outdoors in the orchard gardens. ⊠ *30 km (19 mi) southeast of Visby, Ala* ☎ *0498/55055* ⊟ *MC, V.*

Where to Stay

$–$$ ⊞ **Strand Hotel.** An environmentally friendly hotel with efficient heating and cooling systems, the Strand may ease your conscience with its approach. In any case, the lap pool, sauna, and bright, comfortable rooms will ease your spirit. The clubby, relaxing bar has large leather sofas and a smoking area in an adjoining library. All things considered, the Strand is a good deal. ⊠ *Strandg. 34, 621 56* ☎ *0498/258800* 🖷 *0498/258811* ⊕ *www.strandhotel.net* ⇥ *110 rooms, 2 with bath, 6 suites* ⌕ *Restaurant, bar, indoor lap pool, sauna* ⊟ *AE, DC, MC, V* ⑉ *BP.*

$–$$ ⊞ **Wisby Hotell.** The tall, thin building that's now the Wisby dates from the 1200s and is at the junction of two narrow streets. A hotel since 1855, the ocher-color walls, light floral-patterned fabrics, dark wood, and vaulted ceilings give it old European grandeur. There are two excellent bars in the hotel, one a glassed-in courtyard that serves cocktails and the other a cozy pub with a good beer selection. ⊠ *Strandg. 6, 621 24* ☎ *0498/257500* 🖷 *0498/257550* ⊕ *www.wisbyhotell.se* ⇥ *134 rooms, 94 with bath, 10 suites* ⌕ *Restaurant, 2 bars, no-smoking rooms* ⊟ *AE, DC, MC, V* ⑉ *BP.*

$ ⊞ **Hotell Solhem.** A hotel that resembles a beach house, the Solhem offers wonderful views of Visby Harbor and the sea beyond. The rooms and public areas are small, but the hotel is very bright and simply furnished, making up for the lack of space. ⊠ *Solhemsg. 3, 621 58* ☎ *0498/ 259000* 🖷 *0498/259011* ⇥ *94 rooms, 1 with bath* ⌕ *Bar, sauna* ⊟ *AE, DC, MC, V* ⑉ *BP.*

$ ⊞ **Toftagården.** Nestled among the trees near the Gotland coast about 20 km (12 mi) from Visby, the placid verdant grounds here are ideal for strolling, lazing about, and reading in the shade. The long sandy beach in Tofta is also nearby, as is the Kronholmen Golf Course. Most of the brightly furnished rooms, all on the ground floor, have their own terrace. There are also a number of cottages with kitchens—a two-night minimum stay is required for these. If the seawater at the beach is too cold, take a dip in the outdoor heated pool. The restaurant serves very good regional fare. ⊠ *Toftagården, 621 98* ☎ *0498/297000* 🖷 *0498/ 265666* 📑 *50 rooms, 15 cottages* ♨ *Restaurant, some kitchenettes, pool, sauna* ═ *AE, DC, MC, V* ⦿ *BP.*

¢ 🖪 **Hotel St. Clemens.** Four buildings make up the St. Clemens, in Visby's Old Town. They range in age from a relatively young sixty-something years to about four centuries, dating to the 1600s. Rooms are simple and modern with private baths; some have small kitchens. There are two gardens on the property, one of which is shared with St. Clemens Church, one of Visby's oldest. ⊠ *Smedjeg. 3, 621 55* ☎ *0498/219000* 🖷 *0498/279443* 📑 *32 rooms* ♨ *Breakfast room, some kitchenettes, sauna* ═ *AE, DC, MC, V* ⦿ *CP.*

¢ 🖪 **Kronholmens Gård.** This charming little complex has its own small beach a short walk from Kronholmen's acclaimed 27-hole golf course. There are two cabins. One has four rooms, each with five small beds. Inside the other is a common kitchen and living room that all cabin guests share. For families hoping to save a little money that enjoy cooking for themselves, this is a great spot on the island. Weekly discounts are available. ⊠ *Västergarn, 620 20 Klintehamn* ☎ *0498/245004* 🖷 *0498/ 245023* 📑 *1 4-bedroom cabin* ♨ *Sauna* ═ *AE, DC, MC, V.*

★ ¢ 🖪 **Villa Alskog.** A short drive from the sandy beaches to the south of Gotland, Villa Alskog is a delightful inn surrounded by beautiful open spaces, stone fences, and small groves of trees. The building dates to 1840 and was originally a residence for the local priest. Its 10 guest rooms are bright and simply furnished, with hardwood floors. Most have a private bath; when you reserve a room, verify that it's one that has its own bath. The location is ideal for swimming, hiking, and horseback riding. ⊠ *620 16 Alskog* ☎ *0498/491188* 🖷 *0498/491120* ⊕ *www.villa-alskog.se* 📑 *10 rooms, 7 with bath* ♨ *Restaurant, café, sauna, meeting room* ═ *AE, DC, MC, V* ⦿ *BP.*

Nightlife & the Arts

Medeltidsveckan (Medieval Week), celebrated in early August, is a city-wide festival marking the invasion of the prosperous island by Danish king Valdemar on July 22, 1361. Celebrations begin with Valdemar's grand entrance parade and continue with jousts, an open-air market on Strandgatan, and street-theater performances re-creating the period.

In the ruins of **St. Nicolai,** the old dilapidated church in Visby, regular concerts are held throughout the summer months. Everything from folk to rock to classical is available. The tourist office has details.

There are many bars and drinking establishments on Gotland, but the best are in Visby. **Skeppet** (⊠ Strandv. ☎ 0498/210710), a lively bar playing both live and recorded rock music, attracts a frantic young crowd.

Graceland (☎ 0498/215500) is on a boat moored in Visby's harbor. As the name suggests, it's a magnet for Elvis fans. The 35-and-over crowd fills its Priscilla Bar and dances to the King's finest until 2 AM.

Sports & the Outdoors

Bicycles, tents, and camping equipment can be rented from **Gotlands Cykeluthyrning** (⊠ Skeppsbron 2 ☎ 0498/214133 ⊕ www.gotlandscykeluthyrning.com). **Gotlandsleden** is a 200-km (120-mi) bicycle route around the island; contact the tourist office for details.

For an aquatic adventure, **Gotlands Havskajakcenter** (☎ 0498/223012 📧 Kr 150 for three hours) will rent you a canoe and a life jacket from its center at Valleviken, on the northeast coast of the island. From here you can explore the 15 uninhabited islands nearby. Many have beautiful rock formations.

If you do nothing else on Gotland, go for a swim. The island has miles and miles of beautiful golden beaches and unusually warm water for this part of the world. The best and least-crowded beaches are at Fårö and Själsö to the north of the island.

Shopping

Barbro Sandell (✉ Längsv. 146, Norrlanda ☎ 0498/39075) is a bright shop with one of the island's best selections of fabrics printed with local patterns.

G.A.D (Good Art and Design; ✉ Södra Kyrkog. 16 ☎ 0498/249410) sells stunningly simple modern furniture that has been designed and made on Gotland. Just as at its shop in Stockholm, the firm sells high-end pieces with a cosmopolitan flair.

Gotland A to Z

BOAT & FERRY TRAVEL Car ferries sail from Nynäshamn, a small port on the Baltic an hour by car or rail from Stockholm; commuter trains leave regularly from Stockholm's central station for Nynäshamn. Ferries depart at 11:30 AM year-round. From June through mid-August there's an additional ferry at 12:30 PM. A fast ferry operates from mid-April until mid-September, departing three times a day. The regular ferry takes about five hours; the fast ferry takes 2½ hours. Boats also leave from Oskarshamn, farther down the Swedish coast and closer to Gotland by about an hour. Call Gotland City Travel for more information.

🚢 **Gotland City Travel** ✉ Kungsg. 57 ☎ 08/4061500 ✉ Nynäshamn ☎ 08/5206400 ✉ Visby ☎ 0498/247065.

CAR RENTAL 🚗 Agencies **Biltjänst** ✉ Endrev. 45, Visby ☎ 0498/218790. **Budget** ✉ Visby ☎ 0498/279396.

CONTACTS & RESOURCES 🏥 Doctors & Dentists **Visby Hospital** ☎ 0498/268009.

TOURS Guided tours of the island and Visby, the capital, are available in English by arrangement with the tourist office.

VISITOR INFORMATION The main tourist office is *Gotlands Turistförening* (Gottland Tourist Association) in Visby. Gotlands Turistservice at Österport in Visby is a private tour operator. They can help you plan trips in the region. You can also contact Gotland City Travel in Stockholm for lodging or ferry reservations.

ℹ️ Tourist Information **Gotland City Travel** ☎ 08/4061500. **Gotlands Turistförening** ✉ Hamngatan 4 Visby ☎ 0498/201700 🌐 www.gotland.info. **Gotlands Turistservice** ✉ Österväg 3A Visby ☎ 0498/203300 🌐 www.gotlandsturistservice.com.

Uppsala

6 *67 km (41 mi) north of Stockholm.*

Sweden's principal university, Uppsala has only one rival for the title: Lund, to the south. August Strindberg, the nation's leading dramatist, studied here—and by all accounts hated the place. Ingmar Bergman, his modern heir, was born in town. It is also a historic site where pagan (and extremely gory) Viking ceremonies persisted into the 11th century. Uppsala University, one of the oldest and most highly respected institutions in Europe, was established in 1477 by Archbishop Jakob Ulfson. As late as the 16th century nationwide *tings* (early parliaments) were convened here. Today it is a quiet home for about 170,000 people. Built along the banks of the Fyris River, the town has a pleasant jumble of old buildings that is dominated by its cathedral, which dates from the early 13th century.

The last day of April never fails to make the town become one big carnival—the Feast of Valborg. To celebrate the arrival of spring (and the end of the school year), students of the university don sailorlike hats and charge down the hill from the university library (try not to get in their way). The university chorus then sings traditional spring songs on the steps of the main building. And finally the whole town slips into mayhem. Thousands descend on the city as the streets are awash in champagne and celebrations. It's an age-old custom worth seeing, but it's not for the fainthearted.

Ideally you should start your visit with a trip to **Gamla Uppsala** (Old Uppsala), 5 km (3 mi) north of the town. Here under three huge mounds lie the graves of the first Swedish kings—Aun, Egil, and Adils—of the 6th-century Ynglinga dynasty. Close by in pagan times was a sacred grove containing a legendary oak from whose branches animal and human sacrifices were hung. By the 10th century Christianity had eliminated such practices. A small church, which was the seat of Sweden's first archbishop, was built on the site of a former pagan temple.

Today the archbishopric is in Uppsala itself, and **Gamla Uppsala Kyrka,** the former seat, is largely kept up for the benefit of tourists. The whitewashed walls and simple rows of enclosed wooden pews make the church plain but calming. The tomb of Anders Celsius, the inventor of the temperature scale that bears his name, and some faded panels depicting the life of St. Erik are about the only other thing to look at inside.

need a break? To sample a mead brewed from a 14th-century recipe, stop at the **Odinsborg Restaurant** (☎ 018/323525), near the Gamla Uppsala burial mounds.

The Gamla Uppsala **Historiskt Center** (Historical Center) contains exhibits and archaeological findings from the Viking burial mounds that dominate the local area. The museum distinguishes between the myth and legends about the area and what is actually known about its history. Next to Gamla Uppsala Church, the ultramodern building made of wood and copper will change color as it ages. Its aggressive design inspires either admiration or dislike among Uppsala's populace. ☎ 018/239300 ☑ SKr 50 ⊙ May–Sept., daily 11–6; Oct.–Apr., Tues.–Sun. 10–5.

★ Back in Uppsala, your first visit should be to **Uppsala Domkyrka** (Uppsala Cathedral). Its 362-foot twin towers—whose height equals the length of the nave—dominate the city. Work on the cathedral began in the early 13th century; it was consecrated in 1435 and restored between 1885 and 1893. Still the seat of Sweden's archbishop, the cathedral is also the site of the tomb of Gustav Vasa, the king who established Sweden's independence in the 16th century. Inside is a silver casket containing the relics of St. Erik, Sweden's patron saint. ☎ 018/187177 ⊕ www.uppsalacathedral.com ☑ Free ⊙ Daily 8–6.

The **Domkyrka Museet,** in the north tower, has arts and crafts, church vestments, and church vessels on display. ☎ 018/187177 ☑ SKr 20 ⊙ May–Aug., daily 9–5; Sept.–Apr., Sun. 12:30–3.

Gustav Vasa began work on **Uppsala Slott** (Uppsala Castle) in the 1540s. He intended the building to symbolize the dominance of the monarchy over the church. It was completed under Queen Christina nearly a century later. Students gather here every April 30 to celebrate the Feast of Valborg and optimistically greet the arrival of spring. Call the tourist center for information. ⊠ *Ingång C, 75310 Uppsala* ⊕ *www.uppsalaslott. com* 🖃 *Castle SKr 60* ⊙ *Guided tours of castle mid-Apr.–Sept., daily at 11 and 2; Oct.–mid-Apr., weekdays at 11 and 2, weekends at 10, 11, 2, and 3.*

In the excavated Uppsala Slott ruins, the **Vasa Vignettes,** scenes from the 16th century, are portrayed with effigies, costumes, light, and sound effects. 🖃 *SKr 40* ⊙ *Mid-Apr.–Aug., daily 11–4; Sept., weekends 10–5.*

One of Uppsala's most famous sons, Carl von Linné, also known as Linnaeus, was a professor of botany at the university during the 1740s. He created the Latin nomenclature system for plants and animals. The **Linné Museum** is dedicated to his life and works. ⊠ *Svartbäcksg. 27* 🕾 *018/ 136540* 🖃 *SKr 20* ⊙ *Late May and early Sept., weekends noon–4; June–Aug., Tues.–Sun. 1–4.*

The botanical treasures of Linnaeus's old garden have been re-created and are now on view in **Linnéträdgården.** The garden's orangery houses a pleasant cafeteria and is used for concerts and cultural events. ⊠ *Svartbäcksg. 27* 🕾 *018/109490* 🖃 *SKr 25* ⊙ *May–Aug., daily 9–9; Sept.–Apr., daily 9–7.*

Uppsala Universitetet (Uppsala University; 🕾 018/4710000 ⊕ www.uu. se), founded in 1477, is known for the **Carolina Rediviva** university library, which contains a copy of every book published in Sweden, in addition to a large collection of foreign works. Two of its most interesting exhibits are the *Codex Argentus,* a Bible written in the 6th century, and Mozart's original manuscript for his 1791 opera *The Magic Flute.*

Completed in 1625, the **Gustavianum,** which served as the university's main building for two centuries, is easy to spot by its remarkable copper cupola, now green with age. The building houses the ancient anatomical theater—one of only seven in the world to function on natural light—where human anatomy lectures and public dissections took place. The Victoria Museum of Egyptian Antiquities is in the same building. ⊠ *Akademig. 3* 🕾 *018/4717571* 🖃 *SKr 40* ⊙ *June–Aug., daily 11–3; Anatomical Theater June–Aug., daily 11–3; Sept.–May, weekends noon–3.*

Where to Stay & Eat

$$–$$$ ✕ **Domtrappkällaren.** In a 14th-century cellar near the cathedral, Domtrappkällaren serves excellent French and Swedish cuisines. Game is the specialty, and the salmon and reindeer are delectable. ⊠ *Sankt Eriksgränd 15* 🕾 *018/130955* ⚛ *Reservations essential* 🖃 *AE, DC, MC, V.*

$–$$ ✕ **Hambergs Fisk.** As the name suggests, this is a fish restaurant, the one slightly odd concession to nonfish eaters being several dishes made from goose liver. After sampling the wonderful menu you can head to the in-house deli counter to bring away fresh fish, pâtés, and other fine foods. ⊠ *Fyris Torg 8* 🕾 *018/710050* 🖃 *AE, DC, MC, V.*

¢–$$ ✕ **Katalin.** You can eat and watch the trains rattle by in this converted warehouse behind the main station. Just as the interior is simple and modern, Katalin serves classic versions of such Swedish favorites as salmon and meatballs. There is often a jazz band in the evenings, and on weekends the bar is one of the most popular in town. ⊠ *Östra Station* 🕾 *018/140680* 🖃 *AE, DC, MC, V.*

¢–$ ✕ **Al Harem.** Authentic cushion seating, ornate gilded arches, vibrant purples and golds, and even a belly dancer add an authentic eastern touch to the delicious Lebanese food at Al Harem. Beef and chicken dishes are a highlight, complimented by flavors of garlic, parsley, olive oil, and chickpeas. ⊠ *Kungsg. 25* 🕾 *018/100903* 🖃 *AE, DC, MC, V.*

¢ ✕ **Café Alma.** A huge hit with local students, this lunch-only restaurant is in the basement of the main university building. The delicious and varied buffet (SKr 60) is overflowing with soups, salads, quiche, and bread. Everything's made in-house by the two wonderfully friendly owners. No à la carte is offered. ⊠ *Övre Slottsg.* ☎ *018/4712330* ☐ *MC, V* ☻ *No dinner.*

$–$$$ ▥ **Gillet.** Operated by the Radisson SAS group, Uppsala's largest hotel first opened in 1971. Rooms are bright and large, with pleasant watercolors, soft furnishings, and hardwood floors. The hotel is only a short walk from Uppsala's most famous buildings. The public areas are a little bland and standardized, but very comfortable. ⊠ *Dragarbrunnsg. 23, 751 42* ☎ *018/681800* ☐ *018/681818* ⊕ *www.radissonsas.com* ⇥ *160 rooms, 48 with bath* ♨ *2 restaurants, pool* ☐ *AE, DC, MC, V* ⦿ *BP.*

$–$$ ▥ **Grand Hotel Hörnan.** A castlelike creation from 1906, the Hörnan's city-center location means that it's near the train station and has views of both the castle and the cathedral. The rooms are spacious and have antique furnishings and soft lighting. ⊠ *Bandgårdsg. 1, 753 20* ☎ *018/139380* ☐ *018/120311* ⊕ *www.eklundshof.se* ⇥ *37 rooms* ☐ *AE, DC, MC, V* ⦿ *BP.*

$ ▥ **Scandic Hotel Uplandia.** This branch of the giant Nordic chain has the usual modern comforts and high-tech amenities expected of an international business hotel. There's also the pleasing design that's found in the best Scandinavian hotels. Blond wood accented with moss-green and aquamarine fabrics gives the decor a sophisticated edge. ⊠ *Dragarbrunnsg. 32, 751 40* ☎ *018/4952600* ☐ *018/4952611* ⊕ *www.scandic. se* ⇥ *133 rooms, 93 with bath, 2 suites* ♨ *Restaurant, room service, in-room data ports, sauna, bar, meeting rooms, no-smoking rooms* ☐ *AE, DC, MC, V* ⦿ *BP.*

¢ ▥ **First Hotel Linné.** The namesake of this white-stone town-house hotel with lush gardens is the botanist Linnaeus (Carl von Linné). The hotel's interior is in harmony with the gardens outside: soft floral prints and warm reds dominate. In winter, a huge open fire is lighted. Rooms are done in a bright, modern Scandinavian design, with earth and red tones. Most of the floors and furniture are made of wood. ⊠ *Skolg. 45, 750 02* ☎ *018/102000* ☐ *018/137597* ⊕ *www.firsthotels.com* ⇥ *116 rooms, 28 with bath, 6 suites* ♨ *Restaurant, minibars, sauna, bar, no-smoking rooms* ☐ *AE, DC, MC, V* ⦿ *BP.*

Nightlife & the Arts

Svenssons (⊠ Sysslomansg. 15 ☎ 018/553310) is Uppsala's most popular nightspot. The two-floor building houses a bar, a restaurant, and a nightclub. The restaurant is nothing to speak of. But after 9, when food is no longer being served, on come the '80s tunes and out comes the roulette table. Downstairs are two more bars, with loads of chrome, mirrors, and people, all of them gyrating to contemporary dance music. Arrive early to avoid lines. For a relaxed evening head to **Alex Vinbar** (⊠ Skolg. 45 ☎ 018/102000), a dark, comfortable wine bar that sells many wines by the glass and plays mainly jazz. **Uppsala Stadsteater** (town theater; ⊠ Kungsg. 53 ☎ 018/160300) is a local theater known for its high-quality productions, many directly from Stockholm and a fair number in English.

Shopping

★ **Jaber** (⊠ Fyris Torg 6 ☎ 018/135050) is something of a draw for the area's wealthy elite. It is a family-run clothes shop with a line of gorgeous international designs, matched only by the personal service it provides. **Trolltyg** (⊠ Östra Åg. 25 ☎ 018/146304) has an exclusive selection of the sort of clean-line clothes and household furnishings for which Scandinavian design is known. The shop is wonderfully laid out and is a joy to explore, especially the fabrics section. Out in Old Uppsala, **Gamla Uppsala Keramik** (Gamla Uppsala Pottery; ⊠ Ulva Kvam ☎ 018/322060) makes all its own pottery and china, much of it with ancient local designs from Viking graves and stone carvings.

Uppsala A to Z

SIGHTSEEING TOURS

You can explore Uppsala easily on your own, but English-language guided group tours can be arranged through the Uppsala Guide Service. 🚹 **Uppsala Guide Service** ☎ 018/7274818.

TRAIN TRAVEL

Trains between Stockholm and Uppsala run twice hourly throughout the day all year-round. The cost of a one-way trip is SKr 75. For timetables and train information contact SJ.
🚹 **SJ** ☎ 0771/757575 ⊕ www.sj.se.

VISITOR INFORMATION

The main tourist office run by the Uppsala Convention and Visitors Bureau is in the town center; in summer a small tourist information office is also open at Uppsala Castle.
🚹 **Tourist Information Main Tourist Office** ⊠ Fyris Torg 8 ☎ 018/7274800 ⊕ www. uppland.nu. **Information Office at Uppsala Castle** ☎ 018/554566.

THE BOTHNIAN COAST

Indented with shimmering fjords, peppered with pine-clad islands, and lined with sheer cliffs, the Bothnian Coast is a dramatic sliver of land on Sweden's east coast.

Its history and prosperity come from the sea and the forest. This is as true of the grand 19th-century stone houses built from the profits of international sea trading and the paper industry as it is of the ancient fishing villages, which are now used mainly as holiday homes for urban Swedes. The Bothnian Coast has both kinds of dwellings in abundance. In the north of the region you can see traces of the religious fervor that took hold in past centuries, evident in the small religious communities and the many ancient, well-preserved churches and artifacts in towns such as Umeå and Skellefteå.

Many of the original wood cottages that dotted this coastline have been destroyed by fires over the years. The worst damage, caused by Russia's many incursions through the area in the 18th century, prompted many of the towns along the coast to rebuild themselves in grand styles more befitting a capital than a local fishing town. Aided by the burgeoning shipping trade in the 1800s, port towns such as Gävle, Sundsvall, and Umeå created cities of wide boulevards, huge central squares, and monumental stone buildings partly to discourage future fires from spreading.

Traveling up the Bothnian Coast is a simple task, mostly involving a single road or railway track. All the major towns are on the coast and are relatively evenly spread, making it easier for you to plan your rests. The coastline is rocky and rugged in places and is bordered by the beautiful forests and lakes of Hälsingland. By car, the E4 highway quickly eats up the miles, and takes in all the major sights. By train, the coastal line that links Stockholm to the north of Sweden does the same.

Gävle

⚐ ❶ *180 km (111 mi) north of Stockholm (via E4).*

Gävle, the capital of the county (*land* in Swedish) Gästrikland, is considered by many Swedes a gateway to the northern wildernesses. The town was granted its charter in 1446. This great age is not evident in the mix of grand 19th-century boulevards and parks and modern, bland shopping centers that make up much of the small downtown area. The original town was destroyed in a great fire in the mid-1800s, and the only part that survives today is the small enclave that lay south of the river, a watery barrier that kept the flames at bay. The grand architectural style of much of the town reflects the wealth it once enjoyed as a major trading port. Today it is better known as home of Gevalia, Sweden's largest coffee producer, which is quite evident on the days the town is filled with the delicious aroma of roasting beans drifting from the factory chimneys.

The **Joe Hill Museet,** dedicated to the Swedish emigrant who went on to become America's first well-known protest singer and union organizer, is in Hill's former home in the oldest section of Gävle. Once a poor working-class district, this is now the most highly sought-after residential part of town, with art studios and crafts workshops nearby. The museum—furnished in the same style as when Hill lived there—contains very few of his possessions but does display his prison letters. The house itself bears witness to the poor conditions that forced so many Swedes to emigrate to the United States (estimated to be between 850,000 and 1 million between 1840 and 1900). Hill, who was born Joel Hägglund, was a founder of the International Workers of the World and was executed for the murder of a Salt Lake City grocer in 1914. He maintained his innocence, an opinion shared by many, right up to the end. ⊠ *Nedre Bergsg. 28* ☎ *026/613425* ✉ *Free* ☉ *June–Aug., daily 11–3.*

The **Skogsmuseet Silvanum** (Silvanum Forestry Museum) is on the west end of town, by the river. Silvanum, Latin for "forest," was inaugurated in 1961; it was the first such museum in the world and is one of the largest. The museum provides an in-depth picture of the forestry industry in Sweden, still the backbone of the country's industrial wealth: trees cover more than 50% of Sweden, and forest products account for 20% of national exports. Silvanum includes a forest botanical park and an arboretum that contains an example of every tree and bush growing in Sweden. ⊠ *Kungsbäcksv. 32* ☎ *026/614100* ✉ *Free* ☉ *Tues. 10–2, Wed. 10–7, Thurs.–Fri. 10–4, weekends 1–5.*

For a glimpse of Gävle's past, go to the **Länsmuseet** (County Museum). Inside this impressive redbrick building is a museum celebrating the history of the town and area. On the ground floor are changing exhibits on local artists and photographers. Upstairs there are old farm implements, clothes, and re-creations of local house interiors that extend from the 12th century to the 1930s. The largest part of the museum is dedicated to the town's maritime history and includes model ships as well as trinkets and treasures brought back from sea voyages long ago. ⊠ *Strandg. 20* ☎ *026/655635* ✉ *SKr 40* ☉ *Tues.–Sun. noon–4.*

Housed in what used to be the local train storage shed, the **Sveriges Järnvägsmuseum** (Swedish Railway Museum) has many different engines and coach cars on display. The royal hunting car from 1859 is thought to be the world's oldest. ⊠ *Rälsg. 1* ☎ *026/106448* ✉ *SKr 40* ☉ *Tues.–Sun. 10–4.*

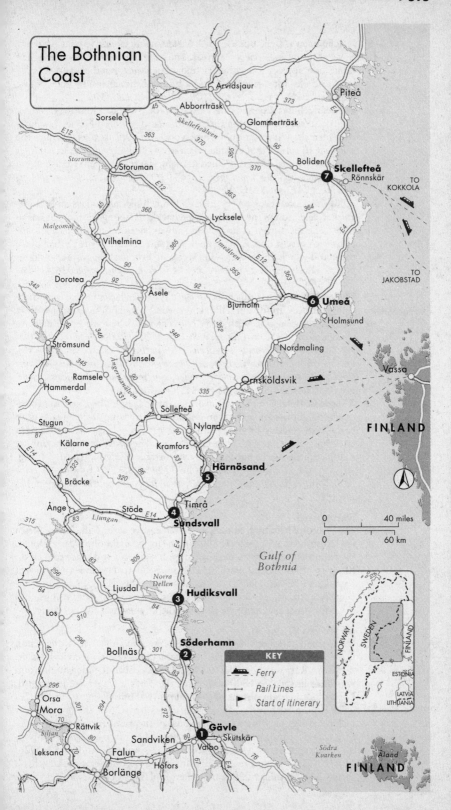

The Bothnian Coast

Arvidsjaur

Abborrträsk

Piteå

Sorsele

Glommerträsk

Storuman

Boliden

Skellefteå ⑦

Rönnskär

TO KOKKOLA

Vilhelmina

Lycksele

TO JAKOBSTAD

Dorotea

Åsele

Bjurholm

⑥ **Umeå**

Strömsund

Junsele

Holmsund

Ramsele

Hammerdal

Nordmaling

Vassa

Örnsköldsvik

Stugun

Sollefteå

Kälarne

Nyland

FINLAND

Bräcke

Kramfors

Ånge

Stöde

Härnösand ⑤

Ljusdal

Timrå

④ **Sundsvall**

Los

Gulf of Bothnia

Bollnäs

Norra Dellen

③ **Hudiksvall**

Orsa

Mora

Söderhamn ②

Rättvik

Leksand

Falun

Sandviken

① **Gävle**

Skutskär

Borlänge

Hofors

Valbo

Södra Kvarken

Åland

FINLAND

KEY

⛴ *Ferry*

— *Rail Lines*

▶ *Start of itinerary*

0 — 40 miles

0 — 60 km

NORWAY · SWEDEN · FINLAND · ESTONIA · LATVIA · LITHUANIA

Where to Stay & Eat

★ **$-$$** ✕ **Johansson's.** Delicious local fish dishes and an extensive wine list make this restaurant in Gävle a real treat. The interior of dark wood and white tablecloths appears somewhat flat and sober at first, but the warm, friendly staff and elegant service will add a brighter dimension to your dining experience. ✉ *Nyg. 7* ☎ *026/100734* ▭ *AE, DC, MC, V.*

$-$$ ✕ **Söderhjelmska Gården.** This classic Swedish wooden house dates from 1773 and stands out from the rest of mostly modern Gävle. The interior, furnished in traditional white wood and blue linen, is split into the same small rooms that existed when it was still a residence. In summer you can also eat in the tree-lined garden. The traditional Swedish menu emphasizes fish. ✉ *S. Kungsg. 23* ☎ *026/613393* ⌖ *Reservations essential* ▭ *AE, DC, MC, V.*

¢-$ ✕ **Järnvägsrestaurangen.** Very good daily lunch specials and a simple home-cooked selection in the evening are what the Railway Restaurant has to offer. The restaurant is in the old railway station building, which adjoins the current one. A large glass veranda in front is the perfect place to sit and watch Gävle go by. On weekend evenings the restaurant doubles as a lively bar and music venue. ✉ *Stora Esplanadg.* ☎ *026/514495* ▭ *AE, DC, MC, V.*

$ 🏨 **Hotel Winn.** What this hotel in the city center lacks in charm and design, it makes up for in facilities. Aimed at conventiongoers, the Winn has very large rooms with every convenience. The leisure facilities are also excellent. ✉ *Norra Slottsg. 9, 801 38* ☎ *026/5958400* 🖷 *026/647009* 🛏 *200 rooms, 6 suites, 20 rooms with bath* ⌂ *Restaurant, room service, in-room data ports, in-room fax, in-room safes, minibars, indoor pool, gym, sauna, bar, laundry service, concierge, meeting rooms, parking (fee), no-smoking rooms* ▭ *AE, DC, MC, V.*

Fodor's Choice
★

$ 🏨 **Scandic Hotel Grand.** Built in 1836, this is Gävle's best attempt to recreate the glories of yesteryear. Behind the imposing stone facade is an early-20th-century interior with some art deco features, including a sweeping lobby bar with huge chandeliers. The bedrooms are beginning to look a little worn, but they are comfortable and good-sized. ✉ *Nyg. 45, 801 04* ☎ *026/129060* 🖷 *026/124499* 🛏 *220 rooms, 95 with bath, 7 suites* ⌂ *Restaurant, sauna, gym, bar, convention center* ▭ *AE, DC, MC, V.*

Shopping

★ The beautiful furniture, clothes, and kitchenware at the **Gefle Design Forum** (✉ Drottningg. 25 ☎ 026/188008) come from Stockholm Design House, the capital's well-known design group. It's also a good place to pick up fun gift items. For something classic, head to **Prylboden** (✉ Norra Kungsg. 11 ☎ 026/189761) a small, friendly shop selling 19th- and 20th-century antiques, especially housewares. Drink trays, coffee cups, and large furniture pieces all vie to catch the attention of the nostalgic.

Nightlife & the Arts

In the small park between Norra Rådmansgatan and Norra Kungsgatan is the grand stone building that contains **Gävle Teatren** (Gävle Theater; ✉ Norra Råmansg. 23 ☎ 026/129200). Its beautiful gilded auditorium was built in the late 1800s. Many of the plays it stages are in English. For a raucous night out, head to **O'Learys** (✉ Södra Kungsg. 31 ☎ 026/652920), an Irish pub that's also a sports bar. Catch the latest soccer or baseball game while sampling some of the excellent beers available. Friday and Saturday nights the place becomes a disco and the most popular nightspot in town. **Heartbreak Hotel** (✉ Norra Strandg. 15 ☎ 026/183020) is a bar and nightclub with a 1950s American rock-and-roll theme. Memorabilia of Elvis and others is plastered on the walls. If you're lucky, you may catch one of the many Elvis impersonators who perform periodically.

Söderhamn

② *75 km (47 mi) north of Gävle (via E4).*

Söderhamn is a town with a lot of space. Besides the extensive open countryside that borders the town, the center is awash with parks, gardens, and wide boulevards. In summer Swedes come from all over to enjoy the pretty public spaces. The many trees help to remove air pollution, making sitting in an open-air café here exceptionally pleasing. The town's architecture is a mix of monumental 18th-century buildings, erected through fortunes made by fishing, and modern shopping precincts built to replace areas devastated by numerous fires. This coastal town is also close to one of the finest archipelagos in the region: more than 500 islands, islets, and skerries are near.

For stunning panoramic views of the town and the surrounding forest and sea, climb **Oscarborg**, a 75-foot tower at the edge of town. Built in 1895, the white tower and attached building resemble a Disney-esque fairy-tale castle.

Dating to the 1600s, **Smedjan** (Blacksmiths) is a living, working museum where you can watch craftsmen use traditional methods to make horseshoes and other items. ⊠ *Kungsgården* ☎ *027/035031* ⊡ *Free* ⊙ *June–Aug., Mon. and Thurs. 2–8. All other times by appointment.*

Where to Stay & Eat

$–$$ ✕ **Restaurang Albertina.** This converted red wooden barn is on the water's edge, just north of Söderhamn, in the old fishing village of Skärså. Inside, scrubbed wooden walls and beamed ceilings blend with the crisp, white table linens. Fish is the specialty here. The locally caught salmon that they serve here is among the best in the region. ⊠ *Skärså* ☎ *027/032010* ⊟ *AE, MC, V.*

¢–$ ✕ **RådhusKonditoriet.** Inside an uninspiring building is a restaurant that doubles as one of the few photographic galleries in the north of Sweden. The gallery and the excellent selection of sandwiches, specialty teas, and light meals make it worth the trip. ⊠ *Kykog. 10* ☎ *027/012457* ⊟ *AE, MC, V* ⊙ *Closed Sun.*

$–$$ ⊞ **First Hotell Statt.** The oldest hotel in town is also the most luxurious. All the rooms are individually furnished and have wooden floors and a comfortable mix of blond wood and pastel furnishings. The public areas have their original chandeliers, stucco-work ceilings, and large open fireplaces, giving the hotel a feel of old luxury. ⊠ *Oxtorgsg. 17, 826 22* ☎ *027/073570* ⊟ *0270/13524* ⊲ *78 rooms without bath* ⌂ *Restaurant, sauna, bar, nightclub, convention center* ⊟ *AE, DC, MC, V.*

¢ ⊞ **Centralhotellet.** As the name suggests, it's the central location that makes this hotel worth the stay. The rooms are quite dark and small, but are well furnished with antique-style fittings and wooden floors. ⊠ *Rådhustorget, 826 32* ☎ *027/070000* ⊟ *027/016060* ⊲ *13 rooms without bath* ⌂ *Restaurant, bar, nightclub* ⊟ *AE, DC, MC, V.*

Nightlife & the Arts

Inside the Folkets Hus (People's House), a 1950s building built for town gatherings, **Café August** (⊠ Rådhusparken ☎ 065/038450) is a lively nightspot. Although the building isn't glamorous, the interior has original paintings on the walls and a pleasingly quiet color scheme throughout. As night falls, the place comes alive with two floors of modern dance music, live bands, and an outdoor bar area for cooling off. **Pub Tre Bockar** (⊠ Bankgränd 1 ☎ 065/099994) is a traditional English pub.

The dark-wood interior is jammed with people on weekend evenings. They all want to sample the live music, disco sound, and good beer.

Sports & the Outdoors

Söderhamn is the perfect place for a boat trip out to the nearby archipelago. The **MS Sandskär** (☎ 027/012254) is one of many boats that offer day trips with fishing and swimming. For an energetic inland-water adventure, there are myriad lakes and rivers around Söderhamn that are perfect for canoeing. For more information contact **Fritidskontoret** (leisure office; ☎ 027/075000).

Shopping

There are real bargains to be found at **Albert and Herbert** (⊠ Sannahedsv. 11 ☎ 065/017777), an outlet store that sells clothes, household items, and furniture. The range is huge, and the quality is excellent.

Hudiksvall

❸ *60 km (37 mi) north of Söderhamn via E4.*

Granted its town charter in 1582, Hudiksvall's history is bound up with the sea. Having been partially destroyed by fire 10 times, Hudiksvall is now an interesting mix of architectural styles. The small section of the old town that remains is built around a central harbor and contains some fine examples of flower-strewn courtyards and traditional wood-panel buildings built along narrow, cobbled streets.

The **Fiskarstan** (Fishertown; ☎ 065/019100 tourist office) neighborhood is tightly packed with striking streets of fishermen's huts and houses and boardwalks of wooden fish stores that hang precariously over the water. Lilla Kyrkogatan, the oldest street in town, leads to Hudiksvall's Church, which is still marked by cannonballs from a Russian invasion in 1721. Guided tours, maps, and information can be arranged through the town's tourist office.

Inside a former bank building in the middle of town, the **Hälsinglands Museum** offers insight into the development of Hudiksvall and the surrounding region. Furniture, house reconstructions, religious artifacts, local textiles, and art are all organized and displayed thoughtfully. It's a revealing picture of life in the area. ⊠ *Storg. 31* ☎ *065/019600* 🖾 *Free* ☉ *Mon. noon–6, Tues.–Thurs. 9–4, weekends 11–3.*

Where to Stay & Eat

$–$$ ✕ **Bruns VS.** This very relaxed, informal restaurant offers a wildly diverse choice of foods, from traditional Swedish to Polynesian and beyond. There's a pub area, for those seeking only liquid refreshment, and in the summer there's a huge terrace for outside dining. ⊠ *Brunnsg. 2* ☎ *065/010402* 🍽 *AE, DC, MC, V.*

¢–$$ ✕ **Gretas Krog.** Built right by the fishing docks, this restaurant is rarely empty and seldom disappoints. The interior trades predictably on fishing history through sepia photographs of weather-beaten fishermen and old nets strung from the ceiling, but there is something undeniably cozy about it all. The menu is packed with good local specialties and traditional Swedish cuisine. ⊠ *Västra Tväkajen* ☎ *065/096600* 🍽 *Reservations essential.*

¢–$$ 🏨 **First Hotell Statt.** From the outside the grand 19th-century yellow-stone facade of this hotel, with its pillars and arches, looks like a typical Swedish town hall. Once you've gone inside, the more familiar marble floor and pastel shades confirm that you have arrived at your hotel. Rooms here are nothing special; most are in need of redecoration. But the hotel is central. ⊠ *Storg. 36, SE-824 22* ☎ *065/015060* 📠 *065/096095*

↩ *106 rooms, 26 with bath, 8 suites* ᗷ *Restaurant, pool, gym, sauna, pub, nightclub, convention center* ▤ *AE, DC, MC, V* ⫯◯⫯ *BP.*

Sports & the Outdoors

Hudiksvall's archipelago is centered around the peninsula of **Hornslandet**, north of the town. As well as the usual fishing, swimming, and boating, the peninsula has Europe's second-largest system of mountain caves, which can be explored by experts and beginners alike. Call **Alf Siden** (☎ 065/070492), who arranges and conducts official tours of the caves.

Shopping

Slöjd i Sjöboden (⊠ Möljen ☎ 065/012041) is a series of old fishing huts now housing stalls where 15 local craftspeople sell their wares. Locally inspired textiles, jewelry, ceramics, and glassware can all be bought at very good prices.

Sundsvall

❹ *80 km (50 mi) north of Hudiksvall via E4.*

Sundsvall also goes by the name of *Stenstan* (Stone Town), and rightly so. When the town was razed by fire in 1888, it was rebuilt entirely out of stone, which is atypical for this part of Sweden. The reconstruction added more parks and widened roads to prevent later fires from spreading. Add to these Sundsvall's impressive limestone and brick buildings and it begins to resemble Sweden's largest cities, Stockholm and Göteborg.

The best place to get a feel for the city and its history is at the **Kulturmagasinet** (Culture Warehouse), a series of four 19th-century waterfront warehouses that now include a museum, library, archives, a children's culture center, art exhibitions, and street music. The museum, which traces the town's history, is built over an old street, where tram tracks and cobbles are still in place. It gives a good sense of what Sundsvall was like when it was still a busy trading port. ⊠ *Packhusg. 8* ☎ *060/191803* ▨ *June–Aug. SKr 20, Sept.–May free* ⊗ *Mon.–Thurs. 10–7, Fri. 10–6, weekends 11–4.*

Sundsvall is a good city to walk around, as most of the points of interest are woven into the streets, boulevards, and squares of **Storgatan and Stora Torget**. History comes to life here with churches, the town hall, and grand porticoed stone buildings all flexing their architectural muscles. Guided tours and maps can be arranged through the **tourist office** (☎ 060/610450).

Gustav Adolfs kyrka, at the far end of Storgatan, is Sundsvall's main church. In keeping with much of the city, it's a grand 19th-century affair that's built of red brick. There is a pleasing order about the interior, its vaults and pillars all constructed from smooth square stones that look like children's building blocks.

Where to Stay & Eat

★ **$$–$$$** ✕ **Restaurang Grankotten.** The food here, described as modern Swedish with a French influence, has won praise from all over. Dishes such as veal with truffles and anything that uses the delicious local elk are worth traveling for. The views of Sundsvall from the turn-of-the-19th-century building are stunning, especially if you dine outside in the summer. ⊠ *Norra Stadsberget* ☎ *060/614222* ᗷ *Reservations essential* ▤ *AE, DC, MC, V* ⊗ *Closed Sun.*

$–$$ ✕ **Skeppsbrokällaren.** Classic Swedish design and furnishings and good Scandinavian cuisine are the main attractions at this quiet basement restaurant, on the site of the original boat entrance to the city. For a more calming dining experience book a table in the Röda Rummet (Red Room), a smaller, darkened dining area at the back of the restaurant. ⊠ *Sjög. 4* ☎ *060/173660* ⚱ *Reservations essential* ☰ *AE, DC, MC, V.*

★ **$–$$** ▥ **Elite Hotel Knaust.** The Knaust family opened this art nouveau hotel in 1860, and it has lost none of its original glory. The sweeping marble staircase and black-and-white-tile lobby is extraordinary and worth a look even if you are not staying. Comfort and luxury are watchwords in the rooms, which have warm, lush fabrics and artworks. The hotel is downtown, conveniently near Sundsvall's shops and other attractions. ⊠ *Storg. 13, 85 105* ☎ *060/6080000* ◳ *060/6080010* ↩ *94 rooms, 4 suites* ⚱ *Restaurant, in-room data ports, minibars, cable TV, gym, sauna, bar, business services, convention center* ☰ *AE, DC, MC, V* ⦿ *BP.*

$ ▥ **Comfort Hotel Sundsvall.** Grand stone arches and portals give an impression of stately luxury to this central hotel. The interior doesn't quite live up to the grand facade, but the rooms are large, comfortable, and individually furnished in earth and red tones and have wooden floors. ⊠ *Sjög. 11, 852 34* ☎ *060/150720* ◳ *060/123456* ↩ *52 rooms, 3 with bath* ⚱ *Restaurant, in-room data ports, cable TV, pool, sauna, bar* ☰ *AE, DC, MC, V.*

Nightlife & the Arts

Bars and pubs provide the best source of evening entertainment in Sundsvall. **Spegelbaren** (⊠ Nybrog. 10 ☎ 060/156006), with its large mirrors, glass ceilings, and 19th-century paintings, is one of the best. If you have spare vacation money to use up, then head for **Casino Cosmopol** (⊠ Södermalmsg. 7 ☎ 060/156289). Housed in the old railway station, built in 1875, it is Sweden's oldest international-style casino. The **Kulturmagasinet** (⊠ Packhusg. 8 ☎ 060/191803) is a museum with art exhibitions (mostly of Swedish artists); a children's theater; and live music, readings, and debates.

Sports & the Outdoors

The nearby river of Ljungan is an excellent spot for rafting. Tours include one hour of white-water rafting, beautiful scenery, and lunch on a small island. Contact the tourist office (☎ 060/610450) for more information.

Shopping

Northern Sweden's largest shopping mall, **Ikano Huset,** is 8 km (5 mi) north of Sundsvall, along Route E4. There are shops of every type, from branches of large, internationally known companies such as IKEA to local handicraft stores. **Sköna Ting** (⊠ Nybrog. 15 ☎ 060/170501), meaning "beautiful things," is a crafts store selling gifts and trinkets: dolls, linen and lace, and handblown glass. Everything is locally made and of good quality.

Härnösand

❺ *40 km (25 mi) north of Sundsvall via E4.*

Dating from 1585, Härnösand is a town rich in history. Narrow ancient streets lined with wood-panel houses contrast with 18th- and 19th-century boulevards and squares. The town has a long history as an administrative center for local government, a history hinted at in its orderly layout and infrastructure as well as in the grandness of its buildings. In the center of town is Sweden's smallest—and only—white cathedral.

With works by both Chagall and Matisse on display, **Härnösands Konsthall** is an art museum of considerable note. The museum has works by many of Sweden's prominent painters and sculptors and puts on around 20 exhibitions per year. ⊠ *Stora Torget 2* ☎ *061/1348142* ☒ *Free* ⊙ *Tues.–Fri. 11–3, weekends noon–3.*

Länsmuseet Västernorrland is an excellent, well-thought-out history museum that covers Härnösand and the surrounding area. The museum also has one of the country's largest collections of weapons. ⊠ *Murberget* ☎ *061/188600* ☒ *Free* ⊙ *Daily 11–5.*

Where to Stay & Eat

$–$$ ✕ **Spjutegåden.** Stark-white walls are broken up by small local paintings at this very traditional restaurant in a building from the early 1800s. The floor and ceiling are both made of white wood, and a huge, open fireplace makes the room cozy. The menu consists of very good traditional Swedish food with international touches. As in most Swedish restaurants, the fish dishes are delicious. ⊠ *Murberget* ☎ *061/1511090* ⌂ *Reservations essential* ▤ *AE, MC, V.*

¢–$ ✕ **Highlander.** At this Celtic-theme pub all the requisite details are in place— even a staff dressed in kilts. There are Irish beer and a good selection of wines. The food is hearty and filling, with lots of beef and other meat dishes on the menu. ⊠ *Nybrog. 5* ☎ *061/1511170* ▤ *AE, MC, V* ⊙ *Closed Sun.*

$–$$ 🏨 **First Hotel.** Of the three hotels in Härnösand, this is the best choice. Large, functional rooms in cream, green, and purple all have wooden floors, armchairs, a desk, and generally very good views of the harbor. ⊠ *Skeppsbron 9, 871 30* ☎ *061/1554440* 🖷 *061/1554447* ⇌ *95 rooms, 7 suites* ⌂ *Restaurant, cable TV, gym, sauna, bar, pub, meeting room, no-smoking rooms* ▤ *AE, DC, MC, V.*

Nightlife & the Arts

The place to be seen in Härnösand is **Apothequet** (⊠ Köpmang. 5 ☎ 061/ 1511717), a nightclub and bar popular with those in their late twenties and thirties. Modern hits are mixed with classics in this darkened lounge. When you can dance no more, the bar does great cocktails.

Shopping

Hantverksboden (⊠ Järnvägsg. ☎ 061/116607) is an old wooden building next to the water where local craftsmen rent stalls to sell their wares. Silverware, jewelry, handicrafts, glassware, and pottery are all in abundance.

Umeå

❻ *225 km (140 mi) north of Härnösand (via E4).*

Built on the River Ume, Umeå is the largest city in northern Sweden. Because it's a university town with inhabitants whose average age is the youngest of anywhere in the country, there are many bars, restaurants, festivals, and cultural events to visit.

Aside from taking a walk around the city's open squares and wide boulevards, the best way to get to know Umeå is by visiting **Gammlia,** a series of museums that focus on the city and surrounding area. The open-air museum has a living village made up of farmhouses and working buildings. Actors in period costumes demonstrate how people lived hundreds of years ago. You can wander around amid farm animals of all kinds and learn about baking bread, preserving meat, and harvesting grain. There are also a church and historic gardens. The indoor museums, which have exhibitions on Umeå's history, consist of the fishing and maritime museum, the Swedish ski museum, and a modern art museum that shows work from major Swedish and international artists. A sort of intellectual theme park, it can take the better part of a day to see everything in Gammlia. ⊠ *Gammliav.* ☎ *090/171800* ☜ *Free* ☼ *Daily 10–5.*

> **off the beaten path**
>
> **NORBYSKÄ** – Around 1800 this island had Europe's largest sawmill, and an ambitious group of Swedes attempted to set up a utopian commune around this industry. The attempt at good living didn't work, and the commune broke up around 1830. However, much of what they built remains today as a monument to their dreams. By walking around the island you can see the remains of the houses, school, and work buildings the commune created. The island is also perfect for picnics, fishing, swimming, and safaris to view the local seal population. Norbyskä is a 15-minute boat trip from Umeå. For details and prices contact the **Umeå tourist office** (☎ 090/161616).

Where to Stay & Eat

$$ ✕ **Greta & Co.** Housed inside a somewhat indifferent hotel, Greta's is a must for those seeking out authentic regional specialties. Food from around northern Sweden is served in a dining room of simple, classic Swedish design. The reindeer, rabbit, and salmon are exceptional. ⊠ *Skolg. 62* ☎ *09/0100730* ☐ *AE, DC, MC, V.*

$–$$ ✕ **Lottas Krog.** On the site of a former Italian bistro, this Swedish eating house has kept some of its Mediterranean feel. The food, though, is unashamedly local, with such classics as meatballs and salmon dishes. ⊠ *Nyg. 22* ☎ *090/129551* ☐ *AE, DC, MC, V.*

¢–$$ ✕ **Grottan.** This restaurant and bar is very popular with the local student population and comes alive at night. The dining room is pretty basic, with red-checked tablecloths and plain wood chairs, but the simple menu is well executed and full of café classics such as lasagna, beef bourguignonne, and steaks. ⊠ *Axtorpsv.* ☎ *090/779600* ☐ *AE, DC, MC, V.*

$–$$ 🏨 **Scandic Hotel Plaza.** A clean, modern glass-and-brick structure that dominates the city skyline, the Scandic is one of the most stylish hotels in the region. The huge open lobby has a staircase of marble and steel, copper-tone pillars, and tile floors. A lounge, restaurant, bistro, and bar all lead off from the lobby. At the very top of the hotel is a luxury health suite and spa, which has exceptional views of the city. Rooms are large, well equipped, and decorated in pastel shades. ⊠ *Storg. 40, 903 04* ☎ *090/ 2056300* 🖷 *090/2056311* ☜ *196 rooms, 58 with bath, 1 suite* ⚓ *2 restaurants, minibars, gym, sauna, spa, bar, lounge, convention center, no-smoking rooms* ☐ *AE, DC, MC, V.*

$ 🏨 **Hotel Winn.** The beautiful powder-blue clapboard exterior of this hotel
Fodor'sChoice encloses a modern, officelike reception area, but one that is comfort-
★ able and welcoming nonetheless. Rooms are very stylishly furnished with paintings and lots of dark wood and asymmetrical fittings. The Mucky Duck, a classic English-style pub on the premises, serves roughly 40 types of beer and is always busy in the evening. ⊠ *Vasaplan, 901 06* ☎ *090/ 711100* 🖷 *090/711150* ☜ *87 rooms, 5 with bath, 5 suites* ⚓ *Sauna, bar, pub, no-smoking rooms* ☐ *AE, DC, MC, V.*

¢ 🏨 **Strand Hotell.** Although this hotel is a severe redbrick blob from the '70s, it is right on the water and is well priced. The rooms are large and basically furnished with notably comfortable beds. ⊠ *Västra Strandg. 11, 903 26* ☎ *090/51444* 🖷 *090/704090* ☜ *41 rooms, 15 with bath* ⚓ *Restaurant, bar, meeting rooms* ☐ *AE, DC, MC, V.*

Nightlife & the Arts

Being a student town, Umeå is never short of a good night out. The nightlife scene here, as in many Swedish towns, revolves around bars and pubs. The stylish **Blå** (⊠ *Rådhusesplanden* ☎ *090/135660*) is full of chrome, glass, and people with attitude. It's the place to see and be seen in town. For an informal night out try **Rex** (⊠ Rådhustorget ☎ 090/126050), a friendly and popular haunt that attracts a young crowd. For those who prefer something a little more sedate and traditional, **Äpplet** (⊠ Vasaplan ☎ 090/156200) puts on fox-trot, cha-cha, and tango for all comers.

Shopping
Designers Guild (⊠ Kungsg. 49 ☎ 090/131300), the fabric and print shop started by English designer Patricia Guild, sells beautiful English-, French-, and Italian-inspired fabrics, clothes, and household goods.

Skellefteå

❼ *140 km (87 mi) northeast of Umeå via E4.*

In 1324 King Magnus Eriksson invited anyone who believed in Jesus Christ, or anyone who wanted to convert to Christianity, to settle a town near the River Skellefte. Thus was Skellefteå born, and for hundreds of years it was a devout Christian township. Today the town makes a living from the electronics and computer industries and from nearby gold and silver mining.

Fodor'sChoice ★ The focus of the town's religious beliefs still stands today, in the form of **Skellefteå Landskyrka.** Inside the area known as Bonnstan—a 400-room "village" built to house traveling churchgoers in the 17th century when attendance was compulsory—the striking neoclassical Skellefteå County Church has a dome roof. It has some exquisite medieval sculptures, including an 800-year-old walnut wood carving of the Virgin Mary, one of only a handful of Romanesque Maria carvings left anywhere in the world.

One of the very few art museums in the world dedicated to female artists, **Anna Nordlander Museum** displays about 80 of this Swedish painter's portraits and landscapes. Born in 1843, Nordlander found that success came quickly and increased steadily until her death from tuberculosis at the age of 36. ⊠ *Kanalg. 73* ☎ *0910/736100* ⊠ *Free* ☉ *Daily 10–5.*

Where to Stay & Eat

$–$$ ✕ **Kriti.** An authentic Greek restaurant in the north of Sweden is not what you may expect, but you won't be disappointed. Garish yellow tablecloths with red napkins, rickety wooden chairs, white concrete walls, and a small tile roof over the bar make this the real deal. Huge portions of good meat and fish dishes are hearty and satisfying. ⊠ *Kanalg. 51* ☎ *0910/779535* ⊟ *AE, DC, MC, V.*

$–$$ ✕ **Värdshuset Disponenten.** This beautiful green colonial-style wooden mansion has wrought-iron balconies and ivy creepers on the walls. The smörgåsbord that's offered here is generous and well prepared. Cold and hot fish, meat, and vegetable dishes are almost all made using local ingredients—some as local as the kitchen garden. ⊠ *Skelleftehamnsv. 63* ☎ *0910/30930* ⚘ *Reservations essential* ⊟ *AE, DC, MC, V* ☉ *No dinner Sat.*

$–$$ ⬚ **Scandic Hotel.** This modern building is shaped like an upturned boat, half of which is made of glass. This huge glassed portion is the Winter Garden, which houses the lobby, lounges, restaurants, and an extraordinary collection of huge trees, tropical palms, and flowers. The large rooms are furnished in blond wood and come with all the modern additions you would expect of an international hotel. ⊠ *Kanalg. 75, SE-931 78* ☎ *0910/752400* 🖷 *0910/752411* ⊕ *www.scandic.se* ⮑ *111 rooms without bath, 4 suites* ⚬ *2 restaurants, indoor pool, gym, sauna, bar, convention center* ⊟ *AE, DC, MC, V.*

$ 🏨 **Rica Hotel.** Each room is individually furnished in this modern hotel. The building's low light, candles, and dark furnishings are very restful. ✉ *Torget 2, SE-931 31* ☎ *0910/732500* 🖷 *0910/732529* 🌐 *www. rica.se* ⇌ *123 rooms, 25 with bath, 2 suites* ⏶ *Restaurant, in-room data ports, 2 pools, sauna, bar, parking (fee)* ☰ *AE, DC, MC, V.*

Nightlife & the Arts

Underbar (✉ Torget ☎ 0910/732530) means wonderful, and if you asked the locals, that's exactly how most would describe this dark and smoky nightclub. The three underground floors become unbelievably packed on weekends. There are two bars and dance floors, a disco, and a stage where live bands play the very popular local sound known as *Skelletepop*.

Locally sponsored and managed **Pinkerton** (✉ Magasingränd 3 ☎ 091085060) has the promotion of Skellefteå music very much on its mind. The dark, cool club serves up cold beer, snacks, and lots of local pop, blues, jazz, and rock bands.

Shopping

The market stalls arranged under the large roof of the **Handelsgården** (✉ Storg. 46 ☎ 09/10779924) mean that the place offers one-stop shopping for ceramics, glass, jewelry, woodwork, woven textiles, prints and artwork, and delicatessen foods.

The Bothnian Coast A to Z

AIR TRAVEL

CARRIERS The only carrier to Sundsvall Airport is SAS, which operates nine flights a day from Stockholm.
🚩 **SAS** ☎ 0770/727727 🌐 www.scandinavian.net.

AIRPORTS

Sundsvall Airport (20 km [12 mi] west of Sundsvall) is the area's main airport. Local flight connections can be made to Umeå and Skellefteå. A bus service to Sundsvall runs in connection with arriving and departing SAS flights and costs SKr 80. A taxi will cost SKr 275–SKr 320.
🚩 **Sundsvall Airport** ☎ 060/6088000. **Taxi Sundsvall** ☎ 060/199000.

BUS TRAVEL

Swebus operates a twice-daily service from Stockholm to Gävle. Y-Buss operates daily from Stockholm to Hudiksvall, Sundsvall, Härnösand, and Umeå.
🚩 **Swebus** ☎ 020/0218218. **Y-Buss** ☎ 020/0334444.

CAR RENTAL

Avis and Hertz have offices in Gävle, Sundsvall, and Umeå. Europcar has offices in Gävle and Umeå.
🚩 **Major Agencies Avis** ✉ Gävle ☎ 026/186880, ✉ Sundsvall ☎ 060/570210, ✉ Umeå ☎ 090/131111. **Europcar** ✉ Gävle ☎ 026/621095, ✉ Umeå ☎ 090/153960. **Hertz** ✉ Gävle ☎ 026/644938 ✉ Sundsvall ☎ 060/669080 ✉ Umeå ☎ 090/177140.

CAR TRAVEL

From Stockholm take E4 directly north 174 km (108 mi) to Gävle. From Göteborg take E20 284 km (177 mi) to Örebro, Route 60 north 164 km (102 mi) to Borlänge, and Route 80 west 70 km (43 mi) to Gävle. From Gävle the E4 runs the entire length of the Bothnian coast through every major town north to Skellefteå.

EMERGENCIES

For emergencies dial 112. There are several hospitals in the area and emergency dental care is available at Sundsvall and Umeå. There are late-night pharmacies in Gävle and Sundsvall that stay open until 11.

? Hospitals **Gävle Hospital** ☎ 026/154000. **Hudiksvall Hospital** ☎ 065/092000. **Söderhamn Hospital** ☎ 0270/77000. **Umeå Hospital** ☎ 090/7850000.

? Dental Care ☒ Sundsvall ☎ 060/613135 ☒ Umeå ☎ 070/3992480.

? Late-Night Pharmacies ☒ Gävle ☎ 026/149200, ☒ Sundsvall ☎ 060/181117.

TOURS

The Bothnian coast covers many miles, and tours of the entire area are not available. Individual towns and cities usually offer their own tours, either of the town or of points of interest in the surrounding area. The Umeleden Way is a waterside cycling path with many stops, including Europe's largest hydroelectric power station. Details of tours can be obtained from an individual town's tourist information offices.

? Gävle City Tour ☎ 026/147430. **Hudiksvall Town Walk** ☎ 0650/19100. **Skellefteå Countryside Tours** ☎ 091/0711210. **Umeleden Way** ☎ 090/161616.

TRAIN TRAVEL

SJ operates hourly train services from Stockholm to Gävle, Söderhamn, Hudiksvall, Sundsvall, and Härnösand. Tågkompaniet operates a night train from Stockholm to Umeå, with connections to Skellefteå.

? SJ ☎ 0771/757575. **Tågkompaniet** ☎ 020/444111.

VISITOR INFORMATION

? Tourist Information **Gävle** ☒ Drottningg. 37 ☎ 026/147430. **Härnösand** ☒ Järnvägsg. 2 ☎ 061/188140 ⊕ www.turism.harnosand.se. **Hudiksvall** ☒ Möljen ☎ 0650/19100 ⊕ www.hudiksvall.se. **Skellefteå** ☒ Trädgårdsg. ☎ 0910/736020 ⊕ turistinfo.skelleftea.se. **Söderhamn** ☒ Resecentrum ☎ 0270/75353 ⊕ www.turism.soderhamn.se. **Sundsvall** ☒ Stora Torget ☎ 060/610450 ⊕ www.sundsvallturism.com. **Umeå** ☒ Renmarkstorget 15 ☎ 090/161616 ⊕ www.umea.se.

GÖTEBORG

If you are passing through Göteborg (Gothenburg) on the way to your coastal vacation spot, do try to spend a day or two exploring this attractive port. Quayside cranes and warehouses attest to the city's industrial might, yet within a 10-minute walk of the waterfront is an elegant, modern city of broad avenues, green parks, and gardens. This is not to slight the harbor along both banks of the Göta Älv (river): it comprises 22 km (14 mi) of quays with warehouses and sheds covering more than 1.5 million square feet, making Göteborg Scandinavia's largest port. The harbor is also the home of Scandinavia's largest corporation, the automobile manufacturer Volvo (which means "I roll" in Latin), as well as of the roller-bearing manufacturer SKF and the world-renowned Hasselblad camera company.

Historically, Göteborg owes its existence to the sea. Tenth-century Vikings sailed from its shores, and a settlement was founded here in the 11th century. Not until 1621, however, did King Gustav II Adolf grant Göteborg a charter to establish a free-trade port on the model of others already thriving on the Continent. The west-coast harbor would also allow Swedish shipping to avoid Danish tolls exacted for passing through Öresund, the stretch of water separating the two countries. Foreigners were recruited to realize these visions: the Dutch were its builders—hence the canals that thread the city—and many Scotsmen worked and settled here, though they have left little trace.

Today Göteborg resists its second-city status by being a leader in attractions and civic structures. The Scandinavium, with a capacity of 14,000 people, is one of Europe's largest indoor arenas; the Ullevi Stadium stages some of the Nordic area's most important concerts and sporting events; Nordstan is one of Europe's biggest indoor shopping malls; and Liseberg, Scandinavia's largest amusement park in the area, attracts some 3 million visitors a year. Above the Göta River is Älvsborgsbron, at 3,060 feet the longest suspension bridge in Sweden.

Exploring Göteborg

Göteborg is an easy city to explore: most major attractions are within walking distance of one another, and the streetcar network is excellent—in summer you can take a sightseeing trip on an open-air streetcar. The heart of Göteborg is Kungsportsavenyn (more commonly referred to as Avenyn, "the Avenue"), a 60-foot-wide, tree-lined boulevard that bisects the city along a northwest–southeast axis. Avenyn links Göteborg's cultural heart, Götaplatsen, at the southern end, with the main commercial area, now dominated by the modern Nordstan shopping center. Beyond lies the waterfront, busy with all the traffic of the port, as well as some of Göteborg's newer cultural developments.

To the west are the Haga and Linné districts. Once home to the city's dockyard, shipping, and factory workers, these areas are now alive with arts-and-crafts galleries, antiques shops, boutiques selling clothes and household goods, and street cafés and restaurants. Most of these shops are inside the original wood-and-brick cottages that line the narrow streets.

Cultural Göteborg

A pleasant stroll will take you from Götaplatsen's 1930s architecture along the Avenyn—the Boulevard Kungsportsavenyn lined with elegant shops, cafés, and restaurants—to finish at Kungsportsplats. At the square the street becomes Östra Hamngatan and slopes gently up from the canal.

a good walk

Start your tour in **Götaplatsen** ❶ ►, a square dominated by a fountain statue of Poseidon; behind him is the **Konstmuseet** ❷. Stroll downhill past the cafés and restaurants along Avenyn to the intersection with Vasagatan. A short way to the left down Vasagatan, at the junction with Teatergatan, you can visit the **Röhsska Museet** ❸, one of the few galleries dedicated to Swedish design.

Continue down Vasagatan. If the weather's good, have a look in at the Vasa Parken (Vasa Park). Then turn right to go north on Viktoriagatan, cross the canal, and make an immediate left to visit one of the city's most peculiar attractions, **Feskekörkan** ❹, whose name is an archaic spelling of *Fisk Kyrkan,* the Fish Church. It resembles a place of worship but is actually an indoor fish market.

You may now feel inspired to visit the city's principal place of worship, **Domkyrkan** ❺. Follow the canal eastward from Feskekörkan and turn left onto Västra Hamngatan; walk about four blocks to the church. Continue northward on Västra Hamngatan and cross the canal to get to Norra Hamngatan, where you'll find the **Stadsmuseet** ❻, housed in the 18th-century Swedish East India Company.

TIMING   Depending on how much time you want to spend in each museum, this walk may take anywhere from a couple of hours to the better part of a day. Note that many sites close Monday off-season.

WHAT TO SEE **Domkyrkan** (Göteborg Cathedral). The cathedral, in neoclassic yellow
5 brick, dates from 1802, the two previous cathedrals on this spot having been destroyed by fire. Though disappointingly plain on the outside, the interior is impressive. Two glassed-in verandas originally used
for the bishop's private conversations run the length of each side of the
cathedral. The altar is impressively ornate and gilt laden. Next to it stands
a post-Resurrection cross, bare of the figure of Jesus and surrounded
by his gilded burial garments strewn on the floor. ✉ *Kyrkog. 28, Centrum* ☎ *031/7316130* ✉ *Free* ☉ *Weekdays 8–6, Sat. 9–4, Sun. 10–3.*

4 **Feskekörkan** (Fish Church). Built in 1872, this fish market gets its nickname from its Gothic-style architectural details. The beautiful arched
and vaulted wooden ceiling covers rows and rows of stalls, each offering silvery, slippery goods to the shoppers who congregate in this vast
hall. ✉ *Fisktorget, Rosenlundsg, Centrum.*

off the
beaten
path
FISKHAMNEN (Fish Docks) – An excellent view of **Älvsborgsbron**
(Älvsborg Bridge), the longest suspension bridge in Sweden, is
available from Fiskhamnen, west of Stigbergstorget. Built in 1967,
the bridge stretches 3,060 feet across the river and was built high
enough for ocean liners to pass beneath. Also look toward the sea to
the large container harbors—Skarvikshamnen, Skandiahamnen, and
Torshamnen—which today welcome most of the city's cargo.

▶ **1** **Götaplatsen** (Göta Place). This square was built in 1923 in celebration
FodorsChoice of the city's 300th anniversary. In the center is the Swedish-American sculp-
★ tor Carl Milles's fountain statue of Poseidon choking a codfish. Behind
the statue stands the Konstmuseet, flanked by the **Konserthuset** (Concert Hall) and the **Stadsteatern** (Municipal Theater), three contemporary
buildings in which the city celebrates its important contribution to
Swedish cultural life. The **Stadsbiblioteket** (Municipal Library) maintains
a collection of more than half a million books, many in English.

2 **Konstmuseet** (Art Museum). This impressive collection of the works of
leading Scandinavian painters and sculptors encapsulates some of the
moody introspection of the artistic community in this part of the world.
The museum's Hasselblad Center devotes itself to showing the progress
in the art of photography. The Konstmuseet's holdings include works
by Swedes such as Carl Milles, Johan Tobias Sergel, impressionist Anders Zorn, Victorian idealist Carl Larsson, and Prince Eugen. The 19th-
and 20th-century French art collection is the best in Sweden, and there's
also a small collection of old masters. ✉ *Götaplatsen, Götaplatsen*
☎ *031/612980* ✉ *SKr 40* ☉ *Tues. and Thurs. 11–6, Wed. 11–9,
Fri.–Sun. 11–5.*

off the
beaten
path
LISEBERG NÖJESPARK – Göteborg proudly claims Scandinavia's
largest amusement park. The city's pride is well earned: Liseberg is
one of the best-run, most efficient parks in the world. In addition to a
wide selection of carnival rides, Liseberg also has numerous
restaurants and theaters, all set amid beautifully tended gardens. It's
about a 30-minute walk east from the city center or a 10-minute ride
by bus or tram; in summer a vintage open streetcar makes frequent
runs to Liseberg from Brunnsparken, in the middle of town.
✉ *Örgrytev. 5, Liseberg* ☎ *031/400100* ✉ *SKr 50* ☉ *Mid-
Apr.–mid-May, Sat. noon–9, Sun. noon–8; mid-May–July, weekdays
3–10, Sat. noon–11, Sun. noon–8; Aug., weekdays and Sun. 11–11,
Fri.–Sat. 11 AM–midnight; Sept., Thurs.–Fri. 4 PM–10 PM, Sat.
noon–10, Sun. noon–8* ⊕ *see www.liseberg.se for deviations to
schedule around holidays.*

Göteborg

3 **Röhsska Museet** (Museum of Arts and Crafts). This museum's fine collections of furniture, books and manuscripts, tapestries, and pottery are on view. Artifacts date back as far as 1,000 years, but it's the 20th-century gallery, with its collection of many familiar household objects, that seems to provide the most enjoyment. ⊠ *Vasag. 37–39, Vasastan* ☎ *031/ 613850* ⊠ *SKr 40* ☼ *Year-round, Tues. noon–9, Wed.–Sun. noon–5.*

6 **Stadsmuseet** (City Museum). Once the warehouse and auction rooms of the Swedish East India Company, a major trading firm founded in 1731, this palatial structure dates to 1750. Today it contains exhibits on the Swedish west coast, with a focus on Göteborg's nautical and trading past. One interesting exhibit deals with the East India Company and its ship the *Göteborg*. On its 1745 return from China, she sank just outside the city while crowds there to greet the returning ship watched from shore in horror. ⊠ *Norra Hamng. 12, Centrum* ☎ *031/612770* ⊠ *SKr 40* ☼ *Weekdays 10–5, weekends 11–8.*

Commercial Göteborg

Explore Göteborg's port-side character, both historic and modern, at the waterfront development near the town center, where the markets and boutiques can keep you busy for hours.

a good walk

Begin at the harborside square known as Lilla Bommen Torg, where the **Utkiken** **7** ▶ offers a bird's-eye view of the city and harbor. The waterfront development here includes the ship-turned-restaurant *Viking*, the Opera House, and the **Maritima Centrum** **8**.

From Lilla Bommen Torg take the pedestrian bridge across the highway to **Nordstan** **9**. Leave the mall at the opposite end, which puts you at Brunnsparken, the hub of the city's streetcar network. Turn right and cross the street to Gustav Adolfs Torg, the city's official center, dominated by **Rådhuset** **10**. On the north side of the square is **Börshuset** **11**, built in 1849.

Head north from the square along Östra Hamngatan and turn left onto Postgatan to visit **Kronhuset** **12**, the city's oldest secular building, dating from 1643. Surrounding the entrance to Kronhuset are the **Kronhusbodarna,** carefully restored turn-of-the-20th-century shops and arts-and-crafts boutiques.

Return to Gustav Adolfs Torg and follow Östra Hamngatan south over the Stora Hamnkanal to Kungsportsplats, where the Saluhall (Market Hall) has stood since 1888. A number of pedestrians-only shopping streets branch out through this neighborhood on either side of Östra Hamngatan. Crossing the bridge over Vallgraven from Kungsportsplats brings you onto Kungsportsavenyn and the entrance to **Trädgårn** **13**.

TIMING The walk itself will take about two hours; allow extra time to explore the sites and to shop. Note that the Kronhusbodarna is closed Sunday. Trädgårn is closed Monday off-season.

WHAT TO SEE **Börshuset** (Stock Exchange). Completed in 1849, the former Stock Exchange building houses city administrative offices as well as facilities for large banquets. The fabric of the large, opulent banqueting halls and blue-stucco anterooms is under considerable strain through age. The building is not open to the public, but if you can get in, you won't be disappointed. ⊠ *Gustav Adolfs Torg 5, Nordstan.*

Kronhusbodarna (Historical Shopping Center). Glassblowing and watchmaking are among the arts and crafts offered in this area of shops that adjoin the Kronhuset. There is also a nice, old-fashioned café. ⊠ *Kronhusg. 1D, Nordstan* ☼ *Closed Sun.*

⑫ Kronhuset (Crown House). Göteborg's oldest secular building, dating from 1643, was originally the city's armory. In 1660 Sweden's Parliament met here to arrange the succession for King Karl X Gustav, who died suddenly while visiting the city. The building is now used for classical concerts and the City Museum's annual Christmas market. ⊠ *Postg. 68, Nordstan* ☎ *031/612770, City Museum.*

❽ Maritima Centrum (Marine Center). In the world's largest floating maritime museum you'll find modern naval vessels, including a destroyer, submarines, lightship, cargo vessel, and various tugboats, providing insight into Göteborg's historic role as a major port. The main attraction is a huge naval destroyer, complete with a medical room in which a leg amputation operation is graphically re-created, with mannequins standing in for medical personnel. ⊠ *Packhuskajen 8, Nordstan* ☎ *031/105950* ⊠ *SKr 60* ⊙ *May–July, daily 10–6; Aug.–Apr., daily 10–4.*

❾ Nordstan. Sweden's largest indoor shopping mall—open daily—is replete with a huge parking garage, pharmacy open until 10 PM, post office, several restaurants, entertainment for children, a branch of the department store Åhlens, and a tourist information kiosk. ⊠ *Entrances on Köpmansg., Nils Ericsonsg., Kanaltorgsg., and Östra Hamng., Nordstan.*

❿ Rådhuset. Though the town hall dates from 1672, when it was designed by Nicodemus Tessin the Elder, its controversial modern extension by Swedish architect Gunnar Asplund is from 1937. The building therefore offers two architectural extremes. One section has the original grand chandeliers and trompe l'oeil ceilings; the other has glass elevators, mussel-shape drinking fountains, and vast expanses of laminated aspen wood. Together they make a fascinating mix. ⊠ *Gustav Adolfs Torg 1, Nordstan.*

⑬ Trädgårdsföreningens Park (Horticultural Society Park). Here you'll find
FodorśChoice beautiful open green spaces, a magnificent rose garden with 5,000
★ roses of 2,500 varieties; the Butterfly House, with butterflies flying free, and the Palm House, whose late-19th-century design echoes that of London's Crystal Palace. ⊠ *Just off Kungsportsavenyn, Centrum* ☎ *031/611804* ⊠ *Park SKr 15; Palm House SKr 20; Butterfly House SKr 35* ⊙ *Park May–Aug., daily 7 AM–9 PM; Sept.–Apr., daily 7 AM–7:30 PM. Palm House May–Aug., daily 10–5; Sept.–Aug., daily 10–4. Butterfly House Apr., May, and Sept., daily 10–4; June–Aug., daily 10–5; Oct.–Mar., daily 10–3.*

▶ **❼ Utkiken** (Lookout Tower). This red-and-white-stripe skyscraper towers 282 feet above the waterfront, offering an unparalleled view of the city and skyscrapers from the viewing platform at the top. ⊠ *Lilla Bommen, Lilla Bommen* ☎ *031/609670.*

off the beaten path

GULLBERGSKAJEN – For an interesting tour of the docks, head northeast from Lilla Bommen about 1½ km (1 mi) along the riverside to the Gullbergskajen, just off Gullbergsstrandgatan. Today this is the headquarters of a local boating association, its brightly colored pleasure craft contrasting with the old-fashioned working barges either anchored or being repaired at Ringön, just across the river.

NYA ELFSBORGS FÄSTNING – Boats leave regularly from Lilla Bommen to the Elfsborg Fortress, built in 1670 on a harbor island to protect the city from attack. ☎ *031/609660* ⊠ *SKr 85* ⊙ *Early May–Aug., 7 departures daily; Sept., weekends.*

SJÖFARTSMUSEET & AKVARIET – This museum combines maritime history with an aquarium. The museum has model ships, cannons, a ship's medical room, and a collection of figureheads. The adjacent aquarium contains a good selection of Nordic marine life and a more exotic section with, among other animals, two alligators and some piranhas. ⊠ *Karl Johansg. 1–3, 2 km (1 mi) west of city center, Majorna* ☎ *031/612901* ⊠ *SKr 40* ☉ *Sept.–Apr., Tues., Thurs., and Fri. 10–4, Wed. 10–9, weekends 11–5; May–Aug., daily 10–5.*

VIKING. – This four-masted schooner, built in 1907, was among the last of Sweden's sailing cargo ships. The ship is now used as a hotel and restaurant, with cabins for two without bath starting at SKr 650. The restaurant serves up traditional Swedish fare starting at 79 SKr. ⊠ *Gullbergskajen, Lilla Bommen, Hamnen* ☎ *031/635800.*

Haga & Linné Districts

Just west of the main city, the Haga and Linné districts are at the forefront of the new cosmopolitan Göteborg. These areas once housed the city's poor and were so run-down that they were scheduled for demolition. They now make up some of the city's most attractive areas. The older of the two neighborhoods, the Haga district is full of cozy cafés, secondhand stores, and artist shops along cobbled streets. The Linné district is the trendiest neighborhood in which to live in Göteborg, and real estate prices have shot up accordingly. Corner restaurants, expensive boutiques, and stylish cafés cater to neighborhood residents and to Göteborg's wealthy young elite, there to see and be seen.

a good walk

Set off from the east end of **Haga Nygatan** ⑭ ☞ and stroll west past the busy cafés and boutiques selling art-deco light fixtures and antique kitchenware. Turn left onto Landsvägsgatan and walk up to join Linnégatan, the Dutch-inspired street that's now considered Göteborg's "Second Avenyn." There is an air of quiet sophistication about Linnégatan, with small antiques and jewelry shops competing for attention against secluded street cafés and high-end design and crafts shops.

Walk south along Linnégatan for five minutes to get to **Slottskogen** ⑮. If relaxing is your thing, you can spend some time lounging in this huge, tranquil expanse of parkland. Alternatively, you can make use of your time here and visit the **Naturhistorika Museet** ⑯, Göteborg's oldest museum, or the **Botaniska Trädgården** ⑰, on the south side of the park.

Depart the park the same way you came in, and wind your way north up Nordenhemsgatan. At the end of this road turn right onto Första Långgatan and then onto Södra Allégatan. Here you can find the beautiful and tranquil oasis of the **Haga Badet** ⑱, a superbly renovated bathhouse.

TIMING At a gentle pace the walk alone will take about one hour. If you allow yourself to be tempted by the great shopping, superb cafés, and both museums, you could spend almost a whole day in this part of the city.

WHAT TO SEE **Botaniska Trädgården** (Botanical Gardens). With 1,200 plant species this ⑰ is Sweden's largest botanical garden. Herb gardens, bamboo groves, a Japanese valley, forest plants, and tropical greenhouses are all on display. ⊠ *Carl Skottsbergs Gata 22A, Slottsskogen* ☎ *031/7411101* ⊠ *Greenhouses SKr 20; Park free* ☉ *Park daily 9–sunset; greenhouses May–Aug., daily 10–5; Sept.–Apr., daily 10–4.*

⑱ **Haga Badet.** This stunning bathhouse was built at the end of the 19th
FodorsChoice century by the Swedish philanthropist Sven Renström. Originally used
★ by local dock- and factory workers, it now plays host to Göteborg's leisure-hungry elite. It's well worth a visit. The pretty pool is art nouveau, with

wall paintings, an arched ceiling, and lamps with a diving-lady motif. The Roman baths and the massage and spa area all exude relaxation, but the architecture alone is worth a visit, even if you don't intend to take the plunge. ⊠ *Södra Allég. 3, Haga* ☎ *031/600600* ⊠ *SKr 320 for day pass to use facilities, otherwise free* ☉ *Mon.–Thurs. 7 AM–9:30 PM, Fri. 7 AM–8:30 PM, Sat. 9–6, Sun. 10–6.*

▶ **⑭ Haga Nygatan.** The redbrick buildings that line this street were originally poorhouses donated by the Dickson family, the city's British industrialist forefathers. ROBERT DICKSON can still be seen carved into the facades of these buildings. Like most buildings in Haga, the buildings' ground floors were made of stone in order to prevent the spread of fire (the upper floors are wood). The Dickson family's impact on the architecture of the west of Sweden can also be seen in the impressive, fanciful mansion that belonged to Robert's grandson James, in Tjolöholm, to the south of Göteborg. ⊠ *Haga Nyg, Haga.*

⑯ Naturhistoriska Museet. Although the Natural History Museum has a collection containing more than 10 million preserved animals, you may be disappointed to discover that the majority are tiny insects that sit unnoticed in rows of drawers. It's worth a visit to see the world's only stuffed blue whale, harpooned in 1865. ⊠ *Slottsskogen, Slottsskogen* ☎ *031/7752400* ⊕ *www.gnm.se* ⊠ *SKr 40* ☉ *Sept.–Apr., Tues.–Fri. 9–4, weekends 11–5; May–Aug., daily 11–5.*

> **off the beaten path**

SKANSEN KRONAN – To the south of Haga is one of Göteborg's two surviving 17th-century fortress towers. Built on a raised mound of land, the tower houses the military museum, containing displays of weapons dating to the Middle Ages and Swedish uniforms from the 19th and 20th centuries. The museum's presentations can be a little dry at times and is probably only for the true enthusiast of military history. But the view northward across the city makes the journey worthwhile.

⑮ Slottsskogen. Spend some time in this stunning area of parkland containing cafés, farm animals, a seal pond, Sweden's oldest children's zoo, and many birds, in summer even pink flamingos. Slottsskogen is one of the best parts of the city in which to take a break. ⊠ *South of Linnég., Slottsskogen* ☉ *Daily dawn–dusk.*

> **off the beaten path**

VOLVO MUSEUM – In Arendal, 8 km (5 mi) west of the city center, the Volvo Museum pays homage to the car company that in one way or another helps support 25% of Göteborg's population. Not surprisingly, exhibits include most of Volvo's cars over the years as well as some prototypes, the first electric car, and an early jet engine, the first one used by the Swedish Air Force. A 20-minute film helps to put the whole history into perspective at this rather well-put-together museum. ⊠ *Avd. 1670 ARU, off Rd. 155 toward Öckerö/Torslanda Arendal* ☎ *031/664814* ⊕ *www.volvo.com* ⊠ *SKr 30* ☉ *June–Aug., Tues.–Fri. 10–5, weekends 11–4; Sept.–May, Tues.–Fri. noon–5, weekends 11–4.*

Where to Eat

You can eat well in Göteborg but expect to pay dearly for the privilege. Fish dishes are the best bet here. Call ahead to be sure restaurants are open, as many close for a month in summer.

$$$$ ✕ **Sjömagasinet.** Seafood is the obvious specialty at this waterfront restaurant. In a 200-year-old renovated shipping warehouse, the dining room has views of the harbor and the suspension bridge. An outdoor terrace opens up in summer. ✉ *Klippans Kulturreservat, Kiel-terminalen* ☎ *031/7755920* ☖ *Reservations essential* ☰ *AE, DC, MC, V.*

★ **$$$–$$$$** ✕ **28+.** Step down from the street into this former wine-and-cheese cellar to find an elegant restaurant owned by two of the best chefs in Göteborg. Finely set tables, flickering candles, and country-style artwork evoke the mood of a rustic French town. Italian and American flavors blend their way into the French dishes; choose a five- or seven-course meal, or take your pick à la carte. Note that one of the best wine cellars in Sweden is at your disposal. ✉ *Götabergsg. 28, Centrum* ☎ *031/202161* ⋔ *Jacket required* ☰ *AE, DC, MC, V* ☽ *Closed Sun.*

$$$ ✕ **Le Village.** Ever been to a restaurant with tables and chairs you liked
Fodor's Choice so much you wished you could take them home? What about the lamps
★ or the paintings on the wall? Well, at Le Village that's exactly what you can do. Everything in this restaurant and the connected **antiques shop** (☎ *031/143833*) is for sale. The food is exceptional, especially the seasonal meat dishes. Try the smaller dining room if you want to avoid some of the prices in the main room. ✉ *Tredje Långgatan 13, Linnéstaden* ☎ *031/242003* ☰ *AE, DC, MC, V* ☽ *Closed Sun.*

$$$ ✕ **Noon.** Swedish and Asian styles fuse to produce innovative, quality seafood and noodle dishes that are served in a simple, modern dining room. Try a few of the smaller, less expensive appetizers, or go all out by ordering the flounder in lemon-ginger sauce with saffron dumplings. ✉ *Viktoriag. 2, Vasastan* ☎ *031/138800* ☰ *AE, DC, MC, V.*

$$$ ✕ **Räkan.** This informal and popular place makes the most of an unusual gimmick: the tables are arranged around a long tank, and if you order shrimp, the house specialty, they arrive at your table in radio-controlled boats you navigate yourself. ✉ *Lorensbergsg. 16, Götaplatsen* ☎ *031/169839* ☖ *Reservations essential* ☰ *AE, DC, MC, V* ☽ *No lunch.*

$$$ ✕ **Trägårn.** Spicy, Asian-influenced cuisine stands out against linen tablecloths in this earth-tone restaurant; the vegetarian menu is extensive. A wall of glass in the two-story dining hall affords a view of Göteborg's beautiful Trägårnpark; another wall is covered in blond-wood paneling, a contrast to the black-slate floor. ✉ *Nya Allén, Centrum* ☎ *031/102080* ☰ *AE, DC, MC, V* ☽ *Closed Sun. No lunch fall–spring.*

$$–$$$ ✕ **A Hereford Beefstouw.** At this, an American steak house in Sweden, the chefs grill beef selections in the center of the three dining rooms, one of which is set aside for nonsmokers. The restaurant is popular in a town otherwise dominated by fish restaurants. Thick wooden tables, pine floors, and landscape paintings give the place a rustic touch. ✉ *Linnég. 5, Linnéstaden* ☎ *031/7750441* ☰ *AE, DC, MC, V* ☽ *No lunch weekends and July.*

$$–$$$ ✕ **Ahlströms Pier.** Across the river from central Göteborg lies Eriksberg, where former dockyards mix with modern buildings. Perched at the end of a pier that juts out into the harbor, this restaurant has a main dining hall in an elegant triangular room on the second floor and a less expensive brasserie on the first floor; contemporary French-inspired Swedish fare is on the menu at both. In summer food is served on an outdoor patio. Finding the pier by car can prove difficult; consider taking a ferry from the city side of the river. ✉ *Dockepiren, Eriksberg* ☎ *031/519555* ☖ *Reservations essential* ⋔ *Jacket and tie* ☰ *AE, DC, MC, V* ☽ *Main dining hall closed Sun.*

$$–$$$ ✕ **Fiskekrogen.** The Fish Inn has more than 30 fish and seafood dishes from which to choose. Lunches are particularly good value, and ideal if you're coming from the Stadsmuseet across the canal. ✉ *Lilla Torget 1, Centrum* ☎ *031/101005* ☰ *AE, DC, MC, V* ☽ *Closed Sun.*

$$–$$$ ✕ **Palace.** In the center of Brunnsparken, the Palace is one of Göteborg's most popular summer spots for eating, dancing, and drinking. Live

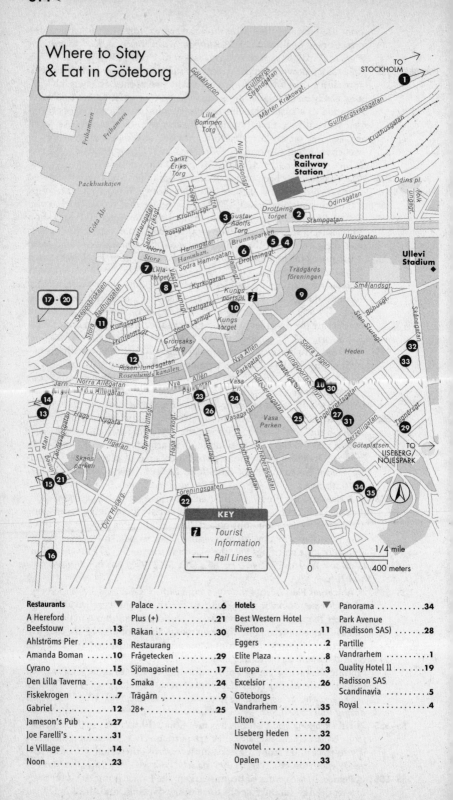

Where to Stay & Eat in Göteborg

KEY

𝑖 Tourist Information

↔ Rail Lines

0 — 1/4 mile

0 — 400 meters

Restaurants ▼

A Hereford Beefstouw	13
Ahlströms Pier	18
Amanda Boman	10
Cyrano	15
Den Lilla Taverna	16
Fiskekrogen	7
Gabriel	12
Jameson's Pub	27
Joe Farelli's	31
Le Village	14
Noon	23
Palace	6
Plus (+)	21
Räkan	30
Restaurang Frågetecken	29
Sjömagasinet	17
Smaka	24
Trägårn	9
28+	25

Hotels ▼

Best Western Hotel Riverton	11
Eggers	2
Elite Plaza	8
Europa	3
Excelsior	26
Göteborgs Vandrarhem	35
Lilton	22
Liseberg Heden	32
Novotel	20
Opalen	33
Panorama	34
Park Avenue (Radisson SAS)	28
Partille Vandrarhem	1
Quality Hotel 11	19
Radisson SAS Scandinavia	5
Royal	4

bands and DJs play the '70s and '80s favorites of the well-dressed forty-somethings who frequent the restaurant and nightclub. The extensive single-malt whiskey collection is known around town: call ahead to arrange a tasting. The menu of mostly traditional Swedish cuisine is extensive. ⊠ *Brunnsparken, Brunnsparken* ☎ 031/807550 ⊟ *AE, DC, MC, V* ☺ *Closed Sun.*

$$ ✕ **Plus (+).** This atmospheric and relaxing restaurant recalls the Sweden of the past. It's inside a beautiful early-1900s ramshackle wooden house whose foundations are attached to the original rock on which the city was built. (As you travel through town, you may see some of this rock poking up through the modern sidewalks and streets.) Eat well-prepared fish and meat dishes with a varied international flavor at polished wood tables, all the while sitting beneath antique chandeliers. ⊠ *Linnég. 32, Linnéstaden* ☎ 031/240890 ⊟ *AE, DC, MC, V.*

$–$$ ✕ **Cyrano.** A little piece of southern France in Sweden, this superb, au-
FodorśChoice thentically Provençal bistro is an absolute must. Inside, the tables are
★ crammed close together, French art hangs on the walls, and French touches extend throughout. Highlights include a sumptuously creamy fish soup, sardines with garlic, and grass-fed lamb with tomatoes and sweet peppers. Laid back and friendly, with helpful service, Cyrano continues to draw in the trendier citizens of Göteborg. ⊠ *Prinsg. 7, Linnéstaden* ☎ 031/143110 ⊟ *AE, DC, MC, V.*

$–$$ ✕ **Joe Farelli's.** Dimly lighted, with booths along the walls and black-and-white photographs of the Big Apple, Joe Farelli's is as close to a New York restaurant as you'll get in Göteborg. Very central, on Avenyn, it's a good place to stop for a dish of pasta or a burger in between sights. ⊠ *Kungsportsavenyn 12, Centrum* ☎ 031/105826 ⊟ *AE, MC, V.*

$–$$ ✕ **Restaurang Frågetecken.** With a name that translates to "Restaurant Question Mark," this spot has attracted a good deal of curiosity. It's just about a minute's walk from Götaplatsen, which also makes it popular with locals and visitors alike. Eat in the busy, bright conservatory in summer or in the relaxing interior, which is decorated in neutral colors. If you don't mind the noise and the hectic pace, dine in the open kitchen to watch the chefs carefully preparing their Balkan-influenced food. Anything with duck is delicious but also pricey. Pasta dishes are homey, comforting, and are the cheaper option. ⊠ *Södra Vägen 20, Götaplatsen* ☎ 031/160030 ⌂ *Reservations not accepted* ⊟ *AE, DC, MC, V.*

$–$$ ✕ **Smaka.** Deep-blue walls and ambient music create Smaka's mellow mood, a perfect backdrop for sampling what the chef calls "modernized" Swedish cuisine. Göteborg's younger crowd tends to stay here for a few extra drinks after eating. ⊠ *Vasaplatsen 3, Vasastan* ☎ 031/132247 ⊟ *AE, DC, MC, V.*

¢–$$ ✕ **Jameson's Pub.** On Tuesday night this English pub on Avenyn comes alive to the beat of live blues, R&B, and rock music. There's live entertainment on the weekends as well; check in to find out who's performing. The food, affordable and surprisingly good, is an eclectic mix of traditional Swedish and international favorites. ⊠ *Kungsportsavenyn 32, Centrum* ☎ 031/187770 ⊟ *AE, MC, V.*

$ ✕ **Amanda Boman.** This little restaurant in one corner of the market hall at Kungsportsplats keeps early hours, so unless you eat an afternoon dinner, plan on lunch instead. The cuisine is primarily Swedish, including fish soup and gravlax. ⊠ *Saluhallen, Centrum* ☎ 031/137676 ⊟ *AE, MC, V* ☺ *Closed Sun. No dinner.*

$ ✕ **Den Lilla Taverna.** A very good, lively, and popular place, this Greek restaurant has paper tablecloths and Greek mythological scenes painted on the walls. Live bouzouki music on Wednesday and Saturday evenings gives the place an authentic feel. ⊠ *Oliver Dahlsg. 17, Linnéstaden* ☎*031/ 128805* ⊟ *AE, MC, V.*

$ ✕ **Gabriel.** A buffet of fresh shellfish and the fish dish of the day draw crowds to this restaurant on a balcony above the fish hall. You can watch all the trading as you eat lunch. ⊠ *Feskekörkan, Centrum* ☎ *031/ 139051* ⊟ *AE, DC, MC, V* ⊙ *Closed Sun. and Mon. No dinner.*

Where to Stay

Some hotels close during the winter holidays; call ahead if you expect to travel during that time. All rooms in the hotels reviewed below are equipped with shower or bath unless otherwise noted. Göteborg also has some fine camping sites if you want an alternative to staying in a hotel.

$$$ ▥ **Opalen.** If you are attending an event at the Scandinavium, or if you have children and are heading for the Liseberg Amusement Park, this RESO hotel is ideally located. Rooms are bright and modern. ⊠ *Engelbrektsg. 73, Box 5106, 402 23 Liseberg* ☎ *031/7515300* 🖷 *031/ 7515311* ⊕ *www.scandic-hotels.com* 🖅 *242 rooms* ♨ *Restaurant, sauna, bar, 2 no-smoking floors* ⊟ *AE, DC, MC, V* ⎢⊙⎟ *BP.*

$$$ ▥ **Radisson SAS Scandinavia.** Across Drottningtorget from the central train station, the Radisson SAS is Göteborg's most modern and spectacular international hotel. The attractive atrium lobby has two restaurants: Frascati, which serves international cuisine, and the Atrium piano bar, with a lighter menu. Rooms are large and luxurious and decorated in pastel shades. Hotel guests receive a discount at the health club on the premises. ⊠ *Södra Hamng. 5965, 401 24 Centrum* ☎ *031/7585000* 🖷 *031/7585001* ⊕ *www.radisson.com* 🖅 *349 rooms* ♨ *Restaurant, in-room data ports, minibars, cable TV, indoor pool, health club, hair salon, bar, shops, casino, convention center, travel services, no-smoking rooms* ⊟ *AE, DC, MC, V* ⎢⊙⎟ *BP.*

$$ ▥ **Best Western Hotel Riverton.** Convenient for people arriving in the city by ferry, this hotel is close to the European terminals and overlooks the harbor. Built in 1985, it has a glossy marble floor and reflective ceiling in the lobby. Rooms are decorated with abstract-pattern textiles and whimsical prints. ⊠ *Stora Badhusg. 26, 411 21 Kungshöjd* ☎ *031/7501000* 🖷 *031/7501001* ⊕ *www.bestwestern.com* 🖅 *191 rooms* ♨ *Restaurant, room service, hot tub, sauna, bar, meeting room, free parking, no-smoking rooms* ⊟ *AE, DC, MC, V* ⎢⊙⎟ *BP.*

★ $$ ▥ **Eggers.** Dating from 1859, Best Western's Eggers has more character and charm than any other hotel in the city. It is a minute's walk from the train station and was probably the last port of call in Sweden for many emigrants to the United States. Rooms vary in size, and all are beautifully decorated, often with antiques. A complimentary buffet breakfast is the only meal served. ⊠ *Drottningtorget, Box 323, SE-401 25 Centrum* ☎ *031/806070* 🖷 *031/154243* ⊕ *www.bestwestern.com* 🖅 *65 rooms* ♨ *Cable TV, meeting room, no-smoking rooms* ⊟ *AE, DC, MC, V* ⎢⊙⎟ *BP.*

★ $$ ▥ **Elite Plaza.** A five-minute walk from the central station, the Plaza is FodorsChoice one of the smartest hotels in the city. The palatial building, an architectural attraction in itself, dates from 1889 and has been modernized ★ with care to give it an air of grandeur, quality, and restfulness. All original features have been retained, from the stucco ceilings to the English mosaic floors, and are tastefully matched with modern art and up-to-date guest facilities. Rooms have earth tones and dark-wood furnishings. The hotel restaurant, Swea Hoff, serves delicious international cuisine, Swedish specialties, and seafood, and there is a very well-chosen wine list. ⊠ *Västra Hamng. 3, Box 110 65, 404 22 Centrum* ☎ *031/7204000* 🖷 *031/7204010* 🖅 *143 rooms, 5 suites* ♨ *Restaurant, in-room data* *ports, in-room safes, minibars, gym, bar, pub, convention center, no-smoking rooms* ⊟ *AE, DC, MC, V* ⑩ *BP.*

★ **$$** ⊡ **Europa.** Large and comfortable, this hotel is part of the Nordstan mall complex, very close to the central train station. The rooms are modern, airy, and colorful. Some rooms have data ports; ask for one of these if it's a consideration. Service throughout is efficient and friendly. ⊠ *Köpmansg. 38, 411 06 Nordstan* ☎ *031/7516500* 🖷 *031/7516511* ⊕ *www.scandic-hotels.com* ⇆ *450 rooms, 5 suites* ♨ *Restaurant, cable TV, indoor pool, sauna, convention center, parking, no-smoking floor* ⊟ *AE, DC, MC, V* ⑩ *BP.*

$$ ⊡ **Panorama.** Within reach of all downtown attractions and close to Liseberg, this Best Western hotel is a quiet, relaxing place to stay. The rooms have dark walls in reds and other earth tones, dark-wood floors, large wall mirrors, and fabrics done in light pastel colors. ⊠ *Eklandag. 5153, Box 24037, 400 22 Johanneberg* ☎ *031/7677000* 🖷 *031/7677070* ⊕ *www.bestwestern.com* ⇆ *339 rooms* ♨ *Restaurant, hot tub, sauna, lounge, meeting room, parking, no-smoking floor* ⊟ *AE, DC, MC, V* ⑩ *BP.*

$$ ⊡ **Park Avenue (Radisson SAS).** Though this modern luxury hotel is sorely lacking in character. It has many facilities though, including an SAS check-in counter. The well-equipped rooms are decorated in earth tones and have good views of the city. ⊠ *Kungsportsavenyn 3638, Box 53233, 400 16 Götaplatsen* ☎ *031/7584000* 🖷 *031/7584001* ⊕ *www.radisson.com* ⇆ *318 rooms* ♨ *2 restaurants, in-room data ports, cable TV, bar, gym, meeting room, no-smoking floors* ⊟ *AE, DC, MC, V* ⑩ *BP.*

$$ ⊡ **Quality Hotel 11.** On the water's edge in Eriksberg, Hotel 11 combines the warehouse style of the old waterfront with a modern interior of multitier terraces. Commonly used by large companies for business conferences, the hotel also welcomes families that want to stay across the harbor from downtown Göteborg. The rooms are clean, bright, and modern; some offer panoramic views of the harbor. Next door is Eriksbergshallen, a theater and conference hall that hosts international performances. To get here from the city, follow signs to Norra Älvstranden. ⊠ *Masking. 11, 417 64 Eriksberg* ☎ *031/7791111* 🖷 *031/7791110* ⊕ *www.hotel11.se* ⇆ *184 rooms, 8 suites* ♨ *Restaurant, in-room data ports, sauna, bar, meeting room, no-smoking rooms* ⊟ *AE, DC, MC, V* ⑩ *BP.*

$ ⊡ **Excelsior.** Although a little worn around the edges, this stylish 1880 building on a road of classic Göteborg houses is the place to stay to get some character and history. The Excelsior has been in operation since 1930, and its guest rooms are full of homey comfort and faded grandeur. Greta Garbo and Ingrid Bergman both stayed here, and more recently, so did musician Sheryl Crow. Classic suites—Garbo's was number 535—with splendid 19th-century style cost no more than ordinary rooms. ⊠ *Karl Gustavsg. 7, 411 25 Vasastan* ☎ *031/175435* 🖷 *031/175439* ⊕ *www.hotelexcelsior.nu* ⇆ *64 rooms, 3 suites* ♨ *Restaurant, cable TV, bar, no-smoking room* ⊟ *AE, DC, MC, V* ⑩ *BP.*

$ ⊡ **Liseberg Heden.** Not far from the famous Liseberg Amusement Park, Liseberg Heden is a popular family hotel in the Sweden Hotels chain. Each of the modern rooms has light-color walls, a satellite television, a minibar, and a large desk, and most have wood floors. Perks include a sauna and a very good restaurant. ⊠ *Sten Stureg., 411 38 Liseberg* ☎ *031/7506900* 🖷 *031/7506930* ⇆ *182 rooms* ♨ *Restaurant, minibars, sauna, meeting room, no-smoking rooms* ⊟ *AE, DC, MC, V* ⑩ *BP.*

$ ⊡ **Novotel.** The redbrick industrial-age architecture of this old brewery belies a mishmash of architectural styles inside. Situated just west of the city on the Göta Älv, the top floors afford spectacular views of Göteborg. There's a very big central atrium, complete with obligatory fake foliage, with an expensive restaurant, Carnegie Kay, attached. ✉ *Klippan 1, 414 51 Majorna* ☎ *031/149000* 🖷 *031/422232* ⊕ *www.novotel. se* ➪ *148 rooms, 5 suites* ⚖ *Restaurant, in-room data ports, cable TV, sauna, bar, free parking, no-smoking rooms* ▤ *AE, DC, MC, V* ❙❍❙ *BP.*

$
Fodor's Choice
★

🏨 **Royal.** Göteborg's oldest hotel, built in 1852, is small, family owned, and traditional. Rooms, most with parquet floors, are individually decorated with reproductions of elegant Swedish traditional furniture. The Royal is in the city center a few blocks from the central train station. ✉ *Drottningg. 67, 411 07 Centrum* ☎ *031/7001170* 🖷 *031/7001179* ⊕ *www.hotel-royal.com* ➪ *82 rooms* ⚖ *Breakfast room, no-smoking floor* ▤ *AE, DC, MC, V* ❙❍❙ *BP.*

¢

🏨 **Göteborgs Vandrarhem.** This hostel is 5 km (3 mi) from the train station in a modern apartment block. Rooms are contemporary, with Swedish-designed furnishings. Breakfast (SKr 50) is not included in the rates, which are per person in a shared apartment. ✉ *Mölndalsv. 23, 412 63 Liseberg* ☎ *031/401050* 🖷 *031/401151* ➪ *150 beds, 4- to 6-bed apartments* ▤ *MC, V.*

¢

🏨 **Lilton.** This unobtrusive bed-and-breakfast-style hotel is inside a small, ivy-covered brick building. Rooms are simple and comfortable, the service friendly and unfussy. ✉ *Föreningsg. 9, 411 27 Vasastan* ☎ *031/828808* 🖷 *031/822184* ➪ *14 rooms* ⚖ *Breakfast room; no smoking* ▤ *AE, MC, V* ❙❍❙ *CP.*

¢

🏨 **Partille Vandrarhem.** This hostel is in a pleasant old house 15 km (9 mi) outside the city, next to a lake for swimming. Rooms have harmonious light- and dark-blue fabrics, simple wood furniture, and rich watercolors of local scenes. You can order meals or prepare them yourself in the guest kitchen. Room rates are per person based on two or more people sharing a room. ✉ *Landvetterv., 433 24, Partille* ☎ *031/446501* 🖷 *031/446163* ➪ *120 beds, 2- to 4-bed rooms* ▤ *No credit cards.*

Nightlife & the Arts

Music, Opera & Theater

Home of the highly acclaimed Göteborg Symphony Orchestra, **Konserthuset** (✉ Götaplatsen, Götaplatsen ☎ 031/7265300) has a mural by Sweden's Prince Eugen in the lobby, original decor, and Swedish-designed furniture from 1935. **Operan** (✉ Christina Nilssons Gata, Packhuskajen ☎ 031/108000), where Göteborg's opera company performs, incorporates a 1,250-seat auditorium with a glassed-in dining area overlooking the harbor. **Stadsteatern** (✉ Johannebergsg. 1, Götaplatsen ☎ 031/615050 tickets, 031/615100 information) puts on high-quality productions of classics by Shakespeare, Molière, Ibsen, and other playwrights. Most of its plays are performed in Swedish.

Nightlife

BARS   As its name implies, **The Dubliner** (✉ Östra Hamng. 50, Inom Vallgraven ☎ 031/139020) is a brave attempt at re-creating what the locals imagine to be old Irish charm. If you're looking for an urbane bar, try **Nivå** (✉ Kungsportsavenyn 9, Centrum ☎ 031/7018090), a popular bar with a stylish tile interior and a crowd to match. **Avenyn 10** (✉ Kungsportsavenyn 10, Centrum ☎ 031/137565) attracts a very young, very loud crowd. **Napoleon** (✉ Vasag. 11, Vasastan ☎ 031/137550) is a dark, mellow hangout crowded with oddities. Even the exterior walls are covered in paintings.

DISCOS &   One of the city's liveliest haunts is **Trädgårn** (✉ Nya Allén, Centrum ☎ 031/
CABARET   102080), a complex of five bars, a disco, and show bands housed in a strange building resembling a half-built sauna. **Bubbles Nightclub** (✉ Kungsportsavenyn 8, Centrum ☎ 031/105820) is big and brash, mainly attracting people in their thirties. Chrome, mirrors, and a white-

tile ceiling like those found in offices make this a memorable place for a drink. At **Rondo** (⊠ Örgrytev. 5, Liseberg ☎ 031/400200) you can dance the night away on Sweden's largest dance floor while surrounded by people of all ages. The crowd is always friendly, and there's a live band. The **Cabaret Lorensberg** (⊠ Park Avenue Hotel [Radisson SAS], Kungsportsavenyn 36, Centrum ☎ 031/206058) plays traditional and contemporary music and has song and dance performances by gifted artists.

FILM As in all Swedish cinemas, the ones in Göteborg show mostly English-language films. The films are subtitled, never dubbed. The strangest movie theater in town is **Bio Palatset** (⊠ Kungstorget, Centrum ☎ 031/174500), a converted meat market turned into a 10-screen cinema. The walls are in various clashing fruit colors, and the floodlighted foyer has sections scooped out to reveal Göteborg's natural rock. **Hagabion** (⊠ Linnég. 21, Linnéstaden ☎ 031/428810) is a good art-house cinema housed in an old ivy-covered school.

JAZZ CLUBS Modern jazz enthusiasts usually head for **Nefertiti** (⊠ Hvitfeldtsplatsen 6, Centrum ☎ 031/7111533), the trendy, shadowy club where the line to get in is always long. Performers at **Jazzhuset** (⊠ Eric Dahlbergsg. 3, Vasastan ☎ 031/133544) tend to play traditional, swing, and Dixieland jazz.

Sports & the Outdoors

Beaches
There are several excellent local beaches. The two most popular—though they're rarely crowded—are Askim and Näset. To reach Askim, take the Express Blå bus from the central station bus terminal. It's a 10-km (6-mi) journey south of the city center. For Näset catch Bus 19 from Brunnsparken for the 11-km (7-mi) journey southwest of Göteborg.

Diving
The water on the west coast of Sweden, although colder than that on the east coast, is a lot clearer: it's great for diving around rocks and wrecks. Wrap up warmly and bring your diving certificate. Among the many companies offering diving is **Aqua Divers** (⊠ Kungsg. 4 ☎ 031/220030).

Fishing
Mackerel fishing is popular here. The **M.S. Daisy** (☎ 031/963018), which leaves from Hjuvik on the Hisingen side of the Göta River, takes expeditions into the archipelago. With plenty of salmon, perch, and pike, the rivers and lakes in the area have much to offer. For details call Göteborg's **Sportfiskarnas fishing information line** (☎ 031/7730700).

Indoor Swimming
Vatten Palatset (⊠ Häradsvägen 3, Lerum ☎ 0302/17020) is a decent indoor pool. As well as regular swimming, this huge complex offers indoor and outdoor adventure pools, water slides, water jets, wave pools, bubble pools, and saunas.

Running
Many running tracks wind their way around Göteborg, but to reach the most beautiful one, hop on Tram 8 at Gamelstadstorget and take it to Angered Centrum. Here the **Angered and Lärjeåns Dalgång** winds its way through 8 km (5 mi) of leafy forests and undulating pastures.

Shopping

Department Stores
Åhléns (☎ 031/3334000) is in the Nordstan mall. Try the local branch of **NK** (⊠ Östra Hamng. 42, Centrum ☎ 031/7101000) for men's and women's fashions and excellent household goods.

Food Markets

There are several large food markets in the city area, but the most impressive is **Salluhallen** (⊠ Kungsgtorget, Centrum). Built in 1889, the barrel-roof, wrought-iron, glass, and brick building stands like a monument to industrial architecture. Everything is available here, from fish, meat, and bakery products to deli foods, herbs and spices, coffee, cheese, and even just people-watching.

Specialty Stores

ANTIQUES **Antikhallarna** (Antiques Halls; ⊠ Västra Hamng. 6, Centrum ☎ 031/7741525) has one of Scandinavia's largest antiques selections. Sweden's leading auction house, **Bukowskis** (⊠ Kungsportsavenyn 43, Centrum ☎ 031/200360), is on Avenyn. For a memorable antiques-buying experience, check out **Göteborgs Auktionsverk** (⊠ Tredje Långg. 9, Linnéstaden ☎ 031/7047700). There's a large amount of very good silver, porcelain, and jewelry hidden among the more trashy items. Viewings on Friday 10–2, Saturday 10–noon, and Sunday 11–noon precede the auctions on Saturday and Sunday starting at noon.

CRAFTS Excellent examples of local arts and crafts can be bought at **Bohusslöjden** (⊠ Kungsportsavenyn 25, Centrum ☎ 031/160072). If you are looking to buy Swedish arts and crafts and glassware, visit the various shops in **Kronhusbodarna** (⊠ Kronhusg. 1D, Nordstan ☎ 031/7110832). As they have since the 18th century, the sheds and stalls at **Crown House** (⊠ Postg. 6–8, Nordstan) sell traditional, handcrafted quality goods, including silver and gold jewelry, watches, and handblown glass.

MEN'S CLOTHING The fashions at **Gillblads** (⊠ Kungsg. 44, Centrum ☎ 031/108846) suit a young and trendy customer. **Ströms** (⊠ Kungsg. 27–29, Centrum ☎ 031/177100) has occupied its street-corner location for two generations, offering clothing of high quality and good taste.

WOMEN'S CLOTHING **Gillblads** (⊠ Kungsg. 44, Centrum ☎ 031/108846) has the most current fashions. **H & M** (Hennes & Mauritz; ⊠ Kungsg. 5557, Centrum ☎ 031/77118262) sells clothes roughly comparable to the choices at flashier Old Navy or Marks & Spencer. **Ströms** (⊠ Kungsg. 27–29, Centrum ☎ 031/177100) offers clothing of high quality and mildly conservative style.

Göteborg A to Z

AIR TRAVEL TO & FROM GÖTEBORG

CARRIERS Among the airlines operating to and from Göteborg are Air Botnia, Air France, British Airways, City Airline, Finnair, KLM, Lufthansa, Malmö Aviation, SAS, SN Brussels Airlines, Sterling, Swiss, and Wideroøe.
⚑ **Air Botnia** ☎ 031/7942020. **Air France** ☎ 031/946505. **British Airways** ☎ 020/781144. **City Airline** ☎ 0200/250500. **Finnair** ☎ 031/131621. **KLM** ☎ 031/942820.

Lufthansa ☎ 031/7942020. **Malmö Aviation** ☎ 020/550010. **SAS** ☎ 020/727727, 08/7972688 from abroad. **SN Brussels Airlines** ☎ 08/58536547. **Sterling** ☎ 08/58769148. **Swiss** ☎ 031/7278132. **Wideroøe** ☎ 031/7942020.

AIRPORTS & TRANSFERS

Landvetter Airport is approximately 26 km (16 mi) from the city.
⚑ **Landvetter Airport** ☎ 031/941100 ⊕ www.lfv.se.

AIRPORT TRANSFERS Landvetter is linked to Göteborg by freeway. Buses leave Landvetter every 15–30 minutes and arrive 30 minutes later at Nils Ericsonsplatsen by the central train station, with stops at Lisebergsstationen, Korsvägen, the Radisson SAS, and Kungsportsplatsen; weekend schedules include some nonstop departures. The price of the trip is SKr 60. For more information call Flygbussarna.

The taxi ride to the city center should cost no more than SKr 310. A shared limousine to the city costs SKr 295.

ℹ Taxi Göteborg ☎ 031/650000. **Scandinavian Limousine** ☎ 031/7942424.

Flygbussarna ☎ 031/272727.

BOAT & FERRY TRAVEL

Traveling the entire length of the Göta Canal by passenger boat to Stockholm takes between four and six days. For details contact the AB Göta Kanalbolaget or Rederi AB Göta Kanal.

ℹ AB Göta Kanalbolaget ☎ 0141/202050 🌐 www.gotakanal.se. **Rederi AB Göta Kanal** ✉ Pusterviksgatan 13, 413 01 Göteborg ☎ 031/806315 🌐 www.gotacanal.se.

BUS TRAVEL TO & FROM GÖTEBORG

All buses arrive in the central city area, in the bus station next to the central train station. The principal bus company is Swebus.

ℹ Swebus ✉ ☎ 031/103800.

CAR RENTAL

Avis, Hertz, and Europcar have offices at the airport and the central railway station. Avis has an office in town also.

ℹ Major Agencies Avis ☎ 031/946030 at airport, 031/805780 at central railway station. **Europcar** ☎ 031/947100. **Hertz** ☎ 031/946020.

CAR TRAVEL

Göteborg is reached by car either via the E20 or the E4 highway from Stockholm (495 km [307 mi]) and the east, or on the E6/E20 coastal highway from the south (Malmö is 290 km [180 mi] away). Markings are excellent, and roads are well sanded and plowed in winter.

CONSULATES

ℹ United Kingdom ✉ S. Hamngatan 23, Centrum ☎ 031/3393300.

EMERGENCIES

Dial 112 for emergencies anywhere in the country, or dial the emergency services number listed below day or night for information on medical services. Emergencies are handled by the Mölndalssjukhuset, Östra Sjukhuset, and Sahlgrenska hospitals. There is a private medical service at CityAkuten weekdays 8–6. There is a 24-hour children's emergency service at Östra Sjukhuset as well.

The national dental-service emergency number and the private dental-service number are listed below. The national service is available 8–8 on weekdays and the private service weekdays between 8 and 5; for after-hours emergencies contact a hospital.

ℹ Doctors & Dentists Folktandvården Dental-Service Emergencies ☎ 031/807800. **Tandakuten Private Dental Services** ☎ 031/800500.

ℹ Emergency Services Medical Services Information (SOS Alarm) ☎ 031/7031500.

ℹ Hospitals After-hours emergencies ☎ 031/7031500. **CityAkuten** ✉ Drottningg. 45, Centrum ☎ 031/101010. **Mölndalssjukhuset** ☎ 031/3431000. **Östra Sjukhuset** ☎ 031/3434000. **Sahlgrenska Hospital** ☎ 031/3421000.

ℹ 24-Hour Pharmacies Vasen ✉ Götg. 12, in Nordstan shopping mall, Nordstan ☎ 031/802053.

ENGLISH-LANGUAGE MEDIA

BOOKS Nearly all bookshops stock English-language books. The broadest selection is at Akademibokhandeln.

ℹ Bookstores Akademibokhandeln ✉ Postgatan 26–32, Nordstan ☎ 031/150284 ✉ Norra Hamngatan 26, Nordstan ☎ 031/617030.

TAXIS

Taxi Göteborg is the main local taxi company.

🔝 **Taxi Göteborg** ☎ 031/650000.

TOURS

BOAT TOURS For a view of the city from the water and an expert commentary on its sights and history in English and German, take one of the Paddan sightseeing boats. *Paddan* is Swedish for "toad," an apt commentary on the vessels' squat appearance. The boats pass under 20 bridges and take in both the canals and part of the Göta River.

🔝 **Paddan** ✉ Kungsportsplatsen, Centrum ☎ 031/609670 ⛴ SKr 85.

BUS TOURS A 90-minute bus tour and a two-hour combination boat-and-bus tour of the chief points of interest leave from outside the main tourist office at Kungsportsplatsen every day from mid-May through August and on Saturday in April, September, and October. Call the tourist office for schedules.

TRAIN TRAVEL

There is regular service from Stockholm to Göteborg, which takes a little over 4½ hours, as well as frequent high-speed (X2000) train service, which takes about three hours. All trains arrive at the central train station in Drottningtorget, downtown Göteborg. For schedules call SJ, the Swedish national rail company. Streetcars and buses leave from here for the suburbs, but the hub for all streetcar traffic is a block down Norra Hamngatan, at Brunnsparken.

🔝 **SJ** ☎ 0771/757575 🌐 www.sj.se.

TRANSPORTATION AROUND GÖTEBORG

Stadstrafiken is the name of Göteborg's excellent transit service. Transit brochures, which are available in English, explain the various discount passes and procedures; you can pick one up at a TidPunkten office.

The best bet for the tourist is the Göteborg Pass, which covers free use of public transport, various sightseeing trips, and admission to Liseberg and local museums, among other benefits. The card costs SKr 175 for one day and SKr 295 for two days; there are lower rates for children younger than 18 years. You can buy the Göteborg Pass as well as regular tram and bus passes at Pressbyrån shops, camping sites, and the tourist information offices.

🔝 **TidPunkten** ✉ Drottningtorget, Brunnsparken, and Nils Ericsonsplatsen, Centrum ☎ 0771/414300.

TRAVEL AGENCIES

See the *Yellow Pages* under "Resor-Resebyråer."

🔝 **Local Agent Referrals Ticket Travel Agency** ✉ Östra Hamng. 35, Centrum ☎ 031/176860. **Carlson Wagonlit Travel** ✉ Kronhusg. 7, Nordstan ☎ 031/7563700

VISITOR INFORMATION

The main tourist office is Göteborg's Turistbyrå. There are also offices at the Nordstan shopping center and in front of the central train station at Drottningtorget.

A free English-language newspaper called *Metro* is available during the summer; you can pick it up at tourist offices, shopping centers, and some restaurants, as well as on the streetcars.

The Friday edition of the principal morning newspaper, *Göteborgs Posten,* includes a weekend supplement with entertainment listings—it's in Swedish but is reasonably easy to decipher.

Göteborg's Turistbyrå's Web site has a good events calendar.

The Göteborg Pass, available from the Göteborg tourist office, and on their Web site, offers discounts and savings for sights, restaurants, hotels, and other services around the city.

🛈 **Tourist Information** **Göteborg's Turistbyrå** ✉ Kungsportsplatsen 2, 411 10 Göteborg ☎ 031/612500 📠 031/612501 ⊕ www.goteborg.com. **Nordstan shopping center** ✉ Nordstadstorget, 411 05 Göteborg ☎ 031/612500.

WHERE TO STAY

CAMPING Göteborg has several fine camping sites.

🛈 **Uddevalla** ☎ 0522/644117 Hafstens Camping. **Göteborg** ☎ 031/840200 Kärralund 📠 031/840500. **Askim** ☎ 031/286261 Askim Strand 📠 031/681335.

BOHUSLÄN

The Bohuslän coastal region north of Göteborg, with its indented, rocky coastline, provides a foretaste of Norway's fjords farther north. It was from these rocky, rugged shores that the 9th- and 10th-century Vikings sailed southward on their epic voyages. Today, small towns and attractive fishing villages nestle among the distinctively rounded granite rocks and the thousands of skerries (rocky isles or reefs) and larger islands that form Sweden's western archipelago. The ideal way to explore the area is by drifting slowly north of Göteborg, taking full advantage of the uncluttered beaches and small rustic fishing villages. Painters and sailors haunt the region in summer.

Kungälv

▶ ❶ *15 km (9 mi) north of Göteborg.*

The trip from Göteborg takes you first along the Göta Älv, a wide waterway that 10,000 years ago, when the ice cap melted, was a great fjord. Some 30 minutes into the voyage the boat passes below a rocky escarpment, topped by the remains of **Bohus Fästning** (Bohus Castle), distinguished by two round towers known as Father's Hat and Mother's Bonnet. It dates from the 14th century and was once the mightiest fortress in western Scandinavia, commanding the confluence of the Göta Älv and Nordre Älv rivers. It was strengthened and enlarged in the 16th century and successfully survived 14 sieges. From 1678 onward, the castle began to lose its strategic and military importance; it fell into decay until 1838, when King Karl XIV passed by on a river journey, admired the old fortress, and ordered its preservation.

Just north of Kungälv along the Trollhätte Canal stretch is the quiet village of **Lödöse,** once a major trading settlement and a predecessor of Göteborg. From here, the countryside becomes wilder, with pines and oaks clustered thickly on either bank between cliffs of lichen-covered granite.

Though today it is something of a bedroom community for Göteborg, Kungälv was an important battleground in ancient times, strategically placed at the confluence of the two arms of the Göta River. The town's several historic sights include a white wooden church, dating from 1679, with an unusual baroque interior. Narrow cobbled streets are full of ancient, leaning, wooden houses.

For a sense of Kungälv's military past, visit the ruins of **Bohus Fästning,** a fortress built by the Norwegians in 1308; it was the site of many battles between Swedish, Norwegian, and Danish armies. ✉ *Kungälv* ☎ *0303/99200* 💰 *SKr 25* ⊙ *Apr., weekends 11–5; May–Aug., daily 10–7; Sept., daily 11–5.*

Sports & the Outdoors

The tiny village of Rönang, on the island of Tjörn, offers excellent **deep-sea fishing**; mackerel and cod are among the prized catches. There are several companies that can take you out, usually in a boat that holds 12 people. One of the best outfitters is **Havsfiske med Hajen** (✉ Hamnen, Marstrand ☎ 0304/672447). Prices range between SKr 100 and SKr 380, depending on how far you go out. All equipment and tackle is included in the price, and you can keep whatever you catch. Most boats leave twice daily. To get to Tjörn, drive over the road bridge from Stenungsund, just north of Kungälv on the E6.

Marstrand

❷ *17 km (11 mi) west of Kungälv (via Route 168).*

Unusually high stocks of herring used to swim in the waters around Marstrand, which is on an island of the same name. The fish made the town extremely rich. But after the money came greed and corruption: in the 16th century Marstrand became known as the most immoral town in Scandinavia, a reputation that reached its lowest point with the murder of a town cleric in 1586. Soon after this the town burned down and the fish disappeared. As Göteborg and Kungälv became major trade centers, in the early 19th century, Marstrand turned to tourism. By 1820 all the town's wooden herring-salting houses had been turned into fashionable and lucrative bathhouses, and people still come to dip into the clear, blue waters and swim, sail, and fish.

Marstrand's main draw is **Carlstens Fästning,** the huge stone-wall castle that stands on the rock above the town. Tours of Carlstens Fortress are not completely in English, but most guides are more than willing to translate. The tours include a morbidly fascinating look at the castle's prison cells, where you can see drawings done in blood and hear tales of Carlstens's most famous prisoner, Lasse-Maja—he dressed up as a woman to seduce and then rob local farmers. ☎ 0303/60265 ✍ SKr 60 ☉ *June–mid-Aug., daily 11–6; mid-Aug.–end of Aug., daily noon–4; Sept.–May, weekends 11–4.*

Where to Stay & Eat

$$ ✕▦ **Grand Hotell Marstrand.** History and luxury abound in this tile-roof hotel, which resembles a French château. Large balconies and verandas open onto a small park, beyond which lies the North Sea. Inside, the hotel is stylishly simple, with bold colors and clean Scandinavian furniture. The rooms are equally light and airy, and the bathrooms have white tiles and brass fittings. A windowed sauna in one of the towers looks out over the harbor. The traditional restaurant ($$) serves excellent local seafood specialties: the garlic-marinated langoustine is a standout. ✉ *Rådhusg. 2, 440 30* ☎ *0303/60322* 🖷 *0303/60053* 🌐 *www.grandmarstrand.se* ➴ *22 rooms, 6 suites* ♨ *Restaurant, sauna, bar, convention center* ⊟ *AE, DC, MC, V* ⧌ *BP.*

$ ▦ **Hotell Nautic.** This basic but good hotel is right on the harbor. The rooms are quite plain but functional, with wood floors and a small desk and chair. The building is a classic white-clapboard construction. ✉ *Långg. 6, 440 35* ☎ *0303/61030* 🖷 *0303/61200* ➴ *29 rooms with shower* ⊟ *AE, DC, MC, V* ⧌ *BP.*

Nightlife

Among the usual peppering of provincial drinking places, **Oscars** (✉ Hamng. 11 ☎ 0303/61554) stands out as one of the best. Sweden's first disco (1964) has retained its silver-and-wood glamour and serves up good music on weekends and great beer all the time.

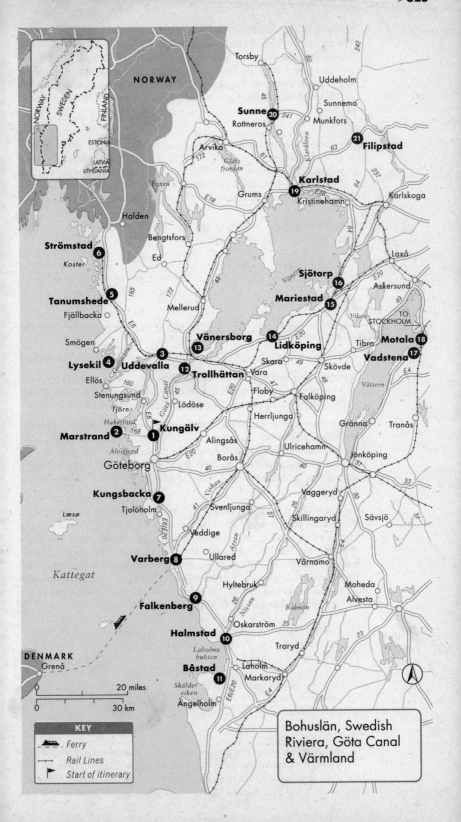

Bohuslän, Swedish Riviera, Göta Canal & Värmland

Sports & the Outdoors

The coastline around Marstrand looks most beautiful from the water. **Franckes Marina** (⊠ Södra Strandg. ☎ 0303/61584 ⊕ www.franckes.se) will rent you a boat, complete with captain, for cocktails, sightseeing, and fishing. It costs about SKr 1,500 for a two-hour excursion and SKr 650 for each additional hour. Fishing equipment is available for SKr 75 per person.

Shopping

The center of Marstrand is full of ancient cobbled streets, pastel-painted wooden houses, and arts-and-crafts shops selling locally inspired paintings, handicrafts, and ceramics. Worth a visit is **Mary Carlsson** (⊠ Kungsg. 2–4 ☎ 0303/60459). Else Langkilde of **Konstnärsateljé Langkilde** (⊠ Myren 29 ☎ 070/3965131 or 0303/60144) paints intriguingly with vivid colors.

off the beaten path

GULLHOLMEN – A frequent ferry from Ellös, on the island of Orust, will take you on the short ride to the windswept, rugged cliff tops of the small island of Gullholmen. In its 13th-century fishing village, tiny, red-painted wooden houses huddle together around a large church. The rest of Gullholmen is set aside as a nature reserve that supports bird life of all kinds. The island of Orust can be reached via Route 160 off E6.

Uddevalla

❸ *64 km (40 mi) north of Kungälv, 79 km (49 mi) north of Göteborg.*

A former shipbuilding town located at the head of a fjord, Uddevalla is best known for a 1657 battle between the Danes and the Swedes. Heavy rains doused the musketeers' tinderboxes, effectively ending hostilities.

The history of the entire Bohuslän region can be seen at the **Bohusläns Museum.** Exhibitions reflect the local culture, countryside, and industries, including, of course, fishing. The museum also traces the history of local inhabitants over the 10,000 years since people first settled this part of Sweden. ⊠ *Museeg. 1* ☎ *0522/656500* ⊠ *Free* ☉ *Mon.–Thurs. 10–8, Fri.–Sun. 10–4.*

Ten thousand years ago receding land ice formed the unique shell banks, the world's largest, just outside Uddevalla. When the 1-km-thick (0.66-mi-thick) ice melted, huge masses of water mixed with saltwater from the sea and left behind fossils from more than 100 species. **Skallbanksmuseet,** the Shell Bank Museum, organizes guided walks in the shell banks every Monday. ⊠ *Kurödsvägen 1* ☎ *0522/656571* ⊠ *Museum free, guided tours SKr 30* ☉ *Apr.–May, weekends 11–5; June–Aug., daily 11–5; Sept., weekends 11–5. Monday tour time varies.*

off the beaten path

GUSTAFSBERG – Adjoining Uddevalla to the west, Gustafberg lays claim to being Sweden's oldest seaside resort, having been mentioned by the botanist Linnaeus in a book he wrote in 1746. There is little left to see of the resort now, save the richly ornamented wooden Society House and a few 18th-century villas, but there is a beautiful little park that leads down to the water's edge, a perfect place for a refreshing swim.

Where to Stay

$ ▦ **Bohusgården.** From its cliff-top location, this modern concrete-block hotel has stunning views of the sea. But even though the rooms are comfortable, they're not that inspiring. The plain, cold, and basic furnishings make them livable but not very welcoming. It is the spa that attracts guests. Pampering treatments include facials, mineral-water baths, massages, and more opulent services. ✉ *Nordens Väg 6, 451 43* ☎ *0522/ 36420* 🖷 *0522/34472* ⊕ *www.bohusgarden.se* ⤷ *97 rooms* ⚒ *Restaurant, pool, spa, bar* ⊟ *AE, DC, MC, V* ⚏ *BP.*

$ ☒ **Carlia.** A hotel by this name has been in Uddevalla for more than 100 years in one form or another. In its latest guise it has large comfortable rooms with furnishings and fabrics that are a touch on the floral side; a homey bar; and a well-equipped reading area with books, newspapers, and periodicals. All the suites have Jacuzzis. ✉ *N. Drottningg. 26, 451 31* ☎ *0522/14140* 🖷 *0522/17081* ⊕ *www.carlia.com* ⤷ *114 rooms, 7 suites* ⚒ *breakfast room, sauna, bar, library* ⊟ *AE, DC, MC, V* ⚏ *BP.*

Lysekil

④ *30 km (19 mi) west of Uddevalla via E6 and Route 161.*

Perched on a peninsula at the head of Gullmarn Fjord, Lysekil has been one of Sweden's most popular summer resorts since the 19th century, when the wealthiest citizens of Sweden would come to take the therapeutic waters. Back then, the small resort was made up mainly of fancy villas painted mustard and brown. Today you can still see the original houses, but among them now are amusement arcades and cotton-candy stalls.

The surrounding coastline has great, rugged walking trails. These trails offer stunning views of the undulating skerries and islets that dot the water below. Guided botanical and marine walks can be organized by the **tourist office** (☎ 0523/13050).

Take any of the many flights of steps that start from Lysekil's main seafront road to get to **Lysekils Kyrka** (Lysekil Church). Probably the town's most impressive landmark, Lysekil Church was carved from the pink granite of the area and has beaten-copper doors. Its windows were painted by Albert Eldh, the early-20th-century artist. ✉ *Stora Kyrkog.*

Havets Hus (House of the Sea) concentrates on the fish and other sea life found in local waters. The giant aquariums contain everything from near-microscopic life-forms to giant cod and even a small but menacing shark. The tour ends with a walk with a stunning view of the fish through a 26-foot glass tunnel. The in-house café has a hole in the floor that looks down into the water above the tunnel. As you sip your coffee, you can watch with amusement as slightly befuddled people wander below you and parents try to stop their children from throwing their cakes in to feed the fish. ✉ *Strandv.* ☎ *0523/19670* 💳 *SKr 10* ⊙ *Daily 10–6.*

Twenty minutes north of Lysekil on Route 162 is **Nordens Ark.** A cut above the usual safari parks, Nordens Ark is a sanctuary for endangered animals. This haven of tranquillity is home to red pandas, lynxes, snow leopards, and arctic foxes. The best way to see the elusive wild animals is to follow the small truck that delivers their food at feeding times. ✉ *Åby Säteri, Hunnebostrand* ☎ *0523/79590* 💳 *SKr 105* ⊙ *Mar.–mid-June, daily 10–5; mid-June–mid-Aug., daily 10–7; mid-Aug.–Oct., daily 10–5; Nov.–Mar., daily 10–4.*

off the beaten path

SMÖGEN – At the very tip of a westerly outcrop of land, Smögen is an ideal point for a quick stop-off. To get here, head north on Route 162 and then west on Route 171 until it stops. The small village's red fishing huts, crystal-blue water, and pretty scrubbed boardwalks appear on many postcards of Bohuslän. Down on the main boardwalk, a stop at the **Bageri Skäret** (⊠ Hamnen 1 ☎ 0523/32317) is a must. As well as having a great ocean view from the upstairs veranda, this small café and bar makes exquisite cakes and bread.

FJÄLLBACKA – Twenty-seven kilometers (16 mi) north of Lysekil, directly along the coast route, is this village with pastel wooden houses nestled in the rock. Fjällbacka, part of an archipelago, was home to actress Ingrid Bergman's summerhouse. In the square named after her, you can see her statue peering out over the water where her ashes were scattered, to the distant island Dannholmen, where her house was. Behind the square is a dramatic ravine known as Kungskliftan (King's Cliff), where, among many others added since, you can find King Oscar II's name, which he etched into the rock in 1887.

Where to Stay & Eat

$–$$ ✕ **Brygghuset.** A short boat ride and a walk through a breathtaking hilltop fishing village on the island of Fiskebäckskil will bring you to this lovely little restaurant. The interior is rustic, with wooden beams and plain wooden tables. Watch the chefs in the open kitchen as they prepare excellent local fish dishes. In the summer there is outdoor eating, or you can just choose a glass of wine from the excellent wine list and watch the boats sail by. The ferry *Carl Wilhelmsson* leaves from outside the tourist office in Lysekil every half hour, bringing you to the restaurant 20 minutes later. ⊠ *Lyckans Slip Fiskebäckskil* ☎ *0523/22222* ⚓ *Reservations essential* ▤ *AE, DC, MC, V.*

$–$$ ✕ **Pråmen.** This modern-looking restaurant has large windows and is propped on legs that allow it to jut out over the water. The view is great; with the windows open you can smell the sea. You can feast on good portions of simply cooked local fish and wash it down with cold beer. ⊠ *Södra Hamng.* ☎ *0523/13452* ▤ *AE, DC, MC, V.*

$ ⬚ **Lysekil Havshotell.** This tall, narrow hotel has great views from atop a cliff. Stripped-wood floors and a miscellany of furnishings and fabrics create relaxed surroundings. Many rooms have sofas and provide bathrobes. Only breakfast is served, and there's a stocked bar (done on the honor system) in each room. For the best view across the water, reserve Room 18, which costs SKr 200 extra. ⊠ *Turistg. 13, 453 30* ☎ *0523/79750* ☒ *0523/14204* ⇗ *15 rooms, 2 suites* ⚒ *Breakfast room, minibars, conference room* ▤ *AE, MC, V* ¶⊙¶ *BP.*

¢ ⬚ **Strand Vandrarhem.** This hostel on the seafront offers simple, friendly accommodations. Unless you stipulate otherwise and pay an additional fee, you may find yourself sharing the room with another guest (the rooms are outfitted with bunk beds). The welcome here is warm, and the breakfast (SKr 50 extra) is excellent. ⊠ *Strandv. 1, 453 30* ☎ *0523/79751* ☒ *0523/12202* ⊕ *www.strandflickorna.se* ⇗ *20 rooms without bath* ⚒ *Breakfast room* ▤ *MC, V.*

Nightlife & the Arts

During July Lysekil comes alive to the sounds of the annual **Lysekil Jazz Festival.** Big-name Swedish, and some international, jazz musicians play in open-air concerts and in bars and restaurants. Contact **Lysekils Turistbyrå** (tourist office; ☎ 0523/13050) for details of events.

Sports & the Outdoors

For a taste of the sea air and a great look at some local nature, take one of the regular seal safaris. Boat trips to view these fascinating, wallowing, slippery mammals leave from the main harbor three times daily between June and August, cost SKr 120, and take about two hours. Details and times are available from **Lysekils Turistbyrå** (☎ 0523/13050).

Tanumshede

5 *45 km (28 mi) north of Lysekil (via Routes 161 and E6).*

From roughly 4000 to 3000 BC, Tanumshede was a coastal settlement. Now it's 5 km (3 mi) from the sea, since sea level is now 50 feet lower than it was then. Although the town itself is not extraordinary, it does hold the largest single collection of **Bronze Age rock carvings** (*hällristningar*) in Europe. People from all over the world flock to this UNESCO World Heritage Site to see the rudimentary scrapings that depict battles, hunting, and fishing.

Most of the carvings are within a short distance of the road, etched onto the weather-worn rocks that were picked up and deposited around the countryside by retreating Ice Age glaciers; the ones that are farther out, carved onto the largest rocks, are best reached by bicycle. Bikes can be rented from **Tanum Strand** (⊠ Tanums Strand Grebbestad ☎ 0525/19000), for SKr 50 per hour or Skr 200 per day.

Heralded for its fantastic architecture, the **Vitlycke Museet** tells the story of the area's famous rock carvings and conveys what life was like between 1500 and 500 BC. It also makes some amusing and seemingly random attempts at decoding the messages held in the stones. ⊠ *Vitlycke 2 Tanumshede* ☎ *0525/20950* ⊠ *SKr 50* ☉ *Apr.–Sept., daily 10–6; Oct.–Mar., by appointment only.*

Strömstad

6 *90 km (56 mi) northwest of Uddevalla, 169 km (105 mi) north of Göteborg.*

This popular Swedish resort claims to have more summer sunshine than any other town north of the Alps. Formerly Norwegian, it has been the site of many battles between warring Danes, Norwegians, and Swedes. A short trip over the Norwegian border takes you to Halden, where Sweden's warrior king, Karl XII, died in 1718.

The **Strömstad Museum,** housed in a beautiful, 18th-century redbrick mansion, has thoughtful, informative displays on the town's history and the importance of fishing as a local industry. Attached to the museum is a good town archive that includes old pictures showing how life was lived here. ⊠ *Södra Hamng. 26* ☎ *0526/10275* ⊠ *SKr 20* ☉ *Mid-June–mid-Aug., Mon. 11–6, Tues.–Fri. 11–4, Sat. 11–2; mid-Aug.–mid-June, weekdays 11–4, Sat. 11–2.*

Although it is of no particular historical importance, **Strömstads Kyrka** is well worth a visit just to marvel at its interior design. The Strömstad Church's seemingly free-form decoration policy throws together wonderfully detailed, crowded frescoes; overly ornate gilt chandeliers; brass lamps from the 1970s; and model ships hanging from the roof. In the graveyard you can find the stone of Adolf Fritiof Cavalli-Holmgren, the eccentric jeweler's son who went on to become a financier and Sweden's richest man for a brief period around 1900. He was responsible for the design of the grand, copper-roof town hall in the middle of Strömstad. He never actually got to see it or to live in its specially created penthouse apartment, since he fell out with the local council over the design. ⊠ *S. Kyrkog. 10* ☎ *0526/10029.*

off the beaten path

KOSTER ISLANDS – There are regular ferryboats from Strömstad to the Koster Islands, Sweden's two most westerly inhabited islands. With no motorized vehicles allowed, the two islands are a perfect place for tranquil bike riding. Bikes can be rented for SKr 50 where you disembark from the boat. Most of the island is a sanctuary for wildlife, so the only sounds you'll hear through the meadows are bird calls. Small, red wooden houses occasionally hold a café or coffee shop. The prawn sandwiches are always superb.

Where to Stay & Eat

$–$$$ ✕ **Göstases.** Somewhat resembling the interior of a wooden boat, this restaurant on the quayside specializes in locally caught fish and seafood. Knots, ropes, life preservers, stuffed fish, and similar paraphernalia abound. But it all pales when you see the low prices for fresh lobster, crab, prawns, and fish, all of which can be washed down with equally affordable cold beer. Sit outside in summer and watch the fishing boats bring in your catch and the pleasure boats float by. ⊠ *Strandpromenaden* ☎ *0526/10812* 🖃 *MC, V.*

$ ✕🏠 **Laholmen.** This huge, sprawling hotel and restaurant offers good-quality food and excellent accommodations on a grand scale. The rooms are a bit garish, with overly vivid color schemes, but they are large and well equipped. The restaurant ($) has a good buffet and an interesting menu of local dishes, including exquisite prawn sandwiches at lunch. The restaurant as well as most guest rooms have views across the pretty harbor and the water beyond, which is scattered with skerries. ⊠ *Laholmen, 452 30* ☎ *0526/197000* 🖨 *0526/10036* ⊕ *www.laholmen.se* 🛏 *150 rooms, 4 suites* ⚘ *Restaurant, bar, lounge, sauna, convention center* 🖃 *AE, DC, MC, V* 🍽 *BP.*

Bohuslän A to Z

BUS TRAVEL
Buses to the region leave from behind the central train station in Göteborg; the main bus company is Västtrafik. The trip to Strömstad takes between two and three hours.
🚍 **Västtrafik** ☎ 0771/414300.

CAR TRAVEL
The best way to explore Bohuslän is by car. The E6 Highway runs the length of the coast from Göteborg north to Strömstad, close to the Norwegian border, and for campers there are numerous well-equipped and uncluttered camping sites along the coast's entire length.

TRAIN TRAVEL
Regular service along the coast connects all the major towns of Bohuslän. The trip from Göteborg to Strömstad takes about two hours, and there are several trains each day. For schedules call SJ.
🚆 **SJ** ⊠ Göteborg ☎ 0771/757575.

VISITOR INFORMATION
🛈 Tourist Information **Göteborg Turistbyrå** ⊠ Kungsportsplatsen 2, 411 10 Göteborg ☎ 031/612500 🖨 031/612501 ⊕ www.goteborg.com. **Kungälv** ⊠ Fästningsholmen ☎ 0303/99200 ⊕ www.kungalv.se/turism. **Kungshamn** ⊠ Hamng. 6 ☎ 0523/665550 ⊕ www.kungshamn.com. **Lysekil** ⊠ Södra Hamng. 6 ☎ 0523/13050. **Marstrand** ⊠ Hamng. ☎ 0303/60087. **Strömstad** ⊠ Torget, Norra Hamnen ☎ 0526/62330 ⊕ www.stromstadtourist.se. **Tanumshede** ⊠ Bygdegårdsplan ☎ 0525/18380. **Uddevalla** ⊠ Kungstorget 4 ☎ 0522/99720 ⊕ www.uddevallaforum.se.

SWEDISH RIVIERA

The coastal region south of Göteborg, Halland—locally dubbed the Swedish Riviera—is the closest that mainland Sweden comes to having a resort area. Fine beaches abound, and there are plenty of sporting activities. But Halland's history is dark, since it was the frontline in the fighting between Swedes and Danes. Evidence of such conflicts can be found in its many medieval villages and fortifications. The region stretches down to Båstad, in the country's southernmost province, Skåne.

Kungsbacka

7 *25 km (15 mi) south of Göteborg.*

This bedroom community of Göteborg holds a market for all sorts of goods on the first Thursday of every month—a 600-year-old tradition.

A break in a high ridge to the west, the **Fjärås Crack,** offers a fine view of the coast. Formed by melting ice 13,000 years ago, the ridge made a perfect transport route for nomadic tribes of 10,000 years ago, who used it to track the retreating ice northward to settle their new communities. Some important archaeological discoveries have been made here, and much of the information learned is on display on signs dotted along the ridge. The signs act as a sort of self-guided outdoor museum, dealing with the geological and anthropological history of the ridge.

FodorsChoice
★

At Tjolöholm, 12 km (7 mi) down the E6/E20 highway from Kungsbacka, is **Tjolöholms Slott** (Tjolöholm Castle), a manor house built by James Dickson, a Scottish merchant and horse breeder. (He was also the grandson of Robert Dickson, the philanthropist and founder of the Swedish East India Trade Company.) The English Tudor–style house, constructed at the beginning of the 20th century, contains many fascinating elements. By and large, they have become a tribute to Dickson's passion for all things modern, including an early version of a pressurized shower and a horse-drawn vacuum cleaner with a very long hose to reach up through the house windows. Dickson died of lead poisoning before the house was completed—he cut his finger while opening a bottle of champagne and wrapped the lead-foil wrapper around the cut. The house he left behind offers much insight into one man's dream. ⊠ *Fjärås* ☎ *0300/ 544200* 🖾 *SKr 60* ☺ *Apr.–mid-June, weekends 11–4; mid-June–Aug., daily 11–4; Sept., weekends 11–4, Oct., Sun. 11–4.*

Near Tjolöholm is the tiny 18th-century village of Äskhult, the site of an open-air museum, the **Äskhults 1700-tals by** (Äskhult's 18th-Century Village). When land reforms forced farmers to combine patches of land into large estates, the four farmers living in Äskhult refused and kept their land separate. This refusal left the village unable to expand while both of the neighboring areas became towns. And so it stayed that way, until the last inhabitants moved away in the mid-19th century. Today you can wander through the houses and farm buildings to get a glimpse of what life was like for 18th-century peasant farmers. ☎ *0300/542159* 🖾 *SKr 25* ☺ *May–Aug., daily 10–6; Sept., weekends 10–6.*

en route

Forty kilometers (25 mi) southeast of Kungsbacka (on E6 and Route 153) is the shopping mecca of **Ullared,** once a single discount store, now a whole town of huge outlet stores and malls visited by 3 million Swedes each year. It's overwhelming, but even the most resolute nonshoppers may find it difficult to resist the selection and the prices.

Varberg

8 *40 km (25 mi) south of Kungsbacka, 65 km (40 mi) south of Göteborg.*

Varberg is a busy port with connections to Grenå, in Denmark. Although the town has some good beaches, it's best known for a suit of medieval clothing preserved in the museum inside the 13th-century

Varbergs Fästning (Varberg Fortress). The suit belonged to a man who was murdered and thrown into a peat bog. The peat preserved his body, and his clothes are the only known suit of ordinary medieval clothing. The museum also contains a silver bullet said to be the one that killed Karl XII. ☎ *0340/18520* ☑ *SKr 40* ☉ *Fortress open yr-round; guided fortress tours June 15–Aug. 9, daily 11–4 every hr on the hr; museum mid-June–mid-Aug., daily 10–6; mid-Aug.–mid-June, weekdays 10–4, weekends noon–4.*

Where to Stay & Eat

$$ ✕ **Societen.** Housed in the cream-and-green carved-wood confection that is the 19th-century Society House, this restaurant presents dining on a grand scale. Two huge, high-windowed dining rooms offer French-influenced dishes such as mussels with eggplant and garlic. There's fox-trot dancing on Friday and live bands and DJs on Saturday. Two separate lively bar areas are on hand if you need to increase your intake of courage before taking to the dance floor. ☒ *Societetsparken* ☎ *0340/ 676500* ♨ *Reservations essential* ☰ *AE, DC, MC, V.*

$$ 🏨 **Kust Hotellet.** A former sanatorium on the beachfront, the grandiose Kust Hotellet stuffs curly pieces of art-nouveau furniture into every room. Guest rooms are a little small but comfortable. There is a large and well-equipped spa and sauna area with hot tubs, a heated seawater pool, a regular pool and a Turkish steam bath. Experienced instructors offer spinning, aerobics, and yoga classes. ☒ *Nils Kreugers Väg 5, 432 24* ☎ *0340/629800* 🖶 *0340/629850* ➷ *106 rooms, 38 suites* ♨ *Restaurant, indoor pool, heath club, sauna, spa, bar* ☰ *AE, DC, MC, V* ⬦ *BP.*

Falkenberg

❾ *30 km (20 mi) south of Varberg, 100 km (60 mi) south of Göteborg.*

With its attractive beaches and the plentiful salmon that swim in the Ätran River, Falkenberg is one of Sweden's most attractive resorts. Its Gamla Stan (Old Town) is full of narrow cobblestone streets and quaint, old wooden houses.

In the middle of Gamla Stan stands the 12th-century **St. Laurentii Kyrka** (St. Laurentii Church). After the construction of a new church at the end of the 19th century, St. Laurentii was deconsecrated and used as a shooting range, a cinema, and a gymnasium, among other things. It was reconsecrated in the 1920s and is now fully restored with its 16th-century font and silver, as well as some awe-inspiring 17th- and 18th-century wall paintings.

Although it does have the usual archaeological and historical artifacts depicting its town's growth and development, the **Falkenberg Museum** also has an unusual and refreshing obsession with the 1950s. The curator here thinks that is the most interesting period of history, and you can make up your own mind once you've learned about the local dance-band scene, visited the interior of a shoe repair shop, and seen a collection of old jukeboxes. ☒ *Skepparesträtet 2* ☎ *0346/86125* ☑ *Free* ☉ *June–Aug., Tues.–Sun. noon–4, Sept.–May, Tues.–Fri. and Sun. noon–4.*

Falkenberg's first movie theater is now home to **Fotomuseum Olympia**, a fascinating display of cameras, camera equipment, and photographs dating to the 1840s. ☒ *Sandg. 13* ☎ *0346/87928* ☑ *SKr 30* ☉ *Mid-June–Aug., Tues.–Thurs. 1–7, Sun. 1–6; Sept.–May, Tues.–Thurs. 5–7, Sun. 2–6.*

When the weather gets hot, what better way to quench that raging thirst than a stroll around a cool brewery, followed by a glass of ice cold beer? At the **Brewery in Falkenberg** groups can do just that. The beer Falcon has been brewed on the premises since 1869, and a tour of the facility takes in both old brewing traditions and modern beer-making technology. The tour ends with dinner and refreshing glasses of the house brew. ✉ *Åstadv.* ☎ *0346/721000 brewery, 0706/977380 to book a group tour* ✇ *Four-hour tour, including dinner and beer tasting, SKr 350 per person in groups of minimum 15* ⊕ *www.alltommalt.se.*

Doktorspromenaden, on the south side of the river in the town center, is a beautiful walk set against a backdrop of heathland and shade trees. The walk was set up in 1861 by a local doctor in an effort to encourage the townsfolk to get more fresh air. ✉ *Doktorspromenaden.*

Where to Stay & Eat

$–$$ ✕ **Restaurant Hertigen.** This beautiful white villa is in wooded grounds on an island just outside the center of town. Dining takes place on a large veranda and garden during the summer. The classic French dishes are prepared with a nod in the direction of local cooking styles. ✉ *Hertings Gård* ☎ *0346/10018* ⌔ *Reservations essential* ▭ *AE, DC, MC, V.*

$$ ▦ **Elite Hotel Strandbaden.** A sprawling, white wood-and-glass building, Elite Hotel Strandbaden sits right on the beach at the south end of town. The rooms here are quite small but well equipped, with amenities and modern, comfortable furnishings. Most have a view of the sea. There is a state-of-the-art spa and health club in the hotel, and a very good restaurant decked out in startling blue and orange. ✉ *Havsbadsallén, 311 42* ☎ *0346/714900* 📠 *0346/16111* ⇥ *135 rooms, 5 suites* ⌔ *Restaurant, brasserie, in-room data ports, minibars, cable TV, health club, sauna, bar* ▭ *AE, DC, MC, V* ⊚ *BP.*

$ ▦ **Grand Hotel Falkenberg.** Not as imposing as the name suggests, this pretty, yellow, 19th-century hotel is comfortable and friendly, with very large rooms. The interior is a jumble of furnishings from the last 30 years, with the odd antique thrown in for good measure. Cherrywood and dark rich fabrics are used throughout. ✉ *Hotellg. 1, 311 31* ☎ *0346/14450* 📠 *0346/14459* ⊕ *www.grandhotelfalkenberg.se* ⇥ *70 rooms, 3 suites* ⌔ *2 restaurants, sauna, 2 bars, lounge* ▭ *AE, DC, MC, V* ⊚ *BP.*

Sports & the Outdoors

BEACHES   A 15-minute walk south from the town center is **Skrea Strand,** a 2-mi stretch of sandy beach. At the northern end of the beach is the huge swimming complex **Klitterbadet** (✉ Klitterv. ☎ 0346/86330 ✇ SKr 35 ⊙ June–Aug., Sun. and Mon. 9–4, Tues. 6 AM–7 PM, Wed. 9–7, Thurs. 6 AM–7 PM, Fri. 9–7, Sat. 9–5; Sept.–May, Mon. 4 PM–8 PM, Tues. 6–9 and noon–8, Wed. noon–8, Thurs. 6–9 and noon–8, Fri. noon–7, Sat. 9–5, Sun. 9–3), with pools (including one just for children), water slides, a sauna, a whirlpool, a 50-meter-long pool with heated seawater, and steam rooms. Farther south the beach opens out onto some secluded coves and grasslands.

FISHING   In the 1800s Falkenberg had some of the best fly-fishing in Europe. This prompted a frenzy of fishermen, including many English aristocrats, to plunder its waters. But despite the overfishing, the Ätran is one of few remaining rivers in Europe inhabited by wild salmon. Fishing permits and rod rentals can be arranged through the local **tourist office** (☎ 0346/86100).

Shopping

Törngrens (✉ Krukmakareg. 4 ☎ 0346/10354 ⊘ Weekdays 9–5) is probably the oldest pottery shop in Scandinavia, and is now owned by the seventh generation of the founding family. Call ahead to make sure the shop is open.

Halmstad

❿ *40 km (25 mi) south of Falkenberg, 143 km (89 mi) south of Göteborg.*

With a population of 55,000, Halmstad is the largest seaside resort on the west coast. The Norre Port town gate, all that remains of the town's original fortifications, dates from 1605. The modern town hall has interior decorations by the so-called Halmstad Group of painters, which formed here in 1929.

Most of Halmstad's architectural highlights are in and around **Stora Torg**, the large town square. In the middle is the fountain *Europa and the Bull*, by the sculptor Carl Milles. Around the square are many buildings and merchants' houses dating from Halmstad's more prosperous days, in the last half of the 19th century.

At the top of Stora Torg is the grand **St. Nikolai Kyrka**, a huge church from the 14th century containing fragments of medieval murals and a 17th-century pulpit.

The **Tropic Centre**, just a few minutes' walk from the center of Halmstad, holds flora and fauna that come from outside Sweden. Tropical plants, birds, snakes, monkeys, spiders, and crocodiles are all safely tucked away behind glass, ready both to amuse and to, perhaps, horrify you. ✉ *Tullhuset, Strandg.* ☎ *035/123333* 🎫 *SKr 60* ⊘ *July, daily 10–6; Aug.–June, daily 10–4.*

No Swedish town would be complete without its local museum, and the **Halmstad Länsmuseet** is more accomplished than most. Everything from archaeological finds to musical instruments to dollhouses is on display. There's also a haunting display of large figureheads taken from ships that sank off the local coastline. ✉ *Tollsg.* ☎ *035/162300* 🎫 *SKr 20* ⊘ *Tues., Thurs., and Sun. noon–4, Wed. noon–9.*

★ The bizarre **Martin Luther Kyrka** is unique among churches. Built entirely out of steel in the 1970s, its exterior resembles that of a shiny tin can. The interior is just as striking, as the gleaming outside gives way to rust-orange steel and art-deco furnishings that contrast with the outside. To some, Martin Luther Church may seem more like a temple to design, not deity. ✉ *Långg.* ☎ *035/151961* ⊘ *Weekdays 9–3, Sun. services at 10.*

In the 1930s the Halmstad Group, made up of six local artists, caused some consternation with their surrealist and cubist painting styles, influenced strongly by artists such as René Magritte and Salvador Dalí. The **Mjellby Konstgård** (Mjellby Arts Center) contains some of the most important works created over the group's 50-year alliance. ✉ *Mjellby (4 km [2½ mi] from Halmstad)* ☎ *035/31619* 🎫 *SKr 40* ⊘ *Hrs vary with exhibits; call for details.*

Where to Stay & Eat

$$–$$$ ✕ **Pio & Co.** Half informal bar and half bistro, this restaurant offers something for all. It's a bright and airy place with good service and excellent Swedish classics on the menu—the steak and mashed potatoes is wonderful. The list of drinks is extensive. ✉ *Storg. 37* ☎ *035/210669* 🚆 *AE, DC, MC, V.*

$$ 🖭 **Scandic Hotel Grand.** A shiny white-tile floor, white ceiling tiles, and a circular podlike lobby create a strange first impression. But don't be alarmed. Rooms here come with all the space, comfort, modernity, and up-to-date technology you would expect from a Scandinavian hotel. ✉ *Rådhusg. 4, 302 43* ☎ *035/2958600* 🖷 *035/2958611* ⬐ *130 rooms, 1 suite* ⚘ *Restaurant, in-room data ports, sauna, spa, bar, convention center* ▭ *AE, DC, MC, V* ⥊ *BP.*

$ 🖭 **Hotel Continental.** Built in 1904 in the national romantic style, the interior of this hotel has been nicely preserved. The sophisticated design includes exposed-brick walls, subtle spotlighting, and light wood fittings. The rooms are bright, modern, and spacious. Five rooms have whirlpool baths. ✉ *Kungsg. 5, 302 45* ☎ *035/176300* 🖷 *035/128604* ⬐ *46 rooms, 3 suites* ⚘ *Bar* ▭ *AE, DC, MC, V* ⥊ *BP.*

Nightlife & the Arts

The nightlife in Halmstad centers around the bars in Storgatan, the main street that runs into Storatorg. **Harry's** (☎ 035/105595) is worth a visit, if only to see its bizarre English phone box with a life-size model of Charlie Chaplin inside. **Pio & Co.** (☎ 035/210669) has a cozy "cognac corner" in the lounge area of the restaurant.

Sports & the Outdoors

There are many good beaches around Halmstad. **Tjuvahålan,** extending west of Halmstad, has an interesting old smugglers' cove that provides pleasant walking. For details contact the **tourist office** (☎ 035/132320).

Båstad

⑪ *35 km (22 mi) south of Halmstad, 178 km (111 mi) south of Göteborg.*

In the southernmost province of Skåne, Båstad is regarded by locals as Sweden's most fashionable resort, where ambassadors and local captains of industry have their summerhouses. Aside from this, it is best known for its tennis. In addition to the **Båstad Open,** a grand prix tournament in late summer, there is the annual **Donald Duck Cup** in July, for children from ages 11 to 15; it was the very first trophy won by Björn Borg, who later took the Wimbledon men's singles title an unprecedented five times in a row. Spurred on by Borg and other Swedish champions, such as Stefan Edberg and Mats Wilander, thousands of youngsters take part in the Donald Duck Cup each year. For details contact the **Svenska Tennisförbundet** (Swedish Tennis Association; ✉ Lidingövägen 75, Stockholm ☎ 08/4504310).

The low-rise shuttered buildings in the center of Båstad give it an almost French provincial feel. In the main square is **St. Maria Kyrka** (St. Maria's Church), which looks much more solidly Swedish. Dating from the 15th century, the plain exterior hides a haven of tranquillity within the cool thick walls. The unusual altar painting depicts Christ on the cross with human skulls and bones strewn beneath him.

Norrviken Gardens, 3 km (2 mi) northwest of Båstad, are beautifully laid out in different styles, including a Japanese garden and a lovely walkway lined with rhododendrons. The creator of the gardens, Rudolf Abelin, is buried on the grounds. A restaurant, shop, and pottery studio are also on the premises. ✉ *Båstad* ☎ *0431/369040* ⊕ *www. norrvikenstradgardar.se* ✆ *May–Aug., SKr 60; Sept.–Apr., free* ⊙ *May–Aug., daily 10–6; Sept.–Apr., daily dawn–dusk.*

Where to Stay & Eat

$$ ✕ **G. Swenson's Krog.** Well worth the 3-km (2-mi) journey out of Båstad, this harbor-front restaurant was originally a fisherman's hut and has been converted into a magnificent dining room with cornflower-blue walls, wooden floors, and a glass roof. The menu is full of Swedish classics such as white asparagus with lemon-butter sauce and the most delicious homemade meatballs. The service is friendly, with the family atmosphere really shining through. ⊠ *Pål Romaresg. 2, Torekov* ☎ *0431/ 364590* ⚙ *Reservations essential* ⊟ *AE, DC, MC, V.*

¢ ✕ **The Wooden Hut.** Actually, this restaurant has no name: it's just a wooden hut on the harbor side. It has no tables either. It has no wine list, no waiters, no interior design, no telephone, and it doesn't accept credit cards. What this restaurant does have is simple and delicious smoked mackerel with potato salad, which will magically take you away from all the pomp and wealth that sometimes bogs Båstad down. Walk past all the hotels and restaurants, smell the fresh sea air, and get ready for a great meal. ⊠ *Strandpromenaden* ☎ *No phone* ⚙ *Reservations not accepted* ⊟ *No credit cards.*

$$ ✕⛐ **Hotel Skansen.** Set in a century-old bathhouse, Skansen's interior reflects the best of modern design. Wonderfully simple earth, cream, and moss green tones create a sense of comfort, simplicity, and relaxation. The rooms are bright, many with glass roof or wall features. Restaurant Sand ($–$$), with a sea view, serves stylish and well-prepared Swedish fare, with fish as a specialty. The bar is well stocked, but the nightclub is nothing special. ⊠ *Kyrkog. 2, 269 21* ☎ *0431/558100* ⛐ *0431/558110* ⊕ *www.hotelskansen.se* ⬦ *112 rooms, 1 suite* ⚙ *Restaurant, sauna, spa, steam room, bar, nightclub* ⊟ *AE, DC, MC, V* ⦿ *BP.*

$ ⛐ **Hjortens Pensionat.** A classic summer resort hotel, Hjortens Pensionat is Båstad's oldest inn. The antiques-filled rooms are light and the common areas cozy. Right in the center of Båstad, the hotel is close to shops, beaches, and tennis courts. ⊠ *Roxmansvägen 23, 269 36* ☎ *0431/ 70109* ⛐ *0431/70180* ⊕ *www.hjorten.net* ⬦ *42 rooms, 37 with bath* ⚙ *Restaurant, bar* ⊟ *DC, MC, V* ⦿ *BP.*

Swedish Riviera A to Z

BUS TRAVEL

Buses to Kungsbacka, Varberg, Falkenberg, Halmstad, and Båstad leave from behind Göteborg's central train station.
🚌 **Hallandstrafiken** ☎ 0346/48600. **Västtrafik** ☎ 0771/414300.

CAR TRAVEL

Simply follow the E6/E20 highway south from Göteborg toward Malmö. It runs parallel to the coast.

TRAIN TRAVEL

Regular train services connect Göteborg's central station with Kungsbacka, Varberg, Falkenberg, Halmstad, and Båstad.
🚆 **SJ** ⊠ Göteborg ☎ 0771/757575.

VISITOR INFORMATION

🚆 Tourist Information **Båstad** ⊠ Stortorget 1 ☎ 0431/75045. **Falkenberg** ⊠ Holgersgatan 9 ☎ 0346/86100. **Halmstad** ⊠ Halmstad Slott ☎ 035/132320. **Kungsbacka** ⊠ Storg. 41 ☎ 0300/834595. **Laholm** ⊠ Rådhuset ☎ 0430/15450. **Varberg** ⊠ Brunnsparken ☎ 0340/88770.

GÖTA CANAL

Stretching 614 km (382 mi) between Stockholm and Göteborg, the Göta Canal is actually a series of interconnected canals, rivers, lakes, and even a stretch of sea. Bishop Hans Brask of Linköping in the 16th century was the first to suggest linking the bodies of water; in 1718 King

Karl XII ordered the canal to be built, but work was abandoned when he was killed in battle the same year. Not until 1810 was the idea again taken up in earnest. The driving force was a Swedish nobleman, Count Baltzar Bogislaus von Platen (1766–1829), and his motive was commercial. Von Platen saw the canal as a way of beating Danish tolls on ships that passed through the Öresund. He also sought to enhance Göteborg's standing by linking the port with Stockholm, on the east coast. At a time when Swedish fortunes were at a low ebb, the canal was also viewed as a way to reestablish faith in the future and boost national morale.

The building of the canal took 22 years and involved 58,000 men. Linking the various stretches of water required 87 km (54 mi) of man-made cuts through soil and rock and building 58 locks, 47 bridges, 27 culverts, and 3 dry docks. Unfortunately, the canal never achieved the financial success that von Platen sought. By 1857 the Danes had removed shipping tolls, and in the following decade the linking of Göteborg with Stockholm by rail effectively ended the canal's commercial potential. The canal has nevertheless come into its own as a modern-day tourist attraction.

You may have trouble conceiving of the canal's industrial origins as your boat drifts lazily down this lovely series of waterways; across the enormous lakes, Vänern and Vättern; and through a microcosm of all that is best about Sweden: abundant fresh air; clear, clean water; pristine nature; well-tended farmland. A bicycle path runs parallel to the canal, offering another means of touring the country. You can bike faster than the boats travel, so it's easy to jump off and on as you please.

Trollhättan

⑫ *70 km (43 mi) north of Göteborg.*

In this pleasant industrial town of about 53,000 inhabitants, a spectacular waterfall was rechanneled in 1906 to become Sweden's first hydroelectric plant. On specific days in the summer the waters are allowed to follow their natural course, a fall of 106 feet in six torrents. This sight is well worth seeing. The other main point of interest is the 82-km-long (51-mi-long) Trollhätte Canal, of which a 10-km (6-mi) stretch runs through the city. The canal's six locks date from 1916. Along the canal are also disused locks from 1800 and 1844, beautiful walking trails, and *The King's Cave,* a rock formation on which visiting monarchs have carved their names since 1754. Trollhättan also has a fine, wide marketplace and waterside parks. The city has become somewhat of a center of the Swedish film industry, earning it the nickname "Trollywood." Lukas Moodyson (*Show Me Love, Together,* and *Lilya 4-Ever*) is just one of the directors who have chosen Trollhättan production studios.

In the summer months the **Trollhättans Turistbyrå** (Tourist Office; ✉ Åkerssjövägen 10 ☎ 0520/488472 ⊕ www.visittrollhattan.se) offers the *Sommarkort* (Summer Pass), with free entrance to the Innovatum, the Innovatum Cableway, Saab Bilmuseum, and the Canal Museum. It costs SKr 100 per day, and accompanying children under 16 are free.

The best way to see the town's spectacular waterfalls and locks is on the **walking trail** that winds its way through the massive system. The walk takes in the hydroelectric power station and the canal museum. Part of the walk is through wooded cliffs that overlook the spectacular cascades of water. The falls flow freely May and June, weekends at 3, and July and August, Wednesday and weekends at 3. In July the falls are also illuminated at 11 PM on Wednesday, Saturday, and Sunday. Details and directions can be found at the tourist office, which will also tell you the best places to watch the waterfall when the waters are allowed to follow their natural course.

The canal and the locks gave Trollhättan its life, and a visit to the **Kanalmuseet** (Canal Museum) tells as full a history of this as you can find. Housed in a redbrick 1893 waterside building, the museum covers the history of the canal and the locks and displays model ships, old tools, and fishing gear. ⊠ *Åkersbergsvägen, Övre Slussen* ☎ *0520/472251* ⊠ *SKr 10* ⊙ *May, weekends noon–5; June–Aug., daily 11–7.*

☺ Kids at the **Innovatum–Kunskapens Hus** (Innovatum–Technology Center) get to touch, examine, and poke at objects illustrating technology, energy, media, design, and industrial history. In the film studio you can edit yourself into contemporary Swedish movies. A big hit are the two robots, Max and Gerda, that spend their days vacuum-cleaning their futuristic apartment. As a reward for their hard work, the staff at Innovatum feeds the robots trash at set times. ⊠ *Åkerssjövägen 10* ☎ *0520/488480* ⊕ *www.innovatum.se* ⊠ *SKr 50* ⊙ *Tues.–Sun. 11–4.*

The **Innovatum Cableway** will take you 400 meters (.25 mi) across the canal at a height of nearly 30 meters (98 feet), with spectacular views of the canal, the town, and the waterfall area. ⊠ *Åkerssjövägen 10* ☎ *0520/488480* ⊠ *SKr 40* ⊙ *June–Aug., daily 10–6.*

The **Saab Bilmuseum** (Saab Car Museum) surveys Saab's automotive output from 1946 to the present. Since the exhibition consists primarily of row upon row of cars, fenced off by rope, there's little here for any but true car enthusiasts. ⊠ *Åkerssjövägen 10* ☎ *0520/84344* ⊠ *SKr 40* ⊙ *Tues.–Fri. 11–4.*

Culture abounds at **Folkets Hus** (People's House), in the pedestrianized downtown area. Part of the building is given over to dramatic, ever-changing displays of contemporary art and art installations. ⊠ *Kungsg. 25* ☎ *0520/422500* ⊠ *Free* ⊙ *Kulturhallen (Culture Hall) at Folkets Hus, Sun.–Mon. noon–4, Tues.–Thurs. noon–7, Sat. 11–2.*

---

en route   Soon after leaving Trollhättan, the Göta Canal takes you past Halleberg and Hunneberg, two flat-top hills that are each more than 500 ft high; the woods surrounding them are extraordinarily rich in elk, legend, and Viking burial mounds. The canal then proceeds through **Karls Grav,** the oldest part of the canal, begun early in the 18th century. It was built to bypass the Ronnum Falls, on the Göta River, which have been harnessed to power a hydroelectric project.

Where to Stay & Eat

¢–$ ✕ **Shangri La.** The large, elegant dining room is decorated in deep brown and gold shades to go with the restaurant's mixed Asian theme. In summer you can sup on the outdoor terrace against a backdrop of humming waterfalls. ⊠ *Storg. 36* ☎ *0520/10222* ⊟ *AC, MC, V.*

¢–$ ✕ **Strandgatan.** This popular, relaxed café is in an 1867 building that once housed canal workers. There's always a good crowd, especially in summer. Locals come to while away the hours over coffee, bagels, home-cooked international cuisine, and beer and wine. ⊠ *Föerningsgatan 1* ☎ *0520/83717* ⊟ *AE, DC, MC, V.*

$ ▥ **Hotel Scandic Swania.** Stunning views over the waterfalls and locks on up to the hills above town are what distinguish this comfortable hotel near Trollhättan's center. Ask for a top-floor room at the front of the hotel and enjoy the sights. If you're up for a party, one of Trollhättan's few clubs is in the basement. ⊠ *Storg. 49, 461 23* ☎ *0520/89000* 🖷 *0520/89001* ⊕ *www.hotel-scandic.com* ↘ *296 rooms, 10 suites*

⑁ *Restaurant, bar, lounge, nightclub, no-smoking rooms* ▤ *AE, DC, MC, V* ⑩ *BP.*

Nightlife

Trollhättan's nightlife mostly revolves around the excellent **KK's Bar & Nightclub** (⊠ Torgg. 3 ☎ 0520/481049), which is always crowded, mostly with those under 25. The bar is comfortable and fun and has a good cocktail selection. On Friday those who are slightly older hit the dance floor.

The Outdoors

Daily boat trips from the center of town take you right into the heart of the lock system and waterfalls. The **MS Strömkarlen** (☎ 0520/32100 ⊠ SKr 162) leaves two times daily (at 10 and 1:30) June 29–August 10.

Vänersborg

⑬ *15 km (9 mi) north of Trollhättan, 85 km (53 mi) north of Göteborg.*

Eventually, the canal enters **Vänern,** Sweden's largest and Europe's third-largest lake: 3,424 square km (1,322 square mi) of water, 145 km (90 mi) long and 81 km (50 mi) wide at one point.

At the southern tip of the lake is Vänersborg, a town of about 30,000 inhabitants that was founded in the mid-17th century. The church and the governor's residence date from the 18th century, but the rest of the town was destroyed by fire in 1834. Vänersborg is distinguished by its fine lakeside park, the trees of which act as a windbreak for the gusts that sweep in from Vänern.

Fans of the esoteric may find the **Vänersborgs Museum** worth a visit. The oldest museum in Sweden outside Stockholm, it has been restored to its 1888 appearance, and as such it has become an unintentional museum of museums. A gloomy apartment in which the museum's janitor once lived is now part of an exhibit—one that preserves the space in all its 1950s glory. The museum's most eccentric collection is one of birds from southwestern Africa—Namibia, Botswana, and Angola. This collection is the most extensive in the world and is the base of an exchange between the museum and the National Museum of Namibia. ⊠ *Östra Plantaget* ☎ *0521/264100* ⊕ *www.alvlanmus.se/museer/vbg/vbgstart.htm* ⊠*SKr 20* ⊙ *June–Aug., Tues.–Thurs. and weekends, noon–4; Sept.–May, Tues., Thurs., and weekends, noon–4.*

A few minutes' walk from the center of town, **Skracklan Park** is a good place to relax. Take a break in the 1930s coffeehouse after walking along the park's promenade. A lake, parkland, and trees are set around the park's centerpiece, a statue of Frida, the muse of a famous local poet named Birger Sjöberg (1885–1929). Frida always has fresh flowers stuffed into her bronze hand.

> **off the beaten path**

HALLEBERG AND HUNNEBERG – Five kilometers (3 mi) east of Vänersborg are the twin plateaus of Halleberg and Hunneberg. Thought to be 500 million years old, these geological wonders are the site of early Viking forts and the resting place of early humans. But they are best known for their stunning natural beauty and the fauna they support: the county's biggest herd of elk. As tradition dictates, the king of Sweden still comes here every October for the royal hunt. To see the animals yourself, head for the walking trail that winds around Halleberg. At dawn or dusk the leggy, long-faced giant elk, inquisitive by nature, will be more than comfortable eating apples from your hand. Whether you'll be so comfortable, once you see the size of them, is another matter. Those less daring can hide behind a guide from the **ÄLGENS BERG & KUNGAJAKTSMUSEUM** (Elk Mountain & Royal Hunt Museum) – ✉ *Vargön* ☎ *0521/277991* 🎫 *Museum SKr 60; private guide 1 hr SKr 795, 30 mins SKr 530* ☉ *May–Aug., daily 10–6; Sept.–Apr., Tues.–Sun. 11–4.*

Where to Stay & Eat

¢–$ ✕ **Pizzeria Roma.** Directly across the road from the hotel Ronnums Herrgård, this small restaurant is perfect for informal meals. The very good and very cheap pizza and pasta served here are worth suffering the somewhat stark and brightly lighted interior. ✉ *Stora Gårdsvägen 2* ☎ *0521/ 221070* 🖃 *MC, V.*

$ 🏨 **Ronnums Herrgård.** A mile outside town, this old manor house has been converted into a hotel of some local repute. Some rooms are a little shabby, so try to get one in the main building. What you do get here is peace, natural beauty, and a very good hotel restaurant. The breakfast offered with the room is worthy of a king. ✉ *Parkvägen, Vargön, 468 30* ☎ *0521/260000* 🖷 *0521/260009* 🛏 *60 rooms, 10 suites* △ *Restaurant, bar, no-smoking rooms* 🖃 *AE, DC, MC, V* ⦿ *BP.*

¢ 🏨 **Hotell Strand.** Lodging choices are limited in Vänersborg, but the Hotell Strand's welcoming staff make it the best in town. ✉ *Hamng. 7, 462 33* ☎ *0521/13850* 🖷 *0521/15900* ⊕ *www.strandhotell.com* 🛏 *28 rooms* △ *No-smoking rooms* 🖃 *AE, DC, MC, V* ⦿ *BP.*

Nightlife

Nightlife is limited here, but at **Club Roccad** (✉ Kungsg. 23 ☎ 0521/61200) there's always good, modern dance music, and the cool, dark interior attracts a young, good-looking crowd that's serious about dancing.

Lidköping

14 *55 km (34 mi) east of Vänersborg, 140 km (87 mi) northeast of Göteborg.*

On an inlet at the southernmost point of Vänern's eastern arm lies the town of Lidköping, which received its charter in 1446 and is said to have the largest town square in Sweden. Nya Stadens Torg (New Town Square) is dominated by the old courthouse building, a replica of the original that burned down in 1960. Lidköping had been razed by fire several times before that, leaving a lot of the old town gone. However, the 17th-century houses around the square Limtorget survived, and are still worth seeing today.

A pleasant enough town, Lidköping's villagelike layout comes from an old rule forbidding buildings from being taller than the street it stands on is wide. The only exception seems to be the ugly industrial park on the northern edge of town, which obscures an otherwise perfect view of Lake Vänern.

The **Rörstrands Porslins Museum** has on display a wealth of pieces that trace the history of china. Rörstrands, Europe's second-oldest porcelain company, also offers tours of its adjoining factory. The factory shop carries a large range of beautiful china at very reasonable prices. ✉ *Fabriksg. 4* ☎ *0510/82300* 🎫 *Free* ☉ *Weekdays 10–6, Sat. 10–2, Sun. noon–4. Factory tours on Thurs. and Fri. for groups; call 0510/82348 for details.*

Väner Museet is dedicated to Lake Vänern's history, the life it supports, and the ways in which it has helped the surrounding area develop. What could be a slightly dull subject is vividly brought to life in this well-planned, modern museum, which has exhibits of meteorites and fossils as well as model ships and maritime photographs. ✉ *Fram-*

näsvägen 2 ☎ *0510/770065* ✐ *SKr 20* ⊙ *Tues.–Fri. 10–5, Thurs. 10–7, weekends noon–5.*

HUSABY HYRKA – This church, 15 km (9 mi) east of Lidköping, is a site of great religious and historical significance. The church itself, dating from the 12th century, houses some fine 13th-century furniture, 15th-century murals, and carved floor stones. But the biggest draw is outside the church, at St. Sigfrid's Well. Here, in 1008, King Olof Skötkonung converted to Christianity—the first Swedish king to do so—and was baptized by the English missionary Sigfrid. Since that time many Swedish kings have come to carve their names in the rock. Most signatures can still be clearly read today.

LÄCKÖ SLOTT – One of Sweden's finest 17th-century Renaissance palaces is 24 km (15 mi) to the north of Lidköping. It's on a peninsula off the site where the eastern arm of Vänern divides from the western. Läckö Castle's 250 rooms were once the home of Magnus Gabriel de la Gardie, a great favorite of Queen Christina. Only the Royal Palace in Stockholm is larger. In 1681 Karl XI confiscated it to curtail the power of the nobility, and in 1830 all its furnishings were auctioned off. Many have since been restored to the palace. ⊠ *Kållandsö* ☎ *0510/10320* ✐ *June–Aug. SKr 70, May and Sept. SKr 50* ⊙ *May–Sept., daily 10–6.*

Where to Stay & Eat

$–$$ ✕ **Götes Festvåning.** Anything with pike (*gädda*) is particularly worth trying at this typical Swedish dining room serving good regional specialties. ⊠ *Östra Hamnen 5* ☎ *0510/21700* ▤ *DC, MC, V.*

$ ▥ **Stadtshotellet.** Like most town-hotels in Sweden, the Stadtshotel offers a faded grandeur with a lot of character. Rooms are a little on the small side but comfortable, with the best ones overlooking the river and the main town square. ⊠ *Gamla Stadens Torg 1, 531 02* ☎ *0510/ 22085* 🖷 *0510/21532* ⊕ *www.stadtlidkoping.se* ⇆ *67 rooms, 2 suites* ⚙ *Restaurant, bar, no-smoking rooms* ▤ *AE, DC, MC, V* ⊙l *BP.*

¢ ▥ **Hotell Rådhuset.** This basic hotel is somewhat oddly located inside a former office building. The rooms are large and have cable TV. There are several computers on which you can access the Internet. ⊠ *Nya Stadens Torg 8, 531 31* ☎ *0510/22236* 🖷 *0510/22214* ⇆ *24 rooms* ⚙ *Breakfast room, cable TV, Internet* ▤ *AE, DC, MC, V* ⊙l *BP.*

On a peninsula 20 km (12½ mi) to the east of Lidköping, the landscape is dominated by the great hill of **Kinnekulle,** towering 900 feet above Lake Vänern. The hill is rich in colorful vegetation and wildlife and was a favorite hike for the botanist Linnaeus.

Mariestad

❶❺ *40 km (25 mi) northeast of Lidköping.*

This town on the eastern shore of Lake Vänern is an architectural gem and an excellent base for some aquatic exploring. The town's center has a fine medieval quarter, a pretty harbor, and houses built in styles ranging from Gustavian (a baroque style named after King Gustav Vasa of the 1500s) to art nouveau. Others resemble Swiss chalets.

Domkyrkan, the late-Gothic cathedral on the edge of the old part of town, stands as a monument to one man's competitiveness. Commissioned at the end of the 16th century by Duke Karl—who named the town after his wife, Maria—it was built to resemble and rival Klara Kyrka in Stockholm, the church of his brother King Johan III, of whom he was insanely jealous. Karl made sure the church was endowed with some wonderfully excessive features, which can still be seen today. The stained-glass windows have real insects (bees, dragonflies, etc.) sandwiched within them, and the silver-and-gold cherubs are especially roly-poly and cute.

Vadsbo Museum is a museum of the local area's industry, which centers not surprisingly around the lake. The museum is just off the old town, on a small island in the River Tidan, which flows off Vänern. Named after the old jurisdiction of Vadsbo, the museum—housed in the medieval judge's residence—has displays on the region from the prehistoric age to the 20th century. ⊠ *Residensö, Marieholmn* ☎ *0501/63214* ⊡ *SKr 20* ⊙ *June–Aug., Tues.–Sun. 1–4, Wed. 1–7; Sept.–May, weekends 1–3.*

off the
beaten
path

GULLSPÅNG – Forty kilometers (25 miles) north of Mariestad, this town is the starting place for 20 km (12 mi) of railway track, originally built to improve Sweden's rail links in the 1960s but now used for leisure purposes. The tracks run through some beautiful countryside and along the Gullspångälv (Gullspång River), which has great swimming. You get to travel the tracks in handcars, which aren't often seen outside cartoons and cowboy movies. The small cars are operated by having two people push a lever up and down. If you've got the energy, it's a great trip.

Where to Stay & Eat

$–$$ ✕ **St. Michel.** The outdoor patio of this old-style restaurant shoots out into Lake Vänern on stilts. Both the indoor and outdoor seating options offer beautiful views of the lake. The traditional Swedish dishes are heavily meat-based, and most come with a side of *rösti* (hash potatoes mixed with grated cheese and chopped onions and shaped to a pancake). ⊠ *Kungsgatan 1* ☎ *0501/19900* ⊟ *MC, V* ⊙ *Closed Sun. No lunch Sat.*

$ ⊡ **Stadtshotellet.** This is the best choice in a town full of below-average hotels. The building is unobtrusive, but the rooms are comfortable, if a little bland in their furnishings. ⊠ *Nygatan 10, 542 30* ☎ *0501/ 13800* ⊟ *0501/77640* ⊅ *29 rooms* ⚲ *Bar, no-smoking rooms* ⊟ *AE, MC, V* ❄ *BP.*

Nightlife & the Arts

Evenings can be fairly quiet and relaxing in Mariestad, but the bar at **Restaurang Björnes Magasin** (⊠ Karlagatan 2 ☎ 0501/18050) can be a lively spot for the young adults in town.

The Outdoors

The nearby island of **Torsö** is perfect for fishing and lying out on the beach. It's reachable by a 1-km-long (½-mi-long) bridge, that makes for a good jog or bike ride. For information on hiring equipment for fishing, contact the **tourist office** (⊠ Hamnplan ☎ 0501/10001).

Sjötorp

❶⑥ *27 km (17 mi) northeast of Mariestad, 207 km (129 mi) northeast of Göteborg.*

At the lakeside port of Sjötorp, the Göta Canal proper begins. A series of locks raises steamers to the village of Lanthöjden—at 304 ft above sea level it's the highest point on the canal. The boats next enter the narrow, twisting lakes of Viken and Bottensjön and continue to Forsvik through the canal's oldest lock, built in 1813. Boats then sail out into **Vättern,** Sweden's second-largest lake, nearly 129 km (80 mi) from north to south and 31 km (19 mi) across at its widest point. Its waters are so clear that in some parts the bottom is visible at a depth of 50 feet. The lake is subject to sudden storms that can whip its normally placid waters into choppy waves.

Vadstena

⑰ *249 km (155 mi) northeast of Göteborg (via Jönköping).*

This little-known gem of a town grew up around the monastery founded by St. Birgitta, or Bridget (1303–1373), who wrote in her *Revelations* that she had a vision of Christ in which he revealed the rules of the religious order she went on to establish. These rules seem to have been a precursor for the Swedish ideal of sexual equality, with both nuns and monks sharing a common church. Her order spread rapidly after her death, and at one time there were 80 Bridgetine monasteries in Europe. Little remains of the Vadstena monastery; in 1545 King Gustav Vasa ordered its demolition, and its stones were used to build **Vadstena Slott** (Vadstena Castle), a huge fortress created to defend against Danish attack. It was later refurbished and used as a home for Gustav's mentally ill son. Many of the original decorations were lost in a fire in the early 1600s. Unable to afford replacement decorations, the royal family had decorations and fittings painted with three-dimensional effect directly onto the walls. Many of the "curtains" that can be seen today come from this period. Swedish royalty held court at Vadstena Slott until 1715. It then fell into decay and was used as a granary. Recent efforts have returned the castle to something approaching its former glory. Today it houses part of the National Archives, the tourist bureau, and is also the site of an annual summer opera festival. ☎ 0143/31570 ⌧ SKr 50, in winter SKr 30 ☉ Mid-May–end of May, daily 11–4; June and Aug., daily 10–6; July, daily 10–7; Sept. 1–Sept. 15, daily 10–4; mid-Sept.–mid-May, daily 11–2; guided tours on the hr in summer.

The triptych altarpiece on the south wall of the **Vadstena Kyrka** (Vadstena Church) shows St. Birgitta presenting her book of revelations to a group of kneeling cardinals. In a cherub-covered tomb are the remains of Gustav Vasa's son. St. Birgitta's bones are here as well, but less grandly stored in a red-velvet box inside a glass case.

Housed in what was once Sweden's oldest mental hospital, the **Hospital Museet** is a fascinating, moving reminder of centuries of misguided treatments and "cures" for the mentally ill. Devices on display include a chair into which patients were strapped and spun until they were sick and a bath in which unruly patients were scalded. Perhaps the most moving display includes photographs of inmates from the 19th century and the drawings they made of the tortures inflicted upon them. The tour also includes **Mården Skinnares Hus,** a very well-preserved private medieval residence once inhabited by the hospital priest. ⌧ Lastköpingsg. ☎ 0143/31570 ⌧ SKr 40 ☉ June and Aug., daily 2–3; July, daily 1–3; 1 guided tour in June and Aug. (2 PM) and 2 in July (1 PM and 2 PM).

A donation of a private doll collection was the start of the **Leksaksmuseet** (Toy Museum). Private donations have now expanded the museum's holdings into one of the largest in Sweden. The museum also has an interesting collection of clocks from the 17th century on. ⌧ Lilla Hamnarmen ☎ 0143/29275 ⌧ SKr 40 ☉ May and Sept., daily 8–6; June–Aug., 8–8; Oct.–Apr., 8–4.

off the
beaten
path

VÄVERSUNDA – This scenic hamlet, 15 km (9 mi) southeast of Vadstena, contains a pretty 12th-century limestone church. Inside there are some fine, restored wall paintings from the 13th century. Next to the church is a very popular bird-watching tower that overlooks a bird sanctuary.

Where to Stay

$$ 🏨 **Vadstena Klosterhotel.** Sweden's oldest secular building, parts of which date from the 13th century, is now a hotel. Rooms are modern and well appointed, and there are three comfortable lounges. You can choose a view of either Lake Vättern or the hotel's courtyard. The former is infinitely more preferable and only SKr 100 extra. ⊠ *Klosterområdet, off Lasarettsg., 592 24 Vadstena* ☎ *0143/31530* 🖷 *0143/13648* ⤶ *31 rooms* ⟲ *Restaurant, lounge, meeting room, no-smoking rooms* ☰ *AE, DC, MC, V* ⟲| *BP.*

$ 🏨 **Kungs-Starby Wärdshus.** This functional guest house, reached via Route 50, is next to a renovated manor house and restaurant. The rooms use light wood throughout and have earth-tone carpets and green, blue, and brown color schemes. The complex is surrounded by a park on the outskirts of town. ⊠ *Ödeshögsv., 592 21 Vadstena* ☎ *0143/75100* 🖷 *0143/75170* ⤶ *61 rooms* ⟲ *Restaurant, indoor pool, hot tub, sauna, spa, meeting room* ☰ *AE, DC, MC, V* ⟲| *CP.*

Motala

⓲ *13 km (8 mi) north of Vadstena, 262 km (163 mi) northeast of Göteborg.*

Before reaching Stockholm, the canal passes through Motala, where Baltzar von Platen is buried. He had hoped that four new towns would be established along the waterway, but only Motala rose according to plan. He designed the town himself, and his statue is in the main square. Motala itself is not an essential sight. Instead, it's the activities along the canal and lake, along with a few very good museums, that make Motala worth a stop.

★ Stop at the **Motala Motormuseum** even if you are not in the slightest bit interested in cars. All the cars and motorcycles on display—from 1920s Rolls Royces, through 1950s Cadillacs and modern racing cars—are presented in their appropriate context, with music of the day playing on contemporary radios; mannequins dressed in fashions of the time; and newspapers, magazines, televisions, and everyday household objects all helping to set the stage. More a museum of 20th-century technology and life than one solely of cars, it makes for a fascinating look back at the last century. ⊠ *Hamnen* ☎ *0141/58888* ⊕ *www.motala-motormuseum. se* ▣ *SKr 50* ⊘ *June–Aug., daily 10–8; May and Sept., daily 10–6; Oct.–Apr., weekdays 8–5, weekends 11–5.*

Europe's most powerful radio transmitter was built in Motala in 1927. In later years radio became an important industry for this little town. The **Rundradiomuseet** uses interactive displays to present the history of radio's birth as well as a glimpse into its future. ⊠ *Radiovägen* ☎ *0141/ 225100* ▣ *SKr 25* ⊘ *May, daily noon–4; June–mid-Aug., daily 10–6; mid-Aug.–Oct., weekends noon–4.*

Where to Stay

$ 🏨 **Palace Hotel.** Ship models decorate the lobby windows of this hotel with a nautical theme. The rooms are designed to look like cabins, though fortunately larger and more comfortable. Paintings of sea motifs and round windows in the bathrooms add to the charm. Just a five-minute walk from the train station, this hotel is close to most of Motala's sights. ⊠ *Kungsgatan 1, 591 30, Motala* ☎ *0141/216660* 🖷 *0141/ 57221* ⇨ *55 rooms, 1 suite* ⚭ *Breakfast room, sauna, bar, free parking* ▤ *AE, MC, V* †⊙| *BP.*

| en route | At Borenshult a series of locks takes the boat down to **Boren**, a lake in the province of Östergötland. On the southern shore of the next lake, Roxen, lies the city of **Linköping**, capital of the province and home of Saab, the aircraft and automotive company. Once out of the lake, you follow a different stretch of canal past the sleepy town of **Söderköping**. A few miles east, at the hamlet of Mem, the canal's last lock lowers the boat into Slätbaken, a Baltic fjord presided over by the **Stegeborg Slottsruin**, the ancient ruins of the Stegeborg Fortress. The boat then steams north along the coastline until it enters **Mälaren** through the Södertälje Canal and finally anchors in the capital at Riddarholmen. |

Göta Canal A to Z

BIKE TOURS

For two-day bike tours along the canal from Sjötorp to Tåtorp and back, contact Resespecialisten utmed Göta Kanal. The price is 1000 SKr for adults and 500 SKr for children under 13. The price includes lodging in a youth hostel in Töreboda, a breakfast, lunch, and dinner, as well as a bike rental for an adult. The same company also has four-day combined bike and boat tours along the canal for 2,500 SKr (all inclusive) for adults.

🛈 **Resespecialisten utmed Göta Kanal** ⊠ Kungsgatan 10 545 30 Töreboda ☎ 0506/ 12500 ⊕ www.gotakanalturer.com.

CAR TRAVEL

From Stockholm follow E18 west; from Göteborg take Route 45 north to E18.

CRUISE TRAVEL

Rolfs Flyg och Buss has one-day cruises along the canal originating in Gothenburg (with bus service to the canal) for 675 SKr (dinner included). The day trip takes 12 hours (7–7). For more details about cruises along the Göta Canal, *see* Göteborg A to Z.

🛈 **Rolfs Flyg och Buss** ⊠ Hjalmar Brantingsg. 1 417 06 Göteborg ☎ 031/511290 🖷 031/ 515060 ⊕ www.rolfsbuss.se.

TRAIN TRAVEL

Call SJ Göteborg for information about service.

🛈 Train Information **SJ** ⊠ Göteborg ☎ 0771/757575.

VISITOR INFORMATION

🛈 Tourist Information **Karlsborg** ⊠ Ankarvägen 2 ☎ 0505/17350. **Lidköping** Götene-Lidköping Turistbyrå ⊠ Bangatan 3 ☎ 0510/770500 **Mariestad** ⊠ Hamnplan ☎ 0501/ 10001 ⊕ www.turism.mariestad.se. **Motala** ⊠ Göta Kanalbolagsmuseet, Hamnen ☎ 0141/225254. **Skövde** ⊠ Sandtorget ☎ 0500/446688. **Uddevalla** ⊠ Kungstorget 4 ☎ 0522/99720 ⊕www.uddevallaforum.se. **Vadstena** ⊠Slottet ☎0143/31572. **Vänersborg** Vänersborgs Turist ⊠ Järnvägsstationen ☎ 0521/271400 ⊕ www.vanersborg.se/turist.

VÄRMLAND

Close to the Norwegian border on the north shores of Vänern, the province of Värmland is rich in folklore. It was also the home of Alfred Nobel and the birthplace of other famous Swedes, among them Nobel Prize–winning novelist Selma Lagerlöf, poet Gustaf Fröding, former prime minister Tage Erlander, and present-day opera star Håkan Hagegård. Värmland's forested, lake-dotted landscape attracts artists seeking refuge and Swedes on holiday.

Karlstad

⑲ *255 km (158 mi) northeast of Göteborg.*

Värmland's principal city (population 80,000) is on Klarälven (Klara River) at the point where it empties into Vänern. Karlstad received its charter in 1684, and the city, then known as Tingvalla, changed its name to Karlstad, meaning Karl's Town, to honor King Karl IX who had extended the charter. In **Residenstorget**, the square in front of the county governor's residence, there is a statue of Karl IX by the local sculptor Christian Eriksson.

Only 11 buildings survived a devastating fire in 1865, but as through a miracle, the fire did not claim a single life. The tourist office organizes free guided walks, in English upon request, during the summer months. The city makes bicycles available for free at Stora Torget in the summertime.

Northeast of Stora Torget, the main square, is **Östra Bron** (East Bridge). Completed in 1811, it is Sweden's longest arched stone bridge, its 12 arches spanning 510 feet across the water. Anders Jacobsson, the bridge's builder, carved his name on a stone in the bridge's center.

Consecrated in 1730, **Karlstads Katedral** (Karlstad's Cathedral; ✉ Kungsg.) fared fairly well in the great fire of 1865. Only one tower was destroyed, and a new, pointier tower was subsequently added. Particular features worth looking for are the angels by the altar, made by sculptor Tobias Sergel, and the altar itself, made of limestone and with a crystal cross, and the font, also made of crystal.

One of the buildings that survived the 1865 fire, the **Biskopsgården** (Bishop's Residence) is a beautiful, two-story, cream-color wooden building with red window trims that was built in 1781. The row of huge elm trees that surrounds the building acted as a natural firebreak and saved it from the flames. The building is now a private home.

The original building of the **Värmlands Museum** has been connected by a glass walkway to a new, red, seven-pointed wing by architect Carl Nyrén. Värmland's history and local notables like sculptor Christian Eriksson and poet Gustaf Fröding make up the base of the exhibits. ✉ *Sandgrun, Karlstad* ☎ *054/143100* 🎟 *SKr 40* ⓢ *Tues.–Fri. 8:30–5, Wed. 8:30 AM–9 PM, weekends 11–5.*

ⓒ In 1920 ten farm buildings were moved to **Marieberg Skogspark** (Marieberg Forest Park) to create an open-air museum. A delight for the whole family, the park has nature trails, a minizoo, a beach, walking trails, minigolf, restaurants, and an outdoor theater. In the middle of the forest there is a "nature room," giving a glimpse of Värmland's flora and fauna. ☎ *0550/86543* ⓢ *Dawn–dusk.*

Karlstad is the site of the **Emigrant Registret** (Emigrant Registry), which maintains detailed records of the Swedes' emigration to America. Those of Swedish extraction can trace their ancestors at the center's research facility. ✉ *Hööksgatan 2, Karlstad* ☎ *054/617720* 🎟 *Free* ⓢ *June–Aug., daily 8:30–3; Sept.–May, Mon. 8:30–8, Tues.–Fri. 8:30–4.*

Where to Stay & Eat

$$–$$$ ✕ **Inn Alstern.** Overlooking Lake Alstern, this elegant restaurant offers Swedish and Continental cuisine, with fish dishes the specialty. ✉ *Morgonv. 4* ☎ *054/834900* 🍽 *AE, MC, V.*

$$–$$$ ✕ **Restaurang Munken.** Walking down the steps into this cellar restaurant is like stepping into a *Three Musketeers* set. Low, arched stone ceilings, long wooden benches, and dim candlelight make this a cozy, informal spot. The food is warming, filling Swedish fare with a heavy Continental hand. Anything with veal is worth trying here. ✉ *Västra Torgg. 17* ☎ *054/185150* 🚇 *AE, DC, MC, V* ☉ *Closed Sun.*

¢–$$ ✕ **Ristorante Alfie.** The three dining rooms are dimly lighted, and the dark-wood tables are close together, making Alfie a very sociable dining experience. The menu includes pizzas and pasta and a huge and varied steak menu. The entrecôte steaks, served extremely rare with béarnaise sauce, are some of the best around. ✉ *Västra Torgg. 19* ☎ *054/216262* 🚇 *AE, DC, MC, V.*

$$ 🏨 **First Hotel Plaza.** The very large rooms here are in soothing neutral tones and come with excellent amenities. There is a sauna and relaxation area on the top floor, which offers great views across the city. ✉ *Västra Torgg. 2, 652 25* ☎ *054/100200* 🖨 *054/100224* ➥ *131 rooms, 5 suites* ♨ *Restaurant, bar, lounge, in-room data ports, minibars, dance club* 🚇 *AE, DC, MC, V* ⎟⊙⎟ *BP.*

$ 🏨 **Comfort Hotel Bilan.** Security will be the least of your worries here since the hotel is in a converted old county jail. Not surprisingly, the outside is a little imposing and uninviting, but once inside, public areas and rooms all have cheery furnishings and fabrics. In the basement there is a museum where you can look at the original cells and see letters and some of the objects—including a hacksaw—once sent to prisoners. ✉ *Karlbergsg. 3, 652 24* ☎ *054/100300* 🖨 *054/219214* ➥ *68 rooms* ♨ *Restaurant, indoor pool, sauna, meeting room, no-smoking rooms* 🚇 *AE, DC, MC, V* ⎟⊙⎟ *BP.*

$ 🏨 **Elite Stadshotellet.** On the banks of the Klarälven, this hotel from 1870 is steeped in tradition. All the rooms are decorated differently, some in modern Swedish style, others in ways that evoke their original look. You can dine at the fancy Matsalen or in the more casual atmosphere of the Bishop's Arms, an English pub offering 50 types of beer. ✉ *Kungsg. 22, 651 08* ☎ *054/293000* 🖨 *054/293031* ➥ *139 rooms* ♨ *Restaurant, sauna, pub, lounge, meeting room, no-smoking rooms* 🚇 *AE, DC, MC, V* ⎟⊙⎟ *BP.*

$ 🏨 **Stay Hotel Karlstad.** In the town center, this small hotel offers nondescript common areas and rather blandly decorated rooms. The hotel's studio apartments, however, are a great deal for visitors staying a week or more. ✉ *Drottningg. 1, 652 24* ☎ *054/150190* 🖨 *054/154826* ➥ *38 rooms, 11 studios* ♨ *Breakfast room, kitchenettes, sauna, meeting room, no-smoking rooms* 🚇 *AE, DC, MC, V* ⎟⊙⎟ *BP.*

Nightlife & the Arts

The choice of bars and pubs in Karlstad is good for a town of this size. **Harry's** (✉ Kungsg. 16 ☎ 054/102020) is an American-style bar with a large wooden interior and good beer on tap. The English-style pub, the **Woolpack Inn** (✉ Järnsvägsg. 1 ☎ 054/158016), is a perennial favorite with the locals.

For late-night dancing try **Plaza Nightclub** (✉ Västra Torgg. 2 ☎ 054/100200), in the basement of the First Hotel Plaza. This is the place to be seen in Karlstad. Those in their mid-20s and beyond dance the night away to the latest club tunes, fueled by lavishly over-the-top cocktails and lots of beer.

Sports & the Outdoors

The Klarälven River runs for 500 km (312 mi) through Scandinavia. The rapid waters used since the 18th century for floating logs downstream to sawmills now offer great opportunities for rafting trips. On the way you can swim, fish, and contemplate the beautiful scenery and wildlife (elk, beavers, wolverines, and bears). At night you camp in tents on the water's edge. Two companies, **Sverigeflottan** (☎ 0564/40227) and **Vildmark i Värmland** (☎ 0560/14040) operate trips along the river on two-person rafts.

You can canoe or boat on Lake Vänern in the center of the city. **Vänerkajak HB** (✉ Östra Rosenlundsvägen 54 Hammarö ☎ 054/521627 ⊕ www.vanerkajak.se) rent boats and offer introductory courses.

Shopping

Stores selling clothes, jewelry, furniture, antiques, and crafts are all concentrated on the streets of **Drotninggatan** and **Östra Torggatan.** All the main national retail brands are here, as are individual boutiques.

> **en route** Värmland is, above all, a rural experience. Drive along the **Klarälven,** through the beautiful Fryken Valley, to Ransater, where author Erik Gustaf Geijer was born in 1783 and where Tage Erlander, the former prime minister, also grew up. The rural idyll ends in **Munkfors,** where some of the best-quality steel in Europe is manufactured.

Sunne

20 *63 km (39 mi) north of Karlstad, 318 km (198 mi) northeast of Göteborg.*

A small village more than a town, Sunne is mainly known for two things. First, the famed Swedish author Selma Lagerlöf has many connections here. Sunne is also known for the prominent spa that dominates the entrance road to the village. It's a haven for stressed executives from all over Sweden.

In the middle of town, **Sundsbergs Gård** is a beautiful building said to have inspired one of the settings in Selma Lagerlöf's novel, *Gösta Berling.* Sundsberg's Manor House (built in 1780) is now a museum charting the last three centuries of Swedish history. ✉ *Ekebyv* ☎ *0565/ 10363* ✎ *SKr 30* ☉ *Museum mid-June–mid-Aug., Tues.–Thurs. and weekends noon–4; art exhibition hall and café year-round, Tues.–Thurs. and weekends noon–4.*

A small collection of old buildings makes up **Sunne Hembygdsgård,** a museum showing how life was lived in the 1800s. The well-preserved buildings include a manor house, school, general store, and courthouse. ✉ *Hembygdsvägen 7* ☎ *0565/12958* ✎ *Free* ☉ *By appointment.*

> **off the beaten path** **MÅRBACKA** – The estate on which Nobel Prize winner Selma Lagerlöf was born in 1858 can be found in this town, 10 km (7 mi) southeast of Sunne. Lagerlöf is considered the best Swedish author of her generation and is known and avidly read by Swedes young and old. The house can be seen by guided tour. Her furnishings, including her study desk and beautiful wood-panel library, have been kept much as she left them at the time of her death in 1940. ✉ *Östra Ämtervik, 686 26* ☎ *0565/31027* ✎ *SKr 60* ☉ *Mid-May–Aug., daily 10–4, tours every hr; July, daily 10–5, tours every ½ hr; Sept., weekends 11–2.*

ROTTNEROS HERRGÅRDS PARK – On the western shore of Fryken Lake, 5 km (3 mi) south of Sunne, is Rottneros Manor, the inspiration for Ekeby, the fictional estate in Lagerlöf's *Gösta Berlings Saga* (*The Tale of Gösta Berling*). The house is privately owned, but you can go to the park, with its fine collection of Scandinavian sculpture. Here there are works by Carl Milles, Norwegian artist Gustav Vigeland, and Wäinö Aaltonen of Finland. The entrance fee covers both the sculpture park and the Nils Holgerssons Adventure Park, an elaborate playground for children. ⊠ *Rottneros* ☎ *0565/ 60295* ☒ *SKr 100* ☉ *May, weekdays 10–4, weekends 10–5; June, daily 10–5; July, daily 10–6; Aug., daily 10–4.*

Where to Stay & Eat

¢–$ ✕ **Köpmangården.** If you blink, you may miss this tiny bar and restaurant that's on a road of private residences. Looking like a derelict old house from the outside, the faded carpet, chipped and frayed furniture, and dingy restrooms on the inside aren't much better. But the food is some of the best around. Everything is homemade. The tomato soup with crème fraîche, huge prawn sandwiches, and inch-thick steaks are all delicious. The warm welcome from the little old lady who runs the place is as good as the food. ⊠ *Ekebyv. 40* ☎ *0565/10121* ▤ *AE, MC, V.*

FodorśChoice ★

$$ ✕▣ **Quality Hotel and Spa Selma Lagerlöf.** This huge complex of a hotel is split onto two sides of the road leading into Sunne. Each side has large rooms furnished in a simple Scandinavian design, public rooms and lobbies, a bar, a restaurant, and a nightclub. The main hotel has a very well-equipped spa and fitness center. Guests can use most of the facilities for free, with a nominal charge for treatments. The restaurants ($$) in each hotel serve good Swedish classics, and French-influenced food. Be sure to try the reindeer if it's available. The extensive grounds of the hotel has many wooded walking and jogging paths. Ask for a room at the front of the hotel, as these have stunning views over the lake. ⊠ *Ekebyvägen, Lagerlöf 686 28 Sunne* ☎ *0565/688810* 🖷 *0565/16631* ⊕ *www.selmaspa.se* ⤳ *156 rooms, 10 suites* ᘒ *2 restaurants, 2 pools, health club, sauna, spa, 2 bars, lounge, 2 nightclubs, convention center* ▤ *AE, DC, MC, V* ⊦O⊦ *BP.*

Shopping

If you're passing through Sunne and feeling a little ravaged by life, you can pick up some pick-me-ups at the local spa resort. **Quality Hotel and Spa Selma Lagerlöf** (⊠ Sundsberget ☎ 0565/688810) offers all manner of wonderful herb, spice, mud, and clay concoctions.

The Outdoors

You're almost guaranteed to see an elk on an **elk safari** (Gräsmarks turistbyrå; ☎ 0565/40016). Departures are every Wednesday and Friday in July and cost SKr 150.

Filipstad

㉑ *63 km (39 mi) northeast of Karlstad via Route 63.*

For hundreds of years Filipstad was the center of the area's mineral mining and metalworking. You can still see many of the ancient mining and stonecutting methods and lifestyles in various working museums and villages such as Nykroppa and Långban. Persberg has the Värmland's only surviving underground mine still producing limestone. Details of mine tours can be obtained from **Filipstad Turistbyrå** (tourist office; ⊠ Stora Torget 3D ☎ 0590/61354). Authorized **city guides** can also be hired through the tourist office, or directly at ☎ 070/2409939.

Visitors to **Hornkullens Silver Mine** (⊠ Nykroppa ☎ 0590/41000 Kroppgårdens Vandrarhem) in Nykroppa can pan for gold after the mine tour, although the finds are not likely to finance any Sweden vacations. A hostel takes care of the tour bookings. Guided tours of the limestone mine **Gåsgruvan** (✉ Persberg ☎ 0590/21377), in Persberg, are arranged through Yngens Café.

Långban is interesting not just for its **Långbans Museum** for mining and minerals, but also as the birthplace of inventor John Ericsson. Ericsson left Sweden for England in 1826 at the age of 23, and emigrated from there to America. During the U.S. Civil War the Union asked him to construct an armored ship. His *Monitor* would ultimately defeat the Confederate ship *Merrimack* at Hampton Roads, Virginia. Tours are available in Swedish, English, and German. Groups of five can call ahead to visit during the off-season. ☎ 0590/22181 or 0590/22115 ⊠ 20 SKr, with tour 30 SKr ☉ Early June–late Aug., weekdays 10–5, weekends noon–4. Guided tours at 11, noon, 2, 3 and 4.

Filipstad's other mainstay is **Wasa** (✉ Konsul Lundströms väg 11 ☎ 0590/18100 ⊕ www.wasa.com), Scandinavia's largest producer of crispbread. The factory runs guided tours, showing the history of the company and how crispbread is produced. Call to arrange a tour.

Where to Stay & Eat

¢ ✕⊡ **Hennickehammars Gård.** Big windows, original wooden floors, and antique furniture define the large and airy guest rooms at this old Swedish manor house. The restaurant ($$$) serves traditional Swedish food in a fresh white-and-blue antique dining room with open fire. After you're full from dinner, a stroll around the peaceful grounds is a delight. ✉ Rte 64, 6.5 km (4 mi) south of Filipstad, Box 52 682 22 ☎ 0590/608500 ᕱ 0590/608505 ⊕ www.hennickehammar.se ⇨ 54 rooms, 3 suites ᕫ Restaurant, bar ⊟ AE, DC, MC, V ⦿ BP.

Värmland A to Z

CAR TRAVEL
From Stockholm follow E18 west; from Göteborg take Route 45 north to E18.

TRAIN TRAVEL
There is regular service to Karlstad from Stockholm and Göteborg on SJ. ⊓ SJ ✉ Göteborg ☎ 0771/757575.

VISITOR INFORMATION
⊓ Tourist Information Karlstad ✉ Tage Erlandergatan 10 ☎ 054/222140 ⊕ www.karlstad. se. **Filipstad** ✉ Stora Torget 3D ☎ 0590/61354 ⊕ www.filipstad.se/main.html. **Sunne** Turistbyrå ✉ Kolsnäsv. 41 ☎ 0565/16460

THE SOUTH & THE KINGDOM OF GLASS

Southern Sweden is considered, even by many Swedes, to be a world of its own, clearly distinguished from the rest of the country by its geography, culture, and history. Skåne (pronounced *skoh*-neh), the southernmost province, is known as the granary of Sweden. It is a comparatively small province of beautifully fertile plains, sand beaches, thriving farms, bustling, historic towns and villages, medieval churches, and summer resorts. These gently rolling hills, extensive forests, and fields are broken every few miles by lovely castles, chronologically and architecturally diverse, that have given this part of Sweden the name Château Country. A significant number of the estates, often surrounded by beautiful grounds and moats, have remained in the hands of the original families, and many are still inhabited.

The two other southern provinces, Blekinge and Halland, are also fertile and rolling and edged by seashores. Historically, these three provinces are distinct from the rest of Sweden: they were the last to be incorporated into the country, having been ruled by Denmark until 1658. They retain the influences of the Continental culture in their architecture, language, and cuisine, viewing the rest of Sweden—especially Stockholm—with some disdain. Skåne even has its own independence movement, and the dialect is so akin to Danish that many Swedes from other regions have trouble understanding it.

Småland, to the north, is larger than the other provinces, with a harsh countryside of stone and woods. A poorer, bleaker way of life here led thousands of peasants to emigrate to the United States in the 19th century. Those who stayed behind developed a reputation for their inventiveness in setting up small industries and are also notorious for being extremely careful—if not downright mean—with money. The area has many small glassblowing firms, and it is these glassworks, such as the world-renowned Kosta Boda and Orrefors, that have given the area the nickname the Kingdom of Glass.

Perhaps the most significant recent event for the South has been the bridge that opened over the Öresund, linking Malmö to Copenhagen in Denmark. At 3 mi (5 km), the bridge is the longest in the world that carries both road and rail traffic. It opened on July 1, 2000, amid hopes that it would bring a windfall to the South. As a tourist, your travel alternatives have improved.

Your itinerary should follow a route that sweeps from the western coastal town of Mölle around the southern loop and along the eastern shore, taking a side trip to the Baltic island province of Öland before heading inland to the finish at Växjö. The entire route can be done by train, with the exception of Mölle, Öland, and most of the glassworks in Småland—the Orrefors factory is the only one on the railway line. Continue your journey in any direction from Växjö.

Since it covers a fairly large area of the country, this region is best explored by car. The coastal road is a pleasure to travel on, with scenic views of long, sandy beaches and the welcoming blue sea. Inland, the hills, fertile plains, and thickly wooded forests are interconnected by winding country roads. The southern peninsula around the province of Skåne has the most urban settlements and, thanks to the spectacular Oresund bridge, fast connections to Denmark and mainland Europe. The rest of the area is more picturesque and slow-paced, inviting you to take your time exploring the pretty fishing villages and ancient castles that dot the landscape.

Mölle

▶ ★ ❶ *35 km (21 mi) northwest of Helsingborg, 220 km (132 mi) south of Göteborg, 235 km (141 mi) southwest of Växjö, 95 km (57 mi) northwest of Malmö.*

Mölle, in the far northwest of Skåne, is a small town set in spectacular isolation on the dramatic headland of the Kulla Peninsula. It is an old fishing village with a beautiful harbor that sweeps up to the Kullaberg Range. You will find beech forests, stupefying views, and rugged shores and beaches, surrounded on three sides by sea.

For those who love nature or want a break from cities and touring, Mölle is perfect. Not only is it a good base from which to explore, but the town itself has a charm that has never been tarnished by an overabundance of tourists or a relentless drive to modernize at all costs.

But Mölle's past isn't all quaintness and tradition. In the late 19th century the town was notorious throughout the country and the rest of Europe as a hotbed of liberal hedonism. This reputation was based on the penchant of locals to enjoy mixed-sex bathing, a scandalous practice at the time. Berliners loved it, and until World War I there was a weekly train that went all the way to Mölle. But as soon as war broke out, the Germans disappeared.

Today it is a relatively wealthy place, as the elaborate residences and the upmarket cars crowding the narrow streets show. Much of this wealth supposedly arrived when the more fortunate men of the sea returned to build mansions. Many of the mansions have local, although perhaps distorted, legends about them.

The **Villa Italienborg** (✉ Harastolsv. 6) was completed in 1910 by a scrap dealer inspired by a trip to the Italian Riviera. The exterior is covered in striking red-and-white tiles that form a checked pattern, which was quite stylish at the time.

The verandas, balconies, and sliding windows all make the two-story **Villa Africa** (✉ N. Brunnsv.) stand out. It was built in a South African colonial style by a local captain to please his South African wife. Legend also has it that while wooing her, he would claim that Mölle's climate was the equal of that of her homeland!

The **Kullaberg** nature reserve is just outside Mölle and covers more than 35 square km (13½ square mi). You can walk, bike, or drive in. This natural playground includes excellent trails through beech forests and along coastal routes. There's a lighthouse here set in stark land that resembles that of the Scottish Highlands—it even has longhaired Highland cattle. The park contains cafés, a restaurant, safe swimming beaches, and a golf course that's one of Sweden's most spectacular. Rock climbers consider the rock structure here to be similar to that of the Himalayas—many climbers planning to travel to that range first train here. ✆ *SKr 25 per car.*

Krapperup Castle was built in 1570 over the ruins of a medieval stronghold dating to the 13th century. The present building was extensively renovated in the late 18th century, although remnants of the stronghold still exist. The garden is among Sweden's best-preserved parks. There's an art gallery and museum inside, and concerts and performance theater are held here in the summer. It is 4 km (2½ mi) from Mölle on the main road to Helsingborg. ☎ *042/344190* ✆ *Castle tours for groups of 10 minimum SKr 70; gallery and museum SKr 30* ☉ *Call to book castle tour for group; gallery and museum May and Sept., weekends 1–6; June–Aug., daily 1–6.*

Just a few kilometers from town, the **Mölle Kapell** is a quaint white church that stands in fields under the Kullaberg. Despite its ancient appearance, the church was built in 1937. Much of the interior—the pulpit, the altar painting, and the pews—was done by local artist Gunnar Wallentin.

The haunting **Nimis** and **Arx** artworks are built of scrap wood and stone and stand on a rugged beach that can be reached only on foot. The artist Lars Vilks has been working on the weird, highly controversial structures since the 1970s. They are the most visited sight in Kullaberg. Vilks has been under constant legal threat because he didn't apply for permission from the local government, which owns the land. ✚ *Head 2 km (1¼ mi) east out of Mölle to a road sign directing you to Him-*

melstorps Hembygdsgård. Following this sign you will reach a parking lot and an old farmhouse. From here it is a 1-km (½-mi) walk marked by small blue N symbols ⊕ *www.turism.hoganas.se.*

off the beaten path

ARILD – This beautiful fishing village of bright fishermen's and sailors' cottages has been important since the Middle Ages. It is 6 km (4 mi) east of Mölle. The nicest place to stay is **Hotel Rusthållargården** (✉ Utsikten 1 ☎ 042/346530), which costs SKr 740 per person. It has an excellent restaurant. If you're looking for a break, continue east from Arild for 2 km (1 mi) to reach the village of **Skäret.** Head for the copper sign shaped like a coffeepot, which marks **Flickorna Lundgren** (☎ 042/346044 ☉ Mid-Apr.–mid-Sept.), one of Sweden's most famous cafés. The outstanding gardens look out onto the sea, and the café's regular visitors have included King Gustav IV as well as Gustav V.

Where to Stay & Eat

Most cafés and restaurants in town are in hotels.

★ **$$**
Fodor'sChoice
★
✕⊡ **Grand Hôtel.** The spectacular Grand Hôtel—a turreted building set high up on in town—has an unrivaled setting, great views, and a helpful staff. The best rooms are those with a sea view, but they are all pleasant. For dining you have a choice of two restaurants, the one in the hotel and the attached Captain's Room. The more expensive ($$) and adventurous meals are from the hotel dining room. ✉ *Bökebolsvägen 11 260 42* ☎ *042/362230* 🖷 *042/362231* ⊕ *www.grand-molle.se* ➷ *44 rooms* ♻ *2 restaurants, sauna, bar, library, meeting rooms* ▤ *AE, D, MC, V* ⦿ *BP.*

$$
✕⊡ **Turisthotellet.** The rooms at this hotel are well appointed, and some have a view of the harbor. The breakfast, included in room rates, is generous and could see you through to dinner. The restaurant ($$$$) serves good food with a Continental flavor, focusing on meat entrées with Swedish side dishes such as lingonberries. The lamb, cooked medium rare with mint sauce, is outstanding. ✉ *Kullabergsv. 32* ☎ *042/347084* 🖷 *042/347100 to Hotel Kullaberg* ⊕ *www.molleturisthotell.se* ➷ *14 rooms* ♻ *Restaurant, bar* ▤ *AE, DC, MC, V* ⦿ *BP* ☉ *Restaurant closed Sept.–May.*

$$$
⊡ **Hotel Kullaberg.** At this luxurious place all the rooms are plush and decorated in themes. One room suggests *Out of Africa,* and another has a large biplane hanging from the ceiling. You may or may not love it, depending on your feelings about kitsch. But the Kullaberg is lush, with views of the sea and the harbor and ornate reading rooms. ✉ *Gyllenstiernas Allé 16* ☎ *042/347000* 🖷 *042/347100* ⊕ *www.hotelkullaberg. se* ➷ *18 rooms* ♻ *Breakfast room, library* ▤ *AE, DC, MC, V* ⦿ *BP.*

Shopping

In the otherwise unremarkable town of Höganäs (south of Mölle) is a good factory outlet store for ceramics and glassware. **Höganäs Keramik** (✉ Norregatan 4, Höganäs ☎ 042/361100 ☉ Sept.–Apr., weekdays 10–6, Sat. 10–4, Sun. 11–4; May–June and Aug., weekdays 9–6, weekends 10–5; July, weekdays 9–7, weekends 10–5 ⊡ Free guided tours in summer) sells brands such as BodaNova at discounts of up to 40%.

Sports

The Skola Mölle Hamn (✉ Special Sports School, Södra Strandvägen 6B ☎ 042/347705, 070/3771210) caters to most outdoor activities. It organizes trips and provides gear and training for mountaineers, scuba divers, and kayakers of all skill levels.

Kullens Hästskjutsar and Turridning (⊠ Himmelstorp 765 ☎ 042/346358) organizes horseback riding.

Mölle Golfklubb (⊠ Kullahalvön ☎ 042/347520 ⊠ Greens fees June–Aug. SKr 320, Sept.–May SKr 220), one of the most spectacular 18-hole courses in Sweden, will slake the most fanatic golfers' thirst for their sport.

en route   **Viken** and **Lerberget** are two small villages on the way from Mölle to Helsingborg. Viken is a preserved fishing village with narrow stone-walled streets, traditional cottages, and a well-kept example of the old windmills once used in Skåne. If you are here between late spring and fall, you can combine dinner at the Gula Boden seafood restaurant in Viken with a stay at the quaint Pensionat Solgården guest house, in nearby Lerberget (a drive of two minutes).

$$ ✕ **Gula Boden.** With a local reputation for excellent fish meals and great views of the boat harbor and sunsets, Gula Boden is quite popular. Reservations are essential in July. ⊠ *Vikens Hamn* ☎ *042/238300* ▤ *AE, DC, MC, V* ⊘ *Closed Oct.–Apr.*

$ ▥ **Pensionat Solgården.** Run by an artistic woman who spends six months of each year at a B&B in Tonga in the South Pacific, this quaint pension hosts poetry readings outside in the summer. ⊠ *Byav. 102 Lerberget* ☎ *042/330430* ⊘ *Closed mid-Sept.–mid-Apr.* ⦿ *BP.*

Helsingborg

❷ *221 km (137 mi) south of Göteborg, 186 km (116 mi) southwest of Växjö, 64 km (40 mi) north of Malmö.*

Helsingborg, with a population of 120,000, may seem to the first-time visitor little more than a small town with a modern ferry terminal (there are about 125 daily ferry connections to Denmark and one a day to Norway). The town sees itself differently, claiming titles as Sweden's "gateway to the Continent," and the "pearl of the Öresund" region. Helsingborg was first mentioned in a letter written by Canute, the king of Denmark, in 1085; later it was the site of many battles between the Danes and the Swedes. Together with its twin town, Helsingør (Elsinore in William Shakespeare's *Hamlet*), across the Öresund, it controlled shipping traffic in and out of the Baltic for centuries. Helsingborg was officially incorporated into Sweden in 1658 and totally destroyed in a battle with the Danes in 1710. It was then rebuilt, and Jean-Baptiste Bernadotte, founder of the present Swedish royal dynasty, landed here in 1810.

Built in 1897, the turreted **Rådhuset** (City Hall) has a richly adorned facade and window paintings by artist Gustav Cederström that depict important dates in Helsingborg's history. Five times a day (at 9 AM, noon, 3, 6, and 9 PM) songs ring from the 216-foot-tall bell tower. ⊠ *Drottninggatan 2* ☎ *042/105000.*

All that remains of Helsingborg's castle is **Kärnan** (the Keep), which was built in the late 14th century. It has walls 15 ft thick. This surviving center tower, built to provide living quarters and defend the medieval castle, is one of the most remarkable relics of its kind in the north. It fell into disuse after the Swedish defeated the Danes in 1658 but was restored in 1893–94. The interior is divided into several floors, which contain a chapel, an exhibition of kitchen implements, old castle fittings, and some weaponry. ⊠ *Slottshagen* ☎ *042/105991* ⊠ *SKr 15* ⊘ *Jan.–Mar., Tues.–Sun. 11–3; Apr.–May, Tues.–Fri. 9–4, weekends 11–4; June–Aug., daily 11–7; Sept., Tues.–Fri. 9–4, weekends 11–4; Oct.–Dec., Tues.–Sun. 11–3.*

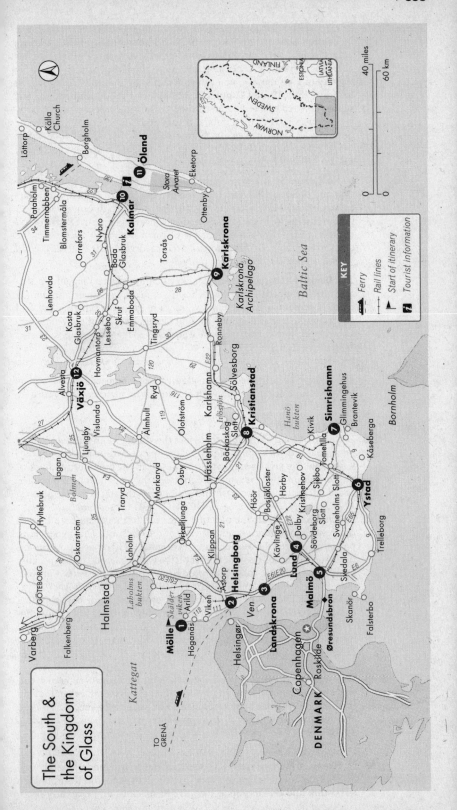

The South & the Kingdom of Glass

KEY

⚓ Ferry
+++ Rail lines
▲ Start of itinerary
🚩 Tourist information

Baltic Sea

Kattegat

NORWAY
SWEDEN
FINLAND
ESTONIA
LATVIA
LITHUANIA

40 miles
60 km

DENMARK

Copenhagen
Roskilde
Ørsundsbron

Helsingør

Bornholm

① Mölle
② Höganäs
③ Helsingborg
④ Lund
⑤ Malmö
⑥ Ystad
⑦ Simrishamn
⑧ Kristianstad
⑨ Karlskrona
⑩ Kalmar
⑪ Öland
⑫ Växjö

Varberg
TO GÖTEBORG
Falkenberg
Halmstad
Laholm
Oskarström
Hylebruk
Lagan
Bolmen
Ljungby
Vislanda
Lenhovda
Löftorp
Källa Church
Borgholm
Stora Alvaret
Eketorp
Ottenby

Pataholm
Timmernabben
Blomstermåla
Orrefors
Nybro
Boda Glasbruk
Glasbruk
Torsås
Kosta Glasbruk
Lessebo
Skruf
Emmaboda
Tingsryd
Ronneby
Karlskrona Archipelago

Hovmantorp
Almhult
Ryd
Olofström
Karlshamn
Sölvesborg
Hanöbukten
Ibbsjön
Bäckaskog Slott
Kivik
Glimmingehus
Brantevik
Käseberga

Alveta
Vislanda
Markaryd
Osby
Hässleholm
Höör
Hörby
Bosjökloster
Sjöbo
Tomelilla
Svaneholms Slott

Oskarström
Traryd
Örkelljunga
Klippan
Åstorp
Kävlinge
Dalby
Krusenhofav
Söderberg Slott
Svedala
Trelleborg

Laholms bukten
Skälderviken
Arild
Vikeń
Ven
Landskrona
Skanör
Falsterbo

TO GRENÅ

In 1865 **Sofiero Slott** (Sofiero Palace) was built in Dutch Renaissance style by Prince Oscar and his wife, Sofia, as a summer home. Half a century later Oscar II gave the palace to his grandson, Gustav Adolf, and his wife, Margareta, as a wedding gift. Since the estate is now owned by the city of Helsingborg, you can gain access to Sofiero's park, a haven for more than 10,000 samples of 300 kinds of rhododendron, various statues donated by international artists, and a large English garden; nearby greenhouses have plant exhibits. A café and fine restaurant are on the grounds. ⊠ *Sofierovägen, on the road to Laröd* ☎ *042/137400* ☟ *SKr 60* ⊙ *Apr., daily 10–5; May–Aug., 10–6; guided tours only. Park, restaurant, and café open year-round.*

Maria Kyrkan (St. Mary's), constructed in the beginning of the 14th century and finished 100 years later, is a fine example of Danish Gothic architecture. St. Mary's has several highlights: the 15th-century reredos, the silver treasure in the sacristy, and a memorial plaque to Dietrich Buxtehude (1637–1707), a prominent German composer as well as the church's organist. ⊠ *Mariatorget, Södra Storgatan 20* ☎ *042/372830* ⊙ *Aug.–June, daily 8–4, July, daily 8–6.*

The **Dunkers Kulturhus** (Henry Dunker Culture Center) includes a theater, the city museum, a music school, a concert hall, an art museum, a cultural center for children and youth, a multimedia center, a bar, and a restaurant. It was designed by Kim Utzon, the son of the controversial architect Jørn Utzon, the Dane who designed the Sydney Opera House. ⊠ *Kungsgatan 11* ☎ *042/107400* ☟ *SKr 60* ⊙ *Mon., Wed., and Fri.–Sun. 11–6, Tues. and Thurs. 11–10* ⊕ *www.dunkerskultuhus.com.*

Helsingborg's refurbished harborside area, **Norra Hamnen** (Northern Harbor), has a pleasant marina with a string of architecturally impressive cafés and restaurants.

Where to Eat

$$$ ✕ **Gastro.** A long leather booth divides this dining room into two halves: one is packed with small tables for groups of two or three, the other with tables for five or six. Larger parties sit in the more formal back of the restaurant, but everyone orders from the same menu of Swedish-based international fare. Fish and seafood are the stars. ⊠ *Södra Storg. 11–13* ☎ *042/243470* ▤ *AE, DC, MC, V* ⊙ *Closed Sun.*

★ $$ ✕ **Pålsjö Krog.** Beside the pier that leads out to the Pålsjö Bath House, this restaurant offers a beautiful view of the Öresund. The owners have partially restored the restaurant to its original 1930s style—note the antique sofa in the lounge and the art on the walls. Seafood is the specialty in summer months, game in winter. Reservations are essential in summer. ⊠ *Drottningg. 151* ☎ *042/149730* ▤ *AE, DC, MC, V.*

$$ ✕ **SS Swea.** Those with a nautical bent or nostalgia for past traveling days will be well served at this restaurant ship modeled after cruise liners of old. The docked boat specializes in fresh seafood and international menus. Enjoy the wide-ranging menu but don't forget to disembark—there are no cabin bunks here. ⊠ *Kungstorget* ☎ *042/131516* ▤ *AE, DC, MC, V.*

$–$$ ✕ **Restaurang La Petite.** If you are yearning for the delicacy of French cuisine and the genuine look and feel of a French restaurant, then look no farther. La Petite has been here since 1975, suggesting success, and can also indulge the diner in Spanish and international meals. ⊠ *Bruksg. 19* ☎ *042/219727* ▤ *AE, DC, MC, V* ⊙ *Closed Sun.*

Where to Stay

$$ ▥ **Elite Hotel Marina Plaza.** This relaxing and stylish modern hotel, with
its enormous central glass atrium, is right next to the Knutpunkten ferry, rail, and bus terminal. Rooms are spacious and elegantly deco-

rated. ⊠ *Kungstorget 6, 251 10* ☎ *042/192100* 🖷 *042/149616* 🖘 *190 rooms* 🖒 *Restaurant, bar, minibars, sauna, meeting rooms, parking, no-smoking rooms* ⊟ *AE, DC, MC, V* ❌ *BP.*

$$ 🏨 **Elite Hotel Mollberg.** Only a short walk from the central station, the Mollberg has spacious rooms with hardwood floors and large windows. Corner rooms have balconies that overlook a cobblestone square. The restaurant offers dining at reasonable prices. ⊠ *Stortorget 18, 251 14* ☎ *042/373700* 🖷 *042/373737* 🖘 *104 rooms* 🖒 *Restaurant, minibars, sauna, bar, meeting room, parking, no-smoking rooms* ⊟ *AE, DC, MC, V* ❌ *BP.*

$$ 🏨 **Hotel Högvakten.** This hotel on the main square has bright, fresh rooms with a mix of modern and antique furniture. Rooms can be a bit small, but the hotel is close to the main shopping street and the central station. ⊠ *Stortorget 14, 251 10* ☎ *042/380490* 🖷 *042/380499* 🖘 *40 rooms* 🖒 *Breakfast room, sauna, meeting rooms* ⊟ *AE, DC, MC, V* ❌ *BP.*

★ $$ 🏨 **Radisson SAS Grand Hotel.** One of Sweden's oldest hotels has been completely renovated, maintaining its long-standing reputation for excellence. Antiques and fresh flowers fill the hotel, and the well-equipped guest rooms have cable TV, a hair dryer, minibar, and trouser press. The hotel is close to the railway station and ferry terminals. ⊠ *Stortorget 8–12, 251 11* ☎ *042/380400* 🖷 *042/380404* 🖘 *117 rooms* 🖒 *Restaurant, gym, sauna, bar, meeting rooms, no-smoking rooms* ⊟ *AE, DC, MC, V.*

$ 🏨 **Villa Thalassa.** This youth hostel 3 km (1.9 mi) from the city center has fine views over Öresund. In the main building and in bungalow-style buildings, all with private patios, there are 172 bunks in two-, four-, and six-bunk rooms. The SKr 45 breakfast is not included. ⊠ *Dag Hammarskjölds väg, 254 33* ☎ *042/380660* 🖷 *042/128792* 🖘 *172 beds in 64 rooms, 24 rooms with private shower facilities* 🖒 *Breakfast room, meeting rooms* ⊟ *No credit cards.*

Nightlife & the Arts

The plush culture and art center, **Dunkers Kulturhus** (⊠ Kungsgatan 11 ☎ 042/107400), stages an array of events in the fields of music, drama, visual arts, and cultural heritage.

Open weekends only, the **Tivoli** (⊠ Kungsgatan 1, Hamntorget ☎ 042/187171 ⊕ www.thetivoli.nu) concentrates on live rock bands, attracting major Swedish and international acts. The moderate-size dance floor has good lighting. If you're looking for a nightclub feel but want to be out of the razzmatazz, check out the vinyl bar. It has a restaurant, too.

Jazz in Helsingborg stages some of its events at a cozy club on Nedre Långvinkelsgatan and some in the culture and arts center Dunkers Kulturhus. If you strike on the right night, you may well find yourself in jazz heaven, since the organizers attract jazz musicians from all over. Admission varies and goes as high as SKr 225. ⊠ *Nedre Långvinkelsg 22* ☎ *042/184900* ⊠ *Dunkers Kulturhus, Kungsgatan 11, Sundstorget* ☎ *042/107400.*

The old-world **Charles Dickens** (⊠ Söderg 43 ☎ 042/135100) is the oldest pub in town.

Sports & the Outdoors

Consider taking a relaxing dip in the sound at the late 19th-century **Pålsjö Baden** (Pålsjö Bath House) just north of town. It's a Helsingborg tradition to sweat in a sauna and then jump into the cool waters of the channel—even in the winter months. After an evening sauna, nearby Pålsjö Krog is a good dinner option. ⊠ *Drottninggatan 151* ☎ *042/149707* 🖃 *Single visit SKr 25.*

Ramlösa Brunnspark (☏ 042/105888) is the source of the famous Ramlösa mineral water, which is served in restaurants and cafés throughout the world. Since it opened in 1707, the park has attracted summertime croquet players and those eager to taste the water (an outdoor café also serves beer and wine). Nearby is the **Ramlösa Wärdshus** (☏ 042/296257), which has been serving authentic Swedish cuisine since 1830. To reach the park by bus, take Bus 2 or 8 going south from the central station (Knutpunkten).

If your bones are weary, visit **Öresundsmassage.** The professionally trained staff offers various massage services and can deal with problems such as cramping or poor blood circulation. ⊠ *Roskildeg. 4* ☏ *042/127042* ✉ *20 min SKr 200, 40 min SKr 350, 55 min SKr 450* ⊙ *Mon. and Wed. noon–7; Tues. and Thurs. 10–6.*

Skåne (☏ 042/104350 Helsingborg Tourist Information) is a golfers' delight. There are more than 60 golf courses in the region in total; within an hour's drive of Helsingborg you can find more than 20.

Shopping

Helsingborg has convenient shopping, and it's a good place to run errands. The best place to head is **Kullagatan,** which was the first pedestrians-only street in Sweden. It's a convenient collection of most of the sorts of shops you might need (e.g., a pharmacy, a photo shop, and a stationery store). If it's cheaper, medium-quality skins, furs, or leathers you want, try the **Skin and Fur Centre** at Kullagatan 7.

Landskrona

❸ *26 km (16 mi) south of Helsingborg (via E6/E20), 41 km (25 mi) north of Malmö, 204 km (127 mi) southwest of Växjö.*

The 17th-century Dutch-style fortifications of Landskrona are among the best preserved in Europe. Though it appears to be a modern town, Landskrona dates from 1413, when it received its charter.

The eclectic **Landskrona Museum** has temporary exhibits as well as permanent coverage of Landskrona history and the Swedish contributions to art, medicine, aviation, and architecture. ⊠ *Slottsg.* ☏ *0418/473123* ⊕ *www.landskrona.se/kultur* ✉ *Free* ⊙ *Mon.–Sun. noon–5.*

Landskrona's **Citadellet** (castle) was built under orders of the Danish king Christian III in 1549 and is all that remains of the original town, which was razed in 1747 by decree of the Swedish Parliament to make way for extended fortifications. The new town was built on land reclaimed from the sea. ⊠ *Slottsg.* ☏ *0418/448250* ✉ *SKr 40* ⊙ *Early June–late Aug., Tues.–Sun. 11–4; guided tours Tues.–Fri. noon, 2, and 4, weekends noon and 2.*

> **off the beaten path**
>
> **VEN –** From Landskrona Harbor there are regular 25-minute boat trips to the island of Ven (✉ SKr 70 round-trip; boats depart every 90 mins 6 AM–9 PM). It's an ideal place for camping; check with **Landskrona's tourist office** (☏ 0418/473000). There are special paths across Ven for bicycling; rentals are available from Bäckviken, the small harbor.
>
> The Danish astronomer Tycho Brahe conducted his pioneering research here from 1576 to 1597. The foundations of his Renaissance castle, **Uranienborg,** can be visited, as can **Stjärneborg,** his reconstructed observatory. The small **TYCHO BRAHE MUSEET –** is

dedicated to Brahe and his work. ✉ *Landsv. 182, Ven* ☎ *0418/ 72530* ✉ *SKr 35* ⊙ *Apr.–June, daily 10–4, July–mid-Aug., 10–5; mid-Aug.–mid-Sept., 11–4.*

Sports & the Outdoors

Three kilometers (2 mi) north of Landskrona lies the **Borstahusen** (✉ 261 61 Landskrona ☎ 0418/10837) recreation area, with long stretches of beach, a marina, and a group of 74 small cabinlike chalets.

Lund

❹ *34 km (21 mi) southeast of Landskrona via E6/E20 and Route 16, 25 km (15 mi) northeast of Malmö, 183 km (113 mi) southwest of Växjö.*

One of the oldest towns in Europe, Lund was founded in 990. In 1103 Lund became the religious capital of Scandinavia and at one time had 27 churches and eight monasteries—until King Christian III of Denmark ordered most of them razed to use their stones for the construction of Malmöhus Castle. Lund lost its importance until 1666, when its university was established—the second-oldest university in Sweden after Uppsala.

Fodor'sChoice ★ Lund's **Domkyrkan** (Cathedral), consecrated in 1145, is a monumental gray-stone Romanesque cathedral, the oldest in Scandinavia. Since the Reformation it has been Lutheran. Its crypt has 23 finely carved pillars, but its main attraction is an astrological clock, Horologum Mirabile Lundense, dating from 1380 and restored in 1923. The "Miraculous Clock of Lund" depicts an amazing pageant of knights jousting on horseback, trumpets blowing a medieval fanfare, and the Magi walking in procession past the Virgin and Child as the organ plays *In Dulci Jubilo*. The clock plays at noon and at 3 Monday–Saturday and at 1 and 3 on Sunday. The oldest parts of the cathedral are considered the finest Romanesque constructions in Sweden. English and Swedish tours are available, and there are concerts at 10 AM on Sunday. ✉ *Free.*

Historiska museet med Domkyrkomuseet (The Cathedral Museum and the Museum of History) are just north of the cathedral. The Cathedral Museum has exhibitions and a slide show about the Domkyrkan's history. The Museum of History has Sweden's second-largest collection of treasures from the Stone, Bronze, and Iron ages. It also houses one of the oldest human skeletal finds, dated to 5000 BC. ✉ *Kraftstorg Sq. 1* ☎ *046/2227944* ✉ *SKr 30* ⊙ *Mid-June–mid-Aug., Tues.–Sat. 11–4.*

One block east of the cathedral is the **Botaniska Trädgården** (Botanical Gardens), which contains more than 7,000 specimens of plants from all over the world, including such exotics as the paper mulberry tree, from the islands of the South Pacific. ✉ *Östra Vallg. 20* ☎ *046/2227320* ✉ *Free* ⊙ *Daily 6 AM–8 PM, greenhouses daily noon–3.*

The Lundagård park separates the Domkyrkan from the oldest parts of **Lund University.** The main building is crisp white and easily spotted among the cobbled streets and traditional cottages. The university was founded in 1666 and today has 30,000 students. Its **History Museum** (☎ 046/350400), part of the **Kulturen** group of museums, exhibits old texts, university regalia, and other items used in the university long ago. ✉ *Kyrkog.*

need a break? Just across from the university is a Lund institution—**Conditori Lund** (✉ Kyrkog. 17), a bakery and coffeehouse. It's easy to imagine the rooms filled with the smoke and loud opinions of intellectuals of the past.

Founded in 1934 in connection with Lund University, **Skissernas Museum** (Sketches Museum) houses more than 20,000 sketches in addition to models and first drafts by major artists. It is scheduled to reopen in 2004 after a major renovation. The international collection contains the early ideas of artists such as Henri Matisse, Pablo Picasso, Fernand Léger, and many others. ⊠ *Finng. 2* ☏ *046/2227283* 🎫 *SKr 30* ☉ *Tues. and Thurs.–Sat. noon–4, Wed. 6:30–8:30, Sun. 1–5.*

Esaias Tegnér, a Swedish poet, lived from 1813 to 1826 in a little house immediately behind the cathedral. The house has since been turned into the **Tegnér Museet**, providing insight into his life and works. ⊠ *Stora Gråbrödersg. 11* ☏ *046/291319* 🎫 *SKr 5* ☉ *July and Aug., Sun. noon–3; Sept.–June, 1st weekend each month noon–3.*

On the southern side of Stortorget, the main square, is **Drottens Kyrko-ruin** (Church Ruins of Drotten), an underground museum showing life as it was in Lund during the Middle Ages. The foundations of three Catholic churches are here: the first was built of wood around AD 1000. It was torn down to make room for one of stone around 1100; this was replaced by a second stone church, built around 1300. ⊠ *Kattensund 6* ☏ *046/141328* 🎫 *SKr 10* ☉ *Tues.–Fri. noon–4, weekends 10–2.*

🐦 **Kulturen** (The Museum of Cultural History) is both an outdoor and an indoor museum; it includes 20 old cottages, farms, and manor houses from southern Sweden, plus an excellent collection of ceramics, textiles, weapons, and furniture. Kulturen's **gardens** have free admission on summer nights, and on many of those nights there is live music and dancing. Call the museum for further details. ⊠ *Tegnérsplatsen* ☏ *046/350400* 🎫 *SKr 50* ☉ *Mid-Apr.–Sept., Fri.–Wed. 11–5, Thurs. 11–9; Oct.–mid-Apr., Tues.–Sun. noon–4.*

The all-brick **Lund Konsthallen** (Lund Art Gallery) may have a rather foreboding iron entrance and few windows, but skylights allow ample sunlight into the large exhibit room full of modern art. ⊠ *Måtenstorget 3* ☏ *046/355000* 🎫 *Free* ☉ *Mon.–Wed. and Fri. noon–5, Thurs. noon–8, Sat. 10–5, Sun. noon–6.*

Fodor'sChoice
★ The **Heligkorskyrkan i Dalby** (Holy Cross Church of Dalby) was founded in 1060, making it the oldest stone church in Scandinavia. It was for a short time the archbishop's seat until this was moved to Lund. Among the hidden treasures is a renowned baptismal font, brought here in 1150. The exposed brick within the church is original and many figures and icons date from medieval times, including a wooden relief at the front of the church called *Veronica's Napkin,* which shows the face of Jesus. The church is on a hill and less than 10 km (8 mi) from Lund. ⊠ *Head east on Rte. 16 and follow signs* ☏ *046/208600* 🎫 *Free* ☉ *May–Aug., daily 9–6; Sept.–Apr., daily 9–4.*

off the beaten path

BOSJÖKLOSTER – About 30 km (19 mi) northeast of Lund via E22 and Route 23, Bosjökloster is an 11th-century, white Gothic castle with lovely grounds on Ringsjön, the second-largest lake in southern Skåne. The castle's original owner donated the estate to the church, which turned it over to the Benedictine order of nuns. They founded a convent school (no longer in operation) for the daughters of Scandinavian nobility and built the convent church with its tower made of sandstone. The 300-acre castle grounds, with a 1,000-year-old oak tree, also have a network of pathways, a children's park, a rose garden, and an indoor-outdoor restaurant. ⊠ *Höör* ☏ *0413/25048* 🎫 *SKr 45* ☉ *Castle grounds, Apr.–Sept., daily 8–sunset; restaurant and exhibition halls Apr.–Sept., daily 10–6.*

Where to Eat

★ $$ ✕ **Bantorget 9.** The restaurant-bar inside this 18th-century building is true to the past, with restored woodwork and paintings on the ceilings, antique flowerpots and candleholders, and classical statues in the corners of the room. The menu offers traditional Swedish dishes plus some more intriguing entrées such as duck breast with pickled red cabbage in apple honey. Bantorget 9 is a short walk from Lund's central train station. ✉ *Bantorget 9* ☎ *046/320200* ☰ *AE, DC, MC, V* ☽ *Closed Sun.*

$$ ✕ **Godset.** Inside an old railroad warehouse right on the tracks near central station, Godset's modern tables and chairs stand on rustic wooden floors between brick walls. On one wall hangs a large 1950s clock taken from Mariakyrkan (Maria Church) in nearby Ystad. The menu is mostly seafood and meat dishes. Try the roasted venison poached in a cream sauce with raspberry vinaigrette. ✉ *Bang. 3* ☎ *046/121610* ☰ *AE, DC, MC, V* ☽ *Closed Sun.*

★ $$ ✕ **Restaurang Café Finn.** Connected to the Lund Konsthallen, Café Finn is an excellent option for lunch or dinner. The creamy lobster soup with mussels is perfect if you're not overly hungry, but for a more substantial meal go for the veal fillet with creamy red-onion sauce and grape jelly. The walls have an extensive collection of museum exhibit posters from the '60s, '70s, and '80s. Just outside is the Krognoshuset; built in the 1300s, it is Lund's best-kept medieval residence. ✉ *Mårtenstorget 3* ☎ *046/130565* ☰ *AE, DC, MC, V.*

$–$$ ✕ **Dalby Gästgifveri.** This is one of Skåne's oldest inns and a gastronomic delight. The many red-meat dishes on the menu follow a tradition of history and quality, but innovative Swedish fare is served, too. Entrées such as the rich, somewhat gamey deer fillet with mushroom spring rolls and cranberry sauce are not for the faint of heart. Be sure to make reservations in the summer. ✉ *Tengsg. 6* ☎ *046/200006* ☰ *AE, MC, V.*

$ ✕ **Ebbas Skafferi.** Just across the central station, Ebbas Pantry serves a number of excellent sandwiches on bagels, baguettes, or *ciabattas* (a flat Italian bread). ✉ *Bytaregatan 5* ☎ *046/127127* ☰ *MC, V.*

Where to Stay

$$ ▨ **Concordia.** Formerly a private residence, this elegant city-center property was built in 1890. Rooms have a modern, clean look but are without much character. ✉ *Stålbrog. 1, 222 24* ☎ *046/135050* ☗ *046/137422* ⇌ *65 rooms* ⚅ *Sauna, meeting room, no-smoking rooms* ☰ *AE, DC, MC, V.*

$$ ▨ **Grand Hotel.** This elegant red-stone hotel is in the heart of the city on a pleasant square close to the railway station. Rooms have turn-of-the-20th-century decor and charm. The fine restaurant serves an alternative vegetarian menu. ✉ *Bantorget 1, 221 04* ☎ *046/2806100* ☗ *046/2806150* ⇌ *84 rooms* ⚅ *Restaurant, hot tub, sauna, meeting room, no-smoking rooms* ☰ *AE, DC, MC, V.*

$$ ▨ **Hotel Lundia.** A few hundred feet from the train station, Hotel Lundia is ideal for those who want to be near the city center. Built in 1968, the modern, four-story square building has transparent glass walls on the ground floor. Rooms are decorated with Scandinavian fabrics and lithographs. ✉ *Knut den Stores torg 2, 221 04* ☎ *046/2806500* ☗ *046/2806510* ⇌ *97 rooms* ⚅ *Restaurant, lounge, nightclub, meeting room, no-smoking rooms* ☰ *AE, DC, MC, V.*

$–$$ ▨ **Djingis Khan.** This English colonial–style Best Western hotel caters to business travelers but is also a great place for families or couples seeking a quiet location. The hotel's unusual name comes from a comedy show that has been performed at Lund University since 1954. With squash, tennis, and badminton courts nearby, along with a large swimming pool, it's ideal if you're looking to keep in shape. ⊠ *Margaretav. 7, 222 40* ☎ *046/333600* 🖷 *046/333610* ➾ *55 rooms* ♨ *Gym, hot tub, sauna, bicycles, meeting room, no-smoking rooms* ☰ *AE, DC, MC, V* ⊙ *Closed July.*

$ 🛏 **STF Vandrarhem Tåget.** So named because of its proximity to the train station (*tåget* means "train"), this youth hostel faces a park in central Lund. ⊠ *Bjerredsparken, Vävareg. 22, 222 37* ☎ *046/142820* ➾ *108 beds without bath* ☰ *No credit cards.*

Nightlife & the Arts

The **Lundia** (⊠ Knut den Stores Torg 2 ☎ 046/2806500) nightclub is in the Hotel Lundia, near the Burger King. Women must be 23 or older to enter, men over 25, and not many attendees are much over 35. It costs SKr 50 to dance to the electronic sounds.

★ **Basilika** (⊠ Stora Söderg. 13 ☎ 046/2116660) has a smallish dance floor and also hosts live bands. On Friday and Saturday things don't get going until 11 and rage on until 3. Basilika draws young hipsters and will cost at least SKr 50 to get in.

The hot spot in town **Stortorget** (⊠ Stortorget 1 ☎ 046/139290) has live music as well as a DJ night and is popular with students. You won't get in here unless you are over 22.

Shopping

About 200,000 secondhand books are stacked in crazy piles in the **Åkards Antikvariat** (⊠ Klosterg. ☎ 046/2112499), making it full of the smells of aged literature. The oldest book dates to about 1500, around the time the printing press was developed. Any sort of book can be found, even an airport thriller.

The oldest coins in Europe date to between 500 and 600 BC, and the coin shop **Lunds Mynthandel** (⊠ Klosterg. 5 ☎ 046/14436) often has specimens going back that far. Lunds Mynthandel also carries books on numismatics.

Saluhalen (⊠ Corner of Mårtenstorget and Botulfsg.), known as Food-hall, is an adventure in itself, an excellent example of the traditional Swedish food house but also one that stocks delicacies from Italy, Japan, and beyond. Cheese, meats, fresh and pickled fish, and pastries are all in great supply. It is the perfect place to get some food for a picnic in one of Lund's many squares and parks. The cheese selection at **Bengsons Ost** (⊠ Klosterg. 9) is hard to surpass. The people are friendly, and it's a great spot to fill your picnic hamper. Bring your own wine and have a tasting session.

Skånae–kraft (⊠ Östra Mårtensg. 5 ☎ 046/144777) carries a wide range of ceramics, crafts, and designer goods that changes frequently. **Teahuset Java** (⊠ Västra Mårtensg.), a well-known tea-and-coffee shop, sells leaves and beans from all over the world. You can also get all the paraphernalia that goes with brewing.

Malmö

❺ *25 km (15 mi) southwest of Lund (via E22), 198 km (123 mi) southwest of Växjö.*

Capital of the province of Skåne, with a population of about 265,000, Malmö is Sweden's third-largest city. It was founded at the end of the 13th century. The remarkable 8-km (5-mi) bridge and tunnel from Malmö to Copenhagen has transformed travel and trade in the area, cutting both time and costs, and replacing the ferries that used to shuttle between the two towns. Eight years in the making, the $3 billion Öresund Bridge has proved to be a success, both environmentally and commercially.

The city's castle, **Malmöhus,** completed in 1542, was for many years used as a prison (James Bothwell, husband of Mary, Queen of Scots, was one of its notable inmates). Today Malmöhus houses a variety of **museums,** including the City Museum, the Museum of Natural History, and the Art Museum, which has a collection of Nordic art. Across the street is the Science and Technology Museum, the Maritime Museum, and a toy museum. ✉ *Malmöhusvägen* ☎ *040/344437* 🎫 *SKr 40 for all museums* ☉ *June–Aug., daily 10–4; Sept.–May, daily noon–4.*

In the same park as Malmöhus is the **Malmö Stadsbibliotek** (Malmö City Library), designed by the famous Danish architect Henning Larsen. Take a walk through the colossal main room—there's a four-story wall of glass that brings seasonal changes of colors inside. ✉ *Kung Oscars Väg* ☎ *040/6608500.*

On the far side of the castle grounds from Malmöhus, the **Aq-va-kul** water park offers a variety of bathing experiences, from water slides to bubble baths. ✉ *Regementsg. 24* ☎ *040/300540* 🎫 *SKr 65* ☉ *Weekdays 9–8:30, weekends 9–5:30; Mon. and Wed. adult sessions 7 PM–9:30 PM.*

A clutch of tiny red-painted shacks called the **Fiskehodderna** (Fish Shacks) is next to a dock where the fishing boats come in every morning to unload their catch. The piers, dock, and huts have been restored and are now a government-protected district. You can buy fresh fish directly from the fishermen Tuesday through Saturday mornings.

★ In Gamla Staden, the Old Town, look for the **St. Petri Church,** on Kalendegatan; dating from the 14th century, it is an impressive example of the Baltic Gothic style, with distinctive stepped gables. Inside there is a fine Renaissance altar.

★ You can learn about Scandinavian art and design at the **Form/Design Center.** The center is run by SvenskForm, a nonprofit association that promotes top-quality design in Sweden; Swedish and other Scandinavian artworks are on display throughout the center. ✉ *9 Lilla Torg* ☎ *040/664510* 🎫 *Free* ☉ *Tues.–Fri. 11–5, Thurs. 11–6, weekends 11–4.*

The **Rådhuset** (Town Hall), dating from 1546, dominates Stortorget, a huge, cobbled market square in Gamla Staden, and makes an impressive spectacle when illuminated at night. In the center of the square stands an equestrian statue of Karl X, the king who united this part of the country with Sweden in 1658. Off the southeast corner of Stortorget is the square Lilla Torg.

The **Idrottsmuseum** (Museum of Sport) occupies Baltiska Hallen (the Baltic Building), next to Malmö Stadium. It traces the history of sports, including soccer and wrestling, from antiquity to the present. ☎ *040/342688* 🎫 *Free* ☉ *Weekdays 8–4.*

One of Sweden's most outstanding art museums, **Rooseum,** is in a turn-of-the-20th-century brick building that was once a power plant. It has exhibitions of contemporary art and a quality selection of Nordic art. ✉ *Gasverksg. 22* ☎ *040/121716* 🎫 *SKr 40* ☉ *Wed.–Fri. 2–8; weekends noon–6. Guided tours in Swedish and English weekends at 2 and Thurs. at 6:30.*

Founded in 1975, the **Malmö Konsthall** (Malmö Art Gallery) is one of the largest contemporary art museums in Europe, with a huge single room that's more than 20,000 square feet. It arranges about 10 exhibitions a year, from the classics of modern art to present-day experiments. Other activities include theater performances, film presentations, and poetry readings. ⊠ *St. Johannesg. 7* ☎ *040/341293* ⊡ *Free* ⊙ *Mon.–Tues. and Thurs.–Sun. 11–5, Wed. 11–9.*

Lilla Torg is a cobblestone square with some of the city's oldest buildings, which date to the 17th and 18th centuries. It is clustered with cafés, restaurants, and bars and is a great place to wander or watch the world go by. Walk into the side streets and see the traditional buildings, which were originally used mainly to store grain and produce. Check out the *Saluhallen* (food hall), which contains one of Sweden's best coffee purveyors.

★ The **Öresundbron** (Öresund Bridge) is an engineering miracle. Its train tracks and four car lanes stretch 8 km (5 mi) from the southern coastal suburbs of Malmö to Copenhagen. Designed under the auspices of Öresund Konsortiet, the bridge is a minimalist beauty. ⊠ *Lookout at Öresund Utställningen at the end of Utställningen Rd. Approach on E20 Hwy.* ⊕ *www.oeresundsbron.com* ⊡ *SKr 275 each way for car.*

The houses and business buildings designed and erected for the 2001 **European Housing Expo** show 58 different types of housing. Wander around the development around the Ribersborgsstranden waterfront, where the expo was held, in order to see the exteriors of more than 500 homes. They were sold as residences after the expo was over. ⊠ *Ribersborgsstranden waterfront.*

> **off the beaten path**

FALSTERBO AND SKANÖR – The idyllic towns of Falsterbo and Skanör are two popular summer resorts on a tiny peninsula, 32 km (20 mi) southwest of Malmö. Falsterbo is popular among ornithologists, who flock there every fall to watch the spectacular migration of hundreds of birds, especially swallows, geese, hawks, and eagles.

TORUPS SLOTT – Built around 1550 near a beautiful beech forest, Torup Castle is a great example of the classic, square fortified stronghold. From Malmö drive 10 km (6 mi) southeast on E65, then head north for another 6 km (4 mi) to Torup. ⊠ *Torup* ⊡ *SKr 60* ⊙ *Sun. tours at 1, 2, and 3* ☎ *040/447050.*

Where to Eat

★ **$$–$$$** ✕ **Årstiderna i Kockska Huset.** Formed by merging two discrete restaurants that were in different locations, the combination is housed in a 16th-century building with beautiful interiors. Several of the dining areas are in an underground cellar. Traditional Swedish dishes, often centered on beef, game, and seafood, are given a contemporary twist. The fried halibut, for example, is served with a crab mousse and a rich shellfish sauce flavored with curry. Like the food, the wine list is excellent. ⊠ *Frans Suellsgatan 3* ☎ *040/230910* ⊟ *AE, DC, MC, V.*

$$–$$$ ✕ **Johan P.** This extremely popular restaurant specializes in seafood and shellfish prepared in Swedish and Continental styles. White walls and crisp white tablecloths give it an elegant air, which contrasts with the generally casual dress of the customers. An outdoor section is open in the summer. ⊠ *Saluhallen, Lilla Torg* ☎ *040/971818* ⊟ *AE, DC, MC, V* ⊙ *Closed Sun.*

$$ ✕ **Hipp.** Distinguishing this bar-restaurant that dates to 1899 are ornate columns that support a high ceiling painted with flower patterns. Heavy chandeliers hang over the dark-wood bar in the center of the restaurant. Hipp's hearty fare is the perfect cap to a night at the city theater, next door. The finely sliced raw salmon with black roe is a standout, as is the vegetable stir-fry. Dry martinis are the specialty of the bar. ⊠ *Kalendeg. 12* ☎ *040/974030* ☰ *AE, DC, MC, V* ☺ *Closed Sun. and Mon.*

$–$$ ✕ **Anno 1900.** This charming little restaurant sits in a former working-class area of Malmö. It is a popular local luncheon place with a cheerful outdoor garden terrace. Head here for such light dishes as salads and fish, as well as for traditional Swedish lunches built around the potato. The bread is outstanding. ⊠ *Norra Bulltoftav. 7* ☎ *040184747* ⌦ *Reservations essential* ☰ *AE, DC, MC, V.*

$–$$ ✕ **Glorias.** This friendly restaurant and sports bar offers a good value. The food is Tex-Mex, with a few international appetizers thrown in. ⊠ *Södra Förstadsgatan 23B* ☎ *040/70200* ☰ *AE, DC, MC, V.*

$–$$ ✕ **Salt & Brygga.** The traditional Swedish kitchen has found some in-
Fodor'sChoice spiration in the Mediterranean at this quayside restaurant. Endive and
★ Gorgonzola toast, and smoked saithe (coalfish) and horseradish *fromage* (cheese) appetizers are followed by rich shellfish casseroles. The restaurant not only uses only organic produce, but also uses ecologically friendly alternatives for everything from the wall paint to the table linens and the staff's clothes. The restaurant's selection of organic wines and beers is unique for the region. ⊠ *Sundspromenaden 7* ☎ *040/6115940* ☰ *AE, DC, MC, V.*

¢–$ ✕ **B & B.** It stands for *Butik och Bar* (Shop and Bar) and is named as such because of its location in the market hall in central Malmö. There's always good home cooking, with dishes like grilled salmon and beef fillet with potatoes. Sometimes there's even entertainment at the piano. ⊠ *Saluhallen, Lilla Torg* ☎ *040/127120* ☰ *AE, DC, MC, V.*

¢ ✕ **Spot.** Reasonable prices and unpretentious food draw a lively group of regulars to this Italian eatery for lunch. ⊠ *Stora Nygatan 33* ☎ *040/120203* ☰ *AE, DC, MC, V* ☺ *Closed Sun. No dinner.*

Where to Stay

$$ ⌂ **Hilton Malmö City.** Ultramodern in steel and glass, the Hilton is the city's only skyscraper—at a modest 20 floors. It provides excellent views all the way to Copenhagen on a clear day. Rooms are plain but comfortable. ⊠ *Triangeln 2, 200 10* ☎ *040/6934700* ☷ *040/6934711* ↭ *216 rooms* ⌕ *Restaurant, in-room data ports, cable TV, gym, sauna, bar, meeting room, no-smoking rooms* ☰ *AE, DC, MC, V.*

★ **$$** ⌂ **Mäster Johan Hotel.** The plain exterior of this Best Western hotel disguises a plush and meticulously crafted interior. A top-to-bottom redesign of a 19th-century building, with the focal point an Italianate atrium breakfast room, the Mäster Johan is unusually personal for a chain hotel. The rooms are impressive, with exposed plaster-and-stone walls, recessed lighting, oak floors, Oriental carpets, and French cherry-wood furnishings. ⊠ *Mäster Johansg. 13, 211 21* ☎ *040/6646400* ☷ *040/6646401* ↭ *69 rooms* ⌕ *Breakfast room, room service, sauna, meeting room, no-smoking rooms* ☰ *AE, DC, MC, V.*

$$ ⌂ **Radisson SAS Hotel.** Only a five-minute walk from the train station, this modern luxury hotel has rooms decorated in several styles: Scandinavian, Asian, and Italian. There are even special rooms for guests with pets. Service is impeccable. The restaurant serves Scandinavian and Continental cuisine, and there's a cafeteria. ⊠ *Österg. 10, S211 25* ☎ *040/6984000* ☷ *040/6984001* ↭ *229 rooms* ⌕ *Restaurant, cafeteria, gym, sauna, spa, meeting room, no-smoking rooms* ☰ *AE, DC, MC, V.*

★ **$** ⌂ **Baltzar.** This turn-of-the-20th-century house in central Malmö makes a small, comfortable hotel. Rooms are modern, with the original hardwood floors. ⊠ *Söderg. 20, 211 34,* ☎ *040/6655700* ☷ *040/236375* ↭ *41 rooms* ⌕ *No-smoking rooms* ☰ *AE, DC, MC, V.*

$ ⊡ **Comfort Hotel.** In a rejuvenated part of Malmö Harbor, this low-over-head, minimal-service hotel has small but comfortable rooms equipped with satellite TV, telephone, and radio. The large front entrance and lobby atrium are inventively created out of a narrow strip between two build-ings. Though the hotel doesn't add a surcharge to the telephone bill, break-fast does cost extra (SKr 65). ⊠ *Carlsg. 10C, 211 20* ☎ *040/330440* ☎ *040/330450* 🖘 *109 rooms* ♨ *Breakfast room, cable TV, parking* ☰ *AE, DC, MC, V.*

Nightlife & the Arts

The Bishop's Arms (⊠ Savoy Hotel, Nora Vallg. 62 ☎ 040/6644888) is a classic and busy English pub. It is in the former grill room of the Savoy Hotel and can hardly fail to impress the pub connoisseur. There's an excellent assortment of old whiskeys.

Étage (⊠ Stortorget 6 ☎ 040/232060 ▤ SKr 50 or more ☉ Mon., Thurs., Fri., and Sat. 11 PM–5 AM) is a centrally located nightclub for hipsters, with two dance floors. It also has a piano bar for relaxing, as well as a restaurant. Dancing begins late under psychedelic lights Thurs-day, Friday, and Saturday. Karaoke, roulette, and blackjack tables are available.

Five rooms of an old patrician apartment make up **Klubb Plysch** (⊠ Lilla Torg 1 ☎ 040/127670 ▤ SKr 60 ☉ Weekends 10 PM–3 AM). Lounge about in the superb velvet chairs with champagne and cigars in the early evening, and join the dance floor around 11.

At **Wallmans Salonger** (⊠ Generalsg. 1 ☎ 040/74945 ▤ SKr 100–Skr 180) the artistic, bohemian staff is part of the entertainment. They may burst into song or start juggling. A dance show with terrific lighting be-gins at 7, and the nightclub proper begins at 11. There are also a casino and a restaurant.

The **Malmö Symfoni Orkester** (☎ 040/343500 ⊕ www.mso.se) is a sym-phony orchestra that has a reputation across Europe as a class act. Each concert is a finely tuned event. Performances are held at many venues, including outdoors; some are at the impressive Malmö Konserthus.

Sports & the Outdoors

From Ribersborg Beach you can walk on a pier to the **Kallbadhuset Ribers-borgsstranden,** which are old baths (the name translates as "cold bath-houses Ribersborg Beach"). Built in 1898, they are a popular place to swim, since a man-made harbor of boulders offers protection from the sea's turbulence. It also hosts cultural events such as poetry readings and has a bar and a café. To get to the beach, follow Citadellsvägen to the west from the central railway station. Walk alongside Öresunds Parken and turn right at the sign for Ribersborg. ⊠ *Ribersborg Beach* ☎ *040/ 260366* ▤ *SKr 40.*

Paddle boating on the canals is a great way to see the city. Each boat takes up to four people. Start paddling from Raoul Wallenberg Park, just southeast of Gustav Adolfs Square along Lilla Nygatan. ⊠ *Raoul Wallenberg Park* ☎ *0704/710067* ▤ *SKr 100 per hr, SKr 70 for 30 mins* ☉ *June–Sept., daily 11–7.*

Shopping

Malmö has many quality housewares and design stores. **Duka** (⊠ Hansacompagniet Centre, Malmborgsg. 6 ☎ 040/121141) is a high-quality housewares shop specializing in glass, crockery, and glass art. Special tables are set up with Swedish products on display, and hand-carved and hand-painted wood Dala horses are for sale. **Cervera** (✉ Södra Förstadsgatan 24 ☎ 040/971230) carries big-name glassware brands such as Kosta and Orrefors. There's an excellent selection of glass art as well as porcelain and china—and almost everything you might need as far as housewares.

The **Form/Design Centre** (✉ Lilla Torg 9 ☎ 040/6645150) sells products related to its changing exhibitions on everything from ceramics to books. Also look here for the very latest in Scandinavian interior design. **Formagruppen** (✉ Engelbrektsg. 8 ☎ 040/4078060) is an arts-and-crafts cooperative owned and operated by its 22 members. It sells high-quality woodwork, including cabinets. Quality ceramics, textiles, metalwork, and jewelry are also for sale. An arts-and-crafts shop with a Nordic twist, **Älgamark** (✉ Östra Rönneholmsvägen 4 ☎ 040/974960) sells many antiques dating from Viking and medieval times up to the 1600s. The shop also sells gold, silver, and bronze jewelry, much of which is also quite old.

Duxiana (✉ Södra Promenaden 63 ☎ 040/305977) sells the world-famous Dux beds, which have elaborate spring systems and are built into wooden frames. Shipping can be arranged. Beds range in price from SKr 25,000 to SKr 57,000. **Outside** (✉ Kyrkog. 3, Stortorget ☎ 040/300910) specializes in high-quality outdoor gear. Everything from sleeping bags, boots, and tents to gas canisters and waterproofing products is stocked here. In addition to such brands as North Face and Patagonia, Outside is the only Scandinavian store to carry products from Mac Pac of New Zealand. At the summer market called **Möllevångstorget,** on the square of the same name, there is usually a wonderful array of flowers, fruit, and vegetables. It is an old working-class area and a nice place to stroll. The market is open Monday–Saturday.

en route   One of Skåne's outstanding Renaissance strongholds, **Svaneholms Slott** lies 30 km (19 mi) east of Malmö, on E65. First built in 1530 and rebuilt in 1694, the castle today features a museum occupying four floors with sections depicting the nobility and peasants. On the grounds are **Gästgiveri** (☎ 0411/40540), a notable restaurant, walking paths, and a lake for fishing and rowing. ✉ *Skurup* ☎ *0411/40012* ✉ *SKr 25* ☉ *May–Aug., daily 11–5; Apr. and Sept., Wed.–Sun. 11–4.*

Ystad

❻ *64 km (40 mi) southeast of Malmö (via E65), 205 km (127 mi) southwest of Växjö.*

A smuggling center during the Napoleonic Wars, Ystad has preserved its medieval character with winding narrow streets and hundreds of half-timber houses built over a span of five centuries. A good place to begin exploring is the main square, Stortorget.

The principal ancient monument, **St. Maria Kyrka** (St. Mary's Church; ✉ Lilla Norregatan) was built shortly after 1220 as a basilica in the Romanesque style, though there have been later additions. The watchman's copper horn sounds from the church tower beginning at 9:15 PM and repeating every 15 minutes until 1 AM. It's to proclaim that "all is well." The church lies behind Stortorget on Lilla Norregatan. The 16th-century Latinskolan (Latin School) is adjacent to the church—it's said to be the oldest schoolhouse in Scandinavia.

Charlotte Berlin's Museum is a well-preserved burgher's home from the 19th century. Charlotte Berlin left the home and the contents to the city upon her death in 1916. It has a variety of displays, including one that shows many antique clocks and watches. ⊠ *Dammg. 23* ☎ *0411/ 18866* ✉ *SKr 20* ✆ *June–Aug., weekdays noon–5, weekends noon–4.*

The Franciscan monastery **Gråbrödraklostret** adjoins St. Peter's church and is one of the best-preserved cloisters in Sweden. The oldest parts date to 1267. Together, the church and monastery are considered the most important historical site in Ystad. ⊠ *Sankt Petri Kyrkoplan* ☎ *0411/577590* ✉ *SKr 20* ✆ *Weekdays noon–5, weekends noon–4.*

Sweden's best-preserved theater from the late 1800s, **Ystads Teater** (⊠ Sjömansg. 13 ☎ 0411/577199) is a beautiful, ornate building. The dramatic interior adds a great deal to any performance seen here. Outside is a battery of cannons first used in 1712 to defend the harbor from its many marauders, especially the Danes.

Ystads Konstmuseum houses a collection of important Swedish and Danish 20th-century art, as well as a photographic collection that includes a daguerreotype from 1845. ⊠ *St. Knuts Torg* ☎ *0411/577285* ⊕ *www. konstmuseet.ystad.se* ✉ *SKr 20* ✆ *Tues.–Fri. noon–5, weekends noon–4.*

> **off the beaten path**

SÖVDEBORGS SLOTT – Twenty-one kilometers (13 mi) north of Ystad on Route 13 is Sövdeborgs Slott. Built in the 16th century and restored in the mid-1840s, the castle, now a private home, consists of three two-story brick buildings and a four-story-high crenellated corner tower. The main attraction is the Stensal (Stone Hall), with its impressive stuccowork ceiling. It's open for tours if booked in advance for groups of at least 10. Otherwise, the grounds are open. ⊠ *Sjöbo* ☎ *0416/16012.*

★ **ALES STENAR –** Eighteen kilometers (11 mi) east of Ystad, on the coastal road off Route 9, is the charming fishing village of Kåseberga. On the hill behind it stands the impressive Ales Stones, an intriguing 230-foot-long arrangement of 58 Viking stones in the shape of a ship. Believed to be between 1,000 and 1,500 years old, the stones and their purpose still puzzle anthropologists.

Glimmingehus – About 10 km (6 mi) east of Ales Stenar and 10 km (6 mi) southwest of Simrishamn just off Route 9 lies Glimminge House, Scandinavia's best-preserved medieval stronghold. Built between 1499 and 1505 to defend the region against invaders, the late-Gothic castle was lived in only briefly. The walls are 8 feet thick at the base, tapering to 6½ feet at the top of the 85-foot-high building. On the grounds are a small museum and a theater. There are concerts and lectures in summer and a medieval festival at the end of August. ⊠ *Hammenhög* ☎ *0414/18620* ✉ *SKr 50* ✆ *Easter–May, daily 11–5; June–mid-Sept., daily 10–6; mid-Sept.–end of Sept., daily 11–5.*

Where to Stay & Eat

$–$$ ✕ **Bryggeriet.** A lovely cross-timbered inn, this restaurant brews its own beer—there are two large copper boilers near the bar. It has a pleasant garden, and the dimly lighted interior is made out of bricks in the curved shape of an underground cavern. Hearty traditional fare, including reindeer and other game, is Bryggeriet's specialty. Try the duck, which is prepared in an elegant port sauce with an herb garnishing. ⊠ *Långg. 20* ☎ *0411/69999.*

$–$$ ✕ **Lottas.** This restaurant is in an interesting two-story building on the
FodorśChoice main square in the heart of town. The food includes several lighter fish
★ dishes, including scallops in season. As is typical in Sweden, there are
many red-meat options; the steaks are cooked and presented with care.
⊠ *Stortorget 11* ☎ *0411/78800.*

$$ ✕⊡ **Hotel Continental.** The Continental opened in 1829 and is a truly
FodorśChoice stunning building, both inside and out. Take a good look at the lobby
★ with its marble stairs, crystal chandelier, stained-glass windows, and mar-
ble pillars. No two guest rooms are alike. The restaurant ($$) gives each
dish its own flair. The meat dishes are served with a selection of root
vegetables, including fresh potatoes, carrots, and what the British call
swedes (rutabagas), when they're in season. ⊠ *Hamng. 13* ☎ *0411/13700*
🖨 *0411/12570* ⊕ *www.hotelcontinental-ystad.se* ⇌ *52 rooms* ⟳ *Restaurant* ☰ *AE, MC, V* ⧵⊙⧸ *BP.*

$ ⊡ **Anno 1793 Sekelgården Hotell.** Centered around a cobblestone court-
yard, this small and comfortable family-owned hotel is in the heart of
Ystad, a short walk from St. Maria's Church and the main square. The
half-timber buildings that make up the hotel date from the late 18th century, and in the summer breakfast is served in the courtyard. ⊠ *Låg-
gatan 18* ☎. *0411/739 00* 🖨 *0411/189 97* ⇌ *18 rooms* ⟳ *Restaurant,
sauna, meeting room* ☰ *AE, DC, MC, V* ⧵⊙⧸ *BP.*

$ ⊡ **Bäckagården.** This homey small hotel is centrally located. It dates from
the 17th century, has a secluded garden, and serves breakfast. ⊠ *Dammg.
36* ☎ *0411/19848* 🖨 *0411/65715* ⇌ *8 rooms* ☰ *AE, MC, V* ⧵⊙⧸ *BP.*

Shopping

Gifts, souvenirs, clothes, and various household items are sold at **Tidlöst**
(⊠ *Bökareg. 12* ☎ *0411/73029*). The items are a mix of old and new.
Head to **Sjögrens–Butikerna** (⊠ *The Mall, Stora Österg. 6* ☎ *0411/
17200*) for an excellent selection of well-priced design ware, including
crystal, jewelry, glassware, china, and pottery.

Simrishamn

❼ *41 km (25 mi) northeast of Ystad via Route 9, 105 km (65 mi) east of
Malmö, 190 km (118 mi) southwest of Växjö.*

This fishing village of 20,000 swells to many times that number during the summer, though for most, Simrishamn doesn't warrant an
overnight stay. Built in the mid-1100s, the town has cobblestone streets
lined with tiny brick houses covered with white stucco. The medieval
St. Nicolia Kyrka, which was once a landmark for local sailors, dominates the town's skyline.

The **Frasses Musikmuseum** contains an eclectic collection of music oddities, such as self-playing barrel organs, antique accordions, children's
gramophones, and what may be the world's most complete collection
of Edison phonographs. ⊠ *Peder Mörks Väg 5* ☎ *0414/14520* ⊠ *SKr
20* ⊙ *Early June–late June and Aug., Sun. 2–6; July, Mon.–Wed. and
Sun. 2–6.*

The construction of **St. Nicolai Kyrka** (St. Nicolai's Church) began around
1161. Inside are models of sailing ships given to the church by sailors
as a token of gratitude for their safe return from the Baltic Sea. The two
sculptures outside the church are by the famous Swedish sculptor Carl
Milles. In July there is a lunchtime concert starting at noon. ⊠ *Stortorget* ☎ *0414/412480* ⊙ *Mar.–June 10 and mid-Sept.–Dec., weekdays
noon–3, Sat. 10–1, Sun. after service; June 11–mid-Sept., weekdays
10:30–6:30, Sat. 9:30–4, Sun. 11–4.*

off the
beaten
path

BRANTEVIK – Less than 10 km (6 mi) south of Simrishamn on the coastal road is this classic but tiny southern fishing village. It has a marvelous harbor, and the homes are small, brightly colored fishermen's cottages. A hundred years ago only 1,100 people lived here, but the village had Sweden's then-largest sailing fleet with 124 ships. The village hasn't changed much since then. A good place for lunch is **Bronterögen,** a café that serves excellent meals and is right beside the harbor. It will cost between SKr 45 and SKr 125 for an entrée. For something a little more formal or even a night's stay, try the old inn **Brantevik's Bykrog and Hotel** (⊠ Mästergränd 2 ☎ 0414/22069). There are seven rooms here, along with a restaurant.

en route

About 20 km (12 mi) north of Simrishamn is the tiny village of **Kivik.** You are now firmly in the heart of Sweden's apple country, a spectacular place to be when the trees are blooming in early to late May. From Kivik follow the signs to the **Äpplets Hus** (the House of Apples; ☎ 0414/71900), a museum that tells the history of apple orcharding. Alongside is the cider brewery and a gift shop full of apple paraphernalia. On the way back from the Äpplets Hus is a small café—and a huge pile of boulders. This is the **Kivik grave,** one of the most remarkable Bronze Age monuments in Sweden. Dating from before 3000 BC, the tomb consists of a cairn nearly 250 feet across. Walk into the tomb and find the cist with eight tombstones engraved with symbols.

If you're in the area between June and August, you might want to stop off at **Kronovall Castle** (☎ 0417/19710), about 20 km (13 mi) northwest of Simrishamn for a tour that features local wines. The castle is now a restaurant run by restaurateur Petri Pumpa. Guided tours of the castle are organized three times a day in the summer. The 18th-century castle was given its baroque appearance through a remodeling in 1890 by architect Isak Gustaf Clason, best known for the Nordic Museum in Stockholm. Surrounding the castle is a beautiful park with a magnificent hedge labyrinth.

Kristianstad

❽ *73 km (45 mi) north of Simrishamn via Routes 9/19 and E22, 95 km (59 mi) northeast of Malmö (via E22), 126 km (78 mi) southwest of Växjö.*

Kristianstad was founded in 1614 by Danish king Christian IV as a fortified town to keep the Swedes at bay. Today its former ramparts and moats are wide tree-lined boulevards. For most, there isn't much of great interest in the town itself.

About 17 km (11 mi) east of Kristianstad and just north of the E22 highway is **Bäckaskog Slott.** Standing on a strip of land between two lakes, Bäckaskog Castle was originally founded as a monastery by a French religious order in the 13th century. Danish noblemen turned it into a fortified castle during the 16th century. It was later appropriated by the Swedish government and used as a residence for the cavalry. The castle was a favorite of the Swedish royalty until 1900. Today the castle is a hotel and restaurant. ⊠ *Fjälkinge* ☎ *044/53250* 🎫 *Free* 🕐 *Year-round.*

off the
beaten
path

ÅHUS – Ten kilometers (7 mi) southeast of Kristianstad is this seaside resort. The town has a medieval center and sandy beaches stretching for 60 km (40 mi) down Hanöbukten. The best-known feature of Åhus is the **Absolut Vodka distillery.** Every drop of Absolut Vodka, the world's third-largest vodka brand, consumed in the world is still made in this little town. The distillery gives 1½-hour guided tours, which must be booked ahead by telephone; tickets must be picked up and paid for at the tourist office by 6 PM the day before the tour. ☎ *044/240106 reservations* ✉ *30 SKr* ☉ *Tour mid-June–mid-Aug., Tues. 12:45.*

en route | Six kilometers (4 mi) east of Kristianstad on E22, take a left turn to Fjälkinge and follow brown signs marked with a white flower. The route, **Humlesingan,** is a scenic drive of 48 km (30 mi) around Skåne's largest lake, Lake Ivösjö. The geology dates from millions of years ago and is rich in minerals. It was a famed hops region until 1959. The old hop houses can still be seen—one is a café. The big mountainous island is Ivö, 440 feet high.

Karlskrona

❾ *111 km (69 mi) east of Kristianstad via E22, 201 km (125 mi) northeast of Malmö, 107 km (66 mi) southeast of Växjö.*

A small city built on the mainland and on 33 nearby islands, Karlskrona achieved great notoriety in 1981, when a Soviet submarine ran aground a short distance from its naval base. The town dates from 1680, when it was laid out in baroque style on the orders of Karl XI. Two churches around the main square, **Trefaldighetskyrkan** and **Frederikskyrkan,** date from this period and were both designed by the architect Nicodemus Tessin the Younger. Because of the excellent state of preservation of the naval museum and other buildings in town, Karlskrona has been designated a World Heritage Site by UNESCO.

Although the archipelago is not as large or as full of dramatic scenery as Stockholm's islands, Karlskrona is still worth the boat trip. One can be arranged through **Skärgårdstrafiken** (☎ 0455/78330).

★ The **Admiralitetskyrkan** (Admiralty Church) is Sweden's oldest wooden church, built in 1685. It is an unusual variant of the Swedish style of churches, which are generally made of stone. Although it was supposed to be temporary, the stone replacement was never built. The wooden statue of constable Matts Rosenborn, who froze to death here one New Year's Eve in the 18th century, stands outside tipping his hat to those who give alms. The church is on Bastionsgatan on the naval island. Walk east a few minutes from Stortorget, the main square to get to the bridge.

★ The **Marinmuseum** (Naval Museum), in a building dating from 1752, is one of the oldest museums in Sweden and has a superb collection perfect for those with a nautical bent. The shed for making rope is ancient (1692) and huge—nearly 1,000 feet long. In the museum are old maps and charts, old navigating equipment, ship designs, and relics from actual ships, as well as weaponry. The museum can also provide you with brochures of the port area, perfect for a pleasant walk. ✉ *Stumholmen* ☎ *0455/53902* ✉ *SKr 50* ☉ *June–Aug., daily 10–6; Sept.–May, daily noon–5.*

Stunning **Kungsholm Fort,** on the island of Kungsholmen, was built in 1680 to defend the town's important naval port. The fortress was on full alert when the Russians blockaded Karlskrona in the 1780s and when the English were cruising the Baltic in 1801. Perhaps the most impressive aspect of the fort is the round harbor, built into the fort itself with only a narrow exit to the sea. The fort is accessible only by a boat booked through the **tourist office** (✉ Stortorget ☎ 0455/303439) on the main island of Trossö.

The **archipelago** is made up of dozens of islands scattered off the coast of Karlskrona's mainland. They are stunning low-lying islands that make excellent places to walk and picnic. Although some are accessible by road, the best way to take it all in is to go by ferry. The cruises take half a day. Contact **Affärsverken Båttrafik** (✉ N. Kungsgatan 36 ☎ 0455/78300 🖪 SKr 40–SKr 110), the ferry operators, with offices at the ferry terminal.

Where to Stay & Eat

¢–$$ ✕ **Lisas Sjökrog.** Floating on the sea, this docked ship is a great place to see a sunset and look out over the archipelago. The emphasis here is on seafood, including herring, halibut, and shellfish in season. You can also try well-prepared meat dishes and the popular summer salads. ✉ Fisktorget ☎ 0455/23465 🖃 AE, MC, V ☉ Closed Sept.–Apr.

¢ ✕ **Eat—The Home Company.** If you like to mix your dining with design, then Eat (placed within a home-design store) is a good choice for lunch. The menu is vaguely nouvelle, with beautiful presentations of small portions. The soups are terrific, ranging from mushroom to pumpkin. Try the lamb, cooked medium rare and served with mint. Trains were once repaired inside the 18th-century building. ✉ Bleklingeg 3 Lokstallarna ☎ 0455/300003 🖃 AE, DC, MC, V ☉ No dinner.

$ 🏨 **First Hotel Statt.** The rooms are well appointed, the decor classic, and the style Swedish traditional. Built around 1900, this immaculate hotel with an ornate stairwell and candelabras in the lobby is in the heart of the city and is fully renovated. ✉ Ronnebygatan 37–39 ☎ 0455/19250 🖶 0455/169 09 ⊕ www.firsthotels.com ⇨ 107 rooms ♨ Restaurant, hot tub, sauna, bar, nightclub, no-smoking rooms 🖃 AE, DC, MC, V.

$ 🏨 **Hotel Carlscrona.** From this seaside hotel, the beach is a 10-minute walk. The town center and the naval museum are even closer. Though the rooms are nothing special, many have good views. ✉ Skeppsbrokajen ☎ 0455/361500 🖶 0455/361509 ⇨ 80 rooms ♨ Dining room, in-room data ports, sauna, parking, no-smoking rooms 🖃 AE, MC, V ❢❢ BP.

¢ 🏨 **Hotel Conrad.** For simple but functional accommodations at a reasonable price, the Hotel Conrad is a good choice. It is a short walk from shopping, restaurants, and entertainment. ✉ V. Köpmansg. 12 ☎ 0455/363200 🖶 0455/363205 ⊕ www.hotelconrad.se ⇨ 58 rooms ♨ Sauna, free parking 🖃 AE, MC, V ❢❢ BP.

Nightlife & the Arts

In a renovated old theater **Bio Bar och Matsalar** (✉ Borgmästareg. 17 ☎ 0455/311100) is an ornate setting with crystal chandeliers. The scene varies greatly, but you're more likely to hear Top 40 hits than the latest dance music. Playing on the town's seafaring heritage with its name, **Piraten Nattklubb** (✉ Ronnebyg. 50 ☎ 0455/81853) serves up good cocktails, but amid a decor that suggests the Middle Ages.

The Outdoors

Karlskrona has a reputation for both saltwater and freshwater fishing. **Senoren's Sportfishing Tours** (☎ 0455/44010) will take you to the outermost archipelago to fish by boat or from cliffs. Kurt Ola Oftedal of **Hasslö Island Tourist and Fishing Service** (☎ 0455/332492 or 0708/332492) organizes fishing in the ocean and in freshwater streams and lakes.

Kalmar

➊ *91 km (57 mi) northeast of Karlskrona via E22, 292 km (181 mi) northeast of Malmö, 109 km (68 mi) southeast of Växjö.*

Fodor's Choice
★

The attractive coastal town of Kalmar, opposite the Baltic island of Öland, is dominated by the imposing **Kalmar Slott**, Sweden's best-preserved Renaissance castle. Part of it dates from the 12th century. The living rooms, chapel, and dungeon can be visited. ⊠ *Slottsvägen* ☎ *0480/451490* ⌦ *SKr 75* ⊙ *Apr.–May and Sept., daily 10–4; June and Aug., daily 10–5; July, daily 10–6; Oct.–Mar., 2nd weekend every month 11–3:30.*

The **Kalmar Läns Museum** (Kalmar District Museum), with good archaeological and ethnographic collections, contains the remains of the royal ship *Kronan,* which sank in 1676. Cannons, wood sculptures, and old coins were all raised from the seabed in 1980. Another exhibit focuses on Jenny Nystrom, a painter famous for popularizing the *tomte,* a rustic Christmas elf. ⊠ *Skeppsbrog. 51* ☎ *0480/451300* ⌦ *SKr 50* ⊙ *Mid-June–mid-Aug., daily 10–6; mid-Aug.–mid-June, Tues.–Fri. 10–4, weekends 11–4.*

Kalmar Domkyrkan is a highly impressive building designed by Nicodemus Tessin the Elder in 1660 in the Italian baroque style. Inside, the massive open spaces create stunning light effects. Strangely, the cathedral is the only one in Sweden without a bishop. Music is played at noon during the week. ⊠ *Stortorget* ☎ *0480/12300* ⌦ *Free* ⊙ *Daily 10–6.*

off the
beaten
path

PATAHOLM AND TIMMERNABBEN – Numerous seaside towns dot the coastline along E22, opposite Öland. **Pataholm** has a cobblestone main square, and **Timmernabben** is famous for its caramel factory. Miles of clean, attractive, and easily accessible—if windy—beaches line this coastal strip.

Where to Stay & Eat

★ **$$** ✕ **Byttan.** In fine weather this restaurant's large outdoor eating area and beautiful gardens are the perfect place for a leisurely meal. Served with a vast range of freshly baked breads, the summer salads, especially the chicken salad with limes, are terrific. You can also choose a heartier entrée of traditional herring with mashed potatoes. ⊠ *Slottsallén* ☎ *0480/ 16360* ⊟ *MC, V* ⊙ *Closed Oct.–Apr.*

$$ ✕ **Källaren Kronan.** Given the quality of the eclectic international dishes here, the meals are surprisingly cheap. Try the pheasant breast with Calvados sauce or the fillet of venison with black currant sauce. The building dates to the 1660s and has been preserved as a cultural heritage site. ⊠ *Ölandsg. 7* ☎ *0480/411400* ⊟ *AE, DC, MC, V.*

¢–$$ ✕ **Ernesto Salonger.** This outdoor Italian restaurant serves everything from pizza to pasta. On Friday and Saturday nights a nightclub and casino are in action. ⊠ *Larmtorget* ☎ *0480/20050* ⊟ *AE, DC, MC, V.*

$$ ▦ **Slottshotellet.** On a quiet street, this gracious old house faces a waterfront park that's a few minutes' walk from both the train station and Kalmar Castle. Guest rooms are charmingly individual, with carved-wood bedsteads, old-fashioned chandeliers, pretty wallpaper, wooden floors, and antique furniture. The bathrooms are spotlessly clean. Breakfast is served year-round, and full restaurant service is available in the summer. ⊠ *Slottsv. 7, 392 33* ☎ *0480/88260* 🖷 *0480/88266* ⌑ *44 rooms* ⌑ *Restaurant, sauna, meeting room, no-smoking rooms* ⊟ *AE, DC, V* ⦿❘ *BP.*

$$ ▦ **Stadshotellet.** In the city center, Scandic's Stadshotellet is a fairly large hotel with traditional English decor. The main building dates from 1907.

Guest rooms are freshly decorated and have hair dryers and radios, among other amenities. There's also a fine restaurant. ⊠ *Stortorget 14, 392 32* ☎ *0480/496900* 📠 *0480/496910* 🛏 *138 rooms* ♨ *Restaurant, hot tub, sauna, bar, meeting room, no-smoking rooms* ☰ *AE, DC, MC, V.*

$–$$ 🏨 **Frimurare.** Set inside a spacious park, the attractive Frimurare radiates calm and peacefulness. Both the rooms and the hotel itself have old-time touches. It's a short walk from here to the castle. ⊠ *Lamtorget 2* ☎ *0480/15230* 📠 *0480/85887* 🌐 *www.frimurarehotellet.gs2.com* 🛏 *34 rooms, 31 with bath* ♨ *Meeting rooms* ☰ *MC, V.*

Öland

★ ⓫ *8 km (5 mi) east of Kalmar via the Ölandsbron Bridge.*

The island of Öland is a magical and ancient place—and the smallest province in Sweden. The area was first settled some 4,000 years ago and is fringed with fine sandy beaches and dotted with old windmills, churches, and archaeological remains. In the 16th century King Gustav Vasa used land he had confiscated from the church to establish farms around the country. These farms were meant to foster the country's agricultural development and supply the court and the army with grain, meat, butter, and wool. The king founded five farms on Öland: Borgholm, Halltorp, Horn, Gärdslösa, and Ottenby. Of these, Ottenby, Bogholm and Horn are still operating farms.

The island also has spectacular bird life—swallows, cranes, geese, and birds of prey. Many migrate to Öland from Siberia. The southern part of the island, known as Stora Alvaret, is a UNESCO World Heritage Site due partly to its stark beauty and unique flora and fauna. Private car travel is prohibited, so let the public bus shuttle you around the island.

To get to Öland, take the 6-km (4-mi) bridge from Kalmar. Be sure to pick up a tourist information map (follow the signs as soon as you get on the island). Most of the scattered sights have no address. Close to the bridge is the popular **Historium,** where slide shows, wax figures, and constructed dioramas illustrate what Öland was like 10,000 years ago.

Head clockwise around the island. **Borgholms Slott,** the largest castle ruin in northern Europe, is just outside the island's principal town, Borgholm (25 km [16 mi] north of the bridge). Nearby is the royal family's summer home at **Solliden.** If you get hungry, try Pappa Blå, a restaurant on Borgholm's pleasant square. It serves a variety of food, from pizzas to sandwiches to steaks, which run about SKr 60–SKr 150. From Borgholm follow the signs north to **Knisa Mosse,** a marshland area that's home to many bird species.

Heading farther north brings you to Löttorp. From here drive west to **Horns Kungsgård,** a nature preserve on a lake that has a bird-watching tower and walking trails. Horns Kungsgård is also a royal estate, meaning "king's farm" or "king's estate." The government maintains its appearance to look as it did in 1900.

Some 5 km (3 mi) north along the coast from Horns Kungsgård is **Byrum,** a nature preserve with striking, wind-carved limestone cliffs. The botanist Linnaeus (Carl von Linné) discussed this area in his writings. Just a few more kilometers on is **Skäftekärr,** which has a culture museum, a café, an Iron Age farm with an arboretum, and walking trails. At the northernmost tip is the Långe Erik lighthouse.

Turning back you will find one of the island's three nature centers, **Trollskogen.** On its trails are some majestic old oaks, prehistoric barrow graves, and pines. A little to the south is northern Europe's longest beach, a great swimming spot with sparkling white sand.

Pass back through **Löttorp,** heading south. Keep an eye out for the signs leading east off the main road for the intriguing **Källa** church ruins, some of the best on the island. Return to the main road and head south to **Kappelludden,** one of the island's best year-round bird sites. A medieval chapel's ruins and a lighthouse make this coastal spot very scenic.

Gärdslösa, to the southwest of Kappelludden, has an excellently preserved medieval church. Look for the Viking inscriptions on its wall.

Continuing south, turn right at Långlöt for the **Himmelsberga Museum** (☎ 0485/561022 or 0485/561011 ▦ SKr 50 ◷ May–Aug., daily 10–6), a farm museum dating from the end of the 18th century. The buildings and furnishings include horse buggies and horse sleds. The old stables were home to the small, swift Öland horses, which were extinct by the beginning of the 19th century. Old documents claim that they could dance to horns and drums and jump through hoops.

Gråborg, a 6th-century fortress with massive stone walls 625 feet in diameter, is a must-see. To get here, turn right at Norra Möckleby.

Return and head south. About 2 km (1 mi) north of Seby are some strings of **rune stones**: engraved gravestones dating from 500 BC to AD 1050, stone circles, and cists and cairns. Continue south to come to the southeastern edge of Stora Alvaret. This bleak and eerie area has been farmed for 1,000 years.

Just before you reach the 5th-century fortified village of **Eketorp,** you'll reach a turnoff for the **Gräsgård,** an important fishing village. Eketorp's castle is partially renovated; the area includes small tenants' fields from the Iron and Middle ages. Admission to the castle and its grounds is SKr 50.

Ottenby is the southernmost tip of Öland and was a hunting area as long as 5,000 years ago. It's now a popular site for bird-watching. The entrance fee to the burial fields is SKr 50 per car or SKr 10 per person arriving by bus.

Now drive north up the west coastal road. Shortly after **Södra Möckleby** you'll come across the impressive burial grounds of **Gettlinge.** More than 200 graves lie across a distance of 2 km (1 mi). The site was in use from the time of Christ into the Viking era, which lasted until 1050. Beginning in late spring, the land north of here blooms with many different wild orchids.

Farther on is **Mysinge Tunukus,** a Bronze Age site. A group of rune stones here is placed in a shape resembling a ship: it's beautiful at sunset. From here continue on back to the bridge and mainland Sweden.

Where to Stay

$ ▦ **Halltorps Gästgiveri.** This 17th-century manor house has modernized duplex rooms decorated in Swedish landscape tones and an excellent restaurant. Driving north from Ölandsbron, it's on the left side of the road. ✉ *387 92 Borgholm* ☎ *0485/85000* ▤ *0485/85001* ⤳ *36 rooms* ↳ *Restaurant, 2 saunas, meeting room, no-smoking rooms* ▤ *AE, DC, MC, V.*

¢ ▦ **Eksgården Värdshus.** The red cottages at this hotel resemble farmhouses. The pleasant dining room often hosts cultural performances. There's even a museum with farm and domestic implements and footwear, and an arts and crafts shop. ✉ *Gårdby 386 93 Färjestaden* ☎ *0485/33450* ▤ *0485/33434* ⤳ *13 rooms* ↳ *Dining room, shop* ◷ *Closed Sept.–Jan.*

¢ ✕⊞ **Guntorps Herrgård.** Spacious parkland surrounds this manor house, which is 2,500 feet from the center of Borgholm. Outside, there's a heated pool. The restaurant has hardwood floors, a grandfather clock along one wall, and copper pots hanging on an other. ⊠ *387 36 Borgholm* ☎ *0485/13000* ⊟ *0485/13319* ⊕ *www.guntorp.oland.com* ↩ *32 rooms* ♨ *Restaurant, sauna, whirlpool* ⊟ *AE, DC, MC, V.*

¢ ⊞ **Värdshuset Briggen Tre Liljor.** Large trees stand alongside this lovely, old stone-clad hotel, which is 25 km (16 mi) north of Borgholm. The rooms are spacious and old-fashioned, making you feel as if you've stepped into the past. The restaurant serves good traditional food. ⊠ *Lofta, 387 91 Borgholm* ☎ *0485/26400* ⊟ *0485/26420* ↩ *17 rooms* ♨ *Restaurant* ⊟ *AE, MC, V.*

The Kingdom of Glass

Stretching roughly 109 km (68 mi) between Kalmar and Växjö.

Småland is home to the world-famous Swedish glass industry. Scattered among the rocky woodlands of Småland province are isolated villages whose names are synonymous with high-quality crystal glassware. This spectacular creative art was at its height in the late 19th century. The conditions were perfect: large quantities of wood to fuel the furnaces and plenty of water from the streams and rivers. At the time demand was such that the furnaces burned 24 hours a day.

The region is still home to 16 major glassworks, many of them created through the merging of the smaller firms. You can still see glass being blown and crystal being etched by craftspeople. You may also be interested in attending a *Hyttsill* evening, a revival of an old tradition in which Baltic herring (*sill*) is cooked in the glass furnaces of the *hytt* (literally "hut," but meaning "the works"). Most glassworks also have shops selling quality firsts and not-so-perfect seconds at a discount.

Though the glass factories generally prospered before and during the 1900s, this wealth didn't filter down to many of their workers or to Småland's other inhabitants. Poverty became so widespread that the area lost vast numbers of people to the United States from the late 19th through the 20th century. If you're an American with Swedish roots, chances are your ancestors are from this area. The Utvandrarnas Hus (Emigrants' House), in Växjö, tells the story of this exodus.

The Kingdom of Glass's oldest works is **Kosta Glasbruk.** Dating from 1742, it was named for the two former generals who founded it, Anders Koskull and Georg Bogislaus Stael von Holstein. Faced with a dearth of local talent, they initially imported glassblowers from Bohemia. The Kosta works pioneered the production of crystal (to qualify for that label, glass must contain at least 24% lead oxide). You can see glass-blowing off-season (mid-August–early June) between 9 and 3. To get to the village of Kosta from Kalmar, drive 49 km (30 mi) west on Route 25, then 14 km (9 mi) north on Route 28. ⊠*Kosta* ☎*0478/34500* ⊙*May and June and Aug.–mid-Sept., weekdays 9–10 and 11–3, Sat. 10–3; July, daily 10–4; mid-Sept.–Apr., weekdays 9–10 and 11–3.*

Orrefors is one of the best-known glass companies. Orrefors arrived on the scene late—in 1898—but set particularly high artistic standards. The skilled workers in Orrefors dance a slow, delicate minuet as they carry the pieces of red-hot glass back and forth, passing them on rods from hand to hand, blowing and shaping them. The basic procedures and tools are ancient, and the finished product is the result of unusual teamwork, from designer to craftsman to finisher. One of Orrefors's special attractions is a magnificent display of pieces made during the 19th century; you can appease bored children in the cafeteria and playground. From early June to mid-August you can watch glass being blown. ⊠ *On Rte. 31, about 18 km (11 mi) east of Kosta Glasbruk* ☎ *0481/34189* ⊕ *www.orrefors. se* ⊙ *July–mid-Aug., weekdays 9–6, Sat. 10–5, Sun. 11–5; mid-Aug.–June, weekdays 10–6, Sat. 10–4, Sun. noon–4.*

Mystical animal reliefs and female figures play a big role in the work at **Målerås,** which was founded in 1890. The glass workers are great to watch; they use classic techniques with names such as "the grail." Overlooking the factory is a pleasant restaurant with panoramic views. ⊠ *12 km (7 mi) north of Orrefors* ☎ *0481/31401* ⊙ *June–Aug., weekdays 9–6, Sat. 10–5, Sun. 11–5; Sept.–May, weekdays 10–6, Sat. 10–4, Sun. 11–4.*

Boda Glasbruk, part of the Kosta Boda Company, is the second-oldest glassworks, founded in 1864. The work here has an ethereal theme, with the designers drawing on cosmic bodies such as the sun and the moon. Much of the work has veils of violet and blue suspended in the crystal. ⊠ *Just off Rte. 25, 42 km (26 mi) west of Kalmar* ☎ *0481/42410* ⊙ *July–mid-Aug., weekdays 9–6, Sat. 10–5, Sun. 11–5; mid-Aug.–June, weekdays 9–6, Sat. 10–4, Sun. noon–4.*

Continue west from Boda Glasbruk for 20 km (12 mi) to the town of Lessebo. From mid-June to mid-August you can visit the 300-year-old **Lessebo Handpappersbruk,** which is the only handmade-paper factory in Sweden. Since the 18th century the craftsmen have been using much the same techniques to produce fine paper, which is available from the shop. Guided tours take place on weekdays at 9:30, 10:30, 2, and 2:15. ⊠ *Storgatan, Lessebo* ☎ *0478/47691* ▭ *Tours free* ⊙ *Jan.–Dec., weekdays 7–4; June–Aug., guided tours at 9:30, 10:30, 1, and 2:15.*

Skruf Glasbruk began in 1896. Today it's a purveyor to the king of Sweden. The royal family, the ministry of foreign affairs, and the parliament have all commissioned work from Skruf. Local farmers encouraged the development of the glassworks because they wanted a market for their wood. The museum takes you through the historic eras of fine glass craft in Småland. The factory specializes in lead-free crystal, which has a unique iridescence and form. ⊠ *10 km (6 mi) south of Lessebo. Turn left at Åkerby* ☎ *0478/20133* ⊙ *Weekdays 9–5, weekends 10–4.*

★ ☺ Founded in 1889, **Bergadala Glasbruk** is one of the most traditional glassworks. Alongside the main road are the former workers' homes, now used mainly as long-term rentals. Note the impressive circular furnace that stands in the middle of the wooden floor. Bergadala is often called the blue glassworks, since many of its pieces have a rich cobalt hue. A stone's throw from the smelter is a children's playground and a glass-painting workshop that will keep them occupied for hours. From here you are 10 km (6 mi) from Växjö. ⊠ *About 15 km (9 mi) northwest of Lessebo, toward Växjö* ☎ *0478/31650* ⊙ *Weekdays 9–5, weekends 10–4.*

Where to Stay

¢ ▥ **Hotell Björkäng.** Set in a park that will give you plenty of opportunity to take evening strolls, the Björkäng has well-kept rooms. They have some rustic decorations, such as traditional ornaments, wood carved by nature, and glass pieces. You also have the opportunity to spend an evening in the glassblowing room. The dining room offers a range of good traditional Swedish food. ⊠ *Stora Vägen 2, Kosta* ☎ *0478/50000* ▤ *0478/ 50437* ⊶ *24 double and 2 single rooms* ⌂ *Dining room, sauna, billiards* ▭ *MC, V* ⑩ *BP.*

¢ ▥ **Orrefors.** The rooms are cozy, and the hotel is set in the authentic center of the Kingdom of Glass. The restaurant and bar offer good dining and a pleasant atmosphere. ✉ *Kantav. 29, Orrefors* ☎ *0481/30035* 🖨 *0481/30056* 📞 *10 rooms* 🍴 *Restaurant, bar* 🖃 *MC, V* 🍽 *BP.*

¢ 🏨 **Wärdhusset Flustret.** With a big garden, trees, and a forest surrounding you, this countryside inn can't help but be relaxing. It's a great place from which to head out for a walk. ✉ *Storg. 83, Lessebo* ☎ *0478/10100* 🖨 *0478/10103* 📞 *13 rooms, 5 with bath* 🖃 *MC, V.*

Växjö

⑫ *109 km (68 mi) northwest of Kalmar via Route 25, 198 km (123 mi) northeast of Malmö, 228 km (142 mi) southeast of Göteborg, 446 km (277 mi) southwest of Stockholm.*

Some 10,000 Americans visit this town every year, for it was from this area that their Swedish ancestors departed in the 19th century. A large proportion of those emigrants went to Minnesota, attracted by the affordable farmland and a geography reminiscent of parts of Sweden. On the second Sunday of every August, Växjö celebrates Minnesota Day: Swedes and Swedish-Americans come together to commemorate their common heritage with American-style square dancing and other festivities. Beyond this, the city is really just a stopover.

The **Utvandrarnas Hus** (Emigrants' House), in the town center, tells the story of the migration, when more than a million Swedes—one quarter of the population—departed for the promised land. The museum exhibits provide a vivid sense of the rigorous journey, and an archive room and a research center allow Americans with Swedish blood to trace their ancestry. The archives are not open for genealogy research on weekends. ✉ *Vilhelm Mobergsg. 1* ☎ *0170/20120* 🌐 *www. svenskaemigrantinstitutet.g.se* ✉ *SKr 40* 🕐 *June–Aug., weekdays 9–6, Sat. 11–4; Sept.–May, weekdays 9–4, weekends 11–4.*

★ The **Smålands Museum** is famous for its presentation of the development of glass and has the largest glass collection in northern Europe. Its excellent display puts the area's unique industry into perspective and explains the different styles of the various glass companies. ✉ *Södra Jarnvägsg. 2* ☎ *0470/704200* 🌐 *www.smalandsmuseum.se* ✉ *SKr 40* 🕐 *Jun.–Aug., weekdays 10–5, weekends 11–5; Sept.–May, Tues.–Fri. 10–5, weekends 11–5.*

off the beaten path

KRONOBERGS SLOTTSRUIN – About 5 km (3 mi) north of Växjö, this 14th-century castle ruin lies on the edge of the Helgasjön (Holy Lake). The Småland freedom fighter Nils Dacke used the castle as a base for his attacks against the Danish occupiers during the mid-1500s; now it's an idyllic getaway. In summer you can eat waffles under the shade of birch trees by the café, or take a dinner or sightseeing cruise around the lake on the small toylike *Thor,* Sweden's oldest steamboat. ☎ *0470/63000 Café Ryttmästargården, 0470/704200 boat tours* ✉ *Castle ruins SKr 10, dinner cruise SKr 400, 2½-hr canal trip to Årby and back SKr 125, 1-hr lake trip SKr 100 incl. coffee* 🕐 *Castle tours offered late June–late Aug.; dinner cruise Sun.*

Where to Stay

$$ 🏨 **Hotel Statt.** Now a Best Western hotel, the Statt is popular with tourist groups. It has a convenient, central location. The building dates from 1853, but the rooms are up to modern standards. The hotel has a cozy pub, bistro, and café. ✉ *Kungsg. 6, 351 04* ☎ *0470/13400* 🖨 *0470/ 44837* 📞 *124 rooms* 🍴 *Restaurant, café, sauna, gym, pub, meeting room, no-smoking rooms* 🖃 *AE, DC, MC, V.*

$ ▦ **Esplanad.** In the town center, the Esplanad is a small family-run hotel with basic amenities. ✉ *Norra Esplanåden 21A, 352 31* ☎ *0470/22580* 🖷 *.0470/26226* ⤴ *23 rooms, 20 with bath* ⚬ *No-smoking rooms* 🝙 *MC, V* ❤️ *BP.*

The South & the Kingdom of Glass A to Z

AIR TRAVEL

CARRIERS Five airlines serve the Malmö airport (Sturup).
🇸 **Direktflyg** ☎ 021/800645. **KLM** ☎ 040/500530. **Malmö Aviation** ☎ 020/550010. **RyanAir** ☎ 0900/2020240 in Sweden ⊕ www.ryanair.com when booking from abroad. **SAS** ☎ 0770-727727.

CUTTING COSTS SAS offers discounts on trips to Malmö year-round; ask for the "Jackpot" discount package.

AIRPORTS

Malmö's airport, Sturup (MMX), is approximately 30 km (19 mi) from Malmö and 25 km (15 mi) from Lund. Buses for Malmö and Lund meet all flights at Sturup Airport. The price of the trip is SKr 90 to either destination. A taxi from the airport to Malmö or Lund costs about SKr 470. 🇸 ☎ 040/6131100. **Taxi and Limousine Service** ☎ 020/979797 in Sweden, (46)8/797-5025 from abroad. **Sturup** ☎ 040/6131100.

BOAT & FERRY TRAVEL

Since the inauguration of the Öresund bridge, between Malmö and Copenhagen, it is no longer possible to travel by ferry between the two cities, but there is still regular ferry service between Helsingborg in Sweden and Helsingoør in Denmark (by Scandlines, HH-Ferries, and Sundsbussarna). From Ystad there is ferry service to Swinoujscie in Poland (by Polferries), and from Trelleborg ferries run to Sassnitz and Rostock in Germany (by Scandlines). Stena Line ferries run between Karlskrona and Gdynia in Poland.
🇸 **HH-Ferries** ☎ 042/198000. **Polferries** ☎ 08/52018101. **Scandlines** ☎ 0410/65000. **Sundsbussarna** ☎ 042/216060. **Stena Line** ✉ Danmarksterminalen, Masthuggskajen, Göteborg ☎ 031-7040300 in Göteborg, 0455/366300 in Karlskrona.

CUTTING COSTS The Malmökortet (Malmö Card) entitles the holder to, among other benefits, free travel on the city buses, free parking, discounts on tours, and free admission or discounts to most museums, concert halls, nightclubs, and theaters; the Royal Cab company; and many shops and restaurants. A one-day card costs SKr 120, a two-day card SKr 150, and a three-day card SKr 180. Cards are available from the tourist office in Malmö.

CAR RENTAL

If you are coming from Denmark and want to rent a car as soon as you arrive, several rental companies have locations at Malmö Harbor, including Avis, Hertz, and Europcar. Hertz car rentals are available for less than SKr 600 a day on weekends (less during the summer) if you book an SAS flight.
🇸 **Major Agencies Avis** ☎ 040/77830. **Europcar** ☎ 040/71640. **Hertz** ☎ 040/330770.

CAR TRAVEL

Copenhagen and Malmö are connected by the Öresund bridge. It costs SKR 275 one-way.

Malmö is 620 km (386 mi) from Stockholm. Take the E4 Highway to Helsingborg, then the E6/E20 to Malmö and Lund. From Göteborg take the E6/E20.

Roads are well marked and well maintained. Traveling around the coast counterclockwise from Helsingborg, you take the E6/E20 to Landskrona, Malmö, and Lund, then the E6/E22 to Trelleborg; Route 9 goes along the south coast from there all the way to Simrishamn and then heads north until just before Kristianstad. It's there that you can pick up E22 all the way through Karlshamn, Ronneby, Karlskrona, and on across the east coast to Kalmar. From Kalmar, Route 25 goes almost directly west through Växjö to Halmstad, on the west coast between Helsingborg and Göteborg.

EMERGENCIES

As elsewhere in Sweden, call 112 for emergencies.

TRAIN TRAVEL

The major towns of the south are all connected by rail.

There is regular service from Stockholm to Helsingborg, Lund, and Malmö. Each trip takes about 6½ hours, and about 4½ hours by high-speed (X2000) train. All three railway stations are centrally located in their respective towns.

Trains between Malmö and Copenhagen take 35 minutes and run three times an hour during the day and once an hour at night. A one-way ticket is SKr 80.

🚆 Train Companies **Skånetrafiken** ☎ 0771/777777.

TRANSPORTATION AROUND THE SOUTH

A special 48-hour Öresund Runt (Around Öresund) pass is available from the Malmö Tourist Office or any train station in Skåne. Costing between SKr 199 and SKr 249, depending on where you start your trip, the ticket covers a train ticket from the Skåne province to Malmö, a train from Malmö to Helsingborg, a ferry to Helsingør; a train to Copenhagen, and a ferry back to Malmö (or if you so prefer, the same trip clockwise).

VISITOR INFORMATION

🚆 Tourist Information **Helsingborg** ✉ Södra Storgatan 1 ☎ 042/104350 ⊕ www. helsingborgsguiden.com. **Jönköping** ✉ Järnvägsstationen (central train station) ☎ 036/105050. **Kalmar** ✉ Ölandskajen 9 ☎ 0480/417700 ⊕ www.kalmar.se/turism/index2. html. **Karlskrona** ✉ Stortorget 2 ☎ 0455/303490. **Kristianstad** ✉ Stora Torg ☎ 044/121988 ⊕ www.kristianstad.se. **Landskrona** ✉ Storgatan 36 ☎ 0418/473000 ⊕ www. tourism.landskrona.se. **Lund** ✉ Kyrkog. 11 ☎ 046/355040 ⊕ www.lund.se. **Malmö** ✉ Centralstationen (Central Train Station) ☎ 040/341200 ⊕ www.malmo.se. **Öland** ✉ Träffpunkt Öland, Färjestaden ☎ 0485/560600. **Ronneby** ✉ Västra Torggatan 1 ☎ 0457/18090. **Simrishamn** ✉ Tullhusgatan 2 ☎ 0414/819800 **Växjö** ✉ Stationen, Norra Järnvägsgatan 3 ☎ 0470/41410. **Ystad** ✉ St. Knuts Torg ☎ 0411/577681 ⊕ www. visitystad.com.

DALARNA: THE FOLKLORE DISTRICT

A place of forests, mountains, and red-painted wooden farmhouses and cottages by pristine, sun-dappled lakes, Dalarna is considered the most traditional of all the country's 24 provinces. It is the favorite sight for celebrations on Midsummer Day, when Swedes don folk costumes and dance to fiddle and accordion music around maypoles covered with wild-flower garlands.

Dalarna played a key role in the history of the nation. It was from here that Gustav Vasa recruited the army that freed the country from Danish domination during the 16th century. The region is also important artistically, both for its tradition of naive religious decoration and for producing two of the nation's best-loved painters, Anders Zorn (1860–1920) and Carl Larsson (1853–1915), and one of its favorite poets, the melancholy, mystical Dan Andersson (1888–1920). He sought inspiration in the remote forest camps of the old charcoal burners, who spent their days slowly burning wood to make the charcoal for factory furnaces.

Dalarna offers very little in the way of restaurants and accommodation. Visitors to the area—many from elsewhere in Scandinavia or from Germany—make use either of the region's many well-equipped campsites or of *stugbyar* (small villages of log cabins, with cooking facilities), usually set near lakesides or in forest clearings.

Our itinerary circles Siljan, the largest of the 6,000 lakes in the province and the center of Dalarna's folklore. The main points can all be reached by train, except for the southern side of Lake Siljan.

Dalarna is a gloriously compact region, mostly consisting of a single road that rings Lake Siljan, the area's main attraction. A drive round the lake will take in most of the highlights, leaving you only to decide whether to travel clockwise or counterclockwise. The lake itself provides a focal point for the region, providing fish to eat, and swimming and boating to entertain. The tiny villages and towns strung around the lake each have their own particular attraction to offer, making Dalarna a well-ordered, neat little package of a region to explore.

Falun

▶ ❶ *230 km (143 mi) northwest of Stockholm via E18 and Route 70.*

Falun is the traditional capital of Dalarna, though the adjacent nondescript railway town of Borlänge has grown in importance as a business center. Falun's history has always been very much bound to its copper mine, worked since 1230 by Stora Kopparbergs Bergslags AB (today just Stora), which claims to be the oldest limited company in the world. During its great period of prosperity in the 17th century, it financed Sweden's "Age of Greatness," when the country became the dominant Baltic power. In 1650, Stora produced a record 3,067 tons of copper; probably as a result of such rapid extraction, 37 years later its mineshafts caved in. The collapse was on Midsummer Day, when most miners were off duty, and as a result no one was killed. The mine eventually closed in 1992.

★ Today the major part of the mine is an enormous hole in the ground that, in combination with the adjoining **Storamuseum**, has become Falun's principal tourist attraction. The one-hour tour through a network of old shafts and tunnels begins with a hair-raising 150-foot descent in an old elevator. Wear old shoes and warm clothing, since the copper-tinged mud can stain footwear and it's cold down there. The Stora Museum puts into perspective the lives of the men who worked the mines and has eye-opening displays on just how bad working conditions were below ground. ☎ 023/711475 ☒ Mine SKr 90, museum free with mine tour ☉ Mine May–Aug., daily 10–5; Sept.–mid-Nov. and Mar.–Apr., weekdays 11–5, weekends 11–4; museum May–Aug., daily 10–5; Sept.–Apr., weekdays 11–5, weekends 11–4.

The folk art, folklore, clothing, and music of the area are all well covered at **Dalarnasmuseet** (the Dalarnas Museum). There is also a grand reconstruction of the study in which Selma Lagerlöf (1858-1940), the celebrated Swedish author, worked after she moved to Falun in 1897. ⊠ Stigareg. 2–4 ☎ 023/765500 ☒ SKr 40 ☉ May–Aug., Mon.–Thurs.

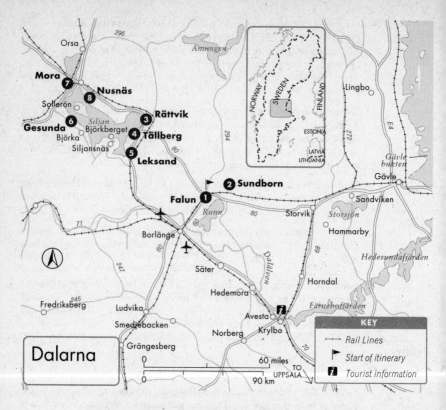

Dalarna

10–5, Fri.–Sun. noon–5; Sept.–May, Mon.–Tues. and Thurs. 10–5, Wed. 10–9, Fri.–Sun. noon–5.

Where to Stay & Eat

$$ ✕ **MS Slussbruden.** This restaurant on a boat offers "prawn cruises." For a set price you can feast on as many prawns as you can shell during the three-hour cruise. Live music acts serenade you all the while. Limitless bread and butter, cheese, fruits, and coffee are included. Wine and drinks are extra, and the choice is a little limited but good nonetheless. Combined with the beautiful scenery, the dinner cruise is a great hit. ⊠ *Strandv.* ☎ *023/63850* ⚓ *Reservations essential* ▤ *AE, DC, MC, V* ☉ *Closed Nov.–Apr.*

$–$$ ✕ **Blå Apelsinen.** The Blue Orange serves up what's known as *husman-skost* (homey) Swedish food. Simple, hearty pork, beef, and fish dishes are all offered here in straightforward surroundings at reasonable prices. ⊠ *Bergskolegränd 8A* ☎ *023/29111* ▤ *AE, MC, V.*

$$ ▥ **Scandic.** Outside Falun, the ultramodern Scandic was built for the 1993 World Skiing Championships that took place in the Lungnet sports and recreation center. The building itself looks like a giant ski jump made of Legos. The comfortable rooms have good views of the giant ski jump that's still used for competitions. ⊠ *Svärdsjög. 51, 791 31 Falun* ☎ *023/ 6692200* 🖷*023/669211* ⇖*153 rooms* ⚘ *Restaurant, indoor pool, sauna, pub, meeting room, no-smoking rooms* ▤ *AE, DC, MC, V.*

$ ▥ **Grand.** Part of the First Hotel chain, this conventional modern hotel is close to the town center. The bright rooms are decorated with Chippendale-style furniture. ⊠ *Trotzg. 9–11, 791 71* ☎ *023/794880* 🖷 *023/ 14143* ⇖*153 rooms* ⚘ *Restaurant, minibars, indoor pool, gym, sauna, bar, convention center, no-smoking rooms* ▤ *AE, DC, MC, V.*

$ 🏨 **Hotel Winn.** This small, cozy hotel in the town center is built in rus-
Fodor'sChoice tic Dalarna style and filled with antique furnishings. There is a pleas-
★ ant relaxation area where the hot tub and sauna will let you unwind
from the day's stresses. ✉ *Bergskolegränd 7, 791 12* ☎ *023/701700*
📠 *023/701709* 🛏 *88 rooms, 84 with bath* ⚒ *Restaurant, hot tub,
sauna, meeting room, no-smoking rooms* ⊟ *AE, DC, MC, V.*

¢–$ 🏨 **Hotel Falun.** Margaretha Eriksson runs this small, friendly, but bland-
looking hotel just 1,300 feet from the railway station. The five rooms
that share baths are offered at a lower rate. The front desk closes at 9
PM. ✉ *Centrumhuset, Trotzg. 16, 791 30* ☎ *023/29180* 📠 *023/13006*
🛏 *22 rooms, 17 with bath* ⚒ *No-smoking rooms* ⊟ *AE, DC, MC, V.*

¢ 🏨 **Birgittagården.** The Dalarna Sisters of Birgitta religious order runs this
small hotel, 8 km (5 mi) outside town. It's smoke- and alcohol-free and
set in a fine park. ✉ *Uddnäsv. 58, 791 46* ☎ *023/32147* 📠 *023/32471*
🛏 *20 rooms* ⚒ *Meeting room; no smoking, no room phones, no room
TVs* ⊟ *No credit cards.*

Sports & the Outdoors

A 25-minute walk from the center of Falun, east on Svärdsjögatan, takes
you to **Lungnet** (☎ 023/83500), Falun's sports complex and national ski
stadium. Horseback riding, swimming, bowling, an indoor sports center, and running tracks are all available. The ski stadium is home to the
260-foot ski jump (used only in competitions). In the winter you can
watch the daredevil jumpers fly through the air, and in the summer, when
the snow has gone, you can go to the top yourself and admire the view
across Falun and beyond.

SKIING At the **Bjursås Ski Center** (☎ 023/774177 ⊕ www.bjursas.com), 25 km
(15 mi) northwest of Falun on Route 80, you can make use of the resort's seven lift systems and 18 varied pistes. It's open between December
and April and has numerous hotels, restaurants, and cafés.

Sundborn

❷ *10 km (6 mi) northeast of Falun off Route 80.*

★ In this small village you can visit **Carl Larsson Gården,** the lakeside home
of the Swedish artist (1833–1915). Larsson was an excellent textile designer and draftsman who painted scenes from his family's busy domestic
life. The house itself was creatively painted and decorated by Larsson's
wife, Karin, also trained as an artist. Their home's turn-of-the-20th-cen-
tury fittings and furnishings have been carefully preserved; their great-
grandchildren still use the house on occasion. Waits for guided tours in
summer can take two hours. You'll receive a timed ticket and can visit
the café or stroll around the garden or lake while you wait. ☎ *023/60053*
🎫 *Guided tours only, SKr 80* ⊙ *May–Sept., daily 10–5; Oct.–Apr., 1
guided tour every Tues.; call for details.* ⊕ *www.clg.se.*

Rättvik

❸ *48 km (30 mi) northwest of Falun via Route 80.*

On the eastern tip of Lake Siljan, Rättvik is a pleasant town of timbered
houses surrounded by wooded slopes. A center for local folklore, the
town has several shops that sell handmade articles and produce from
the region.

Every year in June, dozens of people wearing traditional costumes arrive in longboats to attend midsummer services at the town's 13th-cen-
tury church, **Rättviks Kyrka,** which stands on a promontory stretching
into the lake. Its interior contains some fine examples of local religious

art. Next to the church are 90 stables, the oldest from the 1400s, where churchgoers once rested their horses.

The open-air museum **Rättvik Gammelgård,** a 20-minute walk along the banks of the lake north of Rättvik, reconstructs peasant life of bygone days. More than 3,500 pieces of art, clothing, ceramics, tools, and furniture are on display in the old buildings. Tours in English can be arranged through the Rättvik tourist office. ⊠ *Free, guided tour SKr 20* ☉ *Mid-June–mid-Aug., daily 11–6; tours at 1 and 2:30.*

Just to the west of Rättvik in the forest is **Vidablick.** The top of this tall wooden tower, more than 100 years old, will give you some of the most stunning views across Lake Siljan that you can find.

★ Once a lucrative open chalk mine, the huge multitier quarry left at **Dalhalla** (7 km [4½] mi north of Rättvik) has become one of the world's most beautiful outdoor stages. One side is banked with seats, and the stage, surrounded with water and supported on pillars, appears to float on the cobalt-blue lake at the quarry's bottom. Opera, rock concerts, and amazing light shows are all presented here, where the sound is enhanced by the quarry's incredible acoustics. There is also a museum covering the meteor crash that formed Lake Siljan 360 million years ago, the chalk mining that still takes place, and the history of mining. Guided tours of the more remote parts of the quarry can be booked year-round. ⊠ *Stationshuset, Rättvik* ☎ *0248/797950* ⊠ *SKr 45 for museum and tour* ☉ *Museum mid-May–Sept., daily 10–5; July, daily 10–6.*

Where to Stay & Eat

¢ ✕ **Strandrestaurangen.** A family-style restaurant with a huge outdoor seating area by the lake, Strandrestaurangen serves such standard Swedish fare as meatballs, sausages, and pork chops. It's all well cooked and filling. Kids enjoy the beach, miniature golf, the ice cream bar, and the swimming pool. For the adults, there's a pub attached, which has live music in the evening. ⊠ *Rättvik* ☎ *0248/13400* ⊟ *AE, MC, V* ☉ *Summer months only.*

¢ ▦ **Hotell Vidablick.** Set on its own grounds, with a pleasant view of the lake from the veranda, this small hotel makes a welcome, relaxing stop. Rooms are modern and sparsely furnished, and there's a small private beach where you can take to the water, if it's warm enough. ⊠ *Hantverksbyn, 795 36* ☎ *0248/30250* 🖶 *0248/30660* ⇴ *50 rooms* ⚭ *Bar, beach* ⊟ *AE, DC, MC, V* ⊙ *BP.*

Tällberg

❹ *9 km (5 mi) south of Rättivk via Route 70 57 km (35 mi) northwest of Falun via Route 80.*

Tällberg is considered by many to be the real Dalarna. Once a sleepy town that few knew about, an 1850 visit from Hans Christian Andersen put an end to all that. He extolled its virtues—tiny flower-strewn cottages, sweet-smelling grass meadows, stunning lake views—to such an extent that Tällberg quickly became a major tourist stop. This tiny village, one of the smallest in the region with only about 200 permanent residents, is packed with crowds in summer.

The farm buildings that make up **Klockargården** have become a living museum of handicrafts and local industry. Artists and craftsmen work in the old buildings, performing such skills as blacksmithing, baking flat bread, making lace, and weaving textiles. ⊠ *Tällberg* ☎ *0247/50265* ⊠ *Free* ☉ *June–Aug., daily 10–7.*

Where to Stay & Eat

★ $ ✕🏠 **Åkerblads.** A sprawling, low-built hotel, with parts dating from the 1400s, Åkerblads is known primarily for its gourmet achievements. The restaurant ($$) serves an interesting blend of Swedish and French cuisine, including such dishes as pork roasted with eggplants and blueberries, and salmon with asparagus, truffle, and burgundy wine sauce. The hotel rooms are comfortable, and most have very good views of Lake Siljan. ⊠ *Sjögattu 2, 793 70* 🕾 *0247/50800* 🖷 *0247/50652* ⊕ *www.akerblads-tallberg.se* ⥱ *67 rooms, 25 suites* ♨ *Restaurant, pool, sauna, spa, bar* 🖃 *AE, DC, MC, V* 🍴 *BP.*

$ 🏠 **Tällbergsgården.** A classic Dalarna redwood building, this one claiming to be the oldest in the village, is home to a small hotel with lake views. The guest rooms are light and airy, with neutral shades and wooden floors. ⊠ *Holgattu 1, 793 70* 🕾 *0247/50850* 🖷 *0247/50200* ⊕ *www.tallbergsgarden.se* ⥱ *38 rooms, 6 suites* ♨ *Restaurant, sauna, bar, meeting rooms* 🖃 *AE, DC, MC, V* 🍴 *BP.*

¢ ✕🏠 **Hotel Dalecarlia.** There's a homey feel to this first-class hotel, which has exacting standards and good lake views. The lobby's comfy sofas and darkened corners are welcoming spots to sink into. Rooms are large and done in soft colors, and there is a spa and fitness center with pool, sauna, and beauty treatments. The restaurant ($$) is candlelighted and reminiscent of a farmhouse. It has oak beams, crisp white linen, and a large open fireplace perfect for warming your after-dinner brandy. The food is well presented and emphasizes local and regional specialties. The game is especially good. ⊠ *Tällberg, 793 70* 🕾 *0247/89100* 🖷 *0247/50240* ⊕ *www.dalecarlia.se* ⥱ *80 rooms, 5 suites* ♨ *Restaurant, pool, gym, sauna, spa, bar, convention center* 🖃 *AE, DC, MC, V* 🍴 *BP.*

FodorsChoice ★

Leksand

⑤ *9 km (5½ mi) south of Tällberg via Route 70, 66 km (41 mi) northwest of Falun via Rättvik.*

Thousands of tourists converge on Leksand every June for the Midsummer celebrations; they also come in July for *Himlaspelet* (*The Play of the Way that Leads to Heaven*), a traditional musical with a local cast that's staged outdoors near the town's church. It is easy to get seats; ask the local tourist office for details.

Leksand is also an excellent vantage point from which to watch the "church-boat" races on Siljan. These vessels are supposedly the successors to the Viking longboats. They were used in the 13th and 14th centuries to take peasants from outlying regions to church on Sunday. On Midsummer Eve the longboats, crewed by people in folk costumes, skim the lake once more.

In the hills around Leksand and elsewhere near Siljan are many *fäbodar,* small settlements in the forest where cattle were taken to graze during the summer. Less idyllic memories of bygone days are conjured up by **Käringberget,** a 720-foot-high mountain north of town where alleged witches were burned to death during the 17th century.

FodorsChoice ★ The oldest parts of **Leksands Kyrka** date from the 13th century, and the current exterior dates from 1715. The Leksand Church's interior contains some interesting touches: a German font from the 1500s, a crucifix from 1400, and Dalarna's oldest organ. But what makes this church really shine is its location, perhaps one of the prettiest in the country. The peaceful tree-lined churchyard and the view across the entire lake are both breathtaking. ⊠ *Kyrkudden* 🕾 *0247/80700.*

At the **Leksands Hembygdsgårdar,** the site of the oldest farm buildings in Dalarna, you can find out more about the famous red structures that dot the region's landscape. Other displays look at building techniques that arose in the Middle Ages as well as the history of country living in Dalarna. ⊠ *Kyrkallén* ☎ *070/4095044* ✉ *SKr 20* ⊙ *June–Aug., daily noon–4.*

Famous local doctor and author Axel Munthe built **Munthes Hildasholm** as a present for his English wife in 1910. The house and gardens, filled with exquisite antiques, paintings, and furniture from across Europe, can now be visited and seen exactly as they were left. You can have coffee and cake in the café, set in beautifully manicured gardens and lawns. ⊠ *Klockaregatan 5, Kyrkudden* ☎ *0247/10062* ✉ *SKr 60* ⊙ *June–Sept., Mon.–Sat. 11–6, Sun. 1–6.*

Where to Stay & Eat

¢–$$ ✕ **Bosporen Restaurang.** The large terrace outside this restaurant is a great place to dine in summer. The menu is long and interesting, with some great Swedish classics. The best bet is the selection of pizzas, which make use of such ingredients as arugula, pine nuts, Gorgonzola, and pears. Wine by the glass is of good quality, and the beers are wide-ranging and cheap. ⊠ *Stortorget 1* ☎ *0247/13280* ▤ *AE, MC, V.*

¢ 🏨 **Hotell Korstäppan.** The beautiful rooms, many with traditional tile fireplaces and all with wooden floors, are the main attraction at this large, yellow wooden hotel. All the rooms are spacious and simply furnished with stylish antiques and beautiful old rugs. ⊠ *Hjortnäsv. 33, 793 31* ☎ *0247/12310* 🖨 *0247/14178* ➶ *30 rooms* ♤ *Breakfast room, convention center* ▤ *AE, MC, V* ⊙l *BP.*

¢ 🏨 **Leksands Gasthem.** Simplicity bordering on minimalism is the theme at this converted old school near a farmyard just outside Leksand. The bedrooms have plain, scrubbed wooden floors, large windows, and pale-blue chairs. Each bathroom is shared by several rooms. In the hallway—where you can still see the low coat hooks for the schoolchildren—is a sweeping wood staircase that leads to a TV and lounge area. Wonderful breakfasts are included in the rate; everything is homemade. ⊠ *Krökbacken 5, 793 90* ☎ *0247/13700* 🖨 *0247/13737* ⊕ *www.leksandsguesth. nu* ➶ *13 rooms* ♤ *Breakfast room, lounge* ▤ *AE, DC, MC, V* ⊙l *BP.*

Sports & the Outdoors

Leksand is the perfect base for a bike ride around Lake Siljan. There are many paths and tracks to choose from, and maps and rental bikes are available from the **tourist office** (☎ 0247/796130).

Gesunda

❻ *38 km (24 mi) northwest of Leksand*

A chairlift from Gesunda, a pleasant little village, will take you to the top of a mountain for unbeatable views over the lake. The large island of **Sollerön** is connected to the mainland by a bridge at Gesunda. The island has fine views of the mountains surrounding Siljan. Several excellent beaches and an interesting Viking gravesite are also here. The church dates from 1775.

🎅 **Tomteland** (Santa World), on Gesundaberget, claims to be the home of Santa Claus, or Father Christmas. Toys are for sale at Santa's workshop and at kiosks. There are rides in horse-drawn carriages in summer and sleighs in winter. ⊠ *Gesundaberget, Sollerön* ☎ *0250/21200* ✉ *SKr 125* ⊙ *Mid-June–late Aug., daily 10–5; late Nov.–early Jan., daily 10–4* ⊕ *www.santaworld.se.*

Mora

❼ *50 km (31 mi) northwest of Leksand, 40 km (25 mi) northwest of Rättvik via Rte. 70.*

To get to this relaxed lakeside town of 20,000, you can follow the northern shore of Lake Silja (there is a bridge at Färnäs, or follow the lake's southern shore through Leksand and Gesunda to get a good sense of Dalarna.

Mora is best known as the finishing point for the world's longest cross-country ski race, the Vasalopp, which begins 90 km (56 mi) away at Sälen, a ski resort close to the Norwegian border. The race commemorates a fundamental piece of Swedish history: the successful attempt by Gustav Vasa in 1521 to rally local peasants to the cause of ridding Sweden of Danish occupation. Vasa, only 21 years old, had fled the capital and described to the Mora locals in graphic detail a massacre of Swedish noblemen ordered by Danish king Christian in Stockholm's Stortorget. Unfortunately, no one believed him, and the dispirited Vasa was forced to abandon his attempts at insurrection and take off on either skis or snowshoes for Norway, where he hoped to evade King Christian and go into exile.

Just after he left, confirmation of the Stockholm bloodbath reached Mora, and the peasants, already discontented with Danish rule, sent two skiers after Vasa to tell him they would join his cause. The two men caught up with the young nobleman at Sälen. They returned with him to Mora, where an army was recruited. Vasa marched south, defeated the Danes, and became king and the founder of modern Sweden.

The commemorative race, held on the first Sunday in March, attracts thousands of competitors from all over the world, including the Swedish king. There is a spectacular mass start at Sälen before the field thins out. The finish is eagerly awaited in Mora, though since the start of live television broadcasts the number of spectators has fallen.

You can get a comfortable glimpse of the Vasalopp's history in the **Vasaloppets Hus,** which contains a collection of the ski gear and photos of competitors, news clippings, and a short film detailing some of the race's finer moments. ✉ *Vasag.* ☎ *0250/39225* 🎫 *SKr 20* 🕐 *Mid-June–mid-Aug., daily 10–5; mid-Aug.–mid-June, weekdays 10–5.*

Mora is also known as the home of Anders Zorn (1860–1920), Sweden's leading impressionist painter, who lived in Stockholm and Paris before returning to his roots here and painting the local scenes for which he is now known. His former private residence—Zorngården— a large, sumptuous house designed with great originality and taste by the painter himself, has retained the same exquisite furnishings, paintings, and decor it had when he lived there with his wife. Next door, the

★ **Zorn Museet** (Zorn Museum), built 19 years after the painter's death, contains many of his best works. ✉ *Vasag. 36* ☎ *0250/16560* 🎫 *Museum SKr 35, home SKr 45* 🕐 *Museum mid-May–mid-Sept., Mon.–Sat. 9–5, Sun. 11–5; mid-Sept.–mid-May, Mon.–Sat. noon–5, Sun. 1–5; home (guided tours only) mid-May–mid-Sept., Mon.–Sat. 10–4, Sun. 11–4; mid-Sept.–mid-May, Mon.–Sat. noon–4, Sun. 1–4.*

On the south side of town is **Zorns Gammalgård,** a fine collection of old wooden houses from local farms, brought here and donated to Mora by Anders Zorn. One of them holds the **Textil Kammare** (Textile Chamber), a collection of textiles and period clothing. ✉ *Yvradsv.* ☎ *0250/ 16560 June–Aug. only* 🎫 *SKr 20* 🕐 *June–Aug., daily 11–5.*

off the
beaten
path

SILJANSFORS SKOGSMUSEUM (Siljansfors Forest Musuem) – Partly because there's always been a lot of wood available for firing furnaces, the area around Mora is well known for its metalworking. This outdoor museum shows the smithies' many connections to local forestry, in particular with the art of charcoal burning. A track through the forest will take you to smithies, ironworks, woodcutting sheds, and charcoal-burning towers. The walks are all linked together at the information center near the entrance. ✉ *12 mi southwest of Mora on Rte. 45* ☎ *0250/20331.*

off the
beaten
path

ORSA – Fifteen kilometers (9 mi) north of Mora on Route 45 is a small sleepy town that becomes a big chaotic symphony every Wednesday in July. It's then that the **Orsa Spelmän**, groups of traditional folklore music players, take part in what's called the Orsayran (Orsa rush). The musicians take over the streets of the town, wandering and playing their instruments. This soon becomes a free-for-all in which all the people in town, whether accomplished or not, bring out their instruments and play. It's great fun.

ORSA GRÖNKLITTS BJÖRNPARK – Just outside Orsa is the wildlife reserve inhabited by Sweden's native brown bears and other animals, including wolves. There's a limited chance of spotting one of these shy creatures, but if you do, it is an unforgettable sight. (Be sure to follow common sense safety rules, being sure not to approach the bears too closely. It's important to not make them feel threatened— that's when bears tend to attack).

Where to Stay & Eat

★ $$ ✕ **Jernet Bar & Matsal.** In one of Mora's oldest industrial buildings (1879), Jernet serves high-quality Swedish and international dishes, which may include roast elk with mustard potatoes and lingonberries and breast of chicken stuffed with Brie and apricots. The tables are bare antique oak, the wooden chairs are of a traditional Leksand style, and the crisp linen napkins are woven locally. In the bar area, furnished in birch and stainless steel, the large windows allow for great views over the lake. ✉ *Strandg. 6* ☎ *0250/15020* ▤ *AE, DC, MC, V.*

$ ▦ **Kung Gösta.** This modern, reasonably sized hotel is 2 km (1 mi) from the town center and only 330 feet from the Mora train station. The small rooms are brightly furnished, with wood floors and large windows. ✉*Kristinebergsg. 1, S792 32* ☎*0250/15070* ▤*0250/17078* ⇆*47 rooms* ⌂*Restaurant, indoor pool, gym, sauna, meeting room, no-smoking rooms* ▤ *AE, DC, MC, V* ⧖ *BP.*

$ ▦ **Mora.** This pleasant little hotel, a part of the First Hotel group, is in the town center 5 km (3 mi) from the airport. Its comfortable rooms are brightly decorated. ✉*Strandg. 12, S792 30* ☎*0250/592650* ▤*0250/18981* ⇆ *135 rooms* ⌂ *Restaurant, indoor pool, sauna, gym, meeting room, no-smoking rooms* ▤ *AE, DC, MC, V* ⧖ *BP.*

$ ▦ **Mora Parken.** This modern hotel sits in a park by the banks of the Dala River, not far from the town center. Rooms are small and simply furnished with pastel fabrics and plain wood furniture and floors. ✉ *Parkgatan 1, 792 37* ☎ *0250/27600* ▤ *0250/27615* ⇆ *75 rooms* ⌂ *Restaurant, sauna, convention center, no-smoking rooms* ▤ *AE, DC, MC, V* ⧖ *BP.*

$ ▦ **Siljan.** Part of the Sweden Hotel group, this small modern hotel has views over the lake. Rooms are standard, with radio and television. ✉ *Morag. 6, 792 22* ☎ *0250/13000* ▤ *0250/13098* ⊕ *www.swedenhotels.se* ⇆*44 rooms* ⌂ *Restaurant, sauna, bar, dance club, meeting room, no-smoking floor* ▤ *AE, DC, MC, V* ⧖ *BP.*

Sports & the Outdoors

SKIING Dalarna's principal ski resort is **Sälen,** starting point for the Vasalopp, about 80 km (50 mi) west of Mora. Snow here is pretty much guaranteed from November to May, and there are more than 100 pistes from which to choose, from simple slopes for the beginner to challenging black runs that weave through tightly forested slopes. For more information contact any of the tourist offices in Dalarna.

WALKING For the energetic traveler it's possible to walk the 90-km (56-mi) **track from Sälen to Mora** that's used for the Vasalopp ski race in March. Along the way you may very well see some elk wandering through the forest. Day shelters, basic night shelters, fireplaces, tables, signposts, and restrooms are set up along the trail. Facilities are free, but a donation of SKr 25 is suggested for the night shelters. Maps and other details can be obtained from the **Mora tourist office** (⊠ Stationsvägen ☎ 0250/592020).

Nusnäs

❽ *6 km (4 mi) southeast of Mora via Route 70, 28 km (17 mi) northwest of Falun.*

The lakeside village of Nusnäs is where the small, brightly red-painted, wooden Dala horses are made. These were originally carved by the peasants of Dalarna as toys for their children, but their popularity rapidly spread with the advent of tourism in the 20th century. Mass production of the little horses started at Nusnäs in 1928. In 1939 they achieved international popularity after being shown at the New York World's Fair, and since then they have become a Swedish symbol (although today some of the smaller versions available in Stockholm's tourists shops are actually made in East Asia). At Nusnäs you can watch the genuine article being made, now with the aid of modern machinery but still painted by hand.

Shopping

Shops in the area are generally open every day except Sunday. The best place to buy painted horses is **Nils Olsson** (⊠ Edåkersvågen 17 ☎ 0250/37200).

Dalarna A to Z

AIRPORTS

There are six flights daily from Stockholm to Dala Airport, which is 8 km (5 mi) south of Borlänge. Flights also arrive from Gothenburg. There are half-hourly bus connections on weekdays between Dala Airport and Falun, 26 km (16 mi) away. Bus 601 runs every half hour from Dala Airport to Borlänge; the trip costs SKr 15. Mora Airport has three Skyways flights daily from Stockholm on weekdays, fewer on the weekends. The airport is 6 km (4 mi) from Mora; no buses serve the airport.

A taxi from Dala Airport to Borlänge costs around SKr 125, to Falun approximately SKr 275. A taxi into Mora from Mora Airport costs SKr 100. Order taxis in advance through your travel agent or when you make an airline reservation. Book a cab by calling the Borlänge taxi service. ⌗ **Dala Airport** ☎ 0243/64510 ⊕ www.dalaairport.se. **Borlänge Taxi** ☎ 0243/13100. **Mora Airport** ☎ 0250/30175.

BUS TRAVEL

Swebus runs tour buses to the area from Stockholm on weekends. The trip takes about four hours one-way. ⌗ **Swebus Express** ☎ 020/218218, 8/50309400 from outside Sweden ⊕ www.swebusexpress.se.

CAR RENTAL

Avis has offices in Borlänge and Mora. Europcar has an office in Borlänge. Hertz has an office in Falun, and independent company Bilkompaniet, formerly a part of Hertz, rents cars in Mora.

🚗 Major Agencies **Avis** ⊠ Borlänge ☎ 0243/87080 ⊠ Mora ☎ 0250/16711. **Europcar** ⊠ Borlänge ☎ 0243/19050. **Hertz** ⊠ Falun ☎ 023/58872. **Bilkompaniet** ⊠ Mora ☎ 0250/28800.

CAR TRAVEL

From Stockholm take E18 to Enköping and follow Route 70 northwest. From Göteborg take E20 to Örebro and Route 60 north from there. Villages are well sign-posted.

EMERGENCIES

For emergencies dial 112. There are no late-night pharmacies in the area. Vasen Pharmacy, in Falun, is open 9–7 weekdays and 9–noon on Saturday.

🏥 **Falun Hospital** ☎ 023/492000. **Mora Hospital** ☎ 023/493000. **24-hour medical advisory service** ☎ 023/492900. **Vasen Pharmacy** ⊠ Åsg. 25 Falun ☎ 023/20000.

TOURS

Call the Falun tourist office for English-speaking guides to Falun and the region around Lake Siljan; guides cost about SKr 900 per day.

BOAT TOURS Next to the Falun train station, on the quay in the center of town, is the MS *Gustaf Wasa*, a beautiful old steamship that's used for sightseeing tours of Lake Siljan. Trips can take from two to four hours and range in price from SKr 80 to SKr 120. It's a good way to see the stunning countryside from another perspective.

🚢 **MS *Gustaf Wasa*** ☎ 010/2523292.

TRAIN TRAVEL

There is regular daily train service from Stockholm to both Mora and Falun.

VISITOR INFORMATION

On the approach to the area from the south via Route 70, a 43-feet, bright orange-red Dala horse marks a rest stop just south of Avesta. It has a spacious cafeteria and a helpful tourist information center.

🛈 Tourist Information **Falun** ⊠ Trotzgatan 10-12 ☎ 023/83050 ⊕ www.visitfalun.se. **Leksand** ⊠ Stationsgatan 14 ☎ 0247/796130. **Ludvika** ⊠ Fredsgatan 10 ☎ 0240/86050. **Mora** ⊠ Stationsvägen ☎ 0250/592020 ⊕ www.siljan.se. **Rättvik** ⊠ Riksvägen 40 ☎ 0248/797210. **Sälen** ⊠ Sälen Centrum ☎ 0280/18700.

NORRLAND & NORRBOTTEN

The north of Sweden, Norrland, is a place of wide-open spaces where the silence is almost audible. Golden eagles soar above snowcapped crags; huge salmon fight their way up wild, tumbling rivers; rare orchids bloom in Arctic heathland; and wild rhododendrons splash the land with color.

In the summer the sun shines at midnight above the Arctic Circle. In the winter it hardly shines at all. The weather can change with bewildering speed: a June day can dawn sunny and bright; then the skies may darken and the temperature drops to around zero as a snow squall blows in. Just as suddenly, the sun comes out again and the temperature starts to rise.

Here live the once-nomadic Lapps, or Sámi, as they prefer to be known. They carefully guard what remains of their identity while doing their best to inform the public of their culture. Many of the 17,000 Sámi who live in Sweden still earn their living herding reindeer, but as open space shrinks, the younger generation is turning in greater numbers toward the allure of the cities. As the modern world makes its incursions, the Sámi often exhibit a sad resignation to the gradual disappearance of their way of life. A Sámi folk poem says it best: "Our memory, the memory of us vanishes/We forget and we are forgotten."

Yet there is a growing struggle, especially among younger Sámi, to maintain their identity, and, thanks to their traditional closeness to nature, they are now finding allies in Sweden's Green movement. They refer to the north of Scandinavia as *Sapmi,* their spiritual and physical home, making no allowance for the different countries that now rule it.

Nearly all Swedish Sámi now live in ordinary houses, having abandoned the *kåta* (Lapp wigwam), and some even herd their reindeer with helicopters. Efforts are now being made to protect and preserve their language, which is totally unlike Swedish and bears a far greater resemblance to Finnish. The language reflects their closeness to nature. The word *goadnil,* for example, means "a quiet part of the river, free of current, near the bank or beside a rock."

Nowadays many Sámi depend on the tourist industry for their living, selling their artifacts, such as expertly carved bone-handle knives, wooden cups and bowls, bark bags, silver jewelry, and leather straps embroidered with pewter thread.

The land that the Sámi inhabit is vast. Norrland stretches 1,000 km (625 mi) from south to north, making up more than half of Sweden; it's roughly the same size as Great Britain. In the west there are mountain ranges, to the east a wild and rocky coastline, and in between boundless forests and moorland. Its towns are often little more than a group of houses along a street, built around a local industry such as mining, forestry, or hydropower utilities. Thanks to Sweden's excellent transportation infrastructure, however, Norrland and the northernmost region of Norrbotten are no longer inaccessible. Even travelers with limited time can get at least a taste of the area. Its wild spaces are ideal for open-air vacations. Hiking, climbing, canoeing, river rafting, and fishing are all popular in summer; skiing, ice-skating, and dogsledding are winter activities.

A word of warning: in summer mosquitoes are a constant nuisance, even worse than other parts of Sweden, so be sure to bring plenty of repellent (you won't find anything effective in Sweden). Fall is perhaps the best season to visit Norrland. Roads are well maintained, but be careful of *gupp* (holes) following thaws. Highways are generally traffic free, but keep an eye out for the occasional reindeer.

Dining and lodging are on the primitive side in this region. Standards of cuisine and service are not nearly as high as prices—but hotels are usually exceptionally clean and staff scrupulously honest. Accommodations are limited, but the various local tourist offices can supply details of bed-and-breakfasts and holiday villages equipped with housekeeping cabins. The area is also rich in campsites—but with the highly unpredictable climate, this may appeal only to the very hardy.

Norrbotten is best discovered from a base in Kiruna, in the center of the alpine region that has been described as Europe's last wilderness. You can tour south and west to the mountains and national parks, east and south to Sámi villages, and farther south still to Baltic coastal settlements.

Exploring the vast wilderness of Norrland and Norbotten can be extremely rewarding, but it must be done with care. The harsh plains and rugged mountains of this region are best taken under advisement, with someone who has experience in these matters. Having said that, by using one of the larger towns as your base, it is perfectly possible to explore the extreme beauties that the region has to offer without having to make any additional arrangements for your overnight accommodations.

Kiruna

❶ *1,352 km (840 mi) north of Stockholm.*

About 250 km (155 mi) north of the Arctic Circle, and 1,804 feet above sea level, Kiruna is Sweden's northernmost municipality. Although its inhabitants number only around 26,000, Kiruna is Sweden's largest city geographically—it spreads over the equivalent of half the area of Switzerland. Until an Australian community took the claim, Kiruna was often called "the world's biggest city." With 20,000 square km (7,722 square mi) within the municipal limits, Kiruna boasts that it could accommodate the entire world population with 43 square feet of space per person.

Kiruna lies at the eastern end of Lake Luossajärvi, spread over a wide area between two mountains, Luossavaara and Kirunavaara, that are largely composed of iron ore—Kiruna's raison d'être. Here is the world's largest underground iron mine, with reserves estimated at 420 million tons. Automated mining technology has largely replaced the traditional miner in the Kirunavaara mine, which is some 500 km (280 mi) long and has an underground network of 400 km (249 mi) trafficable roads. Of the city's inhabitants, an estimated fifth are Finnish immigrants who came to work in the mine in the 1950s.

The city was established in 1900 as a mining town, but true prosperity came only with the building of the railway to the Baltic port of Luleå and the northern Norwegian port of Narvik in 1902.

Like most of Norrland, Kiruna is full of remarkable contrasts, from the seemingly pitch-black, months-long winter to the summer, when the sun never sets and it is actually possible to play golf round-the-clock for 50 days at a stretch. Here, too, the ancient Sámi culture exists side by side with the high-tech culture of cutting-edge satellite research. Since the 1960s the city has supported the Esrange Space Range, about 40 km (24 mi) east, which sends sounding rockets and stratospheric balloons to probe the upper reaches of the earth's atmosphere, and the Swedish Institute of Space Physics, which has pioneered the investigation of the phenomenon of the northern lights. The city received a boost in 1984 with the opening of Nordkalottvägen, a 170-km-long (106-mi-long) road to Narvik.

One of Kiruna's few buildings of interest is **Kiruna Kyrka** (Kiruna Church; ✉ Gruvvägen), near the center of the city. It was built in 1921, its inspiration a blending of a Sámi kåta with a Swedish stave church. The altarpiece is by Prince Eugen (1863–1947), Sweden's painter prince.

Where to Stay & Eat

$ ✕🏨 **Kebne och Kaisa.** These twin modern hotels—named after the local mountain, Kebnekaise—are close to the railway station and the airport bus stop. Rooms are bland but modern and comfortable. The restaurant is one of the best in Kiruna; it's open for breakfast and dinner. ✉ *Konduktörsg. 3, 981 34* ☎ *0980/12380* 🖨 *0980/68181* 🌐 *www.hotellkebne. com* 🛏 *54 rooms* ♨ *Restaurant, 2 saunas, no-smoking rooms* ▭ *AE, DC, MC, V.*

$$ 🏨 **Ferrum.** Part of the Scandic Hotels chain, this late-1960s-vintage hotel is near the railway station. Rooms have wood floors and modern

standard furniture. ⊠ *Lars Janssonsg. 15, 981 31* ☎ *0980/398600*
🖶 *0980/398611* ⊕ *www.scandic-hotels.com* ➹ *171 rooms* ♨ *3 restau-*
rants, gym, sauna, 2 bars, dance club, meeting room, no-smoking rooms
🖃 *AE, DC, MC, V.*

¢ 🖻 **Järnvägshotellet.** Dating from 1903, this small hotel has the advantage of being close to the railway station. ⊠ *Bangårdsv. 7, 981 34*
☎ *0980/84444* ⊕ *www.jarnvagshotellet.com* ➹ *20 rooms* ♨ *Restau-*
rant, breakfast room, no-smoking rooms 🖃 *DC, MC, V* ⫯◉⫯ *BP.*

en route Driving south from Kiruna toward Muddus National Park, you'll
pass several small former mining villages before coming into the
Kalixälv (Kalix River) Valley, where the countryside becomes more
settled, with small farms and fertile meadows replacing the wilder
northern landscape.

Jukkasjärvi

❷ *16 km (10 mi) east of Kiruna.*

The history of Jukkasjärvi, a Sámi village by the shores of the fast-flow-
ing Torneälven (Torne River), dates from the early 16th century, when
a market was already here. There is a wooden church from the 17th century and a small open-air museum that evokes a sense of Sámi life in
times gone by.

If you are gastronomically adventuresome, you may want to sample
one of the most unusual of all Sámi delicacies: a cup of thick black coffee with *kaffeost*, small lumps of goat cheese. After the cheese sits in
the coffee for a bit, you fish it out with a spoon and eat it, then drink
the coffee.

Where to Stay & Eat

¢ ✕🖻 **Jukkasjärvi Wärdshus.** The restaurant specializes in Norrland cui-
Fodor's Choice sine—characterized by reindeer, wild berries, mushrooms, dried and
★ smoked meats, salted fish, fermented herring, and rich sauces using thick
creams—and is the lifework of its manager, Yngve Bergqvist. The manor
has one large honeymoon suite with wood floors and antique furniture;
there are 45 cabins around it, 30 with bathroom, kitchen, and two bedrooms with bunk beds. Breakfast is not included. River-rafting and canoeing trips can be arranged. ⊠ *Marknadsv. 63, 981 91* ☎ *0980/66800*
🖶 *0980/66890* ➹ *1 suite, 30 cabins* ♨ *Restaurant, sauna, meeting*
room 🖃 *AE, DC, MC, V.*

★ $ 🖻 **Ice Hotel.** At the peak of winter, tourists are drawn by the annual con-
struction of the world's largest igloo, which opens for business as a hotel
in mid-December continuing through April, after which it melts away,
until being revised and built again nine months later. Made of snow, ice,
and sheet metal, the Ice Hotel offers rooms for 40 guests, who spend
the night in specially insulated sleeping bags on top of layers of reindeer skins and spruce boughs. At the Absolute Icebar, colored electric
lights liven up the solid-ice walls. Breakfast is served in the sauna, with
a view of the (nonelectric) northern lights. The entire hotel is designated
nonsmoking, as it takes only a few puffs to tarnish the snow-white interiors. ⊠ *Marknadsv. 63, 981 91 Jukkasjärvi* ☎ *0980/66800* 🖶 *0980/*
66890 ⊕ *www.icehotel.com* ➹ *120 beds without bath, 18 suites*
♨ *Restaurant, sauna, cross-country skiing, snowmobiling, chapel, bar,*
meeting room, no smoking 🖃 *AE, DC, MC, V* ⊘ *Closed May–Nov.*

Sports & the Outdoors

A challenging local activity is riding the rapids of the Torne River in an
inflatable boat. In winter Jukkasjärvi also offers dogsled rides and snow-

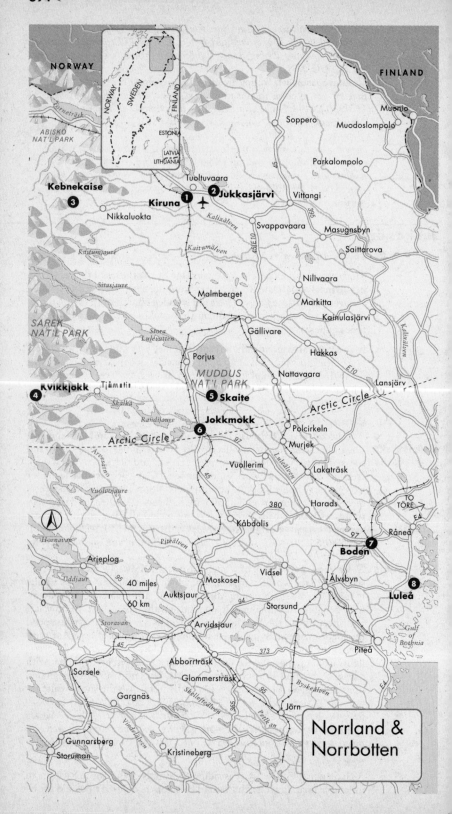

Norrland & Norrbotten

mobile safaris. For more information call the **Ice Hotel** (☎ 0980/66800) or the Kiruna Lappland Tourist Office. .

Kebnekaise

❸ *85 km (53 mi) west of Kiruna.*

At 7,000 feet above sea level, Kebnekaise is Sweden's highest mountain, but you'll need to be in good physical shape just to get to it. From Kiruna you travel about 66 km (41 mi) west to the Sámi village of Nikkaluokta (there are two buses a day from Kiruna in the summer). From Nikkaluokta it is a hike of 19 km (12 mi) to the Kebnekaise Fjällstation (mountain station), at the foot of Kebnekaise, though you can take a boat 5 km (3 mi) across Lake Ladtjojaure. Kebnekaise itself is relatively easy to climb, provided there's good weather and you're in shape; extensive mountaineering equipment is not necessary. If you feel up to more walking, the track continues past the Kebnekaise Fjällstation to become part of what is known as Kungsleden (the Royal Trail), a 500-km (280-mi) trail through the mountains from Abisko National Park, in the north, to Hemavan, in southern Lappland.

Where to Stay

$ ⊡ **Kebnekaise Fjällstation.** This rustic, wooden mountain station consists of six buildings. Choose between the main building, with its heavy wood beams, wood floors, and wood bunk beds—five per room—and the newer annexes, where more modern rooms each contain two or four beds. All guests share the use of a service house, with toilets, showers, and sauna. Though the main lodge is closed in fall and winter, one annex stays open year-round. The facility is 19 km (12 mi) from Nikkaluokta and can be reached by footpath, a combination of boat and hiking, or helicopter. Guided mountain tours are available. ⊠ *981 29 Kiruna* ☎ *0980/55000, off-season, contact Abisko tourist office* ⊟ *0980/55048* ⤶ *196 beds without bath* �ዼ *Restaurant, sauna, bar* ⊟ *AE, V* ⊘ *Closed mid-Aug.–mid-Mar.*

Sports & the Outdoors

All the regional tourist offices can supply details of skiing holidays, but never forget the extreme temperatures and weather conditions. For the really adventuresome, the **Kebnekaise mountain station** (☎ 0980/55000) offers combined skiing and climbing weeks at around SKr 8,700, including lodging and all meals. It also offers weeklong combined dogsledding, skiing, and climbing holidays in the mountains. Because of the extreme cold and the danger involved, be sure to have proper equipment. Consult the mountain station well in advance for advice.

Kvikkjokk & Sarek National Park

❹ *310 km (193 mi) southwest of Kiruna via Route 45.*

Sarek is Sweden's largest high-mountain area and was molded by the last ice age. The mountains have been sculpted by glaciers, of which there are about 100 in the park. The mountain area totals 487,000 acres, a small portion of which is forest, bogs, and waterways. The remainder is bare mountain that is either totally vegetation free or is covered by low-growing alpine vegetation. The park has 90 peaks some 6,000 feet above sea level.

The Rapaätno River, which drains the park, runs through the lovely, desolate Rapadalen (Rapa Valley). The area is marked by a surprising variety of landscapes—luxuriant green meadows contrast with the snowy peaks of the mountains. Moose, bears, wolverines, lynx, ermines, hares, arctic foxes, red foxes, and mountain lemmings inhabit the terrain. Bird life includes ptarmigan, willow grouse, teals, wigeon, tufted ducks, blue-throats, and warblers. Golden eagles, rough-legged buzzards, and merlins have also been spotted here.

Visiting Sarek demands a good knowledge of mountains and a familiarity with the outdoors. The park can be dangerous in winter because of avalanches and snowstorms. In summer, however, despite its unpredictable, often inhospitable climate, it attracts large numbers of experienced hikers. At Kvikkjokk, a major overnight base for visitors, hikers can choose between a trail through the Tarradalen (Tarra Valley), which divides the Sarek from Padjelanta National Park, to the west, or part of the Kungsleden Trail, which crosses about 15 km (9 mi) of Sarek's southeastern corner.

Skaite & Muddus National Park

⑤ *225 km (140 mi) south of Kiruna via E10 and Route 45.*

Established in 1942, Muddus National Park is less mountainous and spectacular than Sarek. Its 121,770 acres are mainly taken up by virgin coniferous forest, some of whose trees may be as much as 600 years old. The park's 3,680 acres of water is composed primarily of two huge lakes at the center of the park and the Muddusjåkkå River, which tumbles spectacularly through a gorge with 330-foot-high sheer rock walls and includes a waterfall crashing 140 feet down. The highest point of Muddus is Sör-Stubba Mountain, 2,158 feet above sea level. From Skaite, where you enter the park, a series of well-marked trails begins. There are four well-equipped, overnight, communal rest huts and two tourist cabins. The park is home to bears, lynx, wolverines, moose, ermines, weasels, otters, and many bird species. A popular pastime is picking cloudberries (a member of the raspberry family) in autumn.

Jokkmokk

⑥ *225 km (140 mi) south of Kiruna via E10 and Route 45.*

Jokkmokk is an important center of Sámi culture. Each February it is the scene of the region's largest market, where everything from frozen reindeer meat to Sámi handcrafted wooden utensils is sold. If you're an outdoor enthusiast, Jokkmokk may be the best base in Norrland for you. The village has good campsites and is surrounded by wilderness. The local tourist office sells fishing permits, which cost SKr 50 for 24 hours, SKr 100 for three days, SKr 175 for one week, and SKr 350 for the entire year. The office can also supply lists of camping and housekeeping cabins.

Where to Stay

$ 🏨 **Hotel Jokkmokk.** A modern hotel this luxurious seems incongruous

FodorśChoice in this remote region but is welcome nevertheless. The hotel is in the ★ town center, but the staff can arrange dogsled rides and helicopter trips to the Sarek and Muddus national parks; there is excellent fishing nearby. ⊠ *Solg. 45, S962 23* ☎ *0971/77700* 🖷 *0971/77790* ⊕ *www. hoteljokkmokk.se* ⤋ *75 rooms* ♨ *Restaurant, sauna, meeting room, no-smoking rooms* ⊟ *AE, DC, MC, V.*

¢ 🏨 **Gästis.** This small hotel in central Jokkmokk opened in 1915. Rooms are standard, with television, shower, and either carpeted or vinyl floors. ⊠ *Herrev. 1, S962 31* ☎ *0971/10012* 🖷 *0971/10044* ⤋ *30 rooms* ♨ *Restaurant, room TVs, sauna, meeting room, no-smoking rooms* ⊟ *AE, DC, MC, V.*

¢ ⊞ **Jokkmokks Turistcenter.** This complex is in a pleasant forest area near Luleälven, 3 km (2 mi) from the railway station. ✉ *Nortudden, Box 75, S962 22* ☎ *0971/12370* 🖷 *0971/12476* ⇝ *59 cabins with bath* ⚱ *4 pools, sauna, meeting room* ▤ *DC, MC, V.*

Boden

❼ *290 km (180 mi) southeast of Kiruna, 130 km (81 mi) southeast of Jokkmokk on Route 97.*

Boden, the nation's largest garrison town, dates from 1809, when Sweden lost Finland to Russia and feared an invasion of its own territory. The **Garrisonsmuseet** (Garrison Museum) contains exhibits from Swedish military history, with an extensive collection of weapons and uniforms. ✉ *Sveav. 10* ☎ *0921/68399* 🎫 *Free* ⊙ *Mid-June–late Aug., Mon.–Sat. 11–4, Sun. noon–4.*

Luleå

❽ *340 km (211 mi) southeast of Kiruna via E10 and E4.*

The northernmost major town in Sweden, Luleå is an important port at the top of the Gulf of Bothnia, at the mouth of the Luleälv (Lule River). The town was some 10 km (6 mi) farther inland when it was first granted its charter in 1621, but by 1649 trade had grown so much that it was moved closer to the sea. Gammelstad Church Town, at the site of the original city, is now protected by the UNESCO World Heritage list. The development of Kiruna and the iron trade is linked, literally, by a railway, with the fortunes of Luleå, where a steelworks was set up in the 1940s. Like its fellow port towns farther south—Piteå, Skellefteå, Umeå, and Sundsvall—Luleå is a very modern and nondescript city, but it has some reasonable hotels. A beautiful archipelago of hundreds of islands hugs the coastline. Many of these islands can be reached by car in the wintertime through a 250-km (166-mi) network of roads on the frozen sea. Wintertime visitors with kids shouldn't miss the iceslide in the city park: each year it's in the shape of a different indigenous animal.

The **Norrbottens Museum** has one of the best collections of Sámi ethnography in the world. ✉ *Hermelinsparken 2* ☎ *0920/243502* 🎫 *Free* ⊙ *Weekdays 10–4, weekends noon–4.*

Where to Stay & Eat

★ $–$$ ✕⊞ **Arctic.** Right in the town center, the Arctic is known locally for its restaurant, which serves local specialties. The hotel is warm and cozy, with tastefully decorated rustic rooms. ✉ *Sandviksg. 80, 972 34* ☎ *0920/10980* 🖷 *0920/60787* ⊕ *www.arctichotel.se* ⇝ *94 rooms* ⚱ *Restaurant, hot tub, sauna, meeting room, no-smoking rooms* ▤ *AE, DC, MC, V.*

$$$ ⊞ **Elite Stads Hotellet.** This large, central Best Western hotel has nightly—sometimes boisterous—dancing. Rooms in the building dating to 1903 are spacious and carpeted, with turn-of-the-20th-century furnishings. ✉ *Storg. 15, 97128* ☎ *0920/67000* 🖷 *0920/67092* ⇝ *135 rooms, 3 suites* ⚱ *Restaurant, café, minibars, sauna, lounge, dance club, meeting room, no-smoking rooms* ▤ *AE, DC, MC, V* ⦿ *BP.*

$$ ⊞ **Scandic.** This hotel on a small tarn has an extremely pleasant setting and is 2 km (1 mi) from the railway station. ✉ *Banv. 3, 973 46* ☎ *0920/ 276400* 🖷 *0920/276411* ⊕ *www.scandic-hotels.com* ⇝ *160 rooms* ⚱ *Restaurant, indoor pool, gym, sauna, meeting room, no-smoking rooms* ▤ *AE, DC, MC, V.*

$ 🏨 **Aveny.** Rooms are of varying sizes and colors, but all are spotless and fresh. It's close to the railway station. ✉ *Hermelinsg. 10, 973 46* ☎ *0920/221820* 🖷 *0920/220122* 🛏 *24 rooms* ♿ *No-smoking rooms* 🖃 *AE, DC, MC, V.*

¢   🏨 **Amber.** A particularly fine old building listed on the Historic Register, this hotel is close to the railway station. Rooms are modern. ✉ *Stationsg. 67, 972 34* ☎ *0920/10200* 🖷 *0920/87906* 🛏 *16 rooms* ♿ *Minibars, cable TV, no-smoking rooms* 🖃 *AE, DC, MC, V.*

Norrland & Norrbotten A to Z

AIR TRAVEL

CARRIERS   There are two nonstop SAS flights a day from Stockholm to Kiruna Airport and three additional flights via Luleå. Check SAS for specific times.
🛪 **SAS** ☎ 0770/727727, from outside Sweden: 8/7972688.

AIRPORTS

In summer buses connect Kiruna Airport, which is 5 km (3 mi) from Kiruna, to the city center; the fare is about SKr 50. A taxi from the airport to the center of Kiruna costs about SKr 200; book through the airline or call the taxi directly.
🛪 **Kiruna Airport** ☎ 0980/68001 🌐 www.lfv.se. **Taxi Kiruna** ☎ 0980/12020.

CAR RENTAL

🛪 **Major Agencies Avis** ✉ Kiruna Airport, Kiruna ☎ 0980/13080. **Europcar** ✉ Forv. 33, Kiruna ☎ 0980/80759. **Hertz** ✉ Industriv. 5, Kiruna ☎ 0980/19000.

CAR TRAVEL

Since public transportation is nonexistent in this part of the country, having a car is essential. The few roads are well built and maintained, although spring thaws can present potholes. Keep in mind that habitations are few and far between in this wilderness region.

EMERGENCIES

For emergencies dial 112. A medical advisory service in Luleå is available 24 hours a day.

There are no late-night pharmacies in Norrbotten. The pharmacy at the Gallerian shopping center in Kiruna is open weekdays 9:30–6 and Saturday 9:30–1.
🛪 **Gallerian Pharmacy** ✉ Föreningsg. 6, Kiruna ☎ 0980/18775. **Jokkmokk Health Center** ✉ Lappstav. 9, Jokkmokk ☎ 0971/44444. **Kiruna Health Center** ✉ Thuleg. 29, Kiruna ☎ 0980/73000. **Sunderbu Hospital Luleå** ✉ Luleå ☎ 0920/282000.

TOURS

Local tourist offices have information on guided tours involving dogsledding, snowmobiling, and ice fishing. Samelands Resor arranges tours to points of interest in Lappland. Call the Swedish Sámi Association for Sámi tours.
🛪 **Samelands Resor** ✉ Hermelinsg. 20, 962 33, Jokkmokk ☎ 0971/10606 🌐 www.samelandsresor.com. **Swedish Sámi Association** ✉ Brog. 5, 903 25, Umeå ☎ 090/141180.

TRAIN TRAVEL

The best and cheapest way to get to Kiruna is to take the evening sleeper from Stockholm on Tuesday, Wednesday, or Saturday, when the fare is reduced to SKr 595 for a single. The regular one-way price is SKr 600 when sharing a cabin with six people and SKr 700 when sharing a cabin with three people, twice that for round-trip. You'll arrive at around lunchtime the next day. To book a train, call Tåg Kompaniet, the rail company that handles northern Sweden.
🛪 **Tåg Kompaniet** ☎ 020/444111, 690/691017 from outside Sweden.

VISITOR INFORMATION

Norrbottens Turistråd is the regional tourist office. Local tourist offices are listed below by town.

Tourist Information Abisko ✉ 980 24 Abisko ☎ 0980/40200. **Gällivare** ✉ Centralplan 3 ☎ 0970/16660. **Jokkmokk** ✉ Stortorget 4 ☎ 0971/22250. **Kiruna** ✉ Folkets Hus ☎ 0980/18880. **Luleå** ✉ Storgatan 43B ☎ 0920/293500.

SWEDEN A TO Z

To research prices, get advice from other travelers, and book travel arrangements, visit www.fodors.com.

AIR TRAVEL

CARRIERS All major cities and towns are linked with regular flights by Scandinavian Airlines System (SAS). Malmö Aviation also has service between Stockholm, Göteborg, and Malmö. Most Swedish airports are a long way from city centers but are served by fast and efficient bus service. From North America, American, Delta, Finnair, Iceland Air, Lufthansa, SAS, United, and other major airlines serve Stockholm's Arlanda International Airport and Göteborg's Landvetter Airport. From the United Kingdom, Stockholm and Göteborg are served by SAS, British Airways, British Midland, and Ryan Air.

American ☎ 800/433-7300. ⊕ www.aa.com. **British Airways** ☎ 020/88974000 ⊕ www.british-airways.com. **British Midland** ☎ 01332/854000 in U.K ⊕ www.flybmi. com. **Delta** ☎ 800/221-1212 ⊕ www.delta.com. **Finnair** ☎ 800/950-5000 ⊕ www. finnair.com. **Iceland Air** ☎ 800/223-5500 ⊕ www.icelandair.com. **Lufthansa** ☎ 800/ 645-3880 ⊕ www.lufthansa.com. **Ryan Air** ☎ 0871/2460000 in U.K., 0155/202240 in Sweden ⊕ www.ryanair.com. **SAS** ☎ 0770/727727 in Sweden, 020/77344020 in U.K., 800/433-7300 in the U.S. ⊕ www.scandinavian.net. **United** ☎ 800/241-6522 ⊕ www. united.com.

BIKE TRAVEL

Cycling is a very popular sport in Sweden and the south of the country, with its low-lying, flat landscape, is perfect for the more genteel cyclist. All major towns and cities are well provided with cycle paths and designated cycle lanes. Bike-rental costs average around SKr 100 per day. Tourist offices and the Swedish Touring Association have information about cycling package holidays that include bike rentals, overnight accommodations, and meals. The Swedish bicycling organization, Cykelfrämjandet (National Cycle Association), publishes a free English-language guide to cycling trips.

Cykelfrämjandet ✉ Thuleg. 43, 113 53 Stockholm ☎ 08/54591030 Mon.-Thurs. 9-noon 🖷 08/54591039 ⊕ www.cykelframjandet.a.se. **Swedish Touring Association (STF)** ✉ Box 25, 101 20 Stockholm ☎ 08/4632200 🖷 08/6781938 ⊕ www.meravsverige.se.

BOAT & FERRY TRAVEL

A rewarding way to see Sweden is from the many ferryboats that ply the archipelagos and main lakes. In Stockholm visitors should buy a special *Båtluffarkort* (Inter Skerries Card, SKr 385) from Waxholmsbolaget. This card allows you 16 days of unlimited travel on the archipelago ferryboats. There are excellent links between Harwich, in the United Kingdom, and Göteborg, and between Newcastle, also in the United Kingdom, and Göteborg, aboard DFDS Seaways ferries. The Viking Lines and Silja Lines also have overnight ferries to Helsinki, Finland, both of them offering great bargains for one- and two-day round-trips. A word of warning though—the Helsinki boats are often filled with graduating students and other young Swedes taking right-of-passage cruises. If you are looking for a peaceful boat crossing, a quick glass of wine and a quiet night, find another route.

Taking a ferry is not only fun; it is often necessary in Scandinavia. Many companies arrange package trips, some offering a rental car and hotel accommodations as part of the deal. The word *ferry* can be deceptive; generally, those vessels so named are more like small-scale cruise ships, with several dining rooms, sleeping quarters, shopping, pool and sauna, and entertainment.

Ferry crossings often last overnight. The trip between Copenhagen and Oslo, for example, takes approximately 16 hours; most lines leave about 5 PM and arrive about 9 the next morning. The direct cruise between Stockholm and Helsinki takes 12 hours, usually leaving about 6 PM and arriving the next morning at 9. Trips from Germany to Oslo and Helsinki generally take about 20 hours; crossings to Reykjavík from Bergen tend to last about two days (25 hours to the Faroe Islands, and another 24 hours to Iceland). The shortest ferry route runs between Helsingør, Denmark, and Helsingborg, Sweden; it takes only 20 minutes.

🚢 **Color Line** ✉ Box 30, DK-9850 Hirsthals, Denmark ☎ 45/99-56-20-00 📠 45/99-56-20-20 ✉ Hjortneskaia, Box 1422 Vika, N-0115 Oslo, Norway ☎ 47/22-94-44-00 📠 47/22-83-04-30, ✉ Color Scandi Line, Torksholmen, S-45 200 Strømstad, Sweden ☎ 46/52662000 📠 46/52614669, ✉ Color Line GmbH, Postfach 6080, 24121 Kiel, Germany ☎ 49/431-7300-300 📠 49/431-7300-400 🌐 www.colorline.no. **ScandLines** ✉ Box 1, DK-3000 Helsingør, Denmark ☎ 45/33-15-15-15 📠 45/33-15-10-20, ✉ Knutpunkten 43, S-252 78 Helsingborg, Sweden ☎ 46/42186100 📠 46/42186049, 🌐 www.scandlines.com.

BUSINESS HOURS

BANKS & OFFICES Banks are officially open weekdays 9:30–3, but many stay open until 5 on most weekdays and until 6 on Thursday. The bank at Arlanda International Airport is open every day with extended hours, and the Forex and Valuta Specialisten currency-exchange offices also have extended hours. Most banks operate a numbered-ticket system for lining up: take a number and wait your turn. Ticket machines are always somewhere near a bank's doors. Make exchanging money your first task to avoid a frustratingly long wait. More and more Swedes use Internet banking for daily cash transactions, and, strange as it may seem, it is not uncommon to come across cashless bank branches. These are more often found in smaller towns and villages, so it is worth checking before traveling.

MUSEUMS & SIGHTS The opening times for museums vary widely, but most are open from 10 to 4 Tuesday–Sunday. Consult the guide in *På Stan,* the entertainment supplement published in *Dagens Nyheter's* Friday edition, or *What's On,* a monthly entertainment listings guide published in Swedish and English by the Swedish tourism authorities. It's available for free at hotels, tourist centers, and some restaurants.

🌐 **Web Sites På Stan** 🌐 www.dn.se/pastan. **What's On** 🌐 www.stockholmtown.se.

SHOPS Shops are generally open weekdays from 9, 9:30, or 10 until 6 and Saturday from 10 to 1 or 4. Most large department stores stay open later in the evening, and some open on Sunday. Several supermarkets open on Sunday, and there are a number of late-night food shops such as the 7-Eleven chain. Systembolaget, Sweden's liquor monopoly and therefore the only place to buy alcohol, is open weekdays from 10 to 6, with extended hours until 7 on Thursday and Saturday from 10 to 2. Most Sytembolagets display their product behind glass. Customers take a numbered ticket and order at a counter from which their choice is collected when their number is called. Unless time is very definitely on your hands, avoid buying alcohol on a Friday, when the wait can be as long as an hour.

BUS TRAVEL

There is excellent bus service between all major towns and cities. Consult the *Yellow Pages* under "Bussresearrangörer" for the telephone numbers of the companies concerned. Recommended are the services offered to different parts of Sweden from Stockholm by Swebus. For local bus journeys, when buying a single ticket only, it is usual to pay the driver on boarding. Longer journeys and coupons or multiple tickets should be purchased before your journey from the relevant bus company.
Interbus ☎ 08/7279000. **Svenska Buss** ☎ 0771/676767 ⊕ www.svenskabuss.se. **SwebusExpress** ☎ 0200/218218 ⊕ www.express.swebus.se.

CAR RENTAL

Major car-rental companies such as Avis, Bonus, Budget, Europcar, and Hertz have facilities in all major towns and cities as well as at airports. Various service stations also offer car rentals, including Q8, Shell, Statoil, and Texaco. See the *Yellow Pages* under "Biluthyrning" for telephone numbers and addresses. Renting a car is a speedy business in Sweden with none of the usual lengthy documentation and vehicle checks; show your passport, license, and credit card, pick up the key, and away you go. Although this is a plus if you are in a hurry, if you feel more comfortable being shown around your car before you drive, just ask and most companies will oblige.

Rates in Stockholm begin at $75 a day and $190 a week for a manual-drive economy car without air-conditioning and with unlimited mileage. This does not include tax on car rentals, which is 25% in Sweden. A service charge also is usually added, which ranges from $15 to $25.

CAR TRAVEL

The Øresundsbron, the new 8-km (5-mi) bridge between Malmö and Copenhagen, simplifies car travel and makes train connections possible between the two countries. Ferry service is cheaper but slower—it takes 45 minutes to make the crossing.

Sweden has an excellent highway network of more than 80,000 km (50,000 mi). The fastest routes are those with numbers prefixed with an *E* (for "European"), some of which are the equivalent of American highways or British motorways. The size of the country compared to its population means that most roads are relatively traffic free. However, rush hour around major cities can bring traffic jams and holdups of frustrating proportions.

Also be aware that there are relatively low legal blood-alcohol limits and tough penalties for driving while intoxicated in Scandinavia; Sweden, Iceland, and Finland have zero-tolerance laws. Penalties include license suspension and fines or imprisonment, and the laws are sometimes enforced by random police roadblocks in urban areas on weekends. In addition, an accident involving a driver who has an illegal blood-alcohol level usually voids all insurance agreements, making the driver responsible for all medical bills and collision damage.

In a few remote areas in northern Sweden, road conditions can be unpredictable, and careful planning is required for safety's sake. Several mountain and highland roads in these areas close during winter—when driving in such remote areas, especially in winter, it is best to let someone know your travel plans. It is also wise to **use a four-wheel-drive vehicle** and to **travel with at least one other car** in these areas.

EMERGENCY SERVICES The Larmtjänst organization, run by a confederation of Swedish insurance companies, provides a 24-hour breakdown service. Its phone numbers are listed in the *Yellow Pages*.

GASOLINE Sweden has some of the highest gasoline rates in Europe, about SKr 10 per liter (about SKr 38 per gallon). Lead-free gasoline is readily available. Gas stations are self-service: pumps marked SEDEL are automatic and accept SKr 20 and SKr 100 bills; pumps marked KASSA are paid for at the cashier; the KONTO pumps are for customers with credit cards.

PARKING Parking meters and, increasingly, timed ticket machines operate in larger towns, usually between 8 AM and 6 PM. The fee varies from about SKr 6 to SKr 35 per hour. Parking garages in urban areas are mostly automated, often with machines that accept credit cards; LEDIGT on a garage sign means space is available. Many streets in urban areas are cleaned weekly at a designated time on a designated day, during which time parking is not allowed, not even at meters. Times are marked on a yellow sign at each end of the street. Try to avoid getting a parking ticket, which can come with fines of SKr 300–SKr 700.

ROAD CONDITIONS All main and secondary roads are well surfaced, but some minor roads, particularly in the north, are gravel.

ROAD MAPS If you plan on extensive road touring, consider buying the *Vägatlas över Sverige,* a detailed road atlas published by the Mötormännens Riksförbund, available at bookstores for around SKr 300.

RULES OF THE ROAD Drive on the right, and—no matter where you sit in a car—seat belts are mandatory. You must also have at least low-beam headlights on at all times. Cars rented or bought in Sweden will have automatic headlights, which are activated every time the engine is switched on. Signs indicate five basic speed limits, ranging from 30 kph (19 mph), in school or playground areas, to 110 kph (68 mph), on long stretches of E roads.

CRUISE TRAVEL

You can go on one of the highly popular four-day cruises of the Göta Canal, which traverse rivers, lakes, and, on the last lap, the Baltic Sea. A lovely waterway, the Göta Canal with its 65 locks links Göteborg, on the west coast, with Stockholm, on the east. Cruise participants travel on fine old steamers, some of which date almost to the canal's opening, in 1832. The oldest and most desirable is the *Juno*, built in 1874. Prices start at SKr 6,100 for a bed in a double cabin. For more information contact the Göta Canal Steamship Company.

To learn how to plan, choose, and book a cruise-ship voyage, check out Cruise How-To's on www.fodors.com.

🇫 **Göta Canal Steamship Company** ✉ Box 272, S401 24 Göteborg ☎ 03/1806315 🖷 03/1158311 ⊕ www.gotacanal.se.

CUSTOMS & DUTIES

Travelers 21 or older entering Sweden from non-EU countries may import duty-free 1 liter of liquor and 2 liters of fortified wine; 2 liters of wine or 15 liters of beer; 200 cigarettes or 100 grams of cigarillos or 50 cigars or 250 grams of tobacco; 50 grams of perfume; ¼ liter of aftershave; and other goods whose total value does not exceed SKr 1,700. Travelers from the United Kingdom or other EU countries may import duty-free 1 liter of liquor or 3 liters of fortified wine; 5 liters of wine; 15 liters of beer; 300 cigarettes or 150 cigarillos or 75 cigars or 400 grams of tobacco; and other goods, including perfume and aftershave, of any value.

EMBASSIES

🇫 Australia ✉ Sergels Torg 12 ☎ 08/6132900.
🇫 Canada ✉ Tegelbacken 4, Box 16129, 10323 Stockholm ☎ 08/4533000.
🇫 New Zealand ✉ Nybrog. 34, Stockholm ☎ 08/50632000.

🚹 United Kingdom ⊠ Skarpög. 68, 11593 Stockholm ☏ 08/6713000.
🚹 United States ⊠ Strandv. 101, 11589 Stockholm ☏ 08/7835300.

EMERGENCIES
Anywhere in Sweden, dial 112 for emergency assistance.

LANGUAGE
Swedish is closely related to Danish and Norwegian. After *z*, the Swedish alphabet has three extra letters, *å*, *ä*, and *ö*, something to bear in mind when using the phone book. Another phone-book alphabetical oddity is that *v* and *w* are interchangeable; Wittström, for example, comes before Vittviks, not after. And after all that, you'll be happy to know that most Swedes are happy to speak English.

LODGING
Sweden offers a variety of accommodations, from simple bed-and-breakfasts, camp sites, and hostels to hotels of the highest international standard.

APARTMENT &
VILLA RENTALS
With 250 chalet villages with high standards, Sweden enjoys popularity with its chalet accommodations, often arranged on the spot at tourist offices. Many are organized under the auspices of the Swedish Touring Association (STF). DFDS Seaways in Göteborg arranges package deals that combine a ferry trip from Britain across the North Sea and a stay in a chalet village.
🚹 Rental Contacts **DFDS Seaways** ☏ 031/650600, 01912/936262 within the U.K. **Swedish Touring Association** ☏ 08/4632200 🖷 08/6781938 ⊕ www.meravsverige.se.

CAMPING
There are 760 registered campsites nationwide, many close to uncrowded swimming places and with fishing, boating, or canoeing; they may also offer bicycle rentals. Prices range from SKr 70 to SKr 130 per 24-hour period. Many campsites also offer accommodations in log cabins at various prices, depending on the facilities offered. Most are open between June and September, but about 200 remain open in winter for skiing and skating enthusiasts. Sveriges Campingvårdernas Riksförbund (Swedish Campsite Owners' Association or SCR) publishes, in English, an abbreviated list of sites; contact the office for a free copy.
🚹 **Sveriges Campingvårdernas Riksförbund** ⊠ Box 255, 451 17 Uddevalla ☏ 0522/642440 🖷 0522/642430 ⊕ www.camping.se.

FARM & COTTAGE
HOLIDAYS
The old-fashioned farm or countryside holiday, long a staple for Scandinavian city dwellers, is becoming increasingly available to tourists. In general, you can choose to stay on the farm itself and even participate in daily activities, or you can opt to rent a private housekeeping cottage. Contact the local tourist board or Swedish Farm Holidays for details.
🚹 **Swedish Farm Holidays** ⊠ Box 8, S-668 21 Ed, Sweden ☏ 46/53412075 🖷 46/53461011 ⊕ www.bopalantgard.org.

HOME
EXCHANGES
If you would like to exchange your home for someone else's, **join a home-exchange organization,** which will send you its updated listings of available exchanges for a year and will include your own listing in at least one of them. It's up to you to make specific arrangements.
🚹 Exchange Clubs **HomeLink International** ⊠ Box 47747, Tampa, FL 33647 ☏ 813/975-9825 or 800/638-3841 🖷 813/910-8144 ⊕ www.homelink.org ✉ $106 per year. **Inter-vac U.S.** ⊠ Box 590504, San Francisco, CA 94159 ☏ 800/756-4663 🖷 415/435-7440 ⊕ www.intervacus.com ✉ $93 yearly fee includes one catalog and online access.

HOSTELS
No matter what your age, you can **save on lodging costs by staying at hostels.** In some 4,500 locations in more than 70 countries around the world, Hostelling International (HI), the umbrella group for a number of national youth-hostel associations, offers single-sex, dorm-style beds

and, at many hostels, rooms for couples and family accommodations. Membership in any HI national hostel association, open to travelers of all ages, allows you to stay in HI-affiliated hostels at member rates; one-year membership is about $25 for adults (C$26.75 in Canada, £9.30 in the U.K., $30 in Australia, and $30 in New Zealand); hostels run about $10–$25 per night. If a hostel has nearly filled up, members have priority over others; members are also eligible for discounts around the world, even on rail and bus travel in some countries.

🇫 Organizations **Hostelling International–American Youth Hostels** ✉ 733 15th St. NW, Suite 840, Washington, DC 20005 ☎ 202/783-6161 🖷 202/783-6171 ⊕ www. hiayh.org. **Hostelling International–Canada** ✉ 400–205 Catherine St., Ottawa, Ontario K2P 1C3, Canada ☎ 613/237-7884, 800/663-5777 in Canada 🖷 613/237-7868 ⊕ www.hostellingintl.ca. **Youth Hostel Association of England and Wales** ✉ Trevelyan House, 8 St. Stephen's Hill, St. Albans, Hertfordshire AL1 2DY, U.K. ☎ 0870/8708808 🖷 01727/844126 ⊕ www.yha.org.uk. **Youth Hostel Association Australia** ✉ 10 Mallett St., Camperdown, NSW 2050, Australia ☎ 02/9565-1699 🖷 02/9565-1325 ⊕ www.yha.com.au. **Youth Hostels Association of New Zealand** ✉ Level 3, 193 Cashel St., Box 436, Christchurch, New Zealand ☎ 03/379-9970 🖷 03/365-4476 ⊕ www.yha.org.nz.

HOTELS All hotels listed have private baths unless otherwise noted.

Major hotels in larger cities cater mainly to business clientele and can be expensive; weekend rates are more reasonable and can even be as low as half the normal price. Prices are normally on a per-room basis and include all taxes and service charges and usually breakfast. Apart from the more modest inns and the cheapest budget establishments, private baths and showers are standard.

Whatever their size, almost all Swedish hotels provide scrupulously clean accommodations and courteous service. Since many Swedes go on vacation during July and through early August, make your hotel reservations in advance, especially if staying outside the city areas during that time. Some hotels close during the winter holidays as well; call ahead for information.

An official annual guide, *Hotels in Sweden,* published by and available free from the Swedish Travel and Tourism Council, gives comprehensive information about hotel facilities and prices. Countryside Hotels comprises 35 select resort hotels, some of them restored manor houses or centuries-old inns. Hotellcentralen is an independent agency that makes advance telephone reservations for any Swedish hotel at no cost. The Sweden Hotels group has about 100 independently owned hotels and its own classification scheme—with a letter assigned according to a hotel's facilities.

Major hotel groups like Best Western, Radisson SAS, RESO, Scandic, and Sweden Hotels also have their own central reservations services.

🇫 **Best Western** ☎ 020/792752. **Countryside Hotels** ✉ Box 69, 830 13 Åre ☎ 06/4751860 🖷 06/4751920. **Hotellcentralen** ✉ Centralstation, 111 20 ☎ 08/7892425 🖷 08/7918666. **Radisson SAS** ☎ 02/0797592. **RESO** ☎ 08/4114040. **Scandic** ☎ 08/51751700. **Sweden Hotels** ☎ 020/770000.

MAIL & SHIPPING

POSTAL RATES Postcards and letters up to 20 grams can be mailed for SKr 8 within Sweden, SKr 10 to destinations within Europe, and SKr 10 to the United States and all other countries.

MONEY MATTERS

Here is an idea what you'll pay for food and drink in Sweden: a cup of coffee, SKr 25–SKr 35; a beer, SKr 40–SKr 55; a mineral water, SKr 12–SKr

25; a cheese roll, SKr 25–SKr 50; pepper steak à la carte, SKr 120–SKr 190; a cheeseburger, SKr 60; and pizza, starting at SKr 40.

You can reduce the cost of food by planning. Opt for a restaurant lunch instead of dinner, since the latter tends to be significantly more expensive. Instead of beer or wine, drink tap water—liquor can cost four times the price of the same brand in a store—but do specify tap water, as the term *water* can refer to soft drinks and bottled water, which are also expensive. Throughout Scandinavia the tip is included in the cost of your meal.

In most of Scandinavia, liquor and strong beer (over 3% alcohol) can be purchased only in state-owned shops, at very high prices, during weekday business hours, usually 9:30–6, and in some areas on Saturday until mid-afternoon. A midsize bottle of whiskey in Sweden, for example, can easily cost SKr 250 (about $35). Weaker beers and ciders are usually available in grocery stores in Scandinavia.

ATMS   The 1,200 or so blue Bankomat cash dispensers nationwide have been adapted to take some foreign cards, including MasterCard, Visa, and bank cards linked to the Cirrus network. You may encounter some complications on remote machines. It's best to use those that are next to major bank offices. For more information contact Bankomatcentralen in Stockholm or your local bank. American Express has cash and traveler's check dispensers; there's also an office at Stockholm's Arlanda Airport.

American Express ✉ Birger Jarlsg. 1 ☎ 020/793211 toll-free. **Bankomatcentralen/ CEK AB** ☎ 08/7255700.

CURRENCY   The unit of currency is the krona (plural kronor), which is divided into 100 öre and is written as SKr or SEK. Coins come in SKr 1, SKr 5, and SKr 10. Bank notes come in denominations of SKr 20, SKr 50, SKr 100, SKr 500, and SKr 1,000. At press time (winter 2003) the exchange rates for the krona was SKr 9 to the U.S. dollar, SKr 6 to the Canadian dollar, SKr 13 to the British pound sterling, SKr 9 to the Euro, SKr 6 to the Australian dollar, SKr 5 to the New Zealand dollar, and SKr 1 to the South African rand.

CURRENCY   Traveler's checks and foreign currency can be exchanged at banks all EXCHANGE   over Sweden and at post offices displaying the NB EXCHANGE sign. Be sure to have your passport with you when exchanging money at a bank.

SPORTS & OUTDOORS

BOATING &   Swedes love to be on the water, whether sailing in the Stockholm SAILING   archipelago or kayaking along the rocky west coast. STF publishes a Swedish-language annual guide to all the country's marinas. Svenska Kanotförbundet (Swedish Canoeing Association) publishes a similar booklet. For information on sailing throughout the country, including information on how to rent or charter boats yourself, contact the Svenska Seglarförbundet (Swedish Sailing Association).

Svenska Kanotförbundet (Swedish Canoeing Association) ✉ Idrotts Hus, 123 87 Farsta ☎ 08/6056565 ⊕ www.svenskidrott.se/kanot. **Svenska Seglarförbundet** (Swedish Sailing Association) ✉ af Pontins väg 6, 115 21 Stockholm ☎ 08/4590990 ⊕ www.ssf.se.

GOLF   Sweden has 365 golf clubs; you can even play by the light of the midnight sun at Boden, in the far north, and there are a number of ice courses, too, offering winter challenges. Wherever you play, all Swedish golf courses require you to show a handicap certificate. Svenska Golfförbundet (the Swedish Golfing Association) publishes an annual guide in Swedish; it costs around SKr 100, including postage.

Svenska Golfförbundet ✉ Box 84, 182 11 Danderyd ☎ 08/6221500 ☎ 08/7558439 ⊕ www.golf.se.

SKIING There are plenty of downhill and cross-country facilities in Sweden. The best-known resorts are in the country's western mountains: Åre, in the north, with 29 lifts; Idre Fjäll, to the south of Åre, offering accommodations for 10,000; and Sälen, in the folklore region of Dalarna. You can ski through May at Riksgränsen, in the far north. Most of Sweden's skiing resorts also offer a host of other winter activities, from skating to ice fishing, for the nonskiers in the family.

TAXES

VALUE-ADDED TAX (V.A.T.) All hotel, restaurant, and departure taxes and the value-added tax (V. A.T.; called *moms* all over Scandinavia) are automatically included in prices. The V.A.T. is 25%; non-EU residents can obtain a 15% refund on goods of SKr 200 or more. To receive your refund at any of the 15,000 stores that participate in the tax-free program, you'll be asked to fill out a form and show your passport. The form can then be turned in at any airport or ferry customs desk. Keep all your receipts and tags; occasionally, customs authorities ask to see your purchases, so pack them where they will be accessible.

TELEPHONES

Post offices do not have telephone facilities, but there are plenty of pay phones. Long-distance calls can be made from special telegraph offices called *Telebutik,* marked TELE.

AREA & COUNTRY CODES Sweden's country code is 46. When phoning Sweden from outside the country, drop the first 0 from the number. Swedish phone numbers vary in their number of digits.

DIRECTORY & OPERATOR ASSISTANCE ⓕ **Directory Assistance** ☎ 118118, 118119 for international calls. **Operator Assistance** ☎ 90200, 0018 for international calls.

INTERNATIONAL CALLS To make an international call, dial 00, followed by the country code and then your number. Access codes for various international companies are listed below.

LONG-DISTANCE SERVICES AT&T, MCI, and Sprint access codes make calling long distance relatively convenient, but you may find the local access number blocked in many hotel rooms. First ask the hotel operator to connect you. If the hotel operator balks, ask for an international operator, or dial the international operator yourself. One way to improve your odds of getting connected to your long-distance carrier is to travel with more than one company's calling card (a hotel may block Sprint, for example, but not MCI). If all else fails, call from a pay phone.
ⓕ **Access Codes AT&T USADirect** ☎ 020/795611. **MCI Call USA** ☎ 020/895438. **Sprint Express** ☎ 020/799011.

LOCAL CALLS A local call costs a minimum of SKr 2. For calls outside the locality, dial the area code (see telephone directory). Public phones are of three types: one takes SKr 1 and SKr 5 coins (newer public phones also accept SKr 10 coins); another takes only credit cards; and the last takes only the prepaid *Telefonkort* (telephone card).

PHONE CARDS A Telefonkort, available at Telebutik, Pressbyrån (large blue-and-yellow newsstands), or hospitals, costs SKr 35, SKr 60, or SKr 100. If you're making numerous domestic calls, the card saves money. Many pay phones in downtown Stockholm and Göteborg take only these cards; so it's a good idea to carry one.

TIPPING

In addition to the 12% value-added tax, most hotels usually include a service charge of 15%; it is not necessary to tip unless you have received extra services. Similarly, a service charge of 13% is usually included in restaurant bills. It is a custom, however, to leave small change when buying drinks. Taxi drivers and hairdressers expect a tip of about 10%.

TOURS

Stockholm Sightseeing runs a variety of sightseeing tours of Stockholm. Also contact local tourist offices.

🚩 **Stockholm Sightseeing** ✉ Skeppsbron 22 ☎ 08/57814020.

TRAIN TRAVEL

From London the British Rail European Travel Center can be helpful in arranging connections to Sweden's SJ (Statens Järnvägar), the state railway.

SJ has a highly efficient network of comfortable electric trains. On nearly all long-distance routes there are buffet cars and, on overnight trips, sleeping cars and couchettes in both first- and second class. Seat reservations are advisable, and on some trains—indicated with *R*, *IN*, or *IC* on the timetable—they are compulsory. An extra fee of SKr 15 is charged to reserve a seat on a trip of less than 150 km (93 mi); on longer trips there is no extra charge. Reservations can be made right up to departure time. The high-speed X2000 train has been introduced on several routes; the Stockholm–Göteborg run takes just under three hours. Travelers younger than 19 years travel at half fare. Up to two children younger than 12 years may travel free if accompanied by an adult.

CUTTING COSTS   SJ cooperates with a number of local traffic systems, allowing you to buy one ticket, called a *Tågplusbiljett*, that works on trains, buses, and subways. Speak with the reservations people about what kind of combination you are interested in and where you'd like to travel. The Eurail and InterRail passes are both valid in Sweden. SJ also organizes reduced-cost package trips in conjunction with local tourist offices. Details are available at any railway station or from SJ.

🚩 **British Rail European Travel Center** ✉ Victoria Station, London ☎ 020/78342345. **DER Travel Services** ☎ 800/782-2424. **Rail Europe** ☎ 800/848-7245. **Statens Järnvägar, or SJ** ✉ Central Station, Vasag. 1 ☎ 08/7622000 or 0771/757575.

VISITOR INFORMATION

🚩 Tourist Information **Stockholm Information Service** (Sverigehuset) ✉ Hamng. 27, Box 7542, 103 93 Stockholm ☎ 08/7892490. **Swedish Travel & Tourism Council** ✉ 73 Welbeck St., London W15 8AN ☎ 020/79359784 in U.K. 🖷 020/79355853 ✉ 655 3rd Ave., 18th fl., New York, NY 10017 ☎ 212/885-9700 🖷 212/697-0835 ✉ Box 3030, Kungsg. 36, 103 61 Stockholm ☎ 08/7255500 🖷 08/7255531 ⊕ www.visitsweden.org. **City of Stockholm** ⊕ www.stockholm.se/english.

🚩 U.S. Government Advisories **U.S. Department of State** ✉ Overseas Citizens Services Office, Room 4811 N.S., 2201 C St. NW, Washington, DC 20520 ☎ 202/647-5225 for interactive hot line ⊕ travel.state.gov/travel/html; enclose a business-size SASE.

UNDERSTANDING SCANDINAVIA

FAIRY TALES & FJORDS

THE ISLANDS OF STOCKHOLM mirrored in the water, the ships and Little Mermaid of Copenhagen, Oslo and its majestic fjord, the bay and peninsulas of Helsinki, Reykjavík with its busy deep-blue harbor: the capitals of Scandinavia are unthinkable without the water that surrounds and sustains them.

What is true of the capitals is equally true of the countries. Denmark consists of one peninsula and more than 400 islands, half of them inhabited. Finland and Sweden used to dispute which country was really "the land of a thousand lakes." Finland settled it, after counting almost 190,000. An island summer in the archipelago is part of every Stockholmer's childhood memory. The mail packets of Norway's *Hurtigruten* sail north from Bergen along the fjord-indented coast and turn around at Kirkenes on the Russian border, 2,000 km (1,242 mi) later. Iceland is so dependent on the surrounding sea that it has been known to take on the British navy to protect its fishing limits.

Water has never separated the Scandinavian nations. In the early days it was far easier to cross a stretch of water than it was to penetrate dense and trackless forests. It was their mastery of shipbuilding that enabled the Vikings to rule the waves 1,000 years ago. Their ocean-going ships could be beached, and this gave them the advantage of surprise.

Viking exploration and conquests ranged from North America to the Black Sea and from Greenland to Majorca. These voyagers developed the angular Runic alphabet, ideal for carving in stone. In Sweden alone, more than 2,000 runic stones still stand, in memory of Vikings who fell in faraway battles. The Vikings also devised a complex mythology and created literature of such realism and immediacy that even today the Icelandic sagas can be read with admiration and enjoyment.

You might think that, with so much in common, the Scandinavians would keep peace among themselves, but this was not so. By the 11th century the passion that had inflamed the Vikings was spent, and Christianity defeated the old beliefs. The Swedes departed on a dubious crusade to conquer the Finns and annex their land. The Norwegians, having colonized Iceland, squabbled among themselves and disappeared as a nation for 500 years. By the 16th century, Scandinavia was divided between Denmark and Sweden, bound together by mutual antagonism. The two countries were at war with one another for a total of 134 years, and the conflict was perpetuated by history books written from nationalistic points of view.

What happened in the distant past has acquired the status of myth and deeply influenced the Scandinavians' self-image. Modern history has left more obvious marks. Allegiances and dependencies were reshuffled early in the 19th century as a consequence of the Napoleonic Wars, which transformed the European landscape. Sweden lost Finland, which spent the next 100 years as a czarist province. Norway declared its independence from Denmark but was thrust into a union with Sweden.

Scandinavian cultures thrived throughout these years. Artist Akseli Gallen-Kallela painted the scenes of a mythical past that Jean Sibelius then fashioned into tone poems. Norway experienced a cultural renaissance, led by artists such as Edvard Grieg, Henrik Ibsen, and Edvard Munch. From Denmark came philosopher Søren Kierkegaard, writer Hans Christian Andersen, and the composer Carl Nielsen. Sweden produced the painters Anders Zorn and Carl Larsson and dramatist August Strindberg. Icelandic poets Bjarni Thorarensen and Jónas Hallgrímsson wrote nationalistic prose inspired by the Viking Sagas, a collection of 12th-century tales written down by anonymous Icelandic scribes, and by the writings of the historian Snorri Sturluson (1178–1241) who compiled ancient Norse poetry and mythology.

Large-scale emigration to the United States (including a million Swedes) peaked during the latter half of the century, only decades before new industries transformed the old farming economy.

In the early 1900s the Norwegians finally became masters in their own house. This could not have happened without strong nationalist sentiment, and it is to the credit of both Norway and Sweden that the separation was amicable. The Russian revolution brought civil war to Finland, followed by independence in 1917, for the first time in that nation's history. Finland was attacked again in 1939, by Stalin's forces, and was eventually defeated but never occupied. Denmark and Norway, attacked by Germany in 1940, were not spared that fate. With Denmark overtaken by Nazi Germany, Iceland, although considered by many in the Third Reich to be an Aryan stronghold, declared its independence from Denmark and was supported by thousands of Allied troops.

Denmark, Norway, and Iceland are members of NATO. Denmark is also a fully paid member of the European Union. Sweden and Finland joined the EU in January 1995. Norwegians, however, turned down the government's proposal for EU membership in a referendum in 1994, and did not join with its neighbors.

Scandinavians, like the British, often talk of Europe as though they were not part of it. They see themselves as different. They dream of the joie de vivre that they believe all southerners enjoy, but maintain that the moral fiber and know-how of the Scandinavians is superior to anything you'd find south of the border.

It used to be said that sick-leave levels were so high in Sweden that there were more sick people in a factory than in a hospital. Scandinavians in all five countries have become so used to high levels of social services that the political coloration of the government seems to matter less, as long as the services are delivered. This requirement is not easily squared with the vociferous demand for lower taxes, but compromises are being made. In Sweden, for example, the government and labor unions agreed to make the first day of sick leave an unpaid day and absences from the second day on reimbursed at 80 percent of the pay, virtually evaporating the absenteeism that led to the old factory-hospital joke.

More than the rest of Europe, Scandinavia has been influenced by the American lifestyle and its ethos of professionalism. This coexists, sometimes precariously, with the "socialism with a human face" doctrines that these societies have followed for the past 50 years or more. Among the measures introduced is Sweden's 12-month maternity–paternity leave, which requires fathers to take at least 30 days for themselves—an idea that was decried as madness but has done wonders for marriage and fatherhood.

The English language has brought together Scandinavians, who are not bound by a native language. Iceland was settled by disgruntled Vikings from Norway, but though once the universal Nordic tongue, little-changed Icelandic is, ironically, virtually incomprehensible to most other Scandinavians. Finnish, like Hungarian, is one of the enigmatic Finno-Ugric languages. Danish, a language rich in glottal stops, is not understood by many Swedes, and Danish TV programs have to be subtitled. Norwegian, in pronunciation and vocabulary halfway between Danish and Swedish, sometimes serves as an intra-Scandinavian mode of communication. But get a group of Scandinavians together and what are they most likely to speak? English.

* * *

THERE IS STILL MUCH TRUTH in the myth of the taciturn Scandinavian. Once there were two Danes, two Norwegians, and two Swedes marooned on a desert island. When a rescue party arrived six months later, they found that the two Danes had started a cooperative and that the two Norwegians had founded a local chapter of the patriotic society Sons of Norway. The two Swedes were waiting to be introduced.

Stereotypes about national characteristics abound among Scandinavians. Danes believe the saving grace of humor will take the sting out of most of life's vicissitudes. The Finns attribute their survival to their *sisu,* or true grit. Icelanders are known as a nation of hard workers, singers, writers, and drinkers, who (living on active volcanoes) stoically think there is always a way to pull things out of the fire. The Norwegians find virtue in being, like Ibsen's Peer Gynt, *sig selv nok,* which means self-reliant in all things. The Swedes, the most introspective of the lot, take pride in their reliability and admit to "Royal Swedish envy" as their principal vice.

The strain of melancholy that runs through the Scandinavian character becomes pronounced in the lonely north. In Finland, the most popular dance—one in which dance halls specialize to the exclusion of all others—is the tango, precisely because it is so sad and yet sultry. But there's no need to look only to Argentine imports: Virtually all Scandinavian folk music, even when rhythms are rapid and joyous, is in a minor key.

Perhaps this tendency to melancholia is natural in a region where solitude abounds. In northern Scandinavia the woods close in, pine and spruce mingling with white-trunked birches, with a clearing or a field here and there. Farther north the hegemony of the forest becomes complete, challenged only by the lakes. On a clear night, from an aircraft, the moonlight is reflected in so many lakes that it seems to cut a shining path to the horizon.

But the forest is not as silent or as lonely as you might think. Walk along a Scandinavian country road on an evening in early summer, and you will hear the barking of roe deer at your approach and the forlorn calling of loons from the lakes. You will see stately moose coming out of the woods to graze in the marshlands. Juniper bushes cast long, eerie shadows, and on a hilltop skeletal pines are silhouetted against a still clear sky. No wonder that in ages past, popular imagination peopled these forests with sprites and trolls and giants.

Having a summer home is not a great luxury in Scandinavia. On Friday afternoons there are traffic jams in Oslo and Reykjavík as Norwegians and Icelanders escape to their cabins in the mountainous interior. In Stockholm the waterways are clogged with motorboats heading for summer cottages in the archipelago. The Finns, less urbanized than their neighbors, almost always have a village or isolated farmstead they consider their real home.

Modern Scandinavia is largely a secular society, but woods and lakes hold a special mystique. A midnight boat ride on an island-studded lake, with the moon suspended just above the treetops, is very close to a religious experience for the people of the north, as their souls fill with a tremendous wistfulness and a sense of simultaneous sadness and joy.

— Eric Sjogren, a Swedish travel writer based in Brussels, is a frequent contributor to the New York Times and other publications.

CHRONOLOGY

ca. 12,000 BC   The first migrations into Sweden.

ca. 10,000 BC   Stone Age culture develops in Denmark.

ca. 8,000 BC   The earliest settlers reach the coast of Norway.

ca. 7,000 BC   First nomadic settlers come to Finland.

ca. 2,000 BC   Tribes from southern Europe, mostly Germanic peoples, migrate toward Denmark.

ca. 500 BC   Migration of Celts across central Europe impinges on Denmark's trade routes with the Mediterranean world. Trade becomes less economically crucial because of the increased use of abundant iron.

ca. AD 100   Ancestors of present-day Finns move to Finland.

ca. 770   The Viking Age begins. For the next 250 years, Scandinavians set sail on frequent expeditions stretching from the Baltic to the Irish seas, and even to the Mediterranean as far as Constantinople and to North America, employing superior ships and weapons and efficient military organization.

ca. 800–1000   Swedes control river trade routes between the Baltic and Black seas; establish Novgorod, Kiev, and other cities.

830   Frankish monk Ansgar makes one of the first attempts to Christianize Sweden and builds the first church in Slesvig, Denmark.

ca. 870   The first permanent settlers arrive in Iceland from western Norway.

911   A Scandinavian, Rollo, rules Normandy by treaty with the French king.

930   Iceland's parliament, the Alþingi, is founded. It's still functioning.

ca. 940–980   King Harald Bluetooth imposes Christianity on the people of Denmark. In less than a century, virtually the whole population is converted.

995   King Olaf I Tryggvason brings Christianity to Norway.

1000   Icelander Leif Eiríksson visits America. Olaf I sends a mission to Christianize Iceland.

1016–35   Canute (Knud) the Great is king of England, Denmark (1018), and Norway (1028). The united kingdom crumbles shortly after Canute's death in 1035.

1070   Adam of Bremen composes *History of the Archbishops of Hamburg-Bremen*, the first important contemporary source for Danish history.

1100   Christianity has diffused throughout Sweden as a result of German missionaries in the 800s and English in the 1000s. The 11th-century destruction of a pagan temple at Uppsala, a center for resistance, helped spread the new religion.

1167   Copenhagen is founded.

1169   King Valdemar, who was acknowledged as the single king of Denmark in 1157 and undertook repeated crusades against the Germans, captures Rugen and places it under Danish rule, marking the beginning of the Danish medieval empire. It culminates in 1219 when Valdemar marches to Estonia and builds a fortress at Ravel.

In 1225, Valdemar, after being kidnapped by a German vassal, is forced to give up all his conquests, except for Rugen and Estonia, in exchange for freedom.

1217   Haakon IV becomes king of Norway, beginning its "Golden Age." His many reforms modernize the Norwegian administration; under him, the Norwegian empire reaches its greatest extent when Greenland and Iceland form unions with Norway in 1261.

1248   In Sweden, Erik Eriksson appoints Birger as Jarl (Earl), in charge of military affairs and expeditions abroad. Birger improves women's rights, makes laws establishing peace in the home and church, and begins building Stockholm.

1250   Stockholm, Sweden, is officially founded.

1282   At a meeting of the Hof, or Danish Parliament, King Erik Glipping signs a coronation charter that becomes the first written constitution of Denmark.

1319   Sweden and Norway form a union that lasts until 1335.

1323   The Treaty of Päkinäsaari divides Finland between Sweden and Novgorod.

1349   The Black Death strikes Norway and kills two-thirds of the population.

1362   Volcanic eruption from beneath the glacier Öræfajökull desolates the adjacent countryside in south central Iceland and is the worst of a dozen Icelandic eruptions in the 1300s.

1370   The Treaty of Stralsund gives the north German trading centers of the Hanseatic League free passage through Danish waters and full control of Danish herring fisheries for 15 years. German power increases throughout Scandinavia.

1397   The Kalmar union is formed by Queen Margrethe as a result of the dynastic ties between Sweden, Denmark, and Norway, the geographical position of the Scandinavian states, and the growing influence of Germans in the Baltic. Erik of Pomerania is crowned king of the Kalmar Union.

1477   University of Uppsala, Sweden's oldest university, is founded.

1479   University of Copenhagen is founded.

1520   Christian II, ruler of the Kalmar Union, executes 82 people who oppose the Scandinavian union, an event known as the "Stockholm bloodbath." Sweden secedes from the Union three years later. Norway remains tied to Denmark and becomes a Danish province in 1536.

1523   Gustav Ericsson founds the Swedish Vasa dynasty as King Gustav I Vasa.

1534   Count Christoffer of Oldenburg and his army demand the restoration of Christian II as king of Denmark, initiating civil war between supporters of Christian II and supporters of Prince Christian (later King Christian III).

1588–1648   King Christian IV's reign is one of the longest and most influential in Danish history. Known as the "Building King," many of the buildings he began still stand. His lavish spending leaves the country nearly bankrupt.

1593   The Swedish national church becomes Lutheran.

1611–16   The Kalmar War: Denmark wages war against Sweden in hopes of restoring the Kalmar Union.

1611–60   Sweden's Gustav II Adolphus (1594–1632), the great warrior king, rules the beginning of this crucial era. During this time, Sweden defeats Denmark in the Thirty Years' War and becomes the greatest power in Scandinavia as well as northern and central Europe.

1640   Finland's first university is founded in Turku.

1660   Peace of Copenhagen establishes modern boundaries of Denmark, Sweden, and Norway.

1666   Lund University, Scandinavia's largest university, is founded in Sweden. Denmark takes possession of St. Thomas in the West Indies.

1668   Bank of Sweden, the world's oldest central bank, is founded.

1700–21   Sweden, led by Karl XII, first broadens then loses its position to Russia as northern Europe's greatest power in the Great Northern War. The country is forced to cede southeastern Finland and the Baltic provinces of Livonia, Estonia and Ingria to Russia.

1733   Denmark buys St. Croix in the West Indies from France.

1754   Royal Danish Academy of Fine Arts is established.

1762   The duke of Gottorp becomes czar of Russia and declares war on Denmark. Catherine, the czar's wife, overrules her husband's war declaration and makes a peaceful settlement.

1763   The first Norwegian newspaper is founded.

ca. 1780   A volcanic eruption, the Skaftárgos, causes a famine in Iceland that kills one-fifth of the population.

1791   The United States and Denmark start diplomatic relations, making Denmark the country with which the United States has had the longest uninterrupted diplomatic relationship.

1792   Denmark abolishes slave trade.

1801–14   The Napoleonic wars are catastrophic for Denmark economically and politically: the policy of armed neutrality fails; the English destroy the Danish fleet in 1801; Copenhagen is devastated during the bombardment of 1807; and Sweden, after Napoléon's defeat at the Battle of Leipzig, attacks Denmark and forces the Danish surrender of Norway. The Treaty of Kiel, in 1814, calls for a union between Norway and Sweden despite Norway's desire for independence. The Danish monarchy is left with the Kingdom of Denmark; the duchies of Schleswig and Holstein; and Iceland, Greenland, and the Faroe Islands.

1807   During the Napoleonic wars, Swedish king Gustav III joins the coalition against France and reluctantly accepts war with France and Russia.

1809   Sweden surrenders the Åland Islands and Finland to Russia; Finland becomes a grand duchy of the Russian Empire; and the Instrument of Government, Sweden's constitution, is adopted.

1810–30   The Golden Age of Danish literature and art, when both Hans Christian Andersen and Søren Kirkegaard made their mark.

1811   University of Oslo is established.

1812   Helsinki becomes the capital of the Grand Duchy of Finland.

1818 Sweden takes a Frenchman as king: Karl XIV Johann establishes the Bernadotte dynasty. National Library of Iceland is founded.

1835 The first compilation of *Kalevala*, the Finnish national epic, is published.

1848 All slaves in the Danish West Indies are emancipated.

1849 Denmark's absolute monarchy is abolished and replaced by the liberal June Constitution, which establishes freedom of the press, freedom of religion, the right to hold meetings and form associations, and rule by Parliament with two elected chambers as well as the king and his ministers.

ca. 1850 The building of railroads begins in Scandinavia.

1863 National Museum of Iceland is established.

1864 Denmark goes to war against Prussia and Austria; the hostilities end with the Treaty of Vienna, which forces Denmark to surrender the duchies of Schleswig and Holstein to Prussia and Austria.

1864–1914 320,000 Finns emigrate to North America during these years.

1865 The company later known as Nokia is founded in Finland. Its first production: lumber and rubber boots.

1874 Iceland adopts a constitution on the 1,000th anniversary of its settlement.

1884 A parliamentary system is established in Norway.

1885 The Art Gallery of Iceland is founded.

1887 The Norwegian Labor Party is founded.

1889 The Swedish Social Democratic Party is founded.

1901 Alfred Nobel, the Swedish millionaire chemist and industrialist, initiates the Nobel prizes.

1903 Norwegian explorer Roald Admundsen finds the Northwest Passage, a sailable passageway from North America to Asia through the Arctic Ocean.

1904 The first Icelandic minister takes office. Home rule by parliamentary majority is introduced.

1905 Norway's union with Sweden is dissolved.

1906 Women in Finland gain the right to vote in national elections.

1911 Norwegian explorer Roald Admundsen is the first man to reach the South Pole.

1913 Norwegian women gain the right of suffrage.

1914 At the outbreak of World War I, Germany forces Denmark to lay mines in an area of international waters known as the Great Belt. Because the British fleet makes no serious attempts to break through, Denmark is able to maintain neutrality. Norway and Sweden also declare neutrality but are effectively blockaded.

1915 Danish and Icelandic women win the right to vote.

1916 Iceland establishes a national organization of trade unions.

1917 Finland declares independence from Russia. Danish writer Henrik Pontoppidan is awarded the Nobel prize for literature. The United States buys the Virgin Islands from Denmark for US$25 million.

1918   Iceland becomes a separate state under the Danish crown; only foreign affairs remain under Danish control. Civil war breaks out in Finland between the "Reds" (Bolshevik sympathizers) and the "Whites" (government forces). The Whites win.

1919   A republican constitution is adopted by Finland. Kaarlo Juho Stahlberg is elected president. Swedish women win the right to vote.

1920   Scandinavian countries join the League of Nations.

1929–37   The first social democratic governments take office in Denmark, Sweden, and Finland. During this period, Norway is ruled by a labor government.

ca. 1930   The Great Depression causes unemployment, affecting 40% of the organized industrial workers in Denmark. The age of the Social Democrats begins, and lays a foundation for the welfare state that still exists in the nation today.

1932   Social Democrats win the Swedish elections and Per Albin Hansson becomes prime minister. The Social Democrats will hang on to power for 44 straight years.

1939   Denmark and the other Nordic countries declare neutrality in World War II. Finnish novelist Frans Eemil Sillanpaa wins the Nobel prize for literature. Finland falls under the Soviet "sphere" through the Molotov-Ribbentrop pact.

1939–40   Russia defeats Finland in the Winter War. Russia invades Finland primarily for its larger strategic interests in the area.

1940   Germany occupies Norway and Denmark. Denmark makes a trade-off, partly cooperating in order to retain a certain amount of self-governance. British forces occupy Iceland until 1941, when U.S. forces replace them.

1941–44   The Continuation War begins when Finland joins Nazi Germany in attacking the Soviet Union. After Russia defeats Finland, an agreement is signed calling for Finnish troops to withdraw to the 1940 boundary lines of Finland and for German troops on Finnish soil to disarm.

1944   The Icelandic Republic, with British and U.S. support, is founded on June 17. Sveinn Björnsson becomes Iceland's first president.

1945   Norway joins the United Nations. Swedish diplomat Raoul Wallenberg disappears into the Soviet gulag. Two years later Soviet officials report that Wallenberg has died in captivity, but evidence remains inconclusive.

1947   Norwegian explorer and anthropologist Thor Heyerdahl sets out from Peru on a balsa-wood raft called KonTiki. One hundred and one days later he reaches Polynesia, proving that people from South America could have first populated the islands. Finland declines Marshall aid after pressure from the Soviet Union.

1948   Treaty of Friendship, Cooperation, and Mutual Assistance between Finland and the Soviet Union obligates Finland to defend the U.S.S.R. in the event of an attack through Finnish territory. The Faroe Islands get home rule.

1949   Denmark, Norway, and Iceland become members of NATO. Sweden and Finland decline membership.

1952   The Nordic Council, which promotes cooperation among the Nordic parliaments, is founded. The Olympic Games take place in Helsinki.

1953   Greenland becomes an independent country, instead of a colony of Denmark.

1955   Finland joins the United Nations and the Nordic Council. Halldor Laxness of Iceland receives the Nobel prize for literature.

1956   Urho Kekkonen assumes office in Finland. He will hold on to the presidency for 25 years.

1958   Birgit Nilsson, Sweden's most well known and acclaimed female opera singer, becomes the first non-Italian to open the season at Milan's La Scala.

1963   An undersea volcano off Iceland erupts in November and the newest Westman Isle, Surtsey, is born. The eruption lasts another four years.

1967   Oil is found in the North Sea outside of Norway.

1970   Finland hosts the Strategic Arms Limitation Talks (SALT). Fueled by the efforts of renowned concert pianist/conductor Vladimir Ashkenazy, a Russian defector married to an Icelandic woman, Reykjavík hosts the first of the city's international Arts Festivals, which becomes a biennial event. Iceland's Mt. Hekla erupts.

1972   Sweden, on the basis of its neutral foreign policy, and Norway decline membership in the EU; Denmark becomes a member in 1973. Queen Margrethe II ascends the throne of Denmark.

1974   The Swedish pop group ABBA win the Eurovision Song Contest with the song "Waterloo," beginning a long international career.

1975   Sweden's Instrument of Government of 1809 is revised and replaced with a new Instrument of Government. This constitution reduces the voting age to 18 and removes many of the king's powers and responsibilities.

1976   The "cod wars," between Britain and Iceland over the extent of Iceland's fishing waters, end. Björn Borg wins his first of five Wimbledon titles, only 20 years old. King Carl XIV Gustaf of Sweden marries Silvia Sommerlath of Germany. A right wing coalition wrings the power from Sweden's Social Democrats after an uninterrupted 44-year reign.

1979   Greenland is granted home rule.

1980   Fifty-eight percent of Sweden's voters advocate minimizing the use of nuclear reactors at Sweden's four power plants. Iceland elects as president Vigdís Finnbogadottir, the world's first popularly elected female president.

1981   Gro Harlem Brundtland, a member of the Labor party, becomes Norway's first female prime minister.

1982   Poul Schluter becomes Denmark's first Conservative prime minister since 1894.

1983   In Finland, the Greens gain parliamentary representation, making them the first elected environmentalists in the Nordic region.

1985   The Alingi, Iceland's Parliament, unanimously approves a resolution banning the entry of nuclear weapons into the country.

1986   U.S. president Ronald Reagan and Soviet premier Mikhail Gorbachev discuss nuclear disarmament at a summit meeting in Reykjavík,

Iceland. Sweden's prime minister, Olof Palme, is assassinated for unknown reasons. Ingvar Carlsson succeeds him.

1988　Due to U.S. pressure, Iceland consents to reducing its quota of whales caught for "scientific purposes." The United States argues that Iceland is acting against a moratorium imposed by the International Whaling Commission.

1989　Tycho Brahe Planetarium opens in Copenhagen. Denmark becomes the first NATO country to allow women to join front-line military units. Denmark becomes the first country in the world to recognize marriage between citizens of the same sex.

1990　Finland becomes the fourth major route for Jewish emigration from the Soviet Union. Helsinki hosts the summit meeting between George Bush and Mikhail Gorbachev.

1991　The Karen Blixen Museum, in Rungstedlund, Denmark, is founded. Norway's King Olav V dies. King Harald V ascends the throne. His wife, Queen Sonja, becomes the first queen since the death of Maud in 1938. Sweden's Social Democrats are voted out of office and the new government launches a privatization policy. Iceland's Mt. Hekla erupts. Linus Torvalds writes the kernel for the Linux operating system while still a student at Helsinki University. Ten years later the freely distributed system has more users than Mac OS and Windows NT.

1992　Denmark declines to support the Maastricht Treaty setting up a framework for European economic union. Denmark wins the European Soccer Championships. Sweden's Riksbank (National Bank) raises overnight interest rates to a world record of 500% in an effort to defend the Swedish krona against speculation. Some 200 years after becoming a chartered city, Reykjavík finally gets its own city hall.

1993　In a second referendum, Denmark votes to support the Maastricht Treaty, as well as its own modified involvement in it. Tivoli celebrates its 150th year, Legoland celebrates its 25th birthday, and the Little Mermaid turns 80. Denmark also commemorates the 50th anniversary of the World War II rescue of Danish Jews, in which they were smuggled into Sweden.

Norway's minister of foreign affairs, Thorvald Stoltenberg, is appointed peace negotiator to war-torn Bosnia-Herzegovina. In secret meetings near Oslo, Norwegian negotiators help bring about a historic rapprochement between Israel and the Palestine Liberation Organization.

1994　The XVII Olympic Winter Games are held in Lillehammer, Norway, from February 12 to February 27. Sweden wins the Olympic gold medal for ice hockey, and later makes its biggest soccer achievement, winning the bronze medal in the World Cup. Sweden and Finland accept membership in the EU, while Norway again declines. The ferry *Estonia*, en route from Tallinn to Stockholm, sinks in the worst maritime disaster in Europe since World War II. 852 people die. Sweden's right wing coalition government loses the elections to the Social Democrats and Ingvar Carlsson steps up as prime minister.

1995　The 50th anniversary of the end of World War II in Europe is celebrated, especially in Denmark and Norway, where May 5 marks the end of the German occupation. Finland and Sweden join the EU in January. Finland holds parliamentary elections in March; the government is presided over by Prime Minister Paavo Lipponen, a Social Democrat. Prince Joachim of Denmark marries Alexandra Manley of Hong Kong.

1996 After her fourth four-year term in office, Iceland's president Vigdís Finnbogadóttir does not seek reelection; the new appointee is Ólafur Ragnar Grímsson. A subglacial crater near Grímsvatn erupts under Iceland's glacier Vatnajökull. In its own blaze of glory, Iceland's Mt. Hekla erupts under the glacier Vatnajökull. Norway's longtime prime minister, Gro Harlem Brundtland, announces her resignation; she is succeeded by the Labor Party's Thorbjorn Jagland.

1997 Copenhagen's venerable Carlsberg Brewery, one of the largest supporters of the arts in Denmark, celebrates its 150th anniversary.

1998 Iceland mourns the passing of First Lady Guðrún Katrin Káradóttir after she loses a heroic struggle against acute leukemia. The celebrity Orca whale Keiko (of *Free Willy* fame) is returned to Icelandic waters after more than 20 years away. Sweden's Social Democrats, led by Göran Persson win the parliamentary elections.

1999 Iceland's Prime Minister Davið Oddsson continues his term as the longest-serving Icelandic prime minister when his Independence Party and the Progressive Party decide to continue their governing coalition. Norway, although not a member of the EU, signs the Schengen Agreement, allowing its citizens to travel without checks between Iceland and the 13 EU countries who have ratified the agreement.

2000 The Øresund Bridge, which links Sweden to Denmark and therefore to the rest of continental Europe, opens for trains and cars. In a national referendum, Danish voters reject full membership in the European Economic Union by voting against replacing the krone with the euro. The Norwegian Labour Party's Jens Stoltenberg becomes Prime Minister. A new constitution is adopted in Finland, increasing the influence of parliament.

2001 Norway's Crown Prince Haakon marries Mette-Marit Tjessem Høiby, a commoner and single mom.

2002 Finland, as the only Scandinavian EU member to do so, enters the euro zone. Sweden's Prime Minister Göran Persson wins a second term in the parliamentary elections. Princess Märtha Louise of Norway weds writer Ari Behn. Norwegian explorer Thor Heyerdahl dies.

2003 Denmark supports the United States and United Kingdom by sending a warship and submarine to Iraq, while the other Nordic governments' foreign policies vary from to cautious to critical. The Centre Party stands as the winner in the Finnish parliamentary elections. Iceland goes to the polls for parliamentary elections on May 10. Swedish foreign minister Anna Lindh is assassinated at a department store in Stockholm. The Swedish people reject the euro in a referendum in September.

BOOKS & MOVIES

Books

For a historical background of the Nordic countries, try *A History of the Vikings* (Oxford University Press, 1984). The book recounts the history of the seafaring traders and plunderers whose journeys stretched as far from Scandinavia as Constantinople and North America. Gwyn Jones's lively account makes learning the history enjoyable.

Myth and Religion of the North, by E. O. G. Turbille-Petre, explains the evolution of the diverse mythological tales and pagan religions of the Nordic countries.

One of the most exhaustive and comprehensive studies of Sweden published in English in recent years is *Sweden: The Nation's History,* by Franklin D. Scott (University of Minnesota Press, 1977). Chris Mosey's *Cruel Awakening: Sweden and the Killing of Olof Palme* (C. Hurst, London 1991) gives an overview of the country's recent history with focus on the events surrounding the assassination of Palme and the fruitless hunt for his killer.

For Norway's past, turn to *Norway: A History from the Vikings to Our Own Times* (1998); Karsten Alnaæs's *A History of Norway in Words and Pictures* (2001); and T. K. Derry's *A History of Scandinavia* (1996). Stunning images of the Norwegian landscape have been captured in the coffee-table books *The Magic of Fjord Norway* (2000), by Per Eide and Olav Grinde; *Panorama Norway* (1996), by Pål Hermansen; and Trym Ivar Bergsmo's *Lofoten* (2001).

Danish thinker Søren Kierkegaard's writings, most of which have been translated into English, transcend the traditional boundaries of philosophy, theology, psychology, literary criticism, devotional literature and fiction. Sometimes referred to as the "Father of Existentialism", his writings have been explored and redeployed by thinkers for 150 years. A great social critic, Kierkegaard also sought to revitalize Christian faith by pointing out its modern relevance.

Danish fiction translated into English ranges from fairy tales to social critique.

Hans Christian Andersen's fairy tales, including such classics as *The Little Mermaid, The Ugly Duckling, Thumbelina,* and *The Princess and the Pea,* have entertained generations of children. The release of a movie about Andersen's life, directed by Bille August, is set to coincide with the 200th anniversary of the writer's birthday, in 2005.

Karen Blixen's (under the pseudonym Isak Dinesen) most important works, *Out of Africa* (1937) and *Shadows on the Grass* (1960) chronicle her years on a coffee farm in British East Africa purchased for her by her family. Blixen lived in Africa together with her husband, a Swedish nobleman, for 18 years, and returned to Denmark in 1931. Originally written in English, and later translated into Danish by the author, Blixen's accounts of her years in Africa are highly selective autobiographical descriptions. Her *Letters from Africa 1914–1931* (1978), published after her death, stay a bit closer to the truth, but that doesn't make her previous publications any less enjoyable to read.

Pelle the Conqueror by Martin Andersen Nexø, follows a young Swedish boy and his father as they leave Sweden to work on a stone farm on the Danish island of Bornholm under hateful Danish landowners. Nexø, a self-described born proletarian, uses the novel to trace the history of common people from the Middle Ages to urban industrialism. Bille August's film adaptation of Nexø's four-volume epic came in 1988.

"Nothing we experience later in life will ever erase the memories of childhood," said Tove Ditlevsen. Her poetic inspiration came from her childhood in the poor working-class district of Vesterbro in Copenhagen. Works by Ditlevsen translated into English include *The Faces* (1968), and *Complete Freedom and Other Stories* (1944).

Peter Høeg's acclaimed novel, *Smilla's Sense of Snow,* is a compulsive page-turner that paints a dark and foreboding picture of Copenhagen and the waters around Greenland. When a small boy leaps to his death from a snow-covered roof, the police assume it was an accident. But Smilla, a Greenlander with a particular "sense" for snow, doesn't buy the explanation and sets out to discover the real reason boy died. The book was turned into a movie, starring Julia Ormond, in 1997. Other novels by Peter Høeg translated into English include *The History of Danish Dreams, Borderliners, Tales of the Night,* and *The Woman and the Ape.*

Suzanne Brøgger is one of Denmark's best-selling authors. Her family saga *The Jade Cat,* about the descendants of a Polish-Jewish immigrant was met by great acclaim in 1997. Other excellent fiction reading on Denmark includes *Laterna Magica* by William Heinesen set in the Faroe Islands, the satirical trilogy by Hans Scherfig— *Stolen Spring, The Missing Bureaucrat,* and *Idealists,* and Wallace Stegner's *The Spectator Bird,* which follows a man's exploration of his Danish heritage.

The first compilation of *Kalevala,* the Finnish national epic, was published in Finland in 1835. The work has been translated into English and offers an interesting poetic account of the history and traditions of the Finns.

Väinö Linna's *The Unknown Soldier* (1954) might be the most famous Finnish work of fiction outside of Finland. Set during the Continuation War (1942–45), *The Unknown Soldier* shows war through the eyes of enlisted men, portraying soldiers realistically without ostentatious heroism by using dialect and sometimes even humor. Linna's approach does not mean a lighthearted end result however; the horrors of war are duly shown.

Finnish writer Tove Jansson's wonderful children's books about a family of trolls, *the Moomintrolls,* are enchanting and inspiring for both young and old. Jansson wrote and illustrated nine books about the little trolls in Moominvalley. The stories have been translated into 34 languages and have been dramatized for TV, film, radio, theater and even opera. English-language titles include *Tales from Moominvalley, Moominpappa at Sea, Moominsummer Madness, Moominpappa's Memoirs,* and *Moominland Midwinter.*

Linus Torvalds' *Just for Fun: The Story of an Accidental Revolutionary* (2001) is the autobiographical account of the inventor of Linux. The life of a computer programmer might not sound like a particularly fun read, but Torwald's wit and humor makes the book an interesting look at the debate over open source code and Finland's booming technology industry.

Mika Waltari (1908–79) is one of Finland's best-known 20th century writers. His historical novels *The Egyptian, The Etruscan,* and *The Roman* have all been translated into English.

The Icelandic Sagas, the Nordic countries' most valuable contribution to world literature, have been translated into many languages. They tell of the lives, characters, and exploits of Icelandic heroes during the 10th and 11th centuries in an intricate combination of fantasy and history. The best-known are *Grettir's Saga,* about the outlaw Grettir the Strong; *Laxdæla Saga,* a tragedy spanning four generations in which women play a prominent role; *Egil's Saga,* about the truculent Viking-poet Egill Skallagrímsson; and *Njáls Saga,* generally considered the greatest, about two heroes, one young and brave, the other old and wise. Told in simple language, with an emphasis on dialogue, these epic poems are about family feuds, vengeance, loyalty, and tragic destiny.

In 1936 two young poets, W. H. Auden and Louis MacNeice, summering in Iceland, wrote a miscellany of poetry and prose that were later collected in Auden's *Letters from Iceland.* Full of insights on the country, its people, and its politics, they are an unorthodox and witty introduction to Iceland even 60 years later. Oscar Wilde also visited Iceland, and in his wit claimed Icelanders were indeed clever to have discovered America—before Columbus—but even more clever to have lost it to the Americans. He is one of many who have interpreted the apparent name-switch between Iceland and Greenland as an Icelandic ploy to keep their island to themselves.

The *Nonni og Manni Books* are charming children's classics set in Iceland. Written by Jesuit Jón Sveinsson, the tales are the embellished experiences of Sveinsson and his brother, Manni. The two brothers, separated during their education abroad, saw each other only once afterward before Manni died of tuberculosis, early in the 20th century. Another modern work of at least peripheral interest to those traveling to Iceland is Jules Verne's classic science-fiction novel *Journey to the Center of the Earth*, in which the heroes begin their subterranean adventure with a descent into Iceland's majestic glacier Snæfellsjökull.

Ólafur Jóhann Ólafsson's books have all become bestsellers in Iceland, and several have been translated to English. In *The Journey Home* (1999),a woman named Asdis returns to the island she left 20 years earlier in search of the life she left behind.

The Grey Moss Glows (1986), by Thor Vilhjálmsson, is a touching story of love between a half-brother and half-sister set in19th-century Iceland, and the couple's prosecution by the authorities.

Einar Már Guðmundsson's lyrical prose and humorous style have made him the most widely-translated post-war Icelandic author. His acclaimed *Footprints on the Heavens* (1997), was followed up by the independent sequel *Dreams on Earth* in 2000.

Þorarinn Eldjarn's *The Blue Tower* (1996), is based on the real-life story of Gudmundur Andresson, an Icelander who provoked and outraged Iceland's spiritual and secular authorities in the 17th century. Accused of encouraging immorality, Andresson was sent to prison in Copenhagen's notorious Blue Tower.

Best known in Iceland for her children's book, Guðrún Helgadóttir published her first novel in 2000. *Family Bonds* is a dramatic saga of four generations of women and the men in their lives.

More than 50 different volumes on Iceland—including poetry, biographies, travel guides, and picture books in English—can be ordered from the **Iceland Review,** (☎ 354/512–7575 in Reykjavík ⊕ www. icenews.is)a quarterly magazine covering tourism and cultural events.

One of the greatest influences on 20th-century drama and literature, Norwegian poet and dramatist Henrik Ibsen is best known for *Peer Gynt* (1867), *A Doll's House* (1879), and *Hedda Gabler* (1890).

His classic plays are still being performed in theaters from Berlin to Beijing. *A Doll's House* challenged both the tradition of how to write a play and the view of women as dependents when it premiered in 1879. The play's main character, Nora, is a young Norwegian housewife treated like a doll by her husband. Her rejection of marriage and motherhood at the end of the play scandalized contemporary audiences to such degree that an alternate ending had to be written for performances in Germany.

Hedda Gabler is a strong woman who marries the wrong man after her father's death and is quickly crushed by her husband's dullness. When a former suitor becomes a literary success and finds love in a girl that Hedda has always despised, her bitterness leads her to manipulate the man to such a degree that he commits suicide.

Three Norwegian novelists were awarded the Nobel Prize for Literature in the 20th century: Bjørnstjerne Bjørnson, Knut Hamsun, and Sigrid Undset. Bjørnson was renowned for his lyric poetry and authored the Norwegian national anthem, *Ja, vi elsker*. Hamsun won for *Growth of the Soil* in 1920, but might be most famous for *Hunger* (1890), an internal monologue by a struggling writer, wretched by anguish at the thought of possible death in a world indifferent to his existence. After publicly supporting the Nazis during World War II, Hamsun was conceived as a traitor, something that has often overshadowed his literary contributions.

Undset was honored for her masterpiece *Kristin Lavransdatter* (1928), a historical saga set in 14th-century Norway. The novel follows the life of Kristin through engagement and an illicit affair, marriage and marital discord. It shows the fragility of reputation and the importance of status in tightly-knit rural communities.

Cora Sandel's *Alberta and Jacob* (1926) is a quiet, intense story of girl who struggles to gain autonomy against the confines of the bourgeoisie; she rebels against her oppressive family in a small town in the far north of Norway.

More recently, Jostein Gaarder achieved international literary acclaim for his bestseller *Sophie's World* (1997). The book was originally intended as a narrative introduction to the history of philosophy for young people. A 14-year-old girl, Sophie, enters a discussion of philosophy with a faceless correspondent. At the same time, she solves a mystery involving another young girl with the knowledge she has gained, only to find out that the truth is much more complicated than she could have imagined.

Classic Swedish authors include 1909 Nobel Prize laureate Selma Lagerlöf, whose *The Wonderful Journey of Nils Holgersson,* written on request as a geography textbook for schoolchildren, takes the reader on an adventure through the entire country with a little boy called Nils Holgersson.

The plays of Swedish writer August Strindberg greatly influenced modern European and American drama. Perhaps the most enduringly fascinating of these, *Miss Julie* (1888), mixes the explosive elements of sex and class to stunning effect.

Vilhelm Moberg's series of novels about a poor Swedish family that emigrated to America, *The Emigrants* (1949), *Unto a Good Land,* (1956), and *The Last Letter Home* (1956–59), gives insight into what life was like in the second half of the 19th century, when Sweden was one of the most backward agrarian countries in Europe and one-quarter of its population left for North America.

Proletarian writer Moa Martinson rose from illegitimacy and poverty to become an acclaimed novelist. Her debut novel, *Women and Appletrees* (1933), and the novel often regarded as her best, *My Mother Gets Married* (1936), have been translated into English. Both novels tell of the struggles of working-class women in a time when women had little say in the decisions affecting their lives.

Eyvind Johnson's semi-autobiographical four-volume epic (1934–37) about a lonely logger named Olaf in the Swedish north blends a sense of fairy tale with realism. The series was the basis for the author's 1974 Nobel Prize award and consists of *The Year was 1914, Here is Your Life!, Don't Look Back!,* and *Postlude to Youth.*

1951 Nobel Prize laureate Pär Lagerkvist's novels are as refined as they are timeless.

Told through the story of the man whom Jesus replaced on Golgata, *Barabbas* (1950) is about humankind's desire to believe. Staying close to the Biblical story, Lagerkvist still manages to subtly question many truths.

Lagerkvist's *The Dwarf* (1944) is both a war protest and a warning about what can happen when evil is unleashed. A servant at a medieval court, the title character is a heartless, Machiavellian figure who takes no responsibility for the deeds he carries out on behalf of his master, the prince. Despite its medieval setting, The Dwarf's themes continue to resonate.

Lagerkvist's mythical *The Sibyl* (1956) portrays the struggles between good and bad and the divine and the human. A man who has been cursed seeks the help of an oracle who shows him that God is both love and hate, and that the two are not contradictory.

Only one of poet and novelist Karin Boye's novels, the masterly futuristic *Kallocain* (1940), has been translated into English. Often compared to George Orwell's *1984,* it is a depiction of a world under totalitarian rule, seen through the eyes of an idealistic scientist Leo Kall. Whereas Orwell is purely political, Boye's take on totalitarianism is much more existential.

Göran Tunström's *The Christmas Oratorio* (1983) spans three generations of the Nordensson family. Incredible journeys, doomed love, and strange misfortunes fill the lives in this story, which, like most of Tunström's novels, starts in the province of Värmland. With his amazing prose, fluctuating from poetic to fantastic to realistic, Tunström has secured his place in Swedish literature.

Captain Nemo's Library (1991), by Per Olov Enquist, is a fine family drama set in the 1940s on the northern coast of Sweden.

Hugely popular in Sweden and exported abroad are the TV dramatizations of the police thrillers written by the husband and wife team of Maj Sjöwall and Per Wahlöö from 1965 until Wahlöö's death in 1975. One of their thrillers, *The Terrorists,* was somewhat prophetic with a scene in which a Swedish prime minister is shot, a precursor to the assassination of

Olof Palme in 1986. All of Sjövall-Wahlöö's books (*The Laughing Policeman, Roseanna, The Locked Room, The Man on the Balcony, The Man Who Went Up in Smoke,* and *The Terrorists*) have been translated into English.

Movies

One of the most interesting Scandinavian directors is the ambitious and visually distinctive Danish director Lars von Trier, whose "Dogma manifesto," a set of restrictions that pares filmmaking down to little more than a camera and actors, has created new rules for directors and sparked a renaissance for Danish film.

Von Trier's 1996 *Breaking the Waves* is set in a deeply religious community in the north of Scotland. Bess, a naive young woman, falls in love with a Danish oil rig worker. When he goes to sea, she begs God to bring him back. When he returns with a broken neck after an accident, Bess believes that she is to blame.

Dancer in the Dark (2000), starring Icelandic pop star Björk, is the second in von Trier's trilogy about women's lives. Here, a woman from Eastern Europe sacrifices everything, including her eyesight, for her son.

In Thomas Vinterberg's *The Celebration* (1998), a 60th birthday turns into a family drama after a horrendous secret is revealed. Bewildered guests watch as the conflict between the birthday celebrant and his oldest son intensifies. *The Celebration* was made in the Dogma tradition for primitive cinematography pioneered by von Trier.

Babette's Feast, which won the Oscar for Best Foreign Language Film in 1987, is a movie adaptation of Karen Blixen's novel of the same title and was produced in Denmark.

Denmark's best-known director abroad is without doubt Bille August. His filmography includes such titles as *Les Misérables* (1998), *Smilla's Sense of Snow* (1997), *The House of Spirits* (1993) and *Pelle the Conqueror* (1988). August's next project is a movie about the life of Hans Christian Andersen, and its release is set to coincide with the 200th anniversary of the writer's birthday, in 2005. Andersen's life has been portrayed before, in the 1952

film *Hans Christian Andersen,* starring Danny Kaye. In fact, his crooning of *Wonderful Copenhagen* became Denmark's official tourism slogan. Several of Andersen's fairy tales have been animated, including Disney's *The Little Mermaid* (1989)—a great way to get your children interested in Andersen's fairy tales.

The list of Finnish directors making a name for themselves abroad has long been limited to Renny Harlin, director of *Die Hard II, Cutthroat Island,* and *The Long Kiss Goodnight,* the latter two starring Harlin's ex-wife Geena Davis.

Finnish director Aki Kaurismäki's *Man Without a Past* was nominated for an Academy Award for Best Foreign Language Film in 2003. The movie is the first Finnish production to get that nomination. In the movie, a man travels to Helsinki in search of work, gets mugged, and loses his memory. He finds love and without the knowledge of who he is, finds a completely new set of values.

The biggest-grossing Finnish movie of all times is *The Unknown Soldier* (1955), based on the novel by Väinö Linna about the Continuation War between Finland and Russia, and adapted for the screen by Edwin Laine.

Viking life in Iceland is compellingly portrayed in Hrafn Gunnlaugsson's trilogy: *When the Raven Flies* (1984), *In the Shadow of the Raven* (1988), and *The White Viking* (1991). The latter deals with turmoil at the arrival of Christianity.

Friðrik Friðriksson's poignant *Children of Nature* was an Oscar finalist for Best Foreign LanguageFilm in 1992. Though it didn't win, it garnered a dozen other film festival awards, including a Felix for its musical score. Another Friðriksson drama, *Cold Fever* (1996), follows a young Japanese man who, out of duty to his parents' memory, finds himself in Iceland. Friðriksson's 1999 *Angels of the Universe,* based on the book by Einar Már Guðmundsson, explores the uneasy border zone where the comic and the tragic fuse. Humor and mental illness blend in this portrayal of a schizophrenic and the people close to him. Hilmar Oddsson's award-winning *Tears of Stone* (1996), chronicles the life of Iceland's major classical music composer, Jón Leifs, whose promising career in Germany took a fateful turn when he was forced back to Iceland with his Jewish wife and two daughters during World War II.

Liv Ullmann first came to the world's attention as a star of several of Ingmar Bergman's best-known films, including *Persona* (1966), and *Autumn Sonata* (1978). Her directorial debut came in 1995 with *Kristin Lavransdatter* (1995), an adaptation of Sigrid Undset's trilogy set in 14th-century Norway. Her two consequent movies *Private Confessions* (1996), and *Faithless* (2000), were both written by Bergman, her one-time lover.

Mention Swedish film, and most people automatically think of Ingmar Bergman. A mainstay of the Swedish cultural scene for fifty years, Bergman has shaped Swedish filmmaking like no other director. From his first triumph in Cannes in 1956 with *Smiles of a Summer Night*, Bergman has continued to please his critics. Three of his movies have won the Oscar award for Best Foreign Language Film over the years: *The Virgin Spring* in 1960, *Through a Glass, Darkly* in 1961 and *Fanny and Alexander* in 1983.

If Bergman gave Swedish directors a reputation for seriousness (some might say gloom), the younger generation is altering that image. Beirut-born Swedish director Josef Fares' *Jalla Jalla* (2000) is a hilarious low-budget production with a cast of Fares' friends and family about a sudden arranged engagement that causes friction between a young immigrant park worker, the girl his father has picked out for him, and the girlfriend he already has. Only 25 when he made *Jalla Jalla,* Fares has been dubbed the wonder child of Swedish film.

Equally funny is Måns Herngren's and Hannes Holm's 1997 *Adam and Eve*. Four years into their relationship, Adam and Eve find out that eternity is a very long time, and sometimes a bit boring. They both realize change is needed, but classic gender differences lead them to seek change in very different ways.

Sometimes the best perspective is offered at a distance. For a decade, British-born director Colin Nutley has amazed Swedish moviegoers with his discerning depictions of their society. His big breakthrough came in 1993 with *House of Angels,* where

a cabaret singer and her gay best friend show up at a funeral in a small Swedish village. The man in the casket, the villagers find out, was the singer's grandfather, and as the sole relative she moves into his house. The pair's perceived decadence causes unease in the community, and they are told to leave town. Avoiding the usual stereotypical pitfalls, Nutley explores bias and fears without becoming preachy or overbearing.

Nutley made headlines overseas again in 2000, when his *Under the Sun* was nominated for an Oscar for Best Foreign Language Film. There is nothing new about this sweet and subtle love story, set against a 1950s countryside backdrop, and this is on purpose. The movie borrows its title from Ecclesiastes: "What was will be again; what has been done will be done again; and there is nothing new under the sun."

Another Swedish director to win recognition abroad is Lasse Hallström. Although *My Life as a Dog* (1985) failed to win an Oscar, it received the New York Film Critics Circle award for Best Foreign Language Film in 1987. Hallström's big break in the United States came with *What's Eating Gilbert Grape* (1993), starring Johnny Depp and Leonardo DiCaprio. His most remarkable movies since then have been *The Cider House Rules* (1999), *Chocolat* (2000), and *The Shipping News* (2001).

Human trafficking is the topic of Lukas Moodysson's latest movie, *Lilya 4-ever.* Based on a true story, the movie tells the disconcerting tale of a teenage girl who, trying to escape hardship in the former Soviet Union, finds herself forced into prostitution and trafficked to Sweden. Shot in an in-your-face, documentary style, the movie leaves no one unaffected. It swept most of the awards at the annual Swedish film awards ceremony in 2003, but failed to get an Oscar nomination.

Moodysson's 1998 debut *Show Me Love* was called "a young master's first masterpiece" by none other than Ingmar Bergman. Shot in a grainy, home-movie-like quality, *Show Me Love* is a story of love between two teenage girls in a small Swedish town where nothing ever happens. The conventional plot line of the love that can't be, at least in a small town, and the deeper themes of suburban alienation, teen angst, and the disconnect between well-meaning parents and their children, avoid becoming cliché through Moodysson's subtle storytelling.

His 2001 follow-up to *Show Me Love*, the charming *Together*, solidified Moodysson's reputation as one of Sweden's brightest new filmmakers. In the film, the leader of a mid-'70s commune tries to keep the community together after his sister and her children move in, introducing such evils as toy guns, television, and Pippi Longstocking.

FINNISH VOCABULARY

	English	Finnish	Pronunciation
Basics			
	Yes/no	Kyllä/ei	kue-leh/ay
	Please	Olkaa hyvä	**ol**-kah **hue**-veh
	Thank you very much.	Kiitoksia paljon.	**kee**-tohk-seeah **pahl**-yon
	You're welcome.	Olkaa hyvä.	**ol**-kah **hue**-veh
	Excuse me. (to get by someone)	Anteeksi suokaa	**ahn**-tehk-see **soo**-oh-kah
	(to apologize)	Anteeksi	**ahn**-teek-see
	Sorry.	Sori.	**sor**-ee
	Hello	Hyvää päivää terve	**hue**-veh **paee**-veh **tehr**-veh
	Hi	Hei	hay
	Goodbye	Näkemiin	**neh**-keh-meen
	Today	Tänään	**teh**-nehn
	Tomorrow	Huomenna	**who**-oh-men-nah
	Yesterday	Eilen	**ay**-len
	Morning	Aamu	**ah**-moo
	Afternoon	Iltapäivä	**ill**-tah-**pay**-va
	Night	Yö	**ue**-uh
Numbers			
	1	yksi	**uek**-see
	2	kaksi	**kahk**-see
	3	kolme	**kohl**-meh
	4	neljä	**nel**-yeh
	5	viisi	**vee**-see
	6	kuusi	**koo**-see
	7	seitsemän	**sate**-seh-men
	8	kahdeksan	**kah**-dek-sahn
	9	yhdeksän	**ueh**-dek-sen
	10	kymmenen	**kue**-meh-nen
Days of the Week			
	Monday	maanantai	mah-nahn-tie
	Tuesday	tiistai	**tees**-tie
	Wednesday	keskiviikko	**kes**-kee-veek-koh
	Thursday	torstai	**tohrs**-tie
	Friday	perjantai	**pehr**-yahn-tie
	Saturday	lauantai	**lou**-ahn-tie
	Sunday	sunnuntai	**soon**-noon-tie

Useful Phrases

Do you speak English?	Puhutteko englantia?	poo-hoot-teh-koh ehng-lahn-tee-ah
I don't speak . . .	En puhu suomea . . .	ehn **poo**-hoo **soo**-oh-may-ah
I don't understand.	En ymmärrä.	ehn **eum**-mehr-reh
I don't know.	En tiedä.	ehn **tee**-eh-deh
I am American/ British.	Minä olen amerikkalainen/ englantilainen.	**mee**-neh **oh**-len **ah**-mehr-ee-kah-lie-nehn/**ehn**-glahn-tee-lie-nehn
I am sick.	Olen sairas.	**oh**-len **sigh**-rahs
I need a doctor.	Tarvitsen lääkäri.	**tar**-vitt-sen **leh**-keh-rieh
Do you have a vacant room?	Onko teillä vapaata huonetta?	**ohn**-koh **tay**-leh **vah**-pah-tah **who**-oh-neht-tah?
How much does it cost?	Paljonko tämä maksaa?	**pahl**-yohn-koh **teh**-meh **mahk**-sah
It's too expensive.	Se on liian kallis.	**say** ohn **lee**-ahn **kahl**-lees
Beautiful	Kaunis	**kow**-nees
Help!	Auttakaa!	**ow**-tah-kah
Stop!	Seis!/Pysähtykää!	**say**(s) **peu**-seh-teu-keh
How do I get to . . .	Voitteko sanoa miten pääsen . . .	**voy**-teh-koh **sah**-noh-ah **mit**-ten **peh**-sen
. . . the train station?	asema (. . . pääsen asemalle?)	**ah**-seh-mah (**peh**-sen **ah**-say-mah-leh)
. . . the post office?	posti (. . . paasen-postiin?)	**pohs**-tee (**peh**-sen **pohs**teen)
. . . the tourist office?	matkatoimisto (. . . pääsen matkatoimistoon?)	**maht**-kah-**toy**-mees-toh (**peh**-sen **maht**-kah-**toy**-mees-tohn)
. . . the hospital?	sairaala (. . . pääsen sairaalaan?)	**sigh**-rah-lah (**peh**-sen **sigh**-rah-lahn)
Does this bus go to . . . ?	Kulkeeko tämä bussi-n . . . ?	**kool**-kay-koh **teh**-meh **boo**-see-n
Where is the bathroom?	Missä on W.C.?	**mihs**-seh ohn **ves**-sah
On the left	Vasemmalle	**vah**-say-mahl-leh
On the right	Oikealle	**ohy**-kay-ah-leh
Straight ahead	Suoraan eteenpäin	**soo**-oh-rahn **eh**-tayn-pa-een

Dining Out

Please bring me . . .	Tuokaa minulle . . .	too-oh-kah mee-new-leh
menu	ruokalista	**roo**-oh-kah-lees-tah
fork	haarukka	**hahr**-oo-kah
knife	veitsi	**vayt**-see

spoon	lusikka	**loo**-see-kah
napkin	lautasliina	**lou**-tahs-lee-nah
bread	leipä	**lay**-pa
butter	voi	**voh**(ee)
milk	maito	**my**-toh
pepper	pippuri	**peep**-poor-ee
salt	suola	**soo**-oh-lah
sugar	sokeri	**soh**-ker-ee
water/bottled	vesi/ kivennäisvesi	**veh**-see/**kee**-ven-water eyes-veh-see
mineral water	Vichy	**vis**-soo
The check, please.	Lasku, olkaa hyvä/ Haluan maksaa.	**lahs**-kew, **ohl**-kah **heu**-va/**hah**-lu-ahn **mahk**-sah

ICELANDIC VOCABULARY

English	Icelandic	Pronunciation
Basics		
Yes/no	Já/nei	yow/nay
Thank you very much.	Þakka þer Kær lega fyrir.	**thah**-kah thyehr **kire**-leh-gah fih-rihr
You're welcome.	Það var ekkert.	**thath** vahr **eh**-kert.
Excuse me. (to get by someone)	Afsakið	**ahf**-sah-kith
(to apologize)	Fyrirgefðu	**fih**-rihr-**gef**-thoo
Hello	Góðan dag	**goh**-than **dahkh**
Goodbye	Bless	bless
Today	Í dag	ee **dahkh**
Tomorrow	Á morgun	ow **mohr**-gun
Yesterday	Í gær	ee **gire**
Morning	Morgun	**mohr**-gun
Afternoon	Eftirmiðdagur	**ehf**-teer-mihth-dahg-ur
Night	Nótt	noht
Numbers		
1	einn	ayd'n
2	tveir	tvayr
3	þrír	threer
4	fjórir	**fyohr**-eer
5	fimm	fim
6	sex	sex
7	sjö	syooh
8	átta	**owt**-tah
9	níu	**nee**-ooh
10	tíu	**tee**-ooh
Days of the Week		
Monday	mánudagur	mown-oo-dah-gur
Tuesday	þriðjudagur	**thrith**-yoo-dah-gur
Wednesday	miðvikudagur	mith-vik-uh dah-gur
Thursday	fimmtudagur	fim-too-dah-gur
Friday	föstudagur	**fuhs**-too-dah-gur
Saturday	laugardagur	**loy**-gahr-dah-gur
Sunday	sunnudagur	**soon**-noo-dah-gur
Useful Phrases		
Do you speak English?	Talar þú ensku?	tah-lahr thoo ehn-skoo

I don't speak Icelandic.	Ég tala ekki. islensku	**yeh** tah-lah **ehk**-kih **ees**-lehn-skoo
I don't understand.	Ég skil ekki.	yeh skil **ehk**-kih
I don't know.	Ég veit ekki.	yeh **vayt ehk**-kih
I am an American/ British.	Ég er Bandaríkjamaður/ breskur.	yeh ehr **bahn**-dah-reek-yah-**mah**-thuhr/ brehs-koor
I am sick.	Ég er veik(ur).	yeh ehr vayk(uhr)
Please call a doctor.	Viltu hringja í lækni, takk.	vil-too hring-yah ee like-nee takk
Do you have a vacant room?	Áttu laust herbergi?	**ow**-too laysht **hehr**-behr-ghee
How much does it cost?	Hvað kostar það?	kvath kohs-tahr thath
It's too expensive.	Það er of dýrt	thahth ehr ohf deert
Beautiful	Fallegur/t	fa'-dleh-guhr
Help!	Hjálp	hyowlp
Stop!	Stopp	stohp
How do I get to . . .	Hvernig kemst ég . . .	kvehrd'-nikh kehmst **yehg**
. . .the post office?	á pósthúsið?	ow pohst-hoos-ith
. . .the tourist office?	á ferðamálaráð?	ow **fehr**-tha-mow-lah-rowth
. . .the hospital?	á sjúkrahúsið?	ow **syoo**-krah-hoo-sith
Does this bus go to . . . ?	Fer þessi vagn . . . ?	fehr **thehs**-see vahg'n
Where is the bathroom?	Hvar er salernið?	kvahr ehr sahl-ehr-nihth
On the left	Til vinstri	til **vin**-stree
On the right	Til hægri	til **high**-gree
Straight ahead	Beint áfram	baynt **ow**-frahm

Dining Out

Please bring me . . .	Get ég fengið . . .	geht yehg fehn-gihth
the menu	matseðil	**maht**-seh-thil
fork	gaffal	**gah**-fahd'l
knife	hníf	hneef
spoon	skeið	skayth
napkin	servíettu	**sehr**-yee-eh-too
bread	brauð	broythe
butter	smjör	smyuhr
milk	mjólk	myohlk
pepper	pipar	**pih**-pahr
salt	salt	sahlt
sugar	sykur	**say**-koor
water/bottled water	vatn/bergvatn	vaht'n/**behrg**-vahtn
Can I get the check, please?	Má ég fá reikninginn?	Mow yeh fow **rake**-ning-inn ghihn

NORWEGIAN VOCABULARY

	English	Norwegian	Pronunciation
Basics			
	Yes/no	Ja/nei	yah/nay
	Please	Vær så snill	**vehr** soh snihl
	Thank you very much.	Tusen takk.	**tews**-sehn tahk
	You're welcome.	Vær så god.	**vehr** soh goo
	Excuse me.	Unnskyld.	**ewn**-shewl
	Hello	God dag	goo **dahg**
	Goodbye	Ha det	**ha** day
	Today	I dag	ee **dahg**
	Tomorrow	I morgen	ee **moh**-ern
	Yesterday	I går	ee **gohr**
	Morning	Morgen	**moh**-ern
	Afternoon	Ettermiddag	**eh-terr**-mid-dahg
	Night	Natt	naht
Numbers			
	1	en	ehn
	2	to	too
	3	tre	treh
	4	fire	**feer**-eh
	5	fem	fehm
	6	seks	sehks
	7	syv, sju	shew
	8	åtte	**oh**-teh
	9	ni	nee
	10	ti	tee
Days of the Week			
	Monday	mandag	mahn-dahg
	Tuesday	tirsdag	**teesh**-dahg
	Wednesday	onsdag	**oonss**-dahg
	Thursday	torsdag	**tohsh**-dahg
	Friday	fredag	**fray**-dahg
	Saturday	lørdag	**loor**-dahg
	Sunday	søndag	**suhn**-dahg
Useful Phrases			
	Do you speak English?	Snakker De engelsk?	snahk-kerr dee ehng-ehlsk
	I don't speak Norwegian.	Jeg snakker ikke norsk.	yay **snahk**-kerr **ik**-keh nohrshk

I don't understand.	Jeg forstår ikke.	yay fosh-**tawr ik**-keh
I don't know.	Jeg vet ikke.	yay veht **ik**-keh
I am American/ British.	Jeg er amerikansk/ engelsk.	yay ehr ah-mehr-ee-kahnsk/ehng-ehlsk
I am sick.	Jeg er dårlig.	yay ehr **dohr**-lee
Please call a doctor.	Vær så snill og ring etter en lege.	vehr soh snihl oh ring **eht**-ehrehn **lay**-geh
Do you have a vacant room?	Har du et rom som er ledig?	yay vil **yehr**-neh hah eht room
How much does it cost?	Hva koster det?	vah **koss**-terr deh
It's too expensive.	Det er for dyrt.	deh ehr for **deert**
Beautiful	Vakker	**vah**-kehr
Help!	Hjelp!	yehlp
Stop!	Stopp!	stop
How do I get to . . . . . . the train station?	Hvor er . . . jernbanestasjonen	voor ehr yehrn-bahn-eh sta-**shoon**-ern
. . . the post office?	posthuset	**pohsst**-hewss
. . . the tourist office?	turistkontoret	tew-**reest**-koon-toor-er
. . . the hospital?	sykehuset	**see**-keh-hoo-seh
Does this bus go to . . . ?	Går denne bussen til . . . ?	gohr **den**-nah boos teel
Where is the bathroom?	Hvor er toalettene?	voor ehr too-ah-**leht**-te-ne
On the left	Til venstre	teel **vehn**-streh
On the right	Til høyre	teel **hooy**-reh
Straight ahead	Rett fram	reht **frahm**

Dining Out

menu	meny	meh-new
fork	gaffel	gahff-erl
knife	kniv	kneev
spoon	skje	shay
napkin	serviett	ssehr-vyeht
bread	brød	brur
butter	smør	smurr
milk	melk	mehlk
pepper	pepper	pehp-per
salt	salt	sahlt
sugar	sukker	sook-kerr
water	vann	vahn
The check, please.	Jeg vil gjerne betale.	yay vil **yehr**-neh beh-**tah**-leh

SWEDISH VOCABULARY

	English	Swedish	Pronunciation
Basics			
	Yes/no	Ja/nej	yah/nay
	Please	Var snäll; vahr vehn-leeg	vahr snehll; Var vänlig
	Thank you very much.	Tack så mycket.	tahk soh **mee**-keh
	You're welcome.	Var så god.	vahr shoh **goo**
	Excuse me. (to get by someone)	Ursäkta.	oor-**shehk**-tah
	(to apologize)	Förlåt.	fur-**loht**
	Hello	God dag	goo **dahg**
	Goodbye	Hej dä	ah-**yoo**
	Today	I dag	ee **dahg**
	Tomorrow	I morgon	ee **mor**-ron
	Yesterday	I går	ee **gohr**
	Morning	Morgon	**mohr**-on
	Afternoon	Eftermiddag	**ehf**-ter-meed-dahg
	Night	Natt	naht
Numbers			
	1	ett	eht
	2	två	tvoh
	3	tre	tree
	4	fyra	fee-rah
	5	fem	fem
	6	sex	sex
	7	sju	shoo
	8	åtta	oht-tah
	9	nio	nee-ah
	10	tio	tee-ah
Days of the Week			
	Monday	måndag	mohn-dahg
	Tuesday	tisdag	tees-dahg
	Wednesday	onsdag	ohns-dahg
	Thursday	torsdag	tohrs-dahg
	Friday	fredag	freh-dahg
	Saturday	lördag	luhr-dahg
	Sunday	söndag	suhn-dahg

Useful Phrases

Do you speak English?	Talar du engelska?	tah-lahr doo ehng-ehl-skah
I don't speak Swedish.	Jag talar inte svenska.	yah tah-lahr **een**-teh **sven**-skah
I don't understand.	Jag förstår inte.	yah fuhr-**stohr** **een**-teh
I don't know.	Jag vet inte.	yah **veht een**-teh
I am American/ British.	Jag är amerikan/ engelsman.	yah air ah-mehr-ee-**kahn ehng**-ehls-mahn
I am sick.	Jag är sjuk.	yah air **shyook**
Please call a doctor.	Jag vill skicka efter en läkare.	yah veel **shee**-kah **ehf**-tehr ehn **lay**-kah-reh
Do you have a vacant room?	Har Ni något rum ledigt?	hahr nee noh-goht **room leh**-deekt
How much does it cost?	Vad kostar det?/ Hur mycket kostar det?	vah **kohs**-tahr deh/ hor **mee**-keh **kohs**-tahr deh
It's too expensive.	Den är för dyr.	dehn ay foor **deer**
Beautiful	Vacker	**vah**-kehr
Help!	Hjälp	yehlp
Stop!	Stopp!/Stanna!	stop, **stahn**-nah
How do I get to . . .	Kan Ni visa mig vägen till	kahn nee **vee**-sah may**vay**-gehn teel
. . . the train station?	stationen	stah-**shoh**-nehn
. . . the post office?	posten	**pohs**-tehn
. . . the tourist office?	en resebyrå	ehn-**reh**-seh-**bee**-roh
. . . the hospital?	sjukhuset	**shyook**-hoo-seht
Does this go to . . . ?	Går den bussen här till . . . ?	gohr dehn bus hehr **boo**-sehn teel
Where is the bathroom?	Var är toalett?/ toaletten?	vahr ay twah-**leht** twah-**leht**-en
On the left	Till vänster	teel **vehn**-stur
On the right	Till höger	teel **huh**-gur
Straight ahead	Rakt fram	rahkt **frahm**

Dining Out

Please bring me . . .	Var snäll och hämta åt mig . . .	vahr snehl oh hehm-tah oht may
menu	matsedeln	maht-seh-dehln
fork	en gaffel	ehn gahf-fehl
knife	en kniv	ehn kneev
spoon	en sked	ehn shehd
napkin	en servett	ehn sehr-veht
bread	bröd	bruh(d)
butter	smör	smuhr

milk	mjölk	myoolk
pepper	peppar	pehp-pahr
salt	salt	sahlt
sugar	socker	soh-kehr
water	vatten	vaht-n
The check, please.	Får jag be om notan.	fohr yah beh ohm **noh**-tahn

INDEX

NOTES

NOTES

FODOR'S KEY TO THE GUIDES

America's guidebook leader publishes guides for every kind of traveler. Check out our many series and find your perfect match.

FODOR'S GOLD GUIDES
America's favorite travel-guide series offers the most detailed insider reviews of hotels, restaurants, and attractions in all price ranges, plus great background information, smart tips, and useful maps.

COMPASS AMERICAN GUIDES
Stunning guides from top local writers and photographers, with gorgeous photos, literary excerpts, and colorful anecdotes. A must-have for culture mavens, history buffs, and new residents.

FODOR'S CITYPACKS
Concise city coverage in a guide plus a foldout map. The right choice for urban travelers who want everything under one cover.

FODOR'S EXPLORING GUIDES
Hundreds of color photos bring your destination to life. Lively stories lend insight into the culture, history, and people.

FODOR'S TRAVEL HISTORIC AMERICA
For travelers who want to experience history firsthand, this series gives in-depth coverage of historic sights, plus nearby restaurants and hotels. Themes include the Thirteen Colonies, the Old West, and the Lewis and Clark Trail.

FODOR'S POCKET GUIDES
For travelers who need only the essentials. The best of Fodor's in pocket-size packages for just $9.95.

FODOR'S FLASHMAPS
Every resident's map guide, with dozens of easy-to-follow maps of public transit, restaurants, shopping, museums, and more.

FODOR'S CITYGUIDES
Sourcebooks for living in the city: thousands of in-the-know listings for restaurants, shops, sports, nightlife, and other city resources.

FODOR'S AROUND THE CITY WITH KIDS
Up to 68 great ideas for family days, recommended by resident parents. Perfect for exploring in your own backyard or on the road.

FODOR'S HOW TO GUIDES
Get tips from the pros on planning the perfect trip. Learn how to pack, fly hassle-free, plan a honeymoon or cruise, stay healthy on the road, and travel with your baby.

FODOR'S LANGUAGES FOR TRAVELERS
Practice the local language before you hit the road. Available in phrase books, cassette sets, and CD sets.

KAREN BROWN'S GUIDES
Engaging guides—many with easy-to-follow inn-to-inn itineraries—to the most charming inns and B&Bs in the U.S.A. and Europe.

BAEDEKER'S GUIDES
Comprehensive guides, trusted since 1829, packed with A–Z reviews and star ratings.

OTHER GREAT TITLES FROM FODOR'S
Baseball Vacations, The Complete Guide to the National Parks, Family Vacations, Golf Digest's Places to Play, Great American Drives of the East, Great American Drives of the West, Great American Vacations, Healthy Escapes, National Parks of the West, Skiing USA.

At bookstores everywhere.   www.fodors.com/books